Applied Industrial/ Organizational Psychology

Fourth Edition

Michael G. Aamodt

Radford University

THOMSON

WADSWORTH

Australia • Canada • Mexico • Singapore • Spain
United Kingdom • United States

This edition is dedicated to the memory of Dr. Wilson Kimbrough,
the role model for a life-long mentor.

THOMSON

✦

WADSWORTH

Editor: Michele Sordi
Assistant Editor: Dan Moneypenny
Editorial Assistant: Chelsea Junget
Technology Project Manager: Darin Derstine
Marketing Manager: Chris Caldeira
Marketing Assistant: Laurel Anderson
Advertising Project Manager: Brian Chaffee
Project Manager, Editorial Production: Paula Berman
Print/Media Buyer: Kris Waller
Permissions Editor: Sarah Harkrader

Production Service: Vicki Moran, Publishing
  Support Services
Text Designer: Andrew Ogus
Photo Researcher: Terri Wright
Copy Editor: Kay Mikel
Cover Designer: Larry Didona
Cover Image: Dennis Harms/Images.com, Inc.
Cover Printer: Quebecor World/Dubuque
Compositor: Carlisle Communications, Ltd.
Printer: Quebecor World/Dubuque

Printed in the United States of America
2 3 4 5 6 7 07 06 05 04

For more information about our products, contact us at:
Thomson Learning Academic Resource Center
1-800-423-0563

For permission to use material from this text, contact us by:
Phone: 1-800-730-2214
Fax: 1-800-730-2215
Web: http://www.thomsonrights.com

Library of Congress Control Number: 2003104058

ISBN 0-534-59688-6

Wadsworth/Thomson Learning
10 Davis Drive
Belmont, CA 94002-3098
USA

Asia
Thomson Learning
5 Shenton Way #01-01
UIC Building
Singapore 068808

Australia/New Zealand
Thomson Learning
102 Dodds Street
Southbank, Victoria 3006
Australia

Canada
Nelson
1120 Birchmount Road
Toronto, Ontario M1K 5G4
Canada

Europe/Middle East/Africa
Thomson Learning
High Holborn House
50/51 Bedford Row
London WC1R 4LR
United Kingdom

Latin America
Thomson Learning
Seneca, 53
Colonia Polanco
11560 Mexico D.F.
Mexico

Spain/Portugal
Paraninfo
Calle/Magallanes, 25
28015 Madrid, Spain

Contents

Chapter 5   Employee Selection: Recruiting and Interviewing   127

Chapter 8   Designing and Evaluating Training Systems   259

Chapter 9 Employee Motivation 291

Chapter 14 Organization Development 445

Chapter 15 Stress Management: Dealing with the Demands of Life and Work 474

Chapter 16   Working Conditions and Human Factors   502

Preface

I can't imagine a career better than industrial/ organizational psychology; it has something for everyone. You can be a scientist, a detective, a lawyer, an adviser, a statistician, an inventor, a writer, a teacher, a mentor, a trainer, a high-stakes gambler, a motivator, a humanitarian, and an engineer—all at the same time. In no other field can you experience such challenging opportunities, an excellent salary, and the satisfaction of bettering the lives of others.

I wrote this book because there is a strong need for a text that appeals directly to undergraduates without sacrificing scholarship. Our field is so exciting, yet the existing texts do not reflect that excitement. This book contains many real-world examples that illustrate important points; employment profiles that demonstrate the wide variety of I/O career paths; humor to make your reading more enjoyable; and charts and tables that integrate and simplify such complicated issues as employment law, job satisfaction, work motivation, and leadership.

In writing this book, I tried to strike a balance between research, theory, and application. In addition to the fundamental theories and research in I/O psychology, you will find such practical applications as how to write a resume, survive an employment interview, write a job description, create a performance appraisal instrument, and motivate employees.

For the Student

Three Books in One!

To save you money, the textbook and workbook are combined under one cover. A CD containing exercises, practice test questions, and data that can be analyzed is also included with your textbook. Using this larger, soft-cover format means that the price for the integrated textbook, workbook, and study guide is less than the price of a new hard-cover textbook by itself. In fact, the cost of a new copy of *Applied Industrial/ Organizational Psychology* (4th edition) is still cheaper than purchasing a used copy of a competing text and its separate workbook and study guide.

Each chapter comes with exercises to help you apply what you have learned. Thus, not only will you read about I/O psychology, you will get the opportunity to experience it as well. You will take psychological tests, conduct the critical incident technique, solve case studies, analyze situations, write a resume, prepare for an interview, and create a structured interview.

The CD-ROM includes additional materials to help you study: a list of key terms, a practice exam, and information on postgraduate programs for I/O psychology.

Perforated Pages!

Notice that the pages in the text are perforated. This will make it easier for you to turn in assignments and tear out chapters so that you don't have to carry the entire book to class or home on the weekend. If you plan to work out using a stepmaster, stationary bike, or treadmill, tear out a few pages and take them along; what could be more exciting reading?

Student Friendly!

To make your reading easier, humor, stories, and real-world examples are used. The text is written at a level designed to help you understand the material rather than at a level designed to show off the author's vocabulary. The feedback I have received indicates that students actually *enjoy* reading this text!

To help you learn, innovative charts such as those found in Chapters 3, 8, 9, 10, and 13 integrate the main points of the chapter. At the beginning of each chapter, a list of *learning objectives* helps organize your thinking for what you are about to read. At the end of each chapter, a *chapter summary* reminds you of the important points you learned, *critical thinking questions* test the depth of your new knowledge, and *key terms* to expand your knowledge using InfoTrac® College Edition are provided.

For the Instructor

Videos That Bring Material to Life!

To make teaching easier, two videos will be provided to qualified adopters. The first video was created by the author and contains a series of 3- to 15-minute segments that demonstrate the concepts discussed in the text. For example, one video segment contains a structured interview in which students can rate the answers given by two applicants. The necessary rating forms are included in the workbook portion of the text. Another video segment depicts four situations involving sexual harassment and FMLA issues to which students respond by indicating if the organization broke the law. Yet another segment depicts a job analysis interview. These and other short segments help bring the text material to life!

The second video contains 12 short segments from CNN. The segments cover such topics as empowerment, workplace safety, computer eyestrain, and sexual harassment. These segments demonstrate how the media have covered material related to the book and should increase student discussion. The instructor's guide accompanying the text helps integrate each segment with the text material.

An Instructor's Manual to Make Teaching Easier!

The instructor's manual will make teaching *Applied I/O Psychology* easier by providing help in three areas: constructing tests, grading student exercises, and delivering classroom lectures. To help in constructing tests, the instructor's manual contains multiple-choice and short-answer test questions for each chapter. The multiple-choice items are also included in an *electronic test bank*.

To help in grading student exercises, the instructor's manual contains answers to exercises for which there are objective answers. This section also contains information to help interpret the psychological tests contained in the textbook, which include the following:

- Personality
- Leadership style (self-monitoring; LPC; task orientation; and needs for achievement, power, and affiliation)
- Predisposition to job satisfaction (core evaluation, life satisfaction, vocational interest)
- Predisposition to work motivation (self-esteem, intrinsic versus extrinsic motivation)
- Communication style (listening skills, listening style)
- Predisposition to stress (Type A, optimism, lifestyle)

To help make lectures more interesting, I have provided the most useful instructor's manual in the field. The manual contains:

- *Transparency* masters for each topic (these PowerPoint slides are also included on a CD-ROM)
- *Lecture outlines* for each topic
- Suggestions for *demonstrations* and *examples*
- Information to tie the *video segments* to text material
- *Humorous examples* to lighten up material (for example, Top 10 Stupid Interviewer Tricks, Strange Cover Letters)

New to this Edition

- The chapter on job analysis has been moved in front of the chapter on legal issues
- The chapter on motivation now comes before the chapter on job satisfaction
- Updated references and material in every chapter
- A substantial increase in cross-cultural comparisons. Examples of this include comparisons of employment law in different countries, international differences in job satisfaction, leadership styles, and international differences in paid time off.
- A substantial increase in the discussion of work–life balance in Chapter 15
- A major reorganization of Chapter 6 (employee selection), Chapter 7 (performance appraisal), and Chapter 8 (training)
- Increased discussion on resolving conflict in Chapter 13
- Added discussion of focus groups, phone etiquette, and email etiquette in Chapter 11
- Majority of the discussion on need for achievement and needs theories moved from Chapter 10 (satisfaction) to Chapter 9 (motivation).
- Majority of discussion on operant conditioning principles moved from Chapter 7 (performance appraisal) to Chapter 9 (motivation)
- Increased discussion of feedback and better description of stock options in Chapter 9
- Greater emphasis on correlates of job satisfaction (Exhibit 10.01), reorganization of absenteeism coverage, increased coverage on turnover in Chapter 10
- Complete reorganization of Chapter 8 (training)
- Increased coverage on training motivation, extensive new coverage on how to deliver a training presentation, and extensive new coverage on how to develop a training program in Chapter 8
- Reorganized Chapter 7 (performance appraisal) with an applied emphasis on how to create a good performance appraisal system and a reduced emphasis in listing techniques of historical, but not practical, interest

- New discussion on the use of training and education as selection tools in Chapter 6 (employee selection)
- Expanded coverage on recruitment (including a discussion on the use of nontraditional populations) and structured interviewing in Chapter 5 (employee selection)
- Chapter 2 (job analysis) is reorganized with a more applied structure, increased discussion on writing task statements and linking KSAOs to tasks, new discussion of O*NET, more applied discussion of job evaluation, and new discussion on salary equity
- New material on alternative dispute resolution and increased emphasis on sexual harassment in Chapter 3 (legal issues)
- Better discussion of research methods in Chapter 1 (introduction)
- Reduction in the number of statistical formulas throughout the text
- A CD-ROM containing study materials and data from a hypothetical organization is included with each textbook

Acknowledgments

I am grateful to the excellent staff at Wadsworth, including Senior Editor Michele Sordi, Editorial Assistant Chelsea Junget, Assistant Editor Dan Moneypenny, Project Manager Paula Berman, and Marketing Manager Laurel Anderson. Michele, your enthusiasm for this book was greatly appreciated. Thanks also to production service, Vicki Moran, of Publishing Support Services, and manuscript editor Kay Mikel, of WordWorks, for their help with this edition. The quality of the text was greatly enhanced by the thoughtful responses of reviewers Laurie Lankin, Mercer University; Marc Pratarelli, University of Southern Colorado; Donald Hantula, Temple University; Todd Thorsteinson, University of Idaho; Daniel DeNeui, University of Southern Oregon; Charles Pierce, Montana State University; James Mitchel, Central Connecticut State University; Keith Syrja, Owens Community College; Jean Kirnan, The College of New Jersey; and Linda Butzin, Owens Community College.

I would also like to thank my family, friends, and students for accommodating my time spent writing and for all their ideas and support. I appreciate my colleagues Mark Nagy, Dave Cohen, Nora Reilly, Tom Pierce, Al Harris, Sean Robson, and Michael Surrette who patiently allowed me to bounce ideas off them, vent, and ask dumb questions. I want to especially thank Chris Moyse for her work in putting together the index and Sarah Krieger for her help with the glossary. Thanks also to my SIOP, IPMA, IPMAAC, and SHRM colleagues for their insight and stories. There is no way I can properly express my gratitude to my mentor, Dr. Wilson W. Kimbrough, who taught me much more than facts and theories.

Finally, I thank my wife Bobbie and son Josh for their love and emotional support. Most of the time, writing a book is an enjoyable process. However, during the times I was stressed or confused, my family was always patient and understanding. I could not have done this, or much of anything, without them. I would also like to thank Bobbie for her contributions in helping write the stress chapter and the section on organizational culture.

Michael G. Aamodt

1 Introduction to I/O Psychology

WOULDN'T IT BE wonderful if all employees loved their jobs so much that they couldn't wait to get to work and were so well suited and trained that their performances were outstanding? Well, this is the ultimate goal of industrial psychology. Unfortunately, not every employee will enjoy his or her job, and not every employee will do well on a job. In this book you will learn the techniques developed by industrial/organizational (I/O) psychologists that show the way toward the goal of a happy and productive workforce.

Before we can talk about these techniques, several areas must be discussed so that you will have the basics to help you better understand the rest of the book. In this chapter, you will find two distinct sections. The first section provides a brief overview of the field of I/O psychology, and the second section discusses the research methods that will be mentioned throughout the text. By the end of this chapter you will

- be able to describe I/O psychology and what I/O psychologists do.
- have learned about the history of I/O psychology.
- know the requirements for graduate programs in I/O psychology.
- understand the importance of conducting research.
- understand how to conduct research.
- be able to differentiate the various research methods.

The Field of Psychology

Differences Between I/O and Business Programs

Perhaps the best place to begin a textbook on I/O psychology is to look at the field itself. **Industrial/ organizational psychology** is a branch of psychology that applies the principles of psychology to the workplace.

The definition used by the Canadian Psychological Association includes the statement, "Industrial-Organizational psychologists are able to apply psychological theories to explain and enhance the effectiveness of human behavior and cognition in the workplace" (Kline, 1997, p. 206). For example, principles of learning are used to develop training programs and incentive plans, principles of social psychology are used to form work groups and understand employee conflict, and principles of motivation and emotion are used to motivate and satisfy employees. The application of psychological principles is what best distinguishes I/O psychology from related fields typically taught in business colleges. Although many of the topics covered in this text are similar to those found in human resource management (HRM) or organizational behavior texts, the techniques and the reasons behind the techniques are often different. For example, many HRM texts advocate the interview as an excellent solution for selecting the best employees. I/O psychologists consider unstructured interviews to be of less value than more suitable alternatives such as psychological tests, work samples, biodata, and assessment centers (Berry, 2003).

A second difference between I/O psychology and business fields is that I/O psychology examines factors that affect the *people* in an organization as opposed to the broader aspects of running an organization such as marketing channels, transportation networks, and cost accounting (Feldman, 1986). As you can see from the typical graduate courses listed in Exhibit 1.01, business programs examine such areas as accounting, marketing, and transportation, whereas I/O programs focus almost exclusively on issues involving the people in an organization (Murphy, Watson-El, Williams, & Wood, 2003; Verdi, 1999).

I/O psychology relies extensively on research, quantitative methods, and testing techniques. I/O psychologists are trained to use empirical data and statistics rather than clinical judgment to make decisions. I/O psychologists are not clinical psychologists who happen to be in industry, and they do not conduct therapy for workers. There are psychologists who work for

Exhibit **1.01** Comparison of MBA and I/O master's degree coursework

Typical I/O Coursework

Time	Day	Course Name
1:00–3:00	M	Statistics
2:00–3:00	T-Th	Experimental Methodology
11:00–12:00	M-W	Psychometric Theory
9:30–11:00	MWF	Employee Selection and Placement

Time	Day	Course Name
8:00–10:00	T-Th	Organizational Psychology
4:00–5:30	W-F	Employee Training and Development
10:00–12:00	M-W	Performance Appraisal
11:30–1:00	Th-F	Job Analysis

Typical MBA Coursework

Time	Day	Course Name
1:00–3:00	M	Statistics
2:00–4:00	T-Th	Business Research
10:00–11:00	MWF	Organizational Behavior
9:30–11:30	M-W	Administrative Policy

Time	Day	Course Name
10:00–11:00	TThF	Managerial Economics
8:00–9:30	MWF	Financial Management
10:00–11:30	M-W	Marketing Management
1:00–2:30	T-Th	Managerial Accounting

organizations and help employees with such problems as drug and alcohol abuse, but these are counseling psychologists rather than I/O psychologists.

I/O psychology continually increases in popularity, perhaps more than any other field, because professionals in the field can have a positive impact on the lives of other people. To support this last statement, look at a typical day in the life of a typical person:

Work	8 hours
Commute to work	1 hour
Watch TV	3 hours
Sleep	8 hours
Prepare and eat meals	2 hours
Other	2 hours

With the possible exception of sleeping, people spend more time at their jobs than at any other activity in life (and sometimes these two activities overlap!). Thus, it makes sense that people who are happy with and productive at their jobs will lead more fulfilling lives than people unhappy with their jobs. If a person is unhappy at work for 8 hours a day, the residual effects of this unhappiness will affect the quality of that person's family and leisure life as well.

From a societal perspective, I/O psychologists can also improve the quality of life by increasing employee effectiveness, which in turn reduces the cost of goods sold by improving product quality, which in turn reduces repair and replacement costs by improving organizational efficiency, which can result in decreases in activities such as waiting in line.

Thus, I/O psychology can improve the quality of life at levels equal to, and often exceeding, those of fields such as counseling psychology and medicine. So even though I/O psychologists make a good salary, the real benefits to the field involve the positive impacts on the lives of others.

Major Fields of I/O Psychology

Personnel Psychology

I/O psychologists and human resource management professionals who are involved in **personnel psychology** study and practice in such areas as analyzing jobs, recruiting applicants, selecting employees, determining salary levels, training employees, and evaluating employee performance. Professionals working in these areas choose existing tests or create new tests that can be used to select and promote employees. These tests are then constantly evaluated to ensure that they are both fair and valid.

Personnel psychologists also analyze jobs to obtain a complete picture of what each employee does, often assigning monetary values to each position. After obtaining complete job descriptions, professionals in personnel psychology construct performance-appraisal instruments to evaluate employee performance.

Organizational Psychology

Psychologists involved in **organizational psychology** are concerned with the issues of leadership, job satisfaction, employee motivation, organizational communication, conflict management, organizational change, and group processes within an organization. Organizational psychologists often conduct surveys of employee attitudes to get ideas about what employees believe are an organization's strengths and weaknesses. Usually serving in the role of consultant, an organizational psychologist makes recommendations on ways problem areas can be improved. For example, low job satisfaction might be improved by allowing employees to participate in making certain company decisions, and poor communication might be improved by implementing an employee suggestion system.

Exhibit 1.02 Important events in I/O psychology

Year	Event
1903	Walter Dill Scott publishes *The Theory of Advertising*
1913	Hugo Munsterberg publishes *Psychology and Industrial Efficiency* (German version published in 1910)
1917	*Journal of Applied Psychology* first published
1918	World War I provides I/O psychologists with first opportunity for large-scale employee testing and selection
1921	First Ph.D. in I/O Psychology awarded to Bruce Moore and Merrill Ream at Carnegie Tech
1932	First I/O text written by Morris Viteles
1933	Hawthorne studies published
1937	American Association for Applied Psychology established
1945	Society for Industrial and Business Psychology established as Division 14 of APA with 130 members
1951	Marion Bills elected as first woman president of Division 14
1960	Division 14 renamed Society for Industrial Psychology, membership exceeds 700
1963	Equal Pay Act passed
1964	Civil Rights Act passed
	First issue of *The Industrial-Organizational Psychologist* (TIP) published
1970	Division 14 membership exceeds 1,100
1971	B. F. Skinner publishes *Beyond Freedom and Dignity*
1980	Division 14 membership exceeds 1,800
1982	Division 14 renamed Society for Industrial and Organizational Psychology
1986	Society for Industrial and Organizational Psychology (SIOP) holds first annual national conference separate from APA meeting
1989	Supreme Court sets conservative trend and becomes more "employer friendly"
1990	Americans with Disabilities Act passed
	SIOP membership exceeds 2,500
1991	Civil Rights Act of 1991 passed to overcome 1989 conservative Supreme Court decisions
1997	SIOP celebrates Golden Anniversary at its annual conference in St. Louis
2000	SIOP membership exceeds 3,600

Training and Development

Psychologists interested in training and development examine various methods that can be used to train and develop employees. People within this subfield usually work in a training department of an organization and are involved in such activities as identifying the training needs of an organization, developing training programs, and evaluating training success. Professionals in organization development implement organization-wide programs designed to improve employee performance. Such programs might include team building, restructuring, and employee empowerment.

Human Factors/Ergonomics

Psychologists in the area of **human factors** concentrate on workplace design, human–machine interaction, ergonomics, and physical fatigue and stress. These psychologists frequently work with engineers and other technical professionals to make the workplace safer and more efficient. Sample activities in this subfield include designing the optimal way to draw a map, designing the most comfortable chair, and investigating the optimal work schedule.

Brief History of I/O Psychology

Considering that the field of psychology itself has been around for only a relatively short time (since 1879), it is not surprising that I/O psychology has a relatively short history. Although various experts disagree about the exact starting date of I/O psychology (Exhibit 1.02), it is generally thought to have started either in 1903 when Walter Dill Scott wrote *The Theory of Advertising,* in which psychology was first applied to business, or in 1910 when Hugo Munsterberg wrote *Psychology and Industrial Efficiency,* which was first published in

English in 1913 (Landy, 1997). Regardless of the official starting date, I/O psychology was born in the early 1900s. Pioneers in I/O psychology include Munsterberg, Scott, James Cattell, Walter Bingham, John Watson, Marion Bills, and Lillian Gilbreth (DiClemente & Hantula, 2000; Koppes, 1997; Landy, 1997).

I/O psychology made its first big impact during World War I. Because of the large number of soldiers who had to be assigned to various units within the armed forces, I/O psychologists were employed to test recruits and place them in appropriate positions. The testing was mainly accomplished through the **Army Alpha** and **Army Beta** tests of mental ability. The Alpha test was used for recruits who could read and the Beta test for recruits who could not read. The more intelligent recruits were assigned to officer training, and the less intelligent to the infantry. Interestingly, John Watson, who is better known as a pioneer in behaviorism, served as a major in the U.S. Army in World War I and developed perceptual and motor tests for potential pilots (DiClemente & Hantula, 2000). I/O psychologists, especially Henry Gantt, were responsible for increasing the efficiency with which cargo ships were built, repaired, and loaded (Van De Water, 1997).

Two of the most interesting figures in the early years of I/O psychology are the husband and wife team of Frank Gilbreth and Lillian Moller Gilbreth. The Gilbreths were among the first, if not the first, scientists to improve productivity and reduce fatigue by studying the motions used by workers. Frank began his career as a contractor and became famous for developing improvements in brick laying that reduced the number of motions needed to lay a brick from 18 to 4½. Lillian, the much more educated of the two, received her Ph.D. from Brown University in 1915—a rare achievement for a woman at that time. As a couple, they had 12 children, and the efficiency methods they used to raise their children while having busy careers was the inspiration for the book and movie, *Cheaper by the Dozen*. After Frank's death in 1924 at the age of 55, Lillian continued her consulting with industry as the pressure of the Great Depression forced companies to find ways to reduce costs and be more productive. In 1935, she became a professor of management and engineering at Purdue University, the first woman to hold such a position.

In the 1930s, I/O psychology greatly expanded its scope. Until then, it had been primarily involved in personnel issues such as the selection and placement of employees. However, in the 1930s, when the findings from the famous **Hawthorne studies** were published, psychologists became more involved in the quality of the working environment as well as in the attitudes of employees. The Hawthorne studies, conducted at the Hawthorne plant of the Western Electric Company, demonstrated that employee behavior was complex and that the interpersonal interactions between managers and employees played a tremendous role in employee behavior. The Hawthorne studies were designed to investigate such issues as the effect of lighting levels on employee performance. The real contribution of the studies, however, was that employees changed their behavior and became more productive because they were being studied and received attention from their managers.

The 1960s were characterized by the passage of several major pieces of civil rights legislation, which are discussed in Chapter 3. These laws focused the attention of human resource professionals on developing fair selection techniques. As a result, the need for I/O psychologists greatly increased. The 1960s were also characterized by the use of sensitivity training and T-groups for managers (Carson, Lanier, Carson, & Guidry, 2000).

The 1970s brought great strides in the understanding of many organizational psychology issues that involved employee satisfaction and motivation. The decade also saw the development of many theories about employee behavior in organizations. B. F. Skinner's (1971) book, *Beyond Freedom and Dignity*, resulted in the increased use of behavior modification techniques in organizations.

The 1980s and 1990s brought four major changes to I/O psychology. The first involved an increased use of fairly sophisticated statistical techniques and methods of analysis. This change is evident if one compares journal articles written in the 1960s with those written since 1980. More recent articles use such complex statistics as path analysis, meta-analysis, multivariate analysis of variance (MANOVA), and causal modeling. Prior to the 1970s, simpler statistics such as *t*-tests and analysis of variance were used. (Unless you are wearing a pocket protector or have taken a statistics course, these methods probably are not familiar to you.) This reliance on statistics explains why students enrolled in an I/O psychology doctoral program take at least five statistics courses as part of their education.

A second change concerned a new interest in the application of cognitive psychology to industry. For example, articles written about performance appraisal in the 1970s primarily described and tested new methods for evaluating employee performance. In the 1980s and early 1990s, however, many articles approached the performance-appraisal issue by examining the thought process used by managers when they conduct performance appraisals.

The third change was the increased interest in the effects of work on family life and leisure activities (McCarthy, 1998). Though stress had long been of interest to psychologists, it was during these two decades that employee stress received attention; especially stress resulting in workplace violence.

The final major change in the 1980s and 1990s was that I/O psychologists took a more aggressive approach in developing methods to select employees. In the 1960s and 1970s, the courts were still interpreting the major civil rights acts of the early 1960s, with the result that I/O psychologists took a cautious approach in selecting employees. By the mid-1980s, however, the courts became less strict, and a wider variety of selection instruments was developed and used. Examples of these instruments include cognitive ability tests, personality tests, biodata, and structured interviews. Other changes during the 1980s and 1990s that had

Exhibit **1.03** Employment settings of I/O psychologists

Employment Setting	Highest Degree Obtained	
	M. A.[a]	Ph.D.[b]
Education	0.8	36.4
Private sector	36.7	23.2
Public sector	25.0	6.3
Consulting	27.5	31.9
Other	10.0	2.2

Source: [a] Gonder and Walker (2000); [b] Katkowski and Medsker (2001).

significant effects on I/O psychology included massive organizational downsizing, greater concern for diversity and gender issues, an aging workforce, increased concern about the effects of stress, and the increased emphasis on such organization development interventions as total quality management (TQM), reengineering, and employee empowerment.

In the new millennium, perhaps the greatest influence on I/O psychology is the rapid advance in technology. Many tests and surveys are now administered through computers and the Internet, employers recruit and screen applicants online, employees are being trained using e-learning and distance education, and managers are holding meetings in cyberspace rather than in person.

Employment of I/O Psychologists

Throughout this text, you will find Employment Profiles, which look at specific jobs done by people with degrees in I/O psychology. However, it is useful to examine some of the broad areas in which I/O psychologists work as well. As shown in Exhibit 1.03, the greatest number of Ph.D. I/O psychologists work at universities, followed by consulting firms and private industry (Katkowski & Medsker, 2001). Also, master's level I/O graduates have a different employment profile, with most master's level graduates working in industry (Ekeberg, Switzer, & Siegfried, 1991; Gonder & Walker, 2000; Rentsch, Lowenberg, Barnes-Farrell, & Menard, 1997). Compared to Ph.D.'s, master's level graduates are more often employed as human resource generalists, data analysts, trainers, and compensation analysts and less often as academicians (Schippman, Schmitt, & Hawthorne, 1992).

I/O professionals who work in industrial settings are involved in a wide range of activities including training, research, work conditions, performance appraisal, productivity enhancement, test construction, test validation, job analysis, employee motivation, recruiting, and personnel selection (Cederbloom, Pence, & Johnson, 1984; Schippman et al., 1992). Those employed by state and local governments are usually involved in job analysis and test construction but also perform other human resource–related functions.

A master's degree is usually required to work in the field of I/O psychology. As of 2000, the median salary was $67,000 for master's level positions and $90,000 for doctoral level positions (Katkowski & Medsker, 2001). The top 10% of I/O psychologists with doctoral degrees earned more than $200,000! Current information about I/O salaries can be found on the Internet at www.siop.org.

Educational Requirements and Types of Programs

To obtain reasonable employment in I/O psychology, a master's degree is required for most jobs and a Ph.D. for some. Obtaining a master's takes between 1 and 2 years after the completion of the bachelor's degree. Admissions requirements vary greatly from school to school, but an undergraduate grade point average (GPA) of at least 3.0 and a score of 1,000 on the **Graduate Record Exam (GRE)**—the graduate school version of the Scholastic Aptitude Test, or SAT, that you took after high school—are not uncommon (Koppes, 1991). Advice for getting into graduate school can be found in Exhibit 1.04.

Types of Graduate Programs

Master's degree programs come in two varieties: those that are part of a Ph.D. program and terminal master's degree programs. Schools with **terminal master's degree programs** do not have Ph.D. programs. Thus, a master's degree is the highest that can be earned at such a school. Schools with doctoral programs have both the master's degree and the Ph.D. Terminal programs are best suited for students wanting an applied human resource position in an organization. These programs usually have less stringent entrance requirements and provide more financial aid and individual attention to master's students than do Ph.D. programs. Doctoral programs, on the other hand, usually have

Exhibit **1.04** Getting into graduate school

This section may seem out of place in an I/O textbook, but the information contained here is often not learned by students until it is too late. This information can be applied to fields other than I/O psychology.

Although different graduate programs often emphasize different entrance requirements, most place some weight on GRE scores, GPA, letters of recommendation, and previous research or professional experience. With this in mind, following the advice below should increase your chances of being selected for a graduate program.

1. Take extra mathematics and English courses. The GRE consists of four parts: quantitative, verbal, analytic, and psychology. The quantitative portion requires knowledge of algebra, geometry, and some trigonometry. Thus, often the only way to do well on this section is to take extra courses in these subjects. Taking English courses in reading comprehension and vocabulary will help your score on the verbal section.

It is important to understand that the GRE is a test of knowledge, not intelligence. Thus, with extra coursework, you can improve your scores. Remember, it will have been a long time since you took these courses in high school.

2. Take at least one psychology course in each of the areas of statistics, experimental methods, abnormal psychology, personality, social psychology, physiological psychology, learning, perception, and cognitive psychology; each area is covered in the GRE's psychology portion. Although courses in sex and group dynamics are interesting and will help you in the future, they will not help you to score well on the GRE.

3. Make sure that you have at least three people who can write good letters of recommendation for you. Getting an A in a professor's class is not enough to expect a good letter that will carry weight with the admissions committee. Let the

professors get to know you as both student and person. Talk with different professors and become involved with their research; not only will this allow you to have research of your own to show prospective graduate programs, but also it will result in better and more complete letters of recommendation.

4. Get involved! Conduct independent research projects, join professional clubs, get a summer job. Anything to demonstrate your desire to be a professional.

5. Study for your GRE and get a good night's sleep before you take the test. You may not be able to learn much new material by studying, but you can at least refresh your memory about material that you have already learned but may have forgotten. Remember that the GRE will determine your future and is probably the most important test that you will ever take. Treat it as such and prepare.

more well-known faculty members as well as better facilities and research funding. Doctoral programs are best suited for students who eventually want to teach, do research, or consult.

Most master's programs require about 40 hours of graduate coursework to complete (Koppes, 1991). Although 15 to 18 hours is considered a full undergraduate semester load, 9 to 12 hours is considered a full graduate load. In addition to coursework, many programs require a student to complete a thesis, which is usually an original research work created and conducted by the student. The thesis is completed in the second year of graduate school.

Most programs also allow the student to complete an **internship** or **practicum** with a local organization (Lowe, 1993). These internship requirements vary by program. For example, at some universities students work 10 hours per week at an organization during their last semester of graduate school, at others students do their internships in the summer between their first and second year, and at still others students take a semester off to work full time with an organization.

Finally, most programs require a student to pass a comprehensive oral or written examination before graduation (Lowe, 1993). These exams usually are taken during the final semester and cover material from all of the courses taken during the graduate program. As you can see, completing a master's degree program in I/O psychology is tough, but it can lead to excellent employment and professional benefits. Obtaining a Ph.D. is more difficult than obtaining a master's, with the typical doctoral program taking 5 years to complete (Rentsch et al., 1997). Common entrance requirements are a 3.5 GPA and a GRE score of 1,200 (Lowe, 1993).

The first 2 years of a doctoral program involve taking a wide variety of courses in psychology. In most programs, the student does not concentrate on I/O courses until the third and fourth years. In addition to a thesis, a student working toward a Ph.D. must complete a **dissertation.** No formal definition distinguishes a thesis from a dissertation, but the major differences are that the dissertation is broader in scope, longer, and requires more original and independent effort than the thesis (Riddle & Foster, 1997). Doctoral programs also involve a series of comprehensive exams that are similar to, but more extensive than, the exams taken in a master's program. A complete list of I/O psychology graduate programs can be found in Appendixes A and B at the end of this chapter. Information on programs is available at the Society for Industrial and Organizational Psychology (SIOP) home page at www.siop.org.

Research in I/O Psychology

Now that you have a good idea about the field of I/O psychology, it is time to learn the essentials of one of the foundations of the upcoming chapters: research. This section does not provide an in-depth discussion of research techniques and procedures, but it gives you enough information so you can understand the method used when a study is mentioned in the text.

Why Conduct Research?

Though most of you will probably not go on to careers as researchers, understanding research and statistics is important for several reasons.

Answering Questions and Making Decisions

As mentioned earlier in the chapter, one of the characteristics of I/O psychology is its extensive use of research and statistics. Although there are many reasons for this reliance on research, the most important is that research ultimately saves organizations money. To many of you, this last statement may seem a bit insensitive. Keep in mind, however, that for most organizations, the most important thing is the bottom line. If I/O psychologists are not able to save the company considerably more money than it pays for their salary and expenses, they will be without a job.

These monetary savings can result from many factors, including increased employee satisfaction, increased productivity, and fewer accidents. Perhaps an excellent example of how research can save organizations money involves the employment interview. For years, many organizations relied on the employment interview as the main method for selecting employees (most still do). But researchers have shown that the unstructured employment interview is not the best predictor of future behavior on the job (Schmidt & Hunter, 1998). Thus, without research, an organization might still be spending money on a method that actually lowers its profits rather than raises them.

Research and Everyday Life

Research confronts us on an almost daily basis, both at home and on the job. As a student, you will encounter research throughout this and other courses. As a professional, you will receive advertisements and sales pitches containing references to research supporting a particular product. At home, you read the results of political polls in the newspaper and are bombarded with TV commercials trumpeting the results of the *Pepsi Challenge* or claiming that "9 out of 10 dentists" recommend a product. Understanding research helps you to critically listen and analyze results of these studies to make more intelligent decisions. After all, you would hate to buy a soft drink based on the results of poorly conducted research!

When I was an undergraduate at Pepperdine University in Malibu, California (yes, the surf was always up), the students attempted to hold the first dance ever at the university. Until this point, dancing had been prohibited, and the students wanted the prohibition removed. The dance proposal came under heavy attack by the church sponsoring the university as well as by several administrators. An opponent of the dance proposal wrote a letter to the school newspaper citing research "that in a study of Catholic confessionals, nine out of ten fallen women had their downfall on the dance floor."

When confronted with this devastating piece of research, we pulled out our trusty experimental psychology books and, using our finely honed research skills, challenged the validity of the study on such grounds as the poorly defined dependent variable (what is a fallen woman?), the sample size (how many women fell?), and the question of whether the study actually existed (there is no way the Catholic Church would allow a study of confessionals). After our impressive critique, the administration gave in; we were allowed to hold our dance off campus but to advertise it on campus. If you consider allowing 200 students with no rhythm to dance a victory, then our superior knowledge of research made us victors.

A crazy story? Sure. But the fact that intelligent people actually used such research to support their point underscores the importance of understanding research.

Common Sense Is Often Wrong

Often, there is a temptation not to conduct research because the answer to a question is "common sense." Unfortunately, common sense is not so common and is often wrong. Until the end of the 15th century, it was common sense that the world was flat and that a person sailing toward the horizon would fall off the earth. Until late in this century, common sense said that women employees could not perform as well as men. In other words, many of our commonsense policies have been, and continue to be, wrong.

As a more recent example, imagine taking a multiple-choice test. After finishing the test, you go back and read question 32 but can't decide if you should stick with your original response of "b" or change it to "c." What would you do? Most students respond with what they have always been told: *Stick with your first answer*. If you stuck with this piece of common advice, you probably would miss the question. Contrary to common sense, five studies investigating this question all concluded that 70% of the time an answer will be changed from wrong to right. Another victory for research over common sense!

Exhibit **1.05** Hypothesis example 1

Does all this noise affect my employees' performance?	High levels of noise will increase the number of errors made in assembling electronic components	Noise causes a distraction making it difficult to concentrate.
Idea or question	*Hypothesis or prediction*	*Theory or explanation*
	What will happen	**Why it will happen**

Considerations in Conducting Research

Ideas, Hypotheses, and Theories

The first step in conducting research is to decide *what to research*. Though the majority of I/O psychology research is conducted to test the accuracy of theories, many research ideas stem from a person starting a sentence with "I wonder." For example, a manager might say, "I wonder why some of my employees can't get to work on time"; an employee might say, "I wonder if I could assemble more parts if my chair were higher"; or a supervisor might ask, "I wonder which of my employees is the best to promote." All three seem to be ordinary questions, but each is just as valid and important in research as those asked by a professor in a university. Thus, everyone is a researcher at heart, and conducting some form of research to answer a question will undoubtedly lead to a better answer than could be obtained by guesswork alone.

Once a question has been asked, the next step is to form a **hypothesis**—an educated prediction about the answer to a question. This prediction is usually based on a **theory**, previous research, or logic. For example, as shown in Exhibit 1.05, a researcher is curious about the effect of noise on employee performance (the question) and believes high levels of noise will result in decreased performance (the hypothesis). The prediction is based on the theory that distracting events reduce the ability to concentrate. To see if the hypothesis is correct, the researcher would need to conduct a study.

If the results support the hypothesis, it becomes important to test the theory. In psychology, there are often competing theories that predict the same outcome, but for different reasons. Take the situation depicted in Exhibit 1.06 as an example. An I/O psychologist wants to know which method of recruiting employees is best. She predicts that employee referrals will result in longer employee tenure (employees staying with the company) than will the other recruitment methods. Though she is sure about her hypothesis, she is not sure about the reason as there are four possible theories or explanations for her hypothesis:

1. Applicants referred by a current employee will stay with the company longer because they were given an accurate picture of the job and the company by the person telling them about the job (realistic job preview theory).

2. The personalities of applicants using employee referrals are different from the personalities of applicants using other methods to find jobs (differential recruitment source theory).

3. Friends have similar personalities; thus, if one person has the type of personality that makes her want to stay with her current job, her friend should also like the job in question (personality similarity theory).

4. Employees who know someone in a workplace are more quickly absorbed into the information system, receive coaching, and have their social needs met (socialization theory).

Thus, even though a study might support a hypothesis, it is still important to determine *why* the hypothesis is true. In this example, it would be necessary to conduct further studies to determine which of the four theories, if any, best explains the results. This is important because our ability to understand and use the best theory allows us to develop new methods to improve productivity in the workplace. In this example, if the first theory were true, we would give every applicant a realistic job preview. If the third theory were true, we would encourage current successful employees to recruit their friends.

At times, forming a hypothesis can be difficult. In some cases, no previous research has been conducted or theory proposed that would suggest a clear hypothesis about the answer to a question. For example, a student of mine wanted to see if personality was related to handwriting neatness. She couldn't find any research on handwriting neatness much less on the relationship between personality and handwriting. There were also no theories or logical reasons to predict what types of personalities would write a particular way. So she conducted an *exploratory study* without a hypothesis—a practice that is not uncommon but is generally frowned on by scientists.

In other cases, it is difficult to form a hypothesis because a prediction could go either way. For example, another of my students was curious about whether a recommendation letter written by an important person (such as a senator) would be more influential than one

Exhibit 1.06 | Hypothesis example 2

	What employee recruitment source is best?	Employee referrals will result in employees who stay with the company longer than will the other recruitment methods.	1. Realistic job preview theory 2. Differential source theory 3. Personality similarity theory 4. Socialization theory
	Idea or question	**Hypothesis or prediction**	**Theory or explanation**
		What will happen	**Why it will happen**

written by a professor (Hey, I thought professors were important!). She had trouble forming a hypothesis because there were as many reasons that a reference by an important person would be more influential as there were reasons that such a reference would be less influential.

At times, a hypothesis may not be supported by a study even though the logic and theory behind it are correct. Often, a poor research design is the culprit. Other times, it is because the topic is more complicated than originally thought. When studying a topic, psychologists wish for simple answers. Unfortunately, most situations in life are not simple. For example, psychologists have been trying for years to understand aggression and violence. They have postulated many theories for why people are violent: genetics, brain abnormalities, learning, and frustration, to name a few. Some studies support these reasons, but others don't. Why the lack of consistency? Because no one theory by itself is the answer. Each of the theories is partially true in that each explains violence in certain people under certain circumstances. Furthermore, violent behavior may be the result of a cumulation of several factors, each of which by itself will not result in violence.

Confused? I hope not. The purpose of the preceding discussion is to show you the complexity of research. At times, many theories may explain a particular behavior. At other times, behavior can be predicted but the reason for the behavior may not be known. At still other times, we have questions but can't predict what the answer will be. This complexity of life is what makes research fun.

Literature Reviews

Once a research idea has been created, the next step is to search the literature for similar research. This search is important because if the question you are interested in answering has already been researched in 20 studies, it is probably not necessary for you to conduct a new study. As a graduate student, it took me a while to realize that most of my research ideas that were "so brilliant no one else could have thought of them" had already been conducted several times over. I guess the

moral of this story is don't forget about your university library, even after you have finished school. I would venture to say that most of the questions you will have can be answered by a quick trip to the library; it is not necessary, or smart, to constantly reinvent the wheel.

Even if your specific question has not been researched before, the probability is high that similar research has been conducted. This research is useful even though it does not directly answer your question, because it can provide some good ideas on how to conduct your study.

Literature reviews can be conducted in many ways, the most common of which are using such subject indexes as PsycINFO and InfoTrac® College Edition, browsing through journals, searching the reference sections of related articles, and asking other researchers (Tubré, Bly, Edwards, Pritchard, & Simoneaux, 2001).

When reviewing the literature, you are likely to encounter four types of periodicals: journals, bridge publications, trade magazines (listed in Exhibit 1.07), and magazines. **Journals** consist of articles written by researchers directly reporting the results of a study. Journals can be difficult to read (and boring) but are the best source of unbiased and accurate information about a topic. The leading journals in I/O psychology are the *Journal of Applied Psychology, Personnel Psychology, Academy of Management Journal, Academy of Management Review*, and *Organizational Behavior and Human Decision Processes* (Zickar & Highhouse, 2001). Fortunately, many journals are available online, making them much easier to obtain.

Bridge publications are designed to "bridge the gap" between academia and the applied world. Articles in these publications are usually written by professors about a topic of interest to practitioners, but they are not as formal nor as statistically complex as articles in journals. Examples of bridge publications are *Academy of Management Executive, Harvard Business Review*, and *Organizational Dynamics*.

Trade magazines contain articles usually written by professional writers who have developed expertise in a given field. The main audience for trade magazines is practitioners in the field. Trade magazines present the research on a topic in an easy to understand

Popular reading in I/O psychology.

format; however, the articles in these publications do not cover all the research on a topic and can be somewhat biased. *HR Magazine* and *Training* are examples of I/O-related trade magazines.

You are already familiar with **magazines** such as *People*, *Time*, and *Cat Fancy*. These periodicals are designed to entertain as well as inform. Magazines are good sources of ideas but terrible sources to use in support of a scientific hypothesis. Magazine articles are written by professional writers, many of whom do not have training in, and thus have little expertise in, the topic on which they are writing. As a result, the "scientific" information in magazines is often wrong.

An increasingly popular source of information is the Internet. As most of you have already discovered, the Internet contains a wealth of information on just about every topic. As useful as the Internet is, a word of caution is in order. There is no review of information placed on the Internet to ensure that it is accurate. For example, I recently was involved with a project in which we were trying to profile the people who were setting church fires. Because our first step was to get a list of church fires, we searched the Internet and found three church-burning home pages. One was from *USA Today* and had a rather complete listing of church burnings, one was from a left-wing group, and the other was from a right-wing group. As you can imagine, the left- and right-wing pages only listed churches that confirmed their hypotheses about why the churches were burned. Had we used only one of the home pages, we would have made an inaccurate profile.

The Location Where the Study Will Be Conducted

Once a research idea has been created and a hypothesis formed, you must decide whether to conduct the study in the laboratory or in the field.

Laboratory Research. Often when one hears the word *research*, the first thing that comes to mind is an experimenter in a white coat running subjects in a basement laboratory. Few experimenters actually wear white coats, but 29% of I/O psychology research *is* conducted in a laboratory (Dipboye, 1990). Usually, this is done at a university, but research also is conducted by such organizations as AT&T, Office of Personnel Management, and Microsoft.

One disadvantage of laboratory research is **external validity,** or **generalizability** of results to organizations in the "real world." An example of this issue involves research about employee selection methods. It is not uncommon in such research for subjects to view a resume or a videotape of an interview and make a judgment about a hypothetical applicant. The problem: Is the situation similar enough to actual employment decisions made in the real world, or is the laboratory environment so controlled and hypothetical that the results will not generalize? Although the answers to these questions have not been resolved, research often is conducted in laboratories because researchers can control many variables that are not of interest in the study.

Field Research. Another location for research is away from the laboratory and out in the "field," which could be the assembly line of an automotive plant, the secretarial pool of a large insurance company, or the interviewing room at a personnel agency. **Field research** has a problem opposite to that of laboratory research. What field research obviously gains in external validity it loses in control of extraneous variables that are not of interest to the researcher (*internal validity*).

Does the location of a study make a difference? It can. A meta-analysis by Sadri and Robertson (1993) found that self-efficacy predicts performance in laboratory

Exhibit **1.07** List of I/O psychology periodicals

Journal

Academy of Management Journal

Academy of Management Review

Administrative Science Quarterly

Applied Ergonomics

Applied H.R.M. Research

Applied Psychological Measurement

Applied Psychology: An International Review

Ergonomics

Human Factors

Human Performance

International Journal of Selection and Assessment

Journal of Applied Psychology

Journal of Applied Social Psychology

Journal of Business and Psychology

Journal of Consulting Psychology: Practice & Research

Journal of Management

Journal of Occupational and Organizational Psychology

Journal of Organizational Behavior

Journal of Vocational Behavior

Organizational Behavior and Human Decision Processes

Personnel Psychology

Public Personnel Management

Bridge Publications

Academy of Management Executive

Harvard Business Review

Organizational Dynamics

Trade Magazines

HR Magazine

Personnel

Personnel Journal

Training

Training & Development

studies more than in field studies; Miller and Monge (1986) found a stronger relationship between participation and job satisfaction in field studies than in laboratory studies; and Mullen and Copper (1994) found that group cohesion was related to performance more in field studies of real groups than in laboratory studies of groups created for the experiment.

Field research also provides researchers with an ethical dilemma. Psychologists require that subjects participate in studies of their own free will—a concept called **informed consent**. In laboratory studies, informed consent is seldom an issue because potential subjects are told the nature and purpose of a study, their right to decline participation or withdraw from participation, the risks and benefits of participating, limits of confidentiality, and who they can contact with questions (Smith, 2003). They are then asked to sign an informed consent form indicating they understand their rights as a subject and have chosen to voluntarily participate. In field studies, however, obtaining informed consent cannot only be difficult but can change the way people behave.

For example, suppose we think making a supervisor's office more pleasant looking will increase the number of employees who visit the supervisor's office. After decorating five supervisors' offices with plants and paintings and making five other supervisors' offices look messy and cold, we use a video camera to record the number of office visitors. Would the results of our study be affected if we told our employees that they were going to be part of a study? Probably so.

On the basis of our ethical guidelines, informed consent can be waived only when the research involves minimal risk to the participants, the waiver will not adversely affect the rights of the participants, and the research could not be carried out without the waiver (Ilgen & Bell, 2001a).

When studies involve negative consequences for a subject, as would be the case if we subjected employees to intense heat to study the effects of temperature, informed consent can only be waived if the importance of the study outweighs the negative consequences. Universities have **Institutional Review Boards** to monitor research to ensure ethical treatment of research participants. One area to which these review boards pay close attention is *confidentiality*. Because the data collected in research can be of a sensitive nature (e.g., performance ratings, salaries, test scores), researchers ensure confidentiality by using subject ID numbers rather than names and by avoiding discussion of individual participants. Interestingly, authors of studies conducted in organizations submitted their research plans to institutional review boards only 44% of the time (Ilgen & Bell, 2001b).

The Research Method to Be Used

After deciding the location for the research, the researcher must determine which type of research method to use. The choices include experiments, quasi-experiments, archival research, observations, surveys, and meta-analyses.

Exhibit 1.08 Example of an experimental design

Received Customer-Service Training in September	Average Customer Sales Per Employee		
	August	October	Change
Yes	$3,200	$4,700	$1,500
No	$3,100	$3,500	$400

Experiments. As you might recall from your general psychology course, the experimental method is the most powerful of all research methods because it is the only method that can determine **cause-and-effect relationships.** Thus, if it is important to know whether one variable produces or causes another variable to change, then the **experiment** is the only method that should be used.

Two characteristics define an experiment: **manipulation** of one or more independent variables, and random assignment of subjects to experimental and control conditions. If either of these characteristics is missing, a research project cannot be called an experiment; instead, it is called a *quasi-experiment*, a *study*, a *survey*, or an *investigation*.

In an experiment, the researcher intentionally manipulates one or more aspects of the question of interest, called the **independent variable,** and measures the changes that occur as a result of that manipulation, called the **dependent variable.** For example, as shown in Exhibit 1.08, a researcher might randomly assign 100 employees to receive customer service training and 100 employees to receive no training. Following the training program, the researcher looks at the change in customer spending. In this example, training is the independent variable (what was manipulated) and customer spending is the dependent variable (what was expected to change as a result of the independent variable). The employees who received the training are collectively called the **experimental group**, and the employees who did not receive the training are collectively called the **control group.**

As another example, suppose we were interested in finding out whether wearing a suit to an interview is better for men than wearing a coat and slacks. We could study this issue by observing job applicants at a specific company and comparing the interview scores of people with suits with those of people wearing coats and slacks. We might find that the better-dressed applicants received higher scores, but we could not conclude that wearing a suit *caused* the higher scores; something other than the suit may be at work. Perhaps applicants who own suits are more assertive than other applicants; it then might have been assertiveness and not dress style that led to the higher interview scores.

If we want to determine that dress style affects interview scores, we have to manipulate the variable of interest and hold all other variables as constant as possible. How could we turn this into an experiment? Let

us take 100 people and give 50 of them suits to wear and the other 50 sports coats and slacks. Each subject then goes through an interview with a human resource director. Afterward, we compare the interview scores of our two groups. In this case, the independent variable is the type of dress, and the dependent variable is the interview score.

Even though this particular research design is not very sophisticated and has some problems (see if you can spot them), the fact that we manipulated the applicant's dress style gives us greater confidence that dress style was the cause of higher interview scores. Even though the results of experiments provide more confidence regarding cause-and-effect relationships, ethical and practical considerations do not always make experimental designs possible.

Suppose we wish to study the effect of loud noise on worker performance. To make this an experimental design, we could have 50 subjects work on an assembly line while being subjected to very loud noise and 50 subjects work on an assembly line with no noise. Two months later we compare the productivity of the two groups. But what is wrong with this study? In addition to having lower productivity, the high-noise group now has poorer hearing—not a very ethical-sounding experiment (yes, the pun *was* intended).

Quasi-experiments. Even though researchers prefer to use an experiment, it is not always possible. **Quasi-experiments** are then used. As an example, let's go back to our noise study. Because we cannot manipulate the level of noise, we will instead test the noise level of 100 manufacturing plants and compare the average productivity of plants with lower noise levels with that of plants with higher noise levels. As you can easily see, this is not as good a research design as the unethical experiment created earlier. There are too many variables other than noise that could account for any differences found in productivity; however, given the circumstances, it still provides more information than we had before the study.

Quasi-experiments are often used to evaluate the results of a new program implemented by an organization. For example, an organization that had instituted a child care center wanted to see whether the center had any effect on employee absenteeism. To find the answer, the organization compared absenteeism levels

Exhibit 1.09		Why nonexperimental studies are difficult to interpret: The child care center	

Date	Absenteeism	External Factor	Internal Factor
1/00	2.8%		
2/00	3.1		
3/00	4.7	Unemployment rate at 4.1%	
4/00	4.7		
5/00	4.8		
6/00	6.7	Main highway closed	
7/00	6.5		
8/00	4.9	Highway reopens	
9/00	4.5		
10/00	4.4		
11/00	8.7	Terrible snowstorm	
12/00	5.3		
1/01	5.3		Child care center started
2/01	5.2		
3/01	5.1		Flextime program started
4/01	2.0	Local unemployment rate hits 9.3%	
5/01	2.0		
6/01	2.0		
7/01	1.8		Wellness program started
8/01	1.8		
9/01	2.0		New attendance policy
10/01	2.1		
11/01	4.0	Mild weather	
12/01	4.2	Mild weather	

Note: Absenteeism rate in 2000 before child care center = 5.09%; rate in 2001 after child care center = 3.01%

from the year before the center was introduced with the absenteeism levels for the year following the implementation; the organization found that both absenteeism and turnover had decreased.

Although it is tempting to conclude that the child care center was a success, such a conclusion would not be prudent. Many other variables might have caused the reduction. As shown in Exhibit 1.09, the organization implemented several other progressive programs during the same period. Thus, the decrease in absenteeism and turnover could have been the result of other programs or some combination of programs. Furthermore, the economy changed and jobs became more difficult to obtain. Workers may have reduced their absentee rates out of fear of being fired, and turnover may have been reduced because employees realized few jobs were available. In addition, the weather improved in the second year, which meant workers were rarely unable to get to work.

Taken by itself, we would certainly not want to bet the mortgage on the results of our quasi-experiment.

But if 10 other researchers conduct separate quasi-experiments to study the same question and find similar results, we might feel confident enough to make changes or reach conclusions based on the available research evidence.

Archival Research. Another research method that is commonly used in I/O psychology is **archival research.** Archival research involves using previously collected data or records to answer a research question. For example, if we want to know what distinguishes good workers from poor workers, we could look in the personnel files to see whether the backgrounds of good workers have common characteristics not shared by poor workers. Or, if we want to see if people on the night shift had more turnover than people on the day shift, we could get information on shift and turnover from the company records. Archival research has many nice features such as being unobtrusive and being relatively inexpensive, but it also has severe drawbacks.

Records in files are not always accurate, and they are not always kept up to date. Furthermore, the type of data needed by a researcher may not be in the archives because the data were never recorded in the first place.

As an undergraduate (this was before the big dance), I was involved with an archival study designed to determine why some students in an executive Master of Business Administration (M.B.A.) program dropped out while others completed their coursework. What was supposed to be an easy job of getting records from a few files turned into a nightmare. The records of more than 300 students were scattered in storage rooms in three locations in southern California and were not filed in any order. Furthermore, almost every student had at least one important item missing from his or her file. Needless to say, these problems kept the results of the study from being as accurate as desired. Now, however, the computerization of information has greatly increased the potential for archival research.

Surveys. Another method of conducting research is to *ask* people their opinion on some topic. Surveys might ask employees about their attitudes toward the organization, human resource directors about their opinions regarding the best recruitment method, or managers about the success of their child care centers.

Survey Method. Surveys can be conducted by mail, personal interviews, phone, fax, email, and magazines. The method chosen depends on such factors as sample size, budget, amount of time available to conduct the study, and need for a representative sample. For example, mail surveys are less expensive and time-consuming than personal interviews but result in lower response rates and, at times, lower-quality answers. Email surveys are inexpensive but are limited to people who have email (not a representative sample), are more subject to size and format restrictions, and result in lower response rates (Kittleson, 1995) than mail surveys. Surveys contained in magazines and professional publications are common (e.g., *HR Magazine, Training and Development Journal*), but as with email, they may not result in a representative sample.

The importance of the survey method used cannot be overstated. For example, in 1998 *The Roanoke Times and World News* conducted a survey of the top motion pictures in history. People who mailed in their votes chose *Gone With the Wind, The Sound of Music, The Wizard of Oz, It's a Wonderful Life,* and *To Kill a Mockingbird* as their top five; people who responded by email chose *Gone With the Wind, Star Wars, Schindler's List, The Wizard of Oz,* and *The Shawshank Redemption.*

Another example of differences in survey samples occurred in February 1998. Nykesha Sales was one point short of setting the University of Connecticut career scoring record in women's basketball when she ruptured an Achilles' tendon, an injury that ended her season. Her coach arranged a deal with their next opponent (Villanova) to allow Sales to score an uncontested basket so that she could break the record. In the days after the Villanova game, the media debated whether allowing Sales to score was a class act designed to honor a great player or a strike at the integrity of the game. In separate surveys, 60% of respondents to ESPN's Internet site thought the gesture was a class act compared to only 47% of the respondents to *USA Today's* Internet site (Patrick, 1998).

A multinational study by Church (2001) found some interesting results regarding survey methods. Employees from the United States, Japan, and France preferred automated phone response technology whereas employees in Germany, Italy, and the United Kingdom preferred the traditional paper-and-pencil method. Employees completing the survey online were more likely to leave items blank than were employees using a paper-and-pencil format.

A high response rate is essential for trust to be placed in survey results. Response rates for a survey mailing can be increased by providing either monetary or non-monetary incentives; making the incentive contingent on returning the survey does not greatly improve response rates (Church, 1993). Response rates can also be increased by making several contacts with respondents; providing a stamped, return envelope; and personalizing the survey request letter (Yammarino, Skinner, & Childers, 1991).

Survey Questions. Well-designed survey questions are easy to understand, use simple language, do not ask about hypothetical situations, and are relatively short in length (Converse & Presser, 1986). Extreme care must be taken in choosing the words used in each question (Schwarz, 1999). An excellent example of this comes from the polls conducted during the impeachment of former president Bill Clinton. First, accurate poll results were hindered by the fact that nearly one third of adults didn't understand the word "impeachment" (Morin, 1999). Second, the wording of the different polls resulted in substantially different results. Consider the following examples provided by Morin (1999):

- Should Clinton resign if he is impeached or should he *fight the charges* in the Senate?
- Should Clinton resign if he is impeached or should he *remain in office to stand trial* in the Senate?

In the first question, 59% said that Clinton should resign. For the second question, only 43% said he should resign.

Accuracy of Responses. A final issue involving surveys is the extent to which responses to the survey questions are accurate. This issue is especially important when asking about sensitive or controversial issues. That is, if I ask if you "believe males and females are equally qualified to be managers," would you tell the truth if you thought men were better qualified? Would people honestly respond to questions about their former drug use, poor performance at work, or unethical behavior? Probably not. But they do seem to be accurate when reporting such things as height and body weight (Imrhan, Imrhan, & Hart, 1996). A good example of people not being truthful in surveys occurred when researchers asked 1,000 adults if they regularly washed their hands after using a public restroom; 94% said yes. However, when researchers observed people in restrooms, less than 70% washed their hands (Mattox, 1997).

Inaccurately responding to survey questions is not always an intentional attempt to be dishonest. Instead, inaccurate responses can be the result of a person not actually knowing the correct answer to a question. For example, an employee might respond to a question about attendance by stating she has missed 3 days of work in the past year when in fact she missed 5 days. Was she lying, or just mistaken about her attendance record?

Meta-Analysis. The newest research method, **meta-analysis**, is a statistical method of reaching conclusions based on previous research. Prior to meta-analysis, a researcher interested in reviewing the literature on a topic would read all of the available research and then make a rather subjective conclusion based on the articles. With meta-analysis, the researcher goes through each article, determines the **effect size** for each article, and then finds a statistical average of effect sizes across all articles. A meta-analysis results in one number, called the **mean effect size**, which indicates the effectiveness of some variable.

Correlation coefficients (r) are used as the effect size when researchers are interested in the *relationship* between two variables, and the majority of studies use correlation as their statistical test. Examples include studies looking at the relationship between personality and job performance, integrity test scores and employee theft, or the relationship between job satisfaction and performance.

A difference score (d) is used as the effect size when researchers are looking at the *difference* between two groups. Examples are studies looking at the effectiveness of a training method, the effect of goal setting, or the effects of shift work. Effect sizes can be interpreted in two ways: by comparing them to norms or directly applying them to a particular situation. When using norms, effect sizes (d) less than .40 are considered to be small, those between .40 and .80 are moderate, and those higher than .80 are considered large (Cohen, 1988). Of course, these numbers are "rules of thumb"; the actual **practical significance** of an effect size depends on many factors—formulas are available to be more precise. The average effect size for an organizational intervention is .44 (Guzzo, Jette, & Katzell, 1985).

When directly applying an effect size to a particular situation, you need to know the standard deviation of the variable in question. This standard deviation is then multiplied by the effect size from the meta-analysis to yield a meaningful score. Confused? Perhaps an example would help.

Suppose employees at a John Deere manufacturing plant miss an average of 9.5 days of work per year with a standard deviation of 3.6 days. John Deere is considering a new incentive system to improve attendance that a meta-analysis indicates has an effect size of .32 in reducing absenteeism. What can John Deere expect to gain from this incentive system? By multiplying their absenteeism standard deviation (3.6 days) by the effect size from the meta-analysis (.32), John Deere can expect the incentive system to reduce absenteeism by an average of 1.15 days per employee ($3.6 \times .32 = 1.15$). If the attendance data for General Motors were an average of 10.4 days per year missed with a standard deviation of 5.6, it could expect an annual reduction in absenteeism of 1.79 days per employee ($5.6 \times .32 = 1.79$). John Deere and General Motors would each have to decide if the predicted reduction in savings is worth the cost of the incentive system.

A complete discussion of meta-analysis is beyond the scope of this book and probably beyond your interest as well. It is important, however, that you be able to interpret the outcomes of meta-analyses because they are used in this text and are the current standard when reviewing previous research. A more in-depth discussion of meta-analysis can be found on the CD-ROM accompanying this text.

To help you understand the various research designs you just learned about, complete Exercise 1–1 at the end of this chapter.

Sample

Decisions also must be made regarding the size, composition, and method of selecting the subjects who will serve as the sample in a study. Although it is nice to have a large sample for any research study, a large sample size is not necessary if the experimenter can choose a random sample and control for many of the extraneous variables. In fact, properly conducted surveys need only about 1,000 participants to generalize survey results to the entire U.S. population (Deane, 1999).

The method of selecting the sample is certainly dependent on the nature of the organization. A small organization will probably be forced to use all of its employees, which means the sample will be small but highly representative of the intended population. For economical and practical reasons, a large organization will select only certain employees to participate in a study rather than use the entire workforce. The problem then becomes one of which employees will participate.

If the study involves a questionnaire, it is no problem to randomly select a desired number of employees and have them complete the survey. If, however, the study is more elaborate, such as investigating the effects of lighting on performance, it would be difficult to randomly select employees. That is, it would not be practical to have one employee work under high levels of light while the person next to her was uninvolved with the experiment. If we decide to have one plant work with high levels of light and another with lower levels, what we gain in practicality we lose in randomness and control. So we try to strike a balance between practicality and experimental rigor.

To increase experimental rigor and decrease the costs of conducting research, many studies are conducted at universities using students as subjects rather than employees. In fact, college students serve as subjects in 87% of all published I/O research (Gordon, Slade, & Schmitt, 1986). This use of students has led to considerable debate regarding the generalizability of university research: That is, do students behave in the same fashion as employees? Some authors (e.g., Sears, 1986) point out that, compared to adults, college students are younger, more educated, and more egocentric; possess a less formulated sense of self; and have a stronger need for peer approval. Because of these differences, it makes sense that students would behave differently than adults in the working world.

Research on this issue, however, is mixed. Some researchers have found differences between student subjects and professional subjects, but others have not (Bordens & Abbott, 2002). In general, the preponderance of research indicates that college student samples behave differently than do real world or nonacademic samples (Barr & Hitt, 1986; Burnett & Dunne, 1986; Gordon et al., 1986; Jawahar & Williams, 1997). Furthermore, some research suggests that results will differ based on the *major* of the college sample. For example, both Staw and Ross (1985) and Forst (1987) found that business students rated managers differently than did psychology students. These findings suggest that, in certain cases, using students for research subjects may not generalize to the real world.

A final important issue concerns the method used to recruit subjects. To obtain the best research results, it is essential to use a **random sample** so that the sample will be as representative as possible. This means that if a survey is randomly sent to 100 employees, the research will be most accurate only if all employees return the survey. The problem is that researchers are unlikely to get a 100% return rate if study participation is voluntary. The ethics of the American Psychological Association (APA) require voluntary participation, but accurate research often requires compulsory participation. How do researchers resolve this dilemma? In some organizations, employees are required to sign a statement when they are hired agreeing to participate in any organizational research studies. To underscore this agreement, research participation is listed in each employee's job description.

Proponents of this method argue that participation in research is still voluntary because the individual had the choice of either not taking the job or taking it with the advance knowledge of research requirements. Opponents argue that taking a job or not taking a job in order to make a living does not constitute a proper and completely free choice. Similarly, in some universities students have the option of participating in a few research studies or writing a term paper. Even though the students are given an alternative to research participation, some psychologists argue that the choice between writing a term paper that will take several days and participating in two or three experiments that will take a few hours is not a legitimate choice (Sieber & Saks, 1989).

Because obtaining random samples is very difficult, especially in industry, many studies use a **convenience sample** and then randomly assign subjects to the various experimental conditions. A convenience sample, such as students in a psychology class, is easily available to a researcher. With **random assignment**, each subject in a nonrandom sample is randomly *assigned* to a particular experimental condition. For example, in a study designed to test the effectiveness of a training method, 60 subjects agree to participate in the study. Thirty of the subjects are randomly assigned to the group receiving training and another 30 are randomly assigned to the control group that does not receive training. Random assignment is important when using convenience samples as research indicates that random and nonrandom assignment result in different outcomes (Shadish & Ragsdale, 1996).

Running the Study

When all of these decisions have been made, it is finally time to run the study and collect data. To ensure that data are collected in an unbiased fashion, it is important that all instructions to the subjects be stated in a standardized fashion and at a level that is understandable. Once the subject is finished with her participation, she should be **debriefed**, or told the purpose of the experiment and be given a chance to ask questions about her participation.

Statistical Analysis

After all data have been collected, the results are statistically analyzed. A discussion of statistics is beyond the scope of this book, but it is important to understand why statistics are used. Statistical analysis helps us determine how confident we are that our results are real and did not occur by chance alone. For example, if we conducted a study in your classroom in which we compared the average age of students on the left side of the room with that of students on the right side of the room, we would no doubt get a difference. That is, the average age of the students on the right would not be exactly the same as that for students on the left. If we did not conduct a statistical analysis of our data, we would conclude that people on the right side are older than people on the left side. Perhaps we could even develop a theory about our results!

Does this sound ridiculous? Of course it does. But it points out the idea that any set of numbers we collect will in all probability be different. The question is, are they *significantly* different? Statistical analysis provides the answer by determining the probability that our data were the result of chance. In psychology, we use the .05 level of significance; if our analysis indicates the probability that our data resulted from chance is 5% or less, we consider our results to be statistically significant. Although the .05 level of significance is the most commonly used, some researchers have suggested that we should be more flexible and use either more conservative or more liberal levels, depending on the situation (Bordens & Abbott, 2002).

At this point, a caution must be made about the interpretation of significance levels. Significance levels only indicate the level of confidence we can place on a result being the product of chance. They say nothing about the strength of the results. Thus, a study finding results significant at the .01 level does not necessarily

Statistical skills are important to good research.

PhotoDisc, Inc.

show a stronger effect than a study with results significant at the .05 level of confidence.

To determine the strength of a finding, we use the effect size discussed earlier in the section on meta-analysis. Significance levels tell us the *statistical significance* of a study, and effect sizes (combined with logic) tell us the *practical significance* of a study.

For example, suppose we conduct a study comparing the SAT scores of male and female high school students. Based on a sample of 5 million students, we find that males average 490 and females 489. With such a huge sample size, we will probably find that the two means are statistically different. However, with only a 1-point difference between the two groups on a test with a maximum score of 800, we would probably not place much practical significance on the difference.

Correlation. It is necessary to discuss one particular statistic—correlation—because it is so widely used in I/O psychology and throughout this book. **Correlation** is a statistical procedure that enables a researcher to determine the *relationship* between two variables— for example, the relationships found between an employment test and future employee performance, or job satisfaction and job attendance, or performance ratings made by workers and supervisors. It is important to understand that correlational analysis does not necessarily say anything about causality.

The result of correlational analysis is a number called a **correlation coefficient**. The values of this coefficient range from −1 to +1; the further the coefficient is from zero, the greater the relationship between two variables. That is, a correlation of .40 shows a stronger relationship between two variables than a correlation of .20. Likewise, a correlation of −.39 shows a stronger relationship than a correlation of +.30. The + and − signs indicate the *direction* of the correlation. A positive (+) correlation means that as the values of one variable increase so do the values of a second variable. For example, we might find a positive correlation between intelligence and scores on a classroom exam. This would mean that the more intelligent the student, the higher her score on the exam.

A negative (−) correlation means that as the values of one variable increase the values of a second variable decrease. For example, we would probably find a negative correlation between the number of beers that you drink the night before a test and your score on that test. In I/O psychology, we find negative correlations between job satisfaction and absenteeism, age and reaction time, and nervousness and interview success.

Why does a correlation coefficient not indicate a cause and effect relationship? Because a third variable, an **intervening variable,** often accounts for the relationship between two variables. Take the example often used by psychologist David Schroeder. Suppose there is a correlation of +.80 between the number of ice cream cones sold in New York during August and the number of babies that die during August in India. Does eating ice cream kill babies in another nation? No, that would not make sense. Instead, we look for that third variable that would explain our high correlation. In this case, the answer is clearly the summer heat.

Another interesting example was provided by Mullins (1986) in a presentation about the incorrect interpretation of correlation coefficients. Mullins pointed out that data show a strong negative correlation between the number of cows per square mile and the crime rate. With his tongue firmly planted in his cheek, Mullins suggested that New York City could rid itself of crime by importing millions of head of cattle. Of course, the real interpretation for the negative correlation is that crime rates are greater in urban areas than in rural areas.

A good researcher should always be cautious about variables that seem related. Several years ago, *People* magazine reported on a minister who conducted a "study" of 500 pregnant teenage girls and found that rock music was being played when 450 of them became pregnant. The minister concluded that because the two are related (i.e., they occurred at the same time) rock music must cause pregnancy. His solution? Outlaw rock music and teenage pregnancy would disappear. In my own "imaginary study," however, I found that in all 500 cases of teenage pregnancy a pillow also was present. To use the same logic as that used by the minister, the real solution would be to outlaw pillows, not rock music. Although both "solutions" are certainly strange, the point should be clear: Just because two events occur at the same time or seem to be related does not mean that one event or variable causes another.

To put together everything you have learned about research in Chapter 1, complete Exercise 1–2 at the end of this chapter and Exercise 1–3 on the CD-ROM.

Chapter Summary

In this chapter you learned:

- The field of I/O psychology consists of four major subfields: personnel psychology, training, organizational psychology, and human factors. Industrial psychologists work in a variety of settings including industry, government, education, and consulting firms.

- The field of I/O psychology began in the early 1900s and has grown rapidly since then.

- At least a master's degree is required to find employment in the field, and median salaries are around $67,000 at the master's level and $90,000 at the Ph.D. level.

- Research is important so that I/O psychologists can make the best decisions.

- Decisions must be made regarding what to research; the location of the research (laboratory or field); the research method that will be used (experimental method, nonexperimental method, survey, archival research, meta-analysis); the sample that will be selected; and the statistics that will be used to analyze the research data.

Critical Thinking Questions

1. If you wanted to pursue a career in I/O psychology, what would you need to do between now and graduation to make this career possible?

2. How are theories and hypotheses different?

3. Is a random sample really better than a convenience sample?

4. When would you use a quasi-experiment rather than an experiment?

5. Why don't correlations between two variables indicate that one caused the other?

To learn more about the issues discussed in this chapter, point your browser to

http://www.infotrac-college.com/wadsworth and enter one of these search terms:

Lillian Gilbreth

Frank Gilbreth

human factors

ergonomics

Hawthorne studies

research ethics

survey response rate

statistical hypothesis testing

United States

University	State	Average GRE	Average GPA	Jr/Sr GPA	Number Applied	Number Admitted	Number Enrolled	Program Chair	Phone	Email
California State University, Long Beach	CA	1050		3.50	50	18	11	Diane Roe	(562) 985-8685	psygrad@csulb.edu
California State University, Sacramento	CA	1160		3.60	70	15	10	Larry Meyers	(916) 278-6365	Youngl@csus.edu
California State University, San Bernardino	CA		3.50	3.70	80	15	12	Janelle Gilbert	(909) 880-5587	Janelle@csusb.edu
Claremont Graduate University	CA				30	20	15	Donna Monika	(909) 607-3286	hrd@cgu.edu
Golden Gate University	CA							Kit Carman	(415) 442-6517	kcarman@ggu.edu
San Diego State University	CA	1180	3.71		48	18	10	Keith Hattrup	(619) 594-1876	khattrup@sunstroke.sdsu.edu
San Francisco State University	CA	1050			55	18	12	Kathleen Mosier	(415) 338-1059	kmosier@sfsu.edu
San Jose State University	CA	1150	3.30		60	12	10	Howard Tokunaga	(408) 924-5649	httokunaga@aol.com
University of Colorado, Denver	CO	1200	3.60		75	15	11	Michael Cook	(303) 556-8567	mcook@carbon.cudenver.edu
Fairfield University	CT				15	13	11	Faith-Anne Dohm	(203) 254-2000	fdohm@fairl.fairfield.edu
University of Hartford	CT	1025	3.31		26	18	8	Kristi Davison	(860) 768-4544	psych@mall.hartford.edu
University of New Haven	CT	1000	3.30	3.50	120	75	35	Tara L'Huereux	(203) 932-7341	Lheureux@charger.newhaven.edu
Carlos Albizu University, Miami	FL				78	41	38	Alberto Ramirez	(305) 593-1223	aramirez@albizu.edu
Florida Institute of Technology	FL	1063	3.30		40	18	8	Richard Griffith	(407) 768-8000	griffith@fit.edu
University of Central Florida	FL	1089	3.50		100	13	12	William Wooten	(407) 823-2552	wwooten@pegasus.cc.ucf.edu
University of West Florida	FL	1098	3.60		65	30	15	Steven Kass	(850) 474-2363	skass@uwf.edu
Valdosta State University	GA	1043	3.30		16	12	8	Larry Wiley	(229) 333-5930	Lwiley@valdosta.edu
University of Northern Iowa	IA	1000			8	6	4	Michael Gasser	(319) 273-7178	michael.gasser@uni.edu
University of Idaho	ID	1096	3.37		11	8	5	Todd Thorsteinson	(208) 885-6324	tthorste@uidaho.edu

University	State	Average GRE	Average GPA	Jr/Sr GPA	Number Applied	Number Admitted	Number Enrolled	Program Chair	Phone	Email
United States										
Chicago School of Professional Psychology	IL							Nancy Newton	(800) 721-8072	nnewton@csopp.edu
Elmhurst College	IL				35	24	16	Elizabeth Kuebler	(630) 617-3069	betsyk@elmhurst.edu
Illinois Institute of Technology	IL				32	15	7	Roya Ayman	(312) 567-3516	ayman@iit.edu
Illinois State University	IL	1100	3.40	3.50	70	12	8	John Binning	(309) 438-8020	jbinning@ilstu.edu
Roosevelt University	IL				46	42	24	Edward Wygonik	(312) 341-3760	
Southern Illinois University, Edwardsville	IL	1000	3.40		32	12	8	Debbie Brueggeman	(618) 692-2569	druegg@siue.edu
Indiana University–Purdue University	IN	1180	3.60		55	5	5	John Hazer	(317) 274-6950	jthazer@iupui.edu
Emporia State University	KS				20	12	6	Brian Schrader	(620) 341-5818	schrader@emporia.edu
Eastern Kentucky University	KY	1000	3.50		25	10	9	Laura Koppes	(859) 622-1105	Laura.Koppes@eku.edu
Northern Kentucky University	KY							George Goedel		
Western Kentucky University	KY	1110	3.30		40	14	9	Betsy Shoenfelt	(270) 745-4418	betsy.shoenfelt@wku.edu
Louisiana Tech	LA							Ram Aditya	(318) 257-4315	psychology@latech.edu
University of Baltimore	MD	990	3.44		90	59	27	Paul Mastrangelo	(410) 837-5310	pmastrangelo@ubmail.ubalt.edu
Springfield College	MA		3.20	3.30	102	30	18	Michael Surrette	(413) 748-3091	msurrett@spfldcol.edu
Central Michigan University	MI	1132	3.65		45	10	2	Terry Beehr	(517) 774-3001	tbeehr@cmich.edu
Western Michigan University	MI	1110	3.25		45	7	5	Alyce Dickinson	(616) 387-4500	alyce.dickinson@wmich.edu
Minnesota State University	MN	1050	3.40	3.60	55	15	10	Dan Sachau	(507) 389-5829	sachau@mankato.msus.edu
Saint Cloud State University	MN							Jody Illies	(320) 229-5772	jiillies@stcloudstate.edu
Southwest Missouri State University	MO	1024			30	16	10	Donald Fischer	(417) 836-4164	carolshoptaugh@mail.smsu.edu
Montana State University	MT	1114	3.51		30	8	5	Jennifer Boldry	(406) 994-3801	jboldry@montana.edu
University of Nebraska, Omaha	NE	1160	3.60		45	12	7	Roni Reiter-Palmon	(402) 554-4810	roni@mail.unomaha.edu
Fairleigh Dickinson University	NJ	1060	3.25		25	20	18	Robert Chell	(973) 443-8547	chell@mailbox.fdu.edu
Kean University	NJ	1000	3.20		25	14	12	Henry Kaplowitz	(908) 527-2170	
Montclair State University	NJ				30	15	10	Jennifer Bragger	(973) 655-5206	
Baruch College	NY	1200	3.30		100	60	40	Richard Wiener	(212) 387-1530	
Columbia University	NY		3.25	3.50	245	177	154	Amy Taylor	(212) 678-3866	ast5@columbia.edu

University	State	Average GRE	Average GPA	Jr/Sr GPA	Number Applied	Number Admitted	Number Enrolled	Program Chair	Phone	Email
Hofstra University	NY	1110	3.30		80	46	33	William Metlay	(516) 463-6344	psy_wzm@vaxc.hofstra.edu
New York University	NY	1140	3.30		211	104	51	Scott Eggebeen	(212) 998-7920	se17@nyu.edu
Rensselaer Polytechnic University	NY	1160	3.37		60	19	14	Jean Bestle	(518) 276-6472	osgain@rpi.edu
Appalachian State University	NC	1150	3.40		80	20	7	Timothy Ludwig	(828) 262-2712	ludwigtd@appstate.edu
East Carolina University	NC	1099	3.42		27	18	7	John Cope	(252) 328-6497	copej@mail.ecu.edu
University of North Carolina, Charlotte	NC				100	30	15	Jo Ann Lee	(704) 687-4753	jolee@email.uncc.edu
Cleveland State	OH	1150	3.50	3.50	20	12	10	Chieh-Chen Bowen	(216) 687-2544	c.c.bowen@csuohio.edu
University of Akron	OH	1169	3.70		30	7	5	Paul Levy	(330) 972-8369	plevy@uakron.edu
Wright State University	OH	1200	3.50		25	2	1	Debra Steele-Johnson	(937) 775-2391	debra.steele-johnson@wright.edu
Xavier University	OH	990	3.46		50	20	10	Mark Nagy	(513) 745-1958	nagyms@xu.edu
University of Oklahoma	OK	1145	3.80		30	5	3	Jorge Mendoza	(405) 325-4568	jmendoza@ou.edu
University of Tulsa	OK	1140	3.77		50	32	20	Kurt Kraiger	(918) 631-2894	kurt-kraiger@utulsa.edu
Portland State University	OR	1039	3.40		20	1	1	Leslie Hammer	(503) 725-3971	hammer@pdx.edu
West Chester University	PA	1090	3.30		35	20	12	Deanne Bonifazi	(610) 436-3143	dbonifazi@wcupa.edu
Austin Peay	TN	900	3.20		15	10	6	Linda Campos	(931) 221-7233	camposL@apsu.edu
Middle Tennessee State University	TN	1100	3.40		80	24	12	Michael Hein	(615) 898-2320	mhein@frank.mtsu.edu
University of Tennessee, Chattanooga	TN	1030	3.40		70	35	15	Michael Biderman	(423) 755-4268	Michael-Biderman@utc.edu
Lamar University	TX	1080	3.11		33	15	10	Oney Fitzpatrick	(409) 880-8285	fitzpatrod@hal.lamar.edu
University of Houston, Clear Lake	TX							Michael McCormick	(281) 283-3372	
Christopher Newport University	VA	950						Sheila Greenlee	(757) 594-7929	psycgrad@cnu.edu
George Mason University	VA	1186	3.40		77	29	16	Richard Klimoski	(703) 993-1367	rklimoski@gmu.edu
Radford University	VA	1052	3.41	3.62	64	32	14	Mike Aamodt	(540) 831-5513	maamodt@radford.edu
Central Washington University	WA	1100	3.40		30	16	12	Anthony Stahelski	(509) 963-2368	stahelsa@cwu.edu
Marshall University	WV							Christopher LeGrow	(304) 697-2780	legrow@marshall.edu
University of Wisconsin, Oshkosh	WI	1000	3.40		35	15	8	Gary Adams	(920) 424-2300	psychology@uwosh.edu
University of Wisconsin, Stout	WI							Richard Tafalla	(715) 232-1662	tafallar@uwstout.edu

Australia

University	State	Average GRE	Average GPA	Jr/Sr GPA	Number Applied	Number Admitted	Number Enrolled	Program Chair	Phone	Email
Curtin University								Roy Payne	(61-8) 9266-7279	r.payne@curtin.edu.au

University	State	Average GRE	Average GPA	Jr/Sr GPA	Number Applied	Number Admitted	Number Enrolled	Program Chair	Phone	Email
Deakin University									(61-3) 9251-7777	hsb.info@deakin.edu.au
Griffith University								Ian Glendon	(61-7) 5594 8964	l.Glendon@mailbox.gu.edu.au
Macquarie University								Rachelle Louison	(61-2) 9850-8087	rlouison@psy.mq.edu.ac
Murdoch University								Max Sulley	(61-8) 9360-2750	msully@murdoch.edu.au
University of Melbourne									(61-3) 8344-6377	jenkins@psyc.unimelb.edu.au
University of New South Wales								James Kehoe	(61-2) 9385-3826	J.Kehoe@unsw.edu.au
University of Queensland									(61-7) 3365-6426	louisew@psy.uq.edu.au
University of South Australia								Anthony Winefield	(61-8) 8302-2204	
Canada										
Saint Mary's University		1100	3.40		32	6	4	Victor Catano	(902) 420-5845	vic.catano@stmarys.ca
University of Waterloo		1260			30	5	3	John Michela	(519) 885-1211	jmichela@watarts.uwaterloo.ca
University of Western Ontario		1200			40	5	3	John Meyer	(519) 661-3679	meyer@sscl.uwo.ca
United Kingdom										
City University, London	England							Jo Silvester	44-20-7477-8019	enqs@igu.ac.uk
London Guildhall University	England								44-20-7320-1616	L.Randerson@psy.hull.ac.uk
University of Hull	England							Martin Chawshaw		
University of London	England							Phillip Corr	44-20-7631-6307	P.Corr@gold.ac.uk
University of Sheffield	England							Fiona Patterson		F.Patterson@sheffield.ac.uk
Queens University of Belfast	Ireland								44-28-9033-5081	
Cardiff University	Wales								44-29-2087-4432	internat@cf.ac.uk
University of Glamorgan	Wales								44-14-4348-0480	
New Zealand										
University of Canturbury								Chris Burt	(03) 364-2902	office@psyc.canterbury.ac.nz
University of Waikato								Michael O'Driscoll		m.odriscoll@waikato.ac.nz

APPENDIX 1B — List of I/O Ph.D. programs

University	State	Average GRE	Average GPA	Jr/Sr GPA	Number Applied	Number Admitted	Number Enrolled	Program Chair	Phone	Email
United States										
Auburn University	AL	1110	3.60		49	6	4	Phillip Lewis	(334) 844-6478	lewispm@mail.auburn.edu
Alliant International University, Fresno	CA							Toni Knott	(559) 456-2777	tknot@alliant.edu
Alliant International University, Los Angeles	CA				40	20	17	Cal Hoffman	(626) 284-2777	choffman@alliant.edu
Alliant International University, San Diego	CA	1090	3.20		9	7	5	Herbert Baker	(858) 623-2777	hbaker@alliant.edu
Alliant International University, San Francisco Bay	CA							Kathryn Schuyler	(510) 523-2300	kgschuyler@alliant.edu
Claremont Graduate University	CA	1180			63	15	5	Dale Berger	(909) 621-8084	cgupsych@cgu.edu
University of California, Berkeley	CA			5	1	1		Sheldon Zedeck	(510) 643-8586	zedeck@socrates.berkeley.edu
Colorado State University	CO	1275	3.30	3.40	130	12	5	Jack Hautaloma	(970) 491-6383	jackh@lamar.colostate.edu
University of Connecticut	CT	1210		3.80	80	10	4	Janet Barnes-Farrell	(860) 486-5929	barnesf@uconnvm.uconn.edu
George Washington University	DC	1213	3.60		100	8	3	Lynn Offerman	(202) 994-6320	psychoff@gwu.edu
Florida Institute of Technology	FL	1200	3.30		25	4	2	Richard Griffith	(407) 768-8000	griffith@fit.edu
Florida International University	FL	1170	3.50	3.50	40	6	4	Chockalingam Viswesvaran	(305) 348-2880	vish@fiu.edu
University of South Florida	FL	1290		3.90	130	23	9	Walter Borman	(813) 974-0379	WallyB@pdi-corp.com
Georgia Institute of Technology	GA	1300	3.40		60	6	2	Jim Dunton	(404) 894-3102	jd234@prism.gatech.edu
University of Georgia	GA	1250			70	10	5	Chuck Lance	(706) 542-2174	clance@arches.uga.edu
DePaul University	IL	1208	3.70		100	15	4	Alice Stuhlmacher	(773) 325-7887	astuhlma@depaul.edu
Illinois Institute of Technology	IL	1174			50	28	5	Roya Ayman	(312) 567-3516	ayman@iit.edu
Northern Illinois University	IL							Christopher Parker	(815) 753-0372	cparker@niu.edu

University	State	Average GRE	Average GPA	Jr/Sr GPA	Number Applied	Number Admitted	Number Enrolled	Program Chair	Phone	Email
United States										
University of Illinois, Urbana–Champaign	IL	1406	3.90		70	8	4	Fritz Drasgow	(217) 333-2169	fdrasgow@uiuc.edu
Purdue University	IN	1267	3.67		93	4	2	Charlie Reeve	(765) 496-2141	creeve@psych.purdue.edu
Kansas State University	KS	1220	3.70		60	8	4	Patrick Knight	(785) 532-0612	knight@ksu.edu
Louisiana State University	LA	1260	3.60		50	3	3	Gary Greguras	(225) 578-9039	ggregur@lsu.edu
Tulane University	LA	1250	3.50		60	8	4	Ronald Landis	(504) 862-3306	rlandis@tulane.edu
University of Maryland	MD	1350	3.80		100	5	3	Benjamin Schneider	(301) 405-5927	ben@psyc.umd.edu
Central Michigan University	MI	1178	3.66		50	15	6	Terry Beehr	(517) 774-3001	tbeehr@cmich.edu
Michigan State University	MI	1350			85	8	4	Rick DeShon	(517) 353-4624	deshon@msu.edu
University of Michigan	MI				40	3	3	Fiona Lee		fionalee@umich.edu
Wayne State University	MI	1220	3.60	3.70	50	10	5	Sebastiano Fisicaro	(313) 577-2812	fisicaro@sun.science.wayne.edu
Western Michigan University	MI	1110	3.40		15	5	3	Alyce Dickinson	(616) 387-4500	alyce.dickinson@wmich.edu
University of Minnesota	MN	1350	3.50		80	8	4	Paul Sackett	(612) 624-9842	psackett@tc.umn.edu
Saint Louis University	MO	1100	3.30	3.40	20	6	3	David Munz	(314) 977-2294	Munzdc@slu.edu
University of Southern Mississippi	MS	1200	3.50		50	4	3	Jeffrey Kudisch	(601) 266-4609	j.kudisch@usm.edu
University of Missouri–St. Louis	MO	1225	3.50		75	9	4	Paul Paese	(314) 516-5384	paul.paese@umsl.edu
North Carolina State University	NC	1260	3.80		100	8	4	Mark Wilson	(919) 515-1718	mark_wilson@ncsu.edu
University of Nebraska, Omaha	NE	1205	3.70		25	3	3	Roni Reiter-Palmon	(402) 554-4810	roni@mail.unomaha.edu
Rutgers University	NJ	1244	3.51		32	9	6	Clayton Alderfer	(732) 445-5233	alderfer@rci.rutgers.edu
Baruch College, CUNY	NY	1240			90	8	5	Joel Lefkowitz	(646) 312-3789	joel_lefkowitz@baruch.cuny.edu
Teachers College, Columbia University	NY	1290	3.60		75	15	8	Debra Noumair	(212) 678-3395	dn28@columbia.edu
University at Albany, SUNY	NY	1120	3.50		50	10	4	Kevin Williams	(518) 442-4849	kevinw@csc.albany.edu

University	State	Average GRE	Average GPA	Jr/Sr GPA	Number Applied	Number Admitted	Number Enrolled	Program Chair	Phone	Email
Bowling Green State University	OH	1220	3.80		100	8	6	Mike Zickar	(419) 372-9984	mzickar@bgnet.bgsu.edu
Ohio University	OH	1260	3.45		36	7	3	Jeffrey Vancouver	(740) 593-1072	psychology@ohiou.edu
Ohio State University	OH									
University of Akron	OH	1260	3.80		100	16	8	Paul Levy	(330) 972-8369	plevy@uakron.edu
Wright State University	OH	1200	3.50		40	8	4	Debra Steele-Johnson	(937) 775-2391	debra.steele-johnson@wright.edu
University of Oklahoma	OK	1145	3.80		60	7	4	Jorge Mendoza	(405) 325-4568	jmendoza@ou.edu
University of Tulsa	OK	1250	3.50		60	6	2	Kurt Kraiger	(918) 631-2894	kurt-kraiger@utulsa.edu
Portland State University	OR	1220	3.40		70	7	5	Leslie Hammer	(503) 725-3971	hammer@pdx.edu
Penn State University	PA	1350	3.70	3.70	100	10	5	James Farr	(814) 863-1734	jsf@psu.edu
Temple University	PA	1300	3.50	3.70	90	4	4	Donald Hantula	(215) 204-5950	hantula@temple.edu
Carlos Albizu University	Puerto Rico							Miguel Martinez	(787) 725-6500	martinez@prip.edu
Clemson University	SC	1290	3.70		120	20	12	Chris Pagano	(803) 656-4980	cpagano@clemson.edu
University of Memphis	TN	1100						William Dwyer	(901) 678-2149	wdwyer@mail.psyc.memphis.edu
University of Tennessee	TN	1283	3.82	3.93	50	7	4	Robert Ladd	(865) 974-4846	iopsyc@utk.edu
Rice University	TX	1311	3.56	3.80	69	10	6	Miguel Quinones	(713) 348-3418	mickey@rice.edu
Texas A&M University	TX	1333	3.62	3.73	63	7	3	Winfred Arthur	(979) 845-7146	gradadv@psyc.tamu.edu
University of Houston	TX	1300	3.50		50	10	5	James Campion	(713) 743-8520	jcampion@uh.edu
University of North Texas	TX	1258	3.50	3.70	46	10	6	Amy Gray	(940) 565-2671	amyg@unt.edu
George Mason University	VA	1238	3.70		53	12	6	Richard Klimoski	(703) 993-4439	rklimosk@gmu.edu
Old Dominion University	VA	1210	3.65		60	12	6	Mark Scerbo	(757) 683-4439	mscerbo@odu.edu
Virginia Tech	VA	1220	3.60		70	12	6	Neil Hauenstein	(540) 231-6581	nhauen@vt.edu

Australia

University	State	Average GRE	Average GPA	Jr/Sr GPA	Number Applied	Number Admitted	Number Enrolled	Program Chair	Phone	Email
Curtin University								Roy Payne		r.payne@curtin.edu.au
Griffith University								Ian Glendon	(07) 5594 8964	l.Glendon@mailbox.gu.edu.au
Macquarie University										
University of Melbourne										Jenkins@psych.unimelb.edu.au

University	State	Average GRE	Average GPA	Jr/Sr GPA	Number Applied	Number Admitted	Number Enrolled	Program Chair	Phone	Email
University of South Wales										
University of South Australia								Jacques Metzer		Jack.Metzer@unisa.edu.au
Canada										
University of Calgary		1200	3.70	3.70	30	5	3	Lorne Sulsky	(403) 220-5050	Lmsulsky@ucalgary.ca
University of Guelph		1250	3.76		60	8	6	Steven Cronshaw	(519) 824-4120	cronshaw@psy.uoguelph.ca
University of Waterloo		1260			10	2	2	John Michela	(519) 885-1211	jmichela@watarts.uwaterloo.ca
University of Western Ontario		1200			40	5	3	John Meyer	(519) 661-3679	meyer@sscl.uwo.ca
Great Britain										
City University of London										
London Guildhall University								Jo Silvester		
Exeter University								Carole Burgoyne		psyadmin@exer.ac.uk
University of Hull								Martin Crawshaw		
University of Nottingham								Tom Cox		tom.cox@nottingham.ac.uk
University of Sheffield								Fiona Patterson		F.Patterson@sheffield.ac.uk
University of Surrey								L. J. Millward		L.Millward@surrey.ac.uk
New Zealand										
University of Waikato								Michael O'Driscoll		psyc0181@waikato.ac.nz

Exercise 1–1
Research Designs

In each of the following examples, determine the type of research design used (experiment, quasi-experiment, survey, correlation, archival, meta-analysis) and then identify the independent variables and the dependent variables (if any). Also identify any problems with the study and offer some suggestions for improvement.

A.   A human resource manager was interested in determining if there was a relationship between employee satisfaction and absenteeism. The professor had 220 employees complete a test of job satisfaction and then compared the scores on this test with the number of days each employee missed work over the past 12 months.

Type of study _____

Independent variable _____

Dependent variable _____

Problems and Suggestions

_____

_____

_____

_____

B.   A study was conducted to determine if men and women were being paid equitably at Raynes Manufacturing. To test this question, company payroll records were examined to compare the average salaries of male and female employees. The results indicated that the average man earned $32,176 per year whereas the average woman earned $30,100.

Type of study _____

Independent variable _____

Dependent variable _____

Problems and Suggestions

_____

_____

_____

_____

_____

C.　　Prior to developing an on-site child care center, Community General Hospital wanted to ensure that enough of its employees would use the center. Amanda Blake, the nursing supervisor, sent a questionnaire to the hospital's employees asking them if they would use the center, and how much they would be willing to pay per week for on-site child care.

Type of study _____

Independent variable _____

Dependent variable _____

Problems and Suggestions

_____

_____

_____

_____

_____

_____

_____

D.　　A supervisor was convinced that the color of the walls at work was drab and that this color made employees depressed. She painted the walls pink and counted the number of days her employees missed during the month before the walls were painted and the month after the walls were painted. She found that 10 days were missed in the month before and 6 days in the month after.

Type of study _____

Independent variable _____

Dependent variable _____

Problems and Suggestions

_____

_____

_____

_____

_____

_____

E.   A professor was interested in discovering the effect of incentives on employee performance. He went back through every issue of the *Journal of Applied Psychology* and the *Journal of Management* and statistically combined the results reported in all of the relevant articles. The mean effect size (*d*) of .63 indicated that incentives did increase employee performance.

Type of study _____

Independent variable _____

Dependent variable _____

Problems and Suggestions

_____

_____

_____

_____

_____

_____

F.   A manager worried that her employees were not happy with the organization. To confirm her fears, she had each of her employees provide written answers to 10 questions about their attitude toward work.

Type of study _____

Independent variable _____

Dependent variable _____

Problems and Suggestions

_____

_____

_____

_____

_____

_____

G.   A police chief was considering the requirement that all new officers must have a college degree. Before doing this, however, he looked at the education level of his current officers and compared their education with their police performance. He discovered that officers with college degrees performed better than their less educated peers.

Type of study _____

Independent variable _____

Dependent variable _____

Problems and Suggestions

_____

_____

_____

_____

_____

_____

_____

H.   A professor hypothesized that people could be trained to detect deception in employment interviews. To test her hypothesis, 50 students were given training on detecting deception and 50 students were given training on interpersonal skills. The 100 students then viewed one of two interviews, one with a person lying and the other with a person telling the truth. After viewing the tape, the students were asked to indicate whether the applicant in the tape was telling the truth about her work history. The professor found that the students who were trained to detect deception were no more accurate than the other students.

Type of study _____

Independent variable _____

Dependent variable _____

Problems and Suggestions

_____

_____

_____

_____

_____

Exercise 1–2
Designing a Study

You are the human resource director for Tyson Earplugs, a company of 10,000 employees specializing in the production of swimming products. Due to the increased complexity of the manufacturing process, you are interested in improving the basic skills (e.g., math, reading, writing) of your employees. Two methods look promising—one involving interactive video and the other involving the use of workbooks. The interactive video approach would cost about $500,000 and the workbooks about $200,000.

Design a study to help you make a decision. Describe your sample and your research method. How would you arrive at a conclusion about what to do?

2 Job Analysis and Evaluation

Job Analysis

IN 1585, 15 English settlers established a colony on Roanoke Island near what is now the Outer Banks of the North Carolina coast. When John White arrived at Roanoke Island in 1590, he found no trace of the colony and only the word *Croatan* carved on a tree. To this day, it is not known what happened to the settlers of the Lost Colony of Roanoke.

Many theories have been put forth to explain the fate of the lost colony—killed by Indians, moved to another location, and so on. One theory is that the members of the colony were not prepared to survive in the new continent; that is, the group consisted of politicians, soldiers, and sailors. Although worthy individuals were sent to the New World, few had the necessary training and skills to survive. In fact, the colony might have survived if settlers with more appropriate skills, such as farmers, had been sent instead of the traditional explorer types. Thus, a better match between job requirements and personnel might have saved the colony.

Does this sound farfetched? Perhaps so, but the story does underscore the importance of a process called **job analysis**—the process of gathering, analyzing, and structuring information about a job's components, characteristics, and job requirements (Sanchez & Levine, 2000). By the end of this chapter, you will

- understand the definition of and uses for job analysis.
- know how to write a job description.
- know how to conduct a job analysis.
- learn when to use the various job analysis methods.
- understand the concept of job evaluation.
- understand the concept of pay equity.

Importance of Job Analysis

Writing Job Descriptions

Often confused with job analysis, **job descriptions** are brief, two- to five-page summaries of the tasks and job requirements found in the job analysis. In other words, the job analysis is the *process* of determining the work activities and requirements, and the job description is the written *result* of the job analysis. Job analyses and job descriptions serve as the basis for many human resource activities including employee selection, evaluation, training, and work design (Brannick & Levine, 2002).

Employee Selection

It is difficult to imagine how an employee can be selected unless there is a clear understanding of the job's requirements. By identifying such requirements, it is possible to select tests or develop interview questions that will determine whether a particular applicant possesses the necessary knowledge, skills, and abilities to carry out the requirements of the job. Although this seems like common sense, the discussion of the unstructured employment interview in Chapter 5 demonstrates that many non-job-related variables are often used to select employees. Examples are height requirements for police officers, firm handshakes for most jobs, and physical attractiveness for airline flight attendants.

Training

Again, it is difficult to see how employees can be trained unless the requirements of the job are known. Job analyses yield lists of job activities that can be systematically used to create training programs.

Personpower Planning

One important, but seldom employed, use of job analysis is to determine *worker mobility* within an organization. That is, if individuals are hired for a particular job, to what other jobs can they expect to eventually be promoted and become successful? Many organizations have a policy of promoting the person who performs the best in the job immediately below the one in question. Although this approach has its advantages, it can result in the so-called **Peter Principle:** promoting employees until they eventually reach their highest level of incompetence (Peter & Hull, 1969). For example, consider an employee who is the best salesperson in the company. Even though this person is known to be excellent in sales, it is not known what type of supervisor he or she will be. Promotion solely on the basis of sales performance does not guarantee that the individual will do well as a supervisor. Suppose, however, that job analysis results are used to compare all jobs in the company to the supervisor's job. Instead of promoting the person in the job immediately below the supervisor, we promote the best employee from the most similar job—that is, a job that already involves much of the same knowledge, skills, and abilities as the supervisor's job. With this approach, there is a better match between the person being promoted and the requirements of the job.

Performance Appraisal

Another important use of job analysis is the construction of a performance appraisal instrument. As in employee selection, the evaluation of employee performance must be job related. Employees are often evaluated with forms that use such vague categories as "dependability," "knowledge," and "initiative." The use of specific, job-related categories leads to more accurate performance appraisals that are not only better accepted by employees but also are accepted more readily by the courts (Werner & Bolino, 1997). In addition, when properly administered and utilized, job-related performance appraisals can serve as an excellent source of employee training and counseling.

Job Classification

Job analysis enables a human resource professional to classify jobs into groups based on similarities in requirements and duties. Job classification is useful for determining pay levels, transfers, and promotions.

Job Evaluation

Job analysis information can also be used to determine the *worth* of a job. Job evaluation will be discussed in greater detail later in this chapter.

Job Design

Job analysis information can be used to determine the optimal way in which a job should be performed. That is, what would be the best way for an employee to sit at her computer or what would be the best way for a warehouse operator to lift boxes? By analyzing a job, wasted motions can be eliminated resulting in higher productivity, and unsafe movements can be eliminated resulting in reduced numbers of job injuries. A good example of job design was mentioned in Chapter 1 when Frank Gilbreth, after studying the inconsistency

in which brick masons did their work, was able to reduce the number of motions needed to lay a brick from 18 to 4½.

Compliance with Legal Guidelines

As will be discussed in greater detail in Chapter 3, any employment decision must be based on job-related information. One legally acceptable way to directly determine job relatedness is by *job analysis*. No law specifically requires a job analysis, but several important guidelines and court cases mandate job analysis for all practical purposes.

First, the *Uniform Guidelines* contain several direct references to the necessity of job analysis. Even though the *Uniform Guidelines* are not law, courts have granted them "great deference" (Brannick & Levine, 2002).

Second, several court cases have discussed the concept of job relatedness. For example, in *Griggs v. Duke Power* (1971), employment decisions were based in part upon applicants' possession of a high school diploma. Because a higher percentage of blacks than whites did not meet this requirement, smaller percentages of blacks were hired and promoted. Thus, a suit was filed against the Duke Power Company charging that a high school diploma was not necessary to carry out the demands of the job. The court agreed with Griggs, the plaintiff, stating that the company had indeed not established the job relatedness of the high school diploma requirement.

Although not specifically mentioning the term *job analysis,* the decision in *Griggs* was the first one that addressed the issue of job relatedness. Subsequent cases such as *Albermarle v. Moody* (1975) and *Chance v. Board of Examiners* (1971) further established the necessity of job relatedness and the link between it and job analysis.

Organizational Analysis

During a job analysis, the job analyst often becomes aware of certain problems within an organization. For example, during a **job analysis interview**, an employee may indicate that she does not know how she is evaluated or to whom she is supposed to report. The discovery of such lapses in organizational communication can then be used to correct problems and help an organization function better. For example, while conducting job analysis interviews of credit union positions, job analyst Deborah Peggans discovered that none of the workers knew how their job performances were evaluated. This let the organization know it had not done an adequate job of communicating performance standards to its employees.

Writing a Good Job Description

As mentioned earlier, one of the most useful results of a job analysis is the job description. A job description is a relatively short summary of a job and should be about two to five pages in length. This suggested length is not really typical of most job descriptions used in industry; they tend to be only one page. But for a job description to be of value, it must describe a job in enough detail that decisions about activities such as selection and training can be made. Such decisions probably cannot be made if the description is only one page long.

Though I/O psychologists believe job descriptions should be detailed and lengthy, many professionals in organizations resist such efforts. These professionals worry that listing each activity will limit their ability to direct employees to perform tasks not listed on the job description. The concern is that an employee, referring to the job description as support, might respond, "It's not my job." This fear, however, can be countered with two arguments. The first is that duties can always be added to a job description, and job descriptions can, and should, be updated on a regular basis. The second is to include the statement "and performs other job-related duties as assigned" on the job description. In fact, Virginia Tech has a policy stating that the university can require employees to perform any duties not on the employees' job descriptions for a period not to exceed 3 months. After 3 months, the duty must either be eliminated or permanently added to the employee's job description, at which time a review will also be made to determine if the addition is significant enough to merit a salary increase.

Job descriptions can be written in many ways, but the format discussed here has been used successfully for many jobs and is a combination of methods used by many organizations and suggested by several researchers. A job description should contain the following eight sections: job title, brief summary, work activities, tools and equipment used, work context, performance standards, compensation information, and personal requirements.

Job Title

A job title is important for several reasons. An accurate title describes the nature of the job. When industrial psychologist David Faloona started a new job at Washington National Insurance in Chicago, his official title was "psychometric technician." Unfortunately, none of the other workers knew what he did. To correct that problem, his title was changed to "personnel assistant," and supervisors then began consulting with him on human resource–related problems. A job analysis that I conducted provides another example. After analyzing the position of "secretary" for one credit union, I found that her duties were actually those of a position that other credit unions label "loan officer." This change in title resulted in the employee receiving a higher salary as well as vindication that she was indeed "more than a secretary."

An accurate title also aids in employee selection and recruitment. If the job title indicates the true nature of the job, potential applicants for a position will be better able to determine if their skills and experience match those required for the job. The "secretary story" is a good example because secretarial applicants might not possess the lending and decision-making skills needed by a loan officer.

When conducting a job analysis, it is not unusual for an analyst to discover that some workers do not have job titles. Job titles provide workers with some form of identity. Instead of just saying that she is a "worker at the foundry," a woman can say that she is a "welder" or a "machinist." At most universities, students receiving financial aid are called "work study students" rather than "clerk," "computer operator," or "mail sorter." This inaccurate title causes many students to think they are supposed to study as they work rather than sort mail or operate a computer.

Job titles can also affect perceptions of the status and worth of a job. For example, job descriptions containing gender-neutral titles such as administrative assistant are evaluated as being worth more money than ones containing titles with a female sex linkage such as executive secretary (Naughton, 1988). As another example, Smith, Hornsby, Benson, and Wesolowski (1989) had subjects read identical job descriptions that differed only in the status of the title. Jobs with higher-status titles were evaluated as being worth more money than jobs with lower-status titles. Some authors, however, have questioned the gender effects associated with titles (Mount & Ellis, 1989; Rynes, Weber, & Milkovich, 1989).

Though many of the .com companies allow their employees to create their own titles, it is important that employees who are doing the same job have the same title, and that the title accurately reflect the nature of the job (Garvey, 2000).

Brief Summary

The summary need be only a paragraph in length but should briefly describe the nature and purpose of the job. This summary can be used in help wanted advertisements, internal job postings, and company brochures.

Work Activities

The work activities section lists the tasks and activities in which the worker is involved. These tasks and activities should be organized into meaningful categories to make the job description easier to read and understand. The category labels are also convenient to use in the brief summary. As you can see in the sample job description in Exhibit 2.01, the 72 work activities performed by the bookkeeper are divided into seven main areas: accounting, clerical, teller, share draft, collections, payroll, and financial operations.

Tools and Equipment Used

A section should be included that lists all the tools and equipment used to perform the work activities in the previous section. Even though tools and equipment may have been mentioned in the activities section, placing them in a separate section makes their identification simpler. Information in this section is primarily used for employee selection and training. That is, an applicant can be asked if she can operate an adding machine, a computer, and a credit history machine.

Exhibit 2.01   Example of a job description

Bookkeeper
Radford Pipe Shop Employee's
Federal Credit Union

Job Summary Under the general supervision of the office manager, the Bookkeeper is responsible for all of the accounting duties of the office. Specifically, the Bookkeeper is responsible for: keeping all financial records accurate and up to date; processing loans; and preparing and posting statements, reports, and bonds.

Work Activities The work activities of the Bookkeeper are divided into seven main functional areas:

Accounting Activities

- Prepares quarterly income statement
- Maintains and posts all transactions in general ledger book
- Pays credit union bills
- Prepares statistical reports
- Updates undivided earnings account
- Prepares and files tax returns and statements
- Completes IRA forms and reports in cooperation with CUNA
- Annually computes Cumis Bond
- Balances journal and cash records

Clerical Activities

- Looks up members' account information when requested
- Answers phone
- Makes copies of transactions for members
- Drafts statements of account to members
- Types certificates of deposit
- Makes copies of letters that are sent to members
- Picks up, sorts, and disperses credit union mail
- Folds monthly and quarterly statements and places into an envelope to be mailed to members

- Processes and mails savings and share draft statements
- Sorts checks or copies of checks in numerical order
- Orders supplies
- Types reports and minutes from board meetings
- Maintains and updates files for members
- Prepares, types, and files correspondence
- Enters change-of-address information into the computer

Teller Activities

- Enrolls new members and opens and closes accounts
- Reconciles accounts
- Issues money orders and traveler's checks
- Conducts history of accounts
- Processes and issues receipts for transactions
- Asks for identification if person making transaction is not known
- Daily enters transaction totals onto a list sent to the bank
- Orders new or replacement checks for members
- Prints and issues checks
- Makes proper referrals

Share Draft Activities

- Deducts fee from member's account when a share is returned
- Processes statements for share draft accounts
- Issues stop payments and sends copy of form to member
- Deducts fee in form of an overdraft when more than three transfers have occurred for any one member in a month
- Checks and records share drafts or additions from previous day
- Receives share draft totals for each member from CUNA data

- Decides on an individual basis whether overdrafts will be covered by credit union
- Determines if overdrafts on account have been paid
- Checks to see if share drafts have cleared
- Telephones Chase-Manhattan Bank when a member does not have enough money to cover a share draft

Collections Activities

- Holds money from member's check in order to meet loan payments
- Decides if a member who has a delinquent loan will be able to take money out of account
- Locates and communicates with members having delinquent loans
- Completes garnishee form to send to courts on delinquent loans
- Resubmits garnishee form once every 3 months until delinquent loan has been paid in full by member
- Makes collection on delinquent loans
- Checks on previous member's address and current job to see if loan payments can be made
- Determines number and length of time of delinquent loans
- Sends judgment form to court, which sends it to delinquent member
- If a member is delinquent, finds out if he or she is sick or on vacation

Payroll and Data-Processing Activities

- Checks and verifies payroll run for all necessary deductions
- Reads and interprets computer printouts
- Computes and subtracts deductions from payroll

continues on next page

Exhibit **2.01** Example of a job description
(continued)

- Sets up and changes deduction amounts for payroll savings plan
- Runs payroll on computer
- Annually sends out backup disk to outside vendor who transfers information to a magnetic tape that is sent to IRS
- Computes payroll
- Runs daily trial balances and transaction registers
- Loads paper into printer
- Makes backup copies of all daily computer transactions
- Runs quarterly and/or monthly statements on computer

Financial Operations Activities

- Scans business/financial environment to identify potential threats and opportunities
- Makes recommendations to the board regarding investments
- Invests all excess money into accounts that will earn interest
- Computes profits and amounts to be used for investments
- Prepares statements of financial condition and federal operating fee report

- Obtains enough funds for day-to-day operation of branch
- Notifies and makes available investment funds to the NCUA

Machines Used The Bookkeeper uses the following machines and equipment

- Adding machine
- Typewriter
- Computer printer
- CRT
- Mainframe computer
- Credit history machine
- Motor vehicle
- Photocopy machine
- Folding machine
- Microfiche reader
- Safe
- Telephone
- Security check writer

Job Context The Bookkeeper spends the majority of time making entries in and balancing journals and ledgers. The work day is spent in a climate-controlled office with four coworkers. Physical demands are minimal and sitting is required for most of the day. Stress is moderate.

Work Performance To receive an excellent performance appraisal, the Bookkeeper should:

- Maintain neat and accurate records
- Meet all deadlines
- Maintain an orderly office
- Make sure all ledgers and journals balance
- Perform duties of other jobs when the need arises

Job Qualifications Upon hire, the Bookkeeper must:

- Have a basic knowledge of math and English
- Understand financial documents
- Be able to make limited financial decisions
- Have completed advanced coursework in accounting and finance
- Have had training in data processing

After hire, the Bookkeeper must:

- Learn general office procedures
- Learn credit union style accounting procedures and regulations
- Learn how to complete the various forms

Some jobs require tremendous attention to detail.

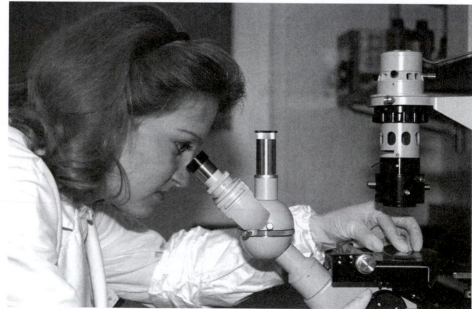

Job Context

This section should describe the environment in which the employee works and should mention stress level, work schedule, physical demands, level of responsibility, temperature, number of coworkers, degree of danger, and any other relevant information. This information is especially important in providing applicants with disabilities with information they can use to determine their ability to perform a job under a particular set of circumstances.

Work Performance

The job description should outline standards of performance. This section contains a relatively brief description of how an employee's performance is evaluated and what work standards are expected of the employee.

Compensation Information

This section of the job description should contain information on the salary **grade**, whether the position is exempt, and information on the compensable factors used to determine salary. These concepts will be described later in the chapter. The employee's actual salary or salary range should *not* be listed on the job description.

Job Competencies

This section contains what are commonly called **job specifications** or **competencies**. These are the knowledge, skills, abilities, and other (KSAOs) characteristics (such as interest, personality, training) that are necessary to be successful on the job. Job specifications are determined by deciding what types of KSAOs are needed to perform the tasks identified in the job analysis. These KSAOs can be determined through a combination of logic, research, and use of specific job analysis techniques discussed later in this chapter. The personal requirements section should be divided into two subsections. The first contains KSAOs that an employee must have at time of hiring. The second subsection contains the KSAOs that are an important part of the job but can be obtained after being hired. The first set of KSAOs is used for employee selection and the second for training purposes (Wooten, 1993).

To apply what you have learned in the preceding pages, complete Exercise 2–1 and Exercise 2–2 at the end of this chapter. Exercise 2–1 will give you a chance to critique a job description, and Exercise 2–2 will provide you with the opportunity to write your own job description.

Preparing for a Job Analysis

Prior to conducting a job analysis, several decisions must be made that will influence how the job analysis is conducted.

Who Will Conduct the Analysis?

Typically, a job analysis is conducted by a trained individual in the human resource department, but it can also be conducted by job incumbents, supervisors, or outside consultants. If job incumbents or supervisors are used, it is essential that they be thoroughly trained in job analysis procedures. The *Uniform Guidelines* state that a job analysis must be "professionally conducted," and a job analyst certainly cannot be called a professional unless she has been trained. In addition, research indicates that analysts who have been trained produce slightly different results from those produced by untrained analysts (Cellar, Curtis, Kohlepp, Poczapski, & Mohiuddin, 1989; Surrette, Aamodt, & Johnson, 1990).

Time is always an issue when using supervisors or incumbents. Telling a supervisor to "write job descriptions in your spare time" is not likely to go over well. Thus, supervisors and employees will need to be released from other duties—a situation that is seldom possible.

The state of Virginia developed a system in which all employees were asked to follow set guidelines and write their own job descriptions. The system itself was well conceived, but employees were not given enough job analysis training, which resulted in substantial confusion and, in some cases, inaccurate job descriptions.

Consultants are a good choice for conducting a job analysis because they are well trained and have extensive experience. The main drawback, though, is their

Should employees in dangerous jobs be compensated for the increased risk?

expense. Consultants typically charge between $50 and $250 per hour based on their degree, experience, and reputation. Given that 10 hours is probably the least amount of time that will be spent analyzing the simplest job, and the most complex jobs can take weeks of analysis, an organization must carefully weigh the benefits of consultants against their cost.

An interesting alternative to consultants is the use of college interns. Graduate students from I/O psychology programs tend to have job analysis training and experience and can be employed for a relatively small cost (often, at no cost). In fact, Radford University operates the Community Human Resource Center in which graduate students obtain job analysis experience by conducting job analyses free of charge to such local nonprofit agencies as school systems, towns, and hospitals. In this way, graduate students obtain experience, and the nonprofit organizations receive professional quality job analyses and job descriptions at no cost. Similar programs can be found at the University of Tulsa and the University of Southern Mississippi.

Which Employees Should Participate?

For organizations with relatively few people in each job, it is advisable to have all employees participate in the job analysis. In organizations in which many people perform the same job (e.g., teachers at a university or assemblers in a factory), every person need not participate. If every incumbent is not going to participate, the question becomes, How many people need to be included in the job analysis? This is a difficult question, one that I normally answer by advising job analysts to keep interviewing incumbents until they don't hear anything new. Anecdotally, this seems to be after the third or fourth incumbent for a particular job.

The answer to this question to some extent depends on whether the job analysis will be committee based or field based. In a committee-based job analysis, a group of subject matter experts (e.g., employees, supervisors) meet to generate the tasks performed, the conditions under which they are performed, and the KSAOs needed to perform them. In a field-based job analysis, the job analyst individually interviews/observes a number of incumbents out in the field. Taken together, the results of four studies (Ash, Levine, Higbee, & Sistrunk, 1982; Maurer & Tross, 2000; O'Leary, Rheinstein, & McCauley, 1990; Tannenbaum & Wesley, 1993) suggest that committee-based job analyses yield similar results to field-based job analyses.

Rouleau and Krain (1975) developed a table to estimate how many incumbents should be included in a job analysis; their recommendation is that a committee-based approach should have one session of 4 to 6 incumbents for jobs having fewer than 30 incumbents and two to three sessions for jobs with higher numbers of incumbents. Green and Stutzman (1986) have suggested a minimum of 3 incumbents and Gael (1988) suggested 6 to 10 incumbents. Unfortunately, no research is available to verify these estimates.

Beatty (1996) compared the results of job analysis samples of 10, 15, 20, and 212 incumbents in a federal law enforcement position. His results indicated that the job tasks and job requirements resulting from the use of 10 versus 212 incumbents were nearly identical. These results support and extend those found by Fletcher, Friedman, McCarthy, McIntyre, O' Leary, and Rheinstein (1993) and Pass and Robertson (1980), who found that job analysis samples of 10 and 20 yielded comparable results.

Mullins (1983) had 97 campus police officers at 13 universities generate critical incidents as part of a job analysis. The results indicated that no new incidents appeared after examining the incidents from the first three universities. Furthermore, after examining the incidents supplied by the first 19 incumbents, no new incidents or categories appeared.

After the number of participants has been determined, a decision needs to be made about which *particular employees* will participate. If every employee will not participate, the same sampling rules used in research should be used in job analysis. That is, as discussed in Chapter 1, participants should be selected in as random a way as practical yet still be representative. The reason for this, according to research, is that employee differences in gender, race, job performance level, experience, job enjoyment, and personality can at times result in slightly different job analysis outcomes.

Job Competence. Sanchez, Praeger, Wilson, and Viswesvaran (1998) and Mullins and Kimbrough (1988) found that high-performing employees generated different job analysis outcomes than low-performing employees, Ansoorian and Shultz (1997) found moderate differences in physical effort made by employees with varying levels of expertise, and Landy and Vasey (1991) found that experienced employees rated tasks differently than less experienced employees. However, Mailhot (1996) did not find any differences in job analysis ratings made by employees of different performance levels.

Race. Aamodt, Kimbrough, Keller, and Crawford (1982); Schmitt and Cohen (1989); Veres, Green, and Boyles (1991); and Landy and Vasey (1991) report small but significant differences in the ways in which white and African American incumbents viewed their jobs. For example, Landy and Vasey found that white police officers administered first aid more often and African American officers were more involved in sweeps and raids related to widespread narcotics use. Interestingly, Veres et al. (1991) found that job analysis ratings were related not only to the race of the incumbent but to the race of the incumbent's coworkers.

Gender. Landy and Vasey (1991) found possible differences in the ways men and women viewed their jobs. Because gender was confounded with experience, they were not able to draw any definite conclusions.

Schmitt and Cohen (1989) found that male middle-level managers were more often involved in budgetary or finance-related tasks than their female counterparts. Ansoorian and Shultz (1997) found no differences in the physical effort ratings assigned by male and female incumbents.

Education Level. Landy and Vasey (1991) found high school educated police officers to be less involved in court activities than their more educated counterparts.

Viewpoint. It should be no surprise that people with different perspectives on the job (e.g., incumbent, supervisor, customer) produce different job analysis results. For example, Mueller and Belcher (2000) found that incumbents (fire captains) and their supervisors (fire chief, deputy fire chiefs, and division chiefs) produced different task ratings during a job analysis of the fire captain position. Wagner (1950) conducted a job analysis of dentists and found that patients generated more patient–dentist relationship critical incidents whereas dentists reported more technical proficiency incidents. Likewise, Fisher and Greenis (1996) and Andersson and Nilsson (1964) found differences in the critical incidents generated by managers, incumbents, and customers.

The consideration of which employees are chosen to participate is an important issue because a job can often be performed in several ways. If males and females perform equally well on a job, yet perform the job in different ways, the job analyses must contain information about both styles. For example, suppose research indicates that male supervisors lead by setting goals and being directive and female supervisors use more of a participative approach. Consequently, a job analysis conducted only on male supervisors would result in a different set of KSAOs than a job analysis using both male and female supervisors. Because job analysis is the basis for every personnel decision, it can be seen that equal opportunity efforts begin as early as the job analysis.

The issue of using the best employees or the typical employees is also important. During a job analysis at a large printing factory, it was discovered that one employee performed his job differently than the employees on the other two shifts. Further investigation revealed that the one employee was also rated much higher in job performance than the other two. Thus, it appeared the logical thing to do was write the job analysis results based on the way the best employee performed the job and then retrain the other two.

What Types of Information Should Be Obtained?

An important decision concerns the *level of specificity*. That is, should the job analysis break a job down into very minute, specific behaviors (e.g., "tilts arm at a 90 degree angle" or "moves foot forward 3 inches"), or should the job be analyzed at a more general level ("makes financial decisions," "speaks to clients")? Although most

PhotoDisc, Inc.

Interviews are a common job analysis technique.

jobs are analyzed at levels somewhere between these two extremes, there are times when the level of analysis will be closer to one end of the spectrum than the other.

For some jobs that involve intricate work, extensive and expensive efforts have been undertaken to identify the optimal way in which tasks should be performed. For example, in a window manufacturing plant, job analysis determined that many more windows could be mounted in frames by lifting the glass just 6 inches and then sliding it into place rather than lifting the glass higher and placing it in the frame. In such a situation, the work obviously must be performed in a specific manner for the greatest financial savings. Thus the job analysis is more effective at a more detailed level.

A related decision addresses the issue of *formal versus informal requirements*. Formal requirements for a secretary might include typing letters or filing memos. Informal requirements might involve making coffee or picking up the boss's children from school. Including informal requirements has the advantages of identifying and eliminating duties that may be illegal or unnecessary. For example, suppose a job analysis reveals that a secretary in one department picks up the boss's children from school and takes them to a day care center. This is an important finding because the company may not want

this to occur. However, because the manager makes $130,000 per year, the company may prefer that the lower paid secretary rather than the higher paid executive take an hour a day to pick up the children. If this task is in the job description, an applicant would know about this duty in advance and could decide at the time of hire if it were acceptable.

In addition, informal requirements, such as picking up the mail, may need to be made more formal to reduce potential confusion regarding who is responsible for the task. At one credit union, a continued source of bickering involved whose job or whose turn it was to pick up the mail, especially when the weather was bad and post office parking became limited. This problem

could have been eliminated if the task was assigned to one individual.

Conducting a Job Analysis

Although there are many ways to conduct a job analysis, the goal of most job analyses is to identify the tasks performed in a job, the conditions under which the tasks are performed, and the KSAOs needed to perform the tasks under the conditions identified. This section will begin with a commonly used strategy for conducting a job analysis and conclude with descriptions of alternative methods.

Cross-sell bank products.
- Study daily rate charts.
- Explain new products to customers.

Balance drawer within 30 minutes at end of day.
- Accurately count money.
- Trial balance drawer during down times.

Comply with federal and state regulations.
- Notify federal government of cash transactions in excess of $10,000.
- Treat customers equally regardless of age, race, gender, or national origin.

Accurately complete paperwork.
- Obtain all necessary information from customers.
- Obtain all necessary signatures.

Make each customer feel a "part of the family."
- Know each customer's name.
- Refer to customers by their first names.
- Smile and greet each customer.

Step 1: Identify Tasks Performed

The first step in conducting a job analysis is to identify the major job dimensions and the tasks performed for each dimension, the tools and equipment used to perform the tasks, and the conditions under which the tasks are performed. This information is usually gathered by obtaining previous information on the job, interviewing job incumbents, observing performance, or actually performing the job itself.

Gathering Existing Information. Prior to interviewing incumbents, it is always a good idea to gather information that has already been obtained. For example, one might gather existing job descriptions, task inventories, and training manuals. This information might come from the organization with which you are working, other organizations, trade publications, and journal articles.

Interviewing Subject Matter Experts. The most common method of conducting a job analysis is to interview **subject matter experts (SMEs).** SMEs are people knowledgeable about the job and include job incumbents, supervisors, customers, and upper-level management. Job analysis interviews differ greatly from employment interviews in that the purpose of the job analysis interview is to obtain information about the job itself rather than about the person doing the job. Job analysis interviews come in two main forms: individual and group. In the individual interview, the **job analyst** interviews only one employee at a time. In the group interview, often called an **SME conference,** a larger number of employees are interviewed together. As mentioned earlier in the chapter, individual interviews tend to yield results similar to group interviews.

Regardless of whether individual or group interviews are used, certain guidelines should be followed that will make the interview go more smoothly (McCormick, 1979).

1. *Prepare* for the interview by announcing the job analysis to the employees well in advance of the interviews and by selecting a quiet and private interview location.

2. *Open* the interview by establishing rapport, putting the worker at ease, and explaining the purpose of the interview.

3. *Conduct* the interview by asking open-ended questions, using easy-to-understand vocabulary, and allowing sufficient time for the employee to talk and answer questions—avoid being condescending and disagreeing with the incumbent.

Most workers are proud of their jobs and are willing to talk about them in great detail. Once the initial apprehensions and jitters are over, most job analysis interviews go well. A good way to start the actual interview is by asking the employee to describe what she does from the moment she first enters the parking lot at work to the moment she arrives back home. A question such as this provides some structure for the employee in recalling the various aspects of her job and also provides the interviewer with many follow-up questions and areas that will provide additional information.

A slightly more formal method for conducting group interviews is the technique described by Kosidlak (1987). With this technique, a committee of SMEs meets to brainstorm the *major duties* involved in a job. Once this has been done, the committee identifies the

Exhibit 2.03   Writing effective task statements

Poorly written task statement	Properly written task statement
Sends purchase requests	Sends purchase requests to the purchasing department using campus mail
Drives	Drives a five-speed truck to make food deliveries within the city of Toledo
Locks hall doors	Uses master key to lock hall doors at midnight so that nonresidents cannot enter the residence hall

tasks (work-related activities) that must be completed for each of the duties. The results are then summarized in job descriptions or a job analysis report.

An excellent job analysis interview technique was developed by Ammerman (1965) and reported by Robinson (1981). The basic steps for the **Ammerman technique** are these:

1. Convene a panel of experts that includes representatives from all levels of the organization.

2. Have the panel identify the objectives and standards that are to be met by the ideal incumbent.

3. Have the panel list the specific behaviors necessary for each objective or standard to be attained.

4. Have the panel identify which of the behaviors from step 3 are "critical" to reaching the objective.

5. Have the panel rank order the objectives on the basis of importance.

The results of these procedures will yield a set of important objectives and the behaviors necessary to meet these objectives. These behaviors can be used to create employee selection tests, develop training programs, or evaluate the performance of current employees. An example of Ammerman-style objectives and behaviors is shown in Exhibit 2.02.

Observing Incumbents. Observations are useful job analysis methods, especially when used in conjunction with other methods such as interviews. During a job analysis observation, the job analyst observes incumbents performing their jobs in the work setting. The advantage to this method is that it lets the job analyst actually see the worker do her job and thus obtain information that the worker may have forgotten to mention during the interview. This is especially important because many employees have difficulty describing exactly what they do; to them, performing their job is second nature and takes little thought. A good demonstration of this point is people's difficulty in naming the location of keys on a typewriter or the

locations of gears when they drive. We all type and shift gears without thinking (well, most of us do), but quickly describing to another person the location of the "v" key on our typewriter or "reverse" in our manual transmission is difficult.

The method's disadvantage is that it is very obtrusive: Observing someone without their knowing is difficult. Think of the jobs at which you have worked: There is seldom any place from which an analyst could observe without being seen by employees. This is a problem because once employees know they are being watched, their behavior changes, which keeps an analyst from obtaining an accurate picture of the way jobs are done. When I was in college and working third shift at a bookbinding factory, the company hired an "efficiency expert" to analyze our performance. The expert arrived in a three-piece suit, armed with a stopwatch and clipboard. He stuck out like a sore thumb! You can bet that for the 2 weeks the efficiency expert observed us, we were ideal employees (I can even remember calling my supervisor "sir") because we knew he was watching. Once he left, we went back to being our normal, time-wasting, soda-drinking, wise-cracking selves.

Job Participation. One can analyze a job by actually performing it. This technique, called **job participation**, is especially nice because it is easier to understand every aspect of a job once you have done it yourself. The technique is easily used when the analyst has previously performed the job. An excellent example would be a supervisor who has worked her way up through the ranks. As mentioned earlier, the problem with using a supervisor or an incumbent is that neither has been trained in job analysis techniques.

A professional job analyst also can perform an unfamiliar job for a short period of time, although this, of course, is limited to certain occupations that involve quick training and minimal consequences from an error. The job of a brain surgeon would probably not be a good one to analyze using this method.

The analyst should spend enough time on the job to properly sample work behavior in addition to job difficulty. Yet spending long periods of time can be very expensive and still not guarantee that all aspects

Exhibit **2.04** Example of task inventory scales

Frequency

0	Task is not performed as part of this job
1	Task is seldom performed
2	Task is occasionally performed
3	Task is frequently performed

Importance

0	Unimportant: There would be no negative consequences if the task was not performed or if the task was not performed properly
1	Important: Job performance would be diminished if this task was not completed properly
2	Essential: The job could not be performed effectively if the incumbent did not properly complete this task

of behavior will be covered. Psychologist Wayman Mullins used job participation techniques to analyze the job of a firefighter. Mullins spent 2 weeks living at the fire station and performing all the duties of a firefighter. The only problem during this 2-week period—no fires. If Mullins had not already had a good idea of what a firefighter did, he would have concluded that the most important duties were sleeping, cleaning, cooking, and playing cards!

Step 2: Write Task Statements

Once the tasks have been identified, the next step is to write the task statements that will be used in the **task inventory** and included in the job description. As shown in Exhibit 2.03, at the minimum, a properly written task statement must contain an *action* (what is done) and an *object* (to what is the action done). Often, task statements will also include such components as *where* the task is done, *how* it is done, *why* it is done, and *when* it is done.

Here are some characteristics of well-written task statements:

- One action and one object. If the statement includes the word "and," it may have more than one action or object. For example, the statement "Types correspondence to be sent to vendors" has one action and one object. However, the statement "Types, files, and sends correspondence to vendors" contains three very different actions (types, files, sends).
- Task statements should be written at a level that can be read and understood by a person with the same reading ability as the typical job incumbent.
- All task statements should be written in the same tense.

- The task statement should include the tools and equipment used to complete the task.
- Task statements should not be competencies (e.g., "Be a good writer").
- Task statements should not be a policy (e.g., "Treats people nicely").
- The statement should make sense by itself. That is, "Makes photocopies" does not provide as much detail as "Makes photocopies of transactions for credit union members," which indicates what types of materials are photocopied and for whom they are copied.
- For those activities that involve decision making, the level of authority must be indicated. This level lets the incumbent know which decisions she is allowed to make on her own and which need approval from a higher level (Degner, 1995).

It has also been suggested that a few tasks not part of a job be placed in the task inventory; data from incumbents who rate these irrelevant tasks as part of their job are removed from the job analysis due to their carelessness (Green & Stutzman, 1986). Including "bogus tasks" is probably a good idea. Pine (1995) included 5 such items in a 68-item task inventory for corrections officers and found that 45% reported performing at least one of the bogus tasks. For example, a task inventory might include "operates a Gonkulator" or "uses PARTH program to analyze data" even though no such machine or computer program actually exists.

Step 3: Rate Task Statements

Once the task statements have been written (usually including some 200 tasks), the next step is to conduct a **task analysis**—using a group of SMEs to rate each

Exhibit 2.05 Example of task analysis ratings

	Raters								
	Scully			Mulder			Combined Average		
Task #	F	+ I	= CR	F	+ I	= CR	F	+ I	= CR
1	2	0	2	3	0	3	2.5	0.0	2.5
2	2	2	4	2	1	3	2.0	1.5	3.5
3	0	0	0	0	0	0	0.0	0.0	0.0
4	3	2	5	3	2	5	3.0	2.0	5.0

task statement on the frequency and the importance or criticality of the task being performed. For example, consider the task, "accurately shoots a gun." For a police officer, this task occurs infrequently, but when it does, its importance is paramount. If a frequency scale alone were used, shooting a gun might not be covered in training. Although many types of scales can be used, research suggests that many of the scales tap similar types of information (Sanchez & Fraser, 1992; Sanchez & Levine, 1989); thus, using the two scales of frequency of occurrence and importance shown in Exhibit 2.04 should be sufficient. In fact, rather than asking for ratings of frequency of occurrence or relative time spent on a task, some researchers advise that the task inventory should simply ask, "Do you perform this task?" (Wilson & Harvey, 1990). Raters tend to agree on ratings of task importance but not on time spent (Lindell, Clause, Brandt, & Landis, 1998).

After a representative sample of SMEs rates each task, the ratings are organized in a format similar to that shown in Exhibit 2.05. Tasks will not be included in the *job description* if their average frequency rating is .5 or below. Tasks will not be included in the final *task inventory* if they have either an average rating of .5 or less on *either* the frequency or importance scales, or an average combined rating (CR) of less than 2. Using these criteria, tasks 1, 2, and 4 in Exhibit 2.05 would be included in the job description, and tasks 2 and 4 would be included in the final task inventory used in the next step of the job analysis.

Step 4: Determine Essential KSAOs

Once the task analysis is completed and a job analyst has a list of tasks that are essential for the proper performance of a job, the next step is to identify the knowledge, skills, ability, and other characteristics (KSAOs) that are needed to perform the tasks. KSAOs are commonly referred to as *competencies* (Shippmann et al., 2000).

- A **knowledge** is a body of information needed to perform a task.

- A **skill** is the proficiency to perform a learned task.

- An **ability** is a basic capacity for performing a wide range of different tasks, acquiring a knowledge, or developing a skill.

- **Other characteristics** include such personal factors as personality, willingness, interest, and motivation and such tangible factors as licenses, degrees, and years of experience.

For example, to correctly shoot a gun (skill), an officer would need to hold the gun properly and allow for such external conditions as the target distance and wind conditions (knowledge), and have the hand strength, steadiness, and vision necessary to hold the gun, pull the trigger, and aim properly (abilities). To carry the gun, the officer would need to have a weapons certification (other characteristic). Determining important KSAOs can be done in one of two ways: logically linking tasks to KSAOs or using prepackaged questionnaires. To practice identifying KSAOs, complete Exercise 2–3 at the end of the chapter.

To logically link KSAOs to tasks, a group of SMEs brainstorm the KSAOs needed to perform each task. For example, a group of police officers might consider the task of "writing accident reports" and determine that grammar skills, spelling skills, legible handwriting, and knowledge of accidents are the KSAOs needed for a police officer to perform this task.

Once the list of essential KSAOs has been developed, another group of SMEs is given the list and asked to rate the extent to which each of the KSAOs is essential for performing the job. If a scale such as that shown in Exhibit 2.06 is used, KSAOs with an average score of .5 or less are eliminated from further consideration.

As you can see in Exhibit 2.06, it is also important for the SMEs to determine when each KSAO is needed. Using the example from Exhibit 2.06, KSAOs that receive average ratings of 2.5 or higher will be part of the employee selection process, KSAOs with average ratings between 1.5 and 2.49 will be taught at the police academy, and KSAOs with average ratings between .5 and 1.49 will be learned on the job during the officer's probationary period.

Exhibit	2.06	Scales used to rate KSAOs for law enforcement

Importance of KSAO

0	KSAO is **not needed** for satisfactory completion of the academy or satisfactory job performance
1	KSAO is **helpful** for satisfactory completion of the academy or satisfactory job performance
2	KSAO is **important/essential** for satisfactory completion of the academy or satisfactory job performance

When KSAO Is Needed

0	KSAO is not needed
1	KSAO is needed after completion of field training
2	KSAO is needed after completion of the academy
3	KSAO is needed at the time of hire

Rather than using the previously discussed process, KSAOs or competencies can be identified using such structured methods as the Job Components Inventory (JCI), Threshold Traits Analysis (TTA), Fleishman Job Analysis Survey (F-JAS), critical incident technique (CIT), and the Personality-Related Position Requirements Form (PPRF). Each of these will be discussed in detail later in the chapter.

Step 5: Selecting Tests to Tap KSAOs

Once the important KSAOs have been identified, the next step is to determine the best method to tap the KSAOs that are needed at the time of hire. These methods will be used to select new employees and include such methods as interviews, work samples, ability tests, personality tests, reference checks, integrity tests, biodata, and assessment centers. These methods, and how to choose them, will be discussed in great detail in Chapters 4, 5, and 6.

The average ratings obtained from step 4 will be used to weight test scores. That is, a test tapping a KSAO with a rating of 2.9 should receive more weight than a test tapping a KSAO with a rating of 2.5.

Using Other Job Analysis Methods

In the previous pages, a particular job analysis strategy was discussed. But many other job analysis methods can be used in conjunction with this strategy or as a replacement for this strategy.

Occupational Information Network (O*NET)

The **Occupational Information Network (O*NET)** is a national job analysis system created by the federal government to replace the **Dictionary of Occupational Titles (DOT)**, which had been in use since the 1930s (Peterson et al., 2001). O*NET is a major advancement in understanding the nature of work, in large part because its developers understood that jobs can be viewed at four levels: economic, organizational, job, and individual. As a result, O*NET has incorporated the types of information obtained in many job analysis techniques, which can be seen in Exhibit 2.07.

O*NET includes information about the occupation (generalized work activities, work context, organizational context) and the worker characteristics (ability, work style, occupational values and interests, knowledge, skills, education) needed for success in the occupation. The O*NET also includes information about such economic factors as labor demand, labor supply, salaries, and occupational trends. This information can be used by employers to select new employees and by applicants who are searching for careers that match their skills, interests, and economic needs.

One advantage of the O*NET is that it yields information similar to that obtained from the job analysis methods discussed in the following pages. The O*NET database is scheduled for completion by 2004 and will be updated annually. Updated information on the O*NET can be viewed at www.doleta.gov/programs/onet/ and at www.onetcenter.org.

Methods Providing General Information About Worker Activities

Using the strategy discussed previously yields *specific* information about the tasks and activities performed by an incumbent in a *particular* job. Though such detailed information is ideal, obtaining it can be both time-consuming and expensive. As an alternative, several questionnaires have been developed to analyze jobs at a more general level. This general analysis saves time and money and allows jobs to be more easily compared

Exhibit 2.07 Comparison of O*NET categories to other job analysis methods

	Job Analysis Method							
	O*NET	F-JAS	TTA	JCI	JAI	PPRF	PAQ	JSP
ABILITY								
Cognitive Abilities								
Verbal abilities	√	√	√	√			√	√
Oral comprehension	√	√	√	√			√	√
Written comprehension	√	√	√	√			√	√
Oral expression	√	√	√	√			√	√
Written expression	√	√	√	√			√	√
Idea generation and reasoning abilities	√	√	√			√	√	√
Fluency of ideas	√	√						
Originality	√	√	√			√		√
Problem sensitivity	√	√						√
Reasoning	√	√					√	√
Deductive reasoning	√	√						√
Inductive reasoning	√	√						√
Information ordering	√	√				√		√
Category flexibility	√	√						
Planning			√				√	√
Decision making			√	√			√	√
Combining information							√	√
Quantitative abilities	√	√	√	√			√	√
Mathematical reasoning	√	√		√				√
Number facility	√	√	√	√			√	√
Use of length, distance, size, weight				√			√	√
Memory	√	√	√					√
Perceptual abilities	√	√	√					
Speed of closure	√	√						
Flexibility of closure	√	√						
Perceptual speed	√	√						
Spatial abilities	√			√				
Spatial orientation		√						
Visualization	√			√				
Attentiveness	√			√				
Selective attention/concentration	√	√	√	√				
Time sharing	√	√		√				
Psychomotor Abilities	√	√		√				
Fine manipulative abilities	√	√		√			√	√
Arm–hand steadiness	√	√		√			√	√
Manual dexterity	√	√		√			√	√
Finger dexterity	√	√		√			√	√
Control movement abilities	√	√		√			√	√
Control precision	√	√					√	√
Multilimb coordination	√	√					√	√
Response orientation	√	√					√	√
Rate control	√	√					√	√
Reaction time and speed ability	√	√	√	√				
Reaction time	√	√		√				
Wrist–finger speed	√	√		√				
Speed of limb movement	√	√						
Physical Abilities	√							
Physical strength	√		√	√				
Static strength	√	√		√				
Explosive strength	√	√		√				

	O*NET	F-JAS	TTA	JCI	JAI	PPRF	PAQ	JSP
Dynamic strength	√	√						
Trunk strength	√	√						
Endurance/Stamina	√	√	√					
Flexibility, balance, coordination	√	√	√	√			√	√
Extent flexibility	√	√		√				
Dynamic flexibility	√	√						
Gross body coordination	√	√		√			√	√
Gross body equilibrium	√	√		√			√	√
Sensory Abilities	√	√						
Visual abilities	√	√	√					
Near vision	√	√		√			√	
Far vision	√	√					√	
Visual color discrimination	√	√		√			√	
Night vision	√	√						
Peripheral vision	√	√						
Depth perception	√	√					√	
Glare sensitivity	√	√						
Sense of color				√				
Auditory and speech abilities	√							
Hearing sensitivity	√	√	√					
Auditory attention		√	√					
Sound localization	√	√						
Sound recognition							√	
Speech localization							√	
Speech recognition	√	√						
Speech clarity	√	√						
Other senses								
Sense of taste				√			√	
Sense of smell				√			√	
Sense of touch				√			√	
Sense of body movement							√	
WORK STYLES								
Achievement Orientation	√			√				
Achievement/effort	√			√		√		
Persistence	√	√		√				
Initiative		√			√			
Social Influence	√							
Energy	√							
Leadership orientation	√					√		
Interpersonal Orientation		√						
Cooperative	√			√		√		
Concern for others	√					√		
Social orientation	√							
Tolerance				√				
Friendliness						√		
Sense of humor					√			
Interest in negotiation						√		
Adjustment	√							
Self-control	√					√		
Stress tolerance	√							
Adaptability/flexibility	√	√	√		√	√		

	O*NET	F-JAS	TTA	JCI	JAI	PPRF	PAQ	JSP
Adaptability to change			√		√			
Adaptability to change			√		√			
Adaptability to repetition			√					
Adaptability to pressure				√		√		
Adaptability to isolation				√				
Adaptability to discomfort			√		√			
Adaptability to hazards/ emergencies			√		√			
Interpersonal adaptability					√			
Cultural adaptability					√			
Problem-solving adaptability					√			
Resilience		√						
Conscientiousness	√					√		
Dependability	√							
Attention to detail		√					√	
Integrity	√		√			√		
Personal appearance			√					
Work ethic						√		
Independence	√							
Practical Intelligence	√							
Innovative	√		√					
Analytical	√							
SKILLS								
Basic Content Skills	√			√				
Active listening	√			√				
Reading comprehension	√			√				
Writing	√			√				
Speaking	√			√				
Mathematics	√		√	√				
Science	√							
Basic Processing Skills	√							
Active learning	√							
Learning strategies	√							
Monitoring	√							
Critical thinking	√							
Problem-solving Skills			√					
Problem identification	√							
Information gathering	√							
Information organization	√							
Synthesis/reorganization	√							
Idea generation	√							
Idea evaluation	√							
Implementation planning	√							
Solution appraisal		√						
Resistance to premature judgment		√						
Planning			√					
Social Skills								
Social perceptiveness	√	√						
Coordination	√							
Persuasion	√	√	√	√			√	√

	O*NET	F-JAS	TTA	JCI	JAI	PPRF	PAQ	JSP
Negotiation	√			√			√	√
Instructing	√						√	√
Advising				√			√	√
Supervising							√	√
Service orientation	√			√			√	√
Oral fact finding (interviewing)		√		√			√	√
Oral defense		√						
Public speaking				√			√	√
Entertaining							√	√
Sales interest		√						
Technical Skills	√							
Operations analysis	√							
Technology design	√							
Equipment selection	√							
Installation	√							
Programming	√							
Testing	√							
Operation monitoring	√							
Operations and control	√							
Product inspection	√							
Equipment maintenance	√			√				
Troubleshooting	√							
Repairing	√							
Electrical/electronic		√						
Mechanical		√						
Tools		√		√			√	√
Map reading		√		√				
Drafting		√						
Reading plans		√		√				
Driving		√					√	√
Typing		√						
Shorthand		√						
Filing				√				
Spelling		√						
Grammar		√						
Computer programming				√				
Craft knowledge			√					
Craft skill			√					
Systems Skills	√							
Visioning	√							
Systems perception	√							
Identification of downstream consequences	√							
Identification of key causes		√						
Judgment and evaluation	√							
Systems evaluation	√							
Resource Management Skills	√							
Time management	√							
Financial resource management	√							
Material resource management	√							
Personnel resource management	√							

Exhibit **2.08** Sample questions from the Position Analysis Questionnaire

RELATIONSHIPS WITH OTHER PERSONS

Code Importance to This Job (I)
N Does not apply
1 Very minor
2 Low
3 Average
4 High
5 Extreme

4 Relationships with Other Persons

This section deals with different aspects of interaction between people involved in various kinds of work.

4.1 Communications

Rate the following in terms of how important the activity is to the completion of the job. Some jobs may involve several or all of the items in this section.

4.1.1 Oral (communicating by speaking)

99 I Advising (dealing with individuals in order to counsel and/or guide them with regard to problems that may be resolved by legal, financial, scientific, technical, clinical, spiritual, and/or other professional principles)

100 I Negotiating (dealing with others in order to reach an agreement or solution, for example, labor bargaining, diplomatic relations, etc.)

101 I Persuading (dealing with others in order to influence them toward some action or point of view, for example, selling, political campaigning, etc.)

102 I Instructing (the teaching of knowledge or skills, in either an informal or a formal manner, to others, for example, a public school teacher, a machinist teaching an apprentice, etc.)

103 I Interviewing (conducting interviews directed toward some specific objective, for example, interviewing job applicants, census taking, etc.)

104 I Routine information exchange: job related (the giving and/or receiving of job-related information of a routine nature, for example, ticket agent, taxicab dispatcher, receptionist, etc.)

105 I Nonroutine information exchange (the giving and/or receiving of job-related information of a nonroutine or unusual nature, for example, professional committee meetings, engineers discussing new product design, etc.)

106 I Public speaking (making speeches or formal presentations before relatively large audiences, for example, political addresses, radio/TV broadcasting, delivering a sermon, etc.)

4.1.2 Written (communicating by written/printed material)

107 I Writing (for example, writing or dictating letters, reports, etc., writing copy for ads, writing newspaper articles, etc,: do not include transcribing activities described in item 43, but only activities in which the incumbent creates the written material)

4.1.3 Other Communications

108 I Signaling (communicating by some type of signal, for example, hand signals, semaphore, whistles, horns, bells, lights, etc.)

109 I Code communications (telegraph, cryptography, etc.)

Source: E. J. McCormick, P. R. Jeannert, & R. C. Mecham, *Position Analysis Questionnaire,* copyright 1969 by Purdue Research Foundation, West Lafayette, Indiana 47907. Reprinted with permission of the publisher.

Exhibit 2.09   Data, people, and things levels

Data	People	Things
0 Synthesizing	0 Mentoring	0 Setting up
1 Coordinating	1 Negotiating	1 Precision working
2 Analyzing	2 Instructing	2 Operating–controlling
3 Compiling	3 Supervising	3 Driving-Operating
4 Computing	4 Diverting	4 Manipulating
5 Copying	5 Persuading	5 Tending
6 Comparing	6 Speaking	6 Feeding–offbearing
	7 Serving	7 Handling
	8 Taking instructions	
	9 Helping	

with one another than is the case if interviews, observations, job participation, or task analysis is used.

Position Analysis Questionnaire (PAQ). The **Position Analysis Questionnaire (PAQ)** is a structured questionnaire developed at Purdue University by McCormick, Jeanneret, and Mecham (1972). The PAQ contains 194 items organized into six main dimensions: information input, mental processes, work output, relationships with other persons, job context, and other job-related variables such as work schedule, pay, and responsibility. In the sample PAQ page shown in Exhibit 2.08, notice that the level of analysis is fairly general. That is, the PAQ tells us if a job involves interviewing but does not indicate the type of interviewing that is performed (interviewing job applicants vs. interviewing a witness to a crime) or how the interview is conducted. Thus, the results would be difficult to use for functions such as training or performance appraisal.

The PAQ offers many advantages. It is inexpensive and takes relatively little time to use (Levine, Ash, & Bennett, 1980). It is one of the most standardized job analysis methods, and its results for a particular position can be compared through computer analysis with thousands of other positions. Furthermore, it is both reliable (McCormick & Jeanneret, 1988) and robust (Jones, Main, Butler, & Johnson, 1982).

Although the PAQ has considerable support, research indicates its strengths are also the source of its weaknesses. The PAQ's instructions suggest that incumbents using the questionnaire have education levels between grades 10 and 12. Research has found, however, that the PAQ questions and directions are written at the college graduate level (Ash & Edgell, 1975); thus, many workers may not be able to understand the PAQ. This is one reason developers of the PAQ recommend that trained job analysts complete the PAQ rather than the employees themselves.

In addition, the PAQ was designed to cover all jobs, but limited to 194 questions and six dimensions, the PAQ has not proven very sensitive. For example, a homemaker and a police officer have similar PAQ profiles (Arvey & Begalla, 1975). Similar profiles also are obtained regardless of whether an analyst actually observes the job or just looks at a job title (Smith & Hakel, 1979) or a job description (Friedman & Harvey, 1986; Jones et al., 1982).

Finally, having a large amount of information about a job yields the same results as having little information (Arvey et al., 1982; Surrette et al., 1990). Although these studies speak favorably about the reliability of the PAQ, they also provide cause for worry because the PAQ appears to yield the same results regardless of how familiar the analyst is with a job.

Job Structure Profile (JSP). A revised version of the PAQ was developed by Patrick and Moore (1985). The major changes in the revision, which is called the **Job Structure Profile (JSP)**, include item content and style, new items to increase the discriminatory power of the intellectual and decision-making dimensions, and an emphasis on having a job analyst, rather than the incumbent, use the JSP. Research by JSP's developers indicates that the instrument is reliable, but further research is needed before it is known whether the JSP is a legitimate improvement on the PAQ.

Job Elements Inventory (JEI). Another method designed as an alternative to the PAQ is the **Job Elements Inventory (JEI)** developed by Cornelius and Hakel (1978). The JEI contains 153 items and has a readability level appropriate for an employee with only a 10th-grade education (Cornelius, Hakel, & Sackett, 1979). Research comparing the JEI with the PAQ indicates that the scores from each method are very similar (Harvey,

Exhibit **2.10** Job components inventory questions

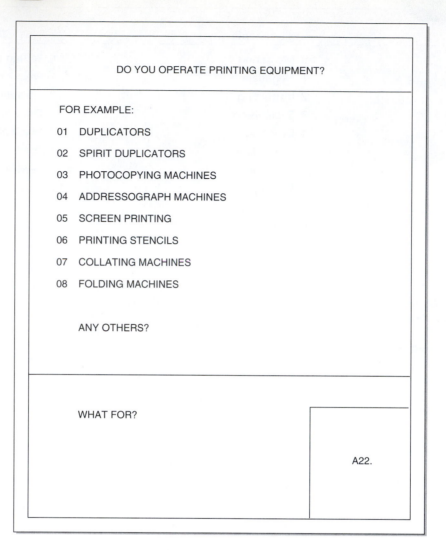

Source: Banks, M. H., Jackson, P. R., Stafford, E. M., & Warr, P. B. (1983). The Job Components Inventory and the analysis of jobs requiring limited skill. *Personal Psychology, 36, 57–66*. Reprinted with permission of the authors.

Friedman, Hakel, & Cornelius, 1988); thus, the JEI may be a better replacement for the difficult-to-read PAQ. But as mentioned with the JSP, much more research is needed before conclusions can be confidently drawn.

Functional Job Analysis (FJA). **Functional Job Analysis (FJA)** was designed by Fine (1955) as a quick method that could be used by the federal government to analyze and compare thousands of jobs. Jobs analyzed by FJA are broken down into the percentage of time the incumbent spends on three functions: data (information and ideas), people (clients, customers, and coworkers), and things (machines, tools, and equipment). An analyst is given 100 points to allot to the three functions. The points are usually assigned in mul-

tiples of 5, with each function receiving a minimum of 5 points. Once the points have been assigned, the highest level at which the job incumbent functions is then chosen from the chart shown in Exhibit 2.09 (Fine, 1988).

Methods Providing Information About Tools and Equipment

Job Components Inventory (JCI). To take advantage of the PAQ's strengths while avoiding some of its problems, Banks, Jackson, Stafford, and Warr (1983) developed the **Job Components Inventory (JCI)** for use in England. The JCI consists of more than 400 questions covering five major categories: tools and equipment, perceptual

Exhibit 2.11 AET dimensions

Part A Work System Analysis

1 Work objects
  1.1 material work objects (physical condition, special properties of the material, quality of surfaces, manipulation delicacy, form, size, weight, dangerousness)
  1.2 energy as work object
  1.3 information as work object
  1.4 man, animals, plants as work objects
2 Equipment
  2.1 working equipment
    2.1.1 equipment, tools, machinery to change the properties of work objects
    2.1.2 means of transport
    2.1.3 controls
  2.2 other equipment
    2.2.1 displays, measuring instruments
    2.2.2 technical aids to support human sense organs
    2.2.3 work chair, table, room
3 Work environment
  3.1 Physical environment
    3.1.1 environmental influences
    3.1.2 dangerousness of work and risk of occupational diseases
  3.2 Organizational and social environment
    3.2.1 temporal organization of work
    3.2.2 position in the organization of work sequence
    3.2.3 hierarchical position in the organization
    3.2.4 position in the communication system

  3.3 Principles and methods of remuneration
    3.3.1 principles of remuneration
    3.3.2 methods of remuneration

Part B Task Analysis

1 Tasks relating to material work objects
2 Tasks relating to abstract work objects
3 Man-related tasks.
4 Number and repetitiveness of tasks

Part C Job Demand Analysis

1 Demands on perception
  1.1 mode of perception
    1.1.1 visual
    1.1.2 auditory
    1.1.3 tactile
    1.1.4 olfactory
    1.1.5 proprioceptive
  1.2 absolute/relative evaluation of perceived information
  1.3 accuracy of perception
2 Demands for decision
  2.1 complexity of decision
  2.2 pressure on time
  2.3 required knowledge
3 Demands for response/activity
  3.1 body postures
  3.2 static work
  3.3 heavy muscular work
  3.4 light muscular work.
  3.5 strenuousness and frequency of movements

Source: Rohmert, W., & Landau, K. (1983). *A new technique for job analysis.* New York: Taylor & Francis. Reprinted with permission of the publisher.

and physical requirements, mathematical requirements, communication requirements, and decision making and responsibility. It is the only job analysis method containing a detailed section on tools and equipment. An example of one JCI question is shown in Exhibit 2.10.

Published research on the JCI is not abundant. But it does appear to be a promising technique, with research indicating that it is reliable (Banks & Miller, 1984), can differentiate between jobs (Banks et al., 1983), can cluster jobs based on their similarity to one another (Stafford, Jackson, & Banks, 1984), and, contrary to the PAQ, is affected by the amount of information available to the analyst (Surrette et al., 1990).

Methods Providing Information About the Work Environment

The techniques discussed so far provide information about the activities that are performed and the equipment used to perform them. The job analyst still needs information about the conditions under which the activities are performed. For example, two employees might perform the task "delivers mail," yet one might do it by carrying 50-pound mail bags in very hot weather while the other delivers mail by driving a golf cart through an air conditioned warehouse. To obtain information about the work environment, a job analyst might use the **AET**, an acronym for "Arbeitswissenschaftliches Erhebungsverfahren zur Tatigkeitsanalyse" (try saying this three times!), which means "ergonomic job-analysis procedure." By *ergonomic*, we mean that it is primarily concerned with the relationship between the worker and work objects. Developed in Germany by Rohmert and Landau (1983), the AET is a 216-item, standardized questionnaire that analyzes a job along the dimensions shown in Exhibit 2.11. Sample items from the AET can be found in Exhibit 2.12. Although the AET appears to be a promising method for obtaining certain types of job analysis information,

Exhibit 2.12   Sample AET Items

CNO	CC	
1.1.7	Weight	
		Answer questions 22–24 indicating the individual proportions of *time* during which the incumbent performs tasks involving work materials of *different weights*.
22	D	*Low* weight
		objects weighing up to 1 kg can normally be manipulated with fingers or hands
23	D	*Medium* weight
		1–10 kg can normally be manipulated with hands
24		*Heavy* weight
		more than 10 kg can partly be manipulated by one person without using additional auxilliaries, partly including the use of handling equipment and hoisting machines
1.1.8	Danger	
		Answer questions 25–30 indicating the individual proportions of time during which the incumbent performs tasks involving *dangerous* work *materials*.
25	D	Work materials that are *explosive*
		e.g., explosives and igniting mixtures, ammunition, fireworks
26	D	Work materials that are *conductive to fire or inflammable*
		e.g., petrol, technical oils, lacquers, and varnishes
27	D	Work materials that are *poisonous or caustic*
		e.g., basic chemicals, chemical-technical materials, plant protectives, cleaning materials
28	D	Work materials that are *radioactive*
		e.g., uranium concentrate, nuclear materials
29	D	Work materials *irritating skin or mucous membrane*
		e.g., quartz, asbestos, Thomas meal, flax, raw cotton
30	D	Work materials *causing other health hazards*
		If characteristic 1 is rated D = 5, continue with characteristic 34.

Source: Rohmert, W., & Landau, K. (1983). *A new technique for job analysis.* New York: Taylor & Francis. Reprinted with permission of the publisher.

there has not been enough published research to draw any real conclusions.

Methods Providing Information About KSAOs

Critical Incident Technique. The **Critical Incident Technique (CIT)** was first developed and used by John Flanagan and his students at the University of Pittsburgh in the late 1940s and early 1950s. The CIT is used to discover actual incidents of job behavior that make the difference between a job's successful and unsuccessful performance (Flanagan, 1954). This technique can be conducted in many ways, but the basic procedure is as follows.

1. Job incumbents each generate between one and five incidents of both excellent and poor performance that they have seen on the job. These incidents can be obtained in many ways—log books, questionnaires, interviews, and so on;

research has shown that the method used makes little difference (Campion, Greener, & Wernli, 1973), although questionnaires are usually used because they are easiest. A convenient way to word requests for critical incidents is by asking incumbents to think of times they saw workers perform in an especially outstanding way and then to write down exactly what occurred. Incumbents are then asked to do the same for times they saw workers perform poorly. This process is repeated as needed. Two examples of critical incidents are shown in Exhibit 2.13.

2. Job experts examine each incident and decide whether it is an example of excellent or poor behavior. This step is necessary because approximately 5% of incidents initially cited as poor examples by employees are actually good examples and vice versa (Aamodt,

Exhibit **2.13** Critical incident examples

About a year ago, I was driving home from school and had a flat tire. I was having trouble changing the tire when the police officer stopped and helped me. He then followed me to the nearest gas station to make sure that I didn't have any more trouble. Most cops probably wouldn't have done a darn thing to help.

I got pulled over for doing 45 in a 25 MPH zone. Instead of just writing me up, the cop told me what a jerk I was for speeding and that if he ever saw me speed again, I would get more than a ticket. He was the one who was the jerk!

Reardon, & Kimbrough, 1986). For example, in a recent job analysis of the position of university instructor, a few students described their worst teachers as those who lectured from material not included in their textbooks. A committee of faculty members and students who reviewed the incidents determined that lecturing from nontext material actually was excellent. Thus, the incidents were counted as examples of excellent rather than poor performance.

3. The incidents generated in the first stage are then given to three or four incumbents to sort into an unspecified number of categories. The incidents in each category are then read by the job analyst, who combines, names, and defines the categories.

4. To verify the judgments made by the job analyst in step 3, three other incumbents are given the incidents and category names and asked to sort the incidents into the newly created categories. If two of the three incumbents sort an incident into the same category, the incident is considered part of that category. Any incident that is not agreed upon by two sorters is either thrown out or placed in a new category.

5. The numbers of both types of incidents sorted into each category are then tallied and used to create a table similar to Exhibit 2.14. The categories provide the important dimensions of a job, and the numbers provide the relative importance of these dimensions.

The CIT is an excellent addition to a job analysis because the actual critical incidents can be used for future activities such as performance appraisal and training. The CIT's greatest drawback is that its emphasis on the difference between excellent and poor performance ignores routine duties. Thus, the CIT cannot be used as the sole method of job analysis. To practice using the CIT, complete the CIT exercise on your CD-ROM.

Job Components Inventory. In addition to information about tools and equipment used on the job, which were discussed earlier, the JCI also provides information about the perceptual, physical, mathematical, communication, decision-making, and responsibility skills needed to perform the job.

Threshold Traits Analysis. An approach similar to the JCI is **Threshold Traits Analysis (TTA)**, which was developed by Lopez, Kesselman, and Lopez (1981). This method is only available by hiring a particular consulting firm (Lopez and Associates), but its unique style makes it worthy of mentioning. The TTA questionnaire's 33 items identify the traits that are necessary for the successful performance of a job. The 33 items cover five trait categories: physical, mental, learned, motivational, and social. Examples of the items and their trait categories can be found in Exhibits 2.15 and 2.07. The TTA's greatest advantages are that it is short and reliable and can correctly identify important traits (Lopez et al., 1981). The TTA's greatest disadvantage is that it is not available commercially. Because the TTA also focuses on traits, its main uses are in the development of an employee selection system or a career plan (Lopez, Rockmore, & Kesselman, 1980).

Fleishman Job Analysis Survey (F-JAS). Based on more than 30 years of research (Fleishman & Reilly, 1992a), the **Fleishman Job Analysis Survey (F-JAS)** requires incumbents or job analysts to view a series of abilities such as the one shown in Exhibit 2.16 and to rate the level of ability needed to perform the job. These ratings are performed for each of the 72 abilities and knowledge shown in Exhibit 2.07. The F-JAS is easy to use, is supported by years of research, and can be used by either incumbents or trained analysts. Its advantages over TTA are that it is more detailed and is commercially available.

Job Adaptability Inventory (JAI). The **Job Adaptability Inventory (JAI)** is a 132-item inventory developed by Pulakos, Arad, Donovan, and Plamondon (2000) that taps the extent to which a job incumbent needs to adapt to situations on the job. The JAI has eight dimensions:

- Handling emergencies or crisis situations
- Handling work stress
- Solving problems creatively

Exhibit 2.14 — Critical incident technique categories and frequencies for excellent and poor resident assistants

Category	Excellent	Poor	Total
Interest in residents	31	19	50
Availability	14	27	41
Responsibility	12	20	32
Fairness	18	10	28
Self-adherence to the rules	0	28	28
Social skills	19	7	26
Programming	13	7	20
Self-confidence	12	8	20
Rule enforcement	4	14	18
Authoritarianism	1	16	17
Counseling skills	12	4	16
Self-control	5	2	7
Confidentiality	1	2	3

- Dealing with uncertain and unpredictable work situations
- Learning work tasks, technologies, and procedures
- Demonstrating interpersonal adaptability
- Demonstrating cultural adaptability
- Demonstrating physically oriented adaptability

Though the JAI is relatively new, it has excellent reliability and has been shown to distinguish among jobs (Pulakos et al., 2000).

Personality-Related Position Requirements Form (PPRF). The **Personality-Related Position Requirements Form (PPRF)** was developed by Raymark, Schmit, and Guion (1997) to identify the personality types needed to perform job-related tasks. The PPRF consists of 107 items tapping 12 personality dimensions that fall under the "Big 5" personality dimensions of openness to experience, conscientiousness, extraversion, agreeableness, and emotional stability. Though more research is needed, the PPRF is reliable and shows promise as a useful job analysis instrument for identifying the personality traits necessary to perform a job.

Evaluation of Methods

In the previous pages, many job analysis methods were presented. But the question left unanswered is: Which of the methods is best? Unfortunately, there is no clear answer to this question. The best method to use in analyzing a job appears to be related to the end use of the job analysis information. That is, different meth-

ods are best for different uses—*worker-oriented methods,* such as CIT, JCI, and TTA, are best for such uses as employee selection and performance appraisal; *job-oriented methods,* such as task analysis, are best for such uses as work design and writing job descriptions. To get the most out of a job analysis, several techniques should be utilized. At least one of these methods should be worker oriented and at least one job oriented (Prien, 1977).

From a legal perspective, courts have ruled that job analysis is necessary (Sparks, 1988) and that acceptable job analyses use several up-to-date sources, be conducted by experts, use a large number of job incumbents, and cover the entire range of worker activities and qualifications (Thompson & Thompson, 1982).

Unfortunately, research directly comparing job analysis methods is not abundant. This is primarily because direct comparison of methods is virtually impossible: Each method yields results that differ in both the number and the type of dimensions (Cornelius, Carron, & Collins, 1979). Thus, the comparative research that has been conducted has focused on opinions of job analysts.

Survey research by Levine, Ash, and their colleagues (Levine, Ash, Hall, & Sistrunk, 1983; Levine et al., 1980) has found the following:

1. The PAQ is seen as the most standardized technique and the CIT the least standardized.
2. The CIT takes the least amount of job analyst training and task analysis the most.
3. The PAQ is the least costly method and the CIT the most.

Exhibit 2.15 Sample from Threshold Traits Analysis questionnaire

Problem Solving

Job Functions Include	Incumbent Must
Processing information to reach specific conclusions, answering problems, adapting and assessing ideas of others, and revising into workable form.	Analyze information and, by inductive reasoning, arrive at a specific conclusion or solution (trait also known as *convergent thinking, reasoning*).

Level	Job Activities That Require Solving	Level	Incumbent Must Solve
0	Very minor problems with fairly simple solutions (running out of supplies or giving directions).	0	Very minor problems with fairly simple solutions.
1	Problems with known and limited variables (diagnosing mechanical disorders or customer complaints).	1	Problems with known and limited variables.
2	More complex problems with many known variables (programming or investment analysis).	2	Problems with many known and complex variables.
3	Very complex and abstract problems with many unknown variables (advanced systems design or research).	3	Very complex and abstract problems with many unknown variables.

Source: Adapted from Lopez, F. M., Kesselman, G. A., & Lopez, F. E. (1981). An empirical test of a trait-oriented job analysis technique. *Personal Psychology, 34,* 479–502. Reprinted with permission of the authors.

4. The PAQ takes the least amount of time to complete and task analysis the most.

5. Task analysis has the highest quality results and TTA the lowest.

6. Task analysis reports are longest and job elements reports the shortest.

7. The CIT was rated as being the most useful and the PAQ the least.

8. Task analysis gave the best overall job picture and the PAQ the worst.

Keep in mind, however, that these findings are based on users' opinions rather than on actual empirical comparison.

Job Evaluation

Job evaluation is the process of determining a job's *worth*. This process is typically done in two stages: determining internal pay equity and determining external pay equity.

Determining Internal Pay Equity

Internal pay equity involves comparing jobs *within* an organization to ensure that people with jobs worth the most money are paid accordingly. The difficulty in this process, of course, is determining the worth of each job. Because a complete discussion of all job evaluation methods is beyond the scope of this text, we will stick to a discussion of the most commonly used method.

Step 1: Determining Compensable Job Factors

The first step in evaluating a job is to decide what factors differentiate the relative worth of jobs. Possible **compensable job factors** include:

- Level of responsibility
- Physical demands
- Mental demands
- Education requirements
- Training and experience requirements
- Working conditions

The philosophical perspective of the job evaluator can affect these factors. Some evaluators argue that the most important compensable factor is responsibility and that physical demands are not important. Others argue that education is most important. The choice of compensable factors thus is often more philosophical than empirical.

Step 2: Determining the Levels for Each Compensable Factor

Once the compensable factors have been selected, the next step is to determine the levels for each

Exhibit **2.16** Fleishman Job Analysis Survey example

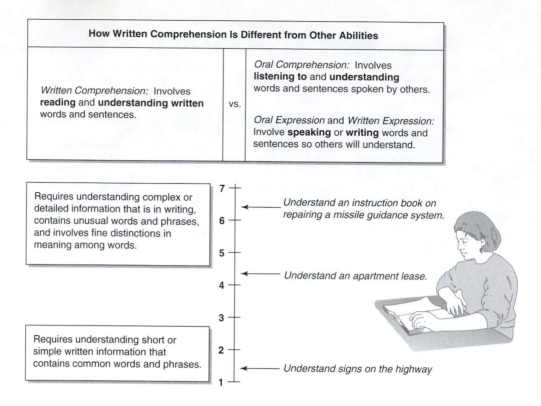

How Written Comprehension Is Different from Other Abilities		
Written Comprehension: Involves **reading** and **understanding written** words and sentences.	vs.	*Oral Comprehension:* Involves **listening to** and **understanding** words and sentences spoken by others. *Oral Expression* and *Written Expression:* Involve **speaking** or **writing** words and sentences so others will understand.

Requires understanding complex or detailed information that is in writing, contains unusual words and phrases, and involves fine distinctions in meaning among words.

Understand an instruction book on repairing a missile guidance system.

Understand an apartment lease.

Requires understanding short or simple written information that contains common words and phrases.

Understand signs on the highway

factor. For a factor such as education, the levels are easy to determine (e.g., high school diploma, associate's degree, bachelor's degree). For factors like responsibility, a considerable amount of time and discussion may be required to determine the levels.

Step 3: Determining the Factor Weights

Because some factors are more important than others, weights must be assigned to each factor and to each level within a factor. Here is the process for doing this:

1. A job evaluation committee determines the total number of points that will be distributed among the factors. Usually, the number is some multiple of 100 (for example, 100, 500, 1,000) and is based on the number of compensable factors. The greater the number of factors, the greater the number of points.

2. Each factor is weighted by assigning a number of points. The more important the factor, the greater the number that will be assigned.

3. The number of points assigned to a factor is then divided into each of the levels. If 100 points had been assigned to the factor of education, then 20

points (100 points/5 degrees) would be assigned to each level. An example of this procedure is shown in Exhibit 2.17. To better understand this process, complete the Job Evaluation Exercise on your CD-ROM.

4. The job evaluation committee takes the job descriptions for each job and assigns points based on the factors and degrees created in the previous steps.

5. The total number of points for a job is compared with the salary currently being paid for the job. This comparison is typically graphed in a fashion similar to the **wage trend line** shown in Exhibit 2.18. Wage trend lines are drawn based on the results of a regression formula in which salary is predicted by the number of job analysis points. Jobs whose point values fall well below the line (as with Job D in Exhibit 2.18) are considered underpaid and are immediately assigned higher salary levels. Jobs with point values well above the line (as with Job H) are considered overpaid and the salary level is decreased once current jobholders leave. To better understand this process, complete Exercise 2–4 at the end of this chapter.

Exhibit 2.17 Example of completed job evaluation results

Factors	Points
Education (200 points possible)	
High school education or less	40
Two years of college	80
Bachelor's degree	120
Master's degree	160
Ph.D.	200
Responsibility (300 points possible)	
Makes no decisions	75
Makes decisions for self	150
Makes decisions for 1–5 employees	225
Makes decisions for more than 5 employees	300
Physical demands (90 points possible)	
Lifts no heavy objects	30
Lifts objects between 25 and 100 pounds	60
Lifts objects more than 100 pounds	90

Determining External Equity

With **external equity,** the worth of a job is determined by comparing the job to the external market (other organizations). External equity is important if an organization is to attract and retain employees. In other words, it must be competitive with the compensation plans of other organizations. That is, a fast food restaurant that pays cooks $6 per hour will probably have trouble hiring and keeping high-caliber employees if other fast food restaurants in the area pay $7 per hour.

To determine external equity, organizations use **salary surveys.** Sent to other organizations, these surveys ask how much an organization pays its employees in various positions. An organization can either construct and send out its own survey or use the results of surveys conducted by trade groups, an option that many organizations choose. On the basis of the survey results such as those shown in Exhibit 2.19, an organization can decide where it wants to be in relation to the compensation policies of other organizations (often called *market position*). That is, an organization might choose to offer compensation at higher levels to attract the best applicants as well as keep current employees from going to other organizations. Other organizations might choose to pay at the "going rate" so that they have a reasonable chance of competing for applicants, even though they will often lose the best applicants to higher paying organizations. Market position is most important in a good economy where jobs are plentiful and applicants have several job options. It may seem surprising that competing organizations would supply salary information to each other, but because every organization needs salary data from other organizations, compensation analysts tend to cooperate well with one another.

Roanoke County (Virginia) provides an excellent example of the importance of market position. The county was concerned about the high turnover rate of its police dispatchers and undertook a study to determine the reason for the problem. Possible reasons were thought to be working conditions, location, reputation, and pay. The study revealed that most of the turnover was due to a neighboring city paying its dispatchers $2,500 more per year. This resulted in Roanoke County dispatchers resigning after a year of experience to take a higher paying job only 5 miles away. Adjusting the salary greatly reduced the turnover rate.

Keep in mind that job evaluation concerns the worth of the *job itself,* not the worth of a *person* in the job. For example, suppose a salary survey reveals that the going rate for a job falls within the range of $20,000 to $30,000, and an organization, deciding to be at the upper end of the market, sets its range for the position at $27,000 to $32,000. Decisions must then be made regarding where in the $5,000 range each particular employee will be paid. This decision is based on such factors as years of experience, years with the company, special skills, education, local cost of living, and performance level.

In the previous few pages, we discussed the amount of money a job is worth: this amount is called **direct compensation.** Employees are also compensated in other ways, such as pay for time not worked (e.g., holidays, vacation, sick days), deferred income (e.g., social

Exhibit 2.18 Example of a wage trend line

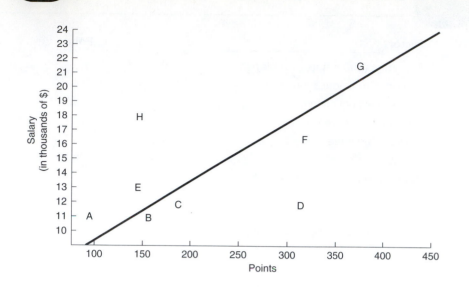

Pay Equity

In addition to internal and external equity, pay audits should also be conducted to ensure that employees are not paid differently on the basis of gender or race. Two types of audits should be conducted: one that looks at pay rates of employees within positions with identical or similar duties (equal pay for equal work) and a second that looks at pay rates of employees in jobs of similar worth as determined by the job evaluation process (comparable worth).

Comparable worth is an issue very much related to the discussion of job evaluation. Comparable worth is often in the news because some groups claim that female workers are paid less than male workers. This perception of pay inequity stems from the statistic that, on average, female workers in 2001 made only 76% of what male workers were paid (U.S. Department of Labor, 2002). However, all but 6.2% of the gap can be explained by such factors as males being in the workforce longer, having a higher percentage of full-time jobs, and working more hours in a year (Wall, 2000). Fortunately, as shown in Exhibit 2.20, pay inequity is decreasing. When males and females just en-

security and pension plans), health protection such as medical and dental insurance, and perquisites (perks) such as a company car (Martocchio, 2001; Milkovich & Newman, 2002). Consequently, a job with a direct compensation of $30,000 might actually be worth more than one at $35,000 because of the indirect compensation package. In fact, any time your author complains to his neighbors about low faculty salaries, they shed few tears as they mention such benefits as 3-week Christmas vacations and 3-month summer holidays.

tering the workforce are compared, this percentage increases to around 91%. Thus, the issue of comparable worth is often less an issue of pay discrimination than one of vocational choice and educational opportunity discrimination. To alleviate gender differences in pay, it is essential that young females be encouraged to enter historically male-dominated fields (assembly lines, management, police) and that young males be encouraged to enter historically female-dominated fields (nursing, clerical, elementary education). Furthermore, because men are more inclined to negotiate such things as starting salaries than are women (Stuhlmacher & Walters, 1999), some of the pay gap can be narrowed by not allowing applicants to negotiate salaries. Although a complete discussion on this topic goes beyond the scope of this text, an excellent assortment of articles and links on this issue can be found at www.swcollege.com/bef/policy_debates/gender.html.

Conducting a Salary Equity Study

The first step in conducting a salary equity analysis for an organization is to see if the average salary for males differs from the average salary for females. This analysis is conducted for each pay grade, not the organization as a whole. If the statistical tests indicate no significant differences between males and females, you can conclude that pay discrimination probably does not exist. If the differences in salaries are statistically significant, you need to determine if these differences can be explained by such merit factors as the amount of time an employee has been with the organization, education level, or performance ratings. If there are at least 30 employees in the grade, this can be done through a statistical technique called *hierarchical regression*.

Exhibit 2.19 Example of salary survey results

Position	Number of orgs with position	Number of employees	Weighted average	Salary Range				
				Low	Q1	Median	Q3	High
Assembly/Production								
Foreperson	18	286	$18.85	9.50	13.24	16.45	20.10	27.51
Machinist	9	419	$13.83	9.00	11.63	14.67	15.36	19.97
Production control planner	9	36	$15.73	7.02	10.28	11.67	17.41	28.36
Production worker	15	3,487	$13.91	6.00	7.71	10.47	13.68	15.30
Quality control inspector	10	45	$12.24	7.00	8.00	9.93	13.38	15.30
Maintenance								
Janitor	10	322	$ 7.08	5.27	6.48	7.62	8.34	12.72
Maintenance person A	17	112	$13.90	7.05	9.62	11.26	13.79	16.65
Mechanic	11	382	$14.80	8.25	10.93	12.41	14.33	16.05

With hierarchical regression, the first step is to enter your merit variables into the equation to determine what percentage of individual differences in pay they explain. The second step is to enter sex (coded 0 for males, 1 for females) into the equation to determine if, after controlling for the merit variables, an employee's sex is still related to pay. That is, suppose the average salary for males in Grade 8 is $27,000 and for females $24,000. It may be that this $3,000 difference can be explained by the fact that the average male in the grade has been with the organization 5 years longer than the average female in the grade. The results of the regression will determine if the $3,000 salary difference can be fully explained, partially explained, or not explained by differences in the merit variables.

If the results of the regression analysis indicate that the merit variables do not explain gender differences in salary, one still cannot conclude that discrimination has occurred. It could be that there are valid explanations for the differences (e.g., the economy at the time of hire) that were not entered into the regression. However, in the absence of a valid explanation, salary adjustments may be in order.

Salary adjustments are determined by entering the merit variables for each employee into a regression equation to estimate what the employees "should" be making. For this approach to be reliable, the merit variables should account for a statistically significant percentage of the individual differences in salary. An employee whose actual salary is two standard errors below his or her predicted salary is a potential candidate for a salary adjustment. I realize this process is complicated and highly statistical, but that is the nature of salary equity analysis. The process can be made substantially easier by using software such as *HREquator* or *Equipay* that is designed for such purposes.

Chapter Summary

In this chapter you learned:

- Job analysis provides the foundation for such areas as performance appraisal, employee selection, training, and job design.

- A properly written job description contains a job title, a brief summary, an extensive list of work activities, a list of tools and equipment used, information about the work context, compensation information, performance standards, and personal requirements.

- Before a job analysis is begun, decisions must be made about the type of information that will be obtained, who will conduct the job analysis, and who will participate in it.

- The typical job analysis involves interviewing and observing subject matter experts (SMEs) to determine tasks that are performed, the conditions under which they are performed, the tools and equipment needed to perform the tasks, and the knowledge, skills, abilities, and other characteristics (KSAOs) needed to perform the tasks.

- Although no job analysis method is always better than others, each is better for certain purposes. For example, the PAQ is an excellent method for compensation uses, and

	1979	1989	1999	2001
Annual v. Hourly Salary				
Annual Salary	59.7	68.7	72.2	76.1
Hourly Salary	64.1	75.4	83.8	84.3
Employee Age				
16–24	78.5	90.7	91.0	90.2
25–34	67.4	78.4	81.9	82.7
35–44	58.3	68.1	71.1	72.3
45–54	56.9	62.7	72.7	73.6
55–64	60.5	63.9	68.5	70.4
65 and older	77.8	74.2	70.5	67.9

Source: U.S. Department of Labor (2002); www.bls.gov/cps/cpswom2001.pdf

the CIT is an excellent method for performance appraisal.

- Job evaluation is the process of assigning a monetary value to a job.
- Internal equity, external equity, and comparable worth are important issues that must be addressed during any job evaluation.

Critical Thinking Questions

1. Why is job analysis so important?
2. Would a job analyst expect to find gender and race differences in the way employees perform the duties of their jobs?
3. Why are there so many job analysis methods?
4. Research indicates that the average salary for females in the United States is about 76% of the average salary for males. Why is this?
5. Is external equity more important than internal equity?

To learn more about the issues discussed in this chapter, point your browser to

http://www.infotrac-college.com/wadsworth

and enter one of these search terms:

Job analysis

Task inventories

Position Analysis Questionnaire

General Aptitude Test battery

Pay equity

Wage surveys

Exercise 2–1
Critiquing Job Descriptions

The purpose of this exercise is to familiarize you with the correct form for the various parts of a job description. On the next two pages, you will find a job description that contains several errors. See if you can identify the errors.

_____

_____

_____

_____

_____

_____

_____

_____

_____

_____

_____

_____

_____

_____

_____

_____

_____

_____

_____

Restaurant Associate

Nora's Scarf 'n Barf Restaurant

Job Summary

The Restaurant Associate is responsible for performing a variety of tasks involved in the preparation and sales of food. Duties include preparing food, cooking food, taking customer orders, and cleaning the restaurant.

Work Activities

Food Preparation

- Removes buns from boxes and places on food preparation table
- Takes meat and chicken from the freezer and places on table to thaw
- Takes condiments from the refrigerator and places them on food preparation table
- Inspects meat and chicken to make sure they are safe to eat
- Handles problems

Cooking

- Places fries and breaded fish patties into vat and removes when high-pitched alarm goes off
- Cooks hamburgers, chicken, and hot dogs on the grill
- Puts grilled food onto bun and adds requested condiments

Cleaning

- Wipes counter and tables as needed
- Cleans the grill at the end of each shift
- Changes cooking oil when the bottom of the vat can't be seen or after several customer complaints
- Uses RK-9 to clean tables after manager indicates a 10–6 has occurred
- Mops
- Cleans cooking utensils at end of shift
- Sweeps and cleans parking lot area

Tools and Equipment Used

- Deep-fat fryer
- Grill
- Cleaning materials (e.g., mop, rags, cleanser)
- Cash register
- Common cooking utensils (e.g., spatulas, tongs)

Materials and Substances Exposed To

- RK-9
- Wesson cooking oil
- Meat, poultry, chicken, fish, potatoes, bread
- Draino

Job Context

The Restaurant Associate works an 8-hour shift, 5 days per week. The actual days and times worked vary based on a rotating schedule. Psychological stress is high when the restaurant is busy or customers get angry. Physical stress is moderate as the Restaurant Associate spends all 8 hours standing, with extensive bending and leaning. At times, crates weighing 80 pounds must be lifted.

Performance Appraisal

The Restaurant Associate is evaluated each month on the standard Scarf 'n Barf performance appraisal instrument. Bonuses can be earned by having few customer complaints, no shrinkage, and no citations for health or safety violations.

Personal Requirements

Upon Hire

- Ability to count change back to customers
- No mental or physical problems
- Bondable
- Excellent communication skills
- Flexible

After Hire

- Knowledge of restaurant menu and recipes
- Knowledge of restaurant policies

Exercise 2–2
Writing a Job Description

In Chapter 2, you learned how to write a job description. This exercise will give you a chance to apply that knowledge. To complete this exercise:

1. Pair up with another person in your class.
2. Take turns interviewing each other about jobs that each of you currently has or has had at one time.
3. Use the information from the interviews to write a job description similar to that found in your text.
4. You will probably want to type your job description so that it looks professional.

Notes

_____

_____

_____

_____

_____

_____

_____

_____

_____

_____

_____

_____

_____

_____

_____

_____

_____

_____

_____

Exercise 2–3
Identifying KSAOs

Part A. For each of the following characteristics, indicate whether the characteristic is a knowledge, skill, ability, or other characteristic.

1. Typing speed _____
2. Finger dexterity _____
3. Driving a car _____
4. Traffic rules _____
5. A driver's license _____
6. A friendly personality _____
7. Ten years of experience _____
8. Basic intelligence _____
9. Physical strength _____
10. Color vision _____
11. Being a nonsmoker _____
12. Customer service experience _____
13. Use of PowerPoint _____
14. Willingness to work weekends _____
15. Spelling and grammar _____
16. Writing reports _____

Part B. For each of the following tasks, list the KSAOs needed to successfully perform the task. Use KSAOs in Exhibit 2.07 as a guide.

Task   **KSAOs**

1. Pulling a citizen from a burning vehicle _____
2. Driving a patrol car in pursuit of motorists _____
3. Writing traffic citations to motorists who violate traffic regulations _____
4. Chasing suspects on foot _____
5. Determining the cause of an automobile accident _____
6. Testifying in court _____
7. Providing a lost motorist with directions _____
8. Searching a car for weapons or evidence _____

Exercise 2–4
Determining Pay Equity

Once a point system has been developed and jobs have been evaluated, the next step in the job evaluation process is to ensure that employees in the jobs with the most number of points are being paid the highest salaries. As discussed in your text, this is usually done by charting the number of points a job is worth with the average current salary of the people in that job. A wage trend line is then drawn that represents where each job should fall if it is paid fairly. Jobs falling well above the line are considered to be overpaid, and those falling well below the line are considered to be underpaid. The line is drawn by using a regression equation to use point values to predict salaries. For the purpose of this exercise, assume that you have performed a regression analysis on the data found on the following page. This analysis yielded the following formula:

$$\text{salary} = -8900 + (67.0 \times \text{the number of points})$$

To draw your wage trend line, enter 400, 500, and 600 points into the equation to obtain their predicted salaries. For example, if you entered 450 points in the equation, the predicted salary would be:

$$\text{salary} = -8900 + (67.0 \times 450) = -8900 + 30,150 = \$21,250$$

You would then plot the points and the predicted salary on the chart on the next page. Now, enter 400, 500, and 600 points into the above equation and place the predicted salaries below.

400 points   _____ (predicted salary)
500 points   _____ (predicted salary)
600 points   _____ (predicted salary)

Plot these three data points on the graph on the next page, and then draw a line through the three points. This line is your wage trend line. When your line is drawn, plot the data found on the next page. Then use your graph to identify which jobs are currently being underpaid and which jobs are currently being overpaid.

Job	Points	Salary
Computer Operator	450	$18,000
Computer Programmer	550	$26,000
Tape Librarian	400	$16,000
Secretary I	500	$17,000
Secretary II	450	$15,000
Computer Analyst	600	$28,000
Clerk	350	$16,000
Supervisor	650	$32,000
Account Representative	500	$18,000
Customer Service Agent	550	$25,000

Salary

35,000	+	+	+	+	+	+	+	+
34,000	+	+	+	+	+	+	+	+
33,000	+	+	+	+	+	+	+	+
32,000	+	+	+	+	+	+	+	+
31,000	+	+	+	+	+	+	+	+
30,000	+	+	+	+	+	+	+	+
29,000	+	+	+	+	+	+	+	+
28,000	+	+	+	+	+	+	+	+
27,000	+	+	+	+	+	+	+	+
26,000	+	+	+	+	+	+	+	+
25,000	+	+	+	+	+	+	+	+
24,000	+	+	+	+	+	+	+	+
23,000	+	+	+	+	+	+	+	+
22,000	+	+	+	+	+	+	+	+
21,000	+	+	+	+	+	+	+	+
20,000	+	+	+	+	+	+	+	+
19,000	+	+	+	+	+	+	+	+
18,000	+	+	+	+	+	+	+	+
17,000	+	+	+	+	+	+	+	+
16,000	+	+	+	+	+	+	+	+
15,000	+	+	+	+	+	+	+	+
14,000	+	+	+	+	+	+	+	+
13,000	+	+	+	+	+	+	+	+
12,000	+	+	+	+	+	+	+	+
11,000	+	+	+	+	+	+	+	+
10,000	+	+	+	+	+	+	+	+
	300	350	400	450	500	550	600	650

Job Evaluation Points

3 Legal Issues in Employee Selection

IN THE FIELD of human resources, it is not a question of *whether* you will get sued by an applicant or former employee but *when* and *how often*. In 2002 alone, 84,442 discrimination complaints were filed with the **Equal Employment Opportunity Commission (EEOC)** resulting in more than $310 million in awards and settlements. This number is up from the 80,840 complaints filed in 2001 and the 79,896 complaints filed in 2000 (updated statistics can be obtained on the Web at www.eeoc.gov/stats/enforcement.html). These statistics should convince anyone entering the human resource field that knowledge of employment law is essential. By the end of this chapter you will

- understand the legal process involving employment law.
- know what classes of people are protected by federal law.
- be able to determine the legality of an employment practice.
- understand the concept of adverse impact.
- understand affirmative action.
- know the important issues involving employee privacy rights.

The Legal Process

To know whether a given employment practice is legal, it is important to understand the legal process as it relates to employment law. The first step in the legal process is for some legislative body, such as the U.S. Congress or a state legislature, to pass a law. If a law is passed at the federal level, states may pass laws that *expand* the rights granted in the federal law; states may not, however, pass laws that will *diminish* the rights granted in federal legislation. For example, if Congress passed a law that gave women 6 months of maternity leave, a state or local government could pass a law extending the leave to 8 months, but they could not

reduce the amount of maternity leave to less than the mandated 6 months. Thus, to be on firm legal ground, it is important to be aware of state and local laws as well as federal legislation.

Once a law has been passed, situations occur in which the intent of the law is not clear. For example, a law might be passed to protect disabled employees. Two years later, an employee is denied promotion because he has high blood pressure. The employee may file a charge against the employer claiming discrimination based on a disability. He may claim that high blood pressure is a disability but that he can still work in spite of the disability and consequently deserves the promotion. The organization, on the other hand, might claim that high blood pressure is not a disability and that even if it were an employee with high blood pressure could not perform the job.

Resolving the Complaint Internally

Before a complaint can be filed with the EEOC, an employee must utilize whatever internal resolution process is available within the organization. As a result, most organizations have formal policies regarding how discrimination complaints will be handled internally. Typically, these policies involve such forms of alternative dispute resolution (ADR) as a grievance process, mediation, and arbitration. ADR will be discussed in greater detail in Chapter 14, but a brief description is provided here. With a **grievance system**, employees take their complaints to an internal committee that makes a decision regarding the complaint. If employees do not like the decision, they can then take their complaints to the EEOC. With **mediation**, employees and the organization meet with a neutral third party who tries to help the two sides reach a mutually agreed-upon solution. If they cannot reach a solution, the complaint can be taken to arbitration or to the EEOC. The EEOC has begun to strongly recommend mediation as a solution to discrimination complaints (Montwieler, 2002).

Exhibit **3.01** Legal process in employment law

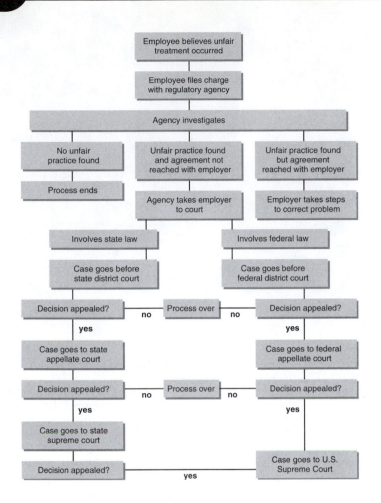

With **arbitration**, the two sides present their case to a neutral third party who then makes a decision as to which side is right. Arbitration and mediation differ in that a neutral third party helps the two sides reach an agreement in mediation whereas in arbitration the neutral third party makes the decision. If **binding arbitration** is used, neither side can appeal the decision. If **nonbinding arbitration** is used, the parties can either accept the decision or take the case to court. The U.S. Supreme Court has ruled (*Circuit City Stores v. Adams*, 2001) that the applicant or employee is not allowed to take the complaint to the EEOC or to court if an organization has a policy of mandatory arbitration.

Filing a Discrimination Charge

As shown in Exhibit 3.01, a charge of discrimination is usually filed with a government agency. A state agency is used if the alleged violation involves a state law, and a federal agency, usually the EEOC, handles alleged violations of federal law. An EEOC complaint must be filed within 180 days of the discriminatory act; 300 days if the complainant has already filed a complaint

with a state or local fair employment practice agency. The government agency will try to notify the employer within 10 days about the complaint, obtain further information from both parties if necessary, and review the charge to determine whether it has merit.

Outcomes of an EEOC Investigation

Charge Does Not Have Merit

If, after reviewing a complaint, the governmental agency does not find merit, one of two things can happen based on whether the person filing the complaint accepts the decision. If the person filing the complaint accepts the decision, the process ends. If the person filing the complaint does not accept the decision, he is issued a "right to sue" letter that entitles him to hire a private attorney and file the case himself.

Charge Has Merit

If the EEOC believes the discrimination charge has merit, it will try to work out a settlement between the claimant and employer without taking the case to court. These settlements might include an employer offering a job or promotion to the person filing the

Discrimination suits are common in business.

complaint, the payment of back wages, and the payment of compensatory or punitive damages. These settlements can range in size from a few dollars to more than $100 million. In 2000, Coca-Cola settled a racial discrimination case for a record $192.5 million. Another large settlement was the $105 million that Shoney's agreed to pay in 1993, mostly to approximately 10,000 African Americans who either worked for or were denied employment with Shoney's over a 7-year period. The size of the settlement was based not only on the high number of victims but also on the severity of the discrimination. For example, the number of African American employees in each restaurant was limited to the percentage of African American customers. When African Americans were hired, they were placed in "low-paying, low-visibility kitchen jobs" (Smothers, 1993). In addition to the $105 million, Shoney's agreed to institute an affirmative action program over the next 10 years. Texaco settled its racial discrimination suit in 1996 by agreeing to pay $176 million to 1,400 current and former African American employees. The settlement was prompted by the public airing of a tape recording of a Texaco executive using a racial slur.

If a settlement cannot be reached, however, the case goes to a federal district court with the EEOC representing (physically and financially) the person filing the complaint. When the court makes a decision, the decision becomes **case law.** Case law is a judicial interpretation of a law and is important because it establishes a precedent for future cases. If one side does not like the decision rendered in a lower court, it may appeal to higher courts, perhaps eventually going to the U.S. Supreme Court. Obviously, a ruling by the U.S. Supreme Court carries more weight than rulings of district courts or state supreme courts.

Determining Whether an Employment Decision Is Legal

At first glance, the legal aspects of making employment decisions seem complicated. After all, there are many laws and court cases that apply to employment decisions. The basic legal aspects, however, are not that complicated. Use the flow chart in Exhibit 3.02 to make the process easier to understand as each stage is discussed.

Does the Employment Practice Directly Refer to a Member of a Federally Protected Class?

An employment practice is any decision that affects an employee. Employment practices include hiring, firing, promoting, assigning employees to shifts, determining pay, sending employees to training, disciplining, and scheduling vacations. Thus, *any* decision made by an employer has the potential for legal challenge.

The first step in determining the legality of an employment practice is to decide whether the employment practice directly refers to a member of a protected class. A **protected class** is any group of people for which protective legislation has been passed. A federally protected class is any group of individuals specifically protected by *federal* law. A list of U.S. federally protected classes is shown in Exhibit 3.03. Exhibit 3.04 shows the similarity of protected classes in the United States and in selected countries. In Canada, there are no federally protected classes; each province makes its own employment law. Thus, the protected classes listed for Canada in Exhibit 3.04 are those protected by law in *all* provinces and territories. A complete list of

Exhibit 3.02 Determining whether an employment practice is legal

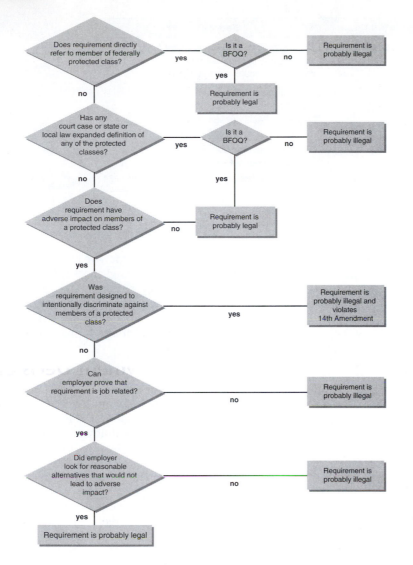

provincially protected classes can be found in Appendix A at the end of this chapter.

Race

On the basis of the Civil Rights Acts of 1866, 1964, and 1991 as well as the Fifth and Fourteenth Amendments to the U.S. Constitution, it is illegal to discriminate against a person based on **race.** According to Congress, but not many anthropologists (Rushton, 1995), the four races are African American, European American (white), Asian American, and Native American Indian.

The *equal protection clauses* of the **Fifth** and **Fourteenth Amendments** mandate that no federal or state agency may deny a person equal protection under the law. Basically, this implies that a government may not *intentionally* discriminate or allow intentional discrimination to take place. Because any suit filed under the Fifth or Fourteenth Amendment must demonstrate intent, they are not often used.

The Civil Rights Acts of 1964 (known as Title VII) and 1991 extended the scope of the Fifth and Fourteenth Amendments to the private sector and to local governments. Title VII makes it illegal for employers with more than 15 employees, labor unions, employment agencies, state and local governmental agencies, and educational institutions to:

1. fail, refuse to hire, discharge any individual, or otherwise discriminate against any individual with respect to his compensation, terms, conditions, or privileges of employment because of the individual's race, color, religion, sex, or national origin; or

2. limit, segregate, or classify employees or applicants for employment in any way that would deprive, or tend to deprive, any individual of employment opportunities or otherwise adversely affect his stature as an employee because of an individual's race, color, religion, sex, or national origin.

Exhibit 3.03 Federally protected classes in the United States

Protected Class	Federal Law
Age (over 40)	Age Discrimination in Employment Act
Disability	Americans with Disabilities Act
	Vocational Rehabilitation Act of 1973
Race	Civil Rights Acts of 1964, 1991
National origin	Civil Rights Acts of 1964, 1991
Religion	Civil Rights Acts of 1964, 1991
Sex	Civil Rights Acts of 1964 and 1991
	Equal Pay Act of 1963
Pregnancy	Pregnancy Discrimination Act
Vietnam veterans	Vietnam-Era Veterans Readjustment Act of 1974

Unlike the Fifth and Fourteenth Amendments, for an employment practice to be potentially illegal under the CRA, the discrimination does not have to be intentional. Instead, proof of discrimination is determined through statistical analysis of selection rates and by the presence or absence of adverse impact, which will be discussed in detail later in the chapter.

The CRA has also been interpreted by the courts to cover the "atmosphere" of the organization, which includes such behavior as sexual harassment (*Broderick v. Ruder*, 1988; *Brundy v. Jackson*, 1971), age harassment (*Louis v. Federal Prison Industries*, 1986), race harassment (*Hunter v. Allis-Chalmers*, 1986), and religious harassment (*Abramson v. William Patterson College of New Jersey*, 2001).

Color

Also protected by the Civil Rights Acts of 1964 and 1991 is color. Though commonly used as a synonym for race, the reference to color protects individuals within one race against discrimination based on variations in skin color. For example, in the 1989 case of *Walker v. Secretary of the Treasury*, a district court found that a darker skinned African American supervisor at the IRS illegally fired a lighter skinned African American employee.

Sex

The Civil Rights Acts of 1964 and 1991 as well as the Equal Pay Act (1963) prohibit discrimination based on sex. The courts have ruled that intentional discrimination against either females or males is illegal (*Diaz v. Pan American Airways*, 1991) but that discrimination against transsexuals is not (*Sommers v. Budget Marketing*, 1991).

National Origin

National origin is protected under the Civil Rights Acts of 1964 and 1991. Note that Hispanics are protected under national origin, not race. Claims of discrimination based on national origin have increased greatly over the past few years. One of the most common complaints is "English only" or "understandable English" speaking requirements. The courts have generally ruled that language requirements are legal if they are job related (Quinn & Petrick, 1993) and limited to communication during "company time" rather than on breaks.

Religion

Also protected under the Civil Rights Acts of 1964 and 1991 is religion. It is illegal to use an individual's religion in an employment decision unless the nature of the job is religious. For example, the Catholic church can require its priests to be Catholic but could not require this of its clerical staff. The Civil Rights Acts also require organizations to make accommodations for religious beliefs unless to do so would be an undue hardship. Three areas most involved with the 3,000 complaints of religious discrimination filed annually with the EEOC are failure to accommodate days of worship, worship practices, and religious attire.

Days of Worship. Many religions forbid their members from working on particular days. For example, Seventh-Day Adventists and Orthodox Jews cannot work from sundown Friday to sundown Saturday, and Greek Orthodox cannot work on Sunday. Such nonwork *requirements* should not be confused with *preferences* for nonwork on days of worship (e.g., Protestants working on Sunday or Christmas; attending a morning rather than an evening worship service) as the courts have ruled that an employee's preference does not need to be accommodated (*Dachman v. Shalala*, 2001; *Tiano v. Dillard Department Stores*, 1998).

Days of worship are often easily accommodated by scheduling employees without religious restrictions to work on those days. When there are few employees, scheduling rotations can be used to reduce, but not eliminate, the number of days of worship that an employee might have to miss. Accommodations become legally unreasonable when

Exhibit 3.04 — International comparison of federally protected classes

Protected Class	U.S.	Canada	Australia	U.K.	E.U.	Mexico	Japan
Race	yes	yes	yes	yes	yes	yes	
National origin	yes		yes	yes	yes	yes	yes
Sex	yes	yes	yes	yes	yes	yes	yes
Age	yes	yes	yes		yes		
Disability	yes	yes	yes	yes	yes		
Color	yes	yes	yes	yes			
Religion	yes	yes	yes		yes	yes	yes
Pregnancy	yes	yes	yes			yes	
Vietnam veteran	yes						
Marital status		yes	yes	yes			
Sexual orientation		yes	yes		yes		
Political beliefs			yes			yes	
Family status			yes				
Transgender status				yes			
Criminal conviction			yes				
National extraction			yes				
Social origin			yes				
Medical record			yes				
Trade union activity			yes				
Social status							yes

there are no coworkers available, overtime will have to be paid to cover an employee's day of worship, or another employee's seniority or collective bargaining rights have been violated. However, with a little ingenuity and proper explanations of an employee's religious requirements, reasonable accommodations can usually be made.

The case of Eddie Kilgore provides an example of a poorly handled case of religious accommodation. Kilgore had been employed for 18 years by Sparks Regional Medical Center when he was suddenly ordered to be on call on Saturdays. As a Seventh-Day Adventist, he was forbidden to work on Saturdays; a requirement long known by his employer. When Kilgore refused the Saturday work, he was fired. Kilgore filed a suit for religious discrimination and a jury awarded him $100,000 and his former job back (Pouliot, 1996).

Worship Practices. Two practices in particular can cause potential problems: prayer and fasting. Some religions require members to pray at certain times. For example, followers of Islam perform the Salat ritual prayer five times daily: sunrise, noon, afternoon, sunset, and night. Because each prayer can take 15 minutes (including preparation such as hand washing), organizations such as fast food restaurants and retail stores often have

difficulty accommodating every prayer request. Fasting requirements can also pose problems. For example, followers of Islam must refrain from food and drink from sunrise to sundown during the 30-day period of Ramadan. Though Islamic employees are available to work, their endurance and performance may be most affected during the later part of the day. Thus, fasting can be accommodated by having dangerous, strenuous, or complicated work performed earlier in the day or scheduling Islamic employees for earlier hours (Pearce, 1994).

Though fasts and prayer are the most common worship practices that need accommodation, they are certainly not the only ones. For example, because Jehovah's Witnesses cannot celebrate birthdays or nonreligious holidays, their lack of participation in an office birthday party or celebration is often viewed by uninformed coworkers as an "attitude problem" (Reid, 1996).

Religious Attire. Several complaints of religious discrimination regarding religious attire have been made by Sikhs, members of a Hindu religious sect (Overman, 1994a). Sikh males are required to wear turbans—head apparel that often conflicts with required job uniforms—and many Sikhs wear a religious bracelet on their right wrists. As long as such attire is not a danger to the employee or others (for example, a bracelet

getting caught in a piece of machinery or a turban preventing the wearing of a safety helmet), it should be allowed.

Age

The **Age Discrimination in Employment Act (ADEA)** and its later amendments forbid an employer or union from discriminating against an individual over the age of 40. In part, this act was designed to protect older workers from employment practices aimed at reducing costs by firing older workers with higher salaries and replacing them with lower-paid younger workers. Such legislation is important because, despite evidence to the

contrary, people often view older workers as being less competent and economically worthwhile than younger workers (Finkelstein & Burke, 1998; Finkelstein, Burke, & Raju, 1995). To file suit under this act, an individual must demonstrate that he or she is in the specified age bracket, has been discharged or demoted, was performing the job adequately at the time of discharge or demotion, and was replaced by a younger worker; even if the younger person is older than 40 (*O'Connor v. Consolidated Coin Caterers*, 1996). Though mandatory retirement ages are allowed in certain circumstances (e.g., 70 for college professors), they are usually illegal because, as research indicates, in general, work performance does not decline with age.

Disability

Discrimination against people with disabilities by the federal government is forbidden by the **Vocational Rehabilitation Act** (1973), and discrimination against the disabled by any other employer with 15 or more employees is forbidden by the Americans with Disabilities Act (1990).

The **Americans with Disabilities Act (ADA)**, signed into law by former President Bush in 1990, is the most important piece of employment legislation since the 1964 Civil Rights Act. The ADA requires organizations with 15 or more employees to make "reasonable accommodation for the physically and mentally disabled, unless to do so, would impose an undue hardship." Though Congress did not provide a list of disabilities, it did define disability as

1. a physical or mental impairment that substantially limits one or more of the major life activities of an individual;

2. a record of such impairment; or

3. being regarded as having such an impairment.

For the first part of the definition, major life activities include such things as walking, hearing, and speaking. A condition that keeps a person from working a *particular* job, as opposed to all jobs or a class of jobs, is not a disability (*Toyota v. Williams*, 2002). Examples of conditions considered disabilities by case law or the Department of Labor are blindness, paralysis, asthma, muscular dystrophy, and various learning disabilities such as dyslexia. Conditions not considered by the courts to be disabilities have included fear of heights, color blindness, hypertension, depression, temporary illnesses such as pneumonia, sprained ankles, being 20 pounds overweight, carpal tunnel syndrome, and wearing glasses.

The second part of the definition was designed to protect people who were once disabled but no longer are. Examples include recovering alcoholics, cancer patients in remission, people who spent time in a mental health facility, and drug addicts who have successfully completed treatment.

The final part of the definition protects individuals who don't have a disability but are treated as if they do. Examples of people protected under this clause are those with facial scarring or severe burns. In an interesting case (*Johnson v. Apland & Associates*, 1997), the U.S. Court of Appeals for the Seventh Circuit ruled that a man missing 18 teeth had a right to file an ADA suit on the grounds he was regarded as having a disability. The case was sent back to the lower court to determine if this perception actually "substantially limits one or more major life activity."

The ADA does not require an organization to hire or give preference to the disabled, only that the disabled be given an equal chance and that reasonable attempts be made to accommodate their disability. Although there are no guidelines regarding what is "reasonable," accommodations can include providing readers or interpreters, modifying work schedules, modifying equipment, and making facilities more

Accommodations, such as providing Braille versions of tests, are sometimes necessary.

accessible. In spite of the fact that two thirds of accommodations cost less than $500 (Cohen, 2002), many employees are reluctant to ask for, and many organizations are reluctant to provide, accommodations (Baldridge & Veiga, 2001).

If a disability keeps a person from performing the "essential functions" of a job identified during a job analysis or poses a direct threat to their own or others' safety, the person does not have to be hired or retained (Zink, 2002). For example, in *Caston v. Trigon Engineering* (1993), a district court ruled that a woman with 44 personalities was unable to perform her job as an environmental engineer. In another case (*DiPompo v. West Point*, 1991), a district court ruled that a dyslexic applicant, though considered disabled, was not able to perform essential job functions such as inspecting vehicles and buildings for the presence of dangerous materials and recording information such as work schedules and emergency calls. In *Ethridge v. State of Alabama* (1994), a district court ruled that a police applicant with restricted use of his right hand could not perform the essential job functions because he was unable to shoot in a two-handed position (Weaver stance).

An interesting and well-publicized ADA case was that of golfer Casey Martin (*Martin v. PGA Tour*, 2000). Martin suffers from Klippel-Trenaunay-Weber syndrome in his right leg. Because this syndrome made it difficult for Martin to walk on the golf course, he requested an accommodation that he be allowed to use a golf cart. The Professional Golfers Association (PGA) denied the request arguing that walking is an "essential function" of golf, and thus, using a cart would not be a reasonable accommodation. The U.S. Supreme Court ruled in favor of Martin's contention that walking was not an essential function of golf and that allowing Martin to use a cart was not an unreasonable accommodation.

Pregnancy

The **Pregnancy Discrimination Act** states that "women affected by pregnancy, childbirth, or related medical conditions shall be treated the same for all employment related purposes, including receipt of benefit programs, as other persons not so affected but similar in their ability or inability to work." Simply put, this act requires pregnancy to be treated as any other disability. For example, in *Adams v. North Little Rock Police Department* (1992), the U.S. Court of Appeals ruled that a police department discriminated against a pregnant police officer when the department denied her "light duty" yet granted light duty to male officers with temporary disabilities such as strained backs.

In the case of *California Federal Savings and Loan Association v. Guerra* (1987), the U.S. Supreme Court expanded the scope of the law. Pregnant women may receive better treatment than other persons with disabilities and cannot receive worse treatment. Many of the rights provided in the Pregnancy Discrimination Act have been greatly expanded by the Family Medical Leave Act (FMLA), which will be discussed later in this chapter.

Vietnam Veteran Status

Due to the large-scale discrimination in the 1960s and 1970s against soldiers returning from duty in Vietnam, in 1974 Congress passed the **Vietnam-Era Veterans Readjustment Act.** This act mandates any contractor or subcontractor with more than $10,000 in federal government contracts to take affirmative action to employ and promote Vietnam-era veterans. This law is one reason that veterans applying for civil service jobs receive credit for their military service as well as for their qualifications.

To test your knowledge of the federally protected classes, complete Exercise 3–1 at the end of this chapter.

Is the Requirement a BFOQ?

Employment decisions based on membership in a protected class (e.g., "We will not hire females because they are not strong enough to do the job") are illegal unless the employer can demonstrate that the requirement is a **bona fide occupational qualification (BFOQ).**

If a job can only be performed by a person in a particular class, the requirement is considered a BFOQ. Actually, some jobs can only be performed by a person of a particular gender; for instance, only a female could be a wet nurse (a woman who breast-feeds another

woman's baby) and only a male could be a sperm donor. However, there are very few jobs in our society that can only be performed by a particular race, gender, or national origin. Take for example a job that involves lifting 150-pound crates. Although it is true that, on average, males are stronger than females, a company could not set a male-only requirement. The real BFOQ in this example is strength, not gender. Thus, restricting employment to males would be illegal.

The courts have clearly stated that a BFOQ must involve the ability to perform the job, not satisfy a customer's or client's preferences. For example, in *Diaz v. Pan American Airways* (1991), the court ruled that even though airline passengers prefer female flight attendants, the nature of the business is to transport passengers safely, and males can perform the essential job functions as well as females. In another interesting case, in 1989 Caesar's Casino in Atlantic City was fined $250,000 for removing African American and female card dealers from a table to appease a high-stakes gambler who preferred white male dealers.

One of the few exceptions to the BFOQ requirement seems to be grooming standards. It is not unusual for an organization to have separate dress codes and grooming standards for males and females. Though different standards based on sex would appear to violate the law, the courts have generally upheld them (Fowler-Hermes, 2001).

Has Case Law, State Law, or Local Law Expanded the Definition of Any of the Protected Classes?

An employment decision may not violate a federal law, but it may violate one of the many state and local laws that have been passed to protect additional groups of people. For example, at the state level,

- 5 states (Hawaii, Illinois, New York, Washington, and Wisconsin) forbid discrimination on the basis of a person's arrest record;
- 12 states (California, Connecticut, Hawaii, Maine, Minnesota, Nevada, New Hampshire, New Jersey, New York, Rhode Island, Vermont, and Wisconsin) and the District of Columbia prohibit discrimination based on sexual orientation;
- 16 states (Alaska, California, Connecticut, Florida, Hawaii, Illinois, Maryland, Michigan, Minnesota, Nebraska, New Hampshire, New Jersey, New York, North Dakota, Oregon, and Virginia) and the District of Columbia forbid discrimination based on marital status.

At the local level,

- Santa Cruz, California, outlaws discrimination based on height and physical appearance;
- 87 cities and counties prohibit discrimination based on sexual orientation; and
- Cincinnati, Ohio, prohibits discrimination against people of Appalachian heritage.

Exhibit 3.05 Adverse impact example

	Sex	
	Male	**Female**
Applicants	50	10
Hires	25	4
Selection ratio	.50	.40

In addition to state and local laws, the definitions of protected classes can be expanded or narrowed by court decisions. As discussed previously, these decisions become case law. For example, in a variety of cases, the courts have ruled that the definition of disability should be expanded to include obesity but not former drug use and that transsexuals are not protected as a gender.

To help you understand the protected classes in your state and locality, complete the Additional Protected Classes Exercise on your CD-ROM.

Does the Requirement Have Adverse Impact Against Members of a Protected Class?

If the employment practice does not refer directly to a member of a protected class, the next step is to determine whether the requirement adversely affects members of a protected class. **Adverse impact** means a particular employment decision results in negative consequences more often for members of one race, gender, or national origin than for members of another race, gender, or national origin. For example, an employee selection requirement of a college degree would lead to a lower percentage of African American applicants being hired when compared to white applicants. Thus, even though such a requirement does not mention African Americans (a protected class), it does adversely impact them because according to 2000 U.S. Census data, 28.1% of whites have bachelor's degrees or higher compared to 16.5% of African Americans.

Though more complicated statistics exist to determine adverse impact (e.g., standard deviation, chi-square), adverse impact is legally determined through the **four-fifths rule.** That is, the percentage of women hired must be at least 80% of the percentage of men who are hired. It is important to keep in mind that adverse impact refers to *percentages* rather than raw numbers. For example, as shown in Exhibit 3.05, if we hire 25 of 50 male applicants, the hiring percentage would be 50%. If we had 10 female applicants, at least 4 would need to be hired to avoid adverse impact. Why 4? Because the hiring percentage for women must be at least 80% of the hiring percentage for men. Because our male hiring percentage was 50%, our hiring percentage for females must be at least four-fifths (80%) of 50%. Thus, .50 × .80

= .40, indicating that we would need to hire at least 40% of all female applicants to avoid adverse impact and a potential charge of unfair discrimination. With 10 applicants, this results in hiring at least 4 of the 10 applicants. Adverse impact is computed separately for race and gender. That is, an organization would not compute hiring rates for white males or African American females. Instead, hiring rates would be computed for males and for females and then be computed separately for whites and for African Americans.

It is illegal to *intentionally* discriminate against whites and males, but employment practices that result in adverse impact against white males although theoretically illegal are not illegal in practice. No court has upheld an adverse impact claim by a white applicant. For example, it was mentioned previously that requiring a college degree adversely impacts African Americans because 28.1% of whites have bachelor's degrees compared to 16.5% of African Americans and 10.6% of Hispanics. Though 44% of Asian Americans have college degrees, a white applicant could not realistically file a discrimination charge based on adverse impact.

To see if you grasp how to determine if adverse impact exists, complete Exercise 3–2 at the end of this chapter.

Was the Requirement Designed to Intentionally Discriminate Against a Protected Class?

If an employment practice does not refer directly to a member of a protected class but adversely affects a protected class, the courts will look closely at whether the practice was initiated to intentionally reduce the pool of qualified minority applicants. For example, suppose a city requires all of its employees to live within the city limits. The city believes this is a justifiable requirement because salaries are paid by tax dollars and town employees should contribute to that tax base. Though such a requirement is not illegal, the court might look deeper to see if the tax base was in fact the reason for the residency requirement. That is, if the city population was 99% white and the population of the area surrounding the town was 90% African American, the court might argue that the residency requirement was a subtle way of discriminating against minorities.

Though such subtle requirements are probably no longer common in the employment sector, they have been used throughout history. For example, before the 1970s, some states required voters to pass a "literacy test" to be eligible to vote. Though the stated purpose of the test was to ensure that voters would make intelligent and educated decisions, the real purpose was to reduce the number of minority voters.

Can the Employer Prove That the Requirement Is Job Related?

As shown in the flowchart in Exhibit 3.02, if our employment practice does not result in adverse impact, it is probably legal. If adverse impact does result, then the burden of proof shifts to the employer to demonstrate that the employment practice is either **job related** or exempt from adverse impact. Before discussing these two strategies, two points need to be made. First, adverse impact is a fact of life in personnel selection. Almost any test is going to have adverse impact against some protected class, though some tests may have less adverse impact than others (Bradburn & Villar, 1992).

Second, the burden of proof in employment law is different than in criminal law. In criminal law, a defendant is innocent until proven guilty. In employment law, both the Civil Rights Act of 1991 and the court's ruling in *Griggs v. Duke Power* (1972) shift the burden of proof: Once adverse impact is established, an employer (the defendant) is considered guilty unless it can prove its innocence by establishing the job relatedness of the test. That employers are treated more harshly than criminals by Congress and the courts is a constant source of frustration among human resource professionals.

Valid Testing Procedures
An employment practice resulting in adverse impact may still be legal as long as the test is job related (valid) and as long as reasonable attempts have been made to find other tests that might be just as valid but have less adverse impact. For example, if an employer uses a cognitive ability test to select employees, there is a strong possibility that adverse impact will occur. If the employer can demonstrate, however, that the cognitive ability test predicts performance on the job and that no other available test with less adverse impact will predict performance as well, the use of the test is probably justified. Validating tests can be quite expensive: Estimates of the average cost to validate a test range from $3,000 to $14,000 per job (Seberhagen, 1996). A more in-depth discussion of validity strategies is found in Chapter 4.

Exceptions
Bona Fide Seniority System. An organization that has had a long-standing policy of promoting employees with the greatest seniority or laying off employees with the least seniority can continue to do so even though adverse impact occurs. For a seniority system to be considered bona fide, the *purpose* of the system must be to reward seniority; not to discriminate (Twomey, 2002). That is, if an organization established a seniority system to protect male employees, it would not be considered bona fide.

National Security. In certain circumstances, it is legal for an employer to discriminate against a member of a particular national origin or other protected class when it is in the best interest of the nation's security to do so. For example, for years Russian citizens living in the United States were prohibited from working for any defense-related industry.

Veteran's Preference Rights. Most civil service jobs provide extra points on tests for veterans of the armed forces. For example, in Fort Worth, Texas, veterans who apply for city jobs get five points added to their exam score. Because most people in the military are male, awarding these extra points for military service results in adverse impact against females. However, according to the Civil Rights Act of 1964, such practices are exempt from legal action. To test your knowledge of these exceptions, complete Exercise 3–3 at the end of this chapter.

Did the Employer Look for Reasonable Alternatives That Would Result in Lesser Adverse Impact?

As shown in Exhibit 3.02, if an employer proves a test is job related, the final factor looked at by the courts is the extent to which the employer looked for other valid selection tests that would have less adverse impact. For example, if an organization wanted to use a particular cognitive ability test, did it explore such alternatives as education level or other cognitive ability tests that would be just as valid but would have less adverse impact? To get experience using the flowchart in Exhibit 3.02, complete Exercise 3–4 at the end of this chapter.

Affirmative Action

Affirmative action is one of the most misunderstood legal concepts concerning employment. Although most people associate affirmative action with hiring goals or quotas, affirmative action can actually involve several strategies (Robinson, Allen, &Abraham, 1992).

Affirmative Action Strategies

Intentional Recruitment of Minority Applicants
A common affirmative action strategy is to target underrepresented groups for more extensive recruitment. Such efforts might include advertising in magazines and newspapers with a minority readership, recruiting at predominantly minority or female

universities, visiting minority communities, or paying current employees a bonus for recruiting a member of a protected class.

A related technique is to establish training programs designed to teach minorities the skills needed to obtain employment with the organization. For example, Hogan and Quigley (1994) found that providing a 6-week exercise program would result in fewer female applicants failing physical agility tests for positions such as firefighter.

Identification and Removal of Employment Practices Working Against Minority Applicants and Employees

A second affirmative action strategy is to identify and remove practices that might discourage minority applicants from applying to an organization or minority employees from being promoted within an organization. Such practices might involve company policy, supervisor attitudes, or the way in which an organization is decorated. For example, an African American employee in a southern city filed a lawsuit alleging race as the reason he wasn't promoted. As evidence, he cited the embroidered Confederate flag hanging in his supervisor's office. The city's affirmative action officer suggested the flag be removed because, even though the supervisor was a Civil War enthusiast rather than a racist, a Confederate flag in a supervisor's office might give the perception of institutional acceptance of racism.

As another example, it is a common practice for police applicants to receive information and obtain employment applications from the police department itself. However, many minorities are uncomfortable with the idea of going to a police station and asking white police officers for information and application materials. As a result, an easy affirmative action strategy would be to have employment applications available only at the city's personnel office.

When your author presented the above example to a meeting of police chiefs, the overwhelming response was "How can someone be a cop if they don't feel comfortable going to a police station?" I responded that it is uncomfortable for anyone to go into a new environment, much less one with the stigma associated with a police station. I then told the group a story of how scared I was when, back in high school, I had to go to a police station to register a car rally that our school group was having. I still recall the icy stare and gruff voice of the desk sergeant, which quickly turned my legs to jelly. When a few others in the crowd joined in with similar stories, it drove home the point that there are many things, seemingly trivial, that deter others from applying for jobs.

Preferential Hiring and Promotion of Minorities

This is certainly the most controversial and misunderstood of the affirmative action strategies. Under this strategy, minority applicants will be given preference over an equally qualified nonminority applicant. It is important to note that in no way does affirmative action

Affirmative action has opened doors for many women and minorities.

require an employer to hire an unqualified minority over a qualified nonminority. Instead, affirmative action requires employers to monitor their employment records to determine whether minority groups are underrepresented. If they are, affirmative action requires that an organization do the best it can to remedy the situation. One such remedy might be preferential hiring and promotion. The legality of preferential hiring and promotion will be discussed later in the chapter.

Reasons for Affirmative Action Plans

Organizations have affirmative action plans for one of four reasons, two of which are involuntary and two voluntary (Robinson et al., 1992).

Involuntary: Government Regulation

Most affirmative action requirements are the result of Presidential Executive Order 11246. This order, as well as sections of several laws, requires federal contractors and subcontractors with more than 50 employees to submit an annual EEO-1 Report and requires federal contractors and subcontractors with contracts in excess of $50,000 to have formal affirmative action plans. Most state and local governments also have such requirements, although the number of employees and dollar amounts of contracts will differ. These required affirmative action plans typically involve analyses of all major job categories that indicate which categories have underrepresentations of the protected classes as well as goals and plans for overcoming such underrepresentations.

Involuntary: Court Order

When a court finds a public agency such as a police or fire department guilty of not hiring or promoting enough members of a protected class, it can order the agency to begin an affirmative action program. As previously discussed, this program may involve increased recruitment efforts or may entail specific hiring or promotion goals.

Voluntary: Consent Decree

If a discrimination complaint has been filed with a court, a public agency can "voluntarily" agree to an affirmative action plan rather than have a plan forced on it by the court. With a consent decree, the agency agrees that it has not hired or promoted enough members of a protected class and is willing to make changes. The specific nature of these changes is agreed upon by the group filing the complaint and the agency that is the subject of the complaint. This agreement is then approved and monitored by the court.

Voluntary: Desire to Be a Good Citizen

Rather than wait for a discrimination complaint, some organizations develop affirmative action programs out of a desire to be good citizens. That is, they want to voluntarily ensure that their employment practices are fair to all groups of people.

Legality of Preferential Hiring and Promotion Plans

Recently, the courts have indicated that any form of preferential hiring or promotion must undergo a "strict scrutiny analysis" in which the plan must be narrowly tailored and meet a compelling government interest (Gutman, 2002). As shown in Exhibit 3.06, the courts use five criteria to "strictly scrutinize" the legality of an affirmative action plan involving preferential hiring. It is always legal to actively recruit minorities and to remove barriers.

History of Discrimination

The first criterion examined is whether there has been a history of discrimination by a particular organization. If no discrimination has previously occurred, then an affirmative action plan is neither necessary nor legal. For example, if 30% of the qualified workforce is African American, as is 30% of a police department's officers, it would be illegal to engage in preferential hiring based on race. However, if 25% of the qualified workforce is African American and there are no African American State Troopers (as was the case in Alabama in 1980), a preferential hiring could be justified (*U.S. v. Phillip Paradise*, 1987). In *Taxman v. Board of Education of the Township of Piscataway* (1996), the Third Circuit Court of Appeals ruled against the use of race as a factor to break a tie between two equally qualified applicants. Sharon Taxman, a white teacher, and Debra Williams, an African American teacher, were tied in seniority.

When the Piscataway School Board decided to lay off a teacher, it kept Williams because she was African American. The Appeals Court ruled the decision to be unconstitutional because there was no racial disparity between the faculty and the qualified workforce. This case was settled in 1997, a few days before it was scheduled to be heard by the U.S. Supreme Court.

Currently, the legality of any type of racial preference is unclear. In *Texas v. Hopwood* (1996), the Fifth Circuit Court of Appeals (Texas, Louisiana, Mississippi) ruled that race is an impermissible factor in considering applicants. The U.S. Supreme Court chose not to review this case, meaning that the circuit court's decision stands. With similar court cases scheduled to be heard in the next few years, the status of preferential hiring may become better defined.

Beneficiaries of the Plan

The second criterion concerns the extent to which the plan benefits people who were not actual victims of discrimination. If the plan only benefits actual victims, it will probably be considered legal, but if it benefits people not directly discriminated against by the organization, other criteria will be considered.

For example, imagine an organization consisting of 100 male but no female managers. Twenty female assistant managers, after being denied promotions for several years, file suit, charging discrimination. The organization agrees to hire 10 of the females to fill the next 10 openings. Because the beneficiaries of this plan were themselves the actual victims of the organization's previous discrimination, the plan would be legal. If the plan, however, involved promoting females who had not previously applied for the management positions, the courts, before determining the legality of the plan, would consider three factors: the population used to set the goals, the impact on nonminorities, and the ending point for the plan.

Population Used to Set Goals

The third criterion concerns which of two types of populations was used to statistically determine discrimination and to set affirmative action goals. With area populations, an organization compares the number of minorities in the general area with the number of minorities in each position in the organization. If a discrepancy occurs, the organization sets hiring goals to remedy the discrepancy. For example, if 80% of the area surrounding an organization is Hispanic but only 20% of the salaried workers in the organization are Hispanic, the organization might set hiring goals for Hispanics at 90% until the workforce becomes 80% Hispanic.

Although the use of area population figures has been traditional, recent Supreme Court decisions have declared them inappropriate. Instead, the population that must be used in goal setting is that of the **qualified workforce** in the area rather than the area population.

For example, several southern states are under court supervision to increase the number of minority faculty in their public universities. Rather than a goal consistent with the percentage of African Americans in the United

Exhibit 3.06   Determining the legality of affirmative action plan

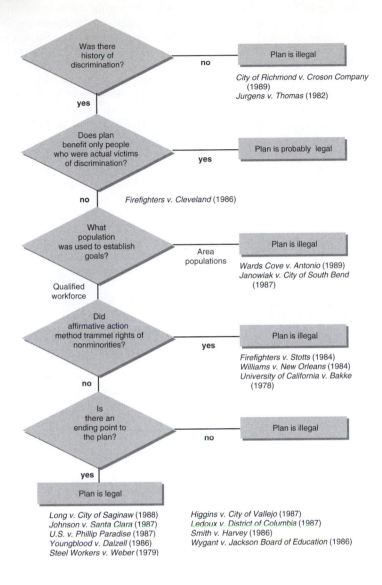

Was there history of discrimination?
no → Plan is illegal

City of Richmond v. Croson Company (1989)
Jurgens v. Thomas (1982)

yes

Does plan benefit only people who were actual victims of discrimination?
yes → Plan is probably legal

no   *Firefighters v. Cleveland* (1986)

What population was used to establish goals?
Area populations → Plan is illegal

Wards Cove v. Antonio (1989)
Janowiak v. City of South Bend (1987)

Qualified workforce

Did affirmative action method trammel rights of nonminorities?
yes → Plan is illegal

Firefighters v. Stotts (1984)
Williams v. New Orleans (1984)
University of California v. Bakke (1978)

no

Is there an ending point to the plan?
no → Plan is illegal

yes

Plan is legal

Long v. City of Saginaw (1988)
Johnson v. Santa Clara (1987)
U.S. v. Phillip Paradise (1987)
Youngblood v. Dalzell (1986)
Steel Workers v. Weber (1979)

Higgins v. City of Vallejo (1987)
Ledoux v. District of Columbia (1987)
Smith v. Harvey (1986)
Wygant v. Jackson Board of Education (1986)

States (roughly 12%), the goal of 2% is based on the qualified workforce: African Americans with doctoral degrees. This example is important because it illustrates that the courts are not unreasonable when it comes to setting affirmative action goals. They realize that a university cannot hire minorities in numbers equal to the national population because a lower percentage of minorities than nonminorities have doctorates.

Another example is the case of *City of Richmond v. Croson* (1989). Because 50% of the Richmond population is minority, the city required that contractors receiving city funds subcontract at least 30% of their work to minority-owned businesses. The J. A. Croson Company received a contract with the city but was unable to subcontract the required 30% because there were not enough minority-owned businesses in the city. The U.S. Supreme Court found Richmond's plan illegal because the goal of 30% was based on the area population rather than the percentage of relevant qualified minority-owned businesses (less than 5%). The U.S. Supreme Court ruled similarly in *Adarand v. Pena* (1995).

Impact on Nonminorities

The fourth criterion used by courts to determine the legality of an affirmative action program is whether the remedy designed to help minorities is narrowly tailored: Does the plan "unnecessarily trammel" the rights of nonminorities. That is, a plan that helps females cannot deny the rights of males. Preference can be given to a qualified minority over a qualified nonminority, but an unqualified minority can never be hired over a qualified nonminority.

Affirmative action becomes controversial when an organization realizes it has discriminated against a particular protected group. For example, police and fire departments have long been staffed by white males. In some cases, this composition has been accidental; in others it has been intentional. To remedy such situations, police and fire departments often set goals for minority hiring. These goals are objectives and are not to be confused with quotas, which *require* a certain percentage of minorities to be hired. This is an important distinction as the Civil Right Act of 1991 forbids the use of quotas.

Should only a small number of minority applicants test highly enough to be considered qualified, the organization is under no obligation to hire unqualified applicants. In fact, if an organization hires unqualified minorities over qualified minorities, hires a lesser-qualified minority over a more qualified minority, or sets unreasonable goals, it can be found guilty of reverse discrimination (Levin-Epstein, 1987). For example, in *Bishop v. District of Columbia* (1986), the U.S. Court of Appeals ruled that reverse discrimination occurred when an African American battalion chief was promoted ahead of five higher ranking white deputy chiefs. The court ruled the promotion to be illegal because it was the result of political pressure rather than qualifications and previous job performance. A similar decision was reached in *Black Firefighters Association v. City of Dallas* (1994) when the U.S. Court of Appeals ruled that "skip promotions" were not legal.

In *Higgins v. City of Vallejo* (1987), however, the U.S. Court of Appeals ruled that promotion of a minority applicant with the third highest score over a nonminority applicant with the highest score was legal. The court's decision was based on the idea that even though the two applicants had different scores, they were close enough to be considered "equally qualified." When two candidates are equally qualified, affirmative action needs can be taken into consideration to decide which of the candidates will be chosen. As one can imagine, the question of how close different qualifications need to be before two candidates are no longer considered equal is difficult to answer. In Chapter 4, methods to answer this question, such as banding and passing scores, will be discussed.

Ending Point for the Plan

The fifth and final criterion concerns the presence of an ending point for the plan. That is, an affirmative action plan cannot continue indefinitely; it must end when certain goals have been obtained. For example, in *Detroit Police Officers Association v. Coleman Young* (1993), the U.S. Court of Appeals ruled that an affirmative action plan that had been utilized for 19 years had resulted in its intended goal: 50% of the Detroit police department was minority. Continuing the plan would be illegal, reasoned the court, because the plan would result in a substantial hardship on nonminority applicants. The court also reasoned that should the percentage of minorities in the department drop in the future, the preferential hiring plan could be reinstated. To test your knowledge of affirmative action, complete Exercise 3–5 at the end of this chapter.

Consequence of Affirmative Action Plans

Though affirmative action programs are an important tool in ensuring equal opportunity, they can result in some negative consequences for people hired or promoted as the result of affirmative action (Kravitz et al., 1997). Research indicates that employees hired due to affirmative action programs are perceived by coworkers as being less competent (Heilman, Block, & Lucas, 1992; Heilman, Block, & Stathatos, 1997), have a tendency to devalue their own performance (Heilman & Alcott, 2001; Heilman, Lucas, & Kaplow, 1990), and behave negatively toward others who are hired based on affirmative action programs (Heilman, Kaplow, Amato, & Stathatos, 1993). These effects can be reduced when applicants are given positive information about their abilities (Heilman et al., 1993; Kravitz et al., 1997). Not surprisingly, women and ethnic minorities hold more positive views toward affirmative action than do males and nonminorities (Kravitz & Platania, 1993).

The previously mentioned studies suggest that affirmative action programs can have negative consequences for their recipients. Affirmative action programs may also have negative consequences for an organization. Silva and Jacobs (1993) found that hiring minorities above their level of representation in the applicant pool (affirmative action) resulted in decreased organizational performance. With these studies in mind, it is essential that an organization weigh the many benefits of affirmative action programs against the programs' unintended side effects.

Privacy Issues

As discussed previously in the chapter, an employment practice is illegal if it results in adverse impact and is not job related. An employment practice can also be illegal if it unnecessarily violates an individual's right to privacy.

The **Fourth Amendment** to the U.S. Constitution protects citizens against unreasonable search or seizure by the government. Its importance to I/O psychology is in the area of drug testing and locker searches. Several courts have ruled that drug testing must be considered a "search" and therefore that, to be legal, drug testing programs must be reasonable and show cause. It is important to understand that the Fourth Amendment is limited to public agencies such as state and local governments. Private industry is not restricted from drug testing by the Fourth Amendment unless government regulations require drug testing (for example, with trucking companies and railroads), but drug testing and searches by a private organization must be conducted in "good faith and with fair dealing."

Generally, employers are free—even encouraged by the government—to test job applicants for current drug use. Drug testing, however, can be illegal when current employees, rather than applicants, are the ones being tested.

Exhibit 3.07

Exhibit 3.07 Do these true-false questions violate an applicant's right to privacy?

I go to church almost every week.

I am very religious.

I believe there is a God.

My sex life is satisfactory.

I like to talk about sex.

I have never indulged in any unusual sex practices.

Drug Testing

Drug testing of current employees by a public agency must be based on "reasonable suspicion" and with "just cause." On the basis of prior cases, reasonable suspicion means that there is reason to suspect that employees are using drugs at work (Goldstein, 2000). Such suspicion can be produced from a variety of sources including "tips" that employees are using drugs (*Copeland v. Philadelphia Police Department*, 1989; *Feliciano v. Cleveland*, 1987; *Garrison v. Justice*, 1995); accidents or discipline problems (*Allen v. City of Marietta*, 1985; *Burnley v. Railway*, 1988); actual observation of drug usage (*Everett v. Napper*, 1987); or physical symptoms of being under the influence (*Connelly v. Newman*, 1990). Traditionally, the courts view as just cause the degree to which an employee's behavior affects the safety and trust of the public. For example, air traffic controllers (*Government Employees v. Dole*, 1987) and teachers (*Knox County Education Association v. Knox County Board of Education*, 1998) have been deemed to be responsible for the safety of the public, but school bus attendants have not (*Jones v. McKenzie*, 1987).

Other factors taken into consideration by the courts include the accuracy of the drug tests and the care and privacy taken during the testing (*Hester v. City of Milledgeville*, 1986; *Triblo v. Quality Clinical Laboratories*, 1982). The issue of privacy is an especially interesting one because employees who use drugs often try to "cheat" on their drug tests (Cadrain, 2003). Attempts at cheating include bringing in "clean" urine that has been taken or purchased from a friend or diluting the urine sample with soap, toilet water, or other chemicals. Strangely enough, to help applicants cheat on their drug test, one company markets a product called the "Whizzinator," a prosthetic penis containing a 4-ounce bag of dehydrated drug-free urine and an organic heating pad to keep the urine at body temperature (Cadrain, 2003). To stop such attempts, some organizations have required employees to strip so that the employee cannot bring anything into the test area; they also may require that the employee be observed while he provides the urine specimen. Testing conditions such as these would be allowed only under the most serious situations involving national security.

Two other important issues are the appeal process (*Harvey v. Chicago Transit Authority*, 1984) and the confidentiality of test results (*Ivy v. Damon Clinical Laboratory*, 1984). Employees must be given the opportunity to have their specimens retested and to explain why their tests were positive even though they may not have taken illegal drugs. Thus, for a drug testing program to be legal, the organization must have reason to suspect drug usage, the job must involve the safety or trust of the public, the testing process must be accurate and reasonably private, the results should be handled in a confidential manner, and employees who test positive must be given opportunities to appeal and undergo rehabilitation. A detailed discussion of the use and validity of drug testing for employee selection can be found in Chapter 6.

Office and Locker Searches

Office and locker searches are allowed under the law as long as they are reasonable and with cause (*O'Conner v. Ortega*, 1987). Allowing employees to place their own locks on lockers, however, removes the right of the organization to search the locker.

Psychological Tests

An employment test may be illegal if its questions unnecessarily invade the privacy of an applicant (O'Meara, 1994). At most risk are psychological tests originally developed to measure psychopathology. These tests often include questions about such topics as religion and sexual preference that some applicants feel uncomfortable answering. In *Soroka v. Dayton Hudson* (1991), three applicants for store security guard positions with Target Stores filed a class action suit after taking a 704-item psychological test (Psychscreen). The applicants believed some of the questions, a few of which are shown in Exhibit 3.07, violated their right to privacy guaranteed by the California Constitution.

Though the two sides reached a settlement prior to the case being decided by the U.S. Supreme Court, the case focused attention on the questions used in psychological testing. Of particular concern to I/O psychologists was that the tests were scored by a consulting firm, and Target Stores never saw the individual answers to the questions. Instead, it only received overall scores indicating the applicant's level of emotional stability, interpersonal style, addiction potential, dependability, and socialization. The finding by courts that use of the test was an invasion of privacy was troubling to psychologists who routinely make decisions based on overall test scores rather than the answers to any one particular question (Brown, 1993).

Electronic Surveillance

Almost 80% of organizations in the United States use video surveillance or monitor their employees' email, Internet usage, or telephone conversations (AMA, 2001). The 1st Circuit Court of Appeals has ruled that video surveillance is not an invasion of privacy because employees do not have an expectation of privacy while working in open areas (*Vega-Rodriguez v. Puerto Rico Telephone*, 1997). Furthermore, several district courts have ruled that organizations can monitor their employees' email or search their computer files (*Gary Leventhal v. Lawrence Knapek*, 2001), especially when the employees have been told that monitoring is part of organizational policy (Raynes, 1997). To be on safe legal ground, organizations should tell employees that they are being monitored and, at the time of hire, have new employees sign consent forms agreeing to be monitored. To test your knowledge of employee privacy issues, complete Exercise 3–6 at the end of this chapter.

Harassment

An issue of growing concern in the workplace is sexual harassment. In 2002, 14,396 complaints of sexual harassment were filed with the EEOC and with state and local agencies. Of these, 14.9% were filed by males. Of harassment claims filed with the EEOC, approximately 45% involve racial harassment, 15% national origin harassment, 34% sexual harassment, and 6% harassment of other protected classes. Research indicates that as many as 44% of women and 19% of men have been victims of sexual harassment (U.S. Merit Systems Board, 1995). These percentages increase when employees are the sole representative of their gender—called gender pioneers—or consist of a small minority of the employees in a particular work setting—called gender isolates (Niebuhr & Oswald, 1992). Though the following discussion focuses on sexual harassment, the courts have ruled that racial, religious, disability, and age harassment are also illegal (*Crawford v. Medina General Hospital*, 1996; Platt, 1994).

Types of Harassment

Legally, sexual harassment can take one of two forms: quid pro quo or hostile environment.

Quid Pro Quo

With **quid pro quo**, the granting of sexual favors is tied to such employment decisions as promotions or salary increases. An example of a quid pro quo case of harassment is a supervisor who tells his secretary that she must sleep with him to keep her job. In quid pro quo cases, a *single* incident is enough to constitute sexual harassment and result in the organization being liable for legal damages.

Hostile Environment

In a **hostile environment** case, sexual harassment occurs when an unwanted *pattern* of conduct related to *gender* unreasonably interferes with an individual's work performance. Though males and females differ in their perceptions of what constitutes harassment (Rotundo, Nguyen, & Sackett, 2001), the courts have ruled that such conduct can include comments, unwanted sexual or romantic advances, or the display of demeaning posters, signs, or cartoons (*Jenson v. Eveleth Taconite Co.*, 1993).

Pattern of Behavior. For conduct to be considered sexual harassment based on a hostile environment claim, the U.S. Supreme Court has ruled that the conduct must be a *pattern* of behavior rather than an isolated incident (*Clark County School District v. Breeden*, 2001). It would not be harassment to ask a coworker for a date, even if the coworker does not agree to the date. It becomes harassment if the employee *continually* makes unwanted romantic or sexual overtures or repeatedly makes inappropriate remarks.

Based on Gender. To be considered sexual harassment, conduct must be due to the *sex* of the employee. That is, but for the sex of the employee, would the conduct have occurred? For example, in *Christopher Lack v. Wal-Mart* (2001), the 4th Circuit Court of Appeals ruled that a supervisor's lewd and vulgar language and jokes were not sexual harassment because they were made to both males and females. Courts of appeal in the 7th (*Holman v. Indiana Department of Transportation*, 2000) and 8th (*Jenkins v. Southern Farm Bureau Casualty*, 2002) circuits have made similar rulings. Members of a police department consistently referring to female officers as "babes" or "honey" would be an example of sexual harassment because the comments are based on gender and are demeaning to the female officers. A male officer calling a female officer "stupid" would be an example of rude behavior, but not sexual harassment because the nature of the comment was not based on gender.

The U.S. Supreme Court recently considered whether an employee can sexually harass a member of the same gender. That is, if a male makes sexual comments or improperly touches another male, is this a case of sexual harassment? In the case of *Oncale v. Sundowner Offshore Services* (1998) the Supreme Court said yes. As a roustabout on an oil platform, Mr. Oncale was subjected to sexual threats and battery by other male roustabouts. After getting no help from his supervisor, Oncale quit his job and filed suit, eventually reaching the Supreme Court.

Negative to the Reasonable Person. The idea is that any pattern of behavior based on gender that causes an employee discomfort might constitute sexual harassment (Egler, 1995). In *Harris v. Forklift Systems* (1993), the court found that a male supervisor's comments, such as "Let's go to the Holiday Inn and negotiate your raise" and "You're just a dumb-ass woman," constituted harassment even though the female employee did not suffer any great psychological damage or have a "nervous breakdown."

Organizational Liability for Sexual Harassment

In cases of quid pro quo harassment, the organization will always be liable for the harassment of its employees (Twomey, 2002). In hostile environment cases, however, the U.S. Supreme Court has ruled that an organization can avoid liability by showing that it "exercised reasonable care to prevent and correct promptly any sexually harassing behavior" (*Burlington Industries v. Ellerth*, 1998; *Faragher v. City of Boca Raton*, 1998) or that the complainant did not take reasonable advantage of the corrective opportunities provided by the organization (Sherwyn, Sturman, Eigen, Heise, & Walwyn, 2001).

Preventing Sexual Harassment

In determining an organization's liability for the sexual harassing behavior of its employees, the courts look first at the organization's attempts to prevent sexual harassment. To avoid liability, the organization must have a well-conceived policy regarding sexual harassment and must have communicated that policy to its employees (*Frederick v. Sprint*, 2001). The policy must explain the types of harassment (*Smith v. First Union National Bank*, 2000) and include a list of the *names* of the company officials to whom an employee should report any harassment (*Gentry v. Export Packaging*, 2001). It is important to note that organizations are also responsible for harassment committed by vendors, customers, and other third parties.

Correcting Sexually Harassing Behavior

If an employee complains of sexual harassment, it is essential that the organization investigate the complaint quickly and then promptly take any necessary action to rectify the situation and punish the offender. To reduce an organization's liability for sexual harassment, Jacobs and Kearns (2001) advise the following:

1. All complaints, no matter how trivial or farfetched they appear, must be investigated.

2. The organization's policy must encourage victims to come forward and allow them multiple channels or sources with which to file their complaint.

3. Complaints must be kept confidential to protect both the accused and the accuser. Information from the investigation should be kept in a file separate from the employee's personnel file.

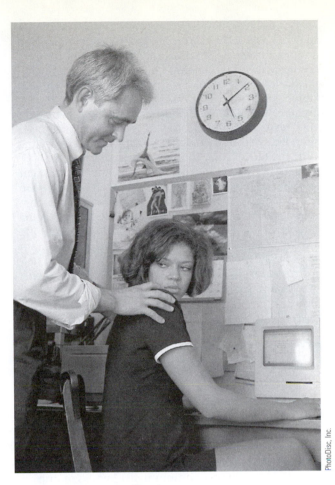

Sexual harassment is illegal.

4. Action must be taken to protect the accuser during the time the complaint is being investigated. Actions might include physically separating the two parties or limiting the amount of contact between them.

5. Both the accused and the accuser must be given due process, and care must be taken to avoid an initial assumption of guilt.

6. The results of the investigation must be communicated in writing to both parties.

7. The severity of the punishment (if any) must match the severity of the violation.

As mentioned previously, the proper handling of a sexual harassment complaint can protect an employer from legal liability. In such cases as *Baskerville v. Culligan International* (1995) and *Rheineck v. Hutchinson Technology* (2001), courts of appeal ruled that the organization was not liable for sexual harassment because it investigated a sexual harassment complaint in a timely manner and then took prompt corrective action against the harasser. In contrast, in *Intlekofer v. Turnage* (1992), the court of appeals found the Veterans Administration liable for the harassment of one of its employees because it ignored nearly two dozen complaints by a female employee and refused to take corrective action against the harasser.

However, the concern for prompt action should not deny the accused due process. In 1997, a jury awarded a man accused of sexual harassment $26.6 million. He was fired by Miller Brewing Company for discussing an episode of the TV show *Seinfeld* in which Jerry Seinfeld forgot the name of a date but remembered that it rhymed with a female body part (Delores). The jury ruled that a reasonable person would not have been offended by the discussion, and thus, Miller Brewing went too far in firing the accused employee.

Rather than being reactive to sexual harassment complaints, it is in the best interests of an organization to be proactive to prevent harassment. Proactive steps include having a strong organizational policy against harassment (*Frederick v. Sprint*, 2001) and training employees about behavior that constitutes harassment (Bronchick, 1997).

In addition to the obvious legal costs, sexual harassment has other financial ramifications for an organization. Sexual harassment results in higher levels of turnover, greater absenteeism, and lower levels of productivity (Munson, Hulin, & Drasgow, 2000; Pratt et al, 2003; Schneider, Swan, & Fitzgerald, 1997). To test your knowledge of sexual harassment, complete Exercise 3–7 at the end of this chapter.

Family Medical Leave Act

In 1993, Congress passed the **Family Medical Leave Act (FMLA)**, which entitles eligible employees (both male and female) to a minimum of 12 weeks of unpaid leave to deal with the following family matters:

- Births, adoptions, or placement for foster care
- To care for a child, parent, or spouse with a serious health condition
- The employee's own serious health condition that make him or her unable to perform the job

All public agencies and private organizations with 50 or more employees physically employed within a 70-mile radius of one another are covered by the act (Kalk, 2000).

Employees are eligible if they

1. work for a covered employer,
2. have worked for the organization for at least one year, and
3. have worked at least 1,250 hours over the previous 12 months.

Because the FMLA allows employees to take leave for the *serious illness* of a child, parent, spouse, or themselves, there has been some debate about how serious an illness has to be to qualify. The Department of Labor defines a serious health condition this way:

- Any period of incapacity of more than 3 consecutive calendar days *and* at least two visits to a healthcare provider *or* one visit and issuance of prescription medicine {or}

- Any period of incapacity due to a chronic serious health condition requiring periodic treatment covering an extended period of time {or}
- Any period of absence to receive multiple treatments for a condition that would result in a 3 or more day period of incapacity if left untreated.

On the basis of this definition, the courts have ruled such conditions as an ear infection (*Juanita Caldwell v. Kentucky Fried Chicken*, 2000) or a cold/flu (*Miller v. AT&T*, 2001; *Rose Rankin v. Seagate Technologies*, 2001) to be serious.

If employees take advantage of family or medical leave, the organization must continue the employees' health care coverage and guarantee employees that when they return they will either have the same or an equivalent position. In return, employees must provide a doctor's certification and give 30 days' notice if the leave is foreseeable (e.g., birth or adoption).

To protect employers from potential problems in complying with the FMLA, Congress allowed employers to exempt their key employees from using the FMLA. Key employees are the highest paid 10% in the organization. Other than record-keeping headaches, however, the FMLA has not resulted in many hardships for most organizations (Martinez, 1994).

The extent of family leave in the United States is similar to that in many countries. For example, laws in other countries mandate *unpaid* leave of 15 weeks in Belgium, 120 days in Brazil, and, depending on the province, 17 to 70 weeks in Canada. Mexico mandates 12 weeks and the European Union 14 weeks of *paid* leave. In England, employees who have been with an organization less than 26 weeks are entitled to 18 weeks of unpaid leave, employees with 26 weeks to 1 year of service are entitled to 18 weeks of paid leave, and employees with more than 1 year of service are entitled to 40 weeks of leave.

To practice what you have learned in this chapter, complete Exercise 3–8. To update some of the EEOC charge statistics found in this chapter, complete The Updating Charge Statistics Exercise on your CD-ROM.

Chapter Summary

In this chapter you learned:

- Discrimination complaints are filed with the EEOC.
- A variety of federal laws forbid discrimination based on sex (male, female); race (African American, European American, Asian American, Native American); national origin; color; religion; disability; age (over 40); pregnancy; and Vietnam-era veteran status.
- The legality of an employment practice is determined by such factors as the presence of adverse impact and the job relatedness of the employment practice.

Protected Class	Province											
	Alb	BC	Man	Ont	NB	NF	NS	NWT	PEI	Queb	SAS	Yukon
Race	yes	yes	yes	yes	yes	yes	yes	yes	yes	yes	yes	yes
Sex	yes	yes	yes	yes	yes	yes	yes	yes	yes	yes	yes	yes
Disability	yes	yes	yes	yes	yes	yes	yes	yes	yes	yes	yes	yes
Color	yes	yes	yes	yes	yes	yes	yes	yes	yes	yes	yes	yes
Religion	yes	yes	yes	yes	yes	yes	yes	yes	yes	yes	yes	yes
Marital status	yes	yes	yes	yes	yes	yes	yes	yes	yes	yes	yes	yes
Pregnancy	yes	yes	yes	yes	yes	yes	yes	yes	yes	yes	yes	yes
National origin	no	no	yes	yes	yes	yes	yes	yes	yes	yes	yes	yes
Age	18+	19–65	all	18–65	all	19–65	all	all	all	all	18–64	all
Sexual orientation	yes	yes	yes	yes	yes	yes	yes	no	yes	yes	yes	yes
Drug/alcohol dependence	yes	yes	yes	yes	yes	yes	yes	no	yes	yes	yes	no
Ancestry/place of origin	yes	yes	yes	yes	no	no	no	yes	no	no	yes	yes
Political beliefs	no	yes	yes	no	no	yes	yes	no	yes	yes	no	yes
Family status	yes	yes	yes	yes	no	no	yes	yes	yes	yes	yes	yes
Association	no	no	yes	yes	yes	no	yes	no	yes	no	no	yes
Criminal conviction	no	yes	no	no	no	no	no	no	yes	yes	no	yes
Language	no	no	no	yes	no	no	no	no	no	yes	no	yes
Social condition	no	no	no	no	no	yes	no	no	no	yes	no	no
Source of income	no	no	no	no	no	no	no	no	yes	no	no	no
Citizenship	no	no	no	yes	no	yes	no	no	no	no	no	no
Receipt of public assistance	no	no	no	no	no	no	no	no	no	no	yes	no

- Adverse impact is usually determined by the four-fifths rule.
- Affirmative action consists of a variety of strategies such as intentional recruitment of minority applicants, identification and removal of employment practices working against minority applicants and employees, and preferential hiring and promotion.
- Employers need to be cautious about violating employee privacy rights regarding drug testing, office and locker searches, psychological testing, and electronic surveillance.
- Organizations can be held liable for the sexual harassment of their employees. This harassment can take the form of quid pro quo or hostile environment.

Critical Thinking Questions

1. What would make an employment practice a BFOQ?
2. Is affirmative action a good idea?
3. Why do public employees have more privacy rights than private employees?
4. If a male employee asks out a female coworker, is this sexual harassment? Would your answer be different if the male were a supervisor rather than a coworker?
5. Would a color-blind person be considered disabled under the ADA?

To learn more about the issues discussed in this chapter, point your browser to

http://www.infotrac-college.com/wadsworth

and enter one of these search terms:

Employment discrimination

Equal Employment Opportunity Commission (EEOC)

affirmative action

Americans with Disabilities Act

bona fide occupational qualification (BFOQ)

minority job applicants

employee privacy

sexual harassment

Family Medical Leave Act

Exercise 3–1
Federally Protected Classes

Your text indicated that several groups were protected by federal equal opportunity legislation. In these examples, indicate whether the group in question would be considered a *federally* protected class. In making your decision, do not take into account whom you think would win the case. Instead, base your answer only on whether the person making the complaint is in a federally protected class.

		Federally Protected Class?	
A.	A World War II veteran claims he was discriminated against because he was in the war.	yes	no
B.	A Mormon says his religion forbids him to work on certain days.	yes	no
C.	A person who is visually impaired claims she is disabled.	yes	no
D.	A gay applicant wasn't hired because of his sexual preference.	yes	no
E.	A male wasn't hired for a sales position in a retail store specializing in female athletic shoes.	yes	no
F.	A 24-year-old female wasn't hired for a managerial job because she was too young.	yes	no
G.	A Norwegian applicant claimed he wasn't hired because a Chinese restaurant hired only Asians.	yes	no
H.	A light-skinned African American would not hire a dark-skinned African American.	yes	no
I.	A store wouldn't hire anyone with a college degree because of the belief that such people had no common sense.	yes	no
J.	A fast food chain refused to hire any males with long hair.	yes	no

Exercise 3–2
Determining Adverse Impact

For several years, Tubalard Bakery has required that all employees hired for cashier positions in their retail bakery store have at least 2 years of college. The company's justification for this requirement is that because their cashiers must add prices in their heads they need to be educated. Even though they are the only food store with this requirement, they are able to attract many applicants because they pay $3 an hour more than any other store.

In May 2002, Sarah Lee applied for a job with Tubalard and was not hired because she had never attended college. Ms. Lee, an African American female, filed charges of discrimination with the EEOC. On the basis of the facts stated above, as well as the data below, will the EEOC investigation reveal adverse impact on the basis of either sex or race?

Applicant	Sex	Race	Years of College
Lee	f	b	0
Amos	m	b	0
Fields	f	b	1
Keebler	m	w	3
Heinz	m	w	3
Smith	f	w	2
Crocker	f	w	2
Hughes	f	w	4
McCormick	f	w	0
Sauer	m	b	3
Chachere	f	b	0
Stubbs	m	b	2
Durkee	f	b	1
Wyler	m	w	3
Godiva	f	w	2
Kerr	m	w	0
Paul	f	w	2
Callander	f	w	0
Dunkin	f	w	3
Kroger	m	w	2
Puck	m	w	0
Roddenbery	f	b	3
Hostess	f	b	3
Kellogg	f	w	1
Mills	m	b	1

Show your work here:

Conclusions:

_____

_____

_____

_____

_____

_____

_____

_____

_____

_____

_____

_____

_____

_____

_____

_____

_____

_____

_____

_____

_____

_____

_____

Exercise 3–3
Responses to Adverse Impact

In the text you learned that, if adverse impact occurs, an employment practice can still be legal if it is job related (valid), is the result of a bona fide seniority system, is in use due to national security concerns, or was implemented to provide veterans with preferential hiring. In these examples, indicate the extent to which you think the employment practice will be found to be legal.

A.   Applicants for patrol officer positions with the City of Fort Worth, Texas, are administered a cognitive ability test. The average score on the test is 70. All applicants who served in the U.S. armed forces automatically get 10 points added to their scores. Adverse impact occurs because 20% of male applicants and 5% of female applicants are veterans. Is this practice legal? Why or why not?

_____

_____

_____

_____

_____

B.   The cognitive ability test described above also results in adverse impact because 80% of white applicants pass the test compared to 60% of African American applicants. Scores on the test correlate significantly ($r = .45$) with performance in the police academy. Is this practice legal? Why or why not?

_____

_____

_____

_____

_____

C.   According to the contract between the union and the company, every employment decision at the Spreewell Box Company is based on seniority. That is, the employees who have been at Spreewell the longest get first opportunity for promotions, working the day shift, and not working overtime. Due to a decline in sales, Spreewell must lay off 30 employees. On the basis of seniority, 25 of these employees are African American and 5 are white. Of the 200 employees who will keep their jobs, 190 are white and 10 are African American. Is this practice legal? Why or why not?

_____

_____

_____

_____

_____

Exercise 3–4
Legality of Employment Practices

Use the legal issues flowchart in Exhibit 3.02 to decide if the following situations would be legal. Be sure to state your logic at *each stage* of the flowchart.

1. An HR director will not hire anyone whose shoes are not well polished when they come to the interview. Is this legal?

2. A court system is about to fill an opening for the position of Victim's Advocate. The position involves working with women who have been sexually assaulted. The court has decided that it will only fill the position with a female because all of the victims are women and the crimes were sexual in nature. Would this be legal?

3. To get a job at the Arsonville Fire Department, applicants must pass a mechanical ability test. An extensive study found that the test correlates significantly ($r = .30$) with performance. During the current testing period, 20% of male applicants and 10% of female applicants passed the test. The Fire Department tried to find a test with less adverse impact but was unable to do so. Would the use of the test be legal?

Exercise 3–5
Understanding Affirmative Action

The personnel director of Tortlaw County thinks she is in big trouble. Ten years ago, 30% of the residents in the county were African American yet only 10% of county employees were African American. To remedy this situation, the county developed an affirmative action program in which at least 40% of all new hires were to be African American. The program had been working well because today 25% of all county employees are African American.

Last week, however, a white employee who wasn't hired for an engineering job filed a lawsuit challenging the legality of the affirmative action plan. Phil Abuster claimed that he was more qualified than the minority applicant who received the job. Abuster had a 3.4 college GPA and 3 years of engineering experience whereas Glen Valley, the minority applicant, had only a 3.2 GPA and 2 years of experience. Should our personnel director be worried? Why or why not?

Exercise 3–6
Employee Privacy Issues

In Chapter 3, you learned that drug testing, office and locker searches, psychological testing, and electronic surveillance can pose potential legal problems due to invasion of privacy. In the following examples, indicate whether you think an invasion of privacy occurred.

A.   A retail store places cameras in each corner of the store to prevent shoplifting and employee theft. The only place the cameras can't see are the dressing rooms. Is this an invasion of privacy? Why or why not?

_____

_____

_____

B.   During a polygraph test, a police department asks applicants how many people they slept with in the past 5 years. Is this an invasion of privacy? Why or why not?

_____

_____

_____

C.   A manufacturing company assigns each employee a locker and requires that the employees provide their own combination locks. The company suspects that several of the employees are drinking on the job, so it cuts the locks and inspects the lockers. Is this an invasion of privacy? Why or why not?

_____

_____

_____

D.   Siesta County has a new drug testing policy in which, weekly, it will require 30 randomly chosen employees to provide a urine sample. To ensure that the employees are not cheating, a monitor will observe the employee as he or she provides the urine specimen. Is this an invasion of privacy? Why or why not?

_____

_____

_____

_____

Exercise 3–7
Sexual Harassment

In Chapter 3, you learned that there are two types of sexual harassment, quid pro quo and hostile environment. In the situations below, indicate if the situation represents a case of quid pro quo, hostile environment, or no sexual harassment.

A.   A supervisor tells his secretary that if she won't sleep with him she will never get a raise or a promotion.

Quid pro quo   Hostile environment   No sexual harassment

_____

_____

_____

B.   Every few days at work, Bill tells Jennifer that she looks nice. Jennifer is a bit of a flirt and seems to like the attention Bill gives her.

Quid pro quo   Hostile environment   No sexual harassment

_____

_____

_____

C.   Judy asks Brian out on a date. He is not really interested in her and he declines. For the next 2 months, Judy asks Brian out every week, and each time he says no. He is so tired of the situation that he brings the matter to his supervisor.

Quid pro quo   Hostile environment   No sexual harassment

_____

_____

_____

D.   John usually addresses his female coworkers as "honey."

Quid pro quo   Hostile environment   No sexual harassment

_____

_____

_____

Exercise 3–8
Testing Your Knowledge

You have just been hired as the employment law expert for a new NBC call-in show, *Can I Sue?* What would you tell the caller asking the following questions? Be sure to include the rationale for your answer as well as the law on which you are basing your answer.

1.   I am one of 25 employees in my company. I want to have a baby but my boss says that the company will not grant me leave. Can they do this?

2.   I was burned badly as a child, and as a result, I have scars all over my face. I can't seem to get a job at McDonald's, Wendy's, or Burger King because they think my looks will turn off the customers. Can they do that to me?

3.   My male supervisor walks behind all of his employees and rubs their shoulders before asking, "How is it going today?" Isn't this sexual harassment?

4.   A female coworker has sent me 15 love letters. After the third letter, I told her to stop. She continued sending the letters that included such statements as "I have enjoyed watching you so much over these past few months" and "I constantly imagine us in bed together." Isn't this sexual harassment?

5.   Nine months ago I was refused a job. I think it was because I am Italian. Can I file a complaint with the EEOC?

4 Evaluating Selection Techniques and Decisions

In Chapter 3, you learned that many laws and regulations affect employee selection methods. In Chapters 5 and 6, recruiting and selecting employees will be discussed. But before we can discuss the available methods for selecting employees, it is important to understand the characteristics of an effective and fair selection system. By the end of this chapter you will learn

- what affects the reliability of a test.
- the three major types of reliability.
- the five ways to validate a test.
- how to find information about tests.
- how to determine the utility of a selection test.
- how to determine the fairness of a test.
- how to use test scores to make personnel selection decisions.

Throughout this chapter, you will encounter the word *test*. Though this word often conjures up an image of a paper-and-pencil test, in I/O psychology we use *test* to mean any technique used to evaluate someone. Thus, employment tests include such methods as references, interviews, and assessment centers.

Characteristics of Effective Selection Techniques

Effective selection techniques have four characteristics. They are reliable, valid, cost efficient, and legally defensible.

Reliability

Reliability is the extent to which a score from a selection measure is stable and free from error. If a score from a measure is not stable or error-free, it is not useful. For example, suppose we are using a ruler to measure the lengths of boards that will be used to build a doghouse. We want each board to be 4 feet long, but each time we measure a board, we get a different number. If the ruler does not yield the same number each time the same board is measured, the ruler cannot be considered reliable and thus is of no use. The same is true of selection methods. If applicants score differently each time they take a test, we are unsure of their actual scores. Consequently, the scores from the selection measure are of little value. Therefore, reliability is an essential characteristic of an effective measure.

Determining the Reliability of a Test

Test reliability is determined in three ways: test–retest reliability, alternate forms reliability, and internal reliability. Each of these techniques will be discussed in the sections that follow.

Test–Retest Reliability. With the **test-retest reliability** method, several people each take the same test twice. The scores from the first administration of the test are correlated with scores from the second to determine whether they are similar. If they are, the test is said to have **temporal stability:** The test scores are stable across time and not highly susceptible to such random daily conditions as illness, fatigue, stress, or uncomfortable testing conditions. There is no standard amount of time that should elapse between the two administrations of the test. The time interval should be long enough, however, so that the specific test answers have not been memorized but short enough so that the person has not changed significantly.

For example, if 3 years have elapsed between administrations of a personality inventory, there may be a very low correlation between the two sets of scores; but the low correlation may not be the result of low test reliability. Instead, it could be caused by personality changes of the people in the sample over time (Kaplan & Saccuzzo, 2001). Likewise, if only 10 minutes separate the two administrations, a very high correlation

Exhibit 4.01 — Design for typical alternate forms reliability study

Subjects	Administration Order	
	First	Second
1–50	Form A	Form B
51–100	Form B	Form A

between the two sets of scores might occur. This high correlation may represent only what the people remembered from the first testing rather than what they actually believe. Typical time intervals between test administrations range from 3 days to 3 months. Usually, the longer the time interval, the lower the reliability coefficient (Anastasi & Urbina, 1997). The typical test reliability coefficient for tests used in industry is .86 (Hood, 2001).

Test–retest reliability is not appropriate for all kinds of tests. It would not make sense to measure the test–retest reliability of a test designed to measure short-term moods or feelings. For example, the *State–Trait Anxiety Inventory* measures two types of anxiety. *Trait anxiety* refers to the amount of anxiety an individual normally has all the time, and *state anxiety* is the amount of anxiety an individual has at any given moment. For the test to be useful, it is important for the measure of trait anxiety, but not the measure of state anxiety, to have temporal stability.

Alternate Forms Reliability. With the **alternate forms reliability** method, two forms of the same test are constructed. As shown in Exhibit 4.01, a sample of 100 people are administered both forms of the test; half of the sample first receives Form A and the other half Form B. This **counterbalancing** of test-taking order is designed to eliminate any effects that taking one form of the test first may have on scores on the second form.

The scores on the two forms are then correlated to determine whether they are similar. If they are, the test is said to have **form stability.** Why would anyone use this method? If there is a high probability that people will take a test more than once, two forms of the test are needed to reduce the potential advantage to individuals who take the test a second time. This situation might occur in police department examinations. To be promoted, most police departments require an officer to pass a promotion exam. If the officer fails the exam one year, the officer can retake the exam the next year. If only one form of the test were available, the officer retaking the test for the seventh time could remember many of the questions and possibly score higher than an officer taking the test for the first time.

Multiple forms also might be used in large groups of test-takers where there is a possibility of cheating. Perhaps one of your professors has used more than one

form of the same test to discourage cheating. The last time you took your written driver's test, multiple forms probably were used, just as they were when you took the SAT or ACT to be admitted to college. As you can see, multiple forms of a test are common.

Recall that with test–retest reliability the time interval between administrations usually ranges from 3 days to 3 months. With alternate forms reliability, however, the time interval should be as short as possible. If the two forms are administered 3 weeks apart and a low correlation results, the cause of the low reliability is difficult to determine. That is, the test could lack either form stability or temporal stability. Thus, to determine the cause of the unreliability, the interval needs to be short. The average alternate form reliability for tests used in industry is .89 (Hood, 2001).

In addition to being correlated, two forms of a test should also have the same mean and standard deviation (Clause, Mullins, Nee, Pulakos, & Schmitt, 1998). The test in Exhibit 4.02, for example, shows a perfect correlation between the two forms. People who scored well on Form A also scored well on Form B. But the average score on Form B is two points higher than on Form A. Thus, even though the perfect correlation shows that the scores on the two forms are parallel, the difference in mean scores indicates that the two forms are not equivalent. In such a case, either the forms must be revised or different standards (norms) must be used to interpret the results of the test.

Any changes in a test potentially change its reliability, validity, difficulty, or all three. Such changes might include the order of the items, examples used in the questions, method of administration, and time limits. Though alternate form differences potentially affect test outcomes, most research indicates that these effects are either nonexistent or rather small. For example, meta-analyses suggest that computer administration (Dwight & Feigelson, 1997; Mead & Drasgow, 1993) or PowerPoint administration (Larson, 2001) of cognitive ability tests results in scores equivalent to paper-and-pencil administration, and changing the order of items does not seem to greatly affect test scores (Aamodt & McShane, 1992). However, research does suggest that African Americans, but not whites, score higher on video-based tests than on traditional paper-and-pencil tests (Chan & Schmitt, 1997).

Exhibit | 4.02 | Example of two parallel but nonequivalent forms

Subjects	Test Scores	
	Form A	Form B
1	6	8
2	9	11
3	11	13
4	12	14
5	12	14
6	17	19
7	18	20
8	19	21
9	21	23
10	24	26
Average score	14.9	16.9

Internal Reliability. A third way to determine the reliability of a test or inventory is to look at the consistency in which an applicant responds to items measuring a similar construct. The extent to which similar items are answered in similar ways is referred to as internal consistency and measures **item stability.**

In general, the longer the test, the higher its internal consistency—that is, the agreement among responses to the various test items (Schmitt, 1996). To illustrate this point, let us look at the final exam for this course. If the final were based on three chapters, would you want a test consisting of only three multiple-choice items? Probably not. If you made a careless mistake in marking your answer or fell asleep during part of the lecture from which a question was taken, your score would be low. But if the test had 100 items, one careless mistake or one missed part of a lecture would not severely affect your total score.

Another factor that can affect the internal reliability of a test is **item homogeneity.** That is, do all of the items measure the same thing, or do they measure different constructs? The more homogeneous the items, the higher the internal consistency. To illustrate this concept, let us again look at your final exam based on three chapters.

If we computed the reliability of the entire exam, it would probably be relatively low. Why? Because the test items are not homogeneous. They are measuring knowledge from three topic areas (three chapters), two sources (lecture and text), and two knowledge types (factual and conceptual). If we broke the test down by chapter, source, and item type, the reliability of the separate test components would be higher because we would be looking at groups of homogeneous items.

When reading information about internal consistency in a journal article or a test manual, you will encounter three terms that refer to the method used to

determine the internal consistency: Split-half method, coefficient alpha, and K-R 20. The **split-half method** is the easiest to use as items on a test are split into two groups. Usually, all of the odd-numbered items constitute one group and the even-numbered items the second group. The scores on the two groups of items are then correlated. Because the number of items in the test has been reduced, the **Spearman-Brown prophecy formula** is used to adjust the correlation.

Cronbach's **coefficient alpha** (Cronbach, 1951) and the **Kuder-Richardson formula 20 (K-R 20)** (Kuder & Richardson, 1937) are more popular and accurate methods of determining internal reliability, although they are more complicated to use and thus are calculated by computer program rather than by hand. Essentially, both the coefficient alpha and the K-R 20 represent the reliability coefficient that would be obtained from all possible combinations of split halves. The difference between the two is that the K-R 20 is used for tests containing dichotomous items (e.g., yes/no, true/false), whereas the coefficient alpha is used for tests containing interval and ratio items such as 5-point rating scales. The typical internal reliability coefficient for tests used in industry is .77 (Hood, 2001).

Scorer Reliability. A fourth way of assessing reliability is **scorer reliability.** A test or inventory can have homogeneous items and yield heterogeneous scores and still not be reliable if the person scoring the test makes mistakes. Scorer reliability is an issue in projective or subjective tests in which there is no one correct answer, but even tests scored with the use of keys suffer from scorer mistakes. For example, Allard, Butler, Faust, and Shea (1995) found that 53% of hand-scored personality tests contained at least one scoring error, and 19% contained enough errors to alter a clinical diagnosis.

When human judgment of performance is involved, scorer reliability is discussed in terms of *interrater reliability*. That is, will two interviewers give an applicant similar ratings, or will two supervisors give an employee similar performance ratings?

Validity

Validity is the degree to which inferences from scores on tests or assessments are justified by the evidence. As with reliability, a test must be valid to be useful. But just because a test is reliable does not mean it is valid. For example, suppose that we want to use height requirements to hire typists. Our measure of height (a ruler) would certainly be a reliable measure; most adults will get no taller, and two people measuring an applicant's height will probably get very similar measurements. It is doubtful, however, that height is related to typing performance. Thus, a ruler would be a reliable measure of height, but height would not be a valid measure of typing performance.

Even though reliability and validity are not the same, they are related. The potential validity of a test is limited by its reliability. Thus, if a test has poor reliability, it cannot have high validity. But as we saw in the example above, a test's reliability does not imply validity. Instead, we think of reliability as having a *necessary but not sufficient relationship* with validity.

Methods for Determining Validity

Content Validity. One way to determine a test's validity is to look at its degree of **content validity**—the extent to which tests or test items sample the content that they are supposed to measure. Again, let us use your final exam as an example. Your instructor tells you that the final exam will measure your knowledge of Chapters 8, 9, and 10. Each chapter is the same length, and your instructor spent three class periods on each chapter. The test will have 60 questions. For the test to be content valid, the items must constitute a representative sample of the material contained in the three chapters; therefore, there should be some 20 questions from each chapter. If there are 30 questions each from Chapters 8 and 9, the test will not be content valid because it left out Chapter 10. Likewise, if there are questions from Chapter 4, the test will not be content valid because it requires knowledge that is outside of the appropriate domain.

In industry, the appropriate content for a test or test battery is determined by the job analysis. A job analysis should first determine the tasks performed and the conditions under which they are performed. Next the KSAOs (knowledge, skills, abilities, and other characteristics) needed to perform the tasks under those particular circumstances are determined. All of the important dimensions identified in the job analysis should be covered somewhere in the selection process, at least to the extent that the dimensions (constructs) can be accurately and realistically measured. Anything that was not identified in the job analysis should be left out.

What would be a valid predictor of performance in a call center?

The readability of a test is a good example of how tricky content validity can be. Suppose we determine that conscientiousness is an important aspect of a job. We find a personality test that measures conscientiousness, and we are confident that our test is content valid because it measures a dimension identified in the job analysis. But the personality test is very difficult to read (e.g., containing such words as *meticulous, extraverted, gregarious*) and most of our applicants are only high school graduates. Is our test content valid? No, because it requires a high level of reading ability, and reading ability was not identified as an important dimension for our job.

Criterion Validity. Another measure of validity is **criterion validity**, which refers to the extent to which a test score is related to some measure of job performance called a **criterion** (criteria will be discussed more thoroughly in Chapter 8). Commonly used criteria include supervisor ratings of performance; actual measures of performance (e.g., sales, number of complaints, number of arrests made); attendance (tardiness, absenteeism); tenure; training performance (e.g., police academy grades); and discipline problems.

Criterion validity is established using one of two research designs: concurrent or predictive. With a **concurrent validity** design, a test is given to a group of employees who are already on the job. The scores on the test are then correlated with a measure of the employees' current performance.

With a **predictive validity** design, the test is administered to a group of job applicants who are going to be hired. The test scores are then compared to a future measure of job performance. In the ideal predictive validity situation, every applicant is hired (or a random sample of applicants), and the test scores are hidden from the people who will later make performance evaluations. If every applicant is hired, a wide range of both test scores and employee performance is likely to be found. Remember that the wider the range of scores, the higher the validity coefficient. But because it is rarely practical to hire every applicant, the ideal predictive design is not often used. Instead, most criterion validity studies use a concurrent design.

Why is a concurrent design weaker than a predictive design? The answer lies in the homogeneity of performance scores. In a given employment situation, very few employees are at the extremes of a performance scale. Employees who would be at the bottom of the performance scale either were never hired or have since been terminated. Employees at the upper end of the performance scale often get promoted. Thus, the **restricted range** of performance scores makes obtaining a significant validity coefficient more difficult.

A major issue concerning the criterion validity of tests focuses on a concept known as **validity generalization (VG)**—the extent to which a test found valid for a job in one location is valid for the same job in a different location. It was previously thought that the job of typist in one company was not the same as that in another company, the job of police officer in one small town was not the same as that in another small town, and the job of retail store supervisor was not the same as that of supervisor in a fast food restaurant.

In the past 2 decades, research (e.g., Schmidt, Gast-Rosenberg, & Hunter, 1980; Schmidt & Hunter, 1998; Schmidt, Hunter, Pearlman, & Hirsh, 1985) indicates that a test valid for a job in one organization also is valid for the same job in another organization. Schmidt, Hunter, and their associates have tested hundreds of thousands of employees to arrive at their conclusions. They suggest that previous thinking resulted from studies with small sample sizes, and test validity in one location but not another was primarily the product of sampling error. With large sample sizes, a test found valid in one location probably will be valid in another, providing that the jobs actually are similar and are not merely two separate jobs sharing the same job title.

The two building blocks for validity generalization are meta-analysis, discussed in Chapter 1, and job analysis, discussed in Chapter 2. Meta-analysis can be used to determine the average validity of specific types of tests for a variety of jobs. For example, several studies have shown that cognitive ability is an excellent predictor of police performance. If we were to conduct a meta-analysis of all the studies looking at this relationship, we would be able to determine the average validity of cognitive ability in predicting police performance. If this validity coefficient is significant, then police departments similar to those used in the meta-analysis could adopt the test without conducting criterion validity studies of their own. This would be especially useful for small departments that have neither the number of officers necessary to properly conduct criterion validity studies nor the financial resources necessary to hire professionals to conduct such studies. Validity generalization should only be used if a job analysis has been conducted and the

results of the job analysis show that the job in question is similar to those used in the meta-analysis.

Construct Validity. Construct validity is the most theoretical of the validity types. Basically, it is the extent to which a test actually measures the construct that it purports to measure (Kaplan & Saccuzzo, 2001). Construct validity is concerned with inferences about test scores, in contrast to content validity, which is concerned with inferences about test construction.

Perhaps a good example of the importance of construct validity is a situation I encountered during graduate school. We had just completed a job analysis of the entry-level police officer position for a small town. One of the important dimensions (constructs) that emerged was honesty. Almost every officer insisted that a good police officer was honest, so we searched for tests that measured honesty and quickly discovered that there were many types of honesty; a conclusion also reached by Rieke and Guastello (1995). Some honesty tests measured theft, some cheating, and others moral judgment. None measured the honesty construct as it was defined by these police officers—not taking bribes and not letting friends get away with crimes. No test measured that particular construct, even though all of the tests measured "honesty."

Construct validity is usually determined by correlating scores on a test with scores from other tests. Some of the other tests measure the same construct, whereas others do not. For example, suppose we have a test that measures knowledge of psychology. One hundred people are administered our Knowledge of Psychology Test as well as another psychology knowledge test, a test of reading ability, and a test of general intelligence. If our test really measures the construct we say it measures—knowledge of psychology—it should correlate highly with the other test of psychology knowledge but not very highly with the other two tests. If our test correlates highest with the reading ability test, our test may be content valid (it contained psychology items), but not construct valid because scores on our test are based more on reading ability than on knowledge of psychology.

Another method of measuring construct validity is **known-group validity** (Hattie & Cooksey, 1984). This method is not common and should be used only when other methods for measuring construct validity are not practical. With known-group validity, a test is given to two groups of people who are "known" to be different on the trait in question.

For example, suppose we wanted to determine the validity of our new honesty test. The best approach might be a criterion validity study in which we would correlate our employees' test scores with their dishonest behavior, such as stealing or lying. The problem is, how would we know who stole or who lied? We could ask them, but would dishonest people tell the truth? Probably not. Instead, we decide to validate our test by administering it to a group known as honest (priests) and to another group known as dishonest (criminals).

After administering the test to both groups we find that, sure enough, the priests score higher on honesty than do the convicts. Does this mean our test is valid?

Not necessarily. It means that the test has known-group validity but not necessarily other types of validity. We do not know whether the test will predict employee theft (criterion validity), nor do we know if the test is even measuring honesty (construct validity). It is possible that the test is actually measuring another construct on which the two groups differ (e.g., intelligence). Because of these problems, the best approach to take with known-group validity is this: If the known groups do not differ on test scores, consider the test invalid. If scores do differ, one still cannot be sure of its validity.

Even though known-group validity usually should not be used to establish test validity, it is important to understand because some test companies use known-group validity studies to sell their tests, claiming that the tests are valid. Personnel analyst Jeff Rodgers once was asked to evaluate a test his company was considering for selecting bank tellers. The test literature sounded impressive, mentioning that the test was "backed by over 100 validity studies." Rodgers was suspicious and requested copies of the studies. After several months of "phone calls and teeth pulling," he obtained reports of the validity studies. Most of the studies used known-group methodology and compared the scores of groups such as monks and priests. Not one study involved a test of criterion validity to demonstrate that the test could actually predict bank teller performance. Thus, if you hear that a test is valid, it is important to obtain copies of the research reports.

Face Validity

Although face validity is not one of the three major methods of determining test validity cited in the *Uniform Guidelines*, it is still important. **Face validity** is the extent to which a test appears to be job related. This perception is important because if a test or its items do not appear valid, the test-takers and administrators will not have confidence in the results. If job applicants do not think a test is job related, their perceptions of its fairness decrease (Gilliland, 1993). Likewise, if employees involved in a training session on interpersonal skills take a personality test and are given the results, they will not be motivated to change or to use the results of the test unless the personality profile given to them seems accurate.

The importance of face validity has been demonstrated in a variety of research studies. For example, Chan, Schmitt, DeShon, Clause, and Delbridge (1997) found that face-valid tests result in high levels of test-taking motivation, which in turn result in higher levels of test performance. Thus, face-valid tests motivate applicants to do well on tests. Face-valid tests that are accepted by applicants decrease the chance of lawsuits (Rynes & Connerley, 1993), reduce the number of applicants dropping out of the employment process (Thornton, 1993), and increase the chance that an applicant will accept a job offer (Hoff Macan, Avedon, & Paese, 1994).

The face validity and acceptance of test results can be increased by telling applicants information about how a test relates to job performance (Lounsbury, Bobrow, & Jensen, 1989) and by administering the test in a multimedia format (Richman-Hirsch, Olson-Buchanan, & Drasgow, 2000). Acceptance of test results also increases when applicants receive honest feedback about their test performance and are treated with respect by the test administrator (Gilliland, 1993).

But just because a test has face validity does not mean it is valid (Jackson, O'Dell, & Olson, 1982). For example, have you ever read a personality description based on your astrological sign and found the description to be quite accurate? Does this mean astrological forecasts are accurate? Not at all. If you also have read a personality description based on a different astrological sign, you probably found it to be as accurate as the one based on your own sign. Why is this? Because of something called **Barnum statements** (Dickson & Kelly, 1985)—statements so general that they can be true of almost everyone. For example, if I described you as "sometimes being sad, sometimes being successful, and at times not getting along with your best friend," I would probably be very accurate. However, these statements describe almost anyone. So face validity by itself is not enough.

With three common ways of measuring validity, one might logically ask which of the methods is the "best" to use. As with most questions in psychology, the answer is that "it depends." In this case, the answer depends on the situation as well as what the person conducting the validity study is trying to accomplish. If it is to decide whether the test will be a useful predictor of employee performance, then content validity will usually be used and a criterion validity study also will be conducted if there are enough employees and if a good measure of job performance is available.

In deciding if content validity is enough, I advise organizations to use the "next door neighbor rule." That is, ask yourself "If my neighbor were on a jury and I had to justify the use of my test, would content validity be enough?" For example, suppose you conduct a job analysis of a clerical position and find that typing, filing, and answering the phone are the primary duties. So you purchase a standard typing test and a filing test. The link between these tests and the duties performed by our clerical worker is so obvious that a criterion validity study is probably not essential to convince a jury of the validity of the two tests. However, suppose your job analysis of a police officer indicates that making decisions under pressure is an important part of the job. To tap this dimension, you choose the Gandy Critical Thinking Test. Because the link between your test and the ability to make decisions under pressure is not so obvious, you may need a criterion validity study.

Why not always conduct a criterion validity study? After all, isn't a significant validity coefficient better than sex? (If you answered yes to this question, consider yourself a true HR nerd and a poor candidate for marriage.) Having the significant validity coefficient is great. But the danger is in conducting the validity study. If you conduct a criterion-validity study and do not get significance, that failure could be deadly if you are taken to court. To get a significant validity coefficient, many things have to go right. You need a good test, a good measure of performance, and a decent sample size. Furthermore, most validity coefficients are small (in the .20 to .35 range). Though assessment experts understand the utility of such small correlations, it can be difficult to convince a jury to share your excitement after you explain that the range for a correlation coefficient is -1 to $+1$, you got a correlation of .20, and that your test explains 4% of the variance.

Finally, a test itself can never be valid. When we speak of validity, we are speaking about the validity of the *test scores* as they relate to a particular job. A test may be a valid predictor of tenure for counselors but not of performance for shoe salespeople. Thus, when we say that a test is valid, we mean that it is valid for a particular job and a particular criterion. No test will ever be valid for all jobs and all criteria.

Finding Reliability and Validity Information

Over the previous pages, we have discussed different ways to measure reliability and validity. But even though most of you will eventually be involved with some form of employee testing, few of you will actually conduct a study on a test's reliability and validity. Consequently, where do you get information about a test's reliability and validity? There are many excellent sources containing reliability and validity information in the reference section of most university libraries.

Perhaps the most common source of test information is the *Fourteenth Mental Measurements Yearbook* (Plake & Impara, 2001). The *Mental Measurements Yearbook (MMY)* contains information about thousands of different psychological tests as well as reviews by test experts. Another excellent source of information is a compendium entitled *Tests* (Sweetland & Keyser, 1991), which contains information similar to the *MMY* without the test reviews. To help you use these test compendia, complete Exercise 4–1 at the end of this chapter.

Cost Efficiency

If two or more tests have similar validities, then cost should be considered. For example, in selecting police officers it is common to use a test of cognitive ability such as the Wonderlic Personnel Test or the Wechler Adult Intelligence Scale (WAIS). Both tests have similar reliabilities and validities, yet the Wonderlic costs only a few dollars per applicant and can be administered to groups of people in only 12 minutes. The WAIS must be administered individually at a time cost of at least an hour per applicant and a financial cost of more than $100 per applicant. Given the similar validities, it doesn't take a rocket scientist (or an I/O psychologist) to figure out which is the better deal. In situations that are not so clear, the utility formula discussed later in this chapter can be used to determine the best test.

A particular test is usually designed to be administered either to individual applicants or to a group of applicants. Certainly, group testing is usually less expensive and more efficient than individual testing, although important information may be lost in group testing. For example, one reason for administering an individual intelligence test is to observe the *way* in which a person solves a problem or answers a question. With group tests, only the answer can be scored.

A recent innovation in the administration of psychological tests involves the use of computers and the Internet. An applicant takes a test at a computer terminal, the computer scores the test, and the test's results and interpretation are immediately available. Because computer-assisted testing can lower testing costs, decrease feedback time, and yield results in which the test-takers can have great confidence, many public and private employers are switching to this method. Many state governments have found considerable cost savings in allowing applicants to take a computerized test near where they live rather than having applicants travel great distances to take a test at a central location. This increase in efficiency does not come at the cost of decreased validity because, as mentioned previously in the chapter, tests administered electronically seem to yield results similar to those administered through the traditional paper-and-pencil format.

An increasingly common use of computer testing is **computer-adaptive testing (CAT)**. In fact, you probably took the SAT in a computer-adaptive format. With CAT, the computer "adapts" the next question to be asked on the basis of how the test-taker responded to the previous question or questions. For example, if the test-taker successfully answered three multiplication questions in a row, the computer would move to another type of math rather than wasting time by asking seven more multiplication questions. When taking a CAT, the computer starts by asking questions of average difficulty. If the test-taker answers these correctly, the computer asks more difficult questions. If the test-taker answers these questions incorrectly, the computer asks easier questions. The logic behind CAT is that if a test-taker can't answer easy questions (e.g., addition and subtraction) it doesn't make sense to ask questions about algebra and geometry. The advantages to CAT are that fewer test items are required, tests take less time to complete, finer distinctions in applicant ability can be made, test-takers can receive immediate feedback, and test scores can be interpreted not only on the number of questions answered correctly but on which questions were answered correctly.

Establishing the Usefulness of a Selection Device

Even though a test is both reliable and valid, it is not necessarily useful. At first, this may not make much sense, but consider a test that has been shown to be valid for selecting employees for a fast food restaurant chain. Suppose there are 100 job openings and 100 job seekers apply for those openings. Even though the test is valid, it will have no impact because the restaurant chain must hire every applicant.

Exhibit 4.03 Typical corrected validity coefficients for selection

Selection Technique	Validity
Structured interview	.57
Work samples	.54
Cognitive ability tests	.51
Job knowledge tests	.48
Biodata	.37
Assessment centers	.38
Integrity tests	.34
College grades	.32
Experience	.27
Reference checks	.26
Personality tests (conscientiousness)	.24
Unstructured interviews	.20
Vocational interest tests	.10
Application blank	.10
Handwriting analysis	.02
Projective personality tests	.00

As another example, imagine an organization that already has a test that does a good job of predicting performance. Even though a new test being considered may be valid, the old test may have worked so well that the current employees are all successful. Or the organization may have such a good training program that current employees are all successful. Thus, a new test (even though it is valid) may not provide any improvement.

To determine how useful a test would be in any given situation, several formulas and tables have been designed. Each formula and table provides slightly different information to an employer. The *Taylor-Russell tables* provide an estimate of the percentage of total new hires who will be successful employees if a test is adopted (organizational success); both *expectancy charts* and the *Lawshe tables* provide a probability of success for a particular applicant based on test scores (individual success); and the *utility formula* provides an estimate of the amount of money that an organization will save if it adopts a new testing procedure.

Taylor-Russell Tables

The **Taylor-Russell tables** (Taylor & Russell, 1939) are designed to estimate the percentage of future employees who will be successful on the job if an organization uses a particular test. To use the Taylor-Russell tables, three pieces of information must be obtained.

The first information needed is the test's *criterion validity coefficient*. There are two ways to obtain this

coefficient. The best would be to actually conduct a criterion validity study with test scores correlated with some measure of job performance. Often, however, an organization wants to know whether testing is useful before investing time and money in a criterion validity study. This is where validity generalization comes into play. On the basis of findings by researchers such as Schmidt and Hunter (1998), we have a good idea of the typical validity coefficients that will result from various methods of selection. To estimate the validity coefficient that an organization might obtain, one of the coefficients from Exhibit 4.03 is used. The higher the validity coefficient, the greater the possibility the test will be useful.

The second piece of information that must be obtained is the **selection ratio**, which is simply the percentage of people an organization must hire. The ratio is determined by the formula

$$\text{Selection ratio} = \frac{\text{number hired}}{\text{number of applicants}}$$

The lower the selection ratio, the greater the potential usefulness of the test.

The final piece of information needed is the **base rate** of current performance—the percentage of employees currently on the job who are considered successful. This figure is usually obtained in one of two ways. The first method is the most simple but the least accurate. Employees are split into two equal groups based on their scores on some criterion such as tenure or performance. The base rate using this method is always .50 because one half of the employees are considered satisfactory.

The second and more meaningful method is to choose a criterion measure score above which all employees are considered successful. For example, at one real estate agency, any agent who sells more than $300,000 in real estate makes a profit for the agency after training and operating expenses have been deducted. In this case, any agent selling more than $300,000 in property would be considered a success because he or she made money for the company. Any agent selling less than $300,000 in property would be considered a failure because he or she cost the company more money than was brought in.

In this example, there is a clear point at which an employee can be considered a success. Most of the time, however, there are no such clear points. In these cases, managers will subjectively choose a point on the criterion that they feel separates successful from unsuccessful employees.

After the validity, selection ratio, and base rate figures have been obtained, the Taylor-Russell tables are consulted (see Exhibit 4.04). To understand how they are used, let us take the following example. Suppose we have a test validity of .40, a selection ratio of .30, and a base rate of .50. Locating the table corresponding to the .50 base rate, we look along the top of the chart until we find the .30 selection ratio. Next, we locate the validity of .40 on the left side of the table. We then trace across the table until we locate the intersection of the selection ratio column and the validity row; we have found .69.

If the organization uses that particular selection test, 69% of future employees are likely to be considered successful. This figure is compared with the previous base rate of .50, indicating a 38% increase in successful employees (.19 ÷ .50 = .38).

Proportion of Correct Decisions

Determining the **proportion of correct decisions** is easier to do but less accurate than the Taylor-Russell tables. The only information needed to determine the proportion of correct decisions is employee test scores and the scores on the criterion. The two scores from each employee are graphed on a chart similar to that in Exhibit 4.05. Lines are drawn from the point on the y axis (criterion score) that represents a successful applicant and from the point on the x axis that represents the lowest test score of a hired applicant. As you can see, these lines divide the scores into four quadrants. The points located in quadrant I represent employees who scored poorly on the test but performed well on the job. Points located in quadrant II represent employees who scored well on the test and were successful on the job. Points in quadrant III represent employees who scored high on the test yet did poorly on the job, and points in quadrant IV represent employees who scored low on the test and did poorly on the job.

If a test is a good predictor of performance, there should be more points in quadrants II and IV because the points in the other two quadrants represent "predictive failures." That is, in quadrants I and III no correspondence is seen between test scores and criterion scores.

To estimate the test's effectiveness, the number of points in each quadrant is totaled, and the following formula is used:

$$\frac{\text{Points in quadrants II and IV}}{\text{Total points in all quadrants}}$$

The resulting number represents the percentage of time that we expect to be accurate in making a selection decision in the future. To determine whether this is an improvement, we use the following formula:

$$\frac{\text{Points in quadrants I and II}}{\text{Total points in all quadrants}}$$

If the percentage from the first formula is higher than that from the second, our proposed test should increase selection accuracy. If not, it is probably better to stick with the selection method currently used.

As an example, look again at Exhibit 4.05. There are 5 data points in quadrant I, 10 in quadrant II, 4 in quadrant III, and 11 in quadrant IV. The percentage of time we expect to be accurate in the future would be:

$$\frac{II + IV}{I + II + III + IV} = \frac{10 + 11}{5 + 10 + 4 + 11} = \frac{21}{30} = .70$$

To compare this figure to the test we were previously using to select employees, we compute the satisfactory performance baseline:

$$\frac{I + II}{I + II + III + IV} = \frac{5 + 10}{5 + 10 + 4 + 11} = \frac{15}{30} = .50$$

Using the new test would result in a 40% increase in selection accuracy [.70 − .50 = .20 ÷ .50] over the selection method previously used.

Lawshe Tables

The Taylor-Russell tables were designed to determine the overall impact of a testing procedure. But we often need to know the probability that a *particular applicant* will be successful. The **Lawshe tables** (Lawshe, Bolda, Brune, & Auclair, 1958) were created to do just that. To use these tables, three pieces of information are needed. The validity coefficient and the base rate are found in the same way as for the Taylor-Russell tables. The third piece of information needed is the applicant's test score. More specifically, did the person score in the top 20%, the next 20%, the middle 20%, the next lowest 20%, or the bottom 20%?

Once we have all three pieces of information, the Lawshe tables, as shown in Exhibit 4.06, are examined. For our example, we have a base rate of .50, a validity of .40, and an applicant who scored third highest out of 10. First, we locate the table with the base rate of .50. Then we locate the appropriate category at the top of the chart. Our applicant scored third highest out of 10 applicants, so she would be in the second category, the next highest one fifth or 20%. Using the validity of .40,

Exhibit **4.04** Taylor-Russell tables

		Selection Ratio									
Employees Considered Satisfactory	**r**	**.05**	**.10**	**.20**	**.30**	**.40**	**.50**	**.60**	**.70**	**.80**	**.90**	**.95**
10%	.00	.10	.10	.10	.10	.10	.10	.10	.10	.10	.10	.10
	.10	.14	.13	.13	.12	.12	.11	.11	.11	.11	.10	.10
	.20	.19	.17	.15	.14	.14	.13	.12	.12	.11	.11	.10
	.30	.25	.22	.19	.17	.15	.14	.13	.12	.12	.11	.10
	.40	.31	.27	.22	.19	.17	.16	.14	.13	.12	.11	.10
	.50	.39	.32	.26	.22	.19	.17	.15	.13	.12	.11	.11
	.60	.48	.39	.30	.25	.21	.18	.16	.14	.12	.11	.11
	.70	.58	.47	.35	.27	.22	.19	.16	.14	.12	.11	.11
	.80	.71	.56	.40	.30	.24	.20	.17	.14	.12	.11	.11
	.90	.86	.69	.46	.33	.25	.20	.17	.14	.12	.11	.11
20%	.00	.20	.20	.20	.20	.20	.20	.20	.20	.20	.20	.20
	.10	.26	.25	.24	.23	.23	.22	.22	.21	.21	.21	.20
	.20	.33	.31	.28	.27	.26	.25	.24	.23	.22	.21	.21
	.30	.41	.37	.33	.30	.28	.27	.25	.24	.23	.21	.21
	.40	.49	.44	.38	.34	.31	.29	.27	.25	.23	.22	.21
	.50	.59	.52	.44	.38	.35	.31	.29	.26	.24	.22	.21
	.60	.68	.60	.50	.43	.38	.34	.30	.27	.24	.22	.21
	.70	.79	.69	.56	.48	.41	.36	.31	.28	.25	.22	.21
	.80	.89	.79	.64	.53	.45	.38	.33	.28	.25	.22	.21
	.90	.98	.91	.75	.60	.48	.40	.33	.29	.25	.22	.21
30%	.00	.30	.30	.30	.30	.30	.30	.30	.30	.30	.30	.30
	.10	.38	.36	.35	.34	.33	.33	.32	.32	.31	.31	.30
	.20	.46	.43	.40	.38	.37	.36	.34	.33	.32	.31	.31
	.30	.54	.50	.46	.43	.40	.38	.37	.35	.33	.32	.31
	.40	.63	.58	.51	.47	.44	.41	.39	.37	.34	.32	.31
	.50	.72	.65	.58	.52	.48	.44	.41	.38	.35	.33	.31
	.60	.81	.74	.64	.58	.52	.47	.43	.40	.36	.33	.31
	.70	.89	.62	.72	.63	.57	.51	.46	.41	.37	.33	.32
	.80	.96	.90	.80	.70	.62	.54	.48	.42	.37	.33	.32
	.90	1.00	.98	.90	.79	.68	.58	.49	.43	.37	.33	.32
40%	.00	.40	.40	.40	.40	.40	.40	.40	.40	.40	.40	.40
	.10	.48	.47	.46	.45	.44	.43	.42	.42	.41	.41	.40
	.20	.57	.54	.51	.49	.48	.46	.45	.44	.43	.41	.41
	.30	.65	.61	.57	.54	.51	.49	.47	.46	.44	.42	.41
	.40	.73	.69	.63	.59	.56	.53	.50	.48	.45	.43	.41
	.50	.81	.76	.69	.64	.60	.56	.53	.49	.46	.43	.42
	.60	.89	.83	.75	.69	.64	.60	.55	.51	.48	.44	.42
	.70	.95	.90	.82	.76	.69	.64	.58	.53	.49	.44	.42
	.80	.99	.96	.89	.82	.75	.68	.61	.55	.49	.44	.42
	.90	1.00	1.00	.97	.91	.82	.74	.65	.57	.50	.44	.42

Exhibit 4.04

Taylor-Russell tables
(continued)

		Selection Ratio										
Employees Considered Satisfactory	r	.05	.10	.20	.30	.40	.50	.60	.70	.80	.90	.95
50%	.00	.50	.50	.50	.50	.50	.50	.50	.50	.50	.50	.50
	.10	.58	.57	.56	.55	.54	.53	.53	.52	.51	.51	.50
	.20	.67	.64	.61	.59	.58	.56	.55	.54	.53	.52	.51
	.30	.74	.71	.67	.64	.62	.60	.58	.56	.54	.52	.51
	.40	.82	.78	.73	.69	.66	.63	.61	.58	.56	.53	.52
	.50	.88	.84	.76	.74	.70	.67	.63	.60	.57	.54	.52
	.60	.94	.90	.84	.79	.75	.70	.66	.62	.59	.54	.52
	.70	.98	.95	.90	.85	.80	.75	.70	.65	.60	.55	.53
	.80	1.00	.99	.95	.90	.85	.80	.73	.67	.61	.55	.53
	.90	1.00	1.00	.99	.97	.92	.86	.78	.70	.62	.56	.53
60%	.00	.60	.60	.60	.60	.60	.60	.60	.60	.60	.60	.60
	.10	.68	.67	.65	.64	.64	.63	.63	.62	.61	.61	.60
	.20	.75	.73	.71	.69	.67	.66	.65	.64	.63	.62	.61
	.30	.82	.79	.76	.73	.71	.69	.68	.66	.64	.62	.61
	.40	.88	.85	.81	.78	.75	.73	.70	.68	.66	.63	.62
	.50	.93	.90	.86	.82	.79	.76	.73	.70	.67	.64	.62
	.60	.96	.94	.90	.87	.83	.80	.76	.73	.69	.65	.63
	.70	.99	.97	.94	.91	.87	.84	.80	.75	.71	.66	.63
	.80	1.00	.99	.98	.95	.92	.88	.83	.78	.72	.66	.63
	.90	1.00	1.00	1.00	.99	.97	.94	.88	.82	.74	.67	.63
70%	.00	.70	.70	.70	.70	.70	.70	.70	.70	.70	.70	.70
	.10	.77	.76	.75	.74	.73	.73	.72	.72	.71	.71	.70
	.20	.83	.81	.79	.78	.77	.76	.75	.74	.73	.71	.71
	.30	.88	.86	.84	.82	.80	.78	.77	.75	.74	.72	.71
	.40	.93	.91	.88	.85	.83	.81	.79	.77	.75	.73	.72
	.50	.96	.94	.91	.89	.87	.84	.82	.80	.77	.74	.72
	.60	.98	.97	.95	.92	.90	.87	.85	.82	.79	.75	.73
	.70	1.00	.99	.97	.96	.93	.91	.88	.84	.80	.76	.73
	.80	1.00	1.00	.99	.98	.97	.94	.91	.87	.82	.77	.73
	.90	1.00	1.00	1.00	1.00	.99	.98	.95	.91	.85	.78	.74
80%	.00	.80	.80	.80	.80	.80	.80	.80	.80	.80	.80	.80
	.10	.85	.85	.84	.83	.83	.82	.82	.81	.81	.81	.80
	.20	.90	.89	.87	.86	.85	.84	.84	.83	.82	.81	.81
	.30	.94	.92	.90	.89	.88	.87	.86	.84	.83	.82	.81
	.40	.96	.95	.93	.92	.90	.89	.88	.86	.85	.83	.82
	.50	.98	.97	.96	.94	.93	.91	.90	.88	.86	.84	.82
	.60	.99	.99	.98	.96	.95	.94	.92	.90	.87	.84	.83
	.70	1.00	1.00	.99	.98	.97	.96	.94	.92	.89	.85	.83
	.80	1.00	1.00	1.00	1.00	.99	.98	.96	.94	.91	.87	.84
	.90	1.00	1.00	1.00	1.00	1.00	1.00	.99	.97	.94	.88	.84

continued on next page

Exhibit 4.04

Taylor-Russell tables
(continued)

Employees Considered Satisfactory	r	Selection Ratio										
		.05	.10	.20	.30	.40	.50	.60	.70	.80	.90	.95
90%	.00	.90	.90	.90	.90	.90	.90	.90	.90	.90	.90	.90
	.10	.93	.93	.92	.92	.92	.91	.91	.91	.91	.90	.90
	.20	.96	.95	.94	.94	.93	.93	.92	.92	.91	.91	.90
	.30	.98	.97	.96	.95	.95	.94	.94	.93	.92	.91	.91
	.40	.99	.98	.98	.97	.96	.95	.95	.94	.93	.92	.91
	.50	1.00	.99	.99	.98	.97	.97	.96	.95	.94	.92	.92
	.60	1.00	1.00	.99	.99	.99	.98	.97	.96	.95	.93	.92
	.70	1.00	1.00	1.00	1.00	.99	.99	.98	.97	.96	.94	.93
	.80	1.00	1.00	1.00	1.00	1.00	1.00	.99	.99	.97	.95	.93
	.90	1.00	1.00	1.00	1.00	1.00	1.00	1.00	1.00	.99	.97	.94

Source: "The relationship of validity coefficients to the practical effectiveness of tests in selection: Discussion and tables," by H. C. Taylor and J. T. Russell, 1939, *Journal of Applied Psychology, 23,* 565–578.

we locate the intersection of the validity row and the test score column and find 59. This means that the applicant has a 59% chance of being a successful employee.

Brogden-Cronbach-Gleser Utility Formula

Another way to determine the value of a test in a given situation is by computing the amount of money an organization would save if it used the test to select employees. Fortunately, I/O psychologists have devised a fairly simple **utility formula** to estimate the monetary savings to an organization. To use this formula, five items of information must be known.

1. *Number of employees hired per year (n).* This number is easy to determine: It is simply the number of employees who are hired for a given position in a year.
2. *Average tenure (t).* This is the average amount of time that employees in the position tend to stay with the company. The number is computed by using information from company records to identify the time that each employee in that position stayed with the company. The number of years of **tenure** for each employee is then summed and divided by the total number of employees.
3. *Test validity (r).* This figure is the criterion validity coefficient that was obtained through either a validity study or validity generalization (Cascio, 1987).
4. *Standard deviation of performance in dollars (SD$_y$).* For many years, this number was difficult to compute. Research has shown, however, that for jobs in which performance is normally distributed, a good estimate of the difference in performance

between an average and a good worker (one standard deviation away in performance) is 40% of the employee's annual salary (Hunter & Schmidt, 1982). The 40% rule yields results similar to more complicated methods and is preferred by managers (Hazer & Highhouse, 1997). To obtain this, the total salaries of current employees in the position in question should be averaged.

5. *Mean standardized predictor score of selected applicants (m).* This number is obtained in one of two ways. The first method is to obtain the average score on the selection test for both the applicants who are hired and the applicants who are not hired. The average test score of the nonhired applicants is subtracted from the average test score of the hired applicants. This difference is divided by the standard deviation of all the test scores.

For example, we administer a test of mental ability to a group of 100 applicants and hire the 10 with the highest scores. The average score of the 10 hired applicants was 34.6, the average test score of the other 90 applicants was 28.4, and the standard deviation of all test scores was 8.3. The desired figure would be:

$$\frac{34.6 - 28.4}{8.3} = \frac{6.2}{8.3} = .747$$

The second way to find *m* is to compute the proportion of applicants who are hired and then use a conversion table such as that in Exhibit 4.07 to convert the proportion into a standard score. This second method is used when an organization plans to use a test, knows the probable selection ratio based on previous hirings, but does not know the average test scores because the organization has never used the test. Using

Exhibit 4.05 Determining the proportion of correct decisions

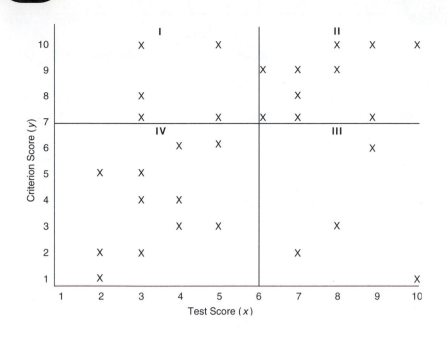

the previous example, the proportion of applicants hired would be:

$$\frac{\text{number of applicants hired}}{\text{total number of applicants}} = \frac{10}{100} = .10$$

From Exhibit 4.07, we see that the standard score associated with a selection ratio of .10 is 1.76. To determine the savings to the company, we use the following formula:

savings = (n) (t) (r) (SD_y) (m) − cost of testing
(# of applicants × the cost per applicant)

As an example, suppose we will hire 10 auditors per year, the average person in this position stays 2 years, the validity coefficient is .30, average annual salary for the position is $30,000, and we have 50 applicants for 10 openings. Thus,

$$n = 10$$

$$t = 2$$

$$r = .30$$

$$SD_y = \$30,000 \times .40 = 12,000$$

$$m = 10/50 = .20 = 1.40 \text{ (.20 is converted to 1.40 by using Exhibit 4.07)}$$

cost of testing = (50 applicants × $10)

Using the above formula, we would have

(10) (2) (.30) (12,000) (1.40) − (50) (10) = $100,300

This means that after accounting for the cost of testing, using this particular test instead of selecting employees by chance will save a company $100,300 over the 2 years that auditors typically stay with the organization.

Because a company seldom selects employees by chance, the same formula should be used with the validity of the test (interview, psychological test, references, and so on) that the company currently uses. The result of this computation should then be subtracted from the first.

This final figure, of course, is just an estimate based on the assumption that the highest scoring applicants accept the job offer. To be most accurate, it must be adjusted by such factors as variable costs, discounting, corporate tax rates, and changes in strategic goals (Boudreau, 1983; Cascio, 1987; Russell, Colella, & Bobko, 1993). Though utility estimates should provide data supporting the usefulness of testing, there is some question about the extent to which managers believe the validity of the estimated financial savings (Carson, Becker, & Henderson, 1998; Latham & Whyte, 1994), especially considering that the size of these estimates is often in the millions of dollars. When one considers the costs of constant poor performance, however, the size of these estimates should not be surprising. The high estimated savings are even more believable when one considers the cost of one employee's mistake. For example:

- An employee of Oxford Organics Inc. mislabeled an artificial vanilla flavoring sent to General Mills resulting in $150,000 in damaged cake frosting.

- A Navy mechanic left a 5-inch wrench inside the wheel compartment of a jet causing the $33 million plane to crash.

- A typo made in a letter by a car dealer told customers to call a 900 number instead of an 800 number. The 900 number turned out to be a sex line, and the dealership had to send out an additional 1,000 letters to apologize and correct the mistake.

Exhibit 4.06 Lawshe individual prediction tables

Percentage of Current Employees Considered Satisfactory	r	Applicant Scores on Selection Test				
		Top 20%	Next 20%	Middle 20%	Next 20%	Bottom 20%
30%	.20	40	34	29	26	21
	.30	46	35	29	24	16
	.40	51	37	28	21	12
	.50	58	38	27	18	09
	.60	64	40	26	15	05
40%	.20	51	45	40	35	30
	.30	57	46	40	33	24
	.40	63	48	39	31	19
	.50	69	50	39	28	14
	.60	75	53	38	24	10
50%	.20	61	55	50	45	39
	.30	67	57	50	43	33
	.40	73	59	50	41	28
	.50	78	62	50	38	22
	.60	84	65	50	35	16
60%	.20	71	63	60	56	48
	.30	76	66	61	54	44
	.40	81	69	61	52	37
	.50	86	72	62	47	25
	.60	90	76	62	47	25
70%	.20	79	75	70	67	59
	.30	84	76	71	65	54
	.40	88	79	72	63	49
	.50	91	82	73	62	42
	.60	95	85	74	60	36

Note: Percentages indicate probability that applicant with a particular score will be a successful employee.

Source: "Expectancy charts II: Their theoretical development," C. H. Lawshe and R. A. Brune, 1958, *Personnel Psychology 11*, 545–599.

Thus, the cost of daily poor performance combined with the cost of occasional mistakes such as these provides support for the validity of high utility estimates. Though utility formulas are useful means for decision making, it is important to consider such factors as adverse impact. For example, Hoffman and Thornton (1997) demonstrated that at times a less valid, more expensive selection method (e.g., an assessment center) can be better than its more valid, less expensive counterpart (e.g., a cognitive ability test) due to the legal cost savings and social value associated with lower adverse impact. To help you understand the utility tables and formulas, complete Exercises 4–2 and 4–3 at the end of this chapter.

Determining the Fairness of a Test

Once a test has been determined to be reliable and valid and to have utility for an organization, the next step is to ensure fairness, the meaning of which has been heavily debated. Though some people argue that a test is unfair if members of a protected class score lower than the majority (e.g., whites, males), most I/O psychologists agree that a test is fair if it can predict performance equally well for all races, genders, and national origins.

Exhibit 4.07 Selection ratio conversion table for utility formula

Selection Ratio	m
1.00	0.00
.90	0.20
.80	0.35
.70	0.50
.60	0.64
.50	0.80
.40	0.97
.30	1.17
.20	1.40
.10	1.76
.05	2.08

Adverse Impact

The first step in determining a test's fairness is finding out whether it will result in **adverse impact.** There are two basic ways to determine this. The most common method is to find the percentage of people in each equal employment opportunity (EEO) group who are hired after taking the test. This procedure was discussed in Chapter 3.

If the selection rate for any of the protected groups is less than 80% of the selection rate for either white applicants or males, the test is considered to have adverse impact. Remember that a legal defense for adverse impact is job relatedness, and that a valid test is a job-related test. Thus, even if the test has adverse impact, it *probably* will be considered a legal test.

But even though the test might be considered legally fair, an organization still might not want to use it. If a test results in adverse impact, the organization may have to go to court to defend itself. Even though a valid test will probably allow the organization to win the case, going to court is expensive. Thus, if the utility of the test is low, potential court costs will outweigh the minimal savings to the organization. Furthermore, a test with adverse impact will lead to poor public relations with minority communities, which could hurt recruitment or marketing efforts by the organization.

Using the 80% rule to determine a test's fairness means that an organization must wait until it has used the test to select employees, at which time damage already has been done. Another method of determining adverse impact compares the average scores of minority applicants with those of white and male applicants. This is most easily done by looking in the test manual to determine whether African Americans and whites or males and females have significantly different test scores. If so, the test prob-

ably will have adverse impact and an alternative test can be sought.

A more sophisticated method of estimating potential adverse impact was suggested by Aamodt, Johnson, and Freeman (1992). These researchers developed a table, based on the normal curve and assuming top-down hiring, that uses selection ratios and effect sizes (*d* scores) obtained from test manual information to determine the ratio of the minority selection rate to the majority selection rate. The table, shown in Exhibit 4.08, is used by finding the point in the table where the selection ratio and the effect size intersect. The number found at this point represents the percentages of minorities that will be selected as a percentage of the nonminority selection ratio. Any number less than .80, or four fifths, indicates that the selection technique will probably result in adverse impact.

Using this table requires two pieces of information. The first is the effect size (*d*) representing the standard difference between the scores of two groups on a test (the effect size can be obtained using the means and standard deviations provided in test manuals). For example, suppose an organization is considering using a mechanical knowledge test to hire maintenance employees. For this type of position, the organization usually has about 10 people applying for each opening (a selection ratio of .10). According to the information in the testing manual supplied by the company marketing the test, the average score for females is 72.1 and the average for males is 80.2. The standard deviation for the test is 33.69. The following formula is used to compute the effect size (*d*):

$$\frac{(\text{minority test mean} - \text{majority test mean})}{\text{overall standard deviation}}$$

For the above data, the effect size (*d*) would be (72.1 − 80.2) / 33.69 = −.24.

Exhibit 4.08 Minority selection ratio as a proportion of the nonminority selection ratio

	Selection Ratio								
Effect Size	.10	.20	.30	.40	.50	.60	.70	.80	.90
.01	.96	.98	.99	.99	.99	.99	.99	.99	.99
.02	.92	.96	.97	.98	.98	.98	.99	.99	.99
.03	.89	.94	.96	.97	.98	.98	.98	.99	.99
.04	.85	.92	.95	.96	.97	.97	.98	.98	.98
.05	.82	.91	.94	.95	.96	.97	.97	.98	.98
.06	.79	.89	.92	.94	.95	.96	.97	.97	.97
.07	.76	.87	.91	.93	.95	.96	.97	.97	.97
.08	.72	.85	.90	.92	.94	.95	.96	.96	.97
.09	.70	.83	.89	.91	.93	.94	.95	.96	.96
.10	.67	.82	.88	.91	.92	.94	.94	.95	.96
.15	.54	.74	.82	.86	.89	.91	.92	.93	.94
.20	.43	.67	.77	.82	.85	.88	.89	.91	.92
.25	.34	.60	.72	.78	.82	.85	.87	.88	.90
.30	.26	.54	.67	.74	.79	.82	.84	.86	.88
.35	.19	.49	.63	.71	.76	.80	.82	.84	.86
.40	.13	.44	.59	.67	.73	.77	.80	.82	.84
.45	.07	.39	.55	.64	.70	.75	.78	.80	.82
.50	.02	.35	.52	.61	.68	.72	.76	.79	.81
.55	.00	.31	.48	.59	.65	.70	.74	.77	.79
.60	.00	.28	.45	.56	.63	.68	.72	.75	.78
.65	.00	.24	.42	.54	.61	.66	.71	.74	.76
.70	.00	.22	.40	.51	.59	.64	.69	.72	.75
.75	.00	.19	.37	.49	.57	.63	.67	.71	.74
.80	.00	.16	.35	.47	.55	.61	.66	.69	.72
.85	.00	.14	.33	.45	.54	.60	.64	.68	.71
.90	.00	.12	.31	.43	.52	.58	.63	.67	.70
.95	.00	.10	.29	.42	.50	.57	.62	.66	.69
1.00	.00	.08	.27	.40	.49	.56	.61	.65	.68
1.10	.00	.05	.24	.37	.47	.53	.59	.63	.66
1.20	.00	.02	.22	.35	.44	.51	.57	.61	.65
1.30	.00	.00	.20	.33	.43	.50	.55	.60	.63
1.40	.00	.00	.18	.31	.41	.48	.54	.58	.62
1.50	.00	.00	.16	.30	.40	.47	.53	.57	.61
1.60	.00	.00	.15	.28	.38	.46	.52	.56	.60
1.70	.00	.00	.14	.27	.37	.45	.51	.56	.60
1.80	.00	.00	.13	.27	.37	.44	.50	.55	.59
1.90	.00	.00	.12	.25	.36	.44	.50	.54	.58

To predict whether this test will result in adverse impact, the intersection of the row containing the effect size of .24 and the column containing the selection ratio of .10 is located in Exhibit 4.08. The number .34 found at this intersection indicates that the selection ratio for females will be 34% of the selection ratio for males, substantially below the 80% figure indicating adverse impact.

Viewing the results from this table indicates how difficult it is to avoid adverse impact if a strict linear selection procedure is used. For example, with a selection ratio of .10, a test in which groups differ by only 6/100ths of a standard deviation ($d = .06$) would result in adverse impact if applicants were hired in a top-down order based on their raw test scores and if the top-scoring applicants accepted the job offer. To practice using this table, complete the Estimating Future Adverse Impact Exercise on your CD-ROM.

Single-Group Validity

In addition to adverse impact, an organization must also determine whether a test has **single-group validity**, meaning that the test will significantly predict performance for one group and not others. For example, a test of reading ability might predict performance of white clerks but not African American clerks.

To test for single-group validity, separate correlations are computed between the test and the criterion for each group. If both correlations are significant, the test does not exhibit single-group validity and it passes this fairness hurdle. If, however, only one of the correlations is significant, the test is considered fair for only the one group.

Single-group validity is very rare (O'Connor, Wexley, & Alexander, 1975) and is usually the result of small sample sizes and other methodological problems (Schmidt, 1988; Schmidt & Hunter, 1978). Where it occurs, an organization has three choices. It can disregard single-group validity because research indicates that it probably occurred by chance; it can stop using the test; or it can use the test for only the one group and find another test to use for other groups.

Disregarding single-group validity probably is the most appropriate choice given that most I/O psychologists believe single-group validity occurs only by chance. As evidence of this, think of a logical reason a test would predict differently for African Americans than for whites or differently for males than for females. That is, why would a test of intelligence predict performance for males but not for females? Or why would a personality test predict performance for African Americans but not for whites? There may be many cultural reasons two groups *score* differently on a test (e.g., educational opportunities, socioeconomic status), but finding a logical reason that the test would *predict* differently for two groups is difficult.

If we do not believe single-group validity is the result of chance, we must adopt one of the other two options. As you can see, even though the third option is statistically correct, many public relations problems may result. For example, if an applicant asks, "Why did I get one test and my friend another?" we could respond that "African Americans get one test and whites get another." Such a response, however, is provocative and ultimately may be counterproductive for an organization.

Differential Validity

The last test of fairness that must be conducted involves differential validity. With **differential validity**, a test is valid for two groups but more valid for one than for the other. Single-group validity and differential validity are easily confused, but there is a big difference between the two. Remember, with single-group validity, the test is valid only for one group. With differential validity, the test is valid for both groups, but it is more valid for one than for the other.

Like single-group validity, differential validity is rare (Katzell & Dyer, 1977; Schmidt & Hunter, 1981). When it does occur, it is usually in single-sex dominated occupations, tests are most valid for the dominant sex, and the tests overpredict minority performance (Rothstein & McDaniel, 1992; Saad & Sackett, 2002). If differential-group validity occurs, the organization has two choices. The first is not to use the test. Usually, however, this is not a good option. Finding a test that is valid is difficult; throwing away a good test would be a shame.

The second option is to use the test with separate regression equations for each group. Because applicants do not realize that the test is scored differently, there are not the public relations problems that occur with use of separate tests. However, the 1991 Civil Rights Act prohibits score adjustments based on race or gender. As a result, using separate equations may be statistically acceptable but would not be legally defensible.

If a test does not lead to adverse impact, does not have single-group validity, and does not have differential validity, it is considered to be fair. If the test fails to pass one of these three fairness hurdles, it may or may not be fair, depending on which model of fairness is followed (Arvey, 1988). But to be used with complete confidence, a test must be valid, have utility, and be fair.

Making the Hiring Decision

After valid and fair selection tests have been administered to a group of applicants, a final decision must be made as to which applicant or applicants to hire. At first, this may seem to be an easy decision—hire the applicants with the highest test scores. But the decision becomes more complicated as both the number and variety of tests increase.

Linear Approaches

Linear approaches assume that the relationship between the test score and the criterion is **linear**. That is, the higher applicants score on the test, the better

T. R. Lin, Ph.D.
Assistant Superintendent, Human Resources Development
Bassett Unified School District

Courtesy of T. R. Lin

My first job out of graduate school was as a Personnel Examiner for the Los Angeles Unified School District, the second largest school district in the nation. While working there, I thoroughly learned public professional human resource management and practices while progressing through the ranks of Senior Personnel Examiner, Principal Personnel Examiner, and for the last 4 years, Assistant Personnel Director, Selection.

As the Assistant Personnel Director, Selection, I directed all the recruitment and selection activities for approximately 35,000 nonteaching employees performing more than 1,000 different jobs. This work was accomplished by a team of 73 full-time and 50 part-time professional HR staff in four geographically dispersed employment offices throughout the City of Los Angeles.

I believe in continued professional development. As an I/O psychologist by training, I frequently attend and present at such I/O psychology-related conferences and workshops as SIOP, Academy of Management, APA, IPMAAC, IPMA, WRIPAC, and regional PTCs. In addition to attending and presenting, I also like to be involved in networking with other professionals. I have been a president for PTC/SC, WRIPAC, and IPMAAC.

After being in recruitment and selection for many years, I decided to expand my HR horizon recently by joining Bassett Unified School District as their newly created Assistant Superintendent, Human Resources Development.

As the Assistant Superintendent, Human Resources Development, I work closely with the Personnel Commission, the Board of Education, and the District Superintendent. My major duties and responsibilities include:

- Administer a comprehensive merit system and human resources development program for certificated and classified employees;

- Develop and recommend short- and long-term human resources strategies, policies, goals, and objectives;

- Serve as the Personnel Commission's secretary;

- Identify appropriate procedures that ensure fair and equal employment opportunity and investigate or assist in the investigation of complaints concerning violations of state or federal law involving fair employment practice;

- Negotiate and administer collective bargaining agreements with the teacher's union and the classified employee's union;

- Plan and coordinate the Personnel Commission agenda;

- Select, assign, train, supervise, and evaluate the performance of HR staff;

- Counsel and consult with certificated and classified employees on various HR issues;

- Serve as the expert adviser to the Personnel Commission, Board of Education, and the Superintendent;

- Serve as a member of the superintendent's cabinet;

- Direct the recruitment, selection, assignment, and compensation activities for both certificated and classified HR programs;

- Direct the credentialing verification and monitoring of certificated personnel;

- Stay abreast of legislative and legal changes in the HR field; and

- Establish and maintain relationship with regulatory agencies, employees, employee associations, community groups, the media, and the public.

As you can see, my new job includes all the human resource topics covered in a typical I/O psychology textbook. Of course, recruitment and selection is one of the areas I know the best. As I am finishing this note, the schools are getting ready for all the new and returning K–12 and adult school students. In preparation for this, the HR department filled every teacher and support staff vacancy over the summer.

My new job enables me to explore many other HR areas that I did not have opportunities to explore previously. Among all the current HR challenges, the biggest one for my department and most of the school districts is to continue to recruit and retain "highly qualified" teachers and paraprofessionals as outlined in the *No Child Left Behind* federal law signed by President Bush in January 8, 2002. To meet this new requirement, we are working on more proactive recruitment and retention strategies.

The other challenging area is to improve the union–management relationship in the school district from a somewhat adversarial to a cooperative one. Our district is planning programs that will promote more teacher and staff involvement in improving student achievement, work productivity, and service quality. To see more participative decision making between teacher and district management is the direction I would like to work on.

One area I would like to commend is that I believe an internship experience should be a part of an I/O graduate program. I remember as a graduate student at Cornell University that I was never able to get real-life internship experience outside of the campus because my foreign student visa limitation prohibited me from obtaining work. I could only get on-campus research assistantships. Although these made my research and data analysis skills quite solid, I missed valuable opportunities to put my classroom lessons to work in the real world.

I promoted the internship program when I joined the Los Angeles USD. Due to budget constraints, I first attracted graduate I/O students as unpaid interns by developing interesting and challenging personnel selection

validation studies for them to work on. When I became the Assistant Personnel Director, I had my own budget and was able to pay interns I hired. Over the years, we successfully "mentored" more than 50 interns, mostly I/O graduate students, several of whom were foreign students. Many of these former interns now work full time in Los Angeles USD and other professional personnel organizations. I plan to introduce the internship project into the Bassett USD.

Maybe because I like people and trust my staff, I am inclined to a participative style of leadership. I like being a mentor and a coach rather than a boss. I use team decision making whenever I can and stress the importance of working as a team. As HR professionals, I believe we need to continue to improve the quality of services and strive for high levels of customer relations, and this is best accomplished by fostering a participative and cooperative working environment.

---

they will do on the job. Usually, tests that are criterion-valid have linear relationships with criteria. Thus, if a criterion-valid test is used, selection decisions are usually based on the highest test scores.

If more than one criterion-valid test is used, the scores on the tests must be combined. Usually, this is done by a statistical procedure known as **multiple regression**, with each test score weighted according to how well it predicts the criterion. Linear approaches to hiring usually take one of four forms: unadjusted top-down selection, rules of 3, passing scores, or banding.

Unadjusted Top-Down Selection

With **top-down selection**, applicants are rank-ordered on the basis of their test scores. Selection is then made by starting with the highest score and moving down until all openings have been filled. For example, for the data in Exhibit 4.09, if we had four openings, we would hire the top four scorers who, in this case, would be Kilborne, Letterman, King, and Williams. Notice that all four are males. If, for affirmative action purposes, we wanted to hire two females, top-down selection would not allow us to do so.

The advantage to top-down selection is that by hiring the top scorers on a valid test, an organization will gain the most utility (Schmidt, 1991). The disadvantages are that this approach can result in high levels of adverse impact and it reduces an organization's flexibility to use nontest factors such as references or organizational fit.

Rule of 3

A technique often used in the public sector is the **rule of 3** (or rule of 5) in which the names of the top three scorers are given to the person making the hiring decision (e.g., police chief, HR director). This person can

then choose any of the three. This method ensures that the person hired will be well qualified but provides more choice than does top-down selection.

Passing Scores

Passing scores are a means for reducing adverse impact and increasing flexibility. With this system, an organization determines the lowest score on a test that is associated with acceptable performance on the job. For example, we know that a student scoring 1,300 on the SAT will probably have better grades in college than a student scoring 800. But what is the lowest score on the SAT that we can accept and still be confident that the student will be able to pass classes and eventually graduate?

Notice the distinct difference between top-down selection and passing scores. With top-down selection, the question is, Who will perform the *best* in the future? With passing scores, the question becomes, Who will be able to perform at an *acceptable level* in the future?

As you can imagine, passing scores provide an organization with much flexibility. Again using Exhibit 4.09 as an example, suppose we determine that any applicant scoring 70 or above will be able to perform adequately the duties of the job in question. If we set 70 as the passing score, we can fill our four openings with any of the eight applicants scoring 70 or better. Because, for affirmative action reasons, we would like two of the four openings to be filled by females, we are free to hire Winfrey and O'Donnell. Use of passing scores allows us to reach our affirmative action goals, which would not have been met with top-down selection. By hiring applicants with lower scores, however; the quality of our future employees will be lower than if we used top-down selection (Schmidt, 1991).

Exhibit 4.09 Hypothetical testing information

Applicant	Sex	Test Score
Kilborne	M	99
Letterman	M	98
King	M	91
Williams	M	90
Winfrey	F	88
Rivera	M	87
Leno	M	72
O'Donnell	F	70 Passing Score
Gibbons	F	68
Philbin	M	62
Springer	M	60
Gifford	F	57
Jones	F	54
O'Brien	M	49
Rose	M	31

Though use of passing scores appears to be a reasonable step toward reaching affirmative action goals, determining the actual passing score can be a complicated process full of legal pitfalls (Biddle, 1993). The most common methods for determining passing scores (e.g., the Angoff and Nedelsky methods) require job experts to read each item on a test and provide an estimation about the percentage of minimally qualified employees that could answer the item correctly. The passing score then becomes the average of the estimations for each question. Legal problems can occur when unsuccessful applicants challenge the validity of the passing score (Cascio, Alexander, & Barrett, 1988).

Banding

As mentioned previously, a problem with top-down hiring is that the process results in the highest levels of adverse impact. On the other hand, use of passing scores decreases adverse impact but reduces utility. As a compromise between top-down hiring and passing scores, **banding** attempts to hire the top test scorers while still allowing some flexibility for affirmative action (Campion et al., 2001).

Banding takes into consideration the degree of error associated with any test score. Thus, even though one applicant might score 2 points higher than another, the 2-point difference might be the result of chance (error) rather than actual differences in ability. The question then becomes, How many points apart do two applicants have to be before we say their test scores are significantly different?

We can answer this question using a statistic called the **standard error (SE)** (Oh God, not another statistic!). To compute this statistic, we obtain the reliability and standard deviation (SD) of a particular test from the test catalog (or we can compute it ourselves if we have nothing better to do on a weekend!). This information is then plugged into the following formula:

$$SE = SD\sqrt{1 - reliability}$$

For example, suppose we have a test with a reliability of .90 and a standard deviation of 13.60. The calculation of the standard error would be:

$$SE = 13.60\sqrt{1 - .90}$$

$$SE = 13.60\sqrt{.10}$$

$$SE = 13.60 \times .316$$

$$SE = 4.30$$

Bands are typically, but do not have to be, determined by multiplying the standard error by 1.96 (the standard score associated with a 95% level of confidence). Because the standard error of our test is 4.30, test scores within 8.4 points (4.3 × 1.96) of one another would be considered statistically the same. If we take this concept a bit further, we can establish a hiring band. For example, look at the applicants depicted in Exhibit 4.09. Suppose that we have four openings and would like to hire at least two females if possible. Because the highest scoring female in our example is Winfrey at 88, a top-down approach would not result in any females being hired. With a nonsliding band, we are free to hire anyone whose scores fall between the top score (Kilborne at 99) and 91 (99 − 8.4). As with top-down selection, use of a nonsliding band in this example would not result in any females being hired. With a sliding band, however, we start with the highest score (Kilborne at 99) and subtract from it the bandwidth (8.4). In this case, 99 − 8.4 = 90.6, meaning that all applicants scoring between 91 and 99 are considered statistically to have the same score. Because no female falls within this band, we hire Snyder and then consider the next score of Letterman at 98. Our next band of 98 through 90 (98 − 8.4) still does not contain a female so we hire Letterman and then consider the next score of King at 94. Our new band of 94 to 86 contains four applicants, one of whom is a female. Because we are free to hire anyone within a band, we would probably hire Winfrey to meet our affirmative action goals. We would then hire King as our fourth person. With banding, one more female was hired than would have occurred under a top-down system. Note, however, that our goal to hire two females was not reached, as it was when we used passing scores. To practice how to construct a band, complete Exercise 4–4 at the end of this chapter.

Though the concept of banding has been approved in several court cases (*Bridgeport Guardians v. City of Bridgeport*, 1991; *Chicago Firefighters Union Local No. 2 v. City of Chicago*, 1999; *Officers for Justice v. Civil Service Commission*, 1992), only selecting minorities in a band would be illegal. Instead, affirmative action goals must be considered as only one factor in selecting applicants from a band. For example, by allowing some flexibility in hiring, the use of banding might allow a police chief to hire a lower-scoring Spanish-speaking applicant or an applicant with computer skills over a higher scoring applicant without these desired, but not required, skills.

Though banding seems to be a good compromise between top-down hiring and passing scores (Zedeck, Cascio, Goldstein, & Outtz, 1996), it is not without its critics (Campion et al., 2001). Research indicates that banding will result in lower utility than top-down hiring (Schmidt, 1991), that it may not actually reduce adverse impact in any significant way (Gutman & Christiansen, 1997), and that its usefulness in achieving affirmative action goals is affected by such factors as the selection ratio and the percentage of minority applicants (Sackett & Roth, 1991).

Nonlinear Approaches

Often employee selection tests do not show a linear relationship between test scores and job performance. For example, suppose that the distance between the floor and the ceiling of an airplane cabin is 6 feet. Because airline attendants must stand while serving meals and assisting passengers, a content-valid requirement might be that the applicants be shorter than 6 feet. Thus, as part of the selection testing process, we measure each applicant. Any applicant taller than 6 feet would be unable to perform the job regardless of other test scores. If we use a linear approach, however, a person 5 feet 3

inches tall would get more points than a person 5 feet 8 inches tall. This would not make sense. Both applicants are able to satisfy the requirement of moving through the aisles of the airplane while standing. Being shorter would not give one person an advantage over another.

In such a situation, we use a **cutoff approach** in which all nonlinear tests are scored on a pass/fail basis. Applicants are administered the complete battery of tests and must pass every nonlinear one. The regression, or standardized composite, method discussed earlier then is used to select applicants on the basis of their scores on the linearly related tests.

For example, suppose that our job analysis finds that a good police officer is intelligent, is confident, is in good health, can lift 100 pounds, is psychologically sound, and does not have a criminal record. Our validity study indicates that the relationships of both intelligence and confidence with job performance are linear: The smarter and more confident the officer, the better he or she performs.

The other tests have a nonlinear relationship with performance. To underscore this point, let us examine good health. Would an applicant with one cold in the last 2 years be a better officer than an applicant who has had two colds in the past 2 years? Probably not, but with a physically active job, we could be confident that an applicant with a bad back would not be able to handle the routine requirements of the job. Thus, physical health would be determined on a pass/fail basis: The applicant is either healthy enough to do the job or not.

Because we have more than one nonlinearly related test, we would adapt our procedure and use a multiple-cutoff approach combined with a linear approach as opposed to either a single-cutoff approach or a strictly linear approach. One problem with a multiple-cutoff approach is the cost. If an applicant passes only three out of four tests, he will not be hired, but the organization has paid for the applicant to take all four tests.

To reduce the costs associated with applicants failing one or more tests, **multiple-hurdle approaches** are often used. With a multiple-hurdle approach, the applicant is administered one test at a time, usually beginning with the least expensive. Applicants who fail a test are eliminated from further consideration and take no more tests. Applicants who pass all of the tests are then administered the linearly related tests; the applicants with the top scores on these tests are hired.

To clarify the difference between a multiple-cutoff and a multiple-hurdle approach, let us look at the following example. Suppose we will use four pass/fail tests to select employees. The tests have the following costs and failure rates:

Test	Cost of Test ($)	Failure Rate (%)
Background check	25	10
Psychological screen	50	10
Medical checkup	100	10
Strength	5	10
Total per applicant:	$180	

If the tests cost $180 per applicant and 100 applicants apply for a position, a multiple-cutoff approach would cost our organization $18,000 (100 applicants × $180 each) to administer the tests to all applicants. But with a multiple-hurdle approach, we can administer the cheapest test (the strength test) to all 100 applicants. Because 10% of the applicants will fail this test, we then can administer the next cheapest test to the remaining 90. This process continues until all tests have been administered. A savings of $3,900 will result based on the following calculations:

Test	Test Cost ($)	Applicants	Total Cost ($)
Strength	5	100	500
Background check	25	90	2,250
Psychological screen	50	81	4,050
Medical checkup	100	73	7,300
Total cost			$14,100

If a multiple-hurdle approach usually saves a company money, why is it not *always* used instead of a multiple-cutoff approach? First, many of the tests cited above take time to conduct or score. For example, it might take a few weeks to run a background check or a few days to interpret a psychological screening. Therefore, the tests usually must be administered on several occasions, and an applicant would have to miss several days of work to apply for a particular job. Because people often cannot or will not take more than 1 day off from one job to apply for another, many potentially excellent applicants are lost before testing begins.

Second, research has shown that in general the longer the time between submission of a job application and the hiring decision, the smaller the number of African American applicants who will remain in the applicant pool (Arvey, Gordon, Massengill, & Mussio, 1975). African American populations have higher unemployment rates than whites, and people who are unemployed are more hurried to obtain employment than people with jobs. Thus, because the multiple-hurdle approach takes longer than multiple-cutoff, it may bring an unintended adverse impact, and affirmative action goals may not be met.

Chapter Summary

In this chapter you learned:

- Test length, item homogeneity, and scorer accuracy can affect the reliability of a test.

- There are three ways to measure reliability: (a) the test–retest method, which measures temporal stability; (b) the alternate forms method, which measures forms stability; and (c) the internal consistency method (split-half, K-R 20, and coefficient alpha), which measures item homogeneity.

- Tests can be validated using five methods: content, criterion, construct, known-group, and face.

- Information about tests can be obtained from such sources as the *Mental Measurements Yearbook* and *Tests*.

- The utility of a test can be determined using the Taylor-Russell tables, the Lawshe tables, proportion of correct decisions, and utility formulas.

- The fairness of a test can be determined by testing for adverse impact, single-group validity, and differential validity.

- Selection decisions can be made in four ways: top-down, rule of 3, top-down with banding, or passing scores.

Critical Thinking Questions

1. What is the difference between reliability and validity?
2. What method of establishing validity is best?
3. Why is the concept of test utility so important?
4. What is the difference between single-group and differential validity?
5. Why should we use anything other than top-down selection? After all, shouldn't we always hire the applicants with the highest scores?

To learn more about the issues discussed in this chapter, point your browser to

http://www.infotrac-college.com/wadsworth

and enter one of these search terms:

criterion validity
Mental Measurements Yearbook
candidate selection technique
hiring decisions
selection utility
computer-adaptive testing

Exercise 4–1
Locating Test Information

You are the personnel assistant for a large corporation. The company I/O psychologist has just completed a job analysis of some supervisory positions and is now looking for tests that will tap the knowledge, skills, and abilities identified in the job analysis. The I/O psychologist has asked you to find information about two types of tests: a math test and a personality test that measures extraversion.

Use the test compendia discussed in the text to do the following:

1.   Identify potential tests to use

2.   List the reliability of each test

3.   List the cost of each test

4.   List the administration time for each test

Math Test

Test Name	Reliability Cost	Administration Time
_____	_____	_____
_____	_____	_____
_____	_____	_____

Personality Test (Extraversion)

Test Name	Reliability Cost	Administration Time
_____	_____	_____
_____	_____	_____
_____	_____	_____

Exercise 4–2
Using the Utility Formula and Tables

Instructions

Below you will find a description of a hypothetical employment situation. Use the information to determine how much money your organization will save if it adopts the proposed selection test.

Situation

You have 500 applicants and 200 job openings. The validity of your proposed test, the Reilly Statistical Logic Test, is .35, and the test costs $4 per applicant to administer. You have 1,000 current employees, 700 of whom are satisfactory. The salary for the position is $42,000, and the typical employee stays for 4 years. Currently, you are using the Robson Math Test with a validity of .25 that costs $8 per applicant to administer. Be sure to show your calculations.

1. On the basis of the Taylor-Russell tables, what percentage of future employees will be successful? _____

2. Using the utility formula, how much money does your current test, the Spearman Math Test, save the company over using no test at all? _____

3. Using the utility formula, how much money does your proposed test, the Reilly Statistical Logic Test, save the company over using no test at all? _____

4. How much money will your proposed test save when compared to the current test? _____

    What would the figures be if no validity data were available but the current method of selection was an unstructured interview costing $15 per applicant and the proposed method was a structured interview also costing $15 per applicant? (Hint: Use the validity charts from this chapter.)

1. On the basis of the Taylor-Russell tables, what percentage of future employees will be successful? _____

2. Using the utility formula, how much money does your current test, the unstructured interview, save the company over using no test at all? _____

3. Using the utility formula, how much money does your proposed test, the structured interview, save the company over using no test at all? _____

4. How much money will your structured interview save when compared to the unstructured interview? _____

Exercise 4–3
Determining the Proportion of Correct Decisions

Instructions

Below you will find two sets of numbers. The first number represents the employee's score on a selection test. Typically, the company must hire half of the applicants who apply for jobs. The second number represents the number of months the employee was employed with the company. To be considered a success, the employee must stay with the company long enough for it to recoup its recruitment and training costs. The company believes this period is 5 months.

Use the data to complete the chart on the following page to determine the proportion of correct decisions that will be made if the company decides to use the test in the future.

Test Score	Tenure
2	4
6	7
9	9
8	6
3	2
7	3
1	4
9	7
4	4
4	6
8	8
2	7
4	5
6	4
4	3
6	6
3	1
4	7
7	6
8	7

	1	2	3	4	5	6	7	8	9
9	-	-	-	-	-	-	-	-	-
8	-	-	-	-	-	-	-	-	-
7	-	-	-	-	-	-	-	-	-
6	-	-	-	-	-	-	-	-	-
5	-	-	-	-	-	-	-	-	-
4	-	-	-	-	-	-	-	-	-
3	-	-	-	-	-	-	-	-	-
2	-	-	-	-	-	-	-	-	-
1	-	-	-	-	-	-	-	-	-

TENURE

Test Score

Exercise 4–4
Using Banding to Reduce Adverse Impact

You are the human resource manager for the law firm of Lie, Cheat, and Steele. On the basis of your most recent employment figures, you would like to hire more female attorneys. You have four openings, and the results of the selection exam are shown on the next page. The reliability of your selection exam is .83 and the standard deviation is 7.43. On the basis of the data, do the following:

1.   Compute the standard error.

2.   Determine the width of a band using a 95% confidence interval (1.96 × the standard error).

3.   If you used a nonsliding band, which four applicants would you hire?

_____   _____

_____   _____

4.   If you used a sliding band, which four applicants would you hire?

_____   _____

_____   _____

5.   If you used a passing score of 80 rather than a band, what four applicants would you hire?

_____   _____

_____   _____

Applicants to the Law Firm of Lie, Cheat, and Steele 2003 Test Scores

Applicant	Score	Gender
Jack McCoy	97	m
Ben Stone	95	m
Paul Robinette	94	m
Adam Schiff	94	m
Abbie Carmichael	91	f
Ron Carver	89	m
Claire Kincaid	89	f
Harmon Rabb	88	m
Jamie Ross	87	f
Alexandra Cabot	86	f
Ben Matlock	86	m
Nora Lewin	85	f
Perry Mason	83	m
Bobby Donnel	80	m
Jimmy Berlutti	78	m
Eleanor Frutt	70	f
Eugene Young	70	m
Rebecca Washington	68	f
Lindsay Dole	65	f
Helen Gamble	65	f

Employee Selection: Recruiting and Interviewing

IN THE TELEVISION version of the motion picture *The Enforcer*, actor Clint Eastwood played police detective Harry Callahan who, upon learning that he had been transferred from homicide to personnel, replied "Personnel—only idiots work in personnel!" Although this statement is a bit strong, it represents the attitude many people held about the field of human resources. That is, if you can't do anything else, you can always work in human resources.

The image of the human resources field has been greatly enhanced in recent years, however, for the most part by its application of modern, scientific principles in employee selection and by the realization that properly designed employee selection procedures can save organizations a lot of money.

In this chapter, we will first explore ways to recruit employees and explain job hunting methods and then discuss interviewing techniques as well as offer some tips that you can use to find and obtain a desired job. By the end of this chapter, you will have learned

- how to recruit applicants.
- how to apply for jobs.
- why the traditional, unstructured interview doesn't work.
- how to construct a valid, structured interview.
- how to perform well when being interviewed.
- how to write a resume and a cover letter.

As shown in Exhibit 5.01, certain steps can be taken to successfully choose employees. Some of the steps are designed to attract excellent applicants to the organization, others are designed to select the best applicants, and still others are designed to give applicants a good image not only of the organization but of the job search process in general. Keep in mind that for most job openings many more people will apply than will be hired. If you multiply the number of people who are not hired by the number of job openings each year, it is clear that a lot of people will be in contact with a particular organization. Those people not hired are potential customers with friends who are also potential customers. Furthermore, applicants not hired for one position may turn out to be well qualified for future positions with the organization. Leaving them with a positive image of the company should be a priority.

Job Analysis

As discussed in Chapter 2, job analysis is the cornerstone of personnel selection. Remember, unless a complete and accurate picture of a job is obtained, it is virtually impossible to select excellent employees. Thus, during the job analysis process, in addition to identifying the important tasks and duties, it is essential to identify the knowledge, skills, and abilities needed to perform the job.

Therefore, the methods used to select employees should tie in directly with the results of the job analysis. In other words, every essential knowledge, skill, and ability identified in the job analysis should be tested, and every test must somehow relate to the job analysis. For example, if a job analysis reveals that an office manager types correspondence and proofreads reports to ensure the reports are grammatically correct, then the battery of selection tests might include a typing test and a grammar test.

Recruitment

An important step in selecting employees is **recruitment**: attracting people with the right qualifications (as determined in the job analysis) to apply for the job. The first decision is whether to promote someone from within the organization (**internal recruitment**) or to hire someone from outside the organization (**external recruitment**). Organizations such as AT&T and Norfolk and Southern Railroad first advertise employment

Exhibit **5.01** Steps in selecting employees

Job analysis

Selection of testing methods

Test validation

Recruitment

Screening

Testing

Selecting

Hiring/ rejecting

openings for 2 weeks to current employees. If no qualified applicants are found, the organizations then advertise outside.

To enhance employee morale and motivation, it is often good to give current employees an advantage in obtaining new internal positions (Joinson, 1997). However, if an organization always promotes employees from within, it runs the risk of having a stale workforce that is devoid of the many ideas that new employees bring with them from their previous employment settings. Heavy reliance on internal sources is thought to perpetuate the racial, gender, and age composition of the workforce. Thus, a balance between promoting current employees and hiring outside applicants is needed.

Exhibit 5.02 | Examples of help-wanted ads

PLUMBER needed immediately in Rocky Mount area. Top pay for experienced person. Call 712-483-2315

LEGAL ASSISTANT

TITLE AGENCY ADMINISTRATOR Downtown law firm seeking experienced real estate legal assistant/title agency administrator with working knowledge of WordPerfect 5.1. All benefits and parking provided. Send résumé in confidence to: Box M262. c/o Poncha Springs Times & World News, P.O. Box 2491, Poncha Springs, Va. 24010

HOTEL DESK CLERK

Afternoon & night shift available. Apply in person at Comfort Inn, Bassville.

Engineering Manager

Highly motivated and professional individual with 10 years performance track record to successfully lead a large engineering department. Must have clear conceptual understanding of the telephone industry including PABX and Key telephone systems. Engineering abilities including analog circuit design, digital logic design, microprocessor, and infrared design. Familiarity with regulatory agencies is necessary. Ability to maintain productivity and quality schedules for timely work completion. Most desirable credentials include BSEE degree plus MBA.

Respond by sending résumé to:

Volcan, Inc.
Attn: Human Resources
2222 Industry Ave.
Sweed, VA 24013

EOE
No agencies or phone calls please.

Media Advertisements

Newspaper Ads

Running ads in periodicals such as local newspapers or professional journals is a common method of recruiting employees. In fact, in a survey of 281 organizations, recruiters rated newspaper advertising as one of the most effective avenues of applicant recruitment (Gere, Scarborough, & Collison, 2002).

As shown in Exhibit 5.02, newspaper advertisements typically ask the applicant to respond in one of four ways: calling, applying in person, sending a resume directly to the organization, or sending a resume to a blind box. Applicants are asked to **respond by calling** when an organization wants either to quickly screen applicants or to hear an applicant's phone voice (e.g., for telemarketing or receptionist positions). Organizations use **apply-in-person ads** when they don't want their phones tied up by applicants calling (e.g., a travel agency or pizza delivery restaurant), want the applicants to fill out a specific job application, or want to get a physical look at the applicant. Applicants are asked to send a resume directly to the company (**send-resume ads**)

when the organization expects a large response and does not have the resources to speak with thousands of applicants.

The fourth type of ad directs applicants to send a resume to a **blind box.** Organizations use blind boxes for three main reasons. First, the organization doesn't want its name in public. This might be the case when a well-known company such as AT&T or IBM has a very specific job opening and is concerned that rumors will spread that there are many openings for a variety of positions. This could result in an avalanche of resumes, many from unqualified applicants. Second, the company might fear that people wouldn't apply if they knew the name of the company. For example, an ad for sales positions would probably not draw a large response if applicants were asked to send their resumes to a funeral home (even though selling burial plots can be a lucrative job). Third, on rare occasions, a company needs to terminate an employee but wants first to find a replacement. As you can imagine, running an ad containing the name of the company would not be smart if the current employee was not aware that he or she was about to be fired.

Exhibit **5.03** How to respond to newspaper ads

Respond-by-Calling Ads

- Practice the first few sentences, such as "I saw your help-wanted advertisement in the local newspaper and would like to get more information." Don't count on being able to ad lib or you might sound as inarticulate as the typical person leaving a message on an answering machine.

- Be prepared for a short interview by making sure you have time to talk, have your resume handy to answer questions, and have paper and pencil close by. Ge Ge Beall, a human resource manager, once received a phone call just as she was stepping out of the shower and before she had time to get dressed. The caller turned out to be an employer who interviewed Beall for the next hour. The employer told Beall that she liked phone interviews because the applicant "didn't have to worry about putting on her interview suit." In this case, she didn't realize just how accurate her statement was!

Apply-in-Person Ads

- Be prepared to interview on the spot. The organization may simply take your resume and call at a later date to schedule an interview. However, it is not unusual for an organization to interview applicants as they drop off their resume.

- Dress as if you were going to an interview. It might be convenient to drop off your resume on your way to the beach, but dressing poorly will leave a bad impression whether you receive an immediate interview or not.

- Bring copies of your resume, and leave one even if you are asked to complete a job application.

- Bring a pen. Many organizations automatically eliminate applicants who do not do this.

- Be nice to the receptionist or any other person with whom you come in contact. The organization's first look at you is probably the most important, and you can be sure that word of a rude or poorly dressed applicant will quickly get back to the person making the actual hiring decision.

Send-Resume Ads

- Always include a cover letter (a concept that will be discussed later in the chapter).

- Type the envelope if possible.

Blind-Box Ads

- Don't be afraid to respond to these types of ads. Most of the time these ads will result in good jobs with respectable organizations.

- Respond promptly as these boxes are assigned to advertisers only for the period in which they run their ad.

Exhibit 5.03 contains information about how to respond to various kinds of ads. To help you identify the types of help-wanted ads, complete Exercise 5–1 at the end of this chapter.

Writing Recruitment Ads. Although little research is available, there is plenty of expert advice on the best way for an employer to write recruitment advertisements. Kaplan and her colleagues (1991) tested some of this expert advice by first determining the characteristics of help-wanted ads and then comparing the design of actual help-wanted ads in 10 newspapers with the quantity and quality of applicants who responded. After examining thousands of ads, Kaplan and her colleagues identified 23 advertising characteristics. After comparing the presence or absence of these 23 characteristics with the quantity and quality of applicants who responded to the ad, the researchers found that ads displaying the company emblem and using creative illustrations attracted the greatest *number* of applicants, but ads that included the salary range and a company phone number attracted the highest *quality* applicants.

In recent years, a new trend in help-wanted advertising has been the use of creative ads such as those shown in Exhibit 5.04 (Martinez, 2001). By using innovative advertising, On-Line Software tripled the number of applicants who responded to its help-wanted ad for secretarial positions. Hyundai's innovative ad cost only $5,000 and had almost 2,000 responses to advertised positions. Some organizations have tried to recruit employees by making fun of the job openings. Here are some examples:

- FH Company, a Norwegian importer and distributor, ran a help-wanted advertisement reading "Tiresome and boring wholesale company seeks indolent people with a total lack of service mindedness for a job that is completely without challenge."

Exhibit 5.04 Creative help-wanted ads

Source: Reprinted with permission of Ad Master, Inc.

- C. Rinker Paving, a Virginia asphalt company, ran a help-wanted advertisement asking for applicants who "have hair short enough to see and hear, are able to gulp down a sandwich in 30 minutes and be able to work at least 30 minutes without going to the restroom or drinking something, and have nose and ear rings light enough not to interfere with their work."

- A national sales company advertised that they were "interested in hiring five semi-obnoxious pushy sales pros for a very boring repetitive job of selling. Our current sales staff is the laziest group of individuals that you'll ever see drag themselves to work 5 days a week to decide whether to complain about the weather, coffee, thermostat or the manager."

Thus, using the same techniques and imagination used in product advertisements may increase the recruitment yield from help-wanted ads. That is one reason major advertising firms such as Bernard Hodes and Austin-Knight are increasingly involved in the development of recruitment ads and campaigns. To practice what you have learned about writing help-wanted advertisements, complete Exercise 5–2 at the end of this chapter.

Electronic Media

Whereas 96% of organizations run recruitment advertisements in newspapers, only 26% use television and radio to advertise job openings (SHRM, 2001b). Perhaps the best use of television recruitment in the private sector has been by McDonald's, whose television commercials show McDonald's to be the ideal place for retirees to work part time. In addition to

Exhibit **5.05** Examples of situation-wanted ads

TOP SPEECHWRITER

Currently writing speeches for Fortune 200 CEO. Background in tech, multi-industry, Wall St., Wash. D.C. Box EA-213, The Wall Street Journal

---

AVAILABLE AUG. 15: Woman religious teacher. College, seminary, adult education. Master's religious ed, PhD, American Lit., Jour. Experience in men's, women's, coed undergrad., grad., adult ed. Retreat work, spir. dir., poet, writer. Interdisciplinary, incarnate person.
Contact: Ad Random, Dept. L-237

---

generating applicants, the commercials are an excellent public relations vehicle.

An interesting twist in television recruiting was developed by Videosearch, a California-based employment agency. Videosearch's 30-minute television program titled "Meet Your Next Employer" is paid for by organizations that advertise their job opportunities. The cost for this service is about $1,500 per minute for national exposure. A similar program called "CareerLine" is broadcast weekly on the Financial News Network. Although television advertising sounds promising, it is an area that needs much more empirical investigation to determine its actual effectiveness.

The potential advantage to using electronic media for recruitment is that 95% of Americans listen to the radio at least weekly, and the average person spends 4 hours a day listening to the radio compared to 45 minutes reading the newspaper (Joinson, 1998). Furthermore, different types of radio stations (e.g., rock, rap, classical, country, oldies, news) reach different types of audiences and thus radio ads can be more easily targeted to the desired audience.

Harris Trucking often advertises its openings for drivers on radio stations playing country music. The radio ads are used not only to recruit new drivers but to thank current drivers for doing such a good job (Gibson, 1997). Reserves Network, a job placement firm in Ohio, and WCLV-FM, a classical radio station in Ohio, also have had great success using radio stations to recruit employees. In fact, WCLV had found radio advertising to be its best method of recruiting minority applicants. In an innovative use of the media, Prudential Insurance advertised its job openings in film clips that ran in local movie theaters prior to the start of major motion pictures (Fernandez, 1997).

Situation-Wanted Ads

Situation-wanted ads are placed by the applicant rather than by organizations. As shown in Exhibit 5.05, these ads take a variety of forms: Some list extensive qualifications, some give applicants' names, and some are generally more creative than others. Two studies (Williams & Garris, 1991; Willis, Miller, & Huff, 1991) investigated the effectiveness of these ads by contacting applicants for white-collar jobs who had placed situation-wanted ads in a variety of daily and professional publications. The results of the two studies are encouraging: 69.4% of those applicants placing ads were contacted. However, not all contacts were from employers. Instead, some were from employment agencies, resume writing services, and even an encyclopedia salesperson (how could the applicant afford an encyclopedia when she doesn't even have a job?). Of the applicants who placed the ads, 21.5% did receive actual job offers. Situation-wanted ads appear to be a useful way of looking for a job, and given that they don't cost an organization any money, they may be a beneficial method of recruitment.

Point-of-Purchase Methods

This **point-of-purchase method** of recruitment is based on the same point-of-purchase advertising principles used to market products to consumers. For example, consider shopping at a local grocery store. As you push your cart through one aisle of the store, you see a special display for potato chips, in the next aisle a display for cookies. When you get to the checkout stand, products such as the *National Enquirer*, candy, and batteries are conveniently placed so you can

Exhibit **5.06** Point-of-purchase recruitment examples

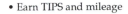

examine them while you wait in line. The idea is to get you to buy more items once you are already in the store.

In employee recruitment, job vacancy notices are posted in places where customers or current employees are likely to see them: store windows, bulletin boards, restaurant placemats, and the sides of trucks. The advantages to this method are that it is inexpensive and it is targeted toward people who frequent the business. The disadvantage is that only a limited number of people are exposed to the sign.

Because of the difficulty in obtaining employees, many fast food restaurants are using unusual point-of-purchase techniques. McDonald's, Arby's, Burger King, and Carl's Jr. have all printed help-wanted ads with application blanks on their paper placemats. To apply for a job, customers (can we now call them McApplicants?) simply wipe the spilled ketchup off the placemat, fill in their name and address, and give the placemat to the manager. Examples of these are shown in Exhibit 5.06.

Wendy's printed the words "Now hiring smiling faces" on their cash register receipts, Domino's Pizza placed help-wanted ads on its pizza boxes, and Kentucky Fried Chicken placed signs on vans that stopped at student gathering places to distribute free sodas and application materials. Because Store 24 had difficulty recruiting manager trainees, it took the unique approach of placing a help-wanted advertisement on one side of its milk cartons. The cost of the recruitment campaign was minimal as the company already bore the expense of creating and printing the milk cartons. Other innovative recruitment methods include Lauriat's Books placing a job posting and mini-resume on a bookmark, and both SmithKline and Prudential Insurance posting help-wanted advertisements on billboards in the Philadelphia area. To record point-of-purchase methods you have seen, complete Exercise 5–3.

Campus Recruiters

Many organizations send recruiters to college campuses to answer questions about their organizations and interview students for available positions. Though campus recruiters are not necessarily effective at selecting the best applicants (Aamodt & Carr, 1988), their behavior can greatly influence applicants' decisions to accept jobs that are offered (Glueck, 1973; Powell, 1991; Rynes, Bretz, & Gerhart, 1991).

Outside Recruiters

Seventy-six percent of organizations use outside recruiting sources such as private employment agencies, public employment agencies, and executive search firms (SHRM, 2001b). Private employment agencies and executive search firms are designed to make a profit from recruitment activities, whereas public employment agencies are operated by state and local public agencies and are strictly nonprofit.

Private Employment Agencies

Employment agencies operate in one of two ways. They charge either the company or the applicant when the applicant takes the job. The amount charged usually ranges from 10 to 30% of the applicant's first-year salary.

From an organization's perspective, there are few risks in using an employment agency that charges the applicant for its services. That is, if the employment agency cannot find an appropriate candidate, the organization has not wasted money. But if the employment agency is successful, the organization gets a qualified employee at no cost.

Employment agencies are especially useful if a human resource department is overloaded with work or if an organization does not have an individual with the skills and experience needed to select employees properly. The disadvantage of employment agencies is that a company loses some control over its recruitment process and may end up with undesirable applicants. Remember, most "counselors" at employment agencies

are hired because of their skill in sales, not because of their solid background in the area of personnel selection. In fact, one employment agency turned down one of its own job applicants because the applicant had earned a degree in personnel management. During the interview the head of the agency told the applicant, "We are not really looking for a personnel professional. What we want is the type of person who could sell aluminum siding to the owner of a brick home."

The applicant can seldom go wrong using an employment agency. If the fee is charged to the company, the applicant gets a job at no cost. However, even if the fee is charged to the applicant, the applicant may still benefit. For example, suppose you are having difficulty finding a job, and an employment agency finds you a good job paying $36,000 per year. Spending $3,600 to obtain a good job might be worthwhile because every month of unemployment is costing you $3,000 in lost income. So the fee is essentially one month's salary that you would not have earned anyway without the job.

Public Employment Agencies

The third type of outside recruitment organization is state and local employment agencies. These **public employment agencies** primarily are designed to help the unemployed find work, but they often offer services such as career advisement and resume preparation. From the organization's perspective, public employment agencies can be of great value in filling blue-collar and clerical positions. Not only is there no cost involved in hiring the applicants, but often government programs are also available that will help pay training costs. In addition, with the advent of standardized testing programs (which will be discussed in Chapter 6), the quality of employees hired through public agencies is now much higher than in the past.

Executive Search Firms

Executive search firms, better known as "head hunters," differ from employment agencies in several ways. First, the jobs they represent tend to be higher paying, non–entry level positions such as executives, engineers, and computer programmers. Second, reputable executive search firms always charge their fees to organizations rather than to applicants. Third, fees charged by executive search firms tend to be about 30% of the applicant's first-year salary.

A word of caution about both employment agencies and executive search firms: Because these firms make their money on the number of applicants they place, they tend to exert tremendous pressure on applicants to take jobs that are offered. But applicants are not obligated to take jobs and should not be intimidated about turning down a position that appears to be a poor match.

Employee Referrals

Another way to recruit is by **employee referral**, in which current employees recommend family members and friends for specific job openings. Surveys investigating this referral method indicate that about 48% of private organizations have formal referral programs and 66% use employee referrals in some way (SHRM, 2001a). Only 1% of public organizations such as state and city governments have such programs, and the few that do use them to encourage minority recruitment of police officers and firefighters (Trice, 1997).

In a survey of 566 human resource executives, employee referrals were rated as the third most effective recruitment method (SHRM, 2001b). Some organizations are so convinced of the attractiveness of this method that they provide financial incentives to employees who recommend applicants who are hired. For example, Integrated Systems Consulting Group gave $3,000 and a chance to win a vacation in Hawaii to employees referring successful applicants. Transaction Information Systems gave $1,000 to employees recommending applicants for a World Wide Web programming position; Temporary Associates in Illinois gave $250 college scholarships to students who recommended applicants for seasonal positions; 7-Eleven offered employees $1,000 for recommending potential field consultants; UPS paid $50 for package handler referrals; Sybase ran a referral campaign in which employees whose referrals resulted in an interview were entered in a raffle for such prizes as a TV, five cases of beer, 36 Baby Ruth bars, and a hammock; and White Memorial Medical Center provided recommenders of successful employees free maid service for a full year. The average amount of such bonuses offered by organizations is less than $1,000 (SHRM, 2001a).

The typical time period that a new employee must stay with the company before the referring employee is eligible for a bonus is 3 months (Stewart, Ellenburg, Hicks, Kremen, & Daniel, 1990). Stewart and his colleagues found no relationship between the size of the bonus and the number of referrals, nor did they find that organizations offering referral bonuses received more referrals than organizations not offering bonuses. Though such a finding might be surprising, 42% of employees said they made a referral to help a friend and another 24% said they made the referral to help their employer. Only 24% reported making the referral for the incentive (Lachnit, 2001).

Although the idea of employee referrals sounds good, not all referrals are the same. Aamodt and Carr (1988) and Rupert (1989) compared the success of employees who had been referred by current successful and unsuccessful employees and found that employees referred by successful employees had longer tenure than did employees who had been referred by unsuccessful employees. Thus, only those referrals made by successful employees should be considered. This finding, explained by social psychology research, indicates that our friends tend to be similar to us in characteristics such as personality, values, and interests. If a particular employee is a good employee, then the same characteristics that make her a good employee are probably shared by her friends and family. The same would be true of an unsuccessful employee.

Even though referrals by successful employees are a good recruitment avenue, the similarity of friends can also pose some problems. The biggest is that our friends also tend to be the same gender, race, national origin, and religion as we are. Thus, if an organization uses employee referrals and the organization consists predominantly of white male Protestants, it will seldom hire African Americans or females. Thus, even though the organization didn't intend to discriminate, the consequences of its recruitment policy may have that effect. However, organizations such as Alpine Banks of Colorado have used this similarity bias to their advantage by asking its bilingual employees to refer bilingual applicants.

Direct Mail

Because **direct mail** has been successful in product advertising, several organizations have used direct mail to recruit applicants, especially those who are not actively job hunting (Woodward, 2000). With direct mail recruitment, an employer typically obtains a mailing list and sends help-wanted letters or brochures to people through the mail. According to direct mailing expert Lewis Shomer, 40% of the success of a direct mail campaign is the mailing list itself, 40% is the offer, and 20% is in the words and look of the brochure (Woodward, 2000). Most mailing lists cost from $15 to $150 per 1,000 names (Woodward, 2000).

One California branch of Allstate Insurance had been using newspaper advertisements and getting limited response. However, from a single mailing of 64,000 letters that explained the career opportunities available at Allstate to current policyholders, the company received more than 500 calls and was able to hire 20 new employees. Union Special, an Illinois manufacturer of sewing machines, had difficulty filling 10 engineering positions, so they direct mailed 3,300 cards to Chicago area engineers at a cost of about $5,000. As a result, the company received 100 responses and conducted 30 interviews. A third company that successfully used direct mail recruitment is the Bank of America. To save money, Bank of America did something different from Allstate and Union Special. Instead of sending a special recruitment mailing, Bank of America included recruitment literature in the regular monthly mailing of bank statements to its customers.

Direct mail recruiting is especially useful for positions involving specialized skills. For example, Minor's Landscape Services in Texas had difficulty finding licensed irrigators, so the company located a list of people in Texas who had irrigation licenses and sent letters to each person on the list. The company found 20 qualified candidates and was able to fill both of its openings (Gruner, 1997). An example of direct mail recruiting can be found in Exhibit 5.07.

Exhibit **5.07** Example of a direct mail recruitment advertisement

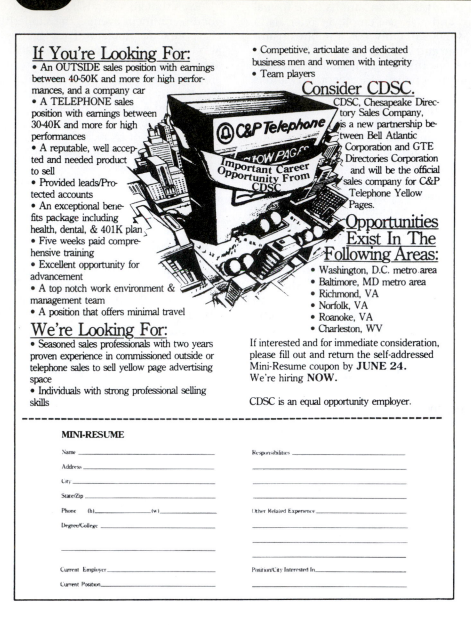

If You're Looking For:
- An OUTSIDE sales position with earnings between 40-50K and more for high performances, and a company car
- A TELEPHONE sales position with earnings between 30-40K and more for high performances
- A reputable, well accepted and needed product to sell
- Provided leads/Protected accounts
- An exceptional benefits package including health, dental, & 401K plan
- Five weeks paid comprehensive training
- Excellent opportunity for advancement
- A top notch work environment & management team
- A position that offers minimal travel

We're Looking For:
- Seasoned sales professionals with two years proven experience in commissioned outside or telephone sales to sell yellow page advertising space
- Individuals with strong professional selling skills

- Competitive, articulate and dedicated business men and women with integrity
- Team players

Consider CDSC.
CDSC, Chesapeake Directory Sales Company, is a new partnership between Bell Atlantic Corporation and GTE Directories Corporation and will be the official sales company for C&P Telephone Yellow Pages.

Opportunities Exist In The Following Areas:
- Washington, D.C. metro area
- Baltimore, MD metro area
- Richmond, VA
- Norfolk, VA
- Roanoke, VA
- Charleston, WV

If interested and for immediate consideration, please fill out and return the self-addressed Mini-Resume coupon by **JUNE 24**. We're hiring **NOW**.

CDSC is an equal opportunity employer.

MINI-RESUME

Name _____

Address _____

City _____

State/Zip _____

Phone (h) _____ (w) _____

Degree/College _____

_____

Current Employer _____

Current Position _____

Responsibilities _____

_____

_____

_____

Other Related Experience _____

_____

_____

_____

Position/City Interested In _____

Internet

The Internet is a fast-growing source of recruitment; in 2000 there were more than 30,000 employment-related Web sites (Leonard, 2000b), and 82% of organizations use them (Gere et al., 2002). The largest Internet recruiter, Monster.com, has more than 5 million unique visitors per month (Lee, 2001) and 294,000 recruiters have access to its 8 million resumes (Szary, 2001). Perhaps the major reason for the increased use in online databases is the cost. A quarter-page help-wanted ad in a major city newspaper might cost an employer $10,000 for one weekend printing, but an organization can list an unlimited number of openings with a major database for about $100,000 per year (Leonard, 2000b). In a few databases, applicants pay a fee to have their resumes listed in an online database, but for most online databases the organization pays the fee to use the database and the applicants list their resumes for free. Though the Internet changes every day, these were the leading recruitment Web sites in early 2003:

- www.CareerMosaic.com
- www.monster.com
- www.CareerBuilder.com
- www.hotjobs.com
- www.futurestep.com
- www.headhunter.net
- www.jobsonline.com

Most major newspapers also have their help-wanted ads online. For example, jobs in Atlanta can be viewed on the Web at http://www.atlantaclassifieds.com and jobs in Chicago can be viewed at http://www.suntimes.com/classified/help.html.

Job Fairs

Job fairs are used by 70% of organizations (SHRM, 2001b) and are designed to provide information in a personal fashion to as many applicants as possible. Job fairs are typically conducted in one of three ways. In the first, many types of organizations have booths at the same location. For example, a multiemployer job fair in Montgomery, Alabama, drew nearly 1,000 applicants and 81 employers (Dugan, 2001). Your college probably has one or two of these job fairs each year in which dozens of organizations send representatives to discuss employment opportunities with students and to collect resumes. In addition, company representatives usually hand out company literature and souvenirs such as T-shirts, yardsticks, and cups. If you haven't been to a campus job fair, contact your career services center to see when they are scheduled on your campus.

Following the September 11, 2001, attack on the World Trade Center, a job fair for displaced workers attracted more than 25,000 job seekers. Similar fairs were held for airline workers in Philadelphia and Pittsburgh (Gelbart, 2001).

The second type of job fair is to have many organizations in the same field in one location. For example, a technology job fair in New York City in 2000 had 83 companies represented and attracted more than 5,000 potential programmers (Maroney, 2000). The advantage to this type of job fair is that, with a single employment field represented, each visitor is a potential applicant for every organization. The drawback, of course, is that each organization must compete directly with the other organizations at the fair.

The third approach is for an organization to hold its own job fair. Here are some examples:

- Gaylord Palms in Kissimmee, Florida, held a job fair attended by more than 12,000 people interested in the resort's 1,400 job openings. The job fair began with an overnight "pajama party" attended by 3,000 applicants (Hunt, 2001).
- First Union Bank held a Thursday job fair that attracted more than 400 people interested in the bank's 70 openings (Gibson, 1997).
- Microsoft held a job fair in Atlanta that attracted 3,000 people (Lewis, 1997), and Concentra Corporation held an "open house" that attracted more than 100 applicants and resulted in four job openings being filled.

Although this approach is certainly more expensive, it has the advantage of focusing the attention of the applicants on only one company. Such an approach was taken by Compaq Computer Corporation. Because of a shortage of applicants with technical skills, Compaq created a traveling job fair called "Compaq, Texas." The job fair traveled from city to city and was set up in hotel ballrooms. Before the job fair arrived in each city, Compaq conducted a media blitz to tell prospective applicants about the fair. Upon arrival at the hotel, each prospective applicant was assigned a personal recruiter who would lead the applicant through "Compaq, Texas" with its product displays, videos, literature, and company representatives. The cost to Compaq for each job fair was about $100,000. This amount seems high, but each job fair draws 1,000 or more applicants; if the company hires at least 5 of the applicants, it spends less than it would if it used outside recruiters (Chauran, 1989).

Incentives

When unemployment rates are low, organizations have to take extra measures to recruit employees. One of these measures is to offer incentives for employees to accept jobs with an organization. Though these incentives often come in the form of a financial signing bonus, usually about $5,000 (Poe, 1999), other types of incentives are increasing in popularity. For example, such organizations as Sears and Starwood Hotels offer employee discounts on company products and services (Woodward, 2001a), and 6% of organizations offer mortgage assistance to lure employees (Tyler, 2001a).

Nontraditional Populations

When traditional recruitment methods are unsuccessful, many organizations look for potential applicants from nontraditional populations. Here are a few examples:

- Manpower, Inc. in Chandler, Arizona, the Chicago Police Department, and the Hackensack, New Jersey, Police Department formed partnerships with local churches that resulted in successful hires (Tyler, 2000b).
- Xerox, J. P. Morgan, Bell Atlantic, and American Express developed recruitment strategies and such gay-friendly benefits as domestic partner benefits to recruit and retain gay and lesbian employees (Armour, 2000).
- Seventy percent of organizations have reported that hiring welfare recipients has been a successful source of recruitment (Minton-Eversole, 2001).
- Due to low wage and benefit costs, TWA, Jostens, and Escod Industries are using prison inmates to perform work. In addition to the financial savings to the employer and the work skills learned by the inmates, 20 cents of every dollar earned by inmates is used to pay the cost of incarceration and another 10 cents goes for victim compensation and support of the inmate's family (Workplace Visions, 1999).

Exhibit 5.08 Evaluating the effectiveness of recruitment strategies

	Recruitment Sources		
Criterion	Advertisements	Referrals	Walk-ins
Number of applicants	40	30	10
Number qualified	10	15	5
Number hired	2	7	1
Number successful	0	4	1

- Denny's and Sheboygan Upholstery have been successful in recruiting ex-cons. In fact, the Kettle Moraine Correctional Institution in Wisconsin held a job fair for 180 soon to be released convicts. The job fair was attended by 15 employers (Jones, 2001).

- Prudential Insurance recruits applicants with cognitive disabilities to fill certain positions (Chafkin, 1999).

Evaluating the Effectiveness of Recruitment Strategies

Considering the number of potential recruitment sources, it is important to determine which source is the best to use. Such an evaluation can be conducted in several ways. As shown in Exhibit 5.08, one method is to examine the *number of applicants* each recruitment source yields. That is, if a newspaper ad results in 100 applicants and an in-store sign results in 20 applicants, newspaper ads could be considered the better method.

But looking only at the number of applicants does not take into account the cost of the recruitment campaign. Thus, a second method for evaluating the success of a recruitment campaign is to consider the **cost per applicant**, which is determined by dividing the number of applicants by the amount spent for each strategy. Continuing with the previous example, suppose our newspaper ad cost $200 and yielded 10 applicants and our in-store sign cost $5 and yielded 2 applicants. The cost per applicant for the newspaper ad would be $20, whereas the cost per applicant for the in-store sign would be just $2.50. Using this method of evaluation, the in-store sign would be best as long as it generated the number of applicants needed by the organization. However, if the organization needs to hire 10 new employees and only 2 applicants apply for jobs, this recruitment strategy by itself is not effective.

Although the cost per applicant evaluation method is an improvement on the applicant yield method, it too has a serious drawback. Even though an organization might receive a large number of applicants at a relatively low cost per applicant, none may be qualified

for the job. Therefore, the third and fourth strategies would be to look at either the *number of qualified applicants* or the **cost per qualified applicant.**

A final method for evaluating the effectiveness of various recruitment sources, and perhaps the best one, looks at the number of successful employees generated by each recruitment source. This is an effective method because, as shown in Exhibit 5.08, every applicant will not be qualified nor will every qualified applicant become a successful employee.

To determine differences in recruitment source effectiveness, a meta-analysis conducted by Zottoli and Wanous (1998) first categorized recruitment methods as being either an inside source (employee referrals, rehires) or an outside source (advertisements, employment agencies, school placement offices, recruiters). Zottoli and Wanous found that employees recruited through inside sources stayed with the organization longer (higher tenure) and performed better than employees recruited through outside sources. Several theories might explain the superiority of inside recruitment sources.

The first theory suggests that rehires or applicants who are referred by other employees receive more accurate information about the job than do employees recruited by other methods (Wanous, 1980). This theory has been supported in research by McManus and Baratta (1992), Conard and Ashworth (1986), Breaugh and Mann (1984), and Quaglieri (1982), who found that applicants referred by current employees received not only more information but also more accurate information about the job than did applicants recruited through other channels.

The second theory postulates that differences in recruitment source effectiveness are the result of different recruitment sources reaching and being used by different types of applicants (Schwab, 1982). Although some research has supported this individual differences theory (Breaugh & Mann, 1984; Ellis & Taylor, 1983; Swaroff, Barclay, & Bass, 1985; Taylor & Schmidt, 1983), other research has not (Breaugh, 1981). In fact, no variables have *consistently* distinguished users of one recruitment method from users of another method. Furthermore, as shown in Exhibit 5.09, the typical person looking for a job uses a wide variety of job search strategies. To underscore this point, think of the

Exhibit 5.09 How applicant Joe Smith was recruited

Position	Recruitment Source
Cook, Burger King	Newpaper ad
Clerk, Kmart	Friend
Waiter, Big Sizzle	Sign in window
Camp counselor	State employment agency

part-time jobs you have held. How did you find out about each one? Was it the same method each time? As you can see, it is unlikely that a certain type of person responds only to newspaper ads, while another type goes only to employment agencies.

A third theory might better explain the finding that employee referrals result in greater tenure than other recruitment strategies. This theory, cited earlier in the discussion on employee referral programs, has its roots in the interpersonal attraction literature, which indicates that people tend to be attracted to those who are similar to themselves (Byrne, 1971). If true—and research strongly suggests that it is—then an employee recommending a friend for a job will more than likely recommend one similar to herself. Thus, it would make sense that a person who is happy with her job would recommend a person who, because of her similarity to the incumbent, should also be happy with the job. Likewise, an unhappy employee would recommend similar friends who would also be unhappy and would probably have short tenure with the organization.

This theory has not been heavily researched but it has been supported by two studies. As discussed earlier, both Aamodt and Carr (1988) and Rupert (1989) found that long-tenured employees referred applicants who, after being hired, stayed on their jobs longer than applicants who were referred by short-tenured employees. No significant differences were found when job performance was examined instead of tenure.

Realistic Job Previews

Because recruitment sources have only a slight effect on tenure of future employees, using other methods during the recruitment process may be helpful in recruiting applicants who will be successful. One such method is the **realistic job preview (RJP).** RJPs involve giving an applicant an honest assessment of a job. For example, instead of telling the applicant how much fun she will have working on the assembly line, the recruiter honestly tells her that although the pay is well above average the work is often boring and there is little chance for advancement.

The logic behind RJPs is that, even though telling the truth scares away many applicants (Saks, Wiesner, & Summers, 1996), especially the most qualified ones (Bretz & Judge, 1998), the ones who stay will not be surprised about the job. Because they know what to expect, informed applicants will tend to stay on the job longer than applicants who did not understand the nature of the job. For example, an RJP at a long-distance trucking company increased job satisfaction and reduced annual turnover from 207% to 150% (S. G. Taylor, 1994).

In a meta-analysis of 21 RJP studies, Premack and Wanous (1985) found that RJPs have only a small effect on future employee tenure: the average effect size for tenure was only .12 (if you don't remember what an effect size is, you may want to review the meta-analysis section in Chapter 1). The relationship between RJPs and performance was more complicated. RJPs administered written or orally to an applicant had almost no effect at all—the mean effect size was $-.04$. But if the RJP was conducted using multimedia methods, the mean effect size was a respectable .32.

In another meta-analysis, Shetzer and Stackman (1991) found that RJPs discussing opportunities for career advancement ($d = .19$) were more effective than ones without a career component ($d = .05$). These two meta-analyses indicate that RJPs, especially if they are conducted using multimedia methods and contain a career component, may be useful in the recruitment process.

To practice developing a recruitment campaign, complete Exercise 5–4 at the end of the chapter.

Effective Employee Selection Techniques

If the recruitment process was successful, an organization will have several applicants from which to choose. At this point, many techniques can be used to select the best person from this pool of applicants. In the remainder of this chapter, we will discuss the employment interview. In Chapter 6, such methods as reference checks, assessment centers, biodata, psychological tests, and physical ability tests will be discussed.

Effective employee selection systems share three characteristics: they are valid, reduce the chance of a legal challenge, and are cost effective. If you recall from Chapter 4, a valid selection test is one that is based on

Rhonda Duffie, M.S., PHR
Manager, Dublin Operations
Pfizer

I am the Manager of Operations for a distribution and fulfillment center in southwestern Virginia. We distribute samples and promotional materials for Pfizer, a large pharmaceutical and consumer health products manufacturer. In addition to my general operations duties, I am responsible for employee relations, employee training and development, compensation, benefits administration, employee recruitment, administration of selection tests, interviewing, employee orientation, and safety. Part of my time is spent recruiting and interviewing applicants for open positions. Recruiting and hiring highly qualified applicants is a critical component in the success of our operation, as well as the reputation of the human resources department.

Whether a position is a new or existing one, the first step is ensuring that an accurate job description exists for the position. Information from this job description is then used for recruitment. In advertising the position, it is important to target the appropriate market, which depends, in large part, on the type of position to be filled and the availability of qualified local applicants.

Because our center is located in a rural area, we sometimes have difficulty attracting qualified applicants for upper level positions. Therefore, it is essential to use a variety of recruitment methods to reach more potential applicants. All open positions are posted on the company's Web site, which includes a searchable database for all open positions. The job posting Web site allows internal and external candidates to search by location, facility, or job category. Candidates can complete an online application and may also attach a resume file to their online application. Pfizer also offers incentives to colleagues who refer candidates who are subsequently hired for positions with the company. In addition to the company Web site, a variety of other advertisement methods are used. For entry-level and mid-level positions, an advertisement is typically placed in a local newspaper. An employment ad is placed with the state employment office as well as with local college placement offices. Recruiting for upper-level positions requires a broader focus. These positions are typically advertised regionally as well as nationally. Particularly for higher-level positions, we often utilize Web-based job posting sites such as Monster.com.

As with most organizations, an important part of the selection process is the employment interview. To increase the effectiveness of the interview as a selection tool, we use a structured interview for all open positions. For each position, a set of essential competencies is identified. Questions for each competency are established and may be either technical or situational in nature. Applicants are interviewed by a member of the HR staff, then by the position's supervisor, and lastly, by another supervisor. Each interviewer takes notes during the interview and completes a standard rating sheet with ratings for each of the identified competencies. Using a structured interview and having several independent interviewers increases the amount of pertinent information received and reduces the bias involved in typical interviews. Depending on the position, applicants also may be required to pass typing, data-entry, or PC skills assessments. Once an offer of employment is made, the candidate is required to complete a physical and substance abuse screening test. In addition, criminal background checks are conducted for all new hires. This is to ensure that there are no criminal record issues, which may preclude a colleague from working in certain positions, such as handling prescription drugs.

a job analysis (content validity), predicts work-related behavior (criterion validity), and measures the construct it purports to measure (construct validity). As you will recall from Chapters 3 and 4, selection tests will reduce the chance of a legal challenge if their content appears to be job related (face validity), the questions don't invade an applicant's privacy, and adverse impact is minimized. As you will recall from Chapter 4, ideal selection tests are also cost efficient in terms of the cost to purchase or create, cost to administer, and cost to score. With these characteristics in mind, let's begin our discussion of selection techniques with the employment interview.

The Structured Employment Interview

Undoubtedly, the most commonly used method to select employees is the **employment interview**. In fact, if you think back to all of the part-time and summer jobs for which you applied, most of those jobs were obtained after you went through an interview process. You might even remember the sweaty palms that went along with the interview. In all likelihood, the interviews you have been through could be labeled "traditional" or "unstructured" and must be distinguished from the structured interviews that will be discussed in this chapter.

A **structured interview** is one in which the interview questions are based on a job analysis (job related), every applicant gets asked the same questions, and there is a standard scoring system for each question. Unstructured interviews are ones in which the questions are not based on a job analysis and there is no standard system of scoring. Though some human resource professionals think they are using a structured interview because they ask the same questions of everyone, it is the job relatedness and standardized scoring that most distinguish the structured from the unstructured interview. The distinction is an important one because meta-analyses (Huffcutt & Arthur, 1994; Hunter & Hunter, 1984; McDaniel, Whetzel, Schmidt, & Maurer, 1994) clearly indicate that interviews high in structure are more valid than unstructured interviews. This is true even when the interview is conducted over the phone (Schmidt & Rader, 1999). Furthermore, research (Campion, Campion, & Hudson, 1994; Cortina, Goldstein, Payne, Davison, & Gilliland, 2000) indicates that structured interviews can add predictive power (called incremental validity) to the use of cognitive ability tests.

From a legal standpoint, structured interviews are viewed more favorably by the courts than are unstructured interviews (Williamson, Campion, Malos, Roehling, & Campion, 1997). There are two probable reasons for this. One, structured interviews are based on a job analysis. A review of interview research by Campion, Palmer, and Campion (1997) concluded that interviews based on a job analysis will be more valid and legally defensible than ones not based on a job analysis. Two, structured interviews result in substantially lower adverse impact than do unstructured interviews (Huffcutt, Conway, Roth, & Stone, 2001). In part, this is due to the fact that unstructured interviews concentrate on general intelligence, education, and training whereas structured interviews tap job knowledge, job skills, applied mental skills, and interpersonal skills (Huffcutt et al., 2001).

Though structured interviews result in less adverse impact, they are not completely immune from potential discrimination. Research by Prewett-Livingston, Feild, Veres, and Lewis (1996) and Lin, Dobbins, and Farh (1992) indicates that when interview panels are racially balanced (e.g., two white interviewers, two African American interviewers), white and African American interviewers assign higher ratings to applicants of their own race. When the interview panel is predominantly white (e.g., three white interviewers, one African American interviewer), white applicants receive higher ratings from both African American and white interviewers. When the interview panel is predominantly African American, the opposite occurs: African American applicants receive higher ratings from white and African American interviewers.

Although structured interviews are considered superior to unstructured ones, applicants perceive structured interviews to be more difficult (Gilmore, 1989). Furthermore, because the interview is so structured, applicants may feel that they did not have the chance to tell the interviewer everything they wanted to (Gilliland & Steiner, 1997).

Problems with Unstructured Interviews

Why does the unstructured interview seem *not* to predict future employee performance? Researchers have investigated this question for several years and have identified eight factors that have contributed to the poor reliability and validity of the unstructured interview: poor intuitive ability, lack of job relatedness, primacy effects, contrast effects, negative information bias, interviewer–interviewee similarity, interviewee appearance, and nonverbal cues.

Poor Intuitive Ability

Interviewers often base their hiring decisions on "gut reactions," or intuition (Goodale, 1992). However, people are not good at using intuition to predict behavior. And contrary to what many human resource professionals think, there are no individual differences in interviewers' ability to predict future performance (Pulakos, Schmitt, Whitney, & Smith, 1996). That is, research does not support the idea that some interviewers are able to predict behavior whereas others are not. Divorce rates provide an excellent example of this poor predictive ability. Couples involved in romantic relationships spend, on average, 2 years together before getting married. In spite of this time together, 50% of all marriages fail—an important reason for which is lack of compatibility. So, if after 2 years of "interviewing" a prospective spouse, we make the wrong choice 50% of the time, is it logical to assume that after spending only 15 minutes interviewing an applicant we can predict how well she will get along with the varied members of an organization?

Lack of Job Relatedness

Research by Bolles (2003) and Biegeleisen (1994) has identified the most common questions asked by interviewers. As you can see in Exhibit 5.10, these questions are not related to any particular job (Overman, 1995). Furthermore, the proper answers to these questions have not been empirically determined. Research has shown which answers personnel managers prefer (Bolles, 2003), but preference for an answer does not imply that it will actually predict future performance on the job. As discussed earlier in this and preceding chapters, information that is used to select employees *must* be job related if it is to have any chance of predicting future employee performance. In addition to not being job related, many questions asked by interviewers are illegal (for example, Are you married? or Do you have any health problems?). Interestingly, most interviewers who ask illegal questions know that they are illegal (Dew & Steiner, 1997).

Primacy Effects

Research indicates that information presented prior to the interview (Dougherty, Turban, & Callender,

Exhibit 5.10   Commonly asked employment interview questions

1. Why should I hire you?
2. What do you see yourself doing five years from now?
3. What do you consider your greatest strengths and weaknesses?
4. How would you describe yourself?
5. What college subjects did you like best? Least?
6. What do you know about our company?
7. Why did you decide to seek a position with the company?
8. Why did you leave your last job?
9. What do you want to earn five years from now?
10. What do you really want to do in life?

1994) or early in the interview carries more weight than does information presented later in the interview (Farr, 1973). Furthermore, it has been suggested that interviewers decide about a candidate within 5 minutes after the start of a 15-minute interview (Dessler, 1984). In fact, of a group of personnel professionals, 74% said they can make a decision within the first 5 minutes of an interview (Buckley & Eder, 1989). Thus, the **primacy effect** may help explain why research has shown no relationship between interview length and outcome (Huegli & Tschirgia, 1975). To reduce the primacy effect, interviewers are advised to make repeated judgments throughout the interview rather than one overall judgment at the end of the interview (Farr & York, 1975). That is, the interviewer might rate the applicant's response after each question or series of questions rather than waiting until the end of the interview to make a single rating or judgment.

Contrast Effects

With the **contrast effect**, the interview performance of one applicant may affect the interview score given to the next applicant (Carlson, 1970; Oduwole, Morgan, & Bernardo, 2000; Wexley, Sanders, & Yukl, 1973). If a terrible applicant precedes an average applicant, the interview score for the average applicant will be higher than if no applicant or a very qualified applicant preceded her. In other words, an applicant's performance is judged in relation to the performance of previous interviewees. Thus, it may be advantageous to be interviewed immediately after someone who has done poorly.

Research by Wexley, Yukl, Kovacs, and Sanders (1972) found that interviewers who were trained to be aware of the occurrence of contrast effects were able to reduce them. Other researchers (Landy & Bates, 1973), however, have questioned whether the contrast effect actually plays a significant role in the interview process.

Negative Information Bias

Negative information apparently weighs more heavily than positive information (Bocketti, Hamilton, & Maser, 2000; Rowe, 1989; Springbett, 1958), and positive information is underweighted (Hollmann, 1972). **Negative information bias** seems to occur only when interviewers aren't aware of job requirements (Langdale & Weitz, 1973). It seems to support the observation that most job applicants are afraid of being honest in interviews for fear that one negative response will cost them their job opportunities.

This lack of honesty may be especially evident in the interview, where the face-to-face nature of the process increases the odds that an applicant would respond in such a way as to look better to the interviewer. In a study conducted to increase the honesty of applicants during the interview process, Martin and Nagao (1989) had applicants interview for a job in one of four conditions. In the first, applicants read written interview questions and then wrote their responses to the questions. In the second condition, applicants were "interviewed" by a computer. In the third condition, applicants were interviewed face to face by an interviewer who behaved warmly; and in the fourth condition, applicants were interviewed by an interviewer who seemed cold. As expected, Martin and Nagao found that applicants were more honest in reporting their GPAs and their SAT scores under the nonsocial conditions that involved paper-and-pencil and computer interviewing. Thus, one might increase the accuracy of information obtained in the interview by reducing social pressure and using written or computerized interviews.

Interviewer–Interviewee Similarity

If an interviewee's personality (Foster, 1990), attitude (Frank & Hackman, 1975), gender (Foster, Dingman, Muscolino, & Jankowski, 1996), and race (Prewett-Livingston, Feild, Veres, & Lewis, 1996) are similar to that of the interviewer, the interviewee will receive a higher score (Howard & Ferris, 1996). Interviewer–interviewee similarity affects interviews other than those for employment. Golightly, Huffman, and Byrne (1972) found that loan officers gave more money to loan applicants with attitudes similar to their own than they did to loan applicants whose attitudes were dissimilar.

Interviewee Appearance

The majority of evidence indicates that, in general, physically attractive applicants have an advantage over less attractive applicants (Dipboye, Fromkin, & Wilback, 1975; Gilmore, Beehr, & Love, 1986; Raza & Carpenter, 1987). Interestingly enough, for females this relationship is moderated by the type of position for which they apply. Attractive females tend to get higher ratings for nonmanagerial jobs than unattractive females, but less attractive females get higher ratings than attractive females for managerial positions (Heilmann & Saruwatari, 1979). The appearance bias extends to weight as research (Pingitore, Dugoni, Tindale, & Spring, 1994; Volker, 1993) indicates that obese applicants receive lower interview scores than their leaner counterparts. Interviewee appearance, it seems, is a potent hiring factor (Posthuma, Morgeson, & Campion, 2002).

Along these same lines, Cash, Gillen, and Burns (1977) found that attractive males received the highest ratings for traditionally masculine jobs and attractive females received the highest ratings for traditionally feminine jobs. When the job was gender-neutral, attractive applicants in general received higher ratings than unattractive applicants.

Interviewers, however, are not as attuned to fashion or dress style as the popular press would suggest. Still, research indicates that a job applicant should dress well and conservatively. That is, for white-collar positions males should wear at least a coat and tie, and females should wear a skirt and blouse. There is no available research providing advice for blue-collar jobs. For females, a more masculine style of dress may lead to higher interview scores (Forsythe, Drake, & Cox, 1985).

Strangely enough, Baron (1983) found that even something as trivial as wearing cologne or perfume can affect interview scores. Male interviewers gave lower scores to applicants who wore a pleasant scent, whereas female interviewers gave higher scores to applicants who wore perfume or cologne.

Nonverbal Cues

Perhaps the one interview variable that accounts most for high or low interview scores is **nonverbal communication.** Amalfitano and Kalt (1977) found that making eye contact led to higher interview scores. Howard and Ferris (1996) found a significant relationship between use of appropriate nonverbal behaviors and interviewer perceptions of interviewee competence. Young and Beier (1977) reported results, which indicate that 80% of the interview score variance can be accounted for by the presence or absence of eye contact, smiling, and head nodding. In contrast to unstructured interviews, structured interviews are not greatly affected by nonverbal cues (Martin & Stockner, 2000; McShane, 1993).

Although many more studies and variables could be listed, this discussion shows that the interview contains many sources of bias that are not job related. Remember that one of the major purposes of the employment interview is to determine which applicant will be the most successful in performing a job. To determine this, decisions must be based on ability to do the job and not on such variables as physical attractiveness and eye contact.

Creating a Structured Interview

To create a structured interview, information about the job is obtained (job analysis) and questions are created that are designed to find out the extent to which applicants' skills and experiences match those needed to successfully perform the job. These questions are incorporated in an interview form used by all interviewers for all applicants. Examples of good and bad answers are located next to the questions to help an interviewer score the answers given by applicants.

Determining the KSAOs to Tap in the Interview

The first step in creating a structured interview is to conduct a thorough job analysis and write a detailed job description. As discussed in Chapter 2, the job analysis should identify the tasks performed, the conditions under which they are performed, and the KSAOs needed to perform the tasks. The second step is to determine the best way to measure an applicant's ability to perform each of the tasks identified in the job analysis. Some of the KSAOs can be appropriately measured in an interview; others will need to be tapped through such methods as psychological tests, job samples, assessment centers, references, background checks, and training and experience ratings (these other methods will be thoroughly discussed in Chapter 6). For example, suppose a job description for a receptionist indicated that the primary tasks included typing reports, filing correspondence, answering the phone, and dealing with people visiting the organization. Typing ability might best be measured with a typing test, filing correspondence through a filing test, answering the phone with a job sample, and customer service through an interview question. The important point here is that not every KSAO can or should be tapped in an interview. To practice this process, use the job description in Exercise 5–5 to determine the KSAOs you would tap in an interview.

Creating Interview Questions

As shown in Exhibit 5.11, there are six types of interview questions: clarifiers, disqualifiers, skill-level determiners, past-focused, future-focused, and organizational fit. **Clarifiers** allow the interviewer to clarify resume, cover letter, and application information, fill in gaps, and obtain necessary information. Because each applicant's resume and cover letter are unique, specific clarifiers are not standard across applicants. For example, an interviewer may need to ask one applicant to explain what she won the McArthur Award for and another applicant what she was doing during a 2-year gap between jobs.

Disqualifiers are questions that must be answered a particular way or the applicant is disqualified. For example, if a job requires that employees work on weekends, a disqualifier might be "Are you available to work on weekends?" If the answer is no, the applicant will not get the job.

Exhibit 5.11 Types of interview questions

Question Type	Example
Clarifier	I noticed a three-year gap between two of your jobs. Could you tell me about that? You were a bench hand at AT&T. What is that?
Disqualifier	Can you work overtime without notice? Do you have a valid driver's license?
Skill-level determiner	Several months after installing a computer network, the client calls and says that nothing will print on the printer. What could be going wrong?
Past-focused (behavioral)	When you are dealing with customers, it is inevitable that you are going to get someone angry. Tell us about a time when a customer was angry with you. What did you do to fix the situation?
Future-focused (situational)	Imagine that you told a client that you would be there at 10:00 a.m. It is now 10:30 and there is no way you will be finished with your current job until 11:30. You are supposed to meet with another client for lunch at noon and then be at another job at 1:15 p.m. How would you handle this situation?
Organizational fit	What type of work pace is best for you? Describe your experience working with a culturally diverse group of people.

Skill-level determiners tap an interviewee's level of expertise. For example, if an applicant says she is proficient in Microsoft Word, an interviewer might ask some questions about the word processing program. If an applicant claims to be fluent in Spanish, the interviewer might want to ask her a few questions in Spanish.

Future-focused questions, also called **situational questions**, ask an applicant what she would do in a particular situation. As shown in Exhibit 5.12, the first step in creating situational questions is to collect critical incidents, a technique that you learned in Chapter 2. These incidents are then rewritten into questions that will be used during the interview. It is important that these questions can be answered with the applicant's current knowledge. That is, asking police applicants situational questions in which they would need knowledge of police procedures would not be appropriate because they won't learn this information until they complete the police academy. After creating the questions, the next step is to create a scoring key. This step will be discussed later in the chapter.

Past-focused questions, sometimes referred to as **patterned behavior description interviews (PBDI)**, differ from situational interview questions by focusing on *previous* behavior rather than on future intended behavior. That is, applicants are asked to provide specific examples of how they demonstrated job-related skills in previous jobs (Janz, Hellervik, & Gilmore, 1986). Although future-focused and past-focused interview questions have different orientations, interviewees who do well on one type typically do well on the other (Campion et al., 1994; Cohen & Scott, 1996). However, scores on past-focused questions are better predictors of performance in higher-level positions than are future-focused questions (Huffcutt, Roth, Conway, & Klehe, 2003; Huffcutt, Weekley, Wiesner, DeGroot, & Jones, 2001; Pulakos & Schmitt, 1995).

Rather than trying to predict future performance, **organizational fit questions** tap the extent to which an applicant will fit into the culture of an organization or with the leadership style of a particular supervisor. For example, some organizations are very policy oriented whereas others encourage employees to use their initiative. Some supervisors are very task oriented whereas others are more person oriented. The idea behind organizational fit questions is to make sure that the applicant's personality and goals are consistent with those of the organization. To practice creating interview questions, complete Exercise 5–6.

Creating a Scoring Key for Interview Answers

Once interview questions are created, the next step is to create a key to score applicants' answers to the questions. Though answers to some questions can be scored as being right or wrong (e.g., "Do you have to pay an employee overtime for working over 8 hours in a day?"), as shown in Exhibit 5.13, there are two main methods of scoring most answers: typical answer approach and key issues approach.

Typical Answer Approach

The idea behind the **typical answer approach** is to create a list of all possible answers to each question, have subject matter experts rate the favorableness of each answer, and then use these ratings to serve as benchmarks for each point on a 5-point scale. Though some scoring keys have only one benchmark answer for each point on the scale, research by Buchner (1990) indicates that increasing the number of **benchmark answers** will greatly increase the scoring reliability. Because the number of possible an-

Exhibit 5.12 Creating situational interview questions

The Critical Incident

A customer entered a bank and began yelling about how the bank had messed up his account. He became so angry that he began to swear, saying that he would not leave the bank until the problem was solved. Unfortunately, the information needed by the teller was not at this branch, so there was nothing she could do.

The Question

You are working as a teller and have a long line of waiting customers. One customer runs to the front of the line and yells that he bounced a check and was charged $20, which caused other checks to bounce. He then swears at you and tells you that he will not leave until the problem is solved. You are unable to check on his account because the information is at another branch. What would you do?

The Benchmark Answers

5 — Because I do not have the information and the line is long, I would call my supervisor and have her talk to the customer in her office away from everyone else.

4 — While trying to calm him down, I would call my supervisor.

3 — I would try to calm him down and explain to him that the computer is down.

2 — I would explain that I cannot help him because the computer is down, and ask him to come back later.

1 — I would tell him to go to the end of the line and wait his turn.

---

swers to any question is probably finite, it might be a good idea at this stage to brainstorm all possible answers to a question and then benchmark each of the answers. This approach would result in 10 or so benchmarked answers per question rather than the traditional 5.

Key Issues Approach

A problem with the typical answer approach is that there are many possible answers to a question, and applicants often provide answers that could fit parts of several different benchmarks. To correct this problem, the **key issues approach** can be used. With this approach, subject matter experts create a list of key issues they think should be included in the perfect answer. For each key issue that is included, the interviewee gets a point. The key issues can also be weighted so that the most important issues get more points than the less important issues.

Psychologist Pete DiVasto uses the key issue approach when he interviews applicants for law enforcement positions. In one of his questions, he asks applicants to imagine that they are a police officer and have received a call about a possible break-in at a store. As the officer arrives at the store, she notices the following: a police car in the parking lot with its lights flashing, an officer on the ground next to the squad car, an alarm going off in the store, and a person running from the store. DiVasto then asks the applicant what he or she would do in that situation. The key issues in a good answer include indicating that a cop is hurt and needs help, an understanding that the person running could be dangerous but could also be a victim, the realization that backup is needed, and articulation of a good rationale for choosing to either help the cop first or attend to the person running.

When scoring interviews, it is appropriate to have a system to evaluate an applicant's nonverbal cues, especially when the job involves interpersonal skills. Such scoring is supported by research demonstrating that an applicant's nonverbal cues in interviews can predict job performance (Burnett & Motowidlo, 1998; Motowidlo & Burnett, 1995). To practice scoring interviews, complete Exercise 5–7.

Conducting the Structured Interview

Though it is common to use a panel interview, research suggests that interviews will best predict performance when one trained interviewer is used for all applicants (Huffcutt & Woehr, 1999). The first step in conducting the interview is to build rapport; do not begin asking questions until applicants have had time to "settle their nerves." Once an applicant feels at ease, set the agenda for the interview by explaining the process. Most applicants have not been through a structured interview, so it is important to explain the types of questions that will be asked and point out that each interviewer will be taking notes and scoring the answers immediately after the interviewee has responded. After the agenda has been established, ask the interview questions. You may want to have only one person ask all of the questions or have each panel member ask some questions. It is important to score each answer after it has been given. Once the questions have been asked, provide information about the job and the organization. Such information might include salary and benefits, the job duties, opportunities for advancement, a history of the organization, and so on. Then, answer any questions the applicant might have. It is a good idea at this point to say something such

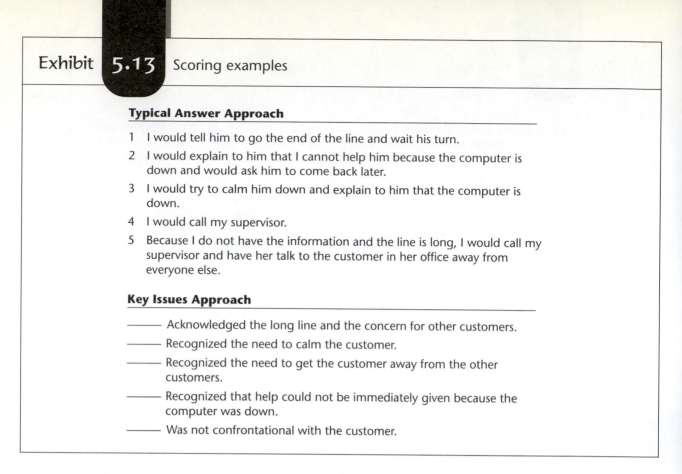

Exhibit 5.13 Scoring examples

Typical Answer Approach

1 I would tell him to go the end of the line and wait his turn.
2 I would explain to him that I cannot help him because the computer is down and would ask him to come back later.
3 I would try to calm him down and explain to him that the computer is down.
4 I would call my supervisor.
5 Because I do not have the information and the line is long, I would call my supervisor and have her talk to the customer in her office away from everyone else.

Key Issues Approach

——— Acknowledged the long line and the concern for other customers.

——— Recognized the need to calm the customer.

——— Recognized the need to get the customer away from the other customers.

——— Recognized that help could not be immediately given because the computer was down.

——— Was not confrontational with the customer.

as "We have asked you a lot of questions but may not have asked you about things you want to tell us. Is there any information you would like to tell us that we did not ask about?" End the interview on a pleasant note by complimenting the interviewee ("It was a pleasure meeting you.") and letting her know when you will contact the applicants about job offers. At the conclusion of the interview, the scores from the questions are summed and the resulting figure is the applicant's interview score.

Job Search Skills

Though the orientation of this and the next chapter is on selecting employees, it is important that you master the skills necessary in obtaining a job. The following three sections provide advice on how to interview, write a cover letter, and write a resume.

Successfully Surviving the Interview Process

Even though the unstructured employment interview has many problems, the odds are high that a person being considered for a job will undergo such an interview. Research and experience both indicate that applicants can take several steps to increase their interview scores. One of the most important of these steps is to obtain training on how to interview. Research by Maurer and his colleagues (Maurer, Solamon, Andrews, & Troxtel, 2001; Maurer, Solamon, & Troxtel, 1998) has shown that such training can increase an applicant's score on structured interviews.

Scheduling the Interview

Contrary to advice given in popular magazines, neither day of week nor time of day affects the interview scores (Aamodt, 1986; Willihnganz & Myers, 1993). What will affect the score, however, is *when* applicants arrive for the interview. If they arrive late, the score will be drastically lower (Lantz, 2001). In fact, in a study I conducted (Aamodt, 1986), no applicant who arrived late was hired. No differences, however, have been found in interview scores based on whether an applicant arrives on time or 5 or 10 minutes early. Therefore, the interview can be scheduled for any time of the day or week, but the applicant must not be late!

Before the Interview

Learn about the company (Crowther, 2001). Recall from Exhibit 5.10 that one of the most commonly asked interview questions ("What do you know about our company?") is used to determine the applicant's knowledge of the organization. Not only does this advice make sense, but research has found that an applicant's knowledge significantly correlated (.32) with the interview rating (Aamodt, 1986) and that interview preparation significantly correlated with being asked back for a second interview (Caldwell & Burger, 1998). Organizations are especially impressed if an applicant knows its products and services, future needs, major problems faced, and philosophy or mission. Statistics such as market share and sales volume are not as valuable (Gardner, 1994).

A former student of mine tells the story about an interview for a managerial position that she had with Allstate Insurance Company. The night before the

Interviews are the most common method of hiring employees.

PhotoDisc, Inc.

interview she read all the available information on Allstate at her local library. During the interview, she was asked why she wanted to work for Allstate. She replied that she was active in the community and was attracted to Allstate because of its "Helping Hands" community program—which she had read about the night before. The interviewer was greatly impressed and spent the next 10 minutes describing the program and its importance. The interview was a success in part because the applicant had done her homework. To see how the career services center at your university can help you prepare for interviews, complete the Finding Career Resources Exercise on your CD-ROM.

On the day of the interview, dress neatly and professionally, and adjust your style as necessary to fit the situation (Sabath, 2001). Avoid wearing accessories such as flashy large earrings and brightly colored ties. Hair should be worn conservatively—avoid "big hair" and colors such as purple and green (impersonating former Chicago Bulls forward Dennis Rodman is not a good interview strategy).

During the Interview

Most suggestions about how best to behave in an interview take advantage of the interviewer biases discussed in this chapter. Nonverbal behaviors should include a firm handshake, eye contact, smiling, and head nodding. Desired verbal behaviors include asking questions, subtly pointing out how you are similar to the interviewer, not asking about the salary, not speaking slowly, and not hesitating before answering questions (DeGroot & Motowidlo, 1999). Keep in mind that first impressions are the most important. If you want to appear similar to the interviewer, look around the office. Kopitzke and Miller (1984) found that the contents of an interviewer's office are often related to her personality and interests.

After the Interview

Immediately following the interview, write a brief letter thanking the interviewer for her time. Although research evidence supports all of the suggestions offered in this section, no research has been done on the effects of thank-you letters. Still, this nice touch certainly cannot hurt. To help you prepare for the employment interview, complete the Surviving the Employment Interview Exercise on your CD-ROM.

Writing Cover Letters

Cover letters tell an employer that you are enclosing your resume and would like to apply for a job. Cover letters should never be longer than one page. As shown in the sample cover letters in Exhibits 5.14 and 5.15, cover letters contain a salutation, three or four basic paragraphs, and a closing signature (Banis, 2001).

Salutation

If possible, get the name of the person to whom you want to direct the letter. If you aren't sure of the person's name, call the company and simply ask for the name of the person (have it spelled) to whom you should send your resume. If the first name leaves doubt about the person's gender (e.g., Kim, Robin, Paige), ask if the person is male or female so that you can properly address the letter to Mr. Smith or Ms. Smith. Do not refer to the person by his or her first name (e.g., Dear Sarah). If you can't get the person's name, a safe salutation is "Dear Human Resource Director." Avoid phrases such as "Dear Sir or Madam" (unless the company is a "house of ill repute") or "To Whom It May Concern" (it doesn't concern me).

Paragraphs

The opening paragraph should be one or two sentences long and communicate three pieces of information: the

Exhibit **5.14** Example of a cover letter

April 18, 2002

Mr. John Smith
Alco, Inc.
217 West Street
Johnson, VA 24132

Dear Mr. Smith

Enclosed is a copy of my resume. Please consider me for the position of welder that was advertised in the *Roanoke Times and World News*.

For several reasons, I believe that I am qualified for your position. First, I have six years of welding experience in an industrial setting. Second, I am a very dependable worker as shown by the fact that I have missed only two days of work in the last five years. Finally, I am available to work any shift at any of your three plants.

I look forward to hearing from you. I can best be reached after 3:00 p.m. on weekdays and anytime on weekends.

Sincerely,

Andrew S. Jones

---

fact that your resume is enclosed, the name of the job you are applying for, and how you know about the job opening (such as a newspaper ad or from a friend). The second paragraph states that you are qualified for the job and provides about three reasons why. This paragraph should be only four or five sentences in length and should not rehash the content of your resume. The third paragraph explains why you are interested in the particular company to which you are applying. The final paragraph closes your letter and provides information on how you can best be reached. Though your phone number will be on your resume, this paragraph is a good place to tell the employer the best days and times to reach you.

Signature

Above your signature, use words such as "cordially" or "sincerely." "Yours truly" is not advised and words such as "Love," "Peace," or "Hugs and snuggles" are strongly discouraged. Personally sign each cover letter; and type your name, address, and phone number below your signature.

Human resource director Ge Ge Beall provides job applicants with the following tips about cover letters:

- Avoid sounding desperate and don't beg (I really need a job bad! Please please please hire me!).

- Avoid grammar and spelling errors. Employers view cover letters and resumes as examples of the best work applicants can produce. If your cover letter contains errors, an employer will be concerned about the quality of your regular work.

- Avoid officious words or phrases. Don't use a 25-cent word when a nickel word will do. Not only will employers be unimpressed by a large vocabulary, but applicants using "big words" often misuse them. As an example, one applicant tried to describe his work productivity by saying that his writings were "voluptuous," rather than "voluminous" as we think he meant to say.

- Don't discuss personal circumstances such as "I find myself looking for a job because I am recently divorced." Employers are only interested in your qualifications.

- If possible, tailor your letter to each company. Standard cover letters are efficient but not as effective as those written specifically for each job you are applying for.

- Don't write your cover letter on the stationery of your current employer.

- Ensure that you have used the correct name of the organization throughout the letter. It is not uncommon when sending out large numbers of cover letters to change the company name in the address but forget to change it in the body of the letter.

Writing a Resume

Resumes are summaries of an applicant's professional and educational background. Although resumes are commonly requested by employers, little is known about their value in predicting employee performance. When an interviewer reads a resume before interviewing an applicant, some studies have found that the validity of the employment interview may actually be *reduced* (Dipboye, Stramler, & Fontenelle, 1984; Phillips & Dipboye, 1989). Beyond these studies, however, it is unclear how much predictive value, if any, resumes have.

Exhibit 5.15 Example of a customized cover letter

July 15, 2002

Ms. Maria Duffie, Director
Human Resource Department
Raynes Cosmetics, Inc.
69 Beall Avenue
Amityville, NY 00312

Dear Ms. Duffie:

Enclosed is a copy of my résumé. Please consider me for the position of sales representative that was advertised this past Sunday in the *Washington Post*. As you can see below, my qualifications are a good match for the requirements stated in your advertisement.

Your Requirements	My Qualifications
Bachelor's degree	B.A. in marketing from Radford University
Two years of sales experience	Five years of sales experience
History of success in sales	Received three sales awards at L.L. Bean
Strong clerical skills	A.A.S. in secretarial science
	Three years of clerical experience
	55 words per minute typing speed

I am especially interested in working for your company because I have used your products for over ten years and thus am familiar with both your product line and the high quality of your cosmetics.

I am looking forward to hearing from you. Please feel free to call me at home after 6:00 p.m. or at work from 8:00 a.m. until 5:00 p.m. Because L.L. Bean is downsizing, my employer will not mind your calling me at work.

Sincerely,

Mable Leane

Mable Leane
2345 Revlon Blvd.
Avon, VA 24132
Home: (540) 555–5678
Work: (540) 555–7676
mimi@aol.com

Resumes may not predict performance partly because they are intended to be advertisements for an applicant. Companies that specialize in resume design openly brag about their ability to "make your strengths more obvious and your weaknesses hard to find." As a result, many resumes contain inaccurate information. For example, Advanced Data Processing found that 40% of the resumes it received contained inaccurate information (Weisser, 2002); Frieswick (2002) reported that between 5 and 15% of executives' resumes contain a falsification, embellishment, or omission; and MacInnis (2002) reported that 25% of the resumes for IT professionals in Canada contained inaccurate information.

Contrary to popular belief, there is no one best way to write a resume. Because people have such different backgrounds, a format that works for one individual may not work for another. Therefore, this section will provide only general advice about writing a resume; the rest is up to you.

Views of Resumes

Resumes can be viewed in one of two ways: a history of your life or an advertisement of your skills. Resumes written as a history of one's life tend to be long and contain every job ever worked as well as personal information such as hobbies, marital status, and personal health. Resumes written as an advertisement of skills tend to be shorter and contain only information that is both positive and relevant to a job seeker's desired career. This latter view of resumes is the most commonly held today.

Characteristics of Effective Resumes

One of the most frustrating aspects of writing a resume is that asking 100 people for advice results in 100 different opinions. However, though there are many *preferences*, there are really only three *rules* that must be followed in writing resumes.

The Resume Must Be Attractive and Easy to Read. To do this, try to leave at least a 1-inch margin on all sides, and allow plenty of white space (Ryan, 1995); that is, do not "pack" information into the resume. An undergraduate student of mine came to me with the "great idea" of typing his resume on a legal sized sheet and then using a photocopy machine to reduce the size to regular paper with a 1-inch margin. Although this technique may look nice, it is probably not advisable because you are still "packing" information into a small space, and personnel directors do not spend much time reading resumes. A resume can have great content, but if the "package" is not attractive, few employers will want to read it.

This rule is hardly surprising as physical attractiveness provides a first impression for many activities such as interviewing, dating, and purchasing products. White is probably the best paper color as it scans, copies, and faxes more clearly than other colors (Ryan, 1995).

The Resume Cannot Contain Typing, Spelling, Grammatical, or Factual Mistakes. When Walter Pierce Jr. was a personnel officer for Norfolk-Southern Corporation, his boss received a resume from an excellent applicant who was applying for a job as a computer programmer. Even though the applicant had outstanding credentials, the personnel director would not even offer him an interview because the applicant had misspelled two words on his resume. A similar story is told by Dick Williams, the General Manager for N & W Credit Union. He once received two cover letters stapled together—both referring to the resume that wasn't there. To make matters worse, four words were misspelled. I could tell you more horror stories but the point should be clear—do not make any careless mistakes!

The Resume Should Make the Applicant Look as Qualified as Possible—Without Lying. This is an important rule in determining what information should be included. If including hobbies, summer jobs, and lists of courses will make you look more qualified for *this particular* job, then by all means, include them.

If a resume follows the above three rules—that is, it looks nice, doesn't contain mistakes, and makes the applicant look as good as possible—then it is an effective resume. Opinions to the contrary (such as "use

boldface type instead of underlining" or "outline your duties instead of putting them in a paragraph") probably represent differences in individual preferences rather than any major problem with the resume.

Types of Resumes

There are three main types of resumes: chronological, functional, and psychological. As shown in Exhibit 5.16, **chronological resumes** list previous jobs in order from the most to the least recent. This type of resume is useful for applicants whose previous jobs are related to their future plans and whose work histories do not contain gaps.

The **functional resume**, as shown in Exhibit 5.17, organizes jobs based on the skills required to perform them rather than the order in which they were worked. Functional resumes are especially useful for applicants who are either changing careers or have gaps in their work histories. The problem with this type of resume is that it takes employers longer to read and comprehend than the other resume types—this problem makes functional resumes the least popular with employers (Toth, 1993).

The **psychological resume** is the style I prefer as it contains the strengths of both the chronological and functional styles and is based on sound psychological theory and research. As shown in Exhibit 5.18, the resume should begin with a short summary of your strengths. This section takes advantage of the impression formation principles of *priming* (preparing the reader for what is to come), *primacy* (early impressions are most important), and *short-term memory limits* (the list should not be longer than seven items).

The next section of the resume should contain information about either your education or your experience—whichever is strongest for you. The design of the education section is intended to provide an organizational framework that will make it easier for the reader to remember the contents. In deciding which information to put into these two sections, three impression-management rules should be used: relevance, unusualness, and positivity. If information is *relevant* to your desired career, it probably should be included. For example, you might mention that you have two children if you are applying for day care or elementary school teaching positions but not if you are applying for a job involving a lot of travel. How far back should one go in listing jobs? Using the principle of relevance, the answer would be far enough back to include all relevant jobs. It is certainly acceptable to list hobbies if they are relevant (Oliphant & Alexander, 1982).

Unusual information should be included when possible as people pay more attention to it than to typical information. A problem for college seniors is that their resumes look identical to those of their classmates. That is, most business majors take the same classes, belong to the same clubs, and have had similar part-time jobs. To stand out from other graduates, an applicant needs something unusual such as an internship, an interesting hobby, or an unusual life experience (for example, spent a year in Europe, rode a bike across the country).

Exhibit **5.16** Chronological resume

CHRISTOPHER R. MILLER

812 Main Street, Gainesville, FL 32789   (904) 645–1001

Objective	Entry-level management position in financial services.
Education	B.S., University of Florida, May 1991
	Major: Business Administration
	GPA: 3.43/4.0
	Minor: Information Systems
	Business-Related Courses: Accounting, Money & Banking, Principles of Marketing, Economics, Statistics
Professional Experience	July 1995–Present
	Assistant Manager. TCBY Yogurt, Gainesville, FL
	Responsible for posting daily receipts and making bank deposits. Further responsible for supervising and scheduling counter personnel, writing progress reports, and handling employee disputes.
	August 1994–July 1995
	Cashier/Customer Service, TCBY Yogurt, Gainesville, FL
	Responsible for assisting customers promptly and courteously, maintaining a balanced cash drawer, and cleaning work station.
	May 1993–August 1994
	Bank Teller: Barnett Bank, Gainesville, FL
	Responsible for assisting and advising customers with financial transactions. Cash drawer balanced 99% of the time. Received excellent performance ratings.
	August 1992–May 1993
	Waiter, Shakers Restaurant, Gainesville, FL
	Responsible for taking food and drink orders from customers and serving them courteously and efficiently. Worked in a high-volume, fast-paced environment.
Activities	Member of Phi Kappa Phi Honor Society
	Member of Phi Beta Lambda Business Organization
	Vice President, Kappa Alpha Pi Social Fraternity
	Member of Circle K Service Organization
	Participated in Intramural Football

Though it is advisable to have unusual information, the information must also be *positive*. It probably would not be a good idea to list unusual information such as "I've been arrested more times than anyone in my class" or "I enjoy bungee jumping without cords." The unacceptability of these two examples is obvious, and few applicants would make the mistake of actually placing such information on their resumes; however, more subtle items can have the same effect. For example, suppose you enjoy hunting and are a member of the Young Democrats on campus. Including these items might make a negative impression on Republicans and those who oppose hunting. Only include information that most people will find positive (such as Red Cross volunteer, worked to help finance education, and so on), and avoid information that may be viewed negatively such as political affiliation, religion, and dangerous hobbies (Bonner, 1993).

Of the many positive activities and accomplishments that you could list, only list your best. Do not list everything you have done; research by Spock and Stevens (1985) found that it is better to list a few great things rather than a few great things and many good things. This finding is based on Anderson's (1965) **averaging versus adding model** of impression formation, which implies that activity quality is more important than quantity. It is neither necessary nor desirable to list all of your coursework (Pibal, 1985). To practice writing a psychological resume, complete the Resume Writing Exercise on your CD-ROM.

Exhibit 5.17 Functional resume

MATTHEW F. JOHNSON

818 Broadway Road, Lexington, KY 63189
(508) 814-7282

Career Objective   Management-level position in banking services.

Banking & Management Experience

Posted receipts and made bank deposits daily for Dunkin' Donuts coffee shop in Lexington, Kentucky. July 1994–present.

Supervised and scheduled cashier personnel for Dunkin' Donuts coffee shop in Lexington, Kentucky. July 1994–present.

Bank teller for Citizen's Fidelity Bank in Lexington, Kentucky. Maintained balanced cash drawer 99% of the time. Trained in various financial transactions of the banking field. May 1995–August 1995.

Customer Service Experience

Customer service/cashier for Dunkin' Donuts coffee shop in Lexington, Kentucky. Assisted customers with placing orders and was responsible for maintaining a balanced cash drawer.

Assisted customers promptly and courteously with financial transactions at Citizen's. Fidelity Bank in Lexington, Kentucky. Received excellent performance ratings. May 1995–August 1995.

Waited on customers at EL Torito Mexican Restaurant in Lexington, Kentucky. After taking customers' orders, served customers promptly and courteously. August 1993–May1994.

Leadership Experience

Vice President of Sigma Epsilon Phi Social Fraternity. Was responsible for assisting pledges with the transition into the fraternity and for raising money for the fraternity philanthropy through various fundraisers.

Coordinated and participated in the actual intramural team for the fraternity.

Community Service and Campus Activities

Member of Key Club Service Organization on campus.

Member of Management Association.

Member of Phi Kappa Phi Honor Society.

Education   B.A., Management University of Kentucky. May 1995.
GPA: 3.44/4.0   Minor: Information Systems
Courses: Accounting, Economics, Marketing, Money & Banking, Principles of Management.

Exhibit **5.18** Psychological resume

ALEXANDER G. BELL
1421 Watson Drive
Ringem, Virginia 24147
(540) 555–5555
abell@runet.edu

PROFESSIONAL STRENGTHS

- Bachelor's degree in business
- Two years of supervisory and leadership experience
- Three years of customer service experience
- Skilled in using spreadsheets (Excel) and presentation software (PowerPoint)
- Conversational in Spanish
- Excellent accounting and statistical skills

EDUCATION

B.S., Business Administration (May, 1999)
Radford University, Radford, VA

Highlights:
– 3.33 G.P.A.
– Extensive coursework in human resource management
– Minored in psychology
– President, Society for the Advancement of Management (SAM)
– Received two academic scholarships
– Worked to finance 50% of own education
– Participated in a variety of college activities including intramurals, two professional organizations, and a fraternity

PART-TIME AND SUMMER EMPLOYMENT

Student Manager (August, 1998–present)
Radford University Dining Services, Radford, VA
    Responsible for supervising 30 students working in the dining hall. Specific responsibilities include scheduling employees, solving customer complaints, balancing the cash drawers, promoting high levels of customer service, and ensuring health regulations are being followed.

Food Server (August, 1997–May, 1998)
Radford University Dining Services, Radford, VA
    Responsible for serving food to students, keeping work area clean, and following health regulations.

Server (Summers 1996, 1997, 1998)
Whale's Tail Restaurant, Redondo Beach, CA.

Chapter Summary

In this chapter you learned

- that employees can be recruited by a variety of methods including help-wanted and situation-wanted advertisements, employee referrals, employment agencies, point-of-purchase methods, direct mail, and job fairs.

- that the traditional, unstructured interview isn't valid because of such factors as lack of job relatedness, poor interviewer intuition, contrast effects, negative information bias, use of nonverbal cues, interviewer–interviewee similarity, and primacy effects.

- how to construct structured interviews that are valid predictors of future performance.
- how to perform well when being interviewed.
- how to write a resume and a cover letter.

Critical Thinking Questions

1. Why are employee referrals an effective means of recruitment?
2. What is the best way to find a job?
3. If the unstructured interview is so bad, why is it still used so often?
4. Is the key issues approach to scoring interview questions better than the typical answer approach?
5. What psychological principles of impression formation are important to consider when writing a resume?

 To learn more about the issues discussed in this chapter, point your browser to

http://www.infotrac-college.com/wadsworth

and enter one of these search terms:

employment recruitment

campus recruiters

executive search firms

employee referrals

job fairs

employment interviews

realistic job preview

nonverbal cues in interviews

resumes—employment

recruitment ads

Exercise 5–1
Reading Help-Wanted Ads

Your text discussed the types of help-wanted advertisements that can be found in a newspaper. From a recent copy of your local newspaper, find examples of each type of ad and tape them to the spaces below.

Send resume

Respond by calling

Apply in person

Blind box

Exercise 5–2
Writing Help-Wanted Ads

The recruitment manager for "Pay 'n Pray," a new fast food chain, has asked you to develop a help-wanted advertisement that will increase the number of applicants who apply for customer service positions with the restaurant. In the space below, design your help-wanted advertisement.

Exercise 5–3
Point-of-Purchase Recruitment

Your text discussed the popularity of point-of-purchase recruitment techniques. As you go to the mall, drive down the road, or eat at restaurants, note the examples of point-of-purchase recruiting that you see. If possible, attach copies of the techniques (such as tray liners) that you encounter. Do not remove things (such as table tents) that are not designed to be taken.

Location   **Point-of-Purchase Technique**

_____   _____

_____   _____

_____   _____

_____   _____

_____   _____

_____   _____

_____   _____

What did you notice about the techniques? What types of applicants did they try to attract?

_____

_____

_____

_____

_____

_____

_____

_____

_____

_____

Exercise 5–4
Employee Recruitment

Your text discussed a number of methods that organizations use to recruit employees. The purpose of this exercise is to provide you with an opportunity to develop a recruitment program.

The Situation

The McBurger King restaurant chain has serious personnel problems. Each franchise is designed to employ 30 employees as cooks and counter helpers. Unfortunately, all of the franchises are having difficulty recruiting employees because they can pay only minimum wage.

As Assistant Personnel Director, you have been asked to develop a novel recruitment strategy to solve this problem. In addition to using the methods discussed in your text, try to design a recruitment strategy that is both practical and creative. Discuss your strategy and provide examples of your ads and your innovative creations.

_____

_____

_____

_____

_____

_____

_____

_____

_____

_____

_____

_____

_____

_____

_____

_____

_____

_____

Exercise 5–5
Identifying KSAOs

On the next page is a job description for an employee in a fast food restaurant. Use this job description, one you wrote in Chapter 2, or one for your current job to begin to create a structured interview. List the essential KSAOs for the job, and then indicate which of the KSAOs would best be tapped in an interview.

KSAO	Best tapped in an interview?	
_____	yes	no
_____	yes	no
_____	yes	no
_____	yes	no
_____	yes	no
_____	yes	no
_____	yes	no
_____	yes	no
_____	yes	no
_____	yes	no
_____	yes	no
_____	yes	no

Restaurant Associate

Nora's Scarf 'n Barf Restaurant

Job Summary

The Restaurant Associate is responsible for performing a variety of tasks involved in the preparation and sales of food. Duties include preparing food, cooking food, taking customer orders, and cleaning the restaurant.

Work Activities

Food Preparation

- Carries 80-pound crates from storage area to food preparation area
- Removes buns from boxes and places on food preparation table
- Takes meat and chicken from the freezer and places on table to thaw
- Takes condiments from the refrigerator and places them on food preparation table
- Inspects meat and chicken to make sure they are safe to eat

Cooking

- Places fries and breaded fish patties into vat and removes when high-pitched alarm goes off
- Cooks hamburgers, chicken, and hot dogs on the grill until they look ready
- Puts grilled food onto bun and adds requested condiments

Customer Service

- Takes customer orders
- Enters the order into the cash register
- Gives the order ticket to cook
- Fills drink order
- Compares order ticket to items on food tray to ensure accuracy
- Gives completed order to customer when food is ready
- Solves any customer problems

Cleaning

- Wipes counter and tables as needed
- Cleans the grill at the end of each shift
- Changes cooking oil when the bottom of the vat can't be seen or after several customer complaints
- Uses RK-9 to clean tables after manager indicates a 10–6 has occurred
- Mops floors and cleans bathrooms
- Cleans cooking utensils at the end of the shift
- Unclogs drains in wash area and bathrooms
- Sweeps and cleans parking lot area

Tools and Equipment Used

- Deep fat fryer
- Grill
- Cleaning materials (e.g., mops, rags, cleanser)
- Cash register
- Common cooking utensils (e.g., spatulas, tongs)

Materials and Substances Exposed To

- RK-9
- Wesson Cooking Oil
- Meat, chicken, fish, potatoes, bread
- Draino

Job Context

The Restaurant Associate works an 8-hour shift, 5 days per week. The actual days and times vary based on a rotating schedule. The restaurant is open 24 hours a day, 7 days a week. Psychological stress is high when the restaurant is busy or customers get angry. Physical stress is moderate as the Restaurant Associate spends all 8 hours standing, with extensive bending, lifting, and leaning. At times, crates weighing 80 pounds must be lifted.

Performance Appraisal

The Restaurant Associate is evaluated each month on the standard Scarf 'n Barf performance-appraisal instrument. Bonuses can be earned by having few customer complaints, no shrinkage, and no citations for health or safety violations.

Personal Requirements

Upon Hire

- Ability to count change back to customers
- Ability to lift 80-pound crates
- Must be bondable
- Customer service orientation
- Must be available to work all shifts

After Hire

- Knowledge of restaurant menu and recipes
- Knowledge of restaurant policies

Exercise 5–6
Developing Interview Questions

After completing Exercise 5–5, you have identified the essential KSAOs for the job and determined which of the KSAOs are best tapped in an interview. To get you started, for each of the examples below, indicate the *type* of structured interview question that it represents.

A. _____ I see on your resume that you belonged to the Ryder Club. What is the Ryder Club?

B. _____ How would you rename an Excel file?

C. _____ Tell me about a time when you had to manage multiple tasks.

D. _____ Suppose a customer told you that he wanted a refund on his meal because it wasn't cooked properly. What would you do?

E. _____ Imagine that you are a teller and the line of customers is getting too long for you to handle before your lunch break. What would you do?

F. _____ What are the components needed to install a telephone?

G. _____ On your resume your job at Sears ended in June 1998 and your next job at Belk started in October 1998. What were you doing between June and October?

H. _____ The job of Research Assistant involves a lot of stress. Tell me how you have handled stressful jobs in the past.

I. _____ Can you work every other weekend?

J. _____ What is the ideal work environment for you?

Now that you can identify different types of questions, the next step is to actually write questions that will tap each KSAO identified in the previous exercise. In the space below, write two examples of each type of interview question.

Disqualifier

1. _____

_____

_____

_____

2. _____

_____

_____

Skill-Level Determiner

1. _____

_____

_____

2. _____

_____

_____

_____

Future-Focused (Situational)

1. _____

_____

_____

_____

_____

2. _____

_____

_____

_____

Past-Focused (Behavioral)

1. _____

_____

_____

_____

2. _____

_____

_____

_____

_____

_____

Organizational Fit

1. _____

_____

_____

_____

_____

2. _____

_____

_____

_____

_____

Clarifiers

Use the resume on the following page to write your clarifiers. You will probably have more than two of these to ask.

1. _____

_____

2. _____

_____

3. _____

_____

4. _____

_____

Matthew "Bucky" Crenshaw

27122 East Bay Ridge Road
Radford, VA 24141
(540) 555–5656

Professional Strengths

- Five years of customer service experience
- Good math skills
- Get along well with people
- Supervisory experience
- Can work any kind of cash register

Work Experience

Sales Associate (January 1997–present)
J. C. Penney, Christiansburg, VA
   Responsibilities include helping customers with their purchases, stocking shelves, and taking inventory.

Salesperson (March 1994–May 1996)
Ties for Guys, Roanoke, VA
   Helped customers find ties that best matched their shirts and suits. Received three raises.

Teller (August 1991–February 1994)
Pulaski Community Bank, Pulaski, VA
   Responsible for opening new accounts, helping customers with transactions, and ensuring that the teller drawer is accurate. Left to take better-paying job.

Education

High School Diploma (1991)
John Wayne High School, Tustin, CA

Exercise 5–7
Scoring Interview Questions

After writing your interview questions in Exercise 5–6, the next step is to develop the key for scoring answers to the questions. To provide you with practice in developing a scoring key, choose two of your questions and use a typical answers approach to score one and a key issues approach to score the other.

Typical Answers Approach

5 _____

_____

_____

4 _____

_____

3 _____

_____

2 _____

_____

1 _____

_____

_____

Key Issues Approach

Employee Selection: References and Testing

IN CHAPTER 5, interviews and resumes were described as the most commonly used methods to screen and select employees. Although these methods are the most commonly used, they are certainly not the best. In this chapter, we discuss several other techniques that are preferred by industrial psychologists to select employees. By the end of this chapter you will

- understand why references typically don't predict performance.
- know how to use the trait approach to score letters of recommendation.
- understand how to choose the right type of employment test for a particular situation.
- be able to describe the different types of tests used to select employees.
- be able to create and score a biodata instrument.
- know how to write a well-designed rejection letter.

References and Letters of Recommendation

In psychology, a common belief is that the best predictor of future performance is past performance. Thus, if an organization wants to hire a salesperson, the best applicant might be a successful salesperson who held jobs that were similar to the one for which he is now applying.

Verifying previous employment is not difficult, but it can be difficult to verify the *quality* of previous performance. I recently watched the National Football League's draft of college players on television (ESPN, of course) and was envious of the fact that professional football teams can assess a player's previous performance by watching game films. That is, they do not have to rely on the opinions of other coaches. Instead, the scouts can watch literally every minute a player has spent on the field while in college.

Unfortunately, few applicants bring "game films" of their previous employment performances. Instead, an employer must obtain information about the quality of previous performance by relying on an applicant's references: either by calling those references directly or by asking for **letters of recommendation** from previous employers.

Reasons for Using References and Recommendations

Confirming Details on a Resume

As mentioned in Chapter 5, it is not uncommon for applicants to engage in **resume fraud**—lying on their resumes about what experience or education they actually have. Thus, one reason to check references or ask for letters of recommendation is simply to confirm the truthfulness of information provided by the applicant. An excellent example of resume fraud is the bizarre 1994 assault against figure skater Nancy Kerrigan arranged by Shawn Eckardt, the bodyguard of Kerrigan's skating rival Tonya Harding. Harding hired Eckardt as her bodyguard because his resume indicated he was an expert in counterintelligence and international terrorism, had graduated from an elite executive protection school, and had spent 4 years "tracking terrorist cells" and "conducting a successful hostage retrieval operation" (Meehan, 1994). After the attack against Kerrigan, however, a private investigator discovered that Eckardt had never graduated from a security school and would have been 16 during the time he claimed he was in Europe saving the world from terrorists. The president of a school he did attend stated that he "wouldn't hire Eckardt as a bodyguard in a lifetime"—an opinion that would have been discovered had Harding checked Eckardt's references.

Resume fraud may not initially seem like a great problem, but consider these examples:

- In October 2002, Kenneth Lonchar was forced to resign after serving as the CFO of Veritas for 5 years when the company discovered he had lied about having an M.B.A. from Stanford.

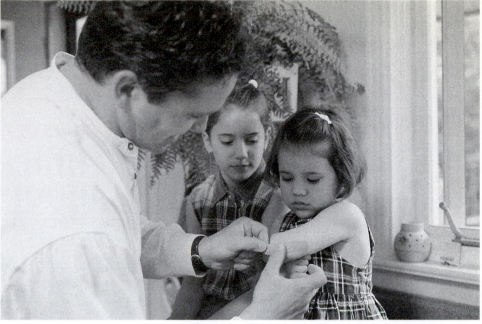

Reference checking is especially important in jobs such as child care.

PhotoDisc, Inc.

- In June 2002, Charles Harris resigned on his first day as the new athletic director at Dartmouth University when a call from a previous employer indicated that Harris had not earned the master's degree in journalism he had listed on his resume.

- In May 2002, Sandra Baldwin was forced to resign as Chair of the U.S. Olympic Committee when it was discovered that she had lied on her resume about having a Ph.D.

- In December 2001, George O'Leary resigned after only a few days as the head football coach at Notre Dame University after it was discovered that he had lied about lettering in high school football and about receiving a master's degree from New York University.

- Paul Crafton used 33 aliases to receive university teaching jobs.

- Abraham Asante, posing as a doctor, improperly gave anesthesia resulting in a patient suffering brain damage; and a man on probation for a felony conviction posed as an electrical engineer and received a $95,000 a year job by falsely claiming he spoke 13 languages.

These stories are tragic and may not be typical of resume fraud cases, but more than 80% of companies believe it is enough of a problem to merit reference checks (Bliss, 2001b).

Checking for Discipline Problems

A second reason to check references or obtain letters of recommendation is to determine if the applicant has a history of discipline problems such as poor attendance, sexual harassment, or violence. Such a history is important for an organization to discover to avoid future problems as well as to protect itself from a potential charge of **negligent hiring.** If an organization hires an applicant without checking his references and background, and he later commits a crime while in the employ of the organization, the organization may be found guilty of negligent hiring if the employee has a criminal background that would have been detected had a background check been conducted.

Negligent hiring cases are typically filed in court as common-law cases, or torts. These cases are based on the premise that an employer has the duty to protect its employees and customers from harm caused by its employees or products. In determining negligent hiring, courts look at the nature of the job. Organizations involved with the safety of the public, such as police departments and day care centers, must conduct more thorough background and reference checks than organizations like retail stores. Such checks are important, as demonstrated by a study done by a reference checking firm, which found that 12.6% of applicants had undisclosed criminal backgrounds (Mayer, 2002).

For example, a child care center in California hired an employee without checking his references. A few months later, the employee molested a child at the center. The employee had a criminal record of child abuse that would have been discovered with a simple call to his previous employer. As one would expect, the court found the employer guilty of negligent hiring because the employer had not taken "reasonable care" in ensuring the well-being of its customers.

In Virginia, an employee of a grocery store copied the address of a female customer from a check she had written to the store. The employee later went to the customer's home and raped her. In this example, a case for negligent hiring could not be made because the company had contacted the employee's previous employment references and had found no reason not to hire him. Because there was nothing to discover and

Exhibit 6.01 Coworkers' attitudes toward employee

Situation	Positive	Neutral	Negative
1	👤👤👤👤👤👤👤👤		
2	👤👤	👤👤👤	👤
3	👤👤		👤👤👤👤👤
4			👤👤👤👤👤👤👤👤

because the store took reasonable care to check its employees, it was not guilty of negligent hiring.

Discovering New Information About the Applicant

Employers use a variety of methods to understand the personality and skills of job applicants; references and letters of recommendation certainly can be two of these methods. Former employers and professors can provide information about an applicant's work habits, character, personality, and skills. Care must be taken, however, when using these methods because the opinion provided by any particular reference may be inaccurate or purposefully untrue. For example, a reference might describe a former employee as "difficult to work with," implying that everyone has trouble working with the applicant. It may be, however, that only the person providing the reference had trouble working with the applicant. This is an important point because every one of us has people we don't get along with even though, all things considered, we are basically good people. Thus, reference checkers should always obtain specific behavioral examples and try to get consensus from several references.

Predicting Future Performance

I/O psychologists use tests to predict future employee performance. As mentioned earlier, however, psychologists believe the best predictor of future performance is past performance. Thus, it makes theoretical sense that performance on previous jobs should be a better predictor of performance on future jobs if the two jobs are similar. It is on this use of references that our discussion will focus.

Even though references are commonly used to screen and select employees, they have not been successful in predicting future employee success. In fact, the average uncorrected validity coefficient for references and performance is only .10 (Reilly & Chao, 1982) and the corrected validity coefficient is .26 (Schmidt & Hunter, 1998). This low validity is largely due to four main problems with references and letters of recommendation: leniency, knowledge of the applicant, low reliability, and extraneous factors involved in writing and reading such letters.

Leniency. Research is clear that most letters of recommendation are positive (Carroll & Nash, 1972; Grote, Robiner, & Haut, 2001; Miller & Van Rybroek, 1988; Whitcomb & Bryan, 1988), especially those written by personal acquaintances (Mosel & Goheen, 1958). Because we have all worked with terrible employees at some point in our lives, it would at first seem surprising that references typically are so positive. But keep in mind that *applicants choose their own references!* Even Nazi leader Adolph Hitler, serial killer Ted Bundy, or terrorist Osama bin Laden would have been able to find three people who could provide them with favorable references.

Exhibit 6.01 shows how coworkers' attitudes toward an employee affect the references they give that person. In the first situation, all of the applicant's eight coworkers have positive feelings about the applicant. Thus, if we ask for references from two coworkers, both would be positive *and* representative of the other six coworkers. In Situation 2, most coworkers have neutral regard for the applicant, with two having positive feelings and two having negative feelings. In this situation, however, both references chosen by the applicant would be positive—and *more favorable* than most coworkers' attitudes. In Situation 3, only two of eight people like the applicant—yet the two reference letters will be the same as in the first and second situations even though most coworkers have negative feelings about our applicant. In Situation 4, no one likes our applicant. In this case, our request for references would either keep the person from applying for our job or force the applicant to find references from somewhere else. But if we *require* work-related references, they probably, but not necessarily, would be negative because research has shown that coworkers *are* willing to say negative things about unsatisfactory employees (Grote et al., 2001; Nash & Carroll, 1970).

A second factor that influences the degree of leniency is the *confidentiality of the reference*. By law, people have the right to see their reference letters. By signing a waiver such as that shown in Exhibit 6.02, however, applicants can give up that right. This may be more beneficial for a potential employer; research by Ceci and Peters (1984) and Shaffer and Tomarelli (1981) indicates that people providing references tend to be less lenient when an applicant waives his right to

Exhibit 6.02 A typical reference waiver

Statement of Release

_____   _____
Name of person asked to write   Date
this recommendation

I request that you complete this recommendation form, which I understand will become a part of my file in the Radford University Graduate College. I further understand:

(1) that this recommendation statement from you will be a candid evaluation of my scholarship, work habits, and potential;

(2) that the completed statement will be sent to the Radford University Graduate College; and

(3) that it will be held in confidence from me and the public by the Radford University Graduate Office.

_____   _____
Applicant's name (print)   Applicant's signature

see a reference letter. That is, when a person writing a reference letter knows that the applicant is allowed to see the letter, the writer is more inclined to provide a favorable evaluation. With this in mind, a colleague of mine almost completely discounts any recommendation letters for which the waiver is not signed.

A third cause of leniency stems from the _fear of legal ramifications_. A person providing references can be charged with defamation of character (slander if the reference was oral, libel if it was written) if the content of the reference is both untrue and made with malicious intent. This fear keeps many organizations from providing references at all (Kleiman & White, 1991). However, people providing references are granted what is called a _conditional privilege,_ which means that they have the right to express their opinion provided they believe what they say is true and have reasonable grounds for this belief (Ryan & Lasek, 1991). Furthermore, many states have passed laws strengthening this conditional privilege. One way to avoid losing a defamation suit is to provide only behavioral information in a reference. That is, rather than saying "This employee is a jerk," you might say "He was warned three times about yelling at other employees and four employees requested that they not have to work with him." A good way to reduce the possibility of a lawsuit is to have the applicant sign a waiver such as those shown in Exhibits 6.03 to 6.05 (Morse, 1988). The waiver in Exhibit 6.03 is used by a reference writer, and the other two are used by the

organization checking references. The one in Exhibit 6.04 waives claims against people providing references to the organization, and the one in Exhibit 6.05 waives future claims against the organization so that the organization can provide references about the employee if he leaves the organization. Waivers are used by 86% of organizations (SHRM, 1998).

Because an employer can be guilty of negligent hiring for not contacting references, a former employer also can be guilty of **negligent reference** if it does not provide relevant information to an organization that requests it. For example, if Dinero Bank fires John Smith for theft and fails to divulge that fact to a bank that is thinking of hiring Smith, Dinero Bank may be found liable if Smith steals money at his new bank.

A number of years ago, on the basis of several letters of recommendation, our department hired a part-time instructor. Two weeks after he started the job we discovered that he had to return to his home in another state to face charges of stealing drugs from his former employer, a psychology department at another university. We were upset because neither of the references from his former job mentioned the charges. After a rather heated conversation with one of the references, we learned that the applicant was the son of the department chairman and that faculty were afraid to say anything that would anger their boss.

These last examples show why providing references and letters of recommendations can be so difficult. On

Exhibit **6.03** Sample waiver used by a reference writer

I, _____, have asked Dr. Marcus Kildare to write a letter of reference to accompany my application to graduate school. I understand that Dr. Kildare has a professional responsibility to write an honest and accurate letter about my past behavior and academic performance and his judgment about my potential for graduate school. Because I understand his need to provide an honest opinion, I waive my right to any future defamation or other legal claims arising from his reference. As a condition of this waiver, Dr. Kildare understands the importance of providing accurate information and agrees to provide what he believes to be an accurate and fair appraisal of my past behavior and potential.

_____   _____
Student's signature / Date   Marcus A. Kildare, Ph.D. / Date

the one hand, a former employer can be charged with slander or libel if it says something bad about an applicant that cannot be proven. On the other hand, an employer can be held liable if it does not provide information about a potentially dangerous applicant. Because of these competing responsibilities, many organizations will only confirm employment dates and salary information unless a former employee has been convicted of a criminal offense that resulted in the termination of the employee. The use of professional reference checking companies can help alleviate this problem (Garvey, 2001).

Three other factors that affect the leniency of references are the *gender of the letter writer,* the *gender of the applicant,* and the *race of the letter reader*. Carroll and Nash (1972) found that female reference letter writers are more lenient when referring female applicants, Kryger and Shikiar (1978) found that letters written about female applicants were rated higher than identical letters written about male applicants, and Bryan (1992) found that African American professionals are more lenient than white professionals in evaluating letter content. Thus, when an applicant chooses his or her own references, retains the right to see reference letters, is referred by a female coworker, or is evaluated by an African American professional, the references are likely to be far more positive than if based solely on the applicant's actual performance.

Knowledge of the Applicant. A second problem with letters of recommendation is that the person writing the letter often does not know the applicant well, has not observed all aspects of an applicant's behavior, or both.

Professors are often asked to provide recommendations for students whom they know only from one or two classes. Such recommendations are not likely to be as accurate and complete as those provided by professors who have had students in several classes and perhaps worked with them outside the classroom setting.

Even in a work setting in which a supervisor provides the recommendation, he often does not see all aspects of an employee's behavior (see Exhibit 6.06). Employees often act very differently around their supervisors than they would around coworkers and customers. Furthermore, as Exhibit 6.06 shows and as will be discussed in greater detail in Chapter 7, those behaviors that a reference writer actually recalls are only a fraction of the behaviors actually occurring in the presence of the person writing the recommendation.

Reliability. The third problem with references and letters of recommendation involves the *lack of agreement* between two people who provide references for the same person. Research reveals that reference **reliability** is less than .30 (Aamodt, Nagy, & Thompson, 1998; Baxter, Brock, Hill, &Rozelle, 1981; Mosel & Goheen, 1952). The reliability problem is so severe that Baxter and his colleagues (1981) and Aamodt et al. (1998) found more agreement between recommendations written *by the same person* for two different applicants than between two people writing recommendations *for the same person*. Thus, letters of recommendation may say more about the person writing the letter than about the person for whom it is being written. To test this idea, complete the Letters of Recommendation Exercise on your CD-ROM.

Exhibit **6.04** Employee's consent to obtain information

I,_____ , authorize the Bundy Shoe Company to contact any or all of my former employers or any or all of the references I have supplied to Bundy Shoe Company for the purpose of verifying any of the information I have provided to Bundy Shoe Company and/or for the purpose of obtaining any information whatsoever, whether favorable or unfavorable, about me or my employment with any former employer.

This low level of reliability probably results from the point cited earlier that a reference writer has not seen all aspects of an applicant's behavior. Thus, a reference provided by a professor who has observed an applicant in a classroom may not agree with a reference provided by a supervisor who has observed the same applicant in a work setting. Although there may be good reasons for the low levels of reliability in reference letters that limit their validity, research has yet to answer this question: If two references do not agree, which one should be taken the most seriously?

Extraneous Factors. The fourth problem with letters of recommendation concerns extraneous factors that affect their writing and evaluation. Research has indicated that the method used by the letter writer is often more important than the actual content. For example:

- Knouse (1983), but not Loher, Hazer, Tsai, Tilton, and James (1997), found that letters that contained specific examples were rated higher than letters that contained generalities.

- Cowan and Kasen (1984) found that male and female writers use different titles when referring to applicants in their letters. Female writers refer to applicants as "Mr." or "Mrs." whereas male writers refer to applicants by their first names.

- Mehrabian (1965) and Weins, Jackson, Manaugh, and Matarazzo (1969) found that even though most letters of recommendation are positive, letters written by references who like applicants are longer than those written by references who do not.

- Loher and colleagues (1997) found that the longer the recommendation letter, the more positively the letter was perceived.

To improve the validity of references, Peres and Garcia (1962) developed, and Aamodt and his colleagues (Aamodt, Bryan, & Whitcomb, 1993; Aamodt, Dwight, & Michals, 1994) refined, the *trait approach*, a unique way to make reference letters more useful by focusing on their relevant content rather than on their positiveness. For examples, see the two letters of recommendation in Exhibit 6.07. Although both describe the applicant in favorable terms, they differ greatly in the content words used to describe the applicant.

After examining thousands of letters of recommendation, Peres and Garcia (1962) found that the adjectives contained in such letters fall into one of five categories: **dependability–reliability, cooperation-consideration, mental agility, urbanity,** and **vigor.** A complete list of the trait words in each category is shown in Exhibit 6.08.

Thus, to use letters of recommendation to accurately predict performance, an employer would use the following five-step process:

1. Determine the importance of each of these five categories to the performance of a particular job.

2. Read each letter of recommendation and underline the traits in each letter used to describe the applicant.

3. Use the list of words in Exhibit 6.08 to place each trait into one of the five categories.

4. Total the number of words for each of the five categories.

5. Divide each category total by the total number of traits.

To demonstrate this process, Exhibit 6.09 shows the traits in the two letters in Exhibit 6.07. The traits have been underlined and summed to provide a score for each of the five categories.

Two studies investigating the validity of the trait approach (Aamodt et al., 1993, 1994) found that the percentage of "mental agility" adjectives mentioned in a letter of recommendation significantly correlated with graduate grade point averages, and the percentage of traits in the "urbanity" category significantly correlated with teaching ratings received by general psychology instructors. Thus, the trait approach may indeed be a useful way to determine the validity of

Exhibit 6.05 Employee's consent to release information

I, _____ , am applying for a position with the Bundy Shoe Company and authorize any of my former employers to provide a representative of Bundy Shoe Company with any and all information pertaining to my previous employment and/or other related behavior. I agree to waive any future defamation or other legal claims arising from information provided to the Bundy Shoe Company.

_____

Signature / Date

letters of recommendation. To practice using the trait approach, complete Exercise 6–1 at the end of this chapter.

As this discussion illustrates, references and letters of recommendation often are unable to predict performance. But with further refinement and research, techniques such as the trait approach may increase the predictive abilities of such references.

Ethical Issues

Because providing references and letters of recommendation is a rather subjective process, several ethical problems can arise involving their use. Let's look at three ethical guidelines referees should follow.

First, *explicitly state your relationship* with the person you are recommending. That is, are you the applicant's professor, boss, coworker, friend, relative, or some combination of the five? This is important because people often have dual roles: a person may be a supervisor as well as a good friend. Without understanding the exact nature of the referee–referent relationship, making judgments about the content of a reference can be difficult. For example, I was told of a situation in which an applicant received a glowing letter of recommendation from a coworker and in which the applicant was hired in part due to the strength of that letter. Within a few months, the new employee was engaged in discipline problems, and it was only then that the organization discovered that the person who wrote the glowing letter was the applicant's daughter. Because the mother's and daughter's last names were different and because the exact relationship between the two was not stated in the letter, the organization never suspected that they were related.

Second, *be honest* in providing details. A referee has both an ethical and a legal obligation to provide relevant information about an applicant (Range, Menyhert, Walsh, Hardin, Craddick, & Ellis, 1991). A good rule of thumb is to ask, "If I were in the reference seeker's shoes,

what would I need to know?" Of course, deciding what information to provide can often be a difficult process. I was once contacted by a secret service agent conducting a reference check on an applicant for a position in a human resource department. My reservations about the student concerned his excessive use of alcohol in social situations and his negative attitude toward women. After some soul searching (as much as can be done with a federal agent staring at you), I decided to provide information about the student's attitude toward women, as I thought it was relevant to a human resource job, but not to mention the social drinking problem. Had the student been an applicant for a position as an agent, I would have mentioned the drinking. I'm not sure that my decision was correct, but the example demonstrates the dilemma of balancing the duty to provide information to the reference seeker with a duty to treat an applicant fairly.

Finally, let the *applicant see your reference* before sending it, and give him the chance to decline to use it. Such a procedure is fair to the applicant and reduces the referee's liability for any defamation charge. Though this last piece of advice seems wise, it can result in some uncomfortable discussions about the content of references that are not positive. After one such discussion, a student told me, "I will get you for this," even though the reference was never sent because the student declined to use the letter. Fortunately, after 2 months of harassment by the student and several calls to campus police to remove the student from the building, the episode finally ended. Thus, being fair and open with former employees or students can have its price.

Predicting Performance Using Applicant Training and Education

For many jobs, it is common that applicants must have a minimum level of education or training to be con-

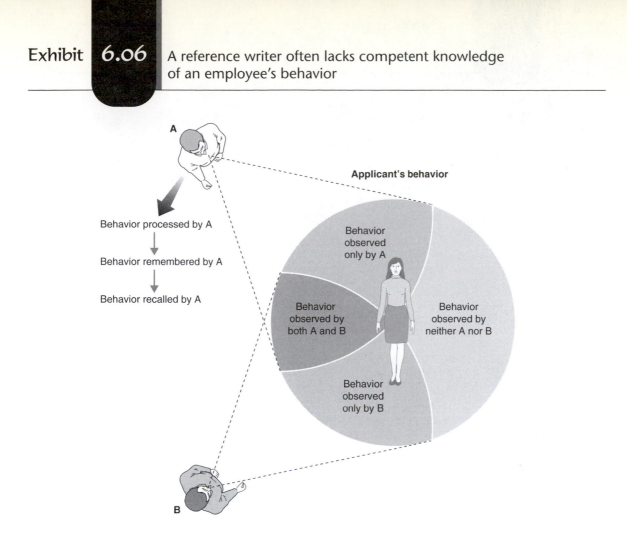

A

Applicant's behavior

Behavior processed by A

Behavior remembered by A

Behavior recalled by A

Behavior observed only by A

Behavior observed by both A and B

Behavior observed by neither A nor B

Behavior observed only by B

B

sidered for the job. That is, an organization might require that managerial applicants have a bachelor's degree to pass the initial applicant screening process. Though degree requirements may seem logical, the research literature has generally not supported their validity. A meta-analysis by Hunter and Hunter (1984) found that the validity of education was only .10 and that it did not add any predictive power (incremental validity) over the use of cognitive ability tests. However, a meta-analysis of the relationship between education and police performance found that education was a valid predictor of performance in the police academy ($r = .41$) and performance on the job ($r = .33$) and added incremental validity to cognitive ability tests (Aamodt, 2002).

Meta-analyses indicate that a student's grade point average can predict job performance (Roth, BeVier, Switzer, & Schippmann, 1996), training performance (Dye & Reck, 1989), promotions (Cohen, 1984), salary (Roth & Clarke, 1998), and graduate school performance (Kuncel, Hezlett, & Ones, 2001). GPA is most predictive in the first few years after graduation (Roth et al., 1996). As with many measures of cognitive ability, the use of GPA will result in high levels of adverse impact (Roth & Bobko, 2000).

Another factor complicating the use of education and GPA to select employees is the increased use of home schooling; more than 1 million children are currently being homeschooled (Grossman, 2001).

Predicting Performance Using Applicant Knowledge

Used primarily in the public sector, especially for promotions, **job knowledge tests** are designed to measure how much a person knows about a job. For example, applicants for a bartender position might be asked how to make a martini or a White Russian, and applicants for a human resource position might be asked how to conduct a job analysis. These tests are similar to the exams given several times a semester in a college class. They are typically given in multiple-choice fashion for ease of scoring, but they also can be written in essay format or given orally in a job interview. Common examples of job knowledge tests include tests of computer programming knowledge, knowledge of electronics, and knowledge of mechanical principles. Standardized job knowledge tests are

Exhibit **6.07** Two letters of recommendation

Dear Personnel Director:

Mr. John Anderson asked that I write this letter in support of his application as an assistant manager, and I am pleased to do so. I have known John for six years as he was my assistant in the accounting department.

John always had his work completed accurately and promptly. In his six years here, he never missed a deadline. He is very detail oriented, diligent in finding errors, and methodical in his problem-solving approach. Interpersonally, John is a very friendly and helpful person.

I have great confidence in John's ability. If you desire more information, please let me know.

Dear Personnel Director:

Mr. John Anderson asked that I write this letter in support of his application as an assistant manager, and I am pleased to do so. I have known John for six years as he was my assistant in the accounting department.

John was one of the most popular employees in our agency as he is a friendly, outgoing, sociable individual. He has a great sense of humor, is poised, and is very helpful. In completing his work, he is independent, energetic, and industrious.

I have great confidence in John's ability. If you desire more information, please let me know.

commonly used by state licensing boards for such occupations as lawyers and psychologists.

Job knowledge tests have excellent content and criterion validity (Schmidt & Hunter, 1998), and because of their high face validity, they are positively accepted by applicants (Robertson & Kandola, 1982).

Even though job knowledge tests do a good job of predicting performance, they often result in adverse impact (Schmidt, Greenthal, Hunter, Berner, & Seaton, 1977) and can only be used for jobs in which applicants are expected to have job knowledge at the time of hire or promotion.

Exhibit 6.08 Complete list of words used in the trait approach

Urbanity

active in class discussions	delightful	member of group	sociable
affable	engaging personality	(pres., secretary)	sophisticated
animated	enjoyable	motivator	sparkling
articulate	expressive	oral	speaks well
assured	friendly	outgoing	talkative
chatty	gregarious	participates in discussion	teaching assistant
cheerful	interacts (interacted)	personable	very involved
commanding	interpersonal (skilled)	pleasant	well bred
confident	jokes	poised	well liked
contributor	leader (a)	polished	well rounded (be aware
conversational	leadership (shown)	refined	of context)
cultured	likable	relates well to others	
delight (to work with)	lively	sense of humor	

Cooperation–Consideration

accommodating	easy-going	incorruptible	restrained
altruistic	emotionally stable	integrity (shows)	sacrificing
attentive	(mature)	kindly	sensitive
big-hearted	empathetic	levelheaded	serious
calm	encouraging (peers)	liberal	sincere
caring	ethical	loyal	sober
clean-cut	even keel emotionally	mature	staid
congenial	faithful	modest	strong character
considerate	fine person	moral	takes suggestions well
compassionate	generous	nonjudgmental	team player
composed	gentle	obliging	teamwork (promotes)
conscientious	genuine	open	thoughtful
(toward a person)	good listener	open-minded	trustworthy
cooperative	good-natured	patient	upstanding
counselor (good)	gracious	placid	volunteer (be aware
courteous	group-centered	professional	of context)
decent	helpful	(in interactions)	warm
desire (to help others)	honest	quiet	well mannered
down to earth	human relations	respectable	willing
earnest	(outstanding)	respectful	works well (with others)

Dependability–Reliability

ability to follow through	decisive	follows through	pride (toward work)
accurate	dedicated	independent (works)	prompt
attended (class)	definite	methodical	proofreads
businesslike	dependable	neat	reliable
careful	detail-minded	never have to remind	responsible
certain	diligent	on time	self-reliant
committed	disciplined	orderly	sure
completed (projects)	efficient	organized	thorough
conscientious	fastidious	practical	well prepared
(toward work)	focused	precise	work completed on
critical	(be aware of context)	prepared	time

Mental Agility

able to apply	common sense (shows)	ingenious	proficient
(information, knowledge)	competent	inquisitive	quick to comprehend
able to use	creative	insightful	research skills (excellent)
common sense	curious (intellectually)	intellectual	retains knowledge
able to use good	did very well	intelligent	resourceful
judgment	discerning	imaginative	sagacious
able to retain information	effective	judicious	sensible
above average	esthetic	knowledgeable	skilled
academic ability (high)	excellent student	learns quickly	skillful (handles material)
adaptable	excels (scholastically)	logical	sound judgment
adventurous	farsighted	on-target	technically competent
alert	fine_____skills	on the ball	thinks clearly
analytical	fluent (in a language)	original	thinker
aptitude	good common sense	perceptive	thoughtful
artistic	good student	performed well	top 10%, etc.
artistic talent	good writing skills	potential	understanding (good)
astute	held in high-regard	(demonstrated, has)	wise
bright	honor roll	practical	
capable	informed	(uses common sense)	

Vigor

achiever	devoted (extra time)	hustling	resolute
active	eager	independent	self-assured
aggressive	ebullient	industrious	self-confident
ambitious	energetic	initiative (shows)	self-directed
assertive	enterprising	interest (high level of)	self-driving
autonomous	enthusiastic	involved (highly)	self-improvement
challenges (an assertion)	fast	pace-setting	self-reliant
compulsion (to achieve)	forthrightness	persevere	self-starting
courageous	forward	persistent	sought opportunities
demanding	frank	probes beyond . . .	(info.)
desire (to succeed)	goal-directed	productive	speedy
determined	hard worker	pursues opportunities	
defends (ideas, positions)	high energy	quick	

Exhibit 6.09 Identified traits in letters of recommendation

Dear Personnel Director:

Mr. John Anderson asked that I write this letter in support of his application as an assistant manager, and I am pleased to do so. I have known John for six years as he was my assistant in the accounting department.

John was one of the most _popular_ employees in our agency as he is a _friendly_, _outgoing_, _sociable_ individual. He has a great _sense of humor_, is _poised_, and is very _helpful_. In completing his work, he is _independent_, _energetic_, and _industrious_.

I have great confidence in John's ability. If you desire more information, please let me know.

U __6__ CC __1__ DR __0__ MA __0__ V __3__

Dear Personnel Director:

Mr. John Anderson asked that I write this letter in support of his application as an assistant manager, and I am pleased to do so. I have known John for six years as he was my assistant in the accounting department.

John always had his work completed _accurately_ and _promptly_. In his six years here, he _never missed a deadline_. He is very _detail oriented_, _diligent_ in finding errors, and _methodical_ in his problem-solving approach. Interpersonally, John is a very _friendly_ and _helpful_ person.

I have great confidence in John's ability. If you desire more information, please let me know.

U __1__ CC __1__ DR __6__ MA __0__ V __0__

Predicting Performance Using Applicant Ability

Ability tests tap the extent to which an applicant has the ability to learn or perform a job-related skill. Ability tests are used primarily in occupations in which applicants are not expected to know how to perform the job at the time of hire. Instead, new employees will be taught the necessary job skills and knowledge. Examples of such occupations include police officers, firefighters, and military personnel. For example, cognitive ability would enable a police cadet to obtain knowledge of search and seizure laws, psychomotor ability (dexterity) would enable a secretary to type fast or an assembler to rapidly assemble electronic components, perceptual ability would enable a mail clerk to distinguish zip codes or a textile worker to distinguish colors, and physical ability would enable a firefighter to learn how to climb a ladder or carry a victim from a burning building.

Cognitive Ability

Cognitive ability includes such dimensions as oral and written comprehension, oral and written expression, numerical facility, originality, memorization, reasoning (mathematical, deductive, inductive), and general learning. Cognitive ability is important for professional, clerical, and supervisory jobs, including such occupations as supervisor, accountant, and secretary.

Cognitive ability tests are commonly used because they are excellent predictors of employee performance (Schmidt & Hunter, 1998), are easy to administer, and are relatively inexpensive. Cognitive ability is thought to predict work performance in two ways: by allowing employees to quickly learn job-related knowledge and by processing information resulting in better decision making. Though cognitive ability tests are thought by many to be the most valid method of employee selection, they have been criticized because they result in high levels of adverse impact (Roth, BeVier, Bobko, Switzer, & Tyler, 2001) and often lack face validity.

One of the most widely used cognitive ability tests in industry is the **Wonderlic Personnel Test.** The short amount of time (12 minutes) necessary to take the test as well as the fact that it can be administered in a group setting makes the test popular. Sample items from the Wonderlic are shown in Exhibit 6.10. Other popular mental ability tests are the Miller Analogies Test, Quick Test, and Raven Progressive Matrices. To better understand cognitive ability tests, complete the short form of the Basic Cognitive Ability Test (BCAT) found in Exercise 6–2 at the end of this chapter.

A type of test related to cognitive ability is the situational judgment test. In these tests, applicants are given a series of situations and asked how they would handle each one. A meta-analysis by McDaniel, Morgeson, Finnegan, Campion, and Braverman (2001) found that situational judgment tests correlated highly with cognitive ability tests ($r = .46$) and with job performance ($r = .34$). Though situational judgment tests are correlated with cognitive ability, the combination of the two is more valid than either test alone (Clevenger, Pereira, Wiechmann, Schmitt, & Harvey, 2001).

Perceptual Ability

Perceptual ability consists of vision (near, far, night, peripheral); color discrimination; depth perception; glare sensitivity; speech (clarity, recognition); and hearing (sensitivity, auditory attention, sound localization; Fleishman & Reilly, 1992b). Abilities from this dimension are useful for jobs involving setting up machines and such occupations as machinist, cabinetmaker, die setter, and tool and die maker. An example of a perceptual ability test is shown in Exhibit 6.11.

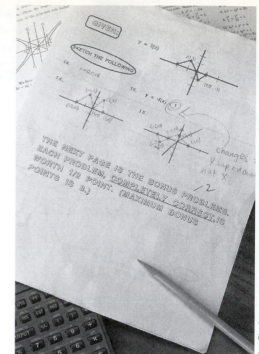

Ability tests are a good predictor of performance.

Psychomotor Ability

Psychomotor ability includes finger dexterity, manual dexterity, control precision, multilimb coordination, response control, reaction time, arm–hand steadiness, wrist–finger speed, and speed-of-limb movement (Fleishman & Reilly, 1992b). Psychomotor abilities are useful for such jobs as carpenter, police officer, sewing machine operator, post office clerk, and truck driver. An example of a psychomotor test is shown in Exhibit 6.12.

Physical Ability

Physical ability tests are often used for jobs that require physical strength and stamina, such as police officer, firefighter, and lifeguard. Physical agility is measured in one of two ways: job simulations and physical agility tests. With a job simulation, applicants actually demonstrate job-related physical behaviors. For example, firefighter applicants might climb a ladder and drag a 48-pound hose 75 feet across a street, police applicants might fire a gun and chase down a suspect, and lifeguard applicants might swim 100 yards and drag a drowning victim back to shore. Though job simulations are highly content valid, from a financial or safety perspective they are often impractical (Hoover, 1992).

Testing the physical agility of police applicants is an excellent example of this impracticality. Job analyses consistently indicate that the physical requirements of police officers can be divided into two categories: athletic and defensive. *Athletic requirements* are easy to simulate because they involve such behaviors as running, crawling, and pulling. *Defensive requirements,*

Exhibit **6.10** Wonderlic Personnel Test

WONDERLIC

PERSONNEL TEST

FORM II

_____   _____

NAME   (Please Print)   Date

READ THIS PAGE CAREFULLY. DO EXACTLY AS YOU ARE TOLD.
DO NOT TURN OVER THIS PAGE UNTIL YOU ARE
INSTRUCTED TO DO SO.

PROBLEMS MUST BE WORKED WITHOUT THE AID OF A CALCULATOR
OR OTHER PROBLEM-SOLVING DEVICE.

This is a test of problem-solving ability. It contains various types of questions. Below is a sample question correctly filled in.

PLACE
ANSWERS
HERE

REAP is the opposite of
    1 obtain.   2 cheer.   3 continue.   4 exist.   5 <u>sow.</u>   [_5_]

The correct answer is "sow." (It is helpful to underline the correct word.) The correct word is numbered 5. Then write the figure 5 in the brackets <u>at the end of the line.</u>

Answer the next sample question yourself.

Paper sells for 23 cents per pad. What will 4 pads cost?   [___]

The correct answer is 92¢. There is nothing to underline so just place "92¢" in the brackets.

Here is another example:

MINER   MINOR — Do these words
    1 have similar meanings?   2 have contradictory meanings?   3 mean neither the same nor opposite? [___]

The correct answer is "mean neither the same nor opposite" which is number 3 so all you have to do is place a figure "3" in the brackets <u>at the end of the line.</u>

When the answer to a question is a letter or a number, put the letter or number in the brackets.
All letters should be printed.

This test contains 50 questions. It is unlikely that you will finish all of them, but do your best. After the examiner tells you to begin, you will be given exactly 12 minutes to work as many as you can. Do not go so fast that you make mistakes since you must try to get as many right as possible. The questions become increasingly difficult, so do not skip about. Do not spend too much time on any one problem. The examiner will not answer any questions after the test begins.

Now, lay down your pencil and wait for the examiner to tell you to begin!

Do not turn the page until you are told to do so.

Source: Wonderlic Personnel Test, Inc. Northfield, Illinois. Reprinted by permission.

however, are difficult to safely and accurately simulate because they involve such behaviors as applying restraining holds, kicking, and fending off attackers. One can imagine the liability and safety problems of physically attacking applicants to see if they can defend themselves.

Because of the difficulty in using simulations to measure these last types of behaviors, physical agility tests are used. Instead of simulating defensive behaviors, tests are developed that measure the basic abilities needed to perform these behaviors. Tests commonly used to measure the abilities needed to perform defensive

Exhibit 6.11 Perceptual ability test

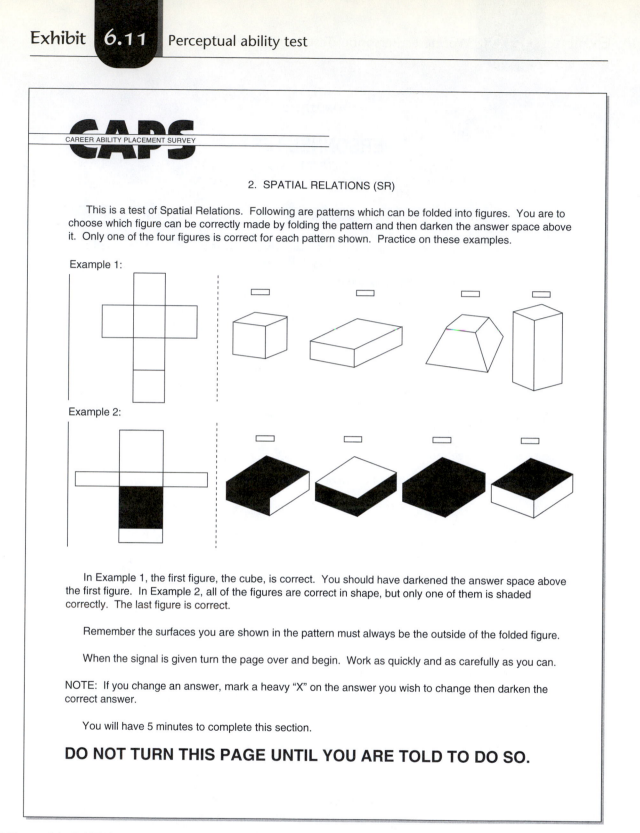

CAPS
CAREER ABILITY PLACEMENT SURVEY

2. SPATIAL RELATIONS (SR)

This is a test of Spatial Relations. Following are patterns which can be folded into figures. You are to choose which figure can be correctly made by folding the pattern and then darken the answer space above it. Only one of the four figures is correct for each pattern shown. Practice on these examples.

Example 1:

Example 2:

In Example 1, the first figure, the cube, is correct. You should have darkened the answer space above the first figure. In Example 2, all of the figures are correct in shape, but only one of them is shaded correctly. The last figure is correct.

Remember the surfaces you are shown in the pattern must always be the outside of the folded figure.

When the signal is given turn the page over and begin. Work as quickly and as carefully as you can.

NOTE: If you change an answer, mark a heavy "X" on the answer you wish to change then darken the correct answer.

You will have 5 minutes to complete this section.

DO NOT TURN THIS PAGE UNTIL YOU ARE TOLD TO DO SO.

behaviors include push-ups, sit-ups, and grip strength. Research has shown that there are nine basic physical abilities (Fleishman & Reilly, 1992b):

1. Dynamic strength (strength requiring repetitions)

2. Trunk strength (stooping or bending over)
3. Explosive strength (jumping or throwing objects)
4. Static strength (strength not requiring repetitions)
5. Dynamic flexibility (speed of bending, stretching, twisting)

Exhibit **6.12** Psychomotor ability test

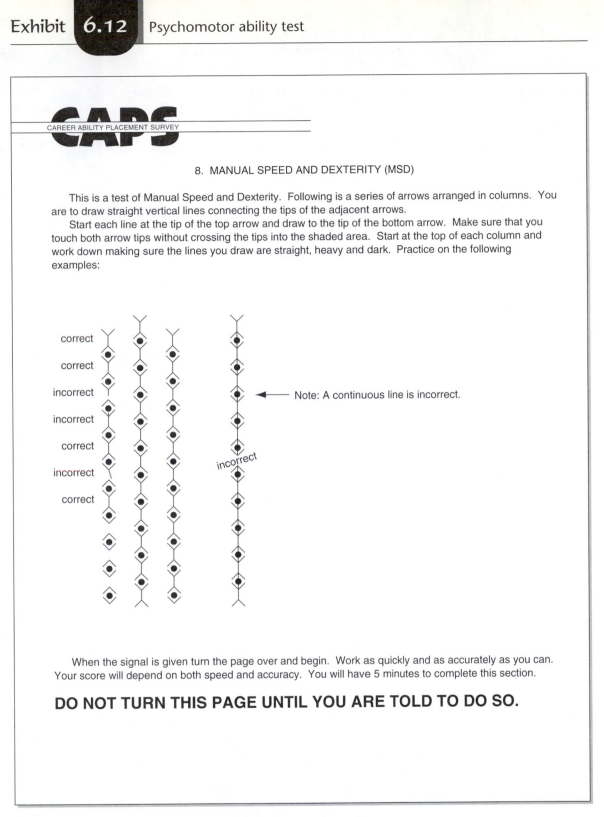

CAPS
CAREER ABILITY PLACEMENT SURVEY

8. MANUAL SPEED AND DEXTERITY (MSD)

This is a test of Manual Speed and Dexterity. Following is a series of arrows arranged in columns. You are to draw straight vertical lines connecting the tips of the adjacent arrows.

Start each line at the tip of the top arrow and draw to the tip of the bottom arrow. Make sure that you touch both arrow tips without crossing the tips into the shaded area. Start at the top of each column and work down making sure the lines you draw are straight, heavy and dark. Practice on the following examples:

correct
correct
incorrect
incorrect
correct
incorrect
correct

incorrect

Note: A continuous line is incorrect.

When the signal is given turn the page over and begin. Work as quickly and as accurately as you can. Your score will depend on both speed and accuracy. You will have 5 minutes to complete this section.

DO NOT TURN THIS PAGE UNTIL YOU ARE TOLD TO DO SO.

6. Extent flexibility (degree of bending, stretching, twisting)
7. Gross body equilibrium (balance)
8. Gross body coordination (coordination when body is in motion)
9. Stamina

Because physical agility tests have tremendous adverse impact against women (Arvey, Nutting, & Landon, 1992; Hoover, 1992; Mijares, 1993), they have been criticized on three major points: job relatedness, passing scores, and the time at which they should be required.

Mark Foster, Ph.D.
Consultant, Carl Vinson Institute of Government
University of Georgia

The Vinson Institute of Government is one of several service units of the University of Georgia. The human services division provides technical assistance to municipal, county, and state government agencies. Within this division, assistance is provided primarily in human resource management.

My position is primarily as a consultant. Our clients are mainly public safety agencies such as police and fire departments. Typical projects range from helping a small city choose a new police chief to helping a state law enforcement agency develop new promotion procedures.

We also develop and administer written job knowledge tests and assessment centers. Much of my time is spent ensuring that these testing instruments are valid predictors of future job performance. The primary strategy we use is content validity. The basis of this approach is ensuring that the questions on the job knowledge tests and the assessment center exercises measure actual duties and responsibilities that are required by the individual who performs the job.

The content validation approach relies heavily on conducting a thorough job analysis. This is a lengthy process in which I will spend time with job incumbents while they perform their jobs. For example, if we are developing test materials for police sergeants, I will ride with a representative sample of police sergeants and observe them while they perform their jobs. During this time, I ask questions and take extensive notes on exactly what they are doing and why. From this information, a task list and a list of necessary knowledges and skills are developed. From these two lists, we know which knowledges to test for on the written examination and which skills to test for during the assessment center.

Examples of knowledge might include basic laws, departmental policy and procedures, and proper collection and handling of evidence. Examples of skills might include recognizing and handling performance problems of a subordinate, making decisions, oral and written communication, and organization and planning.

The development of written examinations is relatively straightforward; the development of assessment centers is much more involved. The assessment center is a series of job simulations that require the candidate to perform skills that are required by the job. These job simulations or exercises can take many forms. We typically use three or four different exercises. These exercises might include a role play, an oral presentation, and a written problem exercise.

Job Relatedness

Though few people would disagree that it is *better* for a police officer to be strong and fit than weak and out of shape, many argue whether it is *necessary* to be physically fit. Critics of physical agility testing cite two reasons for questioning the necessity of physical agility: current out-of-shape cops and technological alternatives. Currently, many police officers are overweight, slow, and out of shape, yet they perform safely and at high levels. Furthermore, there is research to suggest that physical size is not related to police safety (Griffiths & McDaniel, 1993). Thus, critics argue that physical agility is not an essential part of the job. This is especially true due to technological advances in policing. As an example, Sollie and Sollie (1993) presented data showing that the use of "pepper spray" in Meridian, Mississippi, almost completely reduced the need for officers to physically restrain drunk or physically aggressive suspects. However, supporters of physical agility testing cite studies demonstrating significant relationships between isometric strength tests and supervisor ratings of employee physical ability (Blakley, Quinones, Crawford, & Jago, 1994).

Passing Scores

A second problem with physical agility tests is determining passing scores; that is, how fast must an applicant run or how much weight must be lifted to pass a physical agility test? Passing scores for physical agility tests are set based on one of two types of standards: relative or absolute. Relative standards indicate how well an individual scores compared to others in a group such as females, police applicants, or current police officers. The advantage to using relative standards is that adverse impact is eliminated because males are compared with males and females with other females. The problem with relative scales, however, is that a female applicant might be strong compared to other females, yet not strong enough to perform the job. Furthermore, relative standards based on protected classes (e.g., gender or race) were made illegal by the 1991 Civil Rights Act (although technically illegal, the Justice Department has not enforced the ban against gender-specific physical standards).

In contrast, absolute passing scores are set at the minimum level needed to perform a job. For example, if a police officer needs to be able to drag a 170-pound person from a burning car, 170 pounds becomes the passing score. As one can imagine, the problem comes in determining the minimum amounts. That is, how fast does an officer *need* to run to adequately perform the job? Because people come in all sizes, how many pounds does an officer *need* to be able to drag?

When the Ability Must Be Present

A third problem with physical agility requirements is with the point at which the ability must be present. Most police departments require applicants to pass physical agility tests on the same day other tests are being completed. However, the applicant doesn't need the strength or speed until he is actually in the academy or on the job. Showing awareness of this problem, cities such as San Francisco and Philadelphia provide applicants with a list of physical abilities that will be required of them once they arrive at the academy. Applicants are then given suggestions on how they can get themselves into the proper condition. Some cities even hold conditioning programs for applicants! Such policies greatly reduce adverse impact by increasing the physical agility of female applicants.

An interesting example of the importance of monitoring physical ability testing is provided in a study by Padgett (1989), who was hired to determine vision requirements for a municipal fire department. Prior to Padgett's study, national vision standards for firefighters had been set without any empirical research. The standards stipulated that firefighters needed a minimum uncorrected vision of 20/40 and could not wear contact lenses because they might be "blown out of their eyes."

After conducting his study of actual job-related duties, however, Padgett discovered that the minimum vision needed to perform firefighting tasks was 20/100 if the person wore glasses and that there was no minimum if the person wore contacts. The difference in requirements for contacts and glasses was because certain duties might result in a loss of glasses, but it was very unlikely a firefighter would lose contacts while performing a task requiring acute vision. As a result of this study, many qualified applicants who had been turned away because of the archaic vision requirements were now allowed the chance to become firefighters.

Predicting Performance Using Applicant Skill

Rather than measuring an applicant's current knowledge or potential to perform a job (ability), some selection techniques measure the extent to which an applicant already has a job-related skill. The two most common methods for doing this are the work sample and the assessment center.

Work Samples

With a work sample, the applicant performs actual job-related tasks. For example, an applicant for a job as automotive mechanic might be asked to fix a torn fan belt, a secretarial applicant might be asked to type a letter, and a truck driver applicant might be asked to back a truck up to a loading dock.

Work samples are excellent selection tools for several reasons. First, because they are directly related to job tasks, they have excellent content validity.

Second, scores from work samples tend to predict actual work performance and thus have excellent criterion validity (Callinan & Robertson, 2001). Third, because job applicants are able to see the connection between the job sample and the work performed on the job, the samples have excellent face validity and thus are challenged less often in civil service appeals or in court cases (Whelchel, 1985). Finally, minorities tend to score better on work samples than on written exams (Cascio & Phillips, 1979; Schmidt et al., 1977). The main reason for not using work samples is that they can be expensive both to construct and to administer. For this reason, work samples are best used for well-paying jobs for which many employees will be hired.

Assessment Centers

An **assessment center** is a selection technique characterized by the use of multiple assessment methods that allow multiple assessors to actually *observe* applicants perform simulated job tasks (Joiner, 2002). Its major advantages are that assessment methods are all job related, and multiple trained assessors help to guard against many (but not all) types of selection bias. For a selection technique to be considered an assessment center, it must meet the following requirements (Joiner, 2000):

1. The assessment center activities must be based on the results of a thorough job analysis.
2. Multiple assessment techniques must be used, at least one of which must be a simulation.
3. Multiple trained assessors must be used.
4. Behavioral observations must be documented at the time the applicant behavior is observed.
5. Assessors must prepare a report of their observations.
6. The overall judgment of an applicant must be based on a combination of information from the multiple assessors and multiple techniques.
7. The overall evaluation of an applicant cannot be made until all assessment center tasks have been completed.

Development and Components

Although many different techniques may be used in assessment centers, the basic development and types of exercises are fairly standard. The first step in creating an assessment center is, of course, to do a job analysis. From this analysis, exercises are developed that measure different aspects of the job (Joiner, 2000). Common exercises include the in-basket technique, simulations, work samples, leaderless group discussions, structured interviews, personality and ability tests, and business games. Each of these techniques can be used by itself, but only when several are used in combination do they become part of an assessment center. The typical assessment center has four to seven exercises, takes 2 to 3 days to complete, and costs about $2,000 per applicant. Once the exercises have been developed, assessors are chosen to rate the applicants going through the assessment center. These assessors typically hold positions two levels higher than the assessees and spend 4 days being trained (Spychalski, Quinones, Gaugler, & Pohley, 1997)

The In-Basket Technique. The **in-basket technique** is designed to simulate the types of daily information that appear on a manager's or an employee's desk. The technique takes its name from the wire baskets typically seen on office desks. Usually these baskets have two levels: the "in" level, which holds paperwork that must be handled, and the "out" level, which contains completed paperwork.

During the assessment center, examples of job-related paperwork are placed in a basket, and the job applicant is asked to go through the basket and respond to the paperwork as if he were actually on the job. Examples of such paperwork might include a phone message from an employee who cannot get his car started and does not know how to get to work or a memo from the accounting department stating that an expense voucher is missing.

The applicant is observed by a group of assessors, who score the applicant on several dimensions, which can include the quality of the decision, the manner in which the decision was carried out, and the order in which the applicant handled the paperwork—that is, did he start at the top of the pile or did he start with the most important papers? Research on the reliability and validity of the in-basket provides only modest support for its usefulness (Schippmann, Prien, & Katz, 1990).

Simulations. Simulation exercises are the real backbone of the assessment center because they enable assessors to see an applicant "in action." **Simulations,** which can include such diverse activities as role plays and work samples, place an applicant in a situation that is as similar as possible to one that will be encountered on the job (Kaman & Bentson, 1988). To be effective, simulations must be based on job-related behaviors and should be reasonably realistic.

A good example of a role-playing simulation is an assessment center used by a large city to select emergency telephone operators. The applicant sits before a switchboard to handle a distressed caller who is describing an emergency situation. The applicant must properly answer the call, calm the caller, and obtain the necessary information in as little time as possible. Other examples include a police applicant writing a traffic citation for an angry citizen and an applicant for a resident assistant position breaking up an argument between two roommates.

To reduce the high costs associated with actual simulations, many public organizations such as the New York Civil Service Commission and the City of Fairfax, Virginia, have developed situational exercises shown on videotape. Organizations using video simulations administer them to a group of applicants, who view the situations in the tape and then write down what they would do in each situation. The written responses are scored by personnel analysts in a fashion similar to that used with situational interviews. In a series of simulations called the B-PAD, police applicants respond orally as they view tapes of situations encountered by police officers.

The development of simulation exercises can be expensive, but prepackaged exercises can be purchased at a much lower price (Cohen, 1980). Though simulation exercises can be expensive, the cost may be money well spent as simulations result in lower adverse impact than do traditional paper-and-pencil tests (Schmitt & Mills, 2001).

Work Samples. Usually, when a simulation does not involve a situational exercise, it is called a **work sample.** Work samples were discussed earlier in this section but are listed again here because they are common assessment center exercises.

Leaderless Group Discussions. In this exercise, applicants meet in small groups and are given a job-related problem to solve or a job-related issue to discuss. For example, supervisory applicants might be asked to discuss ways to motivate employees, or resident assistant applicants might be asked to discuss ways to reduce noise in residence halls. No leader is appointed, hence the term **leaderless group discussion.** As the applicants discuss the problem or issue, they are individually rated on such dimensions as cooperativeness, leadership, and analytical skills. To better understand leaderless group discussions, complete Exercise 6–3 at the end of this chapter.

Business Games. **Business games** are exercises that allow the applicant to demonstrate such attributes as creativity, decision making, and ability to work with others. A business game in one assessment center used a series of Tinker Toy models. Four individuals joined a group and were told that they were part of a company that manufactured goods. The goods ranged from Tinker Toy tables to Tinker Toy scuba divers, and the group's task was to buy the parts, manufacture the products, and then sell the products at the highest profit in an environment in which prices constantly changed.

Evaluation of Assessment Centers

Research indicates that the assessment center has been successful in predicting a wide range of employee behavior (Gaugler, Rosenthal, Thornton, & Bentson, 1987; Arthur, Day, McNelly, & Edens, 2003). Klimoski and Strickland (1977), however, have questioned the relative value of the assessment center by pointing out that many of the validation criteria (e.g., salary and management level achieved) are measures of survival and adaptation rather than actual performance. Furthermore, other methods can predict the same criteria better and less expensively than assessment centers (Schmidt & Hunter, 1998). Thus, even though an assessment center may be excellent in predicting certain aspects of employee behavior, other, less expensive methods may be as good if not better. Furthermore, there is some question regarding the ability of an assessment center developed at one location to predict performance in similar jobs at other locations (Schmitt, Schneider, & Cohen, 1990).

Exhibit 6.13 Biodata questionnaire

1. Member of high school student government?
   ☐ No   ☐ Yes

2. Number of jobs in past 5 years?
   ☐ 1   ☐ 2   ☐ 3–5   ☐ More than 5

3. Length of time at present address?
   ☐ Less than 1 year   ☐ 1–3 years
   ☐ 4–5 years   ☐ More than 5 years

4. Transportation to work:
   ☐ Walk   ☐ Bike   ☐ Own car
   ☐ Bus   ☐ Ride with a friend   ☐ Other

5. Education:
   ☐ Some high school
   ☐ High school diploma or G.E.D.
   ☐ Some college
   ☐ Associate's degree
   ☐ Bachelor's degree
   ☐ Master's degree
   ☐ Doctoral degree

Predicting Performance Using Prior Experience

Applicant experience is typically measured in one of four ways: experience ratings of application/resume information, biodata, reference checks, and interviews. Because interviews were discussed extensively in Chapter 5 and reference checking was discussed earlier in this chapter, only experience ratings and biodata will be discussed here.

Experience Ratings

The basis for experience ratings is the idea that past experience will predict future experience. Support for this notion comes from a meta-analysis by Quiñones, Ford, and Teachout (1995) that found a significant relationship between experience and future job performance ($r = .27$). In giving credit for experience, one must consider the amount of experience, the level of performance demonstrated during the previous experience, and how related the experience is to the current job. That is, experience by itself is not enough. Having 10 years of low-quality unrelated experience is not the same as 10 years of high-quality related experience. Sullivan (2000) suggests that there be a cap on credit for experience (e.g., no credit for more than 5 years of experience) because knowledge obtained through experience has a shelf life and paying for experience is expensive. For example, given the rapid changes in technology, would a computer programmer with 20 years of experience actually have more relevant knowledge than one with 5 years of experience?

Biodata

Biodata is a selection method that considers an applicant's life, school, military, community, and work experience. Meta-analyses have shown that biodata is a good predictor of job performance as well as the best predictor of future employee tenure (Beall, 1991; Ghiselli, 1966).

In a nutshell, a biodata instrument is an application blank or questionnaire containing questions that research has shown measure the difference between successful and unsuccessful performers on a job. Each question receives a weight that indicates how well it differentiates poor from good performers. The better the differentiation, the higher the weight. Biodata instruments have several advantages:

1. Research has shown that they can predict work behavior in many jobs, including sales, management, clerical work, mental health counseling, hourly work in processing plants, grocery clerking, fast food work, and supervising.

2. They have been able to predict criteria as varied as supervisor ratings, absenteeism, accidents, employee theft, loan defaults, sales, and tenure.

3. Unlike other methods, use of biodata results in higher organizational profit and growth (Terpstra & Rozell, 1993).

Exhibit **6.14**   Biodata weighting process

Variable	Long Tenure (%)	Short Tenure (%)	Differences in Percentages	Unit Weight
Education				
High school	40	80	−40	−1
Bachelor's	59	15	+44	+1
Masters	1	5	−4	0

4. Biodata instruments are easy to use, quickly administered, inexpensive, and not as subject to individual bias as interviews, references, and resume evaluation.

Development of a Biodata Instrument

In the first step, information about employees is obtained in one of two ways: the file approach or the questionnaire approach. With the **file approach**, we obtain information from personnel files on employees' previous employment, education, interests, and demographics. As mentioned in the discussion of archival research in Chapter 1, the major disadvantage of the file approach is that information is often missing or incomplete.

Second, we can create a biographical questionnaire that is administered to all employees and applicants. An example is shown in Exhibit 6.13. The major drawback to the **questionnaire approach** is that information cannot be obtained from employees who have quit or been fired.

After the necessary information has been obtained, an appropriate criterion is chosen. As will be discussed in detail in Chapter 7, a criterion is a measure of work behavior such as quantity, absenteeism, or tenure. It is essential that a chosen criterion be relevant, reliable, and fairly objective. To give an example of developing a biodata instrument with a poor criterion, I was once asked to help reduce absenteeism in an organization by selecting applicants who had a high probability of superior future attendance. When initial data were gathered, it was realized that absenteeism was not an actual problem for this company. Less than half of the workforce had missed more than 1 day in 6 months; but the company perceived a problem because a few key workers had missed many days of work. Thus, using biodata (or any other selection device) to predict a nonrelevant criterion would not have saved the organization any money.

Once a criterion has been chosen, employees are split into two **criterion groups** based on their criterion scores. For example, if tenure is selected as the criterion measure, employees who have worked for the company for at least 1 year might be placed into the "long tenure" group, whereas workers who quit or were fired in less than 1 year would be placed in the "short tenure" group. If enough employees are available, the upper and lower 27% of performers can be used to establish the two groups (Hogan, 1994).

Once employee data have been obtained and the criterion and criterion groups chosen, each piece of employee information is compared with criterion group membership. The purpose of this stage is to determine which pieces of information will distinguish the members of the high criterion group from those in the low criterion group. Traditionally, the **vertical percentage method** has been used to do this. Percentages are calculated for each group on each item. The percentage of a particular response for the low group is subtracted from the percentage of the same response in the high group to obtain a weight for that item. An example of this weighting process is shown in Exhibit 6.14. It is important to ensure that the weights make rational sense. Items that make sense are more face valid and thus easier to defend in court than items that are empirically valid but don't make rational sense (Stokes & Toth, 1996).

Once weights have been assigned to the items, the information is weighted and then summed to form a **composite score** for each employee. Composite scores are then correlated with the criterion to determine whether the newly created biodata instrument will significantly predict the criterion. Although this procedure sounds complicated, it actually is fairly easy although time-consuming.

A problem with creating a biodata instrument is *sample size*. To create a reliable and valid biodata instrument, it is desirable to have data from hundreds of employees. For most organizations, however, such large sample sizes are difficult if not impossible to obtain. In creating a biodata instrument with a small sample, the risk of using items that do not really predict the criterion increases. This issue is important because most industrial psychologists advise that employees should be split into two samples when a biodata instrument is created: One sample, the **derivation sample**, is used to form the weights; the other sample, the **hold-out sample**, is used to double-check the selected items and weights. Although this sample splitting sounds like a great idea, it is not practical when dealing with a small or moderate sample size.

Research by Schmitt, Coyle, and Rauschenberger (1977) suggests that there is less chance of error when a sample is not split. Discussion on whether to split samples is bound to continue in the years ahead, but because many human resource professionals will be dealing with relatively small numbers of employees, it might be best to create and validate a biodata instrument without splitting employees into derivation and hold-out samples.

A final issue to consider is the sample used to create the biodata instrument. Responses of current employees can be used to select the items and create the weights that will be applied to applicants. Stokes Hogan, and Snell (1993) found that incumbents and applicants respond in very different ways, indicating that the use of incumbents to create and scale items may reduce validity. To make the biodata process more clear, complete the Biodata Exercise on your CD-ROM.

Criticisms of Biodata

Even though biodata does a good job of predicting future employee behavior, it has been criticized on two major points. The first holds that the validity of biodata may not be stable—that is, its ability to predict employee behavior decreases with time. For example, Wernimont (1962) found that only three questions retained their predictive validity over the 5-year period of 1954 to 1959. Similar results were reported by Hughes, Dunn, and Baxter (1956).

Other research (Brown, 1978), however, suggests that declines in validity found in earlier studies may have resulted from small samples in the initial development of the biodata instrument. Brown used data from more than 10,000 life insurance agents to develop his biodata instrument, but data from only 85 agents were used to develop the biodata instrument that was earlier criticized by Wernimont (1962). Brown (1978) compared the validity of his original sample (1933) with those from samples taken 6 years later (1939) and 38 years later (1971). The results indicated that the same items that significantly predicted the criterion in 1933 predicted at similar levels in 1971.

A study of the use of a biodata instrument created in one organization and used in 24 others found that the validity generalized across all organizations (Carlson, Scullen, Schmidt, Rothstein, & Erwin, 1999). Thus, biodata may be more stable across time and locations than was earlier thought (Rothstein, Schmidt, Erwin, Owens, & Sparks, 1990; Schmidt & Rothstein, 1994).

The second criticism is that some biodata items may not meet the legal requirements stated in the *Uniform Guidelines*, the federal guidelines that establish fair hiring methods. Of greatest concern is that certain biodata items might lead to racial or sexual discrimination. For example, consider the selection item "distance from work." Applicants who live close to work might get more points than applicants who live farther away. The item may lead to racial discrimination if the organization is located in a predominantly white area. Removal of such discriminatory items, however, should eliminate most legal problems while still allowing for significant predictive validity (Reilly & Chao, 1982). Though biodata instruments are valid and no more prone to adverse impact than other selection methods, the fact that applicants view them and personality tests as being the least job-related selection methods (Smither, Reilly, Millsap, Pearlman, & Stoffey, 1993) may increase the chance of a lawsuit *being filed*, but not the chance of *losing* a lawsuit.

To make biodata instruments less disagreeable to critics, Gandy and Dye (1989) developed four standards to consider for each potential item:

1. The item must deal with events under a person's control (e.g., a person would have no control over birth order but would have control over the number of speeding tickets received).
2. The item must be job related.
3. The answer to the item must be verifiable (e.g., a question about how many jobs an applicant has had is verifiable, but a question about the applicant's favorite type of book is not).
4. The item must not invade an applicant's privacy (asking why an applicant quit a job is permissible, asking about an applicant's sex life is usually not).

Even though these four standards eliminated many potential items, Gandy and Dye (1989) still obtained a validity coefficient of .33. Just as impressive as the high validity coefficient was that the biodata instrument showed good prediction for African Americans, whites, and Hispanics.

The third criticism is that biodata can be faked, a charge that has been made against every selection method except work samples and ability tests. Research indicates that applicants do in fact respond to items in socially desirable ways (Stokes et al., 1993). However, warning applicants of the presence of a lie scale (Kluger & Colella, 1993) and using objective, verifiable items (Becker & Colquitt, 1992; Shaffer, Saunders, & Owens, 1986) will reduce this tendency to lie. Furthermore, it is uncertain if applicants who lie will actually score higher on a biodata instrument (Crosby, 1990).

Predicting Performance Using Personality, Interest, and Character

Personality Inventories

Personality inventories are becoming increasingly popular as an employee selection method, in part because they predict performance better than was once thought, and in part because they result in lower adverse impact than do ability tests. Personality inventories fall into one of two categories based on their intended purpose: measurement of types of normal personality or measurement of psychopathology (abnormal personality).

Tests of Normal Personality

Tests of normal personality measure the traits exhibited by normal individuals in everyday life. Examples of such traits are extraversion, shyness, assertiveness, and friendliness. Tests of normal personality have been criticized in the personnel field, primarily because few personnel professionals have the knowledge to use the tests properly and, until the past decade or so, personality tests had not shown much predictive validity.

Another problem with personality tests is that the thousands of available tests measure thousands of different types of personalities. The problem is not so much in the tests themselves as with the methods used to construct the personality dimensions measured by the tests. The number and type of personality dimensions measured by a test are usually determined in one of three ways: theory based, statistically based, and empirically-based. The number of dimensions in a *theory-based test* is identical to the number postulated by a well-known theorist. For example, the Myers-Briggs has four scales and is based on the personality theory of Carl Jung, whereas the Edwards Personal Preference Schedule, with 15 dimensions, is based on a theory by Henry Murray. The number of dimensions in a *statistically based test* is determined through a statistical process called factor analysis. The most well-known test of this type, the 16-PF, was created by Raymond Cattell and, as its name implies, contains 16 dimensions. The number and location of dimensions under which items fall in an *empirically keyed test* is determined by grouping answers given by people known to possess a certain characteristic. For example, in developing the Minnesota Multiphasic Personality Inventory (MMPI), hundreds of items were administered to groups of psychologically healthy people and to people known to have certain psychological problems such as paranoia. Items that were endorsed more often by paranoid patients than healthy individuals were keyed under the paranoia dimension of the MMPI.

Though there is some disagreement, psychologists today generally agree there are five main personality dimensions. Popularly known as the *Big Five*, these dimensions are openness to experience (bright, inquisitive), conscientiousness (reliable, dependable), extraversion (outgoing, friendly), agreeableness (works well with others, a team player), and emotional stability (not anxious or tense).

Examples of common tests of normal personality used in employee selection include the Hogan Personality Inventory, California Psychological Inventory, NEO, and the 16-PF. To better understand personality tests, complete the Employee Personality Inventory found in Exercise 6–4 at the end of this chapter.

Meta-analyses by Tett, Jackson, and Rothstein (1991), Barrick and Mount (1991), Tett, Jackson, Rothstein, and Reddon (1994), and Hurtz and Donovan (2000) indicate that objective personality tests are useful in predicting performance. However, the meta-analyses disagree regarding which of the Big Five dimensions is most related to performance. Probably the best interpretation of these conflicting meta-analyses is that personality can significantly predict performance, conscientiousness is the best predictor in most situations, and that the validity of the other four personality dimensions is dependent on the type of job and criterion for which the test is being validated.

Tests of Psychopathology

Tests of psychopathology (abnormal behavior) determine if individuals have serious psychological problems such as depression, bipolar disorder, and schizophrenia. Though used extensively by clinical psychologists, these tests are seldom used by I/O psychologists except in the selection of law enforcement officers. Because the courts consider tests of psychopathology to be "medical tests," they can only be administered after a conditional offer of employment has been made to an applicant.

Tests of psychopathology are generally scored in one of two ways: objectively or projectively. **Projective tests** provide the respondent with unstructured tasks such as describing ink blots and drawing pictures. Because projective tests are of questionable reliability and validity (Lilienfeld, Wood, & Garb, 2001) and are time-consuming and expensive, they are rarely used in employee selection. Common tests in this category also include the **Rorschach Ink Blot Test** and the **Thematic Apperception Test (TAT)**.

Objective tests are structured so that the respondent is limited to a few answers that will be scored by standardized keys. By far the most popular and heavily studied test of this type is the revised **Minnesota Multiphasic Personality Inventory (MMPI-2)**. Another test in this category is the Millon Clinical Multiaxial Inventory (MCMI-III).

Interest Inventories

As the name implies, these tests are designed to tap vocational interests. The most commonly used **interest inventory** is the **Strong Interest Inventory (SII)**, which asks individuals to indicate whether they like or dislike 325 items such as bargaining, repairing electrical wiring, or taking responsibility. The answers to these questions provide a profile that shows how similar a person is to people already employed in 89 occupations that have been classified into 23 basic interest scales and six general occupational themes. The theory behind these tests is that an individual with interests similar to those of people in a particular field will more likely be satisfied in that field than in a field composed of people whose interests are dissimilar. Other popular interest inventories include the Minnesota Vocational Interest Inventory, the Kuder Occupational Interest Inventory, and the California Occupational Preference System.

Interest inventories are often used in *vocational counseling* (helping people find the careers for which they are best suited). Even though scores on interest inventories have poor validity in selecting employees (Schmidt & Hunter, 1998), a meta-analysis by Morris and Campion (2003) found that employees whose interests are congruent with those of the job are more satisfied and perform at higher levels than employees whose interests are not congruent with the job. To get a better feel for interest inventories, complete the short form of the Aamodt Vocational Interest Inventory (AVIS) found in Exercise 6–5 at the end of this chapter.

Integrity Tests

Integrity tests (also called *honesty tests*) tell an employer the probability that an applicant would steal money or merchandise. Honesty tests are used mostly in the retail area and more than 9 million are sold each year. Such extensive use is due to the fact that 42% of retail employees, 62% of fast food employees, and

32% of hospital employees have admitted stealing from their employers (Jones & Terris, 1989). One study estimates that 50% of employees with access to cash steal from their employers (Wimbush & Dalton, 1997). Dishonest employees steal $10.37 for every dollar stolen by shoplifters (Washburn, 1997).

Prior to the 1990s, employers used both electronic and paper-and-pencil honesty tests to screen applicants. In 1988, however, the U.S. Congress passed the Employee Polygraph Protection Act making general use of electronic honesty tests, such as the **polygraph** and the **voice stress analyzer,** illegal except in a few situations involving law enforcement agencies and national security. The law did, however, allow the use of paper-and-pencil integrity tests.

Paper-and-pencil integrity tests fall into one of two categories: overt and personality-based (Sackett & Wanek, 1996). **Overt integrity tests** are based on the premise that a person's attitudes about theft as well as his previous theft behavior will accurately predict his future honesty. Overt integrity tests measure attitudes by asking the test-taker to estimate the frequency of theft in society, how harsh penalties against thieves should be, how easy it is to steal, how often he has personally been tempted to steal, how often his friends have stolen, and how often he personally has stolen. **Personality-based integrity tests** are more general in that they tap a variety of personality traits thought to be related to a wide range of counterproductive behavior such as theft, absenteeism, and violence. Overt tests are more reliable and valid in predicting theft and other counterproductive behaviors than are personality-based tests (Ones, Viswesvaran, & Schmidt, 1993; Snyman, et al., 1991). In addition to predicting counterproductive behavior, both overt and personality-based integrity tests have been shown to predict job performance (Ones et al., 1993) and have low levels of adverse impact against minorities (Viswesvaran & Ones, 1997). To see how integrity tests work, complete Exercise 6–6 at the end of this chapter.

There are many integrity tests on the market, several of which do a decent job of predicting either polygraph results or admissions of theft (Ones, et al., 1993; Snyman, et al., 1991). Unfortunately, few studies have attempted to correlate test scores with actual theft. Of course, these would be difficult to conduct. Instead, the validity of honesty tests has been determined by comparing test scores with these indicators:

- Polygraph test results
- Self-admissions of theft
- Shrinkage (the amount of goods lost by a store)
- Known groups (e.g., priests versus convicts)
- Future theft

Unfortunately, all of these measures have problems. If polygraph results are used, the researcher is essentially comparing integrity test scores with the scores of a test—the polygraph—that has been made illegal partly because of questions about its accuracy. If self-admissions are used, the researcher is relying on dishonest people to be honest about their criminal history. If **shrinkage** is used, the researcher does not know which of the employees is responsible for the theft or, for that matter, what percentage of the shrinkage can be attributed to employee theft as opposed to customer theft or incidental breakage. Even if actual employee theft is used, the test may only predict employees who *get caught* stealing as opposed to those who steal and do not get caught. The problems with known-group comparisons were discussed in great detail in Chapter 4.

As indicated in this discussion, integrity tests do a good job of predicting theft, especially when one considers that not all theft is caused by a *personal tendency* to steal (Murphy, 1993). Normally honest people might steal from an employer due to *economic pressure* caused by factors such as high debts or financial emergencies or by an organizational culture in which it is considered *normal to steal* (e.g., "It's OK because everyone takes food home with them"). Employee theft can also be the result of a *reaction to organizational policy* such as layoffs or a change in rules that employees perceive as unfair. To reduce theft caused by situational factors, nontesting methods such as increased security, explicit policy, and availability of appeal and suggestion systems are needed.

Although paper-and-pencil honesty tests are inexpensive and may be useful in predicting theft, they also have serious drawbacks. The most important disadvantage might be that males have higher failure rates than do females, and younger people have higher failure rates than do older people. Adverse impacts on these two groups pose little legal threat, but telling the parents of a 17-year-old boy that their son has just failed an honesty test is not the best way to foster good public relations. Failing an honesty test has a much greater psychological impact than failing a spatial relations test. For these reasons, some legal experts advise against letting applicants know they were not hired because they failed an honesty test (Douglas, Feld, & Asquith, 1989).

Graphology

An interesting method to select employees used by more than 6,000 U.S. organizations (Bianchi, 1996), 8% of United Kingdom, and 75% of French organizations (Leonard, 1999b) is handwriting analysis, or **graphology.** The idea behind handwriting analysis is that the way people write reveals their personality, which in turn should indicate work performance.

To analyze a person's writing, a graphologist looks at the size, slant, width, regularity, and pressure of a writing sample (Leonard, 1999b). From these writing characteristics, information about temperament, mental traits, social traits, work traits, and moral traits is obtained (Currer-Briggs, 1971).

Research on graphology has revealed interesting findings. First, graphologists are consistent in their judgments about script features (Lockowandt, 1976)

Exhibit **6.15** Handwriting analysis research

Study	Year	Country	Sample	Criterion	Validity
Sonnemann & Kernan	1962	Germany	Executives	Supervisor ratings	.74
Keinan & Barak	1984	Israel	Military officers	Training success	.26
Ben-Shakhar et al.	1986	Israel	Bank tellers	Supervisor ratings	.25
Rafaeli & Klimoski	1983	U.S.A.	Salesmen	Sales performance	.04
Rafaeli & Klimoski	1983	U.S.A.	Salesmen	Supervisor ratings	.00
Zdep & Weaver	1967	U.S.A.	Salesmen	Sales commissions	−.05

but not in their interpretation about what these features mean (Keinan & Barak, 1984; Rafaeli & Klimoski, 1983). Second, trained graphologists are no more accurate or reliable at interpreting handwriting samples than untrained undergraduates (Rafaeli & Klimoski, 1983) or psychologists (Ben-Shakhar, Bar-Hillel, Bilu, Ben-Abba, & Flug, 1986; Jansen, 1973). Finally, as shown in Exhibit 6.15, handwriting analysis may predict performance in other countries but not in the United States. This mysterious finding might explain why graphology is used more in Europe than in the United States.

Predicting Performance Limitations Due to Medical and Psychology Problems

As mentioned in Chapter 3, the Americans with Disabilities Act (ADA) limits the consideration of medical and psychological problems to those that keep the employee from performing essential job functions.

Drug Testing

Drug testing certainly is one of the most controversial testing methods used by human resource professionals. The reason for its high usage is that 16% of employees admit to using drugs in the past month (Collins, 2001) and human resource professionals believe that not only is illegal drug use dangerous but also that many employees are under the influence of drugs at work. Their beliefs are supported by research that indicates illegal drug users are more likely to miss work (Bahls, 1998; Normand, Salyards, & Mahoney, 1990), 16 times as likely to use health care benefits (Bahls, 1998), and more likely to be fired (Normand et al., 1990), and they have 3.6 times as many accidents on the job (Cadrain, 2003) as nondrug users. One consulting firm estimates that a substance-abusing employee costs his employer $7,000 per year in lost productivity, absenteeism, and medical costs (Payne, 1997). Though the few available

studies conclude that applicants testing positive for drugs will engage in some counterproductive behaviors, some authors (e.g., Morgan, 1990) believe these studies are terribly flawed.

Because of such statistics, organizations are increasing their drug testing before applicants are hired. In fact, as of 2001, 80% of U.S. companies were testing for drugs (Ozminkowski, Mark, Cangianelli, & Walsh, 2001). The increase in drug testing has resulted in fewer applicants testing positive for drugs: 5% in 1997 compared to 11% in 1990 (Rubis, 1998). According to a survey by the Substance Abuse and Mental Health Services Administration, construction workers (17%), food preparation workers (16.3%), restaurant servers (15.4%), and writers, athletes, and designers (13.1%) are the most common drug users, whereas police officers (1%), clerical staff (2.2%), teachers (2.3%), and child care workers (2.6%) are the least common users of drugs. When applicants test positive for drugs, 98% of their job offers are withdrawn. When current employees test positive, 25% of organizations fire the employee and 66% refer the employee for counseling and treatment (Greenberg, 1996).

In general, applicants seem to accept drug testing as being reasonably fair (Mastrangelo, 1997; Truxillo, Normandy, & Bauer, 2001). Not surprisingly, compared to people who have never tried drugs, current drug users think drug testing is less fair and previous drug users think drug testing is less fair if it results in termination but not when the consequence for being caught is rehabilitation (Truxillo, Normandy, & Bauer, 2001).

Drug testing usually is done in two stages. In the first, an employee or applicant provides a urine or hair sample that is subjected to an initial screening test. The most common initial drug screens for urine are the **Enzyme Multiplied Immunoassay Technique (EMIT)** and **radioimmunoassay (RIA)**. EMIT uses enzymes as reagents, while RIA uses radioactive tagging. Both cost approximately $30 per sample. Hair-follicle testing costs approximately $50 per sample (Overman, 1999).

If the initial test for drugs is positive, then second-stage testing is done. The urine sample undergoes a more expensive confirmation test such as **thin layer**

chromatography or **gas chromatography/mass spectrometry analysis.** These tests can range anywhere from $30 to more than $100 per sample.

When both stages are used, testing is very accurate in detecting the presence of drugs. But drug tests are not able to determine whether an individual is impaired by drug use (Rosen, 1987). An employee smoking marijuana on Saturday night will test positive for the drug on Monday, even though the effects of the drug have long since gone away. Most drugs can be detected 2 to 3 days after they have been used. The exceptions are the benzodiazepines, which can be detected for 4 to 6 weeks after use; P.C.P., which can be detected for 2 to 4 weeks; and marijuana, which can be detected up to 5 days for the casual user and up to 30 days for the frequent user. Testing conducted on hair follicles rather than urine samples can detect drug usage in the past 90 days (Curry, 1997; Thistle, 1997). A disadvantage to testing hair follicles is that it takes a few days before drugs will be detected in the hair; thus it is not a good method to determine if an employee is currently under the influence (Stevenson & Williamson, 1995).

Because positive drug tests have a certain degree of uncertainty, if an applicant fails a preemployment drug test, he can usually reapply 6 months later. With such a policy, there are few legal pitfalls.

In the public sector or in the union environment, however, drug testing becomes complicated when it occurs after applicants are hired. Testing of employees usually takes one of three forms:

1. All employees or randomly selected employees are tested at predetermined times.
2. All employees or randomly selected employees are tested at random times.
3. Employees who have been involved in an accident or disciplinary action are tested following the incident.

The second form is probably the most effective in terms of punishing or preventing drug usage, but the third form of testing is legally the most defensible (Veglahn, 1989).

Psychological Exams

In jobs involving public safety (e.g., law enforcement, nuclear power, transportation), it is common for employers to give psychological exams to applicants after a conditional offer of hire has been made. If the applicant fails the exam, the offer is rescinded. Psychological exams usually consist of an interview by a clinical psychologist, an examination of the applicant's life history, and the administration of one or more of the psychological tests discussed earlier in this chapter.

Medical Exams

In jobs requiring physical exertion, many employers require that a medical exam be taken after a condi-

tional offer of hire has been made. In these exams, the physician is given a copy of the job description and asked to determine if there are any medical conditions that will keep the employee from safely performing the job.

Comparison of Techniques

After reading this chapter, you are probably asking the same question that industrial psychologists have been asking for years: Which method of selecting employees is best?

Validity

As shown in Exhibit 6.16, it is clear that the unstructured interview, education, interest inventories, and some personality traits are not good predictors of future employee performance for most jobs. It is also clear that ability, work samples, biodata, and structured interviews do a fairly good job of predicting future employee performance.

Over the past few years, researchers have been interested in determining which *combination* of selection tests is best. Though much more research is needed on this topic, it appears that the most valid selection battery includes a cognitive ability test and either a work sample, an integrity test, or a structured interview (Schmidt & Hunter, 1998).

Even though some selection techniques are better than others, *all* are potentially useful methods for selecting employees. In fact, a properly constructed selection battery usually contains a variety of tests that tap different dimensions of a job. Take, for example, the job of police officer. We might use a physical ability test to make sure the applicant has the strength and speed necessary to chase suspects and defend himself, a situational interview to tap his decision-making ability, a personality test to ensure that he has the traits needed for the job, and a background check to determine whether he has a history of antisocial behavior.

The late industrial psychologist Dan Johnson likened the selection process to a fishing trip. During our trip, we can try to catch one huge fish to make our meal or we can catch several small fish that, when cooked and placed on a plate, make the same size meal as one large fish. With selection tests, we try for one or two tests that will predict performance at a high level. But by combining several tests with smaller validities, we can predict performance just as well as with one test with a very high validity.

Legal Issues

As you might recall from Chapters 3 and 4, methods used to select employees are most prone to legal challenge when they result in adverse impact, invade an applicant's privacy, and do not appear to be job related (lack face validity). As shown in Exhibit 6.17, cognitive

Exhibit 6.16 Validity of selection techniques

	Observed	True	k	N	Meta-Analysis
Performance					
Work sample		.54			Hunter & Hunter (1984)
Cognitive ability		.51			Schmidt & Hunter (1998)
Job knowledge		.48			Hunter & Hunter (1984)
Biodata	.36	n/a	22	20,905	Beall (1991)
Structured interview	.34	.57	60	6,723	Huffcutt & Arthur (1994)
Behavioral description interviews	.31	.51	22	2,721	Huffcutt et al. (2003)
Situational interviews	.26	.43	32	2,815	Huffcutt et al. (2003)
Situational judgment tests	.26	.34	102	10,640	McDaniel et al. (2001)
Assessment centers	.28	.38	258	83,761	Arthur et al. (2003)
Experience	.22	.27	44	25,911	Quiñones et al. (1995)
Integrity tests	.21	.34	222	68,772	Ones et al. (1993)
Personality (self-efficacy)	.19	.23	10	1,122	Judge & Bono (2001)
Personality (self-esteem)	.18	.26	40	5,145	Judge & Bono (2001)
Grades	.16	.32	71	13,984	Roth et al. (1996)
Personality (locus of control)	.14	.22	35	4,310	Judge & Bono (2001)
Personality (conscientiousness)	.15	.24	42	7,342	Hurtz & Donovan (2000)
Personality (overall)	.12	.17	97	13,521	Tett et al. (1994)
Unstructured interview	.11	.20	15	7,308	Huffcutt & Arthur (1994)
Reference checks	.10	.26			Hunter & Hunter (1984)
Personality (emotional stability)	.09	.15	35	5,027	Hurtz & Donovan (2000)
Personality (agreeableness)	.07	.12	38	5,803	Hurtz & Donovan (2000)
Education		.10			Hunter & Hunter (1984)
Interest inventories		.10			Hunter & Hunter (1984)
Personality (extraversion)	.06	.09	37	5,809	Hurtz & Donovan (2000)
Personality (openness)	.03	.06	33	4,881	Hurtz & Donovan (2000)
Graphology		.02			Schmidt & Hunter (1998)
Tenure					
Biodata	.28	n/a	27	70,737	Beall (1991)
Training Proficiency					
Cognitive ability		.56			Hunter & Hunter (1984)
Integrity		.38			Schmidt et al. (1994)
Biodata		.30			Hunter & Hunter (1984)
Personality (extraversion)	.15	.26	17	3,101	Barrick & Mount (1991)
Personality (openness)	.14	.25	14	2,700	Barrick & Mount (1991)
Personality (conscientiousness)	.13	.23	17	3,585	Barrick & Mount (1991)
References		.23			Hunter & Hunter (1984)
Education		.20			Hunter & Hunter (1984)
Vocational interest		.18			Hunter & Hunter (1984)
Personality (emotional stability)	.04	.07	19	3,283	Barrick & Mount (1991)
Personality (agreeableness)	.04	.06	19	3,685	Barrick & Mount (1991)

Note: Observed = mean observed validity; True = observed validity corrected for study artifacts; k = number of samples in the meta-analysis, N = total number of subjects in the meta-analysis

Selection Technique	*d* score		Meta-Analysis
	White-Black	White-Hispanic	
Cognitive ability	1.10	.72	Roth et al. (2001)
GPA	.78		Roth & Bobko (2000)
Job sample/job knowledge	.38	.00	Schmitt, Clause, & Pulakos (1999)
Biodata	.33		Bobko, Roth, & Potosky (1999)
Structured interview	.23		Huffcutt & Roth (1998)
High school diploma	.20	.52	Aamodt (2002)
Bachelor's degree	.18	.26	Aamodt (2002)
Personality	.09		Schmitt, Clause, & Pulakos (1999)
Integrity tests	.07	−.05	Ones & Viswesvaran (1998)

ability and GPA will result in the highest levels of adverse impact whereas integrity tests, structured interviews, and personality tests will result in the lowest levels (in viewing this table, you might want to review the concept of *d* scores (discussed in Chapter 1). In terms of face validity, applicants perceive interviews, work samples/simulations, and resumes as being the most job related/fair and graphology, biodata, and personality tests as being the least job related/fair (Rynes & Connerley, 1993; Smither et al., 1993; Steiner & Gilliland, 1996).

Rejecting Applicants

Once a decision has been made regarding which applicants will be hired, those who will not be hired must be notified. As mentioned earlier in the chapter, applicants who are rejected should still be treated well because they are potential customers and potential applicants for other positions that might become available in the organization (Brice & Waung, 1995; Waung & Brice, 2003). With this in mind, what is the best way to reject an applicant? Even though specific rules of courtesy will be discussed, only one study has indicated what effect, if any, different kinds of **rejection letters** have on an applicant's attitude or behavior.

The best type of letter to use is not known, but it is believed that a few rules should be followed when rejecting an applicant. First, always respond to an application as quickly as possible. If you think back on your job-hunting experiences, nothing can be more irritating than never hearing from a company or waiting a long period of time before being notified of the status of your application. Once it is known that certain applicants will not be hired, they should be notified so that they can continue their job hunting. Excuses about not having the funds to notify

applicants are probably not justified when one considers the ill feelings that may result from not contacting applicants.

Second, be as personable and as specific as possible in the letter. With the use of mail merge options in word processing programs, it is fairly easy to individually address each letter, express the company's appreciation for applying, and perhaps explain who was hired and what their qualifications were.

Aamodt and Peggans (1988) found that rejection letters differ to the extent that they do or do not contain the following types of responses:

- A personally addressed and signed letter
- The company's appreciation to the applicant for applying for a position with the company
- A compliment about the applicant's qualifications
- A comment about the high qualifications possessed by the other applicants
- Information about the individual who was actually hired
- A wish of good luck in future endeavors
- A promise to keep the applicant's resume on file

Furthermore, it was found that a statement about the individual who received the job actually increased applicant satisfaction with both the selection process and the organization (Aamodt & Peggans, 1988; Gilliand, Groth, Baker, Dew, Polly, & Langdon, 2001).

Perhaps the most important thing to consider when writing a letter of rejection is to be honest. Do not tell an applicant that his resume will be kept on file if the files for each job opening will not be used. Adair and Pollen (1985) think rejection letters treat job applicants like unwanted lovers; they either beat around the bush ("There were many qualified applicants") or stall for time ("We'll keep your resume on file"). A study by Brice and Waung (1995) supports these ideas as most organizations either never formally reject applicants, or when they do, they take an average of almost a month to do so.

Chapter Summary

In this chapter you learned that

- references typically don't predict performance due to such factors as leniency, poor reliability, fear of legal ramifications, and a variety of extraneous factors.
- the trait approach to scoring letters of recommendation is a valid method of predicting future performance.
- reliability, validity, cost, and potential for legal problems should be considered when choosing the right type of employment test for a particular situation.
- personality, interest, ability, job knowledge, integrity, and physical agility tests; biodata; assessment centers; and simulations are potential methods for selecting employees.
- writing a well-designed rejection letter can have important organizational consequences.

Critical Thinking Questions

1. Should an organization provide reference information for former employees?
2. What should be the most important factor in choosing a selection method?
3. What selection methods are most valid?
4. Should employers test employees for drugs?
5. Are integrity tests fair and accurate?

To learn more about the issues discussed in this chapter, point your browser to

http://www.infotrac-college.com/wadsworth

and enter one of these search terms:

resume fraud

negligent hiring

negligent references

employment psychological tests

employment personality tests

vocational counseling

honesty testing

mandatory drug testing

Exercise 6–1
Trait Approach

In Chapter 6, the trait approach to scoring letters of recommendation was discussed. Below, you will find two letters of recommendation. Using the information in your text, score each of the letters using the trait approach by underlining the traits and then counting the number of traits in each of the five categories. Which of the applicants would you hire for the job of an accountant?

Dimension	Elijah Craig	James Beam
Mental Agility	_____	_____
Vigor	_____	_____
Urbanity	_____	_____
Cooperation–Consideration	_____	_____
Dependability–Reliability	_____	_____

Dear Mr. Daniels:

It is a pleasure to write this letter in support of Mr. Elijah Craig. I have known Elijah for 10 years as he was an accounting associate in our firm.

Elijah is a very dependable, careful, and precise person. He amazes all of us at the office with his attention to detail and with the accuracy of his reports. To the best of my knowledge, Elijah always has his work completed on time. Elijah is a considerate employee who is a real team player.

If you have any questions or need more information about Elijah, please let me know.

Dear Mr. Daniels:

It is a pleasure to write this letter in support of Mr. James Beam. I have known Jim for 10 years as he was an accounting associate in our firm.

Jim is one of the most intelligent, original, and creative individuals I have ever met. He is always developing new ideas. In addition to being so smart, Jim has a great sense of humor, is very friendly, and always cheerful.

If you have any questions or need more information about Jim, please let me know.

Exercise 6–2
Cognitive Ability

One of the best predictors of performance is cognitive ability. The following few pages contain sample items from the Basic Cognitive Ability Test (BCAT). The BCAT is used by career advisers to test employees' basic skills.

Section I: Basic Math

Circle the correct answer for each of the math questions. You may NOT use a calculator.

1. A bus is traveling 60 miles per hour. How many miles down the road will the bus be in 5 minutes?
   a) 5 miles   b) 6 miles   c) 12 miles   d) none of the above

2. It takes 25 minutes to cut and style someone's hair. If you cut and styled nine customers' hair in 1 day, how many minutes would you have spent working?
   a) 125   b) 175   c) 225   d) none of the above

3. A pharmaceutical company sells a drug to a store for $9.00 per dose. The store increases the price it charges customers to $20 per dose. How much profit would the store make on 20 doses?
   a) $40   b) $400   c) $580   d) none of the above

4. If it costs 16 cents a minute to call from 5 p.m. to 11 p.m. and 10 cents a minute to call from 11:00 p.m. to 8:00 a.m., how much would it cost if a person talked to a friend from 10:52 p.m. to 11:18 p.m.?
   a) $2.98   b) $3.00   c) $3.08   d) none of the above

5. A customer gives you a Kennedy half-dollar, a five dollar bill, three dimes, six nickels, and four pennies. How much did the customer give you?
   a) $6.04   b) $6.10   c) $6.14   d) none of the above

Section IV: Logic

6. What number would come next?
   46   42   38   34   _____

7. Which of the following words does not fit with the others?
   creek   stream   river   lake   brook   _____

   James King is 5'9" tall. Kelly King is 5'7" tall. Kelly's brother, Steven, is 2 inches taller than James. James's uncle, Dave, is the same height as Kelly. Dave's wife, Patty, is the same height as Steven.

8. Kelly is James's wife.
   a) True   b) False   c) not enough information

9. Dave is taller than Kelly.
   a) True   b) False   c) not enough information

10. Dave is taller than his wife.
    a) True   b) False   c) not enough information

Section III: Vocabulary

For each of the following sentences, indicate which of the three words is most similar in meaning to the word that is bold faced.

11. Airline fares are constantly **fluctuating.**
     a) changing   b) increasing   c) decreasing

12. Hotels are now offering special **amenities.**
     a) prices   b) courtesies   c) schedules

13. Bob and Jane are my **colleagues.**
     a) neighbors   b) associates   c) friends

14. The **impasse** will not be easily settled.
     a) deadlock   b) argument   c) contest

15. He thought of himself as **omniscient.**
     a) all knowing   b) a scholar   c) versatile

Section IV: Grammar

For each of the sentences below, mark the letter of the part of the sentence that contains an error such as a misspelling, a grammatical error, or wrong punctuation. If there are no errors in the sentence, mark the letter "e" for correct.

16. They / were / the boys / books.   correct
         (a)   (b)   (c)   (d)   (e)

17. The car / was / moving / to fast.   correct
         (a)   (b)   (c)   (d)   (e)

18. We / believe she / is their / teacher.   correct
         (a)   (b)   (c)   (d)   (e)

19. He would'nt / stop talking / about the / accident. correct
         (a)   (b)   (c)   (d)   (e)

20. Your going / to be late / for the / meeting.   correct
         (a)   (b)   (c)   (d)   (e)

Exercise 6–3
Leaderless Group Discussion

As discussed in your text, assessment centers are often a useful method for predicting employee success on the job. One of the most common exercises in an assessment center is the leaderless group discussion. With a leaderless group discussion, several applicants are given a problem to discuss. As the group is discussing the problem, a group of assessors listens to the conversation and rates the quality of participation by each applicant.

Instructions

Below you will find a problem to use in a leaderless group discussion. Your professor will assign six students to take part in the discussion while the other students use the rating form on the following pages to evaluate the participation of each group member. Each observer should rate the behavior of two group members. Rather than use students in your class, your instructor might have you watch a video of a leaderless group discussion and rate two of the participants in the video.

Class Discussion Problem

IBM has noticed that their younger employees seem not to be as dedicated to their jobs as are older employees. The young employees tend to miss more work and often refuse to work overtime. Do you think this observation is valid, and if so, what can be done to change the attitudes and behavior of the younger workers?

_____

_____

_____

_____

_____

_____

Rating for Leaderless Group Discussion

Name of Group Member _____

Check all of the behaviors you observed for the person you were designated to watch.

Oral Communication

_____ Made clear and concise comments (did not ramble)

_____ Maintained eye contact

_____ Voice easy to understand

_____ Used proper grammar and vocabulary

_____ Fully expressed thoughts

_____ Was enthusiastic

Direction

____ Got the group started on the task

____ Ensured that the group was making progress

____ Made suggestions

Logic

____ Presented sound arguments

____ Pulled together related ideas

Sensitivity

____ Reinforced positive comments made by group members

____ Encouraged others to talk

Total number of positive behaviors checked _____

Comments

_____

_____

_____

_____

Rating for Leaderless Group Discussion

Name of Group Member _____

Check all of the behaviors that you observed for the person whom you were designated to watch.

Oral Communication

____ Made clear and concise comments (did not ramble)

____ Maintained eye contact

____ Voice easy to understand

____ Used proper grammar and vocabulary

____ Fully expressed thoughts

____ Was enthusiastic

Direction

____ Got the group started on the task

____ Ensured that the group was making progress

____ Made suggestions

Logic

____ Presented sound arguments

____ Pulled together related ideas

Sensitivity

____ Reinforced positive comments made by group members

____ Encouraged others to talk

Total number of positive behaviors checked _____

Comments

_____

_____

_____

_____

Exercise 6–4
Personality Tests

One of the techniques that can be used to select employees is personality tests. These types of tests are especially useful in jobs such as sales and teaching that involve interacting with people.

On the next page you will find the Employee Personality Inventory (EPI), a short personality test that is used mostly for seminars about understanding people but has also been fairly successful in predicting performance in several jobs.

Employee Personality Inventory

Choose the word in each pair that is most like you. Even if both words are like you, you must choose only one word. If neither word is like you, you must still choose one of the words. After completing the test, your instructor will show you how to score the test and then you can read about your personality type on the following few pages. Please note that the EPI may not be reproduced in any format without the written permission of the author of this text.

Thinking	_____
Directing	_____
Communicating	_____
Soothing	_____
Organizing	_____

1.	( ) Calm	( ) Efficient
2.	( ) Accurate	( ) Energetic
3.	( ) Original	( ) Competitive
4.	( ) Introverted	( ) Extraverted
5.	( ) Careful	( ) Bold
6.	( ) Resourceful	( ) Trusting
7.	( ) Empathic	( ) Inquiring
8.	( ) Assertive	( ) Exact
9.	( ) Playful	( ) Dominant
10.	( ) Curious	( ) Detailed
11.	( ) Precise	( ) Tolerant
12.	( ) Ambitious	( ) Helpful
13.	( ) Outgoing	( ) Imaginative
14.	( ) Talkative	( ) Agreeable
15.	( ) Enterprising	( ) Friendly
16.	( ) Persuasive	( ) Sociable
17.	( ) Patient	( ) Convincing
18.	( ) Organized	( ) Inventive
19.	( ) Conversational	( ) Self-disciplined
20.	( ) Confident	( ) Creative
21.	( ) Loyal	( ) Chatty
22.	( ) Outspoken	( ) Soft-spoken
23.	( ) Clever	( ) Socializer
24.	( ) Powerful	( ) Insightful
25.	( ) Dependable	( ) Self-assured
26.	( ) Frisky	( ) Intense
27.	( ) Peaceful	( ) Smart
28.	( ) Spontaneous	( ) Cautious
29.	( ) Innovative	( ) Systematic
30.	( ) Orderly	( ) Cooperative
31.	( ) Daring	( ) Sincere
32.	( ) Methodical	( ) Outgoing
33.	( ) Sharp	( ) Fun
34.	( ) Rebellious	( ) Punctual
35.	( ) Fun-loving	( ) Fearless
36.	( ) Bright	( ) Dynamic
37.	( ) Modest	( ) Perceptive
38.	( ) Detailed	( ) Ingenious
39.	( ) Mingler	( ) Courteous
40.	( ) Supportive	( ) Logical

Thinkers

General Personality

Often called "rebels" or "mavericks" by others, Thinkers are creative, unconventional, insightful, inventive individuals who love the process of thinking, analyzing, and creating. They challenge the status quo, create new products and ideas, and provide new ways to think of things. Though they create new products and ideas, Thinkers consider the idea the end result and seldom get excited about the process of carrying through on a project. Thinkers hate schedules, dislike rules and policy, and have little need for authority. They are free spirits and independent thinkers who value freedom and require the latitude to do things "their way." Thinkers can often be identified by the notion that they always seem to be preoccupied with thought. They can walk right by a person without even seeing him.

Thinkers are interesting people in that of the five personality types they are the most difficult to predict. They are complex people who are not easily understood or categorized. However, they do make excellent artists, writers, computer programmers, troubleshooters, engineers, and marketing analysts.

Communication Style

Thinkers communicate with others by discussing ideas, being sarcastic, creating puns, and dreaming. Their communication style is a combination of the other four styles in that they tend to be friendly like the Communicator, adventurous like the Director, and introverted like the Soother. The best way to communicate with a Thinker is to discuss the "big picture." Do not get caught up in detail. Rather than being provided with solutions to problems up front, Thinkers should be asked what they think a good solution might be.

Leadership Style

Thinkers do not seek leadership positions but can become leaders because they are often the people with the best ideas. When they do become leaders, they lead through motivation and inspiration. Others get carried away by their ideas.

Strengths

- Ability to develop new ideas and systems
- Are not afraid of change
- Can see the "big picture"
- Are good problem solvers

Weaknesses Associated with Very High Scores or Stressful Situations

- May not carry through on their ideas
- Often have problems with rules and structure
- May not always be realistic
- Are easily bored and distracted

Directors

General Personality

Directors are fast-paced, efficient, confident, assertive individuals who are more interested in quantity than quality. Directors set high goals for themselves and for others. They are highly competitive: Doing well is not enough for Directors; they want to do better than everyone else. Directors are fearless and are willing to take chances—"play it safe" is a phrase seldom uttered by a Director. They tend to be independent and are much happier working alone than with others. Their greatest strength to an organization is that, when given a job to do, they will always get the job done ahead of schedule.

More than anything, Directors fear being taken advantage of and thus are not very trusting of others. Directors also tend to be impatient and easily agitated. As a result of this impatience and lack of trust, Directors are often considered to have poor interpersonal skills.

Communication Style

Directors communicate with others in a very direct fashion. They tend to dislike small talk, would prefer to "get right to the point," and prefer executive summaries rather than pages of detail. Directors communicate best if they are told the purpose of the meeting before it occurs. Directors use eye contact when they speak and like to be given more than an average amount of personal communication space. Directors are not good at picking up subtle hints or nonverbal cues, so the best way to communicate with them is to look them in the eye and tell them exactly what you want. Directors should never be told they "must" do something as their automatic reaction is to resist threats to their freedom.

Leadership Style

Directors enjoy being "in charge" but are not always good at leadership. They tend to use a very directive style of leadership and rarely ask for the advice or approval of others. They set goals, provide direction, and expect a high level of performance from everyone. As leaders, Directors are good at quickly making tough decisions, exuding a "can do" attitude, and cutting through red tape.

Strengths

- Ability to get things done

- Willingness to take charge

- Ability to quickly make tough decisions

- Efficient use of time resulting in a high volume of work

Weaknesses Associated with Very High Scores or Stressful Situations

- Often are perceived as being too competitive

- Can be abrasive, impatient, and short with people

- Are often not good followers or team players

- Have a tendency to break rules and regulations

Communicators

General Personality

Communicators are outgoing, friendly, talkative individuals who are much more interested in people than they are in projects or paperwork. They get along well with other people and tend to mingle well in social situations. Because Communicators like fun and excitement, they are easily bored. As a result of their people skills, Communicators make excellent supervisors, teachers, and customer service representatives.

More than anything, Communicators fear not being liked and thus are not as direct with others as they at times need to be. Communicators need a lot of attention and often dislike sharing the limelight. Because of their preference for people as opposed to things, Communicators often delay work that involves data or reports.

Communication Style

Communicators talk with others in a very friendly, animated fashion. They tend to dislike business or serious discussions and would prefer to talk about fun things, exchange stories, and tell jokes. Thus, the best way to talk to a communicator is to start the conversation with an interesting topic and then slowly move toward the actual topic. Communicators are very expressive when they speak.

Leadership Style

Communicators do not necessarily seek leadership positions but often find themselves being chosen as a leader because they are well liked by others. When placed in charge, Communicators will usually adopt a participative leadership style in which they will probably call a meeting and ask for feedback from the people involved with the problem or decision.

Strengths

- Ability to talk with anyone about anything (good mingling skills)
- Good sense of humor
- Are well liked
- Can increase the morale of a group
- Are best at dealing with angry or difficult people

Weaknesses Associated with Very High Scores or Stressful Situations

- Often are late to appointments or miss work and deadlines
- Are easily bored and distracted
- Have trouble getting to the point (ramble)
- Have a tendency to gossip

Soothers

General Personality

Soothers are individuals who are calm and steady and whose greatest strength is their ability to get along with a variety of people. Soothers tend to be warm, caring people who are very loyal to their friends and their organization. Soothers enjoy stability and thus tend to keep the same friends and jobs for long periods of time. Interestingly, some evidence provided by counseling psychologists suggests that Soothers are the least likely personality type to get a divorce. Soothers tend to make excellent counselors, and if they have a high score on Thinking, also tend to be excellent computer programmers.

Soothers most fear conflict and will do almost anything to avoid it. Thus, they are inclined to allow others to take advantage of them because they will not confront others. Soothers are the most likely personality type to develop ulcers, especially if they are working with a Director. Soothers tend to set low goals for themselves, are responsive to praise, and are easily hurt by criticism.

Communication Style

Soothers communicate in a positive fashion with just about everyone. They seldom criticize others and don't want to hear others criticize them. Soothers are the most sensitive about picking up nonverbal cues and emotional states in others. They tend to listen more for the way in which things are said than for what is actually said. Soothers seldom yell, and they react poorly to those who yell at others.

Leadership Style

Soothers seldom seek leadership positions but do occasionally find themselves in leadership roles because they are good compromise candidates. That is, because they seldom have enemies, it is difficult to find a person who dislikes a Soother. When they are thrust into leadership roles, they lead by delegating work to others and then providing the emotional support necessary to complete the project. Soothers utilize a participatory leadership style in which they solicit the opinions of others before making decisions.

Strengths

- Are loyal and trusted

- Are good listeners

- Are well liked and seldom have enemies

- Are good followers, team players, and group members

Weaknesses Associated with Very High Scores or Stressful Situations

- Have difficulty making tough decisions involving people

- Tend to avoid confrontation

- Often deny that problems exist

- Are often walked on

Organizers

General Personality

Organizers are detailed, organized individuals who are more concerned with quality than with quantity. Because Organizers are perfectionists who want everything done perfectly or not done at all, they produce high-quality work. As their name implies, Organizers' greatest strength is their ability to organize people and things; they have a system for everything. Because Organizers are so compulsive, they tend to be critical of others. Due also to their love of detail, Organizers usually would rather work with data than with people.

Organizers believe in the system and in authority. They follow rules, create new regulations and policies, and expect others to also believe in and follow the system. Organizers are hard workers who do what it takes to get a job done properly. Organizers are on time to appointments and expect others to be as well. Unlike Thinkers and Communicators, Organizers enjoy carrying out the details of ideas; they are doers rather than talkers or thinkers.

Communication Style

Organizers communicate with others in a detailed, factual manner. They don't want to chit-chat, and they don't want general ideas. They are basically the Jack Webbs of the world in that they prefer "just the facts." Organizers are poor at noticing nonverbal cues and can be even worse at understanding the real meaning behind what is being said. They pay attention only to the details of the conversation.

Leadership Style

Organizers lead by organization and strategy. They have an uncanny ability to take the knowledge and resources of others and organize them so that a task can be accomplished. Like Soothers, Organizers tend to delegate authority but demand that things be done "by the book."

Strengths

- Have strong organizational skills

- Are good risk managers

- Understand the process

- Produce high-quality work

Weaknesses Associated with Very High Scores or Stressful Situations

- Have difficulty seeing the big picture

- Are resistant to change

- Are overly critical

- Are often inflexible

Exercise 6–5
Interest Inventories

In this exercise, you will get to take a shortened version of the Aamodt Vocational Interest Survey (AVIS). The AVIS is used for adult employees who are thinking about changing careers.

Directions

For each of the activities on the next two pages, rate the extent to which you might enjoy performing the activity often or for long periods of time. On the AVIS answer sheet, rate each statement using the following scale:

1.   I would absolutely hate doing this activity
2.   I would dislike doing this activity
3.   I would neither dislike nor like doing this activity (I'm neutral)
4.   I would enjoy doing this activity
5.   I would very much enjoy doing this activity

Questions

1.   Filing patients' charts in alphabetical order
2.   Calming an angry customer
3.   Testing blood samples for the presence of disease
4.   Appraising the value of real estate
5.   Calling people to determine their interest in a product
6.   Raising livestock
7.   Driving a bus
8.   Overhauling an engine
9.   Arresting a drug dealer
10. Caring for patients in a hospital
11. Evaluating the performance of an employee
12. Baking bread at a deli
13. Creating an advertising campaign

14. Entering information into a computer
15. Helping customers make travel arrangements
16. Taking X rays of an injured foot
17. Predicting the success of stocks and bonds
18. Selling automobiles at a car lot
19. Planting vegetables
20. Picking up passengers in a cab
21. Repairing a broken VCR
22. Giving first aid and CPR in an emergency situation
23. Teaching young people a topic in your favorite area
24. Making tough decisions
25. Sewing clothing
26. Writing a computer program

27. Typing letters and reports
28. Answering questions about products or services
29. Cleaning teeth
30. Appraising the value of a damaged car
31. Asking people to donate money to charity
32. Baling hay
33. Delivering packages to stores
34. Fixing leaks in household plumbing
35. Driving an ambulance through the streets at a high speed
36. Helping people with marital problems
37. Setting production goals
38. Cleaning hotel rooms
39. Designing a floral arrangement

40. Sorting mail
41. Ringing up merchandise on a cash register
42. Testing urine samples for the presence of drugs
43. Determining ways to reduce a client's taxes
44. Calling people to determine their interest in selling their home
45. Plowing a field
46. Driving through heavy traffic
47. Building a house
48. Explaining crime prevention techniques to citizens
49. Working with a physically disabled person
50. Organizing daily work activities
51. Cooking meals at a nice restaurant
52. Playing a musical instrument

53. Scheduling appointments for a business executive
54. Solving customers' problems
55. Filling prescriptions at a pharmacy
56. Forecasting the economy
57. Selling products at a department store
58. Spreading fertilizer over a field
59. Parking cars in a parking garage
60. Assembling electronic components
61. Writing a ticket for a speeding motorist
62. Taking care of young children
63. Setting up employee work schedules
64. Shortening the length of a skirt
65. Coming up with ideas for a new product

AVIS Answer Sheet

(1) absolutely hate   (2) dislike   (3) neutral   (4) enjoy   (5) very much enjoy

Total

1. _____   14. _____   27. _____   40. _____   53. _____   _____

2. _____   15. _____   28. _____   41. _____   54. _____   _____

3. _____   16. _____   29. _____   42. _____   55. _____   _____

4. _____   17. _____   30. _____   43. _____   56. _____   _____

5. _____   18. _____   31. _____   44. _____   57. _____   _____

6. _____   19. _____   32. _____   45. _____   58. _____   _____

7. _____   20. _____   33. _____   46. _____   59. _____   _____

8. _____   21. _____   34. _____   47. _____   60. _____   _____

9. _____   22. _____   35. _____   48. _____   61. _____   _____

10. _____   23. _____   36. _____   49. _____   62. _____   _____

11. _____   24. _____   37. _____   50. _____   63. _____   _____

12. _____   25. _____   38. _____   51. _____   64. _____   _____

13. _____   26. _____   39. _____   52. _____   65. _____   _____

AVIS Profile Sheet

Vocational Interest Area	Low Interest																				High Interest
Clerical	5	6	7	8	9	10	11	12	13	14	15	16	17	18	19	20	21	22	23	24	25
Customer Service	5	6	7	8	9	10	11	12	13	14	15	16	17	18	19	20	21	22	23	24	25
Science	5	6	7	8	9	10	11	12	13	14	15	16	17	18	19	20	21	22	23	24	25
Analysis	5	6	7	8	9	10	11	12	13	14	15	16	17	18	19	20	21	22	23	24	25
Sales	5	6	7	8	9	10	11	12	13	14	15	16	17	18	19	20	21	22	23	24	25
Agriculture	5	6	7	8	9	10	11	12	13	14	15	16	17	18	19	20	21	22	23	24	25
Transportation	5	6	7	8	9	10	11	12	13	14	15	16	17	18	19	20	21	22	23	24	25
Trades	5	6	7	8	9	10	11	12	13	14	15	16	17	18	19	20	21	22	23	24	25
Protective	5	6	7	8	9	10	11	12	13	14	15	16	17	18	19	20	21	22	23	24	25
Helping/Caring	5	6	7	8	9	10	11	12	13	14	15	16	17	18	19	20	21	22	23	24	25
Leadership/ Management	5	6	7	8	9	10	11	12	13	14	15	16	17	18	19	20	21	22	23	24	25
Consumer Economics	5	6	7	8	9	10	11	12	13	14	15	16	17	18	19	20	21	22	23	24	25
Creative	5	6	7	8	9	10	11	12	13	14	15	16	17	18	19	20	21	22	23	24	25

Career Areas

Clerical

Health Care	medical insurance clerk, medical records clerk, medical secretary, medical transcriptionist, admissions clerk
Banking	credit clerk, mortgage clerk, loan interviewer, teller
Hospitality	hotel clerk, ticket agent, reservation clerk
Legal	court reporter, legal secretary, paralegal
Office	administrative assistant, clerk, mail clerk, payroll clerk, secretary
Manufacturing	stock clerk, shipping and receiving clerk
Transportation	toll collector, dispatcher

Customer Service

Health Care	dental assistant, collections, hospital insurance representative
Banking	teller, loan officer, collections, customer service representative
Hospitality	server, caterer, bartender, dietician, dietician's assistant
Office	operator, switchboard, receptionist, personnel assistant
Cosmetology	hair stylist, manicurist, barber
Retail	cashier, sales representative, customer service representative
Travel	travel agent, flight attendant

Science

Dental	dental technician, dental hygienist
Medical	medical technologist, radiographer, sonographer
Optical	optician, optical lab technician, lens grinder
Pharmacy	pharmacist, pharmacy assistant
Science	lab technician
Veterinary	veterinarian, veterinary assistant

Analysis

Accounting	accountant, bookkeeper, financial analyst, economist
Insurance	insurance appraiser, claims adjuster, underwriter
Investments	financial planner, stockbroker
Law	lawyer, paralegal
Real estate	real estate appraiser

Sales

Aggressive	insurance, fundraiser, manufacturer's representative
Real Estate	real estate agent, real estate broker
Retail	sales representative, demonstrator
Telemarketing	telemarketer

Agriculture

Farming
Ranching

Transportation

Public	bus driver, cab driver, chauffeur, car lot attendant
Delivery	delivery truck driver
Long Haul	truck driver, escort driver

Trades

Construction	painter, mason, asphalt paver, heavy equipment operator, carpet layer
Electrical	electrician, electronic repairer, appliance repairer, cable installer, office machine repairer, vending machine repairer
Mechanical	automotive mechanic, truck mechanic, maintenance mechanic, aircraft mechanic, boat mechanic
Metal	welder, sheet metal worker
Physical Labor	logger, miner, jackhammer operator
Plumbing	plumber
Production	assembler, solderer, machinist, foundry worker
Wood	cabinetmaker, carpenter, woodworker, furniture assembler
Other	locksmith

Protective

Dispatch	police dispatcher, 911 operator
Emergency	EMT, paramedic
Fire Science	firefighter
Outdoor	lifeguard, park ranger, fish and game warden
Police Science	police officer, security guard

Helping/Caring

Day Care	babysitter, child care, home companion
Health Care	nurse, nurse's aide, physician's assistant
Banking/Finance	loan counselor, financial counselor
Education	teacher, teacher's aide, special education teacher
Law	parole officer
Outdoor	camp counselor
Social Services	social worker, psychologist, counselor

Management

Education	principal
Hospitality	hotel manager, restaurant manager
Office	office manager, personnel director
Production	supervisor
Retail	store manager, assistant manager

Consumer Economics

Cooking	baker, caterer, cook, chef, dietitian, nutritionist
Housekeeping	janitor, maid
Textiles	tailor, sewing machine operator, weaver, dry cleaner

Creative

Art	painter, sculptor
Business	advertising, marketing
Computers	computer programmer, graphic artist
Fashion	fashion design, fashion buyer
Floral	floral design
Oral	actor/actress, trainer, teacher, disc jockey, broadcaster
Outdoor	landscaper
Photography	photographer
Retail	jeweler
Writing	writer, poet, technical writer, reporter

Exercise 6–6
Integrity Testing

In this chapter you learned that integrity testing has increased in popularity. This exercise will give you a chance to take a sample integrity test. Because of the sensitive nature of these tests, you will not actually receive a test score.

sd = strongly disagree   d = disagree   n = neutral   a = agree   sa = strongly agree

1. Everyone is dishonest at times.   sd d n a sa
2. Most people have stolen things from their employer.   sd d n a sa
3. Most employees in restaurants steal food.   sd d n a sa
4. Dishonesty is just part of life.   sd d n a sa
5. Most police officers would take a bribe.   sd d n a sa

6. I have stolen things from an employer.   sd d n a sa
7. I often do not tell the truth.   sd d n a sa
8. I have shoplifted in the past 5 years.   sd d n a sa
9. I have changed the price tag on an item I wanted to buy.   sd d n a sa
10. I have given a discount to a friend when I shouldn't have.   sd d n a sa

11. I have been tempted to steal from my employer.   sd d n a sa
12. On occasion I have been tempted to shoplift.   sd d n a sa
13. There have been times when I thought about stealing.   sd d n a sa
14. I have cheated on exams in school.   sd d n a sa
15. I have lied to my friends.   sd d n a sa

16. People who steal from an employer should be fired.   sd d n a sa
17. People who shoplift should spend time in jail.   sd d n a sa
18. Stores should always file charges against shoplifters.   sd d n a sa
19. Students who cheat on exams should be suspended.   sd d n a sa
20. Punishment will not deter people from stealing.   sd d n a sa

21. It is easy to shoplift without getting caught.   sd d n a sa
22. My employer would never notice if I took a few things.   sd d n a sa
23. Very few people who steal get caught.   sd d n a sa
24. Very few students who cheat get caught.   sd d n a sa
25. People who steal might get arrested but they won't go to jail.   sd d n a sa

26. My friends shoplift.   sd d n a sa
27. My friends steal things from their employer.   sd d n a sa
28. I have friends who have been arrested.   sd d n a sa
29. Most people I know have been in trouble with the law.   sd d n a sa
30. My parents are not very honest.   sd d n a sa

31. It is OK to steal from someone who has treated you poorly.   sd d n a sa
32. It is OK to steal food if your family is hungry.   sd d n a sa
33. If a store clerk gives you too much change, it is OK to keep it. sd d n a sa
34. Stealing is always wrong.   sd d n a sa
35. Stealing is OK if done for the right reason.   sd d n a sa

What dimensions do you think the sample integrity questions were measuring?

_____

_____

_____

_____

_____

_____

_____

_____

Do you think integrity tests should be used?

_____

_____

_____

_____

_____

_____

_____

_____

Do you think you could successfully fake an integrity test?

_____

_____

_____

Classroom Exercise 6–1

On the next page is a resume of an applicant for an assistant manager position. On the basis of this person's resume, would you hire him? Why or why not?

_____

_____

_____

_____

_____

_____

_____

_____

_____

_____

_____

_____

_____

_____

_____

_____

_____

_____

_____

_____

_____

_____

_____

_____

_____

xxxxxx

8213 Summerdale Avenue

Chicago, IL 60610

Job Objective
Supervisory or management position with a progressive organization

Professional Strengths
- Extensive management experience
- Award-winning sales and promotional skills
- Active in the community
- Excellent construction, remodeling, and maintenance skills

Professional Experience
Owner—PDM Contractors-Chicago, Illinois

Owned and operated a successful general contracting and remodeling business. Responsibilities included bidding for jobs; supervising construction and remodeling; hiring, scheduling, and supervising employees; and handling all financial and accounting duties.

Manager—Kentucky Fried Chicken–Waterloo, Iowa

Responsible for managing three KFC restaurants. High level of performance demonstrated by huge increases in store profits.

Management Trainee—Nunn-Bush Shoes–Springfield, Illinois

Responsibilities included hiring, scheduling, and supervising employees; maintaining inventory; and selling shoes. High level of performance led to several promotions and commendations.

Ambulance Attendant—Palm Mortuary–Las Vegas, Nevada

Grocery Bagger—IGA–Chicago, Illinois

Community Activities
Waterloo, Iowa
- Named "Best Jaycee Chaplain" in Iowa
- Member of the Merchant Patrol

Springfield, Illinois
- Vice president of the Jaycees
- Ran largest Christmas parade in central Illinois
- Named *Outstanding First Year Jaycee* and *Third Outstanding Jaycee Member* in Illinois
- Member Junior Chamber of Commerce

Chicago, Illinois
- Precinct Captain for the Democratic Party
- Member, St. John Berchmans' parish bowling team
- Organizer of annual Snowtillion (church winter dance)
- Directed the annual Polish Constitution Day Parade
- Member of the Moose Lodge

Education
Diploma
Northwestern Business College

7 Evaluating Employee Performance

HAVE YOU EVER received a grade that you did not think was fair? Perhaps you had an 89.6 and the instructor would not "round up" to an A, or the test contained questions that had nothing to do with the class. If so, you were probably upset with the way your professor appraised your performance. In this chapter, we will discuss the process of evaluating and appraising employee performance, which is similar to evaluating a student's performance. By the end of this chapter you will

- learn about the increased use of 360-degree feedback.
- know how to create a performance-appraisal instrument.
- know how to administer a performance-appraisal system.
- understand the problems associated with performance ratings.
- be able to conduct a performance-appraisal review.
- understand how to legally terminate an unproductive employee.

As shown in Exhibit 7.01, the performance-appraisal process can be divided into nine interrelated steps. Each of these steps will serve as a major section in this chapter.

Step 1: Determine the Reason for Evaluating Employee Performance

The first step in the performance-appraisal process is to determine the reasons your organization wants to evaluate employee performance (Cleveland, Murphy,

& Williams, 1989). That is, does the organization want to use the results to improve performance? Give raises on the basis of performance? This determination is important because the various performance-appraisal techniques are appropriate for some purposes but not for others. For example, the forced-choice rating scale (see chapter Appendix) is excellent for determining compensation but terrible for training purposes. Likewise, the use of 360-degree feedback is an excellent source for improving employee performance but is not appropriate for determining salary increases. Surprisingly, most organizations do not have specific goals for their performance-appraisal systems. As a result, it comes as no surprise that several national surveys found that the vast majority of performance-appraisal systems are not successful (Coens & Jenkins, 2000).

Though there are many uses and goals for performance appraisal, the most common include determining salary increases, making promotion decisions, providing employee feedback and training, making termination decisions, and conducting personnel research.

Determining Salary Increases

As mentioned in Chapter 2, a job's worth is determined by many factors, including the degree of responsibility and level of education required to perform the job. But the difference in compensation between two individuals within the same job is a function of both tenure and job performance. That is, it would not seem fair to pay a poorly-performing employee the same amount as an excellently performing one. Thus, one important reason for evaluating employee performance is to provide a fair basis on which to determine an employee's salary increase. If performance-appraisal results are to be used to determine salary increases, a numerical rather than a narrative format is probably needed.

Exhibit 7.01 The performance-appraisal process

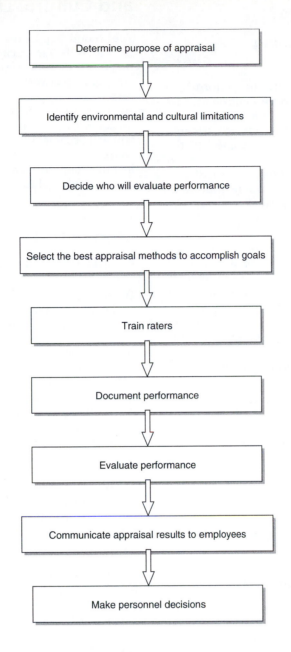

Determine purpose of appraisal

Identify environmental and cultural limitations

Decide who will evaluate performance

Select the best appraisal methods to accomplish goals

Train raters

Document performance

Evaluate performance

Communicate appraisal results to employees

Make personnel decisions

Making Promotion Decisions

Another reason for evaluating performance is to determine which employees will be promoted. Although it would seem only fair to promote the best employee, this often does not occur. For example, the policy in some organizations is to promote employees with the most seniority. This is especially true of organizations whose employees belong to unions. Even though promoting employees on the basis of performance or tenure seems fair, it may not always be smart. The best employee at one level is not always the best at the next level. Promoting the best or most senior employee often results in the so-called Peter Principle—the

promotion of employees until they reach their highest level of incompetence. If performance evaluations are used to promote employees, care should be taken to ensure that the employee is evaluated well on the job dimensions that are similar to the new position's dimensions.

For example, the five important job dimensions of a salesperson might be sales, communication skills, accuracy of paperwork, client rapport, and responsibility. The four important job dimensions of sales manager would be communication skills, accuracy of paperwork, motivational ability, and employee rapport. The salesperson with the highest scores on the overlapping dimensions, which in this case are communication skills and accuracy of paperwork, should be the one promoted. Sales volume might not even be used as a factor in this decision.

Providing Employee Training and Feedback

By far, the most important use of performance evaluation is to improve employee performance by providing feedback about what employees are doing right and wrong. Even though employee training should be an ongoing process (see Chapter 8), the semiannual **performance-appraisal review** is an excellent time to meet with employees to discuss their strengths and weaknesses. But more important, it is the time to determine how weaknesses can be corrected. This process is thoroughly discussed later in the chapter.

Another use of performance-appraisal data is in training-needs analysis, which will be discussed in greater detail in Chapter 8. If many employees score poorly on a performance-appraisal dimension, an increase or change in training is probably necessary for all employees. If only a few employees have low scores, training at an individual level is indicated. Thus, performance appraisal can provide useful information about an organization's strengths and weaknesses.

Making Termination Decisions

Unfortunately, providing feedback, counseling, and training to employees does not always increase performance or reduce discipline problems. When performance management techniques are not successful, the results of a performance review might suggest the best course of action is to terminate the employee. Methods for doing this and the legal issues that surround such decisions will be discussed in great detail at the end of this chapter.

Conducting Personnel Research

A final reason for evaluating employees is for personnel research. As discussed in previous chapters, employment tests must be validated, and one way this can be done is by correlating test scores with some measure of job performance. To do this, however, an accurate and reliable measure of job performance must be available.

The same is true in evaluating the effectiveness of training programs. To determine effectiveness, an accurate measure of performance must be available for use in determining whether performance increases as a result of training.

Although not the most important reason for evaluating employee performance, personnel research is still important, especially in organizations where union contracts forbid the use of performance evaluations in personnel decisions. In those situations, performance evaluations are still needed for effective personnel research.

Step 2: Identify Environmental and Cultural Limitations

The second step in the performance-appraisal process is to identify the environmental and cultural factors that could affect the system. For example, if supervisors are highly overworked, an elaborate, time-consuming, performance-appraisal system will not be successful. In an environment in which there is no money available for merit pay, developing a numerically complex system will become frustrating and the results of the evaluation may not be taken seriously. In an environment in which employees are very cohesive, the use of peer ratings might reduce the cohesiveness.

Step 3: Determine Who Will Evaluate Performance

Traditionally, employee performance has been evaluated solely by supervisors. Recently, however, organizations have realized that supervisors see only certain aspects of an employee's behavior. For example, as shown in Exhibit 7.02, a branch manager might observe only 30% of a teller's work behavior; the rest is observed by customers, peers, and support staff in other parts of the bank. Furthermore, the teller might behave very differently around her supervisor than around other people. Consequently, to obtain an accurate view of the teller's performance, these other sources should provide feedback. The buzzword for using multiple sources to appraise performance is **360-degree feedback.** Depending on the survey conducted, 360-degree feedback is used by between 25% (Towers Perrin survey) and 65% (William Mercer survey) of large U.S. organizations. The SHRM (2000) survey reported 360-degree feedback was used by 18% of organizations for nonexempt positions, 29% for exempt positions, and 32% for executive-level positions. Sources of relevant information about employee performance include supervisors, peers, subordinates, customers, and self-appraisal. As shown in Exhibit 7.03, often there is little agreement in the way two supervisors evaluate an employee or a supervisor and a peer might rate an employee (Viswesvaran, Schmidt, & Ones, 2002). Interestingly, supervisors whose self-ratings agree with others' ratings tend to be better performers than supervisors whose ratings are not consistent with others' (Witt, 1996).

Supervisors

By far the most common type of performance appraisal is the supervisor rating. In fact, Bernardin and Beatty (1984) estimated that more than 90% of all performance appraisals are conducted using supervisors' ratings of performance. Supervisors are best able to evaluate the extent to which an employee contributes to the overall success of the organization. Though supervisors may not see every minute of an employee's

Exhibit 7.02   Who observes employee performance?

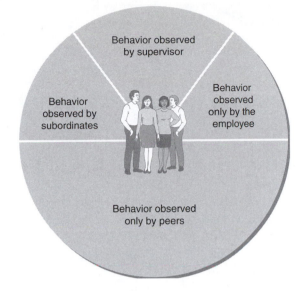

Behavior observed
by supervisor

Behavior
observed
only by the
employee

Behavior
observed by
subordinates

Behavior observed
only by peers

behavior, they do see the end result. A supervisor may not actually see a teller sign up customers for Visa cards but will review the daily sales totals. Likewise, a professor does not see a student actually research and write a paper but infers the levels of these behaviors by viewing the results—the finished term paper.

Peers

Whereas supervisors see the *results* of an employee's efforts, peers often see the actual *behavior*. Peer ratings usually come from employees who work directly with an employee; a bank teller could be rated by other bank tellers. However, other employees in the organization, those who often come in contact with the employee, can also provide useful information. For example, our teller could be rated by employees from the loan support or Visa card departments.

Research has shown that peer ratings are fairly reliable only when the peers who make the ratings are similar to and well acquainted with the employees being rated (Landy & Guion, 1970; Mumford, 1983). Most important, peer ratings have been successful in predicting the future success of promoted employees as they correlate highly with supervisor ratings (Cederbloom, 1989). Although peer ratings appear promising, few organizations use them (DeNisi, Randolph, & Blencoe, 1983). One reason could be that peer ratings are lenient when used for evaluation purposes but not when used only to provide feedback (Farh, Cannella, & Bedeian, 1991).

Research suggests certain employees are more lenient in their peer ratings than are other employees. Saavedra and Kwun (1993) found that high performers evaluate their peers more strictly than do low performers. This difference in ratings is probably because employees compare others to themselves. Thus, the average employee does not appear impressive to a high performer but may to a less productive employee. Though peers may provide a unique view of performance, employees tend to react worse to negative feedback from peers than from experts (Albright & Levy, 1995). Employees who score high in self-esteem, high in self-monitoring, and low in individualism react most favorably to peer ratings (Long, Long, & Dobbins, 1998).

Subordinates

Subordinate feedback (also called upward feedback) is an important component of 360-degree feedback as subordinates can provide a very different view about a supervisor's behavior (Whetstone, 1994). However, with the exception of students rating teachers, formal methods are neither common nor well regarded by managers (McEvoy, 1988, 1990). Subordinate ratings can be difficult to obtain because employees fear a backlash if they unfavorably rate their supervisor, especially when a supervisor has only one or two subordinates. For example, when the supervisors at one mental health facility gave poor performance ratings to their boss, each was "called to the carpet" for having the audacity to rate the boss poorly. After such a brow beating, what do you think is the probability the subordinates will be honest in the future? However, subordinates' feedback can be encouraged if supervisors appear open to employee comments (Baumgartner, 1994), if the ratings are made anonymously (Antonioni, 1994), and if the ratings are used for developmental purposes (Avis & Kudisch, 2000). Interestingly, subordinate ratings correlate highly with upper-management ratings of supervisors' performance (Furnham & Stringfield, 1994; Riggio & Cole, 1992). With some exceptions (e.g., Atwater, Waldman, Atwater, & Cartier, 2000), research generally indicates that subordinate feedback increases managerial performance,

Exhibit 7.03 Correlations between raters

Agreement Between	Correlation
Two supervisors	.50
Two peers	.37
Two subordinates	.30
Supervisors and peers	.34
Supervisor and subordinates	.22
Supervisor and self	.22
Peers and subordinates	.22
Peers and self	.19

Source: Conway & Huffcut, 1997.

especially that of poorly performing managers (Atwater, Roush, & Fischthal, 1995; Reilly, Smither, & Vasilopoulous, 1996; Smither et al., 1995; Walker & Smither, 1999). This increase in performance is especially true for areas targeted for improvement (Clarke, Miklos, & Rogers, 1996). Though supervisor performance might increase from upward feedback, such feedback does not appear to improve the overall performance or stock value of an organization (Pfau & Kay, 2002a).

Customers

Although it would be unlikely that an organization would ask customers to fill out a performance-appraisal instrument on an employee, organizations do value customer feedback. Informally, customers provide feedback on employee performance by filing complaints or complimenting a manager about one of her employees. Formally, customers provide feedback by completing evaluation cards such as that shown in Exhibit 7.04.

Organizations also seek customer feedback in the form of *secret shoppers*—current customers who have been enlisted by a company to periodically evaluate the service they receive. In exchange for their ratings, secret shoppers get a few dollars and a free meal. For years, I have been "employed" by a national marketing company to eat at local restaurants and secretly complete a rating of the quality of food and service. The compensation is only $4 per visit plus reimbursement for the meal, but it is a fun experience. I only wish they would have granted my request for sunglasses and a trench coat!

Self-Appraisal

Allowing an employee to evaluate her own behavior and performance is a technique used by only a small percentage of organizations (Atwater, 1998). Research on self-appraisal, however, has found what we might expect to find: employee self-appraisals tend to suffer from leniency (Beehr, Ivanitskaya, Hansen, Erofeev, & Gudanowski, 2001; Meyer, 1980) and correlate

moderately (.29) with actual performance (Mabe & West, 1982) and poorly with subordinate (Conway & Huffcutt, 1997) and management ratings (Beehr et al., 2001). However, when evaluations are made with clear rating standards and social comparison information, agreement is increased between self- and supervisor ratings (Keeping & Sulsky, 1996; Schrader & Steiner, 1996). When peer ratings are lower than self-ratings, employees react negatively to, and question the accuracy of, negative feedback (Brett & Atwater, 2001).

The leniency found in the self-ratings of U.S. workers may not generalize to other countries. Farh, Dobbins, and Cheng (1991) found that the self-ratings of Taiwanese workers suffered from modesty rather than from leniency. However, Furnham and Stringfield (1994) and Yu and Murphy (1993) found leniency in the self-ratings of Mainland Chinese employees. Further research is still needed to investigate potential cultural differences in self-ratings.

Self-appraisals of performance appear to be most accurate when the self-appraisal is not to be used for such administrative purposes as raises or promotions (Atwater, 1998). They are also more accurate when employees understand the performance-appraisal system (Williams & Levy, 1992) and when employees believe an objective record of their performance is available with which the supervisor can compare the self-appraisal (Farh & Werbel, 1986). To think more about who should evaluate performance, complete Exercise 7–1 at the end of this chapter.

Step 4: Select the Best Appraisal Methods to Accomplish Your Goals

The next step in the performance-appraisal process is to select the performance criteria and appraisal methods that will best accomplish your goals for the system.

Exhibit 7.04 Customer evaluation card

McBurger Queen Restaurants

Dear Customer:

We value your business and strive to make each of your visits a dining pleasure. To help us reach our goal, we would appreciate your completing this card and placing it in our suggestion box on your way out.

1. Was your food cooked properly?   Y N
2. Was your server friendly?   Y N
3. Was your server efficient?   Y N
4. Do you plan to return?   Y N

5. Who was your server? _____

Comments:

_____
_____
_____
_____

Criteria are ways of describing employee success. For example, it might be decided that attendance, quality of work, and safety are the three most important criteria for a successful employee.

After the relevant criteria have been chosen, the methods for measuring the criteria must be chosen and created. That is, how can we measure attendance, quality, and safety?

The choice of the criteria and methods used to measure the criteria are important (Lance, Teachout, & Donnelly, 1992). An excellent example of this importance comes from a study of the relationship between age and job performance. A meta-analysis by Waldman and Avolio (1986) found a correlation of .27 between age and objective measures of job performance. The correlation between age and supervisor ratings, however, was $-.14$. Thus, using the latter ratings would lead to the conclusion that older workers are not as good as younger workers. But using actual performance as the criterion leads to the opposite conclusion: older workers performed better than younger workers.

Prior to developing the actual performance-appraisal instrument, two important decisions must be made: the focus of the performance-appraisal dimensions and whether to use rankings or ratings.

Decision 1: Focus of the Appraisal Dimensions

As shown in Exhibit 7.05, the appraisal dimensions can focus on traits, competencies, task types, or goals.

Trait-Focused Performance Dimensions

A trait-focused system concentrates on such employee attributes as dependability, honesty, and courtesy. Though commonly used, trait-focused performance-appraisal instruments are not a good idea because they provide poor feedback and thus will not result in employee development and growth. For example, think of a performance-review meeting in which the supervisor tells an employee that she received low ratings on responsibility and friendliness. Because traits are personal, the employee is likely to become defensive. Furthermore, the employee will want specific examples the supervisor may not have available. The only developmental advice the supervisor can offer would be to "be more responsible and friendly." Such advice is not specific enough for the employee to change her behavior.

Competency-Focused Performance Dimensions

Rather than concentrating on an employee's traits, competency-focused dimensions concentrate on the employee's knowledge, skills, and abilities. For example, competency-focused dimensions might include writing skills, oral presentation skills, and driving skills. The advantage to organizing dimensions by competencies is that it is easy to provide feedback and suggest the steps necessary to correct deficiencies. That is, if an employee is evaluated as having poor writing skills, the obvious corrective measure would be for the employee to take a writing course.

Exhibit 7.05 Four ways to focus performance dimensions

Competency Focus
- Report-writing skills
- Driving skills
- Public-speaking skills
- Knowledge of the law
- Decision-making skills
- Physical agility skills

Goal Focus
- Prevent crimes from occurring
- Arrest/cite lawbreakers
- Finish shift without personal injury
- Have arrests and citations stand up in court
- Minimize citizen complaints
- Ensure public safety

Task Focus
- Crime prevention
- Arrest procedures
- Court testimony
- Use of vehicle
- Radio procedures
- Following rules and regulations

Trait Focus
- Honesty
- Courtesy
- Responsibility
- Dependability
- Assertiveness
- Cooperation

Task-Focused Performance Dimensions

Task-focused dimensions are organized by the similarity of tasks that are performed. For a police officer, such dimensions might include "Following Radio Procedures" or "Court Testimony." Note that a task-focused dimension usually includes several competencies. For example, to receive a high rating on the dimension of Court Testimony, the officer would need the competencies of public speaking, organization, and knowledge of the law. The advantage of this approach is that, because supervisors are concentrating on tasks that occur together, it is often easier to evaluate performance than with the other dimensions. The disadvantage is that it is more difficult to offer suggestions for how to correct the deficiency if an employee scores low on a dimension. That is, is the low score on Court Testimony due to a lack of knowledge or to poor public speaking skills?

Goal-Focused Performance Dimensions

The fourth type of performance dimension is to organize the appraisal on the basis of goals to be accomplished by the employee. Sticking with our patrol officer example, goals might include preventing crimes from occurring, finishing shift without personal injury, and minimizing the number of citizen complaints. The advantage to a goal-focused approach is that it is easier for an employee to understand why certain behaviors are expected. Take, for example, the behavioral expectations of wearing a seat belt and wearing body armor. If these expectations were listed under the dimension of "Following Department Policy," the officer might not be too concerned about changing behavior about following "some stupid rule." If, however, these two expectations were listed under the goal of "Staying Alive," it would be clearer that these expectations are there for an important purpose.

To better understand how to choose the type of dimension, complete Exercise 7–2.

Decision 2: Use of Employee Comparisons, Objective Measures, or Ratings?

Once the type of dimensions have been considered, the next decision to be made is whether to evaluate performance by comparing employees to one another (ranking), using objective measures such as attendance and number of units sold, or having supervisors rate how well the employee has performed on each of the dimensions.

Employee Comparisons

To reduce leniency, employees can be compared with one another instead of rated individually on a scale. The easiest and most common of these methods is the **rank order.** In this approach, employees are ranked in order by their judged performance for each relevant dimension. As Exhibit 7.06 shows, the ranks are then averaged across each dimension to yield an overall rank.

Rank orders are easily used when there are only a few employees to rank, but they become difficult to use with larger numbers. Ranking the top few and bottom few employees is relatively easy, but deciding which 2 of 50 employees should be placed at the 30th and 31st ranks is more difficult.

To make this process easier, **paired comparisons** can be used. This method involves comparing each possible pair of employees and choosing which one of each pair is the better employee. An example is shown in Exhibit 7.07. You can practice using the

Exhibit 7.06 Ranking method of evaluating performance

| | Dimension | | | |
Employee	Knowledge	Dependability	Quality	Total
Clark	1	1	1	1.00
Cochran	2	3	2	2.33
Bailey	3	2	3	2.67
Darden	4	5	4	4.33
Shapiro	5	4	5	4.67

paired-comparisons method by completing Exercise 7–3 at the end of this chapter.

Even though comparing one pair of employees at a time is easier than simultaneously comparing a large number of employees, it does have its drawbacks. With large numbers of employees, the time necessary to make all of the comparisons becomes prohibitive. For example, to determine how many comparisons must be made, we can use the following formula:

$$\text{number of comparisons} = \frac{n(n-1)}{2}$$

where n = the number of employees. Thus, if we have 10 employees to compare:

$$\text{number of comparisons} = \frac{(10)(10-1)}{2}$$
$$= \frac{(10)(9)}{2} = \frac{90}{2} = 45$$

Thus, we would need to make 45 comparisons for each performance dimension. Although this number is not too bad, evaluating 100 employees would result in 4,950 separate comparisons! And with five performance dimensions, some unfortunate supervisor would have to make almost 25,000 separate comparisons! Obviously, the supervisor would not favor such a task.

The final type of employee comparison system is called the **forced-distribution method.** With this method, a predetermined percentage of employees are placed in each of the five categories shown in Exhibit 7.08. This system is much easier to use than the other two employee comparison methods, but it also has a drawback. To use the method, one must assume that employee performance is normally distributed; that is, that there are certain percentages of employees who are poor, average, and excellent. As we discussed in Chapter 4, employee performance probably is not normally distributed because of restriction of range. There probably are few terrible employees because they either were never hired or were quickly fired. Likewise, truly excellent employees probably have been promoted. Thus, employee performance is distributed in a non-normal fashion.

Perhaps another way to look at this concept is by examining the grades given in a class. When students ask an instructor to "curve" a test, technically they are asking her to force their grades into a normal curve—that is, there will be approximately 10% A's and 10% F's. (Of course, what these students are really often asking for is extra points.)

Suppose that you are at the bottom of your class, yet you still have a 75% average on class exams. Do you deserve an F? What if you are the last person in the D category, and a student withdraws from the class with 2 weeks to go. To keep the distribution normal, you are given an F. Do you consider this fair?

Perhaps the greatest problem with all of the employee comparison methods is that they do not provide information about how well an employee is actually doing. For example, even though every employee at a production plant might be doing an excellent job, someone has to be at the bottom. Thus, it might appear that one worker is doing a poor job (because she is last), when in fact she, and every other employee, is doing well.

Objective Measures

A second way to evaluate performance is to use what are commonly called *objective* or *hard* criteria. Common types of objective measures include quantity of work, quality of work, attendance, and safety.

Quantity of Work. Evaluation of a worker's performance in terms of **quantity** is obtained by simply counting the number of relevant job behaviors that take place. For example, we might judge a salesperson's performance by the number of units she sells, an assembly line worker's performance by the number of bumpers she welds, or a police officer's performance by the number of arrests she makes. Even Oprah Winfrey is evaluated on the number of viewers who watch her show.

Although quantity measures appear to be objective measures of performance, they often are misleading. From our previous discussion of contamination, it should be readily apparent that many factors determine quantity of work other than an employee's ability and

Exhibit **7.07** Example of paired-comparison method

Employees
Green
Briscoe
Rey
Logan
Ceretta

Paired Comparisons: Circle the better employee in each pair.

(Green)	Briscoe
(Green)	Rey
(Green)	Logan
(Green)	Ceretta
(Briscoe)	Rey
(Briscoe)	Logan
(Briscoe)	Ceretta
Rey	(Logan)
(Rey)	Ceretta
(Logan)	Ceretta

Scoring

Employee	Number of Times Name Circled
Green	4
Briscoe	3
Rey	1
Logan	2
Ceretta	0

performance. Furthermore, for many people's jobs it might not be practical or possible to measure quantity. Computer programmers, doctors, and firefighters are examples.

Quality of Work. Another method to evaluate performance is by measuring the **quality** of the work that is done. Quality is usually measured in terms of **errors**, which are defined as deviations from a standard. Thus, to obtain a measure of quality, there must be a standard against which to compare an employee's work. For example, a seamstress's work quality would be judged by how it compares to a "model" shirt; a secretary's work quality would be judged by the number of typos (the standard being correctly spelled words); and a cook's quality might be judged by how her food resembled a standard as measured by size, temperature, and ingredient amounts.

Kentucky Fried Chicken, for example, evaluates the quality of its franchises' food by undercover inspectors. These inspectors purchase food, drive down the road, and after parking, use a thermometer to see whether the food has been served at a standard acceptable temperature and also a scale to determine whether the weight of the mashed potatoes is within the acceptable range.

Note that the definition of an error is *any* deviation from a standard. Thus, errors can even be work quality that is higher than a standard. Why is this an error? Suppose a company manufactures shirts that are sold for $15. To keep down the manufacturing costs of its shirts, the company probably uses cheaper material and has its workers spend less time per shirt than does a company that manufactures $100 shirts (these are not the shirts I buy). Thus, if an employee sews a shirt with 15 stitches per inch instead of the standard 10, the company will lose money because of higher quality!

When I was working my way through school, I held a summer job at an amusement park. The job involved wearing a pink and purple uniform and cooking prefabricated pizza. The standard for the large pepperoni pizza was 2 handfuls of cheese and 15 pieces of pepperoni. Now all pizza lovers recognize this to be a barren pizza. The cooks thus tried to increase the pizza quality by tripling the number of pepperoni pieces. The management quickly explained to the young "gourmet chefs" that exceeding the standards was considered poor work performance and that employees who did so would be fired.

A similar situation developed at a factory that produced parts for telephones. Most of the employees were older and took great pride in their work quality and in

Spelling	Tilly Stone	Roberts Winslet Basinger Silverstone	Paltrow Ryan	Hunt
10% Terrible	20% Below average	40% Average	20% Good	10% Excellent

the fact that their parts had the lowest percentage of errors in the company. They were told, however, that their quality was too high and that the parts were lasting so long that the company was not getting much repeat business. Quality errors can occur in many strange ways!

Attendance. A common method for objectively measuring one aspect of an employee's performance is by looking at attendance (this is discussed in greater detail in Chapter 10). Attendance can be separated into three distinct criteria: absenteeism, tardiness, and tenure. Both absenteeism and tardiness have obvious implications for the performance-appraisal process. The weight that each has in the overall evaluation of the employee largely depends on the nature of the job.

Tenure as a criterion, however, is used mostly for research purposes when evaluating the success of selection decisions. For example, in a job such as cook at McDonald's, there is probably little difference in the quantity and quality of hamburgers or French fries that are cooked. But an employee might be considered a "success" if she stays with the company for at least 4 months and "unsuccessful" if she leaves before that

time. In fact, the importance of tenure can be demonstrated by noting that several major fast food restaurants and convenience stores have established bonus systems to reward long-tenure employees—that is, those who have worked for a company at least 6 months. For each hour the employee works, the company places a specified amount of money into an account that can be used by the employee to pay such education expenses as books and tuition.

Safety. Another method used to evaluate the success of an employee is safety. Obviously, employees who follow safety rules and who have no occupational accidents do not cost an organization as much money as those who break rules, equipment, and possibly their own bodies. As with tenure, safety is usually used for research purposes, but it also can be used for employment decisions such as promotions and bonuses.

Ratings of Performance

The most commonly used option in evaluating performance is to have supervisors rate how well the employee performed on each dimension. Though

Quality is a relevant criterion for many jobs.

Exhibit **7.09** Example of a graphic rating scale

Initiative	Poor	1	2	3	4	5	Excellent
Cooperation	Poor	1	2	3	4	5	Excellent
Dependability	Poor	1	2	3	4	5	Excellent
Attendance	Poor	1	2	3	4	5	Excellent

there are many variations of how these rating scales can be created, the two most common are the graphic rating scale and the behavioral checklist.

Graphic Rating Scales. The most common rating scale is the **graphic rating scale**. An example is shown in Exhibit 7.09. As you can see, such scales are fairly simple, with 5 to 10 dimensions accompanied by words such as "good" and "poor" anchoring the ends of the scale.

The obvious advantage to graphic rating scales is their ease of construction and use, but they have been criticized because of their susceptibility to such rating errors as halo and leniency, which are discussed later in this chapter (Kingstrom & Bass, 1981).

Behavioral Checklists. As shown in Exhibit 7.10, behavioral checklists consist of a list of behaviors, expectations, or results for each dimension. This list is used to force the supervisor to concentrate on the relevant behaviors that fall under a dimension. Behavioral checklists are constructed by taking the task statements from a detailed job description (e.g., "Types correspondence") and converting them into behavioral performance statements representing the level at which the behavior is expected to be performed (e.g., "Correspondence is typed accurately and does not contain spelling or grammatical errors").

When creating the statements for each dimension, one should carefully consider whether to write the statements in the form of behaviors or in the form of results. Examples of behavior-based statements for a bank teller might include "Properly greets each customer," "Knows customers' names," and "Thanks customer after each transaction." The obvious advantage to a behavior-focused system is the increased amount of specific feedback that can be given to each employee.

Result-focused statements concentrate on what an employee *accomplished* as a result of what she did. Result-focused systems are tempting because they evaluate employees on their contribution to the bottom line: Did their behavior on the job result in a tangible outcome for the organization (Planchy & Planchy, 1993)? To practice writing behavioral statements, complete Exercise 7–4.

A problem with result-focused statements is that an employee can do everything asked of her by an organization and still not get the desired results due to factors outside her control. These factors are referred to as **contamination.** For example, in banking a teller might not be successful in getting customers to sign-up for Visa cards because the bank's interest rate is not competitive. In law enforcement, a police officer might not write many traffic citations because she patrols an area in which there are few cars. In retail, a salesperson has poor sales because of her geographic location. For example, two salespersons work in different locations. Mary Anderson sells an average of 120 air conditioners per month, whereas Tamika Johnson averages 93. Is this criterion free from contamination? Definitely not.

The number of sales is based not only on the skills of the salesperson but also on such factors as the number of stores in the sales territory, the average temperature in the territory, and the relations between the previous salesperson and the store owners. Thus, if we used only the number of sales, Mary Anderson would be considered our top salesperson. But if we take into account that sales are contaminated by the number of stores in the territory, we see that Mary Anderson sold 120 air conditioners in 50 possible stores, whereas Tamika Johnson sold 93 air conditioners in 10 stores. Thus, Mary Anderson sold an average of 2.4 air conditioners per store in an area with an average temperature of 93 degrees; Tamika Johnson sold an average of 9.3 air conditioners per store in an area with an average temperature of 80 degrees. By considering the potential areas of contamination, a different picture emerges of relative performance. As this example clearly shows, factors other than actual performance can affect criteria. Therefore, it is essential to identify as many sources of contamination as possible and to determine ways to adjust performance ratings to account for these contamination sources.

After considering the behaviors in the checklist, a supervisor provides an overall rating of the employee's performance on each dimension. As shown in Exhibit 7.11, employees can be rated in three ways: how they compared to other employees, the frequency with which they performed certain behaviors, or the extent to which the behaviors met the expectations of the employer.

Comparison to Other Employees. Supervisors can rate performance on a dimension by comparing the employee's level of performance to that of other employees. It is important to note that, when scale anchors such as "below average," "average," and

Exhibit 7.10   Example of a behavioral checklist

Radio Procedures

Behavior Elements

_____ Uses proper codes and signals when sending information

_____ Understands codes and signals when receiving information

_____ Voice is clear and easy to understand and does not indicate panic in high stress situations

_____ Follows proper radio procedures

_____ Monitors the proper channels

_____ Knows the location of all district officers

_____ Never communicates improper information over the radio

_____ Keeps dispatch informed of current status

_____ Treats communications officers with respect and courtesy

Dimension Rating

_____ 5 Consistently exceeds requirements; no improvements needed

_____ 4 Exceeds most requirements

_____ 3 Usually meets requirements; acceptable performance

_____ 2 Usually meets most requirements but needs improvement

_____ 1 Does not meet minimum requirements; needs immediate and extensive improvement

Comments

_____

_____

_____

_____

_____

"above average" are used, the evaluation involves rating employee performance in comparison to other employees. Though this approach will reduce problems of overly lenient or overly strict ratings, it potentially forces a supervisor to rate employees who are performing well as being worse than other employees.

Frequency of Desired Behaviors. Behaviors can be rated based on the frequency in which they occur. For example, we expect our production workers to follow safety guidelines. As part of our performance-appraisal system, supervisors are asked to decide whether their employees "always," "almost always," "often," "seldom," or "never" follow the rules. As you can imagine, it is often difficult for a supervisor to distinguish between levels such as "almost always" and "often."

Extent to Which Organizational Expectations Are Met. Perhaps the best approach is to rate employees on the extent to which their behavior meets the expectations of the organization. Such an approach allows for high levels of feedback and can be applied to most types of employee behavior. Some behaviors, however, are not suitable for such a scale. Take, for example, the expectation that a police officer always wears her seat belt. If she wears it all the time, she has _met_ expectations (a rating of 3): there is no way to get a higher rating because one cannot wear a seat belt more often than always and thus cannot ever exceed expectations. When such a situation is possible, the scale can be adjusted to be similar to that shown in Exhibit 7.12.

As shown in Exhibits 7.13 through 7.15, in addition to graphic rating scales and behavioral checklists, a variety of methods to rate performance are available, including behaviorally anchored rating scales (BARS), forced-choice scales, and mixed-standard scales. Because these scales are not commonly used, but are historically and psychometrically interesting, information about them has been included in the Appendix to this chapter.

Exhibit 7.11 Examples of three scales to measure behavior

Comparison to Other Employees

Refers to customers by name

_____ Much better than other tellers

_____ Better than other tellers

_____ The same as other tellers

_____ Worse than other tellers

_____ Much worse than other tellers

Frequency

Refers to customers by name

_____ Always

_____ Almost always

_____ Often

_____ Seldom

_____ Never

Extent to Which Organizational Expectations Were Met

_____ Greatly exceeds expectations

_____ Exceeds expectations

_____ Meets expectations

_____ Falls below expectations

_____ Falls well below expectations

Evaluation of Performance-Appraisal Methods

In the previous pages and in the chapter appendix, several methods for evaluating employee performance are offered. Of course, we might now ask, "Is any one of these methods the best?" Probably not (Jacobs, Kafry, & Zedeck, 1980; Kingstrom & Bass, 1981; Schwab, Heneman, & DeCotiis, 1975). Research has shown that such complicated techniques as BARS, forced-choice scales, and mixed-standard scales are only occasionally superior to the inexpensive and uncomplicated graphic rating scale (Giffin, 1989; Guion & Gibson, 1988). In fact, behavioral anchors sometimes bias supervisors' ratings by forcing them to concentrate on specific behaviors (Murphy & Constans, 1987). And yet graphic rating scales are seldom superior to these more complicated rating methods.

Although techniques such as behavioral checklists are only slightly more psychometrically sound, they still have some advantages over graphic rating scales. Because employees are directly involved in creating them, they tend to see performance-evaluation results as being more fair. Furthermore, many supervisors who make such ratings prefer many of the behavioral approaches (Dickenson & Zellinger, 1980). Finally, feedback from behavior-based methods is easier to give and to use to provide suggestions for improvement.

Though many of the behavioral methods yield similar results, the same is not true when comparing subjective and objective methods. A meta-analysis by Bommer, Johnson, Rich, Podsakoff, and Mackenzie (1995) indicates that objective and subjective results are only slightly correlated ($r = .39$). Interestingly, there was a stronger relationship between objective and subjective ratings of quantity ($r = .38$) than between objective and subjective ratings of quality ($r = .24$).

From a legal perspective, courts are more interested in the due process afforded by a performance-appraisal system than in its technical aspects. After reviewing 295 circuit court decisions regarding performance appraisal, Werner and Bolino (1997) concluded that performance-appraisal systems are most likely to survive a legal challenge if they are based on a job analysis, raters receive training and written instructions, employees are allowed to review the results, and ratings from multiple raters are consistent.

Step 5: Train Raters

Although training supervisors to evaluate performance is essential to a sound and legal performance-appraisal system, few organizations spend the time and resources

Exhibit **7.12** Rating behaviors that can only meet expectations

Use of Weapons and Vehicle

Behaviors that can meet or exceed expectations

_____ Effectively handled vehicle in pursuit or emergency situations

_____ Demonstrated marksmanship above minimum requirements

_____ Demonstrated appropriate judgment in determining the use of force

_____ Demonstrated appropriate judgment in making pursuit decisions

Behaviors that can only meet expectations

_____ Weapons ratings are current and meet minimum requirements

_____ Weapons were carried in an appropriate manner

_____ When weapons were used, reports were filed on time

_____ When weapons were used, reports contained accurate information

_____ When driving, seat belts were always worn

_____ Carried only weapons issued and/or authorized by the department

_____ Applied force only when use of force was justified

Dimension Rating

_____ 5 Consistently exceeds requirements; no improvements needed

_____ 4 Exceeds most requirements

_____ 3 Usually meets requirements; acceptable performance

_____ 2 Usually meets most requirements but needs improvement

_____ 1 Does not meet minimum requirements; needs immediate and extensive improvement

---

necessary to do this properly (Hauenstein, 1998). This lack of training is surprising given that research indicates that training supervisors to become aware of the various rating errors and how to avoid them often increases accuracy (Smither, Barry, & Reilly, 1989), reduces rating errors (Bernardin & Buckley, 1981; Fay & Latham, 1982), increases the validity of tests validated against the ratings (Pursell, Dossett, & Latham, 1980), and increases employee satisfaction with the ratings (Ivancevich, 1982). This is especially true when the training technique uses discussion, practice in rating, and feedback about rating accuracy rather than lecture (Smith, 1986). These training effects, however, are short-lived (Noble, 1997) unless additional training and feedback are provided, and they can even reduce the accuracy of ratings by substituting new errors (Bernardin & Pence, 1980).

The effectiveness of rater training also is a function of training format. Raters who receive **frame-of-reference training** make fewer rating errors and recall more training information than do untrained raters or raters only receiving information about job-related behaviors (Athey & McIntyre, 1987; Day & Sulsky, 1995; Sulsky & Day, 1992). Frame-of-reference training provides raters with job-related information, practice in rating, and examples of ratings made by experts as well as the rationale behind those expert ratings (Hauenstein & Foti, 1989; McIntyre, Smith, & Hassett, 1984).

Step 6: Document Performance

The next step in the performance-appraisal process is to ensure that supervisors document employees' behaviors as they occur. Such documentation is usually a written log consisting of **critical incidents**—formal accounts of excellent and poor employee performance that were observed by the supervisor. Documentation is important for four reasons. First, documentation forces a supervisor to focus on employee behaviors rather than on traits and provides behavioral examples to use when reviewing performance ratings with employees.

Second, documentation helps supervisors recall behaviors when they are evaluating performance. As shown in Exhibit 7.16, without documentation, instead of recalling all of an employee's behavior or at least a representative sample of behavior, supervisors tend to recall only a small percentage of an employee's actual behavior. Supervisors tend to remember the following:

- _First impressions._ Research from many areas of psychology indicates that we remember our first impression of someone (primacy effect) more than we remember later behaviors. Consequently, supervisors recall behaviors consistent with their first impression of an employee, even though those first behaviors may not have been representative of the employee's typical performance.

Exhibit 7.13 Example of a behaviorally anchored rating scale

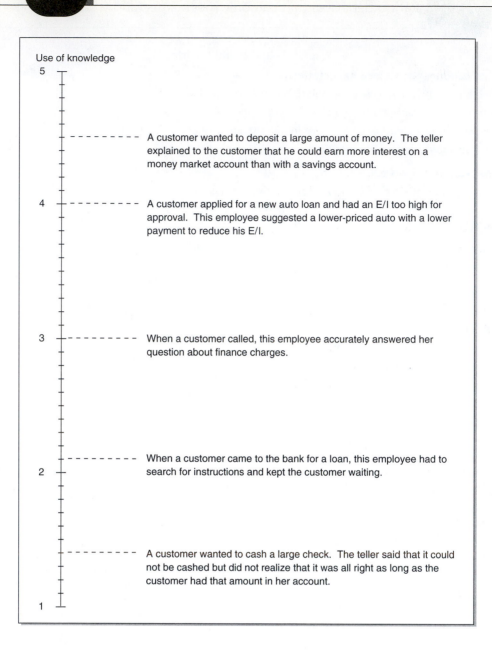

Use of knowledge

5

— A customer wanted to deposit a large amount of money. The teller explained to the customer that he could earn more interest on a money market account than with a savings account.

4 — A customer applied for a new auto loan and had an E/I too high for approval. This employee suggested a lower-priced auto with a lower payment to reduce his E/I.

3 — When a customer called, this employee accurately answered her question about finance charges.

— When a customer came to the bank for a loan, this employee had to search for instructions and kept the customer waiting.

2

— A customer wanted to cash a large check. The teller said that it could not be cashed but did not realize that it was all right as long as the customer had that amount in her account.

1

- *Recent behaviors.* In addition to first impressions, supervisors tend to recall the most recent behavior that occurred during the evaluation period.

- *Unusual or extreme behaviors.* Supervisors tend to remember unusual behaviors more than they remember common behaviors. For example, if an average performing police officer captures an important criminal, the officer's performance evaluations are likely to be inappropriately high. Likewise, a good officer who makes a terrible mistake is likely to receive inappropriately low ratings.

- *Behavior consistent with the supervisor's opinion.* Once we form an opinion of someone, we tend to look for behaviors that confirm that opinion. If a supervisor likes an employee, she will probably only recall behaviors consistent with that opinion. The opposite would be true for a supervisor who dislikes an employee. Once you get on someone's bad side, it is hard to get off it.

Third, documentation provides examples to use when reviewing performance ratings with employees. Instead of telling an employee that she is constantly getting into arguments with customers, a supervisor can use documented critical incidents to show the employee the specific incidents and behaviors that are problematic.

Fourth, documentation helps an organization defend against legal actions taken against it by an

Exhibit 7.14 Example of a forced-choice rating scale

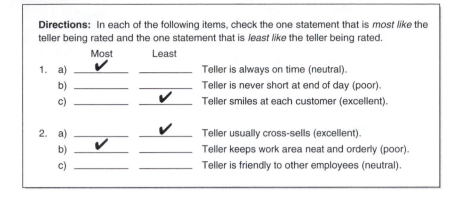

Directions: In each of the following items, check the one statement that is *most like* the teller being rated and the one statement that is *least like* the teller being rated.

		Most	Least	
1.	a)	✔		Teller is always on time (neutral).
	b)			Teller is never short at end of day (poor).
	c)		✔	Teller smiles at each customer (excellent).
2.	a)		✔	Teller usually cross-sells (excellent).
	b)	✔		Teller keeps work area neat and orderly (poor).
	c)			Teller is friendly to other employees (neutral).

employee who was terminated or denied a raise or promotion. As will be discussed later in this chapter, the courts closely examine the accuracy of the performance ratings upon which personnel decisions are based. Judges and juries are not likely to accept a supervisor's rating as proof of poor performance. Instead, they want to see proof of the behaviors that caused the supervisor to rate the employee poorly. Without documentation, employers will seldom win lawsuits filed against them (Foster, 2002). The courts' need for documentation is supported by research indicating that when evaluators must justify their performance ratings their ratings are more accurate (Mero & Motowidlo, 1995).

To use critical incidents to document performance, a supervisor maintains a log of all the critical behaviors she observes her employees performing. These behaviors are then used during the performance-appraisal review process to assign a rating for each employee.

The log refreshes the supervisor's memory of her employees' performance and also provides justification for each performance rating. The use of log books to record behaviors not only provides an excellent source of documentation but also results in more accurate performance appraisals (Bernardin & Walter, 1977). This is especially true if separate logs are kept for each employee rather than maintained as only a random collection of incidents observed on the job (DeNisi & Peters, 1996; DeNisi, Robbins, & Cafferty, 1989).

A more formal method for using critical incidents in evaluating performance was developed by Flanagan and Burns (1955) for use by General Motors. Called the **Employee Performance Record**, this method consists of a two-color form similar to that shown in Exhibit 7.17. Half of the sheet is used to record examples of good behaviors, the other half to record examples of poor behaviors. On each side,

The performance review is the final step in the performance-appraisal process.

Exhibit 7.15 Example of a mixed-standard scale

Directions: Place a "+" after the statement if the typical behavior of the teller is usually better than that represented in the statement, a "0" if the typical behavior of the teller is about the same as that represented in the statement, and a "−" if the typical behavior of the teller is worse than that represented in the statement.

Rating

1. Teller constantly argues with other employees (P).   _____
2. Teller smiles at customers (A).   _____
3. Teller asks customers how their families are doing (E).   _____
4. Teller helps other employees when possible (A).   _____
5. Teller is always friendly to and talks with other employees (E).   _____
6. Teller asks customers what they want (P).   _____

Items 1, 4, and 5 are from the Employee Relations Dimension.
Items 2, 3, and 6 are from the Customer Relations Dimension.

there are columns for each of the relevant performance dimensions. Supervisors have a separate record for each employee and at the end of the day can record the observed behaviors.

The advantage of this format is that supervisors are allowed to record only job-relevant behaviors. At the end of the performance-appraisal period (every 6 months), the supervisor has a record of job-relevant behaviors recorded in an organized fashion.

The Employee Performance Record had several positive effects for General Motors. The number of disciplinary warnings declined, suggestions in the company suggestion box increased, and productivity increased.

When the use of critical incidents was first announced, supervisors at General Motors were opposed, thinking it would take too much time. The actual time per day spent on recording the incidents, however, was only 5 minutes.

Step 7: Evaluate Performance

Obtaining and Reviewing Objective Data

When it is time to appraise an employee's performance, a supervisor should first obtain and review the objective data relevant to an employee's behavior. For example, a police sergeant might review the numbers of tickets an officer wrote, arrests made, and citizen complaints received. A production supervisor might review the number of days an employee was absent, number of units produced, and the tons of material wasted. These data, when combined with critical incident logs, provide a solid basis on which to rate an employee. As mentioned earlier in the chapter, when reviewing objective data, it is essential that potential

sources of contamination (e.g., shift, equipment, training, coworkers, geographic area) be considered. Complete Exercise 7–5 to get experience dealing with contamination problems.

Reading Critical Incident Logs

After obtaining objective data, the supervisor should go back and read all of the critical incidents written for an employee. Reading these incidents should reduce the primacy, recency, and attention to unusual information errors.

Completing the Rating Form

Once critical incident logs have been read and objective data reviewed, the supervisor is ready to assign performance-appraisal ratings. While making these ratings, the supervisor must be careful not to make common rating errors involving distribution, halo, proximity, and contrast.

Distribution Errors

A common type of error in evaluating employee performance involves the distribution of ratings on a rating scale; such errors are known as **distribution errors**. One kind of distribution error is called **leniency error** because certain raters tend to rate every employee at the upper end of the scale regardless of the actual performance of the employee. A related error is **central tendency error**, which results in a supervisor rating every employee in the middle of the scale. Still another error, **strictness error**, rates every employee at the low end of the scale. You have probably encountered such errors in your academic career when you took classes from "easy graders" or "hard graders."

Exhibit **7.16** Information loss in the performance-appraisal system

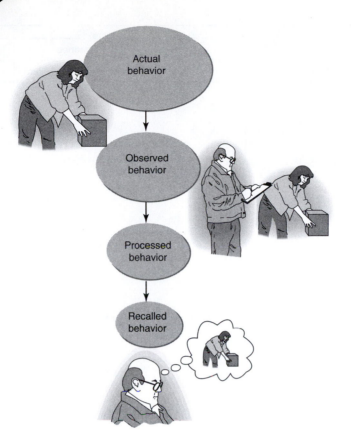

These types of errors pose problems for an organization because two employees doing equal work will receive different ratings if one employee is supervised by a lenient rater and another by a strict rater. This problem can be partially eliminated by having several people rate each employee (Kane & Lawler, 1979), although this is not often feasible, especially in small branch offices with only one manager or supervisor.

Halo Errors

A **halo error** occurs when a rater allows either a single attribute or an overall impression of an individual to affect the ratings that she makes on each relevant job dimension. For example, a teacher might think that a student is highly articulate. Because of that, the teacher might rate the student as being intelligent and industrious when, in fact, the student's grades are below average. In this case, the instructor has allowed the student's articulateness to cloud her judgment of the student's other abilities. Halo effects occur especially when the rater has little knowledge of the job and is less familiar with the person being rated (Kozlowski, Kirsch, & Chao, 1986).

Usually, halo error is statistically determined by correlating the ratings for each dimension with those for the other dimensions. If they are highly correlated, halo error is often said to have occurred. But several industrial psychologists have argued that many times consistent ratings across several dimensions indicate not error but actual employee performance. Thus a teacher who is rated highly in classroom teaching, ability to work with students, knowledge, and fairness of grading actually may excel in those things. But proponents of the halo error explanation would argue that the instructor is friendly and so well liked by her students that she receives high ratings on the other dimensions when, in fact, she may not have shown a high level of knowledge in her subject matter.

Halo errors may or may not be a serious problem (Balzer & Sulsky, 1992), but they can be reduced by having supervisors rate each trait at separate times. That is, the supervisor might rate the employee on attendance one day and then rate him on dependability the next day (Cooper, 1981a, 1981b). Of course, in reality, such a practice is seldom possible. Examples of leniency, strictness, and halo errors are shown in Exhibit 7.18.

Proximity Errors

Proximity errors occur when a rating made on one dimension affects the rating made on the dimension that immediately follows it on the rating scale. The difference between this error and halo error is in the cause of the error and the number of dimensions affected. With halo error, all dimensions are affected by an overall impression of the employee. With proximity error, only the dimensions physically located nearest a particular dimension on the rating scale are affected;

Exhibit **7.17** Employee performance record

	Type of Performance	
Dimension	**Poor**	**Excellent**
Knowledge		
Employee relations		
Customer relations		
Accuracy of work		

the reason for the effect, in fact, *is* the close physical proximity of the dimension rather than an overall impression.

Contrast Errors

The performance rating one person receives can be influenced by the performance of a previously evaluated person (Bravo & Kravitz, 1996). For example, a bank manager has six employees who are evaluated twice a year—on February 5 and again on August 5. The manager makes the evaluations in alphabetical order, starting with Joan Carr and then going to Donna Chan. Joan Carr is the best employee the bank has ever had, and she receives the highest possible rating on each dimension. After evaluating Carr, the manager then evaluates Chan. When compared to Carr, Chan is not nearly as effective an employee. Thus, Chan

receives lower ratings than she might normally receive simply because she has been evaluated immediately after Carr. Her performance has been contrasted to Carr's performance rather than to some objective standard.

Such **contrast errors** can also occur between separate performance evaluations of the same person. That is, the ratings received on one performance appraisal will affect the ratings made on an appraisal 6 months later. For example, an employee's performance during the first 6 months of the year is "excellent," and she receives outstanding performance ratings. For some reason, the employee's actual behavior in the next 6 months is only "good." What type of performance rating will she receive? Based on the results of a study by Murphy, Gannett, Herr, and Chen (1986), the answer probably is that her ratings will be less than "good." In contrast to her initial excellent performance,

Exhibit 7.18   Examples of rating errors

Leniency Error

Norm Nixon							Walt Davis					
Cooperation	1	2	3	4	⑤		Cooperation	1	2	3	4	⑤
Knowledge	1	2	3	4	⑤		Knowledge	1	2	3	4	⑤
Leadership	1	2	3	4	⑤		Leadership	1	2	3	4	⑤

Earvin Johnson							John Lucas					
Cooperation	1	2	3	4	⑤		Cooperation	1	2	3	4	⑤
Knowledge	1	2	3	4	⑤		Knowledge	1	2	3	4	⑤
Leadership	1	2	3	4	⑤		Leadership	1	2	3	4	⑤

Strictness Error

Norm Nixon							Walt Davis					
Cooperation	①	2	3	4	5		Cooperation	①	2	3	4	5
Knowledge	①	2	3	4	5		Knowledge	①	2	3	4	5
Leadership	①	2	3	4	5		Leadership	①	2	3	4	5

Earvin Johnson							John Lucas					
Cooperation	①	2	3	4	5		Cooperation	①	2	3	4	5
Knowledge	①	2	3	4	5		Knowledge	①	2	3	4	5
Leadership	①	2	3	4	5		Leadership	①	2	3	4	5

Halo Error

Norm Nixon							Walt Davis					
Cooperation	1	2	3	4	⑤		Cooperation	1	2	③	4	5
Knowledge	1	2	3	4	⑤		Knowledge	1	2	③	4	5
Leadership	1	2	3	4	⑤		Leadership	1	2	③	4	5

Earvin Johnson							John Lucas					
Cooperation	1	2	3	4	⑤		Cooperation	①	2	3	4	5
Knowledge	1	2	3	4	⑤		Knowledge	①	2	3	4	5
Leadership	1	2	3	4	⑤		Leadership	①	2	3	4	5

the employee's subsequent performance (which may indeed have been "good") appeared to be lower than it actually was.

Contrast effects occur only when the person making the evaluation actually sees the employee perform (Smither, Reilly, & Buda, 1988) and rates the employee (Summer & Knight, 1996) during both rating periods. If a new supervisor reads that an employee's previous evaluations were excellent but she observes poor performance by the employee, she will probably continue to give excellent ratings—even though the employee's performance deteriorated. Smither and his colleagues call this rating error **assimilation.** To get a better feel for rating errors, complete Exercise 7–6 at the end of this chapter.

Low Reliability Across Raters

As shown in Exhibit 7.03, two people rating the same employee seldom agree with one another (Conway & Huffcut, 1997; Viswesvaran, Ones, & Schmidt, 1996). There are three major reasons for this lack of reliability. First, raters often commit the rating errors (e.g., halo, leniency) previously discussed. Thus, if one rater engages in halo error and another in contrast error, it is not surprising that their ratings of the same employee are different.

Second, raters often have very different standards and ideas about the ideal employee. For example, I recently conducted a performance-appraisal workshop for a police department. After viewing a video clip of an officer handling a disturbance call, one sergeant rated the officer's performance as excellent and another rated the officer's performance as being terrible. When asked about their different ratings, one sergeant indicated that he thought officers should be aggressive and take command of a situation whereas the other sergeant thought officers should be more citizen-oriented. Thus, the same employee behavior elicited two very different ratings because each sergeant had a different "prototype" of the ideal cop.

Third, as mentioned earlier in the chapter, two different raters may actually see very different behaviors by the same employee. For example, a desk sergeant may see more administrative and paperwork behaviors whereas a field sergeant may see more law enforcement behaviors. Thus, different ratings by the two sergeants may simply reflect the fact that each has observed the officer perform in very different situations. As mentioned earlier, one way to reduce the number of rating errors and increase reliability is to train the people who will be making the performance evaluations (Hauenstein, 1998).

Sampling Problems

Recency Effect. Performance appraisals are typically conducted once or twice a year. The evaluation is designed to cover all of the behaviors that have taken place during the previous 6 months to a year. Research has demonstrated, however, that recent behaviors are given more weight in the performance evaluation than behaviors that occurred during the first few months of the evaluation period. Such an effect penalizes workers who performed well during most of the period but tailed off toward the end, and it rewards workers who saved their best work until just before the evaluation.

In baseball, the Los Angeles Dodgers had several poor seasons in which they lost many games early in the season, which eliminated them from pennant contention. But several players played well and produced great statistics during the final month of the season; the press called this period the "salary drive" as opposed to the "pennant drive." This suggests that the players may have been aware of the **recency effect.** They hoped that high performance before contracts were renewed would bring better evaluations and thus higher salaries for the next year. It seems that students are well aware of the recency effect when they argue that the high score on their final exam should carry more weight than the lower scores on previous exams!

Infrequent Observation. As shown in Exhibit 7.02, another problem that affects performance appraisals is that many managers or supervisors do not have the opportunity to observe a representative sample of employee behavior. **Infrequent observation** occurs for two reasons. First, managers are often so busy with their own work that they have no time to "walk the floor" and observe their employees' behavior. Instead, they make inferences based on completed work or employee personality traits (Feldman, 1981). A good example involves a teacher who completes a reference form for a student. Reference forms commonly ask

about characteristics such as the applicant's ability to cooperate or to get along with others. The teacher must base her evaluation on the term papers she has seen and the student's test grades. Rarely does she have the opportunity to watch the student "get along with" or "cooperate with" others. Instead, because a group project was turned in on time and received an excellent grade, she surmises that the student must have cooperated and gotten along well with other group members.

Employees often act differently around a supervisor than around other workers, which is the second reason managers usually do not make accurate observations. When the supervisor is absent, an employee may break rules, show up late, or work slowly. But when the boss is around, the employee becomes a model worker. In the eyes of the supervisor, the employee is doing an excellent job; the other workers, however, know better.

As discussed earlier in the chapter, this problem can be alleviated somewhat by having several raters evaluate the employee. Other raters can be other supervisors, fellow workers (peer ratings), and even customers. A meta-analysis by Conway and Huffcutt (1997) indicates that supervisor ratings on the average correlate .34 with peer ratings. Thus, even though the two groups somewhat agree, the agreement is certainly not perfect.

Unfortunately, ratings from these sources are often subject to more errors than the uninformed ratings made by a supervisor. For example, customers may complain about a worker even though she is following policy, and a worker may provide low evaluations of her coworkers so that she will receive a higher raise. Even with these problems, multiple raters remain a good idea.

Cognitive Processing of Observed Behavior

Observation of Behavior. As shown in Exhibits 7.19 and 7.20, just because an employee's behavior is observed does not guarantee that it will be properly remembered or recalled during the performance-appraisal review. In fact, research (Cooper, 1981a; Feldman, 1981; Martell, Guzzo, & Willis, 1995) indicates that raters recall those behaviors that are consistent with their general impression of an employee. And the greater the time interval between the actual behavior and the performance rating, the greater the probability that halo errors (Nathan & Lord, 1983) and distortion errors (Murphy, Martin, & Garcia, 1982) will occur. Furthermore, raters who are familiar with the job being evaluated recall more judgments about performance but fewer behaviors than do raters who are unfamiliar with the job (Harriman & Kovach, 1987; Hauenstein, 1986). The decrease in memory accuracy over time can be reduced if several raters, rather than one, are used to evaluate performance (Martell & Borg, 1993).

But even though memory-based ratings lead to more distortion, in many circumstances they are more accurate than ratings made immediately after the behaviors occur (Murphy & Balzer, 1986). The reason for these increases in halo and accuracy is not yet clear. Supervisors perhaps realize that it will be a long interval

Exhibit 7.19 Factors affecting information loss

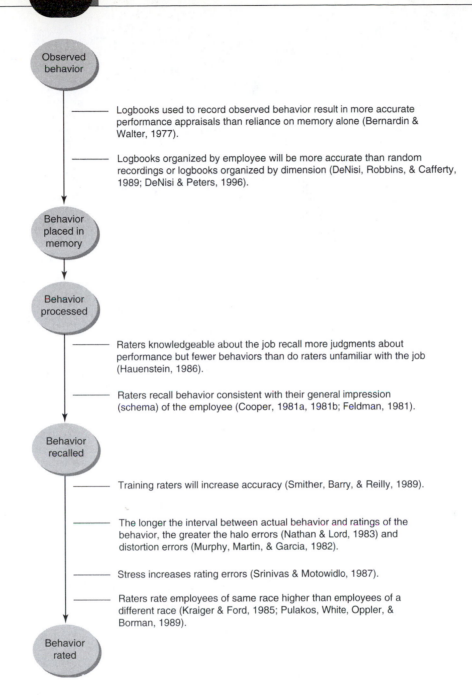

Observed behavior

Logbooks used to record observed behavior result in more accurate performance appraisals than reliance on memory alone (Bernardin & Walter, 1977).

Logbooks organized by employee will be more accurate than random recordings or logbooks organized by dimension (DeNisi, Robbins, & Cafferty, 1989; DeNisi & Peters, 1996).

Behavior placed in memory

Behavior processed

Raters knowledgeable about the job recall more judgments about performance but fewer behaviors than do raters unfamiliar with the job (Hauenstein, 1986).

Raters recall behavior consistent with their general impression (schema) of the employee (Cooper, 1981a, 1981b; Feldman, 1981).

Behavior recalled

Training raters will increase accuracy (Smither, Barry, & Reilly, 1989).

The longer the interval between actual behavior and ratings of the behavior, the greater the halo errors (Nathan & Lord, 1983) and distortion errors (Murphy, Martin, & Garcia, 1982).

Stress increases rating errors (Srinivas & Motowidlo, 1987).

Raters rate employees of same race higher than employees of a different race (Kraiger & Ford, 1985; Pulakos, White, Oppler, & Borman, 1989).

Behavior rated

between observation of employee behavior and the formal evaluation of that behavior and that they will not be able (without great effort or the use of log books) to remember specific behaviors. Thus, they form an overall impression of the employee and an overall impression of an ideal and a poor employee and evaluate the employee based on comparison with the ideal.

Emotional State. The amount of **stress** under which a supervisor operates also affects her performance ratings. Srinivas and Motowidlo (1987) found that raters who were placed in a stressful situation produced

ratings with more errors than did raters who were not under stress. This finding is important because performance evaluations are often conducted hurriedly as supervisors evaluate employee performance so that they can return to their "real" work. Methods for reducing this problem will be discussed later in this chapter.

Bias. Raters who like the person being rated may be more lenient (Lefkowitz, 2000; Varma, DeNisi, & Peters, 1996) and less accurate in rating employees than are raters who neither like nor dislike their employees

Exhibit 7.20 Factors affecting performance

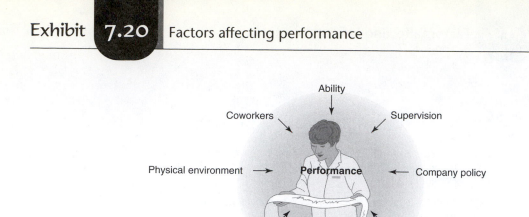

(Cardy & Dobbins, 1986). But this does not mean that a person who is liked will always receive higher ratings than someone who is disliked. The rater may overcompensate in an effort to be "fair." The rater's feelings, or **affect**, toward an employee may interfere with the cognitive processing of actual performance information.

Research has also indicated that **racial bias** exists in performance evaluations. Kraiger and Ford (1985) conducted a meta-analysis of 74 studies and found that white raters gave higher performance ratings to white employees and that African American raters gave higher ratings to African American employees. Interestingly, this bias occurred only with studies involving real organizations—laboratory research seldom reveals racial bias in rating.

A meta-analysis by Bowen, Swim, and Jacobs (2000) and a large data set of 360-degree feedback ratings by Church, Rogelberg, and Waclawski (2000) suggest that gender bias does not seem to be an issue in performance ratings.

Step 8: Communicate Appraisal Results to Employees

As was stated in the beginning of this chapter, perhaps the most important use of performance-evaluation data is to provide feedback to the employee and assess her strengths and weaknesses so that further training can be implemented. Although this feedback and training should be an ongoing process, the semiannual evaluation might be the best time to formally discuss employee performance. Furthermore, holding a formal review interview places the organization on better legal ground in the event of a lawsuit (Feild & Holley, 1982; Malos, 1998).

Normally, in most organizations a supervisor spends a few minutes with employees every 6 months to *tell* them about the scores they received during the most recent evaluation period. This process is probably

the norm because most managers do not like to judge others; because of this dislike, they try to complete the evaluation process as quickly as possible (Grensing-Pophal, 2001a).

Furthermore, seldom does evaluating employees benefit the supervisor. The best scenario is to hear no complaints and the worst scenario is a lawsuit. In fact, one study demonstrated that dissatisfaction and a decrease in organizational commitment occur even when an employee receives an evaluation that is "satisfactory" but not "outstanding" (Pearce & Porter, 1986). Finally, in the "tell and sell" approach to performance-appraisal interviews, a supervisor "tells" an employee everything she has done poorly and then "sells" her on ways she can improve. This method, however, accomplishes little.

Research suggests that certain techniques can be used to make the performance-appraisal interview more effective: time, scheduling, and preparation.

Prior to the Interview

Allocating Time

Both the supervisor and the employee must have time to prepare for the review interview. Both should be allowed at least an hour to prepare before an interview and at least an hour for the interview itself.

Scheduling the Interview

The interview location should be in a neutral place that ensures privacy and allows the supervisor and employee to face one another without a desk between them as a communication barrier (Arthur, 1996). Performance-appraisal review interviews should be scheduled at least once every 6 months for most employees and more often for new employees. Review interviews are commonly scheduled 6 months after an employee begins working for the organization. If this date comes at a bad time (such as during the Christmas season, a busy time for retail stores), the interview should be scheduled for a more convenient time. It is important to note that although the *formal* performance-appraisal review occurs only once or twice a year, informal "progress checks" should be held throughout the year to provide feedback (Rhoads, 1997).

Preparing for the Interview

While preparing for the interview, the supervisor should review the ratings she has assigned to the employee and the reasons for those ratings. This step is important because the quality of feedback given to employees will affect their satisfaction with the entire performance-appraisal process (Mount, 1983). Furthermore, employees perceive and react to the amount of time that a supervisor prepares for the interview (King, 1984).

Meanwhile, the employee should rate her own performance using the same format as the supervisor. The employee also should write down specific reasons and examples that support the ratings she gives herself, as well as ideas for personal development (Falcone, 1999b).

During the Interview

At the outset of the interview, the supervisor should communicate the following: (1) the role of performance appraisal—that making decisions about salary increases and terminations is not its only purpose; (2) how the performance appraisal was conducted; and (3) how the evaluation process was accomplished. It is advisable that the supervisor also communicate her own feelings about the performance-appraisal process (Kelly, 1984).

The review process is probably best begun with the employee communicating her own ratings and her justification for those ratings (Grote, 1998). Research indicates that employees who are actively involved in the interview from the start will be more satisfied with the results (Atwater, 1998; Gilliland & Langdon, 1998).

The supervisor then communicates her ratings and the reasons for them. The supervisor should limit this communication to statements about behavior and performance rather than traits that are or are not possessed by the employee (Arthur, 1996; Ilgen, Mitchell, & Fredrickson, 1981). Of course, it would be nice to avoid negative feedback because employees then are more satisfied with their reviews (Brett & Atwater, 2001) and don't develop negative attitudes toward management (Gabris & Mitchell, 1988). But few employees are perfect, and some negative feedback is inevitable. Because of this, positive feedback generally should be given first (Armentrout, 1993; Stone, Gueutal, & McIntosh, 1984) because employees will likely try to avoid negative feedback to maintain a positive self-image (Larson, 1989). Furthermore, supervisors tend to avoid negative feedback in an effort to reduce the chance of interpersonal conflict (Waung & Highhouse, 1997). Any major differences between the employee's self-ratings and those given

by the supervisor should be discussed until both understand the differences.

The next step is perhaps the most important. Because few employees receive perfect evaluations, it is essential to discuss the reasons an employee's performance is not considered to be perfect. The employee may lack some knowledge as to how to perform the job properly, may have been assigned too many duties, or may have outside problems that affect her work performance.

The supervisor's acknowledgment that there may be external reasons for an employee's poor performance can increase the employee's satisfaction with the review and enable her to perceive the feedback and evaluation as accurate and helpful. In addition, it will help the employee understand and appreciate the supervisor's perceptions (Bannister, 1986; Baron, 1988). Feedback should be candid, specific, and behavioral rather than personal (Hequet, 1994). Awareness and acknowledgment of external factors for performance are especially important because we have a tendency, called the fundamental attribution error, to attribute others' failure or poor performance to personal rather than situational factors.

Once the problems have been identified, the next and most difficult task is to find solutions (Nanry, 1988). What can the supervisor do to help? What can the organization do? What can the employee do? The idea here is that solutions to the problems result from joint effort. Too often we attribute poor performance as being solely the fault of the employee, when, in fact, performance is affected by many factors (see Exhibit 7.20).

At the conclusion of the interview, goals should be mutually set for future performance and behavior, and both supervisor and employee should understand how these goals will be met (Joinson, 2001b). Goals and goal setting will be thoroughly discussed in Chapter 9. For now, however, we should keep in mind that goals should be concrete, reasonable, and set by both employee and supervisor (Ivancevich, 1982). To practice conducting a performance-appraisal review interview, complete Exercise 7–7 at the end of this chapter.

Step 9: Terminate Employees

As discussed in the preceding pages, the primary use of performance-appraisal results is to provide feedback to employees about their behavior. Performance-appraisal results are also used to make positive personnel decisions such as raises and promotions. Unfortunately, there are times when managers have to terminate an employee's employment. Over the next few pages, we will discuss the legal aspects of terminating an employee.

Employment-at-Will Doctrine

There is a big difference between terminating an employee in the public sector versus the private sector.

Exhibit **7.21** Sample employment-at-will statement

> I understand that, if employed, I have the right to end my employment with Sordi Industries. Likewise, I understand that my employment with Sordi Industries is not for any definite period of time, and Sordi Industries has the right to terminate my employment with or without cause and with or without notice. I understand that no representative of Sordi Industries is authorized to imply any contract for permanent employment.

In the private sector, the **employment-at-will doctrine** in most states allows employers freedom to fire an employee without a reason—*at will*. The idea behind employment at will is that because employees are free to quit their jobs at will so, too, are organizations free to terminate an employee at will (Ballam, 1995; Falcone, 1999a). There are some limitations to this doctrine (Falcone, 2002).

- *State law.* Some states such as California and New York have laws that an employee can only be fired for cause—breaking a rule or an inability to perform.

- *Provisions of federal or state law.* Employees cannot be fired for reasons protected by federal or state law. For example, an employer could not fire an employee because she was a female, pregnant, nonwhite, or over the age of 40.

- *Public policy/interest.* Employers cannot terminate an employee for exercising a legal duty such as jury duty or refusing to violate the law or professional ethics. For example, a large savings and loan institution ordered one of its appraisers to appraise homes higher than their actual value so that its customers could qualify to finance property. Citing federal regulations and professional ethics against inflating property values, the employee refused the company order. After being terminated, the employee successfully filed a lawsuit (one of more than 200 filed by employees against this institution) claiming that he had been fired for refusing to violate the law and the ethical standards of his profession.

- *Contracts.* Obviously, if an individual employee has a signed employment contract stipulating a particular period of employment, an organization cannot fire the employee without cause. Likewise, unions enter into collective bargaining agreements (contracts) with employers that also limit or negate employment at will.

- *Implied contracts.* Employment at will is nullified if an employer implies that an employee "has a job for life" or can only be fired for certain

reasons. For example, if an interviewer tells an applicant, "At this company, all you have to do is keep your nose clean to keep your job," the employer will not be able to terminate the employee for minor rule infractions or for poor performance.

- *Covenants of good faith and fair dealing.* Though employers are generally free to hire and fire at will, the courts have ruled that employers must still act in good faith and deal fairly with an employee (Buckley & Weitzel, 1988). These rulings have been based on an item in the Uniform Commercial Code stating "Every contract . . . imposes an obligation of good faith in its performance or enforcement" and the fact that courts consider employment decisions to be a form of a contract.

To protect their right to use a policy of employment at will, most organizations include **employment-at-will statements**, such as that shown in Exhibit 7.21, in their job applications and employee handbooks (Heller, 2001). These statements usually hold up in court (Jenner, 1994) and employees seem not to challenge them (Hilgert, 1991).

Legal Reasons for Terminating Employees

In situations not covered by employment at will, there are only four reasons that an employee can be legally terminated: a probationary period, a violation of company rules, an inability to perform, and an economically caused reduction in force (layoffs).

Probationary Period

In many jobs, employees are given a probationary period in which to prove that they can perform well. Though most probationary periods last 3 to 6 months, those for police officers are usually a year and the probationary period for professors is 6 years! Employees can be terminated more easily during the probationary period than at any other time.

Violation of Company Rules

Courts consider five factors in determining the legality of a decision to terminate an employee for violating company rules. The first factor is that a rule against a particular behavior must actually exist. Though this may seem obvious, organizations often have "unwritten" rules governing employee behavior. These unwritten rules, however, will not hold up in court. For example, a manufacturer fired an employee for wearing a gun under his jacket at work. The employee successfully appealed on the grounds that even though "common sense" would say that guns should not be brought to work, the company did not have a written rule against it.

If a rule exists, a company must prove that the employee knew the rule. Rules can be communicated orally during employee orientation and staff meetings and in writing in handbooks, newsletters, bulletin boards, and paycheck stuffers. Rules communicated in handbooks are the most legally defensible. To prove that an employee knew a rule, organizations require employees to sign statements that they received information about the rule, read the rule, and understand the rule.

The third factor is the ability of the employer to prove that an employee actually violated the rule. Proof is accomplished through such means as witnesses, video recordings, and job samples. Human resource professionals almost have to be detectives because proving rule violations is often not easy. For example, two supervisors saw an employee stagger into work and could clearly smell alcohol on her breath. She was terminated for violating the company rule against drinking. During her appeal of the termination, she claimed that she staggered because she had the flu and what the supervisors smelled was cough syrup rather than alcohol. The employee won the appeal. As a result of this case, the company now has an on-site nurse, and Breathalyzer tests are administered to employees suspected of using alcohol at work.

The fourth factor considered by the courts is the extent to which the rule has been equally enforced. That is, if other employees violated the rule but were not terminated, terminating an employee for a particular rule violation may not be legal. This factor poses a dilemma for many organizations. Because courts look at consistency, lawyers advise organizations to fire any employee who violates a rule. To not fire a rule breaker sets a precedent making termination of future rule breakers more difficult. There are many times when a good employee breaks a rule, a situation that normally would result in termination. However, because the employee is highly valued, the organization does not want to fire the employee.

Such a situation occurred at a bank. In violation of a bank rule, a teller did not ask for the ID of a customer who cashed what turned out to be a forged check. The bank was torn as to what it should do. Because the employee was one of their best tellers, the bank did not want to fire her. However, not firing her in this case would increase the chance that they would lose a future lawsuit if they terminated another employee for doing the same thing. The bank's unusual decision was to terminate the employee, but it called a competitor, told it of the situation, and asked if it would hire her—which it did.

The fifth and final factor is the extent to which the punishment fits the crime. Employees in their probationary period (usually their first 6 months) can be immediately fired for a rule infraction. For more tenured employees, however, the organization must make a reasonable attempt to change the person's behavior through **progressive discipline** (Barth, 2002). The longer an employee has been with an organization, the greater the number of steps that must be taken to correct her behavior. Discipline can begin with something simple such as counseling or an oral warning, progress to a written warning or probation, and end with steps such as reductions in pay, demotions, or terminations.

For violations of some rules, progressive discipline is not always necessary. It is probably safe to say that an employer can terminate an employee who steals money or shoots someone at work.

Inability to Perform

Employees can also be terminated for an inability to perform the job. To do so though, an organization will need to prove that the employee could not perform the job and that progressive discipline was taken to give the employee an opportunity to improve. For an employer to survive a court challenge to terminating a poorly performing employee, it must first demonstrate that a reasonable standard of performance was communicated to the employee. The organization must next demonstrate that there was a documented failure to meet the standard. Such documentation can include critical incident logs and work samples (e.g., poorly typed letters for a secretary, improperly hemmed pants for a tailor).

A properly designed performance-appraisal system is the key to legally terminating an employee (Martin, Bartol, & Kehoe, 2000). Legal performance-appraisal systems (Smith, 1993)

- are based on a job analysis.
- have concrete, relevant standards that have been communicated to employees.
- involve multiple behavioral measures of performance.
- include several raters, each of whom has received training (Rosen, 1992).
- are standardized and formal.
- provide the opportunity for an employee to appeal.

Reduction in Force (Layoff)

Employees can be terminated if it is in the best economic interests of an organization to do so. Reductions in force, more commonly called layoffs, have been used by the vast majority of *Fortune* 500 companies in the past decade (Byrne, 1994; Cameron, Freeman, & Mishra, 1991). In cases of large layoffs or plant closings, the Worker Adjustment and Retraining Notification Act (WARN) requires that organizations provide workers with at least 60 days notice. Though layoffs are designed to save money, research indicates not only that force reductions have a devastating effect on employees (Leana & Feldman, 1992), but that they often do not result in the desired financial savings (Byrne, 1994). Layoffs are extensively discussed in Chapter 14.

The Termination Meeting

Prior to the Meeting

Once a decision has been made to terminate an employee, Connolly (1986) advises that certain steps be taken to prepare for the meeting in which the decision will be communicated to the employee. The first step is to ensure that the legal process has been followed. For example, if an organization is about to terminate an employee for a rule violation, it must be sure that a rule actually existed, that the employee knew the rule, that the organization has proof the rule was violated, that progressive discipline was used, and that the rule was applied equally to all employees. An important responsibility for human resource professionals is to ensure that a termination decision is legally defensible.

The next step is to determine how much help, if any, the organization wants to offer the employee. Forms of help can include references, severance pay, and outplacement assistance. Usually, greater levels of help are given to employees who sign agreements not to sue the organization.

The final step is to schedule an appropriate place and time for the meeting to occur. The meeting should be held in a neutral, private location (DuBose, 1994; Karl & Hancock, 1999). To avoid potential damage caused by a hostile reaction to the termination decision, the meeting should not be held in a supervisor's office. Rather than late on Friday afternoon, as is traditional, the meeting should take place on a Monday or Tuesday so that the employee has an opportunity to seek advice and the organization has a chance to talk to its employees (Karl & Hancock, 1999; Scrivner, 1995). When a termination is made on a Friday afternoon, the employee is unable to contact sources of help over the weekend. Likewise, the terminated employee has all weekend to get on the phone to tell her side of the story to other employees while the organization must wait until Monday to refute the gossip.

During the Meeting

During the meeting, the supervisor should get to the point about terminating the employee. The employee usually knows why she has been called in, and there is no reason to prolong the agony. The supervisor should rationally state the reasons for the decision, express gratitude for the employee's efforts (if sincere), and

offer whatever assistance the organization intends to provide (Nyholm, 1996). Administrative duties such as obtaining copies of keys and completing paperwork are then performed. Finally, the employee is asked to gather personal belongings and is escorted out the door.

I realize that this advice sounds cold. However, terminating an employee is a difficult task, and there is little that can be done to make it pleasant. If you have ever ended a romantic relationship, I think you will understand the feelings that go into terminating an employee. It is an emotional time, and the key is to be brief and professional (Pollan & Levine, 1994).

After the Meeting

Once the meeting is over, the natural reaction of the supervisor is to feel guilty. To relieve some of this guilt, a supervisor should review the facts—she gave the employee every chance to improve, but the employee chose not to. A human resource professional for Valleydale Foods tells employees this: "Through your behavior, you fired yourself. I'm just completing the paperwork."

When an employee is fired, other employees will be tense. Consequently, it is important to be honest with the other employees about what happened (Marchetti, 1997); at the same time, negative statements about the terminated employee's character must be avoided.

Chapter Summary

In this chapter you learned:

- The use of 360-degree feedback is increasing.
- There are five steps in creating a performance-appraisal system: (1) determine the reasons for performance evaluation, (2) create an instrument to evaluate performance, (3) explain the system to those who will use it, (4) evaluate employee performance, and (5) review the results of the evaluation with the employee.
- Common rating errors such as leniency, central tendency, strictness, halo, proximity, contrast, recency, and infrequent observation of behavior hinder the accuracy of performance-appraisal results.
- Important factors in the success of this discussion include scheduling the review to eliminate or minimize interruptions, letting the employee discuss her feelings and thoughts, and mutually setting goals for improvements in future performance.
- In organizations not subject to employment at will, employees can only be terminated for violating a company rule, for inability to perform, or as part of a force reduction.

Critical Thinking Questions

1. What is the most important purpose for performance appraisal?

2. What problems might result from using a 360-degree feedback system?

3. The chapter mentioned a variety of ways to measure performance. Which one is the best?

4. What is the best way to communicate performance-appraisal results to employees?

5. Is the employment-at-will doctrine a good idea?

To learn more about the issues discussed in this chapter, point your browser to

http://www.infotrac-college.com/wadsworth

and enter one of these search terms:

performance appraisals

360-degree feedback

behavioral observation scales

employee dismissals

layoff

terminating employees

Behaviorally Anchored Rating Scales

To reduce the rating problems associated with graphic rating scales, Smith and Kendall (1963) developed **behaviorally anchored rating scales (BARS)**. As shown in Exhibit 7.13, BARS use critical incidents (samples of behavior) to formally provide meaning to the numbers on a rating scale. Although BARS are time-consuming to construct, the process is not overly complicated.

Creating BARS

Generation of Job Dimensions

In the first step in BARS construction, the number and nature of job-related dimensions are determined. If a job analysis already has been conducted, the dimensions can be obtained from the job analysis report. If for some reason a job analysis has not been conducted, a panel of some 20 job experts—the employees—is formed. This panel determines the important dimensions on which an employee's performance should be evaluated. If 15 to 20 employees are not available, several supervisors can meet and develop the job dimensions as a group (Shapira & Shirom, 1980). Usually, 5 to 10 dimensions are generated (Schwab et al., 1975).

Generation of Critical Incidents

Once the relevant job dimensions have been identified, employees are asked to generate examples of good, average, and bad behavior that they have seen for each dimension. Thus, if five dimensions have been identified, each employee is asked to generate 15 critical incidents—a good, an average, and a bad incident—for each of the five dimensions. If the organization is fairly small, employees may need to generate more than one example of the three types of behavior for each dimension.

Sorting Incidents

To make sure that the incidents written for each job dimension are actually examples of behavior for that dimension, three job experts independently sort the incidents into each of the job dimensions. The dimension into which each incident has been sorted by each of the three sorters then is examined. If at least two sorters placed an incident in the same dimension, the incident becomes part of that dimension. But if each sorter has placed the incident in a different category, the incident is considered to be ambiguous and thus is discarded.

As discussed in Chapter 2, 3 sorters achieve results similar to those for 100 sorters. Many developers of BARS, however, use as many sorters as possible so that employees have a part in developing the scales. If many employees are involved, a 60% level of sorter agreement should be used to determine whether an incident is part of a dimension.

Rating Incidents

Another group of job experts is given the incidents and asked to rate each one on a scale that can have from 5 to 9 points as to the level of job performance that it represents (Bernardin, LaShells, Smith, & Alveres, 1976). The ratings from each rater for all of the incidents are then used to determine the mean rating and **standard deviation** for each incident (typically by computer).

Choosing Incidents

The goal of this step is to find one incident to represent each of the points on the scale for each dimension. To do so, the incidents whose mean ratings come closest to each of the scale points and whose standard deviations are small are kept (Maiorca, 1997). This procedure usually results in the retention of less than 50% of the incidents (Green, Sauser, Fagg, & Champion, 1981).

Creating the Scale

The incidents chosen in the previous step are then placed on a vertical scale such as that shown in Exhibit 7.13. Because the mean for each incident is unlikely to fall exactly on one of the scale points, they are often placed between the points, thus serving as anchors for future raters.

Using BARS

To use the scale when actually rating performance, the supervisor compares the incidents she has recorded for each employee to the incidents on each scale. This can be done in one of two ways. The most accurate (and the most time-consuming) method compares each of the recorded incidents to the anchors and records the value of the incident on the scale that most closely resembles the recorded incident. This is done for each recorded incident. The value for each incident is summed and divided by the total number of incidents recorded for that dimension; this yields an average incident value, which is the employee's rating for that particular job dimension.

In the second method (easier, but probably less accurate) all of the recorded incidents are read to obtain a general impression of each employee. This general impression is compared to the incidents that anchor each scale point. The scale point next to the incident that most closely resembles the general impression gained from the incidents then becomes an employee's score for that dimension.

The third way to use BARS (and the least recommended) is to use the incidents contained in the BARS to arrive at a rating of the employee without recording actual incidents. Instead, the BARS are only used to provide meaning to the five scale points. To better understand how to construct a behaviorally anchored rating scale, complete the BARS Exercise in your CD-ROM.

Exhibit **7.22** Original scoring system for mixed-standard scales

Statement Type			
Good	**Average**	**Poor**	**Dimension Score**
+	+	+	7
0	+	+	6
−	+	+	5
−	0	+	4
−	−	+	3
−	−	0	2
−	−	−	1

Source: Adapted from Blanz and Ghiselli (1972).

Forced-Choice Rating Scales

One problem with BARS is that supervisors often do not use the anchors when rating employees. Instead, they choose a point on the scale and then quickly glance to see which anchor is associated with the number. Because of this tendency, BARS do not often reduce leniency in ratings.

To overcome this problem, **forced-choice rating scales** have been developed. These scales use critical incidents and relevant job behaviors as do BARS, but the scale points are hidden. An example of a forced-choice scale is shown in Exhibit 7.14.

In using the forced-choice scale to evaluate employee performance, the supervisor chooses the behavior in each item that appears most typical of that performed by a given employee. The supervisor's choices then are scored by a member of the personnel department to yield the employee's rating on each dimension. The scores on each of the dimensions can be summed to form an overall rating.

The development of a forced-choice rating scale is a long and complicated process, which partly explains why they are not commonly used. However, this method of evaluation does have its advantages. For example, because the supervisor must choose behaviors without knowing "the key," common rating errors such as leniency and halo are less likely. Consequently, performance evaluations should be more accurate.

Creating a Forced-Choice Scale

To create a forced-choice scale, the first step is similar to that for BARS: critical incidents and relevant job behaviors are generated. These incidents, of course, are only available when a job analysis has been conducted.

In the second step, employees rate all of the behaviors on the extent to which excellent employees perform them. After an approximately 1-month interval, the employees again rate the items. This time,

however, they rate the extent to which bad employees perform the behaviors. Finally, after another month, the employees again rate the behaviors, this time for their **desirability.**

In the third step, the actual items for the rating scale are created. This is done by computing a value for each behavior by subtracting the average rating given to each behavior that describes the bad employee from the average rating given to each behavior that describes the good employee. Behaviors with high positive values are considered to discriminate good from bad employees, items with high negative values are considered to discriminate bad from good employees, and behaviors with values near zero are considered neutral.

The next step in creating the items is to pick good, bad, and neutral behaviors that have similar desirability ratings. Thus each rating item has three behaviors: one indicates good performance, one indicates poor performance, and one indicates neither good nor bad performance. Furthermore, all of the behaviors for an item have the same level of desirability. This process is repeated until several items have been constructed for each of the relevant job dimensions.

The disadvantages of the forced-choice scale probably outweigh its advantages. First, evaluations on forced-choice scales can be "faked." A supervisor who wants to give an employee a high rating need only think about a good employee when evaluating the employee in question. Second, supervisors often object to forced-choice scales because the scoring key is kept secret. Not only does this secrecy deprive a supervisor of any control over the rating process, but it can be seen by supervisors as a lack of trust in their abilities to evaluate their employees. Most important, however, because the key must be kept secret, forced-choice scales make feedback almost impossible. Thus they should be used only when the major goal of the performance-appraisal system is accurate employee evaluation for purposes such as promotion and salary increases.

Exhibit **7.23** Revised scoring system for mixed-standard scales

Statement Type			
Good	Average	Poor	Dimension Score
+	+	+	7
0	+	+	6
+	+	0	6
+	0	+	6
−	+	+	5
+	+	−	5
+	0	0	5
+	−	+	5
0	+	0	5
−	+	+	5
−	0	+	4
+	0	−	4
+	−	0	4
0	+	−	4
0	0	0	4
0	−	+	4
−	+	0	4
−	−	+	4
+	−	−	3
0	0	−	3
0	−	0	3
−	+	−	3
−	−	+	3
−	0	0	3
−	−	0	2
0	−	−	2
−	0	−	2
−	−	−	1

Source: Adapted from Saal (1979).

Mixed-Standard Scales

To overcome some of the problems of forced-choice scales, Blanz and Ghiselli (1972) developed **mixed-standard scales**, an example of which is shown in Exhibit 7.15. Mixed-standard scales are developed by having employees rate job behaviors and critical incidents on the extent to which they represent various levels of job performance. For each job dimension, a behavior or incident is chosen that represents excellent performance, average performance, and poor performance. These behaviors then are shuffled and the end results look similar to those shown in Exhibit 7.15.

To evaluate an employee, a supervisor reads each behavior and places a plus (+) next to it when a particular employee's behavior is usually better than the behavior listed, a zero (0) if the employee's behavior is about the same as the behavior listed, or a minus (−) if the employee's behavior is usually worse than the behavior listed. To arrive at a score for each scale, the supervisor uses a chart like the one shown in Exhibit 7.22. An overall score can be obtained by summing the scores from each of the scales.

Although mixed-standard scales are less complicated than forced-choice scales, they also have their drawbacks. The most important is that supervisors often make what are called "logical rating errors." For

Exhibit 7.24   Example of a behavioral observation scale

Job Knowledge

1. _____ Is aware of current interest rates.

2. _____ Offers suggestions to customers about how they can make the most interest.

3. _____ Knows various strategies for converting IRAs.

Employee Relations

1. _____ Offers to help other employees when own workload is down.

2. _____ Praises other employees when they do well.

---

example, it would make no sense for a supervisor to rate an employee as better than the example of excellent performance or worse than the example of poor performance. Yet these types of errors are common. Logical rating errors can still be scored using the revised scoring method developed by Saal (1979; see Exhibit 7.23), but their existence alone casts doubt on the accuracy of the entire performance appraisal.

Behavioral Observation Scales

Behavioral observation scales (BOS), developed by Latham and Wexley (1977), are a more sophisticated method for measuring the frequency of desired behaviors. Even though BOS have no psychometric advantages over BARS (Bernardin & Kane, 1980), they are simpler to construct and easier to use (Latham, Fay, & Saari, 1979). BOS also provide high levels of feedback and are better than simple rating scales at motivating employees to change their behavior (Tziner, Kopelman, & Livnech, 1993).

The development of BOS is relatively straightforward. The first few steps are the same as with BARS: critical incidents and behaviors are obtained from employees, the incidents are placed into categories, and each incident is rated as to the level of job performance it represents.

As shown in Exhibit 7.24, the behaviors are then listed. Supervisors read each behavior on the list and use the following scale to find the frequency for an employee performing that specific behavior:

1 = Employee engaged in behavior less than 65% of the time.

2 = Employee engaged in behavior 65–74% of the time.

3 = Employee engaged in behavior 75–84% of the time.

4 = Employee engaged in behavior 85–94% of the time.

5 = Employee engaged in behavior 95–100% of the time.

After each employee has been rated on each behavior, the scores from each item in each dimension are summed to give the dimension score. Dimension scores are then summed to yield an overall score. The greatest advantage to BOS is that a supervisor can show employees the *specific behaviors* that they currently do correctly and the specific behaviors that they should do to receive higher performance evaluations.

Because supervisors only conduct evaluations once every 6 months, BOS has been criticized for actually measuring only the *recall* of behaviors rather than measuring the actual *observation* of behaviors (Murphy et al., 1982). The importance of this distinction between recall and actual observation comes from research that has demonstrated that after some period of time we cannot recall specific behaviors; instead, we "recall" behaviors that are consistent with sets of traits or **prototypes** we attribute to employees (Feldman, 1981). That is, we assign certain traits or prototypes to employees; 6 months later, we recall behaviors that are consistent with those traits or prototypes. Furthermore, the closer an employee's behavior is to the prototype, the more accurate the performance evaluations (Mount & Thompson, 1987). Thus, as objective and behavioral as BOS appear, they may not be as accurate as initially believed because of cognitive processing distortions.

Exercise 7–1
360-Degree Feedback

Your text indicated that it is increasingly popular to have a variety of sources evaluate an employee's performance. This practice is called *360-degree feedback*. Imagine that you have been asked to design a 360-feedback system for servers (waiters, waitresses) in a restaurant. On the lines below, indicate what sources you would use to gather feedback.

_____

_____

_____

_____

_____

_____

_____

_____

Comments

Exercise 7–2
Creating Performance Dimensions

Imagine that you are the HR manager for a chain of restaurants and have decided to create a performance-appraisal system. You are using the chart from Exhibit 7.01 to guide you and are now trying to decide on your performance dimensions. Using Exhibit 7.05 as a guide, list your performance dimensions for each of the four types of dimensions. To help you, a sample dimension is already listed for each type of dimension. After writing your dimensions, decide which one you like best.

Competency Focused

*Memory*_____

_____

_____

_____

_____

_____

_____

Task Focused

*Taking orders*_____

_____

_____

_____

_____

_____

_____

Goal Focused

*Get food orders correct*_____

_____

_____

_____

_____

_____

Trait Focused

*Friendly*_____

_____

_____

_____

_____

_____

Exercise 7–3
Paired-Comparison Technique

The paired-comparison technique for ranking performance was discussed in your text. With this technique, rather than ranking several employees at one time, employees are compared one pair at a time. This exercise provides you with practice using this technique.

Step 1: List the names of the professors that you have had in your last five classes. (Do not use the name of your professor in this class.)

A. _____

B. _____

C. _____

D. _____

E. _____

Step 2: Write the names of the professors in the appropriate spaces below. Once these names have been written, circle the professor in each pair that you thought was the better professor of the two.

A. _____   B. _____
A. _____   C. _____
A. _____   D. _____
A. _____   E. _____
B. _____   C. _____
B. _____   D. _____
B. _____   E. _____
C. _____   D. _____
C. _____   E. _____
D. _____   E. _____

Step 3: Count the number of times you circled each name above and place that number on the chart below.

Professor	Times Chosen
A. _____	_____
B. _____	_____
C. _____	_____
D. _____	_____
E. _____	_____

Exercise 7–4
Writing Behavioral Statements

One of the steps to creating a performance-appraisal instrument is to convert the task statements from a job description into behavioral expectations. In this list of tasks performed by restaurant servers, convert each of the tasks into a behavioral expectation. The first two have been done for you to serve as examples. Note that few of your behavioral expectations will be as precise as those provided as examples.

Task	Behavioral Expectation
1. Cleans tables after customers leave	*Tables are cleaned within 2 minutes of customer leaving*
2. Gives customers menus	*Customers received menu within 3 minutes of sitting at the table*
3. Suggests appetizers	
4. Takes customers' drink orders	
5. Informs customers of specials	
6. Brings drinks and appetizers to customers	
7. Takes customers' food orders	
8. Places food orders with the kitchen	
9. Prepares salads and soups	
10. Brings salads and soups to customers	
11. Picks up salad plates and soup bowls	
12. Brings food to customers	
13. Refills customers' drinks	
14. Suggests appetizers and deserts	

Exercise 7–5
Evaluating Employee Performance

Your text discussed the use of objective data to evaluate employee performance. Below, you will find data on the number of traffic citations written by police officers. Indicate what performance rating you would give each of the officers. Select the person you think is the best officer and the person you think is the worst officer. Your instructor will discuss your ratings in class.

Officer	Traffic Citations Written	Performance Rating
Malloy	33	_____ 1 = below expectations
Reed	34	_____ 2 = meets expectations
Ho	10	_____ 3 = exceeds
Romano	19	_____ 4 = greatly exceeds
Hooker	23	_____
Williams	09	_____
Boscarelli	17	_____
Fife	14	_____
Friday	08	_____
Yokus	23	_____
Taylor	15	_____
Gannon	08	_____
Lacey	09	_____
Renko	04	_____
Baker	02	_____
Hawk	15	_____
Sullivan	11	_____
Bates	12	_____
Spencer	17	_____
Davis	10	_____
Coffey	03	_____
Cagney	07	_____
Hill	06	_____
Poncherello	05	_____
Department Mean	**13.04**	

Best officer_____ Worst officer_____

Exercise 7–6
Rating Errors

Think of four professors that you had last semester. Write down their names in the places below and then rate each professor on the five dimensions.

PROFESSOR A: _____

Knowledge of Subject	1 2 3 4 5
Fairness of Grades	1 2 3 4 5
Organization	1 2 3 4 5
Speaking Skills	1 2 3 4 5
Interest in Students	1 2 3 4 5

PROFESSOR B: _____

Knowledge of Subject	1 2 3 4 5
Fairness of Grades	1 2 3 4 5
Organization	1 2 3 4 5
Speaking Skills	1 2 3 4 5
Interest in Students	1 2 3 4 5

PROFESSOR C: _____

Knowledge of Subject	1 2 3 4 5
Fairness of Grades	1 2 3 4 5
Organization	1 2 3 4 5
Speaking Skills	1 2 3 4 5
Interest in Students	1 2 3 4 5

PROFESSOR D: _____

Knowledge of Subject	1 2 3 4 5
Fairness of Grades	1 2 3 4 5
Organization	1 2 3 4 5
Speaking Skills	1 2 3 4 5
Interest in Students	1 2 3 4 5

Once you have finished, look at the pattern of ratings that you made. Did your ratings suffer from any of the rating errors discussed in your text?

_____

_____

Exercise 7–7
Performance-Appraisal Interviews

The most important aspect of the performance-appraisal system is the feedback that it provides an employee. This feedback, which should improve employee performance, is usually given during the performance-appraisal review. This exercise provides you with an opportunity to conduct a performance-appraisal review.

Instructions

Think of the last waiter or waitress who served you at a restaurant. Once you have this person in mind, use a 5-point scale to rate the server on the dimensions you identified in the Critical Incidents Exercise from Chapter 2 on your CD-ROM. If you have not yet done that exercise, do it now. Write down comments about specific good and bad behaviors that you saw this server perform.

Pair up with another member of your class and pretend that you are the restaurant owner and the student is actually your server. Using the knowledge you obtained from your text, conduct the performance-appraisal interview with your classmate posing as the server. When you have completed your interview, switch roles and let your classmate conduct his/her interview with you.

What did you do in the performance-appraisal interview? How did the "server" react to what you did and said? What could you do to improve the review?

_____

_____

_____

_____

_____

_____

_____

_____

_____

_____

_____

_____

_____

_____

8 Designing and Evaluating Training Systems

EMPLOYEE PERFORMANCE CAN be improved in many ways. In Chapters 5 and 6, you learned that employee selection procedures often result in higher employee performance. But, as you also learned in Chapter 4, employee selection is not an effective way to improve productivity in situations when only a few applicants compete for a large number of openings or when a job involves only easily learned tasks.

When these situations are encountered, *training* rather than selection techniques must be emphasized (McGlone, 2001). For example, I was once involved in a project designed to develop a selection system for intramural basketball officials. Although we were successful in finding a test that correlated significantly with referee performance, we ran into a problem with the selection ratio. The intramural department needed 35 referees each year but had only 30 applicants. Thus, the selection test could not be used because the intramural department had to hire everyone who applied. The logical solution was to extensively train the referees who did apply.

This does not mean that training should be emphasized only when selection techniques are not appropriate. Instead, training should be used in conjunction with the selection systems discussed in Chapters 5 and 6 and with the motivational techniques that will be discussed in Chapter 9. By the end of this chapter, you will

- know how to conduct a training needs analysis.
- be aware of the various training methods.
- know how to conduct a training program.
- understand the psychological theory behind successful training.
- be able to evaluate the effectiveness of a training program.

Training is the "systematic acquisition of skills, rules, concepts, or attitudes that result in improved performance" (Goldstein & Ford, 2002). Training is

important for several reasons. As shown in the intramural example above, organizations often have difficulty finding applicants with the necessary knowledge and skills to perform a job. Thus, training compensates for the inability to select desired applicants. Also, as discussed in Chapter 2, jobs change. Employees might have the necessary knowledge and skills one year but have deficiencies by the next. Finally, no employee has the "complete package"— every technical and interpersonal knowledge and skill perfected: There is always room for improvement. The ultimate purpose of employee training is to increase an organization's profits.

Collectively, organizations realize the importance of training by spending more than $54 billion on it each year (Galvin, 2002). Major organizations spend an average of 2% of their payroll on training—$704 per employee (Van Buren & Erskine, 2002). In some organizations, including the Palace Hotel in Inverness, Scotland, employee training is viewed as - being so valuable that it is mentioned in the hotel's mission statement. Organizations also demonstrate the importance of training by paying high wages to trainers. Average salaries are $104,359 for executive level training managers, $75,174 for training managers, and $54,825 for corporate trainers (Schettler, 2002).

Determining Training Needs

Conducting a **needs analysis** is the first step in developing an employee training system (Noe, 2002). The purpose of needs analysis is to determine the types of training, if any, that are needed in an organization as well as the extent to which training is a practical means of achieving an organization's goals. As shown in Exhibit 8.01, three types of needs analysis are typically conducted: organizational analysis, task analysis, and person analysis (Goldstein & Ford, 2002).

Exhibit **8.01** The needs analysis process

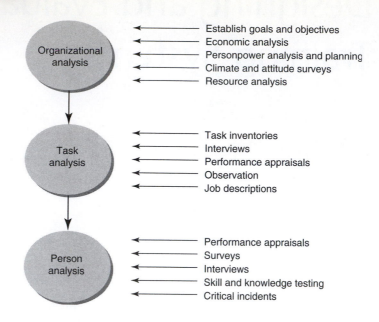

Organizational analysis
- Establish goals and objectives
- Economic analysis
- Personpower analysis and planning
- Climate and attitude surveys
- Resource analysis

Task analysis
- Task inventories
- Interviews
- Performance appraisals
- Observation
- Job descriptions

Person analysis
- Performance appraisals
- Surveys
- Interviews
- Skill and knowledge testing
- Critical incidents

Organizational Analysis

The purpose of **organizational analysis** is to determine those organizational factors that either facilitate or inhibit training effectiveness. For example, an organization may view training as important but may not have the money to fund its training program, may be unable to afford the employee time away from work to be trained, or may not wish to spend money on training because employees leave the organization after a short period of time. A properly conducted organizational analysis will focus on the goals the organization wants to achieve, the extent to which training will help achieve those goals, the organization's ability to conduct training (e.g., finances, physical space, time), and the extent to which employees are willing and able to be trained (e.g., ability, commitment, motivation, stress; McCabe, 2001).

A good example of the importance of organizational analysis comes from an AT&T business center. Employees at the center needed training due to the addition of new technology and a renewed company interest in customer service. However, because of recent layoffs and an increase in business, managers refused to let employees receive training "on the clock." As a result, an expensive series of newly developed training programs sat on the shelf.

An organizational analysis should also include a survey of employee readiness for training. For example, a large organization recently had several rounds of layoffs and had not given its employees salary increases in 3 years. When the organization introduced a new training program, it was surprised to find that the employees were so angry at the company that they were "not in the mood for training." As you can imagine, the training program was a bust! Thus training will

be effective only if the organization is willing to provide a supportive climate for training, it can afford an effective program, employees want to learn, and the goals of a program are consistent with those of the organization (Broadwell, 1993).

Task Analysis

If the results of the organizational analysis indicate that a positive organizational climate for training exists, the next step is to conduct a task analysis. The purpose of a task analysis is to use the job analysis methods discussed in Chapter 2 to identify the tasks performed by each employee, the conditions under which these tasks are performed, and the competencies (knowledge, skills, abilities) needed to perform the tasks under the identified conditions. The most common job analysis methods used for this purpose include interviews, observations, and task inventories. If an organization has detailed and current job descriptions already written, the task analysis process is fairly easy and does not take much time. If such job descriptions are not available, the task analysis process can be expensive and time-consuming.

Once the tasks and competencies for a job have been identified, the next step is to determine how employees learn to perform each task or obtain each competency. For example, due to a rigorous employee selection process, we might expect employees to be able to perform many of the tasks at the time they are hired. Some tasks might be so simple that they can be performed without the need of previous experience or future training. For other tasks, we might have formal training programs to teach employees the necessary competencies needed to perform them.

Exhibit 8.02 | Comparing task analysis results with training programs

Task	How Task Is Learned
Answer customer questions about rates	Daily rate charts
Process customer transactions	Basic teller training
Calm irate customers	
Check loan applications for accuracy	Loan-processing course
Ask customers to complete Visa applications	
Input customer transactions into computer	Basic teller training
Answer customer questions about services	Basic teller training

As shown in Exhibit 8.02, the task analysis process is usually conducted by listing tasks in one column and how the task is learned in a second column. As you can see, the hypothetical bank needs to develop training courses in dealing with difficult customers and in cross-selling because these are competencies not tapped during the selection process nor learned in current bank training programs.

As another example, let's examine the job of a secretary. Obviously, tasks involving typing will be found throughout the job description. If we take just one of these tasks—typing internal memos—we can see that certain knowledge and skills are involved: typing skills, knowledge of the company's word-processing package, knowledge of the computer used to do the word processing, and knowledge of the memo format used by the organization.

In all probability, the company will require that a newly hired secretary already possess typing skills; thus learning how to type will not be a training need. Knowledge of the word-processing program may or may not be required at time of hire. If not required, then learning the program becomes a training need involving extensive training, whereas learning how to use a computer also becomes a training need (this training, however, should take only a short time). Finally, learning the memo format used by the organization is another training need, but one with relatively little time required. With these needs in mind, the supervisor or the training officer must arrange for the new employee to receive needed training.

To practice conducting a task analysis, complete Exercise 8–1 at the end of this chapter.

Person Analysis

The third and final step in the needs analysis process is determining which employees need training and in which areas. **Person analysis** is based on the recognition that not every employee needs further training for every task performed. For example, trainers at Applebee's restaurants test management trainees on essential on-the-job tasks. When the trainees demonstrate proficiency, the training ends. Thus, some trainees complete the management training program

in half the time it takes others (Zuber, 1996). Person analysis uses one or more of the following methods to determine the individual training needs for each employee: performance-appraisal scores, surveys, interviews, skill and knowledge tests, and critical incidents.

Performance-Appraisal Scores

Perhaps the easiest method of needs analysis is to use employees' **performance-appraisal scores**. Low ratings on a particular dimension for most employees may indicate that additional training in that dimension is needed. Conversely, if most employees score high on a particular dimension, relatively little training time is needed. For example, as can be seen in Exhibit 8.03, the employees as a whole need little training in loan processing or data entry, but they do need further training in cross-selling, customer relations, and keeping accurate teller drawers. But even though most employees can accurately process loans, Yamamoto needs further training in this area; both Kerrigan and Thomas probably can skip the training in teller drawer accuracy.

Although using performance-appraisal scores appears fairly easy as a method of needs assessment, three problems can interfere with their use. First, as discussed in the previous chapter, several types of rating errors can reduce the accuracy of performance-appraisal scores. The most relevant here are leniency errors and strictness errors. If the performance-appraisal scores are consistently high because of leniency error, a human resource professional might incorrectly conclude that employees are proficient in a particular area and thus need no training. Likewise, consistently low scores might be interpreted as a need for training when, in fact, the actual cause of the low scores is rater error.

The second problem is that rarely are there situations in which all employees score either high or low on a dimension. Instead, it is more common for only a few employees to score poorly. In this case, a person examining the average performance-appraisal scores might conclude that training in a particular dimension is unnecessary. But that conclusion would be only partially correct. True, not everyone needs training in that dimension, but concluding that training should not be conducted would be incorrect. The

Performance Dimension	Employee					
	Kerrigan	Witt	Hamil	Yarnamoto	Thomas	Average
Cross-selling	2	1	2	5	1	2.2
Loan processing	5	5	5	1	4	4.0
Data input accuracy	5	5	5	5	5	5.0
Customer relations	2	2	2	2	2	2.0
Teller drawer accuracy	5	3	1	2	5	3.2
Average	3.8	3.2	3.8	3.0	3.4	

correct interpretation is that training should be conducted for the few employees who scored low for that dimension.

Third, the current performance-appraisal system may not provide the type of information needed to conduct a training needs analysis (Herbert & Doverspike, 1990). As discussed in Chapter 7, performance-appraisal systems must be specific to be useful. To practice using performance-appraisal scores to conduct a person analysis, complete Exercise 8–2 at the end of this chapter.

Surveys

Another common approach to determine training needs is designing and administering a survey that asks employees what knowledge and skills they believe should be included in future training (Kroehnert, 2000). **Surveys** offer several advantages. First, they eliminate the problems of performance rating errors, which were discussed previously. Second, employees often know best their own strengths and weaknesses. Thus, to determine what employees need, ask them. Finally, training needs can be determined with surveys even when the organization has not previously made an effort to design an effective performance-appraisal system or adequate job descriptions. The main disadvantages to surveys are that employees may not be honest and that the organization may not be able to afford the training suggested by the employees.

As with any type of survey, training needs surveys can be conducted in many ways. The most common method is a questionnaire that asks employees to list the areas in which they would like further or future training. Perhaps a better method was suggested by Graham and Mihal (1986): provide a *list* of job-related tasks and knowledge and have employees rate their need for training on each task and knowledge. The results of these ratings are given to supervisors, who then "validate" the results. This process is used to determine whether the supervisors agree with their employees' perceptions and to prioritize training needs.

Interviews

The third method of needs analysis is the interview, which is usually done with a selected number of employees. Interviews are not used as extensively as surveys, but they can yield even more in-depth answers to questions about training needs (Patton & Pratt, 2002). The main advantage of interviews is that employee feelings and attitudes are revealed more clearly than with the survey approach. The main disadvantage to interviews is that interview data are often difficult to quantify and analyze (Brown, 2002).

Skill and Knowledge Tests

The fourth way to determine training needs is with a **skill test** or a **knowledge test**. Some examples of areas that could be tested to determine training needs include knowledge of lending laws for loan officers, knowledge of company policy for new employees, free-throw shooting for basketball players, and the dreaded midterm exam for this course.

If all employees score poorly on these tests, training across the organization is indicated. If only a few employees score poorly, they are singled out for individual training. The greatest problem with using testing as a method to determine training needs is that relatively few tests are available for this purpose. An organization that wants to use this method will probably have to construct its own tests, and proper test construction is time-consuming and expensive.

Critical Incidents

The fifth method for determining training needs is the critical incident technique discussed in Chapters 2, 5, and 7. Although not a commonly used method, it will be discussed here because it is relatively easy to use, especially if a proper job analysis is available. To use this technique for needs assessment, the critical incidents are sorted into dimensions and separated into examples of good and poor performance, as discussed in Chapter 2. Dimensions with many examples of poor performance are considered to be areas in which many employees are performing poorly and in which additional training is indicated (Glickman & Vallance, 1958).

Developing a Training Program
Establishing Goals and Objectives

Once training needs have been determined, the first step in developing a training program is to establish the goals and objectives for the training (McGlone, 2001). It is important that these goals and objectives be obtainable given the time and resources allocated to the training. For example, if your organizational analysis indicated that due to financial and time constraints one 4-hour training session is all that the organization can afford to teach its supervisors conflict management skills, it would be unreasonable to establish the goal that supervisors will be able to mediate conflicts between employees. Instead, a more reasonable goal might be that by the end of the 4-hour training supervisors will be able to identify the common causes of conflict. When the organization can afford several days of training, the goal of obtaining conflict mediation skills might be more obtainable.

Training goals and objectives should concretely state the following (Mager, 1997):

- What learners are expected to do
- The conditions under which they are expected to do it
- The level at which they are expected to do it

In other words, vague objectives such as "to be a better salesperson" should be replaced with specific objectives such as increasing customer contacts by 10% and increasing new accounts by 5%.

Seminars remain a popular training technique.

PhotoDisc, Inc.

Motivating Employees

For a training program to be effective, employees must be motivated to *attend* training, *perform* well in training, and *apply* their training to their jobs.

Motivating Employees to Attend Training

The most obvious way to "motivate" employees to attend training is to *require* them to attend training "on the clock." However, the majority of training opportunities are optional, and many training opportunities take place on the employee's own time. Here are some strategies to motivate employees to attend training:

- Relate the training to an employee's immediate job. Employees are more likely to attend when the material covered in training will directly affect their immediate job performance. For example, employees would be more motivated to attend a training session on a computer program that the organization will begin using in 2 weeks than a training session on "Future trends in office automation." Thus training should be provided "just in time" rather than "just in case."
- Make the training interesting. Employees are more likely to attend when they know they will have a good time as well as learn something useful.

- Increase employee buy-in. When employees play a role in choosing and planning the types of training offered, they are more likely to attend. Baldwin, Magjuka, and Loher (1991) found that employees given a choice about training programs were more motivated than employees not given a choice. Employees given a choice, but then not given the program they chose, were the least motivated.
- Provide incentives. Common incentives for attending training include certificates, money, promotion opportunities, and college credit.
- Provide food. Medeco Security Locks in Salem, Virginia, has optional monthly training sessions in which a topic is presented while the employees eat lunch provided by the company. Consultants Bobbie Raynes and Ge Ge Beall both have used free pizza as incentives to get employees to attend short training sessions during lunch or dinner.
- Reduce the stress associated with attending. Frequently, employees want to attend training but don't because they can't afford to take time away from their scheduled duties. To encourage employees to attend training, organizations should provide workload reductions or staffing assistance.

Motivating Employees to Perform Well in Training

Providing Incentives for Learning.
Employees motivated to learn perform better in training than their less motivated counterparts (Mathieu, Tannenbaum, & Salas, 1992). This motivation to learn is often related to the perception that there is an incentive (e.g., a pay raise or job advancement) to learn. That is, a coil winder who is taking a course in electronics will probably not study and learn unless he can see how that knowledge will improve his performance enough to result in a desirable outcome such as a salary increase or chance of promotion. Types of incentives that can be used to motivate learning include money, job security, self-improvement, advancement, fun (an interesting training program), and opportunity to enter a new career. The incentives can be made contingent on a variety of factors including completion of a training course, demonstration of new knowledge, demonstration of a new skill, or an increase in actual job performance.

A common financial incentive method is **skill-based pay**, which is used by 60% of major U.S. organizations (Ledford, Lawler, & Mohrman, 1995). With skill-based pay, an employee participates in a training program that is designed to increase a particular skill an employee needs either to be promoted or to receive a pay raise. For example, employees who are currently in the position of Printer III must learn to set their own type before they can be promoted to Printer II. The employees must be able to demonstrate their mastery of the newly taught skill rather than just attend training sessions. Similarly, in situations where promotion is not possible, pay increases alone are given to employees who master new skills. There are four common skill-based pay plans. *Vertical skill plans* pay for skill in a single job, *horizontal skill plans* focus on skills used across multiple jobs, *depth skill plans* reward employees for learning specialized skills, and *basic skill plans* focus on such basic skills as math and English (Recardo & Pricone, 1996).

At Federal Express each year, employees are required to watch 8 hours of interactive video training on customer contact. Employees must score 90% on exams given on this material to pass. Ten percent of the employees' performance review (salary increase) is then based on their test scores (Wilson, 1994).

Skill-based pay not only provides incentives for employees to successfully complete training but also results in increased savings for an organization. For example, a General Foods plant in Kansas found a 92% decrease in its quality reject rate and a 33% decrease in fixed overhead costs after introducing a skill-based pay program (Feuer, 1987).

Interest.
Employees will be more motivated to learn when the training program is interesting. As a result, trainers who are not effective presenters do not last long. Some training topics are naturally interesting and a trainer doesn't need to do much to spice up the material. For example, the topic of detecting deception is intrinsically interesting to most people, but the topic of performance appraisal is not. A topic can be made interesting by making it relevant to the employees' lives, having activities, using a variety of training techniques, using humor, and maximizing audience participation.

Feedback.
Another essential aspect of motivating employees to learn is to provide **feedback**. With some tasks, feedback occurs naturally. For example, in baseball, a batter receives feedback on his swing by seeing how hard and far the ball travels. For other tasks, however, judging the correctness of a behavior without feedback is difficult. For example, if you write a term paper for this class and get a C, your next term paper will probably not improve unless you have been provided feedback about what was right and wrong with the previous paper.

The same is true for training in industry. Our coil winder needs feedback early in the training process to know if the winding is tight enough, if there is an easier way to wind the coil, or if the winding is equally distributed on the coil. A balance, however, must be maintained between giving too little and too much feedback. As shown in Exhibit 8.04, the employee will not learn if too little feedback is given. However, too much or overly detailed feedback causes frustration, and the employee will not learn at an optimal level (Blum & Naylor, 1968).

A final consideration for feedback concerns what type to give. Research and common sense agree that positive feedback should be given when an employee correctly performs a task during training (Kohli & Jaworski, 1994). Praise provides an incentive to continue correct behavior. But if an employee is not performing a task correctly, should he receive **negative feedback**? Probably, even though negative feedback is more complicated than positive feedback. To be most effective, negative feedback should be provided by a trustworthy and knowledgeable supervisor or trainer to employees who are concerned about performing the task correctly (Roberts, 1994). Negative feedback should probably also be accompanied by specific suggestions for how the employee can improve performance.

Motivating Employees to Use Their Training on the Job

Once employees have gathered knowledge and skills from a training program, it is essential that they apply their new knowledge and skill on the job itself. Perhaps the factor that plays the biggest role in employee motivation to apply training is the atmosphere set by management. That is, employees are most likely to apply their new knowledge and skills if supervisors encourage and reward them to do so.

A good example of the importance of management support can be found at a particular fast food restaurant. The employees at three restaurants owned by the same company were given customer service training. At one of the restaurants, the training clearly had an effect as customer complaints were down and secret shopper scores were up. At another of the restaurants, there were no changes in complaints or secret shopper scores. What made the difference? At the one restaurant, the supervisor set goals, provided feedback to the employees, actively encouraged them to use their training, and

Exhibit 8.04 Relationship between feedback specificity and learning

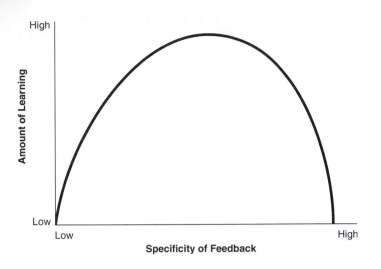

Source: Adapted from Blum and Naylor (1968).

herself modeled the behaviors learned in training. At the other restaurant, the manager hid in the back doing paperwork, a signal to employees that customer service was not important to their boss regardless of what was emphasized in training.

Another important factor in motivating employees is the extent to which they are given the opportunity to apply their skills. This is especially true when an organization pays an employee's college tuition but never provides the employee with an opportunity to use his knowledge or degree. Optimally, employees should be given the opportunity to use their newly acquired knowledge and skills immediately after completing their training.

The use of knowledge and skills learned in training can also be encouraged by having employees set goals (Hamilton, 2001). For example, tellers at a credit union received 2 days of training on cross-selling new products. This training included information about new loans and new loan rates, types of retirement accounts, alternative savings plans, and the advantages to using a new "premium" credit card. Each teller might set a goal of daily asking four credit union members if they would like information about one of the new products. Goal setting works best when goals are individually set by each employee, are concrete rather than vague, and are high enough to be challenging but not so difficult as to be impossible (Locke, 1996). A more comprehensive discussion of goal setting is found in Chapter 9.

Choosing the Best Training Method

Once goals and objectives have been established, the next step in developing a training program is to choose the training method that will best accomplish those goals and objectives. For example, if the goal is for employees to learn an actual skill, some type of hands-on training will be necessary (e.g., role plays, simulations). Because most training programs have multiple

goals and objectives, the best training programs often use a variety of methods so that employees will understand the reasons for doing a certain task, how it should be done, and in what situations it should be done (Lawson, 2000). In the following pages, several training methods will be discussed. Exhibits 8.05 and 8.06 depict the most common training programs and training methods used by organizations.

Conducting Classroom Training

Classroom instruction—commonly called a seminar, lecture, or workshop—is one of the most common training methods (Galvin, 2002). With this approach, either a member of the training staff or an outside consultant provides training, often in the form of a lecture, to a few or many employees at one time.

Initial Decisions

Prior to conducting classroom training, several decisions need to be made by an organization.

Who Will Conduct the Training?

Training seminars can be conducted by a variety of sources including in-house trainers who are employees of the organization, outside trainers who contract with the organization, videotapes, and local universities. In-house trainers are used when a training program will be presented too frequently to justify the cost of an outside trainer or when the training topic is so specific to the organization that finding outside trainers would be difficult.

External trainers are used when the trainers in an organization lack the expertise on a particular topic or when the cost of internally developing a training program exceeds the cost of contracting with an external

Exhibit 8.05 Percentages of organizations often using various training methods

Training Method	1987	1992	1997	2002
Seminars and lectures	83	90	94	90
Workbooks/manuals			77	83
Videotapes	83	92	74	63
Internet				54
Overhead transparencies			64	
Business books			57	
Role plays	53	62	52	42
Computer-based training	35	42	36	
Web-based self-study				36
Self-assessment	36	41	43	32
Case studies	43	41	38	42
Games and simulations	41	54	43	34
Noncomputerized self-study	32	27	44	29
Slides	47	46	29	
Virtual reality			3	1
Teleconferencing	11	11	17	21
Videoconferencing	9	10	10	17
Virtual classroom with instruction				15
Computer-based simulation				12
Outdoor experiential programs			11	7
Audiocassettes	51	44		7
Films	45	43	0	0

Source: Adapted from *Training* magazine's 1987, 1992, 1997, and 2002 Industry Reports (found annually in the October issue).

trainer. For example, an organization needing 2 days of training on communication skills would be better served contracting with an external trainer at $2,000 a day than spending the $20,000 it would take to develop the training program on its own. However, if the training program were to be offered twice a week for 2 years, the organization might be better served using in-house trainers.

Tens of thousands of training consultants around the country offer seminars to industry. In fact, almost 10,000 trainers annually use seminar materials provided by one company alone, Performax Systems International. Thus many types of seminars are conducted by a wide variety of consultants. Needs analysis, however, must be used to determine whether such seminars are actually necessary. Sam Miller, personnel director for Roanoke Electric Steel Company (Roanoke, Virginia), has commented that he receives an average of two brochures each day advertising various seminars. Even though a seminar may sound interesting, it should be used only if it directly relates to some aspect of the job or to the people doing the job. For example, a seminar on communication skills may sound interesting, but it probably would not improve a coil winder's performance whereas a seminar on electronics might. Likewise, a seminar on personal money management may not relate to the coil winder's job,

but it may be useful if it solves outside problems that affect his job performance or attendance.

Rather than using actual trainers, many organizations use videotapes as part of their training programs. Videos have a clear economic advantage over live lecture when the training session is to be repeated many times. A consultant-conducted seminar usually costs between $100 and $500 per hour plus expenses, whereas most videotapes can be purchased for $200 to $600. Thus, a 2-hour videotape will pay for itself if used only two or three times. Developing a seminar in house takes about 30 hours of preparation ($750) for each seminar hour (Zemke, 1997). Developing a custom video costs between $1,000 and $3,000 per finished minute (Sosnin, 2001b). Thus the development of a custom 2-hour training video would cost between $120,000 and $360,000!

Many organizations are beginning to use local colleges and universities to handle their training needs. The advantages of using colleges and universities are lower costs, access to excellent training facilities, access to well-known faculty, and the potential for employees to receive college credit for completing the training (Martyka, 2001). Local universities are typically used for technical (e.g., electronics, computer programming) and leadership training and are most appropriate when only a few employees need training at any given time and the

Exhibit 8.06 Percentages of organizations providing training on a variety of topics

Training Topic	Year			
	1987	1992	1997	2002
New employee orientation	76	91	92	98
New equipment operation	51	76	71	96
Performance appraisal	64	79	79	91
Leadership/supervision	59	75	75	90
Communication				89
Technical training				88
Sexual harassment	n/a	64	74	87
Customer service				87
Conflict resolution				86
Product knowledge	46	66	66	84
Teams	52	68	75	84
Safety issues	46	65	69	81
Problem-solving/decision making	46	66	61	78
Hiring/Employee selection	51	74	71	
Organizational change	43	58	63	
Time management	61	71	62	73
Train-the-trainer	43	66	71	73
Career development				73
Diversity				71
Strategic planning				67
Quality improvement				67
Wellness				59
Public speaking/presentation skills				57
Sales training				53
Personal finance				37
Basic skills				36
English as a second language				16
Foreign language				17

Source: Adapted from *Training* magazine's 1987, 1992, 1997, 2002 Industry Reports (found annually in the October issue).

cost of setting up a training lab is prohibitive. A good example of an organization using a variety of training options can be found at an AT&T manufacturing plant. Seminars on problem solving are conducted by the training staff, communication skills seminars are taught by an outside trainer, and classes on the principles of electronics are offered at a local community college.

Where Will the Training Be Held?

Training can be offered on-site or at an off-site location such as a hotel, university, or conference center. The obvious advantage to conducting training on-site is that it is less expensive. However, many organizations have neither the training space nor the equipment needed for on-site training. Holding training off-site has the advantage of getting the employees away from

the work site and allowing them to concentrate on their training. In some cases, off-site training locations, such as those in Las Vegas, Miami, or New Orleans are chosen as an incentive to get an employee to attend training or as a reward for performing well at work.

How Long Should the Training Be?

Determining the length of a training session is an interesting dilemma. From a cost and efficiency perspective, it is better to conduct a week-long training session rather than divide the training into 10 half-day sessions spread over a 1-month period. However, from an interest perspective, few employees enjoy attending 40 hours of training in a week.

For the highest level of learning, training material should be presented in small, easily remembered chunks distributed over a period of time (distributed learning) rather than learned all at once (massed learning). As shown in a meta-analysis by Donovan and Radosevich (1997), if too much training occurs at one time, employees will not be able to pay attention to all that is being taught or be able to remember that on which they did concentrate. Consequently, training performance will be lower when training is massed rather than distributed.

The best example of the principle of **massed practice** versus **distributed practice** is studying for exams. If we *distribute* the reading over several days, the material is relatively easy to learn. But if we wait until the night before the test to read three chapters—that is, *mass* the reading—we will not retain much at all.

Preparing for Classroom Training

Adjusting for the Audience

The characteristics of the audience play an important role in developing a training program. A trainer must consider the size, demographics, and ability of the audience. For example, with a large audience, not only will the trainer need to use a microphone, but it becomes difficult to supplement lecture material with exercises such as role play, simulation, and group discussion. An audience of female employees often will react differently to certain examples and types of exercises than will an audience of male employees. Likewise, for an older audience, the trainer will often slow the pace, speak more loudly, and use bigger fonts in the PowerPoint slides.

The ability level of the audience members is another important factor. If the audience is low on experience or ability, the training will need to proceed at a slower pace than would be true if the audience were more experienced or more skilled. The toughest situation for a trainer is when the audience has mixed levels of ability. If the trainer sets a slow pace to help the lower-ability trainees, the higher-ability trainees become bored. If the trainer caters to the higher-ability trainees, the other trainees fall behind. For these reasons, most trainers present material at a moderate pace. Not surprisingly, the research evidence is clear that employees who perform well in training are bright, believe they can perform well (high self-efficacy), are motivated, and are goal oriented (Salas & Cannon-Bowers, 2001).

Developing the Training Curriculum

Putting together a training program can take a great deal of time. To develop a training program, the trainer must research a topic, develop a training outline, create visuals (e.g., PowerPoint slides), create handouts, and obtain or create supporting materials such as videos and role-play exercises. Though some authors use an estimate of 30 hours of preparation for every hour of training (Zemke, 1997) and others use 50 hours (Diekmann, 2001), I use an estimate of 16 hours of preparation for every hour of training. Of course the actual time needed to develop a training seminar is a function of how well the trainer knows a topic, how much talking the trainer will be doing, and how readily available are videos, exercises, and role plays related to the topic.

Creating Handouts

An important part of any training presentation is the handouts that are given to the audience. The purpose of these handouts is to provide material that the trainees can take back to their jobs. Providing comprehensive notes is important because people forget about half the training content once they leave the room and then forget another 25% within 48 hours (Nichols & Stevens, 1957). Handouts should include the following:

- A cover sheet with the title of the training program as well as the date and location in which the training took place
- A list of goals and objectives
- A schedule for the training (e.g., breaks, ending times)
- A biographical sketch of the trainer
- The notes themselves in outline form, full text, or copies of the PowerPoint slides
- Activity sheets such as personality tests, free writes, or group activity information
- References and suggestions for further reading
- A form to evaluate the quality of the training program

Delivering the Training Program

Introducing the Trainer and the Training Session

Training sessions usually begin with the introduction of the trainer. The trainer can introduce himself, or another person can make the introduction. The introduction should be short and should establish the credentials of the trainer. The length of the introduction depends on the time allocated for the training and the extent to which the audience already knows the trainer. If necessary, a more complete biography of the trainer can be placed in the training materials so that the audience can see the trainer's credentials without the trainer appearing to be bragging.

After the introduction of the trainer, the objectives of the training seminar, the training schedule (e.g., starting times, break times, meal times, quitting times), and seminar rules (e.g., turning off cell phones, not smoking, not criticizing audience members) are covered. When possible, it is a good idea for the schedule to include a 10-minute break at the end of each hour and $1\frac{1}{2}$ hours for lunch.

Using Icebreakers and Energizers

Following the introduction of the trainer, most training programs start with some sort of icebreaker or energizer (Dahmer, 1992). Types of icebreakers include:

- Introductions such as asking each trainee to introduce the person next to him or her, or having a scavenger hunt in which trainees are given a list of questions (e.g., Who likes baseball? Who has a daughter?) and are asked to mingle with the other trainees to obtain answers to the questions

David Cohen, M.S.
President, DCI Consulting Group Inc.

Courtesy of David Cohen

I am the president of DCI Consulting, a human resources consulting and software-development company that specializes in the area of human resources risk management. We work with clients in assuring compliance with federal employment laws and help them identify and prevent potential liability in employment discrimination issues. Our practice areas include affirmative action compliance; nondiscrimination in hiring promotion, termination, and pay; proactive training; salary equity analysis; and a host of other things. It is our job to keep our clients out of trouble as well as to assist them when they are under investigation by the Department of Labor (DOL) or the Equal Employment Opportunity Commission (EEOC).

As one of the many hats I wear as president of the firm, I conduct training seminars and speaking sessions on HR Risk Management. The training seminars range from highly technical and statistical to nontechnical issues that are softer in content. In addition, I present to all levels of management from chief executives down to line supervisors across numerous types of industries from health care providers to defense contractors. I find training to be one of the most interesting and challenging aspects of my job. Each time I conduct a training program something new and different comes up based on the participants and the organization's culture.

One thing I have learned over the years is that not everyone can be an effective trainer. Some people on our staff are incredible employees and very effective consultants, but they do not perform well in front of a group. In my opinion, you either have the knack for training or you don't.

With that being said, here is my top 10 list of things that will help make you a good trainer.

1. **There is a difference between technical and nontechnical training.**
   Soft skills training and technical training are very different types of training. I find it much more challenging presenting technical material over soft skills material. Eight hours of statistics training can be quite boring. Use exercises, case studies, and other things to keep people engaged. A joke here and there also goes a long way. Know the technical material of your training and plan accordingly.

2. **Trainers are like wine—they get better over time.**
   It takes lots of time and experience to be a really good trainer. Be patient. You will have your fair share of times when you don't perform well. For your first training program, start by practicing in front of a mirror, then making the move to present in front of your friends or family, and finally taking the plunge into your first training. It gets easier as you get more experience and practice.

3. **Get to know your audience prior to the training.**
   It is very important to have a firm understanding of who is going to be in the training session. Prior to your training, find out the knowledge level of the participants, number of participants, their attitude toward attending the seminar, organizational culture, issues within the company that may relate to your training, and so forth. This will help you get an understanding of the company and the participants and will enable you to tailor the training to their needs and skill level.

4. **Know the material.**
   It is very important that you have a thorough understanding of the material prior to presenting. I have been to training sessions that have bombed because the trainer sat and read from notes during the entire session. There is nothing worse than attending a seminar like this. Review your material prior to the training until you know it inside and out. It is one thing to understand material and another to actually teach/present it. Keep practicing until you can do it in your sleep.

5. **Don't make up answers.**
   You will quickly lose the credibility of your participants if you provide answers that are not true. If you are unsure about a question that may come up—and you will be—tell the participant that you don't know the answer to that question but will look into it and get back to him or her with an answer. Or you can always turn the question back to the group to see if anyone in the audience has the answer. Never make up an answer on the spot just to answer the question. This will come back to haunt you!

6. **Use different formats while presenting.**
   I like to use several formats when presenting. I find that variety keeps the participants interested and engaged during the entire training program. Nobody likes attending a seminar where the person lectures to them for 8 hours. Use such things as PowerPoint, group activities, videos, group exercises, round table discussions, Web demos, and case studies. This not only will make your training program more interesting but will help participants learn the materials.

7. Wear good shoes.
It may sound funny, but it's true. I bought a cheap pair of shoes prior to a training program, and I paid the price: back pain and a sore neck. Remember when you train you will be standing for a long period of time. A poor pair of shoes will make for an extremely uncomfortable training experience.

8. Be prepared.
Always check that you have all of your materials and information prior to walking out the door. I like to use a checklist of all the things I need to take with me prior to the training. The one time I did not use a checklist was the last. I showed up to an 8 a.m. training program and forgot to bring with me the training manuals as well as the PowerPoint presentation. As you can imagine, it was quite stressful and embarrassing.

9. Use stories and experiences.
People love to here different war stories and experiences when you present the material. It helps to present the material and apply it to real-life settings. When I conduct a training program on employment discrimination, I share actual cases I have been involved in and the outcomes. This helps me drive home the importance of the training material.

10. Humor goes a long way.
I once asked a colleague what made him such a great trainer. He said, "I may not be the brightest person in the world, but people find me funny." His point was well taken. People like to be amused and entertained when they come to a training session. Effective use of humor can be a great way to engage and entertain your audience. This will help break up the monotony of the session.

Oh, yeah, one more piece of good advice. Always supply good snacks and drinks. The caffeine will keep them awake, and the food will keep them happy.

Every training session you conduct will be different. Different audiences lead to different experiences. This is what makes training so fun. Remember, the most effective way to foster an environment of learning is when you entertain and educate participants at the same time. Your audience will remember you for that!

- Jokes or stories
- Activities in which trainees, either individually or in small groups, are given a question or problem to solve
- Open-ended questions to elicit audience response and encourage discussion
- Free writes in which audience members are asked to write about the topic. For example, in a training seminar on sexual harassment, trainees were asked to write about a time either when they were harassed or when they saw another employee being harassed. In a training seminar on dealing with difficult customers, trainees were asked to write about an angry customer they had to deal with and how they handled the situation.

There are three considerations in choosing an icebreaker: the goal of the icebreaker, the length of the training session, and the nature of the audience.

Goal. For an icebreaker to be successful, it must accomplish a goal. The most common goals for icebreakers are to get people to know one another, to get people talking, to wake up the audience, and to get people thinking about the topic. For example, introductions work well when it is important that the audience members know one another, and free writes work well when the goal is to get the audience thinking about a topic. Having an icebreaker for the sake of having an icebreaker is not a good idea.

Length of the Training Session. If the training session will last only a few hours, the icebreaker should be short—if one is even used. If the training session will last an entire week, time should be spent on introductions and "group bonding" activities.

Nature of the Audience. Certain types of icebreakers work better with some audiences than they do with others. For example, having a group of trainees introduce themselves by saying their name and a trait starting with the first letter of their name (e.g., Friendly Fred, Timid Temea, Zany Zach) is not likely to go over as well with a group of police officers as it might with a group of social workers.

Making the Presentation

Though this is not a public speaking text, here are some tips you might find useful in making a training presentation:

- Make eye contact with the audience.
- Use gestures effectively. That is, don't wave your hands or use other gestures unless they help make a point.

- Don't read your presentation. Use visuals such as your PowerPoint slides to guide you. If you know your material and have practiced your presentation, all you should need is the occasional reminder that can be provided by glancing at your PowerPoint slides projected on the screen.
- Don't hide behind the podium.
- Use a conversational style. A training presentation is not a speech, lecture, or sermon. Talk with your audience, not at them.
- Be confident. Avoid the use of fillers, speak at an appropriate volume, and don't brag about yourself. If you know your stuff, the audience will notice—you don't have to tell them how smart you are.
- Speak at a pace that is not too fast, nor too slow.
- Avoid swearing, making off-color or offensive remarks, and demeaning other people, groups, or organizations.
- Try to make the presentation interesting. This can be done by using fun (e.g., humor, stories), using a variety of activities (e.g., lecture, video, discussion, activity), creating energy either through the speaker's pace or through audience activity, and involving the audience by allowing them to share their opinions, stories, and expertise.
- Don't force humor. If you are a naturally funny person, it will show. When using humor, make sure it meets an objective such as demonstrating a point or keeping the audience awake during a dull topic. Otherwise, humor for the sake of humor can be distracting. Humor should never be at the expense of others—the only safe target is yourself (in moderation).
- When answering audience questions, repeat the question if the room is large. If you are unsure of the question, ask the audience member to repeat the question or try to paraphrase the question (e.g., Is what you are asking . . .). After answering the question, ask whether you have answered the question sufficiently. If you don't know the answer to a question, don't bluff. You can ask if anyone in the audience knows the answer—9 out of 10 times they do.

As with college lectures, many activities can take place within a seminar, including lecture, the use of audiovisual aids such as slides and videotapes, discussion, and question-and-answer periods (Forsyth, 2003). Again, the choice of activities depends on the task or skill to be taught. If the skill is complicated, such as operating a machine or dealing with an angry customer, lecture alone will not be enough. The seminar should also include some type of practice or role play. If the information is not complicated but involves such visual material as building locations, flowcharts, or diagrams, visual aids should be added to the lecture. If the material covered is not comprehensive or if the feelings of the employees toward the material are important, then discussion should be included. Discussion not only helps further learning but also allows employees to feel that their opinions are important.

Using Case Studies to Apply Knowledge

Once employees have received the information they need through lecture, it is important that they be able to apply what they have learned. One way to do this is through the **case study**. Case studies are similar to leaderless group discussions and situational interview problems (which were discussed in Chapters 5 and 6) and are considered to be good sources for developing analysis, synthesis, and evaluation skills (Noe, 2002). With this method, the members of a small group each read a case, which is either a real or hypothetical situation typical of those encountered on the job. The group then discusses the case, identifies possible solutions, evaluates the advantages and disadvantages of each solution, and arrives at what it thinks is the best solution to the problem.

For case studies to be most successful, the cases should be taken from actual situations (Inguagiato, 1993). For example, to make their case study more realistic, Andrews and Noel (1986) had General Electric employees in New York use actual information about a problem within the company. Trainees not only discussed the problem but interviewed employees to gather more information. This use of a **living case** was found to be superior to the typical case study. Not only was the problem relevant, but also the solution could actually be used, thus providing an incentive for the trainees to take the training program seriously. A drawback to the living case study, however, is that trainees may not be the best individuals to solve the problem.

In addition to being realistic, case studies should be interesting. They are best when they are written in the form of a story, contain dialogue between the characters, use realistic details, are descriptive, are easy to follow, contain all information necessary to solve the problem, and are difficult enough to be challenging (Owenby, 1992).

Using Simulation Exercises to Practice New Skills

Whereas case studies are effective in applying knowledge and learning problem-solving skills, simulation exercises allow the trainee to practice newly learned skills. Simulations offer the advantage of allowing the trainee to work with equipment under actual working conditions without the consequences of mistakes (Lierman, 1994). For example, using a cash register or taking a customer's order is easy to learn. But it is a much more difficult task with a long line of angry customers or irritable coworkers. Simulation exercises allow the trainee to feel such pressure but without actually affecting the organization's performance.

Like all training methods, simulation exercises come in many different forms. Some, such as airline simulators, are extremely expensive and complex to use, but others, such as a simulated restaurant counter, are relatively inexpensive. For example, each week at the Salamander Restaurant in Cambridge, Massachusetts, servers role-play such situations as medical emergencies and computer breakdowns (Gruner & Caggiano, 1997). Another good example of an inexpensive simulation exercise is that used by nurses to teach diabetics how to administer their insulin shots—the patients practice by injecting water into oranges.

Whatever the method used, a simulation exercise can be effective only if it physically and psychologically simulates actual job conditions. For example, dummy simulators are a standard part of cardiopulmonary resuscitation (CPR) training provided by the American Red Cross. People practice CPR on the dummies, which simulate the human body and also provide feedback on pressure and location of chest compressions. Although the use of these CPR simulators is probably better than lecture alone, there is some concern that the dummies do not adequately simulate the feel of the human chest. Even worse, practicing CPR on a dummy in front of fellow employees does not involve the pressure or environment that is often encountered in an actual emergency.

Although most simulators do not exactly replicate actual physical and psychological job conditions, they are still better than the single alternatives of either lecture or actual practice. That is, training a pilot is cheaper on a simulator than on a passenger jet, and it is safer for a medical student to practice on a pig than on a sick patient. Rapid advances in virtual reality technology hold tremendous promise for trainers (Hurst, 2000). Virtual reality is already being used to train soldiers, surgeons, air traffic controllers, and police officers. The day that we can exactly simulate real working conditions may not be far away.

Practicing Interpersonal Skills Through Role Play

Whereas simulations are effective for learning how to use new equipment or software programs, **role play** allows the trainee to perform necessary interpersonal skills by acting out simulated roles. For example, when conducting seminars in conflict mediation, consultant Bobbie Raynes has her audience members participate as actors in predetermined situations. The participants are given a conflict situation and are told to use what they have learned to mediate the conflict. When Medtronic, a manufacturer of heart valves, decided to teach its sales force how to use CD-ROM-based demonstrations, it began with an hour of classroom training and then used role plays so that the salespeople could practice their new presentation skills (Webb, 1997).

Role play is used in many types of training situations, from supervisors practicing performance-appraisal reviews to sales clerks taking customer orders. One interesting variation of the role-play exercise has an employee playing the role of "the other person." For example, a supervisor might play the role of an employee, or a sales clerk might play the role of a customer who is frustrated with recently purchased merchandise. In this way, the employee can better understand the reasoning and feelings of the people with whom he works.

Though role plays allow employees to practice what is being taught, they are not for everyone. Many employees feel uneasy and embarrassed about being required to "act" (Becker, 1998). This reluctance can be reduced to some extent by using warm-up exercises and praising employees after they participate (Swink, 1993).

Farber (1994) thinks role play should be replaced by "real play" in which employees practice their skills on actual customers. For example, salespeople can be trained by having the sales staff sit around a conference table and take turns making calls to actual/potential customers. The group then discusses the technique of the person making the call.

Increasing Interpersonal Skills Through Behavior Modeling

One of the most successful training methods has been **behavior modeling** (P. Taylor, 1994). Behavior modeling is similar to role play except that trainees role-play ideal behavior rather than the behavior they might normally perform. The behavior modeling technique begins with a discussion of a problem, why it occurred, and the employee behaviors necessary to correct the problem. Next, employees view a video of another employee who correctly solves a problem involving a customer who claims that a jacket he bought was torn when purchased and who wants to return it. The trainee takes notes during the tape and is given an opportunity to ask questions.

After viewing the video, trainees rehearse the solution to the problem in the way that the employee solved it on the video; they then receive feedback on their performance (Noe, 2002). Employees are also given the opportunity to play the role of the "other" person so that they will gain the same insight they would have by role-play training. Employees then discuss ways to apply their new skills on the job (Pescuric & Byham, 1996). By this procedure, employees will already have had experience dealing with the problem in the proper way when they encounter the same situation on the job. In other words, positive transfer of learning will have occurred.

Of course, for behavior modeling to be successful, the videos must represent commonly encountered problems and situations—thus demonstrating the importance of a thorough job analysis. By observing and interviewing employees and by collecting critical incidents, the necessary problems and situations can be obtained. An important and related issue is whether employees should be trained on specific situational skills or on generic skills that will cover any situation (Hultman, 1986). For example, a specific situational skill would be handling a bank customer who is angry about a bounced check. The related generic skill would be calming *any* angry customer. Obviously, generic skills are more difficult to teach and require the modeling of many different types of behavior in many different situations.

Another issue involves the number and types of models that are viewed in the training video. Russ-Eft and Zucchelli (1987) conducted a study at Zenger-Miller, Inc. (Cupertino, California) in which employees viewed either one or two models. If the employees saw two models, they saw either two models performing correct behaviors or one model performing correctly and the other performing incorrectly. The study results indicated that viewing two models increased training performance more than viewing one but that the addition of a negative model was no more effective in increasing training performance than two positive models. When the proper procedures are followed, behavior modeling can significantly increase employee performance (Meyer & Raich, 1983; Sorcher & Spence, 1982).

Providing Individual Training Through Distance Learning

One disadvantage of classroom instruction is that all employees must be taught at the same pace. This is unfortunate because some employees are brighter or more experienced than others and will be bored if a training seminar moves too slowly. Other employees, however, will become frustrated if the seminar goes too quickly. Thus, to allow employees to learn material at their own pace, at a time and place that is convenient to them, many organizations are using some form of distance learning.

Though distance learning has many advantages, it may result in increased working hours for employees who are already overworked and have family demands. With traditional on-site training programs, employees must take time off from work to attend. With distance learning, however, employees may feel pressured to put in their regular working hours and then engage in self-paced distance learning on their own time.

Most distance learning training takes advantage of the concept of **programmed instruction**. Programmed instruction, whether offered through books or through e-learning, is effective because it takes advantage of several important learning principles (Goldstein & Ford, 2002). First, learning is *self-paced*—that is, each trainee proceeds at his own pace. You have probably been in classes in which the lecturer went too quickly and in others in which the lecturer went too slowly. When the presentation speed of the material does not parallel the comprehension speed of the learner, frustration occurs, and the material will not be learned as well as it might.

Second, each trainee is *actively involved* in the learning. This contrasts sharply with the lecture method, where the employee might sit through 2 hours of lecture without being actively involved. Think of your favorite classes: The instructor probably allowed you to

become involved and actually do things. (That is why some of the chapters in the text are so detailed. By making the text inclusive and complete, your instructor can spend class time on projects instead of straight lecture.)

Finally, programmed instruction presents information in *small units* or chunks because learning smaller amounts of material is easier than learning larger amounts. To demonstrate this point, think of the exam for this class. Would your score on the test be higher if you read and reviewed one chapter each week, or if you waited until the night before the test to read five chapters? (The answer is obvious, and I hope you didn't answer the question from experience!) A meta-analysis by Manson (1989) concluded that programmed instruction can lead to improved performance at relatively low cost.

Programmed Instruction Using Books, Videos, or Interactive Video

With this method, employees are provided with books, videos, or interactive videos that provide the material to be learned as well as a series of exams that measure the employee's knowledge of the material. If employees do not pass the test at the end of each unit, they must reread the material and retake the test until they pass. In this way, employees study at their own pace, and the exams ensure that employees understand the material.

The training program used by Life of Virginia (Richmond, Virginia) is a good example. One problem encountered by the company was that more than 1,000 sales agents were spread over 140 offices throughout the country. Thus, to conduct a training program that would be both effective and practical, consultants Williams and Streit (1986) used sales experts to create seven training modules: marketing and asking for referrals, calling for appointments, interviews, preparing the insurance recommendation, presenting the recommendation, delivering the insurance policy, and periodic review. Each module contained a 5- to 10-page reading assignment, a written exercise on the reading, a videotape showing models performing the appropriate behaviors, a situational problem, and a series of questions to be answered by each insurance agent. Agents study at their own pace, taking between 2 and 4 weeks per module. This training program resulted in a 25% annual increase in sales and a 10% decrease in turnover.

Computer-Based or Web-Based Programmed Instruction

Rather than using books and traditional videos for distance learning, many organizations are using **computer-based training (CBT)** and **e-learning**. The difference between the two is that e-learning is Web-based and CBT is not (Roberts, 2001). With CBT and e-learning, employees can choose from a variety of training programs offered on-site, through the Internet, or through an organization's intranet, and complete the training programs at their own pace. Most CBT and e-learning programs provide material in small chunks and then pose a series of questions to the employee. If the employee does not answer enough questions correctly, the computer informs the employee about the areas in which he needs help and returns him to the appropriate material.

A common method of CBT and e-learning is **interactive video**. With interactive video, employees see a videotaped situation on a television or a computer screen. At the end of each situation, employees choose their response to the situation, and the computer selects a video that shows what would happen based on the employee's response. The H. E. Butt Grocery Company decided to use interactive video at its grocery stores because of the difficulty in getting employee schedules coordinated for group training. Butt's first interactive video training focused on food safety practices and included such features as a virtual notepad, allowing trainees to take notes on the computer, and a bacteria-growth simulator (Zimmerman, 1996).

Captain D's Seafood provides an example of a company that switched from paper-based programmed instruction to CBT. Captain D's spent $2 million to develop CBT programs and install computers in each of its 350 restaurants. As a result of their new training, mystery shopper ratings have increased by 4% (Maurer, 2001).

Similar success was found at Federal Express. Because Federal Express has more than 700 locations, costs for sending trainers to each location are high. As a solution to this high cost, Federal Express placed more than 1,200 interactive video units at their 700 locations. This change from live seminars to interactive video reduced training expenses, reduced customer contact training time from 32 to 8 hours, and resulted in the company's receiving several awards for its innovative program (Wilson, 1994).

Though CBT is more common than e-learning, this is expected to change greatly over the next few years (Fox, 2001; Tyler, 2001b). Because creating an e-learning training program can be expensive—200 hours of development time for each hour of training (Diekmann, 2001)—most organizations contract with a learning portal—a Web site containing a variety of e-courses. For example, TrainSeek.com is a learning portal with more than 2,000 e-courses.

Conducting On-the-Job Training

In the previous section, we discussed how employees can be trained in classroom settings and through distance learning. In this section, we will discuss how employees learn through on-the-job training (OJT). OJT works best for teaching skills that require supervision to learn, are best learned through repetition, and are benefited from role modeling (Gallup & Beauchemin, 2000).

Learning by Modeling Others

Also called *social learning*, **modeling** is a vitally important method of learning for training in organizations. As the name implies, employees learn by watching how other employees perform, or model, a behavior.

Modeling as a learning technique is astoundingly pervasive. Think of how you first learned a sport such as baseball. You probably learned your batting stance by watching a favorite player. Why do you dress the way you do? Mostly because you model the way your peers and idols dress. We are most likely to learn through modeling when we are unsure about how to behave. For example, in our first days on a new job, we watch how others act. Do they take only the allotted time on breaks? Do they treat customers politely? Do they pay attention to their work? We learn how to behave at work by watching others so that we will fit in. A theory of job satisfaction that will be discussed in Chapter 10 hypothesizes that we even decide how satisfied we will be in our job by matching our level of job satisfaction with the levels exhibited by other employees.

Modeling is most effective under certain conditions. These conditions mainly involve characteristics of the employee whose behavior is being duplicated and the characteristics of the person attempting to model that performance.

Characteristics of the Model

Of course, we do not model everyone else's behavior. Instead, we tend to model behavior of people who are *similar* to us, who are *successful*, and who have *status*. For example, if we were deciding what new clothes to purchase, whom would we model? If male, would we pick Barbara Walters or Al Gore? After all, both have status and have been successful. No, instead we would look for someone who was more similar to us in both gender and age.

Likewise, if we are going to model our batting stance after someone, whom would it be? Almost certainly, we would choose someone in the major leagues because of his status and success. But which player would it be? It would not be one of the worst players in either league. Instead, we probably would choose Mike Piazza, Alex Rodriguez, or another successful player. Finally, which successful player would it be? It would probably be the successful player who was most similar to us in terms of race, hair color, home town, position, and so on.

This raises an important point about models in industry. We tend to look for a model who is similar to us. For modeling to be effective, the appropriate role models for employees should be similar to them in significant ways. That is why it is essential that a school faculty have both minority and female teachers, that an organization have both minority and female managers, and that television shows portray all types of people in different occupational roles.

Characteristics of the Observer

For an employee to model another's behavior, three conditions are necessary (Bandura, 1977). First, the employee must pay *attention* to the behavior of other employees. All the role models in the world will be unable to effect a behavior change in an employee if the employee pays no attention to the role model.

Second, the employee must be able to *retain* the information that is being modeled. Have you ever watched a person dance and then later tried the dance yourself? For most of us it is difficult to do if there are many steps to remember (for some of us it is difficult to do if there are only two steps to remember!). Thus, even though we might have been paying close attention, there were too many behaviors to recall or retain. That is why training techniques that use modeling concentrate on only a few behaviors at a time.

Finally, the employee must have the ability or skill to *reproduce* the behavior that is seen. For example, suppose a new employee observes a veteran employee winding coils. If the new employee does not have the proper dexterity, technique alone will not enable the employee to be as successful as the veteran. Thus it is important to limit the scope of the behaviors being modeled so that they are at a skill level that can be reproduced by the observing employee.

Learning Through Job Rotation

Another excellent on-the-job training method is **job rotation** in which an employee performs several different jobs within an organization. Job rotation is especially popular for managerial training because it allows a manager trainee to experience and understand most, if not all, of the jobs within the organization that his subordinates will perform.

Kroger and Wal-Mart train their assistant managers as clerks, stockers, and baggers before promotion to manager. Allstate trains its manager trainees in a similar fashion by having them spend a few months in sales, underwriting, personnel, cash control, and marketing. With job rotation, these organizations believe their managers will perform better by understanding more clearly how each employee performs his job. At Applebee's restaurants, executives exchange positions with restaurant employees so that the executives don't lose touch with routine problems. At Levy Restaurants in Chicago, 20 to 40 selected employees hoping to be managers spend 4 days at their normal job and 1 day working in a new area of the restaurant; 75% eventually get promoted. Also, chef trainees at Levy Restaurants spend their first week in the dining room, 4 weeks in the kitchen, and 1 week performing administrative tasks.

Job rotation is also commonly used to train nonmanagerial employees. Aside from increasing employee awareness, the main advantage of job rotation is that it allows for both lateral transfers within an organization and greater flexibility in replacing absent workers. For example, if two bank tellers are ill, an employee who normally approves loans is able to temporarily take over the tellers' tasks. With the increased use of work teams, job rotation, or **cross-training**, is becoming much more common.

Another advantage, which will be discussed in greater detail in Chapter 10, is that job rotation can improve job satisfaction by reducing the boredom that often comes with a task-repetitive job (Wilbur, 1993). Job rotation works best if a corporate trainer is assigned to supervise employees throughout the duration of their rotations (Nadler, 1993). Such a situation provides more stability than would occur if the employee had a different supervisor for each rotation.

An interesting innovation is taking job rotation training outside the organization and encouraging employees to volunteer for worthwhile charities and nonprofit organizations (Caudron, 1994). For example, GATX Capitol employees helped renovate a day care center, EDS employees helped clean a local beach, and Helene Curtis employees raised funds to battle AIDS. The United Way takes advantage of corporate volunteerism through its "Loaned Executive" program, in which organizations "lend" their executives to the United Way to help raise funds.

Employers report that volunteerism increases morale while also increasing employee communication, time management, and planning skills. Added benefits include increased respect for diversity, self-esteem, and social obligation (Caudron, 1994).

Learning Through Apprentice Training

Apprentice training is used by more than 50,000 people annually and is typically found in crafts and trades such as carpentry and plumbing. With apprentice training, an individual usually takes 144 hours of formal class work each year and works with an expert for several (usually 4) years to learn a particular trade and perhaps become eligible to join a trade union. Although apprenticeships are usually formal agreements between labor and management and are regulated by the U.S. Department of Labor's Bureau of Apprenticeship and Training as well as by state agencies, apprenticeships can also be less formal.

For example, an apprentice working with a plumber will initially help the plumber by carrying supplies, picking up parts from suppliers, and holding tools. But with time, the apprentice is taught the necessary knowledge and skills for plumbing. When the apprenticeship is complete, the apprentice can start his own business.

Apprenticeships are good for both the apprentice and the expert. The apprentice learns a valuable trade, and the expert or the organization gets inexpensive labor—usually one half the cost of expert labor. This is why apprenticeships have become more popular over the last few decades. A novel apprenticeship program was developed by Mid-South Independent Electrical Contractors, Inc., a group of independent contractors formed to increase the quality of new employees (Smith, 1997). Students in the program annually receive 360 hours of classroom training at a local state-run technical institute and 2,000 hours of on-the-job experience with one of the organization's contractors. The apprentice receives $7 an hour to start and $17 an hour toward the end of the program.

PhotoDisc, Inc.

Apprenticeships are common in the trades.

Despite this increased popularity, however, some researchers have criticized apprenticeship programs for two major reasons. First, the emphasis during the apprenticeship often is on the production of work as opposed to teaching new skills to the apprentice (Strauss, 1967). Second, unions use apprenticeships to restrict entry into their trades, which results both in inflated wages, caused by high demand and a lower supply of workers, and in unfair minority hiring practices (Strauss, 1971). Employers often shun apprenticeships for fear that the apprentice will become a competitor or join a competing company (Budman, 1994).

Learning Through Coaching and Mentoring

Coaching

Coaching is another popular method of training new employees. With coaching, a new employee is assigned to an experienced employee who is told to "show the kid the ropes." Coaching can be highly effective, allowing the new employee the chance to learn from a job expert. After all, who knows a job better than a person who has mastered it for several years? Furthermore, new employees report that such coaches are more

empathic and knowledgeable than trainers who are assigned to orient new employees (Comer, 1989). Coaching provides just-in-time training, flexible scheduling, customized training, and a smaller financial commitment than many other types of training (Leeds, 1996).

Coaching, however, has its own problems. First, good workers are not necessarily good trainers, and good trainers are not necessarily good workers (Rae, 1994). Being able to do a job is not the same as explaining it. Sports provide good examples of this point. The best coaches often have been terrible players. Charlie Lau was one of the most successful and best respected batting coaches of all time, yet as a player he hit just .255 over 11 seasons. Ted Williams, arguably the best hitter ever in baseball, was a bust as a manager.

This is not to say, of course, that excellent employees or players will never be good teachers or coaches. For example, in the world of sports we have seen such successful basketball players as Bill Russell, Larry Bird, and John Wooden become excellent coaches. In education, we see successful people leave industry to become fine educators. The key is finding a way to identify those workers who will be good coaches or trainers. One solution has been to establish "train-the-trainer" programs in which future trainers or coaches are taught the skills they will need to train other employees.

A second problem with coaching is that it diminishes the expert's productivity (Wexley & Latham, 2002). That is, while the expert shows the new employee how to do the job, his own production declines. If he is on a bonus system, he may lose money as his production declines, as will the organization if the experienced employee is an outstanding worker. One solution to this problem is for the organization to reward workers who do well in training new employees.

Many organizations such as Pitney-Bowes have also adopted **pass-through programs** in which experienced workers are temporarily assigned to the training department. These workers are taught training techniques and then spend several months training new employees before resuming their old jobs (Geber, 1987).

To overcome the problems mentioned here, many organizations are using "corporate coaches." Corporate coaches are similar to consultants, yet rather than working with the organization as a whole, they are hired to coach a particular employee—usually a manager. The job of a corporate coach goes beyond traditional training as they also help employees identify strengths and weaknesses, set goals, and solve problems (Tyler, 2000c).

Mentoring

Mentoring is a form of coaching that has recently received much attention. A **mentor** is a veteran in the organization who takes a special interest in a new employee and helps him not only to adjust to the job but also to advance in the organization. Typically, mentors are older and at least one level or position above the employee being mentored. American Cyanamid Agricultural Products is a good example of an organization using mentoring. Cyanamid previously had its sales trainees spend 6 months in the classroom but has reduced classroom training to 3 months and now puts the trainees in the field with one of 31 "Master Reps" who serve as mentors. With time, trainees get greater responsibility until they can finally handle calls on their own. This change to mentoring is credited with a substantial increase in sales.

As with coaching, not all employees make good mentors; thus both the mentor and the mentor-employee match must be carefully chosen (Mendleson, Barnes, & Horn, 1989). Interestingly, a study of 609 mentoring relationships found that mentoring was more effective when the relationship was informal rather than formal (Ragins & Cotton, 1999).

Performance Appraisal

As discussed in Chapter 7, one of the major uses for employee performance evaluation is training. One excellent method of on-the-job training is to have a supervisor meet with an employee to discuss his strengths and weaknesses on the job. Once the weaknesses have been identified, the supervisor and employee can determine what training methods would best help the employee to improve his job knowledge or skill.

But using performance appraisal for both training and determining raises and promotions can be difficult. As pointed out by Kirkpatrick (1986), three factors account for this difficulty. First, the focus on salary administration is on *past* behavior, whereas the focus for training is on *future* behavior. Second, performance appraisal for salary administration often is subjective and emotional, whereas such appraisal for training is objective and unemotional. Finally, salary administration looks at overall performance, whereas training looks at detailed performance. Because of these differences, Kirkpatrick (1986) suggests the use of two separate performance-appraisal systems in an organization—one for salary administration and the other for training.

To apply what you have learned about the various training methods, complete the Designing a Training Program Exercise on your CD-ROM.

Ensuring Transfer of Training

When an organization spends time and money on training, it expects that the knowledge will be transferred to the job. Unfortunately, this is often not the case (Broad, 2000). Research in learning has indicated that the more similar the training situation is to the actual job situation, the more effective training will be. In other words, the **transfer of training** will be greater. This principle is extremely important when a training program is being chosen or designed (Garavaglia, 1993). For example, if a restaurant is training its employees to wait on tables, the training will be more effective if the employees can practice in an environ-

ment that is similar to that encountered when they actually work. This realism might even include "customers" complaining and changing their orders.

Another example may be more meaningful if you have ever competed in high school or college sports. During practice, teams try to simulate game conditions by performing in the same way they would expect to during a game. To enhance transfer of training, coaches have been known to have players wear the same colors as their opponents.

Another way to increase *positive* transfer of training is by having the trainee practice the desired behavior as much as possible. Such practice is especially important for tasks that will not be performed on a daily basis after training has been completed. For example, if a firefighter is learning to perform CPR, he must overlearn the task through constant practice. This **overlearning** is essential because it may be months before the firefighter will practice what he has learned. In contrast, once our coil winder learns a task during training, it is time for him to move to another task. Overlearning is not necessary for the coil winder because he will perform the task every hour once training has been completed.

The term *overlearning* does not have the same meaning in training that it has on most college campuses. In training, overlearning means practicing a task even after it has been successfully learned. Many students, however, think of overlearning as the negative consequence of "studying too hard." Although it is commonly believed that one can study too hard and "overlearn" the material, research does not support that this type of overlearning occurs or that it has negative consequences. Therefore, no one will be hurt by studying a little longer. In fact, a meta-analysis by Driskell, Willis, and Copper (1992) indicates that overlearning significantly increases retention of training material.

Finally, to further increase the transfer of training, practice in as many different situations as possible should be provided. For example, we might have our coil winder wind coils as fast as possible, wind them slowly, and wind them in various sizes. In this way, the employee will be better able to deal with any changes that occur in the job.

For information learned in training to transfer to behavior on the job, employees must be given the opportunity and encouraged to apply what they have learned (Broad, 2000; Ford, Quiñones, Sego, & Sorra, 1992; Tracey, Tannenbaum, & Kavanagh, 1995). Employees are more likely to be given opportunities to perform what they learned if their supervisor perceives them to be competent and the organizational climate is supportive (Baldwin & Ford, 1988; Ford et al., 1992). Though this seems obvious, research indicates that many employers are neither supportive nor provide opportunities for employees to apply what is learned—especially if the training was in the form of employees going to school to work on a degree (Posner, Hall, & Munson, 1991). Transfer of training also can be increased by teaching concepts, basic principles, and the "big picture" rather than just specific facts or techniques.

Exhibit **8.07** Determining the success of a training program

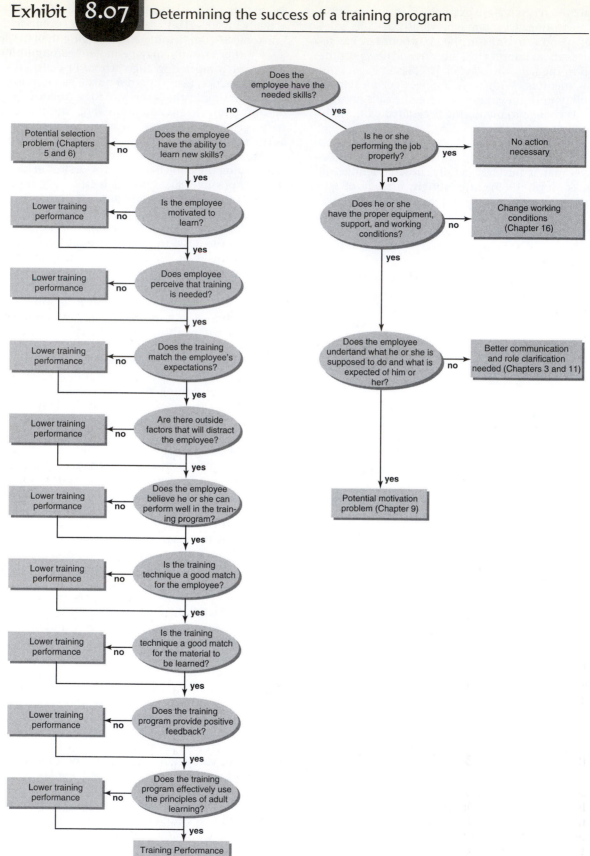

Does the employee have the needed skills?

no → Does the employee have the ability to learn new skills?
- **no** → Potential selection problem (Chapters 5 and 6)
- **yes** → Is the employee motivated to learn?
  - **no** → Lower training performance
  - **yes** → Does employee perceive that training is needed?
    - **no** → Lower training performance
    - **yes** → Does the training match the employee's expectations?
      - **no** → Lower training performance
      - **yes** → Are there outside factors that will distract the employee?
        - **no** → Lower training performance
        - **yes** → Does the employee believe he or she can perform well in the training program?
          - **no** → Lower training performance
          - **yes** → Is the training technique a good match for the employee?
            - **no** → Lower training performance
            - **yes** → Is the training technique a good match for the material to be learned?
              - **no** → Lower training performance
              - **yes** → Does the training program provide positive feedback?
                - **no** → Lower training performance
                - **yes** → Does the training program effectively use the principles of adult learning?
                  - **no** → Lower training performance
                  - **yes** → Training Performance

yes → Is he or she performing the job properly?
- **yes** → No action necessary
- **no** → Does he or she have the proper equipment, support, and working conditions?
  - **no** → Change working conditions (Chapter 16)
  - **yes** → Does the employee undertand what he or she is supposed to do and what is expected of him or her?
    - **no** → Better communication and role clarification needed (Chapters 3 and 11)
    - **yes** → Potential motivation problem (Chapter 9)

Putting it all Together

In this chapter, you have learned many factors that can affect the success of a training program. Before discussing how the success of a training program can be evaluated, let's recap what you have learned. As shown in Exhibit 8.07, the first issue to consider is whether training is the proper solution to a problem. That is, if employees already possess the necessary skills and knowledge but aren't performing well, the problem is probably one of motivation, communication, or work design rather than a lack of training.

If training is to be the desired intervention, several factors will affect its success:

- Employees must have the skills and abilities to complete the training successfully. For example, if an employee is not bright enough to learn a computer program or doesn't have the dexterity to perform intricate microelectronics assembly, no amount of training will improve his performance.
- There should be minimal outside factors (e.g., work or family problems) that might distract the employee and keep him from concentrating on the training program.
- Employees must be motivated to learn. That is, they must perceive that training is needed, that the training program meets their expectations, that they have the ability to complete the training (self-efficacy), and that there will be some reward (e.g., pay, career advancement) for performing well.
- The training method (e.g., programmed instruction, behavioral modeling, lecture) must be a good match for the employee's learning style, ability, and personality.
- The training method must be a good match for the type of material being learned (e.g., knowledge vs. a physical skill).
- The training program must allow for goal setting, positive feedback, distributed practice, overlearning, and the chance to practice and apply the material learned (transfer of training).
- There must be an opportunity and encouragement to use the newly acquired knowledge at work.

Evaluation of Training Results

As discussed in Chapter 1, one important characteristic of industrial psychology is its reliance on research. Evaluating training results is a good example of this reliance. Because training programs can be costly in both time and money, it is essential that they be evaluated to determine if they can be improved and should continue to be offered, and whether they significantly increase performance or effect positive changes in behavior (Kirkpatrick, 2000). A survey of training directors, however, found that 90% claimed that, even though they believed the evaluation of training to be important, they did not conduct evaluations because their organizations did not require them (Bell & Kerr, 1987).

Research Designs for Evaluation

There are many ways to evaluate the effectiveness of a training program, and two factors differentiate the various methods. The first involves *practicality*, and the second is concerned with *experimental rigor*. Although scientifically rigorous research designs are preferred, their use is not always possible. Yet a practical research design without scientific rigor yields little confidence in research findings.

The most simple and practical of research designs implements a training program and then determines whether significant change is seen in performance or job knowledge. To use this method, performance or job knowledge must be measured twice. The first measurement, a **pretest**, is taken before the implementation of training. The second measurement, a **posttest**, is taken after the training program is complete. A diagram of this simple pretest–posttest design is as follows:

Pretest → Training → Posttest

Although this method is fairly simple, its findings are difficult to interpret because there is no control group against which the results can be compared. That is, suppose a significant difference in performance is seen between the pretest and the posttest. If a training program has occurred between the two tests, it would be tempting to credit the training for the increase. The increase, however, may have resulted from other factors such as changes in machinery, changes in motivation caused by nontraining factors, or changes in managerial style or philosophy. Likewise, suppose no significant increase in performance is observed between pretest and posttest. The natural conclusion might be that the training program did not work. Without a control group, that interpretation is not necessarily correct. The same changes noted above for an increase may have caused a decrease in performance in this second case. Thus, it is possible that the training program actually did increase performance but that other factors reduced it, which resulted in no net gain in performance from training.

To overcome these problems, a control group should be used (Kearns, 2001). For training purposes, a control group consists of employees who will be tested and treated in the same manner as the experimental group except that they will not receive training. The control group will be subject to the same policy, machinery, and economic conditions as the employees in the experimental group who receive training. The diagram for a pretest–posttest control group design looks like this:

Experimental group: Pretest → Training → Posttest
Control group   Pretest →   Posttest

The big advantage this second design has is that it allows a researcher to look at the training effect after controlling for outside factors. For example, after going through a training program, employees at R. R. Donnelley & Sons increased their annual commissions by $22,000, and the company increased profits by $34 million. The company was obviously pleased but was worried that the increased performance could have been due to something other than training. So it compared the results to a control group of employees who had not received training. The commissions of the control employees increased by $7,000 over the same period. Thus, the net effect of the training was still sizable—$15,000 per employee—but not as high as the $22,000 originally thought. The control group allowed the company to control for such factors as increased sales agent experience and new company promotions (Montebello & Haga, 1994).

Even though this design is an improvement on the first, it too has its drawbacks. First, except for training manipulation, it is almost impossible to treat a control group the same as the experimental group. Control groups often consist of workers at other plants or on other shifts at the same plant. Such groups are used because there often is no alternative. But the fact that they are in different environments reduces confidence in the research findings.

Even if employees in the same plant on the same shift can be randomly split into control and experimental groups, problems will still exist. The most glaring of these involves the possibility that because the two groups are close to one another, the training effect for the experimental group will spill over to the control group. Employees in the control group also may resent not being chosen for training. This resentment alone may lead to a decrease in performance by employees in the control group. Finally, it is possible that the untrained employees will pressure the newly trained employees to revert to the "old way" of doing things (Spitzer, 1986).

With both of the above designs, the pretest itself presents a problem. That is, the mere taking of a test may itself lead to increases in performance. Because of this, a rather complicated method called the **Solomon four-groups design** can be used (Campbell & Stanley, 1963). With this design, one group will undergo training but will not take the pretest, a second group will undergo training but will take the pretest, a third group will not undergo training but will take the pretest, and a fourth group will neither undergo training nor take the pretest. The diagram for this design is as follows:

Group 1		Training →	Posttest
Group 2	Pretest →	Training →	Posttest
Group 3	Pretest	→	Posttest
Group 4			Posttest

This design allows a researcher not only to control for outside effects but also to control for any pretest effect. This is the most scientifically rigorous of the research designs used to evaluate training, but even it has a serious drawback: It is often not practical. That is, four groups of employees must be used, two of which do not receive training. Thus, to use this design at one organization or plant, ideally a relatively large number of employees must be available and kept from discussing the training with one another.

Evaluation Criteria

In the previous section, we discussed research designs for evaluating training. In each design, a pretest and posttest were included. This section will discuss the types of criteria that can be used for these pre- and posttests. There are five levels at which training effectiveness can be measured: content validity, employee reactions, employee learning, application of training, and bottom-line measures.

Content Validity

At times, the only way that training can be evaluated is by comparing training content with the knowledge, skills, and abilities required to perform a job. In other words, the **content validity** of the training can be examined. For example, if a job analysis indicates that knowledge of electronic circuitry is necessary to perform a job, then a seminar that is designed to teach this knowledge would have content validity. Although content analysis may ensure that a training program is job related, it still does not indicate whether a particular training method is effective. But if a training program is content valid and is conducted by a professional trainer who can *document* previous success with the method in other organizations, it may be a safe assumption that the training program will be successful. Keep in mind, however, that making such an assumption is acceptable only when actually evaluating the effect of training is not possible because there are too few employees.

Employee Reactions

The most commonly used method to evaluate training is measuring **employee reactions** to the training (Tyler, 2002). Thus, when directly measuring training effects is not possible, trainee reactions can be used. Employee reactions are important because employees will not have confidence in the training and will not be motivated to use it if they do not like the training process. However, even though positive employee reactions are necessary for training to be successful, positive employee reactions do not mean that training will lead to changes in knowledge or performance (Pfau & Kay, 2002b). In fact, trainee reactions constitute the lowest level of training evaluation (Birnbrauer, 1987) and can often be misleading. For example, most seminars conducted by outside consultants are informative and well presented, so employee reactions are almost always positive, even though the training may not actually affect knowledge or future performance. For example, as shown in Exhibit 8.08, in a meta-analysis by Alliger,

Exhibit 8.08 — Correlations among training evaluation criteria

	Employee Reactions		Measures of Learning			Application of Training
	E	U	IR	LTR	SD	AT
Employee Reactions						
Enjoyed the training (E)	(.82)	.34	.02		.03	.07
Thought it was useful (U)		(.86)	.26		.03	.18
Measures of Learning						
Immediate retention (IR)			(.77)	.35	.18	.11
Long-term retention (LTR)				(.58)	.14	.08
Skill demonstration (SD)					(.85)	.18
Application of Training (AT)						(.86)

Note: Reliabilities are in parentheses.

Source: Adapted from the meta-analysis by Alliger, Tannenbaum, Bennett, Traver, and Shotland (1997).

Tannenbaum, Bennett, Traver, and Shotland (1997), employee reactions had only a small correlation with learning and application of training.

Employee Learning

Instead of using employee reactions as the criterion in evaluating training performance, actual **employee learning** can usually be measured (Tyler, 2002). That is, if a training program is designed to increase employee knowledge of communication techniques, then creating a test to determine whether an employee actually learned is possible. This test will be administered before training and then again after the training has been completed. The measurements that will be used for the pretest and posttest, as with selection tests, must be both reliable and valid. Thus, if the purpose of a training program is to increase job knowledge, an appropriate job knowledge test must be constructed or purchased. A trainer can spend a great deal of time creating a training program and evaluating its effectiveness, but the whole training effort will be wasted if the measure used to evaluate effectiveness is no good.

The restaurant industry provides many examples of evaluating training effectiveness through employee learning. At Claim Jumpers Restaurants, servers must pass a 100-item menu test before they are released from training. At Rock Bottom Restaurants, learning is measured by requiring new employees to obtain written statements from their peers verifying that they have mastered their new duties; 20% do not perform well enough to get the required verification. To make the testing process more fun, Bugaboo Creek Restaurants hold scavenger hunts to ensure that trainees know where everything is located (Zuber, 1996).

At times, reliable and valid measures of training effectiveness are difficult to obtain. Perhaps a good example of this is seen with the human relations seminars that are common to training programs (Buzzotta, 1986). Typically, an outside consultant conducts a seminar on a topic such as "better communication skills" or "calming irate customers." A seminar may run from 2 hours to 2 days in length. Once completed, however, it is important to measure the effectiveness of the seminar training.

Application of Training

Another criterion for evaluating the effectiveness of training is the degree of **application of training**, or the extent to which employees actually can use the learned material (Geber, 1995). Learning and memorizing new material is one thing, and applying it is another. For example, if employees learn how to deal with angry customers, their ability to apply this material can be measured by observing how they treat an angry customer while they are actually working.

Bottom-Line Measures

The final criterion that can be used to evaluate a training program's effectiveness is a **bottom-line measure** or **return on investment (ROI)**. That is, did the organization actually save money following the training program? For example, imagine that a bank trains its tellers to cross-sell Visa cards. The tellers rate the training session as being enjoyable, all of the employees pass a test on sales techniques, and sales attempts increase by 30%. The bottom-line approach would then ask the question, "If we spent $5,000 training the tellers, how much more revenue was brought in as a result of the training?" If the answer to the question is more than the amount spent on training, then the program would be considered a success (Shelton & Alliger, 1993). For example, Parry (2000) demonstrated that training employees how to conduct effective meetings at Southwest Industries cost $15,538 to implement but saved the organization $820,776 in the first year after the training.

To apply what you have learned about evaluating training programs, complete Exercises 8–3 and 8–4 at the end of this chapter.

Chapter Summary

In this chapter you learned:

- The first step in the training process is to conduct a training needs assessment that includes an organizational analysis, task analysis, and person analysis.

- Training methods take many forms. Classroom learning techniques include seminars, audiovisual aids, programmed instruction, case studies, and critical incidents. Sample job performance techniques include simulation, role play, behavior modeling, and job rotation. Informal training techniques include apprentice training, coaching, and performance appraisal.

- Such psychological principles as modeling, distributed practice, and transfer of training must be considered when conducting a training program.

- It is important to evaluate training success by measuring trainee attitudes, knowledge, ability to apply newly learned material, and improved performance.

Critical Thinking Questions

1. In what type of situations is training most useful? Least useful?

2. What motivates employees to learn during training sessions?

3. What would be the best training technique for teaching computer skills? What would be the best technique for customer service skills?

4. Do all new employees model the behavior of more experienced employees?

5. Why would measures of employees' attitudes about a training program and their actual learning be different?

To learn more about the issues discussed in this chapter, point your browser to

http://www.infotrac-college.com/wadsworth

and enter one of these search terms:

training needs assessment

computer-based training

skill-based pay

employee coaching

employee motivation

evaluating training programs

job rotation

mentoring in the workplace

Exercise 8–1
Needs Assessment: Task Analysis

Below you will find part of a job description for a part-time position in a campus bookstore. Read each task in the job description and identify those tasks for which training (rather than employee selection techniques) would be appropriate. In the next exercise, you will be asked to determine how to train the employees for each of the tasks you identify.

Textbook Clerk

Job Summary

The Textbook Clerk is a university work-study position. The student hired for this job is responsible for assisting the Textbook Supervisor with book inventories, shelving duties, and customer requests. Additionally, the Textbook Clerk performs general clerical and messenger duties and operates the cash register when additional assistance is needed.

Work Activities

Inventory Duties

- Inventories books by section and course number
- Informs supervisor of number of books to be returned
- Writes ISBN on inventory sheet
- Verifies all information as typed on each textbook requisition
- Records price information

Shelving Duties

- Shelves returned books
- Straightens shelves
- Removes previous semester's textbooks from store shelves at the end of each semester
- Shelves used books in the stockroom by title
- Shelves new books in the stockroom by publisher
- Places typed shelf cards on appropriate shelf
- Dusts shelves
- Dusts books

Customer Relations Duties

- Phones professors regarding new textbook editions
- Mails book arrival notices to professors

Clerical Duties

- Types shelf cards
- Types book arrival notices
- Types PU-6 Forms
- Photocopies book orders and notices about book arrivals

Messenger Duties

- Delivers materials or messages to other employees
- Delivers materials to university departments

Cash Register Duties

- Writes name on register tab at beginning and end of shift
- Watches customers entering store to make sure they do not take books and backpacks into store
- Tabulates price of purchases using cash register
- Counts appropriate change and gives it to customers
- Pages employee on register list to assist with checkout when lines are long
- Approves students' checks by validating university ID or by certifying driver's license
- Approves out-of-town checks by verifying name, address, and phone number with driver's license
- Pages supervisor to fill out void slips
- Completes in-slip forms for returns
- Sells laundry tickets, computer disks, and dissection coupons to students
- Verifies textbook tags for price and author codes to ensure that the correct tag is still on the textbook
- Pages supervisor if tag and code are incorrect

Exercise 8–2
Needs Assessment: Person Analysis

On the next page, you will find sample performance appraisal data for ten employees at a bank. A rating of 1 is considered poor, 3 is satisfactory, and 5 is excellent. Due to budget constraints, we want to train any employee whose performance is less than satisfactory. Look at the data and determine:

a) What types of training are needed for all employees?

_____

_____

_____

_____

_____

_____

b) What training is needed by each employee?

Dawson _____

Anderson _____

Barker _____

Trebek _____

Sajak _____

Marshall _____

Eubanks _____

Cullen _____

Clark _____

Ludden _____

Employee	Performance Dimension						
	A	B	C	D	E	F	G
Dawson	5	2	3	5	5	2	5
Anderson	4	5	1	5	5	4	1
Barker	5	4	4	5	5	5	3
Trebek	5	5	2	4	5	4	5
Sajak	5	4	2	5	5	1	4
Marshall	5	2	2	5	5	5	5
Eubanks	4	5	4	5	5	2	4
Cullen	4	5	1	3	5	3	4
Clark	4	1	1	2	1	3	2
Ludden	5	4	3	5	5	1	2

Note: A rating of 5 indicates excellent performance.

A = Accuracy of Data Input
B = Accuracy of Teller Drawer
C = Cross-Selling
D = Friendliness
E = Attendance
F = Knowledge of Bank Services
G = Knowledge of Customer Names

Exercise 8–3
Evaluating Training Programs: 1

As training director for Beavis Enterprises, you are constantly "butting heads" with the other division directors about the need for training. To show these division heads the importance of training, you decide to conduct an experiment. Half of your employees attend a workshop in which information about the company product is presented. The other half do not receive this training. All employees are monitored before the training period on the percentage of correct information they provide to customers and then monitored again 3 weeks after the training program is completed.

On the basis of the data from the following page, did your training program work? In the space below, justify your answer. You might want to draw a chart or table to best represent your findings.

Use the space below to draw any charts or diagrams that might be helpful.

Employee	Training Condition	Pretest Score	Posttest Score
Stevens	no training	68	73
Vessey	training	79	86
Gallo	training	62	73
VanHorn	no training	83	82
DiMuro	no training	63	67
Finch	training	77	84
Crane	training	61	75
Moon	no training	74	74
Doyle	training	84	84
Truman	training	68	70
Adler	no training	70	79
Walker	training	53	58
McFarland	no training	79	88
Heffeman	training	54	71
Spooner	training	93	90
Palmer	no training	71	76
Olchin	no training	76	78
Becker	no training	88	89
Kostas	training	88	92
Wyborn	no training	67	80
Malinak	training	74	80
Hughley	training	64	67
Milsap	no training	61	75
Rogers	training	71	72
Carey	no training	64	73
Lewis	training	85	86
Bobeck	training	70	75
O'Brien	no training	69	68
Oswald	no training	72	79
Wick	no training	68	74

Exercise 8–4
Evaluating Training Programs: 2

In an attempt to increase the performance of its customer service employees, the Clinton Whitewater Canoe Company recently conducted a new training program. The training program involved a series of lectures and discussions to reduce the number of complaints made by customers purchasing a new canoe.

Before spending thousands of dollars on the training, the company allowed three different outside trainers the opportunity to each conduct a training session, with the idea being that the company would then offer a contract to the trainer doing the best job.

On the next page, you will find data for the three training sessions. The effectiveness of the training was evaluated through employee ratings of the trainer, a test of customer service knowledge following training, and the number of customer complaints received by the employee in the 2 weeks following the training session.

The instructor rating was made on a 5-point scale (a rating of 5 is excellent and a rating of 1 is poor) and represents how well the employees thought the trainer conducted the training session. The test score is the percentage of items that each employee got correct on the test of customer service knowledge.

As director of training, your job is to use the data on the next page to make a recommendation about which trainer should be offered the training contract. Justify your reasoning below (hint: you might want to create a chart to help make your decision).

_____

_____

_____

_____

_____

_____

_____

Use the space below to draw any charts or diagrams.

Employee	Trainer	Instructor Rating	Test Score	Customer Complaints
Brooks	Leno	4	71	2
Byrd	Leno	5	78	2
Carpenter	Leno	5	83	3
Dunn	Leno	4	75	1
Hill	Leno	5	94	0
McGraw	Leno	5	97	2
Mattea	Leno	4	80	1
Mesinna	Leno	4	82	3
Times	Leno	4	72	2
Twain	Leno	4	74	1
Bennet	Carson	3	84	2
Cole	Carson	3	77	1
Clooney	Carson	3	85	1
Crosby	Carson	4	78	2
Goulet	Carson	3	88	2
Martin	Carson	3	79	2
Mathis	Carson	5	89	1
Newton	Carson	3	80	0
Sinatra	Carson	3	93	1
Williams	Carson	4	98	1
Badu	Parr	5	81	0
Braxton	Parr	4	77	1
Brown	Parr	3	82	1
Carey	Parr	3	75	0
Dayne	Parr	4	77	0
Houston	Parr	5	84	2
Jackson	Parr	5	85	0
Kelly	Parr	4	76	1
LaBelle	Parr	3	81	1
Turner	Parr	4	79	2

9

Employee Motivation

ONCE AN ORGANIZATION has selected and trained its employees, it is important that employees be both motivated by and satisfied with their jobs. Industrial psychologists generally define work **motivation** as the force that drives a worker to perform well. Ability and skill determine whether a worker *can* do the job, but motivation determines whether the worker *will* do it properly. Although actually testing the relationship between motivation and performance is difficult, psychologists generally agree that increased worker motivation results in increased job performance.

In this chapter, we will explore several theories that seek to explain why workers are motivated by their jobs. None of the theories completely explains motivation, but each is valuable in that it suggests ways to increase employee performance. Thus, even though a theory itself may not be completely supported by research, the resulting suggestions have generally led to increased performance. By the end of this chapter, you will learn

- the types of people who tend to be more motivated than others.
- how to motivate people through goal setting.
- the importance of providing feedback.
- how to use operant conditioning principles to motivate employees.
- the importance of treating employees fairly.
- the types of individual and organizational incentives that best motivate employees.

To get you thinking about motivation in your own life, complete the Free Write Exercise on your CD-ROM.

Individual Differences in Motivation

Psychologists have postulated that some employees are more predisposed to being motivated than are others. That is, some employees come to most jobs with a tendency to be motivated whereas others come to a job with the tendency to be unmotivated. You can probably think of people you know or have worked with who always appear to be motivated and "gung-ho," and you can probably think of others that no amount of money would motivate. Researchers have found three individual difference traits that are most related to work motivation: self-esteem, need for achievement, and an intrinsic motivation tendency.

Self-Esteem

Self-esteem is the extent to which a person views himself as a valuable and worthy person. In the 1970s, Korman (1970, 1976) theorized that employees high in self-esteem will be more motivated and will perform better than employees low in self-esteem. According to Korman's **consistency theory**, there is a positive correlation between self-esteem and performance. That is, employees who feel good about themselves are motivated to perform better at work than employees who do not feel that they are valuable and worthy people. Consistency theory takes the relationship between self-esteem and motivation one step further by stating that employees with high self-esteem actually *desire* to perform at high levels and that employees with low self-esteem desire to perform at low levels. In other words, employees try to perform at levels consistent with their self-esteem level. This desire to perform at levels consistent with self-esteem is compounded by the fact that employees with low self-esteem tend to underestimate their actual ability and performance (Lindeman, Sundvik, & Rouhiainen, 1995). Thus, low-self-esteem employees will desire to perform at lower levels than their actual abilities would allow.

The theory becomes somewhat complicated in that there are three types of self-esteem. **Chronic self-esteem** is a person's overall feeling about himself. **Situational self-esteem** is a person's feeling about himself in a particular situation such as operating a machine or talking to other people. **Socially influenced self-esteem** is how a person feels about himself on the basis of the expectations of others. All three types of self-esteem are important to job performance. For example, an employee might be low in chronic self-esteem but be very high in situational self-esteem. That is, a computer programmer might believe he is a terrible person that nobody likes (low chronic self-esteem) but feel that he can program a computer better than anyone (high situational self-esteem).

If consistency theory is true, we should find that employees with high self-esteem are more motivated, perform better, and rate their own performance as being higher than employees with low self-esteem. Research supports these predictions: Ilardi, Leone, Kasser, and Ryan (1993) found significant correlations between self-esteem and motivation, and a meta-analysis by Judge and Bono (2001) found a significant relationship between self-esteem and job performance ($r = .26$).

On the basis of consistency theory, we should be able to improve performance by increasing an employee's self-esteem. Organizations can theoretically do this in three ways: self-esteem workshops, experience with success, and supervisor behavior.

Self-Esteem Workshops

To increase self-esteem, employees can attend workshops or sensitivity groups in which they are given insights into their strengths. It is thought that these insights raise self-esteem by showing employees that they have several strengths and are good people. For example, in a self-esteem training program called *The Enchanted Self* (Holstein, 1997), employees try to increase their self-esteem by learning how to think positively, discovering their positive qualities that may have gone unnoticed, and sharing their positive qualities with others. More about this approach can be found on the Web at http://www.enchantedself.com.

Outdoor experiential training is another approach to increasing self-esteem (Clements, Wagner, & Roland, 1995). In training programs such as Outward Bound or the "ropes course," participants learn that they are emotionally and physically strong enough to be successful and to meet challenges.

Experience with Success

With this approach, an employee is given a task so easy that he will almost certainly succeed. It is thought that this success increases self-esteem, which should increase performance, then further increase self-esteem, then further increase performance, and so on. This method is based loosely on the principle of the **self-fulfilling prophecy**, which states that an individual will perform as well or as poorly as he or she expects to perform. In other words, if an individual believes he is intelligent, he should do well on tests. If he thinks he is dumb, he should do poorly. So if an employee believes he will always fail, the only way to break the vicious cycle is to ensure that he performs well on a task.

Proper feedback can increase employee motivation.

Supervisor Behavior

Another approach to increasing employee self-esteem is to train supervisors to communicate a feeling of confidence in an employee. The idea here is that if an employee feels that a manager has confidence in him, his self-esteem will increase, as will his performance. Such a process is known as the **Pygmalion effect** and has been demonstrated in situations as varied as elementary school classrooms, the workplace, courtrooms, and the military (Rosenthal, 2002). The Pygmalion effect has also been portrayed in several motion pictures, including *My Fair Lady* and *Trading Places*. In contrast, the **Golem effect** occurs when negative expectations of an individual cause a decrease in that individual's actual performance (Babad, Inbar, & Rosenthal, 1982; Davidson & Eden, 2000).

Two meta-analyses have shown that the Pygmalion effect greatly influences performance. The meta-analysis by McNatt (2000) found an overall effect size of 1.13, and the meta-analysis by Kierein and Gold (2001) found an overall effect size of .81. If you recall the discussion in Chapter 1, effect sizes of this magnitude are considered to be very large. The Pygmalion and Golem effects can be explained by the idea that our expectations of others' performance lead us to treat them differently (Rosenthal, 1994). That is, if we think someone will do a poor job, we will probably treat that person in ways that bring about that result. If a supervisor thinks an employee is intrinsically motivated, he treats the employee in a less controlling way. The result of this treatment is that the employee actually becomes more intrinsically motivated (Pelletier & Vallerand, 1996). Thus, when an employee becomes aware of others' expectations and matches his own with them, he will perform in a manner that is consistent with those expectations (Oz & Eden, 1994; Tierney, 1998).

Sandler (1986) argued that our expectations are communicated to employees through such nonverbal cues as head tilting or eyebrow raising and through more overt behaviors such as providing low-expectation employees with less feedback, worse facilities, and less praise than high-expectation employees. He also stated that employees are quick to pick up on these cues. Along with Korman (1970) and Rosenthal (1994), Sandler argued that employees then adjust their behaviors to be consistent with our expectations and in a way that is self-sustaining.

Though we know the Pygmalion effect is true, efforts to teach supervisors to communicate positive expectations have not been successful. On the basis of seven field experiments, Eden (1998) concluded that there was little support for the notion that teaching the "Pygmalion leadership style" would change the way supervisors treated their employees and thus increase employee self-esteem.

Research on self-esteem and consistency theory has brought mixed results. Laboratory studies have generally supported the theory: subjects who were led to believe they would perform well on a task did so, and subjects who were led to believe they would do poorly on a task also did so (Greenhaus & Badin, 1974). The theory was criticized by Dipboye (1977), however, who believes factors other than self-esteem, such as the need to achieve or the need to enhance oneself, can explain the same results.

But given that consistency theory does have some reasonable research support, the next concern is how it can be used to increase employee performance. If employees do indeed respond to their managers' expectations, then it becomes reasonable to predict that managers who communicate positive and optimistic feelings to their employees will lead employees to perform at higher levels. To determine your level of self-esteem, complete Exercise 9–1.

Intrinsic Motivation

When people are **intrinsically motivated**, they are motivated to perform well because they either enjoy performing the actual tasks or enjoy the challenge of successfully completing the task. When they are extrinsically motivated, they don't particularly enjoy the tasks but are motivated to perform well to receive some type of reward or to avoid negative consequences (Deci & Ryan, 1985). People who are intrinsically motivated don't need external rewards such as pay or praise. In fact, being paid for something they enjoy may reduce their satisfaction and intrinsic motivation (Mossholder, 1980).

An interesting debate has formed between researchers who believe rewards reduce intrinsic motivation and those who don't. A meta-analysis by Cameron and Pierce (1994) concluded that research does not support the idea that rewards reduce intrinsic motivation. However, the meta-analysis has been criticized by Ryan and Deci (1996) as misrepresenting the data. Thus, it appears that this debate will continue for at least a few more years.

Individual orientations toward intrinsic and **extrinsic motivation** can be measured by the **Work Preference Inventory (WPI;** Amabile, Hill, Hennessey, & Tighe, 1994). The WPI yields scores on two dimensions of intrinsic motivation (enjoyment, challenge) and two dimensions of extrinsic motivation (compensation, outward orientation). To determine your own level of intrinsic and extrinsic motivation, complete the WPI found in Exercise 9–2 at the end of this chapter.

Needs for Achievement and Power

A theory developed by McClelland (1961) suggests that employees differ in the extent to which they are motivated by the need for achievement, affiliation, and power. Employees who have a strong **need for achievement** are motivated by jobs that are challenging and over which they have some control, whereas employees who have minimal achievement needs are more satisfied when jobs involve little challenge and have a high probability of success. In contrast, employees who have a strong **need for affiliation** are motivated by jobs in which they can work with and help other people. These types of employees are found more often in people-oriented service jobs than in management or administration (Smither & Lindgren, 1978). Finally, employees who have a strong **need for power** are motivated by a desire to influence others rather than simply to be successful.

Research has shown that employees who have a strong need for power and achievement often make the best managers (McClelland & Burnham, 1976; Stahl, 1983) and that employees who are motivated most by their affiliation needs will probably make the worst managers.

Needs for achievement, affiliation, and power are measured by one of two tests. The first and most popular is the Thematic Apperception Test (TAT), which will be discussed more extensively in Chapter 12. With the TAT, an employee is shown a series of pictures and then asked to tell a story about each one. From the responses, a psychologist identifies the degree to which each theme of power, affiliation, and achievement is present in the stories.

The problem with the TAT is that it is time-consuming and must be administered by a psychologist trained in its use. To avoid these problems, Stahl (1983) developed a more objective and less expensive paper-and-pencil test that measures the same three needs. Although this test has not yet become popular, research seems to indicate that it is as reliable and valid a measure as the TAT (Stahl, 1983).

Employee Values and Expectations

Our work motivation and job satisfaction are determined by the discrepancy between what we *want, value,* and *expect* and what the job actually provides (Lawler, 1973; Locke, 1969). For example, if you enjoy working with people but your job involves working with data, you are not likely to be motivated by or satisfied with your job. Likewise, if you value helping others, yet your job involves selling things people don't really need, you will probably not be motivated to perform well.

Potential discrepancies between what employees want and what the job gives them affect how motivated and satisfied employees will be with their jobs (Knoop, 1994; Rice, Gentile, & McFarlin, 1991). For example, imagine that Jane most values money and Akeem most values flexibility. Both are in jobs that pay well but have set hours and a standard routine. Though the job and the company are the same, one employee (Jane) will be motivated and the other (Akeem) will not be.

Have Employees' Job Expectations Been Met?

A discrepancy between what an employee expected a job to be like and the reality of the job can affect motivation and satisfaction. For example, a recruiter tells an applicant how much fun employees have at a particular company and about the "unlimited potential" for advancement. After 3 months on the job, however, the employee has yet to experience the fun and can't find any signs of potential advancement opportunities. Because these expectations have not been met, the employee will probably feel unmotivated.

Employees compare what the organization promised to do for them (e.g., provide a computer, support continued education) with what the organization actually did. If the organization does less than it promised, employees will be less motivated to perform well and will retaliate by doing less than they promised the organization they would do (Morrison & Robinson, 1997).

As you can guess from these examples, it is important that applicants be given a realistic job preview (a concept that you no doubt remember from Chapter 5). Though being honest about the negative aspects of a job may reduce the applicant pool, it decreases the chances of hiring a person who will later lose motivation or become dissatisfied.

A good example of this comes from an employee who works for a public mental health agency. Prior to accepting her current job, she had worked in the public sector for 10 years in a variety of admini-

strative positions. She was excited about her new opportunity because it was a newly created position with what appeared to be excellent opportunities for personal growth. After a year, however, it became clear that the position was clerical and had no opportunity for advancement, and that the most important decision she could make involved whether to order pizza or sandwiches for executive meetings. To make matters worse, this aspiring professional was asked to shop for food to serve at meetings and then serve the food to the managers. As you can imagine, she was deeply disappointed and angry at having been misled. Because her role as a single mother did not allow her to quit her job, she vented her dissatisfaction by buying stale doughnuts for breakfast meetings, letting the coffee get cold, and "forgetting" to bring mayonnaise for her supervisor's sandwich— behaviors that could not get her fired but allowed her in a passive-aggressive manner to maintain some form of control in her work life.

Have Employees' Needs, Values, and Wants Been Met?

A discrepancy between an employee's needs, values, and wants and what a job offers can also lead to low levels of motivation and satisfaction (Morris & Campion, 2003). Three theories focus on employees' needs and values: Maslow's needs hierarchy, ERG theory, and two-factor theory.

Maslow's Needs Hierarchy

Perhaps the most famous theory of motivation was developed by Abraham Maslow (1954, 1970). Maslow believed employees would be motivated by and satisfied with their jobs at any given point in time if certain needs were met. As Exhibit 9.01 shows, Maslow believed there are five major types of needs and that these needs are hierarchical—that is, lower-level needs must be satisfied before an individual will be concerned with the next level of needs. It is helpful to look at a **hierarchy** as if it were a staircase that is climbed one step at a time until the top is reached. The same is true of Maslow's hierarchy. Each level is taken one step at a time, and a higher-level need cannot be reached until a lower-level need is satisfied. Maslow's five major needs are discussed next.

Basic Biological Needs. Maslow thought that an individual first seeks to satisfy **basic biological needs** for food, air, water, and shelter. In our case, an individual who does not have a job, is homeless, and is on the verge of starvation will be satisfied with any job as long as it provides for these basic needs. When asked how well they enjoy their job, people at this level might reply, "I can't complain, it pays the bills."

Safety Needs. After basic biological needs have been met, a job that merely provides food and shelter will no longer be satisfying. Employees then become concerned about meeting their **safety needs**. That is, they

Exhibit 9.01 Maslow's hierarchy of needs

Self-actualization needs

Ego needs

Social needs

Safety needs

Basic biological needs

may work in an unsafe coal mine to earn enough money to ensure their family's survival, but once their family has food and shelter, they will remain satisfied with their job only if the workplace is safe.

Safety needs have been expanded to include psychological as well as physical safety. Psychological safety—often referred to as job security—can certainly affect job satisfaction. For example, public sector employees often list job security as a main benefit to their jobs—a benefit so strong that they will stay in lower paying public sector jobs rather than take higher paying, yet less secure, jobs in the private sector.

Social Needs. Once these first two need levels have been met, employees will remain satisfied with their jobs only when their social needs have been met. **Social needs** involve working with others, developing friendships, and feeling needed. Organizations attempt to satisfy their employees' social needs in a variety of ways. Company cafeterias provide workers with a place and an opportunity to socialize and meet other employees, company picnics allow families to meet one another, and company sports programs such as bowling teams and softball games provide opportunities for employees to play together in a neutral environment.

It is important that an organization make a conscious effort to satisfy these social needs when a job itself does not encourage social activity. For example, janitors or night watchmen encounter few other people while working. Thus the chance of making new friends is small.

A good friend of mine worked in a large public agency before becoming a writer working out of her home. Prior to working at home, she had seldom accepted invitations to attend parties or socialize. In her words, "Once I get home, I don't want to see another person." However, now that her only social contact during the day is a one-sided conversation with a three-legged, neurotic cat, she socializes every chance she gets.

Ego Needs. When social needs have been satisfied, employees concentrate next on meeting their **ego needs**. These are needs for recognition and success, and an organization can help to satisfy them through praise, awards, promotions, salary increases, and publicity. Ego needs can be satisfied in many ways. For example, former *Tonight Show* host Johnny Carson once commented that the most prestigious sign at NBC is not the salary of the television star or producer but rather whether the person has his or her own parking place. Likewise, many organizations use furniture to help satisfy ego needs. The higher the employee's position, the better her office furniture. Similarly, at one engineering firm in Louisville, Kentucky, engineers are not allowed to mount their diplomas or awards on the wall until they receive their professional certification. At the university where I work (OK, where I am employed; I don't often work), faculty, department chairs, deans, and vice presidents are given furniture that is "commensurate with their status." Perhaps this explains the card table and folding chairs in my office!

Self-Actualization Needs. Even when employees have friends, have earned awards, and are making a relatively high salary, they may not be completely motivated by their jobs because their **self-actualization needs** may not have been satisfied yet. These needs are the fifth and final level of Maslow's needs hierarchy (the top level in Exhibit 9.01). Self-actualization might be best defined by the U.S. Army's recruiting slogan "Be all that you can be." An employee striving for self-actualization wants to reach her potential in every task. Thus, employees who have worked with the same machine for 20 years may become dissatisfied with and less motivated by their jobs. They have accomplished all that can be accomplished with that particular machine and now search for a new challenge. If none is available, they may become dissatisfied and unmotivated.

With some jobs, satisfying self-actualization needs is easy. For example, a college professor always has new

Exhibit 9.02 ERG theory dimensions

withstood the test of time, research has generally not supported its more technical aspects (Soper, Milford, & Rosenthal, 1995; Wahba & Bridwell, 1976). Perhaps the biggest problem with the theory concerns the number of levels. Maslow's model has five needs levels, but research has failed to support that number and suggests instead that there may be only two or three levels (Aldefer, 1972; Lawler & Suttle, 1972; Mitchell & Mougdill, 1976).

A second problem with the theory is that some people do not progress up the hierarchy as Maslow suggests they do. That is, most people move up from the basic biological needs level to safety needs to social needs and so on. Some people, however, have been known to skip levels. For example, bungee jumpers obviously skip the safety needs level and go straight to satisfying their ego needs. Thus, when exceptions to the hierarchical structure occur, the theory loses support.

Another problem is that the theory predicts that once the needs at one level are satisfied, the next needs level should become most important. Research, however, has shown that this does not necessarily happen (Salancik & Pfeffer, 1977).

Even though Maslow's theory has not been supported by research, it may still be useful. Some of the theory's specific assertions may not be true, but it still provides guidelines that organizations can follow to increase motivation and satisfaction. Providing recognition, enrichment, and a safe workplace *does* increase employee motivation. The validity of these suggestions is probably why Maslow's theory still is widely used by human resource professionals even though it is not popular with academicians and researchers, who prefer more complicated models.

A situation at a major university provides an example of how Maslow's general principles can be used. After years of increasing enrollment and prestige, a scandal caused a rapid decline in enrollment, financial backing, and staff morale. To fix these problems, a new president was hired. His first acts were to announce a "spirit day" each Friday on which employees could dress casually, an increased emphasis on diversity issues, and his intention to start a new sports team. Employee satisfaction and motivation continued to drop, faculty left in great numbers, and millions of dollars were cut from the budget.

What went wrong? Among many things, the president's proposals were aimed at Maslow's Level 3 and above, whereas the employees' needs were at

PhotoDisc, Inc.

Money is not the primary motivator for most employees.

research to conduct, new classes to teach, and new clients to consult. Thus, the variety of tasks and the new problems encountered provide a constant challenge that can lead to higher motivation.

Other jobs, however, may not satisfy self-actualization needs. A good example is an employee who welds parts on an assembly line. For 8 hours a day, 40 hours a week, she performs only one task. Boredom and the realization that the job will never change begin to set in. It is no wonder that the employee becomes dissatisfied and loses motivation.

Evaluation of Maslow's Theory

Although Maslow's **needs theory** makes good intuitive sense and is popular with managers and marketing analysts, and although its general components have

Exhibit 9.03 — Examples from Herzberg's two-factor theory

Hygiene Factors	Motivators
Pay	Responsibility
Security	Growth
Coworkers	Challenge
Working conditions	Stimulation
Company policy	Independence
Work schedule	Variety
Supervisors	Achievement
	Control
	Interesting work

Level 2—that is, "Will this university survive?" and "Will I still have a job next year?"

ERG Theory

Because of the technical problems with Maslow's hierarchy, Aldefer (1972) developed a needs theory that has only three levels. As shown in Exhibit 9.02, the three levels are existence, relatedness, and growth—hence the name **ERG theory**. Research by Wanous and Zwany (1977) supports Aldefer's proposed number of levels.

Other than the number of levels, the major difference between Maslow's theory and ERG theory is that Aldefer suggested that a person can skip levels. By allowing for such movement, Aldefer has removed one of the biggest problems with Maslow's theory.

Furthermore, Aldefer's theory explains why a higher-level need sometimes does not become more important once a lower-level need has been satisfied. Aldefer believes that for jobs in many organizations, advancement to the next level is not possible because of such factors as company policy or the nature of the job. Thus the path to the next level is blocked, and the employee becomes frustrated and places more importance on the previous level. Perhaps that is why some unions demand more money and benefits for their members rather than job enrichment. They realize that the jobs will always be tedious and that little can be done to improve them. Thus the previous needs level becomes more important. This idea has received at least some empirical support (Hall & Nougaim, 1968; Salancik & Pfeffer, 1977).

Two-Factor Theory

As shown in Exhibits 9.03 and 9.04, Herzberg (1966) believes job-related factors can be divided into two categories—motivators and hygiene factors—thus the name **two-factor theory**. **Hygiene factors** are those job-related elements that result from but do not involve the job itself. For example, pay and benefits are consequences of work but do not involve the work itself. Similarly, making new friends may result from going to work, but it is also not directly involved with the tasks and duties of the job.

Motivators are job elements that *do* concern actual tasks and duties. Examples of motivators would be the level of responsibility, the amount of job control, and the interest that the work holds for the employee. Herzberg believes hygiene factors are necessary but not sufficient for job satisfaction and motivation. That is, if a hygiene factor is not present at an adequate level (e.g., the pay is too low), the employee will be dissatisfied and less motivated. But if all hygiene factors are represented adequately, the employee's level of satisfaction and motivation will only be neutral. Only the presence of both motivators and hygiene factors can bring job satisfaction and motivation.

Thus, an employee who is paid a lot of money but has no control or responsibility over her job will probably be neither motivated nor unmotivated. But an employee who is not paid enough *will* be unmotivated, even though he may have tremendous control and responsibility over his job. Finally, an employee who is paid well and has control and responsibility will probably be motivated.

Again, Herzberg's is one of those theories that makes sense but has not received strong research support. In general, researchers have criticized the theory because of the methods used to develop the two factors as well as the fact that few research studies have replicated the findings obtained by Herzberg and his colleagues (Hinrichs & Mischkind, 1967; King, 1970).

Do Employees Have Achievable Goals?

To increase motivation, goal setting should be used. With **goal setting**, each employee is given a goal such as increasing attendance, selling more products, or

Exhibit 9.04 Comparison of the Herzberg, Maslow, and ERG theories

Maslow	ERG	Herzberg
Self-actualization	Growth	Motivators
Ego		
Social	Relatedness	Hygiene factors
Safety	Existence	
Physical		

reducing the number of grammar errors in reports. The first goal-setting study that caught the interest of industrial psychologists was conducted by Latham and Blades (1975). Their study was brought about because truck drivers at a logging mill were not completely filling their trucks before making deliveries. Empty space in the trucks obviously cost the company money. To increase each delivery's load, the drivers were given specific weight goals and were told that they would be neither punished for missing the goal nor rewarded for reaching it. A significant increase in the average load per delivery resulted. Although this is the most celebrated study, goal setting has been shown to be effective in a wide variety of situations.

For goal setting to be most successful, the goals themselves should possess certain qualities represented by the acronym SMART: specific, measurable, attainable, relevant, and time bound (Rubin, 2002).

Specific

Properly set goals are concrete and specific (Locke & Latham, 2002; Wood, Mento, & Locke, 1987). A goal such as "I will produce as many as I can" will not be as effective as "I will print 5,000 pages in the next hour." The more specific the goal, the greater the productivity. To underscore this point, we will use an example involving pushups. If a person says he will do as many pushups as he can, does that mean he will do as many as he can until he tires? As many as he can before he begins to sweat? As many as he did his last time? The problem with such a goal is its ambiguity and lack of specific guidelines. Setting more specific subgoals can also improve performance (Klawsky, 1990).

Measurable

Properly set goals are measurable. That is, if one's goal is to improve performance or increase customer service, can performance or customer service be measured?

Difficult But Attainable

Properly set goals are high but attainable (Locke & Latham, 1990). If an employee regularly prints 5,000 pages an hour and sets a goal of 4,000 pages, performance is certainly not going to increase. Conversely, if the goal becomes 20,000 pages, it will also not be effective because the employee will quickly realize that he cannot meet the goal and will quit trying.

A good example of goals set too high comes from the academic retention program at one university. This program is designed to help special students who are having academic trouble and whose GPAs have fallen below the minimum needed to stay in school. The program involves tutoring, study skills, and goal setting. Although it has generally been a success, many students have failed to improve their academic performance. A brief investigation revealed that the goal-setting process was one of the reasons for these failures. Students were allowed to set their own GPA goals for the semester—and students with GPAs of 1.0 were setting goals of 4.0! Obviously, none of the students was able to reach this goal. The problem typically came when students did poorly on their first test and their chance for an A in a class was gone, as was their chance for a 4.0 GPA for the semester. Because their goals could not be attained, the students felt they had failed and they quit trying.

Though setting higher goals generally leads to better performance than does setting lower goals, the level of goal difficulty will most affect performance when employees are committed to reaching the goal (Klein, Wesson, Hollenbeck, & Alge, 1999; Locke & Latham, 2002). For example, if a police chief sets a high goal for a police officer to write traffic citations, the officer will not increase the number of citations he writes unless he is committed to the goal. That is, if he believes he can accomplish the goal, agrees that the goal is worthwhile, and will be rewarded for achieving the goal, his commitment to achieve the goal is likely to be high.

Armand Spoto, M.S.
Senior Consultant, Barnett International

Courtesy of Armand Spoto

Barnett International is the eighth largest consulting firm in Philadelphia. We are a leading provider of consulting, training, and conference planning to pharmaceutical, biotechnology, and life science organizations. I enjoy being a consultant because it allows me to work in a team environment on a variety of projects. For example, in the past 2 years I have assisted in the redesign of a pharmaceutical regulatory department, developed a technology implementation process for consultants, and facilitated training programs for a clinical trial management system.

Currently, I manage a team responsible for training employees to use new corporatewide project management software. In my position, I deal with motivation on a variety of levels. When training participants, my team and I must find ways to motivate individuals to use this new software. Training on any new skill is a challenge, especially new technology. The software assists in estimating human resources allocated across multiple departments in appropriately staffing clinical trials throughout the organization. The software is not difficult to use, but implementing any new technology involves learning new processes, new job responsibilities, and new technical proficiencies. These three factors increase the complexity involved in trying to convey the new skills needed as well as to persuade individuals to use the software regularly. As a trainer, it is important to present the

information in a way that will motivate employees to use the new software.

When I develop a new training program, I use a variety of concepts to assist the class participants not only in acquiring the new skill but in actually using the skill in the workplace. I incorporate expectancy theory in training programs by putting myself in the place of the employees and thinking about how this new skill will help them in their jobs. I ask myself questions that I think participants would ask. For example, I try to develop answers to questions like these:

- How will this help me in my job?

- What makes it better than what I am already doing?

- What activities, or set of activities, will this replace?

- What are the short-term effects compared to the long-term benefits?

- How different is this from what I am currently doing?

This is also referred to as the "What's In It For Me" factor (WIIFM). When developing any soft or hard skills training, you should have a sound rationale for how it will help employees do their job better, faster, or cheaper. To motivate participants, it is essential to identify with their needs and how something new can make them more productive.

Another key responsibility as a senior consultant is motivating my team members to accomplish their work on time with the highest quality possible for our client while incorporating professional development opportunities for each team member. One very effective method to accomplish both of these is goal setting. I have team members determine their professional and personal goals at the beginning of a project. Once these goals are established, I have each team member evaluate these goals using the SMART system: Can the goal be classified as Specific, Measurable, Achievable, Realistic, and Timely? Goals should be concrete and obtainable. Here is one of my SMART goals for this year: "I will follow up on two new business leads every quarter during the next fiscal year." When goals contain SMART characteristics, individuals have confidence that they can accomplish them and are thereby motivated to use their new skills.

Motivation is an important aspect of business at many levels. Applying motivation theory and concepts to training is not easy; nevertheless it is an important aspect of any individual or organizational change initiative. It is important to emphasize that the transfer of new skills to the workplace will increase an employee's job satisfaction, motivation, and performance.

Not surprisingly, people differ in the extent to which they set high goals. Optimists tend to set higher goals than do pessimists (Ladd, Jagacinski, & Stolzenberg, 1997). People scoring high in conscientiousness, extraversion, and openness and low in agreeableness and neuroticism also tend to set high goals (Judge & Ilies, 2002).

Relevant

Properly set goals are also relevant. Setting a goal about increasing public speaking skills will not be as motivating to a person working in a landfill as it would be to a police officer who often testifies in court.

Time Bound

Goals work best when there is a time frame for their completion. For example, a goal to clean one's office would be more motivating if the goal included a date by which the office would be cleaned.

Employee Participation

Until fairly recently, it was generally thought that a goal would lead to the greatest increase in productivity if it was set at least in part by the employee. That is, although performance would increase if the supervisor sets the employee's goal, it would increase even more if the employee participated. However, several meta-analyses have indicated that participating in goal setting does not increase performance (Mento, Steel, & Karren, 1987; Tubbs, 1986). However, a meta-analysis indicates that employee participation in goal setting increased the commitment to reaching a goal (Klein et al., 1999). To practice goal setting, complete the Goal Setting Exercise on your CD-ROM.

Are Employees Receiving Feedback on Their Goal Progress?

To increase the effectiveness of goal setting, feedback should be provided to employees on their progress in reaching their goals (Locke & Latham, 2002; Stajkovic & Luthans, 2003). Feedback is so important that in a survey of information technology (IT) employees 80% said that effective feedback would make them less likely to leave their organization (Joinson, 2001b). Feedback can include verbally telling employees how they are doing, placing a chart on a wall, or using nonverbal communication such as smiles, glares, and pats on the back. Feedback best increases performance when it is positive and informational rather than negative and controlling (Zhou, 1998). To encourage employees to ask for feedback, supervisors should indicate their willingness to provide feedback and then reinforce employees who seek feedback (Williams, Miller, Steelman, & Levy, 1999).

Feedback is constructive when it is given positively with the goal of encouraging and reinforcing positive behavior. For feedback to be effective, it must be given when employees do things properly, not just when they make mistakes. Here are some tips for effective feedback:

- Identify the employee's *behavior* and focus on it rather than on the employee's personality. For example, if an employee is often late for work, a supervisor might say "In the past 2 weeks, you have been late five times" rather than "We are having a problem with your lack of responsibility and commitment to your job."

- Explain how the behavior is impacting others. For example, "When you arrive to work 10 minutes late, customers become angry because there is no one to help them with their purchases. When other employees cover the register for you, it causes them to get behind on their work, resulting in their missing part of their lunch break or being forced to work overtime."

- Ask the employee for suggestions on how the behavior can be changed. If the employee has none to offer, the supervisor can provide some. A sample conversation might go something like this:

   EMPLOYEE: I know I shouldn't be missing work, but I'm so tired in the morning and often don't hear the alarm.

   SUPERVISOR: Can you think of things you can do so that you will not be so tired in the morning?"

   EMPLOYEE: I could go to bed earlier, but I love to watch David Letterman and then Sport Center on ESPN.

   SUPERVISOR: Could you try watching the early edition of Sport Center and tape the David Letterman show so that you can watch it *when you get home from work?*

   EMPLOYEE: I guess I could give that a try.

- After arriving at a solution, the supervisor and employee should then set a specific goal. For example, they could agree that the employee will be on time every day for the next week.

- After an agreed-upon time, the supervisor and employee should meet to see if the goal has been met and to set new goals.

Are Employees Rewarded for Achieving Goals?

An essential strategy for motivating employees is to provide an incentive for employees to accomplish the goals set by an organization. As a result, organizations offer incentives for a wide variety of employee behaviors including working overtime or on weekends, making suggestions, referring applicants, staying with the company (length-of-service awards), coming to work (attendance bonuses), not getting into accidents, and performing at a high level (Henderson, 2003). The basis for these incentive systems are **operant conditioning** principles, which state that employees will engage in behaviors for which they are rewarded and avoid behaviors for which they are punished. Thus, if employees are rewarded for not making errors, they are more likely to produce high-quality work. If employees are rewarded for the amount of work done, they will place less emphasis on quality and try to increase their quantity. Finally, if employees are not rewarded for any behavior, they will search for behaviors that will be rewarded. Unfortunately, these might include absenteeism (which is rewarded by going fishing) or carelessness (which is rewarded by spending more time with friends).

The research and applied literature abound with studies demonstrating the effectiveness of reinforcement. For example:

- Austin, Kessler, Riccobono, and Bailey (1996) provided daily feedback and weekly monetary reinforcement to employees in a roofing crew. This intervention resulted in a 64% labor cost reduction and an 80% improvement in safety.

- Lafleur and Hyten (1995) used a combination of goal setting, feedback, and reinforcement to increase the quality of hotel banquet staff performance.

- Ply Marts, a material supply company in Norcross, Georgia, reduced the number of injuries from 37 per year to 7 by providing daily feedback on injuries and giving employees a bingo number for each day that no employee was injured. Each day, money is added to the pot until an employee gets to "bingo" and wins the pot (Atkinson, 1999).

- Kortick and O'Brien (1996) devised the "World Series of Quality Control" at a package delivery company in New York. The 104 employees were divided into 13 teams of 8 employees each and competed against one another to have the best shipping accuracy and quantity. Performance information and team standings were posted each week with the winning team receiving pizzas. At the end of each month, the winning team received individual plaques and dinner at a local restaurant. The intervention resulted in promising increases in shipping accuracy.

Though the research is clear that rewarding employees will often lead to increased motivation and performance, (Stajkovic & Luthans, 2003) six factors must be considered in determining the effectiveness of incentive programs: timing of the incentive, contingency of the incentive, type of incentive used, use of individual-based versus group-based incentives, use of positive incentives (rewards) versus negative incentives (punishment), and the fairness of the reward system (equity).

Timing of the Incentive

Research indicates that a *reinforcer* or a *punisher* is most effective if it occurs soon after the performance of the behavior. Unfortunately, if the timing of the incentive is too long, the effectiveness of the incentive to improve performance will be hindered. For example, a restaurant employee learning how to wait on tables performs many behaviors in the course of serving a customer. A tip is usually left by the customer after the meal, which provides immediate feedback about the employee's performance. However, if the tip is small, the employee is not sure which particular behavior caused the customer's displeasure. Likewise, if the tip is

large, the employee is unsure which particular behavior or behaviors initiated the large tip. Thus the timing of the consequence by itself may not be enough.

Contingency of Consequence

If it is not possible to immediately reward or punish a behavior, it should at least be made clear that the employee understands the behaviors that brought reward or punishment. To return to our example of the waiter, if he is told the reason for the size of his tip, he will be better able to change his behavior. Have you ever given a waiter or waitress a large tip even though the service was terrible? Most of us have. When this happens, however, the waiter or waitress is reinforced for poor performance and has no incentive to improve unless poor performance has its own consequence. In a similar fashion, if the waiter has done an outstanding job but has received a small tip, the probability of his repeating his outstanding performance is reduced. Furthermore, when tips are pooled at restaurants so that each employee gets a share of all tips received, an individual employee's rewards are not as contingent on his own behavior as when tips are not pooled.

The point of these examples is that reward and punishment must be made contingent upon performance; the contingency of consequence must be clear if learning is to occur. If the reward or punishment cannot be administered immediately, the employee must be told the purpose of the consequence so that the link between behavior and outcome is clear.

Type of Incentive Used

Obviously, it is important to reward employees for productive work behavior. But, as you learned in the discussion of Maslow's hierarchy, different employees have different values, which is why supervisors should have access to and be trained to administer different types of reinforcers. For example, some employees can be rewarded with praise, others with awards, others with interesting work, and still others with money. In fact, a meta-analysis by Stajkovic and Luthans (1997) found that financial, nonfinancial, and social rewards all resulted in increased levels of performance.

The same is true of punishment. Threatening an employee with a 3-day suspension will be effective only if he needs the money or doesn't like being off work; yelling at an employee will be effective only if the employee does not like being yelled at; and threatening to not promote an employee will be effective only if the employee values promotions and perceives he has a reasonable chance of being promoted.

Premack Principle

An interesting method of providing incentives that meet the individual needs of each employee stems from the **Premack Principle** (Premack, 1963), which states that reinforcement is relative and that a supervisor can reinforce an employee with something that on the surface does not appear to be a reinforcer. The

Exhibit **9.05** Premack Principle

Most desired

Money
Time off from work
Lunch time
Working next to Wanda
Supervisor praise
Running the press
Getting printing plates
Throwing out oily rags
Typesetting
Cleaning the press

Reinforcers

Least desired

best way to explain this principle is to construct a **reinforcement hierarchy** on which an employee lists his preferences for a variety of reinforcers.

As Exhibit 9.05 shows, our hypothetical employee most desires money and time off from work and least desires typesetting and cleaning the press. Our employee can enjoy and do a better job of cleaning his press if we give him money for each time he properly completes the task, but such a reward system can become expensive. Thus, according to the Premack Principle, we can get our employee to clean his press properly by allowing him to do one of the activities he likes more than cleaning. From his reinforcement hierarchy, we can see that he ranks throwing out oily rags as more enjoyable because he can take a short break by walking outdoors to the disposal area. Thus all we need for a reward is to let him dispose of the rags.

The Premack Principle may sound silly, but think of the reinforcers you have used to reward yourself for studying. After reading a certain number of pages, you might allow yourself a trip to the water fountain. Certainly, getting a drink of water is hardly anyone's idea of a good time, but it may be more interesting than studying and so can become a reinforcer to increase studying.

When I was in high school, I worked at a printing plant that produced stock reports. All entry level employees were "collators" whose jobs were to place 500 copies of a book page on a piece of wood strapped to their necks and then walk around a room placing a piece of paper in each of 500 slots. This process was repeated about 300 times until a complete book was put together. As you can imagine, the job was extremely boring. To motivate us, our supervisor would "reward" the fastest collators by allowing them to take out the trash, to go pick up lunch (it was kind of cool ordering 100 Whoppers and 100 fries and watching the Burger King employees' expressions), or to move the paper carts from one end of the building to the other. I didn't realize until 10 years later that my boss was using the Premack Principle: rewarding performance of a very boring task by allowing us to perform a less boring task.

As another example, my current boss (the department chair) is a master at using the Premack Principle. Because salary raises are small in size and never a certainty, it is difficult to motivate faculty to do the "little things" by offering financial rewards. Instead, my boss rewards good departmental citizenship by giving the best faculty their most desired schedule (no 8:00 a.m.'s for me!), their favorite classes, and their favorite committee assignments. From what I have seen, these reinforcers work better than money!

Of course, my boss is successful in using the Premack Principle because he has a good sense of every faculty member's reinforcement hierarchy. For example, I hate serving on committees whereas a colleague

PhotoDisc, Inc.

When employees are treated unfairly, they lose motivation.

Exhibit **9.06**   Compensation plan

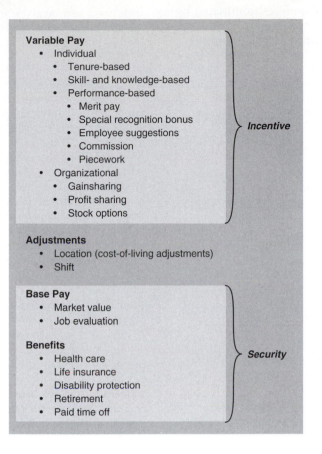

Variable Pay
- Individual
  - Tenure-based
  - Skill- and knowledge-based
  - Performance-based
    - Merit pay
    - Special recognition bonus
    - Employee suggestions
    - Commission
    - Piecework
- Organizational
  - Gainsharing
  - Profit sharing
  - Stock options

Incentive

Adjustments
- Location (cost-of-living adjustments)
- Shift

Base Pay
- Market value
- Job evaluation

Benefits
- Health care
- Life insurance
- Disability protection
- Retirement
- Paid time off

Security

of mine gets his entire self-worth by chairing department and university committees. So my boss reinforces my colleague by putting him on committees and reinforces me by giving me some data to play with. Likewise, some faculty members love early morning classes whereas others would rather teach at night.

In an example from the research literature, Welsh, Bernstein, and Luthans (1992) demonstrated the effectiveness of the Premack Principle with employees at a fast food restaurant. Employees whose errors decreased in a given day were rewarded by being allowed to work in their favorite workstation (e.g., cooking fries vs. flipping burgers). This use of the Premack Principle resulted in a decrease in employee errors.

Even though operant conditioning and the Premack Principle have been successful in improving motivation and performance, a note of caution comes from Deci (1972), who believes that for some people and some jobs work is intrinsically motivating. That is, people are motivated because they enjoy working, not because they are being rewarded. A reasonable body of research, much of it conducted by Deci himself, demonstrates that paying a person for the amount of work done will reduce the degree to which he enjoys performing the task. Thus, when financial incentives are no longer available, the employee will be less motivated to work than before rewards were used. As interesting as this concept sounds, some researchers (e.g., Dickinson, 1989) argue that Deci's conclusions that extrinsic rewards decrease intrinsic motivation are flawed. To apply the Premack Principle to your own life, complete Exercise 9–3 at the end of this chapter.

Financial Rewards

Financial incentives can be used to motivate better worker performance either by making variable pay an integral part of an employee's compensation package (Schuster & Zingheim, 1992) or by using financial rewards as a "bonus" for accomplishing certain goals. As shown in Exhibit 9.06, a compensation plan should include base pay and a benefit package to provide employees with security, salary adjustments to cover such conditions as undesirable shifts and geographic areas with high costs of living, and variable pay to provide an incentive to perform better. Though incentive systems often result in higher levels of performance, when designed poorly, they can result in such negative outcomes as increased stress, decreased health, and decreased safety (Schleifer & Amick, 1989; Schleifer & Okogbaa, 1990).

Financial incentives in the form of bonuses or prizes are also used to motivate employees. For example, Chick-fil-A annually gives more than $13 million in scholarships to employees nominated by their managers for excellent performance (Juergens, 2000). At Net2000 in Herndon, Virginia, employees who stay with the company for 2 years and receive a high performance rating are given a 3-year lease on a BMW, Dodge Durango, or Audi TT, and at Interwoven in the Silicon Valley, employees staying 3 years were given a 3-year lease on a BMW Z-3 (Frase-Blunt, 2001).

Recognition

Rather than providing financial incentives, many organizations reward employee behavior through recognition programs. For example:

- United Airlines holds a special ceremony each year in which employees are given service emblems for each year of service (Renk, 2000).

- Most universities award faculty members the titles of associate professor and professor to recognize years of service as well as quality of performance.

- Restaurants such as Outback Steak House and Chi-Chi's Mexican Restaurant, give "employees of the month" personal parking space.

- Lee Memorial Hospital in Cape Coral, Florida, gives employees a customized key chain that says "Valued employee since . . ." with the year they were hired printed at the end (Leonard, 1999a).

In some organizations, the recognition awards are given by peers. For example, employees at the Angus Barn Restaurant in Raleigh, North Carolina, choose peers to receive the "People's Choice" award, employees at Meridian Travel in Cleveland vote for the "Employee of the Month," and employees at the federal Office of Personnel Management select peers to receive the "Wingspread Award" (Nelson, 2000).

Informal recognition programs, called **social recognition**, can prove to be tremendous sources of employee motivation. Social recognition consists of personal attention, signs of approval (e.g., smiles, head nods), and expressions of appreciation (Stajkovic & Luthans, 2001).

Travel

Many organizations are offering travel awards rather than financial rewards. For example, every executive at McDonald's is allowed to nominate high-performing employees for a chance to spend a week in one of the company's condos in Hawaii, Florida, or Lake Tahoe, Nevada. At Chick-fil-A, sales teams compete for a vacation in Hawaii. At Motorola, managers can nominate employees for travel awards. Nationwide, the average value of these travel awards is $1,750 (Poe, 1997).

Individual-Based Versus Group-Based Incentives

Incentives can be given for either individual performance or group performance.

Individual-Based Incentive Plans

Individual-based incentive plans are designed to make high levels of individual performance financially worthwhile. Individual incentives help reduce such group problems as social loafing, which is discussed in Chapter 13. There are two main problems associated with individual incentive plans. The first is the difficulty in measuring individual performance. Not only are objective measures difficult to find but supervisors are reluctant to evaluate employees, especially when the outcome will determine the amount of money an employee will receive (Schuster & Zingheim, 1992).

The second problem is that individual incentive plans can foster competition among employees. Though competition is not always bad, it is seldom consistent with the recent trend toward a team approach to work. When done right, however, team environments and individual incentive programs can coexist and result in high levels of employee performance (Steers & Porter, 1991).

The two most common individual incentive plans are **pay for performance** and **merit pay**.

Pay for Performance. Also called earnings-at-risk (EAR) plans, pay-for-performance plans pay employees according to how much they individually produce. Simple pay-for-performance systems with which you are probably familiar include commission and piecework.

The first step in creating more complicated pay-for-performance plans is to determine the average or standard amount of production. For example, the average number of envelopes sorted by mail clerks might be 300 per hour. The next step is to determine the desired average amount of pay. We might decide that, on average, our mail clerks should earn $9 an hour. We then compute the piece rate by dividing hourly wage by the number of envelopes sorted (9/300), which is .03. Thus, each correctly sorted envelope is worth 3 cents. If a mail clerk is good and sorts 400 envelopes per hour, he will make $12 per hour. If our clerk is not a good worker and can sort only 200 pieces per hour, he will make $6 per hour. To protect workers from the effects of external factors, minimum wage laws ensure that even the worst employee will make enough money to survive. As suggested in Exhibit 9.06, most organizations provide a base salary to ensure that employees will have at least minimal financial security. In fact, research indicates that employees paid a flat hourly rate plus a performance bonus perform at levels equal to employees who are paid on a piece-rate plan (Dickinson & Gillette, 1993).

A good example of such a plan comes from the Superior Court Records Management Center in Phoenix, Arizona (Huish, 1997). After conducting a study that showed a negative correlation between

Exhibit **9.07** Phoenix, Arizona, hourly rates for pay-for-performance plan

Production as a % of Minimum	Quality Rating			
	1	2	3	4
101	$ 7.20	$ 7.45	$ 7.70	$ 7.95
111	$ 7.56	$ 7.81	$ 8.06	$ 8.31
121	$ 7.92	$ 8.17	$ 8.42	$ 8.67
131	$ 8.28	$ 8.53	$ 8.78	$ 9.03
141	$ 8.64	$ 8.89	$ 9.14	$ 9.39
151	$ 9.00	$ 9.25	$ 9.50	$ 9.75
161	$ 9.36	$ 9.61	$ 9.86	$10.11
171	$ 9.72	$ 9.97	$10.22	$10.47
181	$10.08	$10.33	$10.58	$10.83
191	$10.44	$10.69	$10.94	$11.19
201	$10.80	$11.05	$11.30	$11.55
211	$11.16	$11.41	$11.66	$11.91
221	$11.52	$11.77	$12.02	$12.27
231	$11.88	$12.13	$12.38	$12.63
241	$12.24	$12.49	$12.74	$12.99
251	$12.60	$12.85	$13.10	$13.35

employee salary and productivity ($r = -.49$), the clerk of the court decided to try a pay-for-performance system. Each employee was given a base salary of $7.20 per hour and, on the basis of the quantity and quality of his work (see Exhibit 9.07), could earn incentive pay. This pay-for-performance intervention resulted in an average increase in employee pay of $2.60 per hour, a reduction in cost per unit (a unit was a court document page transferred to microfilm) from 39 cents to 21 cents, and a decreased need for storage space.

Theraldson Enterprises in Fargo, North Dakota, changed its compensation system for the housekeepers employed by its 300 hotels. Rather than being paid by the hour, housekeepers were paid by the number of rooms they cleaned. This change saved the company $2 million per year and resulted in the housekeepers making more money and working fewer hours than under the old hourly rate system (Tulgan, 2001).

Union National Bank in Little Rock, Arkansas, has had tremendous success by paying its workers for the number of customers they serve, the number of new customers gained, the amount of time taken to balance accounts at the end of the day, and so on. The bank's pay-for-performance program has resulted in the average employee making 25% more in take-home pay, and the bank itself has almost doubled its profits.

Nucor in Charlotte, North Carolina, is another company that has used a pay-for-performance plan. By paying its steelworkers for the amount of work they do, Nucor has seen productivity more than double and its workers make more than $30,000 per year while the industry average is some $27,000. Though pay-for-performance plans appear to be successful for both the employee and the employer, some research suggests that employees are not satisfied with such plans (Brown & Huber, 1992).

Merit Pay. The major distinction between merit pay and pay for performance is that merit pay systems base their incentives on performance-appraisal scores rather than on such objective performance measures as sales and productivity. Thus, merit pay is a potentially good technique for jobs in which productivity is difficult to measure.

The actual link between performance-appraisal scores and the amount of merit pay received by an employee varies greatly around the United States. In the state of Virginia's merit pay system, employees' performance-appraisal scores at each office are ranked, and the top 30% of employees each receive a $1,000 annual bonus.

In the merit pay system used by one nonprofit mental health agency, each employee's performance-appraisal rating is divided by the total number of performance points possible, and this percentage is then multiplied by the maximum 3% merit increase that can be received by an employee. With this system, an employee must receive a perfect rating to receive the full 3% increase. Most employees receive between 2% and 2.5%.

The merit pay system used by a California public transit system is similar to that used by the mental health agency, with the exception that the merit increase becomes part of an employee's base salary for the next pay period. Thus increases are perpetuated each year, unlike the mental health system's one-time reward.

Research on merit pay has brought mixed reviews. Some research has shown that employees like the idea of merit pay, but other research has found that it is not popular with all employees and that many employees do not consider the merit ratings to be fair (Hills, Scott, Markham, & Vest, 1987; Wisdom & Patzig, 1987). Employees are most satisfied with merit pay if they help develop the system (Gilchrist & White, 1990).

One of merit pay's biggest problems is that increases are based on subjective performance appraisals. Aware of this, some supervisors will inflate performance-appraisal scores to increase their employees' pay and thus increase the positive feelings of employees toward their supervisors. Managers have also been known to inflate performance-appraisal ratings when they believe the base salaries for certain positions are too low.

Another problem with merit pay is that its availability or amount often changes with each fiscal year. Thus excellent performance one year might result in a large bonus, but the same performance another year might bring no bonus at all. This is especially true in the public sector. For merit pay to be successful, funding must be consistently available, and the amount must be great enough (at least 7%) to motivate employees (Bates, 2003).

Organizational Incentives

The idea behind organization-based incentive plans is to get employees to participate in the success or failure of the organization (Schuster & Zingheim, 1992). Rather than encouraging individual competition, these plans reward employees for reaching group goals. The problems with group incentive plans are that they can encourage social loafing and can get so complicated that they become difficult to explain to employees.

Profit Sharing. Profit sharing was developed in the United States by Albert Gallatin way back in 1794 (Henderson, 2003). As its name implies, profit-sharing programs provide employees with a percentage of *profits* above a certain amount. For example, in addition to their base salary, employees might receive 50% of the profits a company makes above 6%. Organizations will usually not share the initial 5% or so of profits as that money is needed for research and development and as a safety net for unprofitable years. The profits to be shared can be paid directly to employees as a bonus (cash plans) or placed into the employees' retirement fund (deferred plans). Profit sharing will only motivate employees if they understand the link between performance and profits and believe the company has a reasonable chance of making a profit. Research indicates that profit sharing results in greater employee commitment (Fitzgibbons, 1997; Florkowski & Schuster, 1992).

Gainsharing. Used by about 12% of organizations, **gainsharing** ties groupwide financial incentives to *improvements* in organizational performance (Mercer, 2003). The first gainsharing program was developed in 1935 by the Nunn-Bush Shoe Company in Milwaukee, but gainsharing has only become popular in the last 2 decades (Gowen, 1990). Gainsharing programs consist of three important elements: a cooperative/participative management philosophy, incentives based on improvement, and a group-based bonus formula (Gomez-Mejia, Welbourne, & Wiseman, 2000; Hanlon & Taylor, 1992).

The typical gainsharing program works as follows. First, the company monitors performance measures over some period of time to derive a **baseline**. Then productivity goals above the baseline are set, and the employees are told that they will receive bonuses for each period that the goal is reached. To make goal setting more effective, constant feedback is provided to employees on how current performance is in relation to the goal. At the end of each reporting period, bonuses are paid on the basis of how well the group did.

An excellent example of a successful gainsharing program can be found at the Dana Spicer Heavy Axle Division facility in Ohio (Hatcher, Ross, & Ross, 1987). Employees at the Dana plant receive a financial bonus when productivity surpasses the baseline. The gainsharing program has dramatically increased the number of employee suggestions, product quality, and productivity. Employees' bonuses average 14% above their normal pay each month, with year-end bonuses between 11% and 16%.

As another example, Southern California Edison employees agreed to surrender 5% of their base pay. In return, they were given the opportunity to earn 10 to 15% of their base pay in a gainsharing plan. In 1995 alone, this plan generated $96 million in savings—$40 million of which was passed on to the employees.

In general, gainsharing plans seem to be effective. A review of gainsharing studies indicates improvements in productivity, increased employee and union satisfaction, and declines in absenteeism (Gowen, 1990). As with any incentive plan, gainsharing is most effective when employees are formally involved in the design and operation (Bullock & Tubbs, 1990) and when there is not a long delay between performance and the financial payoff (Mawhinney & Gowen, 1990).

Stock Options. Although **stock options** represent the most complicated organizational incentive plan, they are offered to all employees by more than 34% of companies (Brandes, Dharwadkar, & Lemesis, 2003). With stock options, employees are given the opportunity to purchase stock in the future, typically at the market price on the day the options were granted. Usually stock options vest over a certain period of time and must be exercised within a maximum time frame. The idea is that as a company does well the value of its stock increases, as does the employee's profit. For example, suppose AT&T stock is selling for $55 per share on June 1, and the company gives employees the option of purchasing the stock for $55 per share anytime in the next

10 years. Ten years later, the stock is worth $75 per share, and the employee can purchase the stock for the $55 per share option price—a $20 per share profit. However, if the stock had fallen from $55 to $45, the employee would not exercise his option to purchase the stock at $55 per share.

Stock options allow employees to share in the long-term success of an organization. In fact, such organizations as GTE, United Airlines, Home Depot, and Foldcraft Company report not only are their employees making good money through their stock ownership but that organizational productivity has improved as well. At times, stock options may not be good motivators because employees have trouble understanding the concept of stock and because the incentive (profit made on the selling of stock) is psychologically well removed from day-to-day performance. However, having partial ownership in a company can increase performance. For example, in a study of hotel managers, Qian (1996) found a significant correlation between the amount of manager ownership and the hotel's profit margin.

Expectancy Theory

An influential theory of worker motivation that integrates many of the factors discussed previously in this chapter is **expectancy theory**, which was first proposed by Vroom (1964) and then modified by others, including Porter and Lawler (1968). This theory has three components, the definitions of which vary with each modification of the theory. The following definitions are combinations of those suggested by others and make the theory easier to understand:

- **Expectancy (E):** The perceived relationship between the amount of effort an employee puts in and the resulting outcome.
- **Instrumentality (I):** The extent to which the outcome of a worker's performance, if noticed, results in a particular consequence.
- **Valence (V):** The extent to which an employee values a particular consequence.

To understand or predict an employee's level of motivation, these components are used in the following formula:

$$\text{motivation} = E (I \times V)$$

Thus, all possible outcomes of a behavior are determined, the valence of each is multiplied by the probability that it occurs at a particular performance level, and then the sum of these products is multiplied by the expectancy of an employee putting in the effort to attain the necessary level of performance. As can be seen from this formula, the higher the score on each component, the greater the employee's motivation. To expound on this, let us examine each component in more detail.

In terms of *expectancy*, if an employee believes that no matter how hard he works he will never reach the necessary level of performance, then his motivation will probably be low. For *instrumentality*, the employee will be motivated only if his behavior results in some specific consequence. That is, if the employee works extra hours, he expects to be rewarded, or if he is inexcusably absent from work, he expects to be punished. For a behavior to have a desired consequence, two events must occur. First, the employee's behavior must be noticed. If the employee believes he is able to attain the necessary level of performance but that his performance will not be noticed, then his level of motivation will be low. Second, noticed behavior must be rewarded. If no rewards are available, then, again, motivation will be low. As will be discussed in greater detail later in this chapter, if appropriate behavior does not have positive consequences or if inappropriate behavior does not have negative consequences, the probability that a worker will continue undesired behaviors increases, and the probability that an employee will continue desired behaviors decreases.

For *valence*, if an employee is rewarded, the reward must be something he values (Mobaraki, 1996). If good performance is rewarded by an award, then the employee will be motivated only if he values awards. Likewise, if we punish an employee by suspending him, the punishment will be effective only if the employee needs the money. If he does not particularly like his job and would rather spend a few days at the lake, the suspension will obviously not be effective. In an applied study, Fox, Scott, and Donohue (1993) found that in a pay-for-performance environment pay served as an incentive only for employees with a high monetary valence.

This theory can be used to analyze the situation experienced by one bank in Virginia. Concerned that the bank's tellers were averaging only 3 new Visa customers each month, management sought to increase the number of Visa applications taken by each teller. Tellers were expected to ask each customer if he or she had a Visa card. If not, the teller was to give the customer an application. A teller would receive $5 extra per month if he or she increased the number of new Visa customers per month to 25.

The program was a flop, much to management's surprise. Applying expectancy theory, however, would have led an I/O psychologist to predict the program's lack of success. First, let us look at the expectancy component. If the tellers currently averaged only 3 new Visa customers each month, they probably did not believe that, even working hard, they would be able to generate 25 new customers. Thus, the expectancy probability for the program was low.

Second, most tellers probably did not place much value on an extra $5 per month, so the valence component also was low. Thus, with two of three components having low values, the program was destined to fail from the start. The bank later reduced the monthly number of new Visa cards to 10 and increased the teller reward to $20. These simple changes brought the desired increase in new Visa customers.

In addition to predicting employee effort, expectancy theory has been applied successfully to predict speeding by drivers and cheating by students. To demonstrate this last behavior, imagine the typical examination in a typical college class. First, look at the expectancy component. We might ask what the probability is for catching a cheater. Students who cheat most likely believe that it is very low. To determine the instrumentality component, we might ask what the probability is for some negative consequence if a cheater is caught. In many universities, this probability is low. Not only is it difficult to prove that a student cheated, but if it is the first time a student is caught, punishment usually results in no more than a few days' suspension. Finally, we examine the valence component. Even if a student *was* caught and suspended, how terrible would that be? For many students, a few days of vacation may not seem so terrible. Thus, when combining the three components, we should not be surprised that cheating often occurs.

Expectancy theory can also be used to suggest ways to change employee motivation. As we saw with the bank, motivation was increased by making the performance standard more reasonable and by increasing the value of the consequence. Similarly, if we wanted to apply the theory to decrease cheating, we would increase the probability of catching cheaters, make convicting a person who has cheated easier, and make the consequences for cheating more severe.

Although expectancy theory is an interesting and useful method of predicting and increasing employee motivation, some researchers have criticized it. The major criticism involves the components equation. As it is now written, all of the components are multiplied. Some researchers have questioned whether the addition of some components would be more appropriate than their multiplication (Schmidt, 1973). This is because, when the components are multiplied, a zero in any component results in a prediction of zero motivation, even when ratings in the other components are high.

A second criticism involves the values assigned to each component (Ilgen, Nebeker, & Pritchard, 1981). Research has indicated that even though valence and instrumentality can be reliably measured the theory is most predictive when people behave rationally (Stahl & Harrell, 1981), which they often do not, and have an **internal locus of control** (Lied & Pritchard, 1976), which may not always be the case. Despite problems with the equation, however, the theory is still one of the most useful for predicting employee behavior.

Reward Versus Punishment

Rather than rewarding desired behaviors, we can change employee performance by punishing undesired behaviors. That is, instead of rewarding employees who don't miss work, we punish them when they do. Instead of providing monetary incentives for high levels of performance, we suspend employees for low levels of performance. Though many psychologists advise against punishment, it is common, and managers generally believe it to be effective (Butterfield, Trevino, & Ball, 1996).

Proponents of using punishment to change employee behavior argue that if applied properly punishment not only reduces undesired behaviors in a particular employee but also sets an example for other employees. Opponents of punishment argue that punishment changes behavior only in the short run, does not teach an employee proper behaviors, and causes resentment. Furthermore, punishment causes employees to learn new methods to break rules, rather than teaching them not to break rules.

For punishment to be effective, an employee must understand why he is being punished and be shown alternative ways of behaving that will result in some type of desired reinforcement. The punishment must also "fit the crime" in that too severe of a punishment will cause resentment and too lenient a punishment will not motivate a change in behavior. As one would imagine, punishment should usually be done in private rather than in front of other employees.

Are Rewards and Resources Given Equitably?

Another factor related to motivation and job satisfaction is the extent to which employees perceive that they are being treated fairly. The most well known theory on this topic is equity theory. **Equity theory** was developed by Adams (1965) and is based on the premise that our levels of motivation and job satisfaction are related to how fairly we believe we are treated in comparison with others. If we believe we are treated unfairly, we attempt to change our beliefs or behaviors until the situation appears to be fair. Three components are involved in this perception of fairness: inputs, outputs, and input/output ratio.

Inputs are those personal elements that we put into our jobs. Obvious elements are time, effort, education, and experience. Less obvious elements include money spent on child care and distance driven to work.

Outputs are those elements that we receive from our jobs. A list of obvious outputs includes pay, benefits, challenge, and responsibility. Less obvious outputs are benefits such as friends and office furnishings.

According to the theory, employees subconsciously list all their outputs and inputs and then compute an **input/output ratio** by dividing output value by input value. By itself, this ratio is not especially useful. But employees then compute the input/output ratios for other employees and for previous work experiences and compare them to their own. If their ratios are lower than those of others, they become dissatisfied and are motivated to make the ratios equal in one or more ways.

First, employees can seek greater outputs by such means as asking for a raise or for more responsibility. Second, employees can make the ratio more equal by reducing their inputs. Thus they might not work as hard or might reduce their attendance.

A less practical way of equalizing the ratios would be changing the ratios of other employees. For example, employees might try to get another employee to work harder and thus increase that employee's inputs. Or they might try to reduce the outputs of another employee by withholding friendship or finding a way

Exhibit 9.08 Equity theory research

When an employee's inputs are greater than his outputs (underpayment), he

- works less hard (Hauenstein & Lord, 1989)
- becomes more selfish (Harder, 1992)
- has lower job satisfaction (Carr, McLoughlin, Hodgson, & McLachlan, 1996)

When an employee's outputs are greater than his inputs (overpayment), he

- is less likely to be persuaded by his under paid peers (Stewart & Moore, 1992)
- does not feel guilty (Lapidus & Pinkerton, 1995)
- works harder (Adams & Rosenbaum, 1962; Pritchard, Dunnette, & Jorgenson, 1972)
- becomes more team oriented (Harder, 1992)

to reduce the other employee's bonuses. Fortunately, however, strategies to equalize input/output ratios seldom involve reducing others' outputs. Employees can also restore equity by rationalizing the input/output ratio differences, changing the person to whom they are comparing themselves, or leaving the organization.

In general, research has supported the idea that our motivation decreases when our input/output ratios are lower than others'. Research on this was conducted by Lord and Hohenfeld (1979) and Hauenstein and Lord (1989) with major league baseball players. Players who either had their salary cut during their first year of free agency or lost an arbitration case performed at lower levels the following year. Thus players who thought that their *output* (salary) was too low responded by reducing their *inputs* (performance). In a study of professional basketball players, Harder (1992) found that overpaid players responded by being more team oriented (e.g., passing the ball, rebounding), whereas underpaid players responded by being more selfish (e.g., taking shots).

In an interesting study, O'Reilly and Puffer (1989) found that employees' motivation increased when coworkers received appropriate sanctions for their behavior. That is, when a high-performing group member was rewarded or a poor-performing group member was punished, the satisfaction and motivation of the group increased.

The degree of inequity that an employee feels when underpaid appears to be a function of whether the employee chose the actions that resulted in underpayment (Cropanzano & Folger, 1989). That is, if an employee chooses to work harder than others who are paid the same, he will not feel cheated, but if he is pressured into working harder for the same pay, he will be unhappy.

An interesting prediction from this theory is a situation in which an employee's input/output ratio is *higher* than the ratio of others. Because the theory is based on

equity, the prediction would be that the employee would still strive for equal ratios by either increasing his inputs or decreasing his outputs. In other words, he would either work harder or ask to be paid less. In fact, research has indicated that employees often do respond to being "overpaid" by feeling guilty (Lapidus & Pinkerton, 1995) or working harder (Adams & Rosenbaum, 1962; Pritchard, Dunnette, & Jorgenson, 1972). But feelings of inequity caused by being "overpaid" do not last long and probably do not produce long-term changes in behavior (Carrell & Dittrich, 1978).

Exhibit 9.08 summarizes the findings of equity theory research. To practice using expectancy and equity theory, complete the Expectancy Exercise on your CD-ROM.

Motivation Level of Other Employees

Employees observe the levels of motivation and satisfaction of other employees and then model those levels. Thus, if an organization's older employees work hard and talk positively about their jobs and their employer, new employees will model this behavior and be both productive and satisfied. The reverse is also true: If veteran employees work slowly and complain about their jobs, so too will new employees.

Integration of Motivation Theories

As shown in Exhibit 9.09, people come to a job with a predisposition toward motivation. That is, some people, such as those with high self-esteem, are

Exhibit **9.09** Motivation flow chart

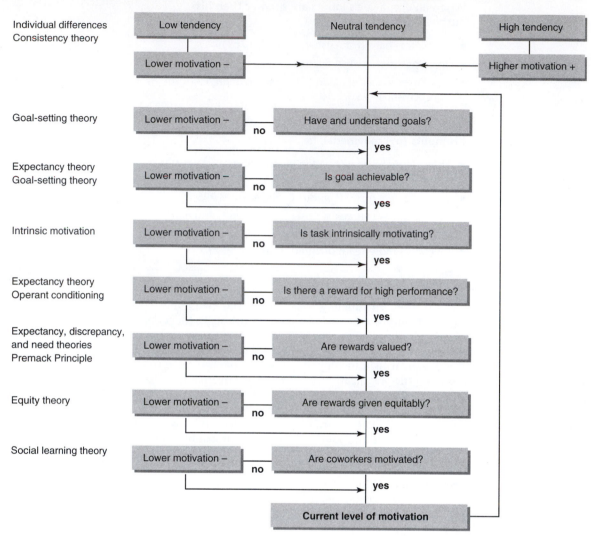

Personal Tendency Toward Motivation

generally more motivated than others. In this chapter, we discussed many theories of work motivation. Let's review what we have learned:

- From the discrepancy and needs theories, we will be motivated in our jobs if the job itself and the organization meet our expectations and values and satisfy our needs.

- From goal-setting theory, we find that employees who have, understand, and agree to goals will be more motivated than those without goals or with unclear goals. From expectancy theory and goal-setting theory, we know that the goals must be challenging but reasonable.

- From operant learning and expectancy theories, it is clear that extrinsically motivated people will be more motivated if behavior results in a reward.

- From these same two theories plus discrepancy theory, the needs theories, and the Premack Principle, we know that the rewards must have value to the employee to be motivating. Because different people value different rewards, care must be taken to ensure that a variety of rewards are available.

- From equity theory, we know that rewards that are valued will be motivating only if they are given in an equitable way. As discussed previously, *perceptions* of equity are as important as the *reality* of equity.

- Social influence theory tells us that if other employees are motivated there is an increased probability that we will model their behavior and be motivated.

The results of these factors are summed to indicate an employee's current level of motivation. As conditions change, so will the motivation level. To practice what you have learned in this chapter, complete the case study in Exercise 9–4 and develop your own theory in Exercise 9–5.

Chapter Summary

In this chapter you learned:

- Employees who have high self-esteem, a high need for achievement, and intrinsic motivation, and who are expected to perform well by others are more motivated than their low self-esteem, low achievement need, extrinsically motivated counterparts.

- Goals are most effective if they are concrete and specific, are of high but reasonable difficulty, and are set with the input of the employee.

- Providing feedback on goal attainment and performance levels will also increase performance.

- Operant conditioning principles can be used to motivate employees.

- It is important to treat employees fairly.

- Common individual incentive plans include pay for performance and merit pay. Common organizational incentive plans include profit sharing, gainsharing, and stock options.

Critical Thinking Questions

1. Does getting paid for a task that one enjoys performing reduce intrinsic motivation?

2. If the right techniques are used, can everyone be motivated to perform well?

3. Which of the individual incentive plans is best?

4. What is the optimal level at which goals should be set?

5. Is the threat of punishment an effective motivator?

To learn more about the issues discussed in this chapter, point your browser to

http://www.infotrac-college.com/wadsworth

and enter one of these search terms:

self-esteem

gainsharing

incentive plans

expectancy theory

intrinsic motivation

goal setting

employee feedback

profit sharing

merit pay

Exercise 9–1
Self-Esteem

The Radford Self-Esteem Inventory

Here is a list of statements about feelings. For each statement, place an "X" in the appropriate column to indicate the extent to which you agree with the statement.

	Strongly disagree	disagree	neutral	agree	Strongly agree
1. Difficult situations usually don't bother me.	1	2	3	4	5
2. I don't like a lot of things about me.	5	4	3	2	1
3. I have good ideas.	1	2	3	4	5
4. I have a low opinion of myself.	5	4	3	2	1
5. I like trying new things.	1	2	3	4	5
6. I am a confident person.	1	2	3	4	5
7. I am not afraid to take risks.	1	2	3	4	5
8. I do most things well.	1	2	3	4	5
9. I am happy with who I am.	1	2	3	4	5
10. I am a likeable person.	1	2	3	4	5
11. There is not much about my personality that I would change.	1	2	3	4	5
12. I am successful at almost everything I try.	1	2	3	4	5
13. I am a good person.	1	2	3	4	5
14. I have a lot of respect for myself.	1	2	3	4	5
15. I am comfortable with who I am.	1	2	3	4	5
16. There is little I cannot accomplish if I set my mind to it.	1	2	3	4	5
17. I am a talented person.	1	2	3	4	5
18. I can overcome any obstacles in my life.	1	2	3	4	5
19. I am as good a person as anyone.	1	2	3	4	5
20. There are so many people I would rather be than me.	5	4	3	2	1

Scoring and Interpreting the Radford Inventory

The Radford Inventory measures your level of self-esteem. To score the inventory, add the points that correspond to the choices you made for each question.

Your self-esteem score is _____.

To interpret your score, look at the chart below and circle where your scores fall.

	Self-Worth
Top 20%	82–100
Next 20%	78–81
Middle 20%	75–77
Next 20%	68–74
Bottom 20%	20–67

On the basis of what you learned about consistency theory, how motivated would your self-esteem score suggest that you would be?

_____

_____

_____

_____

_____

_____

_____

Exercise 9–2
Intrinsic Versus Extrinsic Motivation

Work Preference Inventory (College Student Version; Copyright 1987, Teresa M. Amabile, used with permission of the author.)

Please rate each item in terms of how true it is of you. Please circle one and only one letter for each question according to the following scale:

N = **Never** or almost never true of you
S = **Sometimes** true of you
O = **Often** true of you
A = **Always** or almost always true of you

N S O A   1. I am concerned about what other people think of my work.

N S O A   2. I prefer having someone set clear goals for me in my work.

N S O A   3. The more difficult the problem, the more I enjoy trying to solve it.

N S O A   4. I am keenly aware of the goals I have for getting good grades.

N S O A   5. I want my work to provide me with opportunities to increase my knowledge and skills.

N S O A   6. To me, success means doing better than other people.

N S O A   7. I prefer to figure things out for myself.

N S O A   8. No matter what the outcome of a project, I am satisfied if I feel I gained a new experience.

N S O A   9. I dislike relatively simple, straightforward tasks.

N S O A   10. I am keenly aware of the GPA (grade point average) goals I have for myself.

N S O A   11. Curiosity is the driving force behind much of what I do.

N S O A   12. I'm less concerned with what work I do than what I get for it.

N S O A   13. I enjoy tackling problems that are completely new to me.

N   S   O   A   14. I prefer work that stretches my abilities over work I know I can do well.

N   S   O   A   15. I'm concerned about how other people are going to react to my ideas.

N   S   O   A   16. I often think about grades and awards.

N   S   O   A   17. I'm more comfortable when I can set my own goals.

N   S   O   A   18. I believe that there is no point in doing a good job if nobody else knows about it.

N   S   O   A   19. I am strongly motivated by the grades I can earn.

N   S   O   A   20. It is important to me to be able to do what I enjoy most.

N   S   O   A   21. I prefer working on projects with clearly specified procedures.

N   S   O   A   22. As long as I can do what I enjoy, I'm not that concerned about exactly what grades or awards I earn.

N   S   O   A   23. I enjoy doing work that is so absorbing that I forget about everything else.

N   S   O   A   24. I am strongly motivated by the recognition I can earn from other people.

N   S   O   A   25. I have to feel that I'm earning something for what I do.

N   S   O   A   26. I enjoy trying to solve complex problems.

N   S   O   A   27. It is important for me to have an outlet for self-expression.

N   S   O   A   28. I want to find out how good I really can be at my work.

N   S   O   A   29. I want other people to find out how good I really can be at my work.

N   S   O   A   30. What matters most to me is enjoying what I do.

Interpreting the Work Preference Inventory

The Work Preference Inventory was developed by Dr. Teresa Amabile and measures your predisposition to be intrinsically and extrinsically motivated. To score the WPI, give yourself 1 point if you circled an "N," 2 points if you circled an "S," 3 points if you circled an "O," and 4 points if you circled an "A."

To determine your level of intrinsic motivation, add your points for questions 3, 5, 7, 8, 9, 11, 13, 14, 17, 20, 23, 26, 27, 28, and 30. _____

To determine your level of extrinsic motivation, add your points for questions 1, 2, 4, 6, 10, 12, 15, 16, 18, 19, 21, 24, 25, and 29. _____ On question 22, reverse your score (A = 1, O = 2, S = 3, and N =1), and add this score to the total for the other 14 questions. _____

To interpret your score, look at the chart below and circle where your scores fall. Are you an intrinsically or extrinsically motivated person?

	Intrinsic Motivation	Extrinsic Motivation
Top 20%	46–60	43–60
Next 20%	45–47	39–42
Middle 20%	43–44	37–38
Next 20%	40–42	35–36
Bottom 20%	15–39	15–34

On the basis of what you read in the text, what does your score on the WPI tell you about your personal tendency toward motivation?

_____

_____

_____

_____

_____

_____

_____

_____

_____

_____

_____

_____

_____

_____

_____

_____

_____

_____

_____

_____

_____

_____

_____

Exercise 9–3
Reinforcement Hierarchy

Chapter 9 discussed the idea that it is often difficult to reward employees because each employee values different things in life. This idea is called the Premack Principle. It is the purpose of this exercise to give you the opportunity to create your own reinforcement hierarchy.

Instructions

Think of your current job or one that you have had recently. Once you have this job in mind, create a reinforcement hierarchy for yourself. Use the example in your text as a guide.

Most Liked

1. _____
2. _____
3. _____
4. _____
5. _____
6. _____
7. _____
8. _____
9. _____
10. _____
11. _____
12. _____
13. _____
14. _____
15. _____

Least Liked

Exercise 9–4
Motivation Case Study

For the past 5 months, Vacua Can, a manager at Orion Manufacturing, has come home from work depressed and angry. It seems no matter what she does, she can't motivate her employees to improve their performance. Over the past year, Vacua sent each employee to an extensive training seminar, spent money on new equipment, and transferred out the employees who lacked the ability to do their jobs. Despite these interventions, her department's performance is at the same level it was 2 years ago. Because of this performance stagnation, Vacua is worried that she will be fired.

Vacua thought that a boost in morale might increase performance so she gave each employee a 12% raise. Yet instead of morale being increased, many employees complained even more loudly than before.

Vacua also held a department meeting in which she gave an inspirational appeal for everyone to "work hard and do the very best job you possibly can." Her department seemed enthusiastic for a week, but productivity did not change.

Where did Vacua Can go wrong? What advice can you give her to motivate her employees?

Exercise 9–5
Your Own Motivation Theory

In Chapter 9, you learned about many different theories for why employees are satisfied with their jobs and why they are motivated to perform well. Even though none of the theories has been completely supported, each of the theories has something to offer. On the basis of the various theories, as well as on your experiences, design your own theory of job motivation and satisfaction. Feel free to borrow as much as you want from each of the theories discussed in your text.

_____

_____

_____

_____

_____

_____

_____

_____

_____

_____

_____

_____

_____

_____

_____

_____

_____

_____

10 Employee Satisfaction and Commitment

IMAGINE THE FOLLOWING SITUATIONS:

- Jean Davis and Maria McDuffie have worked as customer service representatives at Fuller Technologies for the past 2 years. Jean loves her job and wants to stay with Fuller until she retires in 10 years. Maria hates her job, uses all of her available sick days, and would leave in a heartbeat if she could only find a job that paid as well.

- Rhonda Beall recently met with a career adviser to chart a new course for her life. She hates her current job and has hated every job she has ever had. She is hoping the career adviser can find "the job" for her.

- David Spoto loves his job and can't wait to get to work in the morning. He loves to work, loves his current job, and has loved every job he has ever had.

- Darnell Johnson, HR director for Simmons Enterprises, is frustrated because his company has the highest turnover rate in the area. Even more frustrating is that employees stay with Simmons just long enough to gain experience and then leave for lower pay with Raynes Manufacturing, another local employer.

Why does Jean Davis love her job and Maria McDuffie hate the same job? Why do Rhonda Beall and David Spoto have such different attitudes about their jobs and careers? What is Raynes Manufacturing doing better than Simmons Enterprises? This chapter will help you answer these questions about **job satisfaction**—the attitude an employee has toward her job and **organizational commitment**—the extent to which an employee identifies with and is involved with an organization. By the end of the chapter, you will learn

- why an employer should even care about job satisfaction and organizational commitment.

- there are individual differences in the predisposition to be satisfied.

- ways to increase employee satisfaction and commitment.

- methods to measure employees' levels of job satisfaction.

- why employees are absent from work.

- why employees quit their jobs.

Why Should We Care About Employee Attitudes?

Many job-related attitudes have been studied by psychologists, but the two most commonly studied are job satisfaction and organizational commitment. Though job satisfaction and organizational commitment are different work-related attitudes, they will be discussed together in this chapter because they are highly correlated (Tett & Meyer, 1993) and result in similar employee behaviors. As shown in Exhibit 10.01, satisfied employees tend to be committed to an organization (Tett & Meyer, 1993), and employees who are satisfied and committed are more likely to attend work (Hackett, 1989), stay with an organization (Tett & Meyer, 1993), arrive at work on time (Kozlowsky, Sagie, Krausz, & Singer, 1997), and perform well (Judge, Thoresen, Bono, & Patton, 2001) than are employees who are not satisfied or committed. Interestingly, there is a stronger relationship between job satisfaction and performance in complex jobs ($r = .52$) than in jobs of low or medium complexity ($r = .29$; Judge et al., 2001).

Though the relationships between job satisfaction and organizational commitment and attendance, performance, tardiness, and turnover are not as large as one would expect, it is important to note that many other factors affect work behavior (Judge et al., 2001). For example, a dissatisfied employee may want to quit her job but not be able to because no other jobs are available. Likewise, a dissatisfied employee may want to miss work but realizes that she will lose pay if she does. Thus we often find that job satisfaction and

Exhibit 10.01 Meta-analysis results of the relationship among job satisfaction, performance, turnover, commitment, and absenteeism

	Performance	Turnover	Absenteeism Frequency	Absenteeism Duration	Commitment Organizational	Commitment Occupational[e]	Intrinsic Motivation	Lateness	OCBs
Job Satisfaction									
Facet									
Pay	.06[a]	−.08[f]	−.08[c]	−.07[c]	.34[i]	.23[e]	.29[j]	−.22[k]	
Supervision	.19[a]	−.13[f]	−.13[c]	−.08[c]	.45[i]		.39[j]		
Coworkers	.12[a]	−.13[f]	−.07[c]	−.07[c]		.23[e]		−.16[k]	
Work	.21[a]		−.21[c]	−.14[c]		.53[e]			
Promotion opportunities	.15[a]		−.09[c]	−.07[c]					
Type									
Intrinsic	.23[a]		−.25[c]	−.01[c]					
Extrinsic	.18[a]		−.24[c]	−.21[c]					
Overall satisfaction	.30[d]	−.22[f]	−.15[c]	−.23[c]	.70[b]	.44[e]	.59[j]	−.11[k]	.24[L]
Turnover									
Intent to leave									
Occupation						−.62[c]		.46[k]	
Organization		.45[f]				−.30[e]			
Actual turnover	−.19[f]				−.27[f]	−.21[e]		.07[k]	
Absenteeism	−.29[g]	.21[f]			−.23[h]		−.25[c]	.40[k]	
Lateness	−.21[k]				−.29[k]				
Performance									
Supervisor ratings			−.32[g]	−.26[g]					
Performance measures			−.22[g]	−.28[g]					
Tardiness		.06[f]							
Stress									
Role clarity		−.24[f]							
Role overload		.12[f]							
Role conflict		.22[f]							
Overall stress		.16[f]						−.21[k]	
Intrinsic Motivation					.67[i]				

Notes: [a]Iaffaldano and Muchinsky (1985); [b]Tett and Meyer (1993); [c]Hackett (1989); [d]Judge, Thoresen, Bono, and Patton (2001); [e]Lee, Carswell, and Allen (2000); [f]Griffeth, Hom, and Gaertner (2000); [g]Bycio (1992); [h]Farrell and Stamm (1988); [i]Mathieu and Zajac (1988); [j]Oldham, Hackman, and Stepina (1990); [k]Koslowsky, Sagie, Krausz, and Singer (1997); [L]LePine, Erez, & Johnson (2002).

organizational commitment are related more to a desire to quit, miss work, or reduce effort than they are to actual behaviors. To get you thinking about job satisfaction in your life, complete the Free Write Exercise on your CD-ROM.

What Causes Employees to Be Satisfied with Their Jobs?

This chapter will explore several theories that seek to explain why workers are satisfied with and committed to their jobs, but none of the theories completely and accurately explains these job-related attitudes. Each is valuable, however, because it suggests ways to increase employee satisfaction and commitment. Thus, even though a theory itself may not be completely supported by research, the resulting suggestions have generally led to increased performance or longer tenure.

Before discussing the various theories, it is important to note that both of these work-related attitudes are multifaceted. That is, employees may be satisfied with one facet of work (e.g., their pay) but not another (e.g., their coworkers). The most commonly studied facets of job satisfaction are pay, supervision, coworkers, work, and promotion opportunities. Many other facets such as satisfaction with equipment, the work facility, the work site, and company policy are also important but have not received as much research attention.

It is thought that there are three facets to organizational commitment (Meyer & Allen, 1997). **Affective commitment** is the extent to which an employee wants to remain with the organization, cares about the organization, and is willing to exert effort on its behalf. For example, an employee of the Red Cross might like her coworkers and her boss, share the altruistic goals of the organization, and realize that her efforts will result in better organizational performance.

Continuance commitment is the extent to which an employee believes she must remain with the organization due to the time, expense, and effort that she has already put into the organization or the difficulty she would have in finding another job. Take, for example, a Chamber of Commerce director who spent 10 years making business contacts, getting funding for a new building, and earning the trust of the local city council. Though she could take a new job with a Chamber in a different city, she would need to spend another 10 years with that Chamber just to make the gains she has already made. As another example, an employee might hate her job and want to leave but realize that no other organization would hire her or give her the salary she desires.

Normative commitment is the extent to which an employee feels obligated to the organization and, as a result of this obligation, must remain with the organization. A good example of normative commitment would be an employee who was given her first job by an organization, was mentored by her manager, and was trained at great cost to the organization. The employee may feel that she is ethically obligated to remain with the organization because of their extensive investment in her.

What Individual Differences Affect Job Satisfaction?

Going back to our examples at the beginning of the chapter, what would explain why David Spoto loves his current job and Rhonda Beall hates hers? According to theories involving individual differences, the key to the answer is the fact that David has been satisfied at every job he has had whereas Rhonda has never been satisfied with a job. Individual difference theory postulates that some variability in job satisfaction is due to an individual's personal tendency across situations to enjoy what she does. Thus, certain types of people will generally be satisfied and motivated regardless of the type of job they hold (Weaver, 1978). This idea also makes intuitive sense. We all know people who constantly complain and whine about every job they have, and we also know people who are motivated and enthusiastic about their every job or task.

For this theory to be true, it would be essential that job satisfaction be consistent across time and situations. Research seems to support this notion. As a demonstration that job satisfaction is fairly consistent across time, significant correlations were found by Staw and Ross (1985) between the job satisfaction levels of employees in 1969 and in 1971 ($r = .33$), by Judge and Watanabe (1993) between job satisfaction levels of employees in 1972 and 1977 ($r = .37$), by Steel and Rentch (1997) between measures of job satisfaction taken 10 years apart ($r = .37$), and by Staw, Bell, and Clausen (1986) between adolescent and adult levels of satisfaction. Complete Exercise 10–1 at the end of this chapter to see how stable your own job satisfaction has been.

Because there seems to be at least some consistency in job satisfaction across time and jobs, the next question concerns the types of people that seem to be consistently satisfied with their jobs. Research in this area has focused on genetic predispositions (Lykken & Tellegen, 1996), core self-evaluations (Judge, Locke, Durham, & Kluger, 1998), and life satisfaction (Tait, Padgett, & Baldwin, 1989).

Genetic Predispositions

An interesting and controversial set of studies (Arvey, Bouchard, Segal, & Abraham, 1989; Keller, Bouchard, Arvey, Segal, & Dawis, 1992) suggests that job satisfaction not only may be fairly stable across jobs but also may be genetically determined. Arvey and his colleagues arrived at this conclusion by comparing the levels of job satisfaction of 34 sets of identical twins who were separated from each other at an early age. If job satisfaction is purely environmental, there should be no significant correlation between levels of job satisfaction for identical twins who were raised in different environments and who are now working at

Exhibit 10.02 Results of Judge and Bono's (2001) meta-analysis

Core-Evaluation Trait	Correlation with Job Satisfaction	Correlation with Job Performance
Self-esteem	.26	.26
Self-efficacy	.45	.23
Internal locus of control	.32	.22
Emotional stability	.24	.19

different types of jobs. But if identical twins have similar levels of job satisfaction despite being reared apart and despite working at dissimilar jobs, then a genetic predisposition for job satisfaction is likely.

On the basis of their analysis, Arvey and his colleagues found that approximately 30% of job satisfaction appears to be explainable by genetic factors. Thus one way to increase the overall level of job satisfaction in an organization would be to hire only those applicants who show high levels of overall job and life satisfaction. Because these findings are controversial and have received some criticism (Cropanzano & James, 1990), more research is needed before firm conclusions can be drawn.

Core Self-Evaluations

Whether the consistency in job satisfaction is due to genetic or environmental factors, a series of personality variables appear to be related to job satisfaction. That is, certain types of personalities are associated with the tendency to be satisfied or dissatisfied with one's job. Judge, Locke, and Durham (1997) have hypothesized that four personality variables are related to people's predisposition to be satisfied with life and with their jobs: emotional stability, self-esteem, self-efficacy (perceived ability to master their environment), and **internal locus of control** (perceived ability to control their environment). That is, people prone to be satisfied with their jobs and with life in general have high self-esteem, have a feeling of being competent, are emotionally stable, and believe they have control over their lives. This view is supported by several meta-analyses and studies:

- As shown in Exhibit 10.02, a meta-analysis by Judge and Bono (2001) found these four variables to be related to both job satisfaction and job performance.
- Judge, Locke, Durham, and Kluger (1998) found a significant correlation between a combination of these four variables and job satisfaction ($r = .41$) and life satisfaction ($r = .41$).
- A meta-analysis by Connolly and Viswesvaran (1998) indicated that 10 to 25% of job satisfaction could be due to affectivity.

- A study by Garske (1990) revealed that employees with high self-esteem are more satisfied with their job than are employees low in self-esteem.
- A meta-analysis by Judge, Heller, and Mount (2002) concluded that emotional stability and extraversion were significantly related to job and life satisfaction.

To get an idea of your own predisposition to be satisfied at work, complete Exercise 10–2 at the end of this chapter.

Life Satisfaction

Judge, Locke, Durham, and Kluger (1998); Judge and Watanabe (1993); and Tait, Padgett, and Baldwin (1989) have theorized not only that job satisfaction is consistent across time but that the extent to which a person is satisfied with all aspects of life (e.g., marriage, friends, job, family, geographic location) is as well. Furthermore, people who are satisfied with their jobs tend to be satisfied with life. These researchers found support for their theory, as their data indicate that job satisfaction is significantly correlated with life satisfaction. Thus people happy in life tend to be happy in their jobs and vice versa.

In an interesting study, Judge and Watanabe (1994) found that for about two thirds of participants, high levels of life satisfaction are associated with high levels of job satisfaction. In other words, satisfaction with one's job "spills over" into other aspects of life and satisfaction with other aspects of life "spills over" into satisfaction with one's job. For the remaining 30% or so of the population, either there is no relationship between life and job satisfaction or there is a negative relationship.

That life satisfaction can influence job satisfaction in the vast majority of people is an important finding. In the 21st century, managers are being asked to work miracles in making even the worst of jobs satisfying. Perhaps a more realistic approach is what I refer to as the "John Travolta Method." If you will recall from those classic films *Saturday Night Fever* and *Urban Cowboy*, John Travolta had boring jobs (as a paint store employee in *Fever* and as an oil refinery worker in *Urban Cowboy*) but made his life meaningful through his dancing. Now I'm not suggesting that disco and

Exhibit **10.03** International differences in job satisfaction

Country	Job Satisfaction Level (1–7 scale)
Denmark	5.69
Cyprus	5.66
Switzerland	5.47
Israel	5.45
Netherlands	5.43
Spain	5.40
U.S.A.	5.34
New Zealand	5.27
Sweden	5.24
Norway	5.22
Italy	5.18
Germany	5.17
Portugal	5.17
Great Britain	5.13
Czech Republic	5.13
France	5.09
Bulgaria	5.05
Slovenia	4.95
Japan	4.87
Russia	4.86
Hungary	4.82

line dancing are the solutions to life's problems. Instead, I am suggesting that an employee's needs can be met in a variety of nonwork activities such as hobbies and volunteer work. A mistake we have made for years has been to assume that a job must satisfy all of a person's needs. Instead, an organization should work toward fulfilling those needs that it can and should help employees find alternative avenues to meet their other needs.

An interesting study by Judge (1993) demonstrates the importance of individual differences. Judge had more than 200 nurses in a medical clinic complete a questionnaire tapping their propensity to gripe about things in everyday life and also asking them to indicate how satisfied they were with their jobs. Judge then compared the nurses' level of job satisfaction with whether or not they quit their jobs with the clinic over the next 10 months. The results of this study indicated that there was no significant relationship between satisfaction and turnover ($r = -.05$) for the people who griped about everything in life. However, for the nurses who were not chronic gripers, satisfaction was significantly correlated with turnover ($r = -.39$). In other words, people who are unhappy in life and unhappy on their jobs will not leave their jobs because they are used to being unhappy. But for people who are normally happy in life, being unhappy at work is seen as a reason to find another job.

To get an idea about your own tendency to be satisfied with work and life, complete Exercise 10–3 at the end of this chapter.

Culture

As shown in Exhibit 10.03, workers in different countries have different levels of job satisfaction. Data from the International Social Survey Program indicates that of 21 countries surveyed, employees in Denmark were the most satisfied and employees in Hungary the least. U.S. employees ranked 7th in the survey, and employees in Great Britain ranked 14th (Sousa-Poza & Sousa-Poza, 2000).

Intelligence

In 1997, a police department in Connecticut created controversy when it announced that applicants who were "too smart" would not be hired. The police chief's reasoning was that really smart people would be bored and have low job satisfaction. Though there has been little research on the topic, a study by Ganzach (1998) suggests that bright people have slightly lower job satisfaction than do less intelligent employees in jobs that are not complex. In complex jobs, the relationship between intelligence and satisfaction is negligible. A meta-analysis of seven studies by Griffeth, Hom, and Gaertner (2000) found that intelligence and turnover were not significantly related.

Are Employees' Job Expectations Being Met?

As was discussed in Chapter 9, employees come to a job with certain needs, values, and expectations. A meta-analysis by Wanous, Poland, Premack, and Davis (1992) concluded that when an employee's expectations are not met lower job satisfaction ($r = -.39$), decreased organizational commitment ($r = -.39$), and an increased intent to leave the organization ($r = .29$) occur. These results support the importance of ensuring that applicants have realistic job expectations. Though the meta-analysis results supported the "met expectations" theory, Irving and Meyer (1994) have criticized the studies that were included in the meta-analysis. In their own study, Irving and Meyer found that an employee's experiences on the job were most related to job satisfaction and that the *difference* between their expectations and experiences was only minimally related to job satisfaction. More studies using methods similar to Irving and Meyer are needed to clarify this issue.

When employees consider how well they "fit" with an organization, they consider three aspects: person–organization fit, needs–supplies fit, and demands–abilities fit (Cable & DeRue, 2002). Person–organization fit is the extent to which an employee's values match those of the organization. Needs–supplies fit is the extent to which the rewards, salary, and benefits received by employees are perceived to be consistent with their efforts and performance. Demands–abilities fit is the extent to which an employee's abilities are consistent with those required by the job. A study by Cable and DeRue (2002) found the following:

- Employees who perceive a good person–organization fit tend to be satisfied with their job, identify with the organization, remain with the organization, and engage in organizational citizenship behaviors.

- Employees who perceive a good needs–supplies fit tend to be satisfied with their jobs and careers and are committed to their occupation.

- There was no relationship between perceived demands–abilities fit and either satisfaction or commitment.

Another factor that has been shown to be related to job satisfaction and commitment is the extent to which employees' desire for a particular work schedule (e.g., shift, number of hours) matches their actual schedule. As one would expect, the better the fit between an employee's desired schedule and his actual schedule, the greater an employee's job satisfaction, organizational commitment, performance, and likelihood to remain with the organization (Holtom, Lee, & Tidd, 2002).

Are the Tasks Enjoyable?

Not surprisingly, research is fairly clear that employees who find their work interesting are more satisfied and motivated than are employees who do not enjoy their jobs (Gately, 1997). Interestingly, though employees rank interesting work as being the most important factor in a job, supervisors rank salary and bonus as being the most important for employees. This discrepancy is why Glanz (1997) advised employers to take innovative steps to make work more interesting.

Do Employees Enjoy Working with Supervisors and Coworkers?

Research indicates that people who enjoy working with their supervisors and coworkers will be more satisfied with their jobs (Newsome & Pillari, 1992; Repetti & Cosmas, 1991). Such findings certainly make sense. We all have had coworkers and supervisors who made our jobs unbearable, and we all have had coworkers and supervisors who made our jobs fun to have. In a study of 500 employees at an apparel manufacturing plant, Bishop and Scott (1997) found that satisfaction with supervisors and coworkers was related to organizational and team commitment, which in turn resulted in higher productivity, lower intent to leave the organization, and a greater willingness to help.

Are Coworkers Outwardly Unhappy?

Social information processing theory, also called **social learning theory**, postulates that employees observe the levels of motivation and satisfaction of other employees and then model those levels (Salancik & Pfeffer, 1977). Thus, if an organization's older employees work hard and talk positively about their jobs and their employer, new employees will model this behavior and be both productive and satisfied. The reverse is also true: If veteran employees work slowly and complain about their jobs, so will new employees.

To test this theory, Weiss and Shaw (1979) had subjects view training videos in which assembly line workers made either positive or negative comments about their jobs. After viewing the videotape, each subject was given an opportunity to perform the job. The study found that those subjects who had seen the positive tape enjoyed the task more than did subjects who viewed the negative tape. In a similar study conducted by Mirolli, Henderson, and Hills (1998), subjects performed a task with two experimenters pretending to be other subjects (these are called confederates). In one condition, the confederates made positive comments about the task (e.g., "Gee, this is fun"), in a second condition they made negative comments about the task (e.g., "This sucks"), and in the control condition

One's coworkers can affect job satisfaction.

they did not make any comments. Consistent with social information processing theory, actual subjects exposed to the confederates' positive comments rated the task as more enjoyable than subjects exposed to negative comments.

In general, the research on social information processing theory supports the idea that the social environment does have an effect on employees' attitudes (Pollock, Whitbred, & Contractor, 2000). As with all of the theories in this chapter, it plays a role in job satisfaction but does not play the only role. One of the appeals of social information processing theory is that it certainly makes intuitive sense. Think of courses you have taken in which one student participated more than anyone else. After a while, the student's level of participation probably decreased to be more in line with the rest of the class. In work as in school, social pressures force individuals to behave in ways that are consistent with the norm, even though the person may privately believe something different (Nail, 1986).

Are Rewards and Resources Given Equitably?

One factor related to both job satisfaction and employee motivation is the extent to which employees perceive that they are being treated fairly. As you hopefully recall from Chapter 9, **equity theory** is based on the premise that our levels of job satisfaction and

motivation are related to how fairly we believe we are treated in comparison with others. If we believe we are treated unfairly, we attempt to change our beliefs or behaviors until the situation appears to be fair.

Research on equity has recently expanded into what researchers call distributive justice, procedural justice, and interactional justice. **Distributive justice** is the perceived fairness of the actual decisions made in an organization, **procedural justice** is the perceived fairness of the methods used to arrive at the decision, and **interactional justice** is the perceived fairness of the interpersonal treatment employees receive. Take, for example, a situation in which three employees are competing for a promotion. The organization has decided that the basis for the promotion decision will be a combination of the employees' performance-appraisal scores (40%), interview with the supervisor (20%), and a score on a managerial assessment center (40%). The extent to which the employees believe that use of the performance appraisal, interview, and assessment center scores is fair would involve their perceptions of procedural justice. Their agreement with who got promoted involves their perceptions of distributive justice.

As shown in Exhibit 10.04, a meta-analysis by Colquitt, Conlon, Wesson, Porter, and Ng (2001) indicates that perceived justice is related to several important factors including job satisfaction, organizational commitment, performance, trust, withdrawal (e.g., turnover, absenteeism), and negative employee

Exhibit 10.04 Organizational justice meta-analysis (Colquitt, Conlon, Wesson, Porter, and Ng, 2001)

Outcome	Correlation with Perceptions of Justice	
	Procedural Justice	Distributive Justice
Job satisfaction	.62	.56
Organizational commitment	.57	.51
Trust	.61	.51
Withdrawal	−.46	−.50
Performance	.36	.15
Negative employee reactions	−.31	−.30

reactions (e.g., theft, sabotage). Because the relationships between perceptions of justice and employee attitudes and behavior are so strong, it is essential that employers be open about how decisions are made, take time to develop fair procedures, and provide feedback to employees who might not be happy with decisions that are made (Jordan, 1997).

One of the greatest problems with the equity and justice theories is that despite their rational sense, they are difficult to implement. That is, based on equity and justice theories, the best way to keep employees satisfied would be to treat them all fairly, which would entail paying the most to those employees who contributed the most. Although few of us would disagree with this approach, it is difficult to implement for several reasons.

The first is *practicality*. An organization certainly can control such variables as salary, hours worked, and benefits, but it cannot easily control other variables such as how far an employee lives from work or the number of friends an employee makes on the job.

The second reason that equity is difficult to achieve is that the employee's *perception* of inputs and outputs determines equity, not *actual* inputs and outputs. For example, two students of equal ability receive the same grade on an exam. One student knows that she studied 10 hours for the exam but never saw the other student in the library. She may feel that the scores are unfair because she studied harder than but received the same grade as the student whom she never saw study. Of course, the other student may have studied 20 hours while at work, but the other student would not know that. In this case, the student's perception of input level may not match reality.

It is important that employees base their judgments on factual information. Of course, this may be easier said than done. Although one way to do this would be by open and public information on salaries, many organizations keep such information confidential and even include statements in their employee manuals that forbid employees from divulging their salaries to one another. Such policies, however, encourage employees to speculate about how much other people make. This speculation usually results in employees thinking the worst and believing others make more than they do. It is probably in the best interests of an organization to make salary and performance information available to all employees, although each employee's permission must be obtained before such information is released.

Even if an organization were able to maintain complete internal equity, employees would then compare their ratios with those of employees from other organizations. The problem with such comparisons is that an organization has little or no control over another's policies. Furthermore, perceptions of wages and benefits at other organizations most likely will be more distorted than internal perceptions. Thus, even if equity theory were completely accurate, maintaining a high level of employee satisfaction would still be difficult.

Is There a Chance for Growth and Challenge?

For many employees, job satisfaction is affected by opportunities for challenge and growth. As discussed in Chapter 9, Maslow thought that the need for growth and challenge, which he labeled *self-actualization*, is only important after low-level needs (e.g., safety, social) have been met. To help satisfy employee self-actualization needs, organizations can do many things. The easiest and most common are job rotation, **job enlargement**, and **job enrichment**. With job rotation and job enlargement, an employee learns how to use several different machines or conduct several different tasks within an organization. With job rotation, the employee is given the same number of tasks to do at one time, but the tasks change from time to time. With job enlargement, an employee is given more tasks to do at one time.

A job can be enlarged in two ways: knowledge used and tasks performed. With knowledge enlargement, employees are allowed to make more complex

Some jobs are not intrinsically interesting.

PhotoDisc, Inc.

decisions. With task enlargement, they are given more tasks of the same difficulty level to perform. As one might imagine, satisfaction increases with knowledge enlargement and decreases with task enlargement (Campion & McClelland, 1993).

Job rotation and job enlargement accomplish two main objectives. First, they challenge employees by requiring them to learn to operate several different machines or perform several different tasks. Thus, once employees have mastered one task or machine, they can work toward mastering another.

Second, job rotation helps to alleviate boredom by allowing an employee to change tasks. Thus, if an employee welds parts one day, assembles bumpers on another, and tightens screws on a third, the boredom caused by performing the same task every day should be reduced.

Perhaps an even better way to satisfy self-actualization needs is through job enrichment. The main difference between job rotation and job enrichment is that with job rotation an employee performs different tasks, and with job enrichment the employee assumes more responsibility over the tasks (Ford, 1973).

In their **job characteristics model**, Hackman and Oldham (1975, 1976) theorized that enriched jobs are the most satisfying. Enriched jobs allow a variety of skills to be used, allow employees to complete an entire task (e.g., process a loan application from start to finish) rather than parts of a task, involve tasks that have meaning or importance, allow employees to make decisions, and provide feedback about performance. Hackman and Oldham developed the **Job Diagnostic Survey (JDS)** to measure the extent to which these characteristics are present in a given job.

If we look again at the job of college professor, job enrichment is clearly an inherent part of the job. That is, the professor decides what she will research and what she will teach in a particular course. This authority to make decisions about her own work leads to higher job satisfaction.

With an assembly line worker, however, responsibility is something that must be added because the employee has minimal control over the way a job is done. After all, bumpers must be assembled in the same way each time and welded to the same place. So what can be done to enrich the typical factory worker's job?

One method is to give workers more responsibility over their jobs. For example, when an employee first begins working for a company, her work is checked by a quality control inspector. After the employee has been with the company long enough for the first four needs levels to be satisfied, the employee is given responsibility for checking her own quality. Likewise, more control can be given to the employee about where and when she will eat lunch, when she will take vacation time, or how fast she will accomplish her work. At one Kaiser Aluminum production plant, for example, time clocks were removed so that the workers could assume more responsibility for their performance by keeping track of their own hours.

It may seem strange to suggest that allowing an employee to make such trivial decisions as lunch times will result in higher job satisfaction. But research has shown that allowing residents in a nursing home to make such decisions resulted in lower death rates, as did allowing them to own pets (Langer & Rodin, 1976; Schulz, 1976). Thus, it is not farfetched to think that allowing control even in limited areas can increase one's level of job satisfaction.

Even when increased decision-making responsibilities are not possible, job enrichment ideas can still be implemented. For example, many organizations have or work with credit unions whose credit committees and boards of directors consist of company employees. These committees and boards provide excellent opportunities to increase employees' decision-making powers even though the decisions are not directly related to their jobs.

Another method to increase the level of job enrichment is by showing employees that their jobs have meaning and that they are meeting some worthwhile goal through their work (Hackman & Oldham, 1975). At some automobile factories, for example, this is accomplished by having employees work in teams to build cars. Instead of an employee performing a single task all day, she does several tasks, as do the other employees in her group. At the end of the day, the employee can see a completed car that she has had a major role in building.

A plant that manufactures transformers provides another example. The training department realized that even though employees spent 8 hours a day manufacturing the product, few understood what it did, who used it, and what would happen if it were not manufactured correctly. To correct this problem, the employees participated in a training session in which they were shown how the transformer was used, who used it, and the consequences that resulted from poor manufacturing.

The final method for increasing employees' self-actualization needs that we will discuss here is the use of **self-directed teams** or **quality circles**. With quality circles, employees meet as a group and make decisions about such quality-enhancing factors as the music played in the work area, the speed of the assembly line, and how to reduce waste. Quality circles are especially effective in increasing employees' job satisfaction when there is little or no chance for advancement. They enable employees to have more control and responsibility.

In an extensive review of the literature, Wagner (1994) concluded that allowing employees to participate in making decisions results in small but significant increases in performance and job satisfaction. Arthur (1994) found lower turnover in steel mills allowing employees to make decisions on their own than in steel mills with a more controlling style. In a more recent study, Rentsch and Steel (1998) found that job enrichment resulted in decreased absenteeism.

Though team approaches are popular, there is considerable debate about their effectiveness. Most quality improvement programs using a team approach fail to provide the desired results (Zemke, 1993).

Integration of Theories

In this chapter, we discussed many theories of job satisfaction. The question you must be asking (other than, When does this chapter end?) is How, then, do we satisfy employees? Unfortunately, the answer to this question is complex and depends on a variety of factors. We can, however, use the theories to design an organizational climate that is more conducive to motivation and satisfaction than the typical climate.

As shown in Exhibit 10.05, individual difference theories say that each of us brings to a job an initial tendency to be satisfied with life and its various aspects such as work. A person with a low tendency toward satisfaction might *start* a job with only 6 hypothetical satisfaction points, a person with a neutral tendency might start with 10 hypothetical points, and a person with a high tendency might bring 14 points.

For example, research indicates that, in addition to genetics, such traits as **internal locus of control** (Stout, Slocum, & Cron, 1987; Surrette & Harlow, 1992), Type A behavior, patience/tolerance (Bluen, Barling, & Burns, 1990), and social trust (Liou, Sylvia, & Brunk, 1990) are related to our tendency to be satisfied with work. Demographically, males and females are equally satisfied with work; whites are more satisfied than African Americans; and older workers are more satisfied than younger workers (Rhodes, 1983).

Surrette and Harlow (1992) found that, people will be most satisfied with a job if they had the *option to choose* that job from other alternatives rather than the job being their only choice. Once people are employed at a job, however, they are most satisfied when they don't have other career alternatives (Pond & Geyer, 1987).

During our years at work, certain events and conditions occur that can add to or decrease our initial level of satisfaction that was due to personal predispositions.

According to discrepancy theories, we will remain satisfied with our job if it meets our various needs, wants, expectations, and values. As discussed previously in the chapter, individuals vary greatly on their needs for such things as achievement, status, safety, and social contact. Thus, not every job can satisfy the needs of every employee during every period of his life. By being aware of employee needs, however, we can select the employees whose needs are consistent with the requirements and characteristics of the job.

According to the intrinsic satisfaction theory and job characteristics theory, we will be more satisfied with our jobs if the tasks themselves are enjoyable to perform. What makes a task enjoyable varies across individuals. For some, working on a computer is fun, whereas for others nothing could be more boring. Many people enjoy making decisions, solving conflicts, and seeing a project through from start to finish, whereas others don't.

Overall satisfaction can be affected by our satisfaction with individual facets of the job. For example, an incompetent boss, terrible coworkers, low pay, or limited opportunities for advancement can lessen overall job satisfaction. Even trivial things can lessen job satisfaction. I once worked at a job where the vending machines never worked and supplies such as paper and pens were often not available. These factors were irritants for most employees—enough to lessen job satisfaction but certainly not enough to make any of us *dissatisfied* with the job. According to social learning theory, we will be more satisfied if our coworkers are satisfied. If everyone else is whining and complaining, it is difficult to be the only person at work who loves his job.

Exhibit 10.05 Satisfaction flowchart

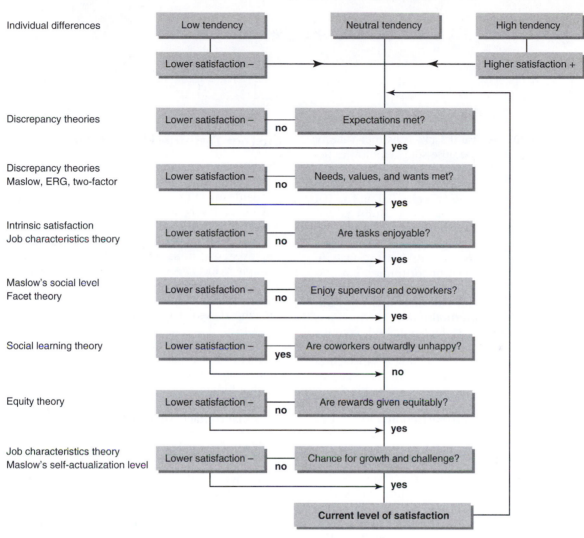

Personal Tendency Toward Satisfaction

No matter how much we intrinsically like our work, equity and justice theories predict we will become dissatisfied if rewards, punishments, and social interactions are not given equitably. If you work harder than a coworker, yet she receives a bigger raise, you are less likely to be satisfied even though money may not be the reason you are working.

On the basis of job characteristics theory and Maslow's level of self-actualization, lack of opportunity for growth, challenge, variety, autonomy, and advancement will decrease satisfaction for many people.

The results of these factors are summed to indicate an employee's current level of satisfaction. As conditions change, so will the level of satisfaction. To apply what you have learned about job satisfaction, complete Exercise 10–4 at the end of this chapter.

Measuring Job Satisfaction

This chapter has discussed several theories that seek to explain job satisfaction. But one important issue that remains is how an employee's level of job satisfaction is determined. Generally, job satisfaction is measured in one of two ways: standard job satisfaction inventories or custom designed satisfaction inventories.

Commonly Used Standard Inventories

One of the first methods for measuring job satisfaction was developed by Kunin (1955) and is called the **Faces Scale** (a simulation is shown in Exhibit 10.06). Although the scale is easy to use, it is no longer commonly

Exhibit 10.06 Simulation of face scale of job satisfaction

Place a check under the face that expresses how you feel about your job in general.

administered partly because it lacks construct validity and sufficient detail, and because some employees believe it is so simple that it is demeaning.

The most commonly used scale today is the **Job Descriptive Index (JDI)** (see Exhibit 10.07). The JDI was developed by Smith, Kendall, and Hulin (1969) and consists of a series of job-related adjectives and statements that are rated by employees. The scales yield scores on five dimensions of job satisfaction: supervision, pay, promotional opportunities, coworkers, and the work itself.

A similar measure of job satisfaction is the **Minnesota Satisfaction Questionnaire (MSQ)**, which was developed by Weiss, Dawis, England, and Lofquist (1967). The MSQ contains 100 items that yield scores on 20 scales. To get experience taking a satisfaction inventory, complete the short form of the MSQ in Exhibit 10.08.

The fact that the JDI has 5 scales and the MSQ 20 underscores the point that job satisfaction is not easy to measure. This is especially true when one considers that employees' responses on the JDI are not highly correlated with their responses on the MSQ (Gillet & Schwab, 1975). Because both the JDI and the MSQ measure specific aspects of job satisfaction, Ironson, Smith, Brannick, Gibson, and Paul (1989) recently developed the **Job in General (JIG) Scale**. The JIG is useful when an organization wants to measure the overall level of job satisfaction rather than specific aspects.

Nagy (1996) criticized many of the standard measures of job satisfaction because these measures ask only if employees are satisfied with a particular aspect of their job but not how important that job aspect is to them. Recall from our previous discussion on discrepancy theories that people differ about what is important to them. With this in mind, imagine that both Sally and Temea think their salaries are lower than they should be. Sally is a real social climber and thinks a person's salary is a measure of one's status in life. Temea, however, has inherited plenty of money and works because she enjoys keeping busy. Although both Sally and Temea think their pay is low, Nagy (1996) argues that only Sally would actually be dissatisfied. To understand these differences, Nagy (1995) created the Nagy Job Satisfaction Inventory, which includes two questions per facet: one asking how important the facet is to the employee, and the other asking how satisfied the employee is with the facet.

Custom-Designed Inventories

Though most research on job satisfaction is conducted using one or more of the previously mentioned standard inventories, most organizations tap their employees' levels of job satisfaction by using custom-designed inventories. The advantage to custom-designed inventories is that an organization can ask employees questions specific to their organization. For example, a local agency recently restructured many of its jobs and wanted to tap how satisfied its employees were with the changes. To do this, they hired a consultant who designed questions that specifically tapped employees' thoughts and feelings about the changes. Using one of the standard inventories would not have provided the needed information. To learn more about custom surveys, read the Employment Profile of Heather King.

Absenteeism

As discussed earlier in this chapter, when employees are dissatisfied or not committed to the organization, they are more likely to miss work and leave their job than are satisfied or committed employees. In the remaining two sections of the chapter, absenteeism and turnover will be discussed and methods to decrease these negative employee behaviors will be presented.

As shown in Exhibit 10.09, depending on which survey data are used, between 1.7% and 2.1% of the U.S. workforce is absent each day, at a cost to employers of $789 per employee each year (Reed, 2003). In 2001, employees in the United States were given an average of 7.6 sick days per year, and on average they took 6.2 of those days (Commerce Clearing House, 2002). Although comparable international data are difficult to come by, a survey by the Confederation of British Industry (CBI) indicates that workers in the United Kingdom miss an average of 7.8 days per year—equivalent to an absenteeism rate of 3.4% (Aldred, 2001). In 2000, the typical worker missed 8 days in Canada (Botchford, 2001), 8.7 days in Ireland (Belfast Telegraph, 2001), and 20 days in the Netherlands (Karaian, 2002). In 2002, the typical employee missed 32 days in Sweden and 20 days in Norway (Karaian, 2002).

Exhibit 10.07 Sample items from the Job Descriptive Index

Think of your present work. What is it like most of the time? In the blank beside each word given below, write

Y for "Yes" if it describes your work
N for "No" if it does NOT describe it
? if you cannot decide

Work on Present Job

_____ Routine
_____ Satisfying
_____ Good
_____ On your feet

Think of the pay you get now. How well does each of the following words describe your present pay? In the blank beside each word, put

Y for "Yes" if it describes your pay
N for "No" if it does NOT describe it
? if you cannot decide

Present Pay

_____ Income adequate for normal expenses
_____ Insecure
_____ Less than I deserve
_____ Highly paid

Think of the opportunities for promotion that you have now. How well does each of the following words describe these? In the blank beside each word put

Y for "Yes" if it describes your opportunities for promotion
N for "No" if it does NOT describe them
? if you cannot decide

Opportunities for Promotion

_____ Promotion on ability
_____ Dead-end job
_____ Unfair promotion policy
_____ Regular promotions

Think of the kind of supervision that you get on your job. How well does each of the following words describe this supervision? In the blank beside each word below, put

Y if it describes the supervision you get on your job
N if it does NOT describe it
? if you cannot decide

Supervision on Present Job

_____ Impolite
_____ Praises good work
_____ Influential
_____ Doesn't supervise enough

Think of the majority of the people that you work with now or the people you meet in connection with your work. How well does each of the following words describe these people? In the blank beside each word below, put

Y if it describes the people you work with
N if it does NOT describe them
? if you cannot decide

People on Your Present Job

_____ Boring
_____ Responsible
_____ Intelligent
_____ Talk too much

Source: *The measurement of satisfaction in work and retirement*, by P. C. Smith, L. M. Kendall, & C. L. Hulin, 1969; Chicago: Rand McNally. The Job Descriptive Index is copyrighted by Bowling Green State University. The complete forms, scoring key, instructions, and norms can be requested from Dr. Patricia C. Smith, Department of Psychology, Bowling Green State University, Bowling Green, Ohio 43403. Used by permission of the authors.

Nutreco, an international supplier of food products, provides an excellent example of international differences in absenteeism. In 2000, the overall absenteeism rate for Nutreco was 4.5%, yet the rate varied tremendously across national borders. Absenteeism was lowest for its plants in Canada (1.6%), Ireland (1.9%), and Poland (2.3%), and highest for its plants in the Netherlands (7.8%), Norway (7.2%), and Belgium (6.3%). The absenteeism rates for Chile (2.7%), the U.K. (3.2%), Spain (3.8%), and France (4.0%) fell in the middle.

Organizations throughout the world are concerned with absenteeism, not only because of the high monetary cost of absenteeism but also because absenteeism is correlated with turnover ($r = .21$) and is thought to be a warning sign of intended turnover (Griffeth et al., 2000).

Exhibit **10.08** Minnesota Satisfaction Questionnaire, short form

*Ask yourself: How **satisfied** am I with this aspect of my job?*

Very Sat. *means I am very satisfied with this aspect of my job.*

Sat. *means I am satisfied with this aspect of my job.*

N *means I can't decide whether I am satisfied or not with this aspect of my job.*

Dissat. *means I am dissatisfied with this aspect of my job.*

Very Dissat. *means I am very dissatisfied with this aspect of my job.*

On my present job, this is how I feel about...	Very Dissat.	Dissat.	N	Sat.	Very Sat.
1. Being able to keep busy all the time	☐	☐	☐	☐	☐
2. The chance to work alone on the job	☐	☐	☐	☐	☐
3. The chance to do different things from time to time	☐	☐	☐	☐	☐
4. The chance to be "somebody" in the community	☐	☐	☐	☐	☐
5. The way my boss handles employees	☐	☐	☐	☐	☐
6. The competence of my supervisor in making decisions	☐	☐	☐	☐	☐
7. Being able to do things that don't go against my conscience	☐	☐	☐	☐	☐
8. The way my job provides for steady employment	☐	☐	☐	☐	☐
9. The chance to do things for other people	☐	☐	☐	☐	☐
10. The chance to tell people what to do	☐	☐	☐	☐	☐
11. The chance to do something that makes use of my abilities	☐	☐	☐	☐	☐
12. The way company policies are put into practice	☐	☐	☐	☐	☐
13. My pay and the amount of work I do	☐	☐	☐	☐	☐
14. The chances for advancement on this job	☐	☐	☐	☐	☐
15. The freedom to use my own judgment	☐	☐	☐	☐	☐
16. The chance to try my own methods of doing the job	☐	☐	☐	☐	☐
17. The working conditions	☐	☐	☐	☐	☐
18. The way my coworkers get along with each other	☐	☐	☐	☐	☐
19. The praise I get for doing a good job	☐	☐	☐	☐	☐
20. The feeling of accomplishment I get from the job	☐	☐	☐	☐	☐
	Very Dissat.	Dissat.	N	Sat.	Very Sat.

Source: *Minnesota Satisfaction Questionnaire* (short form), copyright 1967, Vocational Psychological Research, University of Minnesota. Used with permission.

Because of the high costs of absenteeism and turnover, organizations expend great effort to reduce the number of unscheduled absences. For these efforts to be effective, it is important that we understand why employees miss work. That is, punishment will reduce absenteeism only if employees make conscious decisions about attending. Likewise, wellness programs will increase attendance only if absenteeism is mostly the result of illness. As can be seen in Exhibit 10.10, in the most recent Commerce Clearing House (CCH) survey on unscheduled absenteeism, 67% of absences were due to reasons other than employee illness.

Heather King Foster, M.A.
SE Leader, Organizational & Employee Research
Towers Perrin

Towers Perrin is an international human resources and management consulting firm whose vision is to be the supplier of choice for financial and actuarial services, benefits and retirement services, people strategy and research, communication, change, and total rewards. Our firm has 135 years of experience in several of these service areas, allowing us to bring value-added consulting expertise to our clients. As a firm, our mission is to build relationships with and improve business performance results for our clients.

I am a consultant in our Organizational and Employee Research line of business. In this line of business we conduct research through surveys, focus groups, and interviews. These data are used in a variety of ways to solicit input, understand perceptions, improve performance, and gain buy-in. Our research is generally used to help organizations align their spending on employee programs with what employees value, decrease turnover, increase employee engagement or satisfaction, and improve communication or productivity.

Although we can conduct a variety of research on any given project, we work with our clients to determine which method, or combination of methods, would best meet their budget, timing, and overall project needs. On some projects we suggest that the client simply conduct an employee survey or focus groups. With others, we recommend they also interview key executives and possibly use ongoing feedback to collect data periodically as changes are implemented.

An organization that decides to undergo the full range of employee research may decide to develop an integrated plan for involving key stakeholders over a period of time. This integrated approach typically starts by engaging the top executives through an interview process. Our research team will partner with the client team and our own colleagues in other lines of business,

such as change, communication, benefits, and compensation, to develop a guide to be used during the interviews. The questions in this guide explore executives'

- perceptions of the business and the role employees play in business success.

- philosophy of the rewards programs—what they should be designed to do or not do; for example, should rewards programs be a factor in an employee's decision to join the organization? Stay with an organization? Become fully engaged in his or her work?

- assessment of the impact major changes have had on the organization and its employees.

- views of where the organization's programs should rank against other organizations.

- guidance for the current project team and measures of success.

The data gathered from executives are typically used to set the direction for the project, and input gathered from other groups along the way is compared to these data.

Another core group often targeted for research efforts is line managers. These leaders are typically closest to employees and have the greatest influence on the communication employees receive. By involving managers early in the process, typically through focus groups, we gain an understanding of their needs and challenges as managers; the role that rewards programs play in their ability to attract, retain, and engage employees; and how their views align with those of executives.

Employees often participate in a major change effort through a survey. Input from the executive interviews and manager focus groups are combined with data gathered through employee focus groups to develop the survey. The survey is then administered either to the entire employee population or to a sample of employees. The more

sensitive and pervasive the change effort, the more likely the client will want to provide every employee with a chance to participate. We conduct surveys using a variety of methods: Web, paper, email, and telephone. Once the survey is administered and data are received, we conduct a number of statistical analyses to understand the data. We look at differences across demographic groups, create indices of items to understand "drivers" of employee perceptions, and look for general trends in the data. Our analyses are then used to write a detailed report of the results, where we pull together all the data that has been gathered thus far on the project. We explain the point of view from executives, to managers, to employees, and we compare and contrast their perceptions on various issues.

Often we follow an employee survey with focus groups. These focus groups are used to further explore issues identified in the survey and can be used to test ideas for change or communication with employees. Another form of gathering additional data from employees is through pulse surveys. These surveys are often administered online to just a sample of employees and are brief in nature. Pulse surveys allow the client to gather quick, "real time" data to gauge employees' perceptions and understanding of changes and communication messages that have been introduced. These results are tracked over time to monitor progress that has been made within the organization as a result of a major change.

The most critical component of any form of research is the client's willingness to use the data. Organizations that are the best examples for using employee research ask their employees for feedback on a regular basis, have a good track record for using the data, and constantly keep employees informed of its use.

	1994	1995	1996	1997	1998	1999	2000	2001	2002
Absenteeism rate									
CCH survey data	2.69	2.80	2.80	2.85	3.25	2.70	2.10	2.20	2.10
BNA data			1.60	1.50	1.60	1.70	1.70	1.70	
Annual cost per employee	$593	$662	$603	$572	$757	$602	$610	$755	$789
Reason for missing work (%)									
Employee illness		45	28	26	20	21	40	32	33
Employee stress		6	11	12	16	19	5	19	12
Personal needs		13	20	22	24	20	20	11	21
Family issues		27	26	26	21	21	21	21	24
Sense of entitlement		9	15	14	19	19	14	9	10
Other (e.g., bad weather, transportation)								8	

Source: CCH Annual Unscheduled Absence Survey

Linking Attendance to Consequences

The basis behind rewarding attendance and punishing absenteeism is that employees make a decision each day as to whether they will or will not attend work. Although the decision-making process is not clearly understood, it probably includes weighing the consequences of going to work (or to class) against the consequences of not going. For example, imagine that you have an 8:00 a.m. class and are deciding whether you will attend this morning. By missing class, you can sleep a few hours longer, watch the *Today Show*, and stay out of the rain. By attending class, you will get the notes that you know will be on the test but aren't in the book, get to listen to the instructor's terrific sense of humor, and get to sit next to the great-looking student you think is interested in you. If a good test grade and a chance at a date are most important, you will attend class. If sleep is most important, you will miss class.

If in fact employees make conscious decisions about attending work, attendance can be increased in several ways: rewarding attendance, disciplining absenteeism, and keeping accurate attendance records.

Rewards for Attending

Attendance can be increased through the use of financial incentives, time off, and recognition programs.

Financial Incentives. Financial incentive programs use money to reward employees for achieving certain levels of attendance. One of these programs, **well pay**, involves paying employees for their unused sick leave. For example, Starmark International in Fort Lauderdale, FL, pays employees $100 for each unused absence. Mercy Medical Center in Baltimore, MD, gives employees a $100 bonus for 6 months of perfect attendance and enters them into a drawing for $3,000 after 1 year of perfect attendance. (Armour, 2003). Some reward the employee by paying the equivalent of her daily salary, whereas others might split the savings by paying the employee an amount equal to half her daily salary for each unused sick day. As shown in Exhibit 10.10, a meta-analysis by Johnson (1990) found that well pay programs were the top method for reducing absenteeism.

A second method provides a **financial bonus** to employees who attain a certain level of attendance. With this method, an employee with perfect attendance over a year might receive a $1,000 bonus, and an employee who misses 10 days might receive nothing.

A third financial incentive method is to use **games** to reward employees who attend work. There are many examples. One company used poker as its game, giving a playing card each day to employees who attended. At the end of the week, employees with five cards compared the value of their hands, and the winning employee would be given a prize such as dinner for two at the best restaurant in town or a gas barbecue grill. Although some studies have reported success in using such games, the meta-analysis by Johnson (1990) found that the mean effect size for games was close to zero.

Time Off. Another approach is the **paid time off program (PTO)** or paid leave bank (PLB). With this style of program, vacation, personal, holiday, and sick days are combined into one category—paid time off. For example, in a traditional system, an employee might be given 10 vacation days, 3 personal days, 5 holidays, and 10 sick days, for a total of 28 days. With a PTO program, the employee might be given 28 days in total for the year. An employee who is seldom sick has more days to use for vacation and is protected in case of a long-term illness, and the organization saves money by reducing

Exhibit 10.10 Reducing absenteeism: Effect sizes of various methods

Method	Number of Studies	Effect Size
Well pay	4	.86
Flextime	10	.59
Compressed work schedules	5	.44
Discipline	12	.36
Recognition	6	.30
Wellness programs	6	.18
Financial incentives	7	.17
Games	6	.08

Source: Adapted from Johnson (1990) with permission.

the total number of unscheduled absences (Markowich, 1994). As shown in Exhibit 10.11, HR directors rate PTO programs as the most effective absence control method.

In 51% of PTO programs, an employee can "bank" time off to use at a later date, and 17% of organizations with a PTO program allow employees to donate unused leave to a leave bank for employees who are stricken by a catastrophic illness such as cancer (CCH, 2001). My neighbor provides an excellent example of a PTO in which employees can bank their time off. She works for a hospital and has not missed a day of work in 5 years. As a consequence, she now has 3 months' extra vacation time, which she plans to spend with her newborn son.

Recognition Programs. One other way that we can make work attendance more rewarding is through recognition and praise. Formal recognition programs provide employees with perfect attendance certificates, coffee mugs, plaques, lapel pins, watches, and so forth. In an award-winning study, Scott, Markham, and Robers (1985) directly compared recognition with other techniques such as incentives and discipline. The results of their investigation supported the effectiveness of recognition, as did Johnson's meta-analysis. However, as shown in Exhibit 10.11, HR directors do not perceive these programs to be as effective as many other programs. Though incentive programs can be an effective means of increasing attendance, many organizations are eliminating perfect attendance incentives out of a concern that such programs might violate the Family Medical Leave Act (Tyler, 2001a).

Discipline for Not Attending

Absenteeism can be reduced by punishing or disciplining employees who miss work. Discipline can range from giving a warning or a less popular work assignment to firing an employee. As shown in Exhibits 10.10 and 10.11, discipline works fairly well, especially when combined with some positive reinforcement for attending.

Unclear Policy and Poor Record Keeping

Another way to increase the negative consequences of missing work is through policy and record keeping. Most organizations measure absenteeism by counting the number of days missed, or *frequency*. Perhaps a better method would be to record the number of *instances* of absenteeism rather than the number of days. For example, instead of giving employees 12 days of sick leave, they are given three or four instances of absenteeism. Missing 1 day or 3 consecutive days each counts as one instance of absenteeism.

As shown in Exhibit 10.12, the number of days missed and the instances of absenteeism often yield different results. By decreasing the number of times that a person can miss, the odds increase that the employee will use sick leave only for actual illness. These odds can further be increased by requiring a doctor's excuse for missing a certain number of consecutive days.

Absenteeism can be decreased by setting attendance goals and by providing feedback on how well the employees are reaching those goals. An interesting study by Harrison and Shaffer (1994) found that almost 90% of employees think their attendance is above average and estimate the typical absenteeism of their coworkers at a level two times higher than the actual figures. Similar results were found by Johns (1994). Thus, one reason employees miss work is that they incorrectly believe their attendance is at a higher level than their coworkers'. Providing feedback to employees about their absenteeism levels may be one way to reduce absenteeism.

Increasing Attendance by Reducing Employee Stress

Absenteeism can be reduced by removing the negative factors employees associate with going to work. One of the most important of these factors is *stress*. The greater the job stress, the greater the probability that most people will want to skip work. As will be discussed in great

Exhibit 10.11 CCH Survey of absenteeism control policies

Absence Control Policy	Percent Using Method					Effectiveness Rating			
	1998	1999	2000	2001	2002	1999	2000	2001	2002
Disciplinary action		77	88	93	93	3.5	3.5	3.4	3.4
Performance appraisal			58	81	81		3.2	3.0	3.0
Paid leave bank	25	27	21	58	59	3.9	3.9	3.6	3.6
Personal recognition			33	62	59		3.1	2.5	2.7
No-fault systems	29	50	31	58	57		3.7	2.9	3.0
Bonus programs			21	56	54		3.1	3.3	3.0
Buy-back programs	23	29	17	17	50	3.6	3.4	3.4	3.4

detail in Chapter 15, there are many sources of stress at work including physical danger, boredom, overload, conflict, and bad management practices.

To increase attendance, then, negative factors must be eliminated. The first step in this elimination, of course, is to become aware of the negative factors that bother employees. These can be determined by asking supervisors or by distributing employee questionnaires. Once the problems are known, it is important that management diligently work to eliminate the identified problems from the workplace. As will also be discussed in Chapter 15, employers engage in a variety of programs designed to reduce job-related stress as well as stress from family and personal issues.

To help employees cope with stress and personal problems, 68% of employers offer some form of Employee Assistance Program (EAP; SHRM, 2002). EAPs use professional counselors to deal with employee problems. An employee with a problem can either choose to see a counselor on her own or be recommended by her supervisor. Some large organizations have their own EAP counselors, but most use private agencies, which are often run through local hospitals.

The motivation for EAPs may be good, but little if any empirical evidence supports their effectiveness. Still, many organizations have used EAPs and have been quite pleased with them. Independently operated EAPs typically claim a 3-to-1 return on the dollars invested through increased productivity and reduced absenteeism and turnover.

Increasing Attendance by Reducing Illness

As shown in Exhibit 10.09, about 33% of absenteeism is due to employee illness—a percentage that mirrors that of college students missing class. Kovach, Surrette, and Whitcomb (1988) asked more than 500 general psychology students to anonymously provide the reason for each day of class they missed. Less than 30% of the missed days were the result of illness!

To reduce absenteeism related to illness, organizations are implementing a variety of wellness programs. According to the 2002 SHRM Benefit Survey,

- 61% provide on-site vaccinations.
- 58% have some form of wellness program.
- 42% have on-site health screening (e.g., blood pressure, cholesterol).
- 29% have a smoking cessation program.
- 28% subsidize the cost of off-site fitness center dues.
- 26% have on-site fitness centers.
- 22% offer a weight-loss program.
- 21% offer stress reduction programs.
- 14% offer on-site medical care.

Two meta-analyses suggest that worksite fitness programs have a small, but significant effect in reducing absenteeism. The meta-analysis of 16 studies by Berry and Lagerstedt (2001) found an effect size of −.25, and the meta-analysis by Bonner (1990) found an effect size of −.18. Results found by Erfurt, Foote, and Heirich (1992) did not support the effectiveness of wellness programs in reducing health problems.

Reducing Absenteeism by Not Hiring "Absence Prone" Employees

One interesting theory of absenteeism postulates that one reason people miss work is the result of a particular set of personality traits they possess. That is, certain types of people are more likely to miss work than are other types. In fact, in one study, only 25% of the employees were responsible for all of the unavoidable absenteeism (Dalton & Mesch, 1991).

Although little research has tested this theory, Kovach, Surrette, and Whitcomb (1988) did find that the best predictor of student attendance in general psychology courses was a compulsive, rule-oriented

Exhibit **10.12** Frequency and instance methods of measuring absenteeism

Frequency Method
Patricia Austin
Days missed:

March	4		
April	9		
May	2		
May	30	Days Missed	= 8
June	7	Instances	= 8
July	2		
Sept	3		
Nov	24		

Instance Method
Christine Evert
Days missed:

April	3		
April	4		
April	5		
July	15	Days Missed	= 8
July	16	Instances	= 3
Dec	2		
Dec	3		
Dec	4		

personality. Research by Judge, Martocchio, and Thoresen (1997) supports these findings. Judge and his colleagues found that individuals high in the personality trait of conscientiousness and low in extraversion were least likely to miss work. If more research supports this theory, then a new strategy for increasing employee attendance might be to screen out "absence prone people" during the selection stage.

Uncontrollable Absenteeism Caused by Unique Events

Many times an individual will miss work because of events or conditions that are beyond management's control. One study estimated that 40% of absenteeism is unavoidable (Dalton & Mesch, 1991). For example, bad weather is one reason absenteeism is higher in the Northeast than in the South. Although an organization can do little to control weather, the accessibility of the plant or office can be considered in the decision of where to locate. In fact, this is one reason many organizations have started in or moved to the so-called Sunbelt in the last two decades. Organizations may also want to offer some type of shuttle service for their employees to avoid not only weather problems but also any resulting mechanical failures of employees' automobiles.

Bad weather can certainly be a legitimate reason for an employee to miss work, but one study found that job satisfaction best predicted attendance on days with poor weather. That is, in good weather, most employees attended, but in inclement weather, only those employees with high job satisfaction attended. Thus, even in bad weather, the degree to which an employee likes her job will help to determine her attendance. As the late industrial psychologist Dan Johnson has asked: "How come we hear about employees not being able to get to work and students not being able to attend class because of bad weather, yet we don't ever hear about an employee or a student who can't get home because of bad weather?" It certainly makes one think!

The Absenteeism Exercise on your CD-ROM gives you the opportunity to apply theories of absenteeism.

Turnover

Cost of Turnover

As mentioned previously in this chapter, employees with low job satisfaction are more likely to quit their jobs (Griffeth et al., 2000; Tett & Meyer, 1993) and change careers (Lee, Carswell, & Allen, 2000) than are employees with high job satisfaction. Though turnover rates fluctuate from year to year, about 1.4% of an organization's employees leave each month (16.8% per year). Turnover is a problem because the cost of losing an employee is estimated at 1.5 times the employee's salary (Bliss, 2001). Thus, if an employee's annual salary is $40,000, the cost to replace the employee will be $60,000. Both visible and hidden costs determine this estimate.

Visible costs of turnover include advertising charges, employment agency fees, referral bonuses, recruitment travel costs, salaries and benefits associated with the employee time spent processing applications and interviewing candidates, and relocation expenses for the new employee. Hidden costs include the loss of productivity associated with the employee leaving, other employees trying to do extra work, no productivity occurring from the vacant position, and the lower productivity associated with a new employee being trained. Additional hidden costs include overtime of employees covering the duties of the vacant position and training costs once the replacement is hired.

The actual cost of turnover for any given position can be more accurately estimated using a formula such as those found on the Internet at www.advantagehiring.com/calculators/calc_turnover.shtml or www.uwex.edu/ces/cced/publicat/turn.html.

Reducing Turnover

Because of the high cost of turnover, organizations make tremendous efforts to reduce the number of quality employees that quit their jobs. An organization reducing the number of employees leaving by one per month will save $360,000 a year for a $20,000 job and $720,000 a year for jobs with a $40,000 annual salary.

The first step in reducing turnover is to find out why your employees are leaving. This is usually done by administering attitude surveys to current employees and conducting exit interviews with employees who are leaving. Salary surveys can also be useful because they allow you to compare your organization's pay and benefit practices to those of other organizations.

Employees typically leave their jobs for one of five reasons: unavoidable reasons, advancement, unmet needs, escape, and unmet expectations.

Unavoidable Reasons

Unavoidable turnover includes such reasons as school starting (e.g., quitting a summer job) or ending (e.g., a student quits her job as a part-time receptionist because she has graduated and will be moving), the job transfer of a spouse, employee illness or death, or family issues (e.g., employees staying home to raise their children or take care of their parents). Though employers are taking steps to reduce turnover due to family issues, there is little an organization can do to prevent turnover due to these other reasons.

Advancement

Employees often leave organizations to pursue promotions or better pay. When an organization has few promotion opportunities, there is little it can do to reduce turnover for those employees seeking advancement. A solution used by an increasing number of police departments who have limited promotion opportunities is to allow officers with extensive experience and skills to advance to positions called something such as Master Officer or Senior Officer. Such positions have no supervisory responsibility but do bring an increase in pay and status.

At times, employers can reduce turnover by offering more pay; however, this will only work if a low compensation or an inadequate benefits package is the prime reason for employees leaving the organization. Furthermore, any increase in pay must be a meaningful amount. That is, if an organization increases pay by $3,000, yet other organizations are paying $6,000 more, the increase in pay most probably will not decrease turnover.

Unmet Needs

Employees whose needs are unmet will become dissatisfied and perhaps leave the organization. For example, if an employee has high social needs and the job involves little contact with people, or if an employee has a need for appreciation and recognition that is not being met by the organization, the employee might leave to find a job in which her social needs can be met. To reduce turnover caused by unmet needs, it is important that an organization consider the **person–organization fit** when selecting employees. That is, if an applicant has a need for structure and close supervision, but the culture of the organization is one of independence full of "free spirits," the applicant should not be hired because there would be a poor fit between the employee's need and the organization.

Escape

A common reason employees leave an organization is to escape from people, working conditions, and stress. When conflict between an employee and her supervisor, a coworker, or customers becomes unbearable, the employee may see no option other than to leave the organization. Therefore, it is important to effectively deal with conflict when it occurs (this is covered in detail in Chapter 13). Likewise, if working conditions are unsafe, dirty, boring, too strenuous, or too stressful, there is an increased likelihood that the employee will seek employment in an organization with better working conditions.

Unmet Expectations

Employees come to an organization with certain expectations about a variety of issues such as pay, working conditions, opportunity for advancement, and organizational culture. When reality does not match these expectations, employees become less satisfied, and, as a result, are more likely to leave the organization (Griffeth et al., 2000). As discussed in Chapter 5, turnover due to unmet expectations can be reduced by providing applicants with realistic job previews.

To summarize, organizations can reduce turnover in these ways:

- Conduct realistic job previews during the recruitment stage.
- Look for a good person–organization fit during the selection interview.
- Meet employee needs (e.g., safety, social, growth).
- Mediate conflicts between employees and their peers, supervisors, and customers.

- Provide a good work environment.
- Provide a competitive pay and benefits package.
- Provide opportunities to advance and grow.

Chapter Summary

In this chapter you learned:

- Satisfaction is moderately related to turnover and absenteeism, slightly related to performance, and very much related to organizational commitment.
- Certain types of people have a predisposition to being satisfied or dissatisfied with work and life.
- Job satisfaction can be maximized by meeting employee needs, values, and expectations and ensuring that employees are treated equitably.
- Job satisfaction is typically measured by such attitude surveys as the Faces Scale, the Job Descriptive Index (JDI), the Minnesota Satisfaction Questionnaire (MSQ), the Job in General (JIG) Scale, and the Nagy Satisfaction Inventory (NSI).
- Absenteeism is the result of such factors as a conscious decision not to attend, adjustment to stress, illness and personal problems, individual differences, and unique events.

Critical Thinking Questions

1. Are some employees "destined" to always be dissatisfied with their job?
2. What do most employees value and need in a job?
3. Is it possible to treat all employees equitably?
4. What is the best way to improve employee attendance?
5. Which measure of job satisfaction is best?

To learn more about the issues discussed in this chapter, point your browser to

http://www.infotrac-college.com/wadsworth

and enter one of these search terms:

job satisfaction

employee attitudes

hierarchy of needs

self-actualization needs

social information processing

job turnover

worker absenteeism

paid time off

Exercise 10–1
Stability of Job Satisfaction

In the space below, write down all of the jobs you have had. Then rate the extent to which you were satisfied with each of those jobs. Are your ratings consistent? Do your ratings support the idea that job satisfaction is consistent across jobs?

VD = very dissatisfied   D = dissatisfied   N = neutral   S = satisfied   VS = very satisfied

Job		Level of Job Satisfaction				
_____		VD	D	N	S	VS
_____		VD	D	N	S	VS
_____		VD	D	N	S	VS
_____		VD	D	N	S	VS
_____		VD	D	N	S	VS
_____		VD	D	N	S	VS

Exercise 10–2
Core Self-Evaluation

Circle the number corresponding to the extent to which you agree with each of the following statements.

sd = strongly disagree
d = disagree
n = neutral
a = agree
sa = strongly agree

		sd	d	n	a	sa
1.	Difficult situations usually don't bother me	1	2	3	4	5
2.	I don't like a lot of things about me	5	4	3	2	1
3.	I have good ideas	1	2	3	4	5
4.	I worry a lot	5	4	3	2	1
5.	I have a low opinion of myself	5	4	3	2	1
6.	I like trying new things	1	2	3	4	5
7.	Life is fun	1	2	3	4	5
8.	If I work hard, I will be successful	1	2	3	4	5
9.	I don't seem to be able to control my life	5	4	3	2	1
10.	I am a confident person	1	2	3	4	5
11.	It seems as if my life is controlled by everyone but me	5	4	3	2	1
12.	I am not afraid to take risks	1	2	3	4	5
13.	I do most things well	1	2	3	4	5
14.	People would describe me as being anxious	5	4	3	2	1
15.	I am happy with who I am	1	2	3	4	5
16.	I handle pressure well	1	2	3	4	5
17.	I am successful at most things I try	1	2	3	4	5
18.	I am usually in a good mood	1	2	3	4	5
19.	I am a good person	1	2	3	4	5
20.	I have a lot of respect for myself	1	2	3	4	5
21.	I am as good a person as anybody	1	2	3	4	5
22.	I can overcome any obstacles in my life	1	2	3	4	5
23.	There is not much I worry about	1	2	3	4	5
24.	I am comfortable with who I am	1	2	3	4	5
25.	People who work hard will succeed	1	2	3	4	5
26.	I am responsible for my success and failure	1	2	3	4	5
27.	I get depressed a lot	5	4	3	2	1
28.	I am often nervous	5	4	3	2	1
29.	I control my own destiny	1	2	3	4	5
30.	I am a talented person	1	2	3	4	5
31.	I am a likeable person	1	2	3	4	5
32.	Others would describe me as being enthusiastic	1	2	3	4	5
33.	There are so many people I would rather be than me	5	4	3	2	1
34.	There is little I cannot accomplish if I set my mind to it	1	2	3	4	5
35.	Most of what happens in life is uncontrollable	5	4	3	2	1
36.	There is not much about my personality that I would change	1	2	3	4	5

Scoring and Interpreting the Core Evaluation Inventory

Add the numbers associated with the answers you circled for each question.

Your total score is _____. The higher your score, the greater your predisposition to be satisfied at work and in life. The chart below will help you compare your score to those of other college students.

If your score was	Your core evaluation is higher than _____ of other college students
159–180	95%
152–158	90%
145–151	80%
142–144	70%
137–141	60%
132–136	50%
129–131	40%
126–128	30%
123–125	20%
117–122	10%
36–116	5%

Exercise 10–3
Your Level of Life Satisfaction

Circle the number next to each question that best indicates how you currently feel.

		Not at all like me				Very much like me
1.	My life situation is better than most people's.	1	2	3	4	5
2.	Most days I am very happy.	1	2	3	4	5
3.	I seldom get depressed these days.	1	2	3	4	5
4.	There is not much about my life that I want to change.	1	2	3	4	5
5.	The world is treating me pretty well.	1	2	3	4	5
6.	Things seem to be going my way.	1	2	3	4	5
7.	At my current age, I am about where I want to be in life.	1	2	3	4	5
8.	If I could relive the last few months, there is very little that I would change.	1	2	3	4	5
9.	My thoughts are usually very positive.	1	2	3	4	5
10.	I don't see how my life could get much better.	1	2	3	4	5

Scoring the Life Satisfaction Inventory

Add the numbers that you circled for each question and write that number here _____.

For example, if you had circled the bold-faced numbers in the three questions below, your total would be 7 (2 + 3 + 2).

2.	Most days I am very happy.	1	**2**	3	4	5
3.	I seldom get depressed these days.	1	2	**3**	4	5
4.	There is not much about my life that I want to change.	1	**2**	3	4	5

Interpreting the Life Satisfaction Inventory

If your score was	Your core evaluation is higher than _____ of other college students
48–50	95%
44–47	90%
42–43	80%
40–41	70%
38–39	60%
35–37	50%
33–34	40%
31–32	30%
27–30	20%
21–26	10%
10–20	5%

Exercise 10–4
Case Study

Juan Estoban was eating lunch at Anderson's Restaurant one Thursday when he noticed a help-wanted ad for the restaurant on his placemat. The ad indicated that most servers made over $10 an hour and that the restaurant atmosphere was fun, exciting, and a place to meet new friends. As a college student, Juan thought the job opportunity was perfect: The money was good, and because most of his friends were back in Arizona, the chance to have a good time and make new friends was highly appealing.

During his job interview, the restaurant manager promised Juan that he wouldn't have to work more than 20 hours a week and that he could always have one Friday or Saturday off each week. Juan accepted the job offer and began work on the following Monday.

The first week at work was spent learning the menu, restaurant rules, and serving techniques. Juan was one of five new servers, but was the only one who was also attending college. As one would expect, the second week was a bit stressful as the new servers began waiting tables. The first day was filled with mistakes, but by the end of the week the five new servers were performing like experts.

As the weeks passed, Juan began to feel stressed as he tried to balance his 15-hour courseload with the demands of his new job. Most weeks he worked 30 hours, and he had not had a Friday or Saturday night off in the past 2 months. During the next month, Juan called in sick one Friday and then again a week later on a Saturday. Juan was also feeling a financial pinch. Even though he was working more hours than he expected, his base pay and tips averaged only around $7.00 an hour. Though he liked his coworkers, Juan always seemed to be arguing with his supervisor, who Juan thought was giving the best hours to employees with less seniority than he had. Even worse, the restaurant was constantly busy, and there was never any time to joke around or have fun. Juan's grades began to drop, and after failing a test in his 8:00 a.m. history class, Juan finally quit his job.

On the basis of the theories discussed in the text, what caused Juan to become so dissatisfied and quit?

_____

_____

_____

_____

_____

_____

_____

_____

11 Organizational Communication

Picture the following situations:

- A male employee cannot understand why he was reprimanded for referring to female employees as the "girls in the office."
- A supervisor has tried everything to communicate with her employees, but they still seem lost.
- Customers don't like Sheila because she appears cold and aloof, though she is actually a very caring person.
- A supervisor is frustrated because her employees never read the notices posted on the bulletin board in the break room.

All four situations represent common communication problems. This chapter looks at the ways employees communicate within an organization, problems in the communication process, and ways communication can be improved. By the end of this chapter, you will

- know the types of organizational communication.
- understand why interpersonal communication often is not effective.
- learn how to increase your listening effectiveness.
- learn ways to improve your communication skills.

To get you thinking about communication, complete the Free Write Exercise on your CD-ROM.

Types of Organizational Communication

To be an effective employee, manager, client, or consultant, it is essential to be able to communicate effectively with others. Having ideas, knowledge, or opinions is useless unless you can communicate those concepts to others. Most communication in organizations can

be classified into four types: upward communication, downward communication, business communication, and informal communication.

Upward Communication

Upward communication is communication of subordinates to superiors or of employees to managers. Of course, in ideal upward communication, employees speak directly to management in an "open door" policy environment. In fact, the quality of upward communication is a significant factor in employee job satisfaction (Miles, Patrick, & King, 1996). Such a policy, however, is often not practical for several reasons. Perhaps the most important reason involves the potential volume of communication if every employee communicated with a specific manager. Direct upward communication also may not be workable because employees often feel threatened by managers and may not be willing to openly communicate bad news or complaints (Ettorre, 1997).

To minimize the number of different people communicating with the top executive, many organizations use **serial communication**. With serial communication, the message is relayed from an employee to her supervisor, who relays it to her supervisor, who relays it to her supervisor, and so on until the message reaches the top. Although this type of upward communication relieves the top executive of excessive demands, it suffers several serious drawbacks.

The first is that the message's content and tone change as it moves from person to person. As will be discussed later in the chapter, messages are seldom received the way they were sent—especially if the message is being passed verbally from person to person.

The second drawback to serial communication is that bad news and complaints are seldom relayed, in part due to the stress associated with delivering bad news (McKee & Ptacek, 2001). Rosen and Tesser (1970) have labeled this reluctance to relay bad news the **MUM (minimize unpleasant messages) effect**. The MUM

348

effect negatively affects the organization by keeping important information from reaching the upper levels. But for an employee, the MUM effect is an excellent survival strategy—no one wants to be the bearer of bad news. When bad news is passed on to supervisors, employees tend to use politeness to soften the news (Lee, 1993). Interestingly, people have no problem passing on bad news to peers, especially when the organizational climate is generally negative (Heath, 1996).

Serial communication's third drawback, especially with informal **communication channels**, is that it is less effective the farther away two people are from one another. That is, a supervisor is more likely to pass along a message to another supervisor if the two are in close physical **proximity**. It is unlikely, therefore, that an informal message originating with an employee at a plant in Atlanta will reach another employee at the corporate office in Phoenix. The importance of physical proximity cannot be overstated. In fact, a major source of power often comes from being physically near an executive. Seasoned executives have been known to place rising executives in distant offices to reduce their potential power. And going to lunch "with the guys" has long been recognized as a means of obtaining new information and increased power.

As one would imagine, proximity does not play a role when messages are communicated electronically using email (Valacich, Parantia, George, & Nunamaker, 1993). Thus, email may reduce the power of proximity when communication is formal.

Because of these problems with serial communication, organizations use several other methods to facilitate upward communication: attitude surveys, focus groups, suggestion boxes, and third parties.

Attitude Surveys

Attitude surveys are usually conducted annually by an outside consultant who administers a questionnaire asking employees to rate their opinions on such factors as satisfaction with pay, working conditions, and supervisors. Employees are also given the opportunity to list complaints or suggestions that they want management to read. The consultant then tabulates the responses and reports the findings to management.

Although attitude surveys are commonly used, they are useful only if an organization takes the results seriously. If an organization finds that its employees are unhappy and does nothing to address the problem areas, the survey results will not be beneficial. Furthermore, to increase trust, an organization should share survey results with employees (Sahl, 1996).

If survey results are to be shared, then management must share *all* of them. While proposing a project to a local police department, I encountered a great deal of hostility from many of the senior officers. After a little probing, the officers revealed that several years earlier they had completed an attitude survey for the city. A few months later, the results were made public. The city cited five main complaints by the officers and promised that action would be taken to solve these problems. The officers were happy until they realized

that none of their complaints about pay and working conditions were included in the report—the city was ignoring them. The officers became so resentful and mistrustful of consultants and management that they vowed never again to participate in a project.

Focus Groups and Exit Interviews

A second method of upward communication is to hold focus groups in which an outside consultant meets with groups of current employees to get their opinions and suggestions. This information is then passed on to management. To spur candid responses, the consultant is not told the names of the employees in the focus group, and no direct quotes that could potentially identify a particular employee are passed on (Ettorre, 1997). Exit interviews with employees voluntarily leaving an organization also provide an excellent source of information.

Suggestion Boxes

A third method for facilitating upward communication is the **suggestion box** or a **complaint box**. Theoretically, these two boxes should be the same, but a box asking for suggestions is not as likely to get complaints as a box specifically labeled *complaints* and vice versa. The biggest advantage of these boxes is that they allow employees to immediately communicate their feelings in an anonymous fashion. Suggestion boxes provide a voice for subordinates and customers and essential feedback to the organization as well (Opt, 1998).

For these boxes to be beneficial, management must respond to the suggestions and complaints in a timely manner (DuPont, 1999). Management can respond to every suggestion or complaint by placing it on a bulletin board or the organization's intranet along with management's response. In this way, employees receive feedback about their ideas, which further encourages other employees to use the boxes to communicate.

Some organizations take employee suggestions quite seriously and reward employees who provide useful ideas. Hercules, Inc., for example, provides cash awards up to $10,000 for employees who suggest money-saving ideas, Texas Industries in Dallas provides bonuses that can reach 20% of an employee's salary, and Ingersoll-Rand gives plaques to employees who submit cost-saving ideas that are ultimately adopted by the company.

Third Party Facilitators

The use of a third party such as a **liaison** or an **ombudsperson** is another method that can increase upward communication. Both are responsible for taking employee complaints and suggestions and personally working with management to find solutions. The advantage of this system is that the ombudsperson is neutral and works for a solution that is acceptable to both employees and management (Hirschman, 2003). Furthermore, the ombudsperson is typically supervised at the vice presidential level, so she is not concerned about being fired if she steps on a few toes while looking for a solution.

I am the owner and president of Square Peg Consulting, Inc., an organization and training development consulting company. After earning my master's degree in I/O psychology, I spent 7 years working in the pharmaceutical industry as both a training and development specialist and an organization development consultant. At Glaxo, I designed and delivered management development training programs as well as provided organization development consultation to senior management teams. I also helped launch Glaxo's Total Quality Management (TQM) and process improvement programs in their Technical Operations division. While employed at Merck and Co. Inc., I designed and delivered training and employee involvement programs including facilitating employee involvement teams.

After leaving the pharmaceutical industry, I worked at Nortel Networks. I began as a senior manager in Human Resources and Organization Development, leading the effort in starting up two new businesses for Nortel, one of which is now a significant part of Nortel's strategic data business portfolio. This included benchmarking Silicon Valley technology companies and developing and aligning HR and organization systems to business goals to create a new entrepreneurial culture that positioned Nortel as a competitive business and employer.

I then served as a Senior Manager in several areas including Customer Value Management, Sales and Marketing, and Human Resources and Organization Development. My last position involved working directly with Nortel customers and Nortel Account Management teams to align Nortel's organization processes with identified customer value drivers to achieve full customer potential.

I left Nortel to start my own consulting firm, Square Peg Consulting, Inc., where I work with clients to improve the effectiveness of their organizations. I use a whole-systems approach to organization development (OD), focusing on organization alignment as the key to organization effectiveness. A systems approach includes viewing the organization as a living organism, influenced by external and internal elements. There is a cause and effect relationship between each element, and organizations are most effective when all the systems within it align. My approach to enabling organizations to better perform is to assess alignment gaps and opportunities and develop interventions that align resources, systems, and processes to better position the organization to achieve business results. Because organizations grow and evolve through their natural organizational life cycle, it is important that they continue to shift and realign themselves to ensure all their efforts are going in the same direction for maximum efficiency and effectiveness.

One important element of organizational effectiveness is communication. From a diagnostic perspective, one can tell much about an organization's culture from assessing both what and how communication is shared throughout the organization. For example, if an organization claims to have a culture of "empowerment," yet employees are not aware of the organization's goals or vision, there is a potential gap between leadership's intention and the reality in which employees live. As a result, dysfunctional behavior may occur, leading to mistrust and poor performance.

Confusion and dissatisfaction arise when an organization's communication and governance practices are incongruent with the culture they espouse. For instance, a company aspiring to *engage employees in the business* while restricting employee access to information about its financial performance may be viewed cynically by employees. A company proclaiming *to trust and empower employees* while limiting delegation of authority may be perceived as disingenuous.

Think of the organization's communications strategy as a three-legged stool. One leg is its *external communications* strategy—the messages sent to the outside world about the organization's product or service offerings, including competitive differentiators, market space and positioning, and financial performance. This type of communication helps brand the company in the eyes of current and future customers, shareholders, and job candidates. It includes such things as the company's external Web site, its marketing materials, and its media relation's activities.

The second leg represents the *internal communications* strategy. This communication strategy ensures that employees stay informed about the performance of the company, important changes to policies and practices, and can serve as a vehicle for recognizing employee and team accomplishments. The company newsletter, its intranet site, and its approach to organizing employee meetings are all components of an internal communications strategy.

The third leg is the *organization alignment* strategy, the organized method by which the organization's strategy and tactics are developed and communicated to employees. This helps drive the daily activities of employees and ensures that they are all working in support of the organization's priorities. This usually takes the form of objective setting and performance management and is where the strategic and operational elements of an organization meet. For organizations to be effective, all three legs of the communications stool must be strategically aligned and working together.

Organizations are living organisms whose systems and structures are set up to accomplish a goal. A publicly traded company's goal may be to grow shareholder value, a sports team's goal may be to win the game, and a symphony's goal may be to master a piece of music. An effective communication strategy, one that takes into account the information needs of all constituents in each part of the system, is a critical and often overlooked element for ensuring alignment and, ultimately, organizational success.

Unfortunately, the ombudsperson method is often not used because organizations do not want the expense of an employee who "does not produce." To overcome this problem, Moore Tool Company in Springdale, Arkansas, started its "Red Shirt" program in which selected senior employees wear red shirts that identify them as informal ombudspeople. If an employee has a problem, she can seek help from a Red Shirt who has authority to help find a solution. This system not only opens communication channels but also provides job enrichment for an employee who works at an otherwise boring job.

In organizations that have their employees represented by unions, the job of the ombudsperson is typically handled by the **union steward**. But management–union relationships are often adversarial, so the union steward has a difficult time solving problems because she is not perceived by management or union members as being neutral.

Downward Communication

Downward communication is that of superior to subordinate or management to employees. The downward communication process in organizations has changed greatly over the years (Brandon, 1997). Originally, downward communication involved newsletters designed to bolster employee morale by discussing happy events such as the "3 B's"—babies, birthdays, and ballgame scores. Now, however, downward communication is considered a key method not only of keeping employees informed but of communicating vital information needed by employees to perform their jobs.

Such communication can be accomplished in many ways including bulletin boards, policy manuals, newsletters, and intranets.

Bulletin Boards

The **bulletin board** is yet another method of downward communication. The next time you visit an organization, look around for bulletin boards. You will see them everywhere. Their main use, however, is to communicate non-work-related opportunities such as scholarships, optional meetings, and items for sale.

Important information is seldom seen because the bulletin board is not the appropriate place to post a change of policy or procedure. Still, bulletin boards have the advantage of low cost and wide exposure to both employees and visitors. This is especially true if the boards are placed in high-traffic areas such as outside restrooms and cafeterias or near time clocks. Electronic bulletin boards, also called *in-house message networks*, allow the display of even more current information (Ladio, 1996).

Policy Manuals

The **policy manual** is the place for posting important changes in policy or procedure. This manual contains all the rules under which employees must operate. Most manuals are written in highly technical language, although they should be written in a less technical style to encourage employees to read them as well as to make them easier to understand. Furthermore, the contents of these manuals are considered binding contracts by courts, so the manuals must be updated each time a policy changes (Sosnin, 2001c). This usually is done by sending updated pages to employees so that they can replace older material with newer. To make this process easier, many organizations punch binder holes in the pages to facilitate their replacement. Sosnin (2001c) advises that policy manuals contain the following six disclaimers:

- Employment with the organization is at-will (refer to Chapter 7 for a discussion on employment at-will).
- The handbook does not create either an expressed or an implied contract.
- The handbook is a set of guidelines and should not be considered all-inclusive.
- The material in the handbook supercedes material in previous handbooks.
- The handbook can only be changed in writing by the president of the organization, and it can be changed unilaterally at any time.
- Employees are subject to any amendments, detentions, and changes in the handbook.

Exhibit 11.01 Tips for effective writing

Rather Than	Try
Trying to impress someone with your vocabulary	Using a more conversational style
personnel	employees
utilize	use
urban mass-transit vehicle	bus
cognizant	aware
Writing in generalities	Writing what you mean
I wasn't gone long	I was gone for 5 minutes
A survey said that most of our employees . . .	A survey said that 54% of our employees . . .
Using an entire phrase	Using a single word
Enclosed please find . . .	Enclosed is . . .
Motivation is the idea that . . .	Motivation is . . .
Should it come to pass that you . . .	If you . . .

The typical company manual is hundreds of pages long, so it is not surprising that many employees do not want to read it. To reduce length problems, most organizations have two types of company manuals. The first, called a *policy manual*, is very specific and lengthy, containing all of the rules and policies under which the organization operates. The second type, usually known as the *employee handbook*, is much shorter and contains only the most essential policies and rules, as well as general summaries of less important rules.

An example that supports the need for two manuals involved security guards at a manufacturing plant. The security guards were paid minimum wage and had an average tenure of about 3 months before quitting. The company became concerned for two reasons. First, 3 months was not enough time for the guards to learn all of the policies in the 300-page emergency procedures manual. Second, the manual was written by an engineer, and none of the security guards were able to understand the writing. The organization thus had I/O graduate student interns develop a short, easy-to-read procedure manual that could be read and understood in a day or two. Tips for effective manual writing are shown in Exhibit 11.01.

Newsletters

As mentioned earlier, **newsletters** are designed to bolster employee morale by discussing happy events such as the "3 B's"—babies, birthdays, and ballgame scores. Newsletters are good sources of information for celebrating employee successes, providing feedback on how well the organization is doing, introducing a new employee, and providing reminders about organizational changes. Though many organizations provide newsletters in print format, the trend is to send them

electronically through either email or an intranet (Sosnin, 2001a). This use of cyber-publications saves printing expenses, allows for faster dissemination of information, and provides greater flexibility for making changes and updates.

Intranets

To replace bulletin boards, newsletters, and company manuals, an increasing number of organizations are turning to **intranets**—organization-wide versions of the Internet (Hoffman, 2001). For example, Fletcher Challenge, a Canadian paper and pulp company, designed FletcherNet to improve employee communication. One of the most useful aspects of this intranet is the speed at which the company can survey employees about new ideas (Cohen, 1998). Other advantages include employee self-service; convenience and 24-hour support; and reduced paper, printing, and postage costs (Gray, 1997).

Though the potential for intranets has barely been tapped, here are some common current uses (Grensing-Pophal, 2001b):

- Online employee handbooks
- Answers to frequently asked questions
- Employee activity calendars
- Forms that can be completed online and then emailed
- Programs to write job descriptions or performance appraisals
- Job postings
- Online benefit information
- Training courses
- Information about reward and incentive programs

Business Communication

Business communication is the transmission of business-related information among employees, management, and customers. Business communication methods include memos, telephone calls, and email and voice mail.

Memos

One of the most common methods of business communication is the memorandum or *memo*. Memos have the advantage of providing detailed information to a large number of people in a short period of time. With the widespread use of photocopy machines and computer printers, however, employees (especially office workers) now receive so many memos that they often do not read them. In fact, the executive of a major company once stated that he never read a memo when it first came to him. If the message were really important, he believed the person would talk to him about it later. Although such an attitude probably is not a good one, it does underscore the excessive use of memos and their diminishing effectiveness in communication.

Telephone Calls

Another method of business communication is the *telephone call*. In the past, this method was appropriate only when the message was short and when only a few people needed to receive the communication. But with the advent of conference calls, the number of people who can be reached by this method has certainly increased. Furthermore, telephone calls were previously appropriate only for messages that did not involve detail. But the facsimile, or fax, machine now allows detailed sketches or numbers to be sent to people in different locations in a matter of seconds, and these then can be discussed by telephone. It also has been shown that phone calls, even when long distance, can be less expensive in communicating a message than most memos or letters (Fulger, 1977).

One limitation of phone calls, of course, is that nonverbal cues are not available. Thus, a major portion of the message is often not communicated. For important calls, however, video-enhanced teleconferencing (videoconferencing) can now be used. In fact, many organizations save interview expenses by having job applicants across the country participate in such teleconferences, which allow both parties to see one another. A second limitation to phone calls is that conversations are not documented. For example, one department recently had a problem with an administrator who continually provided incorrect information over the phone or at meetings, denied that she had done so, and then blamed another department for errors that resulted from the use of the information. To correct this problem, employees quit talking to the administrator over the phone and stuck to email where every "conversation" was documented.

Proper phone etiquette includes the following elements:

- Use speakerphones properly. Don't use your speakerphone if you share your office or listening space with others. If you want to place a caller on speakerphone, ask the caller's permission and be sure to tell the caller who else is in the room.
- Do not use your cell phone to hold conversations in public.
- Turn off the ringer on your cell phone or pager when attending meetings or when in public places (e.g., restaurant, church, theater).
- Do not answer the phone when you have someone in your office.
- Use voice mail rather than call waiting during a business conversation. Putting someone on hold so that you can answer another call communicates that your current conversation is not important. If you are expecting an important call that can't wait, let the person you are talking with know that you might be interrupted and apologize for the inconvenience.

Email and Voice Mail

Many memos and telephone calls have been replaced with *email* and *voice mail* (sophisticated phone-answering systems). Voice mail and email are primarily used to exchange general information, ask questions, and exchange *timely* information; they are not meant as a substitute for important conversation (Poe, 2001). The ability to easily document the sending and receiving of email gives it an advantage over voice mail in many situations (Reinsch & Beswick, 1990). The advantages to email and voice mail include a reduction in the use and filing of paper and time saved by avoiding "small talk" when communicating a short message by phone. A survey of human resource managers found that 80% thought that email increased productivity (Thompson, 1997).

On the downside, voice mail often results in "phone tag," and both email and voice mail reduce opportunities for personal contact. In fact, Carillon Health Care Systems recently got rid of its voice mail system because employees and customers were tired of getting answering machines and wanted to talk to "a real person." Voice mail systems should probably be limited to simple tasks (Pospisil, 1997). Well-designed voice mail systems have short menus and allow a caller to talk to a real person at any time during the call (Packard, 1997).

Before writing an email message, decide if email is the appropriate communication channel. Email is appropriate for preparing people for meetings, scheduling meetings, communicating common news, distributing memos, and summarizing a conversation (Poe, 2001). Because email eliminates such factors as body language and tone, it is easy to misinterpret the meaning of an email message.

A good rule of thumb is to never put something in email that you would not want to see published. Examples of material better left unsent include comments about other people, complaints, and offensive

Exhibit **11.02** Grapevine patterns

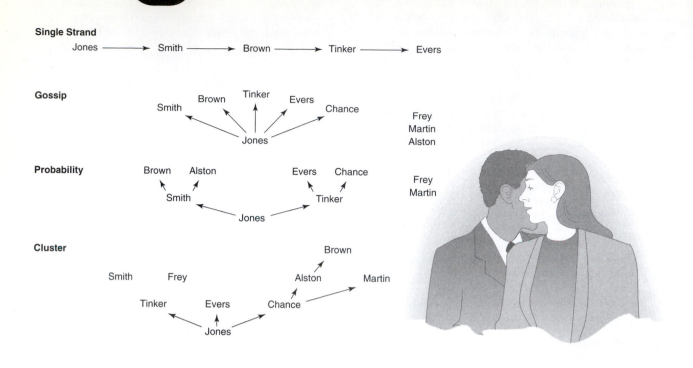

Single Strand

Jones → Smith → Brown → Tinker → Evers

Gossip

Smith Brown Tinker Evers Chance
Jones

Frey
Martin
Alston

Probability

Brown Alston Evers Chance
Smith Tinker
Jones

Frey
Martin

Cluster

Brown
Smith Frey Alston Martin
Tinker Evers Chance
Jones

jokes. Because of the increased use and misuse of email, many organizations, including Merrill Lynch, send their employees through email training. Casperson (2002) and Poe (2001) offer the following email etiquette commonly provided in such training:

- Include a greeting (e.g., "Hi Mark") and a closing (e.g., "Take care.").
- Include a detailed subject line.
- Don't write in all caps. It is difficult to read and comes across as if you are screaming.
- If you are going to forward an email message, change the original subject line and delete the long list of previous messages or names of people to whom the email had been previously forwarded.
- Take the same care in writing (e.g., spelling and grammar) that you would take in writing a formal memo.
- Don't spend company time on personal email unless your organization specifically allows you to do so.
- Allow ample time for the receiver to respond; many people don't believe email requires an immediate response.

When leaving a message on someone's voice mail, follow these guidelines:

- Speak slowly.
- Give your name at the beginning of the message, and then repeat it at the end of the message.

- Spell your name if the person is not familiar with you or if your name is difficult to spell.
- Leave your phone number, even if you think the person already has it.
- To avoid phone tag, indicate some good times the person can return your call.
- Don't ramble. Anticipate the possibility of getting voice mail rather than talking to the actual person and have a short message ready.
- Don't include information that you don't want other people to hear.

Informal Communication

An interesting type of organizational communication is **informal communication**. Often, informal information is transmitted through the **grapevine**, a term that can be traced back to the Civil War when loosely hung telegraph wires resembled grapevines. The communication across these lines was often distorted. Because unofficial employee communication is also thought to be distorted, the term has become synonymous with an informal communication network (Davis, 1977). Grapevines are common because they provide employees with information, power, and entertainment (Kurland & Pelled, 2000; Laing, 1993). Not surprisingly, the increased use of email has increased the importance of the grapevine (Smith, 2001).

Davis (1953) studied the grapevine and established the existence of four grapevine patterns: single strand, gossip, probability, and cluster. As Exhibit 11.02 shows,

Rumors are common in organizations.

PhotoDisc, Inc.

in the **single strand grapevine**, Jones passes a message to Smith, who passes the message to Brown, and so on until the message is received by everyone or someone "breaks the chain." This pattern is similar to the children's game of "telephone." In the **gossip grapevine**, Jones passes the message only to a select group of people. Notice that with this pattern only one person passes the message along, and not everyone has a chance to receive, or will receive, it. In the **probability grapevine**, Jones tells the message to a few other employees, and they in turn randomly pass the message along to other employees. In the **cluster grapevine**, Jones tells only a few select employees who in turn tell a few select others.

Research on the grapevine has supported several of Davis's (1953) findings. Sutton and Porter (1968) studied 79 employees in a state tax office and reached several interesting conclusions. They found that employees could be placed into one of three categories. **Isolates** were employees who received less than half of the information, liaisons were employees who both received most of the information and passed it to others, and **dead-enders** were those who heard most of the information but seldom passed it on to other employees.

Managers tended to be liaisons because they had heard 97% of the grapevine information and most of the time passed this information on. Nonmanagerial employees heard 56% of the grapevine information but seldom passed it on. Only 10% of nonmanagerial employees were liaisons; 57% were dead-enders and 33% were isolates.

Although most people consider the grapevine to be inaccurate, research has shown that information in the grapevine often contains a great deal of truth (Zaremba, 1988). Walton (1961) found that 82% of the information transmitted across the grapevine in one company was accurate. Such a statistic, however, can be misleading. Consider the following hypothetical

example: A message travels through the grapevine that "the personnel director will fire 25 people on Monday morning at 9 o'clock." The truth, however, is that the personnel director will *hire* 25 people on Monday morning at 9:00 a.m. Thus, even though four out of five parts of the message (80%) are correct, the grapevine message paints a picture quite different from reality.

People who hear information about the actions of another person rate that person's behavior more extremely than do the people who actually saw the behavior (Inman, Reichl, & Baron, 1993). This is especially true when the person telling the story is disorganized and when noise interferes with the listener's ability to consider other reasons for the behavior (Baron, David, Brunsman, & Inman, 1997).

Not to be confused with the grapevine, **rumor** is poorly substantiated information that is transmitted across the grapevine. Usually, rumor will occur when the available information is both interesting and ambiguous (Allport & Postman, 1947). The most common topics for rumor are personnel changes, job security, and the external reputation of the organization (DiFonzo & Bordia, 2000). Rumor and gossip are often ways in which employees can relieve stress (Mishra, 1990), respond to perceived organizational wrongs in a nonaggressive way (Tucker, 1993), maintain a sense of control (Waddell, 1996), and increase their power in an organization (Kurland & Pelled, 2000).

Certainly, horizontal communication is not always informal. Employees at the same level often exchange job-related information on such topics as customers and clients, the status of projects, and information necessary to complete a particular task. To increase the amount of job-related horizontal communication, many organizations have adopted the practice of self-managed work groups (Overman, 1994b).

Exhibit **11.03** The interpersonal communication process

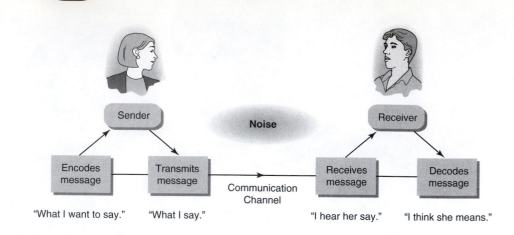

Sender | Noise | Receiver

Encodes message | Transmits message | Communication Channel | Receives message | Decodes message

"What I want to say." | "What I say." | "I hear her say." | "I think she means."

For example, at Columbia Gas Development in Houston, 12-person drilling teams were formed. The team approach greatly increased communication between geologists, engineers, and other staff members who had previously been located in separate departments. As another example, the use of teams at Meridian Insurance in Indianapolis increased communication and efficiency so much that a 29-step process for handling paperwork was reduced to four steps. To apply what you have learned about horizontal communication, complete Exercise 11–1 at the end of this chapter.

Interpersonal Communication

Interpersonal communication involves the exchange of a message across a communication channel from one person to another. As shown in Exhibit 11.03, the interpersonal communication process begins with a sender encoding and transmitting a message across a communication channel (e.g., memo, orally, nonverbally) and ends with another person (the receiver) receiving and decoding the message. Although this seems like a simple process, there are three main problem areas where things can go wrong and interfere with the accurate transmission or reception of the message.

Problem Area 1: Intended Message Versus Message Sent

For effective communication, the sender must know what she wants to say and how she wants to say it. Interpersonal communication problems can occur when the message a person sends is not the message she intended. There are three solutions to this problem: thinking about what you want to communicate, practicing what you want to communicate, and learning better communication skills.

Thinking About What You Want to Communicate

Often the reason we don't say what we mean is that we are not really sure what we want to say. For example, think of using the drive-through window at a fast food restaurant. As soon as you stop, but before you have a chance to read the menu board, a voice booms "Can I take your order?" You intelligently reply something such as "Uhhhhhhh, could you hang on a minute?" and then quickly try to place an order as the pressure builds. As you drive off, you realize that you did not really order what you wanted.

Does this scenario sound familiar? If so, you are not alone. Foster and his colleagues (1988) found that many fast food restaurant customers have so little time to think about their order that they make ordering mistakes. They found that placing a menu sign before the ordering station gave customers more time to think about their order and that this decreased average ordering times from 28 seconds to 6 seconds and ordering errors from 29% to 4%.

As another example, think about calling a friend and unexpectedly getting an answering machine. Have you ever left a message in which the first few sentences sounded reasonably intelligent? Did the first sentence again begin with "Uhhhhhhhhh"? Or have you ever made a call expecting to get an answering machine and instead had an actual person answer the phone? These examples show the importance of thinking about what you want to communicate.

Practice What You Want to Communicate

Even though you may know what you want to say, communication errors can occur if you do not actually say what you meant to say. Thus, when communication is important, it should be practiced. Just as consultants practice before giving a training talk and actors rehearse before a performance, you too need to practice what you want to say in important situations. Perhaps you can remember practicing how you were going to ask a person out on a date:

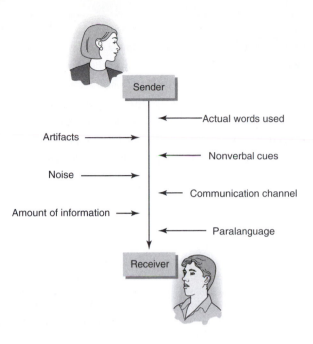

Sender

Actual words used

Artifacts

Nonverbal cues

Noise

Communication channel

Amount of information

Paralanguage

Receiver

changing the tone of your voice, altering your first line, or thinking of topics to discuss so that you would appear spontaneous.

Learn Better Communication Skills

Even if you know what you want to say and how you want to say it, communication errors can still occur if you do not have the proper communication skills. It is essential to take courses in public speaking, writing, and interpersonal communication so that you will be better prepared to communicate effectively. Because of the importance of communication skills, many organizations offer a wide range of communication training programs for their employees.

Problem Area 2: Message Sent Versus Message Received

Even though an individual knows what she wants to say and says it exactly as she planned, as shown in Exhibit 11.04, many factors affect how that message is received.

The Actual Words Used

A particular word may mean one thing in one situation but something else in another. Take the word *fine* as an example. If I told you that you had *"fine* jewelry," you would probably take the statement as a compliment. If the word were used to describe the weather—"The weather here in California is just *fine*"—it would still have a positive connotation. However, if a spouse asked "How was the dinner I cooked?" or "How did you like our evening of romance?" an answer of *"Fine"* would probably result in a very lonely evening.

A particular word may also mean one thing to one person and something different to another. For example, a 60-year-old man with a rural background may use the word *girl* as a synonym for *female*. He may not understand why the women at work get upset when he refers to them as the "girls in the office." When I conduct training sessions for police officers, we discuss how such words as *boy, son,* and *pretty little lady* can be emotionally charged and should thus be avoided.

Even within English speaking countries, a particular word can have different meanings. For example, if someone said, "He was pissed," in the United States we would interpret that the person was angry, yet people in Ireland would interpret that the person was drunk. If someone in Ireland said, "Where is the crack?" they would be asking the location of a party, not asking about drugs.

Words or phrases that are vague can also cause problems. For example, you need a set of data by the end of the day, so you tell your assistant that you need the data immediately. At the end of the day, however, the data are not there. The next morning, the employee proudly brings you the data that she has compiled in "less than a day" and is confused about why you are angry. In this example, you encoded the message as "I need it by five o'clock," you transmitted the message as "I need it immediately," and the employee decoded it as "She needs it tomorrow."

If someone told you, "I won't be gone long," when would you expect her back? When I ask this question of my classes or seminar audiences, the answers usually range from 10 minutes to 3 hours. Interestingly, at one seminar I conducted, a woman responded that her husband said that very phrase and came back 4 days later.

Exhibit **11.05** Gender differences in communication

Men		Women	
Talk about major global events		Talk about daily life	
Tell the main point		Provide details	
Are more direct		Are more indirect	
Use "uh-huh" to agree		Use "uh-huh" to listen	
Are comfortable with silence		Are less comfortable with silence	
Concentrate on the words spoken		Concentrate on meta-messages	
Sidetrack unpleasant topics		Focus on unpleasant topics	

Source: Adapted from Tannen 1986, 1990.

As the previous examples demonstrate, it is important to be more concrete in the words we use. Why, then, are we often vague in the way we communicate? One reason is that we want to avoid confrontations. If a husband tells his spouse that he will be gone for 4 hours, he may know that she will object. By being vague, he avoids the initial confrontation and hopes that she will not notice how long he has actually been gone—a common ploy used by us males but one that never seems to work.

Another reason for vagueness is that it gives us a chance to "test the water" and see what a person's initial reaction might be before we say what we really want. Asking someone out on a date is a perfect example. Instead of being direct and saying, "Do you want to go out this Friday?" we often say something such as "So, what are you up to this weekend?" If the response is positive, we become a bit more bold.

Gender is another factor related to the use of words. As shown in Exhibit 11.05, Deborah Tannen (1986, 1990, 1994) believes men and women speak very different languages and have different communication styles. By understanding these differences, communication in the workplace as well as in the home can be dramatically improved.

Communication can be improved if we choose our words carefully and ask, How might the other person interpret what I am about to say? If I use the word *girl*, will anyone be upset? If so, what word could I use that would be better?

Communication Channel

Problems in communication can occur as a result of the **channel** through which the message is transmitted. Information can be communicated a variety of ways such as orally, nonverbally, through a second party, or through a written medium such as a letter or memo. The same message can be interpreted in different ways based on the channel that was used to communicate it. For example, an employee being reprimanded will receive the message very differently if it is communicated in a memo or an email rather

than face to face. An employee who gives the "cold shoulder" to another employee will receive a different response than if she yelled at the employee or discussed the anger with her.

Another example of the channel's importance would be that of a supervisor criticizing an employee in front of other employees. The employee might be so embarrassed and angered that the criticism was made in front of others that she would not hear the content of the message. Again, transmitting a message through an inappropriate channel interferes with the message's meaning and accurate interpretation.

Often, the communication channel is the message itself. For example, if top management sends a "gofer" to deliver a message, it is essentially communicating that either the message or the receiver is not important. A colleague at another university tells about a former boss who always personally delivered good news (e.g., promotions, raises) as well as donuts on Friday. But lower level management always had to communicate the bad news, a practice that was resented by employees.

Noise

The **noise** surrounding a transmission channel can also affect the way a message is received. Noise can be defined as any interference that affects proper reception of a message. An obvious example is *actual* noise, such as the sound of a subway, interfering with conversation. Other examples are the appropriateness of the channel, the reputation of the person sending the message, and other information being received at the same time.

Nonverbal Cues

Much of what we communicate is conveyed by nonverbal means. Our words often say one thing while our actions say another. For example, a supervisor may tell an employee that she is interested in hearing her opinions, but at the same time she is frowning and looking out the window. The verbal message from the supervisor may be "I care," but the nonverbal message is "I'm bored." Which message will the employee pay attention to? Most likely, it will be the nonverbal one, even though nonverbal cues often lead to incorrect impressions (Malandro & Barker, 1983). Nonverbal cues can be divided into five categories: body language, use of space, use of time, paralanguage, and artifacts.

Body Language. How we move and position our body—our *body language*—communicates much to other people. For example:

- When one's body faces another person, it often is interpreted as a sign of liking, whereas when a person's body is turned away from another, it often is interpreted as a sign of dislike or lack of interest.
- Superiority is communicated by interrupting others, leaning back in a chair, moving closer to someone, or sitting while others stand.
- Making eye contact implies interest. In a casual conversation, increased eye contact is interpreted as a sign of liking, in a bar it may be a sign of flirting, and on a football field it may be interpreted as a sign of aggression. Lack of eye contact can mean many things including disinterest, discomfort, or embarrassment (Taylor, Peplau, & Sears, 1994). A person who makes eye contact while speaking but not while listening is often perceived as being powerful or dominant.
- Raising or lowering the head or the shoulders may indicate superiority or inferiority, respectively.
- Touching someone usually indicates liking, friendship, or nurturance (Brehm & Kassin, 1996). In fact, one study has shown that a waitress who touches her customers will receive a larger tip than one who does not (Crusco & Wetzel, 1984). Another study found that library clerks who briefly touched patrons as they were being handed books were rated by the patrons as being better employees than clerks who did not touch (Fisher, Rytting, & Heslin, 1976). Men initiate contact more often than women (Major, Schmidlin, & Williams, 1990).
- A meta-analysis by DePaulo and her colleagues (2003) found that people are more likely to purse their lips, raise their chin, fidget, and show nervousness when telling a lie than when not telling a lie.

As one might expect, gender differences occur in the use of nonverbal cues. For example, Dolin and Booth-Butterfield (1993) found that females use nonverbal cues such as head nodding to show attention more often than do males. In social situations, females touch, smile, and make eye contact more than males do (DePaulo, 1992).

Not surprisingly, there are many cultural differences in nonverbal communication. Here are a few examples:

- In the United States a thumbs up indicates agreement. In Australia, it is considered a rude gesture.
- In Japan, bowing is preferred to shaking hands.

- In the United States people point at objects with their index finger. Germans point with their little finger, and Japanese point with the entire hand. In Japan and in the Middle East, pointing with your index finger is considered rude.
- Showing the soles of one's feet is common in the United States but considered offensive in Thailand and Saudi Arabia.
- Sitting with one's legs crossed shows relaxation in the United States but is considered offensive in Ghana and Turkey.
- Prolonged eye contact is the norm in Arabic cultures, but it shows a lack of respect in many African, Latin American, and Caribbean countries.
- Touching another person is common in Latin and Middle Eastern countries but not in Northern European or Asian countries.

Research has shown that body language can affect employee behavior. For example, Forbes and Jackson (1980) found that effective use of nonverbal cues resulted in a greater probability of being hired for a job. Similarly, Rasmussen (1984) found that the use of nonverbal cues during an interview will help if the applicant gives the correct answer to an interview question but will hurt the applicant if an incorrect answer is given.

Though body language can be a useful source of information, it is important to understand that the same nonverbal cue can mean different things in different situations and cultures. So be careful and try not to read too much into a particular nonverbal cue.

Use of Space. The ways people make use of space also provides nonverbal cues about their feelings and personality. Dominant people or those who have authority are given more space by others and at the same time take space from others. For example, people stand farther away from such status figures as executives and police officers (and even college professors) and stand in an office doorway rather than directly entering such a person's office. These same status figures, however, often move closer as a show of power. Police officers are taught that moving in close is one method of intimidating a person.

On the other hand, status figures also increase space to establish differences between themselves and the people with whom they are dealing. A common form of this use of distance is for an executive to place a desk between herself and another person. An interesting story is told by a sports agent who was negotiating a player's contract with George Steinbrenner, owner of the New York Yankees baseball club. When the agent arrived at Steinbrenner's office, he noticed that Steinbrenner sat at one end of a long desk. At the other end was a small chair in which the agent was to sit. Recognizing the spatial arrangement to be a power play, the agent moved his chair next to Steinbrenner's. As the story goes, the Yankee owner was so rattled by this ploy that the agent was able to negotiate an excellent contract for his player client.

Exhibit 11.06   Inflection changes and meaning

Inflected Sentences		Meaning
I did not say Bill stole your car.		**Someone else** said Bill stole your car.
I **did not** say Bill stole your car.		I **deny** I said Bill stole your care.
I did not **say** Bill stole your car.		I **implied** that Bill stole your car.
I did not say **Bill** stole your car.		**Someone else** stole your car.
I did not say Bill **stole** your car.		He **borrowed** your car.
I did not say Bill stole **your** car.		Bill stole **someone else's** car.
I did not say Bill stole your **car.**		Bill stole **something else** of yours.

The following example also illustrates how the use of space can enhance a person's status by adding an image of importance. Recently, the psychology building at Radford University was renovated, and with efficient use of attic space, every faculty member was given an office. Students who visited during office hours had been accustomed to faculty members sharing offices. Many of these students commented on how important a psychology faculty member must be to receive his or her own office. (Of course, we never told them that we all had our own offices and that faculty members in other departments would also soon have their own.)

Four major spatial distance zones have been recognized and defined (Hall, 1963): intimacy, personal distance, social distance, and public distance. The size of these zones differ among cultures, and the numbers given here are those recognized to be U.S. cultural norms.

The **intimacy zone** extends from physical contact to 18 inches away from a person and is usually reserved for close relationships such as dates, spouses, and family. When this zone is entered by strangers in crowded elevators and the like, we generally feel uncomfortable and nervous. The **personal distance zone** ranges from 18 inches to 4 feet away from a person and is the distance usually reserved for friends and acquaintances. The **social distance zone** is from 4 to 12 feet away and is the distance typically observed when dealing with businesspeople and strangers. Finally, the **public distance zone** ranges from 12 to 25 feet away and is characteristic of such large group interactions as lectures and seminars.

The way an office is furnished also communicates a lot about that person. As mentioned earlier, certain desk placements indicate openness and power; visitors and subordinates prefer not to sit before a desk that serves as a barrier (Davis, 1984). People whose offices are untidy are perceived as being busy, and people whose offices contain plants are perceived as being caring and concerned.

Use of Time. The way people make use of time is another element of nonverbal communication. If an employee is supposed to meet with a supervisor at 1:00 p.m. and the supervisor shows up at 1:10, the supervisor is communicating an attitude about the employee, the importance of the meeting, or both. Tardiness is more readily accepted from a higher status person than from a lower status person. Dean Smith, the great former basketball coach at the University of North Carolina, suspends any player who is even a minute late for a practice because he believes tardiness is a sign of arrogance and works against the team concept.

In a similar fashion, before a meeting a supervisor sets aside 30 minutes and tells others that she is not to be disturbed because she is in conference. A definitive message thus is conveyed, one that is likely to prevent constant interruptions by telephone calls or people stopping by to say hello because they saw an open door.

Paralanguage

Paralanguage involves the way we say things and consists of variables such as tone, tempo, volume, number and duration of pauses, and rate of speech (Martin, 1995). A message that is spoken quickly will be perceived differently from one that is spoken slowly. In fact, research (e.g., Pearce & Conklin, 1971) has shown that people with fast speech rates are perceived as more intelligent, friendly, and enthusiastic (Hecht & LaFrance, 1995) than people with slow rates of speech. People who use many "uh-hums," "ers," and "ahs" are also considered less intelligent. Men with high-pitched voices are considered to be weak, but females with high-pitched voices are considered to be petite. People telling lies talk less, provide fewer details, repeat words and phrases more often, have more uncertainty and vocal tension in their voice, and speak in a higher pitch than do people telling the truth (DePaulo et al., 2003).

Simple changes in the tone used to communicate a message can change the entire meaning of the message. To demonstrate this point, consider this sentence: "I didn't say Bill stole your car." At first reading, it does not seem unusual, but what does it actually mean? As Exhibit 11.06 shows, if we emphasize the first word, *I*, the implication is that *someone else* said, "Bill stole your car." But if we emphasize the word *Bill*, the meaning changes to "someone else stole your car." And so on. Thus, a simple written message can be interpreted in seven different ways. As you can see, many messages are better communicated orally than through memos or email.

Artifacts

A final element of nonverbal communication concerns the objects, or **artifacts**, that a person wears or with which she surrounds herself. A person who wears bright and colorful clothes is perceived differently from a person who wears conservative white or gray clothing (Arthur, 1995). Similarly, the manager who places all of her awards on her office wall, the executive with a large and expensive chair, and the student who carries a briefcase rather than a book bag are all making nonverbal statements about themselves. To help you apply your new knowledge of nonverbal communication, complete Exercise 11–2 at the end of this chapter.

Amount of Information

The amount of information contained in a message can affect the accuracy with which it is received. When a message contains more information than we can hold in memory, the information becomes leveled, sharpened, and assimilated. For example, suppose a friend told you the following message over the phone:

John Atoms worked for Mell South Corporation. He came to work on Tuesday morning wearing a brown shirt, plaid pants, white socks, and dark shoes. He leaned forward, barfed all over the floor, and then passed out. He was obviously intoxicated. He had worked for the company for 13 years, so they didn't want to fire him, but they had to do something. The company decided to suspend him for a few days and place him on probation. They were especially sensitive to his problems because he was on his eighth marriage.

What would the story sound like if you passed it on to a friend? When you **level** some of the information, unimportant details are removed. For example, information about the color of the employee's shirt and socks would probably not be passed along to the next person. When you **sharpen** the information, interesting and unusual information is kept. In the example here, the employee's "barfing" and his eight marriages would probably be the story's main focus as it is passed from you to your friend. When you **assimilate** the information, it is modified to fit your existing beliefs and knowledge. Most of us have never heard the last name Atoms, but we probably have known someone named "Adams." Likewise "Mell South" might be passed along as Bell South. You would probably use the word *drunk* rather than *intoxicated*.

Reactions to Communication Overload

With many jobs, communication overload can occur when an employee receives more communication than he can handle. When an employee is overloaded, he can adapt or adjust in one of several ways to reduce the

Communication overload can cause job stress.

stress (Miller, 1960): omission, error, queuing, escape, using a gatekeeper, or using multiple channels.

Omission. One way to manage communication overload is **omission**: a conscious decision not to process certain types of information. For example, a busy supervisor may let the phone ring without answering it so that she can finish her paperwork. Although this technique can work if the overload is temporary, it will be ineffective if the employee misses an important communication.

Error. In the **error** type of response, the employee attempts to deal with every message she receives. But in so doing, each processed message includes reception error. The processing errors are not intentional but result from processing more than can be handled.

Perhaps a good example of this would be a student who has 2 hours in which to study four chapters for a test. A student using the error method would attempt to read and memorize all four chapters in 2 hours. Obviously, her test score will probably indicate that even though she did all of her reading, much of it was not remembered or not remembered correctly.

The probability of error occurring can be reduced in two ways. First, the message can be made *redundant*. That is, after communicating an important message over the telephone, it is a good idea to write a memo to the other person summarizing the major points of the conversation. Furthermore, after sending an important memo, it is wise to call its recipient to ensure that the memo was not only received but also read.

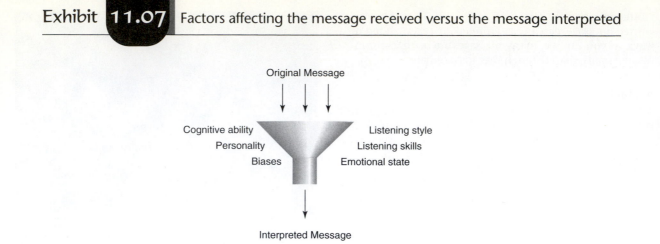

Second, error can be reduced by having the recipient *verify* the message. Ask the person to repeat the message or to acknowledge that she has read and understood it. For example, after a customer has placed an order at the drive-through window of a fast food restaurant, the employee repeats the order to the customer to make sure she heard it correctly. (Of course, with the poor-quality intercoms used by such places, most people still cannot understand the employee.)

Queuing. Another method of dealing with communication overload is **queuing**—placing the work into a *queue*, or waiting line. The order of the queue can be based on such variables as the message's importance, timeliness, or sender. For example, a memo sent by the company president will probably be placed near or at the beginning of the queue, as will an emergency phone message. On the other hand, a message to return the phone call of a salesperson most likely will go at the end of the queue.

With this method of handling communication overload, all of the work will usually get done. Queues are only effective, however, if the communication overload is temporary. If the employee is constantly overloaded, she will never reach the work at the end of the queue.

Escape. If communication overload is prolonged, a common employee response is to **escape**, usually through absenteeism and ultimately through resignation. This response certainly is not beneficial to an organization, but it can be beneficial to an employee if it protects her mental and physical health by relieving stress.

An example of the escape response is often seen with students who withdraw from college courses. A student may enroll in six classes and realize after 2 months that she does not have enough time to do all of the reading and writing required for six classes. Rather than choosing the error or omission strategies, both of which would result in lower grades, the student withdraws from one of her classes to reduce her overload.

Use of a Gatekeeper. A response to communication overload used by many executives is the use of a **gatekeeper**, a person who screens potential communication and allows only the most important to go through. Receptionists and secretaries are the most obvious examples of gatekeepers.

Use of Multiple Channels. The final coping response to communication overload is the use of **multiple channels**. With this strategy, an organization reduces the amount of communication going to one person by directing some of it to another. For example, in a small restaurant, all of the problems involving customers, employees, finances, and vendors are handled by the owner. But as the business grows, the owner may not be able to handle all of the communication and thus may hire others to deal with finances (a bookkeeper) and vendors (an assistant manager).

Knowing and understanding this list of responses to communication overload is important. When communication overload occurs, employees will react in ways that reduce the increased stress. Some of these strategies (omission, error, escape) result in negative consequences for the organization. Thus, the organization must recognize when overload occurs and aggressively adopt an acceptable strategy to deal with it. To look at how you react to communication overload, complete the Communication Overload Exercise on your CD-ROM.

Problem Area 3: Message Received Versus Message Interpreted

Even though a person knows what she wants to say, and says it the way she wants, and even though another individual properly receives the intended message, its meaning can change depending on the way in which the receiver interprets the message that was received. As shown in Exhibit 11.07, this interpretation is affected by a variety of factors, such as listening skills, listening style, emotional state, cognitive ability, and personal biases.

Listening Skills

Listening is probably the most important communication skill that a supervisor should master. In a study of managers, Nichols and Stevens (1957) found that 70% of the white-collar workday is spent communicating. Of that, 9% is spent in writing, 16% is spent in reading, 30% is spent in speaking, and 45% is spent in listening. Thus, a manager spends more time listening than doing any other single activity. This is an important point for two reasons.

First, listening is a skill, and our formal education in high school and college does not prepare us for managerial communication (Burley-Allen, 2001). We are required to take English courses to improve our reading and writing and are usually required to take one speech course to improve our oral communication skills, but we spend little, if any, time learning how to listen. Thus, the amount of time spent learning about various types of communication is inversely related to the actual amount of time spent by managers on the job.

Second, listening effectiveness is poor. It has been estimated that immediately after a meeting, we retain only 50% of the material we have heard and only 25% of the material 48 hours later (Nichols & Stevens, 1957). Although much of this loss can be attributed to poor memory practices, some is the result of poor listening habits.

Styles of Listening

What can be done to increase listening effectiveness? Perhaps the most important thing we can do is to recognize that every person has a particular "listening style" that serves as a communication filter. Geier and Downey (1980) have developed a test, the **Attitudinal Listening Profile**, to measure an employee's listening style. Their theory postulates six main styles of listening: leisure, inclusive, stylistic, technical, empathic, and nonconforming (LISTEN).

Leisure listening is practiced by "good-time" people who listen only for words that indicate pleasure. For example, a student who is a leisure listener will pay attention only when the teacher is interesting and tells jokes. As an employee, she is the last one to "hear" that employees are needed to work overtime.

Inclusive listening is the style of the person who listens for the main ideas behind any communication. In an hour-long meeting full of details and facts about a decline in sales, the only information this type of listener will "hear" is the main point that sales are down and that things had better improve. This listening style can be an advantage when cutting through a jungle of detail, but it can be a disadvantage when detail is important.

Stylistic listening is practiced by the person who listens to the *way* the communication is presented. Stylistic listeners will not listen unless the speaker's style is appropriate, the speaker "looks the part," or both. For example, when speaking to a stylistic listener, a lecturer on finance will find an attentive ear only if she wears a nice suit. After all, this listener reasons, if the lecturer cannot afford a nice suit, why listen to what she has to say about investing money? Similarly,

if the speaker says that an event will be fun, she must *sound* as if she means it. And if an employee calls in sick to a manager who is a stylistic listener, she had better "sound" sick.

Technical listening is the style practiced by the "Jack Webbs" of the listening world—"just the facts, ma'am." The technical listener hears and retains large amounts of detail, but she does not hear the *meaning* of those details. In the earlier example of the meeting in which employees are told that sales have decreased, the technical listener will hear and remember that sales last year were 12.3% higher than this year, that profits are down by 21%, and that six employees will probably be laid off—but she will miss the point that unless sales improve, she could be one of those six.

Empathic listening tunes in to the feelings of the speaker and, of the six listening types, this listener is the most likely to pay attention to nonverbal cues. Thus, an empathic listener will listen to an employee complain about her boss and is the only one of the six types of listeners who will not only pay attention but also understand that the employee's complaints indicate true frustration and unhappiness.

Nonconforming listening is practiced by the individual who attends only to information that is consistent with her way of thinking. If the nonconforming listener does not agree with a speaker, she will not listen to what the speaker says. Furthermore, the nonconforming listener will pay attention only to those people whom she considers to be strong or to have authority.

How Listening Styles Affect Communication

The following example will demonstrate the importance of the six listening styles in a work setting. Suppose an employee approaches a supervisor and tells her that she has a temperature of 106 degrees. How would each of the six listeners react?

The leisure listener would pay little attention to the employee because she does not like to hear about unpleasant things and illness certainly is not pleasant. The inclusive listener would probably tell a story about when she had a high temperature, thinking that the topic of conversation is fever. You may have friends who often say things that are not related to your conversation; as this example points out, they are probably inclusive listeners who mistake the main points of a conversation. In this case, the employee is communicating that she does not feel well; she is not discussing "temperatures I have had."

The stylistic listener would pay attention only if the employee sounded and looked ill. You may have also called a professor or a date and tried to sound ill in order to cancel an appointment or a date. Few people actually sound ill even when they are, but we understand the importance of style in listening and behave accordingly.

The technical listener would hear every word but would not realize their meaning. That is, 10 minutes later, when another employee asked whether Sue is sick, the supervisor would respond, "She didn't say. She has a temperature of 106, but I'm not sure how she is feeling."

Listening skills are important for effective communication.

PhotoDisc, Inc.

The nonconforming listener would pay little attention to the employee. After all, if she actually had a temperature of 106 degrees, she would be dead, and because she is not dead, she must be lying. Of course, the employee exaggerated her temperature because she was emphasizing the point that she is sick. But the nonconforming listener would not "hear" anything once she recognized that an initial statement was incorrect.

In this example, the empathic listener would be the only one who would understand the real point of the communication. The employee is mentioning her temperature because she does not feel well and wants to go home.

Understanding each of the six styles can make communication more effective in two ways. First, becoming aware of your own style allows you to understand the filter you use when listening to others. For example, a student who uses a leisure style may need to recognize that if she listens only to lectures that she finds interesting, she probably will miss a lot of important information. She might want to learn how to concentrate on lectures even when they are boring. Second, understanding the six styles can lead to better communication with others. For example, when speaking to an inclusive listener, we must either write down relevant details that we want her to remember or have her repeat the details. Otherwise, the inclusive listener will remember only the main point: "I know that there is a party tonight, but I'm not sure when or where." On the other hand, when we speak to a technical listener, it is important to tell her what the details mean. For example, if you tell a technical listener there will be a party at your house on Thursday at 8:00 p.m., you should also add that she is invited, or she will understand only that there is a party and not that she has been invited.

Of course, the million-dollar question is, How can we tell what style of listener is listening to us? The best way might be to test the listener on the Attitudinal Listening Profile mentioned earlier, but this is hardly practical. The most practical method is to use the person's speaking style as an indicator of listening style. If the person usually mentions how she feels about things, she is probably an empathic listener, but if she speaks with a lot of detail, she is probably a technical listener.

Someone speaking to a group, of course, must relate to all styles of listeners. The best communicators will have something for everyone. A good instructor will provide jokes and humorous stories for leisure listeners, use an outline format and provide main points for inclusive listeners, provide specific facts and details for technical listeners, discuss her feelings about the topic for empathic listeners, have good speaking skills and appropriate dress for stylistic listeners, and be confident and accurate for nonconforming listeners. To examine your own listening style, complete Exercise 11–3 at the end of this chapter and the Listening Styles Exercise on your CD-ROM.

Tips for Effective Listening. In addition to understanding how your listening style serves as a filter, you can improve your listening effectiveness in many other ways. The best tips I have seen are in a booklet prepared for the Sperry Corporation by Steil (1980). These tips are shown in Exhibit 11.08.

Other authors have also offered tips for more effective listening. For example, Davis (1967) provided these suggestions:

1. Stop talking.
2. Put the speaker at ease.
3. Show the speaker that you want to listen.
4. Remove distractions.
5. Empathize with the speaker.

Exhibit 11.08 Ten keys to effective listening

Keys	The Bad Listener	The Good Listener
1. Find areas of interest.	Tunes out dry subjects.	Opportunitizes; asks, "What's in it for me?"
2. Judge content, not delivery.	Tunes out if delivery is poor.	Judges content, skips over delivery errors.
3. Hold your fire.	Tends to enter into argument.	Doesn't judge until comprehension is complete.
4. Listen for ideas.	Listens for facts.	Listens for central themes.
5. Be flexible.	Takes intensive notes using only one system.	Takes fewer notes. Uses 4–5 different systems, depending on speaker.
6. Work at listening.	Shows no energy output. Attention is faked.	Works hard, exhibits active body state.
7. Resist distractions.	Is distracted easily.	Fights or avoids distractions, tolerates bad habits, knows how to concentrate.
8. Exercise your mind.	Resists difficult expository material; seeks light, recreational material.	Uses heavier material as exercise for the mind.
9. Keep your mind open.	Reacts to emotional words.	Interprets color words; does not get hung up on them.
10. Capitalize on the fact that thought is faster than speech.	Tends to daydream with slow speakers.	Challenges, anticipates, mentally summarizes, weighs the evidence, listens between lines to tone of voice.

Source: Adapted from Steil (1980). Prepared by Dr. Lyman K. Steil for the Sperry Corporation. Reprinted with permission of Dr. Steil and UNISYS Corporation.

6. Be patient.
7. Hold your temper.
8. Go easy on argument and criticism.
9. Ask questions.
10. Stop talking.

Blodgett (1997) has these further suggestions:

1. Let the other person finish speaking.
2. Don't ask excessive questions.
3. Use appropriate nonverbal cues, paralanguage, and verbals to show that you are paying attention.
4. Be silent for a few seconds after the person has finished speaking; this will encourage her to talk more.
5. Focus on what the person is saying, not on your next response.
6. Don't judge; keep an open mind.
7. Try to understand what the other person means.

Golen (1990) found that bad listeners are lazy, closed-minded, opinionated, insincere, bored, and inattentive. To test your own listening skills, complete Exercise 11–4 at the end of this chapter.

Emotional State

The interpretation of a message can certainly be affected by the receiver's emotional state (Martin, 1995). When we are mad, anxious, depressed, elated, or upset, we do not think as clearly as when our moods are more moderate. Think of the last time you had an argument with someone. How rational and intelligent was your conversation? After the argument was over, did both of you remember what was said in the same way?

Likewise, have you ever attended a class when your mind was somewhere else? My guess is that neither your attention span nor your comprehension of the material was as high as normal.

Cognitive Ability

Cognitive ability is another factor that can affect the way in which a received message is interpreted. That is, a person can receive a message exactly as it was sent yet not be bright enough to understand it. For example, have you ever attended a class where you had no idea what the professor was talking about? You heard her words and saw her diagrams, but the message still made no sense. Likewise, have you ever told a great pun, only to be disappointed that the person on the receiving end of the joke did not understand it? If so, then you have

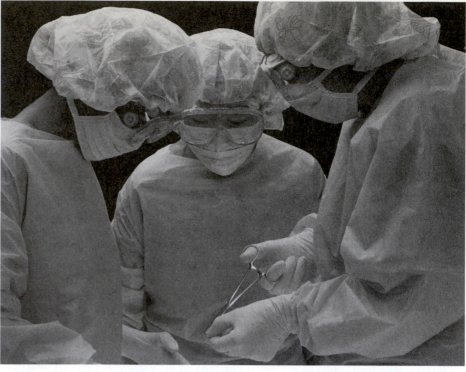

For some jobs, effective communication might be the difference between life and death.

firsthand experience in understanding how cognitive ability can affect the way in which information is interpreted.

Bias

Our biases obviously affect our ability to interpret information we receive. For example, we can hate a political candidate so much that we can refuse to process any of the positive information we hear about her. We do, however, process every piece of information that is consistent with our opinion.

Improving Employee Communication Skills

Organizations are always looking for employees with excellent communication skills. The difficulty in finding such employees was recently exemplified by the experience of a national insurance company. The company was having difficulty with a position that required employees to respond to customer complaints. The company had hired expensive consultants to teach its employees how to write effective letters, but performance had not improved. The company then constructed sample letters so that an employee could read a customer complaint, find a standard response form, and add a few personal lines. This also did not work. Finally, the company tried using a standardized writing test before hiring its employees. Although the test showed significant prediction for the performance of black employees, it did not predict the performance of white employees. This case of single-group

validity made the test risky to use. Thus, the question remains: How can an organization increase the communication skills of its employees?

Interpersonal Communication Skills

One of the most common methods used to increase interpersonal communication skills is the training workshop conducted by an outside consultant. Although a large number of consultants lead communication workshops, such workshops often bring only short-term improvement in skills.

An exception to this general failure to produce long-term improvements was reported by Freston and Lease (1987) from their work with Questar Corporation in Salt Lake City. As the personnel manager at Questar, Freston believed that the organization's managers were not properly trained in communication. Questar thus hired Lease as a communications consultant, and together Freston and Lease designed a new training program that included seminars on awareness, nonverbal communication, assertiveness, and listening. In addition to the seminars, Freston and Lease also used role play and group discussion. The revised training program brought more positive attitudes for supervisors and increased performance quality in tasks such as performance appraisal and training.

Written Communication Skills

Attempts to improve the quality of written communication have generally taken two paths. One approach concentrates on improving the writer's skills, and the other concentrates on making material easier to read.

Exhibit 11.09 Graph for estimating readability—extended

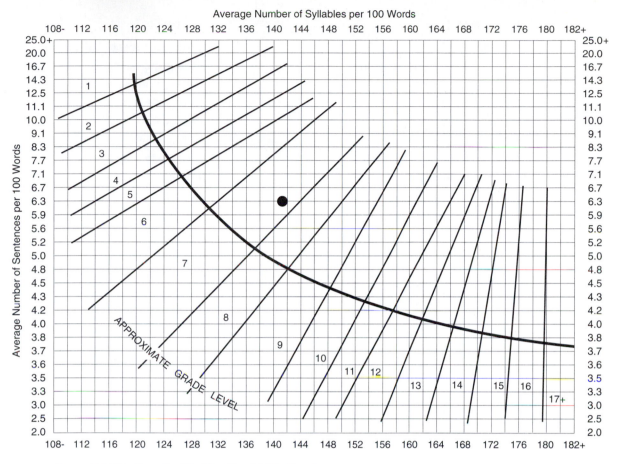

Average Number of Syllables per 100 Words

Expanded Directions for Working Readability Graph

1. Randomly select three sample passages and count out exactly 100 words each, beginning with the beginning of a sentence. Do count proper nouns, initializations, and numerals.
2. Count the number of sentences in the 100 words, estimating length of the fraction of the last sentence to the nearest one-tenth.
3. Count the total number of syllables in the 100-word passage. If you don't have a hand counter available, simply put a mark above every syllable over one in each word. Then when you get to the end of the passage, count the number of marks and add 100. Small calculators can also be used as counters by pushing numeral 1, then pushing the + sign for each word or syllable when counting.
4. Enter graph with *average* sentence length and *average* number of syllables; plot dot where the two lines intersect. Area where dot is plotted will give you the approximate grade level.
5. If a great deal of variability is found in syllable count or sentence count, putting more samples into the average is desirable.
6. A word is defined as a group of symbols with a space on either side; thus *Joe, IRA, 1945*, and *&* are each one word.
7. A syllable is defined as a phonetic syllable. Generally, there are as many syllables as vowel sounds. For example, *stopped* is one syllable and *wanted* is two syllables. When counting syllables for numerals and initializations, count one syllable for each symbol. For example, *1945* is four syllables, *IRA* is three syllables, and *&* is one syllable.

Improving Writing

With increased use of email, effective writing skills are more essential than ever (Tyler, 2003). It is difficult for an organization to overcome an employee's lack of formal training in writing (or to change bad writing habits). Several consulting firms, however, specialize in the improvement of employee writing by teaching employees the most important concepts of writing. For example, Broadbent (1997) advised that writing can be improved when writers value what they write, set personal standards and goals (e.g., a 12th-grade reading level, no grammar errors,

Exhibit 11.10 Readability levels of selected publications

Document	Readability Level
FAA regulations	Graduate student
Position Analysis Questionnaire	College graduate
Air Line Pilot magazine	College student
Study of Values	12th grade
Time magazine	11th grade
Newsweek	11th grade
Reader's Digest	10th grade
Otis Employment Test	9th grade
Ladies' Home Journal	8th grade
Most comic books	6th grade
Minnesota Multiphasic Personality Inventory	6th grade

each document will be proofread twice), and spend considerable time doing their own editing as well as getting others to edit the document. Employees need to analyze their audience. If a written communication is intended for a blue-collar employee, then the readability must be kept simple. If the intended audience is a busy executive, the message must be kept short.

Readability

Written communication can break down when material is too difficult for many employees to read. Here are some examples:

- Federal Aviation Administration (FAA) regulations and many airline company pilots' association agreements are too difficult for pilots to read (Blumenfeld, 1985).
- Corporate annual reports are too difficult for most adults to understand (Courtis, 1995).
- The Position Analysis Questionnaire (the job analysis instrument discussed in Chapter 2) is also too difficult for most job incumbents to read (Ash & Edgell, 1975).

Thus, providing employees with important material to read will be an effective communication form only if the employees can understand what is written.

To ensure that employees will be able to understand written material, several readability indices are available. When using such an index, an organization analyzes the material to be read and compares its readability level with the typical education of the employees who will read the document. For example, if most employees have high school diplomas but have not been to college,

the document should be written at less than a 12th-grade level.

Each index uses a slightly different formula or method. For example, the **Fry Readability Graph** (Fry, 1977) uses the average number of syllables per word and the average length of sentences to determine readability (see Exhibit 11.09). The **Flesch Index** (Flesch, 1948) uses the average sentence length and number of syllables per 100 words; the **FOG Index** (Gunning, 1964) uses the number of words per sentence and the number of three-syllable words per 100; and the **Dale-Chall Index** (Dale & Chall, 1948) uses the number of words that are not included in a list of words known by 80% of fourth graders.

All of the readability indices show reasonable reliability and correlate highly with one another (Blumenfeld & Justice, 1975). (The readability levels of selected publications are shown in Exhibit 11.10.) As we can see from these indices, an easily read document has short sentences, uses simple rather than complicated words, and uses common rather than unusual words (Grazian, 1996).

Specialized indices have also been introduced by both Flesch (1948), who measured the human interest level of reading material, and Tysinger and Pitchford (1988), who developed a method for determining the readability of trait-based psychological tests. Many word processing packages (e.g., WordPerfect, Microsoft Word) now contain readability indices that make it easier to determine the audience level for which the document was written.

To practice how to measure the readability of a document, complete Exercise 11–5 at the end of this chapter. To apply what you have learned throughout this chapter, complete the case study found on your CD-ROM.

Chapter Summary

In this chapter you learned:

- There are three types of organizational communication: upward, downward, and horizontal.

- There are three main problem areas in interpersonal communication: the intended message versus the message actually sent, the message sent versus the message received, and the message received versus the message interpreted.

- Interpersonal communication can be improved with more effective listening skills; understanding the six different styles of listening (leisure, inclusive, stylistic, technical, empathic, and nonconforming); and considering the emotional state, cognitive ability, and personal biases of the sender and the receiver.

- Written communication can be improved by learning better writing skills and by writing organizational documents at a reading level that matches the reading level of most employees.

Critical Thinking Questions

1. Why do people hate to communicate bad news?

2. When is email an inappropriate method of communication?

3. What is the best way to stop a rumor?

4. Which is most important: nonverbal cues, paralanguage, or the actual words chosen to communicate?

5. Can people be taught to be effective listeners?

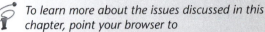 To learn more about the issues discussed in this chapter, point your browser to

http://www.infotrac-college.com/wadsworth

and enter one of these search terms:

employee attitude surveys

upward communication

employee suggestion

ombudsperson

horizontal communication

nonverbal cues

exit interviews

email etiquette

Exercise 11–1
Informal Communication

As discussed in your text, horizontal communication is communication between employees at the same level of the organization. Some of this communication is formal, while the rest is informal and is said to be communicated through the grapevine. The purpose of this exercise is to provide you with the opportunity to study the grapevine in your own life.

Instructions

Think of an interesting piece of information (rumor, gossip, etc.) that you have recently heard and write down that information below.

_____

_____

_____

_____

_____

_____

Now write down the name of the person who told you that piece of information.

_____

Go to that person and ask him/her where he/she got the piece of information.

Write that name here _____.

Continue to track these people down until you come to a dead end. Also, ask each person who they told the information to.

_____

_____

_____

_____

After reaching the end, discuss the type of grapevine pattern that you found. Was it single strand, gossip, probability, or cluster? Also, how would you classify each of the people to whom you talked? Are they isolates, liaisons, or dead-enders?

_____

_____

_____

_____

_____

_____

_____

_____

_____

_____

_____

_____

_____

_____

_____

_____

_____

_____

_____

_____

_____

Exercise 11–2
Nonverbal Communication

Much of what is communicated is communicated nonverbally through cues such as body language, use of space, use of time, paralanguage, and artifacts. The purpose of this exercise is to provide you with the opportunity to study the extent to which nonverbal cues exist in normal conversation.

Instructions

Outside of class, go somewhere where people talk. It might be the cafeteria, the library, or a lounge in a residence hall. Quietly observe the people who are talking, and use the form below to record your observations. Write down what you saw as well as the impression that you got from each of the cues.

Observation Record

Body Language

Eye Contact

_____

_____

_____

_____

_____

_____

Arms

_____

_____

_____

_____

_____

_____

Legs

_____

_____

_____

_____

_____

Body Angles

_____

_____

_____

_____

_____

Touching

_____

_____

_____

_____

_____

Use of Space (How far apart were the people?)

_____

_____

_____

_____

_____

_____

_____

Paralanguage

Tempo of Speech

_____

_____

_____

_____

_____

Volume of Speech

_____

_____

_____

_____

_____

Number of Pauses

_____

_____

_____

_____

_____

Artifacts (How was each person dressed? What impression did this style of dress leave?)

_____

_____

_____

_____

_____

Overall Observation

Exercise 11–3
Your Listening Style

Your text described six listening styles: leisure, inclusive, stylistic, technical, empathic, and nonconforming. To get an idea of your own style, look at the Employee Personality Inventory you took back in Exercise 6–4. Your scores on the five personality scales will give you a rough idea of your listening style. The EPI scales and their listening styles are as follows:

EPI Scale	Listening Style
Thinking	Inclusive
Directing	Nonconforming
Communicating	Leisure, stylistic
Soothing	Empathic
Organizing	Technical

On the basis of your EPI scores, what type of listener are you? Do you agree?

_____

_____

_____

_____

_____

_____

_____

_____

_____

_____

_____

_____

_____

_____

Exercise 11–4
Listening Quiz

On the following pages, you will find three tests in which you will get the opportunity to rate yourself as a listener. There are no correct or incorrect answers. Your responses, however, will extend your understanding of yourself as a listener. This series of quizzes is provided for you courtesy of UNISYS.

Quiz 1

A.   Place a check next to the term that best describes you as a listener.

    _____   Superior
    _____   Excellent
    _____   Above average
    _____   Average
    _____   Below average
    _____   Poor
    _____   Terrible

B.   On a scale of 0–100 (100 = highest), how would you rate yourself as a listener?

    _____

Quiz 2

How do you think the following people would rate you as a listener? (0–100)

    Your best friend _____

    Your boss _____

    A coworker _____

    Your spouse or girl/boyfriend _____

Quiz 3

As a listener, how often do you find yourself engaging in these ten bad listening habits? First, check the appropriate columns: Almost Always (AA), Usually (U), Sometimes (ST), Seldom (S), or Almost Never (AN). Then tabulate your score using the key below.

Listening Habit	AA	U	ST	S	AN
1. Calling the subject uninteresting	—	—	—	—	—
2. Criticizing the speaker's delivery or mannerisms	—	—	—	—	—
3. Getting overstimulated by something the speaker says	—	—	—	—	—
4. Listening primarily for facts	—	—	—	—	—
5. Trying to outline everything	—	—	—	—	—
6. Faking attention to the speaker	—	—	—	—	—
7. Allowing interfering distractions	—	—	—	—	—
8. Avoiding difficult material	—	—	—	—	—
9. Letting emotion-laden words arouse personal antagonism	—	—	—	—	—
10. Wasting the advantage of thought speed (daydreaming)	—	—	—	—	—

Key: For every "AA" checked, give yourself a score of 2.
For every "U" checked, give yourself a score of 4.
For every "ST" checked, give yourself a score of 6.
For every "S" checked, give yourself a score of 8.
For every "AN" checked, give yourself a score of 10.

TOTAL SCORE _____

PROFILE ANALYSIS

Quiz 1

A. Eighty-five percent of all listeners questioned rated themselves as Average or less. Fewer than 5% rated themselves as Superior or Excellent.

B. On the 0–100 scale, the extreme range is 10–90, the general range is 35–85, and the average rating is 55.

Quiz 2

When comparing the listening self-ratings and projected ratings of others, most respondents believe that their best friend would rate them highest as a listener and that this rating would be higher than the one they gave themselves in Quiz 1.

How come? We can only guess that best friend status is such an intimate, special kind of relationship that you can't imagine it ever happening unless you were a good listener. If you weren't, you and he or she wouldn't be best friends to begin with.

Going down the list, people who take this test usually think their bosses would rate them higher than they rated themselves. Now part of that is probably wishful thinking. And part of it is true. We do tend to listen to our bosses better—whether it's out of respect or fear or whatever doesn't matter. The grades for coworker work out to be just the same as the listener rated him/herself—that 55 figure again.

But when you get to your spouse or boy/girlfriend, something really dramatic happens. The score here is significantly lower than the 55 average that previous profile takers gave themselves. And what's interesting is that the figure goes steadily downhill. Newlyweds tend to rate their spouse at the same high level as their best friend, but as the marriage goes on, the rating falls. So in a household where the couple has been married 50 years, there could be a lot of talk, but maybe nobody is really listening.

Quiz 3

The average score is a 62 which is 7 points higher than the average test taker gave him/herself in Quiz 1. This suggests that when listening is broken down into specific areas of competence, we rate ourselves better than we do when listening is considered only as a generality. Of course, the best way to discover how well you listen is to ask the people to whom you listen most frequently, such as your boss, spouse, and best friend. They'll give you an earful.

Exercise 11–5
Readability

It is important for a piece of writing to be written at a level that can be understood by the people who will read it. This exercise provides you with an opportunity to use the Fry Readability Graph to determine the reading level of any material.

Below, is a sample of writing. Use the instructions found in your text to count the number of sentences and syllables in the writing sample. Once you have obtained these numbers, use the Fry Readability Graph to determine the readability level of the passage.

It is essential that all employees conduct themselves in a proper fashion, both on and off of company property. Company property includes the factory floor, the lunchroom, the parking lot, and all unpaved roads leading to the factory.

Proper conduct entails smiling at customers, not cursing, wearing conservative clothing and bathing daily. If a customer asks a question of an employee, the employee will answer the question to the best of his/her ability. Should the employee not know the answer to the inquiry, he/she will locate another employee who might know the answer to the question. Any employee found to violate any of these essential behaviors will be provided with a warning. Should another violation occur, the employee will be terminated.

Number of total words   _____

Number of sentences   _____

Number of syllables   _____

Sentences per 100 words   _____

Syllables per 100 words   _____

Readability level   _____

Notes:

_____

_____

_____

_____

_____

12 Leadership

IMAGINE A COMPANY with thousands of workers that has seen sales drop in each of the past 5 years. The president of the company steps down, and a new president is installed. Several years later, the company makes a profit, and everyone hails the new president as the reason for the improvement.

Now imagine a football team with a winning record in each of the last 10 years. The team's coach leaves for another school, and the team loses the majority of its games in the next few years.

In both of these examples, a new leader took over. In the first example, the organization became more successful; in the second example, the team went into decline. How much of the organization's performance can be attributed to the leader? If the leader *was* the major cause of the changes in performance, why was one leader successful and the other a failure? These types of questions will be addressed in this chapter. By the end of the chapter, you will

- learn what types of people become good leaders.
- understand the importance of leaders adapting their behavior to each situation.
- know what skills are essential for effective leadership.
- understand the theories of leadership.
- learn how leaders use power and influence.

To get you thinking about leadership, complete Exercise 12–1 at the end of this chapter.

An Introduction to Leadership

Many different theories about leadership have been developed over the last few decades. Although none of the theories "tells the whole story" about leadership, each has received at least some empirical support. Understanding the theories and research behind leadership is important because the theory that company executives believe about leadership will, for the most part, determine how an organization selects or develops its managers.

For example, if we believe certain people are "born to be leaders" because of their personal traits, needs, or orientation, then managers could be selected partially on the basis of their scores on certain tests. But if we believe leadership consists of specific skills or behaviors, then theoretically we should be able to train any employee to become an outstanding leader. If we believe good leadership is the result of an interaction between certain types of behaviors and particular aspects of the situation, then we might choose certain types of people to be leaders at any given time, or we might teach leaders how to adapt their behavior to meet the situation.

The following pages provide brief explanations of the most popular leadership theories. When reading about each theory, think about what the theory would imply about the selection or development of leaders for an organization. In addition, think of how you manage and the type of leader you wish to be.

Personal Characteristics Associated with Leadership

In the last 100 years, many attempts have been made to identify the personal characteristics associated with leader emergence and leader performance.

Leader Emergence

Leader emergence is the idea that people who *become* leaders possess traits or characteristics different from people who do not become leaders. That is, people who become leaders, such as Presidents George W. Bush and John Kennedy and CEOs Carly Fiorina and Michael Dell, share traits that your neighbor or a cook at McDonald's does not. If we use your school as an example, we would predict that the

What makes a good leader?

in his life. Some people consistently emerge as leaders in a variety of situations whereas others never emerge as leaders (Kenny & Zaccaro, 1983; Sabini, 1995).

Perhaps one explanation for the lack of agreement on a list of traits consistently related to leader emergence is that the motivation to lead is more complex than originally thought. In a study using a large international sample, Chan and Drasgow (2001) found that the motivation to lead has three aspects (factors): affective identity, noncalculative, and social normative motivation. People with an **affective identity motivation** become leaders because they enjoy being in charge and leading others. Of the three leadership motivation factors, people scoring high on this one tend to have the most leadership experience and are rated by others as having high leadership potential. Those with a **noncalculative motivation** seek leadership positions when they perceive that such positions will result in a personal gain. For example, becoming a leader may result in an increase in status or in pay. People with a **social normative motivation** become leaders out of a sense of duty. For example, a member of the Kiwanis Club might agree to be the next president because it is "his turn," or a faculty member might agree to chair a committee out of a sense of commitment to the university.

Individuals with high leadership motivation tend to obtain leadership experience and have confidence in their leadership skills (Chan & Drasgow, 2001). Therefore, after researching the extent to which leadership is consistent across life, it makes sense that Bruce (1997) concludes that the best way to select a chief executive officer (CEO) is to look for leadership qualities (e.g., risk taking, innovation, vision) and success early in a person's career. As support for his proposition, Bruce cites the following examples:

- Harry Gray, the former chair and CEO of United Technologies, demonstrated vision, risk taking, and innovation as early as the second job in his career.

- Ray Tower, former president of FMC Corp., went way beyond his job description as a salesperson in his first job to create a novel sales training program. Tower continued to push his idea despite upper management's initial lack of interest.

- Lee Iacocca, known for his heroics at Ford and Chrysler, pioneered the concept of new car financing. His idea of purchasing a 1956 Ford for monthly payments of $56 ("Buy a '56 for $56") moved his sales division from last in the country to first. What is most interesting about this success is that Iacocca didn't even have the authority to implement his plan—but he did it anyway.

The role of gender in leader emergence is complex. Meta-analyses indicate that men and women emerge as leaders equally often in leaderless group discussions (Benjamin, 1996), men emerge as leaders more often in short-term groups and groups carrying out tasks with

students in your student government would be different from students who do not participate in leadership activities.

Though some reviews of the literature suggest that the relationship between traits and leader emergence is not very strong (Kenny & Zaccaro, 1983; Lord, De Vader, & Alliger, 1986), a more recent review suggests that people high in openness, conscientiousness, and extraversion and low in neuroticism are more likely to emerge as leaders than their counterparts (Judge, Bono, Ilies, & Gerhardt, 2002). Other research suggests that high self-monitors (people who adapt their behavior to the social situation) emerge as leaders more often than low self-monitors (Buchanan & Foti, 1996; Day, Schleicher, Unckless, & Hiller, 2002; Kolb, 1998).

It is especially perplexing that some of the early reviews concluded that specific traits are seldom related to leader emergence because both anecdotal evidence and research suggest that leadership behavior has some stability (Law, 1996). To illustrate this point, think of a friend whom you consider to be a leader. In all probability, that person is a leader in many situations. That is, he might influence a group of friends about what movie to see, make decisions about what time everyone should meet for dinner, and "take charge" when playing sports. Conversely, you probably have a friend who has never assumed a leadership role low social interaction (Eagly & Karau, 1991), and women emerge as leaders more often in groups involving high social interaction (Eagly & Karau, 1991). Though women often emerge as leaders, historically they have been excluded from the highest levels of leadership and power in politics and business. Thus, it is said that there is a "glass ceiling" for women in leadership and management. This glass ceiling is slowly breaking as the vast majority of women leaders at the highest levels achieved their positions since 1990 (Carli & Eagly, 2001).

Leader Performance

In contrast to leader emergence, which deals with the likelihood that a person will *become* a leader, **leader performance** involves the idea that excellent leaders possess certain characteristics that poor leaders do not. For example, an excellent leader might be intelligent, assertive, friendly, and independent, whereas a poor leader might be shy, aloof, and calm. Research on the relationship between personal characteristics and leader performance has concentrated on three areas: traits, needs, and orientation.

Traits

A meta-analysis by Youngjohn (1999) found that individual difference variables were reasonably good predictors of leadership performance. More specifically, individuals who were charismatic, dominant, energetic, and high in self-monitoring (people who constantly change their behaviors to meet the demands of the situation or the person with whom they are dealing) were more effective as leaders than were people scoring lower on these four traits. In another meta-analysis, Judge, Bono, Ilies, and Gerhardt (2002) found that extraversion, openness, agreeableness, and conscientiousness were positively related to leader performance and that neuroticism was negatively related to leader performance. The meta-analysis by Youngjohn also found that management, decision-making, and oral communication skills were highly correlated with leadership effectiveness.

The concept of **self-monitoring** is especially interesting as it focuses on what leaders *do* as opposed to what they *are*. For example, a high self-monitoring leader may possess the trait of shyness and not truly want to communicate with other people. She knows, however, that talking to others is an important part of her job, so she says hello to her employees when she arrives at work, and at least once a day stops and talks with each employee. Thus, our leader has the trait of shyness but adapts her outward behavior to appear to be outgoing and confident. To determine your level of self-monitoring, complete Section A in Exercise 12–2 at the end of the chapter.

An interesting extension of the trait theory of leader performance suggests that certain traits are necessary requirements for leadership excellence but that they do not guarantee it (Simonton, 1987). Instead, leadership excellence is a function of the right person being in the right place at the right time. The fact that one person with certain traits becomes an excellent leader while another with the same traits flounders may be no more than the result of timing and chance.

For example, Lyndon Johnson and Martin Luther King, Jr. were considered successful leaders because of their strong influence on improving civil rights. Other people prior to the 1960s had the same thoughts, ambitions, and skills as King and Johnson, yet they did not become successful civil rights leaders, perhaps because the time was not right.

Needs

A personal characteristic that has received some support pertains to a leader's need for power, achievement, and affiliation. Research by McClelland and Burnham (1976) and McClelland and Boyatzis (1982) demonstrates that high-performance managers have a **leadership motive pattern**, which is a high need for power and a low need for affiliation. The need is not for personal power but for organizational power.

This pattern of needs is thought to be important because it implies that an effective leader should be concerned more with results than with being liked. Leaders who need to be liked by their subordinates will have a tough time making decisions. A decision to make employees work overtime, for example, may be necessary for the organization's survival, but it will probably be unpopular with employees. Leaders with high affiliation needs may decide that being liked is more important than being successful, causing conflict with their decision.

This theory would also explain why internal promotions often do not work. Consider, for example, a person who worked for 6 years as a loan officer. He and 10 coworkers often went drinking together after work and went away on weekends. One day he was promoted to manager, and he had to lead the same people with whom he had been friends. The friendships and his need to be liked hindered the new manager when giving orders and disciplining his employees. When he tried to separate himself from his friends, he was quickly thought of as "being too good for his friends"— a tough situation with no apparent solution, according to this theory.

This does not mean a leader should not be friendly and care about subordinates. But successful leaders will not place their need to be liked above the goals of the organization. President Richard Nixon was thought to have a high need for being liked. He would often make a tough decision and then apologize for it because he wanted to be liked by both the public and the press.

Needs for power, achievement, and affiliation can be measured through various psychological tests. The most commonly used is the Thematic Apperception Test (TAT), a projective test in which a person is shown a series of pictures and asked to tell a story about what is happening in each picture. A trained psychologist then analyzes the stories, identifying the needs themes contained within them. Obviously, this technique is time-consuming and requires a great deal of training.

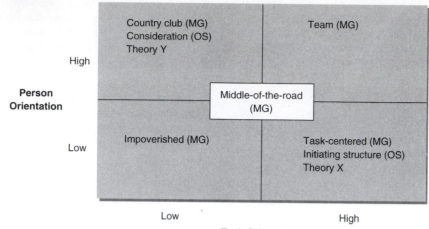

Another commonly used measure is the **Job Choice Exercise (JCE)**, developed by Stahl and Harrell (1982). With the JCE, the person reads descriptions of jobs that involve varying degrees of power, achievement, and affiliation needs, and rates how desirable she finds each particular job. These ratings are then subjected to a complicated scoring procedure that uses regression analysis to reveal scores on the three need categories. To find your own need-for-achievement, need-for-power, and need-for-affiliation levels, complete Section D of Exercise 12–2.

Another method to determine leaders' needs is to examine the themes that occur in their writing and speeches. In one interesting use of this method, it was found that Presidents Franklin Roosevelt, Kennedy, and Reagan had high needs for power; Presidents Harding, Truman, and Nixon had high needs for affiliation; and Presidents Wilson, Hoover, and Carter had high needs for achievement (Winter, 1988).

Gender

As with leader emergence, meta-analyses suggest that the role of gender in leader effectiveness is complex. When all studies are combined, men and women appear not to differ in leadership effectiveness (Eagly, Karau, & Makihijani, 1995). However, men were more effective as leaders in situations traditionally defined in masculine terms and in situations in which the majority of subordinates were men. Women were more effective as leaders in situations traditionally defined in less masculine terms. In a large-scale study of leaders, women were more likely than men to engage in behaviors associated with high-quality leadership (Eagly & Johannesen-Schmidt, 2001).

Task Versus Person Orientation

Over the last 45 years, three major schools of thought—Ohio State Studies (Fleishman, Harris, &

Burtt, 1955), Theory X (McGregor, 1960), and **Managerial Grid** (Blake & Mouton, 1984)—have postulated that differences in leader performance can be attributed to differences in the extent to which leaders are task versus person oriented. As shown in Exhibit 12.01, though the three schools of thought use different terms, they say similar things.

Person-oriented leaders, such as **Country club leaders, Theory Y leaders**, and leaders high in **consideration**, act in a warm and supportive manner and show concern for their subordinates. Person-oriented leaders believe that employees are intrinsically motivated, seek responsibility, are self-controlled, and do not necessarily dislike work. Because of these assumptions, person-oriented leaders consult their subordinates before making decisions, praise their work, ask about their families, do not look over their shoulder, and use a more "hands-off" approach to leadership. Under pressure, person-oriented leaders tend to become socially withdrawn (Bond, 1995).

Task-oriented leaders, such as **task-centered leaders, Theory X leaders**, and leaders high in **initiating structure**, define and structure their own roles and those of their subordinates to attain the group's formal goals. Task-oriented leaders see their employees as lazy, extrinsically motivated, wanting security, undisciplined, and shirking responsibility. Because of these assumptions, task-oriented leaders tend to manage or lead by giving directives, setting goals, and making decisions without consulting their subordinates. Under pressure, task-oriented leaders become anxious, defensive, and dominant (Bond, 1995). Interestingly, task-oriented leaders tend to produce humor (e.g., tell jokes and stories) whereas person-oriented leaders tend to appreciate humor (e.g., listen to others' jokes) (Philbrick, 1989). As shown in Exhibits 12.01 and 12.02, the best leaders (**team**) are both task and person oriented, whereas the worst (**impover-**

Exhibit **12.02** Consequences of leader orientation

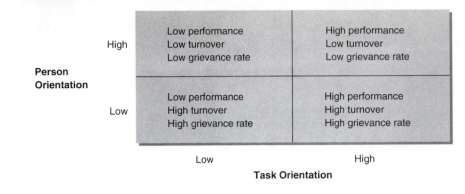

ished) are neither task nor person oriented. Some leaders (**middle-of-the-road**) have moderate amounts of both orientations.

A leader's task or person orientation can be measured by several instruments, two of which are the **Leadership Opinion Questionnaire (LOQ)** and the **Leader Behavior Description Questionnaire (LBDQ)**. The LOQ is filled out by supervisors or leaders who want to know their own behavioral style. The LBDQ is completed by subordinates to provide a picture of how they perceive their leader's behavior. A meta-analysis by Eagly and Johnson (1990) indicates that in laboratory studies women were more likely to have a person orientation and less likely to have a task orientation than were men. They did not find any such difference in studies that were conducted in actual organizations. They did, however, find small gender differences in that women were more likely to use a more participative approach and men were more likely to use a more autocratic approach.

Research on the consequences of using a task or person orientation has brought interesting findings. As shown in Exhibit 12.02, person-oriented leaders tend to have satisfied employees (Wofford & Liska, 1993), whereas task-oriented leaders tend to have productive employees. Leaders scoring high in both (called team leadership) have satisfied and productive employees, whereas leaders scoring low in both (called impoverished leadership) tend to have unhappy and unproductive employees (Fleishman & Harris, 1962; Hutchison, Valentino, & Kirkner, 1998; Korman, 1966; Pool, 1997).

These results certainly make sense, but the relationship between person and task orientation is probably more complex than was first thought. Several studies have shown that leader experience and knowledge and such external variables as time pressures and work importance tend to moderate the relationship between person-orientation scores and satisfaction and between task-orientation scores and subordinate performance. To find your own level of task orientation, complete Section C of Exercise 12–2.

Unsuccessful Leaders

In a departure from research to identify characteristics of successful leaders, Hogan (1989) attempted to identify traits of unsuccessful leaders. Hogan was interested in investigating poor leaders because, according to both empirical research and anecdotal accounts, most employees report that one of the greatest sources of stress in their jobs is their supervisors' poor performance, strange behavior, or both. This finding should come as no surprise: You can probably quickly recall many examples of poor performance or strange behavior with current or former supervisors.

Lack of Training. On the basis of years of research, Hogan (1989) concludes that poor leader behavior has three major causes. The first is a *lack of leadership training* given to supervisors. The armed forces are among the few organizations that require supervisors to complete leadership training before taking charge of groups of people. The norm for most organizations, however, is either to promote a current employee or hire a new employee and place him directly into a leadership role. If training is ever provided, it is usually after the promotion and well after the supervisor has begun supervising. The serious consequences of this lack of training can best be understood if we imagine allowing doctors to perform surgery without training or truck drivers to drive the highways without first learning how to drive.

Cognitive Deficiencies. The second cause of poor leadership stems from *cognitive deficiencies*. Hogan (1989) believes poor leaders are unable to learn from experience and are unable to think strategically (i.e., to plan ahead). They consistently make the same mistakes and do not plan ahead.

The manager of a local convenience store that I frequent is an example of a person who does not learn from his mistakes. The manager did not give employees their work schedules until 1 or 2 days before they had to work. The employees complained because the hours always changed and they could not schedule their personal, family, and social lives. But the manager continued to do it his way, and most of the employees quit. Eight years later, he still does it his way, and his employees still leave at a high rate.

Personality. The third, and perhaps most important, source of poor leadership behavior involves the *personality* of the leader. Hogan (1989) believes many unsuccessful leaders are insecure and adopt one of three personality types: the paranoid/passive-aggressive, the high-likability floater, and the narcissist.

The source of insecurity for leaders who are paranoid, passive-aggressive, or both is some incident in their life in which they felt betrayed. This *paranoid/passive-aggressive* leader has deeply rooted, but perhaps unconscious, resentment and anger. On the surface, these leaders are charming, quiet people who often compliment their subordinates and fellow workers. But they resent the successes of others and are likely to act against subordinates in a passive-aggressive manner; that is, on the surface they appear to be supportive, but at the same time they will "stab" another person in the back.

The type of leader who is insecure and seldom rocks the boat or causes trouble is known as a *high-likability floater*. This person goes along with the group, is friendly to everyone, and never challenges anyone's ideas. Thus, he travels through life with many friends and no enemies. The reason he has no enemies is because he never does anything, challenges anyone, or stands up for the rights of his employees. Such leaders will be promoted and never fired because even though they make no great performance advances, they are well liked. Their employees have high morale but show relatively low performance.

Narcissists are leaders who overcome their insecurity by overconfidence. They like to be the center of attention, promote their own accomplishments, and take most, if not all, of the credit for the successes of their group—but they avoid all blame for failure.

Interaction Between the Leader and the Situation

As already indicated, a leader's effectiveness often depends on the particular situation in which the leader finds herself. In the past few decades, several theories have emerged that have sought to explain the situational nature of leadership.

Situational Favorability

The best-known and most controversial situational theory was developed by Fred Fiedler in the mid-1960s (Fiedler, 1967). Fiedler believes an individual's leadership style is the result of a lifetime of experiences and thus is extremely difficult to change. **Fiedler's contingency model** holds that any individual's leadership style is effective only in certain situations. The way to increase leader effectiveness, then, is

to help people understand their style of leadership and learn how to manipulate a situation so that the two match. To help people understand their leadership style, Fielder developed the **Least-Preferred Coworker (LPC) Scale.**

To complete the LPC Scale, leaders identify the subordinate or employee with whom they would least want to work. Leaders then rate that person on several semantic differential scales that range from *nice* to *nasty* and from *friendly* to *unfriendly*. The higher the leaders rate their least-preferred coworker, the higher the LPC score. This score is then compared to the favorableness of the situation to determine leader effectiveness. Low-scoring LPC leaders tend to be task oriented, whereas high-scoring LPC leaders tend to be more concerned with interpersonal relations (Fiedler, 1978; Rice, 1978). High-LPC leaders would fall in the same quadrant in Exhibit 12.01 as Theory Y and Consideration leaders. Low-LPC leaders would fall in the same quadrant as Theory X and Initiating Structure leaders. To find your own LPC score, complete Section B of Exercise 12–2.

The favorableness of a situation is determined by three variables. The first is **task structuredness**. Structured tasks have goals that are clearly stated and known by group members, have only a few correct solutions to a problem, and can be completed in only a few ways. The more structured the task, the more favorable the situation.

The second variable is **leader position power**. That is, the greater the position or legitimate power of the leader, the more favorable the situation. Thus, a group or organizational setting in which there is no assigned leader is not considered to be a favorable leadership situation. The third variable is **leader–member relations**. The more that subordinates like their leader, the more favorable the situation. The leader–member relationship is considered the most important of the three variables.

As shown in Exhibit 12.03, the relationship between LPC scores and group performance is complex. Basically, low-scoring LPC leaders (those who rate their least-preferred coworker low) function best in situations that are either favorable or unfavorable, whereas high-scoring LPC leaders function best when the situation is only of moderate favorability.

In spite of psychometric problems with the LPC Scale (Kennedy, Houston, Korsgaard, & Gallo, 1987; Stewart & Latham, 1986), research generally has supported Fiedler's theory. Strube and Garcia (1981) conducted a meta-analysis of 145 independent studies that investigated Fiedler's model as well as 33 of Fiedler's own studies and conclude that the ideas were well supported by the research. Schriesheim, Tepper, and Tetrault (1994) found support for the general predictions of leader behavior but not for some of the specific predictions.

Fiedler's training program, called **Leader Match**, has also been supported by research (Strube & Garcia, 1981). This program is based on Fiedler's belief that an individual's leadership style is not easily changed. Thus, to improve their abilities, leaders learn through

Exhibit 12.03 — Relationship between LPC scores and group success

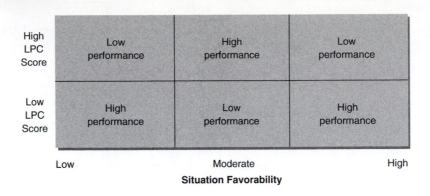

	Low	Moderate	High
High LPC Score	Low performance	High performance	Low performance
Low LPC Score	High performance	Low performance	High performance

Situation Favorability

4-hour workshops how to diagnose situations and then change these situations to fit their particular leadership styles (Csoka & Bons, 1978). Leader Match is probably the only training program in the country concentrating on changing the situation rather than the leader.

Organizational Climate

A more recent situational theory, known as **IMPACT theory**, was developed by Geier, Downey, and Johnson (1980), who believe each leader has one of six behavioral styles: *informational, magnetic, position, affiliation, coercive,* or *tactical.* Each style is only effective in a particular situation, or in what the researchers call an *organizational climate.* As shown in Exhibit 12.04, the six styles are similar to the five bases of power suggested several years ago by French and Raven (1959; also Raven, 1965).

Informational Style in a Climate of Ignorance

The leader who has an **informational style** provides information in a climate of **ignorance**, where important information is missing from the group. For example, if a car containing four college professors and a mechanic broke down on the side of the road, who would become the leader? Almost certainly it would be the mechanic because he would probably be the one who had the most knowledge or information needed to solve the problem.

For many years in the U.S. Senate, Sam Nunn was one of the most powerful and respected congressional leaders. He became powerful because of his expertise in defense matters, an area that was important and that few in Congress knew much about. Thus, Nunn used an informational style in a climate of ignorance to become a powerful leader.

Magnetic Style in a Climate of Despair

A leader with a **magnetic style** leads through energy and optimism and is effective only in a climate of **despair**, which is characterized by low morale. Ronald Reagan is perhaps the best example of a magnetic leader. As president, he was optimistic and well liked, even by people who may not have agreed with him politically. He was elected at a time when the national mood was depressed because of high inflation, high unemployment, and the Iran hostage situation. The chances of successful leadership increase in a situation of general despair when a magnetic or charismatic individual assumes control (Latham, 1983).

Position Style in a Climate of Instability

A person who uses the **position style** leads by virtue of the power inherent in that position. Such a person might lead through statements like these: "As your captain, I am ordering you to do it" or "Because I am your mother—that's why." Individuals who use a position style will be effective only in climates of **instability**. This style is especially effective during corporate mergers, particularly when people are not sure what actions to take. However, there are often questions about a leader's legitimate scope of power (Yukl, 1989).

Affiliation Style in a Climate of Anxiety

A person with an **affiliation style** leads by liking and caring about others. This style is similar to that of the person-oriented leader discussed previously. A leader using affiliation will be most effective in a climate of **anxiety** or when worry predominates. Former president Jimmy Carter provides an excellent example of the affiliation style. Carter was elected president shortly after the Watergate affair when many voters were worried that they could not trust politicians or their government. Carter campaigned successfully with statements such as "I care" and "I'm not part of that Washington crowd."

Coercive Style in a Climate of Crisis

A person using the **coercive style** leads by controlling reward and punishment and is most effective in a climate of **crisis**. Such a leader will often use statements such as "Do it or you're fired" or "If you can get the package there on time, I will have a little something for you." This style is typical in war. If soldiers disobey an

Exhibit **12.04** Comparison of IMPACT styles and bases of power

MPACT Style (Geier et al., 1980)	Base of Power (French & Raven, 1959)
Informational	Expert
Magnetic	Referent
Position	Legitimate
Affiliation	
Coercive	Coercive/Reward
Tactical	

order, an officer can have them shot. Conversely, if soldiers behave with bravery and distinction, an officer can reward them with a medal or promotion.

Mulder, de Jong, Koppelaar, and Verhage (1986) found support for the situational appropriateness of coercive styles of leadership. They studied the behavior of bankers whose leadership styles had been measured by the Influence Analysis Questionnaire. Mulder and his colleagues found that in crisis situations bankers tend to use more formal and coercive types of power than they do in noncrisis situations.

Tactical Style in a Climate of Disorganization

A leader with a **tactical style** leads through the use of strategy and is most effective in a climate of **disorganization**. A good example is a class that breaks into small groups to complete an assignment. Ideally, every student knows the material well enough to complete the assignment, but normally there is a limited amount of time and too much work to do. The person who becomes the leader is the one who is best able to organize the group.

Becoming an Effective Leader According to IMPACT Theory

If IMPACT theory is correct, people can become effective leaders by one of the four methods shown in Exhibit 12.05. The first is by finding a climate that is consistent with their behavioral style. This method, however, involves either a great deal of luck or a lot of patience as the leader must be in the right place at the right time.

In the second method, leaders change their style to meet a particular climate (Suedfeld & Rank, 1976). That is, if the climate is one of ignorance, individuals change their behavior and use information to lead. On the other hand, if the climate is one of despair, individuals become more outgoing and positive. Thus, people who are willing to adapt their behavior and who have the ability to "play" each of the six leadership styles should be effective leaders.

Although there is continual debate about whether a person can be trained to be a leader, a study by Manz and Sims (1986) suggests that leaders can indeed be

taught different styles of leadership. Manz and Sims used a behavioral modeling approach to successfully teach 40 leaders how to use positive-reward behavior, reprimand behavior, and goal-setting behavior. Thus, those who are willing to use different leadership styles can learn the necessary skills and behaviors through training programs.

The third method by which a person can become an effective leader is to change followers' perception of the climate so that the perception matches the leader's behavioral style. This tactic is common in politics, in which each candidate tries to convince the voting public that he or she is the best person for an office.

The fourth method by which a leader can become effective is by actually changing the climate itself rather than simply changing followers' perceptions of the climate. Obviously, this is difficult to do, but it is the strategy advocated in Fiedler's Leader Match training. Such a strategy is difficult but can be successful.

Subordinate Ability

House (1971) believes a leader's behavior will be accepted by subordinates only to the extent to which the behavior helps the subordinates achieve their goals. Thus, leaders will be successful only if their subordinates perceive them as working with them to meet certain goals and if those goals offer a favorable outcome for the subordinates.

Because the needs of subordinates change with each new situation, supervisors must adjust their behavior to meet the needs of their subordinates. That is, in some situations subordinates need a leader to be directive and to set goals; in others, they already know what to do and need only emotional support. Leaders who adapt their behavior to match the needs of their subordinates will be more effective than leaders who stick to one leadership style (Foster, 1999).

According to House's **path-goal theory**, a leader can adopt one of four behavioral leadership styles to handle each situation: instrumental, supportive, participative, or achievement-oriented.

Exhibit **12.05** Four leadership strategies

- Find a climate consistent with your leadership style.
- Change your leadership style to better fit the existing climate.
- Change your followers' perception of the climate.
- Change the actual climate.

The **instrumental style** calls for planning, organizing, and controlling the activities of employees. The **supportive style** leader shows concern for employees, the **participative style** leader shares information with employees and lets them participate in decision making, and the leader who uses the **achievement-oriented style** sets challenging goals, and rewards increases in performance.

Each style will only work in certain situations and depends on subordinates' abilities and the extent to which the task is structured. In general, the higher the level of subordinate ability, the less directive the leader should be. Likewise, the more unstructured the situation, the more directive the leader should be (Schriesheim & DeNisi, 1981).

House and Mitchell (1974) further advise that, to be effective, a leader should

- recognize the needs of subordinates and work to satisfy those needs.
- reward subordinates who reach their goals.
- help subordinates identify the best paths to take in reaching particular goals.
- clear those paths so that employees can reach their goals.

Path-goal theory is intuitively appealing because it gives a manager direct advice about how to behave in certain situations. Furthermore, because it is behavior based rather than trait based, the theory could be used in training. Research thus far, however, has not supported application of this theory (Hammer & Dachler, 1975; Schriesheim & Schriesheim, 1980; Wofford & Liska, 1993). If path-goal theory is to have real impact, it will need further revision.

Another theory that focuses on the relationship between leader and follower is the **situational leadership theory** developed by Hersey and Blanchard (1988). Hersey and Blanchard postulate that a leader typically uses one of four behavioral styles: delegating, directing, supporting, or coaching. Hersey and Blanchard term the most important follower characteristic *follower readiness*, or the ability and willingness to perform a particular task. The degree of follower readiness can be measured by either the manager's rating form or the self-rating form developed by Hersey and Blanchard. Scores from these forms place followers into one of four categories, or readiness (R) levels:

R1: Unable and unwilling or insecure
R2: Unable but willing or confident
R3: Able but unwilling or insecure
R4: Able and willing or confident

As shown in Exhibit 12.06, for R1 followers, the most effective leader behavior is the *directing approach*. That is, the leader directs the follower by telling him what to do and how to do it. A *coaching approach* should be used with R2 followers because they are willing to do the work but are not sure *how* to do it. Leaders using this approach explain and clarify how work should be done. R3 followers are given plenty of emotional support as well as opportunities for two-way communication. This approach is successful because these followers already know what to do but are not sure whether they *want* to do it. R4 followers are most productive and happy when a delegating leadership style is used. These followers are both willing and able to perform the task. Thus, the only real job for the leader is to delegate specific tasks to subordinates and then let them complete those tasks with minimal supervision or guidance.

Under this theory, effective leaders first diagnose the competency and motivation levels of employees for each goal or series of tasks and then adapt their leadership style to fit the employee's level. As the employee makes developmental progress, the leader changes styles and becomes less directive. It is important for leaders to discuss this strategy with each employee so that employees will understand why they are being treated a particular way (Blanchard, Zigarmi, & Zigarmi, 1985).

As with many theories of leadership, situational leadership theory has excellent intuitive appeal and has been successful in some organizational applications (Gumpert & Hambleton, 1979) but not others (Goodson, McGee, & Cashman, 1989; Norris & Vecchio, 1992). In general, however, a meta-analysis by Shilobod, McMullen, and Raymark (2003) provides support for situational leadership theory by demonstrating a moderate relationship between leader adaptability and leadership performance.

Relationships with Subordinates

Leader–member exchange (LMX) theory was developed by Dansereau, Graen, and Haga (1975) and was originally called **vertical dyad linkage (VDL) theory**.

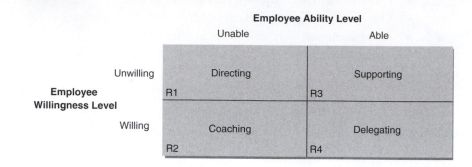

Employee Ability Level

	Unable	Able
Unwilling	Directing R1	Supporting R3
Willing	Coaching R2	Delegating R4

Employee Willingness Level

LMX theory is a unique situational theory that makes good intuitive sense. The situational theories discussed earlier concentrate on interactions between leaders and situations and between leaders and employees with differing levels of ability. LMX theory, however, concentrates on the *interactions* between leaders and subordinates. These interactions are called leader–member exchanges (LMX). The theory originally took its name from the relationship between two people (a *dyad*), the position of the leader above the subordinate (*vertical*), and their interrelated behavior (*linkage*).

LMX theory states that leaders develop different roles and relationships with different subordinates and thus act differently with different subordinates. Dansereau and his colleagues believe subordinates fall into one of two groups—the *in-group*, characterized by a high-quality relationship with the leader, or the *out-group*, characterized by a low-quality relationship with the leader.

In-group subordinates are those who have developed trusting, friendly relationships with the leader. As a result, the leader deals with in-group members by allowing them to participate in decisions and by rarely disciplining them. Out-group subordinates are treated differently from those in the in-group and are more likely to be given direct orders and to have less say about how affairs are conducted (Graen & Uhl-Bien, 1995). As one would imagine, employees with a high-quality LMX are more satisfied with their jobs, less likely to leave the organization, and perform at higher levels than do employees with a low-quality LMX (Colella & Varma, 2001; Griffeth et al., 2000). To become members of the in-group, employees often engage in such ingratiation behaviors as complimenting their leader. The extent to which these ingratiation attempts work is a function of such factors as the number of employees being supervised (Schriesheim, Castro, & Yammarino, 2000) and whether the employee is disabled (Colella & Varma, 2001).

In general, research on LMX theory has been supportive (Gerstner & Day, 1997; Scandura, Graen, & Novak, 1986; Schriesheim, Castro, & Cogliser, 1999; Vecchio, Griffeth, & Hom, 1986; Wakabayashi & Graen, 1984). Though in-group employees often receive higher performance ratings than out-group employees, the relationship between performance and LMX is complicated. Supervisors and employees often have different perceptions of the leader–member exchange, and such factors as the number of employees being supervised and impression management attempts by employees moderate the relationship between LMX and performance (Schriesheim et al, 2000).

Specific Leader Skills

Another way to think about leadership is that excellent leaders possess specific behaviors or skills that poor leaders do not. After observing thousands of leaders in a variety of situations, Yukl (1982), Carter (1952), Hemphill and Coons (1950), and Gibbs (1969) have proposed a behavioral "theory." According to these researchers, leaders do the following:

1. Initiate ideas
2. Informally interact with subordinates
3. Stand up for and support subordinates
4. Take responsibility
5. Develop a group atmosphere
6. Organize and structure work
7. Communicate formally with subordinates
8. Reward and punish subordinates
9. Set goals
10. Make decisions
11. Train and develop employee skills
12. Solve problems
13. Generate enthusiasm

In a job analysis of first-line supervisors at the Maryland Department of Transportation, Cooper, Kaufman, and Hughes (1996) found the following skills to be essential:

Adapting to the needs of subordinates is an essential component of leadership.

PhotoDisc, Inc.

- Organizing
- Analysis and decision making
- Planning
- Communication (oral and written)
- Delegation
- Work habits (high-quality work)
- Carefulness
- Interpersonal skill
- Job knowledge
- Organizational knowledge
- Toughness
- Integrity
- Development of others
- Listening

This theory is not particularly exciting and is the least described in textbooks, but it is the way leadership is most often practiced in industry. If this theory is true, then leadership and management are something learned; if the specific behaviors and skills important for effective leadership can be identified, then almost anyone can be trained to become an effective leader. There are many examples of such training programs currently in use.

The city of San Diego has its own management academy that provides interested employees with the skills necessary to become managers. On weeknights and weekends, employees learn skills such as oral communication, report writing, decision making, conflict management, and performance appraisal. After an employee is trained and tested in each of these important skill areas, he or she receives a certificate of completion. Even though graduates of the management academy are not promised managerial positions, more often than not they are the employees who are promoted.

If you have ever attended a leadership conference, you probably have noticed that the training involves specific leadership skills such as time management, goal setting, persuasion, and communication. Such an agenda typifies the idea that leadership consists of specific and learnable skills and behaviors.

Although it is beyond the scope of this chapter to discuss each of the behaviors and skills listed in Exhibit 12.07, many are covered throughout this text. A discussion of a few additional skills follows.

Leadership Through Decision Making

Decision making is a specific behavior or skill that is important for a leader to possess. Vroom and Yetton (1973), however, point out that previous research has shown that only in certain situations are decisions best made by the leader; in other situations, decisions are best made with the participation of a leader's subordinates, colleagues, or both. Because of this situational aspect to decision making, Vroom and Yetton believe leadership performance can be improved by teaching

Exhibit 12.07 Specific behaviors taught in leadership training programs

Specific Behavior	Corresponding Chapter in This Text
Communication skills	11
Conflict management	13
Decision-making skills	14
Delegation	
Discipline	7, 10
Motivation	9
Persuasion	12
Planning and organizing	
Problem solving	
Providing performance feedback	7
Public speaking, oral communication	
Reward and punishment	9
Running a meeting	
Soothing and supporting	9
Stress management	15
Team building	13, 14
Time management	15
Training and mentoring	8
Understanding people	
Writing	

leaders to become better decision makers. To aid this process, Vroom and Yetton developed a decision tree to help leaders decide when decisions should be made alone and when they should be made with the help of others. Of course, developing a chart that would tell a leader what to do in every possible situation is impossible. But the **Vroom-Yetton model** does provide a flowchart that can tell a leader what *process* to go through to make a decision in a particular situation. This theory will be discussed in further detail in Chapter 14.

Leadership Through Contact: Management by Walking Around

Management by Walking Around (MBWA) is another popular specific behavioral theory. This one holds that leaders and managers are most effective when they are out of their offices, walking around and meeting with and talking to employees and customers about their needs and progress. Many industry leaders such as the late Sam Walton of Wal-Mart have used this approach with great success. MBWA is thought to increase communication, build relationships with employees, and encourage employee participation (Amsbary & Staples, 1991; Miller, 1998).

In an interesting series of studies by Komaki and her associates (Komaki, 1986; Komaki, Zlotnick, & Jensen, 1986), the behavior of bank managers was observed to determine the differences between effective and ineffective managers. The results of the investigations indicate that the main difference between the two is that effective managers spend more time walking around and monitoring the behavior and performance of their employees. Empirical evidence thus seems to support the MBWA concept.

Leadership Through Power

Another strategy leaders often use is management by power. Power is important to a leader because as it increases so does the leader's potential to influence others (Nesler, Aguinis, Quigley, Lee, & Tedeschi, 1999). Leaders who have power are able to obtain more resources, dictate policy, and advance farther in an organization than those who have little or no power.

Earlier in this chapter, French and Raven's bases of power were alluded to in terms of their relationships to Geier et al.'s IMPACT theory. These authors (French & Raven, 1959; Raven, 1992) identified five basic types of power: expert, legitimate, reward, coercive, and referent.

Expert Power

As mentioned earlier in the chapter, in certain situations, leaders who know something useful—that is, have expert knowledge—will have power. But there are two requirements for **expert power**. First, the knowledge must be something that others in an organization need. In a university's psychology department, a researcher with an excellent grasp of statistics has power over those who do not. Similarly, a soldier who knows how to get around the military bureaucracy has more power than those who only know how to follow established channels and procedures.

Second, others must be aware that the leader knows something. Information is powerful only if other people know that the leader has it or if the leader uses it (Benzinger, 1982).

Legitimate Power

Leaders obtain **legitimate power** on the basis of their position. For example, a sergeant has power over a corporal, a vice president has power over a supervisor, and a coach has power over players on a football team. Leaders with legitimate power are best able to get employees to comply with their orders (Rahim & Afza, 1993) but have low follower satisfaction (Rahim, 1989).

Reward and Coercive Powers

Leaders also have power to the extent that they can reward and punish others. **Reward power** involves having control over both financial—salary increases, bonuses, or promotions—and nonfinancial rewards—praise or more favorable work assignments (Ward, 2001).

For a leader to have **coercive power**, it is important that others believe she is willing to use her ability to punish; she cannot maintain coercive power if employees believe she is bluffing. Punishment includes such actions as firing or not promoting and the more subtle actions of giving a "cold shoulder."

Referent Power

Another source of power for a leader may lie in the positive feelings that others hold for him. Leaders who are well liked can influence others even in the absence of reward and coercive power. Leaders can obtain such **referent power** by complimenting others, doing favors, and generally being friendly and supportive (Kipnis, Schmidt, & Wilkinson, 1980). Employees of leaders with referent power are most committed to their organizations and satisfied with their jobs (Rahim & Afza, 1993).

Leadership Through Vision: Transformational Leadership

In the past 20 years, it has become popular to separate leadership styles into two types: transactional and transformational. **Transactional leadership** consists of many of the task-oriented behaviors mentioned throughout this chapter—setting goals, monitoring performance, and providing a consequence to success or failure. **Transformational leadership** focuses on long-term goals (Bass, 1990; Howell & Avolio, 1993). Transformational leaders are often labeled as being "visionary," "charismatic," and "inspirational." They lead by developing a vision, changing organizations to fit this vision, and motivating employees to reach the vision or long-term goal. Transformational leaders are confident, have a need to influence others, and hold a strong attitude that their beliefs and ideas are correct (Bryman, 1992). They innovate, challenge the status quo, focus on people, are flexible, look to the future, carefully analyze problems, and trust their intuition (Bass, 1997; Nanus, 1992; Yukl, 1994). Transactional leaders tend to score highly on the personality traits of agreeableness, extraversion, and openness to experience (Judge & Bono, 2000).

A good example of a transformational leader is Herb Kelleher, the CEO who turned Southwest Airlines into one of the top airlines in the world. Kelleher is charismatic (on one occasion he settled a dispute by arm wrestling, on another he came to work dressed as Elvis); employee oriented (his employees come first, the customers second); visionary (his concept of a low-cost airline was designed to compete as much with ground transportation as with other airlines); and a great motivator of people.

Yukl (1994) offered the following guidelines for transformational leadership:

- Develop a clear and appealing vision.
- Develop a strategy for attaining the vision.
- Articulate and promote the vision.
- Act confident and optimistic.
- Express confidence in followers.
- Use early success in small steps to build confidence.
- Celebrate successes.
- Use dramatic, symbolic actions to emphasize key values.
- Lead by example.
- Create, modify, or eliminate such cultural forms as symbols, slogans, and ceremonies.

The research on transformational leadership has yielded positive results. Two separate meta-analyses (Fuller, Patterson, Hester, & Stringer, 1996; Lowe, Kroeck, & Sivasubramaniam, 1996) found strong correlations between transformational leadership and leader effectiveness. Further research on transformational leadership suggests that it is the most effective form of leadership, is used on every continent, and is best liked by employees (Bass, 1997).

After studying a variety of successful and unsuccessful leaders, Hunt and Laing (1997) concluded that too much effort has been expended trying to label leaders as "transformational" or "charismatic." Instead, they proposed that excellent leadership should be defined by exemplar—that is, does a leader have characteristics similar to successful leaders and dissimilar to unsuccessful leaders? On the basis of their research, Hunt and Laing hypothesize that good leaders possess five characteristics not shared by poor leaders: vision, differentiation, values, transmission, and flaws.

Vision

Consistent with the notion of transformational leadership, good leaders have a vision of where they want the organization to go, and provide direction toward that end. Hunt and Laing (1997) found that 72% of high-performing leaders were described by their subordinates as being visionary compared to only 34% of the least successful leaders.

Differentiation

Successful leaders are somehow different from their followers. In some cases, the difference might be one of personality; in others, it might be one of charisma, knowledge, or skill. Though successful leaders are somehow different from their followers, they are also similar enough to relate to and empathize with their followers. A good example of this point can be found in presidential elections. Candidates travel the country trying to relate to the people by wearing regional attire (e.g., cowboy hats in Texas, a John Deere cap in Iowa) but still trying to "look presidential."

Values

Successful leaders have strong values. For example, Wal-Mart founder Sam Walton strongly valued customer service, whereas Southwest Airlines CEO Herb Kelleher strongly values employee relations.

Transmission of Vision and Values

Successful leaders are able to communicate their vision and values to others. In a study of speeches given by U.S. presidents, it was found that presidents who communicated their messages using imagery were considered more charismatic and had higher ratings of "greatness" than were presidents who engaged in content-based rhetoric (Emrich, Brower, Feldman, & Garland, 2001).

Flaws

Interestingly, successful leaders typically have a major flaw and they know it. This flaw makes the leader more human and provides a target that followers can focus on when they are upset with the leader. A look at recent presidents shows many with flaws: Ronald Reagan tended to ramble and forget, Bill Clinton had his affairs, and George W. Bush mangled the English language. Our attention to these flaws often kept us from criticizing these presidents on more important problems (e.g., ethics, economy, foreign relations).

Leadership Through Persuasion

One skill that is commonly needed by leaders is the ability to persuade others. Supervisors often need to persuade upper-level managers that a new program will work; politicians need to persuade fellow politicians to vote a particular way; and public relations executives often want to persuade the public to change its perception of an organization or a product. We will only briefly discuss two important aspects of persuasion here—the communicator and the message.

Persuasion by Communication

Considerable research indicates that people who have certain characteristics can communicate through persuasion more easily than people who lack these characteristics. Let's look at three of them: expertise, trustworthiness, and attractiveness.

Expertise. Research has found that, in general, a leader who either has or is perceived as having **expertise** about a topic will be more persuasive than a leader who does not (Libo, 1996; Maddux & Rogers, 1980; Wilson & Sherrell, 1993). Thus, for leaders to persuade their followers, they must be the most knowledgeable about their common interest. In many high-technology fields, technical knowledge is an essential characteristic for a leader. If, however, those who are to be persuaded also are knowledgeable about a topic, the leader's expertise plays a smaller role (Rhine & Severance, 1970).

Trustworthiness. Another leader characteristic that is important in persuasion is **trustworthiness**. Used-car salespeople, for example, have difficulty persuading customers to buy cars because customers do not trust them. And in many corporations, management is distrusted by its employees and thus has trouble convincing union members, especially, that the organization does not have the money available to grant raises. Support for the importance of trust can be found in an interesting study of college basketball coaches. Dirks (2000) found a strong relationship between the level of trust players had in their coach and the success of the team.

To improve his trustworthiness, a leader can do several things. First, he can occasionally argue against what appears to be his own self-interest (Walster, Aronson, & Abrahams, 1966). For example, he can sometimes tell his employees not to work as hard, or he can disagree with other managers. In doing so, he will not appear to be one-sided.

A leader also can communicate to those he hopes to persuade not only that he is similar to them (Dembroski, Lasater, & Ramirez, 1978; Deshande & Stayman, 1994) but also that his goals are the same as theirs (Cantor, Alfonso, & Zillman, 1976). For example, a manager trying to increase his department budget can explain to the vice president that his goal includes saving the company money, but to do so he needs a larger recruiting budget so that better quality employees can be hired.

Attractiveness. Chapter 5 briefly observed that attractive people tend to receive higher interview scores than do unattractive people. **Attractiveness** has the same effect with persuasion: Attractive people are more persuasive than unattractive people (Chaiken, 1979; DeBono, 1992). This is why television commercials generally use attractive people and why attractive politicians are considered to be ideal candidates.

The Message

In addition to the leader's personal attributes, the type of message that is presented also has a role in persuasion. Research has focused on three aspects of the message: message discrepancy, one-sided versus two-sided arguments, and the use of threats.

Message Discrepancy. Suppose that you are representing a group of employees in a labor negotiation. The employees currently are paid $8 per hour, but you think they deserve $10 per hour. What strategy would best achieve an increase to $10? Would it be to ask for $20 an hour and hope that management will actually give you more than $10? Or would the best strategy be honesty—that is, ask for exactly what you want—$10 per hour? Or would the best strategy be to ask for $13 an hour so that you appear reasonable but still have room to "give in" when management offers $8.50 per hour?

According to persuasion research, the third choice would be best. Ask for more than you want and then back down during negotiations (Cialdini, 1985; Jaccard, 1981). Asking for too much, or making an argument that is too far away from that of the other side, will diminish your credibility. Asking for the amount you actually desire leaves no room for negotiation.

Can effective leadership be taught?

PhotoDisc, Inc.

One-Sided Versus Two-Sided Arguments. Another question that arises concerning the persuasive message is whether giving only one side of an argument is better than giving both sides. The answer is, "It depends." If the person being persuaded already is positive about an idea, it is usually better to argue only one side of an issue. If, however, the other person disagrees with the reasoning, it is better to argue both sides (Sawyer, 1973). When the other side is presented, the other person's perspective is acknowledged as legitimate and understood. But after the other side of the issue has been argued, it can be refuted, and the favored side can then be reargued. If you know that an opponent will bring up negative information about you or your position, it is better to bring it up yourself to "steal their thunder" (Williams, Bourgeois, & Croyle, 1993).

Threats. The threat is another method of persuasion a leader can use when appropriate. For a threat to be effective, however, the person being persuaded must actually believe it will be carried out—that is, that the consequences of not complying *are* undesirable and inevitable (Tedeschi, Bonoma, & Schlenker, 1972).

For example, a supervisor tells an employee that he will be fired if he does not work overtime. For the threat to be effective, the employee must believe the supervisor has both the authority and the willingness to fire him. Even then, the threat will be effective only if the employee values his job.

Threats certainly can be effective in persuasion, but they also can have negative consequences. Few people like being threatened, and many will resent the person who makes the threat (Heilman, 1974; Rubin & Lewecki, 1973). Some may even so react against the threat that they do the opposite of what the leader wants (Brehm, 1966).

Cultural Differences in Leadership: Project Globe

Over the past few years, an extensive international project involving approximately 150 researchers has been undertaken to study cultural differences in leadership. This endeavor, called Project GLOBE (Global Leadership and Organizational Behavior Effectiveness), has two goals: (1) discover differences and similarities in cultures and (2) determine why these differences exist (House, Javidan, Hanges, & Dorfman, 2002). Project GLOBE researchers have concluded that cultures can differ on these nine dimensions:

- Uncertainty avoidance: The extent to which a culture avoids uncertainty by using social norms and rituals
- Power distance: The extent to which power is unequally shared
- Social collectivism: The extent to which a culture encourages collective distribution of resources
- In-group collectivism: The extent to which individuals express pride in their organizations and families
- Gender egalitarianism: The extent to which a culture tries to minimize differences in gender roles and prevents discrimination
- Assertiveness: The extent to which individuals in a culture are assertive and challenging in social relationships
- Future orientation: The extent to which a culture plans for and invests in the future

Exhibit 12.08 Project GLOBE: Cultural differences in leadership

	Leadership Style Raw Scores					
	Charisma	Team	Self-Protective	Participative	Humane	Autonomous
All Countries						
Mean	5.83	5.76	3.45	5.35	4.77	3.86
Standard deviation	0.33	0.26	0.41	0.41	0.38	0.45
Latin Europe (Israel, Italy, Portugal, Spain, France, French speaking Switzerland)	5.74	5.83	3.19	5.48	4.24	3.70
Eastern Europe (Hungary, Russia, Greece, Poland, Georgia, Slovenia, Albania, Kazakhstan)	5.73	5.50	3.67	5.09	4.75	4.18
Germanic Europe (Austria, Switzerland, Netherlands, Germany)	5.93	5.62	3.03	5.85	4.71	4.16
Arab Cultures (Qatar, Morocco, Turkey, Egypt, Kuwait)	5.35	5.55	3.79	4.98	4.80	3.69
Anglo Cultures (United States, England, Australia, Canada, New Zealand, Ireland, South Africa (white sample)	6.04	5.74	3.82	5.72	5.08	3.82
Southern Asia (India, Indonesia, Philippines, Malaysia, Thailand, Iran)	5.97	5.86	3.82	5.06	5.68	3.99
Latin America (Argentina, Bolivia, Brazil, Colombia, Costa Rica, Ecuador, El Salvador, Guatemala, Mexico, Venezuela)	5.91	5.91	3.65	5.25	4.85	3.68
Sub-Saharan Africa (Namibia, Zambia, Zimbabwe, Nigeria, South Africa (black sample)	5.63	5.57	3.74	5.19	5.22	3.69
Confucian Asia (Taiwan, Singapore, Hong Kong, South Korea, China, Japan)	5.64	5.62	3.73	4.99	5.04	4.03
Nordic Europe (Denmark, Finland, Sweden)	5.88	5.76	2.77	5.64	4.59	3.97

	Leadership Style Standard Scores					
Culture Cluster	Charisma	Team	Self-Protective	Participative	Humane	Autonomous
Latin Europe	−0.27	0.27	−0.63	0.32	−1.39	−0.36
Eastern Europe	−0.30	−1.00	0.54	−0.63	−0.05	0.71
Germanic Europe	0.30	−0.54	−1.02	1.22	−0.16	0.67
Arab Cultures	−1.45	−0.81	0.83	−0.90	0.08	−0.38
Anglo Cultures	0.64	−0.08	0.90	0.90	0.82	−0.09
Southern Asia	0.42	0.38	0.90	−0.71	2.39	0.29
Latin America	0.24	0.58	0.49	−0.24	0.21	−0.40
Sub-Saharan Africa	−0.61	−0.73	0.71	−0.39	1.18	−0.38
Confucian Asia	−0.58	−0.54	0.68	−0.88	0.71	0.38
Nordic Europe	0.15	0.00	−1.66	0.71	−0.47	0.24

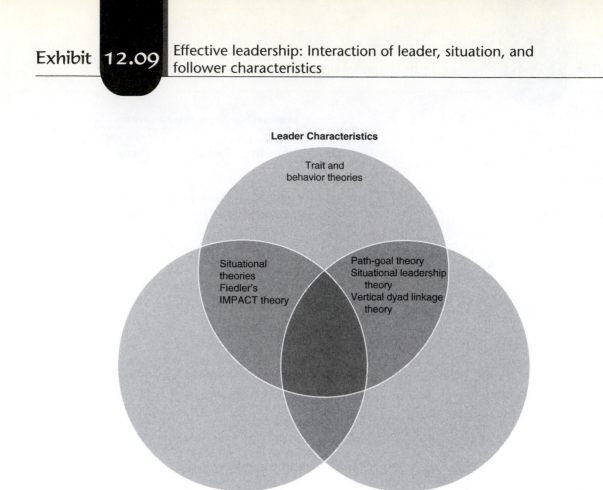

- **Performance orientation:** The extent to which a culture encourages and rewards improvement in performance
- **Humane orientation:** The extent to which a culture encourages and rewards people for being fair, caring, and giving

A comparison of the data from 61 nations revealed that each nation could be placed in one of 10 clusters (Gupta, Hanges, & Dorfman, 2002). These clusters are shown in Exhibit 12.08.

Project GLOBE researchers also determined that six main leadership styles distinguish cultures: charismatic, self-protective, humane, team oriented, participative, and autonomous (Den Hartog, House, Hanges, Ruiz-Quintanilla, & Dorfman, 1999). A *charismatic* style involves vision, inspiration, integrity, and a performance orientation. A *self-protective* style involves following procedure, emphasizing status differences, being self-centered, and saving face. A *humane* style involves being modest and helping others. A *team-oriented* style involves being collaborative, building teams, and being diplomatic. A *participative* style involves getting the opinions and help of others. An *autonomous* style involves being

independent and individualistic and making one's own decisions.

Project GLOBE researchers found that the 10 culture clusters differed on the six main leadership styles. For example, compared to other clusters, leaders from countries in the Anglo cluster are more self-protective and participative, leaders from countries in the Nordic Europe cluster are more participative and less self-protective, and leaders from the Southern Asia cluster are more humane and less participative.

Leadership: Where Are We Today?

Most of this chapter has described leadership theories. Of course, when several theories address the same topic, the question comes to mind: Which of the theories are true? The answer probably is that each is somewhat true and that the best "theory" about leadership is some combination.

As Exhibit 12.09 shows, if we combine all of the theories discussed in this chapter, leadership emerges

Exhibit 12.10 Situational leadership flowchart

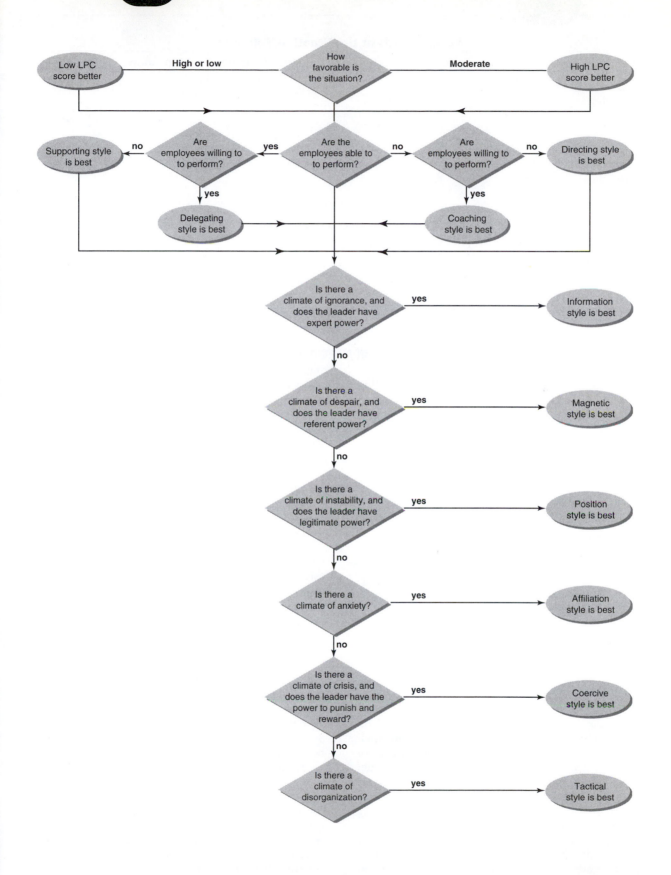

Exhibit 12.11 Effective leadership skills

Leadership Skill	Requirements of the Situation/Follower				
	Information	Direction	Empathy/Support	Motivation	Persuasion
Decision making		X			
Goal setting		X			
Persuasion	X	X		X	X
Team building			X	X	
Stress management			X		
Friendliness			X	X	
Empathy			X		
Energy				X	
Time management		X			
Technical knowledge	X				
Intelligence	X	X			

as a set of interactions: between a leader's traits and skills, between a situation's demands and characteristics, and between followers' needs and characteristics. If we begin with a leader's traits and skills, a summary of the theories would suggest that individuals would be more likely to be successful leaders if they

- have received leadership training and mastered the behaviors listed in Exhibit 12.07.
- are high self-monitors.
- are high in both task and person orientations.
- have the leadership motive pattern (high need for power, low need for affiliation).
- are intelligent.
- are emotionally stable (don't possess such problem personalities as the high-likeability floater, narcissist, or passive-aggressive personality).
- possess the skills and personality to be transformational leaders.

If individuals have these skills and traits, their leadership performance will depend on the characteristics of the situation. Thus, as shown in Exhibit 12.10, certain people will be effective leaders in certain situations when particular types of people are followers. For example, in a structured situation in which the leader has both legitimate and referent power (a highly favorable situation), a low-LPC leader will perform better than a high-LPC leader. If subordinates are unwilling and unable to perform a task, a directing leadership style will work better than a supporting style. If there is a climate of despair and the leader has referent power, a magnetic leadership style will work better than an informational style. Unfortunately, we are not yet at the stage where we can determine the exact matches that result in the best leadership for every situation. But it is probably safe to make the following assumptions.

First, because different situations require different leadership styles and skills, individuals who have a wide variety of relevant skills will be best able to be effective leaders in a larger variety of situations. That is, a person who only has excellent planning skills will be an effective leader only in situations that require planning. But a leader who has excellent skills in planning, persuasion, people, goal setting, and motivation will be able to lead in many different types of situations.

The advice that flows from this assumption is obvious. As Exhibit 12.11 shows, an individual interested in becoming an effective leader should obtain as many leadership skills as possible. By attending leadership conferences, taking college courses, and gaining a variety of experiences, a leader can gain most of these skills.

Second, because individuals have different needs and personalities, leaders who are able to adapt their interpersonal styles to fit the needs of followers will be better leaders than those who stick to just one behavioral style. It is much easier for a leader to adapt his style to fit the individual needs of his followers than for 30 people with different needs and styles to adapt their behavior to fit their leader's needs and style.

Finally, because a leader must use different skills in different situations and act differently with different followers, it is important that she be able to understand the needs of the situation, the follower, or both and then behave accordingly. Thus, leaders who accurately recognize situational and follower needs will be more effective than those who are unable to distinguish one situation from another.

Why is the study of leadership so important? Research demonstrates that leader performance affects organizational performance. In addition, when employees trust their leaders, the employees perform better, are more satisfied with their jobs, are more committed to the organization, are less likely to quit, and are more likely to engage in organizational citizenship behaviors (Dirks & Ferrin, 2002).

Chapter Summary

In this chapter you learned:

- Intelligence, interpersonal adjustment, self-monitoring, a leadership motive pattern (high power, low affiliation), and the combination of a task and person orientation are related to high levels of leadership performance.

- Leadership effectiveness is also a function of the interaction between the leader and the situation. Important situational aspects include situational favorability (Fiedler); organizational climate (IMPACT theory); subordinate ability (path-goal theory, situational leadership theory); and the relationship between leaders and their subordinates (vertical dyad linkage, LMX theory).

- Effective leaders possess specific skills such as persuasion, motivation, and decision making that ineffective leaders do not.

Critical Thinking Questions

1. Do those who seek leadership roles, those who emerge as leaders, and those who are successful leaders share similar traits?

2. Which of the situational theories seems to provide the best explanation for successful leadership?

3. Hogan identified three main reasons for unsuccessful leadership. Are there others that he did not mention?

4. Can effective leadership actually be taught?

5. How can a leader be more persuasive?

To learn more about the issues discussed in this chapter, point your browser to

http://www.infotrac-college.com/wadsworth

and enter one of these search terms:

workplace leadership

persuasion

Theory X leaders

transformational leadership

job choice exercise

organizational climate

Exercise 12–1
Thinking About Leadership

Think of the leader that you respect more than any other leader. This person can be an international, national, or local person. Describe what it is about this person that caused you to choose him/her as your top leader.

_____

_____

_____

_____

_____

_____

_____

_____

_____

_____

_____

_____

_____

_____

_____

_____

_____

_____

_____

_____

_____

Now think of the leader who is your least respected leader. Again, this person can be international, national, or local. What is it about this leader that you do not like?

_____

_____

_____

_____

_____

_____

_____

_____

_____

_____

_____

_____

_____

_____

_____

_____

_____

_____

_____

_____

_____

_____

_____

_____

_____

_____

Exercise 12–2
Understanding Your Leadership Style

The following pages contain four tests of leadership styles that are discussed in this chapter. Before reading any further in the text, follow the instructions for each of the four sections below. After you have completed the tests, continue reading the chapter.

Section A: Answer true or false for the next 18 questions.

1.	I find it hard to imitate the behavior of others.	T	F
2.	At parties and social gatherings, I do not attempt to do or say things that others will like.	T	F
3.	I can only argue for ideas that I already believe.	T	F
4.	I can make impromptu speeches even on topics about which I have almost no information.	T	F
5.	I guess I put on a show to impress or entertain people.	T	F
6.	I would probably make a good actor.	T	F
7.	In a group of people, I am rarely the center of attention.	T	F
8.	In different situations with different people, I often act like very different people.	T	F
9.	I am not particularly good at making other people like me.	T	F
10.	I am not always the person I appear to be.	T	F
11.	I would not change my opinions to please someone else or win their favor.	T	F
12.	I have considered being an entertainer.	T	F
13.	I have never been good at games like charades or improvisational acting.	T	F
14.	I have trouble changing my behavior to suit different people and different situations.	T	F
15.	At a party, I let others keep the jokes and stories going.	T	F
16.	I feel a bit awkward in company and do not show up quite as well as I should.	T	F
17.	I can look anyone in the eye and tell a lie with a straight face (if for the right end).	T	F
18.	I may deceive people by being friendly when I really dislike them.	T	F

Section B: Think of the person with whom you can work least well. He/she may be someone you work with now, or he/she may be someone you knew in the past. He/she does not have to be the person you like least well, but should be the person with whom you had the most difficulty in getting a job done. Describe below how this person appears to you by placing a check in the appropriate place on the scale.

Pleasant	8	7	6	5	4	3	2	1	Unpleasant
Friendly	8	7	6	5	4	3	2	1	Unfriendly
Rejecting	1	2	3	4	5	6	7	8	Accepting
Helpful	8	7	6	5	4	3	2	1	Unhelpful
Unenthusiastic	1	2	3	4	5	6	7	8	Enthusiastic
Tense	1	2	3	4	5	6	7	8	Relaxed
Distant	1	2	3	4	5	6	7	8	Close
Cold	1	2	3	4	5	6	7	8	Warm
Cooperative	8	7	6	5	4	3	2	1	Uncooperative
Supportive	8	7	6	5	4	3	2	1	Unsupportive
Boring	1	2	3	4	5	6	7	8	Interesting
Quarrelsome	1	2	3	4	5	6	7	8	Harmonious
Self-assured	8	7	6	5	4	3	2	1	Hesitant
Efficient	8	7	6	5	4	3	2	1	Inefficient
Gloomy	1	2	3	4	5	6	7	8	Cheerful
Open	8	7	6	5	4	3	2	1	Guarded

Section C: For each statement, circle the number corresponding to the extent to which you agree.

SD = strongly disagree
D = disagree
N = neutral
A = agree
SA = strongly agree

	SD	D	N	A	SA
1. Most employees need to be told what to do.	1	2	3	4	5
2. Most employees will take advantage of a friendly supervisor.	1	2	3	4	5
3. Most decisions should be made by management rather than by employees.	1	2	3	4	5
4. When a supervisor leaves the room, employee effort goes down.	1	2	3	4	5
5. Most employees who call in sick are probably faking their illness.	1	2	3	4	5
6. The decline in productivity is mostly due to employees not caring about their work.	1	2	3	4	5
7. If welfare and work paid the same, few people would choose to work.	1	2	3	4	5

Section D: For each item below, rate the extent to which the statement is true for you. The rating is on a 5-point scale with a rating of 1 indicating that the statement is not at all true of you and a rating of 5 indicating that the statement is very true of you.

	not true at all				very true of me
1. It is important for me to accomplish many things in life.	1	2	3	4	5
2. It is important for me to have many friends.	1	2	3	4	5
3. I like to be better than others.	1	2	3	4	5
4. I feel hurt when people don't like me.	1	2	3	4	5
5. I always try to get an "A" in every class.	1	2	3	4	5
6. Failure greatly upsets me.	1	2	3	4	5
7. I enjoy being in charge of other people.	1	2	3	4	5
8. I hate to be alone.	1	2	3	4	5
9. Awards are important to me.	1	2	3	4	5
10. I would feel uncomfortable going to a movie alone.	1	2	3	4	5
11. I am much more of a leader than a follower.	1	2	3	4	5
12. It is important for me to be in control.	1	2	3	4	5
13. I need to have close friends.	1	2	3	4	5
14. I hate having people in charge of me.	1	2	3	4	5
15. I have high standards and goals for myself.	1	2	3	4	5

Section E: To give you an idea about your IMPACT leadership styles, go back to Exercise 6-4 and get your scores for the Employee Personality Inventory. Scores on these dimensions roughly correspond with the IMPACT styles.

EPI Category	Your EPI Score	IMPACT Equivalent
Thinking	_____	Informational
Directing	_____	Position/Coercive
Communicating	_____	Magnetic
Soothing	_____	Affiliation
Organizing	_____	Tactical

Scoring and Interpreting Your Leadership Inventories

Section A

This is the Self-Monitoring Scale. To get your score:

_____ Count the number of times you chose "false" for Questions 1, 2, 3, 7, 9, 11, 13, 14, 15, & 16

_____ Count the number of times you chose "true" for Questions 4, 5, 6, 8, 10, 12, 17, & 18

Add the two numbers to get your self-monitoring score _____.

Section B

This inventory is the Least Preferred Coworker (LPC) Scale. To get your score, add the numbers below each of your checkmarks. For example, your total from the two questions below would be 10 (3 + 7). Your LPC score is _____.

Boring   —   —   ✓—   —   —   —   —   —   Interesting

     1   2   3   4   5   6   7   8

Quarrelsome   —   —   —   —   —   —   ✓—   —   Harmonious

     1   2   3   4   5   6   7   8

Section C

This inventory measures the extent to which you are a task- or person-oriented leader. To score this test, add the points from each of the numbers you circled.

Your task orientation score = _____

Section D

This inventory provides scores on need for achievement, need for affiliation, and need for power. To get your scores, add the numbers you circled for the following questions:

Need for achievement (Questions 1, 5, 6, 9, 15) _____

Need for power (Questions 3, 7, 11, 12, 14) _____

Need for affiliation (Questions 2, 4, 8, 10, 13) _____

Putting It All Together

Transfer your scores from Sections A, B, C, and D onto the chart below.

Leadership Profile

Percentile	Need for power	Need for achievement	Need for affiliation	Self-monitoring	LPC	Task orientation	Percentile
99	25	25	25	15	119	30	99
95	24	24	24	14	103	28	95
90	21	23	22	13	92	26	90
85	20		21	12	83	25	85
80	19				80	24	80
75	18	22	20	11	75		75
70		21	19	10	72	23	70
65	17				70		65
60	16		18	9	67	22	60
55		20			65	21	55
50	15	19	17	8	62		50
45				7	60	20	45
40		18	16		55		40
35			15	6	54	19	35
30	14	17	14		51	18	30
25				5	49		25
20	13	16	13		46	17	20
15	12	15	12		44	16	15
10	10	14	11	4	35	15	10
5	8	12	9	3	28	14	5

_____ _____ _____ _____ _____ _____

Transfer your scores from Section E onto the chart below.

IMPACT Leadership Profile

Percentile	Information (Thinking)	Magnetic (Communication)	Position/Coercive (Directing)	Affiliation (Soothing)	Tactical (Organizing)	Percentile
99	14	16	13	16	15	99
95	12	15	11	14	14	95
90	11	14	10	13	13	90
85	10		9	12	12	85
80	9	13	8	11	11	80
75					10	75
70		12	7	10	9	70
65						65
60	8	11		9	8	60
55			6			55
50	7	10		8	7	50
45			5			45
40		9		7		40
35	6	8			6	35
30			4	6		30
25	5	7			5	25
20		6	3	5	4	20
15		5		4		15
10	4	4	2	3	3	10
5	3	3	1	2	2	5

Information (Thinking)   Magnetic (Communication)   Position/Coercive (Directing)   Affiliation (Soothing)   Tactical (Organizing)

_____   _____   _____   _____   _____

Your Leadership Style

Are you a task- or person-oriented leader?　　　　　　　＿＿＿＿＿＿＿＿＿

Are you a high- or low-LPC leader?　　　　　　　　　　＿＿＿＿＿＿＿＿＿

Do you have the leadership motive pattern?　　　　　　　＿＿＿＿＿＿＿＿＿

Are you a high or low self-monitor?　　　　　　　　　　＿＿＿＿＿＿＿＿＿

What is your IMPACT style?　　　　　　　　　　　　　　＿＿＿＿＿＿＿＿＿

On the basis of your scores, how would you describe your leadership style? In what situations would you perform best? Worst?

_____

_____

_____

_____

_____

_____

_____

_____

_____

_____

_____

_____

_____

_____

_____

_____

_____

13 Group Behavior and Conflict

WITH FEW EXCEPTIONS, most employee behavior takes place in groups. Firefighters work together when fighting fires, managers make decisions in committee meetings, and bank tellers work together to deal with customers. Because employees tend to work in groups, it is important for a manager or a leader to understand group dynamics. This understanding is especially important in light of the increasing use of teams by organizations (Lawler, 2001). By the end of this chapter you will

- understand what constitutes a group.
- learn why people join groups.
- know how to increase group performance.
- be able to decide when groups perform better than individuals.
- understand the causes of conflict.
- know how to reduce conflict.

To get you thinking about group dynamics, complete Exercise 13–1 at the end of this chapter.

Definition of a Group

We begin our discussion of group behavior by defining what constitutes a group. For a collection of people to be called a group, the following four criteria must be met (Gordon, 1998): (a) The members of the group must see themselves as a unit; (b) the group must provide rewards to its members; (c) anything that happens to one member of the group affects every other member; and (d) the members of the group must share a common goal.

Multiple Members

The first criterion is that the group must have multiple members. Obviously, one person does not constitute a group (even if he is a multiple personality). Therefore, at least two people are necessary to form a group (a person with multiple personalities would not be considered a group). Usually we refer to two people as a dyad, three people as a triad, and 4 to 20 people as a small group (Forsyth, 1998). To be considered a group, these two or more people must also see themselves as a unit. Thus, three individuals walking down the sidewalk would be considered a group only if they knew one another and were together. Eight separate customers shopping at a store would not be considered a group.

Group Rewards

The second group criterion is that membership must be rewarding for each individual in the group. In the next section we will discuss the reasons people join groups, but for now it is important to remember that people will join or form a group only if it provides some form of reward.

To demonstrate this point, imagine four students studying for an exam. If the four study in separate rooms and do not share information, they are not a group. Likewise, consider if the same four people sat at one desk in the library. If each person studies the book separately and never communicates with the other three, then the four still will not be a group because none of the individuals is rewarded by the others. But if none of the four would have studied independently otherwise, then the four students would be considered a group because being together was rewarding. Even though they did not talk with one another during their time in the library, the fact that they were together provided the structure for each of them to study.

Corresponding Effects

The third group criterion is that an event that affects one group member should affect all group members. That is, if something significant happens to one person and does not affect any of the other people gathered with her, then the collection of people cannot be considered a group. This requirement is called **corresponding effects.** For example, suppose five bank tellers work side by side, and one teller becomes ill and goes home. If the activities of the other four change as a result of one teller leaving, the five might be considered a group. But if the activities of the other four do not change after one teller leaves, then the tellers cannot be considered a group.

Common Goals

The fourth and final criterion is that all members must have a **common goal.** In the teller example, if the goal of one of the tellers is to meet only young, single customers, and the goal of another teller is to serve as many customers as possible, the tellers are not considered to be a group because they work in different ways and for different reasons.

Why do we care if a collection of people meets the technical definition of a group? The answer lies within your ability to change employee performance. Over the course of this chapter, you will learn many factors affecting group performance. If you apply what you learn, you will be effective in changing performance only if the collection of individuals is actually a *group*.

Reasons for Joining Groups

Affiliation

Affiliation involves our need to be with other people. Thus, one reason people join groups is to be near and talk to other people. Research has demonstrated that our need for affiliation is very strong. Mayo (1946), for example, found that employees at a textile plant who worked separately from other employees were not as satisfied with their jobs as were employees at the same plant who had the opportunity to work with others. Likewise, Burling, Lentz, and Wilson (1956) found that turnover rates in a hospital could be reduced by assigning maids to work in teams rather than alone.

Perhaps the most interesting demonstrations of the strength of the human affiliation need come from the writings of Schein (1956) and Naughton (1975). These researchers were interested in the reasons American prisoners of war (POWs) in World War II behaved so differently from those in the Korean and Vietnam conflicts. POWs in World War II made more escape attempts, suffered fewer deaths, and provided information less frequently to the enemy than did their counterparts in Korea and Vietnam.

Although the American public attributed the differences to a postwar decline in the American character (Hampton, Summer, & Webber, 1978), both Schein and Naughton pointed out the differences from a perspective of group dynamics. In World War II, the POWs were kept in groups that remained together for long periods of time. Thus, these men were able to receive emotional support from one another, they could work together to plan escapes, they were able to hear what

each POW said to the enemy, and they knew about and supported a strong group norm about not talking to the enemy.

In the two Asian conflicts, the situations were entirely different. Rather than living in groups, these POWs were isolated and not allowed to communicate with one another. Naughton (1975) reports that the men were so in need of contact and communication with others that they scraped their cell walls to make noise and establish contact and informal communication with one another. This behavior is similar to that reported by hostages held in Beirut and Syria.

If people are not allowed the opportunity for affiliation, they make attempts to secure at least minimal contact. When even minimal contact is not possible, morale and perhaps even the will to live are lessened. Such is the concern about the new supermaximum prisons being built for inmates who behave violently while incarcerated. In these new prisons, inmates will spend 23 hours each day alone in concrete stalls without air conditioning. There will be no books, magazines, or television, and only minimal contact with guards (Johnson, 1997). During the remaining hour each day, inmates will be placed alone in an 18- by 20-foot cage where they can pace or toss a basketball at an iron hoop. As one might imagine, prisoners' rights advocates are concerned about the long-term effects of such isolation. Similar concerns were expressed after several suspected al-Qaeda terrorists housed in Guantanamo Bay, Cuba, attempted suicide in February 2003.

Of course, people are not equal in their desire or need to affiliate with others (Ray & Hall, 1995). For example, computer programmers have lower needs and desires to affiliate than do people in many other occupations (Shneiderman, 1980). This point is especially interesting because a trend in the computer-programming industry is to place programmers and analysts in groups to debug programs and solve problems (Shneiderman, 1980). Although research is not yet available on the effects of such groupings, putting such strong individualists into groups does not sound like a promising idea. However, people with a high need for affiliation perform better in groups than alone (Klein & Pridemore, 1992). It is especially important to consider the need for affiliation and the negative consequences of isolation given such trends as having employees work from home (telecommuting) and sending employees to work in different countries (expatriates).

Identification

Another reason we join groups is our desire for **identification** with some group or cause. There are many examples of this need to identify with others. In the 1960s and 1970s, young men wore their hair long; although some thought it attractive and comfortable, many others grew long hair because it helped them identify with other males of their generation and separated them from adult males of previous generations. Many of us still know someone who wears his hair long and refers to the 1960s and 1970s, thus identifying himself with an earlier period. In the 1980s and 1990s, so-called punk and grunge styles of hair and clothes were worn by students in much the same way that long hair and tie-dyed shirts were worn by people in the 1960s. In each case, the purpose may have been separating oneself from a more conservative majority and identifying with a more liberal or radical group.

Around your school you may notice that many students wear T-shirts with logos or messages. Students wearing "U2," "Los Angeles Lakers," or "Spring Break Cancun 2003" shirts are all identifying with particular groups and thus making statements about themselves.

A study by Cialdini and his associates (1976) investigated clothing as a means of identification. At several universities, Cialdini et al. observed the number of students who wore school-related clothing such as T-shirts and sweatshirts on the Monday following a school football game. They found that following a football victory many more students wore school-related clothing than on Mondays following football losses. In a second study, Cialdini et al. also asked students who won the football game. As we might expect, when the football team won, the students answered by saying, "We won." When the team lost, the students answered by saying, "They lost." On the basis of these two studies, Cialdini called this identification process "basking in reflected glory."

Another example of the identification process comes from a major manufacturing plant in Virginia. Several months before union contract talks began, the company gave each employee several nice shirts with the company name printed on the front. The company did this because it had previously noticed that in the months before contract negotiations began, the employees began to wear more union caps and shirts. The company believed that this clothing helped increase the employees' level of identification with the union. To counter this effect, the company hoped that its shirts would influence the negotiation process. Although we cannot determine the exact effect of this strategy, that year was the only one in a decade in which union members did not strike.

Emotional Support

We also join groups to obtain emotional support. Alcoholics Anonymous, Gamblers Anonymous, and Weight Watchers are good examples of groups that provide emotional support for their members.

Assistance or Help

People often join groups to obtain assistance or help. For example, students having problems with an algebra class might form a study group.

Common Interests

People often join groups because they share a common interest (Greenberg & Baron, 1999). At school, students joining a geology club share an interest in geology, students joining a fraternity share an interest in socializing, and students joining a service club such as Circle K or Alpha Phi Omega share an interest in helping people.

It is an interesting side note that most campus clubs based on common academic interests, such as a psychology club or a Latin club, are smaller and less active than other campus groups. Apparently, college students have many needs, and common academic interests are usually not as strong as the social needs satisfied by the Greek organizations. For example, a service club on the Radford University campus was having difficulty attracting members, so several advisers suggested that it increase its number of social activities to attract people who had both community service and social needs. This slight change in activities increased membership from 15 to 45.

Common Goals

People who join political parties are examples of people in pursuit of a common goal. These people may also share common interests, but their primary purpose is to get a particular person or members of a particular party elected to office.

Physical Proximity

One especially strong reason a person might join a particular group, especially if the group is informal, is physical proximity (Forsyth, 1998). That is, people tend to form groups with people who either live or work nearby. For example, think of the intramural teams on your campus. Most teams consist of students who live in the same dorms or have classes together. At work, employees tend to form groups that consist of those who work in the same general area. And some employees seek close physical proximity to people in power, hoping they will become part of an elite group.

The "bomber wing" provides an interesting example of how physical proximity can create an unlikely group. The bomber wing is a small section of the federal maximum security prison in Florence, Colorado, whose 1999 residents included Ted Kaczynski (the Unabomber), Ramzi Yousef (World Trade Center bomber), and Timothy McVeigh (Oklahoma City bomber). Though the three only had access to one another for 2 hours a week and had to shout across the hall to communicate, they formed quite the social group. Without this proximity, it is unlikely that the three would ever have belonged to the same group (Chua-Eoan, 1999).

Assignment

In the workplace, the most common reason for joining groups is that employees are assigned to them. For example, a new employee might be assigned to a department with five other employees, all of whom are asked to work together as a team. Other examples might include employees assigned to committees or quality improvement teams.

To apply the material you just learned about why people join groups, complete Exercise 13–2 at the end of this chapter.

Factors Affecting Group Performance

Group Cohesiveness

Group cohesiveness is the extent to which group members like and trust one another. In general, the more cohesive the group, the greater its productivity (Gully, Devine, & Whitney, 1995; Mullen & Copper, 1994; Reizenstein & Burke, 1996), decision quality (Mullen, Anthony, Salas, & Driskell, 1994), member satisfaction (Brawley, Carron, & Widmeyer, 1993; Deluga & Winters, 1991), member interaction (Shaw & Shaw, 1962), and employee courtesy (Kidwell, Mossholder, & Bennett, 1997).

Group cohesion is most strongly related to increased group performance when

- group members agree with the goals of their group (Podsakoff, MacKenzie, & Ahearne, 1997).
- the group being studied is an actual working group, especially a sports team (Mullen & Copper, 1994).
- cohesion is defined as group commitment to the task rather than the extent to which group members get along or take pride in their group (Mullen & Copper, 1994).

In its 1989 strike against Pittston Coal Co., the United Mine Workers union realized the importance of cohesiveness and identification needs by adopting a unique strategy. Each union member as well as his or her family members and supportive friends wore camouflage shirts and fatigues as a sign of unity. Every time miners looked around, they saw others dressed alike. The union members thus developed a sense of unity and cohesiveness that helped them last through a lengthy strike. Groups such as the Boy Scouts and the Guardian Angels also wear uniforms to increase group cohesiveness.

But cohesiveness can also lower group performance, especially in a work setting. When employees become too cohesive, they often lose sight of organizational goals. For example, it is common for restaurant employees to put the needs of other employees above those of their customers. Similarly, police departments tend to be highly cohesive—so much so that anyone who is not a police officer is considered an outsider, which can make community relations difficult.

Although the majority of research supports the conclusion that cohesiveness results in better group performance, it is not always necessary to have cohesion to have high group performance. For example, the Oakland A's in the early 1970s and the New York Yankees in the mid-1970s were baseball teams that won championships despite constant fighting among the players.

Research has also demonstrated that employees in cohesive work groups will conform to a norm of lower production even though they are capable of higher performance (Forsyth, 1998). An excellent example of this conformity to a group norm involved the Hollywood Division of the Los Angeles Police Department in the early 1980s. Many of the division's officers and detectives were extensively involved in property crimes. They would break into various retail stores and radio that they were responding to the ringing burglar alarms. They then placed the stolen goods in their car trunks and proceeded as if they were investigating the break-ins. The officers later met at specific locations to hide and sell the stolen goods. Officers who did not participate in the crimes saw the merchandise and knew what was going on, but they did not report the offenders. Instead, they put their loyalty to their fellow officers above their loyalty to the city or the police department.

Group Homogeneity

The homogeneity of a group is the extent to which its members are similar. A **homogeneous group** contains members who are similar in some or most ways, whereas a **heterogeneous group** contains members who are more different than alike. An important question for a leader to consider when developing a group is which composition, homogeneous or heterogeneous, will lead to the best group performance. Many research studies have sought to answer this question, but only mixed results have been found, with some studies finding homogeneous groups most effective and others finding heterogeneous groups most effective.

Neufeldt, Kimbrough, and Stadelmaier (1983) sought to explain these mixed results by predicting that certain types of groups would do better with certain types of tasks. Neufeldt and his colleagues thus had homogeneous and heterogeneous groups each perform several different tasks. They expected the homogeneous groups to perform better on simple tasks and the heterogeneous groups to perform better on more complex tasks, but they found that the type of task did not moderate the relationship between group composition and performance.

Aamodt, Kimbrough, and Alexander (1983) then hypothesized that previous research yielded mixed results because the compositions of the best-performing groups were actually somewhere between completely homogeneous and completely heterogeneous. These authors labeled them **slightly heterogeneous groups.**

To test their hypothesis, Aamodt and his colleagues separated 202 NCAA Division I basketball teams into three categories based on the racial composition of the starting five players. Heterogeneous groups were teams with three whites and two blacks or three blacks and two whites (3–2), homogeneous groups had five blacks or five whites (5–0), and slightly heterogeneous groups had either four blacks and one white or four whites and one black (4–1). The study results supported the notion that slightly heterogeneous groups were superior—they won 60% of their games. Both heterogeneous and homogeneous teams won about 53% of their games (all winning percentages are above 50% because Division I teams played and usually beat many non-Division I teams).

These results were later supported by a study that divided contestants on the television game show *Family Feud* into the same three kinds of groups using gender rather than race as the variable. The results indicated that the slightly heterogeneous teams won more money than the other two group types. The slightly heterogeneous families won an average of $330, heterogeneous families won an average of $278, and homogeneous families won an average of $254. A meta-analysis by Aamodt, Freeman, and Carneal (1992) found support for the superiority of slightly heterogeneous groups.

This research appears to support the conclusion that the best working groups consist primarily of people who are similar but with a dissimilar person adding tension and a different vantage point. But it is not yet clear which variable is most important in determining group composition. For example, a group might be homogeneous in terms of race but heterogeneous in gender. Researchers have studied race, gender, personality, intelligence, attitudes, and background, but more research is needed to clarify this issue. Research does indicate, however, that homogeneous groups result in the greatest member satisfaction and the lowest amount of turnover (Aamodt, Freeman, & Carneal, 1992; Jackson et al., 1991; Nolan, Lee, & Allen, 1997).

Although group performance is best in slightly heterogeneous groups, the group member who is "different" (e.g., the only female, the only African American) may not have the same level of satisfaction as the rest of the group members.

Stability of Membership

The greater the **stability** of the group, the greater the cohesiveness. Thus, groups whose members remain in the group for long periods of time are more cohesive and perform better than groups that have high turnover. A good example again can be found on a college campus. At most colleges, fraternities and sororities usually are the most active organizations and have high levels of performance; professional clubs and honorary societies such as Psi Chi and Lambda Alpha Beta tend to be the least active. Why is this? Certainly, it cannot be the abilities of the members—honorary societies have more intelligent members than most fraternities and sororities. Instead, the answer might be in the stability of the groups. Students tend to join Greek organizations in their freshman or sophomore year, whereas students tend to join professional clubs in their junior year and honorary societies in their senior year, often to help "pad" their resume. The Greek organizations thus have more stable memberships than the other organizations.

Isolation

Physical **isolation** is another variable that tends to increase a group's cohesiveness. Groups that are isolated or located away from other groups tend to be highly cohesive. A good example is the New River Valley (Virginia) branch of the AT&T Credit Union. The credit union has 15 branches, most located within a few miles of one another and within a few miles of the main branch in Winston-Salem, North Carolina. The New River Valley branch is 100 miles from the next closest branch; physically and psychologically, the branch is isolated from the main part of the organization. The New River Valley branch, however, is the only one to have no turnover in 5 years. It also is the branch where the employees are most cohesive.

Outside Pressure

Groups who are pressured by outside forces also tend to become highly cohesive. To some degree, this response to **outside pressure** can be explained by the phenomenon of *psychological reactance* (Brehm, 1966). When we believe someone is trying to intentionally influence us to take some particular action, we often react by doing the opposite (Van Leeuwen, Frizzell, & Nail, 1987). Consider, for example, a teenaged dating couple. As the boy arrives to pick up his date, the girl's father notices the young man's beard and Harley-Davidson motorcycle and forbids his daughter to go out. Before this order, the daughter may not have been especially interested in the boy, but after being told she cannot go on the date, she reacts by liking the boy more.

An interesting example of psychological reactance comes from a study by Ruback and Juieng (1997), who observed drivers leaving their parking spots at a local mall. There were four conditions in the study. In the control condition, the researchers timed how long it took from the moment the driver opened her door to the moment she completely left the parking space when no other cars were present. In the distraction condition, they noted how much time was taken when a car drove past the parking space. In the low-intrusion condition, an experimenter pulled up next to the parking spot, indicating that she was waiting for the spot. In the high-intrusion condition, the waiting driver honked her horn. Consistent with psychological reactance, when a driver honked, it took 42.75 seconds for the parked driver to leave versus 26.47 seconds when there was no driver waiting for the spot (control) and 31.09 seconds when a car drove by (distraction).

On a larger scale, such reactions are commonly seen in labor negotiations. Company managements and unions tend to disagree with and criticize one another. But often such criticism backfires because attacking another group may serve to strengthen that group. In fact, if a company or group wants to increase the cohesiveness of its membership, it can artificially create pressure and attribute it to another group. This tactic involves building a *straw man*—an opponent who does not actually exist but to whom negative statements about the group can be charged (Schweitzer, 1979).

Exhibit 13.01 Examples of task types

Task Type	Group Activity
Additive	Typing pool
	Relay race
	Bowling team
	Car washing
Disjunctive	Problem solving
	Brainstorming
	Golf tournament
Conjunctive	Assembly line
	Hiking

Group Size

Groups are most cohesive and perform best when **group size** is small. Studies have shown that large groups have lower productivity (Mullen, Johnson, & Drake, 1987); have less coordination and lower morale (Frank & Anderson, 1971); and are less active (Indik, 1965), less cohesive (Carron, 1990), and more critical (Valacich, Dennis, & Nunamaker, 1992) than smaller groups. In fact, research suggests that groups perform best (Kaplan, 2002; Manners, 1975) and have greatest member satisfaction (Hackman & Vidmar, 1970) when they consist of approximately five members. Thus, a large organization probably works best when it is divided into smaller groups and committees and when work groups contain approximately five people.

This does not mean, however, that small groups are always best. Although small groups usually increase cohesiveness, high performance is only seen with certain types of tasks. **Additive tasks** are those for which the group's performance is equal to the sum of the performances by each group member. **Conjunctive tasks** are tasks for which the group's performance depends on the least effective group member (a chain is only as strong as its weakest link). **Disjunctive tasks** are those on which the group's performance is based on the most talented group member. Examples of the three task types are shown in Exhibit 13.01. Large groups are thought to perform best on disjunctive and additive tasks (Littlepage, 1991), whereas small groups perform best on conjunctive tasks (Frank & Anderson, 1971; Steiner, 1972).

The addition of more members has its greatest effect when the group is small. Latane (1981) first investigated this idea when he formulated **social impact theory.** Imagine that a four-person committee is studying safety problems at work. If the group is stable and cohesive, adding a fifth person may be disruptive. But in a factory of 3,000 employees, hiring one new employee is not likely to change the complexion of the company. That is why sport experts have observed that a single great player can turn around a poor basketball team—as occurred with Bill Walton and the Portland Trailblazers,

Kareem Abdul-Jabbar and the Milwaukee Bucks, Jason Kidd with the New Jersey Nets, and Alan Iverson with the Philadelphia 76ers—but not a football or baseball team.

More recent research indicates that groups working through a computer behave differently from groups working face to face. When computers are used, large groups appear to perform best and have the most satisfied members (Dennis, Valacich, & Nunamaker, 1990; Valacich, Dennis, & Connolly, 1994; Valacich, Dennis, & Nunamaker, 1992). Interestingly, when groups work via a computer, minority members are more likely to express opinions. However, these same minority members are more persuasive when the group meets face to face (McLeod, Baron, Marti, & Yoon, 1997).

Group Status

The higher the group's status, the greater its cohesiveness. This is an important point: A group can be made more cohesive by increasing **group status.** The group does not actually have to *have* high status, but it is important that its members *believe* they have high status.

Again, look around campus and notice the methods used by various groups to artificially increase their status. On our campus, one fraternity advertises itself as the "Porsche of fraternities," another claims to be the "fraternity of distinction." Of course, there is little difference between the actual status and performance of most organizations, so effective leaders try to increase the cohesiveness of group members by claiming high status—and apparently it works.

One way leaders can increase their group's status is by increasing the perception that the group is difficult to join but that, once in, members will find that the group's activities are special. In most high schools, "two-a-day" practices are typical during the week before football practice begins. During this period, each prospective team member is worked close to exhaustion. Coaches have such "hell weeks" to increase the team's status and thus its cohesion and performance. Obviously, a player cannot get into shape in a week, so the purpose of two-a-day practices is not conditioning—it is to build

Exhibit 13.02 Possible communication networks for small groups

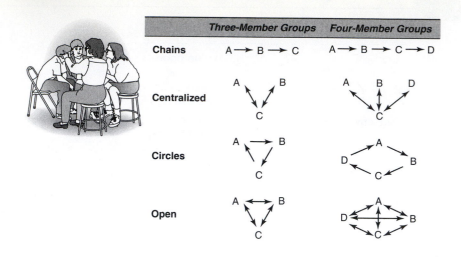

	Three-Member Groups	Four-Member Groups
Chains	A → B → C	A → B → C → D
Centralized		
Circles		
Open		

the status of the group members who survive the week. A similar approach is taken by the Marine Corps. By its tough basic training, the Corps builds the status of its enlistees so that Marines and non-Marines alike will believe that the Corps consists of just the "few, the proud."

Fraternities and sororities are also notorious for hazing during their pledge weeks. Aside from the illegality and cruelty of this behavior, hazing serves the purpose of increasing the effort required for a potential member to join, thus increasing the group's cohesiveness and status. Football players, Marines, and fraternity or sorority members are not likely to quit a group that they have worked so hard to join.

Group Ability and Confidence

Not surprisingly, groups consisting of high ability members outperform those with low ability members (Devine & Phillips, 2001). Furthermore, groups whose members believe their team can be successful both at a specific task (high team efficacy) and at tasks in general (high team potency) perform better than groups whose members aren't as confident about their probability for success (Gully, Incalcaterra, Joshi, & Beaubien, 2002).

Communication Structure

Another variable that can affect a group's performance is its **communication structure** or network. For a group to perform successfully, good communication among members is essential. As shown in Exhibit 13.02, a variety of communication networks can be used by small groups, and even more complex networks are possible with larger groups. Each network has advantages and disadvantages, but the best networks depend on the situations and goals of their groups. For example, if the goals of fraternities and singles clubs are to encourage members to get to know one another, then a centralized structure will be less conducive than

a completely open one. Conversely, if the goal of a group is to solve a problem as quickly as possible, then the centralized network will be the best structure. A good leader carefully chooses the communication network that best facilitates the goals of his group.

Group Roles

Another factor that affects the performance of a group is the extent to which its members assume different roles. For a group to be successful, its members' roles must fall into one of three categories: task oriented, maintenance oriented, and individual (Benne & Sheets, 1948). *Task-oriented roles* involve behaviors such as offering new ideas, coordinating activities, and finding new information; *maintenance-oriented roles* involve encouraging cohesiveness and participation; and *individual roles* include blocking group activities, calling attention to oneself, and avoiding group interaction. Individual roles seldom result in higher group productivity.

Group members will often naturally assume these roles on the basis of their individual personalities and experiences, although sometimes leaders must assign roles to certain individuals. For example, if a leader notices that every group member is filling a task-oriented role, he may either recruit a new group member or assign a current member to fill a maintenance role.

Presence of Others

Social Facilitation and Inhibition

In 1898, Triplett noticed that cyclists rode faster when competing against other cyclists than when competing against a clock. Intrigued by this observation, Triplett conducted a study in which children completed a task either alone or while competing against other children. As expected, Triplett found that children who worked against others completed their tasks faster than did children who worked alone.

Exhibit 13.03 Tasks affected by social facilitation and social inhibition

Skill Level	Facilitation: Increased Performance	Inhibition: Decreased Performance
Well learned	Bicycle racing	—
	Pool shooting	—
	Simple mathematics	—
	Ant nest building	—
	Cockroaches running	—
Novice	—	Pool shooting
	—	Learning nonsense syllables
	—	Completing a maze
	—	Complex mathematics
	—	Cockroaches running

Since that first study, psychologists have studied what we now call social facilitation and social inhibition. **Social facilitation** involves the positive effects of the presence of others on an individual's behavior; **social inhibition** involves the negative effects of others' presence (research examples are listed in Exhibit 13.03). Social facilitation and social inhibition can be further delineated by audience effects and coaction.

Audience Effects. The phenomenon of **audience effects** takes place when a group of people passively watches an individual. An example would be a sporting event held in an arena. The strength of the effect of having an audience present is a function of at least three factors. Latane (1981) hypothesized these factors to be an audience's size, its physical proximity to the person or group, and its status. Thus, groups are most likely to be affected by large audiences of experts who are physically close to the group (Jackson, 1986; Tanford & Penrod, 1984). Not surprisingly, the presence of an audience increases performance in extraverts but not introverts (Graydon & Murphy, 1995).

Coaction. The effect on behavior when two or more people are performing the same task in the presence of one another is called **coaction**. Examples would be two runners competing against each other without a crowd present or two mail clerks sorting envelopes in the same room. Shalley (1995) found that coaction decreased creativity and productivity. Two other studies provide interesting examples of coaction-influenced behavior. In the first study, Sommer, Wynes, and Brinkley (1992) found that when people shopped in groups they spent more time in a store and purchased more goods than when alone. In the second study, de Castro and Brewer (1992) discovered that meals eaten in large groups are 75% larger than those eaten when alone.

Explaining Social Facilitation Effects. More than 200 studies of social facilitation have indicated that performance does not always increase in the presence of others. Performance increases only when the task being performed is easy or well learned; performance decreases when the task is difficult or not well learned (Bond & Titus, 1983; Platania & Moran, 2001; Zajonc, 1965). Social facilitation and coaction effects occur not only with humans but also with cockroaches running a maze (Zajonc, Heingartner, & Herman, 1969), chickens eating food (Tolman, 1968), and ants building nests (Chen, 1937). See Exhibit 13.03 for research examples.

Although researchers have not agreed on the exact reason for these findings, four explanations have received some empirical support. The first explanation holds that the **mere presence** of others naturally produces arousal (Zajonc, 1980). This arousal, or increase in energy, helps an individual perform well-learned tasks but hinders him on poorly learned or unpracticed tasks.

The second explanation states that a coacting audience provides a means for **comparison**. If an individual is working on a task with another individual, he can directly compare his performance to the other person's (Seta, 1982). In some jobs, this comparison effect may increase competition and production quantity, whereas in other jobs comparison effects may cause employees to slow down to be in line with the working norm.

The third explanation—**evaluation apprehension**—hypothesizes that judgment by others causes the differential effects of social facilitation (Cottrell, 1972). That is, individuals are aware that the presence of others can be rewarding (e.g., when a crowd cheers) or punishing (when a crowd boos). On well-learned tasks, the individual knows that he normally performs well and thus expects a rewarding experience when in the presence of others. When the task is not well learned, however, the individual may believe she will not perform well and will be embarrassed; thus she performs even worse than if she were alone.

One example of this phenomenon was seen in an experiment by Michaels, Blommel, Brocato, Linkous, and Rowe (1982), who observed students shooting pool and found that good players increased their shot accuracy from 71% to 80% when watched by an audience, whereas poor players' accuracy decreased from 36% to 25% when they were watched. In another study, Thombs, Beck, and Mahoney (1993) found that high-intensity drinkers were more likely than low-intensity drinkers to drink in social situations.

The evaluation apprehension explanation has special application to industry and training settings. Imagine a waiter who must carry five plates of food to a table. For a new waiter, this is not a well-learned task, and in the presence of others he is likely to be anxious. When the lack of practice in carrying plates is combined with a large restaurant crowd, the chance of an accident increases. So what is the solution? The waiter should practice carrying several plates before the restaurant opens. Evaluation apprehension also occurs when performance is being monitored electronically rather than in person (Aiello & Svec, 1993; Davidson & Henderson, 2000). Thus, supervisors who remotely monitor employee performance over a computer must be aware of the potential effects on performance.

The fourth explanation proposes that the presence of others is **distracting** to the individual who is trying to perform a task (Sanders, 1981). On well-learned tasks, the individual is able to perform despite the distraction because the behaviors are almost automatic. On a novel or complicated task, however, the distraction caused by other people's presence keeps the individual from concentrating and learning the task. For example, Baxter, Manstead, Stradling, and Campbell (1990) found that drivers with passengers were less likely to signal than were drivers without anyone else in the car.

An example that demonstrates the effects emphasized by both the evaluation apprehension and distraction theories is that of coaching children in sports. In a typical Little League practice, one coach must teach an 8-year-old how to bat while 10 other children stand in the field and wait for a ball to be hit to them. Each time the child at the plate fails to hit the ball, the others tease him. After a while, the children in the field are bored and begin to throw rocks and talk with one another. What is the probability of success in teaching this child to hit under these circumstances? For the coach to be successful, he must teach the child alone and away from other children.

Social facilitation effects also have been examined in the sports world by investigating the advantage that a team might have by playing its game at home. In general, having a home crowd behind a team or an individual athlete such as a wrestler increases the probability of winning (McAndrew, 1993); this is especially true with indoor sports (Schwartz & Barsky, 1977). The effect increases immediately after a crowd cheers a play or boos a referee's decision (Greer, 1983).

Social Loafing

Whereas the social facilitation and social inhibition theory explains increases and decreases in performance when others are present and either watching the individual or working with her, the **social loafing** theory considers the effect on individual performance when people work together on a task. Social loafing was first investigated by Ringleman (reported in Moede, 1927) in a study in which subjects singly pulled as hard as possible on a rope while he measured their exerted force. Ringleman then had his subjects perform the task in pairs. He expected the force exerted by two subjects to be approximately twice that exerted by a single subject, but to his surprise he found that both subjects exerted less force than when they worked alone.

More recent research has supported the theory and has found that social loafing occurs with many tasks. For example, one study found that restaurant customers tipped about 19% of the bill when they dined alone, 16% of the bill when they dined with another person, and 13% when they dined with five others (Latane, 1981). This explains why tips, or gratuities, often are automatically added to a bill when six or more people dine at a table.

Although it is clear that social loafing occurs, especially in poor performers (Hardy & Crace, 1991), it is not clear *why* it occurs. One theory is that because group members realize their individual efforts will not be noticed there is little chance of individual reward. A second theory, called the *free-rider theory* (Kerr & Bruun, 1983), postulates that when things are going well a group member realizes that his effort is not necessary and thus does not work as hard as he would if he were alone. If this explanation is true, social loafing should occur only when a group project is going well.

The third theory, called the *sucker-effect theory* (Kerr, 1983), hypothesizes that social loafing occurs when a group member notices that other group members are not working hard and thus are "playing him for a sucker." To avoid this situation, the individual lowers his work performance to match those of the other members. This theory, however, does not explain the loafing of other members.

Social loafing is an important variable to keep in mind; having employees work together on a project may not be as productive as having them work individually. Fortunately, social loafing can be reduced by identifying individual performance and providing feedback to each worker on how hard he works when rated against some goal or standard (Williams, Harkins, & Latane, 1981), explaining the link between individual effort and group performance (Shepperd & Taylor, 1999), and rewarding those who achieve (George, 1995; Shepperd, 1993). Punishing social loafers has unpredictable effects—sometimes it works, sometimes it doesn't (George, 1995; Miles & Greenberg, 1993).

Individual Dominance

Another variable that can affect group performance is **individual dominance** by a leader or single group member. If the leader or group member has an accurate solution to a problem the group is trying to solve, the group will probably perform at a high level. But if the leader or group member has an inaccurate solution, he will lead the group astray, and it will perform poorly.

Bobbie Raynes, M.S.
Virginia State Supreme Court Certified Mediator
Director of Training and Development
Personnel Research Associates, Inc.

I work for a small human resources consulting company that offers public and private organizations a variety of services, including employee selection and performance evaluation instruments, salary and compensation studies, career assessment, employee and supervisory trainings, and conflict management through mediation or conflict management workshops.

The part of my job I enjoy most is mediating workplace conflicts and teaching others how to better manage conflict. In today's business world, with all of the additional demands placed on employees and supervisors as a result of downsizing, reduced funding, and other organizational changes, conflict is inevitable. However, if these conflicts can be acknowledged and addressed quickly, it is much less likely that lawsuits will arise and more likely that employee morale and productivity will remain at an acceptable level. At least 90% of conflict situations that I have handled have been resolved through mediation.

Mediation can work for almost any type of conflict, including conflicts arising from employment issues (e.g., discrimination or sexual harassment) between employees and their supervisors, team members, and coworkers. However, for mediation to be most successful, certain criteria must be met, which include willingness from all parties to try the process, their desire to solve their problem without litigation, time to mediate (because mediation may take several days or weeks), and the perception that the mediator is impartial and the process will be confidential.

A good example of how important these criteria are involves one of my recent cases, which consisted of a team of 13 members who weren't getting along. I met individually with all 13 members

and asked about their perceptions of the problem. All but one stated that one particular team member was the source of the problem. Apparently this one member yelled a lot (they called him a "blow hard" who didn't take constructive criticism about his work performance well). Can you guess which team member didn't give this response? Of course, it was the alleged "blow hard" who was unable to see his role in the conflict. His answer instead was, "I don't know what the problem is. Everyone just seems mad at each other." After talking to him, I was sure he really didn't have a clue about the problems some of his behaviors were causing!

I asked each team member if they would like to try mediation, which meant they all had to sit down at the same table and talk about what they felt was the source of the conflict and then brainstorm some ideas on how to resolve the problem. No one wanted to sit at the same table with the problem employee. Apparently, because this team member was a physically big man with a tendency to act out, other people were intimidated by him and felt he would retaliate in some way. For that reason, mediation wasn't the best strategy because parties weren't willing to meet to discuss their problems. Instead, we conducted an all day training session, which included role plays on how to communicate to each other about perceptions of behavior. In this way, no one person was singled out, and during the role play we were able to talk about what were good communication behaviors and what kind of verbal or nonverbal communication could become a source of conflict. This gave the problem team member an opportunity to learn what behaviors he may have that were causing problems. I knew this training was successful when he spoke up after a role play and said, "Hey, I do that

sometimes. I didn't realize how intimidating that can be." You could just see the relief on the other team members' faces when he made this announcement!

In another team situation involving five school teachers, there were two main sources of conflict. The first was that their new principal was not good at directing the teachers and explaining his expectations, so they weren't sure what they were supposed to be doing. The second source was the fact that the team had a fairly new teacher, fresh out of college, who had many new and innovative ideas she had learned in school and wanted to try out. The other four teachers had been there for many years and were comfortable with what they had been doing—they weren't real receptive to any type of change!

I often see this in mediations that involve employees and organizational change. Because most of us fear the unknown that change brings, it is easier not to try anything new. The key is to talk about what fears individuals have and then try to determine if those fears are real and, if they are, how to overcome those fears.

Mediation was very successful with this group because they were all friends and wanted to preserve their relationships, they were eager and willing to try the process, and there weren't any time constraints (which means we were able to have two or three different sessions in which they were able to air their concerns and then talk about how to resolve the conflict). Two basic solutions resulted from these mediation meetings. One was that the five teachers would ask the new principal to meet with them as a group to help them develop a set of clear expectations he had of them.

The second was that they would be more open to trying new ideas any of them might have. They asked that the next time the new teacher had an idea she wanted to try that she make sure she was able to clearly tell them how to go about implementing the new idea and what role each of them would have in it.

Another good example of where mediation can be helpful is in employment issues, such as sexual harassment cases. Your text talks about the role perceptions play in causing or resolving conflict. In this particular case, a woman perceived that one of her coworkers was harassing her by patting her on the rear end whenever she did a good job. It happened several times before she went to her supervisor and said she was being sexually harassed. The supervisor talked to both parties and asked if they would be willing to mediate this conflict. They were

both willing, and I was called in as the mediator. I had the woman start the session by telling her coworker what she felt was the situation. After she talked, he simply hung his head and said, "I swear to you, I never meant anything by it. I guess I've always done that, and not just to women, but to my buddies. I never knew it bothered you. I grew up in a big family where we did that to each other all the time." In this situation, you can see that the woman's perception of being harassed was a misperception. However, just because it is a misperception doesn't mean it never should have been resolved. Probably 80% of my cases are based on misperceptions that, if not corrected, would have resulted in litigation. Once this woman was offered a safe environment in which to discuss her concerns, she was able to communicate her feelings and her desire that the behavior stop. Her

coworker apologized to her, and she thanked him for being willing to listen to her and stop his behavior. She also acknowledged that it helped her to understand why he did that behavior. Last I heard, they have remained on good terms with each other.

Being a mediator has been challenging, but rewarding. Knowing that I have been instrumental in helping people preserve their relationships and resolve their differences has made all the hard work and hours I put into training for this position worthwhile.

I have been seeing more and more human resource specialists pursue training in this area so they can better manage their organization's day-to-day conflict. If you are interested in this area, contact the National Institute for Dispute Resolution (NIDR), 1726 M Street, NW, Suite 500, Washington, DC, 20036–4502, (202) 466–4764, for general information.

For example, a study by LePine, Hollenbeck, Ilgen, and Hedlund (1997) found that a group of highly intelligent members perform poorly when their leader is not very intelligent. The same relationship was found for the personality variable of conscientiousness.

Groupthink

The term **groupthink** was coined by Janis (1972) after studying the disastrous Bay of Pigs invasion of 1961. The Bay of Pigs was the Cuban landing site for 1,400 Cuban exiles who sought to overthrow the government of Fidel Castro. The plan called for the U.S. Navy and Air Force to covertly protect the invasion force and its supply ships. The invaders, however, were met unexpectedly by 20,000 Cuban troops and were quickly killed or captured. The help promised by the U.S. government never appeared. Janis (1972) proposed the concept of groupthink to explain how some of the nation's brightest men could hatch such an ill-conceived plan.

With groupthink, members become so cohesive and likeminded that they make poor decisions despite contrary information that might reasonably lead them to another decision. Groupthink most often occurs when the group

- is cohesive (Bernthal & Insko, 1993).
- is insulated from qualified outsiders.
- has an illusion of invulnerability, infallibility, or both.
- believes it is morally superior to its adversaries.
- is under great pressure to conform (Shafer & Crichlow, 1996).
- has a leader who promotes a favorite solution.
- has gatekeepers who keep information from other group members.

Groupthink can be reduced in several ways. First, the group leader should not state his own position or beliefs until late in the decision-making process. Second, the leader should promote open discussion and encourage group members to speak. Third, a group or committee can be separated into subgroups to increase the chance of disagreement. Finally, one group member can be assigned the job of **devil's advocate**—one who questions and disagrees with the group. Though groupthink is commonly written about, a comprehensive evaluation of it by Aldag and Fuller (1993) and subsequent research by Choi and Kim (1999) has questioned its validity as a phenomenon as well as its negative effect.

Most jobs involve working in groups.

To apply what you have learned about the factors affecting group productivity, complete the Group Performance Exercise on your CD-ROM.

Individual Versus Group Performance

When several people individually work on a problem but do not interact, they are called a **nominal group.** When several individuals interact to solve a problem, they are called an **interacting group.** An important decision a leader must make is when to assign tasks to individuals, nominal groups, or interacting groups. This decision should be based on both the type of task and the outcome desired. If the *quality* of the task is most important, it should be assigned to a group or committee. Research has shown that groups generally produce higher quality results than do individuals or nominal groups (Kanekar, 1987; Martell & Borg, 1993). Group superiority in performance probably is due to the fact that a group encourages its members to work on a task more seriously, provides emotional support, and provides a broader knowledge base.

The importance of the difference between nominal and interacting groups can be found in an interesting study by Liden, Wayne, Judge, Sparrowe, Kraimer, and Franz (1999). Liden and his colleagues had managers, nominal groups of employees, and interacting groups of employees read scenarios about a group member's poor performance and then determine how the employee should be disciplined. The interacting groups and the managers decided on more severe levels of discipline than did the nominal groups.

If the task involves *creating* ideas, individuals should be asked to independently create ideas and then meet as a group. Although **brainstorming** is a commonly used technique, it is not an effective one. In brainstorming, group members are encouraged to say aloud any and all ideas that come to mind and are not allowed to comment on the ideas until all have been given. When research compares a brainstorming group's creativity with that of a single individual, the brainstorming group will almost always be more creative. However, when comparing the number and quality of ideas created by nominal groups to the quality and number of ideas created by an interacting group in a brainstorming session, the ideas of nominal groups are more creative and of higher quality than ideas of the interacting group (Diehl & Stroebe, 1987; Gratias & Hills, 1997). This difference may partially be due to interacting groups setting lower goals than individuals (Larey & Paulus, 1995).

The superiority of nominal groups over interacting groups may depend on the type of task. Brophy (1996) found nominal groups to be most effective with a single brainstorming problem and interacting groups to be most effective in complex problems. Similar results were reported by Davis and Harless (1996), who found that in complex problems groups take better advantage of feedback and learning and thus outperform nominal groups.

If the task involves *taking chances* or *being risky*, then the task should be assigned to an interacting group or committee. Although the results are somewhat mixed, research has generally shown that interacting groups make more decisions that require risk than do individuals or nominal groups (Clark, 1971; Johnson & Andrews, 1971). This increased riskiness is thought in part to be due to group polarization, the tendency for group members to shift their beliefs to a more extreme version of what they already believe individually (Greenberg & Baron, 1999). In a particularly interesting piece of research, Cromwell, Marks,

Olson, and Avary (1991) found that burglars committed more crimes when working as part of a group than when working alone.

An example of increased group riskiness comes from a brokerage firm that was interested in getting its brokers to make riskier but higher yielding investments. A consulting firm was asked to develop a way to select such brokers. Using its knowledge of group dynamics, the consulting firm told the brokerage company that it could obtain better results by having its brokers make investment decisions in groups rather than individually. Implementing this suggestion, the company later reported that its brokers were indeed making riskier investments.

Group Conflict

As discussed early in this chapter, there are many reasons for joining groups and many factors that influence group performance. When individuals work together in groups, however, there is always potential for conflict. **Conflict** is the psychological and behavioral reaction to a perception that another person is either keeping you from reaching a goal, taking away your right to behave in a particular way, or violating the expectancies of a relationship. For example, Bob might perceive that Lakisha is trying to get the promotion that is "rightfully his" (keeping him from his goal), Andrea might perceive that Jon is trying to pressure her to hire a particular applicant (taking away the right to behave in a particular way), or Carlos might perceive that when Jill goes to lunch with her male colleagues she is violating their agreement not to date other people (violation of a relationship expectation).

It is important to note that one of the key components to conflict is *perception*. For example, two people may share the same goals, but if one person perceives that their goals are different, the possibility of conflict increases. Thus, conflict is often the result of one person's misperception of another's goals, intentions, or behavior. Because conflict can often be attributed to misperceptions, an important part of conflict resolution is for each party to discuss his or her perceptions of a situation.

The level of conflict that occurs is a function of the importance of the goal, behavior, or relationship. That is, one person's behavior may force a change in another's, but if the change in behavior is not important to the individual (e.g., waiting in line for a few minutes), conflict will be less severe than in a situation in which the change is important (e.g., a promotion or a person's reputation).

Dysfunctional conflict keeps people from working together, lessens productivity, spreads to other areas, or increases turnover. Dysfunctional conflict usually occurs when one or both parties feel a loss of control due to the actions of the other party. **Functional conflict**, however, involves a moderate degree of conflict and often results in increased performance (Van Slyke, 1999). The energy resulting from moderate levels of conflict can

stimulate new ideas, increase friendly competition, and increase team effectiveness (Berglas, 1997; Jehn & Mannix, 2001; Rahim, Garrett, & Buntzman, 1992; Sessa, 1994). Furthermore, moderate conflict can reduce the risk of much larger conflicts.

As an example of these types of conflict, imagine two employees competing for a promotion. Each thinks she deserves the promotion and doesn't really like the other person. If the conflict causes the employees to withhold information from each other that is necessary for each to do her job, the conflict would be considered dysfunctional. If however, the conflict caused each person to work harder to show who is best, the conflict would be considered functional.

Types of Conflict

Interpersonal Conflict

Interpersonal conflict occurs between two individuals. In the workplace, interpersonal conflict might occur between two coworkers, a supervisor and a subordinate, an employee and a customer, or an employee and a vendor.

Individual–Group Conflict

Conflict can occur between an individual and a group just as easily as between two individuals. **Individual-group conflict** usually occurs when the individual's needs are different from the group's needs, goals, or norms. For example, a Marine might want more independence than the corps will give him, a basketball player might want to shoot when the team needs him to set picks, a faculty member might be more interested in teaching when his university wants him to publish, and a store employee might be more interested in customer relations when the store wants him to concentrate on sales.

Group–Group Conflict

The third type of conflict occurs between two or more groups. In academia, such **group–group conflict** occurs annually as departments fight for budget allocations and space. In industry, company divisions often conflict for the same reasons. A good example of group–group conflict occurred between two branches of the same bank located in the same town. The branches competed not only with other banks for customers but also with each other. To make matters worse, the two branches were to be consolidated, so their staffs were involved in even more conflict as they tried to establish who would be in charge of the new and unified branch.

Causes of Conflict

Competition for Resources

In the marketplace, when customer demand exceeds product supply, prices increase. Similarly, in groups, when demand for a resource exceeds its supply, conflict occurs. This often occurs in organizations, especially when there is not enough money, space, personnel, or

Conflict can occur when working with others.

PhotoDisc, Inc.

equipment to satisfy the needs of every person or every group (Smith & Mackie, 1999).

A good example of this cause of conflict, **competition for resources**, occurs annually when Congress decides on the nation's budget. With only limited tax revenues and many worthy programs, tough choices must be made. But often, instead of working together to solve the country's problems, our representatives come into conflict over whose favorite programs will be funded.

Another example of this competition occurs in colleges and universities across the country. There are probably few universities where parking and office spaces are not a problem. Faculty and students argue about who gets the parking places, and once that argument is settled, seniors and juniors argue over what is left.

I once belonged to an organization that initially had no conflict over resources because there were none to fight over. There were no extra offices, no equipment, and no supplies. Organization members even had to supply their own paper! After several years, however, the organization received a large amount of money and a new building with plenty of space. But as expected, conflict increased. All the employees wanted more space, their own computers, and so on. What had once been a very cohesive group was now characterized by conflict because of competition for new resources.

Task Interdependence

Another cause of conflict, **task interdependence**, comes when the performance of some group members depends on the performance of other group members (Lulofs & Cahn, 2000). For example, a group is assigned to present a research report. The person who is assigned to type the report cannot do his job unless he can read what others have written, the person assigned to write the conclusion cannot do so until others have written their sections, and no member of the group is finished until every member has completed the assigned work.

Conflict caused by task interdependence is especially likely when two groups who rely on each other have conflicting goals. For example, the production department in a factory wants to turn out a high volume of goods, whereas the quality control department wants the goods to be of high quality. Neither department can do its job without the help of the other, yet a production department with high quantity goals probably will have lower quality standards than those desired by quality control. By insisting on high quality, the quality control department is forcing the production department to slow down. When this happens, conflict is likely to occur.

Jurisdictional Ambiguity

A third cause of conflict, **jurisdictional ambiguity**, is found when geographical boundaries or lines of authority are unclear. For example, two employees might argue over whose job it is to get the mail, two supervisors might fight over who is in charge when the vice president is out of town, or two secretaries might disagree about who controls the conference room. When lines of authority are not clear, conflict is most likely to result when new situations and relationships develop (Deutsch, 1973). Thus, to some extent, turf wars can be avoided through the use of thorough job descriptions and up-to-date organizational charts.

On an international level, jurisdictional ambiguity is a cause for many wars and conflicts. For example, in the early 1990s Iraq invaded Kuwait under the pretense that Kuwait actually belonged to Iraq, and in the 1980s, England and Argentina fought over who had the right to the Falkland Islands. In cities, jurisdictional ambiguity is often a cause for gang wars.

Communication Barriers

Communication barriers are the fourth cause of conflict. The barriers to interpersonal communication can be *physical*, such as separate locations on different floors or in different buildings; *cultural*, such as different languages or different customs; or *psychological*, such as different styles or personalities. An in-depth discussion of the communication process can be found in Chapter 11.

Personality

A fifth cause of conflict is the **personalities** of the people involved in conflict. Such conflict is often the result of two incompatible personalities who must work together. For example, a person who is very quality oriented will probably have conflicts with a person who is very quantity oriented. Likewise, a "big picture" person is likely to have conflicts with a "nuts and bolts" person.

Though it is probably true that most of the conflict that can be attributed to personality is the result of incompatible personalities, it is also very true that certain people are generally more difficult to work with than others. For example, it has been suggested that people who are dogmatic and authoritarian and have low self-esteem are involved in conflict more often than open-minded people who feel good about themselves (Bramson, 1981; Brinkman & Kirschner, 1994). Little research has investigated "difficult people" who are most likely to cause conflict, but a fair amount has been written about the topic in the popular press. For example, Bernstein and Rozen (1992) describe in great detail three types of *Neanderthals at Work*—rebels, believers, and competitors—and how conflict with each can be managed.

The most commonly referred to classification of difficult people was developed by Bramson (1981) and enhanced by Brinkman and Kirschner (1994). Brinkman and Kirschner postulate that abnormally high needs for control, perfection, approval, or attention form the basis for the difficult personality.

People with high needs for control are obsessed with completing a task and take great pride in getting a job done quickly. The *Tank* gets things done quickly by giving orders, being pushy, yelling, and at times being too aggressive. The *Sniper* controls people by using sarcasm, embarrassment, and humiliation. The *Know-It-All* controls others by dominating conversations, not listening to others' ideas, and rejecting arguments counter to her position.

People with high needs for perfection are obsessed with completing a task correctly. They seldom seem satisfied with anyone or any idea. *Whiners* constantly complain about the situation but never try to change it. The *No Person* believes that nothing will ever work and thus disagrees with every suggestion or idea. The *Nothing Person* responds to difficult situations by doing and saying nothing; she simply gives up or retreats.

People with high needs for approval are obsessed with being liked. Their behavior is often centered on gaining approval rather than completing a task

correctly or quickly. The *Yes Person* agrees to everything and, as a result, often agrees to do so much that she cannot keep her commitments. The *Yes Person* seldom provides others with feedback because she is afraid of getting someone mad at her. The *Maybe Person* avoids conflicts by never taking a stand on any issue. She delays making decisions, seldom offers opinions, and seldom commits to any course of action.

People with high needs for attention are obsessed with being appreciated. They behave in a manner that will get them noticed. When she doesn't feel appreciated, the *Grenade* throws a tantrum: she yells, swears, rants, and raves. The *Friendly Sniper* gets attention by poking fun at others. Unlike the *Sniper*, the *Friendly Sniper* aims to get attention rather than control. The *Think-They-Know-It-All* exaggerates, lies, and gives unwanted advice to gain attention.

Do you recognize any of these people? A summary of how to deal with each type of difficult person can be found in Exhibit 13.04. Though early writings on difficult people suggested that their behavior is due to low self-esteem or a high need for control, a study by Raynes (2001) indicated that the cause is much more complicated. For example, Raynes found that *high* self-esteem and confidence were correlated with behaviors associated with the Think-They-Know-It-All and the No Person; the personality variable of extraversion was correlated with gossiping; and a high level of work interest was positively correlated with behaviors associated with the Yes Person, and negatively correlated with whining.

To apply what you have learned about the causes of conflict, complete Exercise 13–3 at the end of this chapter.

Conflict Styles

It is generally believed that most people have a particular style they use when faced with conflict. Although a variety of names are assigned to these styles, the consensus among experts is that there are five common styles: avoiding, accommodating, forcing, collaborating, and compromising (Wilmot & Hocker, 2001).

Avoiding Style

Employees using an **avoiding style** choose to ignore the conflict and hope it will resolve itself. When conflicts are minor and infrequent, this style may be fine, but obviously it is not the best way to handle every type of conflict. When conflict occurs, **withdrawal** from the situation is one of the easiest ways to handle it. A person can leave a difficult marriage by divorce, an employee can avoid a work conflict by quitting the organization, or a manager can avoid a turf battle by letting another manager win. Common withdrawal behaviors include avoiding the source of conflict, quitting, talking behind the other person's back, and forming alliances with others (Martin & Bergmann, 1996). Even though withdrawal can make one feel better, often it only postpones conflict rather than prevents it.

Exhibit 13.04 Types of difficult people

Type	Need	Obsession	Description	Best Way to Handle
Tank	Control	Task completion	Pushes, yells, gives orders, intimidates	Don't counterattack or offer excuses, hold your ground.
Sniper	Control	Task completion	Uses sarcasm, criticizes, humiliates others	Call them on their sarcasm and have them explain what was really behind their comment.
Know-It-All	Control	Task completion	Dominates conversations, doesn't listen	Acknowledge their knowledge, make your statements appear as if they are in agreement.
Whiner	Perfection	Task quality	Constantly complains	Focus their complaints on specifics and solutions.
No Person	Perfection	Task quality	Disagrees with everything	Don't rush them or argue; acknowledge their good intentions.
Nothing Person	Perfection	Task quality	Doesn't do anything	Be patient and ask them open-ended questions.
Yes Person	Approval	Being liked	Agrees to everything	Talk honestly and let the person know it is safe to disagree with you.
Maybe Person	Approval	Being liked	Won't commit or make a decision	Help them learn a decision-making system, and then reassure about the decisions they make.
Grenade	Attention	Being appreciated	Throws tantrums	Don't show anger, acknowledge their complaint, and give them a chance to cool down.
Friendly Sniper	Attention	Being appreciated	Uses jokes to pick on people	Give them attention when they are not making fun of you.
Think-They-Know-It-All	Attention	Being appreciated	Exaggerates, lies, gives advice	Give them attention and ask them for specifics; don't embarrass them.

An interesting form of avoidance, called **triangling**, occurs when an employee discusses the conflict with a third party, such as a friend or supervisor. In doing so, the employee hopes that the third party will talk to the second party and that the conflict will be resolved without the need for the two parties to meet (Ruzich, 1999). When triangling occurs, supervisors are advised to have the two parties meet to resolve the issue or to use a formal third-party approach such as mediation.

Accommodating Style

When a person is so intent on settling a conflict that he gives in and risks hurting himself, he has adopted the **accommodating style.** People who use this style when the stakes are high are usually viewed as cooperative but weak. I observed an example of this style at a self-

serve gas station. Two drivers parked their cars next to the same pump at roughly the same time. Both drivers got out of their cars and simultaneously reached for the only pump. Obviously, one person had to give in to avoid conflict and would have to wait 5 minutes longer than the other. Yet one driver quickly told the other to "go ahead." Why did this person so quickly accede to the other? Probably because he had an accommodating reaction to potential conflict and because, in this case, the stakes were low.

Forcing Style

A person with a **forcing style** handles conflict in a win–lose fashion and does what it takes to win, with little regard for the other person. This style is appropriate in emergencies or when there is the potential for a

Exhibit **13.05** Negotiating territory and conflict resolution

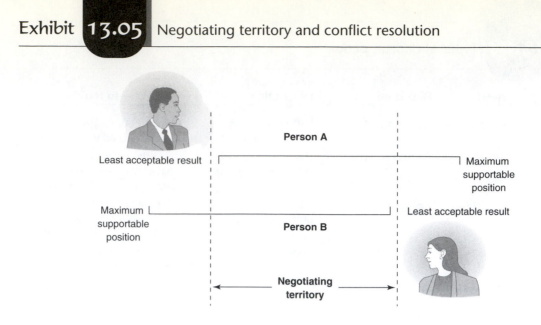

policy, ethical, or legal violation if the other party does not agree to your proposal. Though this style can be effective in winning, it also can damage relations so badly that other conflicts will result. This strategy of **winning at all costs** occurs especially when a person regards his side as correct and the other person is regarded as the enemy whose side is incorrect. This reaction often occurs when each side needs a victory to gain or retain status. Union–management conflicts provide good examples of this need for status. For a union to survive, its members must perceive it as being useful. Thus, during contract negotiations, union leadership must force management to "give in" or run the risk of losing status with its membership.

But the problem with putting status on the line is that it makes backing down to resolve a conflict very difficult. As a conflict escalates, each side "digs in" and becomes less willing to compromise. Unless one side has the resources to clearly win, the win-at-all-costs reaction is likely to prolong conflict. Thus, this strategy is only appropriate if the position holder is actually correct and if winning the conflict is more important than the probable damage to future relationships.

Collaborating Style

An individual with a **collaborating style** wants to win but also wants to see the other person win. These people seek win–win solutions—that is, ways in which both sides get what they want. Though this style is probably the best to use whenever possible, it can be time-consuming and may not be appropriate in emergencies (e.g., determining how best to treat a person having a heart attack).

Compromising Style

The final strategy is the **compromising style.** The user of this type adopts give-and-take tactics that

enable each side to get some of what it wants but not everything it wants. Most conflicts are resolved through some form of compromise so that a solution benefits both sides. Compromising usually involves a good deal of **negotiation and bargaining.** The negotiation process begins with each side making an offer that asks for much more than it really wants. For example, union leaders might demand $10 an hour while management offers $5 an hour. Each side understands what the other is doing, so the union might lower its demand to $9 and management might raise its offer to $6. This process continues until an acceptable compromise has been reached.

An *acceptable compromise* is one that falls within the settlement range for both sides (Schatzki, 1981). According to Schatzki, a settlement range is between the **least acceptable result (LAR)** and the **maximum supportable position (MSP)** for each side. The LAR is the lowest settlement that a person is willing to accept; it must be realistic and satisfy the person's actual needs. The MSP is the best possible settlement that a person can ask for and still reasonably support with facts and logic. A short-order cook's proposal for $30 an hour would not be reasonably supportable and thus would not be a proper MSP.

As shown in Exhibit 13.05, negotiations usually begin with each side offering its MSP as an opening bid. The actual negotiating territory is the area between both sides' LARs. Each side then bargains for a settlement closest to its own MSP and the other's LAR. The final settlement will be a function of the skill of each negotiator as well as time pressures. Such pressures may be exerted by customers who cannot wait for a settlement or by union members who cannot financially afford prolonged negotiations.

Seitz and Modica (1980) have suggested four indicators that tell when negotiations are coming to an end so that each side can prepare its final offer:

1. The number of counterarguments is reduced.
2. The positions of the two sides appear closer together.
3. The other side talks about final arrangements.
4. The other side appears willing to begin putting things in writing.

Although this conflict resolution strategy appears to be the best approach to take, it often is not. Sometimes, compromise results in a bad solution. For example, if Congress wants to include $100 million in the federal budget to construct a new nuclear power plant and the president wants to budget only $50 million, then the two are likely to agree on a median figure such as $75 million. But if the project cannot be completed for less than $100 million, then the compromise may waste millions of dollars that could be spent elsewhere.

Determining Conflict Styles

A person's method of dealing with conflict at work can be measured by the Rahim Organizational Conflict Inventory II (Rahim & Magner, 1995) or the Cohen Conflict Response Inventory (Cohen, 1997). To determine your own conflict style, complete Exercise 13–4 at the end of this chapter.

Resolving Conflict

Prior to Conflict Occurring

An organization should have a formal policy on how conflict is to be handled. Usually such a policy will state that employees should first try to resolve their own conflicts, and if that is not successful, they can utilize a third-party intervention. Employees should receive training on the causes of conflict, ways to prevent conflict, and strategies for resolving conflict. An example of such training occurred at the Timken plant in Alta Vista, Virginia. Each employee received 12 hours of training on how to resolve conflicts, which included role plays to practice what they learned.

When Conflict First Occurs

When conflict first occurs between coworkers or between a supervisor and a subordinate, the two parties should be encouraged to use the conflict resolution skills they learned in training to resolve the conflict on their own. These skills include expressing a desire for cooperation, offering compliments, avoiding negative interaction, emphasizing the similarities of two groups, and pointing out common goals. A key to resolving conflict is to reduce tension and increase trust between two parties. This can be accomplished by stating an intention to reduce tension, publicly announcing what steps will be taken to reduce tension, inviting the other side also to take action to reduce tension, and making sure that each initiative offered is unambiguous. By taking these steps early on, minor conflict can be resolved quickly, and serious conflict can be resolved through negotiation.

The two parties meet in a private location to address the problem—prior to this meeting the two parties should not talk to others about the problem. During the meeting, the employee who arranged the meeting explains his perception of the problem, when it occurred, and the impact it has had on that person (e.g., anxiety, anger, depression, lower productivity). For example, an employee might say, "When you made fun of my accent at lunch last week, it made me feel that you were putting me down and didn't respect me." Or an employee might tell a supervisor, "When the promotion was given to John instead of me, I thought it was because he is a male and I am a female." It is important that the employee address the behavior of the other person rather than address such aspects as the person's values, personality, and ability. For example, an employee would not want to say, "You demonstrated what a racist you are by giving the promotion to Henry instead of me." In other words, the focus should not be on whom an employee *is* but rather on what he has *done*.

The second party then responds to what was said by the first party. If the second party agrees, he might apologize and then agree to stop the behavior. If the second party doesn't agree, she would explain her perception of what happened. The two parties would then exchange views and suggestions until they have reached an agreement on how to resolve the issue. If the two can't agree, the conflict is labeled a **dispute**, and the parties should seek third-party intervention (Lulofs & Cahn, 2000).

An interesting aspect of this idea is **cooperative problem solving**. An example of this approach is when the president of an organization forms a task force or committee with representatives from all of the departments or divisions that will be affected by the solution. Together these representatives work to define the problem, identify possible solutions, and arrive at the best solution.

This process doesn't always go smoothly, but it is important that employees try to resolve their own conflicts before seeking help from a third party. Employees who resolve their own conflicts are more likely to buy into a resolution than employees who use a third party. Furthermore, bringing in a supervisor makes it more difficult for employees to admit that they have done something wrong. Of course, employees should not be forced to try to resolve all conflicts on their own. When emotions are high, alcohol or drugs are involved, or one party feels threatened by the other, a third-party intervention is in order.

Third-Party Intervention

If conflict cannot be resolved by the parties involved, it is often a good idea to seek help—that is, to ask for **third-party intervention**. This third party usually is provided through mediation, and if that doesn't work, through arbitration.

Mediation. With **mediation**, a neutral third party is asked to help both parties reach a mutually agreeable solution to the conflict. Mediators are not there to make decisions. Instead, their role is to facilitate the communication process by providing the parties with a safe and equitable venue so that they are more willing and able to reach a solution. Mediators can be employees of the organization (e.g., team leader, supervisor, HR manager), or they can be professional mediators who work with a variety of organizations. Mediators are most successful when two parties do not trust one another (Kressel & Pruitt, 1985; Ross & Wieland, 1996), and they provide the best results when both sides consider the mediator to be competent and trustworthy (Rubin & Brown, 1975). For mediation to be successful, both parties must agree that there is a conflict and that a solution can be found by working together (Van Slyke, 1997).

Mediation has been effective in resolving even the most difficult conflicts. For example, in 2000, 65% of the employment discrimination claims that were sent to mediation by the EEOC were resolved. Furthermore, the mediation process took substantially less time than did the typical lawsuit. Interestingly, 81% of charging parties were willing to accept mediation, yet only 31% of employees agreed to mediation (Janove, 2001).

According to Lovenheim (1996), mediation is better than filing a lawsuit in these situations:

- When you need to solve a problem with a person with whom you do not want to end your relationship (e.g., coworker, boss, neighbor)
- When you don't want your problems publicized in the newspaper
- When you want to save the costs associated with paying a lawyer
- When you want to settle your dispute promptly

Arbitration. With **arbitration**, a neutral third party listens to both sides' arguments and then makes a decision. Within an organization, this neutral party is often the manager of the two employees in conflict. However, if that manager just served as a mediator, then an HR director might be used.

Organizations are increasingly using outside arbitrators to handle discrimination claims by employees (Hirschman, 2001). This increase in the use of arbitrators represents organizational attempts to avoid the negative publicity associated with discrimination suits and to reduce the costs that come with lengthy litigation. In 2001, the U.S. Supreme Court ruled that employers can require employees to use arbitration rather than litigation (*Circuit City Stores v. Adams*). However, arbitration works best when it is provided as an option rather than being a requirement (Hirschman, 2001).

Though mandatory arbitration can be effective, arbitration is more expensive than mediation; so much so that mandatory arbitration policies discourage employees from making formal disputes, or cause financial hardships if they do (Armour, 2001).

Arbitration decisions can be either *binding* or *nonbinding*. If the decision is binding, the two sides have agreed to abide by the arbitrator's decision regardless of how displeased one or both sides may be with that decision. If the decision is nonbinding, then one or both sides can reject an unfavorable decision. Even though arbitration can end conflicts quickly, usually neither side is as satisfied with the outcome as both would be if they had settled the conflict themselves or used mediation. Employees are most willing to use arbitration when they perceive that a conflict was the result of intentional behavior by another, resolution of the conflict has important consequences, and the conflicting employees are of equal power (Arnold & Carnevale, 1997).

Some research suggests that performance may drop (Sommers, 1993) and turnover increase (Bretz & Thomas, 1992) as a result of an arbitrator's decision. Further, a third party may be viewed suspiciously, as having his own agenda or goals and even as being more disruptive of the relationship between the parties involved in the conflict (Rubin, 1994). As you might imagine, an individual's performance is most likely to drop after losing and most likely to improve after winning an arbitration hearing (Hauenstein & Lord, 1989).

To apply what you have learned about reactions to conflict, complete Exercises 13–5 and 13–6 at the end of this chapter. To apply what you have learned throughout the entire chapter, complete the case study found on your CD-ROM.

Chapter Summary

In this chapter you learned:

- Groups consist of multiple members who perceive themselves as a unit and share a common goal or goals.
- People join groups due to a need for affiliation, a need to identify with success, a need for emotional support, a need for assistance, common goals, physical proximity, and assignment.
- Factors that influence a group's success include its level of cohesiveness, the composition of its membership, the stability of the membership, and the group's size, status, and communication structure.
- Conflict usually results from factors such as competition for resources, task interdependence, jurisdictional ambiguity, communication barriers, and personality.
- People react to conflict by ignoring the conflict through withdrawal, trying to win at all costs, trying to persuade the other side to resolve the conflict in their favor, bargaining for an agreement, or asking for third-party help.

Critical Thinking Questions

1. How can you use the knowledge of why people join groups to increase group effectiveness?
2. When are interacting groups better than nominal groups or individuals?
3. Why does the presence of others cause increased performance in some situations and decreased performance in others?
4. When can a group be too cohesive?
5. How are mediation and arbitration different?

 To learn more about the issues discussed in this chapter, point your browser to

http://www.infotrac-college.com/wadsworth

and enter one of these search terms:

group conflict in the workplace

interpersonal conflict

group cohesiveness

social loafing

groupthink

employee mediation

Exercise 13–1
Focused Free-Write

To get you thinking about the relevance of group dynamics in your own life, think of a group that you currently belong to or recently belonged to (e.g., a committee, club, team). Describe why you joined that group and why you think the group performed as well or as poorly as it did.

_____

_____

_____

_____

_____

_____

_____

_____

_____

_____

_____

_____

_____

_____

_____

_____

_____

_____

_____

_____

_____

_____

Exercise 13–2
Increasing Group Membership

People join groups for a variety of reasons, and a leader who understands this is better able to attract members to the group. To apply what you learned, think of a group that you belong to. Why do people join this group? On the basis of the discussion in the chapter, what could you do to attract more members?

_____

_____

_____

_____

_____

_____

_____

_____

_____

_____

_____

_____

_____

_____

_____

_____

_____

_____

_____

_____

_____

Exercise 13–3
Competition and Conflict

One of the factors involved in organizational conflict is competition. This exercise provides you with an opportunity to see how complex conflict can be.

Instructions

First, pair up with another student and read the situation described here. Then individually decide what each of you will do.

Both of you are employees working for separate branches of a national bank. There are seven employees in each branch: a branch manager who manages the branch and recruits new business; a customer service representative who helps customers with loans, IRAs, and special banking problems; a teller supervisor who supervises the tellers; and four tellers.

You are the customer service representative for the Hollow Valley Branch, and your partner is the customer service representative for the Steeple Peak Branch. Both branches are in the same town but usually deal with different customers.

Both of you have heard a rumor that the two branches are going to be merged in a year, that one of the managers will be transferred to another area, and that one of the customer service representatives will be promoted to be the assistant branch manager. You both figure that the customer service representative with the highest volume of loans will be the one promoted.

Each of you must make a decision and will not be allowed to talk with the other about this decision. If both of you compete and try to increase the loan volume by going into the other's geographic area, the area manager will be angry and will promote one of the teller supervisors. If neither of you competes and if instead you both try to increase the volume of loans by staying in your own area, the most productive will be promoted and the other will receive a raise. If one of you competes and the other does not, the person who competes will be guaranteed the promotion while the other person will be demoted to teller because his/her loan volume dropped.

Without talking to the other person, decide what you are going to do, and write this choice below.

_____

_____

_____

_____

_____

_____

_____

What did the other person do? If you were the area manager, should you have seen this situation coming? What could you have done to prevent competition?

_____

_____

_____

_____

_____

_____

_____

_____

_____

_____

_____

_____

_____

_____

_____

_____

_____

_____

_____

_____

_____

_____

_____

Exercise 13–4
Cohen Conflict Response Inventory (short version)

Read the items below and circle the number under the category that indicates how much the item is like you. Answer the questions in terms of how you handle conflict situations. There are no wrong answers to these questions.

	very unlike me	unlike me	neutral	like me	very like me
1. I try to find the best solution to a problem that is acceptable to both parties.	1	2	3	4	5
2. I try to find a middle of the road solution to conflicts.	1	2	3	4	5
3. I try to keep myself out of disagreements.	1	2	3	4	5
4. I usually give in to other people's needs.	1	2	3	4	5
5. I tend to use my power or authority to get my way in a conflict situation.	1	2	3	4	5
6. I share ideas with others so that we may collaborate and come up with a final solution.	1	2	3	4	5
7. I try to find a middle ground solution to a problem.	1	2	3	4	5
8. I try to avoid argument situations.	1	2	3	4	5
9. I try to make other people happy.	1	2	3	4	5
10. I will use threats if I have to in order to get people to see it my way.	1	2	3	4	5
11. I share resources with others so that we may come up with the best possible solution.	1	2	3	4	5
12. I try to negotiate with people to find an acceptable solution.	1	2	3	4	5
13. I tend to avoid engaging in conversations about differences.	1	2	3	4	5
14. I usually go along with the solutions offered by the other party.	1	2	3	4	5
15. I often get very angry and hostile when others do not agree to my solution to a problem.	1	2	3	4	5
16. I try to investigate problems with others so we can get to the root of the problem.	1	2	3	4	5
17. I try to put all other things aside so that a solution can be reached that is acceptable to all.	1	2	3	4	5

18. I pretend or deny the fact that a conflict situation exists between myself and another.	1	2	3	4	5
19. I try to satisfy the needs of others.	1	2	3	4	5
20. I sometimes bully my way to get others to agree with me.	1	2	3	4	5
21. I try to meet the needs and goals of both parties to come up with a final solution.	1	2	3	4	5
22. I tend to give up some of my own needs to come up with a mutually acceptable decision.	1	2	3	4	5
23. I usually withdraw from a disagreement.	1	2	3	4	5
24. I feel it is important to satisfy others' needs.	1	2	3	4	5
25. I try to show my expertise and knowledge to get others to agree with me.	1	2	3	4	5

Scoring: Add the numbers you circled for each statement in each group, and record the total on the blank under Conflict Response Style.

Statement Number and Score	Conflict Response Style
1, 6, 11, 16, and 21	_____ Sage
2, 7, 12, 17, and 22	_____ Diplomat
3, 8, 13, 18, and 23	_____ Ostrich
4, 9, 14, 19, and 24	_____ Philanthropist
5, 10, 15, 20, and 25	_____ Warrior

The style under which you recorded your highest score is your preferred way of dealing with conflict. Descriptions of the style follow.

Descriptions of Conflict Response Styles

Sage Sages have a high concern for both themselves and the other party involved in a conflict situation. They use an integrating, cooperative conflict style and view conflict in a positive light. This style is solution oriented where an open exchange of information is used. It is associated with problem solving and brainstorming with others that leads to the best possible solution to a conflict. This entails a solution that is mutually beneficial to all parties. Overall, this is the best way to effectively resolve conflict.

Diplomat The Diplomat uses a compromising conflict style. This involves a give and take style to derive a mutually acceptable solution to all parties. Solutions are reached that involve the least amount of personal loss. This occurs from both parties negotiating, splitting the differences, or seeking a middle ground solution to a conflict. Most likely, the end result is not the best solution, but a solution that both parties can live with. Diplomats are concerned with getting their own needs met first.

Ostrich The Ostrich tends to avoid conflict situations at all costs and views conflict in a negative fashion. This style is used to steer clear of conflict situations or to remove oneself from an existing conflict. Ostriches tend to ignore the needs of themselves and others. Sometimes Ostriches will procrastinate when they have to deal with a conflict situation and generally won't deal with it if possible. Most likely they do so because they don't like the stress and tension that conflict creates and feel intimidated by it.

Philanthropist The Philanthropist uses an obliging or peaceful coexistence conflict style. This involves giving up one's own needs to satisfy the needs of others. This style attempts to play down differences and emphasize commonalities to satisfy the concerns of the other party. Philanthropists try to keep other people complacent and will sacrifice their own needs to achieve this. Using this style may send messages to others that they are pushovers and can be easily persuaded.

Warrior Warriors view conflict as a win–lose situation and will use a dominating, forcing style to get what they want. They view conflict as a positive challenge and an opportunity to win something for themselves. They commonly use threats, aggression, and anger to win. The other party may view Warriors negatively and have resentment and hostility toward them because their focus is so much on themselves that they totally negate the feelings of others.

Do you think this inventory accurately portrays how you handle conflict? Explain. Which style would you feel least comfortable with?

_____

_____

_____

_____

_____

_____

_____

_____

_____

_____

_____

_____

_____

_____

_____

Exercise 13–5
Reactions to Conflict

The latter part of this chapter discussed the types and causes for conflict as well as how people react to conflict. This exercise asks you to apply this material to conflicts you have had in your work experience.

Instructions

Think of the last time that you had a conflict with someone at work. Once you have this situation in mind, answer the following questions. Try to use the terms from the text in your answers.

1.   What do you think caused the conflict?

_____

_____

_____

_____

_____

_____

_____

_____

_____

2.   What type of conflict was it?

_____

_____

_____

_____

_____

_____

_____

3.   How did you react to the conflict?

_____

_____

_____

_____

_____

_____

_____

_____

_____

_____

_____

_____

_____

_____

_____

_____

_____

_____

_____

_____

Exercise 13–6
Reacting to Conflicts

The end of this chapter discussed ways in which people react to conflicts. Some of these reactions are beneficial to a person or an organization, but others can be harmful. This exercise provides you with the opportunity to practice these methods and to decide which methods are most appropriate in a given situation.

Instructions

Read the situation below and then write how you would react to the situation if you were using each of the common reactions to conflict.

Joe Hunter has been with the San Angeles Police Department for the past 6 years. After graduating second in his class at the state police academy, Hunter was hired as a patrol person with San Angeles. He quickly moved up in the ranks to corporal in his second year and sergeant in his fourth. All of the officers considered Hunter to be the best cop on the force because of his high level of intelligence as well as his uncanny ability to work with the public by anticipating problems in the community.

Everything was going along well for Sergeant Hunter until the spring of 1988. During this time, he started dating a woman that he quickly fell in love with. What he didn't know until 5 months after they began dating was that she had once been engaged to his captain.

When Hunter's captain discovered the relationship, he was furious with Hunter but knew that legally he could not control the private life of his employees. However, even though he could not directly tell Hunter what to do, he decided to make his life miserable at work. Captain Webb constantly gave Hunter the worst assignments, kept him away from the public contact that made him such a good officer, and started to lower Hunter's performance evaluations.

Hunter was frustrated at first, then hurt, and finally angry. He reached a point where one day he was so angry that he had to do something. If Hunter were to take each of the common reactions to conflict in this situation, what would he do in each case? Which would be the most appropriate?

Withdrawal

_____

_____

_____

_____

_____

_____

Win at All Costs

_____

_____

_____

_____

_____

_____

Persuasion

_____

_____

_____

_____

_____

_____

Smoothing and Conciliation

_____

_____

_____

_____

_____

_____

_____

Negotiation and Bargaining

_____

_____

_____

_____

_____

_____

_____

_____

Cooperative Problem Solving

_____

_____

_____

_____

_____

_____

_____

Third-Party Interventions

_____

_____

_____

_____

_____

_____

_____

_____

Which of these reactions to conflict do you think would be the most effective in this situation?

_____

_____

_____

_____

_____

_____

_____

_____

_____

_____

_____

_____

_____

_____

_____

_____

_____

_____

_____

_____

14

Organization Development

You learned about increasing an individual employee's skills through training in Chapter 8. In this chapter, you will learn about organization development—the process of improving organizational performance by making organization-wide changes. Though there are many aspects to organization development, this chapter will focus on four major issues: managing change, empowering employees, developing teams, and downsizing. By the end of this chapter, you will

- know how and why organizations change.
- understand how to increase employee acceptance of change.
- understand the importance of organizational culture.
- know how to handle change.
- know when empowering employees is a good idea.
- understand the levels of employee input.
- know what makes a group a team.
- understand how teams operate.
- know why the team approach is not always best.
- know how to avoid layoffs.
- know how to properly conduct a layoff.
- understand the effects of layoffs on victims, survivors, the organization, and the community.

Managing Change

In organizations, change occurs for many reasons and takes on many forms. Some changes are due to organization development efforts such as downsizing, reorganization, or the introduction of teams. Some changes are the result of external mandates like managed care or new government regulations. Still other changes occur due to new leadership or new personnel.

Sacred Cow Hunts

Perhaps the first step toward organizational change is what Kriegel and Brandt (1996) call a **sacred cow hunt.** Organizational sacred cows are practices that have been around for a long time and invisibly reduce productivity. A sacred cow hunt, then, is an organization-wide attempt to get rid of practices that serve no useful purpose. Merck Pharmaceutical and Tractor Supply Stores have periodic sacred cow hunts in which cowbells are rung when a sacred cow is found, monthly sacred cow barbecues are held, and employees receive awards and money for finding a sacred cow. In a sacred cow hunt, an organization looks at all its practices and policies and asks questions like these:

- Why are we doing it? Does it add value, improve quality, improve service, or improve productivity?
- What if it didn't exist?
- Is it already being done by someone else?
- How and when did we start doing this?
- Can it be done better by another person, department, or company?

According to Kriegel and Brandt, common types of sacred cows include the **paper cow**, the **meeting cow**, and the **speed cow.**

The Paper Cow

Paper cows are unnecessary paperwork—usually forms and reports that cost organizations money to prepare, distribute, and read. To determine if something is a paper cow, consider the extent to which the paperwork increases efficiency, productivity, or quality. Ask if anyone actually reads the paperwork. A unique strategy tried by employees at one company was to stop sending a monthly report that had been distributed for years. The employees' thinking was that if the report was actually needed, they would receive complaints. Three months and three missing reports later, no one had complained.

A good annual practice is to review all forms and reports and determine whether they are still needed and, if they are, whether they are needed in their current format. To demonstrate the importance of this practice, review the forms used by your university or organization. How many of them are a third of a page or a quarter of a page? Probably none. There seems to be an unwritten rule that all forms must ask questions until the bottom of the page is reached. I was recently preparing contracts for our graduate assistants and noticed that I was being asked questions about the university from which the students had received their undergraduate degrees, their undergraduate GPA, and their work histories. Note that these were contracts, not application forms, where this information was already contained. So, in the spirit of a good sacred cow hunt, I called the graduate college to ask why this information was necessary. Their reply? No one knew. Did anyone actually need this information? No. Will you change the form for next year? No. This is an example of a sacred cow hunt—but no sacred cow barbecue. To apply what you have learned about paper cow hunts, complete Exercise 14–1 at the end of this chapter.

The Meeting Cow

Another area ripe for change is the number and length of meetings. Think about meetings you have attended recently. How much meeting time was spent doing business as opposed to socializing? Was the meeting really necessary? To reduce the number and length of meetings, some organizations ask the person calling the meeting to determine the cost of the meeting (e.g., 1 hour's salary of each attendee, cost of meeting room, cost of refreshments and supplies) and consider whether the cost will exceed the potential benefits. In some of these organizations, the meeting costs are actually posted at the beginning of the meeting! Needless to say, when people are forced to consider the benefits of most meetings against their cost, most meetings will not be held.

The Speed Cow

Unnecessary deadlines are another source for potential change. Requiring work to be done "by tomorrow" is sometimes necessary. However, unnecessary deadlines cause employees to work at a faster than optimal pace, resulting in decreased quality, increased stress, and increased health problems.

In addition to sacred cow hunts, Kriegel and Brandt (1996) suggest that effective change can be encouraged by using these strategies:

- Think like a beginner: Ask stupid questions, constantly ask "why" things are being done a certain way, and don't assume anything makes sense.
- Don't be complacent with something that is working well. Keep looking for ways to improve, new markets to enter, new products to introduce.

- Don't play by everyone else's rules, make your own. Domino's Pizza is a great example of this type of thinking. While all the other pizza chains competed for ways to increase the number of customers entering their restaurants, Domino's decided to change the rules and bring the restaurant to the people rather than bringing the people to the restaurant.
- Rather than penalizing mistakes, reward employees for making the attempt to change or to try something new.

Employee Acceptance of Change

Though change can be beneficial to organizations, employees are often initially reluctant to change. This reluctance is understandable, as employees are comfortable doing things the old way. They may fear that change will result in less favorable working conditions and economic outcomes than what they are used to. According to consultant William Bridges (1985), it is common for employees undergoing change to feel out of control and as if they are losing their identity ("Who am I? What am I supposed to do?"), meaning ("How do I fit into the newly changed

It is important to plan organizational change.

organization?"), and belonging ("Why do I have to work with a bunch of new people I don't even know?").

Stages

Carnall (1990) suggests that employees typically go through five stages during major organizational changes: denial, defense, discarding, adaptation, and internalization.

Stage 1: Denial. During this initial stage, employees deny that any changes will actually take place, try to convince themselves that the old way is working, and create reasons why the proposed changes will never work (e.g., "We tried that before and it didn't work, something like that won't work in a company like ours").

Stage 2: Defense. When employees begin to believe that change will actually occur, they become defensive and try to justify their positions and ways of doing things. The idea here is that if an organization is changing the way in which employees perform, there is an inherent criticism that the employees must have previously been doing things wrong.

Stage 3: Discarding. At some point, employees begin to realize not only that the organization is going to change but that the employees are going to have to change as well. That is, change is inevitable, and it is in the best interest of the employee to discard the old ways and start to accept the change as the new reality.

Stage 4: Adaptation. At this stage, employees test the new system, learn how it functions, and begin to make adjustments in the way they perform. Employees spend tremendous energy at this stage and can often become frustrated and angry.

Stage 5: Internalization. In this final stage, employees have become immersed in the new culture, become comfortable with the new system, and accepted their new coworkers and work environment.

Important Factors

The extent to which employees readily accept and handle change is dependent on the reason behind the change, the leader making the change, and the personality of the person being changed.

The Reason Behind the Change. Employee acceptance of change is often a function of the reason behind the change. For example, employees understand (but don't necessarily like) change that is due to financial problems, external mandates, or attempts to improve the organization. Acceptance is lower when employees perceive the change to be a change in organizational philosophy, a whim on the part of the person making the change ("Hey, let's do teams"), or a change because everyone else is changing ("Everyone else has teams, so we need to create them now before we get left behind"). Employees are least likely to accept change if they don't understand or were not told the reasons behind the change.

The Person Making the Change. Another factor affecting employee acceptance of change is the person making or suggesting the change. Changes proposed by leaders who are well liked and respected and who have a history of success are more likely to be accepted than changes proposed by leaders whose motives are suspect (Dirks, 2000; Lam & Schaubroeck, 2000). Let me provide two very different examples.

In the first example, the head of a small consulting firm decided to change the focus of her business from delivering training seminars to helping companies switch from a traditional organizational approach to a flatter, team-based approach. Though the consultant's employees were apprehensive about the change in focus, they quickly accepted the change because the consultant was well respected for her knowledge, treated her employees as family, and had on a prior occasion changed the company's focus, resulting in a 30% increase in revenue.

In the second example, due to financial and regulatory reasons, a local mental health agency was forced to move its 120 employees from their current buildings to a new location. A management committee was formed to determine the location for the new building. When the new location was announced, the employees were very upset. The new building was expensive, in a highly congested traffic area, and located far away from most of the agency's clients. The employees' unhappiness was not due to the relocation but to the choice of buildings. It just didn't make sense. That is, it didn't make sense until several of the employees realized that the new building was only 5 minutes from where each of the deciding committee members lived. I don't think I have to finish the story for you to understand the importance of motive.

The differences in these two stories are clear. In the first story, employees quickly accepted change because they trusted the person making the change. In the second story, the employees did not accept the change because the decision makers were not well respected and acted in a manner inconsistent with the well-being of the majority of employees.

For organizational change of any type to work, it is essential that employees trust the organization as a whole as well as the specific individuals making the change. Viking Glass in Sioux Falls, South Dakota, realized the importance of trust when it decided to change the organization to foster more employee participation. Viking Glass spent more than a year laying the foundation to increase the extent to which its employees trusted the company. After gaining employees' trust, the company successfully increased the level of employee empowerment (Andrews, 1994).

The Person Being Changed. As one would imagine, there is considerable variability in the way in which people instigate or react to change. **Change agents** are people who enjoy change and often make changes just for the sake of change. A change agent's motto might best be expressed as "If it ain't broke, break it." Though many people like to call themselves change agents, it may not be such a compliment. That is, reasoned change is good, but change for the sake of change is disruptive.

Let me give you an example. When I was about 30, I was president of our local Kiwanis Club. Now before you get too impressed, I was asked to be president because I was the only person in the club who had not yet been president and one of only five or so members under the age of 60. My first act as president was to restructure all of the committees and create an impressive-looking matrix to depict these changes. When I presented this matrix at our board meeting, each member just stared at me (some were already asleep) until one person said, "Mike, you can't change committees. It's in the national bylaws." My response was to say "whoops" and move on to the next topic. Though this story is not an example of good leadership skills, it is a perfect example of being a change agent. By the way, with some maturity, I hope I have become a change analyst.

Change analysts are not afraid to change or make changes but want to make changes only if the changes will improve the organization. Their motto might be "If it ain't broke, leave it alone; if it's broke, fix it." Change analysts are people who constantly ask such questions as "Why are we doing this?" and "Is there a better way we could be doing this?" But in contrast to the change agent, they are not driven by a need to change constantly.

Receptive changers are people who probably will not instigate change but are willing to change. Their motto is "If it's broke, I'll help fix it." Receptive changers typically have high self-esteem, optimistic personalities, and the belief that they have control over their own life (Wanberg & Banas, 2000). Receptive changers are essential for any major organizational change to be successful.

Reluctant changers will certainly not instigate or welcome change, but they will change if necessary. Their motto is "Are you sure it's broken?" **Change resisters** hate change, are scared by it, and will do anything they can to keep change from occurring. Their motto is "It may be broken, but it's still better than the unknown."

Implementing Change

Another important factor in employee acceptance of change is the way the change is implemented. That is, how and when will details be communicated? How long will the implementation take? Does the organization have the right personnel for the change? What types of training needs does the organization have?

Creating an Atmosphere for Change

According to Denton (1996), one of the first steps in organizational change is to create the proper atmosphere for change. This process begins by creating

dissatisfaction with the current system. Employees should be surveyed to determine how satisfied they are with the current system. If things go as normal, the results of the survey will indicate that many employees are unhappy with the ways things are currently done and have suggestions for improvement. By sharing these results with employees, an organization can protect itself from employees reacting to change by remembering the "good old days." Instead, employees will focus on the "bad old days" and be more willing to change.

Perhaps a good example of this comes from some friends of mine who had been dating for several years. For the last few months of their relationship, each of the two would privately tell me how stale their relationship had become and say that it was time for a change. "Jill" made the decision to end the relationship and told "Jack" of her decision on a Friday night. The following week, Jill was energetic and enthusiastic, talked of dating new people, and even asked if I knew any good-looking single guys. Jack, however, whined all week about how good a relationship he and Jill had had and how he would never be able to find another woman he would love so much. What was the sudden difference in their attitudes? Jill kept the "bad old days" in mind when she made the decision to end the relationship, and Jack remembered only the "good old days" after the relationship ended.

Some of this "pining for the good old days" seems inevitable. A colleague of mine had been complaining for years about his college president. The president eventually was fired and replaced by a new president who made many strange changes. It didn't take a year before my colleague lamented about how much he missed his former boss. It took only a few reminders of the horror stories he had told me about his previous boss to quiet this lamenting.

After creating dissatisfaction with the status quo, Denton (1996) advised organizations to work hard to reduce the fear of change by providing emotional support, allowing employees to vent and discuss their feelings, and providing employees with a safety net that allows them to make mistakes during the transition period. Fear can also be reduced by having someone in the organization describe the benefits of change.

Communicating Details

Employees are most responsive to change when they are kept well informed (Wanberg & Banas, 2000). Unless there is a need for secrecy (e.g., a merger), employees should be aware of and involved in all aspects of the change from initial planning to final implementation. If employees are kept in the dark until the very end, they usually suspect that something bad is happening. It seems to be human nature to think the worst when we don't know something. After undergoing a major restructuring, staff at the Educational Testing Service (ETS) in Princeton, New Jersey, reported that poor communication was responsible for many of the difficulties encountered in the change process (Wild, Horney, & Koonce, 1996). During their restructuring, ETS learned these important lessons:

1. *Communicating change is hard work.* Early in the change process, ETS thought it had done a good job communicating the reasons for and details of their restructuring. However, a change readiness survey that ETS administered to its employees indicated that many employees didn't understand the change or were still resisting the change. The survey results told ETS that it still had a ways to go in communicating important information to its employees.

2. *Training is needed.* The employees who were given the responsibility for communicating the change had not been properly trained in such areas as dealing with employee hostility and resistance.

3. *Two-way communication is essential.* Employees must have the opportunity to provide feedback to the people making the changes.

4. *Honesty is the best policy.* Be honest with employees and tell them information as it arises rather than waiting until all aspects of the change are completed.

Time Frame

Most successful organizational changes occur in a timely fashion. The longer it takes to change, the greater the opportunity for things to go wrong and the greater the chance that employees will become disillusioned. Many consultants advise that organizations should not remain in a "change mode" for longer than 2 years.

Training Needs

After an organization has made a major change, it is often necessary to train employees. For example, if an organization changes to a new computer system, all employees working with computers will need to be trained in the use of the new system. Likewise, if an organization is changing to a self-directed team environment, employees will need to be trained in such areas as goal setting, teamwork, presentation skills, and quality analysis. To apply what you have learned about acceptance of change, complete the Acceptance of Change Exercise on your CD-ROM.

Organizational Culture

Another important consideration in organizational change is organizational culture. Often referred to as corporate culture or climate, **organizational culture** is the shared values, beliefs, and traditions that exist among individuals in organizations (Nwachucwu & Vitell, 1997; Schein, 1985; Weber, 1996). It is this culture that establishes workplace norms of appropriate behavior (what's wrong or right) and defines roles and expectations that employees and management have of each other (Nwachukwu & Vitell, 1997; Sackman, 1991; Weber, 1996). Most cultures have a subculture. For example, the environment in which you were raised is a subculture of a bigger culture, the American culture.

In organizations, each department or office can be a subculture with norms of behaviors that may be different from those of the overall organization. How each department reacts to change is a result of that subculture. Most major changes, such as changing management philosophies, will require a culture and a subculture change to support the implementation of new ideas throughout the entire organization. This is discussed in more detail later in this section.

Think of your university as an organization with its own culture and your classroom as a subculture. Your university probably has created a culture of honesty and trust where each student is expected to adhere to honor codes. To enforce or maintain that culture, it uses sanctions such as taking you before the judicial board if you are caught cheating or violating some other rule.

From the first day of class, norms such as good attendance and participation in class have been established that create a subculture. These norms were probably established by rules that your professor orally communicated or were written in your class syllabus. If you know that the classroom culture is one where you may be expected to discuss your reading material, you are more likely to read your text each week prior to class. Your professor may use certain rewards (such as giving points for classroom participation) or sanctions (such as taking off points) to maintain the culture. Eventually, this culture, which includes the expectations of the professor, gets communicated to other students, who at that point decide whether they want to be members of that culture or not. In other words, if the class and expectations are too hard, the students will sign up for a different class with a more compatible culture.

Culture and norms also result from observing, or modeling, the behaviors of others. Just like your individual personal cultures, which contained role models such as your parents, church, and friends who significantly influenced you over the years, organizational culture also has role models who influence your work behavior and teach you norms (Nwachukwu & Vitell, 1997; Weber, 1996). Going back to the classroom example, if you observe your professor coming in late every class or several of your classmates consistently arriving late or leaving early without negative consequences, this may begin to create a culture of irresponsibility or unaccountability. You may eventually become one of those students with poor attendance because this has become the accepted "norm." To transform that culture into one of accountability and responsibility, the leader (your professor) needs to model appropriate behavior and to use some strategy (such as taking off points for tardiness) to maintain the better culture.

As you can see, organizational culture can aid employees in behaving optimally. However, it can also be a contributing factor in many undesirable behaviors such as unethical decision making. For example, if an organization's top management consistently engages in unethical behaviors and decision making, it is likely that its employees will learn those norms and incorporate them into their own professional value system and

Susan Worrell, B.S.
Human Resources Manager
New River Valley Community Services Board

I work at a Virginia Community Services Board. This agency is one of 40 in Virginia whose purpose is to plan and operate community-based services dealing with mental health, mental retardation, and substance abuse. We have a staff of approximately 270 including both full time and part time workers. The human resources department was formed in 1988. Since that time, the agency has grown from 125 employees to its current level of 270. The HR department has grown to two employees, me and a human resources assistant.

Our department is committed to being employee focused. Our mission is to ask ourselves daily: "What can we do to make this a better workplace for the employees of the agency?" This mission is in line with the agency's philosophy of being person centered.

Our department stays quite busy. I conduct both orientations and exit interviews for employees. They see me both coming and going! I am also responsible for developing and administering the fringe benefits, and this involves frequent contact with insurance companies. In addition, I am available to assist and advise the executive director and supervisors on personnel-related matters to ensure compliance with employment law. I also oversee the maintenance of personnel records and files to ensure compliance with licensure requirements.

My most important responsibility is providing a safe place for employees to vent. This has been particularly useful over the last several years. Our agency recently went through a major reorganization. As with any reorganization, regardless of the magnitude, the stress level of employees increased. I provided empathy and guidance to employees to help them through this trying time. Their stress levels increased mainly from the thought of the change as opposed to the change itself. In other words, they feared the unknown. To address the many concerns and questions of employees, we implemented a communications team that provided a positive communication link for and between employees and a source for answers to rumors and fears.

We involved employees in this reorganization from the beginning. We believed that their insight and input were essential factors for a successful reorganization. Focus groups, involving all levels of employees, were formed a year prior to the implementation of changes. From the focus groups, action steps were developed and explained to everyone so that everyone could see what had been done and what still needed to be done. The transition to the reorganization was a slow, difficult, but beneficial process. Even after we were "officially" reorganized, there was, and still is, fine-tuning of the process.

Team development was a core concept for the reorganization. This process began 2 years ago with the development of facility teams at seven of our locations. We have currently expanded to eight more self-directed teams within the agency. Training was provided to all employees involved regarding their roles and responsibilities on their team. In addition, we reviewed some effective communication and conflict skills they could use.

There continue to be some adjustment issues for both administrators and employees regarding these changes. For example, the employees on the facility teams have new responsibility for specific areas of the operation of the facility to ensure the continuity of not only the quality of services but a clean and safe work environment. These teams are also responsible for a portion of their facility's budget. This level of responsibility and decision making is new, and we have had to help them develop skills in this area. For example, we had to teach them not only how to read a budget but how to manage and understand one.

As the agency moves more into the team concept, I will continue to find more creative ways to support the employees and help them make successful changes. I am constantly striving to provide the best services and support to our hardworking, dedicated staff. My goal is to anticipate the changing needs and to be proactive in establishing programs and plans to meet these needs, such as training programs and other methods of employee development.

---

behave accordingly (Chen, Sawyers, & Williams, 1997; Nwachukwu & Vitell, 1997). To change that behavior, the cultural norms that hinder change must be eliminated (e.g., unethical supervisors, positive consequences of unethical behavior such as financial rewards; Van Slyke, 1996).

As important as it is, organizational culture has traditionally been ignored during restructuring and other changes. This is either because there is a general belief that culture can't be changed or because many organizations do not know how to change their cultures. In fact, in a recent survey of 500 corporations, 70% stated that they did not have the knowledge to address cultural issues (Sherriton & Stern, 1997). Without such knowledge, changes in the way the company operates, and thus the way its employees behave, will not be long lasting. Consequently, it is important that an organization knows how to include culture in its change process.

Changing Culture

Making organizational changes doesn't necessarily mean that everything about the existing culture must change. According to one manager, "The change process includes holding on to the successful elements of the present culture and adding new elements that are important" (Laabs, 1996, p. 56). Consequently, the first step in changing culture is assessing the desired culture and comparing it with the existing one to determine what needs to change. Two additional steps are creating dissatisfaction with the current culture to create support for the new one and maintaining the new culture.

Assessing the New Culture

Assessment of the new culture involves a great deal of discussion and analysis and should include the following steps (Sherriton & Stern, 1997).

Step 1: Needs Assessment. Because parts of the existing culture may actually support certain organizational changes, the current culture must be analyzed and compared with the desired culture to determine what might need to change. For example, if an organization wants to move from a traditional hierarchical management philosophy to a more empowering one where employees share more decision-making responsibilities, systems, procedures, and policies will have to be changed to fully support the new culture. Areas such as role expectations, job descriptions identifying the new decision-making responsibilities, accountability, rewards, and employee selection systems must be reviewed. Data for an analysis are usually collected through observations, review of existing documentation, and employee interviews and surveys consisting of questions that ask for potential recommendations of changes.

Step 2: Determining Executive Direction. Management must then analyze the needs assessment to determine the decisions or actions that will reinforce the culture and to assess the feasibility of certain changes. Using the previous example, if most of the supervisors and managers in an organization are unwilling to share their decision-making authority, a true "empowering" culture cannot be maintained. Consequently, that change will not be reinforced by the culture. In fact, according to research, it takes the wholehearted support of top management to implement an empowering philosophy (Schuster, Morden, Baker, McKay, Dunning, & Hagan, 1997). Addressing possible obstacles to culture change during the transformation process can usually minimize unintended consequences (Gilmore, Shea, & Useem, 1997).

Step 3: Implementation Considerations. This area addresses how the new culture will be implemented. Will committees or ad hoc groups be set up to carry out changes or will management execute the changes? If the organization's desired culture is to encourage more input by employees, employees should be allowed to participate in implementing the empowering organization in order to support the new culture.

Step 4: Training. Culture change means a change of philosophy, and that ultimately means different role expectations. As with any new skill, all organizational members must be trained in a new philosophy for the new culture to thrive and be long lasting. This has often been the biggest barrier in organizations that have declared that their members are now empowered to share in decisions. Employees, both management and lower level, are typically not trained on what that means. As explained later in this chapter, management and employees have a different interpretation of what empowerment culture means and how to carry it out. Training can reduce such ambiguity and confusion.

Step 5: Evaluation of the New Culture. As with any changes, an evaluation mechanism must be established to review the new culture. Issues such as whether the change actually has occurred or whether old norms and procedures still exist should be addressed. If change has not occurred, additional strategies must be identified to establish and support the new culture.

Now that the ideal culture has been determined, the next step is implementing it. This is done by creating dissatisfaction with the existing culture (Van Slyke, 1997).

Creating Dissatisfaction with Existing Culture

Just as creating dissatisfaction with the status quo in general is necessary to promote a change, for employees to accept a new culture, the existing culture and status quo must be "upset." This might mean communicating to employees the future impact of continuing to "do business as usual." For example, many organizations share data that show technological trends and the financial performance of the company. If employees see this information as negatively affecting either them or the organization as a whole, this can create the necessary displeasure with the status quo and be the catalyst for developing a new business strategy.

Another way to create dissatisfaction is to distribute attitude surveys that ask people how satisfied they are with the organization's goal and to suggest ideas for changes. The results of the survey are distributed throughout the organization so that people can see the dissatisfaction level and will begin to buy into a new culture and other organizational changes.

The key at this point is to seek input from employees in the process. A successful culture transformation requires commitment from all levels of the organization. When employees have an opportunity to be an actual part of the change, they are more likely to be committed to it (Van Slyke, 1996). Once you have started the process of transformation, it is important that it be maintained.

Maintaining the New Culture

If the new culture is expected to last, developing new reward systems and selection methods should occur. Rewarding current employees for successfully participating and cooperating with the new system is imperative (Kotter & Cohen, 2002). These rewards can include pay for performance in jobs that have increased responsibilities due to the new culture or other changes. But they also go beyond financial rewards and can include employee recognition and meaningful work.

Selection of Employees

Future employees should be selected on the basis of how well they epitomize the new culture. For example, if the new culture is one of team decision making, new employees should have not only the ability but the willingness and personality to perform in such an environment. As current employees are replaced by new ones, the new culture can become "frozen" into the desired system selected by the leadership (Lewin, 1951). On the other hand, continuing to hire employees who prefer a more structured management philosophy and who work better alone will eventually cause the organization to revert to its old culture.

Finally, the socialization process of new employees must reinforce the new culture. **Organizational socialization** is the process whereby new employees learn the behaviors and attitudes they need to be successful in the organization. It also helps any newcomer to the organization define his role and what is expected of him in his position (Morrison, 1993). Both informal and formal strategies can help with this process. Informal strategies of socialization include such things as hearing the same stories repeated by several different employees. For example, you have probably listened to people in the workforce talk about getting the best stories by hanging around the water cooler or the copier. Usually stories about some "bad decision" are discussed. New employees who hear stories consistently repeated will get an understanding of the type of culture the organization has. If the discussions are negative, the new employee will begin to believe that the organization is incompetent, mistreats its employees, or is unethical.

There are also formal ways organizations can influence the socialization process. One way is through establishing rituals. **Rituals** are procedures in which employees participate to become "one of the gang." Activities such as annual awards banquets or staff picnics are rituals that reinforce the impression of a "caring" organization. Another ritual is requiring all new employees to go through a probationary period before being considered a permanent employee.

Finally, symbols that represent certain attitudes of the organization can be used. **Symbols** are a communication technique that convey a certain message to employees. For example, establishment of an on-site wellness center conveys the organization's interest in health. In addition, communication techniques such as mission and value statements can help acculturate the new person to his environment. To apply what you have learned about organizational culture, complete Exercise 14–2 at the end of this chapter.

Coping with Change

Though organizational change can be traumatic for employees, it can also be exciting and full of new opportunities. Organizational change expert Price Pritchett (1993) offered the following advice to employees involved in organizational change. This advice can be communicated by management to other employees throughout the organization.

Speed Up

It is natural for people faced with a new situation to be cautious and want to take things slowly (Kotter & Cohen, 2002). However, Pritchett (1993) advises employees to get involved, increase the pace of their work, and not get left behind. This advice is analogous to paddling a canoe: If you move faster than the current, you can control where you are going. If you slow down or remain at the same speed as the current, you will be swept wherever the current takes you.

Take the Initiative

Instead of waiting for instructions and for people to tell you what to do, chart your own course. Show initiative, try to solve problems, make suggestions. Don't be afraid to take risks, and don't be afraid to make mistakes. As hockey star Wayne Gretsky once said, "You miss 100% of the shots you don't take."

Spend Energy on Solutions

Instead of spending energy complaining and resisting change, accept change, and then spend your energy trying to solve problems and make the new system work. Take personal responsibility for fixing what doesn't work and making suggestions for ways the system can be improved.

To remove the stress associated with change, some psychologists suggest that organizations do innovative things to make work more fun (Brotherton, 1996). Consultant Matt Weinstein offered these suggestions to managers:

- Post baby pictures of managers so that employees can laugh at them and realize that the people making the change weren't always in powerful positions.

- Create a stress-free zone where employees can go to relax for a few moments. The Brookstar Corporation in Michigan went so far as to put a punching bag in a room so that employees could take out their frustration on the bag rather than on each other.

- Give employees a surprise hour off. Store managers at Crate and Barrel tell one employee each week to take an hour and have fun, go shopping, or take a nap.

- Other suggestions include holding an ugly tie contest, giving employees stuffed animals, and designing personalized fortune cookies.

Though we certainly have no scientific evidence that any of these techniques will work, the idea is that managers should realize the stress inherent in change and take creative measures to reduce that stress.

Empowerment

As discussed in Chapter 9, many employees are more satisfied with their jobs if they feel they have some control over what they do. As a result, many organizations are "empowering" employees to participate in and make decisions. As you will see in the following pages, "empowering" employees can range from asking employees for their opinion to giving them complete decision-making control. However, before discussing ways to empower employees—which I will refer to as ways to increase "levels of employee input"—it might be best to first discuss why and when employees should be involved in decision making.

Making the Decision to Empower

Factors in Making the Decision to Empower

Employees need to be involved in decisions in circumstances in which the quality of the decision is important, the decision affects employees, the supervisor doesn't have the knowledge to make the decision, or the employees don't trust the supervisor. As shown in Exhibit 14.01, Vroom and Yetton (1973) have developed a flowchart to help determine when employees should be involved in making decisions. The flowchart uses the following seven factors.

Importance of Decision Quality. The first concern when making a decision is whether one decision will be better than another. For example, if a supervisor is trying to decide whether to sign a letter with blue ink or black ink, his decision probably will not make any difference to the organization. Thus, the importance of the decision quality is low, and little time or effort should be spent making it.

Leader Knowledge of the Problem Area. The second concern of decision making involves the extent to which leaders have sufficient information to make the decision alone. If they do, then consultation with others is desired only if leaders want their subordinates to feel involved. If leaders lack sufficient knowledge to make a decision, consultation is essential. For example, it would be difficult for managers to select a benefit package without first asking their employees about the types of benefits they need.

Structure of the Problem. The third concern is the extent to which a leader knows what information is needed and how it can be obtained—that is, the problem's structure. If the leader does not know how to obtain this information, the decision-making process will require other people, and the decision will take longer to reach.

Importance of Decision Acceptance. The fourth decision-making concern involves the degree to which it is important that the decision be accepted by others. For example, for a supervisor to decide what hours each employee will work, it is important the employees agree with and have input into the decision-making process. However, if the supervisor is deciding what he wants for lunch, whether others agree with or have input into the decision is not important (unless, of course, the choices involve onions or garlic).

Probability of Decision Acceptance. The fifth decision-making concern is subordinate acceptance. If the leader feels that he can make the decision himself but that acceptance of the decision is important, he must determine whether his subordinates will accept it. If the leader is popular and viewed as being competent, his subordinates will probably accept and follow the decision. But if the leader is not popular, powerful, and competent, he will probably want help from his subordinates and colleagues in making the decision, even though he has the ability to make the decision himself. This is why leaders often ask subordinates and colleagues for their opinions. The leader may already know what he will decide, but gaining the support of others by eliciting opinions and comments increases the chances that they will accept his decision when he announces it.

A colleague told me a story that provides a perfect example of the importance of considering the need for subordinate acceptance. At her university, the graduate college changed the way in which it administered and awarded graduate assistantships. The assistant dean was placed in charge of developing and implementing the new system. A week prior to the end of school, the new system was announced, and the graduate faculty went crazy. The awarding of the assistantships came too late to recruit students, the new application forms did not provide the information needed by departments to make decisions, and the deadlines for paperwork were convenient for the graduate college but not for the students or the departments.

What went wrong? If we look at the Vroom-Yetton model, two problems stand out. First, the assistant dean did not have the information necessary to make the decision. She had never taught a class, been a graduate student, or been involved in the financial aid process. In spite of this lack of experience and information, she chose not to consult any of the stakeholders (e.g., faculty, department chairs, graduate students) who would be affected by the decisions. Second, although acceptance of her decision was certainly important, she made no attempt to communicate the reasons for her decisions or to work with the departments to increase acceptance. Furthermore, the staff at the graduate college was viewed by faculty as being incompetent, not trustworthy, and making

Exhibit 14.01 The Vroom-Yetton decision-making flowchart

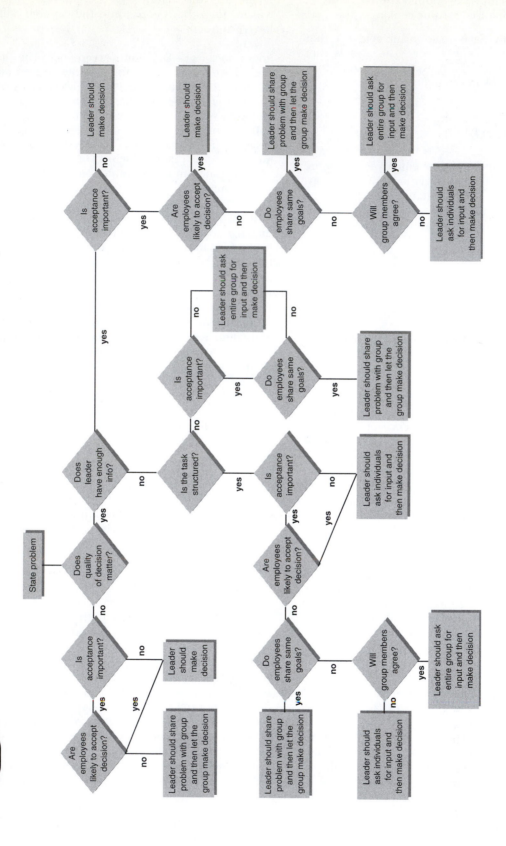

decisions beneficial to the dean's career but not always in the best interest of the students, faculty, or university as a whole.

Subordinate Trust and Motivation. The sixth concern of the decision-making process is the extent to which subordinates are motivated to achieve the organizational goals and thus can be trusted to make decisions that will help the organization. For example, suppose a marketing survey indicates that a bank will attract more customers if it is open on Saturdays. If the branch manager allows his employees to decide whether the branch should be open on Saturdays, can he trust the employees to make the decision on the basis of what is best for the bank and its customers rather than what is best for the employees? If the answer is "no," the branch manager will need to make the unpopular decision after receiving input from his subordinates.

Probability of Subordinate Conflict. The final concern of the decision-making process involves the amount of conflict that is likely among the subordinates when various solutions to the problem are considered. If there are many possible solutions and the employees are likely to disagree about which is best, the leader will be best served by gathering information from employees and then, as in the previous situation, making the decision herself.

Decision-Making Strategies Using the Vroom-Yetton Model

Answering the questions in the flowchart shown in Exhibit 14.01 will lead to one of five possible decision-making strategies: Autocratic I, Autocratic II, Consultative I, Consultative II, or Group I.

With the **Autocratic I strategy**, leaders use the available information to make the decision without consulting their subordinates. This is an effective strategy when the leader has the necessary information, and when acceptance by the group either is not important or is likely to occur regardless of the decision.

With the **Autocratic II strategy**, leaders obtain the necessary information from their subordinates and then make their own decisions. The leader may or may not tell the subordinates about the nature of the problem. The purpose of this strategy is for leaders to obtain information they need to make a decision even though acceptance of the solution by the group is not important.

Leaders using the **Consultative I strategy** share the problem on an individual basis with some or all of their subordinates. After receiving their input, the leader makes a decision that may or may not be consistent with the thinking of the group. This strategy is especially useful in situations in which it is important for the group to accept the decision but in which the group members may not agree regarding the best decision.

Leaders using the **Consultative II strategy** share the problems with their subordinates as a group. After receiving the group's input, the leader makes a decision that may or may not be acceptable to the group. The main difference between this strategy and the

Consultative I strategy is that with Consultative II the entire group is involved, whereas in Consultative I only a few employees are asked to provide input. This strategy is used when acceptance of the decision by the group is important and when the individual group members are likely to agree with one another about the best solution.

With the **Group I strategy**, the leader shares the problem with the group and lets the group reach a solution. The role of the leader is merely to assist in the decision-making process. This strategy is effective when group acceptance of the decision is important and when the group can be trusted to arrive at a decision that is consistent with the goals of the organization.

Although relatively little research has been conducted on the Vroom-Yetton model, the results of a few studies have been encouraging. For example, Field and House (1990) and Jago and Vroom (1977) found that managers who used the decision-making strategy recommended by the model had better quality decisions than managers who used decision-making strategies that the model would not have recommended. Similar results were found by Brown and Finstuen (1993) with military officers and Paul and Ebadi (1989) with sales managers. To practice using the Vroom-Yetton model, complete Exercise 14–3 at the end of this chapter.

Levels of Employee Input

When employers talk about "empowering" employees, they seldom intend to let employees make all of the decisions affecting an organization. Instead, they most often want to give employees "more say" in day-to-day activities. Unfortunately, when employees are told that they are being "empowered," they often apply a different meaning to the word than that intended by the employer. In fact, one organization that went through a change spent fully 2 weeks meeting with employees to hash out what *empowerment* should and would mean in that organization! Thus, it might be useful to set aside the word *empowerment* and talk instead of levels of employee input and control. Let me provide two examples of why *levels of input* might be a better choice of terms than *empowerment*.

Several years ago, I was hired by a large poultry company to help them design a system to empower their employees. In such situations, my first question is always, "Why do you want to empower your employees?" In this case, the response was that they were implementing a total quality management (TQM) system and were at the stage in which they were supposed to empower employees. In other words, the organization was making a change because they thought they were "supposed to do it" rather than because something was actually going wrong. When I asked them if they wanted to actually "empower" their employees to make most of the decisions about their jobs, the company responded that it did not. When I asked what they meant by *empower*, their response was that they weren't sure. I conducted a training workshop in which I discussed the concept of

Exhibit **14.02** Levels of employee input

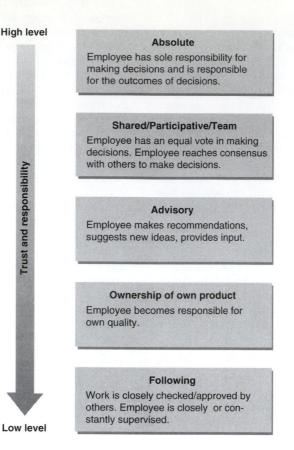

High level

Trust and responsibility

Absolute
Employee has sole responsibility for making decisions and is responsible for the outcomes of decisions.

Shared/Participative/Team
Employee has an equal vote in making decisions. Employee reaches consensus with others to make decisions.

Advisory
Employee makes recommendations, suggests new ideas, provides input.

Ownership of own product
Employee becomes responsible for own quality.

Following
Work is closely checked/approved by others. Employee is closely or constantly supervised.

Low level

empowerment and the levels of employee input discussed in the following paragraphs. At the end of the workshop, I told them to discuss what they had just learned and make a decision about what level of employee input they wanted their employees to have. It took just a short time for the managers to reach consensus that they wanted their employees at the advisory level, that their employees already had one of the best suggestion/advisory systems in the nation, and that there was no real need to change. In other words, the organization was already "empowering" its employees at the optimal level for that particular industry.

The second example comes from a university setting in which a new president appointed a number of committees to study such issues as summer school and student recruitment and "empowered" these committees to make changes to improve the current system. The committees worked diligently for several months and then presented their new systems to the president. After a week of consideration, the president thanked the committees and told them that he appreciated their hard work but had decided not to follow any of their recommendations. The committee members were shocked at this response because, to them, being told they were "empowered" meant that their decisions were final and thus would become the new policy. The

president responded by saying that he had empowered them to "study" the issues and make "recommendations." His intent had never been to allow a committee to make a final decision.

As these two examples demonstrate, *empowerment* means many things to many people. As shown in Exhibit 14.02, there are five main levels of employee input and control.

Following

Employees at the following level have no real control over their jobs. They are given instructions about what to do, when to do it, and how it should be done. Furthermore, their work is often checked by other employees (e.g., quality control) or by their supervisor. Employees at this level can be those who are new or inexperienced to the work being performed or those with weak decision-making skills.

Ownership of Own Product

At this level, employees are still told what to do but are solely responsible for the quality of their output. For example, an employee working on an assembly line would follow a set of procedures in assembling a product but would decide if the quality of the assembled product was good enough. Likewise, a secretary might type a report the way it was submitted by his boss but would be responsible for ensuring that there were no typographical errors.

In essence, this level removes what psychologist Rick Jacobs (1997) calls "redundant systems." With a redundant human system, every person's work is checked by another person. In some organizations, a single piece of work might even be checked by several different people. The logic behind redundant systems is that with more than one person checking quality there is less chance of a poor-quality product reaching a consumer. Furthermore, in many cases, an employee might not have the skill level necessary to check her own work. For example, a secretary might well be an excellent typist but might not have the grammatical skills to know if her memos contain mistakes. Even if she did have the skills, we have all missed typos because we knew what we wanted to say and thus proofread a sentence the way we meant to say it rather than the way we actually wrote it.

Though redundant systems make sense in many cases, they do have their drawbacks. The most relevant of these to this chapter is that satisfaction, motivation, and performance are often lessened when others check our work. Let me provide you with a prime example. At my university, graduate students must submit a program of studies covering the courses they intend to take during their 2 years in graduate school. The student completes the form, signs it, and then gets his adviser to sign it. The adviser must then get his department chair to sign the form, and the department chair must then get the graduate dean to sign the form. Now keep in mind that because 10 of our 12 classes are required and thus standard for all I/O graduate students, theoretically there should be little room for error. However, as an adviser, I often see mistakes made by my students, who then tell me that they didn't bother to read the catalog because they knew I would find any mistakes. The problem is that I seldom read the forms because I figure if there are any mistakes my department chair will catch them. She never reads the forms because she figures the dean will catch them. Thus, the very redundant system designed to prevent errors is actually the cause of errors!

As one can imagine, making employees responsible for their own output does a number of things. It motivates employees to check their work more carefully, provides them with a sense of "ownership" in their product, and provides a greater sense of autonomy and independence. In the Saturn division of General Motors, employees receive feedback on problems that drivers encounter with the cars assembled by a particular group of employees. This feedback helps employees gauge their quality control efforts, and it affects the size of their bonus.

Advisory

At the advisory level, employees are asked to provide feedback, suggestions, and input into a variety of organizational concerns. The key at this level is that there is no guarantee that an organization will follow the advice given by the employees; the only guarantee is that the organization will seriously consider the advice.

The idea behind this level is that employees often have the best knowledge about their jobs so getting their input makes good business sense. As previously discussed, though employees often have the knowledge to make a decision, they are placed at an advisory level because they may not have the "motivation" to make the best decision. In such situations, an organization will ask employees for their opinions and preferences to better understand the employees' positions but will reserve the right to make the actual decision.

Shared/Participative/Team

The fourth level of employee input and control allows an employee to make a decision. However, this decision is made at a group level. For example, an organization might put a team together to find better ways to market its projects or to determine what type of benefits package employees will receive. This level differs from the previous level (advisory) in that only in very rare circumstances will the team's decision not be implemented. At this level, employees must not only be well trained in decision making but also be willing to take on the responsibility of making decisions.

Absolute

The final level of employee input and control gives an employee the absolute authority to make a decision on his own—no group consensus, no supervisory approval. It is important to point out, however, that he is also responsible for the consequences of that decision. So if he makes the wrong decision, he may encounter such negative consequences as being reprimanded or fired. Because of these potential consequences, many employees are leery about being given absolute power. Thus it is important in many circumstances to remove the potential for a negative sanction.

For example, Holiday Inn has empowered each of its employees to take any reasonable means necessary to satisfy a customer. This decision was made so that an unhappy guest can have his problem solved immediately rather than passed on to a manager. So if a guest complains to a housekeeper that there were not enough towels in his room, the housekeeper is empowered to deal with the situation. The housekeeper might opt to apologize, or she might opt to take $25 off the night's stay. Let's imagine that a particular housekeeper comps a night's lodging for each of 10 people who complained about not having enough towels. The manager thinks that these decisions were excessive and fires the housekeeper. What effect will the firing have on future employee decisions?

When employees are empowered to make decisions, they must first receive some training in how to make decisions. If an employee makes a bad decision, rather than punishing the employee it is better for the organization to discuss with the employee what might have been a better decision and to explain why

Exhibit 14.03 Example of employee empowerment chart

Job Component	Following	Ownership	Advisory	Participative	Absolute
Job-Related Tasks					
Opening new accounts	[----J---E----]				
Approving loans	[----J---E----]				
Waiving check fees	[----J---E----]				
Scheduling Issues					
Taking breaks	[--J-E-------------]				
Taking vacations	[--J-E-------------]				
Scheduling hours	[---J-E----]				
Personnel Issues					
Hiring new staff			[-----E----]		
Innovation Issues					
Changing procedures/methods			[-----E----]		
Developing new products			[-----E----]		

J = Jane, E = Emily

the employee's decision was improper. Without such training and coaching, employees are not likely to enthusiastically accept their newly empowered status, especially if their new level of authority is not accompanied by an increase in pay.

Empowerment Charts

Organizations never have just one level of employee input and control that applies to every employee. Instead, levels will differ by employee as well as by task. For example, a bank teller might be placed at the absolute level to decide when she will take her breaks, at the advisory level when it comes to hiring new employees, and at the following level when it comes to scheduling waiving check fees. To reduce confusion, it is a good idea for organizations to develop what I call individual employee **empowerment charts**. An example of such a chart is shown in Exhibit 14.03.

Notice that for each task a range of control/input is allowed. For example, according to our chart, the task of opening new accounts can be performed at the following, ownership, or advisory levels. The "J" in the chart indicates that our new employee, Jane, is at the following level, whereas our experienced teller, Emily, is at the advisory level. In most organizations, a new employee would most likely be placed at the following level until she demonstrated mastery in performing the task. Individual employee empowerment charts reduce confusion and provide a systematic plan

for providing employees with more autonomy as their skills and experience increase. To practice creating an employee empowerment chart, complete the Empowerment Chart Exercise on your CD-ROM.

Consequences to Empowerment

As shown in Exhibit 14.04, being at a higher level of control/input has many positive aspects. For example, research indicates that increased empowerment typically results in increased job satisfaction for employees in the United States, Mexico, and Poland but not for employees in India (Robert, Probst, Martocchio, Drasgow, & Lawler, 2000). The increased responsibility can result in higher skill levels, which in turn can result in higher pay, increased job security, and increased potential to find other employment. However, empowerment can have its downside. With increased responsibility comes increased stress. With the power to make decisions comes the risk of making bad decisions and thus being fired or denied a promotion.

One of the things that is true throughout life is that people are different, and not everything affects everyone the same way. For example, imagine that we place all of the employees in a fast food restaurant at the absolute level in making decisions such as when to "comp" drinks or a meal if the service is slow or the food is bad, or when to allow customers to make substitutions. For many of these employees, this authority will be welcome as it reduces the time taken to get

Exhibit **14.04** Consequences of empowerment

Personal

1. Increased job satisfaction for most
2. Stress
   a. Decreased stress due to greater control
   b. Increased stress due to greater responsibility

Financial

1. Bonuses
2. Pay increases

Career

1. Increased job security
2. Promotions
3. Increased marketability
4. Increased chance of being terminated

permission from a supervisor and provides them with a sense of "power." However, for some employees, the increased stress of making decisions and being accountable far outweighs any feelings of "empowerment."

Teams

Group behavior was discussed extensively in Chapter 13. This section will focus on one kind of group, teams—a popular method of increasing employee empowerment. The concept of employee work teams had been around for decades (they were often called "quality circles" in the 1970s), but the use of work teams greatly increased in the 1990s. Surveys indicate that 72% of *Fortune* 1000 companies use teams (Lawler, 2001).

Unfortunately, this increase in the use of teams is often the result of "keeping up with the Joneses" rather than a strategically planned method of organization development. As with any type of organizational intervention, teams can improve performance in some, but not all, situations. Teams work best in situations in which the job requires high levels of employee interaction, a team approach will simplify the job, a team can do something an individual can not, and there is time to create a team and properly train team members (Kriegel & Brandt, 1996).

What Is a Team?

According to Devine, Clayton, Philips, Dunford, and Melner (1999), a team is "a collection of three or more individuals who interact intensively to provide an organizational product, plan, decision, or service"

(p. 681). At times, putting employees into teams fails because the team is really a "group" or a "committee" rather than a true "team." In fact, according to a survey of practitioners who work with teams, only 48% of work groups would be officially classified as a team (Offermann & Spiros, 2001). Before calling a group of individuals a team, several factors should be considered (Donnellon, 1996).

Identification

Identification is the extent to which group members identify with the team rather than with other groups. For example, suppose a committee was created composed of one representative from each of five different departments (e.g., accounting, engineering, human resources). During the meetings, members use such statements as "Our department won't agree," "This committee just doesn't like us in engineering," or "We didn't even want to be on this committee." Notice that the use of *we, our,* and *us* referred to their departments rather than to the committee. According to Donnellon (1996), for the committee to be considered a team, those same words would need to refer to the committee: for example, "How can we convince the accounting department?" or "Our solution is a good one."

Interdependence

In a team, members need and desire the assistance, expertise, and opinions of the other members. If a team member can perform her job without the assistance of others, the team would not meet the definition of a group (see Chapter 13). For example, some teams, such as a surgical team in a hospital, have very high task **interdependence** in that what one member does greatly

Work teams are becoming more common.

influences what another member does. Other teams (most committees) have low task interdependence in that each member completes a task and the separate parts are then compiled. Though each part is important in completing the final product, the completion of each part is not dependent on another group member. The importance of task interdependence was demonstrated by Liden, Wayne, and Bradway (1996), who found that empowerment increased the performance of teams with high task interdependence but decreased the performance of teams with low task interdependence.

Power Differentiation

In a team, members try to decrease **power differentiation** by treating others as equals and taking steps to ensure equality. In groups that are not teams, members challenge, correct, and interrupt each other, give orders, and use sarcasm. For example, I worked with one organization that had an "administrative team." What I discovered, however, was that one individual in that team was treated differently, had less authority, and had no voting power. Consequently, rather than being a "team," they were a "committee."

In teams, members apologize for overstepping their roles, ask indirect questions to avoid challenges, and are polite to one another (Donnellon, 1996). For example, in a team, a member might disagree with another member by saying something like "I don't know your field as well as you do, but what if we tried. . . ." whereas in a nonteam a member might disagree by saying, "That's so stupid; I'll tell you what will work."

Social Distance

In a team, members try to decrease **social distance** by being casual, using nicknames, and expressing liking, empathy, and common views. Nonteam members use formal language and forms of address, excessive politeness, and impersonal conversations. For example, team members would use such phrases as "Hey, how's it going?" "Thanks, pal." and "I understand your feelings on that." Nonteam members might address another member as "Mr. Jones" rather than "Bob" or agree with someone by saying "I concur with your opinion" rather than "I'm right with you on that one."

Conflict Management Tactics

Team members respond to conflict by collaborating, whereas nonteam members respond by forcing and accommodating (remember our discussion of these styles in Chapter 13). In nonteams, members react to conflict by threatening, directing, or giving in. In teams, members try to understand the others' views, make attempts to compromise, and use nonthreatening tones (Donnellon, 1996).

Negotiation Process

In teams, members negotiate in a win–win style in which the goal is for every person to come out ahead. In nonteams, members negotiate so that they win and the other members lose.

On the basis of the six factors just discussed, Donnellon (1996) placed teams into one of five categories: collaborative teams, emergent teams, adversarial teams, nominal teams, and doomed teams. Collaborative teams and emergent teams are what I have referred to as "true teams," whereas nominal teams and doomed teams are what I have referred to as "nonteams." Adversarial teams are somewhere between a true team and a nonteam.

Though not affecting the extent to which a group is officially a team, teams differ in two other ways.

Exhibit **14.05** Traditional versus team approaches

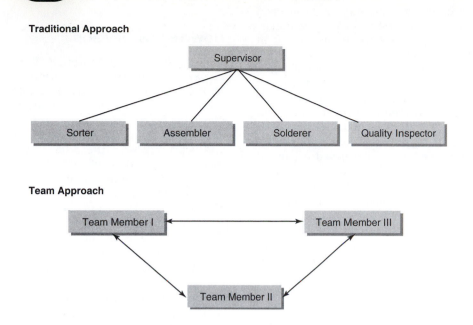

Traditional Approach

Supervisor

Sorter | Assembler | Solderer | Quality Inspector

Team Approach

Team Member I ⟷ Team Member III

Team Member II

Teams differ as to their **permanency.** That is, some teams are designed to work together permanently, whereas others are formed to solve a particular problem and then are expected to dissolve. For example, I was appointed to a university task force designed to create a new system for students to use to evaluate faculty. Once the system was created, our team disbanded.

Teams can also differ in the proximity of their members. Members of surgical teams, baseball teams, and the cast of a Broadway play not only are task interdependent but work physically close to one another. In many instances, however, members of teams may be located across several cities, states, or countries. Because of the expense of bringing such teams to the same location, companies like IBM, USFilter, and KDA Software use **virtual teams** whose members use email, fax machines, and computer-based video conferencing to carry out their team functions (Joinson, 2002). Though virtual teams can certainly be productive, they tend to struggle with building trust, creating synergy, and overcoming feelings of isolation (Kirkman, Rosen, Gibson, Tesluk, & McPherson, 2002).

Types of Teams

Teams come in many shapes and sizes based on the factors discussed earlier in the chapter. For example, Devine, Clayton, Philips, Dunford, and Melner (1999) surveyed organizations and determined that teams differ on two major characteristics: temporal duration (ad hoc versus ongoing) and product type (project versus production). For this chapter, teams will be classified into the four categories determined by Cohen and Bailey (1997): work teams, parallel teams, project teams, and management teams.

Work Teams

Work teams consist of groups of employees who manage themselves, assign jobs, plan and schedule work, make work-related decisions, and solve work-related problems (Kirkman & Shapiro, 2001). They are typically formed to produce goods, provide service, or increase the quality and cost-effectiveness of a product or a system. For example, work teams at

- Monarch Marking Systems in Dayton, Ohio, reduced past due shipments by 70% and doubled productivity.
- GTE Directories in Dallas increased the production of telephone directories by 158%, reduced errors by 48%, and reduced the time to respond to customer complaints from 18.8 days to 2.9 days
- Xerox in Webster, New York, saved $266,000 by discovering the cause of high failure rates in one of its products

As shown in Exhibit 14.05, the traditional method of manufacturing a product is to have employees specialize in performing one particular task. For example, a company might have a supervisor, sorter, assembler, solderer, and quality inspector. The sorter places parts on the assembly line, the assembler puts the parts together, the solderer solders the parts, and the quality control inspector makes sure the part is properly assembled.

In a team approach, there would be no supervisor. Each of the production workers would be called a "team member" and be cross-trained to perform all of the tasks. In this way, if parts were assembled faster than they could be soldered, the sorter might spend some time soldering rather than sorting or waiting. The team would be responsible for checking its own quality, and one of the production workers would probably be appointed as a team leader. The use of production teams saves money by removing management layers and making the team responsible for its own production.

Customer service teams are commonly found in restaurants and retail stores. In the traditional customer service model at a restaurant, each employee is assigned specific tasks (e.g., serving, cooking, bussing tables) in specific areas. With the team approach, each employee may still be assigned a primary duty and area but is expected to "do what it takes" to satisfy ustomers. For example, suppose that Ken is your server at a very busy restaurant. You want a new drink (milk, of course), but Ken is at another table. The closest person to you is Barbie, who is bussing tables. In the traditional system, a request of more milk from Barbie would result in a response such as "I only bus tables; you'll have to wait for your server." In the team approach, Barbie would have been cross-trained in serving beverages and would be able to comply with your request.

Parallel Teams

Parallel teams, also called **cross-functional teams**, consist of representatives from various departments (functions) within an organization (Keller, 2001). For example, a team formed to reduce the time to ship a product might include members from the sales, shipping, production, and customer service departments. For cross-functional teams to be successful, it is important that they have a clear purpose, receive support from each functional area, and take steps to increase the trust levels of committee members. Building trust in cross-functional teams is especially important as members are often torn between representing the interests of their function and doing what is best for the organization as a whole.

Project Teams

Project teams are formed to produce one-time outputs such as creating a new product, installing a new software system, or hiring a new employee. Once the team's goal has been accomplished, the team is dismantled. The temporary nature of project teams is what distinguishes them from parallel and work teams. The environmental consulting firm of Camp Dresser & McKee, Inc. provides an excellent example of a project team. The company needed to replace its human resource information system (HRIS), which tracks employment information for its 3,500 employees. Because such a system was used by a wide variety of departments, Camp Dresser & McKee formed a 40-person team to select and implement the new system. Once the system was in place, the team disbanded (Jossi, 2001b).

Management Teams

Management teams coordinate, manage, advise, and direct employees and teams. Whereas work, parallel, and project teams are responsible for directly accomplishing a particular goal, management teams are responsible for providing general direction and assistance to those teams.

How Teams Develop

Teams typically go through four developmental phases: forming, storming, norming, and performing. In the **forming stage**, team members get to know each other and decide what roles each member will play. During the early part of this stage, team members are on their best behavior as they try to impress and get along with the other team members. Team members are often excited about the potential to accomplish something but are also anxious about working with others in a team. During the later part of this stage, the team concentrates on clarifying its mission, determining the goals it wants to accomplish, deciding on the tasks to be done to accomplish their goals, setting rules and procedures, and developing alternative courses of action to reach their goals (Marks, Mathieu, & Zaccaro, 2001). A meta-analysis by Salas, Mullen, Rozell, and Driskell (1997) indicates that formal team building (training on how to be a team) that focuses on role clarification will slightly improve team performance.

During the **storming stage**, the good behavior disappears. On an individual level, team members often become frustrated with their roles, show the stress of balancing their previous duties with their new team responsibilities, and question whether they have the ability to accomplish the goals set in the forming stage. Interpersonally, team members begin to disagree with one another and to challenge each other's ideas. It is from this tension and conflict that the team often gets the energy to perform well in later stages.

During the **norming stage**, the team works toward easing the tension from the storming stage. Team members begin to acknowledge the reality of the team by accepting the team leader and working directly with other team members to solve difficulties. At this point, team members have either accepted their initial roles or made adjustments to roles for which they are better suited.

In the **performing stage**, the team begins to accomplish its goals. Group members make innovative suggestions, challenge one another without defensive responses, and participate at high levels. During this stage, the team continually monitors its progress toward goals, determines additional resources that might be needed, provides assistance and feedback to team members, and makes necessary strategic adjustments (Marks et al., 2001).

Why Teams Don't Always Work

Given that the failure rate for teams is at least 50% (Joinson, 1999), there has been an abundance of advice in the literature about how to create successful teams. In a study investigating this advice, Hyatt and Ruddy (1997) found that customer service teams were most effective when they received the necessary support from management (e.g., information, technology, training); had confidence in their ability to complete their tasks; were customer oriented; exhibited an open, supportive, and professional communication style; had set appropriate goals; and followed an agreed-upon group process. Moran, Musselwhite, and Zenger (1996) identified 12 common problems encountered by teams. Let's look at the six most important ones.

The Team Is Not a Team

Consistent with the previous discussion, teams often aren't successful because they are teams in name only.

Excessive Meeting Requirements

A common problem with teams is that they either meet too often or waste time when they meet. The key to successful team meetings is to limit the topics to be discussed and to meet only when the entire team is needed to contribute. Furthermore, teams often feel the need to meet for the entire time for which a meeting is scheduled, even though the necessary business could be conducted in much less time. This tendency to "stretch" a meeting can reduce the motivation and enthusiasm of a team.

As an example of the tendency to meet too often, I was placed on one of several teams whose task it was to address specific problems facing the university. Our team leader (committee chair) wanted us to meet every Wednesday at 2 o'clock until our task was completed. Because of the nature of our task, weeks might pass before we had anything new to bring to the group. Yet we still met every Wednesday. After 4 weeks, attendance at the meetings dropped to about 50%. When our angry team leader confronted our team members, she was shocked to hear such comments as "These weekly meetings are a waste of time" and "I always attend the important meetings, just not the worthless ones."

I was on another committee that demonstrated the tendency to stretch meetings. The committee contained 25 people and met one Friday a month from 3:00 to 4:30 p.m. When the dean ran the meetings, they always ended at exactly 4:30 p.m. When the dean was out of town, the committee's vice-chair (the second in command, not the person in charge of vice) would start the meetings by saying, "Let's do our business and get out of here." On these occasions, we never met past 3:45 p.m.

Lack of Empowerment

Many teams are formed to solve problems but are not given sufficient authority to conduct their business. According to Moran et al. (1996), teams aren't empowered because managers worry that the job won't be done correctly, the teams are moving too fast, and the teams will overstep their boundaries such that other parts of the organization will be affected. This last managerial concern is especially important because as teams work to solve problems their solutions often involve many different departments. If the teams are not properly empowered, they will lack the authority to overcome the political resistance of each affected department.

Though empowerment is essential for the success of most teams, it is not uncommon for team members to reject their empowered status. After all, with the advantages of empowerment come the risks of making mistakes and getting others angry. To many employees, these risks override the benefits of empowerment.

Lack of Skill

It is assumed that members assigned to a team have the skills necessary to effectively carry out their assignment. Unfortunately, this is often not the case (Yandrick, 2001b). What is most common is for team members to lack either the skills needed to work in a team (e.g., communication, problem solving) or the expertise to solve the problem itself. As an example, universities typically form committees whose membership consists of representatives from various colleges (e.g., arts and sciences, education) and departments (e.g., history, psychology, economics). Such a membership strategy makes sense if the issue is one on which various departments might differ. That is, a committee asked to determine general education requirements or summer school offerings should have representatives from each department. However, a committee formed to develop fund-raising strategies would be better served with a membership of marketing and psychology faculty rather than history and music faculty.

Research on the personal characteristics of team members has revealed some interesting findings. Teams whose members are bright, conscientious, extraverted, and emotionally stable perform better than do teams whose members do not possess such characteristics (Barrick, Stewart, Neubert, & Mount, 1998; Devine & Phillips, 2001).

Distrust of the Team Process

Many teams don't succeed because management doesn't trust the concept of teams. A study by the consulting firm Zinger Miller found that in organizations in which top management was not enthusiastic about the team approach only 49% of teams made satisfactory progress. However, in teams with supportive management, 84% of teams made satisfactory progress (Moran et al., 1996). Some of this distrust comes from managers being unwilling to give up any authority. Managers, too, need to be trained in the team process if the team concept is going to survive.

Team members must also be receptive to the team process. Research indicates that job satisfaction and organizational commitment are reduced when members are not receptive to the team process (Kirkman & Shapiro, 2001). Another source of team distrust is that not all work is appropriate for teams (Drexler & Forrester, 1998). That is, some tasks (e.g., typing) are better done individually and others, such as kissing, are performed better with the help of others.

Laid off	Restructured	Fired
Downsized	Dejobbed	Separated
Rightsized	Terminated	Canned
Wrongsized	Axed	Given the boot
Reengineered	Furloughed	RIFfed (Reduction in Force)

Unclear Objectives

Teams work best when they know why they were formed, what they are expected to accomplish (what is the team's "charge"), and when they are supposed to be finished. Though this statement sounds obvious, you would be surprised at how many teams aren't sure what they are supposed to do. As an example, I was on a university committee entitled "Committee on Student Evaluation of Faculty." We spent most of the time during our first few meetings asking "What are we supposed to do?" "Are we supposed to design a new evaluation instrument?" and "Do we make decisions or do we just make recommendations?" It took almost a month to get clarification, and during that time the committee made no progress, its members became frustrated, and attendance dropped. To practice what you have learned about teams, complete Exercise 14–4 at the end of this chapter.

Downsizing

When organizations restructure, the result is often a decrease in the size of their workforce (see Exhibit 14.06). For example, in 2002, restructuring resulted in 15,000 fewer jobs at Hewlett-Packard, 22,000 fewer at Kmart, 21,000 fewer at Ford, and 13,000 fewer at Lucent Technologies. These reductions in force are the result of a variety of factors, including economic difficulties, pressure by stockholders for quick profits, new technology replacing humans, mergers, and employee empowerment programs resulting in a lesser need for managers (Adam, 1997). Interestingly, 81% of downsizing organizations were profitable the year prior to downsizing (Cascio, 1995). Thus, economics is not always the major force driving downsizing. The number of layoffs in 2001 and 2002 rose tremendously due primarily to the fallout of the September 11 terrorist attacks and accounting scandals at such organizations as Enron and WorldCom.

Reducing the Impact of Downsizing

Signs of Problems

Short of a catastrophe, organizations usually have some warning that there may be an impending need to downsize. Steps taken at this stage can greatly reduce

the need for, or size of, future downsizing (Cascio, 2002). Unfortunately, less than 5% of organizations considered alternative steps to layoffs (Good, 1996).

A strategy taken by many organizations at this stage is to freeze the hiring of new permanent employees and either not fill vacancies caused by employees leaving or retiring or fill vacancies with **temporary employees.** Typically, these "temps" are hired through temporary employment agencies such as Kelly, Olsten, Bright Services, or Manpower. The advantage to using a temporary agency is that temps are not considered employees of the company and thus have no expectation of a future with the company. If business declines, the company can cancel its contract with the temporary agency. If business remains at a good level, the temp remains with the company.

If temps are going to stay with the organization for a long time, it is essential that they be treated like other employees. That is, they should be given the proper training, receive incentives for excellent performance, be given the supplies they need to do their jobs, and be invited to participate in informal activities such as going to lunch or attending a wedding shower (Vines, 1997).

A related strategy used by more than 80% of organizations is **outsourcing**—using outside vendors to provide services previously performed internally. For example, many organizations have found that it is more cost-efficient and productive to hire an outside vendor to manage their data-processing system than it is to keep five full-time data-processing employees on their payroll. Commonly outsourced functions include employee assistance/wellness programs, benefits and payroll administration, training, data processing, housekeeping, and landscaping.

Another strategy that can be taken at this stage is to encourage employees to change careers and then help these employees learn the skills needed to make the career change. An excellent example of this strategy, called the Alliance for Employee Development and Growth, was developed in the 1980s as a joint venture between AT&T and its union, the Communication Workers of America (CWA). In the 1980s and 1990s, AT&T realized that it would need to lay off many of its employees. To reduce the number of layoffs, the Alliance was created to encourage employees to look at their future, decide if they would be happier in another career, and then take steps toward changing careers. To help this change, the Alliance provided current employees with $1,500 per year to take classes or receive training in any legitimate career area. Thus, an assembly line worker could receive funding to learn to be a cosmetologist, a paralegal, or a computer programmer. Though the Alliance cost AT&T about $15 million per year, the money was easily recovered in decreased downsizing costs when employees left voluntarily or increased productivity resulting from a better-trained workforce.

A fourth strategy for reducing the need for layoffs is to offer early retirement packages. The idea here is to make it financially worthwhile for an employee to retire earlier than planned. For example, in 1996, Arizona Public Service Company offered employees 8 weeks of severance pay plus 2 more weeks for each year of service with the company. They also agreed to add a year of service time and a year to an employee's age. The company's plan was to encourage employees close to retirement to leave a little earlier than planned.

Though early retirement programs are expensive during the first few years, they can save a tremendous amount of money. A drawback to early retirement packages is that only 10 to 20% of eligible employees agree to take early retirement (Wyatt Company, 1993).

A fifth option to layoffs is to ask employees to take pay cuts. This strategy is based on the idea that most economic recessions last less than a year. If an organization lays off a significant number of its employees, it can take years to get production back to normal when the economy recovers. To get employees to agree to a pay cut, many organizations offer their employees company stock worth more than the pay cut. When the economy recovers, the employees are financially better off and the company has employees who are more committed to the success of the organization (Jossi, 2001a).

A final strategy involves adjusting work schedules. A 1992 survey by Right Associates, a Philadelphia-based consulting firm, revealed that 45% of organizations tried to avoid layoffs by restricting overtime, 74% tried job sharing, 9% implemented payless holidays or a shortened work week, and 6% reduced their employees' pay.

Employees can also reduce the effect of downsizing by monitoring their organization's economic health. According to Beyer, Pike, and McGovern (1993), signs of possible trouble include use of any of the workforce reduction strategies previously mentioned, rumors of corporate acquisitions or mergers, loss of a major contract, and increases in the number of "secret" managerial meetings.

Beyer et al. also advised employees to take stock of their personal standing at work to help determine their vulnerability to being laid off. Here are some important questions employees should ask themselves:

- Have I kept up with the latest changes in technology? Have I changed with the times?
- Have I received excellent performance appraisals? Do I actually make a contribution to the organization? Do I have a lot of downtime in which I do nothing?

- Do I hate my job? Does my dissatisfaction show? Does it affect my performance?
- Am I well liked? Do others, especially my manager, include me on both trivial and important decisions? Have I kept a good enough attitude that it would be emotionally difficult for my boss to get rid of me?

Selecting the Employees to Be Laid Off

Should the above measures not be sufficient and a layoff becomes necessary, the next step is to choose which employees will leave the organization. Criteria used to make this decision might include seniority, performance, salary level, or organizational need. To reduce the chances of legal problems, the committee deciding which employees will leave should be diverse in terms of race, sex, and age (Segal, 2001). The committee's decisions should be analyzed to determine potential adverse impact against protected classes (e.g., race, sex) or intentional discrimination against older workers.

The Announcement

The way in which the layoff is announced can affect the success of future programs designed to help employees. Layoff announcements are best done in person. Some organizations opt for a general announcement, whereas others prefer that supervisors notify their employees on a one-to-one basis. At this time, it is essential that employees receive concrete information. A mistake made by many organizations is to announce a downsizing but not to have answers to the hundreds of employee questions and concerns that are bound to follow. Employees need answers to questions like these:

- Why are the layoffs needed?
- Isn't there any other alternative?
- When will the layoffs take place?
- Who will be laid off?
- What type of financial assistance will be available?
- Will we get help writing our resumes?
- How will this affect my pension?

When answers to employees' questions are not available, employees become anxious, angry, and resentful and tend to develop their own answers (rumors).

Outplacement Programs

To help layoff victims move on with their lives, many organizations have some type of outplacement program (Juergens, 2001). These programs typically include emotional counseling, financial counseling, career assessment and guidance, and job search training.

Emotional Counseling. After receiving word of being laid off, employees go through four stages that are similar to the stages of change: denial, anger, fear, and acceptance. In the **denial stage**, employees deny that a layoff will actually occur. They make statements like "I'm sure the company will come to its senses," "There is no way they will actually lay off a person with my seniority," and "This can't be happening." For some employees, this stage will last a few hours; for others, it can last until the minute they are no longer working. When employees are in the denial stage, they will not participate in efforts to help them (e.g., resume writing or interview skills) because they don't see a need to participate in something that is not going to happen.

In the **anger stage**, employees realize that they will be losing their jobs, and they become angry at the organization, their supervisors, and even their coworkers, especially those who will not be losing their jobs. At this stage it is important that employees be given an appropriate avenue to vent their anger and frustration. It is not uncommon to have "support groups" for layoff victims, and the first few meetings of these groups are usually spent venting.

After the anger has subsided, employees move to the **fear stage**. During this third stage, employees start to worry about how they are going to pay bills, feed their families, and find new jobs. At this stage, the emotional counseling moves from a listening stage to one that is more empathic and soothing.

Though layoff victims remain fearful for much of the layoff period, they eventually move to the **acceptance stage**. At this stage, the victims accept that the layoff will occur and are now ready to take steps to secure their future. It is at this last stage that employees are ready for specific offers of assistance.

Financial Counseling. As layoff victims move through the fear stage into the acceptance stage, financial counseling is needed. Layoff victims are under tremendous stress as they worry about how to make their rent, mortgage, and loan payments and how to pay for utilities, insurance, food, tuition, and medical and dental costs. Most banks and credit unions have certified financial counselors who are well trained in helping people with these concerns. The financial counseling process should include the issues of severance pay, unemployment insurance, medical insurance, and any special programs that might be available to help the layoff victims.

Career Assessment and Guidance. Though many layoff victims will search for jobs similar to the ones that they left, many layoff victims will need to consider other careers. Psychologists involved in this process will administer a battery of tests that tap an individual's basic abilities (e.g., math, grammar), transferable skills (e.g., woodworking, typing), career interests, and work values (e.g., status, independence, leadership). In discussing potential careers, such life realities as financial needs, time constraints (e.g., "I can't take 4 years to earn a degree"), and geographic constraints (e.g., "I want to stay near my family" or "My spouse has a good job, and I can't leave the immediate area") need to be considered. For employees willing and able to relocate or go back to school, finding a new job is not as difficult as it is for employees who are limited to a particular geographic area and are not able or willing to be retrained.

A major issue that arises during this process is the ability of a layoff victim to obtain new training. Jobs in the 21st century require higher levels of skill than did their earlier counterparts. So retraining is often necessary to get a new job. However, barriers such as funding and day care problems, the lack of relevant training sites, and fear of going back to school can keep layoff victims from getting the new training they so desperately need.

To help layoff victims find new employment, workshops are conducted on such topics as understanding the job market, finding potential job openings, writing resumes, performing well in the employment interview, and making decisions about job offers.

Effects of Downsizing

Victims

Research is clear that there are many negative consequences to losing one's job. From a health perspective, **victims** of downsizing report increases in headaches, stomach upsets, sleeping problems, cholesterol levels, physical illness, hospitalization rates, heart trouble, hypertension, ulcers, vision problems, and shortness of breath. Emotionally, victims report high levels of stress, increased drug and alcohol abuse, more marital problems, and feelings of depression, unhappiness, anger, frustration, and dissatisfaction with life. Socially, victims are reluctant to share their feelings with friends, avoid family and friends due to feelings of embarrassment and shame, and avoid social situations and entertainment requiring money.

To reduce the effects of downsizing, Beyer and colleagues (1993) advise layoff victims to do the following:

1. Immediately tell their families.
2. Evaluate the reasons for the job loss. That is, was the loss inevitable due to problems with the organization, or could better performance, more current skills, or a better attitude have allowed the employee to keep his job?
3. Deal with the emotions that accompany a layoff (e.g., anger, disbelief, guilt, shame) and to get help if necessary.
4. Prepare for departure by doing such things as securing references, negotiating a severance package, and taking advantage of outplacement opportunities.
5. Take a vacation or a short rest period to help prepare for the journey ahead.
6. Plan a new course of action and go forward with confidence.

Survivors

At first, one might think that an organization need not worry about **survivors**—those employees not laid off. After all, these are people who still have their jobs. However, research indicates not only that survivors suffer psychological trauma but that their future productivity is related to the way in which they and their not so fortunate counterparts are treated during the downsizing process. Research (Cascio, 1993; Marks, 2003) indicates that survivors

- become afraid of taking risks and are more apprehensive and narrow minded.
- are more stressed, anxious, secretive, skeptical, cynical, and distrustful.
- have greater role conflict and ambiguity.
- lose confidence in themselves and in management.
- feel a loss of control.
- have lower levels of morale and job satisfaction.

Survivors will be more productive and feel more secure if they are allowed to participate in decisions and make suggestions, are given a moderate level of job security, are supported by supervisors and the organization, and if the layoff victims were treated well (Kernan & Hanges, 2002; Preston, 2003). It is important that the organization talk positively about the layoff victims, keep an open two-way communication policy with survivors, and communicate the company vision to the survivors. To reduce the negative effects on survivors, organizations must ensure that the procedure used to determine layoffs is fair and that the procedure is clearly communicated both to victims and survivors (Sadri, 1996).

Local Community

Though not often considered, layoffs and plant closings have a tremendous impact on the local community. Local governments suffer as their tax base and revenues are reduced, local charities such as the United Way get fewer donations and often have increased demands for their services, retail stores lose business, banks have greater numbers of loan defaults, crime rates increase, and social problems (e.g., drinking, divorce) increase. On the positive side, layoffs result in an increase in the quality of the available workforce. This increased quality can help other employers and may even result in attracting new industry.

The Organization

Though many organizations continue to downsize, it is not clear that downsizing produces the desired increases in organizational effectiveness. For example:

- Cascio (2002) reports that organizations that downsized between 1982 and 2000 did not improve the financial success of their organizations.
- Henkoff (1990) surveyed almost 1,500 downsized organizations and found that half reported lower productivity.
- A Wyatt Company (1993) survey found that only 46% of downsized organizations reduced expenses, 22% increased productivity, and 9% improved quality.
- The Tierney Group (Peak, 1997) surveyed 300 organizations and found that disability claims and costs increased following downsizing.

To apply what you have learned about downsizing, complete the Downsizing Exercise on your CD-ROM.

Chapter Summary

In this chapter you learned:

- Employees react to change by going through the stages of denial, defense, discarding, adaptation, and finally internalization.
- Employees best accept change if the reason behind the change makes sense and the person making the change is trusted and respected.
- Change is best implemented by creating an atmosphere for change, communicating details, making the change over a reasonable period of time, and training employees. Employees can best accept change if they speed up, take initiative, and spend energy on solutions rather than complaining.
- The five levels of employee input are following, ownership of own product, advisory, shared, and absolute.
- Teams go through four developmental stages: forming, storming, norming, and performing.
- The team approach is not always best.
- Layoffs can be avoided by using temporary employees, outsourcing, offering early retirement programs, and creating alternative work schedules.
- There is a proper way to conduct a layoff.
- Layoffs have negative effects on victims, survivors, the organization, and the community.

Critical Thinking Questions

1. Why are employees reluctant to change?
2. How important is organizational culture on organization development?
3. When organizations talk about "empowering employees," what do they actually mean?
4. How do we build effective teams?
5. Is downsizing a good idea?

 To learn more about the issues discussed in this chapter, point your browser to

http://www.infotrac-college.com/wadsworth

and enter one of these search terms:

change in the workplace

organizational culture

employee empowerment

Vroom-Yetton model

workplace teams

downsizing

employee input

Exercise 14–1
Sacred Cow Hunts

For this exercise, get several forms that you must fill out at your university. These can include applications to graduate, registration forms, and change-of-grade forms. For each of the forms, conduct a "paper cow hunt." That is, determine if the form is really needed. If it is, is all the information and are all of the signatures asked for actually necessary?

Form 1: _____

_____

_____

_____

_____

_____

_____

_____

_____

Form 2: _____

_____

_____

_____

_____

_____

_____

_____

_____

_____

_____

_____

Form 3: _____

_____

_____

_____

_____

_____

_____

_____

_____

_____

_____

_____

Form 4: _____

_____

_____

_____

_____

_____

_____

_____

_____

_____

_____

_____

Exercise 14–2
Organizational Culture

Think about either your current job or one that you held previously. How would you describe the organizational culture? What types of values, beliefs, and traditions were there? What type of climate existed? Compare this culture to that of another job. If you have not had enough work experience, think about the culture of two classes you have had or about two clubs you have belonged to.

_____

_____

_____

_____

_____

_____

_____

_____

_____

_____

_____

_____

_____

_____

_____

_____

_____

_____

_____

_____

_____

_____

Exercise 14–3
Vroom-Yetton Decision-Making Model

The Vroom-Yetton model shown in Exhibit 14.01 provides leaders with a system to help determine how a decision should be made. This exercise will provide you with the opportunity to use the Vroom-Yetton model.

Each of these situations requires a decision to be made. Using the chart in Exhibit 14.01, determine which of the five strategies — Autocratic I, Autocratic II, Consultative I, Consultative II, Group I—the leader should use to make the decision.

Situation A

Jonathon Hancock has been asked to set production goals for his welders and then to return a signed copy of these goals to the plant manager. Mr. Hancock has been a supervisor for 10 years. He always dreads setting goals and does not think they are useful. What strategy should he use?

_____ Autocratic I
_____ Autocratic II
_____ Consultative I
_____ Consultative II
_____ Group I

Why did you choose this strategy?

_____

_____

_____

Situation B

Krista Harrison is the branch manager for a small bank and must schedule vacations for her ten employees. The regional manager wants the vacation lists to her in the next week. What strategy should she use?

_____ Autocratic I
_____ Autocratic II
_____ Consultative I
_____ Consultative II
_____ Group I

Why did you choose this strategy?

_____

_____

_____

Situation C

Kent Clark is an optometrist and has four assistants who work for him. Dr. Clark is considering purchasing a new piece of equipment that will allow him to more accurately measure the vision needs of his patients. What decision-making strategy should he use?

_____ Autocratic I
_____ Autocratic II
_____ Consultative I
_____ Consultative II
_____ Group I

Why did you choose this strategy?

_____

_____

_____

_____

_____

Situation D

Debika Johnson is the vice president of Reilly College. She has been at Reilly for 6 months and must create a policy for student evaluation of faculty. That is, she needs to decide what type of evaluation instrument will be used, how often evaluations will occur, and how much weight the student evaluations should carry in the overall evaluation of a faculty member. What strategy should she use?

_____ Autocratic I
_____ Autocratic II
_____ Consultative I
_____ Consultative II
_____ Group I

Why did you choose this strategy?

_____

_____

_____

_____

_____

Exercise 14–4
Teams

Think of the last team that you were a member of. It could be a work team, an athletic team, or a team assigned to complete a group project. On the basis of what you read in the chapter, answer these questions:

1.   Was your team actually a team?

_____

_____

_____

_____

_____

2.   Did the team go through the forming, storming, norming, and performing stages?

_____

_____

_____

_____

_____

3.   Was the team successful? Why or why not?

_____

_____

_____

_____

_____

15 Stress Management: Dealing with the Demands of Life and Work

AN INFLUENCING FACTOR over your behavior and thus your relations with others at work is stress: more than 75% of workers in the United States consider their jobs to be stressful (Smith, 2003a). Not only does stress affect your interpersonal style, it can have serious health implications if ignored and not properly managed. To properly manage stress, you must first identify and understand what causes your stress and then learn ways to handle that stress. This chapter will identify some of the sources of stress and suggest successful ways for dealing with it. By the end of this chapter you will

- learn the definition of stress.
- be able to name common stressors.
- learn the common consequences of stress (strains).
- understand the effects of stress on behavior.
- learn ways to reduce stress.
- be familiar with the importance of child care and elder care programs.
- learn how stress can at times result in workplace violence.

To get you thinking about stress, complete the focused free write on your CD-ROM.

Stress Defined

Though psychologists cannot agree on one definition for the word *stress* (Beehr, 1996), for the purpose of this chapter, **stress** will be defined as the psychological and physical reaction to certain life events or situations (called **stressors**). Here, the emphasis is on how we respond to the stressor, as opposed to the stressor itself. **Strain** is the physical and psychological consequences of stress.

As you may have already discovered, what is a stressor to you may not be stressful to another person. For example, if you have ever been in a minor car accident in which no one was hurt, you may or may not have experienced stress depending on how your body and mind responded to the incident. Maybe you and the other party, while exchanging phone numbers and insurance information, actually had a good laugh over what happened. Others of you may have experienced extreme fear and suffered from nightmares and body aches for several days or weeks.

Eustress

Contrary to popular belief, not all stress is bad. **Eustress** occurs when stress is converted to positive energy and becomes motivating. You might say it is a desirable outcome of stress. An example of positive stress is the anxiety you feel before taking a test. If you felt no anxiety at all, you might not have the motivation and energy to spend the necessary time studying for the exam. Thus, some stress in this situation is probably helpful. However, if you are too stressed, your performance will decline. This is what is known as the **optimal level of arousal**. As shown in Exhibit 15.01, having no arousal or too much arousal results in poor performance, whereas a moderate level results in the highest levels of performance. Of course, the optimal level of arousal is different for each person.

Distress

Bad or negative stress, known as **distress**, happens when there is too much stress and nothing is done to eliminate, reduce, or counteract its effects. Distress usually occurs in situations or at events on which you place great importance (e.g., interviewing for a job) that put great demands on you and over which you eventually perceive you have little or no control. For example, having to wait in line to drop or add a class may be irritating, but it's usually not a big enough deal to cause distress. But interviewing for a new job or a new position that you really need for financial reasons can be a big source of stress, particularly if you feel you have

Exhibit **15.01** Optimal level of arousal

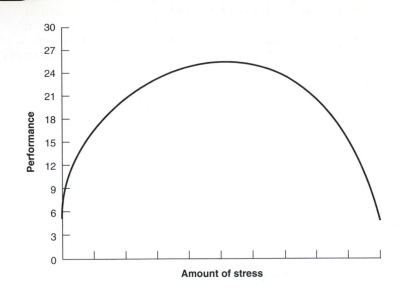

Amount of stress

little control over whether you get the job. Quite simply, negative stress occurs when we perceive an imbalance between the demands (stressors) placed on us and our ability to meet those demands (Davidson, 1997).

The distinction between eustress and distress is important because when employees report being stressed, their performance will not necessarily diminish. For example, in a study of more than 1,800 U.S. managers, the amount of eustress (called challenge-related stress by the researchers) had no relationship to job satisfaction or attempts to leave the organization. However, managers with high levels of distress (hindrance-related stress) were less satisfied with their jobs, left there jobs more often, and made more attempts to find a new job than did managers with low levels of distress (Cavanaugh, Boswell, Roehling, & Boudreau, 2000).

Predisposition to Stress

There appear to be individual differences in the extent to which people are susceptible to stress or are predisposed to tolerate stressors. For example, rates of coronary heart disease, exacerbated by stress, are higher for divorced persons than married people. Married people report higher satisfaction and less stress than unmarried people, top corporation executives have lower mortality rates than second-level executives, and people who live in suburban environments have more stress-related illness than people who live in rural environments. These individual tolerances can be explained by the following factors.

Stress Personalities

Some personalities are more apt to respond negatively to stressors. These include individuals with **Type A** personalities and pessimists. Others, such as **Type B**

personalities and optimists, seem to respond more positively toward stressors.

Do you, or does someone you know, talk and walk fast, get impatient easily, and always seem to be in a hurry? Chances are you or the person you know has a Type A personality. Type A individuals have three main characteristics: achievement striving, impatience and time urgency, and anger and hostility. Type A individuals tend to do many things at one time (called *multitasking*). For example, a Type A individual would read the paper while eating lunch, type on the computer while talking to someone on the phone, and eat breakfast while driving to work. Type A's are fast-paced individuals who talk and walk fast, finish other people's sentences, and always seem to be on the go. They are achievement-oriented, competitive individuals who tend to place work before pleasure. These characteristics become exaggerated when the Type A personality experiences stress (Schaubroeck, Ganster, & Kemmerer, 1994). Type A employees under stress are more likely than others to exhibit high blood pressure and high levels of stress-related hormones. In addition, Type A individuals are slower to recover after the stressor is removed (Schaubroeck et al., 1994).

Type B individuals seem to be more laid back. That is, when a potentially stress-producing event occurs, they are better able to keep it in perspective and use more positive ways to deal with it. They are more relaxed and more agreeable. To determine if you are a Type A personality, complete Exercise 15–1 at the end of this chapter.

Pessimists are very negative people who don't respond appropriately to stress. They tend to ignore the problem or source of the stress, often give up on goals blocked by stress, and do not attempt to develop positive ways to deal with the problem. This type of individual might be the one who, failing in a required class that is causing a great deal of stress, believes it won't do any good to talk to the professor because the professor hates her and life sucks! Does that sound familiar? **Optimists**, on the other hand, deal with stress head on. In fact, they are more likely to seek proactive means of dealing with stress, such as exercise or obtaining advice from others. Optimists have lower blood pressure levels and higher performance levels than do pessimists (Begley, Lee, & Czajka, 2000). To determine if you are a pessimist or an optimist, complete Exercise 15–2.

Dempcy and Tihista (1996) believe there are actually seven types of stress personalities. You may see yourself in one or all of them because most of us have a blend of personalities that influence our behavior. These personalities can actually be the source of stress or the cause of escalating stress. If you understand your stress personality, you may be able to modify your behavior in future stress-producing situations.

Pleasers want to make everyone happy and are usually cooperative and helpful. They tend to take on many demands and responsibilities. Under stress, which occurs when they are no longer able to meet their needs or those of others, they display resentment and perhaps anger. **Internal timekeepers** also seem desirous of taking on a lot of responsibility, perhaps to please or just because of their interest in doing so many things. Under normal situations, they are very energized, efficient, and competent. Under stress, which is often caused by taking on too much, they become inefficient and anxious.

Strivers are ambitious and competitive and are usually their own source of stress. Why? Because they continue to make demands on themselves—some of which they cannot meet. Their goal is to be successful at everything, even if it means to work, work, work until finally they burn out. Then there are the **inner con artists** who convince themselves to not work too hard, to avoid conflict (which usually means avoiding responsibility), or to ignore potentially stress-producing situations. This is self-defeating behavior and ultimately leads to even more stress in the long run as these types of people, also known as "procrastinators," fall behind in both personal and work responsibilities.

Critical judges, when under stress, focus on the negative about themselves and their situation. This type of personality focuses on mistakes, not on learning from mistakes. **Worriers** are as negative as critical judges and are highly influenced by unpredictability and unclear situations. If they don't know what is going to happen next, they predict the worst! Their constant obsessing over the future increases their stress levels. Worriers need others to tell them what they can expect from situation to situation. Finally, **sabertooths** respond to stress with a great deal of anger, which is often expressed through sarcasm or humorous insults. Needless to say, this type of stress personality can also be the source of stress to others!

Gender, Ethnicity, and Race

Much of the research on gender and stress is conflicting. Many studies suggest that women have more stress than men and that depression is twice as common among women as men. Other studies claim that gender is not a contributor to stress (e.g., Guppy & Rick, 1996).

Only minor differences in reactions to stress have been found among racial and ethnic groups. What few differences there are mostly concern physical reactions to stress. For example, African American men seem to experience higher rates of hypertension than white men.

Stress Sensitization

The amount of stress you have experienced throughout your life seems to affect how you will handle future stress. For instance, if you are exposed to high levels of stress (such as abuse) over a long duration, studies suggest that you are likely to react more quickly and more negatively to situations that are potentially stress producing because, in a sense, you have become "trained" to respond in such a way. That is, if you are used to being jumpy because of the stress you experienced earlier in your life, you are more likely to react that way with future stress. This, of course, has implications for your future health and your stress behaviors. Desensitization can occur through learning new behaviors to handle stress and working through your feelings about past stress.

Sources of Stress

Many events and factors could be considered stressors, and, as previously stated, what is stressful for one person may not be for another. Again, what determines whether something will be a stressor depends a great deal on its importance and the amount of perceived controllability. Stressors can be grouped under two broad categories: personal and occupational. Exhibit 15.02 lists common personal and occupational sources of stress.

Personal Stressors

Personal sources of stress deal with such nonwork issues as family and intimate relationships, marriage, divorce, health issues, financial problems, and raising children. Difficult and angry people are also sources of stress because of the conflict they cause in our personal and work life. In addition, having to deal with life's changes can be enormously stressful. In fact, many stressors can be considered as our reaction to change, whether the change is moving to a new home, ending or beginning a new relationship, or changing ourselves.

Exhibit 15.02 shows how teenagers and young adults are "stressed" by the demands of school and the transition from the security of childhood to the demands of adulthood. Throughout high school, teens experience an enormous amount of change. Change is a major contributor to stress, and it affects both your personal life and your professional life. Why do you think that is? For most of us, change gives rise to at least one, if not all, of these three responses—fear,

Exhibit **15.02** Common stressors

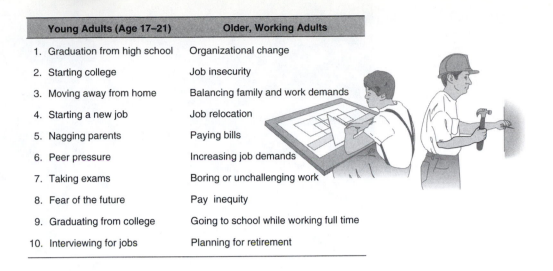

Young Adults (Age 17–21)	Older, Working Adults
1. Graduation from high school	Organizational change
2. Starting college	Job insecurity
3. Moving away from home	Balancing family and work demands
4. Starting a new job	Job relocation
5. Nagging parents	Paying bills
6. Peer pressure	Increasing job demands
7. Taking exams	Boring or unchallenging work
8. Fear of the future	Pay inequity
9. Graduating from college	Going to school while working full time
10. Interviewing for jobs	Planning for retirement

resistance, and resentment—all of which ultimately lead to stress. You may have already experienced one of these emotions upon entering college after graduating from high school.

Fear

When we voluntarily or involuntarily leave a stage of our lives that has become comfortable and predicable, we enter another stage in which we don't know what will happen. The challenge and potential excitement from the change can produce eustress in people who thrive on unpredictability. But to many of us, fear of the unknown produces negative stress. For example, when you were a senior in high school, did you think a lot about what the future would hold? Although anxious to move out of their family home and be on their own, many students respond that they were terrified of what could happen. They didn't know if they would be successful in life—they weren't even sure they could get a job to support themselves. They were sure they would fail in college, which they felt meant failing in life!

Other students respond that they were "psyched" about the thought of moving out and trying a new life! For those of you who are more fearful than challenged by change, you are probably already recognizing that the key to handling "fear of the unknown" is seeing that there aren't the monsters you thought there would be if you made the change. In other words, handling your fears in the future means realizing that most change does not end up being as bad as you first predicted.

Resistance

Let's face it—some of us just don't want to leave the security and structure of that which is known. We like the predictability in our lives, no matter how boring. We like knowing what is going to happen from day to day, and telling us that we have to change our routine

can throw us into a tailspin. Something as minor as having to change brands of toothpaste can be too much for us to handle and send us into a determined stubbornness not to change! A good illustration of resistance to change is holding onto old traditions that are no longer feasible. For example, I met a man at a conference who said that for many years after his divorce he still expected to spend Christmases with his former in-laws! It had been a tradition for him for more than 15 years, and he didn't understand why that tradition should stop just because he was no longer legally part of the family. He continued to call his ex-wife for several Christmases after the divorce, asking to join in the festivities. Of course, he was turned down, and the continued stress from this rejection and his refusal to change eventually led him to seek counseling. He seems to be doing better now and has even begun trying to start his own holiday traditions with the new woman in his life. Resisting change doesn't allow people to cope with inevitable changes that come from living. This resistance leads to stress.

Resentment

Finally, changes that are forced on us, particularly those that we feel we had no control over or input into, can cause resentment. If we don't want the change, don't understand why we have to make the change, and don't like how the change makes us feel (e.g., scared and confused), it raises feelings of resentment. Later in this chapter, we will discuss more about how to deal with life's changes.

Occupational Stressors

Exhibit 15.02 shows how experience and age contribute to what individuals consider sources of stress. Individuals who have been on their own and in the workforce

Stress can be a major problem at work.

PhotoDisc, Inc.

full time seem preoccupied with the stress that work brings. Organizational stressors can be grouped under two broad categories: job characteristics and organizational characteristics (Cordes & Dougherty, 1993).

Job Characteristics

Three main job characteristics cause stress: role conflict, role ambiguity, and role overload.

Role conflict occurs when our work expectations and what we think we should be doing don't match up with the work we actually have to do. For example, a woman who was hired as assistant to the chief executive officer (CEO) of one particular organization was informed upon hire that she would be handling such administrative duties as policy development, participating as an equal partner in management meetings, and serving as a liaison between the CEO and the public. However, after she had been on the job for a while, she heard herself referred to as a "secretary," not only by the CEO but by other department heads too. In fact, the work she ended up doing mainly consisted of taking minutes at various meetings, ensuring that there was food at those meetings, and doing other routine clerical work such as answering the phone and routing interoffice mail. What she expected from the position was incompatible with what she was actually required to do. This role conflict caused her a great deal of stress, and, consistent with research on the effects of role conflict (e.g., Griffeth et al., 2000; Rahim & Psenicka, 1996), she eventually quit her job.

Role conflict can also occur when an employee has competing roles or conflicting roles. For example, an employee's role as manager may require her to work on a Saturday, but her role as a mother requires her to attend her daughter's soccer game on the same day.

Role ambiguity occurs when an individual's job duties and performance expectations are not clearly defined. In the preceding example, the woman experienced not only role conflict but role ambiguity because what her boss expected her to do was different from what the other staff expected her to do. Although her boss referred to her as "secretary," a job title that clearly denotes certain duties, he felt that she should have an equal say in certain decisions affecting the organization. The other directors, however, did not consider her their "peer" and did not feel she should have the same power or authority that they had. Because the director did not, in the 4 years she worked there, ever settle that issue, she was never sure just how she was supposed to act at committee meetings. Needless to say, each day brought more and more stress as she struggled to find out, on her own, just what her job responsibilities should be. Consistent with the research of Frone, Russell, and Cooper (1995), the stress of this role ambiguity caused her to become depressed, and consistent with the meta-analysis by Abramis (1994), her job satisfaction decreased.

Role overload develops when an individual feels he lacks either the skills or workplace resources to complete a task or perceives that the task cannot be done in the required amount of time (Cordes & Dougherty, 1993). Role overload has been cited as one of the primary reasons for job stress. Research indicates that role overload can cause anxiety, depression, and anger (Rahim & Psenicka, 1996); especially when employees have little control over their jobs (Karasek & Theorell, 1990). As suggested in Chapter 14, the negative consequences of role overload can be reduced if organizations actively ensure that employees have increased control over their jobs (Parker & Sprigg, 1999).

The key to minimizing the stress that comes from role conflict, ambiguity, and overload is to get clarification about your job duties. Although you are given a job description upon hire, make sure you sit down with your boss to ensure that you know just what he expects from you. In fact, it is wise to discuss the particulars of the job description prior to hire so that you are clear about work expectations. If you have been assigned a project you don't fully understand or feel you can't complete, let your employer know. Further, if possible, suggest that you be allowed to participate in training that can help you complete the project. Finally, it is sometimes beneficial if your boss explains your job responsibilities to other staff. This explanation should reduce any misunderstanding about your role in the organization.

Organizational Characteristics

Organizational characteristics that are likely to cause stress include such factors as person–organization fit, organizational rules and policies, supervisory relationships, and organizational change.

Person–Organization Fit. The term **person–organization fit** refers to how well such factors as your skills, knowledge, abilities, expectations, personality, values, and attitudes match those of the organization. At one time, organizations were primarily concerned that applicants had the necessary skills and knowledge to perform certain jobs. Now, organizations, as well as workers, realize there are other areas in which compatibility is critical for an employee to "fit" into an organization and perform well. For example, a pro-life individual may not work well in an organization such as Planned Parenthood, a nonsmoker may not feel comfortable working for Phillip-Morris, and an environmentally conscious person may be unhappy working for Exxon because the philosophies of the individual and the organization are not the same. This incompatibility in philosophies and values can cause stress (Lovelace & Rosen, 1996), lower job satisfaction, and increased turnover (Bretz & Judge, 1994).

The management philosophy of an organization may not meet the expectations of some individuals. A person who works best in a very structured environment (e.g., the military) in which everyone must follow a chain of command may not work well in a team-oriented environment where the workers have the opportunity to make and enforce policy. Incompatibilities between personal and management philosophies can quickly become a stressor (Atkinson, 2000). Other stressors include the relationships between supervisors and employees. If an employee's expectation of that relationship differs from the supervisor's, not only will stress result, but conflict between the parties will inevitably arise.

Work Environment. As will be discussed in great detail in Chapter 16, the environment in which you work can produce stress. For example, noise in the workplace can be stressful to some people, which can affect their performance. Research indicates that continued exposure to high levels of noise can raise blood pressure (Evans, Hygge, & Bullinger, 1995), worker illness (Cohen, 1972), and produce more aggressive and irritable behavior in response to the stress noise causes (Donnerstein & Wilson, 1976).

Shift work can also have stressful consequences on individuals. Research shows that working evening and late night shifts have many physical, mental, and work-related effects. These include fatigue (Nicholson, Jackson, & Howes, 1978) and deterioration in physical health (Frese & Semmer, 1986) and mental health (Jamal, 1981).

Change. As discussed in Chapter 14, a major contributor to organizational stress is change, which occurs most often from downsizing and restructuring, trends that are expected to continue into the 21st century (Offermann & Gowing, 1990). Realizing the amount of stress accompanying change, organizations are placing increasing emphasis on workplace wellness by offering programs that teach employees how to cope with change and manage stress.

Relations with Others. Our coworkers and customers can be a major source of workplace stress (see Chapter 13). Though I don't want to rehash material you learned in previous chapters, it is important to understand the stress associated with conflict, working with difficult people, dealing with angry customers, and feeling that you are not being treated fairly. An employee I met at one organization provides a perfect example of this stress. The employee worked at a job she enjoyed, and her personal life was more fulfilling than it had been in years. Despite the positive aspects of her job and life, she had trouble sleeping, lacked energy, and was depressed. What was the source of these strains? A difficult coworker who constantly yelled, used sarcasm, and belittled everyone. Such a story is not unusual and demonstrates the important role interpersonal relationships can play in causing stress. In fact, a study of more than 15,000 employees over a 4-year period found that stress from interpersonal conflict at work resulted in a number of severe psychiatric problems (Romanov, Appelberg, Honsakalo, & Koskenvuo, 1996).

Organizational Politics. A meta-analysis by Chang and Rosen (2003) found that an important source of employee stress is the perceived use of organizational politics. Organizational politics are self-serving behaviors employees use to increase the probability of obtaining positive outcomes in organizations. *Positive politics* are behaviors designed to influence others with the goal of helping both the organization and the person playing the politics (Holden, 1998). Examples of positive politics include portraying a professional image, publicizing one's accomplishments, volunteering, and complimenting others. *Negative politics* are manipulative behaviors designed to achieve personal gain at the expense of others and the organization (Holden, 1998). Examples of negative politics include backstabbing, withholding important information from others, and spreading rumors. In addition to increasing stress, negative organizational politics result in lower performance, lower levels of job satisfaction, and higher turnover (Chang & Rosen, 2003).

Other Sources of Stress

Minor Frustration

Minor frustration is stress we encounter in our daily lives, and it might include irritations such as waiting in traffic or not being able to get some information from the library. Minor frustrations may try our patience, but in and of themselves these daily frustrations may not be a problem and usually last for only a short duration, such as an hour or a few hours. If we do not have a healthy outlet for our frustrations, they may build up over time until they control us. These short-term frustrations may then carry over to the next day and then the next, until finally they become long-term stressors.

Minor frustrations can be managed through perspective taking. **Perspective taking** means rating the frustration on a scale of 1 to 10 with 10 meaning the situation is worthy of high levels of irritation. A friend of mine rates everything on a scale of life and death. He says that during potential stress-producing situations he asks himself the following question: "How bad is this in relation to death?" Because he served in Vietnam, faced death often, and in fact saw many of his buddies killed, most of the situations he confronts get a very low rating. Consequently, he is basically a very peaceful and laid-back individual. Now, most of us can't relate to life's situations on that basis because we have never come close to experiencing death. But we can still ask ourselves: "In the scheme of things, just how important was that incident? Is it important enough for me to have a bad day, increase my chances of a heart attack, or die for?" See how this perspective taking works? Making sure you don't make "mountains out of molehills" can keep you from having to deal with the long-term effects of stress.

Forecasting

The stress from **forecasting** develops from constantly worrying about the future and wasting time and energy on "what ifs?" This continuous fretting about things over which we may have no control (such as the end of the universe from aliens!) or that may never even happen can become very emotionally and physically draining, not to mention debilitating. Forecasting very quickly becomes long-term stress as we continue to keep our minds and body in a fearful and anxious state. Learning how to recognize those areas you can't control and ceasing to worry about them is the key to eliminating stress from forecasting.

Residual Stress

Residual stress is stress that is carried over from previous stressful situations that we refuse to "let go." Minor frustrations can become residual stress if we don't handle those daily problems effectively and rehash them over and over again. Many people continue to carry grudges, hurt, or anger from past situations that keep them in a constant state of stress. For example, have you ever been in a relationship that ended unexpectedly? If you didn't want the relationship to end, you may have been very hurt and then became angry. Now, every time you think of that situation, you get angry and hurt all over again. Many people continue to dredge up those bad feelings long after the relationship is over. All this serves to do is recycle the stress process. Residual stress is almost always long term: If not dealt with, it chips away at our physical and emotional well-being until we become prisoners to its effects. This type of stress eventually leads individuals to therapy and counseling to learn positive ways, such as forgiveness, to cope with past negative experiences.

Consequences of Stress

Personal Consequences

How we respond to stress can have devastating consequences. For instance, responding with anger or rage can lead to family members being hurt, the loss of jobs, and perhaps trouble with the law. Responding with the use of alcohol and drugs can lead to addiction, broken relationships, and even death. Financially, the impaired decisions we make while under stress can have negative consequences. In an interesting study, Repetti and Wood (1997) examined the effects of work stress on the relationships between 30 working mothers and their preschool children. The results of the study indicated that on highly stressful workdays, mothers spoke less often to their children and had fewer expressions of affection.

As shown in Exhibit 15.03, there are numerous physical responses to stress. Some people sweat under extreme stress. For example, many people report that interviewing for a job is very stressful and causes them to sweat. Headaches and body aches are also symptoms of stress. If you are prone to migraines, you may find that your migraines occur more often during stressful situations. Body aches often are the result of tensing up during stressful times. Many people report that when they awake in the morning their back, neck, shoulders, and legs are very sore, which can be attributed to tensing during sleep. Extreme physical responses to stress include hair loss. Although we are supposed to lose several strands of hair a day, which are replaced by new

Exhibit 15.03 The stress process

Stressors	Strains	Behaviors
Personal	**Psychological**	**Health**
Marital problems	Depression	Smoking
Family problems	Anxiety	Drinking
Health problems	Anger	Drug abuse
Financial problems	Sleep problems	
Daily hassles		**Work Related**
Residual stress	**Physical**	Absenteeism
	Illness	Turnover
Occupational	Cardiovascular problems	Lower productivity
Job Characteristics	Headaches	Workplace violence
Role conflict	Joint pain	
Role ambiguity		
Role overload		
Organizational Characteristics		
Person–organization fit		
Work environment		
Change		
Relations with others		
Coworker problems		
Supervisor problems		
Difficult and angry		
customers		
Lack of empowerment		
Personality/Habits		
Type A		
Pessimism		
Tendency to forecast		
Diet		
Exercise		

hair, hair that falls out in clumps is often your body's way of signaling high amounts of stress.

Stress has been labeled the "silent killer" because, as you have already read, it can quietly chip away at your immune system, thereby weakening your body's ability to prevent or fight off illnesses and diseases. It is often the source of debilitating ulcers, escalating blood pressure, heart attacks, strokes, or worse: death. Stress may also increase the symptoms of rheumatoid arthritis because the hormones released in response to stress can cause swelling in the joints (Carpi, 1996). In fact, research suggests that 50 to 70% of all illnesses, such as coronary heart disease, can be attributed to stress. Even minor ailments such as recurring colds can be attributed to recent stressful events.

Depression is another health problem associated with stress. Most of us experience some form of depression from time to time. Usually, a good night's sleep or being with friends and family will lift that depression. Sometimes a few visits to a counselor who can help us sort out our feelings and put things in perspective is helpful. Long-term stress, however, can eventually lead to clinical depression, which often requires medical treatment. In addition, prolonged depression has effects on the body such as stroke-triggering clots, hypertension, and high heart rates (Elias, 1997). Early diagnosis and treatment of depression is the key to managing it. If you feel you are suffering from depression, you may want to consult the counseling center at your college. Or, if your town has a public mental health agency, contact them. Any visit you make to a counselor is confidential.

Organizational Consequences

Job Performance

Studies show a curvilinear relationship between stress and job performance (Robbins, 2001). That is, moderate levels of eustress can actually improve productivity, increase energy levels, and heighten creativity. However, when stress levels exceed that energizing level, job performance declines.

Burnout

Burnout—the state of being overwhelmed by stress—is usually experienced by highly motivated professionals faced with high work demands. Initial studies on burnout targeted people in the health care field as employees most likely to experience burnout. But over the years the definition has expanded to include other types of workers who become emotionally exhausted and no longer feel they have a positive impact on other people or their job. People who feel burned out have a lack of energy and are filled with frustration and tension. Emotional symptoms of burnout include

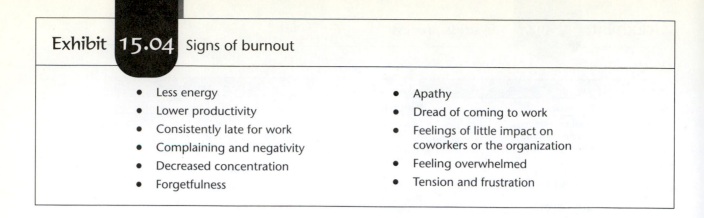

Exhibit 15.04 Signs of burnout

- Less energy
- Lower productivity
- Consistently late for work
- Complaining and negativity
- Decreased concentration
- Forgetfulness

- Apathy
- Dread of coming to work
- Feelings of little impact on coworkers or the organization
- Feeling overwhelmed
- Tension and frustration

dreading coming to work each day (Cordes & Dougherty, 1993). Behavioral signs may include cynicism toward coworkers, clients, and the organization. People who are burned out display detachment toward the people (e.g., clients) with whom they work. Eventually, these people may become depressed and respond to burnout through absenteeism, turnover, and lower performance (Parker & Kulik, 1995).

Absenteeism and Turnover

Absenteeism and turnover, resulting in loss of productivity and, subsequently, revenues, are highest during times of burnout and increased stress as employees struggle to deal with physical and emotional ailments. About 2% of the workforce is absent each day in the United States, and 12% of absenteeism is attributed to stress (CCH Survey, 2002). With this in mind, the question then becomes: Is this absenteeism due to illness brought about by stress, or does it represent "mental health days" in which employees miss work to take a break from stress? From a study by Heaney and Clemans (1995), it appears that the stress–illness relationship best explains absenteeism. Such absenteeism costs employers billions of dollars a year in lost productivity and is thought to be a warning sign of intended turnover (Mitra, Jenkins, & Gupta, 1992).

Interestingly, even when employees take a "mental health day," the strategy apparently is not highly effective. In a study of hospital nurses, Hackett and Bycio (1996) found that stress was lowered immediately following a day of absence but that taking a day off had no longer-term effects.

Drug and Alcohol Abuse

Unfortunately, as stress levels rise and anger increases, so often does the abuse of drugs and alcohol. Most incidents of domestic and other types of violence occur after an individual has been drinking or using drugs. This doesn't excuse the violator's behavior, but it does indicate the relationship between drugs and alcohol and anger and rage. And there are an increasing number of news reports of violence occurring in the workplace. Of those violent events that are carried out

by employees, many are by employees who have abused drugs and alcohol.

Because of the increasing problems of drug and alcohol abuse in organizations, many companies have set up employment assistance programs (EAPs) to which they refer employees suspected of drug or alcohol abuse, as well as those who are depressed and experiencing other problems. EAPs use professional counselors to deal with employee problems. Some large companies have their own EAP counselors, but most use private agencies, which are often run through local hospitals.

Many organizations also offer stress management programs that help people learn how to cope with stress. Having such organizational programs that can be used as a positive outlet for stress and the problems that come from it can often be beneficial in employees' regaining control over their lives.

Because many of our behavioral responses to stress are learned, the negative ones can be unlearned. Stress management teaches us positive and healthy behavioral responses. The key is acknowledging when you use destructive methods and taking measures to correct those negative behaviors. If you don't, you won't like the consequences that result from improperly managed stress.

As organizations recognize the consequences of stress, they are beginning to take better precautions against it. For example, free voluntary counseling is made available by many organizations to all employees exhibiting emotional or discipline problems and particularly to those who have been terminated or laid off (Mantell & Albrecht, 1994).

Health Care Costs

One other organizational, as well as personal, consequence of stress is an increase in health insurance premiums. Because of the high use of medical facilities and options by others suffering from illnesses caused by stress, organizations that at one time paid the full cost for health insurance benefits are passing the increases on to the employees. This additional financial burden to some employees can be a new source of stress! The answer is reducing the number of ailments causing stress, thereby decreasing the need to seek medical attention.

Managing Stress

Managing stress, or better yet, changing your behavior to healthfully respond to stress, should occur before, during, and after stress. Managing stress before it happens means incorporating daily practices (e.g., exercise) that will prepare your mind and body to handle the effects of stress. During stress you should continue with your prestress management techniques (such as reducing caffeine), as well as incorporate some others. Finally, after the stressor is eliminated (if that's even possible!), continue to proactively manage your stress. In addition, there are some other things you should consider. Let's examine some techniques for before, during, and after stress.

Planning for Stress

Some of the techniques suggested to proactively reduce stress should also be considered during times you are actually engaged in stress. These are discussed in the following sections.

Exercise

Exercising not only keeps your heart strong and resistant to the effects of stress, but can also help reduce your stress levels during particular stressful moments. It is a good idea to incorporate some kind of exercise program into your life at least three or four times a week for 20 minutes. You can reap great benefits from walking, swimming, running, playing sports, or climbing stairs because these strengthen your cardiovascular system thereby making you more resistant to the effects of stress. Even such household chores as mowing, vacuuming, or washing your car can help your cardiovascular system. The good news is that not all exercise has to be strenuous. Certain relaxation techniques (explained later in this section) are good prestress techniques that can be used during and after stress.

To begin an exercise program, start with "baby steps." For instance, instead of taking the elevator at work or school, walk the stairs. Or consider this: Stop driving around the mall parking lot 20 times looking for the perfect parking spot! Instead, make a conscious effort to park farther away and walk the distance. From these baby steps, make the transition to a more serious exercise routine. Just remember to pick a program that works for you, which might not be the one your friends use. If you don't like running, don't do it. There is no need to add to your stress by choosing exercises that you absolutely can't tolerate. As a good example, many of my graduate students lift weights to reduce stress. They have repeatedly asked me to join them, but I decline because I know that their plan of "We're going to work on abs for an hour this morning and then shoulders for an hour this evening" involves more time than is practical for my Type A personality. Instead, I stick to the trusty "Bullworker" I purchased in the 1970s.

Organizations realize how important exercise is to managing the effects of stress, as evidenced by the increase of worksite fitness and health programs over the last 15 years. Research shows exercise can reduce coronary heart disease by reducing blood pressure and lowering cholesterol (Gebhardt & Crump, 1990). In addition, absenteeism and turnover are reduced, and morale and job performance improve (Daley & Parfitt, 1996; Gebhardt & Crump, 1990; Heaney & Clemans, 1995).

Laughter

Humor has been shown to buffer stress in several ways (Chubb, 1995; Singer, 2000). First, it can help you put a new perspective on a stressful situation. You have probably heard many jokes about death—many of which are told by police officers, doctors, and morticians! The

Exercise is a good way to reduce stress.

purpose of such jokes is not to hurt feelings or show callousness but to better deal with an uncomfortable topic that we all must face sooner or later. It is better to laugh at it than to dwell over what we can't control. But be careful when telling such jokes: Not everyone will appreciate the humor, and a little sensitivity and common sense should be exercised before sharing the joke.

Second, when you are upset and in what seems to be a difficult situation, going to a funny movie, listening to a comedian, or watching a funny television show can help distance you from the situation until you have calmed down enough to begin thinking rationally again.

Physically, laughter can reduce your blood pressure. Studies show that laughing through a funny movie has the same effect on your heart as 10 minutes on a rowing machine (Stanten, 1997). So next time you have the opportunity to go to a funny movie, go! Or, if you have a favorite comedy show that comes on more than once a week, try to watch as many episodes as possible (but don't forget to study for this class).

Though much has been written about the potential stress reduction benefits of humor, a qualitative literature review by Martin (2001) suggests that more research is needed to determine if humor is as useful as thought. Martin's review does not conclude that humor is not useful, but instead concludes that the jury is still out.

Diet

Foods that have been shown to counteract the effects of stress include fresh fruits and vegetables, whole grains, and nonfat yogurt, which contains the B vitamin considered to be lost during high-stress periods of time (Ornish, 1984). A daily dose of one or more of these can help you meet stress head on! Also, decrease your intake of fat because your body has to work overtime to digest fatty foods, adding to your level of stress (Carpi, 1996). To help reduce the effects of stress, many organizations are including healthier items in their vending machines.

Drinking water helps keep your body hydrated and able to cope with daily stressors (maybe all that running to the bathroom is an added bonus to reducing stress and keeping you fit!). Caffeine should be gradually eliminated from your diet altogether. But before your stress level elevates from thinking about going without your daily caffeine boost, notice I said "should be" eliminated. If you can't eliminate caffeine, at least reduce your daily intake. Any change in that area is better than no change. Be aware of just how much caffeine you are getting: You may be getting more than you think. It's not just cola and coffee products that contain caffeine; chocolate and many types of medicines and other foods have caffeine as well. If you decide to eliminate caffeine from your diet, do it gradually. Most people who are used to large amounts of daily caffeine experience withdrawal symptoms such as nausea, severe headaches, and fatigue if they go "cold turkey."

Smoking Reduction

Though many smokers say smoking decreases their feelings of stress, research indicates that smoking increases the physiological characteristics associated with stress (Kassel, Stroud, & Paronis, 2003). This is an important finding because research also indicates that smokers increase their smoking when they feel stressed (McCann & Lester, 1996). Thus, smoking and stress become a vicious cycle in which people smoke because they are stressed and then become more stressed because they smoke.

Sleep

There is no one study that says absolutely just how much individuals need to sleep. What studies show is that sleep deprivation or lack of sleep can cause negative behavior such as irritability, fatigue, lack of concentration, and even depression. Alcohol can severely affect your sleep, although it may seem that it helps you go to sleep. Studies show that the sleep of people who have had as little as two drinks before bed is interrupted several times a night. In addition, stay away from caffeine at least 6 hours before going to bed. To examine how your own lifestyle prevents or contributes to stress, complete Exercise 15–3 at the end of this chapter.

Support Groups

Studies show that people who have someone to talk to, like a family member or a friend, are better able to manage their stress. You may have already experienced this. When you feel you aren't doing well in class, do you talk to someone about your feelings? Do you feel better afterward? Sometimes talking to someone we trust helps put things in perspective. So if you don't have a good support system, seek one out. This may mean joining certain college groups where you can meet people. Attend campus lectures where meeting friends is possible. And for extreme situations, familiarize yourself with the type of professional help that is available on or off campus that can give you the support you need during stressful times.

Self-Empowerment

In Chapter 14 you learned about empowerment. Most of the literature on empowerment is approached from an organizational, managerial perspective. That is, the literature explains how management can empower employees by giving employees more control over important decisions that affect their lives. This has become important to organizations because research suggests that not having input into matters that affect us can be a big source of stress.

What most of the literature doesn't discuss is how employees can and need to learn to empower themselves. Ninety percent of workers think employers must act to reduce stress. But because employees cannot control what organizations do, it is more important for employees to find their own ways to reduce stress. This is another form of self-empowerment. In addition, instead of complaining about how they don't get to participate in organizational decision making, employees need to take the initiative to volunteer to participate on committees or on group projects; this is one way to take back some control they perceive they have lost.

Individuals can also empower themselves in their personal lives. Instead of playing the victim who believes life has singled him or her out to play dirty tricks on, individuals must learn to find ways to gain control over those situations they can control. This means taking an active role in finding out why something didn't turn out the way they wanted and making changes to prevent the event from occurring again. Chronic complaining about how everyone mistreats you is, to most people, a behavioral response to what is perceived as lack of control in your life. Most of victimization is from learned behavior that we see modeled by family members, friends, coworkers, and even people we don't know, such as those in the news. To break that behavior, attending workshops on assertiveness and decision making can be beneficial. These types of workshops are often offered through colleges, churches, and community groups. If you are interested in attending such training, check with your university to see what may be available.

To apply the concept of self-empowerment, complete Exercise 15–4 at the end of this chapter.

Coping Skills

Improving your coping skills often means learning how to deal with conflict. It also means learning how to accept what you can't change. I often tell workers who participate in stress management classes that they can't change the fact that their organizations are downsizing or that restructuring is the trend for today's companies. Spending energy and time worrying about it or being angry is a waste of time. The best solution for them is finding areas that they can control to meet organizational change. This includes returning to college or taking technical training to make themselves marketable should they be laid off.

This is good advice for you as a college student as well. Worrying about whether you will graduate with a 4.0 GPA is both emotionally and physically stressful. Though setting a goal of high achievement is admirable, worrying about it for the entire 4 years you are in college is unproductive.

During and After Stress

Much of the stress you will have to deal with comes from that experienced during changes in either your personal or your work life. Consequently, this next section focuses on managing change.

According to Pritchett and Pound (1995), people make several mistakes when dealing with change. Three of the most glaring mistakes are expecting somebody else to reduce their stress, deciding not to change, and trying to control the uncontrollable. We already talked above about empowering yourself so that you take responsibility for these areas of your life. Change is going to happen no matter how you resist. To help you better cope with these changes, try these strategies:

- Determine why the change is necessary. At work, ask why your job duties are changing. In your personal life, recognize that you have no choice but to make the change (e.g., graduating from high school or ending a relationship).

- Find out how the change is going to be made. For example, many of you who knew you were going to college sat down and planned some goals. Those goals helped organize how your life would change over the next 4 years. This will reduce the anxiety that comes from fear of the unknown.

- Make a list of positive consequences that will result from the change. There may be some negatives, but focusing on the positives will help keep your spirits up and may even challenge you into action.

- Finally, if you are still having trouble with the change and seeing any positive consequences, ask someone you trust to talk you through it. Sometimes when we are too close to a situation that we don't like, we are unable to be objective or positive. Turning to others can help us with our perspective taking.

All of the above steps are giving you some amount of control. Also, when you feel out of control in one area, try to find control in others. I use the example of a woman who, when she feels stressed because of not having control, cleans her house from top to bottom—no matter what time of day it is. She says she may not have control over her job, but she can at least control how her house looks!

Relaxation Techniques

Another stress-reducing technique you can use is relaxation. Here are some relaxation techniques the American Red Cross recommends.

Abdominal breathing is especially helpful for emotional calming. This requires that you get into a comfortable position, either sitting or lying on your back. Close your eyes and place your left hand on your abdomen and your right hand on your chest. Breath normally, mentally counting from one to four as you inhale through your nose. Pause for two counts. Then open your mouth and mentally count from one to six as you exhale through your mouth. After several minutes of slow, rhythmic breathing, let your hands slowly move to your sides as your abdomen continues to move freely in and out with each breath. When you are finished, open your eyes and sit quietly.

Progressive muscle relaxation is used to relax the body. In a sitting or prone position, close your eyes and tense the following muscle groups: hands and arms, face, neck and shoulders, stomach and abdomen, buttocks and thighs, calves, and feet. Tense each group separately for a few seconds while breathing normally. Slowly release the tension as you focus on the pleasant contrast between tight and relaxed muscles.

Meditation is helpful for quieting a chaotic mind. Sit in a comfortable position and close your eyes. Breathe slowly from the abdomen. Focus your mind on a single word (e.g., calm), phrase (peace, love, joy), or sound (ooommm). Mentally repeat the chosen sound over and over. Adopt a passive attitude toward the process. When intruding thoughts occur, as they will, slowly and gently redirect your mind back to your repetitive sound. After 15 to 20 minutes, slowly open your eyes.

Your local library or hospital has additional information about relaxation methods. This is a good place to begin if you are interesting in finding out more.

Time Management

Because a general feeling of "being out of time" can be a big source of stress, using time management techniques before and during stress can be helpful (Jex & Elacqua, 1999). Here is a small sample of the many time management techniques suggested by Mayer (1990):

- Take several hours to clean your desk. I have a ritual in which at the end of the semester, I take almost a full day to clean my desk and office. For the 2 or 3 weeks that they stay uncluttered, I feel much more relaxed—as do the visitors to my office.

- Place a dollar amount on your time and then determine if any activity is worth the money. For example, if you value your time at $100 per hour and you spend 30 minutes each morning gossiping with a coworker, ask yourself, "Was the conversation worth $50?" If the answer is "no," the conversation was a time-waster.

- Make "to do" lists, and cross out tasks once they have been accomplished.

- Keep a daily time log in which you schedule your appointments, even appointments for yourself. For example, you might schedule 10:00 a.m. to 11:00 a.m. to return phone calls or to read your mail. Treat these self-appointments as you would any other meeting, and don't let people interrupt you.

- To avoid waiting in line, do things at times when nobody else is doing them. For example, eat lunch at 11:00 a.m. rather than noon, go to the bank in the middle of the week rather than on Friday, or do your grocery shopping in the evening rather than right after work or on Saturday morning.

Though many of these suggestions seem reasonable, the empirical literature is unclear regarding the actual stress-reduction benefits of such time management techniques as making lists (Adams & Jex, 1999).

Stress Reduction Interventions Related to Life/Work Issues

As shown in Exhibit 15.05, due to the combination of an increasing number of duel-income and single-parent families, a tight job market, and a trend toward longer workdays, many organizations have made efforts to ensure that their employees maintain a balance between work and life. Such efforts are important as research suggests that employees with work–family conflicts are several times more likely to suffer from mood, anxiety, and substance-abuse disorders than are employees without such conflicts (Frone, 2000). Though organizational efforts to reduce life–work conflicts are designed to help employees reduce their stress levels and thus increase their mental and physical health, they are also motivated by the fact that employees with such outside concerns as child and elder care are more prone to miss work and are less productive than employees without such concerns.

Easing the Child Care Burden

More than 40% of employees in the labor force have children under the age of 18 and thus have a variety of child care needs (Vincola, 1999). To help employees meet these needs, an increasing number of organizations have become involved with child care issues. This increase is due in part to research demonstrating that the lack of regular child care options causes employees with children to miss an additional 8 days of work per year and costs an organization with 300 employees an average of $88,000 per year in lost work time (Woodward, 1999). Organizational child care programs usually fall into one of three categories: on-site care, voucher systems, and referral services. In the first category, organizations such as AFLAC Insurance and Cisco built **on-site child care facilities.** In 2001, 6% of organizations in the United States had on-site child care centers, 5% sponsored off-site programs, 5% helped subsidize the cost of child care, and 20% offered a child care referral service (SHRM, 2002). On-site facilities allow a parent to save commuting time because a separate stop at a child care center is avoided; this also permits the parent to visit the child during breaks.

Some organizations fully fund the cost of child care, whereas others charge the employee the "going rate." There are advantages to both the employee and the organization that pays the full cost of a child enrolled in its facility. For example, the child care cost can be used as a benefit, meaning that neither the employee nor the organization will have to pay taxes on the amount. Of course, tax laws may eventually change the situation, but until that time, calculating child care as an employee benefit is financially rewarding for both the employee and the organization.

Although the employee response to such on-site programs has been overwhelmingly positive, on-site centers cost nearly $1 million to start and more than $3,000 per child to maintain. Because of such high costs, it is important to determine whether these centers "pay off" by reducing such phenomena as employee turnover and absenteeism. According to Scarr (1998), secure child care results in reduced levels of absenteeism and tardiness.

Positive evidence has been provided from five sources.

- Intermedics, in Freeport, Texas, reported a 23% decrease in turnover and absenteeism.

- Prudential Insurance in Newark, New Jersey, reported $80,000 in annual savings due to their child care center (Vincola, 1999).

Lori Hurley, M.S.
President
Time Savers, Inc.

Courtesy of Lori Hurley

My entire career has been in human resources; however, this year I ventured out and created a new corporation called Time Savers, Inc. Time Savers is a concierge/errand service. I made the decision to start this company in response to a growing need to provide people with one of the hottest commodities around . . . time. I was constantly seeing overworked, stressed employees who never appeared to have time to get everything done, myself included. Many days I dreamed of having a personal assistant who could take care of things like picking up my dry cleaning, which had been at the cleaners for weeks, or getting the birthday gift that needed to be shipped out the same day. Now I do these things for others.

According to a recent study by the Families and Work Institute, employees are spending an average of 44 hours per week on the job, and 45% of workers have daily family responsibilities to go home to. Seventy-eight percent of married workers also have spouses who are also employed (www.entrepeneur.com/article/0,4621,229091,00.html.) So what does everyone do on his or her days off? Relax? No, they run errands. Employers also find that many employees are spending company time to complete personal business. With no time for leisure, stress is abundant. Busy people need more time to release tension, and

concierge/errand services can help them do just that. We can take away a great many of those "to do" items and give them back some time to do the important things like spending time with their families, exercising, or just going out to dinner with friends.

The concierge idea has been around for a long time in the hotel industry. Recently, it has begun to emerge in the corporate world and the private sector. I started thinking about the idea of starting this business after visiting a local company that had an in-house concierge service for its employees. I was very impressed with this concept. Companies today are looking for ways to attract and retain good employees. Concierge services are starting to show up on the list of company benefits. I wanted to be a part of this up and coming trend.

So what did it take for me to get this company off the ground? The first thing I had to do was research. Was this a viable business? Many hours were spent on the Internet, reading books, speaking with others who had existing concierge businesses, talking to my attorney, conferring with my accountant, and asking my friends and acquaintances their thoughts on using concierge services. The results were positive, so I decided to take the chance.

The next several months were spent going through the process of incorporating, developing a

business plan, creating a logo, getting my office ready, getting special permits, deciding on a pricing strategy, identifying my target market, and drafting my brochures and advertisements. Finally, I was ready to advertise.

My first customer came within the first month. I was ecstatic. She was a single executive who commuted to another state. I was asked to do a variety of errands ranging from standing in line at the Division of Motor Vehicles, to dropping off dry cleaning, picking up contact lenses, and shopping for personal items. This customer has become a regular client. Other clients followed. I have retrieved mail, shopped for groceries, identified vendors, and taken items for repair, among other services.

The time that I am not spending fulfilling client requests, I am creating marketing materials, making sales contacts, handling the finances, and making plans for the future. I have learned more in the past few months about business then I have in my entire career.

It's very rewarding knowing that I am in some way helping my clients live a more satisfying life. The sky's the limit for my clients, and so are the possibilities for the business.

- Banc One Corporation in Chicago found that users of on-site child care centers had 7 fewer days of absenteeism than nonusers (Vincola, 1999).

- Scott and Markham (1982) reported an average decrease of 19% in absenteeism for organizations that established on-site centers.

- Tioga Sportswear in New Jersey found a 50% decrease in turnover (LaMarre & Thompson, 1984).

Negative evidence has been provided by Miller (1984), who reviewed published studies and concluded that day care centers may not have the impacts that they were initially thought to have (e.g., reduced absenteeism, increased production). Still, child care centers will probably have their greatest impact on organizations with high percentages of young, married female workers.

A second avenue that can be taken with child care is to provide employees with *vouchers* to be used with private day care centers. For example, the San Antonio, Texas, branch of Levi Strauss provides a $100 monthly

Exhibit 15.05 Percentage of employers offering stress-reducing practices

Stress Reducing Practice	Percent Offering
Provide Alternative Work Schedules	
Flextime	64
Telecommuting	60
Compressed work week	33
Job sharing	24
Assist with Child Care	
Allow employee to bring child to work during emergencies	30
Provide child care referral service	20
Provide emergency/sick child care	9
Provide on-site child care center	6
Provide company-supported child care center	5
Subsidize cost of child care	5
Assist with Elder Care	
Provide an elder care referral service	21
Provide emergency elder care	2
Provide company-supported elder care center	1
Subsidize cost of elder care	1
Provide on-site elder care	1
Increase Employee Wellness	
Offer an employee assistance program (EAP)	68
Provide wellness information	58
Provide health screening programs	42
Sponsor employee sports teams	39
Offer a smoking cessation program	29
Subsidize fitness center dues	28
Provide on-site fitness center	26
Offer a stress-reduction program	21
Offer a weight loss program	22
Provide on-site massage therapy services	13
Allow employee to bring pet to work	4
Assist with Daily Chores	
Provide dry cleaning service	15
Provide concierge services	4
Provide take-home meals	4

Source: SHRM 2002 Benefits Survey

voucher for employees making less than $32,000. NationsBank offers a similar program. From the perspective of the organization, **voucher systems** alleviate both the high start-up costs and the high costs of liability insurance associated with on-site centers. From an employee's perspective, this approach reduces the cost of private child care.

Unfortunately, there are several reasons this approach probably does not reduce employee turnover or absenteeism. First, an employee must still leave work to visit a sick child or to attend parent conferences. Although the FMLA discussed in Chapter 3 allows an employee to take up to 12 weeks of unpaid leave to care for a sick family member, employees that leave work to

Balancing work and family can be difficult.

care for their families leave a void that organizations may find difficult to fill. Furthermore, because only 23% of organizations provide paid family leave (SHRM, 2002), the financial loss to the employee can create tremendous stress and hardship. A second reason off-site child care facilities aren't optimal is that most private child care centers operate from 7 a.m. until 6 p.m. Thus, employees who work swing or night shifts are not helped. Finally, there is a shortage of quality child care in many areas. Some corporations, such as the Fayetteville, Arkansas, branch of Levi Strauss, donate large sums of money to local child care centers to expand hours or services (Harris, 1993). Others, such as Time Warner and SunTrust Bank, contract with outside vendors to provide emergency child care services for children who are ill. Because it can be difficult to find child care centers that will take sick children, employers such as The Principal Financial Group in Des Moines, Iowa, have contracted with local health care agencies to provide in-home care to their employee's sick children. Interestingly, 30% of organizations allow their employees to bring their children to work in emergency situations in which child care is not available (SHRM, 2002).

The final avenue taken by organizations is to provide a **referral service** to quality child care centers. This approach has been taken by both IBM and Digital Corp. Although this is certainly a useful service, nothing about it would suggest that it would reduce either absenteeism or turnover.

Hallmark Cards, Inc. is an excellent example of a company with progressive child care and family benefits. Hallmark allows employees to take 6 months of unpaid maternity and paternity leave, reimburses

employees up to $5,000 for the cost of adopting a child, helps employees locate care for children and aged parents, provides care for mildly ill children, holds parenting seminars, and provides alternative care arrangements for children out of school during holidays, inclement weather, or teacher workdays (Matthes, 1993). An excellent Web site for information on child care issues is www.dol.gov/dol/wb/childcare/ccguide.htm.

Easing the Elder Care Burden

By 2005, more than 40 million people in the United States will be older than 65. As the number of elderly increase, so too does the need for elder care. In 2001 more than one third of employees were providing elder care to a relative (O'Toole & Ferry, 2002): 64% of the people providing elder care also work full or part time jobs, and 41% also care for children. According to statistics generated by the National Council on Aging, 50% of employees taking care of an elderly relative were absent from work, arrived at work late, or left work early to care for their elderly relative. Six percent quit working to spend the necessary elder care time. Given the negative impact on emotional health of working and providing elder care (Lee, Walker, & Shoup, 2001), such statistics are not surprising.

In spite of the great demand for elder care, organizational efforts on this front have lagged behind child care efforts. According to a survey by the Society for Human Resource Management (SHRM, 2002), only 21% of organizations provide elder care referral services and a mere 2% offer a company-sponsored or on-site elder care facility. The most common elder care programs provided by employers include flexible work schedules, resource and referral programs, long-term care insurance, expanded FMLA benefits, flexible spending and dependent care accounts, adult day care, seminars, and support groups.

Fannie Mae is an excellent example of an employer that understands the potential elder care crisis. After a survey of its employees revealed that 70% expected to take on elder care responsibilities within 5 years, Fannie Mae hired a licensed clinical social worker to help employees coordinate elder care. Fannie Mae estimates that it saves $1.50 in absenteeism and turnover costs for every $1.00 it spends on its elder care program. Most important, 28% of the employees said that they would have quit their job had they not had the company-provided help (Wells, 2000).

Easing the Daily Chore Burden

With work, child care, and elder care responsibilities, many employees find it increasingly difficult to complete such basic chores as going to the dentist, getting the car inspected, and picking up dry cleaning. As a result, organizations have implemented a variety of strategies to ease this burden. Popular strategies include increasing the use of flexible working hours, increasing the number of paid personal days off, and providing essential services on-site.

Exhibit 15.06 — Paid time off provided by employers in two employee-benefit surveys

Paid Time Off	Manufacturers in the New River Valley (VA)	Virginia Credit Unions
Paid Holidays		
Lowest	6	5
Median	10	10
Highest	16	14
Paid Vacation Days		
Lowest	0	5
Median	8	10
Highest	27	25
Paid Sick Days		
Lowest	0	0
Median	3	9
Highest	15	20

By providing essential services on-site, employers assume that employees will work more hours because they will not have to take time away from work to complete common chores. For example, Berkshire Associates in Columbia, Maryland, provides its employees with catered breakfasts and lunches so that employees can eat at their desks rather than going out to lunch. This benefit saves employees money and Berkshire gets an additional 30 to 45 minutes of work out of its employees each day.

To ease the daily chore burden, 4% of organizations provide concierge services for their employees (SHRM, 2002). For a cost between $30 and $1,000 per employee per year, these services will perform such tasks as making restaurant reservations, ordering flowers, having food delivered, scheduling car repairs, picking up dry cleaning, and having a person wait at an employee's home for a repairman to come (Taylor, 2000). Examples of concierge services include Les Concierges (www.lesconcierges.com), Best Upon Request (www.bestuponrequest.com), and Circles (www.circles.com).

To make shopping easier for employees, Microsoft, 3M, and Northwest Airlines allow employees to use their computers at work to buy discounted products and services. Thus, employees can purchase a variety of products including groceries and movie tickets without leaving the office. Employees get the benefit of lower prices and ease of shopping and employers get the benefit of employees working longer hours.

Providing Rest Through Paid Time Off

Working long hours is a major factor in employee stress, as one third of U.S. employees feel that they are overworked (Clark, 2001). These long hours are confounded by the fact that 14% of employees don't even take time off for lunch, and another 55% engage in other activities during their lunch break (McCullough, 1998). Likewise, 60% of employees take laptops, pagers, and cell phones with them on vacation so that they can keep in touch with work (Frase-Blunt, 2001).

To help employees balance life and work, the majority of employers provide paid time off, usually in the form of vacations, holidays, sick days, and rest periods. As shown in Exhibit 15.06, the amount of paid time off varies across organizations, and some organizations do not provide any paid vacation days for hourly employees. In contrast to the United States, where organizations are not legally mandated to provide paid vacations, many countries do. For example, the legal minimum number of vacation days is 30 in Sweden, 25 in France, and 22 in Brazil.

Workplace Violence

In the past decade, the issue of workplace violence has received considerable interest from psychologists and human resource professionals. In part this interest has been spurred by statistics such as these:

- In 2001, 677 employees were murdered at work.
- Eleven percent of fatal workplace injuries in the United States are the result of homicide.
- Approximately 1.7 million incidents of violence take place annually in the United States.
- Eighteen percent of violent crimes were committed while the victim was at work.

- Twenty-five percent of workers in the United Kingdom were victims of some form of bullying at work in the past 5 years.

Though the issue of workplace violence has received increasing interest, the homicide rate in the workplace has steadily declined from a high of 17% of all fatal workplace injuries in 1993 to 11% in 2000. Stated another way, 1.6% of employees in the United States were victims of workplace violence in 1993 compared to just under 1% in 2000.

Though more than 75% of homicide victims at work are men, homicide is only the third most common cause of fatal workplace injuries among men (traffic accidents and head injuries are the first two), but it is the most common cause of fatal workplace injuries among women. The gender differences in workplace violence can be explained by the fact that men traditionally work in higher risk occupations such as mining that have high levels of fatalities caused by such other means as driving and construction accidents (Thornburg, 1993).

Though these figures are certainly attention getting, from a human resource perspective they can be misleading as a relatively small portion of the homicides are committed by current or former employees. Incidents of workplace violence can be placed into one of three categories. The first category, representing 71% of job-related homicides, is violence against an employee occurring as a result of a *crime* being committed. The most common examples are employees assaulted during the commission of a robbery. In fact, taxi drivers and convenience store clerks are the two occupations most susceptible to workplace violence (working the graveyard shift at a 7–Eleven store may have more than chronological meaning).

The second category, representing 14% of job-related homicides, is violence against law enforcement officers (e.g., police officers, sheriffs, FBI agents) or security guards while they are in the *line of duty*. Law enforcement officers have a homicide rate of 9.3 per 100,000 employees, and the rate for security guards is 3.6 per 100,000. The average for all workers is 0.7 per 100,000.

The third category, representing 15% of job-related homicides, is violence against an employee or supervisor as an act of *anger or vengeance* by another employee, a customer, or a jilted lover. It is this category of violence that most involves human resource professionals and has captured the imagination of the public. Of the homicides in this category, 44% are committed by current employees, 23% are committed by former employees, 21% involve domestic violence, and 12% involve other causes (Grossman, 2002a).

Employee violence against other employees is usually the result of interpersonal disagreements. For example, an employee of Prescolite, Inc. in Arkansas killed one coworker and wounded seven others because the employee was upset that he was being harassed by his coworkers.

However, employees can be assaulted when coworkers take out their anger on a supervisor. Here are some examples:

- An employee at the Connecticut State Lottery who was upset with his supervisors for not listening to him killed four employees before killing himself (something done by 36% of employees committing workplace violence).
- A Tulsa, Oklahoma, Wendy's employee, angry because his boss asked him to start work early, fired 12 shots from a .380-caliber handgun, wounding his supervisor and five other employees.
- An employee in a Micropure Plant in California killed two and wounded four employees because he was frustrated with his job.

Thirteen percent of workplace violence incidents involve employees seeking revenge against a supervisor as a result of being fired, laid off, or subject to some form of negative personnel action. For example:

- A former employee of the California Department of Transportation killed four former coworkers because he was angry about being fired.
- After being fired, Paul Calden killed three supervisors at Firemen's Fund Insurance before shooting himself.
- Fernando Ruiz shot his supervisor at Dahn's Fresh Herbs in Houston after his boss threatened to fire him.
- Larry Hansel used a 12-gauge shotgun to kill two company executives he believed were responsible for his being fired.

Recently, psychologists have expanded their studies of workplace violence to include behaviors referred to as mobbing and bullying. Mobbing and bullying consist of hostile, alienating, and unethical behavior among employees. Examples of such behavior include intimidating a person, excluding or isolating someone socially, spreading malicious gossip that is not true, yelling, using profanity, and belittling a person's opinions or work. Research suggests that about 1 in 5 employees in the United States, United Kingdom, Australia, and Canada report being the victim of bullying. This expanded definition of workplace violence has been adopted by the Canadian Centre for Occupational Health and Safety, whose definition of workplace violence includes the following actions:

- Threatening behavior
- Physical attacks
- Verbal abuse
- Verbal or written threats
- Harassment (any behavior that demeans, embarrasses, humiliates, annoys, alarms, or verbally abuses a person)

Perpetrators of Workplace Violence

Research on workplace violence by employees reveals a fairly consistent pattern. Perpetrators tend to be males (80%) between the ages of 20 and 50 (usually in their

40s), have their self-esteem tied to their job, are fond of violent films and TV shows, are fascinated by guns, have ready access to guns, often subscribe to *Soldier of Fortune*, and are usually described as loners (Dietz, 1994). Psychologically, they are often classified as suffering from paranoid disorders. About 15% are suffering severe stress due to family problems, 8% are suffering from other severe sources of stress, and another 10% have severe substance abuse problems (Trenn, 1993).

Reducing Workplace Violence

Acts of workplace violence cannot be completely eliminated, but they can be reduced through security measures, employee screening, and management awareness (Epstein, 2003).

Security Measures

Increased security measures can decrease the probability of workplace violence. These measures can include such physical changes as adding surveillance cameras, silent alarms, bright external lighting, bulletproof barriers, sophisticated lock systems, and security guards; making high-risk areas more visible; and using drop safes and posting signs stating that only limited cash is kept on the premises. Staffing changes can include increasing the number of staff on duty; closing during the higher risk late-night and early morning hours; and training employees in how to deal with robberies, conflicts, and angry customers.

Employee Screening

Though the security measures mentioned here are primarily aimed at reducing workplace violence resulting from other crimes such as robbery, they can also aid in reducing violence caused by current and former employees. Another method of reducing violence committed by current and former employees is to use psychological tests, reference checks, and background checks to screen applicants for violence potential.

Background and reference checks can provide information about an applicant's history of violence (Tonowski, 1993). These checks are important because employees who engage in workplace violence are chronically disgruntled, have a history of causing trouble, and frequently change jobs. Dietz (1994) provides two interesting examples. An applicant at a California maintenance company was hired in spite of a history of domestic violence and burglary convictions. He later set fire to a bookkeeper who wouldn't give him his paycheck. Another organization was sued because an employee who had killed a coworker was rehired by the same company in an effort to employ ex-cons. After a short period on the job, the employee killed another coworker.

It is important to note that ex-cons cannot categorically be denied employment. An organization must take into account the length of time that has passed since the crime was committed, the seriousness of the crime, and the relevance of the crime to the job in question.

Psychological tests such as the MMPI and a variety of integrity tests discussed in Chapter 6 can potentially predict violence in people without a history of violence. However, an empirical link between scores on these tests and workplace violence has yet to be made (Tonowski, 1993), in part because the violent event being predicted usually occurs many years after the preemployment testing. Furthermore, incidents of workplace violence are an interaction of a high-risk employee, working for an organization with poor management, who undergoes a stressful event (Habeeb & Prencipe, 2001). Thus, a high-risk employee will only be violent under certain circumstances—circumstances that constantly change and are difficult to measure. Testing for high-risk employees is made even more difficult because the Americans with Disabilities Act (ADA) provides limitations to the use of tests designed to determine psychological problems.

Management Awareness

Workplace violence can be greatly reduced by making managers aware of high-risk situations and empowering them to take immediate action. Most experts on workplace violence (e.g. Dietz, 1994; Turner, 1994) believe that *berserkers*—employees who "go crazy" and shoot people—give indications that they are going to commit future violence. Such indications include threats, acts of violence, comments about wanting to get even, excessive talk of guns, and comments about famous serial and mass murderers. In one survey, 50% of human resource practitioners who had incidents of workplace violence in their organizations observed warning signs prior to the incident (Trenn, 1993).

Take, for example, Thomas McIlvane, a fired postal worker who shot eight postal employees, killing four. Prior to a union hearing appealing his termination, he stated that if he lost his grievance he would make a shooting incident in Oklahoma that took the lives of 14 postal workers "look like a tea party." As another example, prior to being fired and then killing his supervisors, Larry Hansel was reprimanded for excessively talking about a postal worker who killed two coworkers in Escondido, California (Graham, 1991).

Cavanaugh (2001) advises a "zero tolerance" for threats and violence. That is, one act and the employee is terminated (fired, not killed). Dietz (1994) suggests that anyone who makes others feel uncomfortable is potential trouble. Turner (1994) suggests that employees whose behavior makes others feel scared should be screened for violence potential. This screening includes interviews with coworkers and supervisors as well as meetings with a clinical psychologist. From these interviews and meetings, Turner and his associates place the employee into one of five risk categories:

1. High violence potential, qualifies for arrest/hospitalization

2. High violence potential, does not qualify for arrest/hospitalization

3. Insufficient evidence for violence potential, but sufficient evidence for *intentional* infliction of emotional distress upon coworkers

4. Insufficient evidence for violence potential, but sufficient evidence for *unintentional* infliction of emotional distress upon coworkers

5. Insufficient evidence for violence potential, and insufficient evidence for infliction of emotional distress upon coworkers

The potential for workplace violence can also be reduced through careful handling of terminations and layoffs. Refer to the discussion in Chapter 7 for specific ways to fairly evaluate and terminate employees. In addition to these techniques, free voluntary counseling should be made available to all employees, especially those exhibiting emotional, interpersonal, or discipline problems (Mantell & Albrecht, 1994). Information about workplace violence can be found on the Web at http://www.mnsi.net/~wohis/violence.htm and http://www.nvc.org/ddir/info54.htm.

Chapter Summary

In this chapter you learned:

- Stress is the psychological and physical reaction to certain life events or situations.

- Common sources of stress include personal stressors; such occupational stressors as job characteristics (role conflict, role ambiguity, role overload), organizational characteristics, work environment, and change; and relationships with others (e.g., conflict, difficult people, angry customers).

- At a personal level, stress can affect marriages and relationships with others. At a health level, stress results in a number of psychological (e.g., anxiety, depression) and physical (e.g., joint pain, cardiovascular problems) disorders. At an organizational level, stress results in burnout, increased drug and alcohol use, lower job satisfaction, increased absenteeism, and increased turnover.

- Type A individuals and pessimists are more prone to stress than Type B individuals and optimists.

- Such techniques as exercise, laughter, a healthy diet, not smoking, getting plenty of sleep, joining support groups, self-empowerment, and time management can reduce stress.

- Workplace violence can result from employee stress.

Critical Thinking Questions

1. Why are some people more affected by stress than others?

2. What job characteristics are most likely to result in high levels of stress?

3. Why should organizations be concerned about employee stress?

4. Do stress management techniques actually work?

5. Why does workplace violence occur?

To learn more about the issues discussed in this chapter, point your browser to

http://www.infotrac-college.com/wadsworth

and enter one of these search terms:

Type A personality

eustress

time management

occupational stressors

job burnout

job distress

employer-supported day care

workplace violence

Exercise 15–1
Type A Behavior

To determine if you are a Type A personality, complete the Gardner Personality Test below.

Circle the number that corresponds to the extent to which you never, rarely, sometimes, usually, or always engage in the behaviors below.

N = Never
R = Rarely
S = Sometimes
U = Usually
A = Always

	N	R	S	U	A
1. I walk fast even when I have plenty of time to get where I am going.	1	2	3	4	5
2. I am on time for appointments.	1	2	3	4	5
3. I daydream.	5	4	3	2	1
4. I eat a meal while I am doing other things such as studying or watching TV.	1	2	3	4	5
5. Close friends or relatives tell me to slow down and take it easier when we participate in activities together.	1	2	3	4	5
6. I complete school assignments in as little time as possible.	1	2	3	4	5
7. I must attain all my goals in the time frame I set.	1	2	3	4	5
8. People who speak slowly irritate me.	1	2	3	4	5
9. When I have my mind set on certain tasks, I am easily distracted.	5	4	3	2	1
10. When having a conversation about a topic I am interested in, I let others dominate the conversation.	5	4	3	2	1
11. I keep all of my school notes as orderly as possible.	1	2	3	4	5
12. I relax when others are in control of a situation I am in.	5	4	3	2	1
13. I expect the highest grade in my class on any given project.	1	2	3	4	5
14. On days when I have completed my homework, I have a difficult time relaxing.	1	2	3	4	5
15. When I make a mistake and correct it, I view the experience as a learning experience and don't get upset.	5	4	3	2	1

To get your Type A score, add the numbers you circled for each item. Your score is _____.
The higher your score, the more likely you are to be a Type A personality.

Your Type A Score	Percentile
69–75	99
62–68	95
60–61	90
55–59	80
53–54	70
50–52	60
48–49	50
46–47	40
44–45	30
42–43	20
37–41	10
00–36	5

What does your score say about your personality?

_____

_____

_____

_____

_____

_____

_____

_____

_____

_____

_____

_____

_____

_____

Exercise 15–2
Optimism

For each of the questions below, indicate the extent to which you agree or disagree with the statement.

SD = Strongly disagree
D = Disagree
N = Neutral
A = Agree
SA = Strongly agree

	SD	D	N	A	SA
1. I try to learn from my failures.	1	2	3	4	5
2. Most people are good.	1	2	3	4	5
3. If something can go wrong, it will.	5	4	3	2	1
4. I can handle most of life's difficulties.	1	2	3	4	5
5. It is difficult to trust people.	5	4	3	2	1
6. I enjoy life.	1	2	3	4	5
7. One can find something positive in most bad situations.	1	2	3	4	5
8. I have a great life ahead of me.	1	2	3	4	5
9. I find it hard to find things I enjoy doing.	5	4	3	2	1
10. Life is hard.	5	4	3	2	1
11. I will be very successful in my career.	1	2	3	4	5
12. Most people who meet me will like me.	1	2	3	4	5
13. Most politicians are crooks and liars.	5	4	3	2	1
14. Most people will help you if they can.	1	2	3	4	5
15. Most people would say I have a good attitude.	1	2	3	4	5
16. I am usually happy.	1	2	3	4	5
17. I feel that I control my own destiny.	1	2	3	4	5
18. I make other people happy.	1	2	3	4	5
19. I seldom complain.	1	2	3	4	5
20. I often seem to focus too much on the negative aspects of life.	5	4	3	2	1
21. There are few problems that can't be solved.	1	2	3	4	5
22. Life just seems so boring.	5	4	3	2	1
23. People who want to be successful can be successful.	1	2	3	4	5
24. I can smile in even the worst of situations.	1	2	3	4	5

To get your Optimism score, add the numbers you circled for each item. Your score is _____.
High scores indicate you are an optimist, whereas lower scores indicate you are a pessimist.
Pessimists are more likely to be affected by stress.

Your Optimism Score	Percentile
107–120	99
105–106	95
102–104	90
99–101	80
95–98	70
93–94	60
90–92	50
87–89	40
84–86	30
81–83	20
79–80	10
24–78	5

What does this score say about your stress-related personality?

_____

_____

_____

_____

_____

_____

_____

_____

_____

_____

_____

_____

_____

_____

Exercise 15–3
Lifestyle Questionnaire

Circle the number on the right that best corresponds to your answer for each of the ten questions below.

1. How many cigarettes do you smoke each day?   1   2   3   4   5
   1 = none, 2 = a few cigarettes, 3 = half a pack, 4 = one pack, 5 = more than one pack

2. How often do you drink alcohol?   1   2   3   4   5
   1 = never, 2 = once a month, 3 = once a week,
   4 = 2 to 3 times a week, 5 = more than 3 times a week

3. How often do you drink beverages with caffeine?   1   2   3   4   5
   1 = never, 2 = once a month, 3 = once or twice a week
   4 = 3 to 5 times a week, 5 = more than five times a week

4. How often do you eat fruit?   1   2   3   4   5
   5 = never, 4 = once a month, 3 = once a week, 2 = several times a week, 1 = daily

5. How often do you eat vegetables?   1   2   3   4   5
   5 = never, 4 = once a month, 3 = once a week, 2 = several times a week, 1 = daily

6. How often do you exercise or play sports?   1   2   3   4   5
   5 = never, 4 = once a month, 3 = once a week, 2 = several times a week, 1 = daily

7. How many glasses of water do you drink on a normal day?   1   2   3   4   5
   5 = none, 4 = one, 3 = two, 2 = three or four, 1 = five or more

8. How many hours of sleep do you normally get each night?   1   2   3   4   5
   1 = more than eight, 2 = eight, 3 = seven, 4 = six, 5 = less than six

9. How many times in a week do you take a short nap?   1   2   3   4   5
   1 = five or more, 2 = four, 3 = three, 4 = one or two, 5 = none

10. How cluttered is the room, house, or office where you   1   2   3   4   5
    spend most of your time?
    1 = very neat, 2 = neat, 3 = average, 4 = cluttered, 5 = very cluttered

To get your Lifestyle score, add the numbers you circled for each item. Your score is _____.
The higher the score, the more your lifestyle makes you susceptible to the effects of stress.

Your Lifestyle Score	Percentile
35–50	99
33–34	95
32	90
30–31	80
29	70
27–28	60
26	50
25	40
24	30
23	20
21–22	10
10–20	5

Based on your score, what lifestyle changes can you make to make you less susceptible to the effects of stress?

_____

_____

_____

_____

_____

_____

_____

_____

_____

_____

_____

_____

Exercise 15–4
Empowering and Motivating Yourself:
Gaining Control Over Your Life

1. List those areas in your life over which you want to gain more control. These areas could be in your working situation, personal life, or both. Be sure to write down only those areas you believe you can control (e.g., "More control over where my money goes and how much money I have").

_____

_____

_____

_____

_____

_____

_____

_____

2. Now, for each area you listed above, write down specific steps you are going to take to get better control. If you aren't sure of how to do it, talk with a classmate, friend, or family member for suggestions and ideas. Be specific about how you will empower yourself (e.g., Write down a daily budget; stay within that budget; get a job or ask for a raise; put money into a savings account).

_____

_____

_____

_____

_____

_____

_____

_____

_____

_____

3. Finally, write down those items you want to control but feel you can't. Discuss them with someone you trust. Can you think of ways to take more control (if not complete control) in those areas? If so, using these new items, do Question 2 again.

_____

_____

_____

_____

_____

_____

_____

_____

_____

_____

_____

_____

_____

_____

_____

_____

_____

_____

_____

_____

_____

_____

_____

16 Working Conditions and Human Factors

IN PREVIOUS CHAPTERS, you learned that employee performance can be improved through proper selection and training programs, effective organizational communication, and state-of-the-art incentive and participation systems. In this chapter, you will learn that performance and satisfaction are also affected by working conditions, including work schedules, noise, temperature, office design, technology, and safety. By the end of the chapter you will understand

- the effects of compressed work weeks, flexible work hours, shift work, and other work schedules.
- the impact of child care centers and moonlighting policies.
- the types of noise that most affect performance.
- the effects of temperature on work behavior.
- the human factors associated with computer use.
- the importance of office layout.
- the role psychology can play in increasing the "user friendliness" of products and systems.

Work Schedules

Today, most employees work 8 hours a day, 5 days a week. Usually, the workdays are Monday through Friday, and the work times are from 8 a.m. to 5 p.m. with an hour break for lunch. But these have not always been the typical work hours. In the late 18th century, it was common for employees to work 14 to 16 hours a day, 6 days per week. By the early to mid-19th century, there was a movement to reduce working hours to a maximum of 10 per day. This reduction was opposed by many religious organizations, which feared the trouble that supposedly would be caused by people with idle time. But by 1950, the 5-day, 40-hour work week was fairly standard (Moores, 1990).

Compressed Work Weeks

Although the vast majority of people still work 8 hours a day, 5 days a week, there is a trend toward working fewer days a week but more hours per day (Maiwald, Pierce, Newstrom, & Sunoo, 1997). These deviations from the typical 5-day work week are called **compressed work weeks** and usually involve either 10 hours a day for 4 days or 12 hours a day for 3 days.

The first formal use of a compressed work schedule was in 1940, when both the Mobil Oil and Gulf Oil companies had their truck drivers work 10 hours a day for 4 days and then take 3 days off. The "explosion" in organizations that used compressed schedules came in the early 1970s after Riva Poor (1970) published the first book on the topic. In 2001, 33% of organizations surveyed by the Society for Human Resource Management (SHRM) offered compressed work weeks (SHRM, 2002).

The potential advantages of compressed work schedules are obvious from the employees' perspective. Employees get more vacation days, have more time to spend with their families, have increased opportunities to moonlight, and have reduced commuting costs and times. Furthermore, if parents have different compressed schedules, child care costs are greatly reduced.

Because it appears obvious that the employee's non-work-related life will improve with a compressed schedule, the important question becomes, "What is the effect of a compressed schedule on an employee's performance at work?" Most people answer that a worker will be more tired, causing more mistakes and accidents.

The research thus far, however, does not support such speculation. Although research generally indicates that workers do feel moderately more fatigued, their work behavior and work attitudes generally *improve* once a compressed work schedule has been adopted. As shown in Exhibit 16.01, the results of two meta-analyses (Baltes, Briggs, Huff, Wright, & Neuman, 1999; Moores, 1990) suggest that compressed schedules generally bring a moderate reduction in absenteeism, a small increase in productivity, a large increase

Exhibit 16.01 — Effect sizes for compressed work schedules

Criterion	Moores (1990)		Baltes, Briggs, Huff, Wright, and Neuman (1999)	
	Number of Studies	Mean Effect Size	Number of Studies	Mean Effect Size
Absenteeism	5	−.44	5	.01
Productivity	8	.25	4	.04
Supervisor ratings			4	.42
Satisfaction	5	.73	4	.42
Fatigue	1	.35		

in job satisfaction, and a moderate increase in fatigue. Furthermore, on the basis of 3,800 employees in six studies, Moores (1990) concluded that almost 90% of employees who worked compressed schedules were satisfied with them. The exact effect sizes from Moores's meta-analysis are shown in Exhibit 16.01.

Regarding employee health, Williamson, Gower, and Clarke (1994) found that employees who worked 12-hour shifts were healthier than those working 8-hour shifts. There were no differences in productivity or turnover. Duchon, Keran, and Smith (1994) found even more positive results with underground mine workers. Mine workers changing from an 8- to a 12-hour shift reported higher satisfaction, improved sleep, and no negative health or performance changes.

In addition to these empirically verified benefits to employees, an organization that adopts compressed work schedules may realize other advantages. Perhaps the greatest of these is the reduction in start-up and cleanup times associated with many jobs. For example, a printer spends considerable time inking and setting up a press before beginning work. At the end of the day, the printer must also spend time cleaning the press and putting supplies away. If these beginning and ending activities together take an hour, then at least an hour a week can be saved if the printer works 4 days rather than 5. Extended across a year and multiplied by the number of employees in a company, such savings can be substantial.

A word of caution should be made regarding the length of shifts. Though employees seem to suffer few problems with 12-hour shifts, there is probably an upper limit in shift length. For example, Knauth, Keller, Schindele, and Totterdell (1995) found a 14-hour shift for firefighters to be too long.

To help reduce fatigue associated with long working hours, most organizations provide 20 to 40 minutes of paid breaks during the workday. Research suggests that providing four 9-minute breaks is superior to two 15-minute breaks or twelve 3-minute breaks (Dababneh, Swanson, & Shell, 2001). Interestingly, 44% of companies allow fatigued employees to take naps (Circadian Technologies, 2002).

Flexible Work Hours

A second and increasingly popular alternative work schedule involves flexible work hours and is called **flextime**. Flextime originated in West Germany as a way to alleviate traffic problems by staggering the hours people worked. The plan then spread to North America, where it was used first in Canada and then in the United States in the mid-1970s. Though some form of flextime is formally offered by 64% of organizations (SHRM, 2002), only 33% of employees opt to use it (Clark, 2001).

According to Thornburg (1994), organizations use flexible hours for these reasons:

1. Accommodate employees' family responsibilities
2. Attract employees when the available qualified workforce is small
3. Comply with transportation and air quality regulations
4. Satisfy customer demands for 24-hour-a-day services

With flextime, employees are given greater control over the hours they work. It is believed that this increase in control and flexibility has many advantages for employees. First, an employee can take care of personal tasks such as going to the doctor, picking up children from school, and even sleeping in after a rough night. Furthermore, this increased control should enrich the employee's job, thus theoretically resulting in increased job satisfaction (see Chapter 10).

Flextime can be arranged in many ways, but all share the same three basic components: bandwidth, core hours, and flexible hours. As shown in Exhibit 16.02, the **bandwidth** is the total number of potential hours available for work each day. For example, employees can work their 8 hours anytime in the 12-hour bandwidth between 6 a.m. and 6 p.m. A 10-hour band is used by 45% of organizations, and another 23% use a 12-hour band (Clark, 2001).

Core hours are those that everyone must work and typically consist of the hours during which an organization is busiest with its outside contacts. For example,

Exhibit **16.02** Diagram of a bank's flextime program

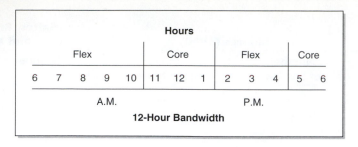

a restaurant might have core hours between 11 a.m. and 1 p.m. to cover its lunchtime business, whereas a bank might have core hours from 12 noon to 1 p.m. and from 5 p.m. to 6 p.m. to cover the periods of highest customer volume.

Finally, **flexible hours** are those that remain in the bandwidth and in which the employee has a choice of working. For example, if the bandwidth is the 12-hour period from 6 a.m. to 6 p.m. and the core hours are from 11 a.m. to 1 p.m., then the employee can schedule the remaining 6 hours (including lunch hour) anywhere from 6 a.m. to 10 a.m. and from 2 p.m. to 6 p.m. The actual degree to which these hours are truly flexible depends on the specific flextime program used by the organization.

The most flexible of these schedules is called **gliding time.** With this system, an employee can choose her own hours without advance notice or scheduling. Employees can come and go as they please as long as they work 8 hours each day and 40 hours each week. With gliding time, there are no core hours. Such a flexible schedule, however, will work only where it is not necessary to always have an employee working, as in typing or accounting. In an organization such as a retail store or a restaurant, such a system would mean that at any given time there might not be *any* employee present—which, of course, is probably not the best way to conduct a business.

Most flexible working schedules are categorized as **flexitour** or **modified flexitour**, with the employee enjoying greater flexibility in working hours, although the hours must be scheduled in advance. With a flexitour system, the employee must submit a schedule on a weekly, biweekly, or monthly basis, depending on the organization. In a modified flexitour, the employee must schedule her hours in advance but can change these hours on a daily basis with some advance notice.

Flexible working schedules are popular with employees and beneficial to organizations. As shown in Exhibits 16.03 and 16.04, meta-analyses by Estes (1990) and Baltes et al. (1999) found that flextime resulted in less absenteeism, less overtime, higher job satisfaction, less role conflict, and increased productivity. These effects were strongest for smaller organizations and for those organizations in which employees

shared limited physical resources such as space and equipment (Estes, 1990).

Peak-Time Pay

A third alternative work schedule is **peak-time pay.** With peak-time pay, certain employees are encouraged to work only part time but are paid at a higher hourly rate for those hours than employees who work full time. Thus, an employee will make more per hour than her full-time counterpart, although she will make less money per day.

The concept of peak-time pay came from the banking and fast food industries, both of which face unique problems (Mahlin & Charles, 1984). Both types of organizations need to be open during the entire day yet have only approximately 4 hours per day that are busy. For example, a McDonald's restaurant might need 20 employees to cover its lunchtime crowd but need only 5 employees from 2 p.m. until 5 p.m., at which time the dinner crowd begins for another 2-hour peak period. Rather than paying 20 employees to sit around for most of the day, it would be better to have 15 employees work for 3 hours a day during peak time and only 5 employees work the full 8 hours.

Unfortunately, few people want to work only 3 hours a day at $7.00 per hour. And those who would be willing, such as students, are often not available during the most crucial hours. Thus, with peak-time pay, 15 people may be paid $9 or $10 per hour to work only the 3 peak hours. Thus, the employee makes a reasonable amount of money per day, and the organization still saves money over what it would have spent had its employees worked the entire 8 hours.

Job Sharing

A fourth alternative working schedule—**job sharing**—is offered by 24% of organizations (SHRM, 2002) and involves two employees who share their work hours. Rather than one person working 40 hours each week, two employees combine their hours so that they total 40. At first glance, job sharing may seem to be little more than part-time work. There are, however, big psychological, if not administrative, differences.

Exhibit 16.03   Estes (1990) meta-analysis of flextime studies

Variable	Effects Observed		
	Positive	None	Negative
Absenteeism	47	6	1
Leave usage	4	3	1
Family/leisure time	21	0	0
Organizational costs	6	5	5
Overtime pay	9	1	0
Productivity	51	8	2
Satisfaction	43	0	0
Transportation ease	23	0	0
Turnover	8	0	0

Source: Adapted with permission from Estes (1990).

First, part-time work usually involves lower-level jobs such as those found in the retail and restaurant industries. But job sharing allows people in such complex occupations as teaching and accounting to enjoy the advantages of fewer work hours.

Second, with part-time work, the performance of one employee rarely affects the performance of another. That is, the work completed by two part-time employees results from two separate jobs. But with job sharing, the work may be done by two different employees who share one job title and one position. Poor-quality work by one employee must be corrected by the other.

From a psychological standpoint, the main difference between job sharing and part-time employment is the level of employee commitment, both to the organization and to the other employee. Job-sharing programs are targeted at employees who have family responsibilities. Thus, an organization can attract a highly qualified employee who would not be able to work full time.

Furthermore, an increasing trend is for husbands and wives in similar professions to share the same position. One such situation recently occurred with a high school teaching position: The wife teaches three morning classes while her husband takes care of their two children; the husband then teaches three afternoon classes while his wife cares for their children.

Work at Home

The fifth and final alternative work schedule is **work at home**. With this schedule, the employee works at home rather than at the workplace. Although working at home has recently received increased attention, it is certainly not a new concept. For more than a century, women have sewn garments at home and then sold them to factories for piece-rate prices. Today, with the increase in computers, other types of work can also be done in the home. With many types of homework, work is completed with little or no contact with a central office or factory. With **telecommuting**, however, an employee uses a computer and modem at home to electronically interact with a central office. Other terms commonly used for telecommuting are *telework* and *mobile working*. Telecommuting is ideal for such tasks as computer programming, data entry, and telemarketing. Though there are many estimates of the frequency of telecommuting, in the United States between 10 million and 28 million employees telecommute (Davis & Polonko, 2001; Wells, 2001b) and 37% of organizations offer some form of telecommuting (SHRM, 2002). Telecommuters feel more social support and less isolation than do their more traditional work-at-home counterparts (Trent, Smith, & Wood, 1994).

An increasingly popular concept in telecommuting is the neighborhood "telebusiness center." At these centers, employees from a variety of organizations share office space close to their homes but are connected electronically to their respective organizations (Verespes, 1994).

For telecommuting to be effective, employees must want to work at home, have the ability to work independently, be dependable, and possess good communication skills (Barnes, 1994; Weiss, 1994). Supervisors of telecommuters must define what they expect, plan and communicate schedules, and determine how often they expect telecommuters to contact the office.

Working at home has many advantages for both the employee and the employer. For the employee, it offers the opportunity to avoid or minimize child care and commuting costs, while allowing flexibility and comfort in working conditions. For the employer, money is saved on both office space and utilities.

Unfortunately, there is little empirical research investigating the consequences of telecommuting.

Exhibit 16.04 Effect sizes for flextime programs

Criterion	Estes (1990)		Baltes, Briggs, Huff, Wright, and Neuman (1999)	
	Number of Studies	Mean Effect Size	Number of Studies	Mean Effect Size
Absenteeism	10	−.59	8	−.93
Productivity	29	.19	4	.45
Satisfaction	9	.27	16	.15
Leave usage	13	−.15		
Role conflict	2	−.48		
Family/leisure time	3	.23		

However, anecdotal evidence has been very positive. For example, Kistner and Zbar (2003) report that telecommuting annually saves KPMG $66 million, Sun $150 million, and Ernst and Young more than $100 million.

But with the advantages come certain disadvantages, which is why most unions oppose home work (Brennan, 1994). First, it is difficult for a union to organize workers when they are scattered around many locations. Second, it is difficult for the government to enforce safety and fair treatment standards when employees are not in a central location. Third, employees cannot be easily supervised when they work at home. Finally, it becomes difficult to disassociate work from home life. Unfortunately, the actual evaluation of the merits of telecommuting will have to wait until more research has been conducted. Until then, working at home sounds like a promising idea when used with controls and checks to ensure employee safety and fair treatment. Information on telecommuting can be found on the Internet at http://www.telecommute.org.

Shift Work

Even though most people work from 8 or 9 a.m. to 5 p.m., approximately 25% of all employees work evening or late night shifts due to economic and safety factors. Police officers and nurses must work around the clock because neither crime nor illness stops at 5 p.m., retail employees must work late hours to accommodate when most people are able to shop, and factory workers work these shifts because one plant can be three times as productive if it operates around the clock.

Because shift work is necessary and affects approximately 25% of all employees, research has attempted to identify its effects as well as ways to reduce any negative effects. As Exhibit 16.05 shows, research clearly indicates that working evening ("swing") and late night ("graveyard") shifts has many physical, mental, and work-related effects.

These negative effects are thought to occur because of disruptions in the **circadian rhythm**, the 24-hour cycle of physiological functions maintained by every person. For example, most people sleep at night and eat in the morning, at noon, and in the evening. Although there are individual differences in the exact times for each function (such as eating or sleeping), people generally follow the same pattern. Working evening and late-night shifts disrupts this pattern and often causes digestive, appetite, and sleeping problems. Unfortunately, we don't "get used to" shift work, and these effects get worse with continued exposure to night shifts (Kaliterna, Vidacek, Prizmic, & Radpsevoc-Vidacek, 1995).

Many of the psychological and social effects of shift work are caused by the incompatibility of an employee's schedule with the schedules of other people. That is, a person who works nights and sleeps mornings may be ready to socialize in the afternoon. Unfortunately, fewer people are around. And when the family is active, the employee is sleeping and thus requires quiet.

As Exhibit 16.06 shows, many factors influence the degree to which shift work will affect an employee. For example, an employee with a family is affected more than a single employee because the employee must adjust his sleeping schedule to those of others in the household (Smith & Folkard, 1993). Other important factors are uniqueness of shift, whether a shift is fixed or rotating, frequency of rotation, and individual differences.

Uniqueness of Shift

The social effects of shift work can be greatly reduced if other organizations in the geographical area also use other shifts. The higher the percentage of organizations with shifts, the greater the number of stores and restaurants that are open during the evening and the greater the number of other people available with whom to socialize. Shift work especially affects male workers who pattern their schedule around leisure concerns; females tend to adjust their schedules to domestic concerns (Chambers, 1986).

Exhibit 16.05 Effects of working evening and late night shifts

Factor	Improved	No Change	Deteriorated
Physical health			Akerstedt & Torsvall (1978)
			Colligan, Frockt, & Tasto (1970)
			Dunham (1977)
			Frese & Semmer (1986)
			Meers, Maasen, & Verhaegen (1978)
			Mott et al. (1965)
			Wolinsky (1982)
Performance			Malaviya & Mariott (1953)
			Mott et al. (1965)
			Smith, Totterdell, & Folkard (1995)
			Wyatt & Mariott (1953)
Attendance		Gannon, Norland, & Robeson (1983)	Colligan et al. (1970)
			Jamal (1981)
			Nicholson, Jackson, & Howes (1978)
Fatigue			Luna, French, & Mitcha (1997)
			Wedderburn (1978)
Social and family life			Akerstedt & Torsvall (1978)
			Bast (1960)
			Dunham (1977)
			Jamal (1977)
			Presser (2000)
			Ulrich (1957)
			Wedderburn (1978)
			Wyatt & Mariott (1953)
Mental health			Colligan et al. (1979)
			Jamal (1981)
			Wedderburn (1978)
Job satisfaction		Dunham (1977)	Frost & Jamal (1979)
			Jamal (1981)
Sleep problems			Smith, Totterdell, & Folkard (1995)

Fixed Versus Rotating Shifts

Shifts can be either fixed or rotated. With **fixed shifts**, separate groups of employees permanently work the day shift, swing shift, and night shift. **Rotating shifts** are those in which an employee rotates through all three shifts, working the day shift for a while, then switching to the swing shift, then working the night shift, and so on. A survey of 623 U.S. and Canadian companies using shifts found that 66% used rotating shifts (Circadian Technologies, 2002).

The rationale for rotating shifts is that the negative effects of working swing and night shifts can be lessened if each employee is allowed to work the day shift part of the time. With fixed shifts, even though two thirds of all workers will have hours that are not compatible with their circadian rhythms, staying permanently on the same shifts will allow them to physically adjust better than if they change shifts, especially when considering that about 2 days are needed to adjust to each shift change.

Research on shift rotation has strongly suggested that fixed shifts result in fewer performance, physical, and psychological problems than do rotating shifts (Buddhavarapu, Borys, Hormant, & Baltes, 2002; Frese & Okonek, 1984; Jamal & Jamal, 1982; Verhaegen, Cober, de Smedt, & Dirkx, 1987). For example, Jamal

Exhibit 16.06 Factors influencing shift work effects

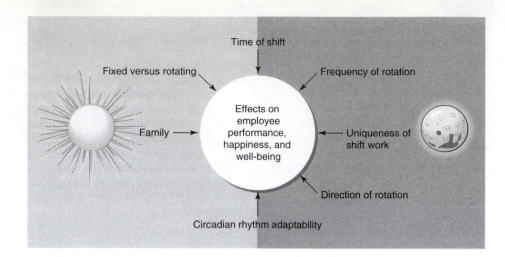

(1981) found that employees on fixed shifts had less absenteeism and tardiness, greater job satisfaction and social participation, and better mental health than did their counterparts working rotating shifts. The results of a meta-analysis (Buddhavarapu et al., 2002) and a traditional review of the literature (Wilkinson, 1992) concluded that fixed shifts were superior to rotating shifts, especially for industrial workers.

Frequency of Rotation

Although fixed shifts are better for individuals than rotating shifts, sometimes shifts must be rotated because employees who feel stuck on swing and night shifts insist on having the opportunity to work days. In such situations, the frequency of the shift rotation must be considered. That is, should the rotation occur daily? Weekly? Monthly? The *2002 Shiftwork Practices Survey* (Circadian Technologies, 2002) found that 47% of organizations that rotate shifts do so weekly, 15% rotate every 2 weeks, and 10% rotate monthly.

Research on this point has been sparse and has not provided a clear and obvious solution. Both Williamson and Sanderson (1986) and Knauth and Kiesswetter (1987) studied changes from 7-day to 3-day rotations and found the faster rotating shifts to result in fewer sleep and eating difficulties. Frese and Semmer (1986), however, found no such effect after controlling for the amount of on-the-job stress. Furthermore, the first two studies compared relatively fast rotations. Research is still needed that compares slower rotations of at least 1 month with the faster rotations before the effects of rotation frequency can be clarified. If shifts are to be rotated, the rotation should be clockwise, with later starting times for the morning shift (Barton & Folkard, 1993; Knauth, 1996). Rest periods of at least 2 days between shift rotations can lessen the negative effects of the rotations (Totterdell, Spelten, Smith, Barton, & Folkard, 1995).

Individual Differences

The final factor concerning the effects of shift work involves individual differences in employees. Obviously, not all employees will react to shift work in the same way because of the differences in their biological time clocks. In fact, we have all probably known people who claimed to be "night people" or to "prefer the morning." These individual differences in time preference are called *chronotypes* (Greenwood, 1994).

Several questionnaires have been developed to distinguish so-called morning people from evening people. Perhaps the best of these was developed by Smith, Reilly, and Midkiff (1988), which contains the 13 most reliable and valid questions from three other available scales (Reilly & Smith, 1988). Such a questionnaire can be used to select and place employees in their optimal shifts. Introverts tend to be "morning people" more than extraverts (Harma, 1993). Males adapt to shift work better than do females, and shift work affects older workers more than younger workers (Oginska, Pokorski, & Oginski, 1993).

To apply your new knowledge of work schedules, complete Exercise 16–1 at the end of this chapter.

Moonlighting

Another interesting problem involving work hours is seen with employees working more than one job, or **moonlighting**. For example, an employee might work the day shift as a machine operator for Ford Motor Co. and then work the night shift as a store clerk for a 7–Eleven convenience store. People moonlight for obvious reasons: They want or need to earn extra money, and they enjoy the second job (Baba & Jamal, 1992). Slightly more than 6% of U.S. employees work more than one job (Hirschman, 2000), and this rate goes as high as 28% for firefighters (Amirault, 1997). Moonlighting employees raise concerns about the effects of extra work on performance and absenteeism for these employees' primary jobs.

Few studies have investigated the effects of moonlighting. Jamal (1981) and Jamal and Crawford (1984) surveyed more than 400 workers at six organizations and found that moonlighters were no different from nonmoonlighters in terms of mental health, quality of life, job performance, and intention to leave their companies. But moonlighters did miss about one day more of work per year than did nonmoonlighters.

Neither Arcuri and Lester (1990), Miller and Sniderman (1974) nor Mott, Mann, McLoughlin, and Warwick (1965) found any negative effects for moonlighting. In fact, Mott and colleagues found that moonlighters were better adjusted and more active in the community than were their nonmoonlighting counterparts. Because there seem to be few negative effects to moonlighting, few organizations prohibit it. Instead, most organizations have moonlighting policies that prohibit moonlighting that might be a conflict of interest (e.g., working for a competitor), that uses company equipment in the outside job, or that requires performing outside jobs during company time.

Work Environment

Noise

If you have ever been upset when someone played his stereo too loudly while you were studying, then you can understand why psychologists are interested in studying the effects of workplace noise. If the "obvious" were true, we could start and end our discussion of noise by stating that high levels of noise reduce performance and make workers unhappy. But as Exhibit 16.07 shows, the relationship between noise and worker behavior is much more complicated than we might first think.

To understand this relationship, we must first realize that not all noise is the same. Two sounds with the same level of loudness can have different frequencies. For example, the sound of a tugboat whistle is much lower in frequency than a train whistle. Lower frequencies do not affect employee performance as much as higher frequencies.

Furthermore, sounds that have the same frequency, intensity, and loudness can differ in their *pleasantness*. For example, noise levels at rock concerts and nightclubs are certainly loud, yet some of us enjoy the sound enough to pay money to hear it. We would probably not pay money to hear a jet engine producing the same sound levels as a rock concert.

This effect can be seen with an employee who listens to music through headphones at work. The noise level of the music is often greater than that of the machines in the environment, but it is considered to be more pleasant. Keep in mind, however, that even though the music may be more interesting than the machine noise, the noise level has the same potential effects: Hearing loss can occur just as easily from music as it can from factory noise.

Noises also differ in whether they are continuous or intermittent. Constant noise has less effect on employee behavior, so environments with steady noise levels are not as disrupting as those in which either noise frequency or noise intensity changes (Teichner, Arees, & Reilly, 1963; Vernon & Warner, 1932).

Another factor that affects the relationship between noise and employee behavior is the *type* and *difficulty* of the task. Noise affects difficult tasks or those that involve cognitive and perceptual skills more than it affects less difficult tasks or those that involve physical performance (Cohen & Weinstein, 1981).

Individual differences in people also determine the degree to which noise will affect performance. Weinstein (1978) examined individual differences in noise sensitivity in college students and found that noise-sensitive students had lower academic performance, were less comfortable in the presence of others, and became more disturbed than their less noise-sensitive peers. Melamed, Harari, and Green (1993) found that Type A personalities' blood pressure and heart rate increased under conditions of high noise but not under conditions of low noise.

The effect of noise also depends on the *necessity* for and *familiarity* of the noise. When certain noises cannot be avoided—for example, the sound of a machine in a manufacturing plant—they are less irritating than unnecessary noises such as an employee talking too loudly or a roommate playing a stereo at full volume (Kjellberg, Landstrom, Tesarz, & Soderberg, 1996).

Likewise, familiar noise is less irritating than unfamiliar noise, probably for two reasons. First, a familiar noise is less distracting or meaningful than one that we hear for the first time. For example, the regular passing of a train outside an office produces less distracting noise than a suddenly dropped glass. Even though the train is louder, it is expected and familiar and thus not as distracting. Soldiers with war experience have often reported they were able to sleep through artillery explosions but would awaken instantly at the sounds of snapped twigs or close footsteps.

Familiar sounds may also be less distracting because our hearing loses sensitivity to loud sounds. For example, on first entering a factory, the noise levels are often very high and distracting. After a few minutes, however, the noise is less noticeable because we have become temporarily less sensitive to it.

Finally, noise affects certain *types* of employee behaviors in different ways. Noise is more likely to decrease the quality of performance rather than its quantity (Broadbent & Little, 1960), cause people to walk faster and make less eye contact (Korte & Grant, 1980), decrease job satisfaction (Sundstrom, Town, Rice, Osborn, & Brill, 1994), and decrease performance on cognitive tasks (Cohen & Weinstein, 1981; Smith & Jones, 1992). But perhaps the greatest effects of noise are not on performance but on employee health and morale.

As Exhibit 16.08 shows, research indicates that in addition to hearing loss, continued exposure to high levels of noise (measured in decibels [db]) can raise blood pressure (Burns, 1979), increase worker illness (Cohen, 1972), cause people to be less helpful (Fisher,

Exhibit 16.07 Factors determining possible noise effects

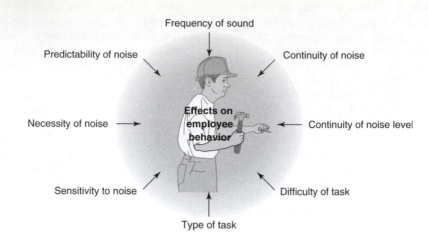

Bell, & Baum, 1984), and produce more aggression and irritability (Donnerstein & Wilson, 1976). Interestingly, even low levels of office noise have been found to increase employee stress and reduce task motivation (Evans & Johnson, 2000).

Noise also causes people to narrow their focus of attention so that they concentrate only on the most important stimuli. In one experiment, Korte and Grant (1980) placed unusual objects (for example, brightly colored balloons tied to a lamppost) and people (a woman wearing a large pink hat) along the sidewalk of a busy shopping district. Korte and Grant then asked shoppers if they had seen anything unusual and read them a list of the unusual people and things they could have seen. When traffic noise was high, only 35% of the shoppers noticed the items, compared to more than 50% when the noise was low. Although such narrowing of attention may decrease the performance levels of employees for whom it is important to notice many stimuli (for example, police officers or safety inspectors), it may help the performance of employees who need only focus on a few different stimuli (Broadbent, 1971).

Noise Reduction

Given that noise affects employee morale, health, and perhaps performance, employers have attempted to solve or minimize the problem of noise by several methods. One has been by setting legal time limits on the exposure to noise at different decibel levels. As you can see from Exhibit 16.09, the legal limits set by the Occupational Safety and Health Administration (OSHA) are not as stringent as those recommended by the National Institute for Occupational Safety and Health (NIOSH).

A second method is to change the environment by using carpeting and acoustically treated ceilings (Sundstrom et al., 1994).

A third method has been by reducing the amount of unwanted noise that reaches an employee. Examples have included employees wearing protective earplugs and muffs or working in soundproof areas away from the sources of noise. In one study, use of hearing protection devices in a noisy factory reduced workers' hostile behaviors (Rabinowitz, Melamed, Feiner, & Weisberg, 1996). Although these methods may limit the effects on employee health, they may also decrease performance in jobs that require detection of or attention to certain types of noise (Mershon & Lin, 1987).

Another method used to limit the problem of noise has been through engineering technology—that is, by reducing the actual amount of noise emitted. For example, rubber pads on machines reduce noise by reducing vibration, and belt drives instead of gears reduce the noise made by many types of machines. In one study, using white noise to mask office noise improved performance on a cognitive task. However, the white noise group still performed worse than the no-noise group (Loewen & Suedfeld, 1992). In offices, airflow from ventilation systems can serve as a source of white noise.

This discussion concentrated on the potential harmful effects of noise, but noise can also be beneficial in the working environment, especially as a warning method. For example, loud noises alert workers that a forklift is backing up, loud whistles tell workers when it is time to go home, and alarms tell workers when a machine has malfunctioned.

Music

One intriguing method for enhancing worker performance and morale has been the use of music during work. The rationale is that music will help reduce the periods of boredom and keep employees alert. More than 10,000 organizations have music played for their employees and customers by subscribing to Muzak (more commonly known as "elevator music").

Rather than playing any type of music, Muzak is highly specific, playing 486 soft instrumental songs per day, each selected so that it can be heard but not be distracting. Furthermore, the music is played in 15-minute programs, with the music at the beginning of the program less stimulating than that played toward the end of the program (is any of Muzak stimulating?).

Exhibit **16.08** Effects of noise at different levels

Cause of Noise	Loudness of Noise (in decibels)	Effect of Noise
Rocket launch	180	
	170	
	160	
	150	
Gunshot blast	140	
Jet takeoff	130	Brief exposure can result in permanent deafness (Trahiotis & Robinson, 1979)
	125	
Disco	120	
Riveting machine	115	Maximum legal exposure to noise
Power lawn mower	110	A person cannot speak over a sound at this level
	105	
Textile-weaving plant	100	Blood pressure increases (Burns, 1979)
Food blender	95	Cognitive performance is reduced (Hockey, 1979) Employees report more illness and somatic complaints (Cohen, 1972)
	93	Angry people become more aggressive (Baron, 1977) Driving performance decreases (Finkelman, Zeitlin, Filippi, & Friend, 1977)
City traffic	90	Legal acceptable noise limit for 8-hour day (OSHA guidelines)
Computer card verifier	85	Helping behavior decreases (Mathews & Canon, 1975)
Train (100 feet away)	80	Reaction time decreases by 3% (Lahtela, Niemi, Kunsela, & Hypen, 1986)
Car	75	
Noisy restaurant	70	Telephone use is difficult
	68	Reduced detection of grammatical errors during proofreading (Weinstein, 1977)
	65	Hearing loss can occur in sensitive individuals
Normal speech	60	
	50	
Normal noise at home	40	
Soft whisper	30	
	20	
	10	
Breathing	0	

Although use of music is popular, questions still remain about its effectiveness. In general, research has shown that employees enjoy listening to music at work and believe that they are more productive because of it (Newman, Hunt, & Rhodes, 1966). Little well-conducted research is available that has tested the actual effects of music on productivity, but what there is has generally been favorable (Fox, 1971). For example, a Japanese study found that worker fatigue was reduced by 32% (Wokoun, 1980); Oldham, Cummings, Mischel, and Schmidtke (1995) found that the use of personal-stereo headsets increased performance and job satisfaction; and Muzak's own research shows a 17% increase in factory productivity, a 13% increase in clerical performance, and a 53% decrease in turnover by airline reservation agents. Furthermore, research has demonstrated that the presence of fast music causes customers in a restaurant to eat faster (Roballey & Gardner, 1986)

and that the presence of slow music causes supermarket customers to spend 38% more money (Milliman, 1986). Thus, music might indeed make working conditions better.

Much more research is necessary, however, because the relationship between music and performance probably depends on several factors. One is undoubtedly the type of music being played. Muzak uses a specific type and sequence of music that it believes is best. But employees often listen to classical, jazz, rock, and country music on their own headphones. What effects do these types of music have? And what if an employee does not like the music being played?

Another issue that needs further investigation is the relationship between music and task type. Music might increase performance in manual tasks that require little thinking, but it is doubtful that the same

Exhibit **16.09** Maximum legal exposure to noise

	Maximum Noise Level (in decibels)	
Hours of Exposure	OSHA Limits	NIOSH Recommendations
8	90	85
7	91	
6	92	
5	93	
4	95	88
3	97	
2	100	91
1.5	102	
1	105	94
0.5	110	97
0.25	115	100

would hold true for complex tasks involving focused mental effort (Gilmer & Deci, 1977; Uhrbrock, 1961). Contrary to what one might expect from this discussion, Wentworth (1991) found no effect for music with production workers who are mentally retarded.

Temperature

Another important issue concerning the working environment is the effect of temperature on employee performance and health. Many jobs such as those in construction and in the steel industry involve working in intense heat, and others such as rescue squad work and meatpacking often involve working in extreme cold.

Perhaps the best place to begin a discussion of the effects of temperature is by describing how the human body tries to maintain an ideal temperature. When body temperature is above normal, we cool down in one of two ways. The first is through **radiation**, with the excess heat radiating away from the body. The second way is by **evaporation**, or by sweating away excess heat.

When body temperature is below normal, blood vessels constrict. Although this process helps protect against cold, it also produces numbness by reducing circulation. That is why our feet and hands are the first parts of the body to feel numb when we are cold. Police officers working a beat can often be seen stomping their feet in cold temperatures to stimulate circulation.

We must next understand how different factors affect what is called the **effective temperature,** or how hot or cold our environment feels to us. In theory, effective temperature has four components—air temperature, humidity, airflow, and temperature of objects in the environment—but it is usually computed by considering only air temperature and humidity. Note that effective temperature is more than simple air temperature. A 90-degree day in a Nevada desert feels cooler than a 90-degree day in a Georgia swamp. As Exhibit 16.10 shows, the higher the humidity, the warmer the air temperature feels, and thus the higher the effective temperature. A table showing the effect of wind on effective temperature (wind chill) can be found on the Web at www.usatoday.com/weather/winter/windchill/wind-chill-chart.htm. Many jobs, such as those in the steel and construction industry, involve working in intense heat, which can affect employee performance and health.

In addition to humidity, airflow is also important. We all can probably recall the feeling of relief from a breeze coming off a lake or off the ocean. The air temperature probably did not change, but discomfort decreased along with the effective temperature. Likewise, we might recall a "biting wind" that made a winter day seem so cold.

Finally, the effective temperature is affected by the heat that radiates from other objects in the environment. For example, the field-level temperature of outdoor sports stadiums that use artificial turf is usually much higher than the air temperature in the stands because heat radiates from the artificial turf. Other examples of this radiation effect include how much hotter it feels when sitting with a group of people than when sitting alone or how much hotter it feels when lying on the sand at the beach than when sitting up.

I can remember many summer days in Los Angeles when the air temperature was already more than 100 degrees but combined with heat radiating from a sidewalk to add 15 degrees and thus make walking uncomfortable. Similarly, a manager who thinks that her outdoor salespeople will be fine in an 85-degree temperature must also account for the effective temperature caused by radiating heat. An air temperature of 85 degrees above a concrete sidewalk is not the same as 85 degrees above a dirt road.

Humidity (%)	Air Temperature (°F)					
	41	50	59	68	77	86
100	41	52	64	78	96	120
80	41	52	63	75	90	111
60	40	51	62	73	86	102
40	40	51	61	72	83	96
20	39	50	60	70	81	91
0	39	50	59	69	77	86

Both air temperature and humidity interact with the body's ability to cool down through radiation and evaporation. When air temperature is higher than body temperature, we are unable to radiate heat. When humidity is high, it is more difficult to lose body heat through evaporation. Thus, high air temperature and high humidity make the body's "natural cooling system" less effective.

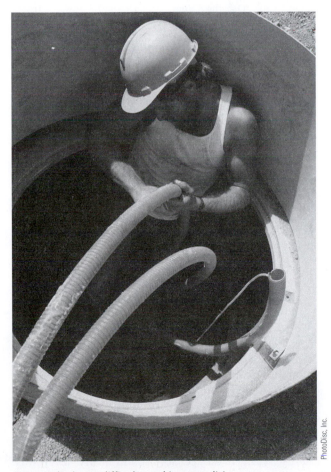

Some jobs have difficult working conditions.

PhotoDisc, Inc.

The relevant question here, of course, is what happens when the effective temperature in the working environment is high or low? As shown in Exhibit 16.11, the answer is that performance usually deteriorates. The degree of deterioration, however, depends on several factors, including the type of task, the workload, and the number and frequency of rest periods that are allowed.

Effects on Tasks

Research indicates that high effective temperatures can affect performance on cognitive, physical, and perceptual tasks. For example, Fine and Kobrick (1978) found that after 7 hours of exposure to 95-degree temperatures with 88% humidity, employees made twice as many errors on a cognitive task as did a control group that worked in a moderate temperature of 75 degrees with 25% humidity.

Beshir, El-Sabagh, and El-Nawawi (1981) also investigated the effects of heat exposure on a perceptual tracking task. Beshir and his colleagues found that subjects' performance did not greatly decrease after working 90 minutes at 68 degrees. At 86 degrees, however, performance decreased significantly within 30 minutes. In a review of 160 studies, Ramsey (1995) found that performance in perceptual motor tasks began to decrease when the temperature rose above 86 degrees.

Though employee comfort and performance are important, heat can also affect the performance of machines and equipment. For example, a California printing and bookbinding company ran into interesting problems involving the airflow in one of its plants. The facility had many different types of printing presses, as well as binders that required the melting of glue chips. As you can imagine, the heat from summer air, binding machines, and employees' bodies combined to make working conditions uncomfortable.

To solve this problem, the managers decided to increase the airflow by opening all of the plant's doors and windows and letting the ocean breezes cool the plant. Unfortunately, the increased airflow not only cooled the plant and made the employees more comfortable, it also caused the mechanical collating machines to malfunction.

Exhibit **16.11** Effects of various temperatures on employee behavior

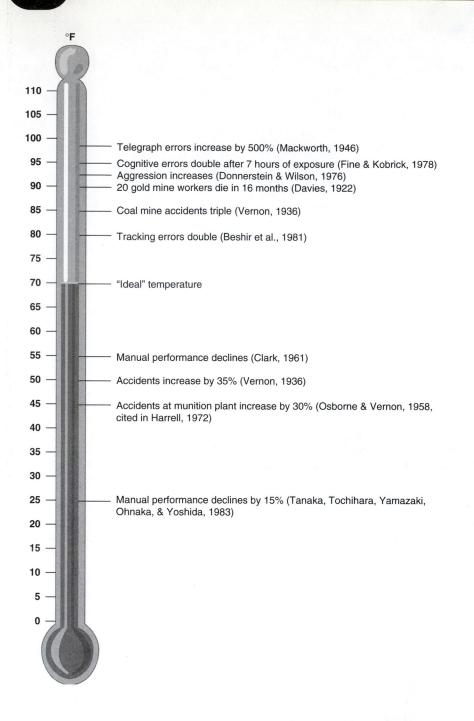

°F

110
105
100 ———— Telegraph errors increase by 500% (Mackworth, 1946)
95 ———— Cognitive errors double after 7 hours of exposure (Fine & Kobrick, 1978)
———— Aggression increases (Donnerstein & Wilson, 1976)
90 ———— 20 gold mine workers die in 16 months (Davies, 1922)
85 ———— Coal mine accidents triple (Vernon, 1936)
80 ———— Tracking errors double (Beshir et al., 1981)
75
70 ———— "Ideal" temperature
65
60
55 ———— Manual performance declines (Clark, 1961)
50 ———— Accidents increase by 35% (Vernon, 1936)
45 ———— Accidents at munition plant increase by 30% (Osborne & Vernon, 1958, cited in Harrell, 1972)
40
35
30
25 ———— Manual performance declines by 15% (Tanaka, Tochihara, Yamazaki, Ohnaka, & Yoshida, 1983)
20
15
10
5
0

The collating machines use sensors that warn their operators when too many or too few sheets of paper have been picked up. The breezes ruffled the sheets and thus set off the sensors. The increased airflow may have made the employees more comfortable and productive, but it reduced the equipment's productivity. Because the potential output of the collating machines was much greater than the outputs of the individual employees, the windows were closed. As a result, the employees became irritable but overall productivity increased.

A similar case occurred at a knitting mill whose owners discovered that yarn tended to snap when humidity was low. Therefore, they made no attempt to dehumidify the air. Unfortunately for the millworkers, the high humidity made working conditions uncomfortable. Thus, a decision had to be made as to the ideal humidity level that would keep the employees happy and productive without causing the yarn to snap. So the humidity level was slightly lowered.

A final example of the differential effects of temperature comes from baseball. When temperatures are high, players are uncomfortable, and pitchers tire more quickly than when temperatures are moderate. But the hotter air allows a baseball to travel farther, and there are often more home runs. Thus, the higher temperatures negatively affect pitchers but positively affect batters.

Effects Related to Workload

High temperatures obviously most affect work performance when workloads are heavy. That is, an effective temperature of 95 degrees would quickly affect a person using a sledgehammer but take longer to affect a person pulling weeds. However, even exposure to moderate levels of heat while performing "light" repetitive-motion work can be dangerous. In a study of female laundry workers, Brabant (1992) found increases in discomfort and cardiac strain—results that were not immediately dangerous but had the potential for future health problems.

Rest Periods

Temperature has the greatest effect on performance when work activity is continuous. With rest breaks, the effects of either heat or cold can be greatly reduced. For example, most people can work for approximately 120 minutes at 90 degrees without impaired performance. At 100 degrees, however, the maximum time for continued performance is approximately 30 minutes; after that time, performance deteriorates (Wing, 1965). Thus, in temperatures of 90 degrees, rest breaks scheduled at a maximum of 2 hours apart will help keep performance (and the employee) from deteriorating. At 100 degrees, rest breaks must occur at intervals of less than 30 minutes.

An interesting problem developed at a large amusement park when its employees were exposed to summer heat. The park had several employees dress in theme costumes, which we will call "gnomes" to protect the park's reputation. The thick and heavy gnome costumes were worn even during summer when temperatures were almost always in the 90s and 100s. The job of each costumed employee was to walk around the park and greet customers, especially children.

Problems, however, began when children punched the gnomes and knocked them over (a rolling gnome was actually a fairly funny sight). Normally, the gnomes kept their sense of humor and laughed, but after an hour in costume in 100-degree temperatures, they sometimes lost their humor and began punching back. And when they were not hitting children, the gnomes were passing out from the heat. Obviously, something had to be done.

To solve the problem, the park's management had the gnomes work 4-hour shifts instead of 8. As we might expect from the previous discussion, this solution was ineffective. Why? Because the outside temperature was 100 degrees and the effective temperature inside the costume was at least 20 degrees higher. At such high temperatures, continuous activity brought decreased performance in less than 30 minutes. The solution that worked, of course, was to have the gnomes work for 20 minutes and then take short breaks in an air-conditioned room, thus taking advantage of what we know about exposure limits to heat as well as frequency of breaks.

An interesting adaptation to extreme temperature can be found at the Ice Hotel, located above the Arctic Circle in Sweden. The Ice Hotel is a fascinating structure made completely of ice—the walls, floors, beds, chairs, and even the chandeliers! During the winter, the temperature outside the hotel falls to 30 degrees below zero and the inside temperature stays at a constant 30 degrees. How do the employees and guests handle these temperatures? By wearing snowsuits, gloves, and hats while indoors, everyone stays rather toasty. Because the people at the reception desk are exposed to the bitter outside cold each time someone opens the door, the receptionists work 30 minutes at the reception desk and then 30 minutes in a "warmer" part of the hotel before rotating back to the reception desk for another 30 minutes. Thus, through the use of proper clothing and rest periods, the Ice Hotel is able to keep its employees safe and productive (and from what we could see, very happy as well).

To apply what you have learned about working conditions, complete Exercise 16–2 at the end of this chapter.

Office Design

Landscaped Offices

In the past decade or so, 70% of organizations have adopted what is formally called an "open" or "landscaped" office design and informally called a "cube farm" (Grossman, 2002a). Originally developed by furniture manufacturers in West Germany, the design uses large, open office areas without walls. Individual work units are separated into cubicles by such items as plants, bookcases, desks, and partitions. The idea behind this design is that employees will communicate better with one another and be easier to supervise and help without the physical barriers of walls (Poe, 2000).

There are three common designs for open or landscaped offices (Martinez, 1990). In a *freestanding* design (also called a *bullpen* design), all desks are placed in a large area that is completely open. With *uniform* plans, desks are placed at uniform distances and are separated by panels into cubicle areas. *Free-form workstations* use a combination of designs so that the different needs of each worker can be accommodated.

Two interesting trends in office design are "boulevards" and portable offices. A boulevard is a wide hallway that runs through several departments. The width of the boulevard allows space for impromptu employee communication, and the path of the boulevard through, rather than around, departments encourages employee interaction. Because landscaped or "open" office environments reduce privacy, many organizations have "portable offices" containing an employee's computer, files, and supplies that can be wheeled into a walled office or cubicle when privacy is needed.

The design of an office can affect employee productivity and satisfaction.

The landscaped office may be appealing, but as Exhibit 16.12 shows, the research has not generally been especially supportive. Landscaped offices can increase contact and communication and are less expensive than regular offices, but often they lessen productivity and job satisfaction (Sundstrom et al., 1994). In a study of more than 500 employees in 14 organizations, O'Neill (1994) found that storage space and the ability to adjust or control one's office space were the best predictors of satisfaction with workspace. Variables such as partition type, panel height, and square footage were not related to satisfaction or performance.

Office Furniture

Given that private offices are more common than, and probably superior to, open office environments, research has sought to determine the factors that affect the placement and perception of furniture within the private office. In particular, this research has concentrated on visitors' perceptions of certain office characteristics as well as on the personalities of office occupants.

Research on visitors' perceptions of certain office characteristics has brought several interesting but not necessarily surprising findings. One line of research examined the perceptions of visitors to offices that used either open or closed desk arrangements. As shown in Exhibit 16.13, an **open desk arrangement** faces a desk against a wall so that a visitor can sit next to the person who sits behind the desk. A **closed desk arrangement** places a desk so that a visitor must sit across from the person behind the desk.

Visitors to offices that use open rather than closed desk arrangements perceive the offices to be more comfortable and their occupants as friendlier and more trustworthy, open, interested, and extraverted (Campbell, 1979; McElroy, Morrow, & Wall, 1983; Widgery & Stackpole, 1972). Visitors rate people with messy offices as being active and busy, those with clean offices as being organized and introverted, and those with organized offices (lots of papers placed in stacks) as being active and achievement oriented (McElroy, Morrow, & Wall, 1983; Morrow & McElroy, 1981). Finally, visitors rate offices with plants and posters as more comfortable, inviting, and hospitable than offices without plants and posters (Campbell, 1979).

This line of research is not only interesting but also important. A supervisor with a messy office and a closed desk arrangement is sending the message that he does not want to be bothered. This may not be his intended message, but it is the one perceived by his subordinates. Thus, a manager who wants to be more open and improve communication with his employees might start by changing the appearance of his office.

Clearly, people make judgments about others based on their office, and the next logical step is to determine whether people with different types of offices actually have different types of personalities. Limited research, in fact, does seem to show that the appearance of an office provides insight into the personality of the occupant.

McElroy, Morrow, and Ackerman (1983) looked at the personalities of faculty members who had open desk arrangements and those who had closed desk arrangements and found that those with open desk

| Exhibit 16.12 | Effects of landscaped office environments |

Study	Employee effects
Brooks and Kaplan (1972)	Increased socialization
T. R. Davis (1984)	
Allen and Gertsberger (1973)	Increased communication
	Decreased construction costs
	Decreased relocation costs
	Decreased lighting and electrical costs
	Decreased office attractiveness
Sundstrom, Burt, and Kamp (1980)	Decreased privacy
	Decreased productivity
	Decreased satisfaction
Oldham and Brass (1979)	Decreased motivation
	Decreased satisfaction
	Decreased concentration
	Increased noise

arrangements were more extraverted and "people oriented" than their closed desk counterparts. Furthermore, faculty members who used open desk arrangements had lower external locus of control and scored higher on the Least-Preferred Coworker (LPC) Scale, which was discussed in Chapter 12.

In another study, Zweigenhaft (1976) compared desk placement using several variables and found that older, higher status faculty members used closed desk arrangements more than did younger members. Even more interesting was the finding that faculty members who used closed desk arrangements were also evaluated less favorably in the classroom. Thus, desk placement was able to partially predict the effectiveness of a faculty member, providing support for the idea that different types of people arrange their offices in different ways.

In a study of personnel managers, Cochran, Kopitzke, and Miller (1984) compared the office characteristics used by managers with their personality. Cochran et al. found that dominant, achievement-oriented managers did not decorate their offices with anything other than standard furniture; more outgoing managers had photographs of their vacations to remind them of good times and a clock to let them know when it was quitting time; introverted managers had plants and paintings so that their office would remind them of home; and organized managers had cartoons to show that even though they were neat and compulsive they also had a sense of humor.

The presence of windows is another factor that seems to affect the way an office is decorated. Heerwagen and Orians (1986) examined the ways people decorate both windowed and windowless offices and found that occupants of windowless offices use twice as

many decorative items such as posters, pictures, and paintings. Not surprisingly, the posters in windowless offices contained more landscapes and fewer cityscapes than do offices with windows.

To apply what you have learned about office environments, complete Exercise 16–3 at the end of this chapter.

Ergonomics and Human Factors

Ergonomics and human factors are areas of study in which psychologists and engineers try to produce products and systems that are easy to use, are safe, maximize efficiency, and minimize physical and psychological strain. Though there are many areas involved in ergonomics and human factors, only four will be highlighted over the next few pages: injury reduction, product design, system efficiency, and transportation.

Providing Ergonomically Correct Work Environments

There is little doubt that the emergence of computers over the last three decades has greatly changed the work environment. Word processing programs allow material to be typed faster and without spelling errors, statistical programs and spreadsheets make research and accounting duties easier, and desktop publishing systems allow material to be attractively produced at a fraction of the cost of using a professional typesetter. But with the improvements in efficiency and quality have come certain health problems.

Exhibit 16.13 Open and closed desk placements

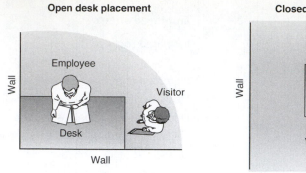

Open desk placement

Closed desk placement

Computer Monitors

In the last 20 years, employees who use computers have complained about health problems. These complaints have even been voiced by students, half of whom believe that computer monitors are dangerous (Trinkaus, 1986). As shown in Exhibit 16.14, these complaints have ranged from simple fatigue to increased numbers of miscarriages suffered by pregnant employees.

Even though employees may report such symptoms, it is unclear how accurate the reports are. For example, Dainoff, Happ, and Crane (1981) believe that the symptoms result from increased stress brought on by the lack of control an employee feels when using a computer as well as by the increased amount of work that can be done on the computer. Thus, the terminal or computer itself does not cause problems, but the loss of control and increased workload does.

Research indicates that 14% of patients seeing an optometrist do so because of problems with computer monitors (Willen, 1996). However, the National Research Council (1983) has indicated that computer monitor use may cause eyestrain but it does not result in permanent eye damage. Furthermore, eyestrain can be greatly reduced by eliminating the glare from the terminal screens. This can be done in several ways, including changing the angle of the screen to limit light reflection, using hoods to screen the terminal from overhead light, using antiglare screens, and changing the lighting in the room in which the terminal is located.

Eyestrain can also be reduced by using large screens with good resolution. Early computer screens tended to be small (the first models of the Kaypro computer) and had print that was difficult to read (the early Apple monitors). Today, however, it is rare for a computer monitor to be less than 17 diagonal inches or to have a resolution greater than .28 dpi.

Proper Work Station Design

Many of the physical symptoms reported by office workers are caused by poorly designed workstations (Willen, 1996). When employees are provided with proper furniture and workstations, performance increases and injuries decrease (Grossman, 2002c). Employees often use the same desk and chair for both their terminal and their typing, writing, and other work. Kroemer and Price (1982) and Grandjean, Hunting, and Pidermann (1983) have conducted extensive research on the optimal design of a computer workstation and how a computer user should sit. For example, the optimal elbow angle when using a terminal is 99 degrees, with a 104-degree trunk incline. Obviously, few computer users are going to measure their elbow angles, but they can be trained to sit in a particular way and be provided with equipment such as detachable keyboards and adjustable tables. The National Institute for Occupational Safety and Health (NIOSH) recommends these features for an ergonomically correct workstation:

- Chairs set at a height allowing the employee's thighs to be horizontal, lower legs to be vertical, and feet placed flat on the floor or on a footrest
- Chairs that have padded seats, armrests, rounded fronts, and provide lumbar support and that are easily adjustable and mobile (with castors)
- Sufficient space for knees and feet
- A table height allowing for straight, relaxed wrists
- A detachable keyboard

Preventing Repetitive Stress Injuries

As a result of the amount of precision and computer work performed by employees, the number of hand and wrist injuries has greatly increased over the last decade. The most common of these repetitive-stress injuries (RSIs) or cumulative trauma disorders (CTDs) are carpal tunnel syndrome (CTS) and tendonitis. RSIs affect 1.8 million workers each year, annually costing employers more than $20 billion in workers' compensation claims and absenteeism (Grossman, 2000).

RSIs are the result of physical stress placed on the tendons and nerves that pass through a tunnel connecting the wrists and hands. The normal stress associated with repeated finger and hand movements is complicated by the awkward angle at which many employees must hold their wrists. Early symptoms of RSI include numbness and tingling in the hands and forearms. Later

Exhibit **16.14**   Research showing problems from computer monitor use

Study	Finding
Mason (1984)	VDT users have 550% more vision-related complaints
Rice (1983)	33% of VDT users are anxious; 5% show symptoms of nausea, high blood pressure, and dizziness
DeGroot and Kamphois (1983)	VDT users report increased eyestrain, migraine headaches, and back problems
Dainoff et al. (1981)	VDT users complain about sore arms, sore backs, and headaches
Harris (1981)	Increased eyestrain, migraines, and back problems
Smith, Cohen, and Stammerjohn (1981)	Increased strain, boredom, workload, and back pains
Savage (1988)	
Nussbaum (1980)	High percentages of miscarriages for women using VDTs
Gunnarson and Ostberg (1977)	VDT typists report twice as much fatigue
	Increased monotony and loss of control for VDT users

stages involve pain severe enough to make opening a door or holding a pen difficult if not impossible.

Treatments for carpal tunnel syndrome include taking anti-inflammatory drugs, wearing wrist braces, and undergoing surgery (more than 100,000 surgeries are performed annually). The healing process can take up to 6 months at a cost per case of $29,000 in medical expenses and lost wages (Heilbroner, 1993). Many RSIs can be prevented by learning ergonomically proper work techniques, performing warm-up exercises, using wrist rests and special keyboards, taking breaks, and stopping work when numbness or pain begins.

A good example of an intervention to reduce RSIs is provided by Pratt & Whitney in Middletown, Connecticut. After employees complained of the physical stress caused by repetitively using their finger to open plastic bags containing machine parts, the company placed a small letter opener on the top of the carts used to move the parts. The cost for this intervention was only $3 a cart. A more complicated intervention was implemented at a Goldkist plant in Alabama. To eliminate the need for employees to repetitively push crates of chicken along a series of rollers, the company installed a moving conveyor belt (Grossman, 2000).

Organizations that have trained employees on ways to prevent RSIs have seen excellent results (Smith, 2003b). For example, Mitsubishi reported a 45% decrease in RSIs over a 2-year period following training, and 3M reported that its training program resulted in a 50% decrease in workers' compensation claims (Tyler, 1998). The training provided by 3M not only reduced the number of worker's compensation claims by 50% but also decreased absenteeism by 13% (Tyler, 1998).

Product Design

Human factors psychologists are often employed by organizations to improve the "user friendliness" of products. Examples might include determining the best layout for a computer keyboard, choosing the optimal size for the finger holes in a pair of scissors,

or designing an automobile dashboard to reduce the distance a driver needs to reach to play the car stereo.

A good example of product design comes from a study by Dempsey, Ayoub, Bernard, Endsley, Karwowski, Lin, and Smith (1996), who were asked to help design the ideal satchel to be carried by postal workers. To do this, they tested four different satchels to determine which one was most comfortable, worked best in diverse climates, was easiest to use, and provided the best protection against attacking dogs. The results of their study indicated that the most comfortable bag also provided the worst protection against attacking dogs and had some problems with ease of mail retrieval.

A similar study was conducted by Pascoe, Pascoe, Wang, Shim, and Kim (1997) in designing book bags. Pascoe and his colleagues compared the effect that three types of bags—two-strap backpack, one-strap backpack, and one-strap athletic bag—had on the posture and gait of the student wearing the book bag. When compared to no book bag, all three types reduced stride length and increased stride frequency. Furthermore, the one-strap backpack and one-strap athletic bag resulted in uncomfortable changes in posture. However, the two-strap backpack did not result in such changes. Thus, the practical aspects of this study suggest that students should buy a backpack with two straps and, even though it is not as cool as slinging one strap over one shoulder, use both straps.

The search for the ideal work glove provides another example of product design studies. This search took two paths: one that investigated the effects of wearing gloves and another that compared the advantages of certain types of gloves over others. Though gloves clearly increase worker safety, their effect on work performance depends on the type of task performed. For example, researchers have found that wearing gloves increases muscle fatigue (Fleming, Jansen, & Hasson, 1997) and decreases the amount of turning force (the authors of the study called this "maximum volitional torque exertion of supination") that can be exerted by a worker (Shih & Wang, 1997), but does not affect the ability to discriminate weights (Shih & Wang, 1996).

Russ Branaghan, Ph.D.
Industrial Psychologist
Fitch, Inc.

Courtesy of Russ Branaghan

I work for Fitch, Inc., an international design firm located in Worthington, Ohio. It is my job to make products more user-friendly.

Just a few short years ago, the lion's share of the high technology market went to the product with the most features, lowest price, and slickest appearance. As consumers have become more technologically savvy, usability has arisen as one of technology's most important issues. Now, product review articles dedicate about 30% of their text to usability issues. Usable products share five characteristics:

1. Learnability: Usable products enable the user to get up to speed and accomplish meaningful work in a relatively short period of time.

2. Efficiency: Efficiency refers to the ease with which users perform their work once they have learned the system.

3. Memorability: What happens when users take a long break from using the product? When they return to it, do they remember how it works, or must they relearn it?

4. Error Minimization: The product should be designed so that users make few errors, and all errors should be easy to recover from.

5. Satisfaction: How pleasurable is the product to use? Users should feel productive, entertained, or satisfied after using it. Satisfaction is perhaps the most important usability factor in a commercial sense.

Usability is accomplished by ensuring that designs fit the user rather than forcing the user to fit the design. This is accomplished by adhering to three principles:

1. Focus on the users, their tasks, and their environment.

2. Measure ease of use by scientific observational methods.

3. Improve the design in an iterative manner, making changes until users can easily and satisfactorily perform their tasks.

A good grasp of psychology is needed because successful design requires an understanding of the user's learning, memory, and judgment capabilities. Further, experimental design and analysis skills are needed to conduct usability tests. In these tests, users conduct realistic tasks with a prototype of the product while the researcher records whether the user was successful at the task, how long it took him or her to complete the task, and problems and design issues experienced along the way. The following case study illustrates how Fitch, Inc. employs usability techniques to improve its clients' products.

Case Study: Teledyne Brown Engineering

Teledyne Brown asked Fitch to work on the design of an aircraft loader for the Air Force (Figure 1). The challenge was to design an interior for the cab that would enable the user to operate the vehicle safely, comfortably, and efficiently. The overall size and components of the cab were predetermined. Fitch assembled a team of designers, cognitive psychologists, and ergonomists to conduct field research to determine how users operate the current equipment, the difficulties they had, and what they liked and disliked about the product.

The field research showed that although aircraft loaders are currently designed to be operated while one is looking out through the front window (like an automobile or truck), operators actually lean their upper body out of the right side window 70% of the time to monitor the loads and communicate with people on the cargo deck. This made it difficult for operators to keep their eyes on the cargo and the airplane.

On the basis of this research, Fitch built a "Velcro" model of the interior of the cab (Figure 2). Fake knobs, dials, and controls were attached so that they could be moved anywhere in the cab depending on the user's input. This enabled the team to work on the model itself rather than rely on

Courtesy of the author

Figure 1 The Teledyne Brown aircraft loader.

drawings for design. The usability research provided invaluable feedback from the users. For example, one user relocated two controls so that a frequently performed operation that had previously required two hands could now be done with one. Further, the users suggested a slanted wall and raised seat that made it easier for operators to lean out of the cab and greatly enhanced visibility. The participatory, user-oriented approach allowed users, designers, and engineers to work together throughout the design process. The result was a smooth and rapid development of a superior product (Figure 3).

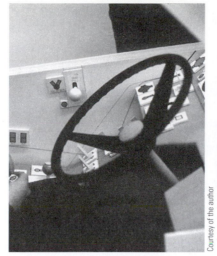

Figure 2 A "Velcro" model of the cab interior of the new aircraft loader.

Figure 3 The redesigned cab interior for the aircraft loader.

Psychologists have conducted studies to identify the optimal work glove.

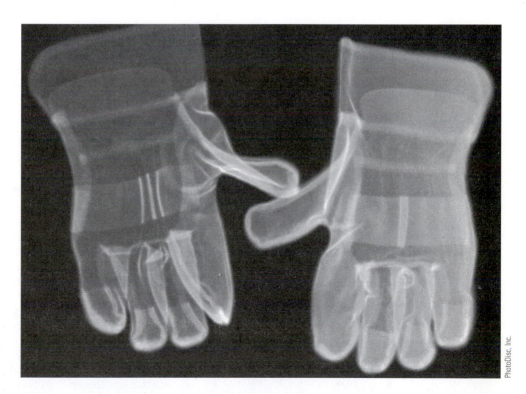

An example of a study searching for the optimal glove comes from Nelson and Mital (1995), who investigated the optimal thickness for examination gloves used by physicians (ouch!). Their study was conducted because although thicker gloves provide greater protection against needle sticks, they might also reduce the ability of the physician to perform sensitive work. The researchers tested five gloves ranging in thickness from 0.21 mm to 0.83 mm. Nelson and Mital found that the 0.83 mm glove not only resisted routine impacts but provided the same level of dexterity and tactility as a bare hand. Though neither bags nor gloves are particularly exciting topics, these examples show the meticulous human factors research that goes into the development of good products.

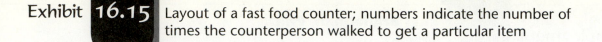

Exhibit 16.15 — Layout of a fast food counter; numbers indicate the number of times the counterperson walked to get a particular item

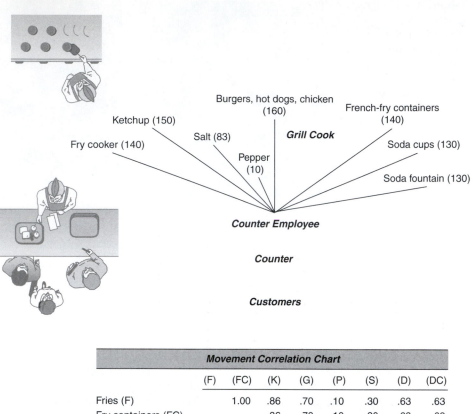

Ketchup (150) Salt (83) Pepper (10) Burgers, hot dogs, chicken (160) — **Grill Cook** French-fry containers (140) Soda cups (130) Soda fountain (130) Fry cooker (140)

Counter Employee

Counter

Customers

	(F)	(FC)	(K)	(G)	(P)	(S)	(D)	(DC)
Movement Correlation Chart								
Fries (F)	1.00	.86	.70	.10	.30		.63	.63
Fry containers (FC)			.86	.70	.10	.30	.63	.63
Ketchup (K)				.70	.30	.60	.45	.45
Grilled food (G)					.10	.40	.65	.65
Pepper (P)						.50	.20	.20
Salt (S)							.29	.29
Drinks (D)								1.00
Drink cups (DC)								

System Efficiency

A major human factors area, at times referred to as "time and motion studies," is making systems more efficient. These studies usually begin with a job analysis to determine how employees perform their jobs. These job analyses tend to be much more specific than the ones you learned about in Chapter 2. For example, suppose you were trying to reduce the time it took for a counterperson at a fast food restaurant to perform his job. As shown in Exhibit 16.15, the employee reached for ketchup packets 150 times, pepper packets 10 times, French fry containers 140 times, and French fries 140 times. What is wrong with the current layout? As you probably guessed, one of the most frequently retrieved items (ketchup) is farthest away, and the least frequently retrieved item (pepper) is closest. Also note from the correlation table that each time the employee retrieved a French fry container, he also retrieved French fries, yet the two are located in different areas. To improve efficiency, the most often retrieved items should be moved closer to the employee, and items that are retrieved together should be located near one another.

As another example, due to the high number of musculoskeletal complaints (for example, back pain or sore wrists) by grocery store cashiers, extensive research has gone into designing a check stand that is both efficient and comfortable. According to a literature review and new data by Grant and Habes (1995), these are the features of the ideal check stand:

• The cashier would face the customer.
• The height of the work surface would be no taller than the cashier's elbows.
• The scanner and keyboard would be in front of the cashier and the cash drawer to the side (less than 18 inches away) of the cashier.

Exhibit 16.16 Some highway signs are easier to understand than others

- Groceries would be presented to the cashier on a conveyor belt that is narrow (to reduce reach) and that runs from the scanner to the back of the check stand.
- Stools, footrests, and antifatigue mats would be present to allow the cashier the choice of sitting or standing.

Transportation

Putting the Brakes on Rear-End Collisions

The goal of human factors research in this area is to make driving safer and easier. For example, human factors researchers have conducted several studies to reduce rear-end collisions. The first step is to study the driving process and create a process chart that diagrams the events that take place, the order in which they occur, and their duration. Such a process chart might show that the amount of time needed to avoid a collision is a function of the time it takes for the lead driver to scan the environment, determine if there is a reason to brake, make the decision to brake, and then apply the brake, and the amount of time it takes for the trailing driver to notice cues (brake lights, turn indicators, slowing of speed), distinguish one cue from another, make a decision to brake, and then apply the brakes. To reduce rear-end collisions, human factors psychologists look for ways to reduce the processing time at each of the steps shown in the process chart. For example, talking on a cellular phone (Alm & Nilsson, 1995) or listening to loud music (Turner, Fernandez, & Nelson, 1996) while driving increases the time it takes to notice such cues as brake lights and traffic signals.

Sivak, Flanagan, Sato, and Traube (1994) found that neither neon or LED brake lights resulted in better reaction times than either a standard or an enhanced incandescent light.

Researchers in another study focused on the step of distinguishing one cue from another. They hypothesized that because both your brake lights and your turn indicators are red, a driver following behind you must spend fractions of a second interpreting whether you are braking or using your turn signal (Luoma, Flanagan, Sivak, Aoki, & Traube, 1997). These fractions of a second could be the difference in avoiding an accident in the case of an immediate stop. Luoma and his research team found that changing the color of the turn signal from red to yellow reduced the time taken to react to a brake signal. This study supports European and Japanese requirements that turn signals be yellow (in the United States both red and yellow are allowed). In another study focusing on the ability to discriminate brake lights from other lights, Theeuwes and Alferdinck (1995) found that a brake light mounted in the rear window is more effective if it is located higher on the window rather than toward the bottom of the window.

Another study sought to reduce the time between the lead driver taking his foot off the accelerator and moving it to the brake. To do this, Shinar (1995) developed an advance brake warning (ABW) system in which a sudden release in the accelerator pedal would activate the brake light for one second. If the driver actually hit the brake pedal, the brake light would stay on. If the driver did not brake, the brake light would go off. Though this system provides an early warning system, it could potentially result in false alarms. To study this possibility, Shinar (1995) studied 95,394 times in

Exhibit **16.17**   What lane should you get into to travel to Roanoke?

Courtesy of the author

which six drivers applied their brakes. The ABW was activated during 820 of the 95,394 instances of braking and provided a following driver an average of one fifth of a second more warning. The false alarm rate was 23% of ABW activations but accounted for only 2% of all brake light activations of less than a second. Thus, the extra warning time did not appear to result in an excessive number of false alarms.

Reducing Speeding

Human factors experts have also conducted research to determine ways to reduce speeding by changing the driving environment. For example, De Waard, Jessurum, Steyvers, Raggatt, and Brookhuis (1995) hypothesized that drivers would speed less often if speeding were made perceptually uncomfortable (as opposed to traffic citations, making speeding financially uncomfortable). To do this, De Waard et al. removed the white lines on the right side of a single-lane road and replaced them with intermittent chippings that made noise when run over by a speeding car. The idea behind this intervention was that speeding drivers often touch the lines on each side of the lane because they are going too fast to keep their vehicle in the center of the lane. "Penalizing" the speeding driver with a noxious noise reduced average speeds by 3 kilometers per hour—enough of a reduction to increase safety.

In another attempt to reduce speeding, one group of researchers believed that some instances of speeding

were the result of drivers being unaware of the speed limit. To reduce this possibility, three researchers at the University of Helsinki in Finland (Lajunen, Hakkarainen, & Summala, 1996) tested three different types of signs telling drivers to slow down as they were entering a "built-up area" (densely populated) in which the national speed limit was 50 kilometers per hour. The first sign contained the symbol for the built-up area, the second the built-up area sign plus the symbol for danger, and the third the built-up area symbol plus the number "50" in a circle. As you might expect, drivers reduced their speed most often with the explicit speed limit sign and least often with the two signs in which one had to "know" the speed limit in a built-up area. In the United States, these findings might be generalized to replace signs that say "School Zone" with ones that say "School Zone: Speed Limit 25 MPH."

Although this study seems to suggest that signs with text are superior to those with icons and symbols, this is not usually the case. Research indicates that icon/symbol highway signs are easier to read and result in lower reaction times than do text-based highway signs (Long & Kearns, 1996). Why the contradictory findings? It is clear that icon/symbol signs are easier to read than signs containing text. However, seeing a symbol and understanding its meaning are two different things. Look at the highway signs in Exhibit 16.16. All of them are easy to read, yet some of them may not be familiar to you. If you aren't familiar with the meaning, or if you are familiar with the meaning ("slow down") but don't know what you are supposed to do (not exceed 25 MPH), the increased viewing distances of the iconic signs are counterbalanced by the increased time to interpret the signs.

This use of icons will be effective only if people have knowledge about the meaning of the icons. Let me provide you with a great example of this point. Our interstate highway system is actually very well designed and marked in most locations. However, many people can't take full advantage of these well-designed and marked highways because they aren't familiar with the codes appearing on the signs. For example, suppose you were driving on I-81 or I-77. That both of these highways end in an odd number tells you the highway runs north–south; even numbered highways run east–west. Or suppose that you were driving up the street, wanted to take the highway to Roanoke, and saw the sign in Exhibit 16.17. What does that sign tell you? Because the arrow is on the left side of the word "Roanoke," you would need to get in the left lane and take a left turn onto the highway. If the arrow was on the right side or beneath the word "Roanoke," you would get in the right lane and take a right turn onto the highway. How many people do you think know these rules?

To apply what you have learned about ergonomics and human factors, complete the Human Factors Exercise on your CD-ROM.

Chapter Summary

In this chapter you learned:

- Compressed work schedules and flextime increase job satisfaction and decrease absenteeism.

- Although shift work often is economically necessary, research indicates that it has negative effects on physical health, performance, and leisure time.

- Noise can reduce job performance and satisfaction, depending on its frequency, pleasantness, purpose, familiarity, and continuity, as well as on the type of task being performed.

- Temperature will affect work behavior depending on the type of task being performed, the workload, and the number and length of rest periods that are allowed.

- Computer terminals increase eyestrain and levels of stress, although the latter probably results from the loss of control one feels when working with a computer as well as a fear of technology. Eyestrain can be corrected through the proper design and construction of computer workstations.

- Private offices are superior to open or landscaped offices. An interesting finding is that the way in which a person decorates his office not only indicates his personality but also affects the behavior of office visitors.

- Ergonomics and human factors are areas in which psychologists and engineers try to produce products and systems that are easy to use, are safe, maximize efficiency, and minimize psychological and physical strain.

Critical Thinking Questions

1. What is the best work schedule?
2. Should employees be allowed to moonlight?
3. What effect does music have on people's behavior at work?
4. How much attention should organizations pay to noise and temperature?
5. How much impact does ergonomics have on employee performance?

To learn more about the issues discussed in this chapter, point your browser to

http://www.infotrac-college.com/wadsworth

and enter one of these search terms:

flextime

compressed work week

telecommuting

shift work

office design

supplemental employment

work environment

ergonomics

job sharing

Occupational Safety and Health Administration (OSHA)

Exercise 16–1
Work Schedules

The first part of Chapter 16 discussed alternative work schedules. The purpose of this exercise is to provide you with an opportunity to apply your new knowledge.

Instructions

Read the situation described below and then use your knowledge of work schedules to create a state-of-the-art scheduling program for the organization.

The computer services department at Taflinger University consists of 38 employees in several divisions. The administrative division consists of a vice president for computer services, a director of administration, two administrative assistants, a receptionist, and two student workers. It is the job of the administration division to administer the computing center and to coordinate all computing activities in the university. Currently, the administrative division is open from 8:00 a.m. to 5:00 p.m., Monday through Friday, and has constant contact with the other departments in the university.

The programming division employs a director of programming, six programmers, three programmer/analysts, and one student worker. The function of the programming division is to write the programs needed to operate the university. For example, they write and update programs for the registrar's office and the payroll office. Employees in this division have occasional contact with employees in other departments.

The computer operations division consists of a director of operations, six computer operators, one tape librarian, two technicians, two clerks, and two student workers. This division is in operation 24 hours a day, 7 days a week. With the exception of the two technicians, none of the employees has contact with people outside of the computing center. Even though they are scheduled from 8:00 a.m. to 5:00 p.m., the technicians are basically "on call" and work whenever computing equipment needs to be fixed.

The academic computing division is staffed by a director for academic computing, two full-time lab assistants, and three part-time student workers. It is the job of this division to serve the computing needs of the various academic departments by operating the student computer lab, helping professors with computer problems, and recommending academic software to be purchased.

Given this wide range of jobs and duties, how would you design a work schedule?

_____

_____

_____

_____

_____

_____

Exercise 16–2
The Work Environment

Several factors involving noise and temperature in the work environment that can affect worker behavior. The purpose of this assignment is to make you more aware of factors such as these in your own work environment.

Instructions

If you are currently working, use your current workplace. If you are not currently employed, visit any local organization and take a tour.

Look around the workplace that you chose. What types of work conditions do you see, hear, smell, and feel? For example, what type of noise do you hear? Is it constant, necessary, loud? Is the workplace hot or cold? How are the employees dressed?

_____

_____

_____

_____

_____

_____

_____

_____

_____

_____

_____

_____

_____

_____

_____

Exercise 16–3
Office Environments

The way in which an office is arranged and decorated not only reflects the person in the office but can also affect the perceptions and behaviors of people visiting the office. The purpose of this exercise is to make you aware of the ways in which people arrange and decorate their offices.

Instructions

Part 1

Go visit several of your professors' offices. Write down what you see. How do their offices compare with their personalities and teaching styles?

Professor _____

Office Environment

_____

_____

_____

_____

_____

_____

_____

Comparison with Personality

_____

_____

_____

_____

_____

_____

_____

Professor _____

Office Environment

_____

_____

_____

_____

_____

Comparison with Personality

_____

_____

_____

_____

_____

Professor _____

Office Environment

_____

_____

_____

_____

_____

Comparison with Personality

_____

_____

_____

_____

_____

Part 2

For each of the following occupations, how would you advise them to decorate their offices to create the right atmosphere?

Professor

_____

_____

_____

_____

_____

_____

_____

_____

_____

Prison Warden

_____

_____

_____

_____

_____

_____

_____

_____

_____

_____

Human Resource Director

_____
_____
_____
_____
_____
_____
_____

Computer Programmer

_____
_____
_____
_____
_____
_____
_____

Dentist

_____
_____
_____
_____
_____
_____
_____
_____

Glossary

Ability A basic capacity for performing a wide range of different tasks, acquiring knowledge, or developing a skill.

Absolute amount The actual salary paid for a particular job.

Acceptance stage The fourth and final stage of emotional reaction to downsizing, in which employees accept that layoffs will occur and are ready to take steps to secure their future.

Accommodating style The conflict style of a person who tends to respond to conflict by giving in to the other person.

Achievement-oriented style In path-goal theory, a leadership style in which the leader sets challenging goals and rewards achievement.

Adaptation The fourth stage of change, in which employees try to adapt to new policies and procedures.

Additive tasks Tasks for which the group's performance is equal to the sum of the performances of individual group members.

Adverse impact An employment practice that results in members of a protected class being negatively affected at a higher rate than members of the majority class. Adverse impact is usually determined by the four-fifths rule.

AET An ergonomic job analysis method developed in Germany.

Affect Feelings or emotion.

Affective commitment The extent to which an employee wants to remain with an organization and cares about the organization.

Affective identify motivation The motivation to lead as a result of a desire to be in charge and lead others.

Affiliation style A leadership style in which the individual leads by caring about others and is most effective in a climate of anxiety.

Affirmative action The process of ensuring proportional representation of employees based on variables such as race and sex. Affirmative action strategies include intentional recruitment of minority applicants, identification and removal of employment practices working against minority applicants and employees, and preferential hiring and promotion of minorities.

Age Discrimination in Employment Act (ADEA) A federal law that, with its amendments, forbids discrimination against an individual over the age of 40.

Alternate forms reliability The extent to which two forms of the same test are similar.

Americans with Disabilities Act (ADA) A federal law, passed in 1990, that forbids discrimination against the physically and mentally disabled.

Ammerman technique A job analysis method in which a group of job experts identifies the objectives and standards to be met by the ideal worker.

Anger stage The second stage of emotional reaction to downsizing, in which employees become angry at the organization.

Anxiety An organizational climate in which worry predominates.

Application of training Measurement of the effectiveness of training by determining the extent to which employees apply the material taught in a training program.

Apply-in-person ads Recruitment ads that instruct applicants to apply in person rather than to call or send resumes.

Apprentice training A training program, usually found in the craft and building trades, in which employees combine formal course work with formal on-the-job training.

Arbitration A method of resolving conflicts in which a neutral third party is asked to choose which side is correct.

Archival research Research that involves the use of previously collected data.

Army Alpha An intelligence test developed during World War I and used by the army for soldiers who can read.

Army Beta An intelligence test developed during World War I and used by the army for soldiers who cannot read.

Artifacts The things people surround themselves with (clothes, jewelry, office decorations, cars, and so forth) that communicate information about the person.

Assessment center A method of selecting employees in which applicants participate in several job-related activities, at least one of which must be a simulation, and are rated by several trained evaluators.

Assimilated A description of a message in which the information has been modified to fit the existing beliefs and knowledge of the person sending the message before it is passed on to another person.

Assimilation A type of rating error in which raters base their rating of an employee during one rating period on the ratings that they gave.

Attitude survey A form of upward communication in which a survey is conducted to determine employee attitudes about an organization.

Attitudinal Listening Profile A test developed by Geier and Downey that measures individual listening styles.

Attractiveness The extent to which a leader is appealing to look at.

Audience effects The effect on behavior when one or more people passively watch the behavior of another person.

Autocratic I strategy Leaders use available information to make a decision without consulting their subordinates.

Autocratic II strategy Leaders obtain necessary information from their subordinates and then make their own decision.

Averaging versus adding model A model proposed by Anderson that postulates that our impressions are based more on the average value of each impression than on the sum of the values for each impression.

Avoiding style The conflict style of a person who reacts to conflict by pretending that it does not exist.

Banding A statistical technique based on the standard error of measurement that allows similar test scores to be grouped.

Bandwidth The total number of potential work hours available each day.

Barnum statements Statements, such as those used in astrological forecasts, that are so general they can be true of almost anyone.

Base rate Percentage of current employees who are considered successful employees.

Baseline The level of productivity before the implementation of a gainsharing plan.

Basic biological needs The first step in Maslow's needs hierarchy, concerning survival needs such as the need for food, air, and water.

Behavior modeling A training technique in which employees observe correct behavior, practice that behavior, and then receive feedback about their performance.

Behavioral observation scales (BOS) A method of performance appraisal in which supervisors rate the frequency of observed behaviors.

Behaviorally anchored rating scales (BARS) A method of performance appraisal involving the placement of benchmark behaviors next to each point on a graphic rating scale.

Benchmark answers Standard answers to interview questions, the quality of which has been agreed on by job experts.

Binding arbitration A method of resolving conflicts in which a neutral third party is asked to choose which side is correct and in which neither party is allowed to appeal the decision.

Biodata A method of selection involving application blanks that contain questions that research has shown will predict job performance.

Blind-box ads Recruitment ads that instruct applicants to send their resume to a box at the newspaper; neither the name nor the address of the company is provided.

Bona fide occupational qualification (BFOQ) A selection requirement that is necessary for the performance of job-related duties and for which there is no substitute.

Bottom-line measure Evaluation of a training program by determining if the organization actually saved money as a result of the training.

Brainstorming A technique in which ideas are generated by people in a group setting.

Bridge publication A publication with the goal of bridging the gap between the research conducted by academics and the practical needs of practitioners.

Bulletin board A method of downward communication in which informal or relatively unimportant written information is posted in a public place.

Burnout The psychological state of being overwhelmed with stress.

Business game An exercise, usually found in assessment centers, that is designed to simulate the business and marketing activities that take place in an organization.

Case law The interpretation of a law by a court through a verdict in a trial, setting precedent for subsequent court decisions.

Case study A training technique in which employees, usually in a group, are presented with a real or hypothetical workplace problem and are asked to propose the best solution.

Cause-and-effect relationship The result of a well-controlled experiment about which the researcher can confidently state that the independent variable caused the change in the dependent variable.

Central tendency error   A type of rating error in which a rater consistently rates all employees in the middle of the scale, regardless of their actual levels of performance.

Change agent   A person who enjoys change and makes changes for the sake of change.

Change analyst   A person who is not afraid of change but makes changes only when there is a compelling reason to do so.

Change resister   A person who hates change and will do anything to keep change from occurring.

Chronic self-esteem   The positive or negative way in which a person views him- or herself as a whole.

Chronological resume   A resume in which jobs are listed in order from most to least recent.

Circadian rhythm   The 24-hour cycle of physiological functions that are maintained by every person.

Clarifier   A type of structured interview question that clarifies information on the resume or application.

Closed desk arrangement   An office arranged so that a visitor must sit across from the person behind the desk.

Cluster grapevine   A pattern of grapevine communication in which a message is passed to a select group of people who each in turn pass the message to a few select others.

Coaching   A method of training in which a new employee receives on-the-job guidance from an experienced employee.

Coaction   The effect on behavior when two or more people are performing the same task in the presence of each other.

Coefficient alpha   A statistic used to determine internal reliability of tests that use interval or ratio scales.

Coercive power   Leadership power that comes from the leader's capacity to punish others.

Coercive style   A leadership style in which the individual leads by controlling reward and punishment; most effective in a climate of crisis.

Cognitive ability   Abilities involving the knowledge and use of information such as math and grammar.

Cognitive ability test   Tests designed to measure the level of intelligence or the amount of knowledge possessed by an applicant.

Collaborative style   The conflict style of a person who wants a conflict resolved in such a way that both sides get what they want.

Common goal   An aim or purpose shared by members of a group.

Communication barriers   Physical, cultural, and psychological obstacles that interfere with successful communication and create a source of conflict.

Communication channel   The medium by which a communication is transmitted.

Communication structure   The manner in which members of a group communicate with one another.

Comparable worth   The idea that jobs requiring the same level of skill and responsibility should be paid the same regardless of supply and demand.

Comparison   The effect when an individual working on a task compares his or her performance with the performance of another person performing the same task.

Compensable job factors   Factors, such as responsibility and education requirements, that differentiate the relative worth of jobs.

Competencies   The knowledge, skills, abilities, and other characteristics needed to perform a job.

Competition for resources   A cause of conflict that occurs when the demand for resources is greater than the resources available.

Complaint box   A form of upward communication in which employees are asked to place their complaints in a box.

Composite score   A single score that is the sum of the scores of several items or dimensions.

Compressed work weeks   Work schedules in which 40 hours are worked in less than the traditional 5-day work week.

Compromising style   A style of resolving conflicts in which an individual allows each side to get some of what it wants.

Computer-adaptive testing (CAT)   A type of test taken on a computer in which the computer adapts the difficulty level of questions asked to the test-taker's success in answering previous questions.

Computer-based training (CBT)   A type of programmed instruction presented through a computer.

Concurrent validity   A form of criterion validity that correlates test scores with measures of job performance for employees currently working for an organization.

Conflict   The psychological and behavioral reaction to a perception that another person is either keeping you from reaching a goal, taking away your right to behave in a particular way, or violating the expectancies of a relationship.

Conjunctive tasks   Tasks for which the group's performance is dependent on the performance of the least effective group member.

Consideration   The degree to which leaders act in a warm and supportive manner toward their subordinates.

Consistency theory   Korman's theory that employees will be motivated to perform at levels consistent with their levels of self-esteem.

Construct validity   The extent to which a test actually measures the construct that it purports to measure.

Consultative I strategy   Leaders share the problem on an individual basis with their subordinates and then make a decision that may or may not be consistent with the thinking of the group.

Consultative II strategy   Leaders share the problem with the group as a whole and then make a decision that may or may not be consistent with the thinking of the group.

Contamination The condition in which a criterion score is affected by things other than those under the control of the employee.

Content validity The extent to which tests or test items sample the content that they are supposed to measure.

Continuance commitment The extent to which employees believe they must remain with an organization due to the time, expense, and effort they have already put into the organization.

Contrast effect When the performance of one applicant affects the perception of the performance of the next applicant.

Contrast error A type of rating error in which the rating of the performance level of one employee affects the ratings given to the next employee being rated.

Control group A group of employees who do not receive a particular type of training so that their performance can be compared to that of employees who do receive training.

Convenience sample A nonrandom research sample that is used because it is easily available.

Cooperation–consideration One of five categories from the trait approach to scoring letters of recommendation.

Cooperative problem solving A method of resolving conflict in which two sides get together to discuss a problem and arrive at a solution.

Core hours The hours in a flextime schedule during which every employee must work.

Correlation A statistical procedure used to measure the relationship between two variables.

Correlation coefficient A statistic, resulting from performing a correlation, that indicates the magnitude and direction of a relationship.

Corresponding effects An event that affects one member of a group will affect the other group members.

Cost per applicant The amount of money spent on a recruitment campaign divided by the number of people that subsequently apply for jobs as a result of the recruitment campaign.

Cost per qualified applicant The amount of money spent on a recruitment campaign divided by the number of qualified people that subsequently apply for jobs as a result of the recruitment campaign.

Counterbalancing A method of controlling for order effects by giving half of a sample Test A first, followed by Test B, and giving the other half of the sample Test B first, followed by Test A.

Country club leadership A style of leadership in which the leader is concerned about the well-being of employees but is not task oriented.

Cover letter A letter that accompanies a resume or job application.

Crisis A critical time or climate for an organization in which the outcome to a decision has extreme consequences.

Criterion A measure of job performance, such as attendance, productivity, or a supervisor rating.

Criterion group Division of employees into groups based on high and low scores on a particular criterion.

Criterion validity The extent to which a test score is related to some measure of job performance.

Critical incident technique The job analysis method developed by John Flanagan that uses written reports of good and bad employee behavior.

Critical incidents A method of performance appraisal in which the supervisor records employee behaviors that were observed on the job and rates the employee on the basis of that record.

Critical judge A person who, when under stress, focuses on negative aspects of him- or herself and the situation.

Cross-functional teams A team consisting of representatives from various departments (functions) within an organization.

Cross-training Teaching employees how to perform tasks traditionally performed by other employees.

Cutoff approach A method of hiring in which an applicant must score higher than a particular score to be considered for employment.

Dale-Chall Index A method of determining the readability level of written material by looking at the number of commonly known words used in the document.

Dead-enders Employees who receive much grapevine information but who seldom pass it on to others.

Debriefing Informing the subject in an experiment about the purpose of the study in which he or she was a participant and providing any other relevant information.

Defense The second stage of change, in which employees accept that change will occur but try to justify the old way of doing things.

Denial The first stage in the emotional reaction to change or layoffs, in which an employee denies that an organizational change or layoff will occur.

Dependability–reliability One of five categories from the trait approach to scoring letters of recommendation.

Dependent variable The measure of behavior that is expected to change as a result of changes in the independent variable.

Derivation sample A group of employees that were used in creating the initial weights for a biodata instrument.

Desirability The extent to which a trait or behavior is valued as being good in society.

Despair An organizational climate characterized by low morale.

Devil's advocate A group member who intentionally provides an opposing opinion to that expressed by the leader or the majority of the group.

Dictionary of Occupational Titles The DOT is a directory published by the federal government that supplies information for almost 30,000 jobs.

Differential validity The characteristic of a test that significantly predicts a criterion for two groups, such as both minorities and nonminorities, but predicts significantly better for one of the two groups.

Direct compensation The amount of money paid to an employee (does not count benefits, time off, and so forth).

Direct mail A method of recruitment in which an organization sends out mass mailings of information about job openings to potential applicants.

Discarding The third stage of change, in which employees accept that change will occur and decide to discard their old ways of doing things.

Disjunctive tasks Tasks for which the performance of a group is based on the performance of its most talented member.

Disorganization A climate in which the organization has the necessary knowledge and resources but does not know how to efficiently use the knowledge or the resources.

Dispute A situation when two parties do not agree.

Disqualifier A type of structured interview question in which a wrong answer will disqualify the applicant from futher consideration.

Dissertation A formal research paper required of most doctoral students in order to graduate.

Distracting The idea that social inhibition occurs because the presence of others provides a distraction that interferes with concentration.

Distress Stress that results in negative energy and decreases in performance and health.

Distributed practice Learning a few things at a time.

Distribution errors Rating errors in which a rater will use only a certain part of a rating scale when evaluating employee performance.

Distributive justice The perceived fairness of the decisions made in an organization.

Downward communication Communication within an organization in which the direction of communication is from management to employees.

Drug testing Tests that indicate if an applicant has recently used a drug.

Dysfunctional conflict Conflict that keeps people from working together, lessens productivity, spreads to other areas, or increases turnover.

Effect size Used in meta-analysis, a statistic that indicates the amount of change caused by an experimental manipulation.

Effective temperature The combination of air temperature, humidity, airflow, and heat radiation that determines how hot or cold the environment feels.

Ego needs The fourth step in Maslow's hierarchy, concerning the individual's need for recognition and success.

e-learning Using computer-based training (CBT) over the Web.

Empathic listening The listening style of a person who listens for the feelings of the speaker.

Employee learning Evaluating the effectiveness of a training program by measuring how much employees learned from the training program.

Employee Performance Record A standardized use of the critical incident technique developed at General Motors.

Employee reactions A method of evaluating training in which employees are asked their opinions of a training program.

Employee referral A method of recruitment in which a current employee refers a friend or family member for a job.

Employment agency An organization that specializes in finding jobs for applicants and finding applicants for organizations looking for employees.

Employment interview A method of selecting employees in which an interviewer asks questions of an applicant and then makes an employment decision based on the answers to the questions as well as the way in which the questions were answered.

Employment-at-will doctrine The opinion of courts in most states that employers have the right to hire and fire an employee at will and without any specific cause.

Employment-at-will statements Statements in employment applications and company manuals reaffirming an organization's right to hire and fire at will.

Empowerment chart A chart made for each employee that shows what level of input the employee has for each task.

Enzyme multiplied immunoassay technique (EMIT) A method of drug testing that uses enzymes to detect the presence of drugs in a urine sample.

Equal Employment Opportunity Commission (EEOC) A branch of the Department of Labor charged with investigating and prosecuting complaints of employment discrimination.

Equity theory A theory of job satisfaction stating that employees will be satisfied if their ratio of effort to reward is similar to that of other employees.

ERG theory Aldefer's needs theory, which describes three levels of satisfaction: existence, relatedness, and growth.

Error Deviation from a standard of quality; also a type of response to communication overload that involves processing all information but processing some of it incorrectly.

Escape A response to communication overload in which the employee leaves the organization to reduce the stress.

Eustress Stress that results in positive energy and improvements in performance and health.

Evaluation apprehension The idea that a person performing a task becomes aroused because he or she is concerned that others are evaluating his or her performance.

Evaporation One way our bodies maintain a normal temperature, in which perspiration reduces excess heat.

Executive search firms Employment agencies, often also called headhunters, that specialize in placing applicants in high-paying jobs.

Expectancy In expectancy theory, the perceived probability that a particular amount of effort will result in a particular level of performance.

Expectancy theory Vroom's theory that motivation is a function of expectancy, instrumentality, and valence.

Experiment A type of research study in which the independent variable is manipulated by the experimenter.

Experimental group In an experiment, the group of subjects that receives the experimental treatment of interest to the experimenter.

Expert power Power that individuals have because they have knowledge.

External equity The extent to which employees within an organization are paid fairly compared to employees in other organizations.

External locus of control The extent to which people believe that their success and failure is determined by external sources (for example, by luck or by other people).

External recruitment Recruiting employees from outside the organization.

External validity The extent to which research results can be expected to hold true outside the specific setting in which they were obtained.

Extrinsic motivation Work motivation that arises from such nonpersonal factors as pay, coworkers, and opportunities for advancement.

Face validity The extent to which a test appears to be valid.

Faces Scale A measure of job satisfaction in which raters place a mark under a facial expression that is most similar to the way they feel about their jobs.

Family Medical Leave Act (FMLA) Passed in 1993, the FMLA provides 12 weeks of unpaid leave for birth, adoption, or serious illness of a child, parent, spouse, or the employee. All organizations with 50 or more employees physically employed within a 70-mile radius of one another are covered by the act.

Fear stage The third emotional stage following the announcement of a layoff, in which employees worry about how they will survive financially.

Feedback Providing employees with specific information about how well they are performing a task or series of tasks.

Fiedler's contingency model A theory of leadership that states that leadership effectiveness is dependent on the interaction between the leader and the situation.

Field research Research conducted in a natural setting as opposed to a laboratory.

Fifth Amendment The amendment to the U.S. Constitution that mandates that the federal government may not deny a person equal protection under the law.

File approach The gathering of biodata from employee files rather than by questionnaire.

Financial bonus A method of absenteeism control in which employees who meet an attendance standard are given a cash reward.

Fixed shift A shift schedule in which employees never change the shifts that they work.

Fleishman Job Analysis Survey (F-JAS) A job analysis method in which jobs are rated on the basis of the abilities needed to perform the jobs.

Flesch Index A method of determining the readability level of written material by analyzing average sentence length and the number of syllables per 100 words.

Flexible hours The part of a flextime schedule in which employees may choose which hours to work.

Flexitour A flextime schedule in which employees have flexibility in scheduling but must schedule their work hours at least a week in advance.

Flextime A work schedule that allows employees to choose their own work hours.

FOG Index A method of determining the readability level of written material by analyzing sentence length and the number of three-syllable words.

Forced-choice rating scales A method of performance appraisal in which a supervisor is given several behaviors and is forced to choose which of the behaviors is most typical of the employee.

Forced distribution method A performance appraisal method in which a predetermined percentage of employees are placed into a number of performance categories.

Forcing style The conflict style of a person who responds to conflict by always trying to win.

Forecasting Constant worrying about the future.

Form stability The extent to which the scores on two forms of a test are similar.

Forming stage The first stage of the team process, in which team members "feel out" the team concept and attempt to make a positive impression.

Four-fifths rule When the selection ratio for one group (for example, females) is less than 80% (four fifths) of the selection ratio for another group (for example, males), adverse impact is said to exist.

Fourteenth Amendment The amendment to the U.S. Constitution that mandates that no state may deny a person equal protection under the law.

Fourth Amendment The amendment to the U.S. Constitution that protects against unreasonable search or seizure; the amendment has been ruled to cover such privacy issues as drug testing, locker and office searches, psychological testing, and electronic surveillance.

Frame-of-reference training   A method of training raters in which the rater is provided with job-related information, a chance to practice ratings, examples of ratings made by experts, and the rationale behind the expert ratings.

Fry Readability Graph   A method of determining the readability level of written material by analyzing sentence length and the average number of syllables per word.

Functional conflict   Conflict that results in increased performance or better interpersonal relations.

Functional Job Analysis (FJA)   A job analysis method developed by Fine that rates the extent to which a job incumbent is involved with functions in the categories of data, people, and things.

Functional resume   A resume format in which jobs are grouped by function rather than listed in order by date.

Future-focused question   A type of structured interview question in which applicants are given a situation and asked how they would handle that situation.

Gainsharing   A group incentive system in which employees are paid a bonus based on improvements in group productivity.

Games   An absenteeism control method in which games such as poker and bingo are used to reward employee attendance.

Gas chromatography/mass spectrometry analysis   A means of analyzing urine samples for the presence of drugs in which the urine sample is vaporized and then bombarded with electrons.

Gatekeeper   A person who screens potential communication for someone else and allows only the most important information to pass through.

Generalizability   Like external validity, the extent to which research results hold true outside the specific setting in which they were obtained.

Gliding time   A flextime schedule in which employees can choose their own hours without any advance notice or scheduling.

Goal setting   A method of increasing performance in which employees are given specific performance goals to aim for.

Golem effect   When negative expectations of an individual cause a decrease in that individual's performance.

Gossip grapevine   A pattern of grapevine communication in which a message is passed to only a select group of individuals.

Grade   A cluster of jobs of similar worth.

Graduate Record Exam (GRE)   A standardized admission test required by most psychology graduate schools.

Grapevine   An unofficial, informal communication network.

Graphic rating scale   A method of performance appraisal that involves rating employee performance on an interval or ratio scale.

Graphology   Also called handwriting analysis, a method of measuring personality by looking at the way in which a person writes.

Grievance system   A process in which an employee files a complaint with the organization and a person or committee within the organization makes a decision regarding the complaint.

Group cohesiveness   The extent to which members of a group like and trust one another.

Group–group conflict   Conflict between two or more groups.

Group I strategy   Leaders share the problem with the group and let the group reach a decision or solution.

Group size   The number of members in a group.

Group status   The esteem in which the group is held by people not in the group.

Groupthink   A state of mind in which a group is so concerned about group cohesiveness that it ignores important information.

Halo error   A type of rating error that occurs when raters allow either a single attribute or an overall impression of an individual to affect the ratings that they make on each relevant job dimension.

Hawthorne studies   A series of studies, conducted at the Western Electric plant in Hawthorne, Illinois, that have come to represent any change in behavior when people react to a change in the environment.

Heterogeneous groups   Groups whose members share few similarities.

Hierarchy   A system arranged by rank.

Hold-out sample   A group of employees that are not used in creating the initial weights for a biodata instrument but instead are used to double-check the accuracy of the initial weights.

Homogeneous groups   Groups whose members share the same characteristics.

Hostile environment   A type of harassment characterized by a pattern of unwanted conduct related to gender that interferes with an individual's work performance.

Human factors   A field of study concentrating on the interaction between humans and machines.

Hygiene factors   In Herzberg's two-factor theory, job-related elements that result from but do not involve the job itself.

Hypothesis   An educated prediction about the answer to a research question.

Identification   The need to associate ourselves with the image associated with other people, groups, or objects.

Ignorance   An organizational climate in which important information is not available.

IMPACT theory   A theory of leadership that states that there are six styles of leadership (informational, magnetic, position, affiliation, coercive, and tactical) and that each style will be effective only in one of six organizational climates.

Impoverished leadership   A style of leadership in which the leader is concerned with neither productivity nor the well-being of employees.

In-basket technique   An assessment center exercise designed to simulate the types of information that daily come across a manager's or employee's desk in order to observe the applicant's responses to such information.

Inclusive listening   The listening style of a person who listens only for the main points of a communication.

Independent variable   The manipulated variable in an experiment.

Individual dominance   When one member of a group dominates the group.

Individual–group conflict   Conflict between an individual and the other members of a group.

Industrial/Organizational (I/O) psychology   A branch of psychology that applies the principles of psychology to the workplace.

Informal communication   Communication among employees in an organization that is not directly related to the completion of an organizational task.

Informational style   A style of leadership in which the leader leads through knowledge and information; most effective in a climate of ignorance.

Informed consent   The formal process by which subjects give permission to be included in a study.

Infrequent observation   The idea that supervisors do not see most of an employee's behavior.

Initiating structure   The extent to which leaders define and structure their roles and the roles of their subordinates.

Inner con artist   A person who procrastinates.

Input/output ratio   The ratio of how much employees believe they put into their jobs to how much they believe they get from their jobs.

Inputs   In equity theory, the elements that employees put into their jobs.

Instability   An organizational climate in which people are not sure what to do.

Institutional Review Board   A committee designated to ensure the ethical treatment of research subjects.

Instrumental style   In path-goal theory, a leadership style in which the leader plans and organizes the activities of employees.

Instrumentality   In expectancy theory, the perceived probability that a particular level of performance will result in a particular consequence.

Integrity test   Also called an honesty test, a psychological test designed to predict an applicant's tendency to steal.

Interacting group   A collection of individuals who work together to perform a task.

Interactional justice   The perceived fairness of the interpersonal treatment that employees receive.

Interactive video   A training technique in which an employee is presented with a videotaped situation and is asked to respond to the situation and then receives feedback based on the response.

Interdependence   The extent to which team members need and rely on other team members.

Interest inventory   A psychological test designed to identify vocational areas in which an individual might be interested.

Internalization   The fifth and final stage of organizational change, in which employees become comfortable with and productive in the new system.

Internal locus of control   The extent to which people believe that they are responsible for and in control of their success or failure in life.

Internal pay equity   The extent to which employees within an organization are paid fairly compared to other employees within the same organization.

Internal recruitment   Recruiting employees already employed by the organization.

Internal reliability   The extent to which responses to test items measuring the same construct are consistent.

Internal timekeepers   A type of stress personality who takes on too much work because he or she enjoys doing a variety of things.

Internship   A situation in which a student works for an organization, either for pay or as a volunteer, to receive practical work experience.

Interpersonal communication   Communication between two individuals.

Interpersonal conflict   Conflict between two people.

Intervening variable   A third variable that can often explain the relationship between two other variables.

Intimacy zone   A distance zone within 18 inches of a person where only people with a close relationship to the person are allowed to enter.

Intranet   A computer-based employee communication network used exclusively by one organization.

Intraorganizational communication   Communication within an organization.

Intrinsic motivation   Work motivation in the absence of such external factors as pay, promotion, and coworkers.

Isolate   An employee who receives less than half of all grapevine information.

Isolation   The degree of physical distance of a group from other groups.

Item homogeneity   The extent to which test items measure the same construct.

Item stability   The extent to which responses to the same test items are consistent.

Job Adaptability Inventory (JAI)   A job analysis method that taps the extent to which a job involves eight types of adaptability.

Job analysis   The process of identifying how a job is performed, the conditions under which it is performed, and the personal requirements that it takes to perform the job.

Job analysis interviews   Obtaining information about a job by talking to the person performing the job.

Job analyst   The person conducting the job analysis.

Job characteristics model   The theory proposed by Hackman and Oldham that suggests that certain characteristics of a job will make the job more or less satisfying, depending on the particular needs of the worker.

Job Choice Exercise (JCE)   An objective test that is used to measure various need levels.

Job Components Inventory (JCI)   A structured job analysis technique that concentrates on worker requirements for performing a job rather than on specific tasks.

Job descriptions   A written summary of the tasks performed in a job, the conditions under which the job is performed, and the requirements needed to perform the job.

Job Descriptive Index (JDI)   A measure of job satisfaction that yields scores on five dimensions.

Job Diagnostic Survey (JDS)   A measure of the extent to which a job provides opportunities for growth, autonomy, and meaning.

Job Elements Inventory (JEI)   A structured job analysis technique developed by Cornelius and Hakel that is similar to the PAQ but easier to read.

Job enlargement   A system in which employees are given more tasks to perform at the same time.

Job enrichment   A system in which employees are given more responsibility over the tasks and decisions related to their job.

Job evaluation   The process of determining the monetary worth of a job.

Job fair   A recruitment method in which several employers are available at one location so that many applicants can obtain information at one time.

Job in General (JIG) Scale   A measure of the overall level of job satisfaction.

Job knowledge test   A test that measures the amount of job-related knowledge an applicant possesses.

Job participation   A job analysis method in which the job analyst actually performs the job being analyzed.

Job related   The extent to which a test or measure taps a knowledge, skill, ability, behavior, or other characteristic needed to successfully perform a job.

Job rotation   A system in which employees are given the opportunity to perform several different jobs in an organization.

Job satisfaction   The attitude employees have toward their jobs.

Job sharing   A work schedule in which two employees share one job by splitting the work hours.

Job specifications   The knowledge, skills, and abilities needed to successfully perform a job.

Job Structure Profile (JSP)   A revised version of the PAQ designed to be used more by the job analyst than by the job incumbent.

Journal   A written collection of articles describing the methods and results of new research.

Jurisdictional ambiguity   Conflict caused by a disagreement about geographical territory or lines of authority.

Key issues approach   A method of scoring interview answers that provides points for each part of an answer that matches the scoring key.

Knowledge   A body of information needed to perform a task.

Knowledge test   A test that measures the level of an employee's knowledge about a job-related topic.

Known-group validity   A form of validity in which test scores from two contrasting groups "known" to differ on a construct are compared.

KSAOs   Acronym referring to knowledge, skills, abilities, and other characteristics required to perform a job.

Kuder-Richardson Formula 20 (K-R 20)   A statistic used to determine internal reliability of tests that use items with dichotomous answers (yes/no, true/false).

Lawshe tables   Tables that use the base rate, test validity, and applicant percentile on a test to determine the probability of future success for that applicant.

Leader Behavior Description Questionnaire (LBDQ)   A test used to measure perceptions of a leader's style by his or her subordinates.

Leader emergence   A part of trait theory that postulates that certain types of people will become leaders and certain types will not.

Leaderless group discussion   A selection technique, usually found in assessment centers, in which applicants meet in small groups and are given a problem to solve or an issue to discuss.

Leader Match   A training program that teaches leaders how to change situations so that the situations are consistent with their leadership styles.

Leader–member exchange (LMX) theory   A leadership theory that focuses on the interaction between leaders and subordinates.

Leader–member relations   The variable in Fiedler's contingency model that refers to the extent to which subordinates like a leader.

Leader performance   A part of trait theory that postulates that certain types of people will be better leaders than will other types of people.

Leader position power   The variable in Fiedler's contingency model that refers to the extent to which a leader, by the nature of his or her position, has the power to reward and punish subordinates.

Leadership motive pattern   The name for a pattern of needs in which a leader has a high need for power and a low need for affiliation.

Leadership Opinion Questionnaire (LOQ)   A test used to measure a leader's self-perception of his or her leadership style.

Least acceptable result (LAR)   The lowest settlement that a person is willing to accept in a negotiated agreement.

Least-Preferred Coworker (LPC) Scale A test used in conjunction with Fiedler's contingency model to reveal leadership style and effectiveness.

Legitimate power The power individuals have because of their elected or appointed position.

Leisure listening The listening style of a person who listens only for interesting information.

Leniency error A type of rating error in which a rater consistently gives all employees high ratings, regardless of their actual levels of performance.

Letter of recommendation A letter written to a prospective employer in support of an applicant's qualifications for a job.

Leveled A description of a message from which unimportant informational details have been removed before the message is passed from one person to another.

Liaison A person who acts as an intermediary between employees and management; or the type of employee who both sends and receives most grapevine information.

Linear A straight-line relationship between the test score and the criterion of measurement.

Living case A case study based on a real situation rather than a hypothetical one.

Magazine An unscientific collection of articles about a wide range of topics.

Magnetic style A style of leadership in which the leader has influence because of his or her charismatic personality; most effective in a climate of despair.

Management teams Teams that coordinate, manage, advise, and direct employees and teams.

Managerial Grid A measure of leadership that classifies a leader into one of five leadership styles.

Manipulation The alteration of a variable by an experimenter in expectation that alteration will result in a change in the dependent variable.

Massed practice Concentrating learning into a short period of time.

Maximum supportable position (MSP) The highest possible settlement that a person could reasonably ask for and still maintain credibility in negotiating an agreement.

Mean effect size Used in meta-analysis, a statistic that is the average of the effect sizes for all studies included in the analysis.

Mediation A method of resolving conflict in which a neutral third party is asked to help the two parties reach an agreement.

Meeting cow Unnecessary or unnecessarily long meeting.

Mental agility A category referring to intelligence; among the categories developed by Peres and Garcia for analyzing the adjectives used in letters of recommendation.

Mental Measurements Yearbook (MMY) The name of a book containing information about the reliability and validity of various psychological tests.

Mentor An experienced employee who advises and looks out for a new employee.

Mere presence The theory that states that the mere presence of others naturally produces arousal and thus may affect performance.

Merit pay An incentive plan in which employees receive pay bonuses based on performance appraisal scores.

Meta-analysis A statistical method for cumulating research results.

Middle-of-the-road leadership A leadership style reflecting an approach that balances people and task orientation.

Minnesota Multiphasic Personality Inventory (MMPI-2) The most widely used objective test of psychopathology.

Minnesota Satisfaction Questionnaire (MSQ) A measure of job satisfaction that yields scores on 20 dimensions.

Mixed-standard scale A method of performance appraisal in which a supervisor reads the description of a specific behavior and then decides if the behavior of the employee is better than, equal to, or poorer than the behavior described.

Modeling Learning through watching and imitating the behavior of others.

Modified flexitour A flextime schedule in which employees have flexibility in scheduling but must schedule their work hours a day in advance.

Moonlighting Working more than one job.

Motivation The force that drives an employee to perform well.

Motivators In Herzberg's two-factor theory, elements of a job that concern the actual duties performed by the employee.

Multiple channels A strategy for coping with communication overload in which an organization reduces the amount of communication going to one person by directing some of it to another person.

Multiple-hurdle approach When applicants are administered one test at a time and must pass that test before being allowed to take the next test.

Multiple regression A statistical procedure in which the scores from more than one criterion-valid test are weighted according to how well each test score predicts the criterion.

MUM (minimize unpleasant messages) effect The idea that people prefer not to pass on unpleasant information with the result that important information is not always communicated.

Need for achievement According to trait theory, the extent to which a person desires to be successful.

Need for affiliation The extent to which a person desires to be around other people.

Need for power According to trait theory, the extent to which a person desires to be in control of other people.

Needs analysis The process of determining the training needs of an organization.

Needs theory   A theory based on the idea that employees will be satisfied with jobs that satisfy their needs.

Negative feedback   Telling employees what they are doing incorrectly in order to improve their performance of a task.

Negative information bias   The fact that negative information receives more weight in an employment decision than does positive information.

Negligent hiring   An organization's failure to meet its legal duty to protect its employees and customers from potential harm caused by its employees.

Negligent reference   An organization's failure to meet its legal duty to supply relevant information to a prospective employer about a former employee's potential for legal trouble.

Negotiation and bargaining   A method of resolving conflict in which two sides use verbal skill and strategy to reach an agreement.

Newsletters   A method of downward communication typically used to communicate organizational feedback and celebrate employee success.

Noise   Any variable concerning or affecting the channel that interferes with the proper reception of a message.

Nominal group   A collection of individuals whose results are pooled but who never interact with one another.

Nonbinding arbitration   A method of resolving conflicts in which a neutral third party is asked to choose which side is correct but in which either party may appeal the decision.

Noncalculative motivation   Those who seek leadership positions because they will result in personal gain.

Nonconforming listening   The listening style of a person who listens only to information that is consistent with his or her way of thinking.

Nonverbal communication   Factors such as eye contact and posture that are not associated with actual words spoken.

Normative commitment   The extent to which an employee feels an obligation to remain with the organization.

Norming   The third stage of the team process, in which teams establish roles and determine policies and procedures.

Objective tests   A type of personality test that is structured to limit the respondent to a few answers that will be scored by standardized keys.

Observation   A job analysis method in which the job analyst watches job incumbents perform their jobs.

Occupational Information Network (O*NET)   The job analysis system used by the federal government that has replaced the DOT.

Ombudsperson   A person who investigates employees' complaints and solves problems.

Omission   A response to communication overload that involves the conscious decision not to process certain types of information.

On-site child care facility   A child care center that is located on the site of the organization employing the parent.

Open desk arrangement   An office arranged so that a visitor can sit adjacent to rather than across from the person behind the desk.

Operant conditioning   A type of learning based on the idea that humans learn to behave in ways that will result in favorable outcomes and learn not to behave in ways that result in unfavorable outcomes.

Optimal level of arousal   The idea that performance is best with moderate levels of arousal.

Optimist   A person who looks at the positive aspects of every situation.

Organizational analysis   The process of determining the organizational factors that will either facilitate or inhibit training effectiveness.

Organizational commitment   The extent to which an employee identifies with and is involved with an organization.

Organizational culture   The shared values, beliefs, and traditions that exist among individuals in an organization.

Organizational fit questions   A type of structured interview question that taps how well an applicant's personality and values will fit with the organizational culture.

Organizational psychology   The field of study that investigates the behavior of employees within the context of an organization.

Organizational socialization   The process whereby new employees learn the behaviors and attitudes they need to be successful in an organization.

Other characteristics   Such personal factors as personality, willingness, and interest that are not knowledge, skills, or abilities.

Outputs   In equity theory, the things that employees get from their jobs.

Outside pressure   The amount of psychological pressure placed on a group by people who are not members of the group.

Outsourcing   The process of having certain organizational functions performed by an outside vendor rather than an employee at the organization.

Overlearning   Practicing a task even after it has been mastered in order to retain learning.

Overt integrity test   A type of honesty test that asks questions about applicants' attitudes toward theft and their previous theft history.

Paid time off program   An attendance policy in which all paid time off (vacations, sick days, and so forth) are combined.

Paired comparison   A form of ranking in which a group of employees to be ranked are compared one pair at a time.

Paper cow   Unnecessary paperwork found in organizations.

Paralanguage   Communication inferred from the tone, tempo, volume, and rate of speech.

Parallel teams   Also called cross-functional teams, they consist of representatives from various departments (functions) within an organization.

Participative style   In path-goal theory, a leadership style in which the leader allows employees to participate in decisions.

Passing score   The minimum test score that an applicant must achieve to be considered for hire.

Pass-through programs   A formal method of coaching in which excellent employees spend a period of time in the training department learning training techniques and training employees.

Past-focused question   A type of structured interview question that taps an applicant's experience.

Path-goal theory   A theory of leadership that states that leaders will be effective if their behavior helps subordinates achieve relevant goals.

Patterned-behavior description interview (PBDI)   A structured interview in which the questions focus on behavior in previous jobs.

Pay for performance   A system in which employees are paid on the basis of how much they individually produce.

Peak-time pay   A system in which part-time employees who work only during peak hours are paid at a higher hourly rate.

Perceptual ability   Abilities such as spatial relations and form perception.

Performance-appraisal review   A meeting between a supervisor and a subordinate for the purpose of discussing performance-appraisal results.

Performance-appraisal score   A rating representing some aspect of an employee's work performance.

Performing   The fourth and final stage of the team process, in which teams work toward accomplishing their goals.

Permanency   The extent to which a team will remain together or be disbanded after a task has been accomplished.

Person analysis   The process of identifying the employees who need training and determining the areas in which each individual employee needs to be trained.

Person–organization fit   The extent to which an employee's personality, values, attitudes, philosophy, and skills match those of the organization.

Personal distance zone   A distance zone from 18 inches to 4 feet from a person that is usually reserved for friends and acquaintances.

Personality   Relatively stable traits possessed by an individual.

Personality-based integrity test   A type of honesty test that measures personality traits thought to be related to antisocial behavior.

Personality inventory   A psychological assessment designed to measure various aspects of an applicant's personality.

Personality-Related Position Requirements Form (PPRF)   A new job analysis instrument that helps determine the personality requirements for a job.

Personnel psychology   The field of study that concentrates on the selection and evaluation of employees.

Perspective taking   Rating potential stressors by asking: "All things considered, in reality, how bad is this situation?"

Pessimist   A person who looks at the negative aspects of every situation.

Peter Principle   The idea that organizations tend to promote good employees until they reach the level at which they are not competent—in other words, their highest level of incompetence.

Physical ability tests   Tests that measure an applicant's level of physical ability required for a job.

Pleaser   A type of person who wants to make everyone happy and is usually cooperative and helpful.

Point method   A job evaluation system in which jobs are assigned points across several compensable factors to determine the worth of the job.

Point-of-purchase method   A recruitment method in which help-wanted signs are placed so that they can be viewed by people who visit the organization.

Policy manual   A formal method of downward communication in which an organization's rules and procedures are placed in a manual.

Polygraph   An electronic test that is intended to determine honesty by measuring an individual's physiological changes that occur after being asked questions.

Position Analysis Questionnaire (PAQ)   A structured job analysis method developed by McCormick.

Position style   A leadership style in which the leaders influence others by virtue of their appointed or elected authority; most effective in a climate of instability.

Posttest   A measure of job performance or knowledge taken after a training program has been completed.

Power differentiation   The extent to which team members have the same level of power and respect.

Practical significance   The extent to which the results of a study have actual impact on human behavior.

Practicum   A paid or unpaid position with an organization that gives the student practical work experience.

Predictive validity   A form of criterion validity in which test scores of applicants are compared at a later date with a measure of job performance.

Pregnancy Discrimination Act   A 1978 federal law protecting the rights of pregnant women.

Premack Principle   The idea that reinforcement is relative both within an individual and between individuals.

Pretest   A measure of job performance or knowledge taken before the implementation of a training program.

Primacy effect   The fact that information that is presented early in an interview carries more weight than information presented later.

Probability grapevine   A pattern of grapevine communication in which a message is passed randomly among all employees.

Procedural justice   The perceived fairness of the methods used by an organization to make decisions.

Programmed instruction   A training method in which employees learn information at their own pace.

Progressive discipline   Providing employees with punishments of increasing severity to change behavior.

Project teams   Groups formed to produce one-time outputs such as creating a new product, installing a new software system, or hiring a new employee.

Projective tests   A subjective test in which a subject is asked to perform relatively unstructured tasks, such as drawing pictures, and in which a psychologist analyzes his or her responses.

Proportion of correct decisions   A utility method that compares the percentage of times a selection decision was accurate and to the percentage of successful employees.

Protected class   Any group of people for whom protective legislation has been passed.

Prototype The overall image that a supervisor has of an employee.

Proximity   Physical distance between people.

Proximity error   A type of rating error in which a rating made on one dimension influences the rating made on the dimension that immediately follows it on the rating scale.

Psychological resume   A resume style that takes advantage of psychological principles pertaining to memory organization and impression formation.

Psychomotor ability   Abilities such as finger dexterity and motor coordination.

Public distance zone   A distance zone greater than 12 feet from a person that is typical of the interpersonal space allowed for social interactions such as large group lectures.

Public employment agency   An employment service, operated by a state or local government, designed to match applicants with job openings.

Pygmalion effect   The idea that if people believe something is true, they will act in a manner consistent with that belief.

Qualified workforce   The percentage of people in a given geographic area that have the qualifications (skills, education, and so forth) to perform a certain job.

Quality   A type of objective criterion used to measure job performance by comparing a job behavior with a standard.

Quality circles   Employee groups that meet to propose changes that will improve productivity and the quality of work life.

Quantity   A type of objective criterion used to measure job performance by counting the number of relevant job behaviors that occur.

Quasi-experiments   Research method in which either the experimenter does not manipulate the independent variable or the subjects are not randomly assigned to conditions.

Questionnaire approach   The method of obtaining biodata from questionnaires rather than from employee files.

Queuing   A method of coping with communication overload that involves organizing work into an order in which it will be handled.

Quid pro quo   A type of sexual harassment in which the granting of sexual favors is tied to an employment decision.

Race   According to Congress the four races are African American, European American, Asian American, and Native American Indian.

Racial bias   The tendency to give members of a particular race lower evaluation ratings than are justified by their actual performance or to give members of one race lower ratings than members of another race.

Radiation   One way our bodies maintain a normal temperature, by the emission of heat waves.

Radioimmunoassay (RIA)   A method of drug testing that uses radioactive tagging to determine the presence of drugs in a urine sample.

Random assignment   The random, unbiased assignment of subjects in a research sample to the various experimental and control conditions.

Random sample   A sample in which every member of the relevant population had an equal chance of being chosen to participate in the study.

Rank order   A method of performance appraisal in which employees are ranked from best to worst.

Realistic job preview (RJP)   A method of recruitment in which job applicants are told both the positive and the negative aspects of a job.

Recency effect   The tendency for supervisors to recall and place more weight on recent behaviors when they evaluate performance.

Receptive changer   A person who is willing to change.

Recruitment   The process of attracting employees to an organization.

Referent power   Leadership power that exists when followers can identify with a leader and the leader's goals.

Referral service   A system of child care in which an employer maintains a list of certified child care centers that can be used by its employees.

Reinforcement hierarchy   A rank-ordered list of reinforcers for an individual.

Rejection letter   A letter from an organization to an applicant informing the applicant that he or she will not receive a job offer.

Reliability   The extent to which a score from a test or from an evaluation is consistent and free from error.

Reluctant changer   A person who will initially resist change but will eventually go along with change.

Residual stress   Stress that is carried over from previous stressful situations.

Respond-by-calling ads   Recruitment ads in which applicants are instructed to call rather than to apply in person or send resumes.

Restricted range   A narrow range of performance scores that makes it difficult to obtain a significant validity coefficient.

Resume   A formal summary of an applicant's professional and educational background.

Resume fraud   The intentional placement of untrue information on a resume.

Return on investment   The amount of money an organization makes after subtracting the cost of training or other interventions.

Reward power   Leadership power that exists to the extent that the leader has the ability and authority to provide rewards.

Rituals   Procedures in which employees participate to become "one of the gang."

Role ambiguity   The extent to which an employee's roles and expectations are unclear.

Role conflict   The extent to which an employee's role and expected role are the same.

Role overload   The extent to which an employee is able to psychologically handle the number of roles and tasks assigned.

Role play   A training technique in which employees act out simulated roles.

Rorschach Ink Blot Test   A projective personality test.

Rotating shift   A shift schedule in which employees periodically change the shifts that they work.

Rule of 3   A variation on top-down selection in which the names of the top three applicants are given to a hiring authority who can then select any of the three.

Rumor   Poorly substantiated information that is passed along the grapevine.

Sabertooths   People who respond to stress with anger.

Sacred cow hunt   The first step in organizational change in which employees look for practices and policies that waste time and are counterproductive.

Safety needs   The second step in Maslow's hierarchy, concerning the need for security, stability, and physical safety.

Salary survey   A questionnaire sent to other organizations to see how much they are paying their employees in positions similar to those in the organization sending the survey.

Scorer reliability   The extent to which two people scoring a test agree on the test score or the extent to which a test is scored correctly.

Selection ratio   The percentage of applicants that an organization hires.

Self-actualization needs   The fifth step in Maslow's hierarchy, concerning the need to realize one's potential.

Self-directed teams   See *quality circles.*

Self-esteem   The extent to which a person views him- or herself as a valuable and worthy individual.

Self-fulfilling prophecy   The idea that people behave in ways consistent with their self-image.

Self-monitoring   A personality trait characterized by the tendency to adapt one's behavior to fit a particular social situation.

Send-resume ads   Recruitment ads in which applicants are instructed to send their resume to the company rather than call or apply in person.

Serial communication   Communication passed consecutively from one person to another.

Sharpened   A description of a message in which interesting and unusual information has been kept in the message when it is passed from one person to another.

Shrinkage   The amount of goods lost by an organization as a result of theft, breakage, or other loss.

Simulation   An exercise that is designed to place an applicant in a situation that is similar to the one that will be encountered on the job.

Single-group validity   The characteristic of a test that significantly predicts a criterion for one class of people but not for another.

Single strand grapevine   A pattern of grapevine communication in which a message is passed in a chainlike fashion from one person to the next person until the chain is broken.

Situation-wanted ads   Newspaper advertisements run by applicants looking for jobs rather than by organizations looking for applicants.

Situational leadership theory   A theory of leadership that states that effective leaders must adapt their style of leadership to fit both the situation and the followers.

Situational question   A structured-interview technique in which applicants are presented with a series of situations and asked how they would handle each one.

Situational self-esteem   The positive or negative way in which a person views him- or herself in a particular situation.

Skill   Proficiency to perform a particular task.

Skill-based pay   Compensating an employee who participates in a training program designed to increase a particular job-related skill.

Skill level determiner   A type of structured interview question designed to tap an applicant's knowledge or skill.

Skill test   A test that measures an employee's level of some job-related skill.

Slightly heterogeneous groups   Groups in which a few group members have different characteristics from the rest of the group.

SME conference   A group job analysis interview consisting of subject matter experts (SMEs).

Social distance   The extent to which team members treat each other in a friendly, informal manner.

Social distance zone   An interpersonal distance zone from 4 to 12 feet from a person that is typically used for business and for interacting with strangers.

Social facilitation   The positive effects that occur when a person performs a task in the presence of others.

Social impact theory   A theory that states that the addition of a group member has the greatest effect on group behavior when the size of the group is small.

Social information processing theory   A theory that states that employees model their levels of satisfaction and motivation from other employees.

Social inhibition   The negative effects that occur when a person performs a task in the presence of others.

Social learning theory   A theory that states that employees model their levels of satisfaction and motivation from other employees.

Social loafing   The fact that individuals in a group often exert less individual effort than they would if they were not in a group.

Social needs   The third step in Maslow's hierarchy concerning the need to interact with other people.

Social normative motivation.   The desire to lead out of a sense of duty or responsibility.

Social recognition   A motivation technique using such methods as personal attention, signs of approval, and expressions of appreciation.

Socially influenced self-esteem   The positive or negative way in which a person views him- or herself based on the expectations of others.

Solomon four-groups design   An extensive method of evaluating the effectiveness of training with the use of pretests, posttests, and control groups.

Spearman-Brown prophecy formula   A formula that is used to correct reliability coefficients resulting from the split-half method.

Speed cow   The tendency for organizations to require employees to work faster and produce work sooner than needed.

Split-half method   A form of internal reliability in which the consistency of item responses is determined by comparing scores on half of the items with scores on the other half of the items.

Stability   The extent to which the membership of a group remains consistent over time.

Standard deviation   A statistic that indicates the variation of scores in a distribution.

Standard error (SE)   The number of points that a test score could be off due to test unreliability.

Stock options   A group incentive method in which employees are given the option of buying stock in the future at the price of the stock when the options were granted.

Storming   The second stage in group formation in which group members disagree and resist their team roles.

Strain   The physical and psychological consequences of stress.

Stress   Perceived psychological pressure.

Stressors   Events that cause stress.

Strictness error   A type of rating error in which a rater consistently gives all employees low ratings, regardless of their actual levels of performance.

Striver   An ambitious and competitive person whose source of stress is often self-placed demands.

Strong Interest Inventory (SII)   A popular interest inventory used to help people choose careers.

Structured interviews   Interviews in which every applicant is asked the same questions and in which identical answers are given identical scores.

Stylistic listening   The listening style of a person who listens to the way in which words are spoken.

Subject matter experts (SMEs)   Sources such as supervisors and incumbents who are knowledgeable about a job.

Suggestion box   A form of upward communication in which employees are asked to place their suggestions in a box.

Supportive style   In path-goal theory, a leadership style in which leaders show concern for their employees.

Surveys   Questionnaires asking employees about the areas in which they feel they need training.

Survivors   Employees who retain their jobs following a downsizing.

Symbols   Organizational behaviors or practices that convey messages to employees.

Tactical style   A leadership style in which a person leads through organization and strategy; most effective in a climate of disorganization.

Task analysis   The process of identifying the tasks for which employees need to be trained.

Task-centered leaders   Leaders who define and structure their roles as well as the roles of their subordinates.

Task-centered leadership   A leadership style in which the leader is more concerned with productivity than with employee well-being.

Task interdependence   A potential source of conflict that arises when the completion of a task by one person affects the completion of a task by another person.

Task inventory   A questionnaire containing a list of tasks for which the job incumbent rates each task on a series of scales such as importance and time spent.

Task structuredness   The variable in Fiedler's contingency model that refers to the extent to which tasks have clear goals and problems can be solved.

Taylor-Russell tables   A series of tables based on the selection ratio, base rate, and test validity that yield information about the percentage of future employees who will be successful if a particular test is used.

Team leadership   A leadership style in which the leader is concerned with both productivity and employee well-being.

Technical listening   The listening style of a person who listens for facts and details.

Telecommuting   Working at home rather than the office by way of communicating with other employees through the use of such media as phones, computers, and fax machines.

Temporal stability   The consistency of test scores across time.

Temporary employees   Also called "temps," employees hired through a temporary employment agency.

Tenure   The length of time an employee has been employed by an organization.

Terminal master's degree programs   Graduate programs that offer a master's degree but not a Ph.D.

Test–retest reliability   The extent to which repeated administration of the same test will achieve similar results.

Thematic Apperception Test (TAT)   A projective personality test in which test-takers are shown pictures and asked to tell stories. It is designed to measure various need levels.

Theory   A systematic set of assumptions regarding the cause and nature of behavior.

Theory X leaders   Leaders who believe that employees are extrinsically motivated and thus lead by giving directives and setting goals.

Theory Y leaders   Leaders who believe that employees are intrinsically motivated and thus lead with a "hands-off" or a participative approach.

Thin layer chromatography   A method of analyzing urine specimens for drugs that is performed by hand and requires a great deal of analyst skill.

Third-party intervention   When a neutral party is asked to help resolve a conflict.

360-degree feedback   A performance-appraisal system in which feedback is obtained from multiple sources such as supervisors, subordinates, and peers.

Threshold Traits Analysis (TTA)   A 33-item questionnaire developed by Lopez that identifies traits necessary to successfully perform a job.

Top-down selection   Selecting applicants in straight rank order of their test scores.

Trade magazine   A collection of articles about related professional topics, seldom directly reporting the methods and results of new research.

Training   A planned effort by an organization to facilitate the learning of job-related behavior on the part of its employees.

Transactional leadership.   Leadership style in which the leader focuses on task-oriented behaviors.

Transfer of training   The extent to which behavior learned in training will be performed on the job.

Transformational leadership   Visionary leadership in which the leader changes the nature and goals of an organization.

Triangling   An employee discusses the conflict with a third party such as a friend or supervisor. In doing so, the employee hopes that the third party will talk to the second party and that the conflict will be resolved without the need for the two parties to meet.

Trustworthiness   The extent to which a leader is believed and trusted by his or her followers.

Two-factor theory   Herzberg's needs theory that postulates that there are two factors involved in job satisfaction: hygiene factors and motivators.

Type A personality   A stress-prone person who is competitive, impatient, and hurried.

Type B personality   A non-stress-prone person who is relaxed and agreeable.

Typical answer approach   A method of scoring interview answers that compares an applicant's answer to benchmark answers.

Uniform Guidelines   Federal guidelines that are used to guide an employer in establishing fair selection methods.

Union steward   An employee who serves as a liaison between unionized employees and management.

Upward communication   Communication within an organization in which the direction of communication is from employees up to management.

Urbanity   A category referring to social skills and refinement; one of the five dimensions in the trait approach to scoring letters of recommendation.

Utility formula   Formula to ascertain the extent to which an organization will benefit from the use of a particular selection system.

Valence   In expectancy theory, the perceived desirability of a consequence that results from a particular level of performance.

Validity   The degree to which inferences from scores on tests or assessments are justified by the evidence.

Validity generalization (VG)   The extent to which inferences from test scores from one organization can be applied to another organization.

Vertical dyad linkage (VDL) theory   A leadership theory that concentrates on the interaction between the leader and his or her subordinates.

Vertical percentage method   The method for scoring biodata in which the percentage of unsuccessful employees responding in a particular way is subtracted from the percentage of successful employees responding in the same way.

Victims   Employees who lose their jobs due to a layoff.

Vietnam-Era Veterans Readjustment Act   A 1974 federal law that mandates that federal government contractors and subcontractors take affirmative action to employ and promote Vietnam-era veterans.

Vigor   A category referring to energy; one of the five dimensions in the trait approach to scoring letters of recommendation.

Virtual teams   Teams that communicate through email rather than face to face.

Vocational counseling   The process of helping an individual choose and prepare for the most suitable career.

Vocational Rehabilitation Act   Federal act passed in 1973 that prohibits federal government contractors or subcontractors from discriminating against the physically or mentally handicapped.

Voice stress analyzer   An electronic test to determine honesty by measuring an individual's voice changes that occur after being asked questions.

Voucher system   A system of child care in which an organization pays all or some of its employees' child care costs at private child care centers by providing the employees with vouchers.

Vroom-Yetton model   A theory of leadership that concentrates on helping a leader choose how to make a decision.

Wage trend line   A line that represents the ideal relationship between the number of points that a job has been assigned (using the point method of evaluation) and the salary range for that job.

Well pay   A method of absenteeism control in which employees are paid for their unused sick leave.

Winning at all costs   An approach to handling conflict in which one side seeks to win regardless of the damage to the other side.

Withdrawal   An approach to handling conflict in which one of the parties removes him- or herself from the situation to avoid the conflict.

Wonderlic Personnel Test   The cognitive ability test that is most commonly used in industry.

Work at home   A system in which employees work at home rather than in an organization's building.

Work Preference Inventory (WPI)   A measure of an individual's orientation toward intrinsic versus extrinsic motivation.

Work sample   A method of selecting employees in which an applicant is asked to perform samples of actual job-related tasks.

Work teams   Groups of employees who manage themselves, assign jobs, plan and schedule work, make work-related decisions, and solve work-related problems.

Worrier   A person who always thinks the worst is going to happen.

References

Aamodt, M. G. (1986). *Validity of expert advice regarding the employment interview.* Paper presented at the 10th annual meeting of the International Personnel Management Association Assessment Council, San Francisco.

Aamodt, M. G. (2002). *The use of education requirements for employee selection: Validity and adverse impact.* Paper presented at the annual conference of the International Personnel Management Association Assessment Council, New Orleans, LA.

Aamodt, M. G., Bryan, D. A., & Whitcomb, A. J. (1993). Predicting performance with letters of recommendation. *Public Personnel Management, 22*(1), 81–90.

Aamodt, M. G., & Carr, K. (1988). Relationship between recruitment source and employee behavior. *Proceedings of the 12th Annual Meeting of the International Personnel Management Association Assessment Council*, pp. 143–146.

Aamodt, M. G., Dwight, S., & Michals, J. (1994). *Reliability and validity of the trait approach to letters of recommendation.* Paper presented at the annual meeting of the International Personnel Management Association Assessment Council, Charleston, SC.

Aamodt, M. G., Freeman, D. M., & Carneal, D. H. (1992). *Effects of group homogeneity on group performance: Two studies and a meta-analysis.* Paper presented at the annual meeting of the Virginia Psychological Association, Roanoke, VA.

Aamodt, M. G., Johnson, D. L., & Freeman, D. M. (1992). *Estimating future adverse impact using selection ratios and group differences in test scores.* Paper presented at the annual meeting of the International Personnel Management Association Assessment Council, Baltimore, MD.

Aamodt, M. G., Kimbrough, W. W., & Alexander, C. J. (1983). A preliminary investigation of the relationship between team racial heterogeneity and team performance in college basketball. *Journal of Sports Sciences, 1*, 131–133.

Aamodt, M. G., Kimbrough, W. W., Keller, R. J., & Crawford, K. (1982). Relationship between sex, race, and job performance level and the generation of critical incidents. *Educational and Psychological Research, 2*, 227–234.

Aamodt, M. G., & McShane, T. (1992). A meta-analytic investigation of the effect of various test item characteristics on test scores and test completion times. *Public Personnel Management, 21*(2), 151–160.

Aamodt, M. G., Nagy, M. S., & Thompson, N. (1998). *Employment references: Who are we talking about?* Paper presented at the annual meeting of the International Personnel Management Association Assessment Council, Chicago, IL.

Aamodt, M. G., & Peggans, D. (1988). Tactfully rejecting job applicants. *Personnel Administrator, 33*, 58–60.

Aamodt, M. G., Reardon, C., & Kimbrough, W. W. (1986). The Critical Incident Technique revisited. *Journal of Police and Criminal Psychology, 2*, 48–59.

Abramis, D. J. (1994). Work role ambiguity, job satisfaction, and job performance: Meta-analyses and review. *Psychological Reports, 75*(3), 1411–1433.

Adair, B., & Pollen, D. (1985, September 23). No! No! A thousand times no: The declining art of the rejection letter. *Washington Post*, p. C-5.

Adam, P. J. (1997). Downsized up. *Ingram's, 23*(2), 29–31.

Adams, G. A., & Jex, S. M. (1999). Relationships between time management, control, work-family conflict, and strain. *Journal of Occupational Health Psychology, 4*(10), 72–77.

Adams, J. S. (1965). Inequity in social change. In L. Berkowitz (Ed.), *Advances in experimental social psychology* (Vol. 2; pp. 267–299). New York: Academic Press.

Adams, J. S., & Rosenbaum, W. B. (1962). The relationship of worker productivity to cognitive dissonance about wage inequities. *Journal of Applied Psychology, 46*, 161–164.

Aiello, J. R., & Svec, C. M. (1993). Computer monitoring of work performance: Extending the social facilitation framework to electronic presence. *Journal of Applied Social Psychology, 23*(7), 537–548.

Akerstedt, T., & Torsvall, L. (1978). Experimental changes in shift schedules: Their effects on well-being. *Ergonomics, 21*, 849–856.

Albright, M. D., & Levy, P. E. (1995). The effects of source credibility and performance rating discrepancy on reactions to multiple raters. *Journal of Applied Social Psychology, 25*(7), 577–600.

Aldag, R. J., & Fuller, S. R. (1993). Beyond fiasco: A reappraisal of the groupthink phenomenon and a new model of group decision processes. *Psychological Bulletin, 13*(3), 533–552.

Aldefer, C. P. (1972). *Existence, relatedness, and growth: Human needs in organizational settings.* New York: Free Press.

Aldred, C. (2001). Reports link work stress, absence. *Business Insurance, 35*, 17–18.

Allard, G., Butler, J., Faust, D., & Shea, T. M. (1995). Errors in hand scoring objective personality tests: The case of the Personality Diagnostic Questionnaire. *Professional Psychology: Research & Practice, 26*(3), 304–308.

Allen, T. J., & Gertsberger, P. C. (1973). A field experiment to improve communications in a product engineering department: The nonterritorial office. *Human Factors, 15*, 487–498.

Allerton, H. E. (2001). Trend watch. *Training & Development, 55*(3), 14.

Alliger, G. M., Tannenbaum, S. I., Bennett, W., Traver, H., & Shotland, A. (1997). A meta-analysis of the relations among training criteria. *Personnel Psychology, 50*(2), 341–358.

Allport, G. W., & Postman, L. (1947). *The psychology of rumor.* New York: Holt, Rinehart & Winston.

Alm, H., & Nilsson, L. (1995). The effects of a mobile telephone task on driver behaviour in a car following situation. *Accident Analysis and Prevention, 27*(5), 707–715.

AMA. (2001). *2001 workplace monitoring & surveillance.* New York: American Management Association.

Amabile, T. M., Hill, K. G., Hennessey, B. A., & Tighe, E. M. (1994). The Work Preference Inventory: Assessing intrinsic and extrinsic motivational orientations. *Journal of Personality and Social Psychology, 66*(5), 950–967.

Amalfitano, J. G., & Kalt, N. C. (1977). Effects of eye contact on the evaluation of job applicants. *Journal of Employment Counseling, 14*, 46–48.

Amirault, T. (1997). Characteristics of multiple job holders, 1995. *Monthly Labor Review, 120*(3), 9–16.

Ammerman, H. L. (1965). *A model of junior officer jobs for use in developing task inventories* (HumRRO Tech. Rep. 65–10). Alexandria, VA: Human Resources Research Organization.

Amsbary, J. H., & Staples, P. J. (1991). Improving administrator/nurse communication: A case study of "management by walking around." *Journal of Business Communication, 28*(2), 101–112.

Anastasi, A., & Urbina, S. (1997). *Psychological testing* (7th ed.). Upper Saddle River, NJ: Prentice-Hall.

Anderson, N. H. (1965). Adding versus averaging as a stimulus combination rule in impression formation. *Journal of Experimental Psychology, 70*, 394–400.

Andersson, B. E., & Nilsson, S. G. (1964). Studies in the reliability and validity of the critical incident technique. *Journal of Applied Psychology, 48*, 398–403.

Andrews, E. S., & Noel, J. J. (1986). Adding life to the case study method. *Training and Development Journal, 40*(2), 28–33.

Andrews, G. (1994). Mistrust, the hidden obstacle to empowerment. *HR Magazine, 39*(9), 66–70.

Ansoorian, A. E., & Shultz, K. S. (1997). *The influence of expertise and gender on physical effort ratings.* Poster presented at the 12th annual conference of the Society for Industrial and Organizational Psychology, St. Louis, MO.

Antonioni, D. (1994). The effects of feedback accountability on upward appraisal ratings. *Personnel Psychology, 47*(2), 349–356.

Arcuri, A. E., & Lester, D. (1990). Moonlighting and stress in police officers. *Psychological Reports, 66*, 350.

Armentrout, B. W. (1993). Eight keys to effective performance appraisal. *HR Focus, 70*(4), 13.

Armour, S. (2000, February 28). Companies work to be more gay-friendly. *USA Today*, p. B1.

Armour, S. (2001, June 12). Arbitration's rise raises fairness issue. *USA Today*, pp. B1–2.

Armour, S. (2003, February 7). Sick days may hurt your bottom line. *USA Today*, p. A1.

Arnold, J. A., & Carnevale, P. J. (1997). Preferences for dispute resolution procedures as a function of intentionality, consequences, expected future interaction, and power. *Journal of Applied Social Psychology, 27*(5), 371–398.

Arthur, D. (1995). The importance of body language. *HR Focus, 72*(6), 22–23.

Arthur, D. (1996). Performance appraisals: Face-to-face with the employee. *HR Focus, 73*(3), 17–18.

Arthur, J. B. (1994). Effects of human resource systems on manufacturing performance and turnover. *Academy of Management Journal, 37*(3), 670–687.

Arvey, R. D. (1988). *Fairness in selecting employees* (2nd ed.) Reading, MA: Addison-Wesley.

Arvey, R. D., & Begalla, M. E. (1975). Analyzing the homemaker job using the PAQ. *Journal of Applied Psychology, 60*, 513–517.

Arvey, R. D., Bouchard, T. J., Segal, N. L., & Abraham, L. M. (1989). Job satisfaction: Environmental and genetic components. *Journal of Applied Psychology, 74*, 187–192.

Arvey, R. D., Davis, G. A., McGowen, S. L., & Dipboye, R. L. (1982). Potential sources of bias in job analytic processes. *Academy of Management Journal, 25*, 618–629.

Arvey, R. D., Gordon, M. E., Massengill, D. P., & Mussio, S. J. (1975). Differential report rates of minority and majority job candidates due to time lags between selection procedures. *Personnel Psychology, 28*(2), 175–180.

Arvey, R. D., Nutting, S. M., & Landon, T. E. (1992). Validation strategies for physical ability testing in police and fire settings. *Public Personnel Management, 21*(3), 301–312.

Ash, R. A., & Edgell, S. A. (1975). A note on the readability of the Position Analysis Questionnaire (PAQ). *Journal of Applied Psychology, 60*, 765–766.

Ash, R. A., Levine, E. L., Higbee, R. H., & Sistrunk, F. (1982). *Comparisons of task ratings from subject matter experts versus job incumbents.* Paper presented at the annual meeting of the Southeastern Psychological Association, New Orleans, LA.

Athey, T. R., & McIntyre, R. M. (1987). Effect of rater training on rater accuracy: Levels of processing theory and social facilitation perspectives. *Journal of Applied Psychology, 72*, 567–572.

Atkinson, W. (1999). Safety—at a price. *HR Magazine, 44*(12), 52–59.

Atkinson, W. (2000). When stress won't go away. *HR Magazine, 45*(12), 104–110.

Atwater, L. E. (1998). The advantages and pitfalls of self-assessment in organizations. In J. W. Smither (Ed.), *Performance appraisal: State of the art in practice.* San Francisco: Jossey-Bass.

Atwater, L., Roush, P., & Fischthal, A. (1995). The influence of upward feedback on self- and follower ratings of leadership. *Personnel Psychology, 48*(1), 35–59.

Atwater, L., Waldman, D. A., Atwater, D., & Cartier, P. (2000). An upward feedback field experiment: Supervisor's cynicism, reactions, and commitment to subordinates. *Personnel Psychology, 53*(2), 275–297.

Austin, J., Kessler, M. L., Riccobone, J. E., & Bailey, J. S. (1996). Using feedback and reinforcement to improve the performance and safety of a roofing crew. *Journal of Organizational Behavior Management, 16*(2), 49–75.

Avis, J., & Kudisch, J. (2000). *Factors influencing subordinates' willingness to participate in an upward feedback system.* Paper presented at the 21st annual Graduate Student Conference in Industrial-Organizational Psychology and Organizational Behavior, Knoxville, TN.

Baba, V. V., & Jamal, M. (1992). How much do we really know about moonlighters? *Public Personnel Management, 21*(1), 65–73.

Babad, E. Y., Inbar, J., & Rosenthal, R. (1982). Pygmalion, Galatea, and the Golem: Investigations of biased and unbiased teachers. *Journal of Educational Psychology, 74*, 459–474.

Bachler, C. J. (1995). Resume fraud: Lies, omissions and exaggerations. *Personnel Journal, 74*(6), 50–58.

Bahls, J. E. (1998). Drugs in the workplace. *HR Magazine, 43*(2), 81–87.

Baldridge, D. C., & Veiga, J. F. (2001). Toward a greater understanding of the willingness to request an accommodation: Can requesters' beliefs disable the Americans with Disabilities Act? *Academy of Management Review, 26*(1), 85–99.

Baldwin, T. T., & Ford, J. K. (1988). Transfer of training: A review and directions for future research. *Personnel Psychology, 41*, 63–105.

Baldwin, T. T., Magjuka, R. J., & Loher, B. T. (1991). The perils of participation: Effects of choice of training on trainee motivation and learning. *Personnel Psychology, 44*, 51–65.

Ballam, D. A. (1995). The traditional view on the origins of the employment-at-will doctrine: Myth or reality? *American Business Law Journal, 33*(1), 1–50.

Baltes, B. B., Briggs, T. E., Huff, J. W., Wright, J. A., & Neuman, G. A. (1999). Flexible and compressed workweek schedules: A meta-analysis of their effects on work-related criteria. *Journal of Applied Psychology, 84*(4), 496–513.

Balzer, W. K., & Sulsky, L. M. (1992). Halo and performance appraisal research: A critical examination. *Journal of Applied Psychology, 77*(6), 971–986.

Bandura, A. (1977). *Social learning theory.* Englewood Cliffs, NJ: Prentice-Hall.

Banis, W. J. (2001). The art of writing job-search letters. *Planning Job Choices: 2002*, 61–67.

Banks, M. H., Jackson, P. R., Stafford, E. M., & Warr, P. B. (1983). The Job Components Inventory and the analysis of jobs requiring limited skill. *Personnel Psychology, 36*, 57–66.

Banks, M. H., & Miller, R. L. (1984). Reliability and convergent validity of the Job Components Inventory. *Journal of Occupational Psychology, 57*, 181–184.

Bannister, B. D. (1986). Performance outcome feedback and attributional feedback: Interactive effects on recipient responses. *Journal of Applied Psychology, 71*, 203–210.

Barnes, K. (1994). Is your office ergonomically correct? *HR Focus, 71*(6), 17.

Baron, R. A. (1977). *Human aggression.* New York: Plenum.

Baron, R. A. (1983). Sweet smell of success: The impact of pleasant artificial scents on evaluations of job applicants. *Journal of Applied Psychology, 68*, 709–713.

Baron, R. A. (1988). Negative effects of destructive criticism: Impact on conflict, self-efficacy, and task performance. *Journal of Applied Psychology, 73*, 199–207.

Baron, R. S., David, J. P., Brunsman, M., & Inman, M. L. (1997). Why listeners hear less than they are told: Attentional load and the teller–listener extremity effect. *Journal of Personality and Social Psychology, 72*(4), 826–836.

Barr, S. H., & Hitt, M. A. (1986). A comparison of selection decision models in manager versus student samples. *Personnel Psychology, 39*, 599–617.

Barrick, M. R., & Mount, M. K. (1991). The big five personality dimensions and job performance: A meta-analysis. *Personnel Psychology, 44*(1), 1–26.

Barrick, M. R., Stewart, G. L., Neubert, M. J., & Mount, M. K. (1998). Relating member ability and personality to work-team processes and team effectiveness. *Journal of Applied Psychology, 83*(3), 377–391.

Barth, S. (2002). How to conduct defensible employee terminations. *Lodging Hospitality, 58*(5), 14.

Barton, J., & Folkard, S. (1993). Advancing versus delaying shift systems. *Ergonomics, 36*(1), 59–64.

Bass, B. M. (1990). *Bass & Stogdill's handbook of leadership: Theory, research, and application* (3rd ed.). New York: Free Press.

Bass, B. M. (1997). Does the transactional-transformational leadership paradigm transcend organizational and national boundaries? *American Psychologist, 52*(2), 130–139.

Bassi, L. J., & Van Buren, M. E. (1998). The 1998 ASTD state of the industry report. *Training & Development, 52*(1), 21–43.

Bast, G. H. (1960). *Ploegenarbeid in de industry. Arnheim: Contract groepvuoering productiviteit* Van Loghum Slaterus. Cited by P. E. Mott, *Shift work.* (1965). Ann Arbor, MI: University of Michigan Press.

Bates, S. (2003). Top pay for best performance. *HR Magazine, 48*(1), 31–38.

Baumgartner, J. (1994). Give it to me straight. *Training & Development Journal, 48*(6), 49–51.

Baxter, J. C., Brock, B., Hill, P. C., & Rozelle, R. M. (1981). Letters of recommendation: A question of value. *Journal of Applied Psychology, 66*, 296–301.

Baxter, J. S., Manstead, A. S., Stradling, S. G., & Campbell, K. A. (1990). Social facilitation and driving behavior. *British Journal of Psychology, 81*(3), 351–360.

Beall, G. E. (1991). Validity of the weighted application blank across four job criteria. *Applied H.R.M. Research, 2*(1), 18–26.

Beatty, G. O. (1996). *Job analysis sample size: How small is large enough?* Poster presented at the annual meeting of the Society for Industrial and Organizational Psychology, San Diego, CA.

Becker, R. (1998). Taking the misery out of experiential training. *Training Magazine, 35*(2), 78–88.

Becker, T. E., & Colquitt, A. L. (1992). Potential versus actual faking of a biodata form: An analysis along several dimensions of item type. *Personnel Psychology, 45*, 389–406.

Beehr, T. A. (1996). *Basic organizational psychology.* Boston: Allyn & Bacon.

Beehr, T. A., Ivanitskaya, L., Hansen, C. P., Erofeev, D., & Gudanowski, D. M. (2001). Evaluation of 360-degree feedback ratings: Relationships with each other and with performance and selection predictors. *Journal of Organizational Behavior, 22*, 775–788.

Begley, T. M., Lee, C., & Czajka, J. M. (2000). The relationship of Type A behavior and optimism with job performance and blood pressure. *Journal of Business and Psychology, 15*(2), 215–227.

Belfast Telegraph (2001, June 18). One third of absenteeism "not genuine." *Belfast Telegraph.*

Bell, J. D., & Kerr, D. L. (1987). Measuring training results: Key to managerial commitment. *Training & Development, 41*(1), 70–73.

Benjamin, A. J. (1996). *Evaluation of leader emergence in a leaderless group discussion*. Unpublished master's thesis, University of California at Fullerton.

Benne, K. D., & Sheets, P. (1948). Functional roles of group members. *Journal of Social Issues, 4*(2), 41–49.

Ben-Shakhar, G., Bar-Hillel, M., Bilu, Y., Ben-Abba, E., & Flug, A. (1986). Can graphology predict occupational success? Two empirical studies and some methodological ruminations. *Journal of Applied Psychology, 71*, 645–653.

Benzinger, K. (1982, May–June). The powerful woman. *Hospital Forum*, pp. 15–20.

Berglas, S. (1997). Boom! There's nothing wrong with you or your business that a little conflict wouldn't cure. *Inc., 19*(6), 56–58.

Bernardin, H. J., & Beatty, R. W. (1984). *Performance appraisal: Assessing human behavior at work*. Boston: Kent.

Bernardin, H. J., & Buckley, M. R. (1981). Strategies in rater training. *Academy of Management Review, 6*, 205–242.

Bernardin, H. J., & Kane, J. S. (1980). A second look at behavioral observation scales. *Personnel Psychology, 33*, 809–814.

Bernardin, H. J., LaShells, M. B., Smith, P. C., & Alvares, K. M. (1976). Behavioral expectation scales: Effects of developmental procedures and formats. *Journal of Applied Psychology, 61*, 75–79.

Bernardin, H. J., & Pence, E. C. (1980). Effects of rater training: Creating new response sets and decreasing accuracy. *Journal of Applied Psychology, 65*, 60–66.

Bernardin, H. J., & Walters, C. S. (1977). Effects of rater training and diary-keeping on psychometric error in ratings. *Journal of Applied Psychology, 62*, 64–69.

Bernstein, A. J., & Rozen, S. C. (1992). *Neanderthals at work*. New York: Ballantine.

Bernthal, P. R., & Insko, C. A. (1993). Cohesiveness without groupthink: The interactive effects of social and task cohesion. *Group and Organization Management, 18*(1), 66–87.

Berry, L. M. (2003). *Employee selection*. Belmont, CA: Wadsworth.

Berry, S., & Lagerstedt, J. (2001). *Worksite fitness and health promotion programs in relation to absentee levels*. Paper presented at the 22nd annual Graduate Conference in Industrial-Organizational Psychology and Organizational Behavior, Penn State University, State College, PA.

Beshir, M. Y., El-Sabagh, A. S., & El-Nawawi, M. A. (1981). Time on task effect on tracking performance under heat stress. *Ergonomics, 24*, 95–102.

Beyer, C., Pike, D., & McGovern, L. (1993). *Surviving unemployment*. New York: Henry Holt.

Bianchi, A. B. (1996). The character-revealing handwriting analysis. *Inc., 18*(2) 77–79.

Biddle, R. E. (1993). How to set cutoff scores for knowledge tests used in promotion, training, certification, and licensing. *Public Personnel Management, 22*(1), 63–79.

Biegeleisen, J. I. (1994). *Make your job interview a success* (4th ed.). Englewood Cliffs, NJ: Prentice-Hall.

Birnbrauer, H. (1987). Evaluation techniques that work. *Training and Development Journal, 41*(1), 53–55.

Bishop, J. W., & Scott, K. D. (1997). How commitment affects team performance. *HR Magazine, 42*(2), 107–111.

Blake, R. R., & Mouton, J. S. (1984). *The managerial grid III*. Houston: Gulf.

Blakley, B. R., Quiñones, M. A., Crawford, M. S., & Jago, I. A. (1994). The validity of isometric strength tests. *Personnel Psychology, 47*(2), 247–274.

Blanchard, K. H., Zigarmi, P., & Zigarmi, D. (1985). *Leadership and the one minute manager*. New York: William Morrow.

Blanz, F., & Ghiselli, E. E. (1972). The mixed standard scale: A new rating system. *Personnel Psychology, 25*, 185–200.

Bliss, W. G. (2001a). Cost of employee turnover can be staggering. *Fairfield County Business Journal, 40*(19), 20.

Bliss, W. G. (2001b). *Legal, effective references*. Alexandria, VA: SHRM.

Blodgett, P. C. (1997). Six ways to be a better listener. *Training & Development, 51*(7), 11–12.

Bluen, S. D., Barling, J., & Burns, W. (1990). Predicting sales performance, job satisfaction, and depression using the Achievement Strivings and Impatience-Irritability dimensions of Type A behavior. *Journal of Applied Psychology, 75*, 212–216.

Blum, M. L., & Naylor, J. C. (1968). *Industrial psychology*. New York: Harper & Row.

Blumenfeld, W. S. (1985). Appropriateness of readability of a Federal Aviation Agency regulation, a flight crew manual, and a company pilot labor agreement for an airline's pilots. *Perceptual and Motor Skills, 61*, 1189–1190.

Blumenfeld, W. S., & Justice, B. M. (1975). Six replicated investigations of the relationship between Flesch and Gunning readability indices. *Perceptual and Motor Skills, 40*, 110.

Bobko, P., Roth, P. L., & Potosky, D. (1999). Derivation and implications of a meta-analytic matrix incorporating cognitive ability, alternative predictors, and job performance. *Personnel Psychology, 52*(3), 561–589.

Bocketti, S., Hamilton, M., & Maser, S. (2000). *Comparing the effect of negative information on resumes and interviews*. Paper presented at the 21st annual Graduate Student Conference in Industrial-Organizational Psychology and Organizational Behavior, Knoxville, TN.

Bolles, R. N. (2003). *What color is your parachute?* Berkeley, CA: Ten Speed Press.

Bommer, W. H., Johnson, J. L., Rich, G. A., Podsakoff, P. M., & Mackenzie, S. B. (1995). On the interchangeability of objective and subjective measures of employee performance: A meta-analysis. *Personnel Psychology, 48*(3), 587–605.

Bond, C. F., & Titus, L. J. (1983). Social facilitation: A meta-analysis of 241 studies. *Psychological Bulletin, 94*, 265–292.

Bond, G. E. (1995). *Leadership behavior: How personality, stress, and gender affect leader behavior*. Unpublished doctoral dissertation, University of Washington.

Bonner, D. (1990). Effectiveness of wellness programs in industry. *Applied H.R.M. Research, 1*(2), 32–37.

Bonner, J. J. (1993). *Measurement of resume content preference*. Unpublished master's thesis, Radford University, Radford, VA.

Bordens, K. S., & Abbott, B. B. (2002). *Research design and methods: A process approach*. New York: McGraw-Hill.

Botchford, J. (2001, March 17). Stressed, but still working: Canadian firms crack down on staff. *Toronto Sun*, p. News-4.

Boudreau, J. W. (1983). Economic considerations in estimating the utility of human resource productivity improvement programs. *Personnel Psychology, 36*, 551–576.

Bowen, C. C., Swim, J. K., & Jacobs, R. R. (2000). Evaluating gender biases on actual job performance of real people: A meta-analysis. *Journal of Applied Social Psychology, 30*(10), 2194–2215.

Brabant, C. (1992). Heat exposure standards and women's work: Equitable or debatable? *Women and Health, 18*(3), 119–130.

Bradburn, W. J., & Villar, P. (1992). Adverse impact resulting from the use of clerical tests: A meta-analysis. *Applied H.R.M. Research, 3*(1), 65–72.

Bramson, R. (1981). *Coping with difficult people*. New York: Anchor.

Brandes, P., Dharwadkar, R., & Lemesis, G.V. (2003). Effective employee stock option design: Reconciling stakeholder, strategic, and motivational factors. *Academy of Management Executive, 17*(1), 77–95.

Brandon, M. C. (1997). From the three B's to the high C's: The history of employee communication. *Communication World, 14*(5), 18–21.

Brannick, M. T., & Levine, E. L. (2002). *Job analysis*. Thousand Oaks, CA: Sage.

Bravo, I. M., & Kravitz, D. A. (1996). Context effects in performance appraisals: Influence of target value, context polarity, and individual differences. *Journal of Applied Social Psychology, 26*(19), 1681–1701.

Brawley, L. R., Carron, A. V., & Widmeyer, W. N. (1993). The influence of the group and its cohesiveness on perceptions of group goal-related variables. *Journal of Sport and Exercise Psychology, 15*(3), 245–260.

Breaugh, J. A. (1981). Relationships between recruitment sources and employee performance, absenteeism, and work attitudes. *Academy of Management Journal, 24*, 261–267.

Breaugh, J. A., & Mann, R. B. (1984). Recruiting source effects: A test of two alternative explanations. *Journal of Occupational Psychology, 57*, 261–267.

Brehm, J. W. (1966). *A theory of psychological reactance*. New York: Academic Press.

Brehm, S. S., & Kassin, S. M. (1996). *Social psychology* (3rd ed.). Boston: Houghton Mifflin.

Brennan, J. (1994). New outlaws? *Forbes, 151*(4), 70.

Brett, J. F., & Atwater, L. E. (2001). 360-degree feedback: Accuracy, reactions, and perceptions of usefulness. *Journal of Applied Psychology, 86*(5), 930–942.

Bretz, R. D., & Judge, T. A. (1994). Person–organization fit and the theory of work adjustment: Implications for satisfaction, tenure, and career success. *Journal of Vocational Behavior, 44*(1), 32–54.

Bretz, R. D., & Judge, T. A. (1998). Realistic job previews: A test of the adverse self-selection hypothesis. *Journal of Applied Psychology, 83*(2), 330–337.

Bretz, R. D., & Thomas, S. L. (1992). Perceived equity, motivation, and final offer arbitration. *Journal of Applied Psychology, 77*(3), 280–287.

Brice, T. S., & Waung, M. (1995). Applicant rejection letters: Are businesses sending the wrong message? *Business Horizons, 38*(2), 59–62.

Bridges, W. (1985). How to manage organizational transition. *Training, 22*(9), 28–32.

Brinkman, R., & Kirschner, R. (1994). *Dealing with people you can't stand*. New York: McGraw-Hill.

Broad, M. (2000). Ensuring transfer of learning to the job. In G. M. Piskurich, P. Beckschi, & B. Hall (Eds.), *The ASTD handbook of training design and delivery*. New York: McGraw-Hill.

Broadbent, B. (1997). Writing for the 90's. *Training & Development, 51*(3), 11–12.

Broadbent, D. E. (1971). *Decision and stress*. New York: Academic Press.

Broadbent, D. E., & Little, E. A. (1960). Effect of noise reduction in a work situation. *Occupational Psychology, 343*, 133–140.

Broadwell, M. M. (1993). Seven steps to building better training. *Training, 30*(10), 75–81.

Bronchick, W. (1997). Take sexual harassment charges seriously. *Denver Business Journal, 48*(23), 15A.

Brookes, M. J., & Kaplan, A. (1972). The office environment: Space planning and effective behavior. *Human Factors, 14*, 373–391.

Brophy, D. R. (1996). *Matching individual and group creativity to different types of problems*. Poster presented at the 11th annual conference of the Society for Industrial and Organizational Psychology, San Diego, CA.

Brotherton, P. (1996). The company that plays together . . . *HR Magazine, 41*(12), 76–82.

Broussard, R. D., & Brannen, D. E. (1986). Credential distortions: Personnel practitioners give their views. *Personnel Administrator, 31*(6), 129–145.

Brown, D. L. (1993). Target stores settle out of court in *Soroka v. Dayton Hudson. The Industrial Organizational Psychologist, 31*(2), 88–89.

Brown, J. (2002). Training needs assessment: A must for developing an effective training program. *Public Personnel Management, 31*(4), 569–578.

Brown, K. A., & Huber, V. L. (1992). Lowering floors and raising ceilings: A longitudinal assessment of the effects of an earnings-at-risk plan on pay performance. *Personnel Psychology, 45*(2), 279–311.

Brown, S. H. (1978). Long-term validity of a personal history item scoring procedure. *Journal of Applied Psychology, 63*, 673–676.

Brown, W. F., & Finstuen, K. (1993). The use of participation in decision making: A consideration of the Vroom-Yetton and Vroom-Jago normative models. *Journal of Behavioral Decision Making, 6*(3), 207–219.

Bruce, H. J. (1997). Looking for a CEO? Look for early career signs of "leadership without portfolio." *Directors & Boards, 21*(2), 20–21.

Bryan, D. A. (1992). Differences in trait interpretations between black and white professionals when evaluating letters of recommendation. *Applied H.R.M. Research, 3*(2), 130–161.

Bryman, A. (1992). *Charisma & leadership*. Newbury Park, CA: Sage.

Buchanan, L., & Foti, R. J. (1996). *Emergent female leaders: Effects of self-monitoring, priming, and task characteristics*. Poster presented at the 11th annual conference of the Society for Industrial and Organizational Psychology, San Diego, CA.

Buchner, L. M. (1990). Increases in interrater reliability of situational interviews as a function of the number of benchmark answers. *Applied H.R.M. Research, 1*(2), 27–31.

Buckley, M. R., & Eder, R. W. (1989). The first impression. *Personnel Administrator, 34*(5), 72–74.

Buckley, M. R., & Weitzel, W. (1988). Employing at will. *Personnel Administrator, 33*(8), 78–81.

Buddhavarapu, S., Borys, J., Homant, M., & Baltes, B. (2002). *The twenty-four hour dilemma: A meta-analytic review of shift work*. Paper presented at the 17th annual conference of the Society for Industrial and Organizational Psychology, Toronto, Canada.

Budman, M. (1994). Apprentices begin apprenticing in the U.S. *Across the Board, 31*(1), 36–37.

Bullock, R. J., & Tubbs, M. E. (1990). A case meta-analysis of gainsharing plans as organization development interventions. *Journal of Applied Behavioral Science, 26*(3), 383–404.

Burley-Allen, M. (2001). Listen up. *HR Magazine, 46*(11), 115–120.

Burling, T., Lentz, E., & Wilson, R. (1956). *To give and take in hospitals*. New York: Putnam.

Burnett, J. J., & Dunne, P. M. (1986). An appraisal of the use of student subjects in marketing research. *Journal of Business Research, 14*(4), 329–343.

Burnett, J. R., & Motowidlo, S. J. (1998). Relations between different sources of information in the structured selection interview. *Personnel Psychology, 51*(4), 963–983.

Burns, W. (1979). Physiological effects of noise. In C. M. Harris (Ed.), *Handbook of noise control* (pp. 15-1–15-23). New York: McGraw-Hill.

Butterfield, K. D., Trevino, L. K., & Ball, G. A. (1996). Punishment from the manager's perspective: A grounded investigation and inductive model. *Academy of Management Journal, 39*(6), 1479–1512.

Buzzotta, V. R. (1986). Does "people skills" training really work? *Training, 23*(8), 59–60.

Bycio, P. (1992). Job performance and absenteeism: A review and meta-analysis. *Human Relations, 45*(2), 193–220.

Byrne, D. (1971). *The attraction paradigm*. New York: Academic Press.

Byrne, J. A. (1994, May 9). The pain of downsizing. *Business Week*, pp. 60–69.

Cable, D. M., & DeRue, D. S. (2002). Convergent and discriminant validity of subjective fit perceptions. *Journal of Applied Psychology, 87*(5), 875–884.

Cadrain, D. (2003). Are your employee drug tests accurate? *HR Magazine, 48*(1), 40–45.

Caldwell, D. F., & Burger, J. M. (1998). Personality characteristics of job applicants and success in screening interviews. *Personnel Psychology, 51*(1), 119–136.

Callinan, M., & Robertson, I. V. (2001). Work sample testing. *International Journal of Selection and Assessment, 8*(4), 248–260.

Cameron, J., & Pierce, W. D. (1994). Reinforcement, reward, and intrinsic motivation: A meta-analysis. *Review of Educational Research, 64*(3), 363–423.

Cameron, K. S., Freeman, S. J., & Mishra, A. (1991). Best practices in white-collar downsizings: Managing contradictions. *Academy of Management Executive, 5*, 57–73.

Campbell, D. E. (1979). Interior office design and visitor response. *Journal of Applied Psychology, 64*, 648–653.

Campbell, D. T., & Stanley, J. C. (1963). *Experimental and quasi-experimental designs in research*. Chicago: Rand McNally.

Campion, J. E., Greener, J., & Wernli, S. (1973). Work observation versus recall in developing behavioral examples for rating scales. *Journal of Applied Psychology, 58*, 286–288.

Campion, M. A., Campion, J. E., & Hudson, J. P. (1994). Structured interviewing: A note on incremental validity and alternative question types. *Journal of Applied Psychology, 79*(6), 998–1002.

Campion, M. A., & McClelland, C. L. (1993). Follow-up and extension of the interdisciplinary costs and benefits of enlarged jobs. *Journal of Applied Psychology, 78*(3), 339–351.

Campion, M. A., Outtz, J. L., Zedeck, S., Schmidt, F. L., Kehoe, J. F., Murphy, K. R., & Guion, R. M. (2001). The controversy over score banding in personnel selection: Answers to 10 key questions. *Personnel Psychology, 54*(1), 149–185.

Campion, M. A., Palmer, D. K., & Campion, J. E. (1997). A review of structure in the selection interview. *Personnel Psychology, 50*(3), 655–702.

Cantor, J., Alfonso, H., & Zillman, D. (1976). The persuasive effectiveness of the peer appeal and a communicator's first-hand experience. *Communication Research, 3*, 293–310.

Cardy, R. L., & Dobbins, G. H. (1986). Affect and appraisal accuracy: Liking as an integral dimension in evaluating performance. *Journal of Applied Psychology, 71*, 672–678.

Carli, L. L., & Eagly, A. H. (2001). Gender, hierarchy, and leadership: An introduction. *Journal of Social Issues, 57*(4), 629–636.

Carlson, K. D., Scullen, S. E., Schmidt, F. L., Rothstein, H., & Erwin, F. (1999). Generalizable biographical data validity can be reached without multi-organizational development and keying. *Personnel Psychology, 52*(3), 731–755.

Carlson, R. E. (1970). Effects of applicant sample on ratings of valid information in an employment setting. *Journal of Applied Psychology, 54*(3), 217–222.

Carnall, C. A. (1990). *Managing change in organizations*. New York: Prentice-Hall.

Carpi, J. (1996, January–February). Stress: It's worse than you think. *Psychology Today*, pp. 34–42.

Carr, S. C., McLoughlin, D., Hodgson, M., & MacLachlan, M. (1996). Effects of unreasonable pay discrepancies for under- and overpayment on double demotivation. *Genetic, Social, and General Psychology Monographs, 122*(4), 475–494.

Carrell, M. R., & Dittrich, J. E. (1978). Equity theory: The recent literature, methodological considerations, and new directions. *Academy of Management Review, 3*, 202–210.

Carroll, S. J., & Nash, A. N. (1972). Effectiveness of a forced-choice reference check. *Personnel Administrator, 35*, 142–146.

Carron, A. V. (1990). Group size in sport and physical activity: Social psychological and performance consequences. *International Journal of Sport Psychology, 21*(4), 286–304.

Carson, K. P., Becker, J. S., & Henderson, J. A. (1998). Is utility really futile? A failure to replicate and an extension. *Journal of Applied Psychology, 83*(1), 84–96.

Carson, P. P., Lanier, P. A., Carson, K. D., & Guidry, B. N. (2000). Clearing a path through the management fashion jungle: Some preliminary trailblazing. *Academy of Management Journal, 43*(6), 1143–1158.

Carter, J. H. (1952). Military leadership. *Military Review, 32,* 14–18.

Cascio, W. F. (1987, April). *Utility analysis and strategic management.* Paper presented at the 8th annual conference in Industrial/Organizational Psychology and Organizational Behavior, Knoxville, TN.

Cascio, W. F. (1993). Downsizing: What do we know? What have we learned? *Academy of Management Executive, 7*(1), 95–104.

Cascio, W. F. (1995). Whither industrial and organizational psychology in a changing world of work? *American Psychologist, 50*(11), 928–939.

Cascio, W. F. (2002). Strategies for responsible restructuring. *Academy of Management Executive, 16*(3), 80–91.

Cascio, W. F., Alexander, R. A., & Barrett, G. V. (1988). Setting cutoff scores: Legal, psychometric, and professional issues and guidelines. *Personnel Psychology, 41,* 1–24.

Cascio, W. F., & Phillips, N. F. (1979). Performance testing: A rose among thorns. *Personnel Psychology, 32,* 751–756.

Cascio, W. F., Young, C. E., & Morris, J. R. (1997). Financial consequences of employment-change decisions in major U.S. corporations. *Academy of Management Journal, 40*(5), 1175–1189.

Cash, T. E., Gillen, B., & Burns, D. S. (1977). Sexism and "beautyism" in personnel consultants' decision making. *Journal of Applied Psychology, 62,* 361–370.

Casperson, D. M. (2002, December). E-mail etiquette: How to make sure your message gets across. *IPMA News,* p. 25.

Caudron, S. (1994). Volunteer efforts offer low cost training options. *Personnel Journal, 73*(6), 38–44.

Cavanaugh, J. (2001, January 15). Death at work: Some killings can be prevented. *People Weekly, 55*(2), 63.

Cavanaugh, M. A., Boswell, W. R., Roehling, M. V., & Boudreau, J. W. (2000). An empirical examination of self-reported work stress among U.S. managers. *Journal of Applied Psychology, 85*(1), 65–74.

Ceci, S. J., & Peters, D. (1984). Letters of reference: A naturalistic study of the effects of confidentiality. *American Psychologist, 39,* 29–31.

Cederbloom, D. (1989). Peer and supervisor evaluations: An underused promotion method used for law enforcement. *Proceedings of the 13th Annual Meeting of the International Personnel Management Association Assessment Council.*

Cederbloom, D., Pence, E. C., & Johnson, D. L. (1984). Making I/O psychology useful: The personnel administrator's view. *The Industrial-Organizational Psychologist, 21*(3), 9–17.

Cellar, D. F., Curtis, J. R., Kohlepp, K., Poczapski, P., & Mohiuddin, S. (1989). The effects of rater training, job analysis format and congruence of training on job evaluation ratings. *Journal of Business and Psychology, 3*(4), 387–401.

Chafkin, R. E. (1999). People with cognitive disabilities: An untapped labor source. *HR News, 18*(9), 43–45.

Chaiken, S. (1979). Communicator physical attractiveness and persuasion. *Journal of Personality and Social Psychology, 33,* 1387–1397.

Chambers, D. A. (1986). The constraints of work and domestic schedules on women's leisure. *Leisure Studies, 5,* 309–325.

Chan, D., & Schmitt, N. (1997). Video-based versus paper-and-pencil method of assessment in situational judgment tests: Subgroup differences in test performance and face validity perceptions. *Journal of Applied Psychology, 82*(1), 143–159.

Chan, D., Schmitt, N., DeShon, R. P., Clause, C. S., & Delbridge, K. (1997). Reactions to cognitive ability tests: The relationship between race, test performance, face validity perceptions, and test-taking motivation. *Journal of Applied Psychology, 82*(2), 300–310.

Chan, K. Y., & Drasgow, F. (2001). Toward a theory of individual differences and leadership: Understanding the motivation to lead. *Journal of Applied Psychology, 86*(3), 481–498.

Chang, C. H., & Rosen, C. C. (2003). *A meta-analytic review of perceived organizational politics and its outcomes.* Poster presented at the 18th annual meeting of the Society for Industrial and Organizational Psychology, Orlando, FL.

Chauran, T. (1989). Taking Texas on the road. *Recruitment Today, 2*(2), 48–52.

Chen, A. Y., Sawyers, R. B., & Williams, P. F. (1997). Reinforcing ethical decision making through corporate culture. *Journal of Business Ethics, 16,* 855–865.

Chen, S. C. (1937). Social modification of the activity of ants in nest-building. *Physiological Zoology, 10,* 420–436.

Choi, J. N., & Kim, M. U. (1999). The organizational application of groupthink and its limitations in organizations. *Journal of Applied Psychology, 84*(2), 297–306.

Chua-Eoan, H. (1999, March 22). The bomber next door: What are the most dangerous men in America talking about at the Supermax prison in Colorado? *Time,* p. 55.

Chubb, R. (1995). Humor: A valuable laugh skill. *Journal of Child and Youth Care, 10*(3), 61–66.

Church, A. H. (1993). Estimating the effect of incentives on mail survey response rates: A meta-analysis. *Public Opinion Quarterly, 57*(1), 62–79.

Church, A. H. (2001). Is there a method to our madness? The impact of data collection methodology on organizational survey results. *Personnel Psychology, 54*(4), 937–969.

Church, A. H., Rogelberg, S. G., & Waclawski, J. (2000). Since when is no news good news? The relationship between performance and response rates in multirater feedback. *Personnel Psychology, 53*(2), 435–451.

Cialdini, R. B. (1985). *Influence: Science and practice.* Glenview, IL: Scott, Foresman.

Cialdini, R. B., Borden, R., Thorne, A., Walker, M., Freeman, S., & Sloane, L. T. (1976). Basking in reflected glory: Three (football) field studies. *Journal of Personality and Social Psychology, 34,* 366–375.

Circadian Technologies. (2002). *2002 shiftwork practices survey.* Lexington, MA: Circadian Technologies, Inc.

Clark, M. M. (2001). More companies offering flextime: Are scheduling options flexible enough? *HR News, 20*(6), 1–10.

Clark, R. D. (1971). Group-induced shift toward risk: A critical appraisal. *Psychological Bulletin, 76,* 251–271.

Clark, R. E. (1961). *The limiting hand skin temperature for unaffected manual performance in the cold.* Natick, MA: Quartermaster Research and Engineering Command, Technical Rep. EP-147.

Clarke, D. L., Miklos, S. M., & Rogers, V. M. (1996). *Upward appraisal: Does it make a difference?* Paper presented at the 11th annual meeting of the Society for Industrial and Organizational Psychology, San Diego, CA.

Clause, C. S., Mullins, M. E., Nee, R., Pulakos, E. D., & Schmitt, N. (1998). Strictly parallel test forms: A development procedure and example. *Personnel Psychology, 51*(1), 193–208.

Clements, C., Wagner, R. J., & Roland, C. C. (1995). The ins and outs of experiential training. *Training & Development, 49*(2), 52–56.

Cleveland, J. N., Murphy, K. R., & Williams, R. E. (1989). Multiple uses of performance appraisal: Prevalence and correlates. *Journal of Applied Psychology, 74*, 130–135.

Clevenger, J., Pereira, G. M., Wiechmann, D., Schmitt, N., & Harvey, V. S. (2001). Incremental validity of situational judgment tests. *Journal of Applied Psychology, 86*(3), 410–417.

Cochran, A., Kopitzke, K., & Miller, D. (1984). *Relationship between interviewer personality and interior office characteristics.* Paper presented at the 5th annual Graduate Student Conference in Industrial/Organizational Psychology and Organizational Behavior, Norfolk, VA.

Coens, T., & Jenkins, M. (2000). *Abolishing performance appraisals: Why they backfire and what to do instead.* San Francisco: Berrett-Koehler.

Cohen, A. (1972, September). *The role of psychology in improving worker safety and health under the Worker Safety and Health Act.* Paper presented at the annual meeting of the American Psychological Association, Honolulu, HI.

Cohen, D. (1997). *Cohen Conflict Response Inventory.* Washington, DC: author.

Cohen, D., & Scott, D. (1996). *Construct validity of a situational interview and patterned behavior description interview.* Paper presented at the 17th annual Graduate Student Conference in Industrial/Organizational Psychology and Organizational Behavior, Toledo, OH.

Cohen, J. (1988). *Statistical power analysis for the behavioral sciences* (2nd ed.). Hillsdale, NJ: Lawrence Erlbaum.

Cohen, P. (1984). College grades and adult achievement. *Research in Higher Education, 20*, 281–293.

Cohen, S. (1998). Knowledge management's killer app: Here's how an intranet can wire employees to information and knowledge without fragmenting a company's culture. *Training & Development, 52*(1), 50–56.

Cohen, S. (2002). High-tech tools: Lower barriers for disabled. *HR Magazine, 47*(10), 60–65.

Cohen, S., & Weinstein, N. (1981). Nonauditory effects of noise on behavior and health. *Journal of Personality and Social Psychology, 37*, 36–70.

Cohen, S. G., & Bailey, D. E. (1997). What makes teams work: Group effectiveness research from the shop floor to the executive suite. *Journal of Management, 23*(3), 239–290.

Cohen, S. L. (1980). Pre-packaged vs. tailor made: The assessment center debate. *Personnel Journal, 59*(12), 989–991.

Colella, A., & Varma, A. (2001). The impact of subordinate disability on leader–member exchange relationships. *Academy of Management Journal, 44*(2), 304–315.

Colligan, M. J., Frockt, I. J., & Tasto, D. L. (1970). Frequency of sickness absence and worksite clinic visits among nurses as a function of shift. *Applied Ergonomics, 10*, 79–85.

Collins, K. (2001, April). HR must find new ways to battle substance abuse in the workplace. *HR News*, pp. 11–16.

Colquitt, J. A., Conlon, D. E., Wesson, M. J., Porter, O. L. H., & Ng, K. Y. (2001). Justice at the millennium: A meta-analytic review of 25 years of organizational justice research. *Journal of Applied Psychology, 86*(3), 425–445.

Comer, D. R. (1989). Peers as providers. *Personnel Administrator, 34*(5), 84–86.

Commerce Clearing House. (2002). *2002 CCH unscheduled absenteeism survey.* Riverwoods, IL: author.

Conard, M. A., & Ashworth, S. D. (1986). *Recruiting source effectiveness: A meta-analysis and re-examination of two rival hypotheses.* Paper presented at the first annual meeting of the Society for Industrial and Organizational Psychology, Chicago, IL.

Connolly, J. J., & Viswesvaran, C. (1998). *Affectivity and job satisfaction: A meta-analysis.* Paper presented at the 13th annual conference of the Society for Industrial and Organizational Psychology, Dallas, TX.

Connolly, P. M. (1986). Clearing the deadwood. *Training & Development Journal, 40*(1), 58–60.

Converse, J. M., & Presser, S. (1986). *Survey questions: Handcrafting the standardized questionnaire.* Beverly Hills, CA: Sage.

Conway, J. M., & Huffcutt, A. I. (1997). Psychometric properties of multi-source performance ratings: A meta-analysis of subordinate, supervisor, peer, and self-ratings. *Human Performance, 10*(4), 331–360.

Cooper, M., Kaufman, G., & Hughes, W. (1996, December). Measuring supervisory potential. *IPMA News*, pp. 8–9.

Cooper, W. H. (1981a). Conceptual similarity as a source of illusory halo in job performance ratings. *Journal of Applied Psychology, 66*, 302–307.

Cooper, W. H. (1981b). Ubiquitous halo. *Psychological Bulletin, 90*, 218–244.

Cordes, C. L., & Dougherty, T. W. (1993). Review and integration of research on job burnout. *Academy of Management Review, 18*(4), 621–656.

Cornelius, E. T., Carron, T. J., & Collins, M. N. (1979). Job analysis models and job classification. *Personnel Psychology, 32*, 693–708.

Cornelius, E. T., & Hakel, M. D. (1978). *A study to develop an improved enlisted performance evaluation system for the U.S. Coast Guard.* Washington, DC: Department of Transportation.

Cornelius, E. T., Hakel, M. D., & Sackett, P. R. (1979). A methodological approach to job classification for performance appraisal purposes. *Personnel Psychology, 32*, 283–297.

Cortina, J. M., Goldstein, N. B., Payne, S. C., Davison, H. K., & Gilliland, S. W. (2000). The incremental validity of interview scores over and above cognitive ability and conscientiousness scores. *Personnel Psychology, 53*(2), 325–351.

Cottrell, N. B. (1972). Social facilitation. In C. G. McClintock (Ed.), *Experimental social psychology* (pp. 185–236). New York: Holt, Rinehart & Winston.

Courtis, J. K. (1995). Readability of annual reports: Western versus Asian evidence. *Accounting, Auditing and Accountability, 8*(2), 4–17.

Cowan, G., & Kasen, J. H. (1984). Form of reference: Sex differences in letters of recommendation. *Journal of Personality and Social Psychology, 46,* 636–645.

Cromwell, P. F., Marks, A., Olson, J. N., & Avary, D. W. (1991). Group effects on decision-making by burglars. *Psychological Reports, 69*(2), 579–588.

Cronbach, L. J. (1951). Coefficient alpha and the internal structure of tests. *Psychometrika, 16,* 297–334.

Cropanzano, R., & Folger, R. (1989). Referent cognitions and task decision autonomy: Beyond equity theory. *Journal of Applied Psychology, 74,* 293–299.

Cropanzano, R., & James, K. (1990). Some methodological considerations for the behavioral genetic analysis of work attitudes. *Journal of Applied Psychology, 75,* 433–439.

Crosby, M. M. (1990, April). *Social desirability and biodata: Predicting sales success.* Poster presented at the annual conference of the Society for Industrial and Organizational Psychology, Miami Beach, FL.

Crowther, K. N. (2001). How to reach companies. *Planning Job Choices: 2002,* 27–33.

Crusco, A. H., & Wetzel, C. G. (1984). The Midas touch: The effects of interpersonal touch on restaurant tipping. *Personality and Social Psychology Bulletin, 10,* 512–517.

Csoka, L. S., & Bons, P. M. (1978). Manipulating the situation to fit the leader's style: Two validation studies of leader match. *Journal of Applied Psychology, 63,* 295–300.

Currer-Briggs, N. (1971). *Handwriting analysis in business: The use of graphology in personnel selection.* New York: Wiley.

Curry, S. R. (1997). Big brother wants a closer look at your hair. *Fortune, 125*(12), 163.

Dababneh, A. J., Swanson, N., & Shell, R. L. (2001). Impact of added rest breaks on the productivity and well being of workers. *Ergonomics, 44*(2), 164–174.

Dahmer, B. (1992). Kinder, gentler icebreakers. *Training and Development Journal, 46*(8), 47–49.

Dainoff, M. J., Happ, A., & Crane, P. (1981). Visual fatigue and occupational stress in VDT operators. *Human Factors, 23,* 420–437.

Dale, E., & Chall, J. S. (1948). A formula for predicting readability. *Educational Research Bulletin, 27,* 37–54.

Daley, A. J., & Parfitt, G. (1996). Good health—is it worth it? Mood states, physical well-being, job satisfaction and absenteeism in members and non-members of a British corporate health and fitness club. *Journal of Occupational and Organizational Psychology, 69*(2), 121–134.

Dalton, D. R., & Mesch, D. J. (1991). On the extent and reduction of avoidable absenteeism: An assessment of absence policy provisions. *Journal of Applied Psychology, 76*(6), 810–817.

Dansereau, F., Graen, G., & Haga, W. J. (1975). *A vertical dyad linkage approach to leadership within the formal organization.* Unpublished report, State University of New York, Buffalo.

Davidson, J. (1997). *The complete idiot's guide to managing stress.* New York: Simon & Schuster.

Davidson, O. B., & Eden, D. (2000). Remedial self-fulfilling prophecy: Two field experiments to prevent Golem effects among disadvantaged women. *Journal of Applied Psychology, 85*(3), 386–398.

Davidson, R., & Henderson, R. (2000). Electronic performance monitoring: A laboratory investigation of the influence of monitoring and difficulty on task performance, mood state, and self-reported stress levels. *Journal of Applied Social Psychology, 30*(5), 906–920.

Davies, E. (1922). *Transactions of the Institute of Mining Engineering, 63,* 326.

Davis, D. D., & Harless, D. W. (1996). Group v. individual performance in a price-searching experiment. *Organizational Behavior and Human Decision Processes, 66*(2), 215–227.

Davis, D.D, & Polonko, K. A. (2001). *Telework in the United States: Telework America Survey 2001.* Wakefield, MA: International Telework Association & Council.

Davis, K. (1953). Management communication and the grapevine. *Harvard Business Review, 31*(5), 43–59.

Davis, K. (1967). *The dynamics of organizational behavior.* New York: McGraw-Hill.

Davis, K. (1977). *Human behavior at work.* New York: McGraw-Hill.

Davis, T. R. (1984). The influence of the physical environment in offices. *Academy of Management Review, 9,* 271–283.

Day, D. V., Schleicher, D. J., Unckless, A. L., & Hiller, N. J. (2002). Self-monitoring personality at work: A meta-analytic investigation of construct validity. *Journal of Applied Psychology, 87*(2), 390–401.

Day, D. V., & Sulsky, L. M. (1995). Effects of frame-of-reference training and information configuration on memory organization and rating accuracy. *Journal of Applied Psychology, 80*(1), 158–167.

de Castro, J. M., & Brewer, E. M. (1992). The amount eaten in meals by humans is a power function of the number of people present. *Physiology and Behavior, 51*(1), 121–125.

De Waard, D., Jessurun, M., Steyvers, F. J., Raggatt, P. T., & Brookhuis, K. A. (1995). Effect of road layout and road environment on driving performance, drivers' physiology, and road appreciation. *Ergonomics, 38*(7), 1395–1407.

Deane, C. (1999, January 10). Don't worry, we've got your number. *Washington Post,* p. C4.

DeBono, K. G. (1992). Pleasant scents and persuasion: An information processing approach. *Journal of Applied Social Psychology, 22*(11), 910–919.

Deci, E. L. (1972). The effects of contingent and noncontingent rewards and controls on intrinsic motivation. *Organizational Behavior and Human Performance, 8,* 217–229.

Deci, E. L., & Ryan, R. M. (1985). *Intrinsic motivation and self-determination in human behavior.* New York: Plenum.

Degner, J. (1995). Writing job descriptions that work. *Credit Union Executive, 35*(6), 13–17.

DeGroot, J. P., & Kamphois, A. (1983). Eyestrain in VDT users: Physical correlates and long-term effects. *Human Factors, 25,* 409–413.

DeGroot, J. P., & Motowidlo, S. J. (1999). Why visual and vocal interview cues can affect interviewers' judgments and predict job performance. *Journal of Applied Psychology, 84*(6), 986–993.

Deluga, R. J., & Winters, J. J. (1991). Why the aggravation? Reasons students become resident assistants. *Journal of College Student Development, 32*(6), 546–552.

Dembroski, T. M., Lasater, T. M., & Ramirez, A. (1978). Communicator similarity, fear arousing communications, and compliance with health care recommendations. *Journal of Applied Social Psychology 8*, 254–269.

Dempcy, M. H., & Tihista, R. (1996). *Dear job stressed.* Palo Alto, CA: Davies-Black.

Dempsey, P. G., Ayoub, M. M., Bernard, T. M., Endsley, M. R., Karwowski, W., Lin, C. J., & Smith, J. L. (1996). Ergonomic investigation of letter-carrier satchels, I: Field study. *Applied Ergonomics, 27*(5), 303–313.

Den Hartog, D. N., House, R. J., Hanges, P. J., Ruiz-Quintanilla, S. A., & Dorgman, P. W. (1999). Culture specific and cross culturally generalizable implicit leadership theories: Are attributes of charismatic/transformational leadership universally endorsed? *Leadership Quarterly, 10*(2), 219–256.

DeNisi, A. S., & Peters, L. H. (1996). Organization of information in memory and the performance appraisal process: Evidence from the field. *Journal of Applied Psychology, 81*(6), 717–737.

DeNisi, A. S., Randolph, W. A., & Blencoe, A. G. (1983). Potential problems with peer ratings. *Academy of Management Journal, 26*, 457–464.

DeNisi, A. S., Robbins, T., & Cafferty, T. P. (1989). Organization of information used for performance appraisals: Role of diary-keeping. *Journal of Applied Psychology, 74*, 124–129.

Dennis, A. R., Valacich, J. S., & Nunamaker, J. F. (1990). An experimental investigation of the effects of group size in an electronic meeting environment. *IEEE Transactions on Systems, Man, and Cybernetics, 20*(5), 1049–1057.

Denton, D. K. (1996). 9 ways to create an atmosphere for change. *HR Magazine, 41*(10), 76–81.

DePaulo, B. M. (1992). Nonverbal behavior and self-presentation. *Psychological Bulletin, 111*, 203–243.

DePaulo, B. M., Lindsay, J. J., Malone, B. E., Muhlenbruck, L., Charlton, K., & Cooper, H. (2003). Cues to deception. *Psychological Bulletin, 129*(1), 74–118.

DePaulo, B. M., Stone, J. L., & Lassiter, G. D. (1985). Deceiving and detecting deceit. In B. R. Schlenker (Ed.), *The self and social life* (pp. 323–370). New York: McGraw-Hill.

DePaulo, B. M., Zuckerman, M., & Rosenthal, A. R. (1980). Detecting deception: Modality effects. In L. Wheeler (Ed.), *The review of personality and social psychology.* Beverly Hills, CA: Sage.

Deshande, R., & Stayman, D. M. (1994). A tale of two cities: Distinctiveness theory and advertising effectiveness. *Journal of Marketing Research, 31*, 57–64.

Dessler, G. (1984). *Personnel management.* Reston, VA: Reston.

Deutsch, M. (1973). *The resolution of conflict.* New Haven, CT: Yale University Press.

Devine, D. J., Clayton, L. D., Philips, J. L., Dunford, B. B., & Melner, S. B. (1999). Teams in organizations: Prevalence, characteristics, and effectiveness. *Small Group Research, 30*(6), 678–711.

Devine, D. J., & Philips, J. L. (2001). Do smarter teams do better? A meta-analysis of cognitive ability and team performance. *Small Group Research, 32*(5), 507–532.

Dew, A. F., & Steiner, D. D. (1997). *Inappropriate questions in selection interviews: Interviewer knowledge and applicant reactions.* Poster presented at the 12th annual conference of the Society for Industrial and Organizational Psychology, St. Louis, MO.

Dickenson, T. L., & Zellinger, P. M. (1980). A comparison of the behaviorally anchored rating and mixed standard scale format. *Journal of Applied Psychology, 65*, 147–154.

Dickinson, A. M. (1989). The detrimental effects of extrinsic reinforcement on intrinsic motivation. *Behavior Analyst, 12*(1), 1–15.

Dickinson, A. M., & Gillette, K. L. (1993). A comparison of the effects of two individual monetary incentive systems on productivity and piece rate pay versus base pay plus incentives. *Journal of Organizational Behavior Management, 14*(1), 63–82.

Dickson, D. H., & Kelly, I. W. (1985). The "Barnum Effect" in personality assessment: A review of the literature. *Psychological Reports, 57*, 367–382.

DiClemente, D. F., & Hantula, D. A. (2000). John Broadus Watson, I-O psychologist. *The Industrial-Organizational Psychologist, 37*(4), 47–55.

Diehl, M., & Stroebe, W. (1987). Productivity loss in brainstorming groups: Toward the solution of a riddle. *Journal of Personality and Social Psychology, 53*, 497–509.

Diekmann, F. J. (2001, July 23). Everything you wanted to know about e-learning (But didn't know where to log on to ask). *Credit Union Journal, 5*(30), 6–7.

Dietz, P. E. (1994). *Overview of workplace violence.* Seminar presented to the Society for Human Resource Management, Roanoke, VA.

DiFonzo, N., & Bordia, P. (2000). How top PR professionals handle hearsay: Corporate rumors, their effects, and strategies to manage them. *Public Relations Review, 26*(2), 173–191.

Dipboye, R. L. (1977). A critical review of Korman's self-consistency theory of work motivation and occupational choice. *Organizational Behavior and Human Performance,18*, 108–126.

Dipboye, R. L. (1990). Laboratory vs. field research in industrial and organizational psychology. In C. L. Cooper & I. T. Robertson (Eds.), *International review of industrial and organizational psychology* (pp. 1–34). Chichester, UK: Wiley.

Dipboye, R. L., Fromkin, H. L., & Wilback, K. (1975). Relative importance of applicant sex, attractiveness and scholastic standing in evaluation of job applicant resumes. *Journal of Applied Psychology, 60*, 39–43.

Dipboye, R. L., Stramler, C. S., & Fontenelle, G. A. (1984). The effects of the application on recall of information from the interview. *Academy of Management Journal, 27*, 561–575.

Dirks, K. T. (2000). Trust in leadership and team performance: Evidence from NCAA basketball. *Journal of Applied Psychology, 85*(6), 1004–1012.

Dirks, K. T., & Ferrin, D. L. (2002). Trust in leadership: Meta-analytic findings and implications for research and practice. *Journal of Applied Psychology, 87*(4), 611–628.

Dolin, D. J., & Booth-Butterfield, M. (1993). Reach out and touch someone: Analysis of nonverbal comforting responses. *Communication Quarterly, 41*(4), 383–393.

Donnellon, A. (1996). *Team talk: The power of language in team dynamics.* Boston, MA: Harvard Business School Press.

Donnerstein, E., & Wilson, D. W. (1976). Effects of noise and perceived control on ongoing and subsequent aggressive behavior. *Journal of Personality and Social Psychology, 34*, 774–781.

Donovan, J. J., & Radosevich, D. J. (1997). *A meta-analytic review of the distribution of practice effect: Now you see it, now you don't.* Paper presented at the annual meeting of the Academy of Management, Boston, MA.

Dougherty, T. W., Turban, D. B., & Callender, J. C. (1994). Confirming first impressions in the employment interview: A field study of interviewer behavior. *Journal of Applied Psychology, 79*(5), 659–665.

Douglas, J. A., Feld, D. E., & Asquith, N. (1989). *Employment testing manual.* Boston: Warren, Gorham & Lamont.

Drexler, A. B., & Forrester, R. (1998). Teamwork—not necessarily the answer. *HR Magazine, 43*(1), 55–58.

Driskell, J. E., Willis, R. P., & Copper, C. (1992). Effect of overlearning on retention. *Journal of Applied Psychology, 77*(5), 615–623.

DuBose, C. (1994). Breaking the bad news. *HR Magazine, 39*(4), 62–64.

Duchon, J. C., Keran, C. M., & Smith, T. J. (1994). Extended workdays in an underground mine: A work performance analysis. *Human Factors, 36*(2), 258–268.

Dugan, K. M. (2001, October 24). Montgomery, AL fair attracts nearly 1,000 applicants. *Montgomery Advisor.*

Dunham, R. B. (1977). Shiftwork: A review and theoretical analysis. *Academy of Management Review, 2*, 626–634.

DuPont, D. K. (1999). Eureka! Tools for encouraging employee suggestions. *HR Magazine, 44*(9), 134–143.

Dvir, T., Eden, D., & Banjo, M. L. (1995). Self-fulfilling prophecy and gender: Can women be Pygmalion and Galatea? *Journal of Applied Psychology, 80*(2), 253–270.

Dwight, S. A., & Feigelson, M. E. (1997). *An investigation of cross-mode differences in the measurement of social desirability.* Paper presented at the annual meeting of the Academy of Management, Boston, MA.

Dye, D. A., & Reck, M. (1989). College grade point average as a predictor of adult success: A reply. *Public Personnel Management, 18*(2), 239–240.

Eagly, A. H., & Johannesen-Schmidt, M. C. (2001). The leadership styles of women and men. *Journal of Social Issues, 57*(4), 781–797.

Eagly, A. H., & Johnson, B. T. (1990). Gender and leadership style: A meta-analysis. *Psychological Bulletin, 108*(2), 233–256.

Eagly, A. H., & Karau, S. J. (1991). Gender and the emergence of leaders: A meta-analysis. *Journal of Personality and Social Psychology, 60*(5), 685–710.

Eagly, A. H., Karau, S. J., & Makhijani, M. G. (1995). Gender and the effectiveness of leaders: A meta-analysis. *Psychological Bulletin, 117*(1), 125–145.

Eden, D. (1998). *Implanting Pygmalion leadership style through training: Seven true field experiments.* Paper presented at the annual meeting of the Society for Industrial and Organizational Psychology, Dallas, TX.

Egler, T. D. (1995). Five myths about sexual harassment. *HR Magazine, 40*(1), 27–30.

Ekeberg, S., Switzer, F., & Siegfried, W. D. (1991). *What do you do with a master's degree in I/O psychology?* Symposium conducted at the sixth annual conference of the Society for Industrial and Organizational Psychology, St. Louis, MO.

Elias, M. (1997, May). Mood a stroke risk factor: Depression may be prelude. *USA Today*, p. A1.

Ellis, R. A., & Taylor, S. M. (1983). Role of self-esteem within the job search process. *Journal of Applied Psychology, 68*, 632–640.

Emrich, C. G., Brower, H. H., Feldman, J. M., & Garland, H. (2001). Images in words: Presidential rhetoric, charisma, and greatness. *Administrative Science Quarterly, 46*(3), 527–560.

Erfurt, J. C., Foote, A., & Heirich, M. A. (1992). The cost-effectiveness of worksite wellness programs for hypertension control, weight loss, smoking cessation, and exercise. *Personnel Psychology, 45*(1), 5–28.

Estes, R. (1990). Effects of flexi-time: A meta-analytic review. *Applied H.R.M. Research, 1*(1), 15–18.

Ettorre, B. (1997). How to get the unvarnished truth. *HR Focus, 74*(8), 1–3.

Evans, G. W., Hygge, S., & Bullinger, M. (1995). Chronic noise and psychological stress. *Psychological Science, 6*(6), 333–338.

Evans, G. W., & Johnson, D. (2000). Stress and open-office noise. *Journal of Applied Psychology, 85*(5), 779–783.

Falcone, P. (1997). The fundamentals of progressive discipline. *HR Magazine, 42*(2), 90–94.

Falcone, P. (1999a). A legal dichotomy? *HR Magazine, 44*(5), 110–120.

Falcone, P. (1999b). Rejuvenate your performance evaluation writing skills. *HR Magazine, 44*(10), 126–136.

Falcone, P. (2002). Fire my assistant now! *HR Magazine, 47*(5), 105–111.

Farber, B. J. (1994). Sales managers: Get real! Real play, not role play, is the best training you can give your salespeople. *Sales & Marketing Management, 146*(10), 25–26.

Farh, J., Cannella, A. A., & Bedeian, A. G. (1991). Peer ratings: The impact of purpose on rating quality and user acceptance. *Group and Organization Studies, 16*(4), 367–386.

Farh, J., Dobbins, G. A., & Cheng, B. S. (1991). Cultural relativity in action: A comparison of self-ratings made by Chinese and U.S. workers. *Personnel Psychology, 44*(1), 129–147.

Farh, J., & Werbel, J. D. (1986). Effects of purpose of the appraisal and expectation of validation on self-appraisal leniency. *Journal of Applied Psychology, 71*, 527–529.

Farr, J. L. (1973). Response requirements and primacy-recency effects in a simulated selection interview. *Journal of Applied Psychology, 57*(3), 228–232.

Farr, J. L., & York, C. M. (1975). Amount of information and primacy-recency effects in recruitment decision. *Personnel Psychology, 28*, 233–238.

Farrell, D., & Stamm, C. L. (1988). Meta-analysis of the correlates of employee absence. *Human Relations, 41*, 211–227.

Fay, C. H., & Latham, G. P. (1982). Effects of training and rating scales on rating errors. *Personnel Psychology, 35*, 105–116.

Feild, H. S., & Holley, W. H. (1982). The relationship of performance appraisal system characteristics to verdicts in selected employment discrimination cases. *Academy of Management Journal, 25*, 392–406.

Feinstein, D. (2000, November). Drug testing: The things people will do. *IPMA News*, pp. 19–20.

Feldman, D. C. (1986). The MBA-ing of Ph.D. education. *The Industrial-Organizational Psychologist, 23*(4), 43–46.

Feldman, J. (1981). Beyond attribution theory: Cognitive processes in performance appraisal. *Journal of Applied Psychology, 66*, 127–148.

Fernandez, B. (1997, December 6). SmithKline Beecham resorts to unusual job ads to attract applicants. *Knight-Ridder/Tribune Business News*, p. 1206B.

Feuer, D. (1987). Paying for knowledge. *Training, 24*(5), 57–66.

Fey, C. (1987). Engineering good writing. *Training, 24*(3), 49–54.

Fiedler, F. (1967). *A theory of leadership effectiveness*. New York: McGraw-Hill.

Fiedler, F. (1978). Recent developments in research on the contingency model. In L. Berkowitz (Ed.), *Group processes* (pp. 207–223). New York: Academic Press.

Field, R. H., & House, R. J. (1990). A test of the Vroom-Yetton model using manager and subordinate reports. *Journal of Applied Psychology, 75*(3), 362–366.

Fine, B. J., & Kobrick, J. L. (1978). Effects of altitude and heat on complex cognitive tasks. *Human Factors, 20*, 115–122.

Fine, S. A. (1955). What is occupational information? *Personnel and Guidance Journal, 33*, 504–509.

Fine, S. A. (1988). Functional job analysis. In S. Gael (Ed.), *The job analysis handbook for business, industry, and government (Volume II)*. New York: Wiley.

Finkelman, J. M., Zeitlin, L. R., Filippi, J. A., & Friend, M. A. (1977). Noise and driver performance. *Journal of Applied Psychology, 62*, 713–718.

Finkelstein, L. M., & Burke, M. J. (1998). Age stereotyping at work: The role of rater and contextual factors on evaluations of job applicants. *Journal of General Psychology, 125*, 317–345.

Finkelstein, L. M., Burke, M. J., & Raju, N. S. (1995). Age discrimination in simulated employment contexts: An integrative analysis. *Journal of Applied Psychology, 80*, 652–663.

Fisher, J. D., Bell, P. N., & Baum, A. (1984). *Environmental psychology*. New York: Holt, Rinehart & Winston.

Fisher, J. D., Rytting, M., & Heslin, R. (1976). Hands touching hands: Affective and evaluative effects of an interpersonal touch. *Sociometry, 39*, 416–421.

Fisher, S. L., & Greenis, J. L. (1996). *The customer in job analysis*. Poster presented at the 11th annual conference of the Society for Industrial and Organizational Psychology, San Diego, CA.

Fitzgibbons, A. (1997). Employees' perceived importance of profit sharing plays a role in profit sharing's organizational impact. *Proceedings of the 18th Annual Graduate Conference in Industrial/Organizational Psychology and Organizational Behavior, 18*, 43–44.

Flanagan, J. C. (1954). The critical incident technique. *Psychological Bulletin, 51*, 327–358.

Flanagan, J. C., & Burns, R. K. (1955). The employee performance record: A new appraisal and development tool. *Harvard Business Review, 33*, 95–102.

Fleishman, E. A., & Harris, E. F. (1962). Patterns of leadership behavior related to grievances and turnover. *Personnel Psychology, 15*(2), 43–56.

Fleishman, E. A., Harris, E. F., & Burtt, H. E. (1955). *Leadership and supervision in industry*. Columbus: Ohio State University Press.

Fleishman, E. A., & Reilly, M. E. (1992a). *Administrator's guide F-JAS*. Palo Alto, CA: Consulting Psychologists Press.

Fleishman, E. A., & Reilly, M. E. (1992b). *Handbook of human abilities*. Palo Alto, CA: Consulting Psychologists Press.

Fleming, S. L., Jansen, C. W., & Hasson, S. M. (1997). Effect of work glove and type of muscle action on grip fatigue. *Ergonomics, 40*(6), 601–612.

Flesch, R. (1948). A new readability yardstick. *Journal of Applied Psychology, 32*, 221–233.

Fletcher, J., Friedman, L., McCarthy, P., McIntyre, C., O'Leary, B., & Rheinstein, J. (1993). *Sample sizes required to attain stable job analysis inventory profiles*. Poster presented at the 8th annual meeting of the Society for Industrial and Organizational Psychology, San Francisco, CA.

Florkowski, G. W., & Schuster, M. H. (1992). Support for profit sharing and organizational commitment: A path analysis. *Human Relations, 45*(5), 507–523.

Forbes, R. J., & Jackson, P. R. (1980). Non-verbal behaviour and the outcome of selection interviews. *Journal of Occupational Psychology, 53*, 65–72.

Ford, J. K., Quiñones, M. A., Sego, D. J., & Sorra, J. S. (1992). Factors affecting the opportunity to perform trained tasks on the job. *Personnel Psychology, 45*, 511–527.

Ford, R. (1973). Job enrichment lessons at AT& T. *Harvard Business Review, 73*, 96–106.

Forst, J. K. (1987). Factors affecting the evaluation of administrator competence. *Proceedings of 8th Annual Graduate Conference in Industrial/Organizational Psychology and Organizational Behavior*, pp. 165–166.

Forsyth, D. R. (1998). *Group dynamics* (3rd ed.). Pacific Grove, CA: Brooks/Cole.

Forsyth, D. R. (2003). *The professor's guide to teaching: Psychological principles and practices*. Washington, DC: American Psychological Association.

Forsythe, S., Drake, M. F., & Cox, C. E. (1985). Influence of applicant's dress on interviewer's selection decisions. *Journal of Applied Psychology, 70*, 374–378.

Foster, D. A. (1999). *A leader–subordinate fit model of the path-goal theory of leadership*. Unpublished doctoral dissertation, George Washington University.

Foster, M. (1990). A closer look at the relationship between interviewer–interviewee similarity and ratings in a selection interview. *Applied H.R.M. Research, 1*(1), 23–26.

Foster, N., Dingman, S., Muscolino, J., & Jankowski, M. A. (1996). Gender in mock hiring decisions. *Psychological Reports, 79*(1), 275–278.

Foster, P. (2002). Performance documentation. *Business Communication Quarterly, 65*(2), 108–114.

Foster, R. S., Aamodt, M. G., Bodenmiller, J. A., Rodgers, J. G., Kovach, R. C., & Bryan, D. A. (1988). Effect of menu sign position on customer ordering times and number of food-ordering errors. *Environment and Behavior, 20*(2), 200–210.

Fowler, A. (1995). How to decide on training methods. *People Management, 1*(25), 36–37.

Fowler-Hermes, J. (2001). The beauty and the beast in the workplace: Appearance-based discrimination claims under EEO laws. *Florida Bar Journal, 75*(4), 32–46.

Fox, A. (2001, July). E-learning dubbed "next wave" in a sea of training options. *HR News*, p. 8.

Fox, J. B., Scott, K. D., & Donohue, J. M. (1993). An investigation into pay valence and performance in a pay-for-performance field setting. *Journal of Organizational Behavior, 14*, 687–693.

Fox, J. G. (1971). Background music and industrial productivity: A review. *Applied Ergonomics, 2*, 70–73.

Frank, C. L., & Hackman, J. R. (1975). Effects of interviewer–interviewee similarity on interviewer objectivity in college admissions interviews. *Journal of Applied Psychology, 60*, 356–360.

Frank, F., & Anderson, L. R. (1971). Effects of task and group size upon group productivity and member satisfaction. *Sociometry, 34*, 135–149.

Frase-Blunt, M. (2001). Driving home your awards program. *HR Magazine, 46*(2), 109–115.

French, J. R. P., & Raven, B. H. (1959). The bases of social power. In D. Cartwright (Ed.), *Studies in social power* (pp. 150–167). Ann Arbor: University of Michigan Press.

Frese, M., & Okonek, K. (1984). Reasons to leave shiftwork and psychological and psychosomatic complaints of former shiftworkers. *Journal of Applied Psychology, 69*, 509–514.

Frese, M., & Semmer, N. (1986). Shiftwork, stress, and psychosomatic complaints: A comparison between workers in different shiftwork schedules, non-shiftworkers, and former shiftworkers. *Ergonomics, 29*, 99–114.

Freston, N. P., & Lease, J. E. (1987). Communication skills training for selected supervisors. *Training and Development Journal, 41*(7), 67–70.

Frick, R. W. (1985). Communicating emotion: The role of prosodic features. *Psychological Bulletin, 97*, 412–429.

Friedman, L., & Harvey, R. J. (1986). Can raters with reduced job descriptive information provide accurate Position Analysis Questionnaire (PAQ) ratings? *Personnel Psychology, 39*, 779–789.

Frieswick, K. (2002, December). Liar, liar. *CFO, The Magazine for Senior Financial Executives, 18*(13), 84.

Frone, M. R. (2000). Work–family conflict and employee psychiatric disorders: The national comorbidity survey. *Journal of Applied Psychology, 85*(6), 888–895.

Frone, M. R., Russell, M., & Cooper, M. L. (1995). Job stressors, job involvement, and employee health: An identity theory. *Journal of Occupational and Organizational Psychology, 68*(1), 1–11.

Frost, P. J., & Jamal, M. (1979). Shift work, attitudes and reported behaviors: Some associations between individual characteristics and hours of work and leisure. *Journal of Applied Psychology, 64*, 77–81.

Fry, E. (1977). Fry's Readability Graph: Clarifications, validity, and extension to level 17. *Journal of Reading, 21*, 243–252.

Fulger, R. (1977). Which costs less—the phone or the letter? *Management World, 6*, 13–14.

Fuller, J. B., Patterson, C. E., Hester, K., & Stringer, D. Y. (1996). A quantitative review of research on charismatic leadership. *Psychological Reports, 78*, 271–287.

Furnham, A., & Stringfield, P. (1994). Congruence of self and subordinate ratings of managerial practices as a correlate of superior evaluation. *Journal of Occupational and Organizational Psychology, 67*(1), 57–67.

Gabris, G. T., & Mitchell, K. (1988). The impact of merit raise scores on employee attitudes: The Matthew effect of performance appraisal. *Public Personnel Management, 17*, 369–386.

Gael, S. (1988). Subject matter expert conferences. In S. Gael (Ed.), *The job analysis handbook for business, industry, and government* (Vol. 1; p. 434). New York: Wiley.

Gallup, D. A., & Beauchemin, K. V. (2000). On-the-job training. In G. M. Piskurich, P. Beckschi, & B. Hall (Eds.), *The ASTD handbook of training design and delivery*. New York: McGraw-Hill.

Galvin, T. (2001). Industry 2001 report. *Training Magazine, 38*(10), 40–75.

Galvin, T. (2002). 2002 industry report. *Training Magazine, 39*(10), 24–73.

Gandy, J. A., & Dye, D. A. (1989). Development and initial validation of a biodata inventory in a merit system context. *Proceedings of 13th Annual Meeting of the International Personnel Management Association Assessment Council*, pp. 138–142.

Ganzach, Y. (1998). Intelligence and job satisfaction. *Academy of Management Journal, 41*(5), 526–539.

Garavaglia, P. L. (1993). How to ensure transfer of training. *Training and Development, 47*(10), 63–68.

Gardner, J. E. (1994). *Determining focus areas for interview preparation research*. Paper presented at the 15th annual Graduate Student Conference in Industrial-Organizational Psychology and Organizational Behavior, Chicago, IL.

Garske, G. G. (1990). The relationship of self-esteem to levels of job satisfaction of vocational rehabilitation professionals. *Journal of Applied Rehabilitation Counseling, 27*(2), 19–22.

Garvey, C. (2000). Getting a grip on titles. *HR Magazine, 45*(12), 112–117.

Garvey, C. (2001). Outsourcing background checks. *HR Magazine, 46*(3), 95–104.

Gately, R. F. (1997, March). Why motivation is free. *IPMA News*, p. 14.

Gaugler, B. B., Rosenthal, D. B., Thornton, G. C., & Bentson, C. (1987). Meta-analysis of assessment center validity. *Journal of Applied Psychology, 72*, 493–511.

Geber, B. (1987). Who should do the sales training? *Training, 24*(5), 69–76.

Geber, B. (1995). Does training make a difference? Prove it! *Training, 32*(3), 27–34.

Gebhardt, D. L., & Crump, C. E. (1990). Employee fitness and wellness programs in the workplace. *American Psychologist, 45*(2), 262–272.

Geier, J. G., & Downey, D. E. (1980). *Attitudinal Listening Profile System*. Minneapolis, MN: Performax Systems International.

Geier, J. G., Downey, D. E., & Johnson, J. B. (1980). *Climate impact profile*. Minneapolis, MN: Performax Systems International.

Gelbart, M. (2001, October 30). 425 hopefuls attend Philadelphia job fair for airline workers. *Philadelphia Inquirer*.

George, J. M. (1995). Asymmetrical effects of rewards and punishments: The case of social loafing. *Journal of Occupational and Organizational Psychology, 68*(4), 327–338.

Gere, D., Scarborough, E. K., & Collison, J. (2002). *SHRM/Recruit Marketplace 2002 recruiter budget/cost survey*.

Alexandria, VA: Society for Human Resource Management.

Gerstner, C. R., & Day, D. V. (1997). Meta-analytic review of leader-member exchange theory: Correlates and construct issues. *Journal of Applied Psychology, 82*(6), 827–844.

Ghiselli, E. E. (1966). *The validity of occupational tests.* New York: Wiley.

Gibbs, C. A. (1969). Leadership. In G. Lindzey & E. Aronson (Eds.), *Handbook of social psychology* (pp. 205–282). Reading, MA: Addison-Wesley.

Gibson, C. (1997). Creative solutions to worker shortage. *Blue Ridge Business Journal, 9*(9), 1–11.

Giffin, M. E. (1989). Personnel research on testing, selection, and performance appraisal. *Public Personnel Management, 18*, 127–137.

Gilchrist, J. A., & White, K. D. (1990). Policy development and satisfaction with merit pay: A field study in a university setting. *College Student Journal, 24*(3), 249–254.

Gillet, B., & Schwab, D. P. (1975). Convergent and discriminant validities of corresponding Job Descriptive Index and Minnesota Satisfaction Questionnaire scales. *Journal of Applied Psychology, 60*, 313–317.

Gilliland, S. W. (1993). The perceived fairness of selection systems: An organizational justice perspective. *Academy of Management Review, 18*, 694–734.

Gilliland, S. W., Groth, M., Baker, R. C., Dew, A. F., Polly, L. M., & Langdon, J. C. (2001). Improving applicants' reactions to rejection letters: An application of fairness theory. *Personnel Psychology, 54*(3), 669–703.

Gilliland, S. W., & Langdon, J. C. (1998). Creating performance management systems that promote perceptions of fairness. In J. W. Smither (Ed.), *Performance appraisal: State of the art in practice* (pp. 209–243). San Francisco: Jossey-Bass.

Gilliland, S. W., & Steiner, D. D. (1997). *Challenge #6: Interactional and procedural justice.* Paper presented at the 12th annual meeting of the Society for Industrial and Organizational Psychology, St. Louis, MO.

Gilmer, B. V. H., & Deci, E. L. (1977). *Industrial and organizational psychology.* New York: McGraw-Hill.

Gilmore, D. C. (1989). Applicant perceptions of simulated behavior description interviews. *Journal of Business and Psychology, 3*, 279–288.

Gilmore, D. C., Beehr, T. A., & Love, K. G. (1986). Effects of applicant sex, applicant physical attractiveness, type of rater and type of job on interview decisions. *Journal of Occupational Psychology, 59*, 103–109.

Gilmore, T. N., Shea, G. P., & Useem, M. (1997). Side effects of corporate cultural transformations. *Journal of Applied Behavioral Science, 33*(2), 174–189.

Glanz, B. A. (1997, March). Spread contagious enthusiasm. *IPMA News*, pp. 13–14.

Glickman, A. S., & Vallance, T. R. (1958). Curriculum assessment with critical incidents. *Journal of Applied Psychology, 42*, 329–335.

Glueck, W. F. (1973). Recruiters and executives: How do they affect job choice? *Journal of College Placement, 34*, 77–78.

Goldstein, C. H. (2000, July). Employee drug testing in the public sector. *IPMA News*, pp. 13–16.

Goldstein, I. L., & Ford, J. K. (2002). *Training in organizations* (4th ed.). Belmont, CA: Wadsworth.

Golen, S. (1990). A factor analysis of barriers to effective listening. *Journal of Business Communication, 27*, 25–36.

Golightly, C., Huffman, D., & Byrne, D. (1972). Liking and loaning. *Journal of Applied Psychology, 56*(6), 521–523.

Gomez-Mejia, L. R., Welbourne, T. M., & Wiseman, R. M. (2000). The role of risk sharing and risk taking under gainsharing. *Academy of Management Review, 25*(3), 492–507.

Gonder, M. L., & Walker, D. D. (2000). *Master's-level industrial/organizational psychologist survey results.* Paper presented at the annual meeting of the Society for Industrial-Organizational Psychology, New Orleans, LA.

Good, B. (1996). Downsizing disgraced. *BC Business, 24*(9), 93.

Goodale, J. G. (1992). *One to one: Interviewing, selecting, appraising, and counseling employees.* Englewood Cliffs, NJ: Prentice-Hall.

Goodson, J. R., McGee, G. W., & Cashman, J. F. (1989). Situational leadership theory: A test of leadership prescriptions. *Group and Organization Studies, 14*(4), 446–461.

Gordon, J. R. (1998). *Organizational behavior: A diagnostic approach* (6th ed.) Englewood Cliffs, NJ: Prentice-Hall.

Gordon, M. E., Slade, L. A., & Schmitt, H. (1986). The "science of the sophomore" revisited: From conjecture to empiricism. *Academy of Management Review, 11*, 191–207.

Gowen, C. R. (1990). Gainsharing programs: An overview of history and research. *Journal of Organizational Behavior Management, 11*(2), 77–99.

Graen, G., & Uhl-Bien, M. (1995). Relationship-based approach to leadership: Development of leader-member exchange (LMX) theory of leadership over 25 years: Applying a multi-level multi-domain perspective. *Leadership Quarterly, 6*, 219–247.

Graham, J. K., & Mihal, W. L. (1986). Can your management development needs surveys be trusted? *Training and Development Journal, 40*(3), 38–42.

Graham, J. P. (1991). Disgruntled employees—ticking time bombs? *Security Management*, 83–85.

Grandjean, E., Hunting, W., & Pidermann, M. (1983). VDT workstation design: Preferred settings and their effects. *Human Factors, 25*, 161–175.

Grant, K. A., & Habes, D. J. (1995). An analysis of scanning postures among grocery cashiers and its relationship to checkstand design. *Ergonomics, 38*(10), 2078–2090.

Gratias, M. B., & Hills, D. A. (1997). *Social loafing in individuals versus groups: Assessing quantity, quality, and creativity.* Poster presented at the 12th annual conference of the Society for Industrial and Organizational Psychology, St. Louis, MO.

Gray, P. M. (1997). How to become intranet savvy. *HR Magazine, 42*(12), 66–71.

Graydon, J., & Murphy, T. (1995). The effect of personality on social facilitation whilst performing a sports related task. *Personality and Individual Differences, 19*(2), 265–267.

Grazian, F. (1996). Frequently asked questions about readability. *Public Relations Quarterly, 41*(3), 19–20.

Green, S. B., Sauser, W. I., Fagg, F. N., & Champion, C. H. (1981). Shortcut methods for deriving behaviorally anchored rating scales. *Educational and Psychological Measurement, 41*, 761–775.

Green, S. B., & Stutzman, T. (1986). An evaluation of methods to select respondents to structured job-analysis questionnaires. *Personnel Psychology, 39*, 543–564.

Greenberg, E. R. (1996). Drug-testing now standard practice. *HR Focus, 73*(9), 24.

Greenberg, J., & Baron, R. A. (1999). *Behavior in organizations* (6th ed.). Englewood Cliffs, NJ: Prentice-Hall.

Greenhaus, J. H., & Badin, I. J. (1974). Self-esteem, performance, and satisfaction: Some tests of a theory. *Journal of Applied Psychology, 59*, 722–726.

Greenwood, K. M. (1994). Long-term stability and psychometric properties of the composite scale of morningness. *Ergonomics, 37*(2), 377–383.

Greer, D. L. (1983). Spectator booing and the home advantage: A study of social influence in the basketball arena. *Social Psychology Quarterly, 46*, 252–261.

Grensing-Pophal, L. (2001a). *HR and the corporate intranet: Beyond brochureware.* Alexandria, VA: Society for Human Resource Management.

Grensing-Pophal, L. (2001b). Motivate managers to review performance. *HR Magazine, 46*(3), 45–48.

Griffeth, R. W., Hom, P. W., & Gaertner, S. (2000). A meta-analysis of antecedents and correlates of employee turnover: Update, moderator tests, and research implications for the next millennium. *Journal of Management, 26*(3), 463–488.

Griffiths, R. F., & McDaniel, Q. P. (1993). Predictors of police assaults. *Journal of Police and Criminal Psychology, 9*(1), 5–9.

Grossman, R. J. (2000). Make ergonomics. *HR Magazine, 45*(4), 36–42.

Grossman, R. J. (2001). Home is where the school is. *HR Magazine, 46*(11), 58–65.

Grossman, R. J. (2002a). Bulletproof practices. *HR Magazine, 47*(11), 34–42.

Grossman, R. J. (2002b). Offices vs. open space. *HR Magazine, 47*(9), 36–40.

Grossman, R. J. (2002c). Space: Another HR frontier. *HR Magazine, 47*(9), 28–34.

Grote, C. L., Robiner, W. N., & Haut, A. (2001), Disclosure of information in letters of recommendation: Writers' intentions and readers' experiences. *Professional Psychology: Research and Practice, 32*(6), 655–661.

Grote, D. (1998). Painless performance appraisals focus on results. *HR Magazine, 43*(11), 52–58.

Gruner, S. (1997). Help! I can't find local people with the specialized skills I need. *Inc., 19*(5), 95.

Gruner, S., & Caggiano, C. (1997). How can we make training programs more effective? *Inc., 19*(5), 94.

Guion, R. M., & Gibson, W. M. (1988). Personnel selection and placement. *Annual Review of Psychology, 39*, 349–374.

Gully, S. M., Devine, D. J., & Whitney, D. J. (1995). A meta-analysis of cohesion and performance: Effects of level of analysis and task interdependence. *Small Group Research, 26*(4), 497–520.

Gully, S. M., Incalcaterra, K. A., Joshi, A., & Beaubien, J. M. (2002). A meta-analysis of team-efficacy, potency, and performance: Interdependence and level of analysis as moderators of observed relationships. *Journal of Applied Psychology, 87*(5), 819–832.

Gumpert, R. A., & Hambleton, R. K. (1979). Situational leadership: How Xerox managers fine-tune managerial styles to employee maturity and task needs. *Management Review,12*, 9.

Gunnarson, E., & Ostberg, O. (1977). *Physical and psychological working environment in a terminal-based data system* [Research Rep. No. 35]. Stockholm: National Board of Occupational Safety and Health.

Gunning, R. (1964). *How to take the FOG out of writing.* Chicago: Dartnell Corp.

Guppy, A., & Rick, J. (1996). The influences of gender and grade on perceived work stress and job satisfaction in white collar employees. *Work and Stress, 10*(2), 154–164.

Gupta, V., Hanges, P. J., & Dorfman, P. (2002). Cultural clusters: Methodology and findings. *Journal of World Business, 37*, 11–15.

Gutman, A. (2000). *EEO law and personnel practices* (2nd ed.) Thousand Oaks, CA: Sage.

Gutman, A. (2002). Affirmative action: What's going on? *The Industrial-Organizational Psychologist, 40*(2), 59–68.

Gutman, A., & Christiansen, N. (1997). Further clarification of the judicial status of banding. *The Industrial-Organizational Psychologist, 35*(1), 75–81.

Guzzo, R. A., Jette, R. D., & Katzell, R. A. (1985). The effects of psychologically based intervention programs on worker productivity: A meta-analysis. *Personnel Psychology, 38*, 275–291.

Habeeb, K., & Prencipe, L. W. (2001, February 5). Avoiding workplace violence. *InfoWorld*, p. 63.

Hackett, R. D. (1989). Work attitudes and employee absenteeism: A synthesis of the literature. *Journal of Occupational Psychology, 62*(3), 235–248.

Hackett, R. D., & Bycio, P. (1996). An evaluation of employee absenteeism as a coping mechanism among hospital nurses. *Journal of Occupational and Organizational Psychology, 69*(4), 327–338.

Hackman, J. R., & Oldham, G. R. (1975). Development of the job diagnostic survey. *Journal of Applied Psychology, 60*, 159–170.

Hackman, J. R., & Oldham, G. R. (1976). Motivation through the design of work: Test of a theory. *Organizational Behavior and Human Performance, 16*, 250–279.

Hackman, R., & Vidmar, N. (1970). Effects of size and task type on group performance and member reactions. *Sociometry, 33*, 37–54.

Hall, D. T., & Nougaim, K. E. (1968). An examination of Maslow's need hierarchy in an organizational setting. *Organizational Behavior and Human Performance, 3*, 12–35.

Hall, E. T. A. (1963). A system for the notation of promemic behavior. *American Anthropologist, 65*, 1003–1026.

Hamilton, D. (2001, May 25). Avoid the three common traps of training programs. *Orlando Business Journal, 17*(53), 43.

Hammer, T. H., & Dachler, H. P. (1975). A test of some assumptions underlying the path goal model of supervision: Some suggested conceptual modifications. *Organizational Behavior and Human Performance, 14*, 60–75.

Hampton, D. R., Summer, C. E., & Webber, R. A. (1978). *Organizational behavior and the practice of management.* Glenview, IL: Scott, Foresman.

Hanlon, S. C., & Taylor, R. R. (1992). How does gainsharing work? Some preliminary answers following application in a service organization. *Applied H.R.M. Research, 3*(2), 73–91.

Harder, J. W. (1992). Play for pay: Effects of inequity in a pay-for-performance context. *Administrative Science Quarterly, 37,* 321–335.

Hardy, C. J., & Crace, R. K. (1991). The effects of task structure and teammate competence on social loafing. *Journal of Sport and Exercise Psychology, 13*(4), 372–381.

Harma, M. (1993). Individual differences in tolerance to shiftwork: A review. *Ergonomics, 36*(1), 101–109.

Harrell, T. W. (1972). *Industrial psychology.* New York: Rinehart.

Harriman, T. S., & Kovach, R. (1987). The effects of job familiarity on the recall of performance information. *Proceedings of the 8th Annual Graduate Conference in Industrial/Organizational Psychology and Organizational Behavior,* pp. 49–50.

Harris, D. (1993). Big business takes on child care. *Working Woman, 6,* 50–56.

Harrison, D. A., & Shaffer, M. A. (1994). Comparative examinations of self-reports and perceived absenteeism norms: Wading through Lake Wobegon. *Journal of Applied Psychology, 79*(2), 240–256.

Harvey, R. J., Friedman, L., Hakel, M. D., & Cornelius, E. T. (1988). Dimensionality of the Job Element Inventory, a simplified worker-oriented job analysis questionnaire. *Journal of Applied Psychology, 73,* 639–646.

Hatcher, L., Ross, T. L., & Ross, R. A. (1987). Gainsharing: Living up to its name. *Personnel Administrator, 32*(6), 154–164.

Hattie, J., & Cooksey, R. W. (1984). Procedures for assessing the validities of tests using the "known-groups" method. *Applied Psychological Measurement, 8,* 295–305.

Hauenstein, N. M. A. (1986). *A process approach to ratings: The effects of ability and level of processing on encoding, retrieval, and rating outcomes.* Unpublished doctoral dissertation, University of Akron, Akron, OH.

Hauenstein, N. M. A. (1998). Training raters to increase the accuracy of appraisals and the usefulness of feedback. In J. W. Smither (Ed.), *Performance appraisal: State of the art in practice* (pp. 404–442). San Francisco: Jossey-Bass.

Hauenstein, N. M. A., & Foti, R. J. (1989). From laboratory to practice: Neglected issues in implementing frame-of-reference rater training. *Personnel Psychology, 42,* 359–378.

Hauenstein, N. M. A., & Lord, R. G. (1989). The effects of final-offer arbitration on the performance of major league baseball players: A test of equity theory. *Human Performance, 2*(3), 147–165.

Hazer, J. T., & Highhouse, S. (1997). Factors influencing managers' reactions to utility analysis: Effects of SDy method, information frame, and focal intervention. *Journal of Applied Psychology, 82*(1), 104–112.

Heaney, C. A., & Clemans, J. (1995). Occupational stress, physician-excused absences, and absences not excused by a physician. *American Journal of Health Promotion, 10*(2), 117–124.

Heath, C. (1996). Do people prefer to pass along good or bad news? Valence and relevance of news as predictors of transmission propensity. *Organizational Behavior and Human Decision Processes, 68*(2), 79–94.

Hecht, M. A., & LaFrance, M. (1995). How (fast) can I help you? Tone of voice and telephone operator efficiency in interactions. *Journal of Applied Social Psychology, 25*(23), 2086–2098.

Heerwagen, J. H., & Orians, G. H. (1986). Adaptations to windowlessness: A study of the use of visual decor in windowed and windowless offices. *Environment & Behavior, 18,* 604–622.

Heilbroner, D. (1993). The handling of an epidemic. *Working Woman, 2,* 60–65.

Heilman, M. E. (1974). Threats and promises: Reputational consequences and transfer of credibility. *Journal of Experimental Social Psychology, 10,* 310–324.

Heilman, M. E., & Alcott, V. B. (2001). What I think of me: Women's reactions to being viewed as beneficiaries of preferential selection. *Journal of Applied Psychology, 86*(4), 574–582.

Heilman, M. E., Block, C. J., & Lucas, J. A. (1992). Presumed incompetent? Stigmatization and affirmative action efforts. *Journal of Applied Psychology, 77*(4), 536–544.

Heilman, M. E., Block, C. J., & Stathatos, P. (1997). The affirmative action stigma of incompetence: Effects of performance information ambiguity. *Academy of Management Journal, 40*(3), 603–625.

Heilman, M. E., Kaplow, S. R., Amato, M. G., & Stathatos, P. (1993). When similarity is a liability: Effects of sex-based preferential selection on reactions to like-sex and different-sex others. *Journal of Applied Psychology, 78*(6), 917–927.

Heilman, M. E., Lucas, J. A., & Kaplow, S. R. (1990). Self-derogating consequences of preferential selection: The moderating role of initial self-confidence. *Organizational Behavior and Human Decision Processes, 46,* 202–216.

Heilman, M. E., & Saruwaturi, L. R. (1979). When beauty is beastly: The effect of appearance and sex on evaluations of job applicants for managerial and nonmanagerial jobs. *Organizational Behavior and Human Performance, 23,* 360–372.

Heller, M. (2001). A return to at-will employment. *Workforce, 80*(5), 42.

Hemphill, J. K., & Coons, A. E. (1950). *Leader behavior description.* Columbus: Personnel Research Board, Ohio State University.

Henderson, R. I. (2003). *Compensation management in a knowledge-based world* (9th ed.). Englewood Cliffs, NJ: Prentice-Hall.

Henkoff, R. (1990, June 17). Cost cutting: How to do it right. *Fortune,* p. 73.

Hequet, M. (1994). Giving good feedback. *Training, 31*(9), 72–77.

Herbert, G. P., & Doverspike, D. (1990). Performance appraisal in the training needs analysis process: A review and critique. *Public Personnel Management, 19*(3), 253–270.

Hersey, P., & Blanchard, K. H. (1988). *Management of organizational behavior* (5th ed.). Englewood Cliffs, NJ: Prentice-Hall.

Herzberg, F. (1966). *Work and the nature of man.* Cleveland: World.

Hilgert, R. L. (1991). Employees protected by at-will statements. *HR Magazine, 36*(3), 57–59.

Hills, F. S., Scott, K. D., Markham, S. E., & Vest, M. J. (1987). Merit pay: Just or unjust desserts. *Personnel Administrator, 32*(9), 53–59.

Hinrichs, J. R., & Mischkind, L. A. (1967). Empirical and theoretical limitations of the two-factor hypothesis of job satisfaction. *Journal of Applied Psychology, 51,* 191–200.

Hirschman, C. (2000). Do you need a moonlighting policy? *HR Magazine, 45*(10), 46–54.

Hirschman, C. (2001). Order in the hearing! *HR Magazine, 46*(7), 58–64.

Hirschman, C. (2003). Someone to listen. *HR Magazine, 48*(1), 47–51.

Hockey, G. R. (1970). Signal probability and spatial locations as possible bases for increased selectivity in noise. *Quarterly Journal of Experimental Psychology, 22,* 37–42.

Hoff Macan, T., Avedon, M., & Paese, M. (1994). *The effects of applicants' reactions to cognitive ability tests and an assessment center.* Paper presented at the ninth annual conference of the Society for Industrial and Organizational Psychology, Nashville, TN.

Hoffman, C. C., & Thornton, G. C. (1997). Examining selection utility where competing predictors differ in adverse impact. *Personnel Psychology, 50*(2), 455–470.

Hoffman, T. (2001, June 4). Intranet helps workers navigate corporate maze. *Computerworld,* p. 34.

Hogan, J., & Quigley, A. (1994). Effects of preparing for physical ability tests. *Public Personnel Management, 23*(1), 85–104.

Hogan, J. B. (1994). Empirical keying of background data measures. In G. S. Stokes, M. D. Mumford, & W. A. Owens, (Eds.), *Biodata handbook* (pp. 69–107). Palo Alto, CA: CPP Books.

Hogan, R. (1989, June). *The darker side of charisma.* Paper presented at 13th annual meeting of International Personnel Management Association Assessment Council, Orlando, FL.

Holden, M. (1998). *Positive politics: Overcome office politics and fast-track your career.* Warriewood, Australia: Business & Professional Publishing.

Hollmann, T. D. (1972). Employment interviewers' errors in processing positive and negative information. *Journal of Applied Psychology, 56,* 130–134.

Holstein, B. B. (1997). *The enchanted self.* Amsterdam: Harwood.

Holtom, B. C., Lee, T. W., & Tidd, S. T. (2002). The relationship between work status congruence and work-related attitudes and behaviors. *Journal of Applied Psychology, 87*(5), 903–915.

Hood, D. (2001). *A meta-analysis of the reliability levels for selection tests used in industry.* Paper presented at the 22nd annual Graduate Conference in Industrial-Organizational Psychology and Organizational Behavior, Pennsylvania State University, State College, PA.

Hoover, L. T. (1992). Trends in police physical ability selection testing. *Public Personnel Management, 21*(1), 29–40.

House, R. J. (1971). A path-goal theory of leader effectiveness. *Administrative Science Quarterly, 9,* 321–332.

House, R. J., Javidan, M., Hanges, P., & Dorfman, P. (2002). Understanding cultures and implicit leadership theories across the globe: An introduction to Project GLOBE. *Journal of World Business, 37,* 3–10.

House, R. J., & Mitchell, T. R. (1974, Autumn). Path-goal theory of leadership. *Journal of Contemporary Business, 3,* 81–98.

Howard, J. L., & Ferris, G. R. (1996). The employment interview context: Social and situational influences on interviewer decisions. *Journal of Applied Social Psychology, 26*(2), 112–136.

Howell, J. M., & Avolio, B. J. (1993). Transformational leadership, transactional leadership, locus of control, and support of innovation: Key predictors of consolidated-business-unit performance. *Journal of Applied Psychology, 78*(6), 891–902.

Huegli, J. M., & Tschirgia, H. D. (1975). Monitoring the employment interview. *Journal of College Placement, 39,* 37–39.

Huffcutt, A. I., & Arthur, W. (1994). Hunter and Hunter (1984) revisited: Interview validity for entry-level jobs. *Journal of Applied Psychology, 79*(2), 184–190.

Huffcutt, A. I., Conway, J. M., Roth, P. L., & Stone, N. J. (2001). Identification and meta-analytic assessment of psychological constructs measured in employment interviews. *Journal of Applied Psychology, 86*(5), 897–913.

Huffcutt, A. I., & Roth, P. L. (1998). Racial group differences in employment interview evaluations. *Journal of Applied Psychology, 83*(2), 179–189.

Huffcutt, A. I., Roth, P. L., Conway, J. M., & Klehe, U. C. (2003). *Moderators of situational and behavior description interview validity.* Poster presented at the 18th annual meeting of the Society for Industrial Organizational Psychology, Orlando, FL.

Huffcutt, A. I., Weekley, J. A., Wiesner, W. H., DeGroot, T. G., & Jones, C. (2001). Comparison of situational and behavioral description interview questions for higher-level positions. *Personnel Psychology, 54*(3), 619–644.

Huffcutt, A. I., & Woehr, D. J. (1999). Further analyses of employment interview validity: A quantitative evaluation of interviewer-related structuring methods. *Journal of Organizational Behavior, 20*(4), 549–560.

Hughes, J. F., Dunn, J. F., & Baxter, B. (1956). The validity of selection instruments under operating conditions. *Personnel Psychology, 9,* 321–324.

Huish, G. B. (1997, August). Piece-rate play plan in clerk's office motivates quantum leap in quality productivity. *IPMA News,* pp. 22–27.

Hultman, K. E. (1986). Behavior modeling for results. *Training and Development Journal, 40*(12), 60–63.

Hunt, A. (2001, November 13). Central Florida resort's job fair ends on positive note for 11,000th applicant. *Orlando Sentinel.*

Hunt, J. W., & Laing, B. (1997). Leadership: The role of the exemplar. *Business Strategy Review, 8*(1), 31–42.

Hunter, J. E., & Hunter, R. F. (1984). Validity and utility of alternative predictors of job performance. *Psychological Bulletin, 96*(1), 72–98.

Hunter, J. E., & Schmidt, F. L. (1982). Fitting people to jobs: The impact of personnel selection on national productivity. In M. D. Dunnette & E. D. Fleishman (Eds.), *Human performance and productivity: Vol. 1 Human capacity assessment* (pp. 233–284). Hillsdale, NJ: Lawrence Erlbaum.

Hurst, J. (2000, July). Virtual training. *Scientific Computing & Instrumentation, 17*(8), 12.

Hurtz, G. M., & Donovan, J. J. (2000). Personality and job performance: The big five revisited. *Journal of Applied Psychology, 85*(6), 869–879.

Hutchison, S., Valentino, K. E., & Kirkner, S. L. (1998). What works for the gander does not work as well for the goose: The effects of leader behavior. *Journal of Applied Social Psychology, 28*(2), 171–182.

Hyatt, D. E., & Ruddy, T. M. (1997). An examination of the relationship between work group characteristics and performance: Once more into the breach. *Personnel Psychology, 50*(3), 533–585.

Iaffaldano, M. T., & Muchinsky, P. M. (1985). Job satisfaction and job performance: A meta-analysis. *Psychological Bulletin, 97*, 251–273.

Ilardi, B. C., Leone, D., Kasser, T., & Ryan, R. M. (1993). Employee and supervisor ratings of motivation: Main effects and discrepancies associated with job satisfaction and adjustment in a factory setting. *Journal of Applied Social Psychology, 23*(21), 1789–1805.

Ilgen, D. R., & Bell, B. S. (2001a). Conducting industrial and organizational psychology research: Review of research in work organizations. *Ethics and Behavior, 11*, 395–412.

Ilgen, D. R., & Bell, B. S. (2001b). Informed consent and dual purpose research. *American Psychologist, 56*(12), 1177.

Ilgen, D. R., Mitchell, T. R., & Fredrickson, J. W. (1981). Poor performers: Supervisors' and subordinates' responses. *Organizational Behavior and Human Performance, 27*, 386–410.

Ilgen, D. R., Nebeker, D. M., & Pritchard, R. D. (1981). Expectancy theory measures: An empirical comparison in an experimental simulation. *Organizational Behavior and Human Performance, 28*, 189–223.

Imrhan, S. N., Imrhan, V., & Hart, C. (1996). Can self-estimates of body weight and height be used in place of measurements for college students? *Ergonomics, 39*(12), 1445–1453.

Indik, B. P. (1965). Organization size and member participation: Some empirical tests of alternate explanations. *Human Relations, 15*, 339–350.

Inguagiato, R. J. (1993). Case studies: Let's get real. *Training and Development, 47*(10), 20–24.

Inman, M. L., Reichl, A. J., & Baron, R. S. (1993). Do we tell less than we know or hear less than we are told? Exploring the teller–listener extremity effect. *Journal of Experimental Social Psychology, 29*, 528–550.

Ironson, G. H., Smith, P. C., Brannick, M. T., Gibson, W. M., & Paul, K. B. (1989). Construction of a Job in General Scale: A comparison of global, composite, and specific measures. *Journal of Applied Psychology, 74*, 193–200.

Irving, P. G., & Meyer, J. P. (1994). Reexamination of the met-expectations hypothesis: A longitudinal analysis. *Journal of Applied Psychology, 79*(6), 937–949.

Ivancevich, J. M. (1982). Subordinates' reactions to performance appraisal interviews: A test of feedback and goal-setting techniques. *Journal of Applied Psychology, 67*, 581–587.

Jaccard, J. (1981). Toward theories of persuasion and belief change. Journal of Personality and Social Psychology, 40, 260–269.

Jackson, D. E., O'Dell, J. W., & Olson, D. (1982). Acceptance of bogus personality interpretations: Face validity reconsidered. *Journal of Clinical Psychology, 38*, 588–592.

Jackson, J. M. (1986). In search of social impact theory: Comment on Mullen. *Journal of Personality and Social Psychology, 50*, 511–513.

Jackson, S. E., Brett, J. F., Sessa, V. T., Cooper, D. M., Julin, J. A., & Peyronnin, K. (1991). Some differences make a difference: Individual dissimilarity and group homogeneity as correlates of recruitment, promotions, and turnover. *Journal of Applied Psychology, 76*(5), 675–689.

Jacobs, J. A., & Kearns, C. N. (2001). Responding effectively to a claim of sexual harassment in the workplace. *Association Management, 53*(11), 19–20.

Jacobs, R. (1997). *Organizational effectiveness: Downsizing, one of many alternatives*. Keynote address presented at the 18th annual Graduate Student Conference in Industrial Organizational Psychology and Organizational Behavior, Roanoke, VA.

Jacobs, R., Kafry, D., & Zedeck, S. (1980). Expectations of behaviorally anchored rating scales. *Personnel Psychology, 33*, 595–640.

Jago, A. G., & Vroom, V. H. (1977). Hierarchical level and leadership style. *Organizational Behavior and Human Performance, 18*, 131–145.

Jamal, M. (1981). Shift work related to job attitudes, social participation, and withdrawal behavior: A study of nurses and industrial workers. *Personnel Psychology, 34*, 535–547.

Jamal, M., & Crawford, R. L. (1984). Consequences of extended work hours: A comparison of moonlighters, overtimers, and modal employees. *Human Resource Management, 4*, 18–23.

Jamal, M., & Jamal, S. M. (1982). Work and nonwork experiences of employees on fixed and rotating shifts: An empirical assessment. *Journal of Vocational Behavior, 20*, 282–293.

Janis, I. L. (1972). *Victims of groupthink*. New York: Houghton Mifflin.

Janove, J. W. (2001). Soothing the EEOC dragon. *HR Magazine, 46*(5), 137–153.

Jansen, A. (1973). *Validation of graphological judgments: An experimental study*. The Hague, Netherlands: Mouton.

Janz, T., Hellervik, L., & Gilmore, D. C. (1986). *Behavior description interviewing*. Boston: Allyn & Bacon.

Jawahar, I. M., & Williams, C. R. (1997). Where all the children are above average: The performance appraisal purpose effect. *Personnel Psychology, 50*(4), 905–925.

Jehn, K. A., & Mannix, E. A. (2001). The dynamic nature of conflict: A longitudinal study of intragroup conflict and group performance. *Academy of Management Journal, 44*(2), 238–251.

Jenner, L. (1994). Employment-at-will liability: How protected are you? *HR Focus, 71*(3), 11.

Jex, S. M., & Elacqua, T. C. (1999). Time management as a moderator of relations between stressors and employee strain. *Work & Stress, 13*(2), 182–191.

Johns, G. (1994). Absenteeism estimates by employees and managers: Divergent perspectives and self-serving perceptions. *Journal of Applied Psychology, 79*(2), 229–239.

Johnson, D. L., & Andrews, I. R. (1971). The risky-shift hypothesis tested with consumer products as stimuli. *Journal of Personality and Social Psychology, 30*, 382–385.

Johnson, K. (1997, August 4). New prisons isolate worst inmates. *USA Today*, pp. A1–A2.

Johnson, T. L. (1990). A meta-analytic review of absenteeism control methods. *Applied H.R.M. Research, 1*(1), 23–26.

Joiner, D. (2000). Guidelines and ethical considerations for assessment center operations: International task force on assessment center guidelines. *Public Personnel Management, 29*(3), 315–331.

Joiner, D. (2002). Assessment centers: What's new? *Public Personnel Management, 31*(2), 179–185.

Joinson, C. (1997). Multiple career paths help retain talent. *HR Magazine, 42*(10), 59–64.

Joinson, C. (1998). Turn up the radio recruiting. *HR Magazine, 43*(10), 64–70.

Joinson, C. (1999). Teams at work. *HR Magazine, 44*(5), 30–36.

Joinson, C. (2001a). Employee, sculpt thyself . . . with a little help. *HR Magazine, 46*(5), 60–64.

Joinson, C. (2001b). Making sure employees measure up. *HR Magazine, 46*(3), 36–41.

Joinson, C. (2002). Managing virtual teams. *HR Magazine, 47*(6), 69–73.

Jones, A. P., Main, D. S., Butler, M. C., & Johnson, L. A. (1982). Narrative job descriptions as potential sources of job analysis ratings. *Personnel Psychology, 35*, 813–828.

Jones, J. W., & Terris, W. (1989). After the polygraph ban. *Recruitment Today, 2*(2), 24–31.

Jones, M. (2001, September 28). Wisconsin prison hosts first job fair. *Milwaukee Journal Sentinel*, p. B1.

Jordan, K. (1997). Play fair and square when hiring from within. *HR Magazine, 42*(1), 49–51.

Jossi, F. (2001a). Take the road less traveled. *HR Magazine, 46*(7), 46–51.

Jossi, F. (2001b). Teamwork aids HRIS decision process. *HR Magazine, 46*(6), 165–173.

Judge, T. A. (1993). Does affective disposition moderate the relationship between job satisfaction and voluntary turnover? *Journal of Applied Psychology, 78*(3), 395–401.

Judge, T. A., & Bono, J. E. (2000). Five-factor model of personality and transformational leadership. *Journal of Applied Psychology, 85*(5), 751–765.

Judge, T. A., & Bono, J. E. (2001). Relationship of core self-evaluations traits—self-esteem, generalized self-efficacy, locus of control, and emotional stability—with job satisfaction and job performance: A meta-analysis. *Journal of Applied Psychology, 86*(1), 80–92.

Judge, T. A., Bono, J. E., Ilies, R., & Gerhardt, M. W. (2002). Personality and leadership: A qualitative and quantitative review. *Journal of Applied Psychology, 87*(4), 765–780.

Judge, T. A., Heller, D., & Mount, M. K. (2002). Five-factor model of personality and job satisfaction: A meta-analysis. *Journal of Applied Psychology, 87*(3), 530–541.

Judge, T. A., & Ilies, R. (2002). Relationship of personality to performance motivation: A meta-analytic review. *Journal of Applied Psychology, 87*(4), 797–807.

Judge, T. A., Locke, E. A., & Durham, C. C. (1997). The dispositional causes of job satisfaction: A core evaluations approach. *Research in Organizational Behavior, 19*(1), 151–188.

Judge, T. A., Locke, E. A., Durham, C. C., & Kluger, A. N. (1998). Dispositional effects on job and life satisfaction: The role of core evaluations. *Journal of Applied Psychology, 83*(1), 17–34.

Judge, T. A., Martocchio, J. J., & Thoresen, C. J. (1997). Five-factor model of personality and employee absence. *Journal of Applied Psychology, 82*(5), 745–755.

Judge, T. A., Thoresen, C. J., Bono, J. E., & Patton, G. K. (2001). The job satisfaction-job performance relationship: A qualitative and quantitative review. *Psychological Bulletin, 127*(3), 376–407.

Judge, T. A., & Watanabe, S. (1993). Another look at the job satisfaction–life satisfaction relationship. *Journal of Applied Psychology, 78*(6), 939–948.

Judge, T. A., & Watanabe, S. (1994). Individual differences in the nature of the relationship between job and life satisfaction. *Journal of Occupational and Organizational Psychology, 67*, 101–107.

Juergens, J. (2000). Read all about it. *HR Magazine, 45*(10), 142–150.

Juergens, J. (2001). Monitoring the survivors. *HR Magazine, 46*(7), 92–99.

Kaliterna, L., Vidacek, S., Prizmic, Z., & Radosevic-Vidacek, B. (1995). Is tolerance to shiftwork predictable from individual difference measures? *Work and Stress, 9*, 140–147.

Kalk, J. E. (2000, September). What every employer should know about the Family and Medical Leave Act, *IPMA News*, pp. 7–8.

Kaman, V. S., & Bentson, C. (1988). Role play simulations for employee selection: Design and implementation. *Public Personnel Management, 17*, 1–8.

Kane, J. S., & Lawler, E. E. (1979). Performance appraisal effectiveness: Its assessment and determinants. In B. M. Staw (Ed.), *Research in organizational behavior* (Vol. 1; pp. 425–478). Greenwich, CT: JAI.

Kanekar, S. (1987). Individual versus group performance: A selective review of experimental studies. *Irish Journal of Psychology, 8*(1), 9–19.

Kaplan, A. B., Aamodt, M. A., & Wilk, D. (1991). The relationship between advertising variables and applicant responses to newspaper recruitment advertisements. *Journal of Business and Psychology, 5*(3), 383–395.

Kaplan, I. T. (2002, April). *Effects of group size and problem difficulty on decision accuracy.* Paper presented at the 17th annual meeting of the Society for Industrial and Organizational Psychology, Toronto, Canada.

Kaplan, R. M., & Saccuzzo, D. P. (2001). *Psychological testing* (5th ed.). Belmont, CA: Wadsworth.

Karaian, J. (2002, December). Sick of it. *CFO Europe* [Online]. Available: www.cfoeurope.com/200212i.html

Karasek, R., & Theorell, T. (1990). *Healthy work: Stress, productivity and the reconstruction of working life.* New York: Basic Books.

Karl, K. A., & Hancock, B. W. (1999). Expert advice on employment termination practices: How expert is it? *Public Personnel Management, 28*(1), 51–62.

Kassel, J. D., Stroud, L. R., & Paronis, C. A. (2003). Smoking, stress, and negative affect: Correlation, causation, and contest across stages of smoking. *Psychological Bulletin, 129*(2), 270–304.

Katkowski, D. A., & Medsker, G. J. (2001). SIOP income and employment: Income and employment of SIOP members in 2000. *The Industrial-Organizational Psychologist, 39*(1), 21–36.

Katzell, R. A., & Dyer, F. J. (1977). Differential validity revived. *Journal of Applied Psychology, 62*, 137–145.

Kearns, P. (2001). Establish a baseline. *Training, 38*(6), 80.

Keeping, L. M., & Sulsky, L. M. (1996). *Examining the quality of self-ratings of performance.* Poster presented at the 11th annual meeting of the Society for Industrial and Organizational Psychology, San Diego, CA.

Keinan, G. A., & Barak, A. (1984). Reliability and validity of graphological assessment in the selection process of military officers. *Perceptual and Motor Skills, 58*, 811–821.

Keller, L. M., Bouchard, T. J., Arvey, R. D., Segal, N. L., & Dawis, R. V. (1992). Work values: Genetic and environmental influences. *Journal of Applied Psychology, 77*(1), 79–88.

Keller, R. T. (2001). Cross-functional project groups in research and product development: Diversity, communications, job stress, and outcomes. *Academy of Management Journal, 44*(3), 547–555.

Kelly, C. M. (1984). Reasonable performance appraisals. *Training and Development Journal, 38*(1), 79–82.

Kennedy, J. K., Houston, J. M., Korsgaard, M. A., & Gallo, D. D. (1987). Construct space of the Least Preferred Coworker (LPC) Scale. *Educational and Psychological Measurement, 47*(3), 807–814.

Kenny, D. A., & Zaccaro, S. J. (1983). An estimate of variance due to traits in leadership. *Journal of Applied Psychology, 68,* 678–685.

Kernan, M. C., & Hanges, P. J. (2002). Survivor reactions to reorganization: Antecedents and consequences of procedural, interpersonal, and informational justice. *Journal of Applied Psychology, 87*(5), 916–928.

Kerr, N. L. (1983). Motivation loss in small groups: A social dilemma analysis. *Journal of Personality and Social Psychology, 45,* 819–828.

Kerr, N. L., & Bruun, S. E. (1983). Dependability of member effort and group motivation loss: Free-rider effects. *Journal of Personality and Social Psychology, 44,* 78–94.

Kidwell, R. E., Mossholder, K. W., & Bennett, N. (1997). Cohesiveness and organizational citizenship behavior: A multilevel analysis using work groups and individuals. *Journal of Management, 23*(6), 775–793.

Kierein, N., & Gold, M. A. (2001). Pygmalion in work organizations: A meta-analysis. *Journal of Organizational Behavior, 21,* 913–928.

King, N. (1970). Clarification and evaluation of the two-factor theory of job satisfaction. *Psychological Bulletin, 74,* 18–31.

King, P. (1984). *Performance planning and appraisal.* New York: McGraw-Hill.

Kingstrom, P. O., & Bass, A. R. (1981). A critical analysis of studies comparing behaviorally anchored rating scales (BARS) and other rating formats. *Personnel Psychology, 34,* 263–289.

Kipnis, D., Schmidt, S., & Wilkinson, I. (1980). Intraorganizational influence tactics: Exploration in getting one's way. *Journal of Applied Psychology, 65,* 440–452.

Kirkman, B. L., Rosen, B., Gibson, C. B., Tesluk, P. E., & McPherson, S. O. (2002). Five challenges to virtual team success: Lessons from Sabre, Inc. *Academy of Management Executive, 16*(3), 67–79.

Kirkman, B. L., & Shapiro, D. L. (2001). The impact of cultural values on job satisfaction and organizational commitment in self-managing work teams: The mediating role of employee resistance. *Academy of Management Journal, 44*(3), 557–569.

Kirkpatrick, D. L. (1986). Performance appraisal: When two jobs are too many. *Training, 23*(3), 65–68.

Kirkpatrick, D. L. (2000). Evaluating training programs: The four levels. In G. M. Piskurich, P. Beckschi, & B. Hall (Eds.), *The ASTD handbook of training design and delivery* (pp. 133–146). New York: McGraw-Hill.

Kistner, T., & Zbar, J. (2003, February 17). Telework in corporate America: Wonder what the other guys are doing? Take a peek inside 10 firms' remote work programs. *Network World,* p. 31.

Kittleson, M. J. (1995). An assessment of the response rate via the postal service and email. *Health Values: The Journal of Health, Behavior, Education and Promotion, 19*(2), 27–39.

Kjellberg, A., Landstrom, U., Tesarz, M., & Soderberg, L. (1996). The effects of nonphysical noise characteristics, ongoing task and noise sensitivity on annoyance and distraction due to noise at work. *Journal of Environmental Psychology, 16*(2), 123–136.

Klawsky, J. D. (1990). The effect of subgoals on commitment and task performance. *Proceedings of the 11th Annual Graduate Conference in Industrial/Organizational Psychology and Organizational Behavior.*

Kleiman, L. S., & White, C. S. (1991). Reference checking: A field survey of SHRM professionals. *Applied H.R.M. Research, 2*(2), 84–95.

Klein, H. J., Wesson, M. J., Hollenbeck, J. R., & Alge, B. J. (1999). Goal commitment and the goal-setting process: Conceptual clarification and empirical synthesis. *Journal of Applied Psychology, 84*(6), 885–896.

Klein, J. D., & Pridemore, D. R. (1992). Effects of cooperative learning and need for affiliation on performance, time on task, and satisfaction. *Educational Technology Research and Development, 40*(4), 39–47.

Klimoski, R. J., & Rafaeli, A. (1983). Inferring personal qualities through handwriting analysis. *Journal of Occupational Psychology, 56,* 191–202.

Klimoski, R. J., & Strickland, W. J. (1977). Assessment centers—validity or merely prescient? *Personal Psychology, 30,* 353–361.

Kline, T. J. B. (1997). Defining the field of industrial-organizational psychology. *Canadian Psychology, 37*(4), 205–209.

Kluger, A. N., & Colella, A. (1993). Beyond the mean bias: The effect of warning against faking on biodata item variances. *Personnel Psychology, 46,* 763–780.

Knapp, M. L. (1978). *Nonverbal communication in human interaction.* New York: Holt, Rinehart & Winston.

Knauth, P. (1996). Designing better shift systems. *Applied Ergonomics, 27*(1), 39–44.

Knauth, P., Keller, J., Schindele, G., & Totterdell, P. (1995). A 14-hour night-shift in the control room of a fire brigade. *Work and Stress, 9,* 176–186.

Knauth, P., & Kiesswetter, E. (1987). A change from weekly to quicker shift rotations: A field study of discontinuous three-shift workers. *Ergonomics, 30,* 1311–1321.

Knoop, R. (1994). The relationship between importance and achievement of work values and job satisfaction. *Perceptual and Motor Skills, 79*(1), 595–605.

Knouse, S. B. (1983). The letter of recommendation: Specificity and favorability of information. *Personnel Psychology, 36,* 331–341.

Kohli, A. K., & Jaworski, B. J. (1994). The influence of coworker feedback on salespeople. *Journal of Marketing, 58*(4), 82–94.

Kolb, J. A. (1998). The relationship between self-monitoring and leadership in student project groups. *Journal of Business Communication, 35*(2), 264–282.

Komaki, J. L. (1986). Toward effective supervision: An operant analysis and comparison of managers at work. *Journal of Applied Psychology, 71,* 270–279.

Komaki, J. L., Zlotnick, S., & Jensen, M. (1986). Development of an operant-based taxonomy and observational index of supervisory behavior. *Journal of Applied Psychology, 71,* 260–269.

Kopitzke, K., & Miller, D. (1984). *Relationship between personality and office environment.* Paper presented at the annual Graduate Conference in Industrial/Organizational Psychology and Organizational Behavior, Virginia Beach, VA.

Koppes, L. L. (1991). I/O psychology master's-level training: Reality and legitimacy in search of recognition. *The Industrial-Organizational Psychologist, 29*(2), 59–67.

Koppes, L. L. (1997). American female pioneers of industrial and organizational psychology during the early years. *Journal of Applied Psychology, 82*(4), 500–515.

Korman, A. K. (1966). Consideration, initiating structure, and organizational criteria: A review. *Personnel Psychology, 19*, 349–361.

Korman, A. K. (1970). Toward a hypothesis of work behavior. *Journal of Applied Psychology, 54*, 31–41.

Korman, A. K. (1976). Hypothesis of work behavior revisited and an extension. *Academy of Management Review, 1*, 50–63.

Korte, C., & Grant, R. (1980). Traffic noise, environmental awareness, and pedestrian behavior. *Environment & Behavior, 12*, 408–420.

Kortick, S. A., & O'Brien, R. M. (1996). The world series of quality control: A case study in the package deliver industry. *Journal of Organizational Behavior Management, 16*(2), 77–93.

Kosidlak, J. G. (1987). DACUM: An alternative job analysis tool. *Personnel, 64*(3), 17–21.

Koslowsky, M., Sagie, A., Krausz, M., & Singer, A. H. (1997). Correlates of employee lateness: Some theoretical considerations. *Journal of Applied Psychology, 82*(1), 79–88.

Kotter, J. P., & Cohen, D. S. (2002). *The heart of change.* Boston: Harvard Business School Press.

Kovach, R., Surrette, M. A., & Whitcomb, A. J. (1988, January). *Contextual, student, and instructor factors involved in college student absenteeism.* Paper presented at the 10th annual National Institute on the Teaching of Psychology, St. Petersburg, FL.

Kozlowski, S. W., Kirsch, M. P., & Chao, G. T. (1986). Job knowledge, rate familiarity, conceptual similarity and halo error: An exploration. *Journal of Applied Psychology, 71*, 45–49.

Kraiger, K., & Ford, J. K. (1985). A meta-analysis of ratee race effects. *Journal of Applied Psychology, 70*, 56–65.

Kravitz, D. A., Harrison, D. A., Turner, M. E., Levine, E. L., Chaves, W., Brannick, M. T., Denning, D. L., Russell, C. J., & Conard, M. A. (1997). *A review of psychological and behavioral research on affirmative action.* Bowling Green, OH: Society for Industrial and Organizational Psychology.

Kravitz, D. A., & Platania, J. (1993). Attitudes and beliefs about affirmative action: Effects of target and of respondent sex and ethnicity. *Journal of Applied Psychology, 78*(6), 928–938.

Kressel, K., & Pruitt, D. G. (1985). Themes on the mediation of social conflict. *Journal of Social Issues, 41*, 179–198.

Kriegel, R., & Brandt, D. (1996). *Sacred cows make the best burgers.* New York: Warner.

Kroehnert, G. (2000). *Basic training for trainers* (3rd ed.). New York: McGraw-Hill.

Kroemer, K. H. E., & Price, D. L. (1982). Ergonomics in the office: Comfortable work stations allow maximum productivity. *Industrial Engineering, 14*(7), 24–32.

Kryger, B. R., & Shikiar, R. (1978). Sexual discrimination in the use of letters of recommendation: A case of reverse discrimination. *Journal of Applied Psychology, 63*(3), 309–314.

Kuder, G. F., & Richardson, M. W. (1937). The theory of estimation of test reliability. *Psychometrika, 2*, 151–160.

Kuncel, N. R., Hezlett, S. A., & Ones, D. S. (2001). A comprehensive meta-analysis of the predictive validity of the Graduate Record Examination: Implications for graduate student selection and performance. *Psychological Bulletin, 127*(1), 162–178.

Kunin, T. (1955). The construction of a new type of attitude measure. *Personnel Psychology, 8*, 65–78.

Kurland, N. B., & Pelled, L. H. (2000). Passing the word: Toward a model of gossip and power in the workplace. *Academy of Management Review, 25*(2), 428–438.

Laabs, J. J. (1996, July). Expert advice on how to move forward with change. *Personnel Journal*, pp. 54–63.

Lachnit, C. (2001), Employee referral saves time, saves money, delivers quality. *Workforce, 80*(6), 67.

Ladd, D., Jagacinski, C., & Stolzenberg, K. (1997). Differences in goal level set for optimists and defensive pessimists under conditions of encouragement. *Proceedings of the 18th Annual Graduate Conference in Industrial/Organizational Psychology and Organizational Behavior, 18*, 85–86.

Ladio, J. (1996). A primer on in-house message networks. *HR Magazine, 41*(11), 84–91.

LaFleur, T., & Hyten, C. (1995). Improving the quality of hotel banquet staff performance. *Journal of Organizational Behavior Management, 15*(1), 69–93.

Lahtela, K., Niemi, P., Kuusela, V., & Hypen, K. (1986). Noise and visual choice reaction time. *Scandinavian Journal of Psychology, 27*, 52–57.

Laing, M. (1993). Gossip: Does it play a role in the socialization of nurses? *Journal of Nursing Scholarship, 25*(1), 37–41.

Lajunen, T., Hakkarainen, P., & Summala, H. (1996). The ergonomics of road signs: Explicit and embedded limits. *Ergonomics, 39*(8), 1069–1083.

Lam, S. S. K., & Schaubroeck, J. (2000). A field experiment testing frontline opinion leaders as change agents. *Journal of Applied Psychology, 85*(6), 987–995.

LaMarre, S. E., & Thompson, K. (1984). Industry sponsored day care. *Personnel Administrator, 29*(2), 53–65.

Lance, C. E., Teachout, M. S., & Donnelly, T. M. (1992). Specification of the criterion construct space: An application of hierarchical confirmatory factor analysis. *Journal of Applied Psychology, 77*(4), 437–453.

Landy, F. J. (1997). Early influences on the development of industrial and organizational psychology. *Journal of Applied Psychology, 82*(4), 467–477.

Landy, F. J., & Bates, F. (1973). Another look at contrast effects in the employment interview. *Journal of Applied Psychology, 58*(1), 141–144.

Landy, F. J., & Guion, R. M. (1970). Development of scales for the measurement of work motivation. *Organizational Behavior and Human Performance, 5*, 93–103.

Landy, F. J., & Vasey, J. (1991). Job analysis: The composition of SME samples. *Personnel Psychology, 44*, 27–50.

Langdale, J. A., & Weitz, J. (1973). Estimating the influence of job information on interviewer agreement. *Journal of Applied Psychology, 57*(1), 23–27.

Langer, E. J., & Rodin, J. (1976). The effects of choice and enhanced personal responsibility for the aged: A field experiment in an institutional setting. *Journal of Personality and Social Psychology, 34*, 191–198.

Lantz, C. (2001). Essential skills for international careers. *Planning Job Choices: 2002*, 42–44.

Lapidus, R. S., & Pinkerton, L. (1995). Customer complaint situations: An equity theory perspective. *Psychology and Marketing, 12*(2), 105–122.

Larey, T. S., & Paulus, P. B. (1995). Social comparison and goal setting in brainstorming groups. *Journal of Applied Social Psychology, 25*(18), 1579–1596.

Larson, J. J. (2001*). A comparison of performance and attitudes of college students on computer-based versus paper-and-pencil testing*. Paper presented at the 22nd annual Graduate Conference in Industrial-Organizational Psychology and Organizational Behavior, Pennsylvania State University, PA.

Larson, J. R. (1989). The dynamic interplay between employees' feedback seeking strategies and supervisors' delivery of performance feedback. *Academy of Management Review, 14*, 408–422.

Latane, B. (1981). The psychology of social impact. *American Psychologist, 36*, 343–356.

Latham, G. P., & Blades, J. J. (1975). The practical significance of Locke's theory of goal setting. *Journal of Applied Psychology, 60*, 122–124.

Latham, G. P., Fay, C. H., & Saari, L. M. (1979). The development of behavioral observation scales for appraising the performance of foremen. *Personnel Psychology, 32*, 299–311.

Latham, G. P., & Wexley, K. N. (1977). Behavioral observation scales for performance appraisal purposes. *Personnel Psychology, 30*, 225–268.

Latham, G. P., & Whyte, G. (1994). The futility of utility analysis. *Personnel Psychology, 47*, 31–46.

Latham, V. M. (1983). Charismatic leadership: A review and proposed model. *Proceedings of the 4th Annual Graduate Conference in Industrial/Organizational Psychology and Organizational Behavior.*

Law, J. R. (1996). *Rising to the occasion: Foundations, processes, and outcomes of emergent leadership*. Unpublished doctoral dissertation, University of Texas at Austin.

Lawler, E. E. (1973). *Motivation in work organizations*. Pacific Grove, CA: Brooks/Cole.

Lawler, E. E. (2001). *Organizing for high performance*. San Francisco: Jossey-Bass.

Lawler, E. E., & Suttle, J. L. (1972). A causal correlational test of the need hierarchy concept. *Organizational Behavior and Human Performance, 7*, 265–287.

Lawshe, C. H., Bolda, R. A., Brune, R. L., & Auclair G. (1958). Expectancy charts, II: Their theoretical development. *Personnel Psychology, 11*, 545–559.

Lawson, K. (2000). Making training active. In G. M. Piskurich, P. Beckschi, & B. Hall (Eds.), *The ASTD handbook of training design and delivery* (pp. 42–53). New York: McGraw-Hill.

Leana, C. R., & Feldman, D. C. (1992). *Coping with job loss*. New York: Lexington.

Ledford, G. E., Lawler, E. E., & Mohrman, S. A. (1995). Reward innovations in *Fortune* 1000 companies. *Compensation and Benefits Review, 27*(4), 76–80.

Lee, F. (1993). Being polite and keeping MUM: How bad news is communicated in organizational hierarchies. *Journal of Applied Social Psychology, 23*(14), 124–149.

Lee, J. A., Walker, M., & Shoup, R. (2001). Balancing elder care responsibilities and work: The impact on emotional health. *Journal of Business and Psychology, 16*(2), 277–289.

Lee, K., Carswell, J. J., & Allen, N. J. (2000). A meta-analytic review of occupational commitment: Relations with person- and work-related variables. *Journal of Applied Psychology, 85*(5), 799–811.

Lee, M. Y. (2001). Search party. *Entrepreneur, 29*(8), 73–74.

Leeds, D. (1996). Training one-on-one. *Training & Development, 50*(9), 42–44.

Lefkowitz, J. (2000). The role of interpersonal affective regard in supervisory performance ratings: A literature review and proposed causal model. *Journal of Occupational and Organizational Psychology, 73*(1), 67–85.

Leonard, B. (1999a). The key to unlocking an inexpensive recognition plan. *HR Magazine, 44*(10), 26.

Leonard, B. (1999b). Reading employees. *HR Magazine, 44*(4), 67–73.

Leonard, B. (2000a). Employers explore on-site day care options. *HR Magazine, 45*(5), 29.

Leonard, B. (2000b). Online and overwhelmed. *HR Magazine, 45*(8), 37–42.

LePine, J. A., Erez, A., & Johnson, D. E. (2002). The nature and dimensionality of organizational citizenship behavior: A critical review and a meta-analysis. *Journal of Applied Psychology, 87*(1), 52–65.

LePine, J. A., Hollenbeck, J. R., Ilgen, D. R., & Hedlund, J. (1997). Effects of individual differences on the performance of hierarchical decision-making teams: Much more than *Journal of Applied Psychology, 82*(5), 803–811.

Levine, E. L., Ash, R. A., & Bennett, N. (1980). Exploratory comparison study of four job analysis methods. *Journal of Applied Psychology, 65*, 524–535.

Levine, E. L., Ash, R. A., Hall, H., & Sistrunk, F. (1983). Evaluation of job analysis methods by experienced job analysts. *Academy of Management Journal, 26*, 339–348.

Levin-Epstein, M. D. (1987). *Primer of equal employment opportunity*. Washington, DC: Bureau of National Affairs.

Lewin, K. (1951). *Field theory in social science*. New York: Harper & Row.

Lewis, D. E. (1997, October 30). More jobs than candidates present at Boston's Microsoft career fair. *Knight-Ridder/Tribune Business News*, p. 1030B.

Libo, G. M. (1996). *The use and effectiveness of influence tactics in hospital–manager–physician relationships*. Unpublished doctoral dissertation, New Mexico State University.

Liden, R. C., Wayne, S. J., & Bradway, L. (1996). Connections make the difference. *HR Magazine, 41*(2), 73–79.

Liden, R. C., Wayne, S. J., Judge, T. A., Sparrowe, R. T., Kraimer, M. L., & Franz, T. M. (1999). Management of poor performance: A comparison of manager, group member, and group disciplinary decisions. *Journal of Applied Psychology, 84*(6), 835–850.

Lied, T. L., & Pritchard, R. D. (1976). Relationship between personality variables and components of the expectancy-valence model. *Journal of Applied Psychology, 61*, 463–467.

Lierman, B. (1994). How to develop a training simulation. *Training and Development, 48*(2), 50–52.

Lilienfeld, S. O., Wood, J. M., & Garb, H. N. (2001, May). What's wrong with this picture? *Scientific American*, pp. 80–87.

Lin, T. R., Dobbins, G. H., & Farh, J. (1992). A field study of race and age similarity effects on interview ratings in conventional and situational interviews. *Journal of Applied Psychology, 77*(3), 363–371.

Lindell, M. K., Clause, C. S., Brandt, C. J., & Landis, R. S. (1998). Relationship between organizational context and job analysis task ratings. *Journal of Applied Psychology, 83*(5), 769–776.

Lindeman, M., Sundvik, L., & Rouhiainen, P. (1995). Under- or overestimation of self? Person variables and self-assessment accuracy in work settings. *Journal of Social Behavior and Personality, 10*(1), 123–134.

Liou, K. T., Sylvia, R. D., & Brunk, G. (1990). Non-work factors and job satisfaction revisited. *Human Relations, 43*, 77–86.

Littlepage, G. E. (1991). Effects of group size and task characteristics on group performance: A test of Steiner's model. *Personality and Social Psychology Bulletin, 17*(4), 449–456.

Locke, E. A. (1969). What is job satisfaction? *Organizational Behavior and Human Performance, 4*, 309–336.

Locke, E. A. (1996). Motivation through conscious goal setting. *Applied and Preventative Psychology, 5*, 117–124.

Locke, E. A., & Latham, G. P. (1990). *A theory of goal setting and task performance*. Englewood Cliffs, NJ: Prentice-Hall.

Locke, E. A., & Latham, G. P. (2002). Building a practically useful theory of goal setting and task motivation. *American Psychologist, 57*(9), 705–717.

Lockowandt, O. (1976). Present status of the investigation of handwriting psychology as a diagnostic method. *JSAS Catalog of Selected Documents, 6*(4), MS No. 11172.

Loewen, L. J., & Suedfeld, P. (1992). Cognitive arousal effects of masking office noise. *Environment and Behavior, 24*(3), 381–395.

Loher, B. T., Hazer, J. T., Tsai, A., Tilton, K., & James, J. (1997). Letters of reference: A process approach. *Journal of Business and Psychology, 11*(3), 339–355.

Long, G. M., & Kearns, D. F. (1996). Visibility of text and icon highway signs under dynamic viewing conditions. *Human Factors, 38*(4), 690–701.

Long, W. W., Long, E. J., & Dobbins, G. H. (1998). Correlates of satisfaction with a peer evaluation system: Investigation of performance levels and individual differences. *Journal of Business and Psychology, 12*(33), 299–317.

Lopez, F. E., Rockmore, B. W., & Kesselman, G. A. (1980). The development of an integrated career planning program at Gulf Power Company. *Personnel Administrator, 25*(10), 21–29.

Lopez, F. M., Kesselman, G. A., & Lopez, F. E. (1981). An empirical test of a trait-oriented job analysis technique. *Personnel Psychology, 34*, 479–502.

Lord, R. G., De Vader, C. L., & Alliger, G. M. (1986). A meta-analysis of the relation between personality traits and leadership perceptions: An application of validity generalization procedures. *Journal of Applied Psychology, 71*, 402–410.

Lord, R. G., & Hohenfeld, J. A. (1979). Longitudinal field assessment of equity effects in the performance of major league baseball players. *Journal of Applied Psychology, 64*, 19–26.

Lounsbury, J. W., Bobrow, W., & Jensen, J. B. (1989). Attitudes toward employment testing: Scale development, correlates, and "known group" validation. *Professional Psychology: Research and Practice, 20*(5), 340–349.

Lovelace, K., & Rosen, B. (1996). Differences in achieving person–organization fit among diverse groups of managers. *Journal of Management, 22*(5), 703–722.

Lovenheim, P. (1996). *How to mediate your dispute*. Berkley, CA: Nolo.

Lowe, K. B., Kroeck, K. G., & Sivasubramaniam, N. (1996). Effectiveness correlates of transformation and transactional leadership: A meta-analytic review of the MLQ literature. *Leadership Quarterly, 7*, 385–425.

Lowe, R. H. (1993). Master's programs in industrial/organizational psychology: Current status and a call for action. *Professional Psychology: Research and Practice, 24*(1), 27–34.

Lulofs, R. S., & Cahn, D. D. (2000). *Conflict: From theory to action*. Boston: Allyn & Bacon.

Luna, T. D., French, J., & Mitcha, J. L. (1997). A study of USAF air traffic controller shiftwork: Sleep, fatigue, activity, and mood analysis. *Aviation, Space, and Environmental Medicine, 68*(1), 18–23.

Luoma, J., Flannagan, M. J., Sivak, M., Aoki, M., & Traube, E. C. (1997). Effects of turn-signal colour on reaction times to brake signals. *Ergonomics, 40*(1), 62–68.

Lykken, D. T., & Tellegen, A. (1996). Happiness is a stochastic phenomenon. *Psychological Science, 7*(3), 186–189.

Mabe, P. A., & West, S. G. (1982). Validity of self-evaluation of ability: A review and meta-analysis. *Journal of Applied Psychology, 67*, 280–296.

MacInnis, P. (2002). Checking out references: Thinking about fudging your resume to get that coveted IT position? Think again. *Computing Canada, 28*(15), 25.

Mackworth, N. H. (1946). Effects of heat on wireless telegraphy operators hearing and receiving Morse messages. *British Journal of Industrial Medicine, 3*, 145.

Maddux, J. E., & Rogers, R. W. (1980). Effects of source expertness, physical attractiveness, and supporting arguments on persuasion: A case of brains over beauty. *Journal of Personality and Social Psychology, 39*, 235–244.

Mager, R. F. (1997). *Preparing instructional objectives* (3rd ed.). Atlanta, GA: Center for Effective Performance.

Mahlin, S. J., & Charles, J. (1984). Peak-time pay for part-time work. *Personnel, 63*(11), 60–65.

Mailhot, E. K. (1996). *Incumbents as job experts: Effects of individual and group characteristics on job analysis results*. Unpublished doctoral dissertation, University of Connecticut.

Maiorca, J. (1997). How to construct behaviorally anchored rating scales (BARS) for employee evaluations. *Supervision, 58*(8), 15–18.

Maiwald, C. R., Pierce, J. L., Newstrom, J. W., & Sunoo, B. P. (1997). Workin' 8 p.m. to 8 a.m. and lovin' every minute of it. *Workforce, 76*(7), 30–36.

Major, B., Schmidlin, A. M., & Williams, L. (1990). General patterns in social touch: The impact of setting and age. *Journal of Personality and Social Psychology, 58*, 634–643.

Malandro, L. A., & Barker, L. L. (1983). *Nonverbal communication*. Reading, MA: Addison-Wesley.

Malos, S. B. (1998). Current legal issues in performance appraisal. In J. W. Smither (Ed.), *Performance appraisal: State of the art in practice* (pp. 49–94). San Francisco: Jossey-Bass.

Manners, G. E. (1975). Another look at group size, group problem solving, and member consensus. *Academy of Management Journal, 18*, 715–724.

Manson, T. (1989). The effectiveness of computer based training in organizational settings: A meta-analysis. *Proceedings of the 10th Annual Graduate Conference in Industrial/ Organizational Psychology and Organizational Behavior.*

Mantell, M., & Albrecht, S. (1994). *Ticking bombs: Defusing violence in the workplace.* New York: Business Irwin.

Manz, C. C., & Sims, H. P. (1986). Beyond limitation: Complex behavioral and affective linkages resulting from exposure to leadership training models. *Journal of Applied Psychology, 71*, 571–578.

Marchetti, M. (1997). The fine art of firing. *Sales and Marketing Management, 149*(4), 6–7.

Markowich, M. M. (1994). Reengineering sick pay. *HR Focus, 71*(4), 12–13.

Marks, M. A., Mathieu, J. E., & Zaccaro, S. J. (2001). A temporally based framework and taxonomy of team processes. *Academy of Management Review, 26*(3), 356–376.

Marks, M. L. (2003). *Charging back up the hill: Workplace recovery after mergers, acquisitions, and downsizings.* San Francisco: Jossey-Bass.

Maroney. T. (2000, March 20). Web recruiting is fine, but we like a job fair: Hurray for the real world. *Fortune, 141*(6), 236.

Martell, R. F., & Borg, M. R. (1993). A comparison of the behavioral rating accuracy of groups and individuals. *Journal of Applied Psychology, 78*(1), 43–50.

Martell, R. F., Guzzo, R. A., & Willis, C. E. (1995). A methodological and substantive note on the performance-cue effect in ratings of work-group behavior. *Journal of Applied Psychology, 80*(1), 191–195.

Martin, C. L., & Nagao, D. H. (1989). Some effects of computerized interviewing on job applicant responses. *Journal of Applied Psychology, 74*, 72–80.

Martin, D. C., Bartol, K. M., & Kehoe, P. E. (2000). The legal ramifications of performance appraisal: The growing significance. *Public Personnel Management, 29*(3), 379–405.

Martin, G. E., & Bergmann, T. J. (1996). The dynamics of response to conflict in the workplace. *Journal of Occupational and Organizational Psychology, 69*(41), 377–387.

Martin, J., & Stockner, J. (2000). *Does the structured interview control for the effects of applicant gender and nonverbal cues?* Paper presented at the 21st annual Graduate Student Conference in Industrial-Organizational Psychology and Organizational Behavior, Knoxville, TN.

Martin, R. A. (2001). Humor, laughter, and physical health: Methodological issues and research findings. *Psychological Bulletin, 127*(4), 504–519.

Martin, S. (1995). The role of nonverbal communication in quality improvement. *National Productivity Review, 15*(1), 27–39.

Martinez, M. N. (1990). In search of a productive design. *HR Magazine, 35*(2), 36–39.

Martinez, M. N. (1994). FMLA: Headache or opportunity? *HR Magazine, 39*(2), 42–45.

Martinez, M. N. (2001). Breaking the mold. *HR Magazine, 46*(6), 81–90.

Martocchio, J. J. (2001). *Strategic compensation.* Upper Saddle River, NJ: Prentice-Hall.

Martyka, J. (2001, June 8). Colleges customize employee training. *Minneapolis-St. Paul City Business, 19*(1), 17–18.

Maslow, A. H. (1954). *Motivation and personality.* New York: Harper & Row.

Maslow, A. H. (1970). *Motivation and personality* (2nd ed.). New York: Harper & Row.

Mason, R. M. (1984). Ergonomics: The human and the machine. *Library Journal, 15*, 331–332.

Mastrangelo, P. M. (1997). Do college students still prefer companies without employment drug testing? *Journal of Business and Psychology, 11*, 325–337.

Mathews, K. E., & Canon, L. K. (1975). Environmental noise level as a determinant of helping behavior. *Journal of Personality and Social Psychology, 32*, 571–577.

Mathieu, J. E., Tannenbaum, S. I., & Salas, E. (1992). Influences of individual and situational characteristics on measures of training effectiveness. *Academy of Management Journal, 35*(4), 828–847.

Mathieu, J. E., & Zajac, D. M. (1990). A review and meta-analysis of the antecedents, correlates, and consequences of organizational commitment. *Psychological Bulletin, 108*(1), 171–194.

Matthes, K. (1993). Greeting from Hallmark. *HR Focus, 70*(8), 12–13.

Mattox, W. R. (1997, December 30). Cleanliness really is next to godliness. *USA Today*, p. A13.

Maurer, S. A. (2001). Logging on to learn. *Chain Leader, 6*(7), 49–52.

Maurer, T. J., Solamon, J. M., Andrews, K. D., & Troxtel, D. D. (2001). Interviewee coaching, preparation strategies, and response strategies in relation to performance in situational employment interviews: An extension of Maurer, Solamon, and Troxtel (1998). *Journal of Applied Psychology, 86*(4), 709–717.

Maurer, T. J., Solamon, J. M., & Troxtel, D. D. (1998). Relationship of coaching with performance in situational job interviews. *Journal of Applied Psychology, 83*(1), 128–136.

Maurer, T. J., & Tross, S. (2000). SME committee vs. field job analysis ratings: Convergence, cautions, and a call. *Journal of Business and Psychology, 14*(3), 489–499.

Mawhinney, T. C., & Gowen, C. R. (1990). Gainsharing and the law of effect as the matching law: A theoretical framework. *Journal of Organizational Behavior Management, 11*(2), 61–75.

Mayer, J. J. (1990). *If you haven't got the time to do it right, when will you find the time to do it over?* New York: Simon & Schuster.

Mayer, M. (2002). Background checks in focus. *HR Magazine, 47*(1), 59–62.

Mayo, E. (1946). *The human problems of an industrial civilization.* Cambridge, MA: Harvard University Press.

McAndrew, F. T. (1993). The home advantage in individual sports. *Journal of Social Psychology, 133*(3), 401–403.

McCabe, M. J. (2001). The money pit. *The RMA Journal, 83*(10), 18–19.

McCann, N., & Lester, D. (1996). Smoking and stress: Cigarettes and marijuana. *Psychological Reports, 79*(2), 366.

McCarthy, P. M. (1998). *Brief outline of the history of I/O psychology* [Online]. Available: www.mtsu.edu/~pmccarth/io_hist.htm

McClelland, D. C. (1961). *The achieving society*. Princeton, NJ: Van Nostrand.

McClelland, D. C., & Boyatzis, R. E. (1982). Leadership motive pattern and long-term success in management. *Journal of Applied Psychology, 67*, 737–743.

McClelland, D. C., & Burnham, D. H. (1976). Power is the great motivator. *Harvard Business Review, 54*(2), 102–104.

McCormick, E. J. (1979). *Job analysis: Methods and applications*. New York: AMACOM.

McCormick, E. J., & Jeanneret, P. R. (1988). Position Analysis Questionnaire (PAQ). In S. Gael (Ed.), *The job analysis handbook for business, industry, and government* (pp. 825–842). New York: Wiley.

McCormick, E. J., Jeanneret, P. R., & Mecham, R. C. (1969). *Position Analysis Questionnaire*. West Lafayette, IN: Purdue Research Foundation.

McCormick, E. J., Jeanneret, P. R., & Mecham, R. C. (1972). A study of job characteristics and job dimensions as based on the Position Analysis Questionnaire (PAQ). *Journal of Applied Psychology, 56*, 347–368.

McCullough, S. (1998). Take the bite out of the lunch crunch. *HR Magazine, 43*(8), 55–62.

McDaniel, M. A., Morgeson, F. P., Finnegan, E. B., Campion, M. A., & Braverman, E. P. (2001). Use of situational judgment tests to predict performance: A clarification of the literature. *Journal of Applied Psychology, 86*(4), 730–740.

McDaniel, M. A., Whetzel, D. L., Schmidt, F. L., & Maurer, S. D. (1994). The validity of employment interviews: A comprehensive review and meta-analysis. *Journal of Applied Psychology, 79*(4), 599–616.

McElroy, J. C., Morrow, P. C., & Ackerman, R. J. (1983). Personality and interior office design: Exploring the accuracy of visitor attributions. *Journal of Applied Psychology,68*, 541–544.

McElroy, J. C., Morrow, P. C., & Wall, L. C. (1983). Generalizing impact of object language to other audiences: Peer response to office design. *Psychological Reports, 53*, 315–332.

McEvoy, G. M. (1988). Evaluating the boss. *Personnel Administrator, 33*(9), 115–120.

McEvoy, G. M. (1990). Public sector managers' reactions to appraisals by subordinates. *Public Personnel Management, 19*(2), 201–212.

McGlone, L. (2001, August 10). To train or not to train: It's not always a simple question. *Puget Sound Business Journal, 22*(14), 34.

McGregor, D. (1960). *The human side of enterprise*. New York: McGraw-Hill.

McIntyre, R., Smith, D., & Hassett, C. (1984). Accuracy of performance ratings as affected by rater training and perceived purpose of training. *Journal of Applied Psychology, 69*, 147–156.

McKee, T. L., & Ptacek, J. T. (2001). I'm afraid I have something bad to tell you: Breaking bad news from the perspective of the giver. *Journal of Applied Social Psychology, 31*(2), 246–273.

McLeod, P. L., Baron, R. S., Marti, M. W., & Yoon, K. (1997). The eyes have it: Minority influence in face-to-face and computer-mediated group discussion. *Journal of Applied Psychology, 82*(5), 706–718.

McManus, M. A., & Baratta, J. E. (1992). *The relationship of recruiting source to performance and survival*. Paper presented at the annual meeting of the Society for Industrial and Organizational Psychology, Montreal, Canada.

McNatt, D. B. (2000). Ancient Pygmalion joins contemporary management: A meta-analysis of the result. *Journal of Applied Psychology, 85*(2), 314–322.

McShane, T. D. (1993). Effect of nonverbal cues and verbal first impressions in unstructured and situational interview settings. *Applied H.R.M. Research, 4*(2), 137–150.

Mead, A. D., & Drasgow, F. (1993). Equivalence of computerized and paper-and-pencil cognitive ability tests: A meta-analysis. *Psychological Bulletin, 114*(3), 449–458.

Meehan, B. T. (1994, January 16). Ice star, bodyguard a pair who didn't fit in. *Roanoke Times and World News*, pp. A1, A8.

Meers, A., Maasen, A., & Verhaagen, P. (1978). Subjective health after six months and after four years of shift work. *Ergonomics, 21*, 857–859.

Mehrabian, A. (1965). Communication length as an index of communicator attitude. *Psychological Reports, 17*, 519–522.

Melamed, S., Harari, G., & Green, M. S. (1993). Type A behavior, tension, and ambulatory cardiovascular reactivity in workers exposed to noise stress. *Psychosomatic Medicine, 55*(2), 185–193.

Mendleson, J. L., Barnes, A. K., & Horn, G. (1989). The guiding light to corporate culture. *Personnel Administrator, 34*(7), 70–71.

Mento, A. J. (1980). *A review of assessment center research*. Washington, DC: U.S. Office of Personnel Management.

Mento, A. J., Steel, R. P., & Karren, R. J. (1987). A meta-analytic study of the effects of goal setting on task performance: 1966–1984. *Organizational Behavior and Human Decision Processes, 39*, 52–83.

Mero, N. P., & Motowidlo, S. J. (1995). Effects of rater accountability on the accuracy and the favorability of performance ratings. *Journal of Applied Psychology, 80*(4), 517–524.

Mershon, D. H., & Lin, L. (1987). Directional localization in high ambient noise with and without the use of hearing protectors. *Ergonomics, 30*, 1161–1173.

Meyer, H. H. (1980). Self-appraisal of job performance. *Personnel Psychology, 33*, 291–296.

Meyer, H. H., & Raich, M. S. (1983). An objective evaluation of a behavior modeling training program. *Personnel Psychology, 36*, 755–761.

Meyer, J. P., & Allen, N. J. (1997). *Commitment to the workplace: Theory, research, and application*. Thousand Oaks, CA: Sage.

Michaels, J. W., Blommel, J. M., Brocato, R. M., Linkous, R. A., & Rowe, J. S. (1982). Social facilitation and inhibition in a natural setting. *Replications in Social Psychology, 2*, 21–24.

Mijares, T. C. (1993). Selecting police personnel for tactical assignments: Considerations for female officers. *Applied H.R.M. Research, 4*(2), 94–101.

Miki, K., Kawwamorita, K., Araga, Y., Musha, T., & Sudo, A. (1998). Urinary and salivary stress hormone levels while performing arithmetic calculations in a noisy environment. *Industrial Health, 36*(1), 66–69.

Miles, E. W., Patrick, S. L., & King, W. C. (1996). Job level as a systematic variable in predicting the relationship between supervisory communication and job satisfaction. *Journal of Occupational and Organizational Psychology, 69*(3), 277–292.

Miles, J. A., & Greenberg, J. (1993). Using punishment threats to attenuate social loafing effects among swimmers. *Organizational Behavior and Human Decision Processes, 56*(2), 246–265.

Milkovich, G. T., & Newman, J. M. (2002). *Compensation* (7th ed.). New York: McGraw-Hill.

Miller, C. W. (1998, January 18). Managers benefit from walking around, talking with workers. *The Roanoke Times*, p. B2.

Miller, G. W., & Sniderman, M. S. (1974). Multijobholding of Wichita public school teachers. *Public Personnel Management, 3*, 392–402.

Miller, J. G. (1960). Information input, overload, and psychopathology. *American Journal of Psychiatry, 116*, 695–704.

Miller, K. I., & Monge, P. D. (1986). Participation, satisfaction, and productivity: A meta-analytic review. *Academy of Management Journal, 29*(4) 727–753.

Miller, R. K., & Van Rybroek, G. J. (1988). Internship letters of recommendation: Where are the other 90%? *Professional Psychology: Research and Practice, 19*(1) 115–117.

Miller, T. I. (1984). Effects of employee-sponsored day care on employee absenteeism, turnover, productivity, recruitment or job satisfaction: What is claimed and what is known. *Personnel Psychology, 37*, 277–289.

Milliman, R. E. (1986). The influence of background music on the behavior of restaurant patrons. *Journal of Consumer Research, 13*, 290–296.

Minton-Eversole, T. (2001, April). Hiring welfare recipients boosts retention, productivity and moral, survey says. *HR News*, p. 9.

Mirolli, K., Henderson, P., & Hills, D. (1998). *Coworkers' influence on job satisfaction*. Paper presented at the 19th annual Graduate Student Conference in Industrial/Organizational Psychology and Organizational Behavior, San Diego, CA.

Mishra, J. (1990). Managing the grapevine. *Public Personnel Management, 19*(2), 213–226.

Mitchell, V. F., & Mougdill, P. (1976). Measurement of Maslow's need hierarchy. *Organizational Behavior and Human Performance, 16*, 334–349.

Mitra, A., Jenkins, G. D., & Gupta, N. (1992). A meta-analytic review of the relationship between absence and turnover. *Journal of Applied Psychology, 77*(6), 879–889.

Mobaraki, G. R. (1996). *A study to determine effective means to motivate employees*. Unpublished doctoral dissertation, Walden University.

Moede, W. (1927). Die Richtlinien der Leistungs-Psychologie. *Industrielle Pscyhotechnik, 4*, 193–207.

Montebello, H. R., & Haga, M. (1994). To justify training, test, test again. *Personnel Journal, 30*(1), 83–87.

Montwieler, N. (2002). Dominguez sets EEOC agenda, redefines "job applicant." *HR News, 21*(1), 2.

Moores, J. (1990). A meta-analytic review of the effects of compressed work schedules. *Applied H.R.M. Research, 1*(1), 12–18.

Moran, L., Musselwhite, E., & Zenger, J. H. (1996). *Keeping teams on track*. Chicago: Irwin.

Morgan, J. (1990, March). Test negative: A look at the "evidence" justifying illicit-drug tests. *Scientific American*, pp. 18–19.

Morin, R. (1999, January 10). Choice words. *Washington Post*, pp. C1, C4.

Morris, M. A., & Campion, J. E. (2003). *New use for an old tool: Vocational interests and outcomes*. Poster presented at the 18th annual meeting of the Society for Industrial and Organizational Psychology, Orlando, FL.

Morrison, E. W. (1993). Newcomer information seeking: Exploring types, modes, sources, and outcomes. *Academy of Management Journal, 36*(3), 557–589.

Morrison, E. W., & Robinson, S. L. (1997). When employees feel betrayed: A model of how psychological contract violation develops. *Academy of Management Review, 22*(1), 226–256.

Morrow, P. C., & McElroy, J. C. (1981). Interior office design and visitor response: A constructive replication. *Journal of Applied Psychology, 66*, 646–650.

Morse, C. S. (1988). Employer liability for negligent hiring and retention of employees. *PAR Employment Law Update, 5*(1), 1–4.

Mosel, J. N., & Goheen, H. W. (1952). The agreement rate among replies to an employment recommendation questionnaire. *American Psychologist, 7*, 365–366.

Mosel, J. N., & Goheen, H. W. (1958). The validity of the Employment Recommendation Questionnaire in personnel selection: Skilled traders. *Personnel Psychology, 11*, 481–490.

Mossholder, K. W. (1980). Effects of externally mediated goal setting on intrinsic motivation: A laboratory experiment. *Journal of Applied Psychology, 65*(2), 202–210.

Motowidlo, S. J., & Burnett, J. R. (1995). Aural and visual sources of validity in structured employment interviews. *Organizational Behavior and Human Decision Processes, 61*, 239–249.

Mott, P. E., Mann, F. C., McLoughlin, Q., & Warwick, D. P. (1965). *Shift work*. Ann Arbor: University of Michigan Press.

Mount, M. K. (1983). Comparisons of managerial and employee satisfaction with a performance appraisal system. *Personnel Psychology, 36*, 99–110.

Mount, M. K., & Ellis, R. A. (1989). Sources of bias in job evaluation: A review and critique of research. *Journal of Social Issues, 45*(4), 153–167.

Mount, M. K., & Thompson, D. E. (1987). Cognitive categorization and quality of performance ratings. *Journal of Applied Psychology, 72*, 240–246.

Mueller, M., & Belcher, G. (2000). Observed divergence in the attitudes of incumbents and supervisors as subject matter experts in job analysis: A study of the fire captain rank. *Public Personnel Management, 29*(4), 529–555.

Mulder, M., de Jong, R. D., Koppelaar, L., & Verhage, J. (1986). Power, situation, and leaders' effectiveness: An organizational field study. *Journal of Applied Psychology, 71*, 566–570.

Mullen, B., Anthony, T., Salas, E., & Driskell, J. E. (1994). Group cohesiveness and quality of decision making: An integration of the groupthink hypothesis. *Small Group Research, 25*(2), 189–204.

Mullen, B., & Copper, C. (1994). The relation between group cohesiveness and performance: An integration. *Psychological Bulletin, 115*(2), 210–227.

Mullen, B., Johnson, D. A., & Drake, S. D. (1987). Organizational productivity as a function of group composition: A self-attention perspective. *Journal of Social Psychology, 127*(1), 143–150.

Mullins, W. C. (1983). *Job analysis outcomes as a function of group composition.* Unpublished doctoral dissertation, University of Arkansas.

Mullins, W. C. (1986). *A note on the efficacy of the spurious nature of relational causation.* Paper presented at the annual meeting of the Society of Police and Criminal Psychology, Little Rock, AR.

Mullins, W. C., & Kimbrough, W. W. (1988). Group composition as a determinant of job analysis outcomes. *Journal of Applied Psychology, 73,* 657–664.

Mumford, M. D. (1983). Social comparison theory and the evaluation of peer evaluations: A review and some applied implications. *Personnel Psychology, 36,* 867–881.

Munson, L. J., Hulin, C., & Drasgow, F. (2000). Longitudinal analysis of dispositional influences and sexual harassment: Effects on job and psychological outcomes. *Personnel Psychology, 53*(1), 21–46.

Munsterberg, H. (1913). *Psychology and industrial efficiency.* Boston: Houghton Mifflin.

Murphy, C., Watson-El, K., Williams, F., & Wood, R. (2003). *I/O psychology versus M.B.A. programs.* Paper presented at the 24th annual Industrial/Organizational Psychology and Organizational Behavior Graduate Student Conference, Akron, Ohio.

Murphy, K. R. (1993). *Honesty in the workplace.* Pacific Grove, CA: Brooks/Cole.

Murphy, K. R., & Blazer, W. K. (1986). Systematic distortions in memory-based behavior ratings and performance evaluations: Consequences for rating accuracy. *Journal of Applied Psychology, 71,* 39–44.

Murphy, K. R., & Constans, J. I. (1987). Behavioral anchors as a source of bias in rating. *Journal of Applied Psychology, 72,* 573–577.

Murphy, K. R., Gannett, B. A., Herr, B. M., & Chen, J. A. (1986). Effects of subsequent performance on evaluations of previous performance. *Journal of Applied Psychology, 71,* 427–431.

Murphy, K. R., Martin, C., & Garcia, M. (1982). Do behavioral observation scales measure observation? *Journal of Applied Psychology, 67,* 562–567.

Nadler, P. (1993). How to start job-rotation training on the right track. *American Banker, 158*(12), 7.

Nagy, M. S. (1995). *An integrated model of job satisfaction.* Unpublished doctoral dissertation, Louisiana State University.

Nagy, M. S. (1996, April). What to do when you are dissatisfied with job satisfaction scales: A better way to measure job satisfaction. *Assessment Council News,* pp. 5–10.

Nail, P. R. (1986). Toward an integration of some models and theories of social response. *Psychological Bulletin, 100*(2), 190–206.

Nanry, C. (1988). Performance linked training. *Public Personnel Management, 17,* 457–463.

Nanus, R. (1992). *Visionary leadership.* San Francisco: Jossey-Bass.

Nash, A. N., & Carroll, S. J. (1970). A hard look at the reference check: Its modest worth can be improved. *Business Horizons, 13,* 43–49.

Nathan, B., & Lord, R. (1983). Cognitive categorization and dimensional schemata: A process approach to the study of halo in performance ratings. *Journal of Applied Psychology, 68,* 102–114.

National Research Council. (1983). *Video displays, work, and vision.* Washington, DC: National Academy Press.

Naughton, R. J. (1975). Motivational factors of American prisoners of war in Vietnam. *Naval War College Review, 27*(4), 2–14.

Naughton, T. J. (1988). Effect of female-linked job titles on job evaluation ratings. *Journal of Management, 14*(4), 567–578.

Nelson, B. (2000, October). Peer-to-peer recognition. *IPMA News,* p. 25.

Nelson, J. B., & Mital, A. (1995). An ergonomic evaluation of dexterity and tactility with increase in examination/surgical glove thickness. *Ergonomics, 38*(4), 723–733.

Nesler, M. S., Aguinis, H., Quigley, B. M., Lee, S. J., & Tedeschi, J. T. (1999). The development and validation of a scale measuring global social power based on French and Raven's power taxonomy. *Journal of Applied Social Psychology, 29*(4), 750–751.

Neufeldt, D., Kimbrough, W. W., & Stadelmaier, M. F. (1983, April). *Relationship between group composition and task type on group problem solving ability.* Paper presented at the 11th annual Graduation Conference in Personality and Social Psychology, Norman, OK.

Newman, R. L., Hunt, D. L., & Rhodes, F. (1966). Effects of noise on productivity in a skateboard factory. *Journal of Applied Psychology, 50,* 493–496.

Newsome, M., & Pillari, V. (1992). Job satisfaction and the worker–supervisor relationship. *The Clinical Supervisor, 9*(2), 119–129.

Nicholls, J. R. (1985). A new approach to situational leadership. *Leadership and Organization Development Journal, 6*(4), 2–7.

Nichols, R. G., & Stevens, L. A. (1957). *Are you listening?* New York: McGraw-Hill.

Nicholson, N., Jackson, P., & Howes, G. (1978). Shiftwork and absence: A study of temporal trends. *Journal of Occupational Psychology, 51,* 127–137.

Niebuhr, R. E., & Oswald, S. L. (1992). The impact of workgroup composition and other work unit/victim characteristics on perceptions of sexual harassment. *Applied H.R.M. Research, 3,* 30–47.

Noble, S. A. (1997). *Effects of a time delay on frame-of-reference training.* Poster presented at the 12th annual conference of the Society for Industrial and Organizational Psychology, St. Louis, MO.

Noe, R. (2002). *Employee training and development* (2nd ed.). New York: McGraw-Hill.

Nolan, J., Lee, K., & Allen, N. (1997). *Work group heterogeneity, performance, and turnover: Some meta-analytic findings.* Poster presented at the 12th annual conference of the Society for Industrial and Organizational Psychology, St. Louis, MO.

Normand, J., Salyards, S. D., & Mahoney, J. J. (1990). An evaluation of preemployment drug testing. *Journal of Applied Psychology, 75*(6), 629–639.

Norris, W. R., & Vecchio, R. P. (1992). Situational leadership theory: A replication. *Group and Organization Management, 17*(3), 331–342.

Nussbaum, K. (1980). *Race against time.* Cleveland, OH: National Association of Office Workers.

Nwachukwu, S. L., & Vitell, S. J. (1997). The influence of corporate culture on managerial ethical judgments. *Journal of Business Ethics, 16,* 757–776.

Nyholm, S. G. (1996). Firing without getting burned. *Journal of Property Management, 61*(5), 36–39.

O'Connor, E. J., Wexley, K. N., & Alexander, R. A. (1975). Single group validity: Fact or fallacy? *Journal of Applied Psychology, 60,* 352–355.

Oduwole, A., Morgan, A., & Bernardo, M. (2000). *A reexamination of contrast effects in the evaluation of job applicant resumes.* Paper presented at the 21st annual Graduate Student Conference in Industrial-Organizational Psychology and Organizational Behavior, Knoxville, TN.

Offermann, L. R., & Gowing, M. K. (1990). Organizations of the future: Changes and challenges. *American Psychologist, 45*(2), 95–108.

Offermann, L. R., & Spiros, R. K. (2001). The science and practice of team development: Improving the link. *Academy of Management Journal, 44*(2), 376–392.

Oginska, H., Pokorski, J., & Oginski, A. (1993). Gender, aging, and shiftwork intolerance. *Ergonomics, 36*(1), 161–168.

Oldham, G. R., & Brass, D. J. (1979). Employee reactions to an open-plan office: A naturally occurring quasi-experiment. *Administrative Science Quarterly, 24,* 267–284.

Oldham, G. R., Cummings, A., Mischel, L. J., & Schmidtke, J. M. (1995). Listen while you work? Quasi-experimental relations between personal-stereo headset use and employee work responses. *Journal of Applied Psychology, 80*(5), 547–564.

Oldham, G. R., Hackman, R. J., & Stepina, L. P. (1978). *Norms for the Job Diagnostic Survey.* Technical Report no. 16, School of Organization and Management, Yale University.

O'Leary, B. S., Rheinstein, J., & McCauley, D. E. (1990). *Job analysis for test development: Can it be streamlined?* Paper presented at the annual meeting of the American Psychological Association, Boston, MA.

Oliphant, V. N., & Alexander, E. R. (1982). Reactions to resumes as a function of resume determinateness, applicant characteristics, and sex of raters. *Personnel Psychology, 35,* 829–842.

O'Meara, D. P. (1994). Personality tests raise questions of legality and effectiveness. *HR Magazine, 39*(1), 97–100.

O'Neill, M. J. (1994). Work space adjustability, storage, and enclosure as predictors of employee reactions and performance. *Environment and Behavior, 26*(4), 504–526.

Ones, D. S., & Viswesvaran, C. (1998). Gender, age, and race differences on overt integrity tests: Results across four large-scale job applicant data sets. *Journal of Applied Psychology, 83*(1), 35–42.

Ones, D. S., Viswesvaran, C., & Schmidt, F. L. (1993). Comprehensive meta-analysis of integrity test validities: Findings for personnel selection and theories of job performance. *Journal of Applied Psychology, 78*(4), 679–703.

Opt, S. K. (1998). Confirming and disconfirming American myth: Stories within the suggestion box. *Communication Quarterly, 46*(1), 75–87.

O'Reilly, C. A., & Puffer, S. M. (1989). The impact of rewards and punishments in a social context: A laboratory and field experiment. *Journal of Occupational Psychology, 62*(1), 41–53.

Ornish, D. (1984). *Stress, diet, and your health.* New York: Signet.

Osborne, E. E., & Vernon, H. M. (1958). The influence of temperature and other conditions on the frequency of industrial accidents. Cited in T. W. Harrell (1972), *Industrial psychology.* New York: Rinehart.

O'Toole, R. E., & Ferry, J. L. (2002). The growing importance of elder care benefits for an aging workforce. *Compensation & Benefits Management, 18*(1), 40–44.

Overman, S. (1994a). Good faith is the answer (religious beliefs in the workplace). *HR Magazine, 39*(1), 74–76.

Overman, S. (1994b). Teams score on the bottom line. *HR Magazine, 39*(5), 82–84.

Overman, S. (1995). Bizarre questions aren't the answer. *HR Magazine, 40*(4), 56–58.

Overman, S. (1999). Splitting hairs. *HR Magazine, 44*(8), 43–48.

Owenby, P. H. (1992). Making case studies come alive. *Training, 29*(1), 43–46.

Oz, S., & Eden, D. (1994). Restraining the Golem: Boosting performance by changing the interpretation of low scores. *Journal of Applied Psychology, 79*(5), 744–754.

Ozminkowski, R. J., Mark, T., Cangianelli, L., & Walsh, J. M. (2001, September). The cost of on-site versus off-site workplace urinalysis testing for illicit drug use. *Health Care Manager,* pp. 59–69.

Packard, M. (1997). Getting vocal about voice mail and automated phone systems. *RV Business, 48*(1), 29.

Padgett, V. R. (1989). Empirical validation of firefighter vision standards. *Proceedings of the 13th Annual Meeting of the International Personnel Management Association Assessment Council.*

Parker, P. A., & Kulik, J. A. (1995). Burnout, self- and supervisor-related job performance, and absenteeism among nurses. *Journal of Behavioral Medicine, 18*(6), 581–599.

Parker, S. K., & Sprigg, C. A. (1999). Minimizing strain and maximizing learning: The role of job demands, job control, and proactive personality. *Journal of Applied Psychology, 84*(6), 925–939.

Parry, S. B. (2000). Measuring training's return on investment: A case in point. In G. M. Piskurich, P. Beckschi, & B. Hall (Eds.), *The ASTD handbook of training design and delivery* (pp. 147–157). New York: McGraw-Hill.

Pascoe, D. D., Pascoe, D. E., Wang, Y. T., Shim, D. M., & Kim, C. K. (1997). Influence of carrying book bags on gait cycle and posture of youths. *Ergonomics, 40*(6), 631–641.

Pass, J. J, & Robertson, D. W. (1980). *Methods to evaluate scales and sample size for stable task inventory information* [Rep. No. NPRDC TR 80–28]. San Diego, CA: Naval Personnel Research and Development Center.

Patrick, D. (1998, February 26). UConn coach arranged "gift" for Sales. *USA Today,* p. C13.

Patrick, J., & Moore, A. K. (1985). Development and reliability of a job analysis technique. *Journal of Occupational Psychology, 58,* 149–158.

Patton, W. D., & Pratt, C. (2002). Assessing the training needs of high-potential managers. *Public Personnel Mangement, 31*(4), 465–484.

Paul, R. J., & Ebadi, Y. M. (1989). Leadership decision making in a service organization: A field test of the Vroom-Yetton model. *Journal of Occupational Psychology, 62*(3), 201–211.

Payne, K. (1997). Undoing drugs: Setting up a drug free workplace program easier than ever. *South Florida Business Journal, 17*(35), 19–20.

Peak, M. H. (1997). Cutting jobs? Watch your disability expenses grow. *Management Review, 86*(3), 9.

Pearce, J. A. (1994). Dealing with religious diversity in the work place: A managerial guide and religious calendar for 1994. *SAM Advanced Management Journal, 59*(1), 4–12.

Pearce, J. L., & Porter, L. W. (1986). Employee responses to formal performance appraisal feedback. *Journal of Applied Psychology, 71,* 211–218.

Pearce, W. B., & Conklin, F. (1971). Nonverbal vocalic communication and perceptions of a speaker. *Speech Monographs, 38,* 235–241.

Peggans, D., Chandra, L., & McAlarnis, C. (1986). Managers' perceptions of the appropriateness of I/O psychology and M.B.A. coursework. *Proceedings of the 7th Annual Graduate Conference in Industrial/Organizational Psychology and Organizational Behavior.*

Pelletier, L. G., & Vallerand, R. J. (1996). Supervisors' beliefs and subordinates' intrinsic motivation: A behavioral confirmation analysis. *Journal of Personality and Social Psychology, 71*(2), 331–340.

Pendleton, C. S. (1986). Drug abuse strategies for business. *Security Management, 8,* 75.

Peres, S. H., & Garcia, J. R. (1962). Validity and dimensions of descriptive adjectives used in reference letters for engineering applicants. *Personnel Psychology, 15,* 279–286.

Pescuric, A., & Byham, W. C. (1996). The new look of behavior modeling. *Training & Development, 50*(7), 25–30.

Peter, L. J., & Hull, R. (1969). *The Peter Principle: Why things go wrong.* New York: Morrow.

Peterson, N. G., Mumford, M. D., Borman, W. C., Jeanneret, P. R., Fleishman, E. A., Levin, K. Y., Campion, M. A., Mayfield, M. S., Morgeson, F. P., Pearlman, K., Gowing, M. K., Lancaster, A. R., Silver, M. B., & Dye, D. M. (2001). Understanding work using the Occupational Information Network (O*NET): Implications for practice and research. *Personnel Psychology, 54*(2), 451–492.

Petrocelli, W., & Repa, B. K. (1992). *Sexual harassment on the job.* Berkeley: Nolo.

Pfau, B., & Kay, I. (2002a). Does 360-degree feedback negatively affect company performance? *HR Magazine, 47*(6), 55–59.

Pfau, B., & Kay, I. (2002b). HR playing the training game and losing. *HR Magazine, 47*(8), 49–54.

Philbrick, K. D. (1989). *The use of humor and effective leadership styles.* Unpublished doctoral dissertation, University of Florida.

Phillips, A. P., & Dipboye, R. L. (1989). Correlational tests of predictions from a process model of the interview. *Journal of Applied Psychology, 74,* 41–52.

Pibal, D. C. (1985). Criteria for effective resumes as perceived by personnel directors. *Personnel Administrator, 30*(5), 119–123.

Pine, D. E. (1995). Assessing the validity of job ratings: An empirical study of false reporting in task inventories. *Public Personnel Management, 24*(4), 451–460.

Pingitore, R., Dugoni, B. L., Tindale, R. S., & Spring, B. (1994). Bias against overweight job applicants in a simulated employment interview. *Journal of Applied Psychology, 79*(6), 909–917.

Plake, B. S., & Impara, J. C. (2001). *Fourteenth Mental Measurements Yearbook.* Austin, TX: Pro-Ed.

Planchy, R. J., & Planchy, S. J. (1993). Focus on results, not behavior. *Personnel Journal, 72*(3), 28–30.

Platania, J., & Moran, G. P. (2001). Social facilitation as a function of the mere presence of others. *Journal of Social Psychology, 141*(2), 190–197.

Platt, H. A. (1994). Nonsexual harassment claims hit HR's desk. *HR Magazine, 39*(3), 29–34.

Podsakoff, P. M., MacKenzie, S. B., & Ahearne, M. (1997). Moderating effects of goal acceptance on the relationship between group cohesiveness and productivity. *Journal of Applied Psychology, 82*(6), 974–983.

Poe, A. C. (1997). Productivity via paradise. *HR Magazine, 42*(10), 91–94.

Poe, A. C. (1999). Signing bonuses: A sign of the times. *HR Magazine, 44*(9), 104–112.

Poe, A. C. (2000). An office undivided. *HR Magazine, 45*(2), 58–64.

Poe, A. C. (2001). Don't touch that send button. *HR Magazine, 46*(7), 74–80.

Pollan, S. M., & Levine, M. (1994). Firing an employee. *Working Woman, 19*(8), 55.

Pollock, T. G., Whitbred, R. C., & Contractor, N. (2000). Social information processing and job characteristics: A simultaneous test of two theories with implications for job satisfaction. *Human Communication Research, 26*(2), 292–330.

Pond, S. B., & Geyer, P. D. (1987). Employee age as a moderator or the relationship between perceived work alternatives and job satisfaction. *Journal of Applied Psychology, 72,* 552–557.

Pool, S. W. (1997). The relationship of job satisfaction with substitutes of leadership, leadership behavior, and work motivation. *Journal of Psychology, 131*(3), 271–283.

Poor, R. (1970). *4 days, 40 hours.* Cambridge, MA: Bursk Poor.

Porter, L. W., & Lawler, E. E. (1968). *Managerial attitudes and performance.* Homewood, IL: Dorsey.

Pouliot, J. S. (1996). Rising complaints of religious bias. *Nation's Business, 84*(2), 36–37.

Posner, B. Z., Hall, J. L., & Munson, J. M. (1991). A first look at the benefits of educational benefits programs. *Applied H.R.M. Research, 2*(2), 128–152.

Pospisil, V. (1997). Keep it simple: Automated answering. *Industry Week, 246*(12), 8.

Posthuma, R. A., Morgeson, F. P., & Campion, M. A. (2002). Beyond employment interview validity: A comprehensive narrative review of recent research and trends over time. *Personnel Psychology, 55*(1), 1–81.

Powell, G. N. (1991). Applicant reactions to the initial employment interview: Exploring theoretical and methodological issues. *Personnel Psychology, 44,* 67–83.

Pratt, A. K., Burnazi, L., LePlan, L. A., Boyce, A. M., & Baltes, B. B. (2003). *Relationship between sexual harassment and negative outcomes: A meta-analysis.* Poster presented at the 18th annual meeting of the Society for Industrial and Organizational Psychology, Orlando, FL.

Premack, D. (1963). Prediction of the comparative reinforcement values of running and drinking. *Science, 139,* 1062–1063.

Premack, S. L., & Wanous, J. P. (1985). A meta-analysis of realistic job preview experiments. *Journal of Applied Psychology, 70,* 706–719.

Presser, H. B. (2000). Nonstandard work schedules and marital instability. *Journal of Marriage and the Family, 62*(1), 93.

Preston, L. A. (2003). *Coping with downsizing: A quantitative review.* Poster presented at the 18th annual meeting of the Society for Industrial and Organizational Psychology, Orlando, FL.

Prewett-Livingston, A. J., Feild, H. A., Veres, J. G., & Lewis, P. M. (1996). Effects of race on interview ratings in a situational panel interview. *Journal of Applied Psychology, 81*(2), 178–186.

Prien, E. P. (1977). The function of job analysis in content validation. *Personnel Psychology, 30,* 167–174.

Pritchard, R. D., Dunnette, M. D., & Jorgenson, D. (1972). Effects of perceptions of equity on worker motivation and satisfaction. *Journal of Applied Psychology, 56*(1), 75–94.

Pritchett, P. (1993). *Culture shift: The employee handbook for changing corporate culture.* Dallas: Pritchett & Associates.

Pritchett, P., & Pound, R. (1995). *The stress of organizational change.* Dallas, TX: Pritchett & Associates.

Pulakos, E. D., Arad, S., Donovan, M. A., & Plamondon, K. E. (2000). Adaptability in the workplace: Development of a taxonomy of adaptive performance. *Journal of Applied Psychology, 85*(4), 612–624.

Pulakos, E. D., & Schmitt, N. (1995). Experience-based and situational interview questions: Studies of validity. *Personnel Psychology, 48,* 289–308.

Pulakos, E. D., Schmitt, N., Whitney, D., & Smith, M. (1996). Individual differences in interviewer ratings: The impact of standardization, consensus discussion, and sampling error on the validity of a structured interview. *Personnel Psychology, 49*(1), 85–102.

Pursell, E. D., Dossett, D. L., & Latham, G. P. (1980). Obtaining valid predictors by minimizing rating errors in the criterion. *Personnel Psychology, 33,* 91–96.

Qian, Y. J. (1996). *Managers' stock ownership and performance in lodging industry.* Unpublished master's thesis, University of Nevada at Las Vegas.

Quaglieri, P. L. (1982). A note on variations in recruiting information obtained through different sources. *Journal of Occupational Psychology, 55,* 53–55.

Quinn, J. F., & Petrick, J. A. (1993). Emerging strategic human resource challenges in managing accent discrimination and ethnic diversity. *Applied H.R.M. Research, 4*(2), 79–93.

Quiñones, M. A., Ford, J. K., & Teachout, M. S. (1995). The relationship between work experience and job performance: A conceptual and meta-analytic review. *Personnel Psychology, 48*(4), 887–910.

Rabinowitz, S., Melamed, S., Feiner, M., & Weisberg, E. (1996). Hostility and hearing protection behavior: The mediating role of personal beliefs and low frustration tolerance. *Journal of Occupational Health Psychology, 1*(4), 375–381.

Rae, L. (1994). Choose your method. *Training and Development, 48*(4), 19–25.

Rafaeli, A., & Klimoski, R. J. (1983). Predicting sales success through handwriting analysis: An evaluation of the effects of training and handwriting sample content. *Journal of Applied Psychology, 68,* 212–217.

Ragins, B. R., & Cotton, J. L. (1999). Mentor functions and outcomes: A comparison of men and women in formal and informal mentoring relationships. *Journal of Applied Psychology, 84*(4), 529–550.

Rahim, M. A. (1989). Relationships of leader power to compliance and satisfaction with supervision: Evidence from a national sample of managers. *Journal of Management,15*(4), 545–556.

Rahim, M. A., & Afza, M. (1993). Leader power, commitment, satisfaction, compliance, and propensity to leave a job among U.S. accountants. *Journal of Social Psychology, 133*(5), 611–625.

Rahim, M. A., Garrett, J. E., & Buntzman, G. F. (1992). Ethics of managing interpersonal conflict in organizations. *Journal of Business Ethics, 11,* 423–432.

Rahim, M. A., & Magner, N. R. (1995). Confirmatory factor analysis of the styles of handling interpersonal conflict: First-order factor model and its invariance across groups. *Journal of Applied Psychology, 80*(1), 122–132.

Rahim, M. A., & Psenicka, C. (1996). A structural equations model of stress, locus of control, social support, psychiatric symptoms, and propensity to leave a job. *Journal of Social Psychology, 136*(1), 69–84.

Ramsey, J. D. (1995). Task performance in heat: A review. *Ergonomics, 38*(1), 154–165.

Range, L. M., Menyhert, A., Walsh, M. L., Hardin, K. N., Craddock, A., & Ellis, J. B. (1991). Letters of recommendation: Perspectives, recommendations, and ethics. *Professional Psychology: Research and Practice, 22*(5), 389–392.

Rasmussen, K. G. (1984). Nonverbal behavior, verbal behavior, resume credentials, and selection interview outcomes. *Journal of Applied Psychology, 69,* 551–556.

Raven, B. H. (1965). Social influence and power. In I. D. Steiner & M. Fishbein (Eds.), *Current studies in social psychology* (pp. 371–382). New York: Holt, Rinehart & Winston.

Raven, B. H. (1992). A power/interaction model of interpersonal influence: French and Raven thirty years later. *Journal of Social Behavior and Personality, 7*(2), 217–244.

Ray, J. J., & Hall, G. P. (1995). Need for affiliation and group identification. *Journal of Social Psychology, 135*(4), 519–521.

Raymark, P. H., Schmit, M. J., & Guion, R. M. (1997). Identifying potentially useful personality constructs for employee selection. *Personnel Psychology, 50*(3), 723–736.

Raynes, B. L. (1997). Review of employee privacy issues: Implications for law enforcement and other public and private sector agencies. *Journal of Police and Criminal Psychology, 12*(2),19–27.

Raynes, B. L. (2001). The relationship between self-esteem and difficult communication styles. *Applied HRM Research, 6*(1), 33–66.

Raza, S. M., & Carpenter, B. N. (1987). A model of hiring decisions in real employment interviews. *Journal of Applied Psychology, 72,* 596–603.

Recardo, R. J., & Pricone, D. (1996). Is skill-based pay for you? *SAM Advanced Management Journal, 61*(4), 16–21.

Reed, D. (2003, January 9). Don't abuse sick time, American CEO warns. *USA Today,* p. B2.

Reid, M. (1996). Keeping the faith while keeping your job: Harmonize your religious beliefs and the rules of the workplace. *Black Enterprise, 26*(12), 52.

Reilly, C. E., & Smith, C. (1988). Effects of shiftwork and psychometric evaluation of shiftworker selection instruments. *Proceedings of 9th Annual Graduate Conference in Industrial/Organizational Psychology and Organizational Behavior.*

Reilly, R. R., & Chao, G. T. (1982). Validity and fairness of some alternative employee selection procedures. *Personnel Psychology, 35,* 1–62.

Reilly, R. R., Smither, J. W., & Vasilopoulous, N. L. (1996). A longitudinal study of upward feedback. *Personnel Psychology, 49*(3), 599–612.

Reinsch, N. L., & Beswick, R. W. (1990). Voice mail versus conventional channels: A cost minimization analysis of individuals' preferences. *Academy of Management Journal, 33*(4), 801–816.

Reizenstein, R. M., & Burke, M. J. (1996). *Another look at relationships between group cohesion and group performance.* Poster presented at the 11th annual conference of the Society for Industrial and Organizational Psychology, San Diego, CA.

Renk, K. (2000). I want my TV. *HR Magazine, 45*(10), 158–162.

Rentsch, J. R., Lowenberg, G., Barnes-Farrell, J., & Menard, D. (1997). Report on the survey of graduate programs in industrial/organizational psychology and organizational behavior/human resources. *The Industrial-Organizational Psychologist, 35*(1), 49–68.

Rentsch, J. R., & Steel, R. P. (1998). Testing the durability of job characteristics as predictors of absenteeism over a six-year period. *Personnel Psychology, 51*(1), 165–190.

Repetti, R. L., & Cosmas, K. A. (1991). The quality of the social environment at work and job satisfaction. *Journal of Applied Social Psychology, 21*(10), 840–854.

Repetti, R. L., & Wood, J. (1997). Effects of daily stress at work on mothers' interactions with preschoolers. *Journal of Family Psychology, 11*(1), 90–108.

Rhine, R. J., & Severance, L. J. (1970). Ego-involvement, discrepancy, source credibility, and attitude change. *Journal of Personality and Social Psychology, 16,* 175–190.

Rhoads, C. (1997). A year-round schedule said to take sting out of performance reviews. *American Banker, 162*(28), 6.

Rhodes, S. R. (1983). Age-related differences in work attitudes and behavior: A review and conceptual analysis. *Psychological Bulletin, 93,* 328–367.

Rice, B. (1983). Curbing cyberphobia. *Psychology Today, 8,* 79.

Rice, R. W. (1978). Psychometric properties of the esteem for Least Preferred Coworker (LPC) Scale. *Academy of Management Review, 3,* 106–118.

Rice, R. W., Gentile, D. A., & McFarlin, D. B. (1991). Facet importance and job satisfaction. *Journal of Applied Psychology, 76*(1), 31–39.

Richman-Hirsch, W. L., Olson-Buchanan, J. B., & Drasgow, F. (2000). Examining the impact of administration medium on examinee perceptions and attitudes. *Journal of Applied Psychology, 85*(6), 880–887.

Riddle, D., & Foster, L. (1997). You know, I've been wondering. *The Industrial-Organizational Psychologist, 35*(2), 49–56.

Rieke, M. L., & Guastello, S. J. (1995). Unresolved issues in honesty and integrity testing. *American Psychologist, 50*(6), 458–459.

Riggio, R. E., & Cole, E. J. (1992). Agreement between subordinate and superior ratings of supervisory performance and effects on self and subordinate satisfaction. *Journal of Occupational and Organizational Psychology, 65,* 137–158.

Roballey, T. C., & Gardner, E. (1986). Eat to the beat. *Psychology Today, 20*(2), 16.

Robbins, S. P. (2001). *Organizational behavior* (9th ed.). Englewood Cliffs, NJ: Prentice-Hall.

Robert, C., Probst, T. M., Martocchio, J. J., Drasgow, F., & Lawler, J. J. (2000). Empowerment and continuous improvement in the United States, Mexico, Poland, and India: Predicting fit on the basis of the dimensions of power distance and individualism. *Journal of Applied Psychology, 85*(5), 643–658.

Roberts, B. (2001). E-learning: New twist on CBT. *HR Magazine, 46*(4), 99–106.

Roberts, G. E. (1994). Maximizing performance appraisal system acceptance: Perspectives from municipal government personnel administrators. *Public Personnel Management, 23*(4), 525–549.

Robertson, I. T., & Kandola, R. S. (1982). Work sample tests: Validity, adverse impact, and applicant reaction. *Journal of Occupational Psychology, 55,* 171–183.

Robinson, D. D. (1981). Content-oriented personnel selection in a small business setting. *Personnel Psychology, 34,* 77–87.

Robinson, R. K., Allen, B. M., & Abraham, Y. T. (1992). Affirmative action plans in the 1990's: A double edged sword? *Public Personnel Management, 21*(2), 261–272.

Rohmert, W., & Landau, K. (1983). *A new technique for job analysis.* New York: Taylor & Francis.

Romanov, K., Appelberg, K., Honkasalo, M., & Koskenvuo, M. (1996). Recent interpersonal conflict at work and psychiatric morbidity: A prospective study of 15,530 employees aged 24–64. *Journal of Psychosomatic Research, 40*(2), 169–176.

Rosen, D. J. (1992). Appraisals can make or break your court case. *Personnel Journal, 71*(11), 113–116.

Rosen, S., & Tesser, A. (1970). Reluctance to communicate undesirable information: The MUM effect. *Sociometry, 33,* 253–263.

Rosen, T. H. (1987). Identification of substance abusers in the workplace. *Public Personnel Management, 16*(3), 197–208.

Rosenthal, R. (1994). Interpersonal expectancy effects: A 30 year perspective. *Current Directions in Psychological Science, 3*(6), 176–179.

Rosenthal, R. (2002). Covert communications in classrooms, clinics, courtrooms, and cubicles. *American Psychologist, 57*(11), 839–849.

Ross, W. R., & Wieland, C. (1996). Effectiveness of interpersonal trust and the pressure on managerial mediation strategy in a simulated organizational dispute. *Journal of Applied Psychology, 81*(3), 228–248.

Roth, P. L., BeVier, C. A., Bobko, P., Switzer, F. S., & Tyler, P. (2001). Ethnic group differences in cognitive ability in employment and educational settings: A meta-analysis. *Personnel Psychology, 54*(2), 297–330.

Roth, P. L., BeVier, C. A., Switzer, F. S., & Schippmann, J. S. (1996). Meta-analyzing the relationship between grades and job performance. *Journal of Applied Psychology, 81*(5), 548–556.

Roth, P. L., & Bobko, P. (2000). College grade point average as a personnel selection device: Ethnic group differences and potential adverse impact. *Journal of Applied Psychology, 85*(3), 399–406.

Roth, P. L., & Clarke, R. L. (1998). Meta-analyzing the relationship between grades and salary. *Journal of Vocational Behavior, 53,* 386–400.

Rothstein, H. R., & McDaniel, M. A. (1992). Differential validity by sex in employment settings. *Journal of Business and Psychology, 7*(1), 45–62.

Rothstein, H. R., Schmidt, F. L., Erwin, F. W., Owens, W. A., & Sparks, C. P. (1990). Biographical data in employment selection: Can validities be made generalizable? *Journal of Applied Psychology, 75,* 175–184.

Rotundo, M., Nguyen, D. H., & Sackett, P. R. (2001). A meta-analytic review of gender differences in perceptions of sexual harassment. *Journal of Applied Psychology, 86*(5), 914–922.

Rouleau, E. J., & Krain, B. F. (1975). Using job analysis to design selection procedures. *Public Personnel Management, 4,* 300–304.

Rowe, P. M. (1989). Unfavorable information and interview decisions. In R. W. Eder, & G. R. Ferris (Eds.), *The employment interview* (pp. 77–89). Newbury Park, CA: Sage.

Ruback, R. B., & Juieng, D. (1997). Territorial defense in parking lots: Retaliation against waiting drivers. *Journal of Applied Social Psychology, 27*(9), 821–834.

Rubin, J. Z. (1994). Models of conflict management. *Journal of Social Issues, 50*(1), 33–45.

Rubin, J. Z., & Brown, B. R. (1975). *The social psychology of bargaining and negotiation.* New York: Academic Press.

Rubin, J. Z., & Lewecki, R. J. (1973). A three-factor experimental analysis of promises and threats. *Journal of Applied Social Psychology, 3,* 240–257.

Rubin, R. S. (2002). Will the real SMART goals please stand up? *The Industrial-Organizational Psychologist, 39*(4), 26–27.

Rubis, L. (1998). Positive drug tests hit 11-year low. *HR Magazine,43*(6), 20.

Rupert, G. (1989). Employee referrals as a source of recruitment and job performance. *Proceedings of the 10th Annual Graduate Conference in Industrial/Organizational Psychology and Organizational Behavior.*

Rushton, J. P. (1995). Construct validity, censorship, and the genetics of race. *American Psychologist, 50*(1), 40–41.

Russ-Eft, D., & Zucchelli, L. (1987). When wrong is all right. *Training and Development Journal, 41*(11), 78–79.

Russell, C. J., Colella, A., & Bobko, P. (1993). Expanding the context of utility: The strategic impact of personnel selection. *Personnel Psychology, 46,* 781–801.

Ruzich, P. (1999). Triangles: Tools for untangling interpersonal messes. *HR Magazine, 44*(7), 129–136.

Ryan, A. M., & Lasek, M. (1991). Negligent hiring and defamation: Areas of liability related to pre-employment inquiries. *Personnel Psychology, 44,* 293–319.

Ryan, R. (1995). 21 ways to improve your resume. *Journal of Accountancy, 180*(6), 83–86.

Ryan, R. M., & Deci, E. L. (1996). When paradigms clash: Comments on Cameron and Pierce's claim that rewards do not undermine intrinsic motivation. *Review of Educational Research, 66*(1), 33–38.

Rynes, S. L., Bretz, R. D., & Gerhart, B. (1991). The importance of recruitment in job choice: A different way of looking. *Personnel Psychology, 44*(3), 487–520.

Rynes, S. L., & Connerley, M. L. (1993). Applicant reactions to alternative selection procedures. *Journal of Business and Psychology, 7,* 261–277.

Rynes, S. L., Weber, C. L., & Milkovich, G. T. (1989). Effects of market survey rates, job evaluation, and job gender on job pay. *Journal of Applied Psychology, 74*(1), 114–123.

Saad, S., & Sackett, P. R. (2002). Investigating differential prediction by gender in employment-oriented personality measures. *Journal of Applied Psychology, 87*(4), 667–674.

Saal, F. E. (1979). Mixed standard rating scale: A consistent system for numerically coding inconsistent response combinations. *Journal of Applied Psychology, 64,* 422–428.

Saavedra, R., & Kwun, S. K. (1993). Peer evaluation in self-managing work groups. *Journal of Applied Psychology, 78*(3), 450–462.

Sabath, A. M. (2001). Dressing for the job. *Planning Job Choices: 2002,* 88–89.

Sabini, J. (1995). *Social psychology* (2nd ed.). New York: Norton.

Sackett, P. R., & Roth, L. (1991). A Monte Carlo examination of banding and rank order methods of test score use in personnel selection. *Human Performance, 4*(4), 279–295.

Sackett, P. R., & Wanek, J. E. (1996). New developments in the use of measures of honesty, integrity, conscientiousness, dependability, trustworthiness, and reliability for personnel selection. *Personnel Psychology, 49*(4), 787–829.

Sackman, S. (1991). Uncovering culture in organizations. *Journal of Applied Behavioral Science, 27*(3), 294–315.

Sadri, G. (1996). Reflections: The impact of downsizings on survivors—some findings and recommendations. *Journal of Managerial Psychology, 11*(4), 56–59.

Sadri, G., & Robertson, I. T. (1993). Self-efficacy and work-related behavior: A review and meta-analysis. *Applied Psychology: An International Review, 42*(2), 139–152.

Sahl, R. J. (1996). Using tailored employee attitude surveys to measure HR's effectiveness. *Employment Relations Today, 23*(3), 55–63.

Saks, A. M., Wiesner, W. H., & Summers, R. J. (1996). Effects of job previews and compensation policy on applicant attraction and job choice. *Journal of Vocational Behavior, 49*(1), 68–85.

Salancik, G., & Pfeffer, J. (1977). An examination of need-satisfaction models of job satisfaction and job attitudes. *Administrative Science Quarterly, 22,* 427–456.

Salas, E., & Cannon-Bowers, J. A. (2001). The science of training: A decade of progress. *Annual Review of Psychology,* 471–499.

Salas, E., Mullen, B., Rozell, D., & Driskell, J. E. (1997). *The effects of team building on performance: An integration.* Poster presented at the 12th annual conference of the Society for Industrial and Organizational Psychology, St. Louis, MO.

Sanchez, J. I., & Fraser, S. L. (1992). On the choice of scales for task analysis. *Journal of Applied Psychology, 77,* 545–553.

Sanchez, J. I., & Levine, E. L. (1989). Determining important tasks within jobs: A policy-capturing approach. *Journal of Applied Psychology, 74,* 336–342.

Sanchez, J. I., & Levine, E. L. (2000). Accuracy or consequential validity: Which is the better standard for job analysis data? *Journal of Organizational Behavior, 21,* 809–818.

Sanchez, J. I., Prager, I., Wilson, A., & Viswesvaran, C. (1998). Understanding the within-job title variance in job analytic ratings. *Journal of Business and Psychology, 12*, 407–419.

Sanders, G. S. (1981). Driven by distraction: An integrative review of social facilitation theory and research. *Journal of Experimental Social Psychology, 17*, 227–251.

Sandler, L. (1986). Self-fulfilling prophecy: Better management by magic. *Training, 23*, 60–64.

Savage, J. I. (1988). Study refires VDT safety debate: Shows link between heavy use and miscarriages. *Computerworld, 22*(6), 1–2.

Sawyer, A. (1973). The effects of repetition on refutational and supportive advertising appeals. *Journal of Marketing Research, 10*, 23–33.

Scandura, T. A., Graen, G. B., & Novak, M. A. (1986). When managers decide not to decide autocratically: An investigation of leader–member exchange and decision influence. *Journal of Applied Psychology, 71*, 579–584.

Scarr, S. (1998). American child care today. *American Psychologist, 53*(2), 95–108.

Schatzki, M. (1981). *Negotiation*. New York: Signet.

Schaubroeck, J., Ganster, D. C., & Kemmerer, B. E. (1994). Job complexity, Type A behavior, and cardiovascular disorder: A prospective study. *Academy of Management Journal, 37*(2), 426–439.

Schein, E. (1956). The Chinese indoctrination program for prisoners of war. *Psychiatry, 19*, 149–177.

Schein, E. (1985). *Organizational culture and leadership: A dynamic view*. San Francisco, CA: Jossey-Bass.

Schettler, J. (2002). Withering heights: 21st annual salary survey. *Training, 39*(11), 36–48.

Schippmann, J. S., Ash, R. A., Battista, M., Carr, L., Eyde, L. D., Hesketh, B., Kehoe, J., Pearlman, K., Prien, E. P., & Sanchez, J. I. (2000). The practice of competency modeling. *Personnel Psychology, 53*(3), 703–740.

Schippmann, J. S., Prien, E. P., & Katz, J. A. (1990). Reliability and validity of in-basket performance measures. *Personnel Psychology, 43*, 837–859.

Schippmann, J. S., Schmitt, S. D., & Hawthorne, S. L. (1992). I/O work roles: Ph.D. vs. master's level practitioners. *The Industrial-Organizational Psychologist, 29*(4), 35–39.

Schleifer, L. M., & Amick, B. C. (1989). System response time and method of pay: Stress effects in computer-based tasks. *International Journal of Human Computer Interaction, 1*(1), 23–39.

Schleifer, L. M., & Okogbaa, O. G. (1990). System response time and method of pay: Cardiovascular stress effects in computer-based tasks. *Ergonomics, 33*(12), 1495–1509.

Schmidt, F. L. (1973). Implications of a measurement problem for expectancy theory research. *Organizational Behavior and Human Performance, 10*, 243–251.

Schmidt, F. L. (1988). The problem of group differences in ability test scores in employment selection. *Journal of Vocational Behavior, 33*(3), 272–292.

Schmidt, F. L. (1991). Why all banding procedures in personnel selection are logically flawed. *Human Performance, 4*, 265–277.

Schmidt, F. L., Gast-Rosenberg, I., & Hunter, J. E. (1980). Validity generalization results for computer programmers. *Journal of Applied Psychology, 65*, 643–661.

Schmidt, F. L., Greenthal, A. L., Hunter, J. E., Berner, J. G., & Seaton, F. W. (1977). Job sample vs. paper and pencil trades and technical tests: Adverse impact and examinee attitudes. *Personnel Psychology, 30*, 187–197.

Schmidt, F. L., & Hunter, J. E. (1978). Moderator research and the law of small numbers. *Personnel Psychology, 31*, 215–232.

Schmidt, F. L., & Hunter, J. E. (1981). Employment testing: Old theories and new research. *American Psychologist, 36*, 1128–1137.

Schmidt, F. L., & Hunter, J. E. (1998). The validity and utility of selection methods in personnel psychology: Practical and theoretical implications of 85 years of research findings. *Psychological Bulletin, 124*(2), 262–274.

Schmidt, F. L., Hunter, J. E., Pearlman, K., & Hirsh, H. R. (1985). Forty questions about validity generalization and meta-analysis. *Personnel Psychology, 38*, 697–798.

Schmidt, F. L., & Rader, M. (1999). Exploring the boundary conditions for interview validity: Meta-analytic validity findings for a new interview type. *Personnel Psychology, 52*(2), 445–464.

Schmidt, F. L., & Rothstein, H. R. (1994). Application of validity generalization to biodata scales in employment selection. In G. S. Stokes, M. D. Mumford, & W. A. Owens (Eds.), *Biodata handbook* (pp. 237–260). Palo Alto, CA: Consulting Psychologists Press.

Schmitt, N. (1996). Uses and abuses of coefficient alpha. *Psychological Assessment, 8*(4), 350–353.

Schmitt, N., Clause, C., & Pulakos, E. (1996). Subgroup differences associated with different measures of some common job relevant constructs. In C. L. Cooper & I. T. Robertson (Eds.), *International review of industrial and organizational psychology* (Vol. 11; pp. 115–140). New York: Wiley.

Schmitt, N., & Cohen, S. A. (1989). Internal analyses of task ratings by job incumbents. *Journal of Applied Psychology, 74*, 96–104.

Schmitt, N., Coyle, B. W., & Rauschenberger, J. (1977). A Monte Carlo evaluation of three formula estimates of cross-validated multiple correlation. *Psychological Bulletin, 84*, 751–758.

Schmitt, N., & Mills, A. E. (2001). Traditional tests and job simulations: Minority and majority performance and test validities. *Journal of Applied Psychology, 86*(3), 451–458.

Schmitt, N., Schneider, J. R., & Cohen, S. A. (1990). Factors affecting validity of a regionally administered assessment center. *Personnel Psychology, 43*, 1–12.

Schneider, K. T., Swan, S., & Fitzgerald, L. F. (1997). Job-related and psychological effects of sexual harassment in the workplace: Empirical evidence from two organizations. *Journal of Applied Psychology, 82*(3), 401–415.

Schrader, B. W., & Steiner, D. D. (1996). Common comparison standards: An approach to improving agreement between self and supervisory performance ratings. *Journal of Applied Psychology, 81*(6), 813–820.

Schriesheim, C. A., Castro, S. L., & Cogliser, C. C. (1999). Leader-member exchange (LMX) research: A comprehensive review of theory, measurement, and data-analytic practices. *Leadership Quarterly, 10*, 63–113.

Schriesheim, C. A., Castro, S. L., & Yammarino, F. J. (2000). Investigating contingencies: An examination of the impact of span of supervision and upward controllingness on leader–member exchange using traditional and multivariate within- and between-entities analysis. *Journal of Applied Psychology, 85*(5), 659–677.

Schriesheim, C. A., & DeNisi, A. S. (1981). Task dimensions as moderators of the effects of instrumental leadership: A two-sample replicated test of path-goal leadership theory. *Journal of Applied Psychology, 66*, 589–597.

Schriesheim, C. A., Tepper, B. J., & Tetrault, L. A. (1994). Least Preferred Coworker score, situational control, and leadership effectiveness: A meta-analysis of contingency model performance predictions. *Journal of Applied Psychology, 79*(4), 561–573.

Schriesheim, J. F., & Schriesheim, C. A. (1980). A test of the path-goal theory of leadership and some suggested directions for future research. *Personnel Psychology, 33,* 349–370.

Schultz, R. (1976). Effects of control and predictability on the physical and psychological well-being of the institutionalized aged. *Journal of Personality and Social Psychology, 33,* 563–573.

Schuster, F. E., Morden, D. L., Baker, T. E., McKay, I. S., Dunning, K. E., & Hagan, C. M. (1997). Management practice, organization climate, and performance: An exploratory study. *Journal of Applied Behavioral Science, 33*(2), 209–226.

Schuster, J. R., & Zingheim, P. K. (1992). *The new pay.* New York: Lexington.

Schwab, D. P. (1982). Recruiting and organizational participation. In K. M. Rowland & G. R. Farris (Eds.), *Personnel management.* Boston, MA: Allyn & Bacon.

Schwab, D. P., Heneman, H. G., & DeCotiis, T. A. (1975). Behaviorally anchored rating scales: A review of the literature. *Personnel Psychology, 28,* 549–562.

Schwartz, B., & Barsky, S. (1977). The home advantage. *Social Forces, 55,* 641–666.

Schwarz, N. (1999). Self reports: How the questions shape the answers. *American Psychologist, 54*(2), 93–105.

Schweitzer, S. C. (1979). *Winning with deception and bluff.* Englewood Cliffs, NJ: Prentice-Hall.

Scott, K. D., & Markham, S. E. (1982). Absenteeism control methods: A survey of practice and results. *Personnel Administrator, 27*(6), 73–84.

Scott, K. D., Markham, S. E., & Robers, R. W. (1985). Rewarding good attendance: A comparative study of positive ways to reduce absenteeism. *Personnel Administrator, 30,* 72–75.

Scott, W. D. (1903). *The theory of advertising.* Boston: Small Maynard.

Scrivner, T. W. (1995). The art of employment termination. *Credit Union Executive, 35*(6), 18–21.

Sears, D. O. (1986). College sophomores in the laboratory: Influences of a narrow database on social psychology's view of human nature. *Journal of Personality and Social Psychology, 51*(3), 515–530.

Seberhagen, L. W. (1996). How much does a test validation study cost? In R. S. Barrett (Ed.), *Fair employment strategies in human resource management* (pp. 88–93). Westport, CT: Quorum.

Segal, J. A. (2001). Workplace tribal councils. *HR Magazine, 46*(6), 197–209.

Seitz, D. D., & Modica, A. J. (1980). *Negotiating your way to success.* New York: Mentor.

Sessa, V. I. (1994). Can conflict improve team effectiveness? *Issues & Observations, 14*(4), 1–5.

Seta, J. J. (1982). The impact of comparison processes on coactor's task performance. *Journal of Personality and Social Psychology, 42,* 281–291.

Shadish, W. R., & Ragsdale, K. (1996). Random versus nonrandom assignment in controlled experiments: Do you get the same answer? *Journal of Consulting and Clinical Psychology, 64*(6), 1290–1305.

Shafer, M., & Crichlow, S. (1996). Antecedents of groupthink: A quantitative study. *Journal of Conflict Resolution, 40*(3), 415–435.

Shaffer, D. R., & Tomarelli, M. (1981). Bias in the ivory tower: An unintended consequence of the Buckley Amendment for graduate admissions. *Journal of Applied Psychology, 66,* 7–11.

Shaffer, G. S., Saunders, V., & Owens, W. A. (1986). Additional evidence for the accuracy of biographical data: Long-term retest and observer ratings. *Personnel Psychology, 39*(4), 791–809.

Shalley, C. E. (1995). Effects of coaction, expected evaluation, and goal setting on creativity and productivity. *Academy of Management Journal, 38*(2), 483–503.

Shapira, Z., & Shirom, A. (1980). New issues in the use of behaviorally anchored rating scales: Level of analysis, the effects of incident frequency, and external validation. *Journal of Applied Psychology, 65,* 517–523.

Shaw, M. E., & Shaw, I. M. (1962). Some effects of social grouping upon learning in a second grade classroom. *Journal of Social Psychology, 57,* 453–458.

Shelton, S., & Alliger, G. (1993). Who's afraid of Level 4 evaluations? *Training and Development, 43*(6), 43–46.

Shepperd, J. A. (1993). Productivity loss in performance groups: A motivation analysis. *Psychological Bulletin, 113*(1), 67–81.

Shepperd, J. A., & Taylor, K. M. (1999). Social loafing and expectancy-value theory. *Personality and Social Psychology Bulletin, 25*(9), 1147–1158.

Sherriton, J., & Stern, J. (1997). HR's role in culture change. *HR Focus, 74*(4), 27.

Sherwyn, D., Sturman, M. C., Eigen, Z. J., Heise, M., & Walwyn, J. (2001). The perversity of sexual-harassment law: Effects of recent court rulings. *Cornell Hotel & Restaurant Administration Quarterly, 42*(3), 46–56.

Shetzer, L., & Stackman, R. (1991). The career path component in realistic job previews: A meta-analysis and proposed integration. *Applied H.R.M. Research, 2*(2), 153–169.

Shih, Y. C., & Wang, M. J. (1996). The effects of weight levels and gloves on the ability to discriminate weight differences. *Ergonomics, 39*(5), 729–739.

Shih, Y. C., & Wang, M. J. (1997). The influence of gloves during maximum volitional torque exertion of supination. *Ergonomics, 40*(4), 465–475.

Shilobod, T. L., McMullen, L. J., & Raymark, P. H. (2003). *Situational leadership theory: A meta-analysis of the adaptability hypothesis.* Poster presented at the 18th annual meeting of the Society for Industrial and Organizational Psychology, Orlando, FL.

Shinar, D. (1995). Field evaluation of an advance brake warning system. *Human Factors, 37*(4), 746–751.

Shippman, J. S. Ash, R. A., Battista, M., Carr, L., Eyde, L. D., Hesketh, B., Kehoe, J., Pearlman, K., Prien, E. P., & Sanchez, J. I. (2000). The practice of competency modeling. *Personnel Psychology, 53,* 703–740.

Shneiderman, B. (1980). *Software psychology.* Cambridge, MA: Winthrop.

SHRM (1998). *Reference checking survey.* Alexandria, VA: Society for Human Resource Management.

SHRM (2000). *Performance management survey*. Alexandria, VA: Society for Human Resource Management.

SHRM (2001a). *Employee referral programs*. Alexandria, VA: Society for Human Resource Management.

SHRM (2001b). *Search Tactics Poll*. Alexandria, VA: Society for Human Resource Management.

SHRM (2002). *2002 benefits survey*. Alexandria, VA: Society for Human Resource Management.

Sieber, J. E., & Saks, M. J. (1989). A census of subject pool characteristics and policies. *American Psychologist, 44*(7), 1053–1061.

Silva, J. M., & Jacobs, R. R. (1993). Performance as a function of increased minority hiring. *Journal of Applied Psychology, 78*(4), 591–601.

Simonton, D. K. (1987). *Why presidents succeed: A political psychology of leadership*. New Haven, CT: Yale University Press.

Sims, R. R., Veres, J. G., & Heninger, S. M. (1989). Training for competence. *Public Personnel Management, 18*(1), 101–107.

Singer, B. W. (2000). Get goofy now! *Health, 14*(8), 76–79.

Sivak, M., Flannagan, M. J., Sato, T., & Traube, E. C. (1994). Reaction times to neon, LED, and fast incandescent brake lamps. *Ergonomics, 37*(6), 989–994.

Skinner, B. F. (1971). *Beyond freedom and dignity*. New York: Knopf.

Smith, A., & Jones, D. M. (1992). Noise and performance. *Handbook of human performance* (Vol. 1; pp. 1–28). London: Academic Press.

Smith, B. N., Hornsby, J. S., Benson, P. G., & Wesolowski, M. (1989). What is in a name: The impact of job titles on job evaluation results. *Journal of Business and Psychology, 3*(3), 341–351.

Smith, C., Reilly, C., & Midkiff, K. (1988, August). *Psychometric evaluation of circadian rhythm questionnaires with suggestions for improvement*. Paper presented at the annual meeting of the American Psychological Association, Atlanta, GA.

Smith, D. (2003). Five principles for research ethics. *American Psychologist, 34*(1), 56–60.

Smith, D. E. (1986). Training programs for performance appraisal: A review. *Academy of Management Review, 11*, 22–40.

Smith, E. R., & Mackie, D. M. (1999). *Social psychology* (2nd ed.). New York: Worth.

Smith, J. E., & Hakel, M. D. (1979). Convergence among data sources, response bias, and reliability and validity of a structured job analysis questionnaire. *Personnel Psychology, 32*, 677–692.

Smith, L., & Folkard, S. (1993). The perceptions and feelings of shiftworkers' partners. *Ergonomics, 36*(1), 299–305.

Smith, L., Totterdell, P., & Folkard, S. (1995). Shiftwork effects in nuclear power workers: A field study using portable computers. *Work and Stress, 9*, 235–244.

Smith, L. B. (1997). Electrical contractor's apprenticeship program offers option to college education. *Memphis Business Journal, 18*(51), 17.

Smith, M. (2001, September). The employee grapevine: What employers can learn from it. *IPMA News*, pp. 10–11.

Smith, M. (2003a, January). Employee health affects more than the bottom line. *IPMA News*, pp. 8–10.

Smith, M. (2003b, January). Repetitive motion injuries and workers' compensation. *IPMA News*, p. 9.

Smith, M. J., Cohen, B. G., & Stammerjohn, L. W. (1981). An investigation of health complaints and job stress in video display operations. *Human Factors, 23*(4), 387–400.

Smith, M. L. (1993). Defensible performance appraisals. *Journal of Management in Engineering, 9*(2), 128–135.

Smith, P. C., & Kendall, L. M. (1963). Retranslating expectations: An approach to the construction of unambiguous anchors for rating scales. *Journal of Applied Psychology, 47*, 149–155.

Smith, P. C., Kendall, L. M., & Hulin, C. L. (1969). *The measurement of satisfaction in work and retirement*. Chicago: Rand McNally.

Smither, J. W., Barry, S. R., & Reilly, R. R. (1989). An investigation of the validity of expert true score estimates in appraisal research. *Journal of Applied Psychology, 74*, 143–151.

Smither, J. W., London, M., Vasilopoulos, N. L., Reilly, R. R., Millsap, R. E., & Salvemini, N. (1995). An examination of the effects of an upward feedback program over time. *Personnel Psychology, 48*(1), 1–34.

Smither, J. W., Reilly, R. R., & Buda, R. (1988). Effect of prior performance information on ratings of recent performance: Contrast versus assimilation revisited. *Journal of Applied Psychology, 73*, 487–496.

Smither, J. W., Reilly, R. R., Millsap, R. E., Pearlman, K., & Stoffey, R. W. (1993). Applicant reactions to selection procedures. *Personnel Psychology, 46*, 49–76.

Smither, R., & Lindgren, H. C. (1978). Salary, age, sex, and need for achievement in bank employees. *Psychological Reports, 42*, 334.

Smothers, R. (1993, January 31). Settlement commits Shoney's to affirmative action plan. *Roanoke Times and World News*, p. B6.

Snyman, J., Aamodt, M. G., Johnson, D. L., & Frantzve, J. (1991). Pre-employment paper-and-pencil testing: A quantitative review. *Journal of Police and Criminal Psychology, 7*(2), 11–25.

Sollie, D., & Sollie, W. (1993). *Non-lethal weapons: An implementation study*. Paper presented at the annual meeting of the Society of Police and Criminal Psychology, New Orleans, LA.

Sommer, R., Wynes, M., & Brinkley, G. (1992). Social facilitation effects in shopping behavior. *Environment and Behavior, 24*(3), 285–297.

Sommers, P. M. (1993). The influence of salary arbitration on player performance. *Social Science Quarterly, 74*(2), 439–443.

Sonnemann, U., & Kernan, J. (1962). Handwriting analysis—a valid selection tool? *Personnel, 39*, 8–14.

Soper, B., Milford, G. E., & Rosenthal, G. T. (1995). Belief when evidence does not support theory. *Psychology and Marketing, 12*(5), 415–422.

Sorcher, M., & Spence, R. (1982). The Interface Project: Behavior modeling as social technology in South Africa. *Personnel Psychology, 35*, 557–581.

Sosnin, B. (2001a). Digital newsletters 'E-volutionize' employee communications. *HR Magazine, 46*(5), 99–107.

Sosnin, B. (2001b). Is a video in your vision? *HR Magazine, 46*(2), 100–106.

Sosnin, B. (2001c). Packaging your policies. *HR Magazine, 46*(7), 66–72.

Sousa-Poza, A., & Sousa-Poza, A. A. (2000). Well-being at work: A cross-national analysis of the levels and determinants of job satisfaction. *Journal of Socio-Economics, 29*(6), 517–538.

Sparks, C. P. (1988). Legal basis for job analysis. In S. Gael (Ed.), *The job analysis handbook for business, industry, and government* (Vol. 1, pp. 37–47). New York: Wiley.

Spitzer, D. (1986). Five keys to successful training. *Training, 23*(6), 37–39.

Spock, G., & Stevens, S. (1985). A test of Anderson's averaging versus adding model on resume evaluations. *Proceedings of the 6th Annual Graduate Conference in Industrial/Organizational Psychology and Organizational Behavior*, pp. 95–96.

Springbett, B. M. (1958). Factors affecting the final decision in the employment interview. *Canadian Journal of Psychology, 12*, 13–22.

Spychalski, A. C., Quiñones, M. A., Gaugler, B. B., & Pohley, K. (1997). A survey of assessment center practices in organizations in the United States. *Personnel Psychology, 50*, 71–90.

Srinivas, S., & Motowidlo, S. J. (1987). Effects of rater's stress on the dispersion and favorability of performance ratings. *Journal of Applied Psychology, 72*, 247–251.

Stafford, E. M., Jackson, P. R., & Banks, M. H. (1984). An empirical study of occupational families in the youth labor market. *Journal of Occupational Psychology, 57*, 141–155.

Stahl, M. J. (1983). Achievement, power, and managerial motivation: Selecting managerial talent with the job choice exercise. *Personnel Psychology, 36*, 775–789.

Stahl, M. J., & Harrell, A. M. (1981). Modeling effort decisions with behavioral decision theory: Toward an individual differences model of expectancy theory. *Organizational Behavior and Human Performance, 27*, 303–325.

Stahl, M. J., & Harrell, A. M. (1982). Evolution and validation of a behavioral decision theory measurement approach to achievement, power, and affiliation. *Journal of Applied Psychology, 67*, 744–751.

Stajkovic, A. D., & Luthans, F. (1997). A meta-analysis of the effects of organizational behavior modification on task performance, 1975–95. *Academy of Management Journal, 40*(5), 1122–1149.

Stajkovic, A. D., & Luthans, F. (2001). Differential effects of incentive motivators on work performance. *Academy of Management Journal, 44*(3), 580–590.

Stanten, M. (1997, May). Fit tips: Smart talk for active living. *Prevention Magazine*, p. 69.

Staw, B. M., Bell, N. E., & Clausen, J. A. (1986). The dispositional approach to job attitudes: A lifetime longitudinal test. *Administrative Science Quarterly, 31*, 56–77.

Staw, B. M., & Ross, J. (1985). Stability in the midst of change: A dispositional approach to job attitudes. *Journal of Applied Psychology, 70*, 469–480.

Steel, R. P., & Rentsch, J. R. (1997). The dispositional model of job attitudes revisited: Findings of a 10-year study. *Journal of Applied Psychology, 82*(6), 873–879.

Steers, R. M., & Porter, L. W. (1991). *Motivation and work behavior* (4th ed.). New York: McGraw-Hill.

Steil, L. K. (1980). *Your personal listening profile*. Great Neck, NY: Sperry Corp.

Steiner, D. D., & Gilliland, S. W. (1996). Fairness reactions to personnel selection techniques in France and the United States. *Journal of Applied Psychology, 81*(2), 134–141.

Steiner, I. D. (1972). *Group process and productivity*. New York: Academic Press.

Stevenson, J. G., & Williamson, R. (1995). Testing for drugs? Bathrooms or barbershops? *Public Personnel Management, 24*(4), 467–474.

Stewart, D. W., & Latham, D. R. (1986). On some psychometric properties of Fiedler's contingency model of leadership. *Small Group Behavior, 17*(1), 83–94.

Stewart, P. A., & Moore, J. C. (1992). Wage disparities and performance expectations. *Social Psychology Quarterly, 55*(1), 78–85.

Stewart, R., Ellenburg, G., Hicks, L., Kremen, M., & Daniel, M. (1990). Employee references as a recruitment source. *Applied H.R.M. Research, 1*(1), 1–3.

Stokes, G. S., Hogan, J. B., & Snell, A. F. (1993). Comparability of incumbent and applicant samples for the development of biodata keys: The influence of social desirability. *Personnel Psychology, 46*, 739–762.

Stokes, G. S., & Toth, C. S. (1996). Background data for personnel selection. In R. S. Barrett (Ed.), *Fair employment strategies in human resource management*, (pp. 171–179). Westport, CT: Quorum.

Stone, D. L., Gueutal, H. G., & McIntosh, B. (1984). The effects of feedback sequence and expertise of the rater on performance feedback accuracy. *Personnel Psychology, 37*(3), 487–506.

Stout, S. K., Slocum, J. W., & Cron, W. L. (1987). Career transitions of superiors and subordinates. *Journal of Vocational Behavior, 30*, 124–137.

Strauss, G. (1967). Related instruction: Basic problems and issues. In *Research in apprentice training*. Madison: University of Wisconsin, Center for Vocational and Technical Education.

Strauss, G. (1971). *Union policies and the admission of apprenticeships* [Reprint No. 357]. Berkeley: University of California Press.

Strube, M. J., & Garcia, J. E. (1981). A meta-analytic investigation of Fiedler's contingency model of leadership effectiveness. *Psychological Bulletin, 90*, 307–321.

Stuhlmacher, A. F., & Walters, A. E. (1999). Gender differences in negotiation outcome: A meta-analysis. *Personnel Psychology, 52*(3), 653–677.

Suedfeld, P., & Rank, A. D. (1976). Revolutionary leaders: Long-term success as a function of changes in conceptual complexity. *Journal of Personality and Social Psychology, 34*, 169–178.

Sullivan, J. (2000). Experience: It "Ain't what it used to be." *Public Personnel Management, 29*(4), 511–516.

Sulsky, L. M., & Day, D. V. (1992). Frame-of-reference training and cognitive categorization: An empirical investigation of rater memory issues. *Journal of Applied Psychology, 77*(4), 501–511.

Summer, H. C., & Knight, P. A. (1996). Assimilation and contrast effects in performance ratings: Effects of rating the previous performance on rating subsequent performance. *Journal of Applied Psychology, 81*(4), 436–442.

Sundstrom, E., Burt, R. E., & Kamp, D. (1980). Privacy at work: Architectural correlates of job satisfaction and job performance. *Academy of Management Journal, 23*, 101–117.

Sundstrom, E., Town, J. P., Rice, R. W., Osborn, D. P., & Brill, M. (1994). Office noise, satisfaction, and performance. *Environment and Behavior, 26*(2), 195–222.

Surrette, M. A., Aamodt, M. G., & Johnson, D. L. (1990). Effect analyst training and amount of available information on job analysis ratings. *Journal of Business and Psychology, 4,* 439–451.

Surrette, M. A., & Harlow, L. L. (1992). Level of satisfaction and commitment to a decisional choice as mediated by locus of control. *Applied H.R.M. Research, 3*(2), 92–113.

Sutton, H. W., & Porter, L. W. (1968). A study of the grapevine in a governmental organization. *Personnel Psychology, 21,* 223–230.

Swaroff, P. G., Barclay, L. A., & Bass, A. R. (1985). Recruiting sources: Another look. *Journal of Applied Psychology, 70,* 720–728.

Sweetland, R. C., & Keyser, D. J. (1991). *Tests* (3rd ed.). Kansas City, MO: Test Corp. of America.

Swink, D. F. (1993). Role-play your way to learning. *Training and Development, 47*(5), 91–97.

Szary, D. (2001). Online recruiting I. *Detroiter, 23*(7), 26.

Tait, M., Padgett, M. Y., & Baldwin, T. T. (1989). Job and life satisfaction: A reexamination of the strength of the relationship and gender effects as a function of the date of the study. *Journal of Applied Psychology, 74,* 502–507.

Takahashi, K., Sasaki, H., Hosokawa, T., Kurasaki, M., & Saito, K. (2001). Combined effects of working environmental conditions in VDT work. *Ergonomics, 44*(5), 562–570.

Tanaka, M., Tochihara, Y., Yamazaki, S., Ohnaka, T., & Yoshida, K. (1983). Thermal reaction and manual performance during cold exposure while wearing cold-protective clothing. *Ergonomics, 26,* 141–149.

Tanford, S., & Penrod, S. (1984). Social influence model: A formal integration of research on majority and minority influence processes. *Psychological Bulletin, 95,* 189–225.

Tannen, D. (1986). *That's not what I meant!* New York: Ballantine.

Tannen, D. (1990). *You just don't understand: Women and men in conversation.* New York: Ballentine.

Tannen, D. (1994). *Talking 9 to 5.* New York: Morrow.

Tannenbaum, R. J., & Wesley, S. (1993). Agreement between committee-based and field-based job analyses: A study in the context of licensure testing. *Journal of Applied Psychology, 78,* 975–980.

Taylor, H. C., & Russell, J. T. (1939). The relationship of validity coefficients to the practical effectiveness of tests in selection: Discussion and tables. *Journal of Applied Psychology, 23,* 565–578.

Taylor, K. (2000). May I help you please? *HR Magazine, 45*(8), 90–96.

Taylor, M. S., & Schmidt, D. W. (1983). A process-oriented investigation of recruitment source effectiveness. *Personnel Psychology, 36,* 343–354.

Taylor, P. (1994, May). *The effectiveness of behavior modeling training in organizations.* Paper presented at the 4th International Human Resource Management Conference, Queensland, Australia.

Taylor, S. E., Peplau, L. A., & Sears, D. D. (1994). *Social psychology* (8th ed.). Englewood Cliffs, NJ: Prentice-Hall.

Taylor, S. G. (1994). Realistic job previews in the trucking industry. *Journal of Management Issues, 6*(4), 457–473.

Tedeschi, J. T., Bonoma, T. V., & Schlenker, B. R. (1972). Influence, decision, and compliance. In J. T. Tedeschi (Ed.), *The social influence process* (pp. 346–418). Chicago: Aldine-Atherton.

Teichner, W. H., Arees, E., & Reilly, R. (1963). Noise and human performance. *Ergonomics, 6,* 83–97.

Terpstra, D. E., & Rozell, E. J. (1993). Relationship of staffing practices to organizational level measures of performance. *Personnel Psychology, 46,* 27–48.

Tett, R. P., Jackson, D. N., & Rothstein, M. (1991). Personality measures as predictors of job performance: A meta-analytic review. *Personnel Psychology, 44,* 703–742.

Tett, R. P., Jackson, D. N., Rothstein, M., & Reddon, J. R. (1994). Meta-analysis of personality-job performance relations: A reply to Ones, Mount, Barrick, & Hunter (1994). *Personnel Psychology, 47*(1), 157–172.

Tett, R. P., & Meyer, J. P. (1993). Job satisfaction, organizational commitment, turnover intention, and turnover: Path analyses based on meta-analytic findings. *Personnel Psychology, 46*(2), 259–293.

Theeuwes, J., & Alferdinck, J. W. (1995). Rear light arrangements for cars equipped with a center-high mounted stop lamp. *Human Factors, 37*(2), 371–380.

Thistle, W. (1997). Rooting out drug abuse. *Security Management, 41*(3), 56–58.

Thombs, D. L., Beck, K. H., & Mahoney, C. A. (1993). Effects of social context and gender on drinking patterns of young adults. *Journal of Counseling Psychology, 40*(1), 115–119.

Thompson, D. E., & Thompson, T. A. (1982). Court standards for job analysis in test validation. *Personnel Psychology, 35,* 865–874.

Thompson, R. W. (1997, November). Internet, e-mail seen as enhancing productivity. *HR News,* p. 7.

Thornburg, L. (1993). When violence hits business. *HR Magazine, 38*(7), 40–45.

Thornburg, L. (1994). Change comes slowly. *HR Magazine, 39*(2), 46–49.

Thornton, G. (1993). The effect of selection practices on applicants' perceptions of organizational characteristics. In H. Schuler, J. Farr, & M. Smith (Eds.), *Personnel selection and assessment: Individual and organizational perspectives.* Hillsdale, NJ: Lawrence Erlbaum.

Tierney, P. (1998). *The role of the Pygmalion effect in employee creativity.* Poster presented at the annual meeting of the Society for Industrial and Organizational Psychology, Dallas, TX.

Tolman, C. W. (1968). The role of the companion in social facilitation of animal behavior. In E. C. Simmel, R. A. Hoppe, & G. A. Milton (Eds.), *Social facilitation and initiative behavior* (pp. 33–54). Boston: Allyn & Bacon.

Tomei, F., Fantini, S., Tomao, E., Baccolo, T. P., & Rosati, M. V. (2000). Hypertension and chronic exposure to noise. *Archives of Environmental Health, 55*(5), 319.

Tonowski, R. F. (1993, September). Assessing a violent situation: Violence and personnel assessment practices in the U.S. Postal Service. *IPMAAC News,* pp. 3–5.

Toth, C. (1993). Effect of resume format on applicant selection for a job interview. *Applied H.R.M. Research, 4*(2), 115–125.

Totterdell, P., Spelten, E., Smith, L., Barton, J., & Folkard, S. (1995). Recovery from work shifts: How long does it take? *Journal of Applied Psychology, 80*(1), 43–57.

Tracey, J. B., Tannenbaum, S. I., & Kavanagh, M. J. (1995). Applying trained skills on the job: The importance of the work environment. *Journal of Applied Psychology, 80*(2), 239–252.

Trahiotis, C., & Robinson, D. E. (1979). Auditory psychophysics. *Annual Review of Psychology, 30,* 31–61.

Trenn, K. (1993, December). Third of survey respondents report violent episodes. *HR News,* pp. 2–4.

Trent, J. T., Smith, A. L., & Wood, D. L. (1994). Telecommuting: Stress and social support. *Psychological Reports, 74,* 1312–1314.

Trice, E. (1997, October). Referrals to the rescue? *IPMA News,* pp. 12–13.

Trinkaus, J. W. (1986). Perceived hazard of video display terminals: An informal look. *Perceptual and Motor Skills, 62,* 118.

Triplett, N. (1898). The dynamogenic factors in pacemaking and competition. *American Journal of Psychology, 9,* 507–533.

Truxillo, D. M., Normandy, J. L., & Bauer, T. N. (2001). Drug use history, drug test consequences, and the perceived fairness of organizational drug testing programs. *Journal of Business and Psychology, 16*(1), 87–99.

Tubbs, M. E. (1986). Goal setting: A meta-analytic examination of the empirical evidence. *Journal of Applied Psychology, 71,* 474–483.

Tubré, T., Bly, P. R., Edwards, B. D., Pritchard, R. D., & Simoneaux, S. (2001). Building a better literature review: References and information sources for I-O psychology. *The Industrial-Organizational Psychologist, 38*(4), 55–59.

Tucker, J. (1993). Everyday forms of employee resistance. *Sociological Forum, 8*(1), 25–45.

Tulgan, B. (2001). Real pay for performance. *Journal of Business Strategy, 22*(3), 19–22.

Turner, J. T. (1994). *Violence in the work place: First line of defense.* Paper presented at the 23rd annual meeting of the Society of Police and Criminal Psychology, Madison, WI.

Turner, M. L., Fernandez, J. E., & Nelson, K. (1996). The effect of music amplitude on the reaction to unexpected visual events. *Journal of General Psychology, 123*(1), 51–62.

Twomey, D. P. (2002). *Employment discrimination law.* Cincinnati, OH: West.

Tyler, K. (1996). Employees can help recruit new talent. *HR Magazine, 41*(9), 57–60.

Tyler, K. (1998). Sit up straight. *HR Magazine, 43*(9), 124–128.

Tyler, K. (2000a). Recruiting through religious organizations. *HR Magazine, 45*(9), 131–138.

Tyler, K. (2000b). Scoring big in the workplace: Corporate coaches help managers produce the right plays on the job. *HR Magazine, 45*(6), 96–106.

Tyler, K. (2001a). All present and accounted for? *HR Magazine, 46*(10), 101–109.

Tyler, K. (2001b). E-learning not just for E-normous companies anymore. *HR Magazine, 46*(5), 82–88.

Tyler, K. (2001c). A roof over their heads. *HR Magazine, 46*(2), 41–46.

Tyler, K. (2002). Evaluating evaluations. *HR Magazine, 47*(6), 85–93.

Tysinger, A., & Pitchford, L. (1988). *A readability index for trait based psychological tests.* Paper presented at the 9th annual Graduate Conference in Industrial/Organizational Psychology and Organizational Behavior, Toledo, OH.

Tziner, A., Kopelman, R. E., & Livnech, N. (1993). Effects of performance appraisal format on perceived goal characteristics, appraisal process satisfaction, and changes in rated job performance: A field experiment. *Journal of Psychology, 127*(3), 281–292.

Uhrbrock, R. S. (1961). Music on the job: Its influence on worker morale and production. *Personnel Psychology, 14,* 9–38.

Ulrich, E. (1957). Zur frage der belastung des arbeitenden menschen durch nacht-und shicktarbeit. *Psychologische Rundschar, 8,* 42–61.

U.S. Census Bureau. (2000).[Online]. Available: www.census.gov/population/socdemo/race/black/pp1–142/tab07.txt

U.S. Department of Labor. (1989, April). *News.* Washington, DC: Author.

U.S. Department of Labor. (2002). [Online]. Available: http://www.census.gov/income/histinc/p40.html.

U.S. Merit Systems Protection Board. (1995). *Sexual harassment in the federal workplace.* Washington, DC: author.

Valacich, J. S., Dennis, A. R., & Connolly, T. (1994). Idea generation in computer-based groups: A new ending to an old story. *Organizational Behavior and Human Decision Processes, 57*(3), 448–467.

Valacich, J. S., Dennis, A. R., & Nunamaker, J. F. (1992). Group size and anonymity effects on computer-mediated idea generation. *Small Group Research, 23*(1), 49–73.

Valacich, J. S., Parantia, D., George, J. F., & Nunamaker, J. F. (1993). Communication concurrency and the new media: A new dimension for media richness. *Communication Research, 20*(2), 249–276.

Van Buren, M. E., & Erskine, W. (2002). *State of the industry: Report 2002 executive summary.* Alexandria, VA: American Society for Training and Development.

Van De Water, T. J. (1997). Psychology's entrepreneurs and the marketing of industrial psychology. *Journal of Applied Psychology, 82*(4), 486–499.

Van Leeuwen, M., Frizzell, M. D., & Nail, P. R. (1987, April). *An examination of gender differences in response to threatening communications.* Paper presented at the annual meeting of the Oklahoma Psychological Association, Oklahoma City, OK.

Van Slyke, E. J. (1996). Busting the bureaucracy. *HR Focus, 73*(7), 15–16.

Van Slyke, E. J. (1997). Facilitating productive conflict. *HR Focus, 74*(4), 17.

Van Slyke, E. J. (1999). Resolve conflict, boost creativity. *HR Magazine, 44*(12), 132–137.

Varma, A., DeNisi, A. S., & Peters, L. H. (1996). Interpersonal affect and performance appraisal: A field study. *Personnel Psychology, 49*(2), 341–360.

Vecchio, R. P., Griffeth, R. W., & Hom, P. W. (1986). The predictive utility of the vertical dyad linkage approach. *Journal of Social Psychology, 126*(5), 617–625.

Veglahn, P. A. (1989). Drug testing that clears the arbitration hurdle. *Personnel Administrator, 34*(2), 62–64.

Verdi, W. M. (1999). MBAs in I-O psychology: Barbarians at the gate or allies against organizational inertia. *The Industrial-Organizational Psychologist, 37*(2), 41–42.

Veres, J. G., Green, S. B., & Boyles, W. R. (1991). Racial differences on job analysis questionnaires: An empirical study. *Public Personnel Management, 20*(2), 135–144.

Verespes, M. A. (1994). The anytime, anyplace workplace. *Industry Week, 243*(13), 37–40.

Verhaegen, P., Cober, R., de Smedt, M., & Dirkx, J. (1987). The adaptation of night nurses to different work schedules. *Ergonomics, 30,* 1301–1309.

Vernon, H. M. (1936). *Accidents and their prevention.* London: Cambridge University Press.

Vernon, H. M., & Warner, C. G. (1932). Objective and subjective tests for noise. *Personnel Journal, 11,* 141–149.

Vincola, A. (1999, April). Back-up child care: An effective solution to a growing need. *IPMA News,* pp. 16–17.

Vines, L. S. (1997). Make long-term temporary workers part of the team. *HR Magazine, 42*(1), 65–70.

Viswesvaran, C., & Ones, D. S. (1997). Review of the Stanton Survey. *Security Journal, 8,* 167–169.

Viswesvaran, C., Ones, D. S., & Schmidt, F. L. (1996). Comparative analysis of the reliability of job performance ratings. *Journal of Applied Psychology, 81*(5), 557–574.

Viswesvaran, C., Schmidt, F. L., & Ones, D. S. (2002). The moderating influence of job performance dimensions on convergence of supervisory and peer ratings of job performance: Unconfounding construct-level convergence and rating difficulty. *Journal of Applied Psychology, 87*(2), 345–354.

Volker, K. D. (1993). *Obesity and perceived interview performance.* Unpublished master's thesis, Radford University.

Vroom, V., & Yetton, P. W. (1973). *Leadership and decision making.* Pittsburgh, PA: University of Pittsburgh Press.

Vroom, V. H. (1964). *Work and motivation.* New York: Wiley.

Waddell, J. R. (1996). You'll never believe what I heard. *Supervision, 57*(8), 18–20.

Wagner, J. A. (1994). Participation effects on performance and satisfaction: A reconsideration of research evidence. *Academy of Management Review, 19*(2), 312–330.

Wagner, R. F. (1950). A study of the critical requirements for dentists. *University of Pittsburgh Bulletin, 46,* 331–339.

Wahba, M. A., & Bridwell, L. T. (1976). Maslow reconsidered: A review of research on the need of hierarchy theory. *Organizational Behavior and Human Performance, 15,* 212–240.

Wakabayashi, M., & Graen, G. B. (1984). The Japanese career progress study: A seven-year follow-up. *Journal of Applied Psychology, 69,* 603–614.

Waldman, D. A., & Avolio, B. J. (1986). A meta-analysis of age differences in job performance. *Journal of Applied Psychology, 71,* 33–38.

Walker, A. G., & Smither, J. W. (1999). A five-year study of upward feedback: What managers do with their results matters. *Personnel Psychology, 52*(2), 393–423.

Wall, H. J. (2000, October). The gender wage gap and wage discrimination: Illusion or reality? *Regional Economist,* pp. 1–5.

Walster, E., Aronson, E., & Abrahams, D. (1966). On increasing the persuasiveness of a low prestige communicator. *Journal of Experimental Social Psychology, 2,* 325–342.

Walton, E. (1961). How efficient is the grapevine? *Personnel, 28,* 45–49.

Wanberg, C. R., & Banas, J. T. (2000). Predictors and outcomes of openness to changes in a reorganizing workplace. *Journal of Applied Psychology, 85*(1), 132–142.

Wanous, J. P. (1980). *Organizational entry: Recruitment, selection, and socialization of newcomers.* Reading, MA: Addison-Wesley.

Wanous, J. P., Poland, T. D., Premack, S. L., & Davis, K. S. (1992). The effects of met expectations on newcomer attitudes and behavior: A review and meta-analysis. *Journal of Applied Psychology, 77*(3), 288–297.

Wanous, J. P., & Zwany, A. (1977). A cross-sectional test of need hierarchy theory. *Organizational Behavior and Human Performance, 18,* 78–97.

Ward, E. A. (2001). Social power bases of managers: Emergence of a new factor. *The Journal of Social Psychology, 141*(1), 144–147.

Washburn, D. (1997). Study shows rise in employee theft in 1996. *Home Improvement Market, 234*(8), 22.

Waung, M., & Brice, T. S. (2003). *The impact of rejection communication on rejected job applicants.* Poster presented at the 18th annual meeting of the Society for Industrial and Organizational Psychology, Orlando, FL.

Waung, M., & Highhouse, S. (1997). *Feedback inflation: Empathic buffering or fear of conflict?* Poster presented at the 12th annual conference of the Society for Industrial and Organizational Psychology, St. Louis, MO.

Weaver, C. N. (1978). Job satisfaction as a component of happiness among males and females. *Personnel Psychology, 31,* 831–840.

Webb, W. (1997). High-tech in the heartland. *Training, 34*(5), 50–54.

Weber, Y. (1996). Corporate cultural fit and performance in mergers and acquisitions. *Human Relations, 49*(9), 1181–1203.

Wedderburn, A. A. (1978). Some suggestions for increasing the usefulness of psychological and sociological studies of shiftwork. *Ergonomics, 21,* 827–833.

Weins, A. N., Jackson, R. H., Manaugh, T. S., & Matarazzo, J. D. (1969). Communication length as an index of communicator attitude: A replication. *Journal of Applied Psychology, 53,* 264–266.

Weinstein, N. D. (1977). Noise and intellectual performance: A confirmation and extension. *Journal of Applied Psychology, 62,* 104–107.

Weinstein, N. D. (1978). A longitudinal study in a college dormitory. *Journal of Applied Psychology, 63,* 458–466.

Weiss, H. M., Dawis, R. V., England, G. W., & Lofquist, L. H. (1967). *Manual for the Minnesota Satisfaction Questionnaire.* Minneapolis: University of Minnesota, Industrial Relations Center.

Weiss, H. M., & Shaw, J. B. (1979). Social influences on judgments about tasks. *Organizational Behavior and Human Performance, 24,* 126–140.

Weiss, J. M. (1994). Telecommuting boosts employee output. *HR Magazine, 39*(2), 51–53.

Weisser, C. (2002). A job to lie for. *Money, 31*(7), 26.

Wells, S. J. (2000). The elder care gap. *HR Magazine, 45*(5), 39–46.

Wells, S. J. (2001a). A female executive is hard to find. *HR Magazine, 46*(6), 40–49.

Wells, S. J. (2001b). Making telecommuting work. *HR Magazine, 46*(10), 34–45.

Welsh, D. H., Bernstein, D. J., & Luthans, F. (1992). Application of the Premack Principle of reinforcement to the quality performance of service employees. *Journal of Organizational Behavior Management, 13*(1), 9–32.

Wentworth, R. (1991). The effects of music and distracting noise on the productivity of workers with mental retardation. *Journal of Music Therapy, 28*(1), 40–47.

Werner, J. M., & Bolino, M. C. (1997). Explaining U.S. Courts of Appeals decisions involving performance appraisal: Accuracy, fairness, and validation. *Personnel Psychology, 50*(1), 1–24.

Wernimont, P. F. (1962). Re-evaluation of a weighted application blank for office personnel. *Journal of Applied Psychology, 46*, 417–419.

Wexley, K. N., & Latham, G. A. (2002). *Developing and training human resources in organizations* (3rd ed.). Upper Saddle River, NJ: Prentice-Hall.

Wexley, K. N., Sanders, R. E., & Yukl, G. A. (1973). Training interviewers to eliminate contrast effects in employment interviews. *Journal of Applied Psychology, 57*, 233–236.

Wexley, K. N., Yukl, G. A., Kovacs, S. Z., & Sanders, R. E. (1972). Importance of contrast effects in employment interviews. *Journal of Applied Psychology, 56*, 45–48.

Whelchel, B. D. (1985). Use of performance tests to select craft apprentices. *Personnel Journal, 65*(7), 65–69.

Whetstone, T. S. (1994). Subordinates evaluate supervisory and administrative performance. *Police Chief, 61*(6), 57–62.

Whitcomb, A., & Bryan, D. (1988). Validity of the Peres and Garcia method of scoring letters of recommendation. *Proceedings of the 9th Annual Graduate Conference in Industrial/Organizational Psychology and Organizational Behavior.*

Widgery, R., & Stackpole, C. (1972). Desk position, interviewee anxiety, and interviewer credibility: An example of cognitive balance in a dyad. *Journal of Counseling Psychology, 19*, 173–177.

Wilbur, L. P. (1993). The value of on-the-job rotation. *Supervisory Management, 38*(11), 6.

Wild, C., Horney, N., & Koonce, R. (1996). Cascading communications creates momentum for change. *HR Magazine, 41*(12), 94–100.

Wilkinson, R. T. (1992). How fast should the night shift rotate? *Ergonomics, 35*(12), 1425–1446.

Willen, J. L. (1996). Computers' toll on the eyes. *Nation's Business, 84*(2), 64.

William Mercer. (2003). *Mercer 2002/2003 compensation planning survey*. New York: William Mercer, Inc.

Williams, J. R., & Levy, P. E. (1992). The effects of perceived system knowledge on the agreement between self-ratings and supervisor ratings. *Personnel Psychology, 45*, 835–847.

Williams, J. R., Miller, C. E., Steelman, L. A., & Levy, P. E. (1999). Increasing feedback seeking in public contexts: It takes two (or more) to tango. *Journal of Applied Psychology, 84*(6), 969–976.

Williams, K. D., Bourgeois, M. J., & Croyle, R. T. (1993). The effects of stealing thunder in criminal and civil trials. *Law and Human Behavior, 17*(6), 597–609.

Williams, K. D., Harkins, S., & Latane, B. (1981). Identifiability as a deterrent to social loafing: Two cheering experiments. *Journal of Personality and Social Psychology, 40*, 303–311.

Williams, R., & Garris, T. S. (1991). A second look at situation wanted advertisements. *Applied H.R.M. Research, 2*(1), 33–37.

Williams, S. W., & Streit, T. (1986). Learner-driven sales training at Life of Virginia. *Training, 23*(2), 65–68.

Williamson, A. M., Gower, C. G. I., & Clarke, B. C. (1994). Changing the hours of shift work: A comparison of 8- and 12-hour shift rosters in a group of computer operators. *Ergonomics, 37*(2), 287–298.

Williamson, A. M., & Sanderson, J. W. (1986). Changing the speed of shift rotation: A field study. *Ergonomics, 29*, 1085–1089.

Williamson, L. G., Campion, J. E., Malos, S. B., Roehling, M. V., & Campion, M. A. (1997). Employment interview on trial: Linking interview structure with litigation outcomes. *Journal of Applied Psychology, 82*(6), 900–912.

Willihnganz, M. A., & Myers, L. S. (1993). Effects of time of day on interview performance. *Public Personnel Management, 22*(4), 545–550.

Willis, S. C., Miller, T. A., & Huff, G. (1991). Situation-wanted advertisements: A means for obtaining job inquiries and offers. *Applied H.R.M. Research, 2*(1), 27–32.

Wilmot, W. W., & Hocker, J. L. (2001). *Interpersonal conflict* (6th ed.). New York: McGraw-Hill.

Wilson, E. J., & Sherrell, D. L. (1993). Source effects in communication and persuasion research: A meta-analysis of effect size. *Journal of the Academy of Marketing Science, 21*(2), 101–112.

Wilson, M. A., & Harvey, R. J. (1990). The value of relative-time-spent ratings in task-oriented job analysis. *Journal of Business and Psychology, 4*(4), 453–461.

Wilson, W. (1994). Video training and testing supports customer service goals. *Personnel Journal, 30*(10), 47–51.

Wimbush, J. C., & Dalton, D. R. (1997). Base rate for employee theft: Convergence of multiple methods. *Journal of Applied Psychology, 82*(5), 756–763.

Wing, J. F. (1965). Upper tolerance limits for unimpaired mental performance. *Aerospace Medicine, 36*, 960–964.

Winter, D. G. (1988). What makes Jesse run? *Psychology Today, 22*(6), 20–24.

Wisdom, B., & Patzig, D. (1987). Does your organization have the right climate for merit? *Public Personnel Management, 16*, 127–133.

Witt, L. A. (1996). *Listen up! Your upward feedback results are speaking.* Poster presented at the 11th annual conference of the Society for Industrial and Organizational Psychology, San Diego, CA.

Wofford, J. C., & Liska, L. Z. (1993). Path-goal theories of leadership: A meta-analysis. *Journal of Management, 19*(4), 857–876.

Wokoun, W. (1980). *A study of fatigue in industry*. New York: Muzak Board of Scientific Advisors.

Wolinsky, J. (1982). Beat the clock. *APA Monitor, 13*, 12.

Wood, R. F., Mento, A. J., & Locke, E. A. (1987). Task complexity as a moderator of goal effects: A meta-analysis. *Journal of Applied Psychology, 72*, 416–425.

Woodward, N. H. (1999). In case of emergency break glass. *HR Magazine, 44*(8), 83–88.

Woodward, N. H. (2000). Direct mail pushes the recruiting envelope. *HR Magazine, 45*(5), 145–152.

Woodward, N. H. (2001). Discounts not to be discounted. *HR Magazine, 46*(4) 91–96.

Wooten, W. (1993). Using knowledge, skill and ability (KSA) data to identify career pathing opportunities: An application of job analysis to internal manpower planning. *Public Personnel Management, 22*(4), 551–563.

Workplace Visions. (1999). Interest in using prison labor is growing. *Workplace Visions, 4*, 4–6.

Wyatt Company. (1993). *Best practices in corporate restructuring*. Washington, DC: author.

Wyatt, S., & Marriot, R. (1953). Night work and shift changes. *British Journal of Industrial Medicine, 10*, 164–177.

Yammarino, F. J., Skinner, S. J., & Childers, T. L. (1991). Understanding mail survey response behavior: A meta-analysis. *Public Opinion Quarterly, 55*(4), 613–639.

Yandrick, R. M. (2001a). Elder care grows up. *HR Magazine, 46*(11), 72–77.

Yandrick, R. M. (2001b). A team effort. *HR Magazine, 46*(6), 136–141.

Young, D. M., & Beier, E. G. (1977). The role of applicant nonverbal communication in the employment interview. *Journal of Employment Counseling, 14*, 154–165.

Youngjohn, R. M. (1999). *Is leadership trait theory fact or fiction? A meta-analytic investigation of the relationship between individual differences and leader effectiveness?* Unpublished doctoral dissertation, Texas A & M University.

Yu, J., & Murphy, K. (1993) Modesty bias in self-ratings or performance: A test of the cultural relating hypothesis. *Personnel Psychology, 46*(2), 357–363.

Yukl, G. A. (1982, April). *Innovations in research on leader behavior*. Paper presented at the annual meeting of the Eastern Academy of Management, Baltimore, MD.

Yukl, G. A. (1989). *Leadership in organizations*. Englewood Cliffs, NJ: Prentice-Hall.

Yukl, G. A. (1994). *Leadership in organizations*. (3rd ed.) Englewood Cliffs, NJ: Prentice-Hall.

Zajonc, R. B. (1965). Social facilitation. *Science, 149*, 269–274.

Zajonc, R. B. (1980). Compressence. In P. B. Paulus (Ed.), *Psychology of group influence*. Hillsdale, NJ: Lawrence Erlbaum.

Zajonc, R. B., Heingartner, A., & Herman, E. M. (1969). Social enhancement and impairment of performance in the cockroach. *Journal of Personality and Social Psychology, 13*, 83–92.

Zaremba, A. (1988). Working with the organizational grapevine. *Personnel Journal, 67*(6), 38–42.

Zdep, S. M., & Weaver, H. B. (1967). The graphoanalytic approach to selecting life insurance salesman. *Journal of Applied Psychology, 51*, 295–299.

Zedeck, S., Cascio, W. F., Goldstein, I., & Outtz, J. (1996). Sliding bands: An alternative to top-down selection. In R. Barrett (Ed.), *Fair employment strategies in human resource management* (pp. 222–234). Westport, CT: Quorum.

Zemke, R. (1993). Rethinking the rush to team-up. *Training, 30*(11), 55–61.

Zemke, R. (1997). How long does it take? *Training, 34*(5), 69–79.

Zhou, J. (1998). Feedback valence, feedback style, task autonomy, and achievement orientation: Interactive effects on creative performance. *Journal of Applied Psychology, 83*(2), 261–276.

Zickar, M. J., & Highhouse, S. (2001). Measuring prestige of journals in industrial-organizational psychology. *The Industrial-Organizational Psychologist, 38*(4), 29–36.

Zimmerman, D. (1996). H-E-B puts its own spin on training by computer. *Supermarket News, 46*(37), 19–20.

Zink, D. L. (2002). *Chevron U.S.A., Inc. v. Echazabal:* Has the Americans with Disabilities Act become a toothless tiger? *The Industrial-Organizational Psychologist, 40*(2), 70–75.

Zottoli, M. A., & Wanous, J. P. (1998). *A meta-analysis of recruitment source effects on turnover and performance*. Poster presented at the annual meeting of the Society for Industrial and Organizational Psychology, Dallas, TX.

Zuber, A. (1996). Tapping a human resource: Restaurants fight labor crunch with training programs. *Nation's Restaurant News, 30*(26), 33–35.

Zweigenhaft, R. L. (1976). Personal space in the faculty office: Desk placement and the student–faculty interaction. *Journal of Applied Psychology, 61*, 529–532.

Name Index

591

Subject Index

Photo Credits

Chapter 1: p. 10, Courtesy of the author; p. 17, PhotoDisc, Inc. **Chapter 2:** p. 36, PhotoDisc, Inc.; p. 37, PhotoDisc, Inc.; p. 39, PhotoDisc, Inc.; p. 40, Courtesy of Deborah L. Gebhardt **Chapter 3:** p. 72, PhotoDisc, Inc.; p. 76, Courtesy of Victor O. Cardwell; p. 77, PhotoDisc, Inc.; p. 81, PhotoDisc, Inc.; p. 87, Photodisc, Inc. **Chapter 4:** p. 102, PhotoDisc, Inc.; p. 116, Courtesy of T. R. Lin **Chapter 5:** p. 140, Courtesy of Rhonda Duffie; p. 147, PhotoDisc, Inc. **Chapter 6:** p. 169, PhotoDisc, Inc.; p. 180, PhotoDisc, Inc.; p. 184, Courtesy of Mark Foster **Chapter 7:** p. 229, PhotoDisc, Inc.; p. 235, PhotoDisc, Inc. **Chapter 8:** p. 263, Photodisc, Inc.; p. 269, Courtesy of David Cohen; p. 276, PhotoDisc, Inc.; **Chapter 9:** p. 292, PhotoDisc, Inc.; p. 296, PhotoDisc, Inc.; p. 299, Courtesy of Armand Spoto; p. 302, PhotoDisc, Inc. **Chapter 10:** p. 327, PhotoDisc, Inc.; p. 329, PhotoDisc, Inc.; p. 335, Courtesy of Heather King Foster **Chapter 11:** p. 350, Courtesy of Amy Podurgal; p. 355, PhotoDisc, Inc.; p. 361, PhotoDisc, Inc.; p. 364, PhotoDisc, Inc.; p. 366, PhotoDisc, Inc. **Chapter 12:** p. 382, PhotoDisc, Inc.; p. 391 PhotoDisc, Inc.; p. 393, Courtesy of Devon Bryan; p. 396, PhotoDisc, Inc.; **Chapter 13:** p. 421, Courtesy of Bobbie Raynes; p. 423, PhotoDisc, Inc.; p. 425, PhotoDisc, Inc. **Chapter 14:** p. 446, PhotoDisc, Inc.; p. 450, Courtesy of Susan Worrell; p. 460, PhotoDisc, Inc. **Chapter 15:** PhotoDisc, Inc.; PhotoDisc, Inc.; p. 487, Courtesy of Lori Hurley; p. 489, PhotoDisc, Inc. **Chapter 16:** p. 513, PhotoDisc, Inc.; p. 516, PhotoDisc, Inc.; p. 520 top, Courtesy of Russ Branaghan; p. 520 bottom, Courtesy of the author; p. 521 top, Courtesy of the author; p. 521 bottom, PhotoDisc, Inc.; p. 524, Courtesy of the author.